BEST AMERICAN PLAYS

Seventh Series 1967-1973

Best American Plays

SEVENTH SERIES

1967-1973

EDITED, WITH AN INTRODUCTION BY

Clive Barnes

CROWN PUBLISHERS, INC., NEW YORK

Inquiries should be addressed to Crown Publishers, Inc.,
225 Park Avenue South, New York, New York 10003

Represented in Canada by the Canadian MANDA Group

Library of Congress Catalog Card Number: 57-12830
ISBN 0-517-51387-0

MANUFACTURED IN THE UNITED STATES OF AMERICA

10   9   8   7   6   5

Acknowledgment is due to the following for their cooperation in the preparation of this volume: Atheneum Publishers; Toby Cole; The Dial Press; Farrar, Straus, and Giroux, Inc.; Samuel French; Grove Press; Harcourt Brace and Jovanovich; Harper & Row, Publishers, Inc.; Hill & Wang; Random House, Inc.; Flora Roberts; Simon & Schuster, Inc.; and Viking Press, Inc.

CONTENTS

INTRODUCTION

One forgets quite when the theatre started to die, but it must have been around the time of Sophocles or even earlier. Probably they had some kind of mystic theatre in the caves, and after the first week one Neolithic man turned to another Neolithic man and said: "It's not like it used to be!" The theatre has always been growing and always dying. This is true of most art forms, but particularly perhaps of the performing arts. They are more susceptible to fashion and even economic and political change than the more independent fine arts, which are not necessarily social forms and can be pursued by a solitary artist virtually exempt from the immediate demands of his society.

The death of the theatre, or the plight of the theatre, is a continual refrain. Where are the plays, where are the playwrights? Why are all the theatres dark, why are people no longer interested in the theatre, why don't young people go to the theatre, why don't old people go to the theatre? Why is the theatre so expensive? What is wrong with the musical? Where are the good family plays? The threnody continues monotonously.

It is my contention that the English-speaking theatre in general and the American theatre in particular have never previously enjoyed such robust health. To readers accustomed to the thin gruel of the all too common theatrical jeremiads, these may sound like fighting words, even hysterical words. Yet this is a position that I think can be justified by a fair scrutiny of the facts. First what do they mean when they say, "The theatre is dying"? What theatre? What kind of theatre? The new theatre, the classic theatre? We must needs define our theatre.

When many people, perhaps even most people, talk and, particularly, write about the American theatre, they mean the commercial theatre of Broadway. It is by no means my intention to disparage Broadway, which still, on occasion, can offer American theatre at its best. But I do wonder whether today Broadway is not running on borrowed time and, for that matter, often on borrowed plays.

The whole concept of Broadway, its special economic viability, seems to be based on the twenties and the thirties. It is predicated on the idea that the theatre is the great popular mass medium of the public. This is not true now, and indeed has not really been true since the end of the twenties, and even before that its power and influence were being significantly eroded by the growing popularity of silent movies.

The reign of the theatre as a popular medium was not a long one. It can be said to have started with the rise, all over the world, of the urban lower middle class during the latter part of the nineteenth century and with the later introduction of electrical lighting into the theatres, together with comparatively cheap mass transportation. These were the palmy days of the bad old theatre, and the period lasted between fifty and sixty years. And yet many Broadway producers fail to recognize that those days are past.

The quality of theatrical entertainment, ranging from low burlesque to grand opera, from embarrassing melodrama to badly staged Shakespeare, must have been terrible. Read the plays today, and read the reviews of the turn-of-the-century scene in both New York and London. Read Shaw and Beerbohm in London, or Huneker in New York—it is perfectly clear that most of the offerings were intellectually and aesthetically beneath contempt. The theatre then was like the television of today, but, arguably I think, it almost certainly lacked television's undeniable expertise.

The theatre was the big entertainment medium of that period. It was generally meant to be undemanding and escapist. It was a night out, a cause for celebration. Now there is nothing wrong with this attitude, the theatre certainly needs its cakes and ale, and all sensible men are in favor of entertainment and, indeed, escapist entertainment. Let us have as much frivolity as we can get. But it gradually became apparent that, as a pure entertainment medium, the theatre left a lot to be desired.

I suppose the first challenge to the popular theatre's supremacy came in 1928 when Al Jolson first sang "Sonny Boy" in *The Singing Fool.* By the middle of the thirties, talking pictures were the mass entertainment of the industrialized world. They were economically more feasible than theatre, and their distribution was virtually international. Many of the theatre's finest talents gravitated to Hollywood, which became a more potent dream palace than Broadway ever was in its finest hour.

There were still some things Broadway could offer—primarily the person-to-person impact of a live performer, but also a special sense of occasion and, on the whole, a more effective way of dealing with that indigenous American dramatic form, the musical. So Broadway survived quite happily—indeed for a time became associated in the popular mind as the equivalent of a rather classy restaurant, whereas the movie house was something more like a coffee shop or a cafeteria. In this way Broadway and Hollywood somewhat uneasily coexisted, with Hollywood traditionally taking much of its talent and material from its elder brother in New York. Then came television.

The impact and effect of television on Broadway and Hollywood are still enormously difficult to evaluate. In the first place what is often not realized is that the impact of television was a double shock wave, with the second wave, if anything, being more important than the first. Black-and-white television was one thing, but the screens were small, there was comparatively little opportunity for fantasy or glamour, and while this was obviously a potent threat to the live theatre and creative films, the blow was softened. Television, for all its technological brilliance and, if you like, magic, could not compare. A line in F. Hugh Herbert's play *The Moon Is Blue,* written at the beginning of the fifties, puts it prophetically. A character is asked whether he would like to watch television. "Is it in color?" he inquires. "Why no, it won't be in color for years!" "Then I'll wait" came back the then hilarious reply. It was not so hilarious for Broadway and Hollywood, for that character did not have to wait too long, and with color television the writing was really on the wall for old-time Broadway.

For years Broadway had scrambled along with moderately bad but moderately passable situation comedies, faintly colored by the forbidden joys of sex. Then two things happened. First such comedies, perfectly well written and extremely well staged, became generally available on television, and then those forbidden joys suddenly seemed to cease to be forbidden. What was Broadway to do? Well, what it did was nothing. It said, in effect, "See a Live Show." It counted on that earlier one-to-one impact of the star performer and also Broadway's sense of occasion. With those weapons Broadway had, battered but upright, sustained the attacks of the Hollywood hordes. Why should they be less effective against television, when television had many specific disadvantages?

The disadvantages of television can still be spelled out for you by dyed-in-the wool Broadway people. It is, they will say, too "common" a medium, anyone can see it in his own home, and it has an almost negative factor in the sense-of-occasion stakes. It also has commercial breaks, which destroy concentration and continuity—it is altogether inferior. Fundamentally, how wrong Broadway was. That sense of occasion it was so happy with soon began to be associated with an alarmingly large dinner tab and the opportunity of being mugged in the increasingly sleazy Times Square area of New York City. Now both the price of eating and the prospect of sudden death were both vastly exaggerated—largely by TV talk-show hosts—but for many people it took the sense out of that sense of occasion.

Even more interestingly, what many Broadway producers took to be a prime disadvantage of television—the commercial interruption—may indeed be no such thing. There is now a young generation that has grown up in the last twenty years that actually expects narrative dramatic forms to pause every ten minutes or so for a message from their sponsor. To a person who grew up with the conditioning and expectation of a different world this attitude may seem unbelievable, but with younger people I suspect it is instinctively widely held. They are being conditioned to accept entertainment and even art in time slots. It is interesting how often Public Television, even in a children's program such as "Sesame Street," feels impelled to interpolate into its programming simulated commercials. There must be a message there.

The important thing to realize about the theatre is that it has become an elitist art. That itself requires some explanation, for I do not mean to suggest that theatre has become a minority taste enjoyed only by the few—the rich and privileged. In these times of mass education even elitist arts can have a surprisingly large following. But it would be wrong to imagine that the theatre is as popular as baseball—it is like the dance, the symphony, the opera, even, in certain instances, the art cinema, a form that appeals to the culturally aware rather than the culturally deprived. And the theatre has to adapt to its changed circumstances. It would seem easy. But in some ways it is more difficult than it seems.

One confusing aspect of the situation is that, despite everything I have said about the theatre's being a nonmass medium, it just once in a while runs contrary to fact. Every season on Broadway there are two or three shows that make a whopping commercial profit—which indicates to the hopeful that the commercial theatre is not at all dead, merely resting. These shows, these money-spinners, moreover run to no set pattern. Let me submit a recent object lesson. A well-known Broadway producing team was proposing to import to New York a British tearjerker about the Edward VIII abdication crisis, *Crown Matrimonial*. They regarded it as certain to make a lot of money, but being honest men with the good of the theatre at heart, they felt the need to do something "artistic," something apart from the lure of money, indeed something that might honorably lose some of the excess profits they felt certain they would be making on their British import. They chose José Quintero's staging of Eugene O'Neill's *A Moon for the Misbegotten*, starring Colleen Dewhurst and Jason Robards. *Crown Matrimonial* lost its shirt, and the O'Neill made a fortune. Never has theatrical plain dealing been better, or more unexpectedly, rewarded.

What is the secret of these dramatic sports that each year convey the illusion that Broadway is still a fit place for a young man to make a million in? The important thing to remember is that they are "sports": they are, in the biological sense, genetic mysteries. I personally believe that their existence is sociological rather than artistic. They are the preserve of an individual who is remote from the living theatre—the splurge theatregoer.

The splurge theatregoer has nothing to do with the theatregoing public. He may go to the theatre once a year, or maybe a little more, or maybe a little less. He will certainly not attend the theatre more than, say, five times a year. He may live in New York or he may be a visitor. He may go to the theatre in his local community on the same splurge basis—in recent years, outside New York, he has begun to favor that special package-evening of entertainment, the dinner theatre.

His reason for attending the theatre may be one of many. A wedding anniversary to celebrate, an out-of-town client to impress, a country cousin to enchant—the reasons will be diverse. But it is decided to take in a show. Which show? Easily agreed on. It will be the most difficult to get into and therefore the most prestigious. Your splurge-once-a-year theatregoer does not usually want to see a show that no one has heard of, and anyone can see. He wants to see *My Fair Lady* in its first year, or some other superhit that in addition to offering an evening out also confers prestige on the people taken out that evening.

But while splurge theatregoers may make a few producers rich, often on a seemingly irrational chance, they have nothing but a maverick effect on the theatre as a whole. They draw attention from the facts of the case; they disguise the way the theatre really is; and they give false hopes to those who believe that the commercial, profit-making theatre, now virtually defunct throughout the world, may still somehow survive in America. Well, it won't.

By cutting standards, using well-known stars and old properties, it is still possible in suburban music theatres and the like to make a buck. But this is exploitation not art. The thing itself—the play—has passed on to different circumstances and a different audience. And the circumstances have to be subsidized, and the audiences are highly educated. For the interesting thing about the new look in the theatre is that as the audiences get smaller the theatre gets better. The mass-produced rubbish that used to be the staple diet of the Great White Way no longer has any buyers. More and more, serious theatre has a better chance of survival in New York than the theatre of cotton candy. The latter is readily available on television, for nothing, while serious theatre has to be bought with love and money.

The great transition of the New York theatre in the past decade can be summed up in four words. The first two are: David Merrick. The second two are: Joseph Papp. They are two of the most famous New York producers of our time. Quite possibly Mr. Merrick has made more money out of the Broadway theatre than any other producer. He has certainly made a great deal more than Mr. Papp. The buccaneering Mr. Merrick was perhaps the last of an always endangered species. He shares with Mr. Papp many qualities: a nose for publicity, especially personal publicity, a flair for the theatre, a zest for the grand style, and a total commitment to, love for, and belief in what he is doing.

But Mr. Merrick is, together with men such as Alexander H. Cohen, one of the last of the old impresarios, whereas Mr. Papp is one of the first of the new impresarios. Mr. Papp is not in the theatre to make a profit. He makes his living from the theatre, but his main objective is not his living but the theatre. He, in brief, is the new knight errant of the institutional theatre.

Joe Papp is typical of the new pattern of the New York theatre. All over New York we have signs of the growing institutional, nonprofit, subsidized theatre. Mr. Papp himself is legion. It is not for nothing that a short time ago *The New Yorker* magazine showed a cartoon of the New York skyline above which was emblazoned the slogan "Joseph Papp Presents . . ."

Certainly Papp does seem to be everywhere with his free Shakespeare in Central Park, his multitheatre complex at the old Astor Library downtown in Lafayette Street, his periodic invasions of Broadway, and, most recently of all, his takeover of the Repertory Theater of Lincoln Center as a stronghold for the young American playwright. But there is also Theodore Mann's Circle in the Square (both downtown and on Broadway), Wynn Handman's The American Place Theatre, the Negro Ensemble Company, Ellen Stewart's La Mama Experimental Theatre Company, the Roundabout Theatre, the Classic Stage Company, the Chelsea Theatre of Brooklyn (this last bidding fair to rival even Joe Papp in prestige), the Circle Theatre, and many other groups Off-Broadway and Off-Off-Broadway.

The very mention of Off-Off-Broadway raises another question that should be answered by those worthies claiming that the New York theatre is dead. Between Thursday and Sunday (because the Off-Off-Broadway theatre typically has a six-performance-a-week schedule and is dark on Monday, Tuesday, and Wednesday), every week in New York there are something like two hundred to two hundred fifty theatres functioning. Some of them are good, some of them are bad, and most of them are mediocre. But the sheer amount of activity is fantastic. London, the next biggest theatre town in the world, has, by a generous estimate, about fifty theatres functioning, and Paris has about thirty-five. The rest of the world is nowhere. You rapidly get down to the dozen or so in Washington, D.C., or Chicago.

The present collection of *Best American Plays* is the seventh in the series begun many years ago by the great Yale Professor of Drama John Gassner and is the second with which I have been associated. I think the selection represents the period fairly enough.

The very title "best play" is rather off-putting. What may be a best play for me may be an insufferable bore to you, and that is a vice that could also be versa. The very idea of "best" is a tricky one, and I idly wonder whether, grammatically, a best play can have a plural. One might have thought that there was only one *best*. But enough of quibbling, this selection is intended as both a personal choice and also as a representative slice of American theatrical life. John Gassner when he started this series was not merely concerned in demonstrating his own taste, which, incidentally, needed no demonstration. Rather, within the wide range of his own predilections, he was trying to give a representative glimpse of the theatre of his time, and in this I have tried, to the best of my ability, to follow Gassner's catholic taste and incisive insight. The aim of this collection, volume by volume, period by period, is not to offer the idiosyncratic taste of any individual but rather to give a generalized and representative picture of the period seen through one individual eye.

As with Gassner before me, I am certain that my own taste has greatly influenced my choice of plays. Nevertheless I have tried, as did my predecessor, to give a conscientious picture of the American theatre at a certain time through its own typical playwrights. The plays you will find here are all children of circumstance. They all represent the trends of the American theatre which I have been attempting to delineate. This selection is different from every other selection because the American theatre is different, and, indeed, America is different.

Of the seventeen plays in this collection only six were products of Broadway. And of these six, a triple bill by the La Mama playwrights Israel Horovitz, Terrence McNally, and Leonard Melfi, or Edward Albee's bleak threnody to death *All Over,* or even Woody Allen's whimsically surrealistic *Play It Again, Sam,* is hardly typically Broadway fare. And those that remain —the elegant musical *1776* by Peter Stone and Sherman Edwards, Arthur Miller's post-Ibsenite *The Price,* and Neil Simon's typically tortured comedy *The Prisoner of Second Avenue* —assuredly represent Broadway at its best.

Mr. Allen is, of course, a delicious maverick—a brilliant dramatic mind, but whether it will ever settle down in the theatre long enough to leave its mark is debatable. One lives in hope, for his humor has a literary bent to it that will never get full satisfaction in movies. Or belles lettres. And he doesn't even understand how television works.

The La Mama trio have all continued to do their own things. They are three very gifted young men. But *1776* was something very different. It was a genre musical that really worked. These are not good days for the musical, our one indigenous theatrical form. But *1776* stood out partly because it was an extremely literate and dramatically thrilling view of our Founding Fathers, and also because musically it was able to place itself outside pop fashion. Musically it could afford the luxury of distance between it and what is currently happening in pop music. It helped.

The other typical Broadway offerings were not all that typical. Arthur Miller's *The Price* and *The Crucible* are probably Mr. Miller's best couple of plays so far. But Mr. Miller, for all his moral fervor, is not likely to leave an imperishable impression on world drama. He is a sound Broadway playwright, but in the post-O'Neill period he is unlikely to match Tennessee Williams (unhappily but understandably not represented in this collection, but he will be in the next) or Edward Albee, or, in a totally different vein, Neil Simon.

Mr. Albee's *All Over,* despite its chilly reception by most of the New York critics and its disastrously short run, will surely be eventually regarded as Albee's finest play to date. It is by a mile the most distinguished play in this collection, and I am delighted to give it some further life. It was a play that was totally misunderstood at its premiere, and this was a premiere that may well be the final denunciation of Broadway as a serious arena for brand-new plays of moment.

All Over had a downbeat theme—death is not the lightest of our toys—and Mr. Albee himself seems to have irritated his critics, so that little that he can do is right. He is not especially lovable in his public pronouncements and, like Mr. Miller, he has been particularly tough on critics. Both with Mr. Albee and Mr. Miller such antagonism is understandable. But I have noticed that some critics bear long grudges—and the fact the critics are the ones who are finally judged in the hourglass of dramatic history is no help to the playwright struggling to keep his play going or to find a producer and backers for his next. Posthumous glory is the most useless kind.

Neil Simon is also bad news—particulary bad news—among our self-measured highbrow critics. I think he is one of the finest comic writers we have ever had in the American theatre, and quite possibly the finest. His humor is always rooted in character, and while he is capable of the effortlessly slick, even his slickness has a style to it.

The remainder of the plays have all originated from somewhere other than Broadway, and have either been imported to Broadway, or remained, very happily, where they were. In this period Broadway has become no longer the essential emblem of theatrical success. For the first time, in this period, in drama, if you had it, it did not matter where you placed it. The Broadway mystique was fast disappearing. And with that mystique went a whole concept of what the theatre was primarily about. It was the end of the theatre of entertainment, and the beginning of the theatre of refreshment.

Recently, for the first time, there have been more members of Actors Equity employed outside New York than inside. This is a remarkable tribute to the rise of the regional theatre, or, to give it a happier title, the resident theatre. Theatres all over the country have sprung up and are catering to the new hunger for classic theatre that can be seen everywhere across the United States. These resident theatres are generally concerned with classic plays, from Aristophanes to Wilder, but they do, of course, occasionally present new plays. One of the finest resident theatres in the country is the Arena Stage in Washington, D.C., run by Zelda Fichandler.

Many plays and musicals originally given at Washington's Arena Stage have finally found themselves on Broadway. I am thinking of the musical *Raisin,* based on Lorraine Hansberry's *Raisin in the Sun,* and Michael Weller's *Moonchildren.* I am also thinking of two plays in this collection, Arthur Kopit's *Indians* and Howard Sackler's *The Great White Hope.* Both added much to their respective Broadway seasons, but both began in Washington. This use of the regional theatre as an initial stamping ground will, in my opinion, be seen much of in the future. The advantages for all sides are so obvious.

Some of the remaining plays were quite simply Off-Broadway productions. During this period the old barriers between Broadway and Off-Broadway virtually disappeared. Mart Crowley's record-breaking *Boys in the Band* demonstrated that the commercial differences between Broadway and Off-Broadway had narrowed considerably, and many of the Off-

INTRODUCTION

Broadway plays in this collection would probably have been Broadway plays even a few years earlier.

I am thinking not only of *Boys in the Band* but also of John Guare's *The House of Blue Leaves,* Lanford Wilson's *Lemon Sky,* and Bruce Jay Friedman's *Scuba Duba.* All these plays had the feel of Broadway about them. Both the Crowley and the Friedman were avowedly commercial vehicles, and both made a lot of money. Guare and Wilson are different. They are playwrights indoctrinated into the way of a public theatre service, and they both insist on freedom rather than money. (I am not trying to be rude to the admirable Messrs. Crowley and Friedman, for they too are part of the same new theatre movement that is not overconcerned with financial return. But they have not been groveling among the grass roots like many of the others.)

Most of these people have emerged from the institutional theatre of New York City. This can also be seen very easily in this present selection. David Rabe's marvelously controversial *Sticks and Bones* originated at Joe Papp's Public Theater, as did Robert Montgomery's *Subject to Fits.* Other public theatres have also played their part in this, and I am particularly thinking, in the specific context of the collection, of *Tom Paine* by Paul Foster, a play that originated with the La Mama Experimental Theatre Club, and *Little Murders,* the Jules Feiffer inspired joke, which actually started on Broadway and, after a disastrous fiasco, had to be rescued by one of our comparatively new nonprofit ventures, the Circle in the Square.

Finally there is Lonne Elder's play *Ceremonies in Dark Old Men,* a production by the Negro Ensemble Company, which not only indicates the strength of the nonprofit institutional theatre but also highlights the new importance of the black theatre.

Since the previous collection of plays there have been two important general trends, both foreseen earlier, but not really documented. The first has been the significant rise of the black theatre. Black playwrights have found a new voice. In some instances they have adopted the realistic modes of the 1930s, but in other instances—and this will be seen in the next collection —the black playwright has found a new style and identity. The black playwright is writing in a different way, and this could well turn out to be one of the most exciting aspects of the American theatre in our time.

The other trend is permissiveness in language and, of course, in stage nudity. In the last series we used, with some trepidation, our first four-letter words. But it was a mild experiment. This time obscenities will fall upon the readers like autumn leaves. It reflects the theatre of our time. I personally do not mind this new frankness, while recognizing the rights of people who do. For some reason I recall a Norman Mailer story. In his first novel, *The Naked and the Dead,* Mr. Mailer used one of the most common of what President Nixon has taught us to call an "expletive deleted," by changing it very slightly. Soon after publication he was introduced to a revered society matron. The society matron looked him up and down and said: "Ah, Mr. Mailer. You are the young man who cannot spell 'fuck.' " Well, looking through this book, you will discover that we, and our playwrights, now can.

It has been said that "living well is the best revenge." And in my submission the English-speaking theatre, of which the American theatre is a vital part, is today living very well indeed. I think that in literary and dramatic terms, this is by far the most distinguished collection of American plays we have had the pleasure of printing.

Before people say the theatre is dead, let them defeat this contention. The American theatre has never been healthier, and now, in your own hands, you have part of the living proof.

CLIVE BARNES

BEST AMERICAN PLAYS

Seventh Series 1967-1973

THE GREAT WHITE HOPE

Howard Sackler

For REGINA VASQUEZ BELLO

First presented by Herman Levin at the Alvin Theatre in New York City on October 3, 1968, with the following cast:

JACK JEFFERSON James Earl Jones	MRS. BACHMAN Ruth Gregory
ELEANOR BACHMAN Jane Alexander	MR. DIXON Brooks Rogers
CAP'N DAN George Mathews	PASTOR L. Errol Jaye
DISTRICT ATTORNEY Jon Cypher	RUDY Mel Winkler
TICK Jimmy Pelham	MR. EUBANKS Larry Swanson
FRED George Ebeling	MR. TREACHER David Thomas
SMITTY Peter Masterson	HANDLER Lance Cunard
GOLDIE Lou Gilbert	SIR WILLIAM GRISWOLD Thomas Barbour
CLARA Marlene Warfield	MR. COATES Max Wright
MRS. JEFFERSON Hilda Haynes	MRS. KIMBALL Sheila Coonan
POP WEAVER Eugene R. Wood	MR. FARLOW George Curley
BRADY Gil Rogers	OFFICIAL Bob Horen
ROLLER Edward McNally	KLOSSOWSKI Jon Cypher
BETTOR Joseph Hamer	RAGOSY Marshall Efron
TOUT George Harris II	AFRICAN STUDENT Don Blakely
BLACKFACE Hector Elizondo	JUGGLER Lou Meyer
COLONEL COX Dan Priest	PACO Donald Girard
DEACON Garwood Perkins	GOVERNMENT AGENT Edd K. Gasper
YOUNG NEGRO Woodie King	SIGNATURE RECORDER Yvonne Southerland
BARKER David Connell	THE KID Sean J. Walsh
MR. DONNELLY Michael Prince	CUBAN BOY Luis Espinosa

and Burke Byrnes, Ed Lauter, Philip Lindsay, Jerry Laws, Terrance Phillips, Lawrence Cook, Don Blakely, Dave Brown, Judy Thames, Dolores St. Amand, Verona Barnes, Joanna Featherstone, Thomas Anderson, Richard Pittman, Glory Van Scott, Christine Thomas, Danette Small, Terrence O'Conner, Clark Morgan, and Antonio Fargas

Directed by Edwin Sherin
Scenery by Robin Wagner
Costumes by David Toser
Lighting by John Gleason

SYNOPSIS OF SCENES

ACT ONE.

SCENE ONE. *Parchmont, Ohio: Brady's farm.* SCENE TWO. *San Francisco: A small gym.* SCENE THREE. *Reno: outside the Arena.* SCENE FOUR. *Chicago: a street.* SCENE FIVE. *Chicago: the District Attorney's office.* SCENE SIX. *Beau Rivage, Wisconsin: a cabin.* SCENE SEVEN. *Chicago: Mrs. Jefferson's house.*

ACT TWO.

SCENE ONE. *London: a chamber in the Home Office.* SCENE TWO. *Le Havre: a customs shed.* SCENE THREE. *Paris: Vel d'Hiver arena.* SCENE FOUR. *New York: Pop Weaver's office.* SCENE FIVE. *Berlin: a sidewalk cafe.* SCENE SIX. *Budapest: Cabaret Ragosy.* SCENE SEVEN. *Belgrade: railway station.*

ACT THREE.

SCENE ONE. *Chicago: a street.* SCENE TWO. *New York: Pop Weaver's office.* SCENE THREE. *Juarez: a disused barn.* SCENE FOUR. *United States: A street.* SCENE FIVE. *Havana: Oriente Racetrack.*

TIME: The year preceding the First World War.

*(All lines set in **boldface type** are addressed to the audience.)*

It is either the sign of a rare play or a particularly poor season when any play wins what is known on Broadway as "the triple crown." This is the New York Drama Critics' Award, the Tony Award, and the Pulitzer Prize. During the 1968/69 season this feat was pulled off by Howard Sackler's play *The Great White Hope*. Furthermore its star, James Earl Jones, also received a Tony for the best actor of the year.

The Great White Hope opened on Broadway on October 3, 1968, and closed on January 31, 1970, after 556 performances. The play, and its subsequent motion picture version, made James Earl Jones a star. Yet one of the most important aspects of *The Great White Hope* does not turn up in the record books. The play was produced the season previous to its Broadway premiere in Washington, D.C., at the Arena Stage.

For many years London has been supplying New York with plays—and of course this was a two-way traffic, for American plays were always well received in Britain. However, traditionally, American plays on Broadway started on Broadway. To be sure, they would have an out-of-town opening; they would play, say, New Haven, Philadelphia, Boston, or any of those tryout towns in the eastern states. Then, hopefully with all wrinkles ironed out, the show would finally arrive in New York.

However, the cost of Broadway producing rose and rose and rose. It soon became impossible to take a chance on Broadway, impossible to experiment. Adventurous plays that were produced, such as Peter Weiss's *Marat/Sade* or Peter Nichols's *A Day in the Death of Joe Egg,* all originated in England, while, for the most part, the American writer on Broadway was restricted to musicals, light comedies, or casts with three or four actors.

In *The Great White Hope,* Sackler was aiming at an epic tragedy, and he was using a very large cast, or, at least, large according to the meager standards of contemporary Broadway drama. It would have been inconceivable for any producer to have picked it up and tried it there and then on Broadway. The solution—and it was a new one for the American theatre —was for the play to be produced first by one of the country's resident theatres, in this case the remarkable Arena Stage in Washington. There was no specific intention to bring it to Broadway; however, the audience reaction and the reviews (from both Washington and New York critics) encouraged the producers and backers and thus made it possible for *The Great White Hope* to make the Great White Way.

Howard Sackler was born in New York City in 1929, although he nowadays bases himself and his family in London. He studied in New York and got his BA degree from Brooklyn College in 1950. He has written plays for many years, including a couple of screenplays for Stanley Kubrick. In 1954 he won the Maxwell Anderson Award for his play *Uriel Acosta.* He has also received grants from the Rockefeller and Littauer foundations.

For many years he supported himself as a director—he was responsible, for example, for the 1964 NBC television special *Shakespeare: Soul of an Age*—and he is credited with about two hundred recordings for Caedmon records in Britain. These records run the full range of the dramatic repertory with perhaps particular emphasis on Shakespeare, and, over the years, have featured most of Britain's greatest actors. Mr. Sackler also writes poetry, which has not only been published in such magazines as *The Hudson Review* but has also been collected into a volume called *Want My Shepherd.*

The Great White Hope is based on the story of Jack Johnson, who in 1908 became the first black heavyweight champion of the world. The ironic title describes the white community's quest for a champion who could defeat Johnson and restore the white man's supremacist image of himself. Probably because he did not wish to tie himself down too literally to facts, Mr. Sackler calls his hero Jack Jefferson. For all this, it is, fairly accurately, the rise and fall of Jack Johnson.

The playwright handles his material with considerable skill. The play starts in 1908, soon after Johnson had beaten Tommy Burns in Australia, and takes the story up until 1915 in Havana when Jess Willard won the title back for the whites. The play does sprawl—it would be difficult to construct such a documentary chronicle in a tidier fashion—but Mr. Sackler has a fine eye and ear for drama. The final scene, for example, where Jefferson is beaten with rather more battering finality than Willard ever dealt out to the real Johnson, is a superb example of stagecraft.

Apart from the episodic and occasionally repetitive nature of Jefferson's European experiences, the work's aim is evidently the whitewashing of its hero. He is seen as perhaps a shade too noble, a shade too put upon. It seems possible that the real Johnson, while not so long-suffering, might have been more interesting. Yet Mr. Sackler has written a play that not only makes one ponder the role of the black sports star vis-à-vis the birth of racial tensions, but also provides a superb vehicle for its star.

ACT ONE

SCENE ONE

Brady's farm, in Parchmont, Ohio
Enter BRADY, *the heavyweight champion;*
FRED, *his manager;* CAP'N DAN, *a champion*
of earlier days; SMITTY, *a famous sports-*
writer; several other PRESSMEN *and* PHOTOG-
RAPHERS; *a few* TRAINERS, GOLDIE, *Jack*
Jefferson's manager, in the background.

———

BRADY.
Get Burke, or Kid Foster. Big Bill Brain!
I ain't gonna fight no dinge.
    FRED.
Now, Frank—
    CAP'N DAN.
Listen here to me, Franklin—
    BRADY.
You wouldn't fight one when you had the
    belt!
    CAP'N DAN.
Well, let's say none of them came up to it
    then.
It wasn't that I wouldn't, I didn't have to.
    FRED.
He didn't have to, Frank, but you do.
    BRADY.
In your hat I do! I know what retired means,
and that's what I am. All I have to do
is dip the sheep and pay taxes.
    CAP'N DAN.
Hear that, boys? It's old Farmer Brown!
    FRED.
Sure looks retired, don't he! Look at the
    arms on him.
    PRESSMAN 1.
Three months back on the mill, that's all you
    need—
    SMITTY.
How long is it you put away Stankiewiez—
    FRED.
Not even a year! And if you smoked him in
    seven—
    TRAINER 1.
You'll get this one in five—
    PRESSMAN 2.
Four!
    FRED.
Two!
They got glass jaws, right, Cap'n Dan?
    BRADY.
I ain't gonna fight no dinge.

    CAP'N DAN.
Now, Franklin,
when you retired with that gold belt last sum-
    mer,
nobody thought it would work out like this.
Everybody just thought that Sweeney'd fight
    Woods,
and whoever won that would be the new
    Number One, right?
So when the nigger asked could he fight
    Woods first
we figured, what the hell, it'll keep up the
    interest—
nobody, least of all Woods, thought he would
    lick him.
And then when he said he wants to try out
    Sweeney too,
why, Sweeney never puts the gloves on with
    a nigger,
everybody knew that—besides, he was in
    Australia.
Nobody thought the nigger would go all that
    way to him,
and even when he did, who would have
    thought
he could needle old Tommy into taking him
    on?
    SMITTY.
I was down in Melbourne for the paper, Mr.
    Brady,
and let me tell you,
no paper here could print how bad it really
    was.
He'd say, Hit me now, Tommy, and then he'd
    let him,
grinning all the time, and then cuffing him,
    jabbing him,
making smart-ass remarks to the crowd—
    wouldn't
be a man and just knock him out, no,
and then, when they stopped it,
with Tommy there bleeding,
he's still got that big banjo smile on him—
    Jesus.
    PRESSMAN 1.
You're the White Hope, Mr. Brady!
    BRADY.
I'm the what?
    PRESSMAN 2.
The White Hope!
Every paper in the country is calling you that.
    FRED.
Frank, he lands in San Francisco tomorrow
    —come on!
    BRADY (*to* CAP'N DAN).
Honest, I don't like this any more than you
    do.

CAP'N DAN.
How're you going to like it
when he claims the belt's his because you
    won't fight him.
The heavyweight belt, son, yours and mine,
he can say it's his.

SMITTY.
Just grin and put it on.

CAP'N DAN.
How're you going to like it when the whole
    damn country
says Brady let us down, he wouldn't stick a
    fist out
to teach a loudmouth nigger, stayed home
    and let him
be Champion of the World.

SMITTY.
Don't do it, Mr. Brady.

BRADY.
I'll tell you the truth, Cap'n Dan. I hate to say
    it,
but I feel too old. **I mean it, that's the truth.**

FRED.
The doc says different and I do too—

TRAINER 1.
**He's thinkin old because he's worried what to
    do—**

BRADY.
Shut up. Cap'n Dan, you know what I mean.

CAP'N DAN.
I know you trust me and I say you're up to
    it—
and, Franklin, God Almighty hates a quitter!
Listen here, I'll confess something to you,
I had this lots of times when I was your age,
every time I had a fight or a birthday.

BRADY.
How'd you get rid of it?

CAP'N DAN.
The one way there is:
plenty of heat and nice deep massage.
Now, Frank, go inside. Mrs. Brady wants to
    show you
a letter I brought for you. I paid a call in
    Washington
on my way out here, and even though I think
it'll make you so big-headed you won't be fit
    to talk to,
you read it, then come out here and we'll see
    where we stand.
    (*Exit* BRADY; GOLDIE *comes forward.*)

GOLDIE.
Good, so it's fixed?

CAP'N DAN.
Somebody say something?

GOLDIE.
Me. I'm asking, Is it settled please, gentle-
    men?
You tell me Yes I can maybe catch the train.

CAP'N DAN.
The man's in a hurry, Fred.

FRED.
What about terms?

GOLDIE.
What, you expect I'm gonna yell about
    terms?
Look, we're no babies here, you know like I
    know,
my Jackie would fight it for a nickel, tomor-
    row.
But it wouldn't look nice for you to take ad-
    vantage,
so you'll offer me low as you can get away
    with
and I'll say OK.

FRED.
Eighty-twenty, Goldie.

GOLDIE.
What! A world's championship? You can't go
    twenty-five?

FRED.
Eighty-twenty. That's it.

GOLDIE.
Well . . . God bless America.

FRED.
And Cap'n Dan to be the referee.

GOLDIE.
Fred, you're kidding me?

FRED.
Him or forget it. You know how it works.

GOLDIE.
I don't mean no disrespect, but—

CAP'N DAN.
Who'd you have in mind, friend, Booker T.
    Washington?

GOLDIE.
All right, all right. Boy! What else?

FRED.
That's all.

GOLDIE.
He don't have to fight with his feet tied
    together?

FRED.
I said that's all.

CAP'N DAN.
We better set the place.

GOLDIE.
Any place, name it, the Coast, Chicago—

CAP'N DAN.
No big towns, Fred. You'll have every nigger
and his brother jamming in there.

GOLDIE.
For my money they could have it in Iceland!
SMITTY.
How about Tulsa?
Denver? Reno?
PHOTOGRAPHER 1.
Hey, Reno, that's OK!
PRESSMAN 1.
Small.
FRED.
No—wait—
TRAINER 2.
Reno—
CAP'N DAN.
Why not? The good old Rockies.
FRED.
Yeah—
CAP'N DAN.
A white man's country!
GOLDIE.
Sure, but you can find them?
FRED.
They'll come from all over, it's on the main
line now—
SMITTY.
And it's high and dry. Mr. Brady would like
that—
TRAINER 2.
The drier the better!
If that nigger gets a sweat up, one good whiff
and Frank'll be finished.
(Enter BRADY *carrying the gold belt)*
BRADY.
Well, he's not through yet!
CAP'N DAN.
There we are—
BRADY.
Want some photos, boys?
PHOTOGRAPHER 1.
Sure thing, Mr. Brady—
PHOTOGRAPHER 2.
With it on, OK?
*(*PHOTOGRAPHERS *set up cameras.* PRESS-
MEN *ready notebooks.)*
GOLDIE.
A deal?
FRED.
It's a deal.
*(*FRED *and* GOLDIE *shake hands.)*
BRADY.
And it's gonna be a pleasure—
tell your nigger I said so!
PRESSMAN 1.
Pour it on, Mr. Brady—
GOLDIE.
I should miss a train for this?

BRADY *(rolling up his sleeves).*
You tell Mr. Black Boy to give me that smile
when he's inside those ropes—
TRAINER 1 *(to* PRESSMEN).
Get it down, get it down—
BRADY.
I'll appreciate it, tell him—
**my eyes ain't too good these days, you under-
stand,**
I like something nice and shiny to aim at—
(Puts on belt)
OK, boys?
PRESSMAN 1.
Ah!
PHOTOGRAPHER 2.
Stance, please, Mr. Brady—
*(*BRADY *takes stance;* PHOTOGRAPHERS'
magnesium flares till end of scene)
FRED *(leading* GOLDIE *off).*
Don't let your boy take this nigger stuff to
heart, huh?
Explain how it's going to pack em in, that's
all.
GOLDIE.
He knows how it is. Good luck!
(Exits)
FRED *(calling after him).*
You're OK, Goldie!
SMITTY *(to* CAP'N DAN, *looking at* BRADY).
Well, there we are!
CAP'N DAN.
Oh, he's the man all right.
I just don't like the idea of calling it a Hope,
I wish you boys hadn't hung that tag on him.
SMITTY.
It's sure caught on, though!
CAP'N DAN.
That's what bothers me, I guess.
SMITTY.
Can I quote you on that?
CAP'N DAN.
No, lend me a comb.
**I better go stand up with him and get my
picture took!**
(Laughter and BLACKOUT. *Thudding of a
punching bag, then* LIGHTS UP *on—)*

SCENE TWO

A small gym, San Francisco
JACK JEFFERSON *shadow-boxing.* TICK, *his
Negro trainer.* ELEANOR BACHMAN, *a white
girl, watching.*

TICK.

Mix it up, Jack honey, pace him, pace him
out,

hands up higher now, move, he's jabbin—

don't follow them head fakes, you watch his
body,

there you go, jab! jab! Beauty—

fake with the body, not just the head, baby—

feint! jab! hook in behind it—

send him the right now—no! Whut you at?

JACK (continuing his movements).

Givin him a right—

TICK.

An where you givin it?

JACK.

Chin bone—

TICK.

Sucker bone! Boy, you a worry!

He groggy now, right, you jabbin his liver

till he runnin outa gas an his eyes goin
fishy—

Why you knock on dat chin! Could be ya
done whut!

JACK.

Wake him up, wake him up—

TICK.

Watch him! He's bobbin, he's comin to you,
block it—

where you gonna take dat right now?

JACK.

Temple—

TICK.

How!

JACK.

Hook it, hook to de temple—

TICK.

Why!

JACK.

Softes place on his head—

TICK.

Yeah! now you listenin to me, sugar!

Hook him again, a beauty, three now—

(JACK stops.)

Hey, whut you doin—

JACK (to ELEANOR).

Now, honey, you juss know you tired a sittin
here,

whyn't you go buy yourself a pretty or somethin—

ELLIE.

No, let me stay. Unless you mind me here,
Jack.

JACK.

You mah Lady Luck! I don' mine you nowhere—

TICK.

**Oh, long as you lookin at him, he don'
mine—**

JACK.

But ain't this too much roughhouse for ya,
honey?

ELLIE.

Well—I try not to listen.

TICK.

Much obliged!

ELLIE.

Oh, Tick, I'm sorry—

JACK.

She somethin, ain't she!

TICK.

Darlin, you keep sittin there any way you like
it, cause he sure workin happy. OK?

ELLIE.

OK!

TICK (to JACK).

Now, we gonna mooch or we gonna move?

JACK (moves).

Hole me dat bag! **Gonna buss it wide open,
then we all go out an have a champagne
lunch!**

(Enter GOLDIE)

GOLDIE.

Four soft-boiled eggs, that's what you're
gonna have—

(He does not notice ELLIE.)

JACK.

Hey, Goldie!

TICK.

How you doin, boss—

GOLDIE.

Oy, those stairs—

JACK.

Get him a chair, Tick—

GOLDIE.

Cover him up first he shouldn't get ice on
him.

JACK.

Figured you stayin in Reno till tomorrow—

GOLDIE.

What, we got it settled there—how do you
feel?

TICK (puts robe on JACK).

He feel like he look, boss!

GOLDIE.

Not eating too quick?

TICK.

No, sir, chewin good!

JACK.

Ah's chewin till it hurts—

GOLDIE.
Laugh, laugh!
This one you have to watch like a hawkeye!
JACK.
Come on, Goldie, when it gonna be?
GOLDIE.
The Fourth of July. Now the newspaper
    guys—
JACK *(laughing)*.
The Fourth of July?
GOLDIE.
So, it makes a difference?
JACK.
No, it juss tickle mah funny-bone, dassall—
TICK.
Fourth a July and Lawd you knows why!
GOLDIE.
We should worry, listen, will we have a gate
    there—
fifteen thousand! Jack, you know what
    they're callin it?
Already by them it's the Fight of the Cen-
    tury—
twenty years I never seen such a hoopla!
Trains from St. Louis and Chicago, direct
    yet,
tents they have to put up, it's a regular mad-
    house,
and wait, from the ring they're gonna tele-
    graph it, Jack,
straight to every Western Union in the coun-
    try,
so like right away everybody should know,
and on that we make somethin too!
TICK.
Lively times, Ah kin hear you comin!
Boy, you bout to win de Fight of de Century!
JACK.
Yeah, or else lose an be the nigger of the
    minute.
GOLDIE *(noticing* ELLIE*)*.
Listen, come here, Jack—
JACK.
Whut kina odds goin?
GOLDIE.
Brady eight to five. What's the girl doin here?
JACK.
Oh, she looking roun. She don't bother us
    none.
GOLDIE.
Lookin around for what?
JACK.
You be nice now, Goldie—come on over, El-
    lie,
don't be shy now, hon—she a friend of mine,
    you know?

GOLDIE.
Jackie, you gotta bring a girl here when you
    train?
JACK.
Ah guess so, boss!
Ah loves to dance an prance fo de wimmins!
ELLIE.
How do you do.
JACK.
Goldie, shake hands
with Miss Ellie Bachman.
GOLDIE.
Pleased to meetcha, Miss Bachman.
I apologize I didn't notice you before,
such a tumult we got here.
ELLIE.
Oh, sure, I understand.
GOLDIE.
You're a fan of Jack's huh?
JACK.
Ellie was on the same boat from Australia,
she was visitin down there.
GOLDIE.
Well, it's great to be home again, I bet.
You can't beat Frisco!
ELLIE.
Yes, I like it fine.
My home is in Tacoma, though.
GOLDIE.
Oh . . . it's awful damp up there, ain't it?
JACK
Mm-hmm! You know it!
ELLIE.
Yes, I can't say I miss it much.
(Pause)
TICK.
Uncle of mine work up dere in a laundry
    once,
he din like it neither . . .
JACK.
Drizzle on you all the time there!
TICK.
Right!
GOLDIE.
Yeah, well, Mis Bachman,
the guys from the papers are comin any mi-
    nute,
you know what I mean, so if maybe you ex-
    cuse us—
JACK.
She stay where she is.
TICK.
Uh-oh.
GOLDIE.
Jackie, look, what's the matter with you!
JACK.
She stayin where she is.

GOLDIE.

I'm gonna pass out here!

ELLIE.

I'll wait in the room, Jack.

GOLDIE.

In the room! Jesus Christ!

JACK.

You be nice now, hear?

GOLDIE.

I knew it!

Last night in my head it's like a voice—

Dumbbell, go home quick, somethin's goin on
with him!

JACK.

Ain't nobody's business!

GOLDIE.

Grow up, for God's sake—

ELLIE.

Let me go, it doesn't matter—

GOLDIE.

No—please, one second—Tick, go lock the
door.

(TICK *does)*

(To JACK)

So you don't know the score, huh?

Well, I'll tell you the score, right now I'll tell
you.

And you should listen too, miss,

I can see you're a fine serious girl, not a bum,

better you should know, so there's no hard
feelins here.

First, Jack, they hate your guts a little bit—
OK!

You don't put on gloves everybody should
like you.

Then they hate your guts some more—still
OK!

That makes you wanna fight, some kinda pep
it give you.

And then they hate you so much they're
payin through the nose

to see a white boy maybe knock you on your
can—

well, that's more than OK, cash in, after all,

it's so nice to be colored you shouldn't have
a bonus?

But, sonny, when they start in to hate you
more than that,

you gotta watch out. And that means now—

Oh, I got ears, I get told things—

guys who want to put dope into your food
there,

a guy who wants to watch the fight behind a
rifle.

OK, cops we'll get, dogs, that we can handle.

But this on top of it, a white girl, Jack,

what, do I have to spell it on the wall for you,

you wanna drive them crazy, you don't hear
what happens—

JACK.

Whut Ah s'pose to do!

Stash her in a iddy biddy hole someplace in
niggertown

and go sneakin over there twelve o'clock at
night,

carry her roun with me inside a box

like a pet bunny-rabbit or somethin—

ELLIE.

Jack—

JACK.

Or maybe she juss put black on her face,

and puff her mouth up, so's nobody notice

Ah took nothin from em—

(Knock at door)

Let 'em wait!

You know Ah done fool roun plenny, Goldie,

she know it too, she know it all,

but Ah ain't foolin roun now, unnerstand—

(Points to TICK)

an if he say, "Thass whut you said lass time,"

Ah bust his nappy head—

TICK.

I ain't sayin nothin!

(More knocking)

GOLDIE.

Hold on, I'm comin—

Jack, I swear, I'll help you,

just you shouldn't throw it in their face, Jack,

I'm beggin you—

JACK.

See? This whut you fell inta, darlin.

ELLIE.

Do what he says.

JACK.

You go along with him?

ELLIE.

Along with you, any way I can.

(More knocking)

GOLDIE.

Go, sit over there—let em in, for Chrissake—

*(*TICK *admits* SMITTY *and several other*
PRESSMEN)

TICK.

Mornin, gents—

JACK.

Hiya, fellers—Hey there, Smitty—

(Handshaking and greeting)

GOLDIE.

Just a few minutes, fellers, OK?

PRESSMAN 1.

Well, you're sure looking good, Jack.

JACK.

Thanks, boss!

PRESSMAN 2.

Guess you know about the Fourth—

PRESSMAN 1.

You starting to get jumpy?

JACK.

Yeah, Ah scared Brady gonna change his mind!

SMITTY.

Still think you can take him, Jack?

JACK.

Well, Ah ain't sain Ah kin take him straight off—

an, anyway, dat be kina mean, you know,

alla dem people, big holiday fight—

how dey gonna feel Ah send em home early?

SMITTY.

So your only worry is deciding which round.

JACK.

Yeah, an dat take some thinkin, man!

If Ah lets it go too long in dere,

juss sorta blockin an keepin him offa me,

then evvybody say, "Now ain't dat one shif'-less nigger,

why dey always so lazy?" An if Ah chop him down quick,

third or fourth roun, all at once then dey holler,

"No t'ain't fair,

dat po' man up dere fightin a gorilla!"

But Ah gonna work it out.

PRESSMAN 2.

What about that yellow streak Brady talks about?

JACK *(undoing his robe).*

Yeah, you wanna see it?

GOLDIE.

Don't clown aroun, Jackie—

PRESSMAN 3.

Any idea, Jack, why you smile when you're fighting?

JACK.

Well, you know, Ah am a happy person.

Ah always feel good, huh? An when Ah'm fightin

Ah feels double good. So whut Ah wanna put a face on for? An you know,

it's a sport, right, like a game,

so Ah like whoever Ah'm hittin to see

Ah'm still his friend.

PRESSMAN 2.

Going to train in Chicago, Mr. Jefferson?

JACK.

Yeah, Ah wanna see my little ole momma—

PRESSMAN 1.

Fried chicken, Jack?

JACK.

Mmm-mmh! Can't wait!

SMITTY.

I believe that's Miss Bachman there, isn't it, Jack?

You first met on the boat?

ELLIE.

No, not exactly—

GOLDIE.

Miss Bachman is my secretary, we hired her in Australia,

she's from here, but she was over there and we, you know,

we hired her and she came over with the boys.

SMITTY.

I see—

TICK.

Boss, if dey finish Ah wanna rub him down—

PRESSMAN 1.

We got plenty for now, Jack—

PRESSMAN 3.

Thanks—

JACK.

Come again!

PRESSMAN 2.

Jack, one more question?

JACK.

Yeah, go head.

PRESSMAN 2.

You're the first black man in the history of the ring

to get a crack at the heavyweight title.

Now the white folks, of course, are behind the White Hope,

Brady's the redeemer of the race, and so on.

But you, Jack Jefferson, are you the Black Hope?

JACK.

Well, Ah'm black and Ah'm hopin.

SMITTY.

Try and answer him straight, Jack.

JACK.

Oh, Ah guess mah cousins mostly want me to win.

SMITTY.

You imply that some don't?

JACK.

Maybe some a them reckon

they gonna pay a little high for that belt, if Ah take it.

SMITTY.

Won't you try and change their minds, Jack, get them all behind you?

JACK.
Man, Ah ain't runnin for Congress!
Ah ain't fightin for no race, ain't redeemin
    nobody!
My momma tole me Mr. Lincoln done
    that—
ain't that why you shot him?
    (General laughter. CLARA, *a Negro woman,*
bursts in)
    CLARA.
My, oh my!
It de big black rooster and de little red hen!
I got you, you mother!
    JACK.
What you want here!
    CLARA.
I show you what I wants—
    (Goes for ELLIE*)*
    ELLIE.
Jack!
    JACK.
Hey!
    TICK *(restrains* CLARA*).*
You crazy, you bitch—?
    GOLDIE.
A little family quarrel, fellers, see you tomor-
    row, you know how it is—
    *(*THEY *remain.)*
    CLARA.
You leave my man be, girl, you don' leave
    him,
Ah gonna throw you at him in chunks—
    GOLDIE.
You got it all wrong, Clara—
    CLARA.
Yeah? Ah gots it
from de chambermaid at the Park Royal Ho-
    tel,
Ah come all de way from Chicago to got it—
    JACK.
Now you got it you git you black ass outa
    here.
    CLARA.
Don' hit me!
    JACK.
Whut you tyin on, you evil chinch, you!
    GOLDIE.
Jack—fellers—
    CLARA.
Sing it, daddy!
Let de gennumuns hear
how you smirchin your wife—
    GOLDIE.
What do you mean?
    JACK.
She ain't no wife of mine—

    CLARA.
No which of what?
We's common law and Ah's comin home to
    poppa!
    JACK.
Ah's common nothin! Don't you poppa me,
    girl,
or Ah poppa you so you never forget it!
Ah quit on you when you cleared out a De-
    troit
wid Willie de pimp—
    GOLDIE.
Fellers, please, have a heart—Jack—
    CLARA.
Ah know you come after me, Ah know you
    was lookin—
    JACK.
You lucky Ah too busy to fine you, girl,
selling off mah clothes, mah ring, silver
    brushes—
    CLARA.
Gimme nother chance, baby, Ah misses you
    awful—
    JACK.
Don' come on with me! You juss smelling
    bread,
you comin here now cause you Willie's in
    jail—
    CLARA.
How you know where he at!
    JACK.
Ah from de jungle like you is, baby,
Ah hears de drums—
    (To TICK*)*
take her over to Goldie's, give her a twenty
    an carfare back.
    TICK.
Come on, Clara.
    JACK.
Ah tellin you once more, go way and stay
    there.
    CLARA.
You ain't closin up the book so easy,
    daddy—
    (To ELLIE*)*
hear me, Gray Meat? Get it while you can!
    TICK.
Come on, out—
    (Drags her out)
    JACK *(to* ELLIE*).*
You all right, honey?
    GOLDIE.
Fellers, now I'm askin you, man to man,
    please,
for everybody's good, don't write nothin

about it,
if it gets out, God knows what can happen—
I mean, look,
we wanna have a fight, don't we? And besides
the girl has a family, what the hell—
(Pause)

PRESSMAN 3.

OK.

PRESSMAN 1.

Don't worry, Goldie.

GOLDIE.

Thanks, fellers, thanks—let's all have a
    drink—
(Hustles THEM *out;* JACK *has begun punching the bag)*

ELLIE.

Oh, Jack! It gets awful, doesn't it.

JACK.

Well . . .
seems to get worse and better both at once.

ELLIE.

Is there anything I can do?

JACK.

Yeah . . .
Stick around. An don' never call me daddy.
*(*BLACKOUT*—sound of fireworks and band music*—LIGHTS UP *on*—)*

SCENE THREE

Outside the arena, Reno
Across the stage a banner: RENO THE HUB
OF THE UNIVERSE. *Many small American
flags in evidence. Stage milling with* WHITE
MEN *of every sort: at the center a huge crap
game, at the rear a* BLACKFACE *performer
entertaining another* GROUP, *at one side a few
MEN breaking up a fight, at the other a* MAN
supporting a singing DRUNK, *in the foreground a* BETTOR *with a fistful of money looking for a* TOUT.

———

ROLLER.

Ooh, six, get ready, baby from Baltimore—

PLAYER 1.

Shoot em—

TOUT *(to* BETTOR*).*

Sure, how much you bettin—

PLAYER 2.

Boxcars!

PLAYER 1.

Let it ride—

BETTOR.

Ninety simoleons—

TOUT.

Ninety on Brady at eight to five—

BETTOR.

Eight—?

ROLLER.

In or out—

BETTOR.

Up yours eight, mister, they're giving eleven,
they're givin thirteen—

ROLLER.

Who's in, who's in, who's—

BLACKFACE *(bursting in on the crap game).*

Yassuh, yassuh, yassuh—

PLAYER 1.

Hey, look who's here—

BLACKFACE.

Move ovah, bredren, ole Doctuh Wishbone
gwine ta roll dem cubicles—
Uh oh! **Lonesome pockets!**
Kin ah come in wiv a chicken laig, boss?
(Flourishes one. Laughter)

PLAYER 3.

Where's the white meat, Wishbone—

BLACKFACE.

White meat? Oh, he puttin on de belt now—
an dark meat, he shakin in de graby!
(Laughter, jeers. THEY *all gather round.)*
**Lawd, Ah sho hopes dey's mo cullud folks
    den me here—**

ROLLER.

Why's that, Wishbone—

BLACKFACE.

Ah cain't bury all dat nigger bah mahself!
(Laughter)
Gwine ta read de sermon ovuh him, dassall—

BETTOR.

Let's hear it!

BLACKFACE.

"Bredren," it start, "kinely pass de plate"—
    no, dat ain it—
(Laughter)
"Bredren," it start, "come outer dem bushes"
    —no, tain't dat neether—
(Laughter)
"Bredren"—here de one—"de tex for dis po'
    darkie
am foun in de Book ob"—well it roun bout
    de place
where Paul git off de steamboat. "Bredren,"
    it say,
"bressed am dey dat lays down, **cause if dey
    ain gittin up
dey mought jes's well stays down"**—
(Laughter, cheers, SOMEONE *throws him a
tambourine,* HE *sings)*
    Ole Marse Brady ship cullud Jack
    Come fum way down Souf,
    Hair curl on his haid so tight
    He coulden shet his mouf—

(THEY all join in)
Coon, coon, coon, ah wish mah culluh'd fade,
   Coon, coon, coon, Lawd, make me a brahter shade—
   (Enter COLONEL COX *with some* NEVADA RANGERS*)*
COX.
All right, all right, stay where you are—
PLAYER 1.
What the hell, Colonel—
PLAYER 2.
Just having some fun—
COX.
Boys, I got orders to confiscate all firearms—
(Protests)
We'll give em back tonight, after it's over—
RANGER 1 *(collecting weapons).*
Let's go—
RANGER 2.
Thank you!
RANGER 1.
Say, that's a real old one—
PLAYER 1 *(as band strikes up nearby).*
What you fraid of, Colonel, we won't have to shoot him!
BETTOR.
They're comin for the weigh-in!
(Cheering nearby)
COX *(to* BLACKFACE*).*
You'd better scram, Mike.
BLACKFACE.
Sure thing, Colonel—
   (Runs off; more cheering; a scale is wheeled on)
PLAYER 1 *(looks offstage).*
That's Brady's bus—here he comes—
   *(*MUSIC *changes to "Oh, You Beautiful Doll")*
ROLLER.
Whack that nigger, Frank—
PLAYER 2.
You fix him for us—
PLAYER 1.
Wipe that smile off him, boy—
   *(*THEY *all cheer as* BRADY, *in a robe and with his hands taped, scowling, enters with* CAP'N DAN, FRED, *and entourage:* HANDLERS, PRESS, *etc.* HE *gets on the scale. Music stops.)*
BRADY.
Come on, it's hot as hell here. Let's go.
PRESSMAN 1.
What did you have for lunch, Mr. Brady?
(Laughter)
BRADY.
Nothin! A cuppa tea!

FRED.
We'll get a statement in a minute, boys—
CAP'N DAN.
Take it easy, Franklin—
WEIGHER-IN.
Two hundred and four.
   (Cheers. HE *steps off the scale, takes out a paper. Silence)*
BRADY.
When I put on the gloves now and defend this here belt
it's the request of the public, which forced me out of retirement.
But I wanta assure them I'm fit to do my best,
and I don't think I'm gonna disappoint nobody.
   (Applause: JACK *enters with* GOLDIE *and* TICK: *Silence)*
JACK.
How come they's no music when I comes in?
CAP'N DAN.
How do you do, Mr. Jefferson. As you know, of course,
I am your referee.
JACK.
Cap'n Dan, it's a honor.
Ah'm proud to shake the han whut shook the han of the Prince of Wales.
ROLLER.
Don't take that lip from him!
(General "Ssh")
Come on, boog, I'll get it over with right—
(General hubbub)
GOLDIE.
Colonel—
COX.
Quiet down there!
BRADY.
Get him on the scale, willya.
JACK *(stepping on).*
Hey, Frank, how you doin?
   *(*BRADY *turns away, muttering.)*
Look like Frank bout ta walk de plank!
WEIGHER-IN.
One hundred ninety-one.
GOLDIE.
Brady?
WEIGHER-IN.
Two hundred and four.
TICK.
OK, Jack, get down—
JACK.
Hey, Frank, you believe that?
This man here saying Ah lighter then you!
BRADY.
Yeah, very funny.

CAP'N DAN.
Just your statement, please.
JACK.
Huh, Oh, sure.
Ah thank Mr. Brady here for bein such a
    sport,
givin me a shot at the belt today.
They's been plenty a mean talk roun—
    (Jeers)
COX.
Quiet, there—
JACK.
But here we is,
an Ah glad it come down to a plain ole scuffle.
*(A few handclaps at the rear of the crowd,
which parts to reveal a group of Negroes there)*
Mercy me, it's de chillun of Isrel—Hey,
    there, homefolks!
BRADY.
Come on, let's clear out of here—
FRED.
Right—
BRADY.
Keep rootin, boys—
CROWD.
All behind you, Frank—
Kill the coon—
Tear him apart, Frank—
Find that yellow streak—
(The BAND *strikes up "Hot Time in the Old
Town Tonight" as it follows, cheering after*
BRADY *and his entourage,* PRESSMEN *and*
RANGERS *behind them.* GOLDIE *and* TICK *re-
main.* JACK *approaches the* GROUP OF
NEGROES. *Music and cheering gradually
recede.)*
JACK.
Well, how you all today!
DEACON.
Gonna be prayin fo you here, Mr. Jefferson.
JACK.
Couldn't get no tickets, huh.
TICK.
Bess dey don' go in dere, Jack.
JACK.
Yeah, maybe so.
DEACON.
That don' matter none. We juss come to pray
you gonna win for us, son.
JACK.
Well, if "us" mean any you wid cash ridin on
    me,
you prayers gonna pay off roun about the
    fifth.
YOUNG NEGRO.
No, Mr. Jefferson. He mean win fo us cullud.

JACK.
Oh, that what you prayin!
DEACON.
May the good Lawd be guidin your hand for
    us, son!
ALL NEGROES.
Amen, amen.
JACK.
An you traipse all this way here to pray it,
    my, my.
YOUNG NEGRO.
What the Revren mean to signify—
JACK.
I know what he signify. I big but I ain dumb,
    hear?
YOUNG NEGRO.
What you salty wif me for—
DEACON.
We folks just want you to preciate—
JACK *(to* YOUNG NEGRO*).*
Hey, man. What my winnin gonna do for
    you!
YOUNG NEGRO.
Huh? Oh . . . er . . .
DEACON.
Give him self-respeck, that's what!
ALL NEGROES.
Amen!
NEGRO 1.
Tell it, brother!
YOUNG NEGRO.
Yeah—Ah be proud to be a cullud man to-
    morrow!
NEGROES *(general response).*
Amen, that's it.
JACK.
Uh huh.
Well, country boy, if you ain't there already,
all the boxin and nigger-prayin in the world
ain't gonna get you there—
TICK.
Jack, let's go—
DEACON.
You look cullud, son, but you ain't thinkin
    cullud.
JACK.
Oh, Ah thinkin cullud, cullud and then cul-
    lud,
Ah so busy think cullud Ah can't see nothin
    else sometime,
but Ah ain't think cullud-us, like you!
An when you come on wid it, you know what
    Ah see, man?
That ole cullud-us? Juss a basketfulla crabs!
Crabs in a basket—

DEACON.
God send you light, son—

GOLDIE.
Time to go, Jack—

JACK.
Tell me you prayin here! An speck Ah gonna
say
Oh, thankya, Revren! You ain't prayin for
me!
("Star Spangled Banner" in the distance)
It ain't, Lawd, don' let that peck break his
nose,
or, Lawd, let him git outa town and not git
shot at—
Ah ain nothin in it but a ugly black fiss here!
They don' even push on in to see it workin!
(COLONEL COX reenters)

COX.
All set, Jefferson?

JACK (to the NEGROES).
Lay your bets, boys, you still got time.
(HE follows the COLONEL out, GOLDIE and
TICK behind him. Lights begin to fade
very gradually.)

DEACON.
Lawd, when the smoke of the battle clear
away here,
may this good strong man be standin up in
victry.
May them who keep shovin all us people
down
see they can't do it all the time, and take a
lesson.
And may us have this livin man today to
show us
the sperrit of Joshua. Give this to us, Lawd,
we needs it, and give him light to understand
why.
(The anthem ends and a wolfish cry is heard
from the CROWD in the stadium)

NEGRO BOY.
Revren—

DEACON.
Don' worry, boy. We be all right out here.
(THEY move back, singing, as the roar in-
creases and the stage darkens)

NEGROES.
(singing unseen)
It's so high you can't get over it,
It's so low you can't get under it,
It's so wide you can't get around it,
You must come through by the living gate.
(The roar reaches a crescendo, suddenly—
dies out . . . BLACKOUT.
(A match lit upstage: CAP'N DAN in shirt

sleeves and braces, lighting a cigar)
CAP'N DAN (speaking over his shoulder).
They better throw away half those pictures
they took
They'll be worse than the fight . . .
(Comes forward)

I really have the feeling
it's the biggest calamity to hit this country
since the San Francisco earthquake—no, I'm
serious.
That one at least was only in Frisco.
What kind of calamity? Hard to say it, exactly.
Oh, I don't think all the darkies'll go crazy,
try to take us over, rape and all that.
Be some trouble, yes, but it can be managed—
after all, only one of em's a heavyweight
champ . . .
But that's it, I suppose. He is! I hold his hand
up,
and suddenly a nigger is Champion of the
World!
Now you'll say, Oh, that's only your title in
sports—
no, it's more. Admit it. And more than if one
got to be
world's best engineer, or smartest politician,
or number one opera singer, or world's biggest genius
at making things from peanuts. No calamity
there.
But Heavyweight Champion of the World,
well,
it feels like the world's got a shadow across
it.
Everything's—no joke intended—kind of
darker,
and different, like it's shrinking, it's all
huddled down somehow, and you with it, you
want to holler
What's he doin up there,
but you can't because you know . . . that
shadow's on you,
and you feel that smile . . .
Well, so what do we do!
Wet our pants, cry in our beer about it?
No, sir, I'll tell you what we do,
we beat those bushes for another White
Hope,
and if he's no good we find another White
Hope,
we'll find them and we'll boost them up till
one stays—
what the hell is this country, Ethiopia?

(BLACKOUT: music—"Sweet Georgia
Brown." LIGHTS UP immediately on—)

SCENE FOUR

A street, Chicago
Dressed-up NEGROES, *more arriving, great animation; some carry small American flags;* BARKER *among them with megaphone.* BAND *playing on stage before an enormous baroque doorway, over which is spelled* CAFE DE CHAMPION *in lights;* MAN *on ladder installing the last few bulbs,* ANOTHER *distributing yellow handbills.*

———

BARKER *(through megaphone).*
Every Chicago man, woman, and chile,
you all invited, tan, pink, black, yellow,
and beginner brown, get along down,
let's shake the han of the best in the lan
in his fine new place here, celebrate the open-
in,
come in you vehicle, come on you foot,
don' bring money, just be here—
(Auto horns and cheering offstage, then on. JACK *enters at the wheel of an open white touring-car,* ELLIE *at his side,* TICK *and* GOLDIE *in the rear. A group of* POLICEMEN *entering with them begins pushing back the* CROWD.*)*
JACK.
Hey—hey—they all right, Mistah Offisah,
leave them cullud come on—
(Cheers as he dismounts and they mill around him, some with flowers)
NEGROES.
God bless you, Jack—
Ah name mah
    baby aftuh you—
Member me, Jack?
Ah wish dey
    wuz ten dozen—
Reach me that han out—
(The CLARINETIST *aims an arpeggio at the backs of the retreating* POLICE: *laughter)*
JACK *(his arms full of flowers).*
Say . . . lookie here, thank you . . . thank you . . . oh my! . . .
look like Rest in Peace, don't it!
(Laughter)
Well, Ah am all rested up, an like you kin see
Ah bout to make Chicago mah real home sweet home now—
(Cheers)
thass right, permint. Ah don' guess
Ah'll be needin to chase aroun fo work awhile—
(Laughter)
an Ah got this joint fix up so's Ah kin visit with mah frens
an git rich both at once—
(Laughter, jeers)

But wait till you see INside—
NEGRO MAN.
You ain't stuck Brady's head up on the wall, man, has you?
(Hoots, laughter)
JACK.
No, but they's a picture of ole Queen Cleopattera
whut'll make you set straight—
(Laughter)
an blue mirrs,
big chambeliers from Germany—well,
Ah ain't gonna spawl it, but say, better tell you,
them jahnt silver pots on the floors, now they artistic,
but they ain't juss for admirin, you know?
(Laughter. He moves toward the car.)
Tick, you gimme a han with these flowuhs, you too. Ellie—
(Silence as she stands to take them, then a spatter of applause, increasing)
Yeah, evvybody say hello to mah fiancey, Ellie Bachman!
(Cheers, ELLIE *waves, smiling.* TRUMPETER *plays a bit of "Here Comes the Bride.")*
Hole on, don' jump the gun, boy—
(Laughter)
An, hey, while you at it,
Gragulate mah manager here, mah fren Goldie—
(Cheers. GOLDIE *waves)*
An—
TICK.
See? You black, you juss nacheral come in lass—
(Laughter, TICK *springs up, flourishing the gold belt in its plush-lined case.)*
Brung this lil doodad, folks, to hang up ovuh de bar!
(Whoops, cheers, drum rolls)
JACK.
OK, stash that away now—
What you headin at now
is a special brew a mine in there call Rajah's Peg—
don' ass whut's in it, jes come inside and git it—
(Cheers)
Yeah, open house! Les have some lively times!
*(*BAND *strikes up "Shine." Cheering continues as* JACK, *cakewalking around the car, ceremoniously collects* ELLIE *and leads her to the doorway, where she formally cuts the ribbon across it; the* NEGROES, *all cakewalking, follow them in, the* BAND *last, continuing to play inside.* GOLDIE *and* TICK *remain.)*

TICK.
Come on, boss!
GOLDIE.
Oh, boy. Oh, boy!
You heard what he said? His fiancée? You
    heard him?
TICK.
Yeah, but dat don' singify nothin—
GOLDIE.
Nothin! With bills up in seven states
against any kinda mixed-around marriages!
TICK.
Boss, he only juss now say fiancey
so them people don figger she a hooker, thas-
    sall—
GOLDIE.
You hear?
Take a lesson how to be a gentleman!
It's all, he says. Why can't he give them
a chance to boil down, what's he gotta bring
    her
in the open, for what?
TICK.
Juss did it today, boss—
GOLDIE *(gesturing to the car).*
Right down Wabash Avenue—
TICK.
No law gainst dat yet—
    (Bass drum heard in the distance—contin-
ues)
GOLDIE.
What the hell is that?
TICK.
I dunno. Muss be some burial society.
    (Enter SMITTY *and* PRESSMAN 1*)*
GOLDIE.
Go on, take the belt in.
    *(*TICK *goes into the Cafe; cheering, music*
continuing)
SMITTY.
Lively times, eh, Goldie?
GOLDIE.
Yeah, Hiya.
SMITTY.
Wouldn't let you in, huh?
GOLDIE.
Are you kiddin?
PRESSMAN 1.
He came out for some air!
(They laugh; drum gradually approaching)
GOLDIE.
Look, what's goin on?
SMITTY.
They'll be here in a minute, Goldie.
    (Drum very near)
GOLDIE.
They, who's they—?

(Looks in direction of drumming)
What the hell is that—?
SMITTY.
You know how they are
about places like this. Just their meat, Goldie.
GOLDIE.
Oh, Jesus, not here, not down here, I checked
    it!
Not in this part of town!
SMITTY.
Anywhere, Goldie.
It's one big cleanup—
GOLDIE.
Oh, boy!
Listen, Smitty, get the cops—
SMITTY.
Always cops along, take it easy—
GOLDIE.
Smitty—we'll have a riot on our hands
    here—
SMITTY.
Really? I never thought of that.
    (They draw back as a trombone is heard,
raggedly joining the drum with "Onward,
Christian Soldiers," and the PARADE *appears,*
escorted by POLICEMEN. *The* MARCHERS
carry signs reading:

CIVIC REFORM NOW
WOMEN'S LEAGUE FOR TEMPERANCE
SEEK YE OUT INIQUITY
AURORA BIBLE COMMITTEE
THOR WITH HIS HAMMER, NORWEGIANS
AGAINST SALOONS
HEPWORTH UNION
WE HAVE BEEN TOO PATIENT
CHICAGO JOAN OF ARC CLUBS

A lone NEGRO *among them with a sign:*
NO SPIRITS NO VICE
The music within has stopped. Still playing
their anthem, the MARCHERS *range them-*
selves before the doorway. The NEGROES
within have emerged and stand out before
them belligerently. JACK *comes out as the*
trombone and drum conclude the anthem.)
MARCHER 1.
Woe unto the keepers of the Temples of Baal!
Woe unto the swillers in the sinks of
    wretchedness!
Woe unto those whose delight is born of evil!
NEGRO 1.
Woe whoevuh break up a party on Division
    Street!
*(*NEGROES *snarl agreement)*
JACK.
Easy now, ace, let the man preach it—

MARCHER 2.
We aren't here just to preach, Mr. Jefferson.
WOMAN MARCHER.
We tell you to shut this establishment down.
NEGROES.
You what?
Who you squeakin at!
Get outa here, fishbait!
Shut me somma this!
Move—
JACK.
Easy easy—now, mistah, lookie here—
NEGROES.
Don' argue to em, Jack—
Shoo em off—
WOMAN MARCHER.
Shame! Shame, Mr. Jefferson!
MARCHER 1.
Instead of offering these people an example—
NEGRO 2 (*squirts a soda syphon at him*).
Have one on me, chesty!
POLICEMAN 1.
Watch it now, you, they got their permit—
JACK.
Hey—
NEGRO 2.
Don't shove when you talk, man—
MARCHER 1.
Drunkenness, disorder, this is what you offer—
NEGRO 3.
Do somethin bout it!
MARCHER 1.
We shall not allow—
NEGRO WOMAN 1.
Stop beatin on de cullud, hear—
POLICEMAN 2.
Look—
NEGRO 3.
Hands off—
MARCHER 1.
We shall not allow fresh corruption to flourish here—
NEGRO 4.
I know that mother, I work for him once—
MARCHER 1.
We shall not sit by—
NEGRO 3.
We ain't gonna let you—
NEGRO WOMAN 1.
Stop beatin on de cullud—
NEGRO 2.
Show em—
POLICEMAN 3.
I warn you—

NEGRO 1.
Git de wimmins inside—
MARCHER 1.
Sing, friends—
POLICEMAN 1.
Keep back—
NEGRO 1.
Juss you make one teeny noise—
(ANOTHER NEGRO *breaks through, begins wrestling with the* DRUMMER: *shouting and struggling at the police line*)
JACK.
Hey, hey—
MARCHER 1.
Hymn number—
NEGRO 2.
You ain't hittin no drum here—
WOMAN MARCHER.
Help—
(JACK *stops the* POLICE CAPTAIN *from blowing his whistle, then, restraining the* NEGRO, *beats the drum with his hand.*)
JACK.
Order in de court, boys, order in de court!
(*Finally, silence. He picks up the fallen stick and returns it to the* DRUMMER.)
Now, you wanta play this ole drum? You play it.
(*To the* MARCHERS)
An you all wanta sing? Then you lean back an sing.
Maybe us kin come in on it, how bout
"Earth Is Not Mah Home, Ah Juss Passin Through?
(*A few Negroes laugh.*)
Thass my favrite.
MARCHER 2.
We don't regard this as a frivolous matter, Mr. Jefferson.
JACK.
Nossir, me neither! Cause if we kicks off a rumpus
this bran new corruptions a mine here get close up!
Now, I pollgize for any gritty remarks was passed,
an for not bin too symbafetic on you aims—
MARCHER 1.
We are going to witness for the Lord—
JACK.
OK—
MARCHER 1.
On this doorstep as long—
NEGRO 4.
Can't sweet-talk em, Jack!
NEGRO WOMAN 1.
Always beatin on the cullud!

JACK.
Say, is you brains stuck, or what!
These folks been layin down trouble all over,
an here, we's gettin included, ain't we?
Ain't that good enough?
Why, it juss like whut Presden Teddy say,
Square Deal for Evvybody!—come on, les
    treat em right,
git some chairs out here, they gonna stay,
    OK,
no use they standin, some old-timie folks
long with em here—
(NEGROES *begin passing chairs out into the
street)*
Hurry up, they been walkin plenny too,
thass right, Tick, the foldin ones, yeah,
thank you, set em down, couple more, here
    you go—
if you all want some samwidges or fruit-
    punch or somethin,
or if, you know, you jus holler out now, OK?
We be right inside—
(The intimidated MARCHERS *have begun
moving off at the appearance of the chairs, and
as the* NEGROES *begin to re-enter the Cafe, two*
WHITE MEN *and a* WOMAN *enter: They ap-
proach* JACK)
DONNELLY *(the elder of the two).*
Are you Mister Jack Jefferson?
(All movement ceases.)
JACK.
Yeah, what about it?
DONNELLY.
My name is Donnelly. I'm an attorney, from
    Tacoma.
And this is Mrs. Bachman.
(Pause)
JACK.
How do you do, ma'am. Would you care to
    step inside?
MRS. BACHMAN.
No, I would not care to step inside.
Is my daughter in there?
JACK.
Yes, ma'am. She is.
*(*DONNELLY *goes in. Silence)*
Ah think she be awful glad to see you, Miz
    Bachman.
(Long silence)
You like to sit down here fo a minute?
(Long silence)
Ellie tole me all bout her people back
    there . . .
(Silence. DONNELLY *comes out)*

DONNELLY.
She refuses to leave, Mrs. Bachman.
(Pause)
MRS. BACHMAN *(crying out).*
Ellie!
(She crumples, weeping, DONNELLY *support-
ing her.)*
JACK.
She all right, ma'am, she all right, Ah bring
    her out to ya—
MRS. BACHMAN *(as* DONNELLY *begins
drawing her away).*
Ellie . . . my baby . . .
GOLDIE.
Look, Mister Donnelly, where could I reach
    you—
DONNELLY.
The Majestic—
GOLDIE.
OK—
JACK.
Ah see she get there—
DONNELLY.
You'd better see a little further than that, sir.
I strongly advise you to send that girl home.
(The beating of the bass drum resumes, as
HE *and the* OTHER MAN, *followed by the*
PRESS, *help* MRS. BACHMAN *away; the*
MARCHERS *resume their withdrawal, the*
NEGROES *returning to the Cafe.* JACK *is last;
he turns to* GOLDIE, *now alone on the street)*
GOLDIE.
Well . . . lively times.
*(*HE *enters the Cafe as the drumming
recedes and the* LIGHTS FADE OUT.*)*

SCENE FIVE

*Office of the District Attorney, Chicago
A meeting in progress.* CIVIC LEADERS *facing* CAMERON, *the district attorney. They include two* WOMEN *and a distinguished-looking* NEGRO. *In the background* SMITTY, *a* DE-
TECTIVE, *and the man with* DONNELLY *in the
previous scene:* DIXON.

———

CAMERON.
No, we do not think he's a privileged charac-
    ter!
MAN 1.
And still he carries on—
CAMERON.
No wait—

(Consults papers)

Since he opened this Cafe, as he calls it,
we have made no fewer than thirteen arrests—

WOMAN 1.

He wasn't arrested!

CAMERON.

Madam, we have no grounds—

MAN 3.

What about that shooting there—

WOMAN 1.

You arrested that poor common-law wife of his—

WOMAN 2.

He was involved—

CAMERON.

Yes, but, madam, SHE shot at HIM!
We can't prosecute him for being a target.

MAN 1.

Why isn't action taken about the Bachman girl!

CAMERON.

She's over the age of consent, Mr. Hewlett—

MAN 2.

This—

(To the Negro)

Forgive me, Doctor, but I must speak my mind—
This connection between them is an outrage
to every decent Caucasian in America!
Perhaps he thinks his victories entitle him to it,
as part of the spoils—

MAN 1.

You know how niggers are—

MAN 2.

Mr. Hewlett!

MAN 1 *(to the Negro).*

Oh, I'm sorry, sir . . .

NEGRO.

We can't pretend that race is not the main issue here.
And, as you imply, sir, the deportment of this man
does harm to his race. It confirms certain views of it
you may already hold: that does us harm.
But it also confirms in many Negroes the belief
that his life is the desirable life, and that
does us even greater harm. **For a Negro
today, the opportunity to earn a dollar in a
factory should appear to be worth infinitely
more than the opportunity of spending that
dollar in emulation of Mr. Jack Jefferson.**
But this I assert: the majority of Negroes
do not approve of this man or of his doings.
He personifies all that should be suppressed by law,
and I trust that such suppression is forthcoming.

(General agreement)

MAN 2.

Everyone in favor say aye—

ALL.

Aye!

*(*THEY *rise,* CAMERON *with them)*

CAMERON.

Well, I appreciate your coming here to discuss this—

MAN 2.

It will not be to your benefit to let it rest here.

CAMERON.

I don't intend to, sir.

(Sees THEM *out)*

Good night, good night.

(He shuts the door. SMITTY, DIXON, *and* DETECTIVE *come forward.)*

DETECTIVE.

Like a drink?

CAMERON.

Sure could use one.

(Bottle is produced, DIXON *abstains.)*

Smitty?

SMITTY.

I'm in training.

CAMERON.

You know . . . if a good White Hope showed up and beat him
it would take the edge off this.

SMITTY.

Forget it, Al.
The best we got around now is Fireman Riley.

CAMERON.

All right, let's go to work. Bring the girl in.

*(*DETECTIVE *leaves.)*

You want to question her, Dixon? It was your idea.

DIXON.

No, you go ahead, Al. See what you can come up with.

SMITTY.

Why don't you revoke the license on his place,
that's easy enough.

CAMERON.

Sure it's easy!
We could close him, we could rap him on

disorderly conduct,
we could make a dozen misdemeanors stick,
but it's all minor stuff. And you heard them.
They want his head on a plate.

(DETECTIVE *enters with* ELLIE.)

Good evening. Miss Bachman. Take a seat,
   please.

ELLIE.

Thank you.

(DIXON, SMITTY, *and* DETECTIVE *withdraw into the background.*)

CAMERON.

You understand, this is an informal inquiry,
you've come at our request, but of your own
   free will?

ELLIE.

Yes, I understand.

CAMERON.

Good. Now, Miss Bachman—
(Consulting papers)
Yes, I see.
You resumed your maiden name after your
   divorce.

ELLIE.

That's right.

CAMERON.

And you obtained your divorce from Mr.
   Martin in Australia.

ELLIE.

Yes.

CAMERON.

An odd place to go for a divorce.

ELLIE.

I have an aunt there. I wanted to get away.

CAMERON.

You hadn't met Mr. Jefferson before your
   trip.

ELLIE.

No, I had not.

CAMERON.

You did not travel there to be with Mr. Jefferson.

ELLIE.

No, I did not. I met him on the boat.

CAMERON.

How did he approach you?

ELLIE.

He didn't. I asked the captain to introduce us.

CAMERON.

May I ask why.

ELLIE.

Yes. I wanted to make his acquaintance.

CAMERON.

And once you had, Miss Bachman, what did
   he propose to you?

ELLIE.

That I have dinner at his table.

CAMERON.

Which you did for several evenings—

ELLIE.

Yes—

CAMERON.

Until you began taking your meals in his
   stateroom.

ELLIE.

That is correct.

CAMERON *(consulting papers).*

Where a great deal of wine and champagne
   was consumed.

ELLIE.

You might say that.

CAMERON.

Presumably he would keep filling your
   glass . . . ?

ELLIE.

When it was empty, yes.

CAMERON.

Ten times per evening? Six?

ELLIE.

No, I drank very little—

CAMERON.

And how often did he give you medicine or
   pills—

ELLIE.

Never, I wasn't ill—

CAMERON.

But the steward reports that you hardly left
   the stateroom,
and that disembarking you appeared quite—

ELLIE.

Well, the last day at sea we had—

CAMERON.

Weren't you ill in some way?
Did you feel strange, or sleepy—

ELLIE.

I felt uncomfortable at how people looked at
   me.
I wasn't used to it.

CAMERON.

He took you from the boat to the hotel.

ELLIE.

Yes.

CAMERON.

Did you ask to be taken there?

ELLIE.

No, I just went with him.

CAMERON.

And what had he promised you?

ELLIE.

To spend some of his time with me.

CAMERON.

Nothing else?

ELLIE.

Nothing that could interest you.

CAMERON.

But naturally, since you were staying there
with him, he provided you with money.

ELLIE.

I have Mr. Martin's settlement and means of
my own.

He's given me presents, yes—

DIXON.

Miss Bachman,

Your railway ticket to Chicago,

did you buy it yourself? Or was it a sort of
present.

ELLIE.

I honestly don't remember. Yes, I believe I
bought it.

DIXON.

Thank you.

CAMERON.

You're parrying these questions very well!

ELLIE.

I didn't come here to tell lies, Mr. Cameron.

I agreed to come, though Jack was against it,

because I wanted to head off any notions you
have

Of getting at him through me. I hope I've
done that.

CAMERON *(putting away papers).*

Well . . . it seems you have. And frankly I
admire you for it.

Not many women . . . **yes, one has to.**

(Sits on desk)

You're quite devoted to him, aren't you?

ELLIE.

I love him, Mr. Cameron.

CAMERON.

He's a splendid man

in many ways, really. No one doubts that,
you know.

ELLIE.

I've never doubted it.

CAMERON.

A magnificent fighter. I saw him when he—

ELLIE.

That's not all he is. He's generous, he's kind,

he's sensitive—why are you smiling?

CAMERON.

I'm sorry. It's how you shy away from mentioning

the physical attraction. I've embarrassed you,
forgive me—

ELLIE.

I'm not ashamed of wanting Jack for a lover.

I wanted him that way.

CAMERON.

Of course you did,

and of course he'd want you!

ELLIE.

Why, because I'm—

CAMERON.

Oh no, I'm not implying—

ELLIE.

He could have nearly any girl he wanted,
black or—

CAMERON.

Yes, I only meant that any man would be
proud—

ELLIE.

I'm proud that he wanted me! Is that clear?

CAMERON.

Certainly—please don't be distressed, we
needn't—

ELLIE.

Who am I, anyway! I'm no beauty or anything or—

CAMERON.

Now, now, you're being unfair to yourself—

ELLIE.

Why can't they leave us alone, what's the
difference—

(She weeps.)

CAMERON.

Oh, there shouldn't be one, ideally . . . and
besides,

people are so blind about that physical side—

a young woman, divorced, disappointed—

ELLIE.

Please. If you've finished—

CAMERON.

Here, here, now, you mustn't cry, Miss Bachman,

It hasn't turned out all that badly, has it?

You have this wonderful man now to love
you—

why should you cry—

ELLIE.

I'll never give him up, I can't—

CAMERON.

Of course not, but why be ashamed of it—

ELLIE.

I'm not, I swear I'm not—

CAMERON.

You seem to be, you know—

ELLIE.

I'm not—

CAMERON.

Well, if you say so—

ELLIE.

I'm crazy for him, yes! I don't care! It's the
truth!

I didn't know what it was till I slept with him!

**I'll say it to anyone, I don't care how it
sounds—**

CAMERON.
That he makes you happy that way—
ELLIE.
Yes—
CAMERON.
And you love him, you'd do anything for him—?
ELLIE.
Yes—
CAMERON.
And not be ashamed—?
ELLIE.
No, never—
CAMERON.
Even if it—
ELLIE.
Yes—
CAMERON.
Seemed unnatural or—
ELLIE.
Yes—
CAMERON.
And when you have, you only—
ELLIE.
What—?
CAMERON.
Tried to make him happy too, am I right?
(*She freezes. Pause*)
Now, Miss Bachman—
ELLIE (*with Negro inflection*).
You slimy two-bit no-dick mothergrabber.
(*Pause. She rises.*)
If that's all.
CAMERON.
Yes, I believe so—
ELLIE.
Good night, then.
CAMERON.
Yes. Thank you for coming in.
(*Sees her out, shuts the door*)
SMITTY.
That's that.
CAMERON.
Nothing!
Seduction, enticement, coercion, abduction,
not one good berry on the bush!
DETECTIVE.
Too bad, Al.
Nearly did get him on five seventy-one, though.
CAMERON.
Rah!
SMITTY.
Makes your hair stand up, don't it?

DETECTIVE.
Sure does.
She's like a kid with a piece of chocolate cake.
CAMERON.
All right! It's a rotten job . . . !
(*To* DIXON)
So, what do you think?
Any hope of a Federal slap here?
DIXON.
I'm not sure yet, Al.
I'll need to have a word with the fine-print boys.
And I'd like to speak to Donnelly—OK?
(DETECTIVE *leaves.*)
CAMERON.
But what's there to move on? The railway ticket?
DIXON.
Well, maybe not that, exactly.
I doubt if we could prove he actually bought it—
CAMERON.
And say you could—so?
DIXON.
It's occurred to me, Al—
seeing how we've just drawn a blank every-where else—
that we might just nail him with the Mann Act.
CAMERON.
What?
But that's for commercial ass, not this. She's not a pro!
DIXON.
Yes, I know that, Al. But here is a law against
"transporting a person across a state line
for immoral purposes."
CAMERON.
No riders, nothing
about "intent to gain" or "against volition"?
DIXON.
I don't believe so.
(DONNELLY *enters with* DETECTIVE.)
Oh, good evening, Mr. Donnelly.
We've spoken to your young lady—
DONNELLY.
Yes? And—?
DIXON.
You'll remember that our office agreed, at the outset,
not to involve her in any proceedings
unless it was absolutely necessary.
Unfortunately, now, Mr. Donnelly, it may be,
and we shall probably require certain evi-

dence.
We thought you should know this before-
hand, so that you
may return to Tacoma and prepare your prin-
cipal.

DONNELLY.

I understand, sir.

DIXON.

Good. Thank you.

CAMERON.

I'll have that bastard watched day and night!

DIXON.

Don't bother, Al. We've done it right along.
(BLACKOUT. *Sound of crickets chirping.*
LIGHTS UP *on*—)

SCENE SIX

A cabin, Beau Rivage, Wisconsin
ELLIE *sitting up in bed, a sheet around her.*
JACK, *wrapped in a towel, beside her. Kerosene*
lamp.

———

JACK.

Shucks, honey, it ain't cold, this the finest
time for swimmin—

ELLIE.

We have come to a parting of the ways.

JACK.

Aw . . . big silvery moon, pine trees—

ELLIE.

Snapping turtles, moccasins—

JACK.

Lawd, whut to do when romance done gone!

ELLIE.

Oh, Jack, I couldn't make it to the door.

JACK

That right? Sposin Ah carry you down there
then
an sorta—

ELLIE.

No—

JACK.

Ease you in—

ELLIE.

No! No fair—Jack!—don't tickle me—

JACK.

Mmm, she a reglah—

ELLIE.

Please—no!—Ow!—Jack, that hurts—

JACK.

Hey, baby, Ah didn—

ELLIE.

I know, this damn sunburn.

JACK.

Aw, Ah'm sorry—here, lemme pat somethin
on it—
(Takes up a champagne bottle, applies some to
her back)
Yeah . . .

ELLIE.

Oh, thanks . . . ooh . . . oh, yes, it's—Jack?

JACK.

Don' that feel good now?

ELLIE.

What are—?

JACK.

Cool—?

ELLIE.

Not champagne, Jack!

JACK.

Well, thass alright, baby, you worth the bess.

ELLIE.

All over me . . .

JACK.

Get some lake on you, huh?

ELLIE.

No, I—
(Peering at him)
Jack, turn around a little . . .
more, this way . . . Are you feeling all right?

JACK.

Ah ain't feelin no diffrunt.

ELLIE.

Are you sure?

JACK.

Yeah!

ELLIE.

You ate all those clams, maybe you—
(Feels his head)

JACK.

Whut you doin that for, ain't got no fever—

ELLIE.

Well, you look—a little peculiar, Jack.

JACK.

Oh . . . ? Kinda ashy, you mean?

ELLIE.

Yes, a sort of funny—

JACK.

Honey, that ain't sick, that how Ah gets a
sunburn.
(ELLIE *tries not to laugh.*)
Now what you laughin at—

ELLIE.

I thought—I mean—oh!—oh, Jack—

JACK.

Huh?

ELLIE.

I can't help it, I'm sorry—how you—oh—

JACK.

Yeah—come on, that ain't nice—

(He starts to laugh.)

You thought what, honey?

ELLIE.

I—I thought it just—bounces off, that's all—
(Both laugh uproariously.)

JACK.

Bounces off—

ELLIE.

Yes—

JACK.

Well, Miss Medium Rare, meet Mr. Well
  Done!
(Gales of laughter)

**Yeah . . . lotta folks better off in de
  shade.**

ELLIE.

Oh . . . do we have to leave tomorrow?

JACK.

Shouldn't leave the place alone too long,
  honey.

ELLIE.

I know. All right.

JACK.

Case there's any fussin or—

ELLIE.

Ssh, I know.

JACK.

My, you do smell good though.

ELLIE.

Yes?

JACK.

Mm-hmm.

ELLIE.

You're not tired of being alone with me, are
  you?

JACK.

Hey. You kiddin?

ELLIE.

Or tired of me asking questions like that?

JACK.

Oh . . . Ah'm gettin tired of plenny . . . but,
  no,
you ain't in there at all.

ELLIE.

It's lovely to hear you say that . . .

JACK.

Yeah? . . . Well, OK then . . .
(Props himself up)
How you doin for pillers?

ELLIE.

Fine, darling . . .
(JACK hums a little.)
Have a swim if you want to.

JACK.

No, Ah'm cozy here . . . I cozy, an you
  rosy . . .
  (ELLIE *chuckles.* JACK *turns the lamp down*

very low, kisses her, draws away. Sings softly)
> Good morning, blues
> Blues, how do you do,
> Blues say, Ah all right,
> Brother, how are you.
> Woke up dis mornin,
> Blues all round mah head,
> Look down to mah breakfas,
> Blues all in mah bread . . .
> For how long, how long,
> Ah sayin, how long . . .

ELLIE.

Lying in the sun I was, you know, daydreaming . . .
how maybe I'd stay there . . . and it would
  keep on burning me . . .
day after day . . . oh, right through September . . .
And I'd get darker and darker . . . I really
  get dark, you know . . .
and then I'd dye my hair . . . and I'd change
  my name . . .
and I'd come to you in Chicago . . . like
  somebody new . . .
a colored woman, or a Creole maybe . . .
and nobody but you would ever guess . . .

JACK.

Won't work, honey.

ELLIE.

Hm?

JACK.

Evvybody know Ah gone off cullud women.

ELLIE.

Oh, Jack, don't tease . . .

JACK

Ah has, too, 'cep for mah momma.

ELLIE.

Maybe if I . . .

JACK.

Ssh.

ELLIE.

What will we do . . .

JACK.

Ssh . . . try an sleep, honey . . .
(Turns the lamp down a little further)
Creepin up on me a little too—
(Darkness; sings)
> For how long, how long, Ah sayin . . .
> Always callin you honey, ain't Ah.

ELLIE.

Mm.

JACK.

Don' remember Ah call no woman by that.
Call em by their name . . . or juss "baby,"
  you know . . .
Don' ever call you by you name, Ah
  guess . . .

ELLIE.

Hardly ever . . .

JACK.

Muss be some kinda ju-ju Ah fraid of in
 it . . .

like if Ah says it you maybe disappear on
 me . . .

ELLIE.

Oh . . . I don't care about my name . . .

JACK.

Honey . . . hit just right . . .

ELLIE.

Yes . . .

JACK.

Honey fum the bees . . .

(*She sighs.*)

Ever look at it real, real good a while . . . ?

ELLIE.

Can't remember . . .

JACK.

Nothin like that stuff . . .

Used to sit . . . Oh, long time ago, in
 Texas . . .

we-all ud have a lil honey-treat sometime . . .

whole yellah mugful . . . used to set there
 with it

till evvybody come in . . . foolin with it, you
 know . . .

liff up a spoonful . . . tip it a lil bit . . .

watch it start to curve up . . . start in

to sli-i-i-de ovuh . . . oh, takin its time
 . . . slow . . . slow . . .

honey underneath waitin . . . honey hanging
 ovuh it . . .

hundred years up there . . . then down . . .
 stringing down . . . down . . .

tiny lil dent where it touch . . . an then . . .

(*Suddenly embracing her*)

Oh, mah sweet, sweet baby, Ah want to have
 it all—

ELLIE.

Yes—

(*Sound of a door splintered open. Six men
—two with lanterns—burst in. Confusion of
light and bodies*)

MAN 1.

On your feet, Jefferson—

ELLIE.

Jack—

MAN 2.

Get the window, Charlie—

MAN 3.

Hey—

MAN 1.

Look out—

MAN 4.

Oh!

MAN 5.

Grab him—

MAN 4.

He's—chokin me—

MAN 1.

Here, you—

(*Thud.* ELLIE *screams.*)

MAN 1.

Let go or I'll put a hole in you—

MAN 2.

Where is he—

MAN 1.

I said—

(*Thud*)

ELLIE.

Stop it—

MAN 4.

Jesus—

MAN 6.

Light that goddamn lamp—

ELLIE.

Please—

MAN 5.

Sit there, lady—

MAN 1.

We're the law.

(*Kerosene lamp on.* ELLIE *huddled at the
head of the bed,* JACK *crouching in a corner,
grasping a chunk of firewood, the injured*
MAN *nursing his neck, the* OTHERS *facing*
JACK, *immobile—*DIXON *is among them,* ALL
breathing heavily. DIXON *moves forward.*)

DIXON.

I'm a federal marshal, Jefferson.

(*Shows his badge*)

Put that down, please.

(*Pause*)

Come on. We don't want to make this any
 worse.

(*Pause.* JACK *drops wood.*)

At ten A.M. this morning you drove Miss
 Eleanor Bachman

across the Illinois-Wisconsin state line.

Having done so, you proceeded to have relations with her.

Under the Mann Act this makes you liable

and I'm therefore placing you under arrest.

ELLIE.

No . . . no . . .

DIXON.

Get dressed, please, Miss Bachman. We'll
 take you into town.

ELLIE.

Jack—

JACK.

Don't worry—get dress—

(*Handing her her clothes*)

MAN 2.

Here.

DIXON.

Hold a blanket up or something.

ELLIE.

Jack . . .

JACK.

Don't you fret now . . .

(MAN 2 *and* MAN 3 *screen her with a blanket.*
To DIXON)

Thanks, mistah.

DIXON.

Sure.

JACK *(pulling on a sweater).*

How much this carry?

DIXON.

One to three.

JACK.

She clear?

DIXON.

Just you.

JACK.

Yeah. Thanks.

MAN 1 *(showing handcuffs).*

We need these, Jim?

DIXON.

No. Find him his pants and let's get out of
here.

(BLACKOUT. *Soft, woeful singing in the*
darkness, which continues through the follow-
ing. A bizarre-looking colored man comes for-
ward: SCIPIO. HE *wears a shabby purple cloak*
fastened with a gold clasp over a shabby dark
suit, a bowler hat with a long plume hanging
from it, fawn shoes, and several large totemic-
looking rings. His manner is feverish.)

SCIPIO *(speaking over his shoulder into the*
darkness).

Start it up, thassit, brothers, singing and
moanin!

White man juss drag him another away here

so all you black flies, you light down together

an hum pretty please to white man's Jesus—

Yes, Lawd!

(Spits)

Waste a mah times . . .

An Ah don' care to talk to you neither!

But Ah sees two-three out there de same
blood is me,

so Ah says good evenin to em, then Ah askin
em this:

How much white you up to? How much you
done took on?

How much white you pinin for? How white
you wanna be?

Oh, mebbe you done school youself away fum
White Jesus—

but how long you evah turn you heart away
frum WHITE!

How you lookin, how you movin, how you
wishin an figgerin—

how white you wanna be, that whut Ah askin!

How white you gaunta get—you tell me!

You watchin that boy? Nothin white-y bout
him, huh?

But whut he hustle after? White man's sport-
in prize!

Whut he gotta itch for? White man's poon-
tang!

Whut his rich livin like? White man's nigger!

Thinks he walkin and talkin like a natchul
man,

don' know how he's swimmin half-drownded
in the whitewash,

like they is, like you is, nevah done diffrunt,

gulpin it in evvy day, pickled in it, right at
home dere—

tell me that ain't how we living!

Tell me how it better you chokin on dat
whitewash

than wearin a iron colluh roun you neck!

Oh, yeah, you sayin, but whut kin we do,

Whut kin us or dat boy or dem gospellers do,

we passin our days in de white man's world
—well,

make you own, brothers!

Don' try an join em and don' try an beat em,

leave em all at once, all together,

pack up!

Colleck you wages, grab whutevah here
gonna come in handy

an sluff off de ress! Time to get it goin!

Time again to make us

a big new wise proud dark man's world

again! Ah says again! Ah tellin whut we had
once!

Nevah mine that singing—learn, brothers,
learn!

Ee-gyp!! Tambuctoo!! Ethiopya!!

Red'n goldin cities older den Jerusalem,

temples an prayin to sperrits whut stick wid
us,

black men carvin ivory, workin up laws,

chartin em maps for de moon an de sun,

refine' cultured cullud people hansome as
statues dere

when Europe an all was juss woods fulla
hairy cannibals—

dat laughin don' harm us none!

Five hundrid million of us not all together,

not matchin up to em, dat what harmin us!

Dream bout it, brothers—

Five hundrid million on dey own part of de
earth,

am not a one dere evah askin another,
How much white you up to,
how white you wanna be . . .
(Glaring, HE *makes his exit as* LIGHTS COME
UP *on—)*

SCENE SEVEN

Mrs. Jefferson's house, Chicago
Surrounding MRS. JEFFERSON *in her arm-*
chair are the PASTOR *and seven or eight*
BROTHERS *and* SISTERS, *who continue singing*
softly, as the PASTOR *speaks. At one side is*
CLARA, *now dressed rather plainly.* MRS. JEF-
FERSON *wears a nightdress, with a shawl over*
her shoulders and another covering her legs.

————

PASTOR.
Lawd, we prayin longside this sick unhappy
mother here,
she lookin to You, Lawd, she know her boy
been sinful,
an she sorry about that, but she do love him
Lawd,
you give him another chance she nevah ask
you for anythin!
She living by You Book all her days, Lawd,
you seen it!
We prayin you touch them judges' eyes with
mercy.
Let em chastise him today, Lawd,
let em fine him so steep he leff withouta dime,
let em scare him so hard he nevah forgit it,
but, Lawd, don' let em lock this woman's boy
away.
(End singing)
BROTHERS.
Amen.
MRS. JEFFERSON.
An if they does, Oh please, Lawd, let it juss
be fo a little.
BROTHERS.
Amen.
PASTOR.
We callin with you, sister.
MRS. JEFFERSON.
Ah thank ya, Pastor.
Wish Ah could offuh ya some lil hospitality
but honess—
PASTOR.
Don' fret now, sister.
MRS. JEFFERSON.
Ah mean, Ah kin hardly—
SISTER 1.

Nevah you mine, Tiny.
CLARA.
Ah'll put on a potta fresh cawfee—
(Starts to go)
MRS. JEFFERSON.
See if Tick or somebody comin down the
street firss.
*(*CLARA *goes to the window.)*
SISTER 2.
Early yet, sister.
CLARA.
Juss a buncha fellers there gawnta play base-
ball.
MRS. JEFFERSON *(sighs).*
Awright, Clara. Thankya.
PASTOR *(as* CLARA *goes to kitchen).*
Got a guardjin angel with that gal in you
house.
BROTHER 1.
Who deserve one better!
*(*BROTHERS *approve)*
MRS. JEFFERSON.
Should've brung word by this. Caint' took
this long.
PASTOR.
We in de Lawd's hans, sister.
BROTHERS.
Amen.
SISTER 1.
You sit easy . . .
MRS. JEFFERSON.
Fum when he was chile Ah knowed this day
comin.
Looka that, Momma, why cain't Ah,
Momma,
lemme lone, Momma. Nevah stop. Fidgety
feet
an, oh, them great big eyes, roamin an
reachin, all ovuh.
Tried to learn him like you gotta learn a cul-
lud boy,
Dass'nt, dass'nt, dass'nt, that ain't for you!
Roll right off him. Tried to learn it to him
meaner—
Mo chile you got, the meaner you go to
if you lovin you chile. That plain cullud
sense.
Hit him with my han, he say, So what.
Hit him with my shoe, he look up an smile.
Took a razor strop to him, that make him
squint
but then he do a funny dance an ask me fo a
nickel.
Ah prayed to de Lawd put mo strenf in my
arm,
the worse Ah was whippin the bigger he

growed,
leven years old an still woulden hear nothin.
Hit him with a stick till Ah coulden hit no
  mo,
he pull it away fum me, an bust it in two,
an then he run o—
PASTOR.
Sister—
MRS. JEFFERSON.
Lawd fogive me treatin him so mean!
Lawd fogive me not beatin on him young
  enough
or hurtin him bad enough to learn him after,
cause Ah seen this day comin—
(Knock downstairs)
SISTER 1.
Ah let em in, Tiny.
(Goes)
PASTOR.
We hopin with you, sister. Hole onter my han
  now.
MRS. JEFFERSON.
No, thass awright.
SISTER 1 *(offstage).*
But you all muss ain't got de right house—
RUDY *(offstage).*
Two thirty-one?
TEAMMATE *(offstage).*
Miz Jeffson's house, ain't it?
SISTER 1 *(closer).*
Yeah, but—hang on, whole lotta you cain't fit
  here—
RUDY.
OK, set on de stairway, de ress of you—
(SISTER 1 *backs into the room, followed by
  three large* YOUNG NEGROES *wearing
  blue satin jackets and matching baseball
  caps.* THEY *carry valises from which bats
  and other gear protrude. Their leader,
  and the largest,* RUDY, *takes off his cap
  and the* OTHERS *follow suit.* CLARA *re-
  enters from the kitchen.)*
Aftuhnoon, evvybody.
MRS. JEFFERSON.
You all comin fum de courthouse?
RUDY.
No ma'am. Us juss get a message—uh—
askin we pay a call here. We de Blue Jays.
MRS. JEFFERSON.
You de which?
RUDY.
De-troit Blue Jays. You know, de cullud
  baseball club?
Pulvrise de Afro Giants here Sadday?
BROTHER 2.
Oh, yeah, my nephew tend dat game.

RUDY.
My name Rudy Sims, Ma'am.
MRS. JEFFERSON.
Pleased to meet you, Mistah Sims—
CLARA.
Who say you sposeta call in here?
RUDY.
Well, we sorta frens with Jack—
CLARA.
This here no celebratin party, you know!
MRS. JEFFERSON.
Hush, Clara, if they frens with Jack—
CLARA.
Why somebody sen us a baseball team here!
RUDY.
Mebbe we bess wait outside in de hall,
  ma'am—
MRS. JEFFERSON.
Nothin of the kine! Clara—
CLARA.
Ah ain't never seed Jack wid no baseball
  frens!
*(*TICK *enters.)*
RUDY.
Well, Ah nevuh seed him wid you, so we
  even.
TICK.
Don't let her rile you, Rudy. Thanks for
  comin.
RUDY.
Any time, man.
TICK.
Got here fass as I could, Miz Jeffson.
MRS. JEFFERSON.
Well. You here . . . Come on.
TICK.
It ain't good, Miz Jeffson.
SISTER 1.
Lawd have mercy.
MRS. JEFFERSON.
Come on. Finish up.
TICK
**Twenty-thousand-dollar fine and three years
  in Joliet.**
SISTER 2.
Jesus above.
BROTHER 1.
Three years.
CLARA.
Why cain't all dem Jew lawyers do nothin!
  Why cain't—
TICK.
Dey got a week ta try appealin on it—
BROTHER 1.
Three years.
MRS. JEFFERSON.
Ah die they lock him up!

SISTER 2.

Don' take on, sister—

PASTOR.

Bring me them smellin salts—

SISTER 1.

Tiny—

MRS. JEFFERSON.

No, Ah don' want nothin—

TICK.

He do have de week out on bail, Miz Jeff-son—

dey set it kina heavy but we figgered dey might,

an we gonna make it.

MRS. JEFFERSON.

A week. Drive him crazy!

TICK.

Well, we gotta try an see it don't.

CLARA.

That snaky lil wax-face bitch! Where she at now!

Where she bloodsuckin now! Oh, Ah'll smoke her out,

an, man—

PASTOR.

Sister—

CLARA.

What Ah gonna do

be worth a hunnerd three yearses!

MRS. JEFFERSON.

Ain't her fault, Clara.

CLARA.

She knowd this end-up comin,

ain a deaf dumb bline pinhead living din know it,

but, Oh, daddy, she joyin hersel so,

it so good when it goin! Leave it alone?

Oh, but daddy, Ah loves you!

MRS. JEFFERSON.

Could be she do love him, Clara.

CLARA.

She WHAT!

MRS. JEFFERSON.

He brung her down once. She din seem too

bad.

TICK.

Nice an quiet too.

CLARA.

Ah ain't talkin to you!

Could be she love him! Why she scat off

wid her man in trouble, why she—

PASTOR.

Bess unwine dat serpint from you heart, sis-ter—

CLARA.

Love him, my black ass!

PASTOR.

Sister!

MRS. JEFFERSON (as CLARA returns to kitchen).

Poor gal been frettin so—

(JACK and GOLDIE enter)

PASTOR.

Praise de Lawd an welcome.

JACK.

Pastor . . . evvybody . . . good boy, Rudy.

RUDY.

Ready fo ya, Jack.

JACK.

Fine, no rush . . . hiya, Momma Tiny.

MRS. JEFFERSON.

They din hurt you, Jack? You git nuff to eat?

JACK.

Sure, Momma.

GOLDIE.

I should feel as good as he does.

JACK.

Whut about you, Momma?

MRS. JEFFERSON.

Oh . . .

JACK.

Still kina poorly?

MRS. JEFFERSON.

It drain me out some, Ah guess.

JACK.

Oh, Momma.

BROTHER 2.

Hard luck, Jack.

MRS. JEFFERSON.

We been prayin an prayin here, son.

JACK.

Well . . . de Lawd hear anyone he gonna hear you.

MRS. JEFFERSON.

Look like he ain't this time—

but He gonna put me on my feet, Ah kin feel it!

An Ah gonna help Him, gonna ress up an eat good,

an Ah comin down there soon, Jack—

JACK.

Momma—

MRS. JEFFERSON.

Often as they 'low ya to, you wait an see,

bring a big ole picnic basket on my arm—

JACK.

No, Momma, listen—

CLARA (flinging herself upon him).

Oh, baby, baby, Ah cain't let em clap you in there—

JACK.

What she doin here!

GOLDIE.
That's all we need.

JACK.
Git offa me, you! Momma, whut de hell—

MRS. JEFFERSON.
Clara come roun when she hear Ah was ailin—

CLARA.
Ah been doin fo you momma, Jack—

MRS. JEFFERSON.
She tryna menn her ways—

TICK (stealing a look out of window).
Jack.

(JACK looks at him. He nods. Pause)

JACK (to CLARA).
Ah count ten fo you beat it. One—

CLARA.
No!

MRS. JEFFERSON.
She been my helpmeet, Jack!

JACK.
Sister fine ya a housekeeper!

CLARA.
Ah keepin house, baby!

JACK.
Ah up to five, girl—

TICK (tense. At the window).
Let her be for now, Jack.
She in here she cain't spoil it,
screamin in the street or somethin.

GOLDIE (mopping his face).
That's all we need.

RUDY.
Soun like sense, Jack.

MRS. JEFFERSON.
Spoil what? Mistah, what these boys up to?

BROTHER 1.
Yeah, what goin on here?

CLARA (to TICK at window)
Whuffo you playin peekaboo wid dat dere automo-bile?

(He shoos her away.)

PASTOR (to JACK).
You ain't about to make things worse, son, are you?

MRS. JEFFERSON.
Jack—

JACK.
Awright. I gotta truss all you folks now—

PASTOR.
Son, however rough it 'pears today—

TICK.
Oughta stan by the winder now, Jack. They lookin.

MRS. JEFFERSON.
Who? Who lookin?

JACK.
'Tectives in that car, Momma.

MRS. JEFFERSON.
Jack—

JACK.
Momma, listen—

MRS. JEFFERSON.
What they waitin out there for, Mistah Goldie?

GOLDIE.
Well, even though Jack is out on bond, you see—

JACK.
They worried Ah gonna try an jump mah bail, Momma.

GOLDIE.
They're worried. I'm in hock up to here with this.

MRS. JEFFERSON.
Jack . . . you juss got let out.

JACK.
Bess time, Momma. They don' know Ah's ready.

MRS. JEFFERSON.
They follerin you, but!

JACK.
Thinks they is.

MRS. JEFFERSON.
Jack, what if they catches you—

JACK.
Won't never get near me! Now, firss thing what Ah do
is take my coat off—

(Does so, revealing a raspberry-colored shirt)
then I stan here sorta talkin—
"Why heaven sake, no foolin!"—now let em see mah face—

(Looks out)
"Oh, my, it look like rain . . . "—an Ah knows they seen my shirt—
Mm-mm! Don't you wish you had one!
Well, Ah goes on talkin, right? Now over there is Rudy—

(RUDY looks at his watch.)
Uh-oh, he checkin his turnip again!
They hasta hop on the train soon, you know,
Blue Jays playin Montreal nex, ain't you, Rude,
against de Canada Blacks?

RUDY.
Thass right, Jack.

JACK.
Less go, fella—

(RUDY starts peeling off jacket and jersey.)
He look mighty fine, ole Rude here, don' he!

Not pretty is me, but he near is big
an just a half shade blacker an—
Oh, mercy, he got dat shirt on too!
(RUDY *does.*)
SISTER 1.
Lawd proteck us!
JACK *(looks out).*
"Yeah, it clearin up now—"
GOLDIE.
Jack, listen, we should maybe talk it over
more—
MRS. JEFFERSON *(to* GOLDIE).
What you trick him inter!
GOLDIE.
It's his idea, believe me—
JACK.
It be awright, Momma!
Rudy spen de aftuhnoon by the winder
an Ah go rollin cross de border with de Jays!
BROTHER 2.
They fine you out, Jack—
JACK.
Naw! I put on Rudy's cap an his jacket?
Stick in the middle of his boys?
Who all fine me! An who lookin?
**You hear that sayin how all niggers look
alike!**
Ain't that so, team?
PASTOR.
But, son, you fogittin we frens with that
Canada!
I mean, we's hardly a diffrunt place—
TICK.
Fore they cotton to it, man,
We on dat ole boat fo Englin. Right?
GOLDIE.
Right, right.
JACK.
It all fixed, Momma!
MRS. JEFFERSON.
All what fixed ain't gotta juss happen—
PASTOR.
Serious offense to go floutin de law, Jack!
I know they done you real hard but, son,
it gonna hang ovuh you long as—
JACK.
Look!
What hang gonna hang but Ah ain't hangin
with it!
Ah done my kickin roun this country,
Ah serve my one nights and my thirty days
too once,
an Ah ain't gonna rot like no log no three
years!
Or be comin out broke as Ah is now either!
Ah in the prime of mah life! Ah wanna live

like Ah got to,
wanna make me some money again, wanna
fight!
**Ah got my turn to be Champeen of the World
an Ah takin my turn! Ah stayin whut Ah am,
wherever Ah has to do it!**
**The world ain't curled up into no forty-eight
states here!**
MRS. JEFFERSON.
Praise de Lawd for lightin a way fo my boy!
Fogive me Ah say Ah didden love you, Jesus!
JACK *(moving to her).*
Thassit, Momma—
MRS. JEFFERSON *(to* BROTHERS *and* PAS-
TOR).
Well?
BROTHERS & PASTOR *(worried).*
Amen . . .
GOLDIE.
She could put in a word for me too, here.
RUDY *(taking his place at the window).*
Better move it, man.
JACK.
Right.
(Pulls on RUDY*'s jersey)*
GOLDIE.
Oh, boy.
JACK.
You folks stay here till we gone, OK?
Then start runnin in an out like, keep em
busy watchin—
CLARA.
Oh, take me with you, honey—
JACK *(pulls on a jacket).*
Don't you cross me now—
CLARA.
Ah go meet you, baby! Any place!
JACK.
You know the score, girl.
CLARA.
Please!
JACK *(buttoning up).*
Fit awright?
GOLDIE.
Yeah, beautiful.
CLARA.
She comin to ya, ain't she! That where she at!
JACK.
Hope you gettin to that game on time,
Rudy—
CLARA.
You ain't meetin that bitch! I turn you in
firss—
(Runs at the door)
TICK.
Hole her—

CLARA *(shaking loose from him).*

JACK GONNA—

(Struggles with SISTERS *at the door).*

SISTER 1.

Stop her mouf up—

CLARA.

HE RUNNIN FFFF—

(Stopping her mouth, they drag her from the door, kicking)

GOLDIE.

Oh, boy—

BROTHER 1.

Make some noise!

SISTER 2.

Sit on her—

PASTOR.

"Look ovuh, Beulah—"

BROTHER 2.

Which—?

PASTOR.

Ready—

MRS. JEFFERSON.

No "Beulah" now, sen up a glad one—

SISTER 1.

Quick, she bitin me—

MRS. JEFFERSON.

Sing, chillun—

ALL *(but* CLARA, *on whom the three largest* SISTERS *are sitting).*

> Just to talk to Jesus
> Oh, what a joy de-vine
> Ah kin feel de lectric
> Movin on de line,
> All wired up by God de Father
> For his lovin own,
> Put a call to Jesus
> On the Royal Telephone—

JACK *(over the singing).*

Here, where that Jew's harp—

(Finds it)

Plung on it, Rudy, it cover you face up—

(Tosses it to him, RUDY *plays.* JACK *moves among them.)*

Good luck—thank you—thank you—

see you soon—you too—don't worry—

Thank you, Momma Tiny—

Get well, darlin, try, please try—

Say you come an see me—good-bye, my momma,

Good-bye, my sweetheart—

*(*MRS. JEFFERSON *nods and sings right on, clapping to the beat, and with* GOLDIE *mopping his face,* CLARA *kicking and crying,* RUDY *twanging and* ALL THE REST *in full chorus,* JACK *puts on his cap and disappears with the* JAYS.)*

ALL.

> Angel operators
> Waitin for you call,
> Central up in heaven,
> Take no time at all,
> Ring, and God will answer
> In his happy tone,
> Put a call to Jesus
> On the Royal Telephone.

CURTAIN

ACT TWO

SCENE ONE

A chamber in the Home Office, London

Some dozen chairs facing a large desk are arranged for the hearing about to take place. As the scene begins, six men and one woman, all middle-aged and soberly dressed are seating themselves. From a door opposite EU-BANKS, *assistant to the Undersecretary, enters chatting with* TREACHER, JACK's *solicitor. Enter* JACK, ELLIE, GOLDIE, TICK.

———

TREACHER.

Ah, good morning—

EUBANKS.

I'll go and fetch Sir William.

(Goes)

JACK.

Mornin, evvybody. . . . Mornin, Miz Kimball. . . . How you today, Mac . . . ?

(They stare straight ahead.)

Muss be de Wax Museum took a branch here.

TREACHER.

Over there, please, Jack.

GOLDIE.

And let Mr. Treacher do the talking, understand?

TREACHER.

Yes, thank you.

JACK *(to* ELLIE).

We straighten dis out, hon.

ELLIE.

Well, I hope so.

JACK.

Feelin kina edgy, huh.

ELLIE *(takes his hand).*

No.

TICK.

Ah does.

EUBANKS *(entering).*

Sir William Griswold.

JACK *(to* ELLIE).

Hey, you breakin mah han!

(SIR WILLIAM *enters.* GOLDIE, TICK, *and the woman stand up.)*

SIR WILLIAM.

Good morning—no, no need to rise, thank you.

(Sits at desk)

Yes . . . Now, then. Allegations have been made to us

concerning the possible undesirability

of an alien person's continued visit here.

We have of course our own book of rules on the subject, and normally—

COATES.

With due respect, Sir William,

I'm amazed that you find this necessary.

SIR WILLIAM.

Mr.—?

COATES.

Coates.

SIR WILLIAM *(to* EUBANKS).

Representing?

EUBANKS.

British Vigilance Board.

COATES.

Can you really be debating this?

A convicted criminal, a fugitive from justice—

TREACHER.

My client's conviction was known to the authorities.

He was admitted at their discretion.

SIR WILLIAM.

That is true, Mr. Coates.

COATES.

And our discreet authorities are helpless to correct

their initial error, is that what you imply, sir?

SIR WILLIAM.

I implied nothing, I'm sure.

COATES.

Your official silence

indeed implies something! Like official license

for breaches of the peace, for moral deficiency

flaunted at the public—

JACK.

Now wait—

Ah ain't flung no fish at no public!

COATES.

I beg your—

TICK.

Jack, you hush up—

SIR WILLIAM.

Gentlemen, please—

MRS. KIMBALL *(the woman).*

I'll tell them what you did do, you great flash nig-nog!

EUBANKS.

Madam, really—

GOLDIE.

Don't you talk like that, lady—

COATES.

Mrs. Kimball here—

MRS. KIMBALL *(to* COATES).

Do I speak my piece now—?

EUBANKS.

Mr. Coates has the—

COATES.

No, go on, Mrs. Kimball.

MRS. KIMBALL.

I rented him my luxury maisonette, your honor,

Ten Portman Square, and not many would rent to them,

believe you me, a black and white job to boot,

but I thought they at least was married, which they

wasn't,

and I thought she being white they'd be clean, which they wasn't

and I thought maybe them being lovebirds like they are

they'd settle down early nights—nothing of the kind!

Parties, champagne, nigger piano playing—

mind you, I like a bit of music, but I never,

all night, screaming up the stairwell. Oh yes,

I'd see them through the door when I went to shut em up,

doing their dirty dances in there—**Turkey Trot**

and all the rest of them colored steps!

COATES.

The damage to Mrs. Kimball's flat, Sir William,

was appraised at nearly four hundred pounds.

MRS. KIMBALL.

Yes, that's right! Vases, Chippendale,

can't replace it neither—**and rubbish all over too,**

the filthy ape! Undesirable!

TREACHER.

The amount has been paid

in full, Sir William.

SIR WILLIAM.

Who is next, Mr. Coates?

COATES.

Inspector Wainwright.

EUBANKS.

Metropolitan Police.

WAINWRIGHT *(reading from notebook).*
November ninth. Charged with using
obscene language on Coventry Street. Fine,
two pounds.
November fifteenth.
Charged with causing a crowd to collect.
Fine, fifty shillings.
Fined a further five pounds for contempt of
court.
SIR WILLIAM *(to* JACK).
Why the fine for contempt, may I ask.
JACK.
Well, de judge he yell, Ah fine you fifty shil-
lins!
So Ah says, Look, dat crowd's still collectin
so maybe you better take a hundred off me.
WAINWRIGHT.
November twenty-fifth—
SIR WILLIAM *(to* COATES).
If the police offenses are all of this nature—
COATES.
You may skip to January third, Wainwright.
WAINWRIGHT.
January third.
Charged with assault on Mr. M. Bratby.
TREACHER.
The charge has been dropped, Sir William.
COATES.
Sir,
when a man trained in the use of his fists—
JACK.
No, Ah juss shoved him—
(To BRATBY)
Whut you tell this man, Mac?
SIR WILLIAM.
You are—?
BRATBY.
M. Bratby.
EUBANKS.
Olympia Sporting Club.
BRATBY.
Jefferson came to us proposing that we match
him.
We had been unwilling to associate ourselves
with him—
we expressed this position—he became un-
ruly—
COATES.
Attacked you, you mean!
TREACHER.
The affair has been settled, Mr. Jefferson's
apology—
COATES.
Yes, all the affairs are settled,
the popular press delightedly reports them,
and nightly in the music halls they are dealt

with as a joke!
Is any of this desirable? This, when disrup-
tion
is the order of the day, with the ground we
stand on
undermined by socialists, atheists, anarchists,
with anarchy not merely a word but a man
with a bomb in a public building—
SIR WILLIAM.
Mr. Coates—
COATES.
And you're amused, sir, when this lady refers
to these dances
coming into vogue since this man's arrival
here,
but read your Plato, Sir William, read your
Plato—
SIR WILLIAM.
I say—
COATES.
"New modes of music herald upheavals of
state," sir—
SIR WILLIAM.
Now really, Mr. Coates, I have seen the Tur-
key Trot—
COATES.
Let me remind you of the waltz, Sir Wil-
liam—
SIR WILLIAM.
The waltz?
COATES.
The first waltz, sir—
SIR WILLIAM.
Are you asking me to dance—?
TREACHER.
Sir William, may I venture—
JACK.
No, Ah kin talk.
SIR WILLIAM.
Yes, please. Go ahead.
JACK.
Ah come over as a prizefighter, sir.
Figgered Ah could fight Billy Wells here or
Jeannette,
an make me mah livin here the way Ah
knows how.
But we couleln git no decent match fix up,
so Ah was juss gittin fat, and kickin up and
fussin people.
Now, Ah guess Ah shouldn've.
cause whut Ah am, you know, cullud Ah
mean,
some folks here think is a freak anyway,
but it took me some time gittin use to bein
here,
an Ah'm sorry bout all these stories they

brung in,

an whut Ah wanna say is, we like it here fine now,

and now Lord Londsale done set me up a match,

Ah'll git trainin an fightin an we won't have no mo rumpus.

SIR WILLIAM.

Well, Mr. Coates, as I see this at the moment,

the American legalities are none of our concern,

the breaches of the peace you've cited are trivial,

the man's moral character deficient perhaps

by Queen Victoria's standards—**but she of course is gone now**—

and as to the palaver in the press and music halls

these are liberties we simply have to bear—

think of them as part of the White Man's Burden.

So unless Mr. Jefferson commits a crime of some sort—

which I hope none of you will tempt him to further—

I do not see—You have something to add?

COATES.

I should like to correct Mr. Jefferson's assumption

that he does indeed have a match on, Sir William.

JACK.

Whut you talkin bout, Ah sign up wid him dere—

(Points to BRATBY)

fightin Albert Lynch on March de eighteenth—

SIR WILLIAM.

Is this relevant, Mr. Coates—

COATES.

Oh, I think so. Bratby?

BRATBY.

Two weeks ago, at Lord Londsdale's persuasion,

we proposed this match, and Jefferson accepted.

It now appears, however, that the London County Council

refuses to issue a license for this fight.

And enquiries indicate this difficulty elsewhere.

TREACHER.

Refused the license on what grounds?

COATES.

Mr. Farlow?

FARLOW.

I should say that Mr. Coates

has already expressed the Council's position.

JACK.

Goldie, how the hell—

TICK.

Sit easy there, baby—

COATES.

This man entered England with the stated purpose

of pursuing his career as a pugilist. Now, what, sir,

are the grounds for his remaining in England

if this career of his does simply not exist here!

*(*JACK *stands,* ELLIE *holds him by the hand.)*

SIR WILLIAM.

Please sit down, sir.

(To the others)

I shall make no comment

on the principles or motives operating among you.

I shall only inform you that an alien is free

to change his means of livelihood, **he may take up any**—

JACK.

OK. Les go.

TICK.

De guy still—

JACK.

Up!

*(*ELLIE *gets up and* TICK *gets up.)*

SIR WILLIAM *(to* JACK).

It is understood, I hope, that—

JACK.

Come on, Goldie—

(To SIR WILLIAM)

Ah thank you fo you time, sir,

and stickin up fo me—

SIR WILLIAM.

I'm really very sorry—

JACK.

You scuse us now, please—

(To TREACHER)

See you, Mr. Treacher—

ELLIE.

Jack—

COATES *(to* TREACHER).

Your client will be leaving the country, I take it.

JACK.

Yeah, man, you take it. It's all yours.

*(*BLACKOUT. *Boat whistle, train whistle, another boat whistle, crowd, band playing.* LIGHTS UP *on—)*

SCENE TWO

A customs shed, Le Havre

At one side, with the BAND, *a welcoming* CROWD; OFFICIALS, PRESS, *etc., some waving small tricolors. At the other side* TWO UNIFORMED INSPECTORS, *beyond them a sign:* DOUANE. *Some* PORTERS *hurry past them, wheeling trunks, and a* CHEER *goes up behind them. Followed by his* ENTOURAGE, *greeting the* CROWD *with hands clasped triumphantly over his head, appears* KLOSSOWSKI, *a Polish heavyweight. The* PHOTOGRAPHERS' *flares commence, and continue through the scene. The* BAND *stops playing as* KLOSSOWSKI *meets the* OFFICIALS *and* PRESS, *shaking hands and embracing all around.*

OFFICIAL.

Bienvenue encore à la France, Monsieur Klossowski!

CROWD.

Bravo, Klossowski! Bienvenue! Bonne arrivée!

KLOSSOWSKI.

Merci, merci, mes amis, mille mercis—

PRESSMAN 1.

Alors, vous êtes prêt pour votre grand combat

avec le noir Jefferson?

KLOSSOWSKI.

Oho, monsieur—je suis absolument—

PRESSMAN 1.

Confiant?

KLOSSOWSKI.

C'est ça! Con—fi—dent!

Je m'excuse que mon français est terrible—

CROWD.

Mais non, mais non!

PRESSMAN 3.

Mais vous n'êtes pas hésitant à faire la boxe avec le champion du monde? Un petit peu?

KLOSSOWSKI.

Hésitant! Ha, ha, ha!

CROWD.

Bravo, Klossowski!

KLOSSOWSKI.

Écoutez—

Je boxai à Buenos Aires avec Paco Flores!

Zut! Zut! Zut! Trois rounds, je gagne!

Je boxai à Rio avec Pereira!

Zut! Frappe! Deux rounds, je gagne!

Je boxai en Afrique avec un noir gigantesque là—

Zut! Boom! **Pas de conteste, messieurs!**

Et cette Jefferson, qui c'est, qui c'est?

Oh, champion du monde, oui, lalala—

mais il n'a pas boxé pour longtemps!

(Miming it)

Il boit le whiskey, il fume les cigares,

il est gros, il êtes lourde,

il vit comme un—un—

PRESSMAN 1.

Cochon?

(Laughter)

KLOSSOWSKI.

C'est ça!

(Laughter)

Non, messieurs, c'est pas la vie du boxeur!

(Mimes it all)

Moi, je cours chaque jour trente kilomètres, même à la bateau—oui!

Je saute à la corde: cent fois!

Je boxe l'ombre: une heure!

Petit sac, vingt minutes!

Des gymnastiques, quarante minutes, deux fois, matin et soir,

et bain chaud! Douche froid!

Forte massage après midi,

mange bien, dix heures sommeil—

(Laughter)

Vous pensez que j'éxagère?

Attendez le combat Jefferson—

(Acts it out)

et zut! Zut! Gauche à l'estomac!

Droite à la tête! Gauche encore!

Zut! Frappe! Boom! Dix!

Voilà—**vous verrez!**

(Cheering, THEY *hoist him on their shoulders, the* BAND *strikes up, and he is borne off as* LIGHTS FADE: *new* CROWD SOUND *gradually replacing cheering, an arena* CROWD, *distant.* LIGHTS UP *on—)*

SCENE THREE

Jack's dressing room at the Vel d'Hiver arena, Paris

JACK *is sitting on the table.* TICK *taping his hands.* ELLIE. *A French* HANDLER *busy with towels, sponge, salts, etc.*

TICK.

Keep breathin deep, champ, nice an slow now.

JACK.

Ah knows howta breathe.

TICK.
Gonna finish off dat Polack like a chicken dinner!

JACK.
Hurry it up, huh.

TICK.
Ain even gonna muss you wool up on him!

JACK.
Don' talk like that fronna her.

ELLIE.
Jack, don't be silly—

JACK.
An when you start callin me "champ" anyway?

TICK.
Hey, come on. See if that too tight now.
(GOLDIE *enters.*)

ELLIE.
Full house?

GOLDIE.
Girlie, they're hangin from the rafters.

JACK.
Water bottle, Tick. Wanna rinse.

GOLDIE.
You OK?

JACK.
Why you keep askin me?

GOLDIE.
So what, so I'm askin!

JACK.
You worried bout somethin? What you worrying bout!

TICK.
Man, dat Polack sure in for it tonight.

GOLDIE.
Tick, for chrissake—

TICK *(to* HANDLER*).*
Uh—hey, Jim, where that O bottle gone to?

HANDLER.
Comment?

TICK.
The O. You know, O?

HANDLER.
Le—Ah—

TICK.
No, the O—

HANDLER.
La bouteille!

TICK.
Mistah who?

JACK.
Never mine—

HANDLER.
Non?

TICK.
Yeah, the O!

HANDLER.
De l'eau!
(Produces it)

TICK.
Attaboy! See? **Juss be patient with em.**
(Gives it to JACK, *who gargles and spits)*

JACK.
Bad tase in there, thassall.

GOLDIE *(to* TICK*).*
Coupla more minutes.

TICK *(to* JACK*).*
Put em up, baby, we better warm up some. Huh? OK?

JACK.
Ah warm up inside there with the man.

TICK.
Aw, be good now!
Ah ain't gonna get you winded—

ELLIE.
Tick!

JACK.
You don' haveta tell me what wind Ah ain't got.

TICK.
No, man, Ah mean—

JACK.
Ah know what shape is an when Ah ain in it.
Ah know when gettin in it's a waste a my good time too!
Ah don' gotta train to take no fith-rate gee-chee—

GOLDIE.
Jack, who says different—

JACK.
Thass who Ah fightin here, ain it!

GOLDIE.
It's the best they got around here, Jack—

JACK.
Hit him one an shovel up the money, right?
Jump in with the big gole belt, right?

TICK *(sings)*
Niggers is evil
White folks too.
So glad Ah'm a Chinaman,
Don' know whut to do.
(PROMOTER enters.)

PROMOTER.
If you please, messieurs.

ELLIE.
I'll go in to my seat now.

JACK.
Honey—

ELLIE *(kisses him).*
Good luck, darlin—

JACK.
Do me a favor. Stay here.

ELLIE.
Oh, Jack.
JACK.
Nothin in there you wanna see.
PROMOTER.
Come along, please, messieurs—
(To HANDLER)
vite, vite—
(To JACK)
But, oh, Monsieur Jefferson, the smile, the
    famous smile—
You will not deny to our public the smile!
JACK.
No, Ah got it on me.
PROMOTER.
Ha, ha, very good.
TICK.
We won't be too long.
   (THEY *leave.* ELLIE *sits. A few seconds go by*
and the CROWD ROAR *increases in volume.*
ELLIE *stands, wanders aimlessly, spies a news-*
paper, tries to read it, puts it down. Over the
CROWD NOISES *the* ANNOUNCER'S VOICE *is*
heard, incoherent. ELLIE *folds a towel, a jer-*
sey, sits again. SMITTY *enters.)*
SMITTY.
Hi there, Miss Bachman.
ELLIE.
Hello—
SMITTY.
Smith, *Evening Mirror.* Smitty?
ELLIE.
Oh, yes.
SMITTY.
Mind if I—
ELLIE.
Aren't you here for the fight?
SMITTY.
Well, the boys'll dope me in.
He's at it again, that's the main thing.
ELLIE.
Yes.
SMITTY.
I've missed him, Old Jack. How is he, any-
    way?
ELLIE.
Fine.
SMITTY.
Sure is looking good! Oh, a little moody—
ELLIE.
A little.
SMITTY.
That'll pass, don't let it get you down.
Part of it's all this moving around.
ELLIE.
Yes.

SMITTY.
Once you're not, and settle in somewhere—
(A ROAR)
There they go! You know what I mean?
ELLIE.
Yes.
SMITTY.
Makes all the difference.
ELLIE.
Probably.
SMITTY.
Sure—
and how long can it be!
ELLIE.
I don't know, really.
SMITTY.
Bet you can't wait, huh? Either of you!
ELLIE.
We talk about it.
SMITTY.
Yeah, what a feeling—
like to have a little nest here, do you think?
ELLIE.
We haven't made any—
(A ROAR. SHE *shivers.)*
SMITTY.
Listen to em!
No idea?
(SHE *shakes her head.)*
Christ, that must be hard on you now . . .
hm?
(No reply)
Well, leave that all to Jack!
As long as you rest and keep your strength
    up—
(SHE *faces him. A* ROAR)
I've had four myself and let me tell yo—
ELLIE.
Go away, will you.
SMITTY.
Ah, be a sport,
when's it going to be?
ELLIE.
It's not. Go away.
SMITTY.
I mean, you were looking so peaked the other
    day,
I had a hunch—
(A ROAR. SHE *turns away.)*
Say, don't get sore!
Look, the folks back home—
ELLIE.
I told you: no!
SMITTY.
I hate to let you down, folks!
   (A ROAR)

ELLIE.
Now, please—
(A ROAR)
SMITTY.
Something else, maybe?
Wedding bells? Homesick? Hear from your
family?
(A ROAR. SHE *covers her ears, shuddering.)*
ELLIE.
Oh, it's never—
SMITTY.
Are you feeling OK, Miss Bachman?
ELLIE.
Yes—
(A ROAR)
SMITTY.
He's dishing it out, he's not getting it—
ELLIE.
Please—
(A ROAR. SHE *bites her hand.)*
SMITTY.
You don't look too hot—Here, take a swal-
low—
(SHE *shakes her head. The* ROARING *is con-
tinuous now,* SMITTY *is nearly shouting.)*
How long do you think you can take it, any-
way,
living like this! It has to burn you out, Miss
Bachman,
can't you see that? Burn you out!
You're not as tough as he is, you know, you
can't just go on—
(The noise has turned to ANGRY BOOS *and*
CATCALLS; RUNNING FEET, *a* BELL CLANG-
ING. SHOUTS *nearby: "Sauvage! Assassin!"*
JACK, TICK, GOLDIE, *and the* PROMOTER
burst in, blood smears on JACK's *gloves and
chest. Sounds of* POLICE SCUFFLING *in the
corridor)*
GOLDIE.
God, why'd you keep—
PROMOTER.
Quickly, please!
ELLIE.
What happened—Jack—
JACK.
He'll come out of it—
GOLDIE.
Grab that bag—
JACK.
It's all right, honey—
TICK.
Yeah—just!
ELLIE.
No—
PROMOTER.
This way, please—

GOLDIE.
Dress in the car, Jack—
PROMOTER.
I beg of you!
JACK.
Come on, honey. I'm sorry, I'm sorry.
(Leads HER *off,* LIGHTS *and* SHOUTS FAD-
ING. DARKNESS)

SCENE FOUR

Pop Weaver's office, New York
The darkened office suite of POP WEAVER,
promoter. In the flickering light of the film
THEY *are watching sit* POP, CAP'N DAN, *and*
FRED, *formerly Brady's manager.*

———

CAP'N DAN.
How much you say he weighs, Fred?
FRED.
Two thirty-seven. He's six foot five . . .
watch it! Mommer!
POP.
Not bad, Cap'n Dan, eh?
FRED.
Wait, here's Vancouver two weeks ago—hold
on—
there's my boy! The one on the left.
CAP'N DAN.
You couldn't exactly miss him, Fred.
FRED.
Rushes straight in—there! I don't wanna
brag,
but when that kid first—
(The film breaks; only the beam continues.)
Ah, for crying out loud!
VOICE *(offstage).*
Won't take a minute.
FRED.
So? Waddaya say!
**If that's no White Hope I'm Queen Pocahon-
tas.**
POP.
He's the right stuff, Dan. Maybe a little raw
yet—
FRED.
Fresh, fresh is what he is! Big, clean, strong,
a real farmboy! They're waiting on their
knees
for something like him!
(Silence. THEY *stare at the blank screen.)*
FRED *(calling out).*
How about it there!
CAP'N DAN.
I don't think we need to see any more, Pop.

POP.
Lights, please, Harry.
(The room is lit.)
Well, you tell me, Dan.
You want me to promote it, I'm ready to
    promote it,
anytime, anywhere.
          FRED *(to* CAP'N DAN*).*
Right!
          POP.
What do you think, Dan?
          CAP'N DAN.
I think he's a full-grown polar bear, myself.
          FRED.
Well, we have to send over somebody, don't
    we?
The papers are hollerin, all the old bull
    again—
**Honest, it's gettin like Remember the Maine
here!**
          CAP'N DAN.
Oh, he fills the bill all right.
But say we do send him over, and the black
    boy
does it again, Fred. Then where are we.
          POP.
You won't ever have it on a plate, Dan, you
    know.
          CAP'N DAN.
Pop, Fred. Let me tell you a secret.
The next White Hope is the one who gets the
    belt back.
Not means to, or almost does, or gets half-
    killed trying:
he takes it, he finishes right on his feet, with
    a big
horizontal nigger down for good there.
          POP.
What do you mean, Dan? Is it yes or no?
          CAP'N DAN.
I'd like you to meet a friend of mine, Pop.
(Calls)
Mr. Dixon there yet?
          VOICE *(offstage).*
Yeah!
          CAP'N DAN.
Come on in.
(Enter DIXON*)*
Pop Weaver. Fred.
          POP.
Have a chair, Mr. Dixon.
          DIXON *(sits).*
Thanks.
(To CAP'N DAN*)*
All right?

          CAP'N DAN.
Oh, we're hopeful, I think.
(THEY *laugh.*)
Dixon here is with the Bureau in Washing-
    ton.
Like you might expect, they have Mr. Jeffer-
    son
on their minds, too. I've been down there,
we've had some ideas—you explain it to
    them, son.
          DIXON.
When a man beats us out like this, we—the
    law, that is—
suffer in prestige, and that's pretty serious.
How people regard the law is part of its effec-
    tiveness,
it can't afford to look foolish, and this applies
especially now to our Negro population.
I don't mean just the ones who always flout
    the law,
and seeing their hero doing it in style
act up more than usual—those are police con-
    cerns, not ours.
But though you may not be aware of it yet,
a very large, very black migration is in prog-
    ress.
They're coming from the fields down there
    and filling up the slums,
trouble's starting in Europe, and our mills
    and factories
have work for them now. And I'm talking of
    hundreds
of thousands, maybe millions soon—
**millions of ignorant Negroes, rapidly mass-
    ing together,**
**their leanings, their mood, their outlook, sud-
    denly**
**no longer regulated by the little places they
    come from—**
situations have arisen already.
We cannot allow the image of this man
to go on impressing and exciting these people.
          POP.
I'm only a sports promoter, Mr. Dixon.
          CAP'N DAN.
He read the writing on the door, Pop. Go on.
          DIXON.
If this position he enjoys were to be lost,
through the outcome of his next engagement,
    let's say,
the effect of this would be so much in our
    interest
that we would be disposed to reconsider his
    sentence.
          POP.
You'd make it worth his while not to win the
    fight, you mean.

POP.

I think I've said what I mean, Mr. Weaver.

CAP'N DAN *(to* DIXON).

What's the furthest you can go?

DIXON.

We'd reduce it to a year, of which he'd serve six months,

preferred treatment, best facilities, etcetera.

We're willing to make this as attractive as possible.

FRED.

I say my kid can beat him fair and square!

POP.

Don't ride it, Fred.

FRED.

Look, if you won't promote it,

I'll hop on a boat with him and find someone who will!

CAP'N DAN.

You don't want to do that, Fred.

FRED.

What am I, a—

CAP'N DAN.

Fred. I'm tellin you as a friend.

FRED.

I just don't like it.

POP.

It goes against me too, Dan.

CAP'N DAN.

And against me too!

I don't have to make anybody no speech here

about how good I feel working something crooked!

None of us like it—**we wouldn't be the men we are**

if we did, or be where we are! I know it's lousy!

But we got a situation here needs a little bending,

the man's tried to tell you how serious it is,

they're bending with it, I'm bending with it,

who are you to sit there and say it goes against you,

or you either, on your pedestal here!

POP.

What about the champ, though, Dan?

FRED.

He'll never buy it!

Or my kid either, he's straight outa Sunday school,

he's—

CAP'N DAN.

Shut up, Fred—

nobody has to tell your kid a thing!

And Jack, well, after that last one,

nobody there'll fight him any more,

he's down to giving exhibitions, peanuts—

POP.

But serving six months, Dan—

CAP'N DAN.

It can't be much worse

than killing the six months. And he'll step out a free man—

all that fight money! See all his pals!

Besides, his ole mammy ain't been too good,

he'll want to see her before she goes.

Sure he'll take it.

POP.

Dan, why not ask Weiler

or Michel to set it up, someone on the spot there?

CAP'N DAN.

I'm asking you, Pop.

(Pause)

POP *(to* DIXON).

You can't put that deal

in writing, can you, mister?

DIXON.

Sorry, Pop. I wasn't even here.

(Pause)

POP.

What the hell, Fred.

We'll balance it out on the one after this.

Everything back on the gold standard, right?

FRED.

OK, OK.

DIXON *(rising).*

Well, thank you, gentlemen—

(THEY *all rise.)*

CAP'N DAN.

And we thank you!

POP.

I wouldn't count on

results straight off, though.

DIXON.

Oh, I think the country

can hold up a little while.

(THEY *laugh,* DIXON *waves them silent.)*

Excuse me—

You seem to be indignant, sir. Yes, I heard you.

We have that all the time from people like you,

that old Machiavelli crap. Look into it further, sir.

But not in here, or at home. Give it some thought

next time you're alone on the streets late at night.

(To CAP'N DAN)

I'll be in touch with you.

(LIGHTS FADE. BLACKOUT. MUSIC: *German street band, distant.* LIGHTS UP *on—)*

SCENE FIVE

A sidewalk café, Berlin
Jack, Tick, four drunken GERMAN OFFI-
CERS *with them.* Jack *Indian-wrestling the*
largest, OFFICER 4, *on the stein-covered table,*
as the other three encourage their comrade.

———

OFFICER 1.
Jetzt!
OFFICER 2.
Kraft, Hans—
OFFICER 3.
Ringe!
OFFICER 4.
Kann nicht!
OFFICER 1.
Nein!
OFFICER 4.
Himmelsgott!
OFFICER 2.
Ja!
    (JACK *begins to bear his arm down.*)
OFFICER 3.
Aber, Hans—
OFFICER 1.
Nein!
OFFICER 4.
Mutter!
OFFICER 2.
Halt—
OFFICER 1.
Nein—
OFFICER 3.
Nein, nein—
ALL.
A-a-a-h!
OFFICER 1.
Wunderbar! **Herrlich!** Mein herr, you are the
    triumph!
JACK.
Well, thanks for stoppin roun, boys—
OFFICER 2.
Wir müssen die Fahne vom Regiment präsen-
    tieren!
OFFICER 1.
He says we must present to you the flag of our
    regiment!
JACK.
Oh, cain't take that, ahma Mercan citizen—
TICK.
You buy some tickets fo de show, dassall—
OFFICER 4 (*offering his arm*).
Bitte—again, please—
JACK.
Tomorrow, buddy, you done wore me out.
    (ALL OFFICERS *laugh.*)

TICK.
We see you all tomorrow, huh?
OFFICER 1 (*picking up stein*).
Kameradschaft!
    (*The* OTHERS *follow suit.*)
JACK (*standing*).
Camera shaft, OK.
TICK.
Lawd, the drinkin sure hard on the feet here.
OFFICER 4.
Wir müssen ihm etwas geben!
ALL.
Ja! Ja!
OFFICER 1.
Mein herr, we go provide for you the suitable
    mememto.
JACK.
Great, be lookin out for ya.
TICK.
Weenersane, weenersane.
ALL (*leaving*).
Hop, hop, hop, hop . . .
JACK (*yawning and stretching*).
O mah bones, whut you after.
TICK.
Wanna go back to the hotel?
JACK (*sits*).
Naw. Nothin doin there. You ready fo
    anuther?
TICK.
Ah better pass.
(*Sips*)
Wonder how they make it brew up so heavy.
You think they mix a egg in or whut?
JACK.
Beats me, man. Puttin me to sleep, though.
TICK.
Well, thass whut they does after lunch here,
    right?
JACK.
No, man, that were someplace else.
    (ELLIE *enters with* RAGOSY, *an impresario.*)
RAGOSY.
Ah, Meester Jafferson—
JACK.
Whut you bring him for—?
RAGOSY.
Such delights again to see you—
JACK.
Now ain Ah tole you, mistah—
RAGOSY.
Ragosy, excuse—
    (*Gives card*)
ELLIE.
He just tagged along, Jack—
RAGOSY.
I am patient rewarded!

TICK.
Which one wuz he?
JACK.
Huh . . . lemme think now . . .
You ain't the one wanted me to team up with a circus—
RAGOSY.
Please?
JACK.
An it wuzn't you pushin me to start a restrunt with him—
RAGOSY.
No, no—
JACK.
Or the artiss guy gonna hire me an do me in black cement?
RAGOSY.
But you recall Ragosy!
TICK.
Man, he that Hungrarian!
JACK.
Oh yeah, thassright—
(WAITER *enters.*)
RAGOSY.
Please, not speak additional word,
I supply first champagne—
(*To* WAITER)
Abräumen, bitte!
(*To* JACK)
Wait, not to trust here, I consult myself—sit!
(*Goes in*)
JACK (*to* ELLIE).
Why dinya sen him up ta Goldie, Goldie brush him!
ELLIE.
He wasn't there, he had to go out.
TICK.
Oh yeah? Something movin?
ELLIE.
Just meeting that reporter.
JACK.
Smitty?
ELLIE.
Yes, he rang up.
JACK.
Whut he doin here?
TICK.
Must be he onna job an he sayin hello.
JACK.
Nothin goin on here.
TICK.
You ain't the only item in the paper, bighead.
RAGOSY (*reentering with champagne;*
WAITER *sets glasses*).
See, from my own hands! I take it the privilege—
Champion, lovely friends—

TICK.
Ready wid de pumps, men.
RAGOSY.
Oh, Meester Jafferson!
It pains in my heart these nights attending you.
I count there the people and I make totality:
one-quarter business! you do not divert!
JACK.
Mebbe Ah oughta wear a bone through ma nose.
RAGOSY.
No, no!
For the true fisticuff with bleedings they come,
but now you are not doing, you must look otherwise.
I implore again myself, let Ragosy be devising
the spectacle to you—Song! Dancing! **Sentiment!**
The name is on you still like a diamond, my friend,
only let make necessary light and then, then—
JACK (*leaping up: buck and wing*).
Out in San Francisco where de weather's fair
Dey have a dance out dere—
RAGOSY.
Ah, aha—
JACK.
Dey call the Grizzly Bear,
All your other lovin' dances don't compare—
ELLIE.
Jack, please stop it.
JACK.
What?
ELLIE.
Can't you just tell him no and—
JACK.
Ah tell him whut Ah wants to, hon—
ELLIE.
Jack, we're in the street—
JACK.
An where Ah wants to an how, hear?
TICK.
Baby, all she sayin—
JACK.
Who ass you!
(*To* ELLIE)
Talk to me bout streets.
If you so goddam tetchy bout people lookin
you ain't even oughta be here!
ELLIE.
I don't like them looking when you're this way—

JACK.
No? Well, me neither! But Ah's stuck widdit
an you ain't, so any time you wanna—where
    you goin!
RAGOSY *(rising).*
Oh, Madam, I sincerely—
JACK *(to* ELLIE*).*
Git you ass back on there! Man bought cham-
    pagne—
RAGOSY.
Please, Meester Jafferson—
JACK.
You siddown too!
*(*RAGOSY *does.)*
ELLIE.
I'll be in the room.
JACK.
Yeah, then you say you sicka waitin roun
    hotels!
ELLIE.
I never said that.
JACK.
You givin out you misery so hard you don'
    haveta!
You juss don' like nothin no more!
ELLIE.
I won't even answer you—
JACK.
Dassit, give it out!
ELLIE.
What do you want, Jack!
JACK.
Don' like nothin!
ELLIE *(going).*
Excuse me, please—
JACK.
You siddown here, girl—
TICK.
Let her go, man, she got the Fear again—
JACK *(calling after her).* ELLIE!
TICK *(following).*
Ah walk her on back—
    *(*NOISE *of rhythmical clanging and shout-*
ing)
JACK.
Tell that Goldie Ah wants him, hear!
    TICK *(looking in direction of noise).*
Say—
JACK.
Git!
(Holds ears)
Oh, them heavy-foot bastuds.
    TICK *(going).*
He turnin meaner than a red hyena.
    JACK *(toasting* RAGOSY*).*
Happy days, mistah—

RAGOSY.
Prosit, prosit, and I eagerly to hope we—
    *(*RAGOSY *slips off as the* FOUR OFFICERS
*gaily return; one is beating on dustbin lid with
a chair leg, two of the others frog-march be-
tween them a very black young* NEGRO*, who
struggles violently)*
NEGRO.
Lassen mir! Lassen mir absteigen!
JACK.
Hey—
OFFICER 1.
So, we bring you as we promise—halt!
OFFICER 4.
Einen Schwarzen Kameraden—
    (Laughing, THEY *dump* NEGRO. JACK
helps him up.)
JACK.
Here, lemme duss you off—
OFFICER 2.
Is suitable, nein?
NEGRO.
Mutig Soldaten spielen wie Kinder!
    (Jeers and laughter)
JACK.
Don' rile em, man—
NEGRO.
Again, bitte?
JACK.
Whut—where the hell you from, anyway?
OFFICER 1.
Where! He must ask!
    (Gales of laughter)
NEGRO.
Afrika.
OFFICER 2.
Boomboomboom!
OFFICER 4.
Crucrucru!
OFFICER 3.
Authentick, ja!
JACK.
Oh, Jesus.
OFFICER 1.
Here, you observe?
    (Points to scars on NEGRO*'s face.* JACK
gasps. More laughter.)
NEGRO.
Ja. Iss tribe mark.
OFFICER 2.
Walawalawala!
NEGRO.
Here iss custom more large.
(Makes gesture of dueling scar. OFFICER 4
    goes for him.)
OFFICER 4.
Scheissfarbiger Hund—

OFFICER 2 *(as other* OFFICERS *tussle with*
OFFICER 4, *restraining him).*
Nein, Hans, nein—
　JACK.
Go siddown there, Jim—
　NEGRO.
Please?
　JACK *(pushing him toward table).*
Move—
(Going to struggling OFFICERS.)
Well, much obliged, fellahs, thass zackly
　　what Ah wanted—
(OFFICER 4 *breaks away,* JACK *catches him
by arm.)*
Hey, Hands, you know this one?
(Stands with him toe to toe.)
　OFFICERS 1, 2, 3.
Ah!
　OFFICER 2.
Wirf ihn!
　OFFICER 3.
Jetzt! Jetzt!
　OFFICER 1.
Nun, Hans—
　(JACK *pulls him off balance.)*
　ALL OFFICERS.
Bravo!
　OFFICER 2.
Der schaffts immer!
　OFFICER 4 *(to* WAITER).
Herr Ober, Bier für uns alle!
　JACK.
No, Hands—
(Drawing them away.)
Bess leave us darkies get quainted . . . you
　　know,
chomp a few bananas an all—
　OFFICERS 3 *and* 4 *(laughing).*
Er muss eine Banane essen! Ja!
　OFFICER 2.
He pleases you, the new Kamerad, Herr
　　Boxer!
　JACK *(drawing them further).*
Man, Ah'm happy as a cow with six tits.
(Shrieks of laughter. THEY *go.* JACK *waves
　　after them.)*
Weenersane! Donker!
(Returning)
Wish they'd start a war up and keep them
　　boys busy.
　NEGRO *(standing at table).*
You forgiff I am employed in siss, please.
　JACK.
Thass awright, chief. Needed some ex'cise
　　anyway.
　NEGRO.
I am nutt chiff. I am son from ser chiff.

　JACK.
Oh, yeah? Well, take a pew here with the
　　fiel'-nigger's boy.
(THEY *sit,* JACK *pours.)*
　NEGRO.
You are ser Boxer, ja?
　JACK.
Thass me. When Ah workin at it.
　NEGRO.
From Amerika kommen.
　JACK.
Yeah, kommen and goin. You never been
　　there, Ah guess.
　NEGRO.
Nein. I haff nutt zere ser purpose. Iss gutt?
　JACK.
Sometimes. Ain been there a while myself.
　NEGRO.
You learn zere gutt make ser laughink.
　JACK.
Oh, thanks.
　NEGRO.
Please, iss nut uffenz. Must I learn also, I
　　sink.
　JACK *(laughs).*
Seem like you leff it kina late.
　NEGRO.
Iss better, nein?
　JACK.
Yeah, mebbe so . . . Well, here's to us fish
　　outa water.
(THEY *drink.)*
　NEGRO.
Away much long iss to hurt now. You.
　JACK.
Might say that.
　NEGRO.
I am feeling. I haff in Europe sree year so.
　JACK.
Lawd. Lit out for good, huh?
　NEGRO.
Please?
　JACK.
Vamoose fum de ole country, Africa.
　NEGRO.
Ah! You sink I go for nut be zere,
nein, nein. I go so I komm zere back.
　JACK.
How zat?
　NEGRO.
Mit more knowings.
　JACK.
Oh! Ah gotcha.
　NEGRO.
Student.
　JACK.
Yeah. Nevah touch it myself.

NEGRO.
I do nutt tell to giff shame inn.
JACK.
Huh? No. Ah'm with you, man.
What all you studyin?
NEGRO.
Ser Law and ser Finanz and ser Chemikals-
mining.
JACK.
My, my, my.
NEGRO.
Ja, makes ser headache!
(JACK *laughs with him.*)
JACK.
Better go warn de chief bout dis one!
NEGRO.
Please? You haff choke mit ser fazzer?
JACK.
Naw . . .
But Ah thought Mistah White running things
down there.
NEGRO.
Now, ja.
JACK.
They gonna letya help, huh?
NEGRO.
So, I vatch.
JACK.
They ain leavin go, man. No place.
NEGRO.
Zumorrow, nein.
JACK.
Nex Wensdy nine neither.
NEGRO.
Sey make here ser war soon, ja?
JACK.
So?
NEGRO.
Iss like drunken peoples,
Sree mann, fife mann, hitting one ozzer—you
haff see, Boxer?
All ser teess mit bloot, outspitten!
Up all ser eatings, POUAH, POUAH!
Sey make so enough ser war,
plack mann fly out from ser mouss. I sink.
JACK *(takes it in, then lifts his glass).*
Here's to you an me and de "How Long
Blues."
NEGRO.
Please?
JACK.
Drink up.
NEGRO.
Ah, Boxer, Goes like you Pessimismus
in Amerika all plack mann, I am fearing.
JACK.
Well, don't go by me, buddy.

NEGRO.
Ach, aber ja.
Goes plack Champion so, goes klein plack
mann so!
Logik, nein?
JACK.
He a bitch, ain he.
NEGRO.
Bad, stronk peoples to be so.
JACK.
Oh, man, we strong on cryin there, thassall.
NEGRO.
Nein, was slafe. Slafe nutt stronk, he die.
Cry iss from ser life inn.
JACK.
Well, it sure the wrong kina strong to git leff
with
when you ain slavin no more.
NEGRO.
You komm gutt out. You.
JACK.
Outa where.
NEGRO.
Ser slafe. I see.
JACK.
Ah dunno. Juss went the whole hog, man.
NEGRO.
Please?
JACK.
Shoot it all. You know: jump.
NEGRO.
Ja, exakt.
(Points at him)
Ser bekinnink-man.
JACK.
Naw, Ah ain tried ta start nothin.
(NEGRO *bursts out laughing.*)
What so funny bout dat?
NEGRO *(rocking with laughter).*
Oh, Boxer, Boxer, Boxer.
ven I am to chumping in Afrika.
I hope so much nossing vill I make!
(GOLDIE *bursts in.*)
GOLDIE.
Jack! All over town I—oh, you busy?
(NEGRO *rises.*)
JACK.
Don' run off, man—
GOLDIE.
Gotta talk to ya, Jack.
NEGRO.
So, I go.
(JACK *rises,* NEGRO *removes object from
shirt.*)
Please, you take?
JACK.
Oh, hey—

NEGRO.
Please. My fazzer giff.

JACK *(hesitates, then takes it).*
Wish you all the luck in the worl, man, thanks.

NEGRO.
Also you. You keep mit, ja?

JACK.
Sure. Zat what it's for? Luck?

NEGRO.
Nein. For hurt from spirits.

JACK.
Yeah.

NEGRO.
Gootbye, Boxer.

(NEGRO *bows and goes.)*

JACK.
OK, I'm listenin.

GOLDIE.
Well . . . we got a match.

JACK.
How much Ah get for losin it?

GOLDIE.
Huh?

JACK.
Yeh, Ah'm listenin.

GOLDIE.
How the hell does he know!

JACK.
Mah witch-doctor tole me.

GOLDIE.
Look! Lemme first explain what Smitty—

JACK.
Boss, Ah know whut Smitty.
They askin fo a straight fight, they ain't sendin Smitty—

GOLDIE.
Whattaya gettin sore, the guy calls me up—

JACK.
Nobody sore. How much it worth?

GOLDIE.
Fred's got this kid, see—

JACK.
Now, boss, you ain't hearin good.

GOLDIE.
Eighty-twenty split. A hundred G's guarantee.

JACK.
Mm, boy!
Pretty nice fo plain ole layin down, huh!

GOLDIE.
And they'll cut the rap to six months for ya.

JACK.
Well!
See all folks kin do when evvybody pitch in?

GOLDIE.
Jackie, I don't blame you for—

JACK.
Any special roun they like me to dive in?

GOLDIE.
He says we can work all that out.

JACK.
Uh huh. An whut you say?

GOLDIE.
I said it stinks but I'll let him know later.

JACK *(pointing to champagne).*
Right.
Sen him a bottle a this, an tell him suck it through a straw.

GOLDIE.
No thinkin it over.

JACK.
How long you my manager?

GOLDIE.
Five-six years.

JACK.
Then why you gotta ask?

GOLDIE.
Why? Cause I gotta eat, that's why!
What am I managin here, for God's sake!
What else you got in fronta you—

JACK.
Don't try an sell me, boss.

GOLDIE.
Big shot! Send him champagne! On what?
The fights you have with your girl, maybe?
On a ten percent like this my enemies should live!

JACK.
Ah know it, man. Time to fine fresh meat.

GOLDIE.
Well, what the hell you need me for, anyway!

JACK.
Yeah, been thinkin bout that—

(The FOUR OFFICERS *charge in.* THEY *carry a rope.)*

OFFICER 4 *(to* WAITER).
Herr Ober, Bier für uns alle!

GOLDIE.
Jack, let's go talk to him, they're gonna keep after you,
you're getting sick here—

JACK.
No, you call it right—

OFFICER 1 *(giving* JACK *one end).*
We make now to pull, Boxer?

JACK.
Yeah, why not—

GOLDIE.
Listen—

OFFICER 3 *(as* OFFICERS *take other end).*
Erst, Hans!

JACK.
There's no hard feelins, boss—

OFFICER 4 *(as* THEY *all line up).*
Nun gewinnen wir!
GOLDIE.
Jack—
JACK.
Take all you need to get home on—
OFFICER 1.
Prepared, mein herr?
JACK *(getting a grip).*
Anytime!
(Tug of war: JACK *holds.)*
GOLDIE.
Oh, Jackie, oh, look at what you're doin—
JACK *(giving ground).*
It . . . ain't . . . good . . . but . . . it's . . . . the . . .
bess . . . Ah . . . can . . .
OFFICERS *(pulling him out as* LIGHTS FADE).*
Ho-ya! ho-ya! ho-ya! ho-ya!
*(*BLACKOUT. *Cymbal crash, followed by a tinny rendering of "Chiri-biri-bin" as* LIGHTS UP *on—)*

SCENE SIX

Cabaret Ragosy, Budapest
Small stage of a cabaret, audience unseen. A JUGGLER *in tights, working in time to the waltz, is finishing his turn.* LOUD APPLAUSE *as* HE *takes his bow;* RAGOSY, *now in evening dress and beaming, joins him on the stage and boosts the applause. Exit the* JUGGLER. RAGOSY *holds up his hand for silence.*

RAGOSY.
És most, Hölgyeim es Uraim,
amire mindanyian vártak! Bemutatom
a Rágosy Kabaré föattrakcióját,
Amerikai klasszikust
"Uncle Thomas Kunyhóját."
(The saxophone begins playing "My Old Kentucky Home," and the LIGHTING *becomes very roseate, as* TWO STAGEHANDS *position a papier-mâché weeping willow and a patch of grass.* RAGOSY *continues accordingly, describing the scene.)*
A jelenet a Mississippi . . . partjan jatszodik
le . . .
sek sek . . .
Uncle Thomas és a little Éva élvezték a nap-
keltét . . .
(Winding up to bring them on)
Tehát bemutatjuk a vilàgbajnokot Jack
Jeffersont,
elbübölö feleségével és néger barájtával!

(Spatter of applause. ELLIE *comes on as Little Eva, golden curls, etc.* JACK *follows her as Uncle Tom, shabby, gray wig, etc.* SHE *sits under "tree.")*
ELLIE.
Here, Uncle Tom, do come and sit beside me.
JACK.
Deed Ah will, Miss Eva. On dis lubly ole grassy bank.
ELLIE.
See how beautiful the clouds are, Tom. And the water too.
JACK.
An you right widdem, Miss Eva, you de byootifluss of all.
ELLIE.
But, friend, why do you seem sad this evening?
JACK.
Oh, Miss Eva, you and de Massah so kine ter Ole Tom he jus gotta cry bout it now and den.
ELLIE.
Yes. We are happy here.
JACK.
It like a plantation fum de Good Book, yes-sum.
You de brightest lil sperrit Ah evah seed, Miss Eva.
ELLIE.
Oh, Tom, sing about the Spirits Bright, would you?
JACK.
Juss gittin set to.
(Piano gives him a chord and accompanies. Sings.)
  Ah sees a ban uh Sperrits Bright
  Dat tase de glo-ries dere—
(Mock GROAN *from the audience)*
  Dey are all robed in spotliss white
  An wavin palm dey bear.
  Ef Ah had wings—
(Another mock GROAN, *a* TITTER, *a* VOICE *saying "következö";* JACK *stops, the piano stops. A moment of uncertainty)*
ELLIE.
Oh, but look who has come to make us lively, Tom!
(Enter TICK *as Topsy, grinning and prancing)*
TICK.
Hee, hee, hee!
ELLIE.
Dear me, Topsy, why do you behave so!
TICK.
Speck cause Ah jes plain ole wicked, Miss Eva!

JACK.
What dis lil black imp done now?

TICK.
Hee, hee, hee!

ELLIE.
How old are you, Topsy?

TICK.
Ah dunno, missy.

ELLIE.
Don't know how old you are? Who was your mother?

TICK.
Ah dunno, missy. Nevah had no mother.

ELLIE.
What do you mean? Where were you born?

TICK.
Ah dunno, missy. Nevah waz bo'n.

ELLIE.
But Topsy, think a moment. Someone must have made you!

TICK.
Nobody's Ah knows on, missy. Ah specks Ah jes growed!

ELLIE.
Oh, Topsy—

TICK.
Hee, hee, hee!

JACK.
Awright, you shifless heathen, give us a breakdown
an git back to you stinks—

(Piano and drums, assisted by ELLIE, who produces a tambourine, and JACK, a Jew's harp. TICK sings.)

TICK.
 I always think I'm up in Heaven
 When I'm down in Dixieland,
 I've got an angel of a Mammy,
 Out of Alabamy,
 Of the good old fashioned brand;
 She taught me that it's wrong,
 To stay up all night long;
 Go to sleep my baby,
 That's Mammy's little fav'rite song.

(Dances through the next chorus, JACK joining him, ELLIE continuing on the tambourine. The audience seems to like this better, but as TICK, breathless, resumes singing, they again grow more and more restless.)

 Everybody loves somebody
 Down in dear old Dixieland,
 The pretty flowers in the garden,
 Keep their heads a noddin,
 When you walk by hand in hand;
 The gals down there are very plain—
(RAGOSY tries to quiet audience.)
 And every other lane's a lovers lane,
 That's why—

(RAGOSY pulls TICK from the stage, motioning to JACK and ELLIE to continue. ELLIE reclines in a moribund attitude against the tree as the saxophone commences with "Old Black Joe.")

JACK.
Is you feelin . . . weakish agin, Miss Eva?

ELLIE.
Yes. There is something I must tell you, Uncle Tom.
(Protest from the audience)

JACK.
It cain't be, Miss Eva, not yit—

ELLIE.
Do not be gloomy! Look, those clouds, they are like great gates of pearl now.
(More protests)

JACK.
No, Miss Eva, no—

ELLIE.
And I can see beyond them . . . far, far off . . .

VOICE.
Gyorsan, gyorsan!

JACK *(kneeling).*
Oh, Ah knows we cain't speck ta keep ya here wid us—

VOICE.
Milyen unalmas!

ELLIE.
Yes, I am going to a better country—

VOICE.
A következö!
(Laugh)

ELLIE.
And I am going there before long, Uncle Tom . . .
(Groan)

VOICES.
Rémes! Rettentes!

JACK.
Well, ef de Lawd needya back, Miss Eva—

VOICE.
Hozd vissza a néger barátodat—!

JACK.
Ah be hunkydory here—

VOICES.
Rémes! Rémes!

(A slow handclap starts in the audience, quickly building up with foot-stamping and bottle-knocking)

ELLIE.
Oh, dear Tom . . . take a tress of my . . .

VOICES.
Borzasztó! Nevetséges!
(JACK rises slowly, looks out at them.)

ELLIE.
Take a tress of my golden hair . . . to . . .
   to . . .
(She stops as the noise gets louder. RAGOSY
*appears at the side of the stage, trying to quiet
them again, but they grow more angry at this.)*
   VOICES.
Takaradjanak el!
Takaradjanak el!
Fogják meg!
   (RAGOSY *tries to speak but cannot be heard;*
ELLIE *runs from the stage.* JACK *pulls the Uncle Tom wig off and stands immobile, expressionless.* RAGOSY, *frightened, signals desperately—for* JACK *to get off-stage, for the saxo-
phonist to stop playing, for the electrician to
cut the lights . . . the saxophone desists, and
after a few attempts the electrician seems to
find the right switch . . . as the lights dim out
on* JACK *the noise reaches a crescendo, then is
cut off sharply in the blackout as, suddenly, at
the extreme opposite end of the real stage,*
MRS. BACHMAN *appears, white, pained, and
haggard. She looks around at the real audience, then speaks.)*
   MRS. BACHMAN.
I know what most of you watching this believe in,
or think you believe in, or try to believe in.
But I know something else too, I know what
   Black means,
and not just to me because of my daughter,
to everyone in here. All of us know,
though it might take some of you a daughter
   you've cared for
to make you say it, what it means, yes,
   means,
what it is to you truthfully—BLACKNESS!
   —there, feel it,
what it sets off in your heart, in the memories
   and words
and shapes you think with, the dark to be
   afraid of,
pitch black, black as dirt, the black hole and
   the black pit,
what's burned or stained or cursed or hideous,
poison and spite and the waste from your
   body
and the horrors crawling up into your mind—
I hate what I'm saying! As much as you do!
I hate that it's so, I wish to God it weren't!
And if it was God who intended it so,
and still willed that color on a race of human

beings,
and brought us face to face here,
how He must hate all of us! Go on imagining
that time and justice can change it in you
   now,
or that when it disappears in the singing of
   songs
it's being destroyed. Tell yourselves it's only
one more wrong to be righted, and that I'm a
   half-mad woman,
oh, making far too much of it. Wait until it
   is
your every other thought, like it is theirs, like
   it is mine,
Wait until it touches your own flesh and
   blood.
*(As she slowly walks off, the lights on her
fading, a distant rumble of artillery fire is
heard, which continues throughout the next
scene—)*

SCENE SEVEN

Railway station, Belgrade
JACK *and* ELLIE *standing bedraggled in wet
raincoats. Suitcases. Pools of light. Station
empty.*

———

   TICK *(entering).*
Nothin, man. Maybe one pullin out tonight.
   JACK.
Anybody know whut goin on dere?
   TICK.
Porter sey dey just practicin.
   JACK.
Yeah.
   ELLIE
What will we do, Jack?
   JACK.
I dunno yet.
   ELLIE.
Do you think we should—
   JACK.
Ah said Ah dunno yet!
   ELLIE.
All right, I heard you.
   JACK.
Play cards or somethin wid her, willya?
   SMITTY *(offstage).*
Jack!
   *(Entering from a distance, catching his
breath)*
God, I'm glad I caught you . . .
   JACK.
Lay offa me, man.

SMITTY.

It's sort of an emergency, Jack . . . back home.

(Takes out telegram)

Your mother's very low.

JACK *(snatching it from him).*

Gimme dat.

(Reads it. Holds onto it throughout scene)

SMITTY.

I'm sorry about this, feller.

JACK.

Yeah. Thanks.

SMITTY.

Maybe we could work something out for you, Jack.

To go straight over now and then do the rest of it.

I know you want to be there.

(Pause)

You might just make it, Jack.

I've hired a car and I fixed up your passage from—

JACK *(to himself).*

Button comin loose here.

ELLIE.

Yes?

(Pause)

SMITTY.

Christ, deal or no deal,

it's worth a try, isn't it? Even just to let her feel you're on your way, she'd be—

JACK.

Thanks for comin roun, man.

SMITTY.

You can't stay over here now, anyway. Jack! It's finished here. You know that. Where do you go?

JACK.

Don' wan none today, man.

SMITTY.

All right, don't get sore—

I really thought—

JACK.

Ah seeya sometime.

(Pause)

SMITTY.

OK . . .

(Turns to go, stops)

What the hell is it for, though, all this.

I mean, you're not a Boy Scout. What the hell is it, Jack.

Keeping the belt a little bit longer? Staying champ

a little while longer? I can't make you out.

JACK.

Champ don' mean piss-all ta me, man.

Ah bin it, all dat champ jive bin beat clear outa me.

Dat belt a yours juss hardware, woulden even hole mah pants up.

But Ah'm stuck widdit, see, a hunk of junky hardware,

but it don't let go, it turnin green on me,

but it still ain lettin go, Ah'm stuck as bad widdit

as you all stuck wid needin it offa me—

shake it loose, man! Knock me fo ten and take it, understan?

Ah be much oblige!

SMITTY.

Look, you know we'd rather

have it straight—

JACK.

Oh, ya would, huh.

SMITTY.

Sure,

and, Jack, if you weren't so damned good—

JACK *(grabbing him).*

Hunnerd million people ovah dere, ain'tya?

SMITTY.

Yes, but—

JACK.

Picked out de bes Hope ya got dere, ain't-ya—?

TICK.

Jack—

JACK.

Ah wants a match widdim—

SMITTY.

It's our way or nothing, feller—

JACK.

Ah said a match widdim!

An if you don' wanna gimme one, Ah gonna makeya,

same's Ah done before, see—

(Releasing him)

Ah gonna make em!

Gonna take mah funky suitcase an mah three-four hundred dollahs,

an git mahself ta Mexico, howya like dat, man,

right up nex ta ya, **gonna sit on dat line dere an wave you crummy belt atya an sing out Here Ah is—**

SMITTY.

It's not going to work, Jack—

JACK.

Dassall Ah got worth tryin now—

(Crumpling the telegram)

dis ain't, dis ain't,

Ah know dis pass trying, Ah—

TICK.

Easy—

ELLIE.

Jack, I'm so sorry—

JACK.

Took too much outa her, Ah guess, she musta—

musta juss—

(Strikes himself a blow on the forehead, staggers)

ELLIE.

Oh, Jack—

JACK.

Leave me lone.

CURTAIN

ACT THREE

SCENE ONE

A street, Chicago

In the BLACKOUT, *at slow tempo, approaching from the distance, "How Long Blues": bass drum, clarinet, trombone, As the lights come up, Negroes are quietly filling the stage; they arrange themselves as if lining both sides of a street. A few policemen station themselves among them, and a group of pressmen is deployed at one side. The funeral procession appears, the* BANDSMEN *first, followed by the coffin—*GOLDIE *conspicuous as a pallbearer—behind it* CLARA, *supported by* SISTER, *then the* PASTOR. *The music stops as the coffin is set down. The Negroes close in around it and the* PASTOR *addresses them.*

———

PASTOR.

"When thou passes through de waters Ah will be wid thee,

and de rivers, dey shall not overflow thee,

fo Ah am de Lawd thy God, de Holyone of Isrel."

CONGREGATION.

Amen.

PASTOR.

Mosta you ain present today outa respeck to Sistah Tiny here,

you-all here to stan up fo son Jack. An dass fine!

He got a place in you heart, de Lawd muss wan him havin it.

But Bredren, make a place dere fo dis humble woman, his momma, too.

Take Sistah in you heart an let her show you

somethin, Bredren,

Ah know you done took in what Jack bin showin you,

but dis leass as good an mebbe worth more, praise de Lawd.

CONGREGATION.

Amen.

PASTOR.

"When thou passes through de waters Ah will be wid thee."

Dis woman pass through dem all de days of her life.

Born slave, like lotsa you poppas and mommas.

Passed through dem waters. Passed through plain hungry waters,

mean waters, cesspool-y waters. Currents like to swamp you—

CONGREGATION.

Lawd!

PASTOR.

Waters wid blood in em! Even passed through de waters

of dat killer flood down Galveston, passin through one waters

inter de nex one—

CONGREGATION.

Lawd!

PASTOR.

Sweatin in dem waters

fum "cain't see" in de mornin till "cain't see" at night,

an inter de nex one—

CONGREGATION.

Jesus!

PASTOR.

An when she coulden sweat no mo,

passed through em juss shiverin an achin an sick—

but whut wuz going long wid her!

CONGREGATION.

Mah Savior!

PASTOR.

Tell me dat!

CONGREGATION.

Glory comin!

PASTOR.

Amen!

De Lawd say Ah'll be wid thee,

de Lawd was passin through dem waters wid her,

inter de nex one an de nex one an de nex,

holdin her afloatin an liftin up de joy in her—

CONGREGATION.

Hallelujah!

PASTOR.

DASS whut she had, Bredren! Dass whut she show you!

She din cuss dem waters—

CONGREGATION.

No Lawd!

PASTOR.

She know whut evvybody know in deir heart, here,

dere's ALWAYS dem waters, dere ALWAYS tribberlation,

de nex one an de nex

an we ALWAYS passin through—

CONGREGATION.

Can't hurt me!

PASTOR.

Ah is, an you is,

an you chillun gonna, an anybody's chillun till kingdom come—

CONGREGATION.

Oh, yeah!

PASTOR.

She din blame de Lawd

fo not partin dem waters like de ole Red Sea!

She knowed He done said, "Dey shall not overflow thee,"

an she TRUSTED her Lawd.

CONGREGATION.

Jesus!

PASTOR.

She knowed dat fifty year ago

when we wuz nigh to GITTIN overflowed

He give us a Moses and He did part dat sea

an He took us oughta bondage!

CONGREGATION.

Hallelujah!

PASTOR.

She knowed

All de time she pine for her boy

dat de Lawd workin in His own way—

(CLARA *begins sobbing*)

dat He ain't juss on tap evvy time we give a holler—

CONGREGATION.

Oh my!

PASTOR.

She felt de Lawd takin her fore she got ta see him,

but she held on tight to dat—

(Flurry of movement, photo-flashes, jostling)

NEGRO 1.

Whut gawn on dere—

PHOTOGRAPHER 1.

This way, miss—

PHOTOGRAPHER 2.

Excuse me—

GOLDIE.

Say, can't you guys—

CLARA *(going for PHOTOGRAPHER 1).*

Gimmer dat, you mother—

PASTOR.

Sistah—

NEGRO 2.

Who dat—

GOLDIE *(checking her).*

For Godsakes—

POLICEMAN 1.

No shoving there—

PASTOR.

Gennulmen—

CLARA.

Leggo me—

GOLDIE.

Ignore em, just—

CLARA.

You too, ya dirty pinkface pimp—

PASTOR.

Sistah, dis ain no time—

CLARA *(breaking away).*

Yeah, oh yeah

dis de time awright! Whut he doin here,

whut any of em doin here—

SISTER.

Clara—

CLARA.

Look at em!

Howya feelin now, folks! All dress up dere watchin de fewnral? Ain'ttya bought some flowahs?

GOLDIE *(to PASTOR).*

I'm sorry about this—

CLARA.

Sho you is!

You an dat white bitch an de whole pack a ya—

come on ovah to de box here, sugah,

see how good y'all nail de lid down—

PASTOR.

Sistah—

CLARA.

No!

Ah seed mah Momma Tiny's heart gittin busted,

Ah seed her layin dere pinin and sick

till she nothin but bone, Ah heard her beggin fo Jack—

Who set him runnin! Who put de mark on him!

Why she die so bad! Where all her trouble fum!

Dem, dem, dem, dem, an Ah wanna make juss one of em—

(Goes for the audience)

PASTOR.
Sistah—
POLICEMAN 1 *(to* PASTOR*).*
Look, if you can't handle em—
PASTOR.
Bredren—
NEGRO 2.
No, let her, man—
CLARA.
Ah gonna settle wid—
SISTER *(slaps* CLARA*'s face).*
Behave yourself!
CLARA *(falling on the coffin).*
Oh, help me, Momma Tiny, Ah wanna do
    right by ya,
Don' leave me, Momma, Momma, Ah be
    good, please . . .
PASTOR.
Oh, brudders and sistahs!
Look out when Satan start a-lightin dat hate
    fire!
Member who de Lawd say vingeance belong
    ta,
member he fogit not de cry a de oppressed—
SCIPIO *(concealed in the* CROWD*).*
Dass right, chillun, suffer nice an easy—
school em on it, boss!
PASTOR.
Who talkin dere!
SCIPIO *(appearing).*
Me—
ya no-name brudder!
PASTOR.
Take dat off your head here—
SCIPIO.
No! Went inta buy me a hat once, boss,
Man say cover you head wid a hankie
And DEN try it on—
PASTOR.
Shame on you!
SCIPIO.
Yeah, now you sayin it—shame on me, an
    shame on alla us
for BEIN de oppressed, an bein it, an bein it!
Shame on us moanin low two hundred years
    here!
Fo needin a big White Moses fo a daddy!
NEGRO 3.
Amen, brudder!
PASTOR.
Whut—
SCIPIO.
Yeah!
Shame on evvy Goodie-Book thumper like
    you!
White man keep pullin de teeth outa you

head
an preacher here giving you de laughin-gas—
PASTOR.
Ah warnin you, heathen—
SCIPIO.
Ah warnin evvybody!
**Warnin dat white gal an warnin dem po-lice
ain nothin lass foever!**
NEGRO 2.
Tell em!
SCIPIO.
**Warnin dat dead woman
Jesus wuzn't swimmin! Warnin mah people
dat boy juss a shadow an dey livin black men
whut gotta live long—**
NEGRO 3.
Right!
SCIPIO.
Don' Amen me!
Makin believe you de Chillun of Isrel,
fiery-furnacin an roll-on-Jordanin—
you ain no Isrel! Dere—
(Points to GOLDIE*)*
Dass a Jew-man—
see whut ya see! Look in de mirrah once
an see whut ya see! Ah said de MIRRAH,
not a lotta blue eyes you *usin* for a mirrah,
an hatin whut dey hates, de hair you got,
de nose you got, de mouth you got, de—
PASTOR.
Offissah, Ah'm askin you—
POLICEMAN 1.
Right—
NEGRO 3.
Whut dey doin—
SCIPIO.
Hate dat woolly head, you gotta hate de man
    whut got it, brudders,
dat man YOU—
POLICEMAN 2 *(to* SCIPIO*).*
Move—
SCIPIO.
Don' hate it, brudders—
NEGRO 5.
Lemme through—
NEGRO 6.
Stop em—
SCIPIO *(as* POLICE *haul at him).*
Champeen in your heart, but dey ain one a
    you—
NEGRO 4.
Help him—
NEGRO 6.
Dey hurtin him—
NEGRO 7.
Quick—

NEGRO 8.

Dey gonna kill him—

NEGRO 4.

Let em have it—

POLICEMAN 3.

Move—

PASTOR.

Bredren—

NEGRO 1 (holding back CLARA).

Sistah—

NEGRO 5.

No cuttin—

NEGRO WOMAN 1.

Help—

NEGRO 8.

Cut em—

POLICEMAN 3.

There—

NEGRO 4.

Gimme dat—

POLICEMAN 1.

Come on, call em out—!

(Police whistles above the pandemonium; flashing nightsticks and swinging fists; the coffin is hurried off; lights begin fading and hoofbeats are heard, then screams)

NEGRO VOICES.

Look out—

No, dis way—

Brudders—

Pull em off—

No—

You mother—

Here—

Lemme git one—

Move—

Teddy—

Run—

Here—

Mah head, mah head, mah head, mah head—

(DARKNESS. Silence. LIGHTS UP on—)

SCENE TWO

Pop Weaver's office, New York
CAP'N DAN and SMITTY, followed in by POP and FRED. Newspapers.

———

CAP'N DAN.

Look at this, look at this—**I can't even think straight—**

SMITTY.

I told you, he's out for—

CAP'N DAN.

Don't tell me again!

One more lousy picture of him and that belt,

One more newsie sneakin down there to see him—

FRED.

What about the ones on me up here, Dan'l?

CAP'N DAN.

Say you can't promote it! Say he's askin too much!

FRED.

After that piece in the *Journal?*

SMITTY.

Here.

FRED.

Will Fight Kid for Carfare and a Watermelon.

CAP'N DAN.

Christ—

POP.

Maybe we could pay him off to retire, Dan—

CAP'N DAN.

Twenty years, what I'd give for twenty years—

POP.

He wouldn't need to lay down, we'd get the belt back—

CAP'N DAN.

Sure, and have a coon champ retire undefeated!

SMITTY.

What if we promise him a straight fight later on

if he dives on this one.

FRED.

Later on.

SMITTY.

You know.

CAP'N DAN.

He's too goddam smart for that!

FRED.

Just an idea now,

but supposing we sign it, then something gets put

on his sponge, or in his water . . .

SMITTY.

It's worked before, Dan.

POP.

I would hate to hang this on something from a drugstore.

CAP'N DAN.

Jesus, listen to us, **look what that boogie's got us down to here—**

POP.

Don't excite yourself, Dan—

CAP'N DAN.
On the verge, I tell them! You know what I
     look like,
stalling for months and making excuses,
and all he winds up is smack on the border
like a boil on the whole country's ass?
FRED.
All right!
Then why don't we sign it and have it, for
     chrissake!
He'll never be in shape the way he was in
     Reno—
CAP'N DAN.
Get it in writing—
FRED.
Here, look at the gut on him—
And look at that Kid—
POP.
Fred—
FRED.
Honest to God, he's better, every time out,
     listen,
four KO's and three decisions since April,
and I've got him with Brady now,
we've giving him all kinds of angles on the
     nigger,
like how when he smiles—
CAP'N DAN.
Do I have to hear this?
FRED.
Wait, no, I mean it—when you're doin a
     smile, see,
your mouth's kina open and your teeth's not
     clenched,
so you hit him when he's smilin, you can bust
     a guy's jaw—
That's no bull, that's from an osteopath!
CAP'N DAN.
Pop, you try, go down there yourself—
POP.
Dan, I don't discourage very easy,
But I'm afraid there's only one safe bet for us.
It isn't ideal—
CAP'N DAN.
Come on, come on—
POP.
Even if he's still as good as he was, Dan,
the man is no spring chicken any more.
And you know what happens. Maybe not by
     tomorrow,
or the next day either, but it will happen,
     Dan.
The legs'll start to go, like everybody else's—
it's all downhill.
CAP'N DAN.
Two years? Three years?

POP.
Whenever he's ripe we throw him in with
     Fred's boy—
CAP'N DAN.
Pop, can't you help me?
POP.
Taking this on was a real mistake, Dan.
I'd like to follow through but that's the best
     we have.
FRED.
I'd go along—
SMITTY.
We could say we're waiting
on account of the war—
FRED.
**We could give a big play
to the middleweights—**
CAP'N DAN.
Pop—Jesus!
POP.
We can work it,
let's put it on ice—
CAP'N DAN.
There ain't that much ice
in this whole rotten world—
FRED.
What do we do then—
kill him?
(Pause)
CAP'N DAN.
How broke is he, Smitty?
SMITTY.
They live in a flophouse
and he trains in a barn.
CAP'N DAN.
Any dough from outside?
SMITTY.
Friends, a little.
CAP'N DAN.
Find out who, we'll stop it—
anybody sparring with him?
POP.
Dan, what's the point—
SMITTY.
A couple of rubes from Texas—
CAP'N DAN.
Pull them out, send them home.
No exhibitions, nothing, no contact, cut him
     off—
POP.
He's not going to give, Dan—
CAP'N DAN.
He made the last
move he had and now we'll screw him with

it,
now we're gonna show him
what a bad move it was, this time we ain't
     askin,
or offerin, or tryin, or pussyfootin round this
like a bunch of pansies, we got him so close
we can reach out and squeeze—**we're gonna
     squeeze that dinge
so goddam hard soon a fix is gonna look
like a hayride to him!**
     POP.
Dan, don't get him
any madder than he is—
     CAP'N DAN.
Start scouting out
a place we can hold it—
     POP.
We're making us two
mistakes in a row, Dan—
     CAP'N DAN.
Havana, maybe,
the bigger the better—
     POP.
I mean it. Tell your people
we just can't deliver.
     CAP'N DAN.
No, I tell them
we might need a hand—
     FRED.
Say, wait—
     CAP'N DAN.
You get busy,
talk to Goldie—I want all that set!
     POP.
We're way out over our head now, you know.
     CAP'N DAN.
So is he friend. Let's see who goes under.
     (BLACKOUT. *Enter* CLARA *in* SPOTLIGHT,
     as distant BELL *slowly chimes midnight.* SHE
     clutches a flimsy stained garment to her).
     CLARA.
**Do it, soon, soon, goin good now, drag him
on down. Oh won'tya, fo me an mah momma
an evvy black-ass woman he turn his back on,
for evvy gal wid a man longside dreamin him
a piece a what HE got, fo alla his let-down
secon-bess sistahs, all Mistah Number One's
lil ugly sistahs—ssh!
dey' moonin fo de day you does it,
dey's some sleepin an plenny itchin quiet,
dey's me aholda dis, an we drawin him,
drawin him. Oh, where dem rosy
cheeks gonna git him, don' never stop now,
offa dat high horse an on down de whole
long mud-track in fronna him, years gawnta**

**nothin,
feelin em, dere, limpin an slippin
an shrinkin an creepin an sinkin right in—
Call him to ya, Momma!**
     (*Holds out the garment at full length: a night-
     gown, stiff with blood and excrement.*)
Soon, baby, soon.

     (LIGHT *fades slowly into* BLACKOUT; *thud-
     ding of a punching-bag is heard;* LIGHTS UP
     on—)

SCENE THREE

A disused barn, Juarez
By the light of a few kerosene lanterns,
JACK *pounds at a punching-bag, which is
steadied from behind by* PACO, *a Mexican boy.*
TICK *claps his hands in time with him.*

———

     TICK.
Slow it up, slow it up—
     JACK.
Whut—?
     TICK.
Slow it,
let dat sweat out—
     (*Claps at a slower tempo, sings*)
Times is very hard,
Gimme ten-cent worth a lard,
Gonna keep mah skillet greasy
If Ah can, can, can,
Gonna keep mah skillet—
     (JACK *delivers a last impatient slam and turns
     away from it.*)
Nuff?
     JACK.
Yeah, Ah'm pushin.
     TICK.
OK, Paco, dassit.
     JACK.
Six thirty mañana.
     PACO.
Si, Campeón. We ron?
     JACK.
Yeah, we run.
     PACO.
I com for wek op?
     JACK.
No, Ah be up.
     (PACO *starts putting gear in order.*)

TICK *(leading* JACK *to a trestle table).*
Wearin us out, baby, comin on fine . . .
(JACK *sits,* TICK *pulls his gloves off.)*
Oughta raise de bag up higher tomorrer,
   startya liftin em, huh?
(JACK *lies down.)*
Yeah . . .
(Working on him)
bout a foot or so. You know, seein how big
   dat Kid is . . .
(JACK *does not reply.)*
Sho a funny size for a Kid, ain he?
Soun like somethin gone wrong wid his glans!
   JACK.
Don' try unwindin me, man. Juss rub.
   TICK.
Yassuh, shine em up—
   JACK *(to* PACO, *who has picked up his*
gloves).
Leave dose, willya.
   PACO.
Si, Campeón.
   TICK.
You cain work out
tonight no mo, Ah mean—
   JACK.
How much dat guy say
he giveya for em.
   TICK.
Oh.
   JACK.
Fifty?
   (BARKING *is heard)*
   TICK.
You gloves, baby.
   (JACK *doesn't reply.)*
   PACO *(looking out).*
Viene la señorita.
   JACK.
Put em in a piece a paper she don' see em.
   TICK.
Well, you kin work wid de heavy ones, time
   bein.
Bettah fo ya, anyhow.
   (More BARKING. ELLIE *enters, carrying a*
dish with a napkin over it. SHE *wears sun-*
glasses.)
   PACO.
Buenas noches—
   TICK.
Mmm-MM!
Whut dat old lanlady whip up tonight?
   PACO *(at the door shooing away the dogs).*
Andale! Vaya!
   ELLIE.
I wish they would feed their dogs around
   here.

   JACK.
You feedin yours here, ain'tya.
   TICK *(resuming massage).*
Set it down, hon—
how mah gal today?
   ELLIE.
All right. You?
   TICK.
Fine!
Shoulda seed him burn up dat road dis morn-
   in,
right fum de bridge to Pedrilla an up ta—
   JACK *(to* ELLIE, *not looking at her).*
Gonna say it or whut.
   ELLIE.
No, nothing, Jack.
No cables. Nothing.
   JACK.
Thanks.
   TICK.
Man, we be hearing pretty soon.
Worry juss makin you tight, dass why
ya ain sweatin like you oughta—
   JACK.
Juss you rub, man.
   TICK.
Ass me, we's lucky dey ain sign it up yet!
Givin us all dis good gittin-ready time?
   ELLIE.
Let him eat before it gets cold, Tick.
   TICK.
Yeah, switch you brain off a while an—
   JACK.
Leave it.
   TICK.
OK, OK.
   (Long pause)
   ELLIE.
Jack—
   (TRAIN WHISTLE)
   PACO.
Tren from El Paso.
   ELLIE.
Yes?
   TICK.
Yeah . . . Whistle like dat crossin ovah.
   PACO.
Hasta mañana, señores.
   TICK.
So long, kid.
   (PACO *goes.)*
   ELLIE.
Why don't you come back and wash now,
   Jack.
I'll wait here if you like.
   JACK.
Smelling pretty strong, huh?

ELLIE.
You know that's not what I—
JACK *(sitting up)*.
Dass inuff, man.
ELLIE.
Jack, will you talk to me.
JACK.
Tick gawn ovah
on a erran, you kin go walk roun dere
a lil widdim—
ELLIE.
No, I want to talk to you—
JACK.
Mebbe git a ice-cream soda, lookit some
Mericans or somethin—
ELLIE.
Jack—
TICK.
Not wid me, boss—
Ah ain strollin wid no white gal in no Texas!
(To ELLIE, *as he goes out with the package)*
Hole de fort, hon, won' be too long.
(Pause. TRAIN WHISTLE*)*
ELLIE.
Let them go ahead, Jack.
JACK.
Take dem specs off.
Ah cain hardly see ya.
ELLIE *(doing so)*.
I didn't think you wanted to.
JACK.
You readin mah mine now?
ELLIE.
Jack—
JACK.
Ah toleya
keep outa dis, din Ah.
ELLIE.
I can't. Please,
let them, you have to.
JACK.
Finely battin
fo de home team, huh.
ELLIE.
Cable them tonight,
please—
JACK.
Finely come roun to it—
ELLIE.
Jack don't bitch me now—
JACK.
Ah toleya—
ELLIE.
No, I don't care!
Forget what you told me! Say yes and get it
over with, for God's sake! You're letting

them
do this to you, it's worse—
JACK.
Worse fo you, mebbe—
ELLIE.
Jack, it's slow poison here, there's nothing
else to wait for,
just more of it, you've had enough—please,
you're being paralyzed—
JACK.
Wid you mebbe—
ELLIE.
All right, yes, with me too,
with everything but hammering that stupid
bag there!
You're not your own man any more—
JACK.
Now you rollin—
ELLIE.
How can you be your own man, they have
you!
They do and you know it, you're theirs, at
least
you can buy yourself back from them—
JACK.
Sold—
one-buck nigger fo de lady!
ELLIE.
Let it sound the way it is!
Run when they push you and back when they
pull you,
work yourself sick in this hell-hole for noth-
ing,
and tell me you're not theirs—here,
look at the grease you swallow for them,
look at the bedbug bites on your arms,
and the change in your pockets and the
blotches in your eyes—
JACK.
Don't leave de smell out—
ELLIE.
The two of us smell!
Whatever turns people into niggers—there—
(Shows her neck)
it's happening to both of us—
JACK.
Wish comin true, huh—
ELLIE.
No,
never this, it wasn't this—
JACK.
Sing it, sistah!
ELLIE.
I want you there fighting them again,
that's what I wish now, I want to watch
when you're knocking them down for this,

dozens of them,
God help them, wipe it off on all of them—
JACK.
How bout rooster-fightin, plenty right here—
ELLIE.
Listen to me, please—
JACK.
Oughta look inta dat—
ELLIE.
You'd fight them and you'd be with your friends and you'd—
(JACK *crows like a rooster.*)
JACK.
Somebody wanna sign me?
ELLIE.
Maybe we could live then, damn you!
JACK.
Lil frame house,
tree in front?
ELLIE.
Anything!
JACK.
Nice quiet street?
ELLIE.
Anywhere! A place!
JACK.
Lil cozy—
ELLIE.
A kitchen!
JACK.
Put de cat out? Tuck in de kids?
ELLIE.
Oh, you're just hateful!
JACK.
Well Ah gonna tellya whut de livin like, baby,
far as Ah concern—
ELLIE.
Get away from me—
JACK.
Yeah,
Ah put you straight on it—**an alla you too.**
Ah wen into a fair once and dere wuz dis old pug, see,
give anybody two bucks who stan up a roun widdim—
perfessional set-up, reggerlation ring an all,
cep dey had rope juss on three sides, dass right,
de back side wuz de tent. So Ah watches a couple
git laid out real quick in dere, but he don' look
dat red-hot ta me, see, so Ah climbs in wid-dim.
An Ah doin awright fo a youngster, when all
it once
he bulls me up gainss dat tent-side a de ring
an SLAM, WHAM, somebody behine dere conks me,
right through de canvas, musta use a two by four,
an evvy time Ah stands up he shove me back agin,
an SLAM, dere's anudder, down she come—
good story, huh?
ELLIE.
Jack—
JACK.
Dass how it go like Ah knows it, baby—
ELLIE.
Sometimes, sometimes—
JACK.
All de way now!
dass where Ah is and dass whut Ah'm gittin,
gonna git it de same sayin Yassuh, Nossuh,
don' mattah whut Ah does—An in dere, un-nerstan?
An Ah don' wan you watchin, or helpin, or waitin,
or askin, or hannin me you jive bout livin,
or anythin fromya but OUT, Ah mean OUT—
ELLIE.
What—
JACK.
How goddamn plain Ah gotta make it for ya!
ELLIE.
Jack—if you want other girls—
JACK.
Git you stuff ready,
train out ten o'clock.
ELLIE.
No, no, I won't, no—
JACK.
When Tick come Ah sen him ovah—
ELLIE.
Jack—
JACK.
Bettah start movin—
ELLIE.
Stop it—
JACK.
Ah apologize actin so yellah
up ta—
ELLIE.
Wait, you have to stop it—
JACK.
All Ah has to is be black an die, lady—
ELLIE.
I want to stay, even if we—
JACK.
Stay wid you own, lady—

ELLIE.

What are you doing!

JACK.

Quit dat, quit it, short an sweet—

ELLIE.

I won't go—

JACK.

You knowed it comin, start movin—

ELLIE.

Wait—

JACK.

Don' cross me now—

ELLIE.

Jack, I thought we'd
save something, please—

JACK.

Ah said MOVE—

ELLIE.

Please, I only—

JACK.

MOVE! You through widdit now—

ELLIE.

Jack—

JACK.

No mo lousy grub you gotta puke up,
no more a ya lookin like a wash-out rag here,
wid you eye twitchin alla—

ELLIE.

Don't—I don't care—

JACK.

Juss MOVE—

ELLIE.

I'll take better—

JACK.

Hangin on me,
dead weight—

ELLIE.

No, not for you—

JACK.

Start—

ELLIE.

Jack, I'll find a job, please—

JACK.

Ah toleya when mah momma die, Ah toleya
leave me be a while, now—

ELLIE.

Jack, I can't
run anymore, not by myself—

JACK.

You got you people
and you a—

ELLIE.

No, listen—

JACK.

You a young woman
an you gonna—

ELLIE.

Please, I'd never—

JACK.

Gonna fine—

ELLIE.

No one else, I'd—

JACK.

Tough titty—

ELLIE.

Just—

JACK.

Move,
or goddamn you—

ELLIE.

Why can't you wait at least!
Wait till you've given me a chance to make
you happy—
one chance, only one—**I swear I've never had
one—**

JACK.

Too big a order all aroun!

ELLIE.

No, I won't go—

JACK.

Wanna drag it out, huh—

ELLIE.

I won't, I can't—

JACK.

Den Ah gonna wise you up good now, you
gray bitch—

ELLIE.

You can't make me go, stop doing this—

JACK.

Why you think
Ah ain't put a han to yo fo how long, why ya
think
it turn me off juss lookin atya—

ELLIE.

Stop it—

JACK.

You stayin,
stay fo it all. Ya know why?
Does ya, honeybunch? Cause evvy time you
pushes
dat pinch-up face in fronna me, Ah sees
where it done got me, dass whut Ah lookin at,
where an how come an de Numbah One
Who,
right down de line, girl, an Ah mean YOU,
an Ah don' wanna give you NOTHIN, un-
nerstan?
Ah cut it off firss!

ELLIE.

Oh, I despise you—

JACK.

Right, like alla resta ya—

ELLIE.

Oh, I'd like to smash you—

JACK.

Me an evvy udder dumb nigger who'd letya!
Now go on home an hustle one up who don'
     know it yet,
plenny for ya, score em up—**watch out, brud-
     ders!**
Oughta hang a bell on so dey hear you comin.

ELLIE.

You mean this?

JACK.

Look in mah purple eyes.

(Pause)

ELLIE.

You win, daddy.

(She turns and goes. Pause. JACK *takes a
swig from the water-bottle, gargles, spits, then
walks to the punching-bag and starts to jab at
it. For a few moments he does not notice the
entrance of a slightly shabby but imposing-
looking Mexican,* EL JEFE. *Then, sensing
someone behind him,* JACK *stops.)*

EL JEFE.

I leesen you mek beeg denuncio, Campeón.
So I nut com een.

JACK.

Who you, mistah?

EL JEFE.

Ees nut meester, Campeón. I seet now, yes?
(Sits)

JACK.

Whut you want?

EL JEFE *(taking out a bottle and offering it).*
You like?

JACK.

No, Ah'm in trainin.

EL JEFE.

Pliz?

JACK.

Trainin. On a fight.

EL JEFE.

Si, es terrible . . .
for Negro, for peon, for avery poor peoples.
fight from meenit we out from dee modder.

JACK.

Ah astya whut you want, man.

EL JEFE.

I hear, Campeón. Salud.
(Drinks)

JACK.

Look, Ah ain made no trouble wid none a
     you.

EL JEFE *(laughs a bit).*

Where ees dee fadders, compadre.

JACK.

De whut?

EL JEFE.

Dee fadders. Dee weengs. Ees all high ovair
flying like anjel, you think, no? **El hombre
     solo.**

JACK.

Whut you after, man?

EL JEFE.

Maybe you halp soon
pobre black amigos. You show heem ees solo
nut posible . . . Que vida, eh?

JACK *(moving to the door).*

Man, you juss playin wid me, Ah'm gonna—

EL JEFE *(standing).*

No,
I filling to you beeg compassion, my fran.
Dees Mejico my cowntry, I ongry here, I keel
     here,
I am fugitivo like you much times. Bot ul-
     ways to love.
You cowntry you nut love her and she nut
     you,
unly mak bad drims ich odder.

*(A car has been approaching and is heard
     braking)*

VOICE OUTSIDE.

Han venido, Jefe.

EL JEFE.

Déjanlos entrar.

(Pause. Enter DIXON, GOLDIE, *and a young
     AGENT)*

DIXON.

Good evening.

EL JEFE.

Señores.

GOLDIE.

Hello, Jack.

JACK.

Yeah.
OK. Ah'm listenin.

GOLDIE.

Well . . .
(To DIXON)
All right?
(DIXON impassive)
They're makin it easier, Jack. I mean
     it's . . .
They threw in now suspended sentence.

JACK.

Yeah.

GOLDIE.

You fight in Havana, you hand yourself in,
you go to court, one-two-three, and that's all.

JACK.

Go on, boss.

GOLDIE.

Well . . .

JACK.

Don' be shy bout it.

GOLDIE.

Jackie, it's quits now . . .

(Stops pained)

JACK *(to* DIXON*).*

Mebbe you tell me.

DIXON.

Apart from your original conviction, Jefferson,

which carries, you remember, up to three years,

there are quite a few other violations, involving,

for example: jumping bail, using the mails to bribe officials in Canada, tax irregularities, falsifying passports—

GOLDIE.

They'll throw the whole book on you.

Till God knows when.

JACK.

Tell me de ress of it, mistah.

You law up dere an Ah down here. Cain leave dat out—

(To EL JEFE*)*

Can he, man? You country, ain't it, man?

EL JEFE *(downcast).*

Si, compadre.

AGENT.

It is perfectly legal,

once we've ascertained where a wanted man is,

to request cooperation of the parties in charge there.

EL JEFE.

Perdóname, Campeón. We nid from dem, comprende?

We nut like. We nid.

JACK.

Yeah.

EL JEFE.

Go Habana. Ees batter.

DIXON.

I would think so.

GOLDIE.

You finish inside there,

what'll you have, Jack. **An old man he'll be.**

JACK.

Well . . . Ah'm far long awready, boss.

Ah'm stannin here gittin older evvy minnit.

An Ah'm goin right through dat door—

(Moves)

EL JEFE.

No—

(Draws pistol)

compadre!

(Steps in front of JACK*)*

JACK.

Use it if ya got to, man.

EL JEFE.

Hombre, ivin I lat you, where now you—

JACK.

Dassall up to me, man.

(Advances)

EL JEFE.

I tie weeth rope, you do theess—!

JACK.

Oh, Ah killya firss, man.

(Advances)

EL JEFE.

Hijo, averyplace

catch on you, I swear you, all geev you to gringos,

Huerta, Obregón—

JACK *(advancing).*

Ah goin out de door, man—

EL JEFE.

Hombre . . .

(Clicks back hammer)

Hombre—

JACK.

Gimme a break, fo Gawdsake.

EL JEFE.

No!

Who you halpeeng een your life, nadie,

OSS now you halp—

*(*JACK *advances.).*

Cabrón, wan more—

JACK.

Well,

mebbe it be doin me a favor.

(Steps around EL JEFE*, keeps walking).*

GOLDIE.

Jack—

*(*EL JEFE *raises his pistol.)*

DIXON.

In the leg—

AGENT.

Don't—

EL JEFE.

Chíngate, gringo—

(Aims at JACK*'s back, calls)*

You stuppeeng? Hombre, nut stuppeeng, I—

*(*JACK *at the doorway, suddenly stops, the slowly moves backward as* TICK *and* TWO MEXICANS *enter.* THEY *carry in* ELLIE*'s mud-smeared and dripping body.)*

MEXICAN.

Se tiró en el pozo. Acabada.

EL JEFE.

Díos.

JACK.

Whut . . . whut . . . ?

TICK.
Threw hersel down de . . .
JACK.
No, no, Jesus—
TICK.
Down de well, Ah coulden—
JACK.
Git somebody,
gimme de bottle—why she—
TICK.
Busted her neck, man.
JACK.
Honey!
Honey, baby, please, sugar, no—!
Whut Ah—whut Ah—whut Ah—baby,
whut Ah done to ya, whut you done, honey,
honey, whut dey done to us . . .
EL JEFE *(turns away).*
No puedo mirarlo.
GOLDIE.
Jack. Jack. Anything I can . . .
(JACK *nods.*)
Anything. What, Jack.
JACK.
Set dat fuckin fight up! Set it up, set it up!
Ah take it now!
(BLACKOUT. *Sound of* PRESSES *rolling.*
CAP'N DAN *appears in spotlight: he smokes a
cigar, wears a white carnation, carries a small
valise, and is jubilant)*
CAP'N DAN.
Well, there's such a commotion on this
you'd think we just organized the Second
Coming!
Tickets? They're going down without em,
hey,
honest to God, it does your heart good,
songs about the Kid, pictures of the Kid
stuck up in windows, stores, you pass a brick
wall
it has KID painted on it, people on the street
saying
Well we got the Hope, Dan!—cost me two
hundred
in cigars already—and wait, wait,
I bet you can't guess who's refereein—
Brady!
Oh, will they eat that up, when he's givin the
count
and he's—what? No, he ain't in on it,
neither is the Kid, who the hell wants that!
But he's the one who lost it,
and the whole world's gonna see him
take it in his hand again, and hold it up
and pass it on, like the Kid'll pass it—

(Boat whistle interrupts him.)
OK!
This time we'll keep it in the family!
(DAN *exits.*)

SCENE FOUR

*A street, somewhere in the United States
As* DAN *exits a group of Negroes swarms on,
one of them rapidly beating on a bass drum,
another holding up a torch in one hand and a
pail in the other, a third scribbling on a long
sheet of foolscap; the others clamorously surround them, calling out their names and
throwing money into the pail. Drumming
throughout.*

———

NEGRO 1.
Oscar Jones—
NEGRO 2.
Peal Whitney—
NEGRO 3.
Jasper Smollett—
PAIL MAN.
Write em down dere—throw in dem nick-
els—
NEGRO 4.
Charlie Webb—
NEGRO 5.
Bill Montgomery—
PAIL MAN.
More! Who else here—
Sign on de telgram to Jack—fi'cents—
NEGRO 4.
Read out de message, man—
NEGRO 1.
Let em all hear it!
PAIL MAN.
**"HELLO   JACK   BESS   NACHUL
FIGHTER IN DE WORL—"**
(Cheers)
**"HOME   FOLKS   PUNCHIN   RIGHT
WIDYA—SIGNED—"**
*(The cheering drowns him, a voice over it
sings—)*
VOICE.
Hot boilin sun comin ovuh—
NEGRO 6.
Waltuh Peters!
SEVERAL JOINING IN.
Hot boilin sun comin ovuh—
NEGRO 2.
We show ya!
MORE JOINING.
Hot boilin sun comin ovuh—

NEGRO 7.

Ah'm on dere!

ALL *(singing).*

AN HE AIN'T A-COMIN DOWN—

(Whooping and cheering, they run off, the sound of their voices fading into the roar of the crowd as LIGHTS COME UP ON—*)*

SCENE FIVE

Oriente Racetrack, Havana

Entrance gate. Two huge ornate wooden columns; suspended high between them, a banner featuring the simplified figures of a white boxer and a black one locked in combat. A cluster of ticketless white men at the barrier, all feverishly trying to follow the fight by the roars of the crowd and through one of their number perched high on a column. In the fierce heat all coats have been discarded, most shirts as well; heads are bound with handkerchiefs or covered with cheap straw hats—a few of these still left are hawked by a couple of ragged Cuban Negro boys.

———

MAN 1 *(on column).*

No, Kid—block him—you're lettin him—

(Roar)

MAN 2.

Again?

MAN 3.

Sounds like he—

MAN 1.

No—but the dinge

caught him right in the—Kid! Christ—

MAN 4.

What—?

MAN 1.

Don't back up—

MAN 6 *(through paper megaphone).*

Use them arms already—

MAN 7.

**Ten goddam rounds,
ain't took a one yet—**

(Roar, as a PINKERTON MAN *helps* MAN 8, *a sunstroke victim, through the gate).*

PINKERTON MAN 1.

I toldya—

leave the gate clear—

(Roar)

MAN 1.

Another one—

MAN 4.

Just keep him

off you—

*(*POP *appears at a side door.* MAN 8 *doubles over, retching.)*

PINKERTON MAN 1.

Move—it's like an oven here—

MAN 6.

Time, for chrissake—

NEGRO BOY 1 *(shaking a gourd in* MAN 8*'s face).*

Eh! Eh! Eh! Eh!

MAN 1.

Kid, quit clinchin—

MAN 8.

Scram, ya dirty little—

MAN 1.

BELL!

MAN 9.

Thank God!

MAN 2.

How the hell can he take it!

SMITTY *(coming through a side door).*

Jesus, Pop—

POP.

You sure they got the high sign?

SMITTY.

Two rounds ago!

POP.

Then what—

SMITTY.

Pop, I gave it four times, I know they got it, Goldie flicked the towel, Pop, we went over and over it—

MAN 4 *(to* MAN 1*).*

How's it look—

MAN 1.

He's collapsin there

but so is the nigger—puffin like a goddamn buffalo—

MAN 2.

He won't last—

MAN 6.

Start sweatin blood, coon!

*(*FRED, *sweating and frantic, comes through side door.)*

FRED.

I warned you, I warned you—

POP.

Get back inside—

FRED.

Can'tya—

SMITTY.

Ssh!

POP.

They won't cross us—

FRED.

They nothing, it's HIM—

MAN 1.

E-leven!

("Ooh" from crowd as FRED *rushes back in)*
MAN 1.
Right off, a low one—
MAN 7.
You would, ya—
MAN 5.
He can't help it,
the Kid's belly's five feet off the—
(Roar)
MAN 1.
Missed him, nigger—
(Enter the AGENT—*heads for* POP *and*
SMITTY)
(Roar)
MAN 1.
He slipped, the nigger slipped—
(Roar)
Hit him, hit him again—Oh, you—
MAN 3.
What—
(POP *and* AGENT *whisper.)*
MAN 1.
Don't just look at him!
MAN 7.
No instink! No instink!
(AGENT *whispers to* SMITTY; SMITTY *runs
inside.)*
MAN 4.
Let's get mad, Kid—
MAN 7.
A hundred and two degrees—
Chalkasians ain't made for it—
MAN 1.
Oh, them clinches—
MAN 3.
He holdin—?
MAN 1.
Come—on—
(Roar)
No, it's the nigger—! He's leanin, yeah—
MAN 4.
He's wearing down!
MAN 3.
I toleya—
MAN 1.
Break it, ref—
MAN 2.
Don't let him rest—
MAN 1.
Oh, good man—
MAN 3.
He wobblin—?
MAN 1.
Sorta—yeah! Yeah!
He's backin away there, he's wipin his eyes—
MAN 6.
Go in on him—

MAN 1.
He's goin—the nigger ain't—there,
he's tryna dodge him—
(Roar)
MAN 9.
Run, tar-baby,
run back to your barrel—
MAN 1.
Boyoboy, yeah,
he's slowin down, he's—
MAN 2.
Let's go—
MAN 1.
Shit—
move in—
(SMITTY *re-enters with* RUDY, *the baseball
player.)*
AGENT.
OK, Rudy—
RUDY.
Who you, man—
MAN 6.
MOVE IN!
AGENT.
Get your shirt off—
(To SMITTY*)*
get him something to carry—
(SMITTY *dashes back inside.)*
RUDY.
Mah whut?
AGENT *(tugging at the buttons).*
That! Off! Like you put one
on for him, remember—
MAN 1.
No, Kid, chase him,
he's tryna get his wind back—
RUDY.
Whut de hell you—
AGENT.
Get into that corner, Rudy, tell that pal of
    yours—
(Roar—drowns what he says)
MAN 1.
Be care—no, jab him off ya—Christ,
the nigger's all over him, pile-drivin,
whalin at him—cover up, he's—duck—
Oh, Jesus, the Kid just—
RUDY *(as* SMITTY *returns with towel and
bottle).*
Gimme dat, you mother—
*(Seizes towel and bottle, and runs inside, pull-
    ing off his shirt)*
MAN 1.
Cover, Kid, turn, turn—cover, he'll cave
your ribs in—
(Roar)

MAN 2.
Stop the goddamn—
MAN 1.
Wait, no, he's up—Oh
the nigger's right on him, he's after it, he's—
MAN 6.
Kid, don't let him—
MAN 1.
All he's got,
he's workin like a butcher—
MAN 2.
No—
MAN 7.
He's gotta—
MAN 5.
Kid—Kid!—
MAN 9.
Kid—
MAN 1.
Hook in him,
sluggin—oh, that eye—
MAN 6.
Ride him out—
(NEGRO BOY *climbs up the other column to see.*)
MAN 7.
Kid—
MAN 6.
Bust your hand, you—
MAN 1.
Murder, it's murder—
MAN 4.
No more—
MAN 2.
Clinch him—
MAN 1.
Ref—
MAN 6.
Clinch him, dummox—
MAN 2
No more—
MAN 1.
REF!
MAN 5.
Stop it—
MAN 2.
REF, YA—
NEGRO BOY
Eh! Eh! Eh! Eh!
MAN 1.
He's
on the ropes, he can't see, he's rollin,
he's punchy—
MAN 2.
How the hell does he—
(*Roar*)

MAN 6.
Is he—
MAN 1.
No, it's a bell, lemme down . . . lemme
down . . .
(*Slips down the column:* MAN 4 *is helped up to take his place.*)
POP (*to* SMITTY).
Tell Fred to throw in the—
AGENT (*to* SMITTY).
Stay right here!
MAN 4 (*looking ring-ward*).
God Almighty!
MAN 1 (*to* MAN 4).
They workin on the eye?
MAN 4.
Yeah, but the rest of him—!
Blood, welts all over—
MAN 5.
Fifty on the coon the next—
MAN 2.
Shut your hole—
MAN 6.
Don't worry, Kid—
MAN 1.
That eye came up like a grape!
POP (*to* AGENT).
Oh, Mister—
PINKERTON MAN 1 (*offstage*).
Comin through—
(*Movement behind barrier*)
MAN 2.
Jesus, the heat got him—
(PINKERTON MEN 1 *and* 2 *come through the gate carrying* GOLDIE *on a chair; the* AGENT *beckons to them.*)
MAN 6.
How you gonna fight without your Jew,
spook—
GOLDIE (*to* AGENT).
Mister, it's no use, it's—
AGENT.
Ssh!
MAN 4.
Here they go—
(PINKERTON MEN *set* GOLDIE *down at the side door and run back inside.*)
AGENT (*to* GOLDIE).
The boy get to him?
(*Roar*)
MAN 4.
Nigger's slouchin in there—
GOLDIE.
Mister, he don't hear, he—
MAN 4.
Little stiff on his pins there—
the Kid's just waiting for it—

GOLDIE.
Like it's my son, I begged him!
MAN 4.
The nigger's feelin him out—the Kid's sorta
  rockin there—
back up, Kid—please—
(*Roar*)
The nigger roundhoused him—!
MAN 5.
Here it comes—
(*Roar*)
The Kid's still up—
he's still up—tryna shake his head clear—
the nigger don't know where to—
(*Roar changes.*)
MAN 2.
Stay on your feet—
MAN 7.
Kid—
MAN 4.
He is! He is! The nigger can't do it—
**he's hittin but he's outa juice! He's punched
  out!**
MAN 2.
I knew it—
MAN 4.
There! Nothin! Just stingin him,
slappin him—
MAN 1.
Kid—
MAN 6.
He can't hurtya—
MAN 1.
He's arm-heavy—
MAN 9.
Please, Kid—
MAN 4.
Look at him—
He's saggin there, just heavin at you—
MAN 6.
What the hell's he—
(*Roar*)
MAN 4.
He's hitting back!
He's lashin at him—swingin there wild—
MAN 1.
**He can't
see—**
MAN 2.
Kid—
MAN 4.
The coon's givin ground—
MAN 7.
Keep on
swingin—

MAN 4.
There, the coon's lurchin
round him, he's—
MAN 6.
Smell him out, Kid—
MAN 4.
There—Oh—
swiped him half across the ring—
MAN 1 (*pulling down* NEGRO BOY).
Lemme up, you goddamn—
MAN 2.
More—
MAN 3.
It's gonna happen, Kid—
MAN 4.
In on him, no, he's over—yeah—
MAN 7.
Keep swinging—
MAN 4.
Walkin in his sleep but he's after him—
MAN 6.
Press him—
MAN 4.
Just flailin them great big—
(ROAR)
Bango!
MAN 2.
More, Kid!
MAN 7.
Wheee!
MAN 1 (*on column*).
Christ, it's like a noctopus!
MAN 2.
Don't stop, Kid—
MAN 4.
Ya shot it all, coon, can't hurt him!
MAN 9.
Wahooo!
MAN 6.
Can't hurt nobody!
(GOLDIE *totters to his feet and goes back
inside.*)
MAN 1.
Kid, aim it lower—
MAN 4.
Don't have to, he's reelin—
MAN 2.
Lower—
MAN 7.
He'll go under you—
MAN 4.
No—
got no legs left—
MAN 1.
Bango!
MAN 2.
Yippeee!

MAN 6.
Give us the smile, coon—
MAN 1.
He's flounderin—
MAN 2.
Poleax him—
MAN 4.
There—
MAN 1.
Clap for that one, you—
MAN 4.
Now , Kid—
MAN 2.
Finish him—
MAN 1.
The nigger can't hardly
get his guard up—
MAN 2.
Finish him—
MAN 4.
It's comin—
the Kid got him bulled into a corner—
punchin blind—
MAN 1.
The blood's in both eyes—
MAN 2 (and OTHERS).
Now—now—now—
MAN 4.
Just goin like a windmill—
MAN 7.
Oh, flatten him—
MAN 2.
Wipe the rotten—
MAN 4.
There—
    the nigger's grabbin for the rope—
he's bucklin—
he's swingin with his other—
MAN 6.
You're THROUGH—
MAN 4.
The Kid's
poundin right down on him, he's grabbin,
he's hangin, he's holdin, he can't, the Kid's
drivin him down like a big black—
(Great roar: MAN 1 follows the referee's
count with his own arm; his voice barely audi-
ble.)
MAN 1.
Four—five—six—seven—eight—
(The CROWD'S ROAR pulsates with the last
two counts and pandemonium breaks loose:
hugging, dancing, etc.)
MAN 1 (falling into arms below).
I love him, I love him—

(AGENT leaves.)
MAN 2.
Wahooo—
(POP goes inside with SMITTY.)
MAN 6.
We got it—
MAN 2.
Yoweee—
MAN 6.
Where's my fifty—
MAN 5.
Let's get in there—
(THEY all push at the barrier)
MAN 2.
What a Kid—
MAN 1.
Quit the pushing—
(Snatches of band music from within)
MAN 4.
They're bringin the nigger out—
MAN 2.
Who cares—
MAN 6.
Open up—
MAN 7.
We're missin all the—
MAN 6.
Break it in, for—
MAN 2 (as THEY break through).
W-A-A-H-O-O-OH!
(THEY ALL rush in except MAN 9, who stops
to throw a coin to NEGRO BOY 2)
MAN 9.
Here, chico—buy yourself a whitewash!
(HE follows the rest and the BOY runs off.
The sounds of jubilation within rise still
higher: the remaining NEGRO BOY climbs the
column to watch.)
PINKERTON MAN 2 (offstage).
Outa the way, come on, let 'em through
    here—
(JACK, helped along by TICK and GOLDIE
and escorted by four PINKERTON MEN, comes
limping through the gates, the PRESS at his
heels.)
PRESSMAN 1.
Just a word, Jack—
PINKERTON MAN 2.
Let's go boys—
GOLDIE.
Not now—
PRESSMAN 2.
Jack, in the tenth when you were—
(The music and crowd noise suddenly dwin-
dle, and the faint but triumphant sound of the
ANNOUNCER'S VOICE is heard. JACK stops.)

TICK.
Les go, baby.
(JACK *stands listening.*)
PRESSMAN 3.
Jack—why do you think it happened?
(JACK *stands listening.*)
I'm asking—
(The VOICE *rises to its conclusion: great
cheering: the* BOY *climbs down.* JACK *turns to*
PRESSMAN 3)
Why did it, Jack?
JACK.
He beat me, dassall.
Ah juss din have it.
(The BOY *spits on him and darts away.)*
Ain't dat right, boy?
TICK *(moving him on)*.
Take it slow, nice an slow . . .
PRESSMAN 3.
But why, Jack? Really.
JACK *(laughs, stops)*.
Oh, man.

Ah ain't got dem reallies from de Year
One . . .
An if any a you got em, step right down an
say em.
(Looks around at audience: DRUM-BEATING
begins)
No . . . you new here like Ah is—
(MUSIC: *A March Triumphal*)
Come on Chillun!
Let 'em pass by!
(Spreading his arms, HE *sweeps* TICK, GOL-
DIE, *and* 1 *or* 2 PRESSMEN *off to one side,
moving slowly, as the cheering* CROWD *surges
out through the gates. The* KID *rides on their
shoulders: immobile in his white robe, with one
gloved hand extended, the golden belt draped
around his neck and a towel over his head—
his smashed and reddened face is barely visible—*HE *resembles the lifelike wooden saints
in Catholic processions. Joyfully his bearers
parade him before the audience, and with a
final cheer fling their straw hats into the air.)*
CURTAIN

THE PRISONER OF SECOND AVENUE

Neil Simon

First presented on November 11, 1971, by Saint-Subber at the Eugene O'Neill Theater, New York City, with the following cast:

(In order of appearance)

MEL EDISON Peter Falk	HARRY EDISON Vincent Gardenia
EDNA EDISON Lee Grant	JESSIE Tressa Hughes
PEARL Florence Stanley	PAULINE Dena Dietrich

Directed by Mike Nichols
Setting by Richard Sylbert
Lighting by Tharon Musser
Costumes by Anthea Sylbert

THE SCENE: The entire action takes place in a Manhattan apartment, on Second Avenue in the upper eighties.

ACT ONE. SCENE ONE: Two-thirty in the morning on a midsummer's day. SCENE TWO: Late afternoon, a few days later.

ACT TWO. SCENE ONE: Mid-September; about one in the afternoon. SCENE TWO: Midafternoon, two weeks later. SCENE THREE: A late afternoon in mid-December.

In many respects Neil Simon must be the most remarkably successful playwright America has ever known. He has written a succession of hit plays, musicals, films, and television shows. Everything he touches turns to laughter and to gold. Yet if ever a man has struggled against his own success it is Neil Simon—who is not only the most successful contemporary playwright in the United States, he is also the most underestimated.

He was born on July 4, 1927. He began by writing revue sketches with his brother, Danny, and was soon remarkably successful in providing material for Sid Caesar's TV series "The Show of Shows." Working with some of the best TV gag writers in the world, and all of them masters of situation comedy, Mr. Simon soon won his spurs and his nickname, "Doc." He went on to write scripts for Phil Silvers in his "Sergeant Bilko" series. Simon later recalled that this was great training for a comedy writer, "because Phil talks so fast that you need to write a three-quarters-of-an-hour script for a half-hour show."

His first play, *Come Blow Your Horn,* was produced in 1961. It was a success in New York, London, and the movies. Mr. Simon's remarkable reign as the King of Broadway was beginning. In the years to come Mr. Simon would always have one show playing on Broadway, often two, and occasionally three. He was to buy his own theatre—the Eugene O'Neill —and to regard anything less than a two-year run as something of a failure.

Early success not infrequently spoils popular writers. Simon set out quite frankly just to make people laugh, and he was perhaps the first important comedy writer to serve his apprenticeship in television comedy. The results of this on his later work, and people's assessment of that work, have significance. He came to comedy with an instinctive sense for what made the mass audience laugh—and he had the TV ratings to prove it.

At first he was a master of the wisecrack—the sparkling one-liner that careened across the stage like a firecracker. But there was always more to Mr. Simon than that: it should be remembered that he was scriptwriter to Sid Caesar, not Bob Hope. Essential even to Mr. Simon's earliest comedies was a feel for life and a natural gift for dialogue. He has often been called a "laugh machine," and in the sense that the laughs have been consistently produced there is some justice in it. But the laughter itself is never mechanical; indeed, his very best jokes are rarely funny out of context. This is the acid test that draws the line between a playwright who is merely a wisecracker and a playwright who is a comedian.

On the other hand, Mr. Simon's television experience was not always to the good. It has given him a tendency to play for the easy laugh, to go for a caricature rather than a character, and to pull back from anything that might be offensive to his audience. Perhaps this is it: most of the time Mr. Simon measures up his audience a shade too self-consciously. There is nothing wrong with high ratings and good box-office returns, but these should be by-products; there are times when Mr. Simon seems to confuse them with ends.

Mr. Simon's situations are largely autobiographical or, more often, biographical. More than most writers, he feeds on life—his own life and the life of his friends. But, of course, having fed, he digests and, to change a metaphor rapidly getting out of hand, he embroiders. In his plays it is clear that he is becoming increasingly serious. (His musical books, however, such as *Little Me* or *Promises, Promises,* continue to run along happily enough!) Perhaps the first hint of seriousness arrived in 1965 with *The Odd Couple.* This story of two men separated from their wives and setting up house together was both amusing and touching.

From this time on, Mr. Simon has consciously—or so it seems—tried to find a new depth in his comedy. Most comedy deals with losers rather than winners, but increasingly Mr. Simon's losers have been the victims of urban blight, middle-age menopause, and middle-class frustration. To an extent Mr. Simon has been holding up a mirror to his typical Broadway audience, but has taken care to ensure that the lighting was never too harsh.

In the first episode of *Plaza Suite,* for example, we see a man, his wife, and his secretary, and the complications such arrangements occasionally provide. These people are lonely and unfulfilled. Equally lonely was Barney, the fish-restaurateur hero of *The Last of the Red Hot Lovers,* where a married man, feeling desperately as if the sexual revolution had bypassed him at great speed, is desperate to have an affair with another woman. And any "another" woman would do.

With *The Gingerbread Lady,* Mr. Simon perhaps went too far for most of his audience. It told of the trials and tribulations of a possibly reformed alcoholic, with all her jokes and her miseries. It was a finely written play, but unfortunately audiences failed to respond to anything quite so outside the typecasting they had imposed on Simon. Yet the playwright persevered in his quest for serious urban comedy rooted in the New York experience. The results were *The Prisoner of Second Avenue* (which is included in this collection) and, at the time of this writing, his most recent play, *The Sunshine Boys.* The latter is a very pungent bittersweet comedy about two aging vaudevillians who are persuaded to make a television comeback.

Perhaps few plays have so well pinpointed New York, its problems and neuroses, as does *Prisoner.* Recently a Viennese *dramaturg* in New York searching for plays for Vienna turned down my suggestion of *The Sunshine Boys* on the ground that they had tried *Prisoner* and found it "hopelessly New York and impenetrable to Viennese audiences!" Well, perhaps it is. It is also funny and true—a very telling picture of a time, a place, and a people. To be sure, there are incidental sketches that are superfluous to the play itself—its craftsmanship is intuitive rather than classic. Yet there is great quality to the writing and a mixture of fun and compassion that raises it from farce to comedy. We have known these people—and not just on television.

ACT ONE

SCENE ONE

*The scene is a fourteenth-floor apartment in
one of those prosaic new apartment houses that
grow like mushrooms all over New York's
overpriced East Side. This one is on Second
Avenue in the upper eighties. The management calls this a five-and-a-half-room apartment. What is visible to us is the living room–
dining room combination, a small, airless and
windowless kitchen off the dining room, a
French door that leads to a tiny balcony or
terrace off the living room, and a small hallway that leads to two bedrooms and bathrooms. This particular dwelling has been the
home of* MEL *and* EDNA EDISON *for the past
six years. What they thought they were getting
was all the modern luxuries and comforts of
the smart, chic East Side. What they got is
paper-thin walls and a view of five taller buildings from their terrace. The stage is dark. It is
two thirty in the morning and a hot midsummer's day has just begun. It is silent . . . In
pajamas, robe and slippers,* MEL EDISON *sits
alone on the tiny sofa, smoking a cigarette. He
rubs his face anxiously, then coughs . . .*

MEL. Ohhh, Christ Almighty.
(A light goes on in the bedroom. EDNA, *his
wife, appears in her nightgown)*
EDNA. What's wrong?
MEL. Nothing's wrong.
EDNA. Huh?
MEL. Nothing's wrong. Go back to bed.
EDNA. Are you sure?
MEL. I'm sure. Go back to bed. *(*EDNA
turns and goes back into the bedroom)* Oh,
God, God, God.
*(*EDNA *returns, putting on her robe. She
flips the switch on the wall, lighting the room.)*
EDNA. What is it? Can't you sleep?
MEL. If I could sleep, would I be sitting
here calling God at two thirty in the morn-
ing?
EDNA. What's the matter?
MEL. Do you know it's twelve degrees in
there? July twenty-third, the middle of a heat
wave, it's twelve degrees in there.
EDNA. I told you, turn the air-conditioner
off.
MEL. And how do we breathe? *(Points to
the window)* It's eighty-nine degrees out there
. . . eighty-nine degrees outside, twelve de-

grees inside. Either way they're going to get
me.
EDNA. We could leave the air-conditioner
on and open the window. *(She goes into the
kitchen.)*
MEL. They don't work that way. Once the
hot air sees an open window, it goes in.
EDNA. We could leave the air-conditioner
off for an hour. Then when it starts to get hot,
we can turn it back on. *(She comes out, eating
from a jar of applesauce.)*
MEL. Every hour? Seven times a night?
That's a good idea. I can get eight minutes
sleep in between working the air-conditioner.
EDNA. *I'll* do it. *I'll* get up.
MEL. I asked you a million times to call
that office. That air-conditioner hasn't
worked properly in two years.
EDNA. I called them. A man came. He
couldn't find anything wrong.
MEL. What do you mean, nothing wrong?
I got it on Low, it's twelve goddamned degrees.
EDNA *(sits down, sighing).* It's not twelve
degrees, Mel. It's cold, but it's not twelve
degrees.
MEL. All right, seventeen degrees. Twenty-
nine degrees. Thirty-six degrees. It's not six-
ty-eight, sixty-nine. A temperature for a normal person.
EDNA. *(sits on the sofa).* I'll call them again
tomorrow.
MEL. Why do they bother printing on it
High, Medium, and Low? It's all High. Low
is High. Medium is High. Some night I'm
gonna put it on High, they'll have to get a
flamethrower to get us out in the morning.
EDNA. What do you want me to do, Mel?
You want me to turn it off? You want me to
leave it on? Just tell me what to do.
MEL. Go back to sleep.
EDNA. I can't sleep when you're tense like
this.
MEL. I'm not tense. I'm frozen stiff. July
twenty-third. *(He sits down on the sofa.)*
EDNA. You're tense. You were tense when
you walked in the house tonight. You've been
tense for a week. Would you rather sleep in
here? I could make up the cot.
MEL. You can't even sit in here. *(Picks up
the small puff pillows from behind him)* Why
do you keep these ugly little pillows on here?
You spend eight hundred dollars for chairs
and then you can't sit on it because you got
ugly little pillows shoved up your back. *(He
throws one of the pillows on the floor.)*
EDNA. I'll take the pillows off.

MEL. Edna, please go inside, I'll be in later.

EDNA. It's not the air-conditioner. It's not the pillows. It's something else. Something's bothering you. I've seen you when you get like this. What is it, Mel?

MEL *(rubs his face with his hands)*. It's nothing. I'm tired. *(He gets up and goes over to the terrace door.)*

EDNA. I'm up, Mel, you might as well tell me.

MEL. It's nothing, I'm telling you . . . I don't know. It's everything. It's this apartment, it's this building, it's this city. Listen. Listen to this. *(He opens the terrace door. We hear the sounds of traffic, horns, motors, etc.)* Two thirty in the morning, there's one car driving around in Jackson Heights and we can hear it. . . . Fourteen stories up, I thought it would be quiet. I hear the subway up here better than I hear it in the subway. . . . We're like some kind of goddamned antenna. All the sound goes up through this apartment and then out to the city.

EDNA. We've lived here six years, it never bothered you before.

MEL. It's worse now, I don't know why. I'm getting older, more sensitive to sounds, to noise. Everything. *(He closes the door, then looks at himself.)* You see this? I had that door opened ten seconds, you gotta wash these pajamas now.

EDNA *(anything to please)*. Give them to me, I'll get you clean pajamas.

MEL *(pacing)*. Two thirty in the morning, can you believe that's still going on next door? *(He points to the wall.)*

EDNA. What's going on?

MEL. What are you, trying to be funny? You mean to tell me you don't hear that?

EDNA *(puzzled)*. Hear what?

MEL *(closer to the wall, still pointing)*. That! That! What are you, deaf? You don't hear that?

EDNA. Maybe I'm deaf. I don't hear anything.

MEL. *Listen,* for God's sakes . . . You don't hear "Raindrops Falling on His Head"? *(He sings.)* Da dum de dum da dum de da . . . "too big for his feet" . . . You don't hear that?

EDNA. Not when you're singing, I don't hear it.

MEL *(stares at the wall)*. It's those two goddamned German airline hostesses. Every night they got someone else in there. Two basketball players, two hockey players, what-

ever team is in town, win or lose, they wind up in there. . . . Every goddamned night! . . . Somewhere there's a 747 flying around with people serving themselves because those two broads never leave that apartment. *(He grabs* EDNA, *pulls her over to the wall.)* Come here. You mean to tell me you don't hear that?

EDNA *(puts her ear against the wall)*. Yes, now I hear it.

MEL. You see! Is it any wonder I don't sleep at night?

EDNA *(moving away from the wall)*. Don't sleep with your head next to the wall. Sleep in the bedroom.

MEL. Hey, knock it off in there. It's two damn thirty in the lousy morning. *(He bangs on the wall, then stops and looks at it. He points to the wall.)* Look at that, I cracked the wall. I barely touched it, the damned thing is cracked.

EDNA. It was starting to crack before. There's a leak somewhere; one of the pipes upstairs is broken.

MEL. A two-million-dollar building, you can't touch the walls? It's a good thing I didn't try to hang a picture; we all could have been killed.

EDNA. They know about it. They're starting to fix it on Monday.

MEL *(he sits down)*. Not Monday. Tomorrow. I want that wall fixed tomorrow, it's a health hazard. And they're going to repaint the whole wall, and if it doesn't match, they'll paint the rest of the room, and if that doesn't match, they'll do the rest of the apartment. And I'm not paying for it, you understand?

EDNA. I'll tell them.

MEL. And tell them about the air-conditioner . . . and the window in the bedroom that doesn't open except when it rains and then you can't shut it until there's a flood and then tell them about our toilet that never stops flushing.

EDNA. It stops flushing if you jiggle it.

MEL. Why should I have to jiggle it? For the money I'm paying here do I have to stand over a toilet in the middle of the night and have to jiggle every time I go to the bathroom?

EDNA. When you're through, get back into bed, tell me, and *I'll* jiggle it.

MEL *(turns, glares at her)*. Go to bed, Edna. I don't want to talk to you now. Will you please go to sleep?

EDNA. I can't sleep if I know you're up

here walking around having an anxiety attack.

MEL. I'm not having an anxiety attack. I'm a little tense.

EDNA. Why don't you take a Valium?

MEL. I took one.

EDNA. Then take another one.

MEL. I took another one. They don't work any more. *(He sits down in a chair.)*

EDNA. *Two* Valiums? They *have* to work.

MEL. They don't work any more, I'm telling you. They're supposed to calm you down, aren't they? All right, am I calm? They don't work. Probably don't put anything in them. Charge you fourteen dollars for the word "Valium." *(He bangs on the wall.)* Don't you ever fly anywhere? Keep somebody in Europe awake! *(He bangs on the wall again with his fist.)*

EDNA. Stop it, Mel. You're really getting me nervous now. What's wrong? Has something happened? Is something bothering you?

MEL. Why do we live like this? Why do we pay somebody hundreds of dollars a month to live in an egg box that leaks?

EDNA. You don't look well to me, Mel. You look pale. You look haggard.

MEL. I wasn't planning to be up. *(He rubs his stomach.)*

EDNA. Why are you rubbing your stomach?

MEL. I'm not rubbing it, I'm holding it.

EDNA. Why are you holding your stomach?

MEL. It's nothing. A little indigestion. It's that crap I had for lunch.

EDNA. Where did you eat?

MEL. In a health-food restaurant. If you can't eat health food, what the hell can you eat any more?

EDNA. You're probably just hungry. Do you want me to make you something?

MEL. Nothing is safe any more. I read in the paper today two white mice at Columbia University got cancer from eating graham crackers. It was in *The New York Times.*

EDNA. Is that what's bothering you? Did you eat graham crackers today?

MEL. Food used to be so good. I used to love food. I haven't eaten food since I was thirteen years old.

EDNA. Do you want some food? I'll make you food. I remember how they made it.

MEL. I haven't had a real piece of bread in thirty years. . . . If I knew what was going to happen, I would have saved some rolls when

I was a kid. You can't breathe in here. *(He goes out onto the terrace.)* Christ, what a stink. Fourteen stories up, you can smell the garbage from here. Why do they put garbage out in eighty-nine-degree heat? Edna, come here, I want you to smell the garbage.

EDNA *(comes to the door of the terrace).* I smell it, I smell it.

MEL. You can't smell it from there. Come here where you can smell it.

EDNA *(walks to the edge of the terrace and inhales).* You're right. If you really want to smell it, you have to stand right here.

MEL. This country is being buried by its own garbage. It keeps piling up higher and higher. In three years this apartment is going to be the second floor.

EDNA. What can they do, Mel? Save it up and put it out in the winter? They have to throw it out sometime. That's why they call it garbage.

MEL. I can't talk to you. I can't talk to you any more.

EDNA. Mel, I'm a human being the same as you. I get hot, I get cold, I smell garbage, I hear noise. You either live with it or you get out.

(Suddenly a dog howls and barks.)

MEL. If you're a human being you reserve the right to complain, to protest. When you give up that right, you don't exist any more. I protest to stinking garbage and jiggling toilets . . . and barking dogs. *(Yells out)* Shut up, goddamnit.

EDNA. Are you going to stay here and yell at the dog? Because I'm going to sleep.

(The dog howls again.)

MEL. How can you sleep with a dog screaming like that? *(The dog howls again.* MEL *goes to the edge of the terrace and yells down.)* Keep that dog quiet. There are human beings sleeping up here. Christ Almighty!!!!

VOICE *(from above).* Will you be quiet. There are children up here.

MEL *(yelling up).* What the hell are you yelling at me for? You looking for trouble, go down and keep the dog company.

EDNA. Mel, will you stop it! Stop it, for God's sakes!

MEL *(comes back in; screams at* EDNA). Don't tell *me* to stop it! DON'T TELL ME TO STOP IT!

EDNA. I don't know what's gotten into you. But I'm not going to stand here and let you take it out on me. . . . If it's too much for you, take a room in the public library, *but don't take it out on me.* I'm going to sleep, *good night!! (She turns angrily and heads for the bedroom. She gets almost to the bedroom door before* MEL *calls to her.)*

MEL. Edna! *(She stops and turns around.)* Don't go! . . . Talk to me for a few minutes, because I think I'm going out of my mind.

(She stops, looks at him, and comes back into the living room.)

EDNA. What is it?

MEL. I'm unraveling . . . I'm losing touch!

EDNA. You haven't been sleeping well lately.

MEL. I don't know where I am half the time. I walk down Madison Avenue, I think I'm in a foreign country.

EDNA. I know that feeling, Mel.

MEL. It's not just a feeling, something is happening to me . . . I'm losing control. I can't handle things any more. The telephone on my desk rings seven, eight times before I answer it. . . . I forgot how to work the water cooler today. I stood there with an empty cup in my hand and water running all over my shoes.

EDNA. It's not just you, Mel, it's everybody. Everybody's feeling the tension these days.

MEL. Tension? If I could just feel tension, I'd give a thousand dollars to charity. . . . When you're tense, you're tight, you're holding on to something. I don't know where to grab. Edna, I'm slipping, and I'm scared.

EDNA. Don't talk like that. What about seeing the analyst again?

MEL. Who? Doctor Pike? He's dead. Six years of my life, twenty-three thousand dollars. He got my money, what does he care if he gets a heart attack?

EDNA. There are other good doctors. You can see someone else.

MEL. And start all over from the beginning? "Hello. Sit down. What seems to be the trouble?" . . . It'll cost me another twenty-three thousand just to fill *this* doctor in with information I already gave the dead one.

EDNA. What about a little therapy? Maybe you just need someone to talk to for a while.

MEL. I don't know where or who I am any more. I'm disappearing, Edna. I don't need analysts, I need Lost and Found.

EDNA. Listen . . . Listen . . . What about if we get away for a couple of weeks? A two-week vacation? Someplace in the sun, away from the city. You can get two weeks' sick leave, can't you, Mel?

(He is silent. He walks to the window and glances over at the plant.)

MEL. Even the cactus is dying. Strongest plant in the world, only has to be watered twice a year. Can't make a go of it on Eighty-eighth and Second.

EDNA. Mel, answer me. What about getting away? Can't you ask them for two weeks off?

MEL *(makes himself a Scotch).* Yes, I can ask them for two weeks off. What worries me is that they'll ask me to take the other fifty weeks as well. *(He drinks.)*

EDNA. You? What are you talking about? You've been there twenty-two years. . . . Mel, is that it? Is that what's been bothering you? You're worried about losing your job?

MEL. I'm not worried about losing it. I'm worried about keeping it. Losing it is easy.

EDNA. Has something happened? Have they said anything?

MEL. They don't have to say anything. The company lost three million dollars this year. Suddenly they're looking to save pennies. The vice-president of my department has been using the same paper clip for three weeks now. A sixty-two-year-old man with a duplex on Park Avenue and a house in Southampton running around the office, screaming, "Where's my paper clip?"

EDNA. But they haven't actually said anything to you.

MEL. They closed the executive dining room. Nobody goes out to lunch any more. They bring sandwiches from home. Top executives, making eighty thousand dollars a year, eating egg-salad sandwiches over the wastepaper basket.

EDNA. Nothing has happened yet, Mel. There's no point in worrying about it now.

MEL. No one comes to work late any more. Everyone's afraid if you're not there on time, they'll sell your desk.

EDNA. And what if they did? We'd live, we'd get by. You'd get another job somewhere.

MEL. Where? I'm gonna be forty-seven years old in January. Forty-seven! They could get two twenty-three-and-a-half-year-old kids for half my money.

EDNA. All right, suppose something *did* happen? Suppose you *did* lose your job? It's not the end of the world. We don't have to live in the city. We could move somewhere in the country, or even out West.

MEL. And what do I do for a living?

Become a middle-aged cowboy? Maybe they'll put me in charge of rounding up the elderly cattle. . . . What's the matter with you?

EDNA. The girls are in college now, we have enough to see them through. We don't need much for the two of us.

MEL. You need a place to live, you need clothing, you need food. A can of polluted tuna fish is still eighty-five cents.

EDNA. We could move to Europe. To Spain. Two people could live for fifteen hundred dollars a year in Spain.

MEL *(nods).* Spanish people. I'm forty-seven years old, with arthritis in my shoulder and high pressure—you expect me to raise goats and live in a cave?

EDNA. You could work there, get some kind of a job.

MEL. An advertising account executive? In Barcelona? They've probably been standing at the dock waiting for years for someone like that.

EDNA *(angrily).* What is it they have here that's so damned hard to give up? *What is it you'll miss so badly, for God's sakes?*

MEL. I'm not through with my life yet . . . I still have value, I still have worth.

EDNA. What kind of a life is this? You live like some kind of a caged animal in a Second Avenue zoo that's too hot in one room, too cold in another, overcharged for a growth on the side of the building they call a terrace that can't support a cactus plant, let alone two human beings. Is that what you call a worthwhile life? Banging on walls and jiggling toilets?

MEL *(shouts).* You think it's any better in Sunny Spain? Go swimming on the beach, it'll take you the rest of the summer to scrape the oil off.

EDNA. Forget Spain. There are other places to live.

MEL. Maine? Vermont, maybe? You think it's all rolling hills and maple syrup? They have more people on welfare up there than they have pancakes. Washington? Oregon? Unemployed lumberjacks are sitting around sawing legs off chairs; they have nothing else to do.

EDNA. I will go anywhere in the world you want to go, Mel. I will live in a cave, a hut, or a tree. I will live on a raft in the Amazon jungle if that's what you want to do.

MEL. All right, call a travel agency. Get two economy seats to Bolivia. We'll go to Abercrombie's tomorrow, get a couple of pith helmets and a spear gun.

EDNA. Don't talk to me like I'm insane.

MEL. I'm halfway there, you might as well catch up.

EDNA. I am trying to offer reasonable suggestions. I am not responsible. I am not the one who's doing this to you.

MEL. I didn't say you were, Edna.

EDNA. Then what do you want from me? *What do you want from anyone?*

MEL *(buries his face in his hands).* Just a little breathing space . . . just for a little while. *(The phone rings.* MEL *looks up at* EDNA.) Who could that be? *(*EDNA *shakes her head, not knowing.)* It couldn't be the office, could it?

EDNA. At a quarter to three in the morning?

MEL. Maybe they got the night watchman to fire me, they'll save a day's salary.

(It keeps ringing.)

EDNA. Answer it, Mel, I'm nervous.

(MEL *picks up the phone.)*

MEL *(into the phone).* Hello? . . . Yes? . . . Yes, Apartment 14A, what about it? . . . *What??? I'm keeping YOU up???* Who the hell do you think got *me* up to get *you* up in the first place? . . . Don't tell me you got a plane leaving for Stuttgart in the morning. . . . I'll talk as loud as I damn well please. This isn't a sublet apartment, I'm a regular American tenant. . . . Go ahead and bang on the wall. You'll get a bang right back on yours. *(He covers the phone, then says to* EDNA) If she bangs, I want you to bang back.

EDNA. Mel, what are you starting in for?

(From the other side of the wall, we hear a loud banging.)

MEL. Okay, bang back.

EDNA. Mel, it's a quarter to three. Leave them alone, they'll go to sleep.

MEL. Will you bang back?!

EDNA. If I bang back, she's just going to bang back at me.

MEL. Will you bang back!!!?

EDNA. I'll bang, I'll bang! *(She bangs twice on the wall.)*

MEL *(into the phone).* All right? *(From the other side of the wall, they bang again.* MEL *says to* EDNA) Bang back! *(She bangs again. They bang from the other side again. He repeats his instructions to* EDNA.) Bang back! *(She bangs again. They bang again.)* Bang back!

(She bangs. The stage goes black, then the

curtain falls. The house remains in darkness. A screen drops and the News Logo appears. We hear Roger Keating with the Six O'Clock Report.)

VOICE OF ROGER KEATING *(in the darkness).* This is Roger Keating and the *Six O'Clock Report.* . . . New York was hit with its third strike of the week. This time the city employees of thirty-seven New York hospitals walked out at 3 P.M. this afternoon. The Mayor's office has been flooded with calls, as hundreds of patients and elderly sick people have complained of lack of food, clean sheets, and medicines. One seventy-nine-year-old patient in Lenox Hill Hospital fell in the corridor, broke his leg, and was treated by a seventy-three-year-old patient who had just recovered from a gall-bladder operation. . . . Two of the most cold-blooded robbers in the city's history today made off with four thousand dollars, stolen from the New York City Home for the Blind. Police believe it may have been the same men who got away with thirty-six hundred dollars on Tuesday from the New York Cat and Dog Hospital. . . . Water may be shut off tomorrow, says the New York Commissioner of Health, because of an anonymous phone call made to the bureau this morning, threatening to dump fifty pounds of chemical pollutants in the city's reservoirs. The unidentified caller, after making his threat, concluded with, "It's gonna be dry tomorrow, baby." . . . And from the office of Police Commissioner Murphy, a report that the number of apartment house burglaries has risen seven point two percent in August.

SCENE TWO

It is late afternoon, a few days later. At the curtain's rise, the room is in a shambles. Chairs are overturned; drawers are pulled open, their contents scattered all over the floor; the bookcase has been cleared of half of its shelves and articles of clothing are strewn about the room. It is obvious what has happened.

EDNA *is on the phone. She is shaking.*

———

EDNA *(sobbing).* Edison, Mrs. Edna Edison . . . I've just been robbed . . . I just walked in, they took everything . . . Edison . . . I just walked in, I found the door open, they must have just left . . . 385 East 88th Street . . . Two minutes sooner, I could have been killed . . . Apartment 14A . . . I don't know yet. Television, the record player, books, clothing . . . They took lots of clothing. My dresses, my coats, all my husband's suits—there's not a thing left in his closet . . . I haven't checked the drawers yet. . . . Would you, please? Send somebody right away . . . I'm all alone. My husband isn't home from work yet . . . *Mrs. Edna Edison.* I could have been killed. Thank you. *(She hangs up, then turns and looks at the room. She crosses the room, lifts a chair up and sets it right. Then she goes over to the bureau and starts to look through the drawers. As she discovers new things are missing, she sobs louder.)* All right . . . Calm down . . . A drink, I have to have a drink. *(She rushes into the kitchen, gets a glass and a few cubes of ice from the refrigerator, then rushes back out into the living room. She rushes to the bar and looks. There are no bottles.)* The liquor's gone. They took the liquor. *(She puts the glass down, slumps into a chair, and sobs.)* Valium . . . I want a Valium. *(She gets up and rushes down the small corridor, disappearing into the bedroom. We hear noises as she must be looking through ransacked medicine chests. There are a few moments of silence.* EDNA *has probably fallen onto the bed, sobbing, for all we know. The front door is unlocked and* MEL *enters. He carries his suit jacket and the New York* Post. *His shirt sleeves are rolled up and he looks hot. He closes the door and hangs his jacket in the closet. Consumed with his own thoughts, he doesn't seem to even notice the room. He moves over to the chair, falls into it exhausted, puts his head back and sighs. . . . His eyes open, then he looks at the room for almost the first time. He looks around the room, bewildered. From the bedroom we hear* EDNA's *voice.)* Mel? . . . Is that you, Mel?

*(*MEL *is still looking at the room, puzzled.* EDNA *appears cautiously from the bedroom. She comes in, holding a vase by the thin end, and looks at* MEL.*)*

MEL. Didn't Mildred come in to clean today?

EDNA *(puts the vase down).* No today . . . Mondays and Thursdays.

MEL. What happened here? . . . Why is this place such a mess?

EDNA. We've been robbed.

*(*MEL *looks at her in a state of shock. . . .*

He slowly rises and then looks at the room in a new perspective.)

MEL. What do you mean, robbed?

EDNA *(starts to cry)*. Robbed! Robbed! What does robbed mean? They come in, they take things out! *They robbed us!!!*

MEL *(he keeps turning, looking at the room in disbelief—not knowing where to look first).* I don't understand. . . . What do you mean, someone just walked in and robbed us?

EDNA. What do you think? . . . They called up and made an appointment? *We've been robbed!*

MEL. All right, calm down. Take it easy, Edna. I'm just asking a simple question. What happened? What did they get?

EDNA. I don't know yet. I was out shopping. I was gone five minutes. I came back, I found it like this.

MEL. You couldn't have been gone five minutes. Look at this place.

EDNA. *Five minutes,* that's all I was gone.

MEL. Five minutes, heh? Then we'd better call the FBI, because every crook in New York must have been in here.

EDNA. Then that's who was here, because I was only gone five minutes.

MEL. When you came back into the building did you notice anyone suspicious-looking?

EDNA. *Everyone* in this building is suspicious-looking.

MEL. You didn't see anybody carrying any bundles or packages?

EDNA. I didn't notice.

MEL. What do you mean, you didn't notice?

EDNA. I didn't notice. You think I look for people leaving the building with my television set?

MEL. They took the television? *(He starts for the bedroom, then stops.)* A *brand new* color television?

EDNA. They're not looking for 1948 Philcos. It was here. They took it. I can't get a breath out.

MEL. All right, sit there. I'll get a drink.

EDNA *(sitting down)*. I don't want a drink.

MEL. A little Scotch. It'll calm you down.

EDNA. It won't calm me down, because there's no Scotch. They took the Scotch too.

MEL. *All* the Scotch?

EDNA. All the Scotch.

MEL The Chivas Regal too?

EDNA. No, they're going to take the cheap Scotch and leave the Chivas Regal. They took it all, they cleaned us out.

MEL *(gnashing his teeth)*. Sons of bitches. *(He runs to the terrace door, opens it, steps out on the terrace, and yells out.) Sons of bitches! (He closes the door and comes back in.)* All in five minutes, eh? They must have been gorillas to lift all that in five minutes.

EDNA. Leave me alone.

MEL *(gnashing his teeth again)*. Sons of bitches.

EDNA. Stop swearing, the police will be here any minute. I just called them.

MEL. You called the police?

EDNA. Didn't I just say that?

MEL. Did you tell them we were robbed?

EDNA. Why else would I call them? I'm not friendly with the police. What kind of questions are you asking me? What's wrong with you?

MEL. All right, calm down, because you're hysterical.

EDNA. I am not hysterical.

MEL. You're hysterical.

EDNA. You're *making* me hysterical. Don't you understand? My house has just been robbed.

MEL. What am I, a boarder? My house has been robbed too. My color television and my Chivas Regal is missing the same as yours.

EDNA. You didn't walk in and find it. *I* did.

MEL. What's the difference who found it? There's still nothing to drink and nothing to watch.

EDNA. Don't yell at me. I'm just as upset as you are.

MEL. I'm sorry. I'm excited, too. I don't mean to yell at you. *(Starts for the bedroom)* Let me get you a Valium, it'll calm you down.

EDNA. I don't want a Valium.

MEL. Take one. You'll feel better.

EDNA. I'm not taking a Valium.

MEL. Why are you so stubborn?

EDNA. I'm not stubborn. We don't have any. They took the Valiums.

MEL *(stops)*. They took the Valiums?

EDNA. The whole medicine chest. Valiums, Seconals, aspirin, shaving cream, toothpaste, razor blades. They left your toothbrush. You want to go in and brush your teeth, you can still do it.

MEL *(smiles, disbelieving)*. I don't believe you. *I don't believe you!* (MEL *looks at her, then storms off and disappears into the bedroom.* EDNA *gets up and picks up a book from the floor. From the far recesses of the bathroom we hear* MEL *scream:)*

MEL *(offstage)*. DIRTY BASTARDS!!!

(EDNA *is holding the book upside down and shaking it, hoping some concealed item will fall out. It doesn't.* MEL *storms back into living room.*) I hope they die. I hope the car they stole to get away in hits a tree and turns over and burns up and they all die!

EDNA. You read about it every day. And when it happens to you, you can't believe it.

MEL. A television I can understand. Liquor I can understand. But shaving cream? Hair spray? How much are they going to get for a roll of dental floss?

EDNA. They must have been desperate. They took everything they could carry. *(Shakes the book one last time)* They even found my kitchen money.

MEL. What kitchen money?

EDNA. I kept my kitchen money in here. Eighty-five dollars.

MEL. In cash? Why do you keep cash in a book?

EDNA. So no one will find it! Where else am I gonna keep it?

MEL. In a jar. In the sugar. Some place they're not going to look.

EDNA. They looked in the medicine chest, you think they're not going to look in the sugar?

MEL. *Nobody looks in sugar!*

EDNA. Nobody steals dental floss and mouthwash. Only sick people. Only that's who live in the world today. *Sick, sick, sick people! (She sits, emotionally wrung out.* MEL *comes over to her and puts his arm on her shoulder, comforting her.)*

MEL. It's all right. . . . It's all right, Edna. . . . As long as you weren't hurt, that's the important thing. *(He looks through the papers on the table.)*

EDNA. Can you imagine if I had walked in and found them here? What would I have done, Mel?

MEL. You were very lucky, Edna. Very lucky.

EDNA. But what would I have done?

MEL. What's the difference? You didn't walk in and find them.

EDNA. But supposing I did? What would I have done?

MEL. You'd say, "Excuse me," close the door, and come back later. What would you do, sit and watch? Why do you ask me such questions? It didn't happen, did it?

EDNA. It *almost* happened. If I walked in here five minutes sooner.

MEL *(walking away from her)*. You couldn't have been gone only five minutes. . . . It took the Seven Santini Brothers two days to move everything in, three junkies aren't gonna move it all out in five minutes.

EDNA. Seven minutes, eight minutes, what's the difference?

MEL *(opens the door, looks at the lock)*. The lock isn't broken, it's not jimmied. I don't even know how they got in here.

EDNA. Maybe they found my key in the street.

MEL *(closes the door; looks at her)*. What do you mean, "found your key"? Don't you have your key?

EDNA. No, I lost it. I thought it was somewhere in the house, but maybe I lost it in the street.

MEL. If you didn't have your key, how were you going to get back in the house when you went shopping?

EDNA. I left the door open.

MEL. You—left—the—door—open???

EDNA. I didn't have a key, how was I going to get back in the house?

MEL. *So you left the door open?* In a city with the highest crime rate in the history of the world, *you left the door open?*

EDNA. What was I going to do? Take the furniture with me? I was only gone five minutes. How did they know I was going to leave the door open?

MEL. They know! They know! A door opens, it doesn't lock, the whole junkie world lights up. "Door open, fourteenth floor, Eighty-eighth Street and Second Avenue." They know!

EDNA. They don't know anything. They have to go around trying doors.

MEL. And what did you think? They were going to try every door in this house except yours? "Let's leave 14A alone, fellas, it looks like a nice door."

EDNA. If they're going to go around trying doors, they have twenty-three hours and fifty-five minutes a day to try them. I didn't think they would try ours the five minutes I was out of the house. I gambled! I lost!

MEL. What kind of gamble is that to take? If you lose, they get everything. If you win, they rob somebody else.

EDNA. I *had* to shop. There was nothing in the house to eat tonight.

MEL. All right, now you have something to eat and nothing to eat it with. . . . Why didn't you call up and have them send it?

EDNA. Because I shop in a cheap store that

doesn't deliver. I am trying to save us money because you got me so worried the other night. I was just trying to save us money. . . . Look how much money I saved us. (EDNA *starts to pick up things.*)

MEL. What are you doing?

EDNA. We can't leave everything like this. I want to clean up.

MEL. Now?

EDNA. The place is a mess. We have people coming over in a few minutes.

MEL. The *police?* You want the place to look nice for the police? . . . You're worried they're going to put it down in their books, "bad housekeeper"? . . . Leave it alone. Maybe they'll find some clues.

EDNA. I can't find out what's missing until I put everything back in its place.

MEL. What do you mean? You know what's missing. The television, the liquor, the kitchen money, the medicine chest and the hi-fi. . . . That's it, isn't it? *(Pause)* Isn't it? (EDNA *looks away.*) Okay, what else did they get?

EDNA. Am I a detective? Look, you'll find out.

(He glares at her and looks around the room, not knowing where to begin. He decides to check the bedroom. He storms down the hall and disappears. EDNA, *knowing what to soon expect, sits on a chair in the dining area and stares out the window. She takes out a hanky and wipes some dirt from the window sill.* MEL *returns calmly— at least outwardly calm. He takes a deep breath.)*

MEL. Where are my suits?

EDNA. They were there this morning. They're not there now. They must have taken your suits.

MEL *(still trying to be calm).* Seven suits? Three sports jackets? Eight pairs of slacks?

EDNA. If that's what you had, that's what they got.

MEL. I'm lucky my tuxedo is in the cleaners.

EDNA *(still staring out the window).* They sent it back this morning.

MEL. Well, they did a good job of it . . . Cleaned me out. . . . Left a pair of khaki pants and my golf hat. . . . Anybody asks us out to dinner this week, ask them if it's all right if I wear khaki pants and a golf hat. DIRTY BASTARDS!!!! *(In what can only be described as an insane tantrum, he picks up some ashtrays from the sideboard and throws them to the floor of the kitchen, continuing*

uncontrollably until all his energy and his vitriol have been exhausted. . . . He stands there panting.)

EDNA. It's just things, Mel. Just some old suits and coats. We can replace them. We'll buy new ones. Can't we, Mel?

MEL. With what? . . . *With what?* They *fired* me. *(He sits, his back to the wall.)*

EDNA. Oh, my God. Don't tell me.

MEL. Well, I'm telling you. *They fired me!* . . . Me, Hal Chesterman, Mike Ambrozi, Dave Polichek, Arnold Strauss . . . Two others, I can't even remember their names. . . . Seven of us, in one fell swoop. *Fired!*

EDNA *(she is so distraught that she can't even stir in her chair).* Oh, Mel, I'm so sorry . . .

MEL. They called us into the office one at a time. They didn't even have to say it, we knew. We saw it coming. Even the secretaries knew. They couldn't look at you when you said good morning. . . . Eighty-five-dollar-a-week girls were bringing me coffee and Danish and not charging me for it. I knew right away.

EDNA. Oh, Mel, Mel, Mel . . .

MEL. They said they had no choice. They had to make cuts right down the line . . . Seven executives, twelve salesmen, twenty-four in office help—forty-three people in one afternoon. . . . It took three elevators two trips to get rid of all the losers. . . . Wait'll the coffee and Danish man comes in tomorrow, he'll throw himself out the window.

EDNA. And then you come home to this. To get fired and then to come home and find your house has been robbed.

MEL. It didn't happen today. It happened Monday.

EDNA. Monday? You mean you've known for four days and you haven't said a word to me?

MEL. I didn't know how to tell you, I couldn't work up the courage. I thought maybe another job would turn up, a miracle would happen. . . . Miracles don't happen when you're forty-seven. . . . When Moses saw the burning bush, he must have been twenty-three, twenty-four, the most. Never forty-seven. *(He goes into the kitchen, gets a can of beer.)*

EDNA. What have you done since Monday? Where have you been? What did you do all day?

MEL *(comes out of the kitchen, sits down, and drinks).* In the mornings I made phone calls, tried to see a few people. When you're looking for help, you'd be surprised how many people are out to lunch at ten-thirty in the morning. . . . In the afternoons? *(He shrugs.)* I went to museums, an auction, the office-furniture show at the Coliseum . . . I saw an Italian movie, I saw a Polish movie . . . I saw two dirty movies . . . I met Dave Polichek at the dirty movie. We both lied. Said we were killing time until our next appointment. Some important appointments. I went to Central Park and he went to the Ripley Wax Museum.

EDNA. You should have come home, Mel.

MEL. Why? I had a very nice bench in the park near the Wollman Skating Rink. For lunch I had my jelly apple and my Fanta orange drink.

EDNA. Oh, Mel, I can't bear it.

MEL. I came very close to having an affair with a seventy-three-year-old English nanny. We hit it off very well but the baby didn't like me. *(At this point* EDNA *gets up and quickly rushes to* MEL, *who is still sitting. He reaches up and grabs her around the waist, holding on for dear life.)* I'll be all right, Edna. I don't want you to worry about me. I'll be all right.

EDNA. I know you will, Mel. I know it.

MEL. I'll find another job, you'll see.

EDNA. Of course you will.

MEL. You'll take down the living room drapes, make me a suit, and I'll look for another job.

EDNA *(hugs him)*. Oh Mel, we'll be all right. We will. *(They break.)*

MEL. I played two innings of softball yesterday.

EDNA. You didn't.

(He sits on the sofa; she resumes picking up items.)

MEL *(nods)*. Mm-hmm. With a day camp for fourteen-year-olds. . . . Harvey, the right fielder, had to go for a violin lesson, so I played the last two innings.

EDNA. And you hit a home run?

MEL. I struck out, dropped two fly balls and lost the game. . . . They wanted to kill me.

EDNA. I wish I'd been there.

MEL. I know I can make the team, I just have to get my timing back. If I don't find a job maybe I'll go back to camp this summer.

EDNA. It would take me two minutes to sew in your name tapes. You want to think about it while I make you a cup of coffee? *(She starts for the kitchen.)*

MEL. They didn't get the coffee? They left us the coffee? How come?

EDNA. Robbers never go into the kitchen.

MEL. Then why didn't you leave the money in the sugar jar?

EDNA. Mel, we're insured. We'll get all the money back.

MEL. We're lucky if we get half. You think you get two hundred dollars for a two-hundred-dollar coat? They depreciate. You put it on once, button it, it's worth forty dollars.

EDNA. Then we'll get half the money back.

MEL. Then the premiums go up. You get robbed once and it costs you twice as much to protect half of what you used to have.

EDNA *(comes out of the kitchen)*. Mel, please don't worry about the money. We have something put aside. We're not extravagant. We can live comfortably for a while.

MEL. With two girls in college? With our rent, with our food bills, with nothing coming in? . . . We have to get out, Edna. We have to get out of everything. *(He paces around the room.)*

EDNA. I'll go wherever you want, Mel.

MEL. I don't mean out of here. Out of obligations. Out of things we don't need that are choking us. I'm gonna quit the gym. I don't need a gym for two hundred and fifty dollars a year. I'll run around the bedroom, it's the only way to keep warm in there anyway. . . . And we don't need the Museum of Modern Art. We can watch *Duck Soup* on television. *(Picks up some magazines)* And these goddamn magazines. I don't want *Time, Life,* or *Newsweek* any more, you understand. I'm not going to spend my last few dollars to find out that unemployment went up this year. *(He throws them into the wastebasket.)*

EDNA. We don't need *any* of them. We never did, Mel.

MEL *(looking around, throwing some more junk into the basket)*. The garbage! The garbage that we buy every year. Useless, meaningless garbage that fills up the house until you throw it out there and it becomes garbage again and *stinks* up the house. For what? For *what,* Edna?

EDNA. I don't know, Mel.

MEL. Two dollars' worth of food that comes in three dollars' worth of wrapping. Telephone calls to find out what time it is because you're too lazy to look at a clock. . . . The food we never ate, the books we never read, the records we never played. *(He picks up a little thing off the bar.)* Look at this! Eight and a half dollars for a musical whiskey pourer. *Eight and a half dollars!* God forbid we should get a little bored while we're pouring our whiskey! Toys! Toys, novelties, gimmicks, trivia, garbage, crap, HORSESHIT!!! *(He hurls the basket to the floor.)*

EDNA. No more. We'll never buy another thing, Mel. I promise. I promise.

MEL *(he is seething with anger)*. Twenty-two years I gave them. What did I give them twenty-two years of my life for? A musical whiskey pourer? It's my *life* that's been poured down the drain. Where's the music? Where's a cute little tune? They kick you out after twenty-two years, they ought to have a goddamned brass band.

EDNA. All right, don't get upset. You're going to get yourself sick.

MEL. You know where my music is? *(He goes over to the wall and points.)* There! There it is! It's playing on the other side of that wall. *(Screaming) There's my music after twenty-two years. (He grabs his chest, grimacing.)* Ohh!

EDNA. What is it, Mel? What's the matter?

MEL. I got pains in my chest. It's nothing, don't worry. It's not a heart attack.

EDNA *(nervously)*. What do you mean? Why do you say it's not a heart attack?

MEL. Because it's not a heart attack. It's pains in my chest.

EDNA. Why are you having pains in your chest?

MEL. BECAUSE I DON'T HAVE A JOB. BECAUSE I DON'T HAVE A SUIT TO WEAR! BECAUSE I'M HAVING A GOD-DAMNED BREAKDOWN AND THEY DIDN'T EVEN LEAVE ME WITH A PILL TO TAKE! *(He rushes out onto the terrace again and screams.)* BASTARDS! . . . YOU DIRTY BASTARDS!

(Suddenly a VOICE, *probably from the terrace above, yells down.)*

VOICE. Shut up, down there! There are children up here!

MEL *(leans over the terrace wall and yells up)*. Don't you yell at me! They took everything! EVERYTHING! They left me with a goddamned pair of pants *and a golf hat!*

VOICE. There are children up here! Are you drunk or something?

MEL. Drunk? Drunk on what? They got my liquor. . . . You wanna keep your chil-

dren, lock 'em up. Don't you tell me you got children up there.

EDNA. Mel, please. You're going to get yourself sick.

VOICE. Don't you have any respect for anyone else?

MEL *(screaming up)*. Respect? I got respect for my ass, that's what I got respect for! That's all anybody respects . . . *(And suddenly* MEL *gets hit with a torrent of water, obviously from a large bucket. He is drenched, soaked through—completely, devastatingly, and humiliatingly. . . . He comes back into the room. He is too stunned and shocked to be able to say a word.)*

EDNA. Oh, God. Oh, God, Mel.

MEL *(very calmly and quietly, almost like a child who has been hurt)*. That's a terrible thing to do. . . . That's a mean, terrible thing to do. *(And he sits down on a chair and begins to sob. He just quietly sits there and sobs. . . .* EDNA *runs out to the terrace and yells up.)*

EDNA. God will punish you for that. . . . I apologize for my husband's language, but God will punish you for that. *(She is crying too. She runs back to* MEL, *picks up some linens from the floor, and begins to dry his face and his head.)* It's all right, Mel. It's all right, baby . . .

MEL. That's a terrible thing to do to a person. . . . I would never do that to anyone.

EDNA *(wiping him)*. Never. You're too good, Mel, too decent. You would never do that. . . . It's going to be all right, Mel, I promise. You'll get another job, you'll see. . . . And we'll move away from here. Someplace far away. . . . You know what we could do? You're so good with kids, you love being with them, we could start a summer camp. . . . You would be the head of the camp and I would do the cooking and the girls can be the riding instructors and the swimming instructors. You would like that, wouldn't you, Mel? We'll just have to save some money, that's all. And if you don't get another job right away, I can always be a secretary again. I can work, I'm strong, Mel. . . . But you mustn't get sick. You mustn't get sick and die because I don't want to live in this world without you. . . . I don't like it here! . . . I don't want you to leave me alone here. . . . We'll show them, Mel. We'll show them all. *(She continues to wipe his ears as the curtain slowly falls.)*

ACT TWO

SCENE ONE

It is about six weeks later. It is mid-September, about one in the afternoon. A radio is on, playing music. From the bedroom we hear dull, rhythmic, thumping sounds. The thump is repeated every few seconds. MEL *emerges from the bedroom. He is wearing khaki slacks, a pajama top, a bathrobe with the belt half open, and a pair of slippers. He has a baseball glove on his left hand and a baseball in his right. He keeps throwing the ball into the glove . . . thump . . . thump . . . thump . . . Six weeks of unemployment have turned* MEL *into a different man. His eyes seem to be sunken into his sockets; he has rings under his eyes and seems to shave only sporadically. There is also a grimness about him, an anger, a hostility, the look of a man who is suffering from a deep depression coupled with a tendency to paranoia. He comes into the living room aimlessly. He has no place to go and no desire to go there. He wanders around the room not seeming to see anything. He walks in all the available walking spaces in the living room and dining room, like a prisoner taking his daily exercise. He keeps banging the ball into his glove with increasing intensity . . . thump . . . thump . . . thump . . . He throws the ball up against the wall where the banging came from, then he crosses into the kitchen looking for something to eat. Someone puts a key in the door; it opens.* EDNA *rushes in, dressed smartly in a suit and carrying a small bundle of food in a brown paper bag. She throws down a magazine, calls out:*

———

EDNA. Mel? . . . Mel, I'm home. *(She closes the door and enters the living room, turns off the radio, and then goes into the kitchen.)* You must be starved. I'll have your lunch in a second. *(She takes things out of the package.)* I couldn't get out of the office until a quarter to one and then I had to wait fifteen minutes for a bus. . . . God, the traffic on Third Avenue during lunch hour. . . . I got a cheese soufflé in Schrafft's, is that all right? I just don't have time to fix anything today, Mr. Cooperman wants me back before two o'clock, we're suddenly swamped with work this week. . . . He asked if I would come in on Saturdays from now until Christmas but I told him I didn't think I could. *(She goes into the kitchen and gets out some pots.)* I

mean we could use the extra money but I don't think I want to spend Saturdays in that office too. We see each other little enough now as it is. . . . Come in and talk to me while I'm cooking, Mel, I've only got about thirty-five minutes today. *(*EDNA *has put the casserole on the table and is now going into the kitchen, setting up two places with dishes and silverware.)* My feet are absolutely killing me. I don't know why they gave me a desk because I haven't had a chance to sit at it in a month. . . . Hi, love. I bought you *Sports Illustrated.* . . . Mr. Cooperman told me there's a terrific story in there about the Knicks, he thought you might be interested in it. (MEL *tosses the magazine aside with some contempt.)* You just can't move up Third Avenue because there's one of those protest parades up Fifth Avenue, or down Fifth Avenue, whichever way they protest . . . Fifteen thousand women screaming, "Save the environment," and they're all wearing leopard coats . . . God, the hypocrisy. . . . Come on, sit down, I've got some tomato juice first. *(She pours tomato juice into two glasses.* MEL *listlessly moves over to the table and sits down.)* Isn't that terrible about the Commissioner of Police? I mean *kidnapping* the New York Commissioner of Police? Isn't that insane? I mean if the cops can't find him, they can't find anybody. *(She sits down, picks up her glass of juice and takes a sip.)* Oh, God, that's good. That's the first food I've had since eight o'clock this morning. We're so busy there we don't even have time for a coffee break. . . . He's going to ask me to work nights, I know it, and I just don't know what to say to him . . . I mean he's been so nice to me, he buys me sandwiches two or three times a week, not that I don't deserve it, the way I've been working this past month, but I just don't want to spend any nights down there because I don't even have the strength to talk when I get home any more . . . I don't know where I'm getting the energy, I must have been saving it up for the past twenty-two years. *(She sips again.)* I've got to stop talking because I'm wound up and I'll never stop. . . . How are you, darling? You feeling all right? (MEL *sits, staring into his tomato juice.)* Mel? You all right?

MEL *(mumbles something affirmative).* Mmm.

EDNA *(looks at him).* Don't feel like talking much?

MEL. Mmm.

EDNA. Oh, come on, Mel. I've got to leave in about thirty minutes and I probably won't get home until seven o'clock. Talk to me. . . . What did you do today?

MEL. *(He looks at her. He waits a long time before he answers.)* I took a walk.

EDNA. Oh, that's nice. Where?

MEL. From the bedroom to the living room . . .

EDNA *(nervous about his frame of mind, but restrains herself to keep from putting him on edge).* Is that all?

MEL. No. I walked back into the bedroom. . . . Once I went into the kitchen for a glass of water. What else you want to know?

EDNA. Nothing. You don't feel like talking, that's all right.

MEL. I feel like talking. You want to hear about the rest of my morning?

EDNA *(sensing his anxiety).* I said it's all right, Mel.

MEL. I looked out the window three times, listened to Martha Deane and went to the toilet, which is still flushing. I didn't jiggle it, I know you like to do it when you get home.

EDNA *(sighs, puts down her glass).* All right, what's the matter, Mel?

MEL. Nothing. I'm telling you about my terrific morning. You ready for some really exciting news? Martha Deane's guest tomorrow is the Galloping Gourmet. Isn't that exciting? He's going to give the secret recipes of five famous celebrities and we're going to have to guess whose casserole is whose. . . . Too bad you're going to miss it.

EDNA. You didn't sleep well again last night, did you?

MEL. Last night? Was last night the night before this morning? I get them mixed up. I'm so busy with my life.

EDNA. I thought you were going to take a walk in the park this morning.

MEL. There is no place left for me to walk. I have walked on every path, every bridge, and every stone. I know every squirrel in the park and I know where they all hide their nuts.

EDNA. I know how cooped up you feel when you stay in the house all day. Maybe we can have lunch in the zoo tomorrow?

MEL. I am *not* going to the zoo. I've been there every day for a month. When I walk by, the monkeys nudge each other and say, "He's here again."

EDNA. I just thought you might get some exercise. Get into a softball game or something.

MEL. There are no softball games. It's September, my whole team is in school.

EDNA. They get out at three o'clock. You could wait for them.

MEL *(his voice rising).* I'm seven years older than the father of the pitcher. I am not going to wait for kids to get out of school so I can have someone to play with.

EDNA *(controlling herself).* There is no reason to scream at me, Mel.

MEL. I'm sorry. I'm alone a lot, I forgot what the normal voice range is. Is this any better?

EDNA. Never mind, Mel. . . . Did anybody call?

MEL. Your mother. We exchanged recipes.

EDNA *(she drums her fingers on the table, trying to control herself).* Anyone else?

MEL. I am not an answering service. You want me to answer phones, hire me. I need the work.

EDNA. I take it then there was nothing in the paper today.

MEL. About what?

EDNA. You know about what, Mel. About a job.

MEL. Yes. Mount Sinai Hospital is looking for surgical technicians. The problem is my slacks are khaki and they require white.

EDNA. I was just asking, Mel.

MEL. And I'm just answering. There's a Puerto Rican luncheonette in East Harlem that's looking for a bilingual counterman. And Delta Airlines is looking for hostesses, but I don't want to be away from home that much. Don't you agree?

EDNA. Mel, please stop it.

MEL. You know what I think my best bet is? Maurice Le Peu in Queens is looking for a hair stylist. I thought I'd practice on you tonight, and if you didn't go bald, I'd give him a call tomorrow.

EDNA *(throws her napkin down angrily).* What's wrong with you? *What's wrong with you today?*

MEL *(slams his napkin down violently).* Today? Today? . . . How about seven weeks? How about almost two months walking around this apartment like a goddamned prisoner? I used to walk from room to room. Now I walk along the edges of the room so I can have longer walks. . . . I have read every page of every book in this apartment. I have read every label of every can of food in the kitchen. Tomorrow I'm going to read underwear sizes. After that, I'm through. I have nothing left to live for.

EDNA *(gets up)*. I'm sorry, Mel. I know you're bored, I know you're unhappy. Tell me what I can do to help you.

MEL. I'm forty-seven years old. Do you have to come home to make me lunches?

EDNA. I *want* to make you lunches. I'm working, I have a job, I never see you. At least this way we get to spend an hour every day together.

MEL. Don't you see how humiliating it is? Everyone in the building knows you come home to make me lunches. The only ones here who get lunches cooked for them every day are me and the six-year-old girl on the fourth floor.

EDNA. I don't care what people in this building think.

MEL. *I* care! *I CARE!!* . . . They probably think you make me take a nap too. . . . I can make my own lunches. I can go out to eat.

EDNA. I was just trying to save us money.

MEL. What are you going to do in the winter when it snows, come home to put on my galoshes?

EDNA. Is this what you do all morning? Walk around the edges of the apartment thinking of things like that? Torturing yourself?

MEL. I don't have to torture *myself.* I got dogs, flushing toilets and the Red Baron's two sisters in there.

EDNA. All right, what did they do today, Mel? Tell me.

MEL. No, listen. I don't want to bother you. I know you've got your own problems at the office. You've got a living to make, don't worry about the house. That's my concern.

EDNA. I thought we agreed about my working. I thought we agreed it was all right for me to take this job until something came through for you.

MEL. I'm not complaining. You've been very nice to me. You pay the rent, buy the food, bought me a nice new sport jacket. . . . Maybe next year you'll take me to Hawaii on United Airlines.

EDNA. Do you want me to quit, Mel? Do you want me to leave the job? I'll leave the minute you say so, you know I will.

MEL. Not this week. Margaret Truman has Bess Myerson on this Friday, I don't want to miss it. (EDNA *gets up and storms into the kitchen. She stands there over the stove and bangs her fist on it in desperation. Finally,*

after a long silence) You think I haven't been looking? You think I haven't tried? That's what you think, isn't it?

EDNA *(from the kitchen)*. I don't, Mel. I swear I don't. I know how hard you've tried.

MEL. There are *no jobs* for forty-seven-years-old men . . . *Nothing! (Picks up* The New York Times*)* Here! Read it! It's all in *The New York Times.* I went out in the hall and stole it from the people next door. . . . *I steal newspapers, Edna!*

EDNA *(bringing in a pot of hot food from the kitchen)*. Please, let's not talk about it any more.

MEL. You want milk? I can get two quarts of milk every morning. If I wear my slippers they don't hear a thing.

EDNA. Stop it, Mel. I don't think that's funny.

MEL. I'm just trying to contribute, Edna . . . Just trying to do my share.

EDNA *(puts some food onto the plate)*. Please eat your lunch. It's the last time. I promise I won't make it any more.

MEL. Why should you? When you can be in some nice Japanese restaurant eating sukiyaki with Mr. Cooperman sitting around with your shoes off.

EDNA. I have never had sukiyaki with Mr. Cooperman.

MEL. How about fettucini with Mr. Feidelson? Look, I know what goes on in offices. I used to be one of the boys too.

EDNA. Well, I am not "one of the girls."

MEL. How come you get home at seven o'clock when everyone knows nobody works past five o'clock any more.

EDNA. *I* work past five o'clock.

MEL. Where? At Charley O's? Listen, I understand. A little drink to unwind before you go home to face the little man.

EDNA. I don't believe what I'm hearing.

MEL. You used to believe it when *I* came home at seven o'clock. . . . You think it's a picnic sitting home all day wondering what's going on in that office? Try it sometime.

EDNA. I feel like I'm watching my whole life running backwards on a movie screen.

MEL. Maybe that's why I can't get a job. Maybe if I put on a wig, some high heels, and a pair of hot pants, they'd hire me in a second.

EDNA *(puts down the dish)*. I'll leave the soufflé here. Eat it or not, do whatever you want. I'm leaving. I can't talk to you when you're like this.

MEL *(mocking)*. Have a good day, darling. Don't work too hard. Leave me some quarters for the laundromat.

EDNA *(starts for the door, then stops)*. You know what I would suggest, Mel?

MEL. What? What would you suggest, Edna?

EDNA. I suggest you either get a very tight grip on yourself . . . or you look for someone to help you.

MEL. I don't need any help. . . . I'm retired. I got it made.

EDNA. You know what I'm talking about. Medical help. A doctor. Some doctor who can talk to you and straighten you out because I am *running out of energy and patience!*

MEL *(looks at her and smiles)*. You think it's all in my mind, don't you? . . . My God, you don't have the slightest inkling of what's been going on. You are so naïve, it's ridiculous.

EDNA. What are you talking about, Mel? What's been going on?

MEL *(smirking, as though he has some secret)*. You think it's just by accident I can't find any work? You think it's just the breaks? I'm having a bad streak of luck, is that what you think?

EDNA. I think it's the times, Mel. We are going through bad times.

MEL. You have no suspicion of the truth, do you? None at all?

EDNA. What truth? What truth are you talking about, Mel?

MEL. I'm talking about the *plot,* Edna. The *plot.*

(She looks at him for a long time.)

EDNA. What plot, Mel?

MEL *(he stares at her incredulously, then laughs)*. "What plot, Mel?" . . . I'm telling you about the plot and all you can say is, "What plot, Mel?"

EDNA. I don't know what plot you're talking about. You mentioned there's a plot and all I can think of to say is, "What plot, Mel?"

MEL. What plot? Jeez! *(He turns away from her.)*

EDNA *(exasperated)*. What plot? WHAT PLOT??

MEL *(he turns back toward her)*. The-social-economical-and-political-plot-to-undermine-the-working-classes-in-this-country.

EDNA. Oh, that plot.

MEL. Yes, *that* plot! Instead of rushing downtown every morning, stay home and listen to the radio once in a while. Listen to the talk shows. Find out what's going on in this country. Ten minutes of WQXR and you'll want to move to Switzerland.

EDNA. If it depresses you, Mel, don't listen to the talk shows. Listen to some nice music.

MEL. Nice music . . . *(laughs)* Incredible. You're a child. You're an uninformed, ignorant little child. . . . They've taken it over, Edna. Our music, our culture, it's not ours any more, it's *theirs.*

EDNA. They have our music?

MEL. All of it. The arts, the media, every form of mass communication. *They got it, baby!*

EDNA. Don't get mad, Mel . . . Who?

MEL. *Who? . . . WHO?? . . .* Jesus God in heaven! *Who???*

EDNA. Mel, I've got to be in the office in twenty minutes. Please tell me who's taking over so I won't be late.

MEL. All right, sit down.

EDNA. I may not get a cab, Mel. Can't you tell me who's taking over standing up?

MEL. Are you going to sit down?

EDNA. Do I have to, Mel? Is it a long name?

MEL. *Sit down, for Christ sakes!* (EDNA *sits down, while* MEL *paces.)* Now . . . Once you do away with the middle class—what have you got left?

EDNA *(she looks at him; it can't be that easy)*. What's left? After you take away the middle class? (MEL *nods.)* The lower class and the upper class?

*(MEL *stares at her incredulously.)*

MEL. I can't talk to you. You have no understanding at all. Go on. Go to work.

EDNA. You mean there's another class besides the lower, the middle and the upper?

MEL *(he walks to the center of the room and looks around suspiciously)*. Come here.

*(EDNA *looks at him.)*

EDNA. I thought you wanted me to sit down.

MEL. Will you come here. Away from the walls. (EDNA *gets up and goes over to him in the middle of the room.)*

EDNA. If it's that secret, Mel, I don't think I want to know. *(He grabs her by the wrist and pulls her to him.)*

MEL *(in a soft voice)*. There *is* a plot, Edna. It's very complicated, very sophisticated, almost invisible . . . Maybe only a half a dozen people in this country really know about it.

EDNA. And they told it on the radio?

MEL. Yes.

EDNA. Then everyone heard it.

MEL. Did you hear it?

EDNA. No.

MEL. Then everyone didn't hear it. How many people you think listen to the radio at ten o'clock in the morning? Everybody is working. But I heard it . . . And as sure as we're standing here in the middle of the room, there is a plot going on in this country today.

EDNA. Against whom?

MEL. Against me.

EDNA. The whole country?

MEL. Not me personally. Although I'm a victim of it. A plot to change the system. To destroy the status quo. It's not just me they're after, Edna. They're after you. They're after our kids, my sisters, every one of our friends. They're after the cops, they're after the hippies, they're after the government, they're after the anarchists, they're after Women's Lib, the fags, the blacks, the whole military complex. That's who they're after, Edna.

EDNA. Who? You mentioned everyone. There's no one left.

MEL. There's someone left. Oh, baby, there's someone left all right.

EDNA. Well, I'm sure there is . . . if you say so, Mel.

MEL. *(yells)*. Don't patronize me. I know what I'm talking about. I am open to channels of information twenty-four hours a day.

(EDNA *is becoming increasingly alarmed at* MEL*'s obvious paranoiac behavior, but doesn't quite know how to handle it yet.)*

EDNA. Mel, Mel . . . would you come here for a minute. Just sit with me for a minute. *(He sits down.)* Mel . . . You know I love you and believe in you completely. I always have. . . . But I just want to say something, I hope you don't misunderstand this—

MEL. You think I'm paranoiac? You think I'm having some sort of mental, nervous breakdown because I'm out of work? Because of the pressure, the strain I've been under, because I sound like a deranged person because of the personal hell I have gone through these past seven weeks. Is that it?

EDNA. *(nods)*. That's it. That's exactly it, Mel . . . I wouldn't have put it that strongly, but that's more or less it. Exactly.

MEL. Do you want proof, Edna? Do you want me to give you actual, indisputable proof?

EDNA. *(trying to be kinder now)*. Of what, Mel?

MEL. That me, that Dave Polichek, that Mike Ambrozi, Hal Chesterman, twenty-three secretaries, six point seven of the working force in this country today is unemployed not because of a recession, not because of wages and high prices, but because of a well-organized, calculated, brilliantly executed *plot!* Do you want me to give you proof right here and now in this room?

EDNA. *(hesitates)*. Well—all right . . . If you want, Mel.

MEL. I CAN'T GIVE YOU ANY PROOF!!! . . . *What kind of proof do I have?* I'm out of work, that's my proof . . . They won't let me work!

EDNA. Who is it, Mel? Tell me who's behind the plot? Is it the kids? The addicts? The Army? The Navy? The Book-of-the-Month Club? WHO THE HELL IS IT, MEL?

MEL. It is the human race! . . . It is the sudden, irrevocable deterioration of the spirit of man. It is man undermining himself, causing a self-willed, self-imposed, self-evident *self-destruction.* . . . That's who it is.

EDNA. *(looks at him)*. The human race? . . . The human race is responsible for the unemployment?

MEL. *(a little smirk)*. Surprised, aren't you?

EDNA. *(nods, quite shaken)*. I never would have guessed. I kept thinking it was somebody else.

MEL. *(glares at her)*. Don't mock me. Don't patronize me and don't mock me.

EDNA. I'm not mocking you, Mel.

MEL. *You're mocking me!* . . . I know when I'm being mocked. I know what I'm talking about. You're working, you've got a job, you're not affected by any of this.

EDNA. I am so affected by it, Mel, you wouldn't believe it was possible . . .

MEL. You don't know the first thing I'm talking about . . . You don't know what it is to be in my place . . . You've never stood on line for two hours waiting for an unemployment check with a shirt and tie, trying to look like you don't need the money. And some fat old dame behind the counter screaming out so everyone can hear, *"Did you look for a job this week?"* "Yes, I looked for a job." *"Did you turn down any work this week?"* "What the hell am I doing here if I turned down work this week?" . . . You never walked into your own building and had a ninety-one-year-old doorman with no teeth, asthma, and beer on his breath giggle at you because *he's* working . . . You've never been on your own terrace and gotten hit with a bucket of ice-cold ice water . . . I haven't forgotten that son of a bitch! *(He goes to the terrace door, but not out on it, and yells up.)* I haven't forgotten you, you son of a bitch!

EDNA. Mel, don't start in again. Please don't start in again.

MEL. I'm waiting for him. I'm just waiting for him. He's up there now, but one day he's gonna be down there and I'm gonna be up here and then we'll see. One cold, snowy day some son of a bitch in this building is gonna be buried under three feet of snow. They won't find him until the spring. *(Yells up again.)* They won't find you until the spring, you son of a bitch!

EDNA. Mel, listen to me. Listen to me very carefully. I want you to see a doctor. . . . I don't want to put it off any more, Mel, I want you to see a doctor as soon as possible. Today, Mel. Now.

MEL *(disregarding her, he keeps talking through her speeches).* He thinks I don't know what he looks like . . . I know what he looks like, all right . . . I know what they *all* look like. I've got their faces engraved in my brain.

EDNA *(going through her pocketbook).* Mel, someone gave me the name of a doctor. They say he's very good and knows about people who've gone through what you're going through . . . I'm going to call him now, Mel. I'm going to call him and make an appointment now.

MEL *(he hasn't heard her).* They can get your clothes, Edna. They can get your clothes, your Valium, your television, your Red Label whiskey, your job, they can get everything. But they can't get your brains . . . That's my secret weapon . . . That and the snow . . . I pray to God it snows tomorrow, I'll wait for him. I bought a shovel today. Oh, yeah.

EDNA *(finds the number).* I'm calling him, Mel . . . I'm calling him now. *(She goes over to the phone. He goes over to the closet.)*

MEL. Not a little shovel, a big one. The kind they use in airports . . . I'll go without shoes this winter, but I won't go without my shovel. I'll bury him so deep, they'll have to salt him out. *(He takes out a shovel, the bottom part of which is in a box.)*

EDNA *(at the phone).* I won't go to work this afternoon, Mel. If he's free, I'm going to take you myself . . . Don't stand near the window, Mel. *(She begins to dial. He opens the box and takes out a shiny new shovel.)*

MEL *(a wild, joyous look on his face).* I live for it. I live for the first snow of the winter . . . He gets home at five fifteen, I checked with the doorman . . . I gave him a five-dollar tip, it was worth it. *(Yells up.)* I know what time you get home, you bastard. Try using the service entrance, I got that blocked off too.

EDNA *(into the phone).* Hello? . . . Is Doctor Frankel there, please? . . . Mrs. Edna Edison . . .

MEL *(to EDNA, oblivious of her on the phone).* Do you have any idea, any conception of the impact of two pounds of snow falling from a height of fourteen floors . . . They'll find him in the garage. *(Yells up.)* They'll find you in the garage, you bastard . . . I know what you look like.

EDNA. Hello? . . . Doctor Frankel? . . . I'm sorry to disturb you, but it's an emergency. . . . No, for my husband. . . . We've got to see you as soon as possible, Doctor Frankel, as soon as possible . . .

MEL *(he goes out onto the terrace).* And if it doesn't snow this winter, I'll wait till next winter . . . I'm in no hurry, smart ass. *(Yelling up.)* I've got nothing but time . . . Nothing but time, baby . . . *(He laughs. The room goes black as the curtain falls. In the darkness, the News logo appears. We hear the voice of Roger Keating again.)*

VOICE. This is Roger Keating and the *Six O'Clock Report.* . . . No word yet on the unsolved mugging and robbing late last night of New York State Governor Nelson Rockefeller on Sixth Avenue and Forty-eighth Street. The governor will be heard in a special interview on the *Eleven O'Clock News* from his room in Beth Israel Hospital where he is resting, which, incidentally, is entering its fifty-seventh day of the hospital strike. . . . "We will not go back to work" was the cry of forty-seven municipal, state and federal judges today, defying the court order of Federal Judge Myron Ackerman. Speaking for the striking judges, Judge Mario Pecona told this to CBS reporter Bethesda Wayne.

JUDGE'S VOICE. We will not go back to woik.

GIRL'S VOICE. Judge Pecona, isn't this strike unconstitutional?

JUDGE'S VOICE. Yes, but we will not go back to woik.

GIRL'S VOICE. How do you feel about the two hundred and seventy-three people in prisons now awaiting trial?

JUDGE'S VOICE. We are underpaid. We will not go back to woik.

GIRL'S VOICE. Do you still feel this way despite the fact that President Nixon has threatened to bring in the National Guard to run the courts?

JUDGE'S VOICE. He can do what he wants, we will not go back to woik.

VOICE. The *Six O'Clock Report* will follow with a filmed story of how twenty million rats survive under the city. . . . But first, this message from Ultra-Brite toothpaste. *(The News logo fades as the curtain rises.)*

SCENE TWO

It is midafternoon, two weeks later. As the curtain rises, we see three women, all in their late fifties and dressed quite well. Two are on a sofa, one sits in armchair. These are MEL's *sisters:* PAULINE, PEARL, *and* JESSIE. PAULINE *is doing needlepoint. Standing is* MEL's *older brother,* HARRY. *He wears an expensive business suit. He is looking out the window. A pot of coffee and cups are on the table in front of the women. They sit there silently.*

JESSIE. He was always nervous.

PEARL. Always.

JESSIE. As far back as I can remember, he was nervous. Never sat still for a minute, always jumping up and down. Am I lying, Pearl?

PEARL. We're his own sisters, who should know better? Up and down, up and down. . . . You want some coffee, Harry? Take some coffee.

HARRY. I don't drink coffee.

JESSIE. He always used to fidget. Talked a mile a minute. . . . He even chewed fast— remember how fast he used to chew?

PEARL. Wasn't I there? Didn't I see him chew? I remember. . . . Harry, why don't you take some coffee?

HARRY. When did you ever see me drink coffee? You're my sister fifty-three years, you never saw me drink coffee. Why would I drink coffee now?

PEARL. What do I see you, two times a year? I thought maybe you took up coffee.

PAULINE. He wasn't nervous, he was high-strung. Melvin was high-strung.

PEARL. I call it nervous. As a baby he was nervous, as a boy he was nervous, in the Army he was nervous. How long did he last in the Army, anyway?

JESSIE. Two weeks.

PEARL. There you are. He was nervous.

PAULINE. Where do you think nerves come from? From being high-strung.

PEARL. Then why weren't any of us high-strung? We all had the same parents. He was nervous, he was fidgety, he chewed fast . . . I never saw him swallow.

JESSIE. No one could talk to him. Poppa could never talk to him, I remember.

PAULINE. How could Poppa talk to him? Mel was three years old when Poppa died.

PEARL. If he wasn't so nervous, Poppa could have talked to him.

HARRY. I never drank coffee in my life. It's poison. Goes right through the system. *(Looks toward the bedroom)* Who's she on the phone with in there, anyway?

PEARL. He had the same thing in high school. A nervous breakdown. Remember when he had the nervous breakdown in high school?

HARRY *(turning to her)*. Who you talking about?

PEARL. Mel! He had a nervous breakdown in high school. You don't remember?

HARRY. What are you talking about? He didn't have a nervous breakdown, he had a broken arm. He fell in the gym and broke his arm.

PEARL. I'm not talking about that time.

HARRY. And once on his bicycle he broke his tooth.

PEARL. I'm not talking about that time.

HARRY. Then when are you talking about?

PEARL. I'm talking about the time he had a nervous breakdown in high school. I remember it like it was yesterday, don't tell me. Pauline, tell him.

PAULINE. Mel never had a nervous breakdown.

PEARL. Isn't that funny, I thought he had a nervous breakdown. Maybe I'm thinking of somebody else.

HARRY. You can't even remember that I don't drink coffee.

PAULINE. He must have had some terrible experiences in the Army.

HARRY. In two weeks? He wasn't there long enough to get a uniform. None of you know what you're talking about. There was never anything wrong with Mel. Never. His trouble was you babied him too much. All of you.

JESSIE. Why shouldn't we baby him? He was the baby, wasn't he?

HARRY. You babied him, that's his trouble. He never had the responsibilities as a child like I did. That's why he can't handle problems. That's why he flares up. He's a child, an infant.

PEARL. What if I put some milk in the coffee?

HARRY. I DON'T WANT ANY COFFEE!!

JESSIE. He doesn't want any coffee, leave him alone.

PAULINE. Correct me if I'm wrong, but when Mel was a tiny baby, didn't you think his head was too large for his body?

PEARL. Mel? Mel had a beautiful head.

PAULINE. I didn't say his head wasn't beautiful. I said it was too large for his body. It always kept falling over to one side. *(She demonstrates.)*

PEARL. *All* babies' heads fall to one side. *(She demonstrates.)*

PAULINE. I know that, but he had trouble getting his up again. *(She demonstrates.)*

HARRY. I was never babied. Poppa wouldn't allow it . . . I was never kissed from the time I was seven years old.

JESSIE. Certainly you were kissed.

HARRY. Never kissed . . . I didn't need kissing. The whole world kissed Mel, look where he is today. Who's she talking to in there all this time?

PEARL. Remember the summer he ran away?

PAULINE. He didn't run away for the whole summer. He ran away for one night.

PEARL. Who said he ran away for the whole summer?

PAULINE. Who said it? You said it. You just said, "Remember the summer he ran away?"

PEARL. So? He ran away for *one* night *one* summer.

PAULINE. But you should say it that way. Say, "Remember the summer he ran away for one night?" . . . Don't make it sound like he ran away for a whole summer. That crazy he never was.

PEARL. Did I say Mel was crazy? Who heard me mention the word crazy? Jessie, did you hear "crazy" from me?

JESSIE. I heard "crazy" but I wasn't looking where it came.

PEARL *(to* PAULINE). If that's what you believe, *you're* the one that's crazy.

PAULINE. All right, if it makes you happy, I'm crazy. Let me be the crazy one.

PEARL. Fine. Then it's settled. You're the crazy one.

HARRY. Listen, I've got to get back to the office, Jessie's going back to Lakewood tonight, let's try to settle things now. What are we going to do?

PAULINE. About what?

HARRY *(looks at her as though she's deranged).* About *what?* About the Suez Canal. What do you mean, about what? What are we here for? What did Jessie come all the way from Lakewood for? What are we doing in that woman's house *(Points to the bedroom),* where none of us have been invited for nine years? Our brother. Our sick brother who's had a nervous breakdown, for God's sakes.

JESSIE *(sniffles, wipes her eyes with a handkerchief).* Every time I hear it—

HARRY. What are you crying *now* for? You didn't just hear. You've known for a week.

JESSIE. You think I haven't been crying the whole week? He's my brother, it hurts me.

HARRY. It hurts all of us. That's why we're here. To try to do something.

PAULINE. Harry, let her cry if she wants. She came all the way from Lakewood . . . Go on, Harry.

HARRY. Fact number one, Mel has had a nervous breakdown. Fact number two, besides a nervous breakdown, Mel doesn't have a job. The man is totally unemployed.

JESSIE *(sniffles again).* You think that doesn't hurt me too?

PAULINE. Jessie, let him finish, you can cry on the way home.

HARRY. Fact—

PAULINE. Go on with the facts, Harry.

HARRY. Fact number three, besides a nervous breakdown and not having a job, the man is practically penniless. . . . I don't want to pass any comments on how a man and a woman mishandled their money for twenty-seven years. It's none of my business how a man squandered a life's savings on bad investments for which he never asked my advice once, the kind of advice which has given me solvency, security, and a beautiful summer place in the country. Thank God, *I'll* never have a nervous breakdown. . . . None of that is my business. My business is what are we going to do for Mel? How much are we going to give? Somebody make a suggestion. *(The silence is deafening. No one speaks. No one looks at each other. There is a lot of coffee drinking, but no offers as to how much they're going to give . . . After what seems like an hour of silence,* HARRY *speaks again)* Well?

PEARL. You're a businessman, Harry. You make a suggestion. You tell us how much we should all give.

HARRY *(thinks a moment)*. Let me have some coffee. (PEARL *pours him a cup of coffee.*) So let's face the facts. . . . The man needs help. Who else can he turn to but us? This is my suggestion. We make Mel a loan. We all chip in X number of dollars a week, and then when he gets back on his feet, when he gets straightened out, gets a job again, then he can pay us all back. That's my suggestion. What do you all think?

(There is a moment's silence. PAULINE *whispers to* PEARL. PEARL *nods.*)

PEARL. Pauline has a question.

HARRY. What's the question?

PAULINE. How much is X number of dollars?

HARRY. X is X. We have to figure out what X is. We'll talk and we'll decide.

PAULINE. I mean is it a big X or a little x?

HARRY. It's not even an X. It's a blank until we fill X in with a figure.

PAULINE. I'm not complaining. We have to do the right thing. But when you say it like that, "X number of dollars," it sounds like a lot of money. . . . I have limited capital, you know.

JESSIE. Everybody has limited capital. Nobody has *un*limited capital. Pearl, do you have unlimited capital?

PEARL. I wish I did. I'd give Mel X number of dollars in a minute.

PAULINE. All I'm asking is, how much is X. I can't figure with letters, I have to know numbers.

JESSIE. Harry, don't say X any more. We're not businesswomen, we don't know about X. Say a number that we can understand.

HARRY. I can't say a number until I figure out A, how much does Mel need a week, and B, how much are we willing to give. I can't even guess what X is until we figure out how much A and B come to.

PEARL. All right, suppose we figure out what A is and what B is. And if we know that, then we'll figure what X is, right?

HARRY. Right.

PEARL. And now suppose everyone here agrees except one person. She thinks it's too much. She doesn't want to give X. She wants to give M or W, whatever. What do we do then?

HARRY. Forget X. Forget I ever said X. *(He rubs his head and drinks some more coffee.)* Let's figure what Mel needs to get over his nervous breakdown. . . . His biggest expense is the doctor, right? Edna says he's the best and he has to go five times a week.

PAULINE. Five times a week to the best doctor? I'm beginning to see what X is going to come to.

JESSIE. Maybe it's not even a nervous breakdown. Doctors can be wrong, too. Remember your pains last year, Pearl?

PEARL. It's true. They took out all my top teeth, then found out it was kidney stones.

HARRY. I can't believe what I'm listening to. . . . You're a hundred and sixty years old between the three of you and not one of you makes any sense. . . . If you'll all be quiet for a minute, I'll settle this thing.

PEARL. All right, we're quiet. Settle it, Harry.

HARRY. The most important thing is that Mel gets well, agreed?

ALL THREE. Agreed!

HARRY. And that the only way he's going to get well is to see a doctor. Agreed?

ALL THREE. Agreed.

HARRY. And it is our obligation, as his only living relatives—not counting his wife, no disrespect intended—to bear the financial responsibility of that burden. Agreed?

ALL THREE. Agreed.

HARRY. And we'll all see this thing through to the end whether it takes a week or a month or a year or even five years. Agreed? *(There is stony silence.)* Okay. Our first disagreement.

PAULINE. No one's disagreeing. We're all in agreement. Except when you mention things like five years. I don't see any sense in curing Mel and ending up in the poorhouse. If, God forbid, that happened, would he be in any position to help us? He's not too able to begin with.

JESSIE. So what should we do, Harry? You know how to figure these things. What should we do?

HARRY. Well, obviously we can't afford to let Mel be sick forever. We've got to put a time limit on it. Agreed?

ALL THREE. Agreed.

HARRY. What do we give him to get better? Six months?

PAULINE. It shouldn't take six months. If that doctor's as good as Edna says, it shouldn't take six months.

(The door to the bedroom is heard closing.)

PEARL. Shhh . . . She's coming.

PAULINE. We'll let Harry do the talking.

PEARL. And then we'll settle everything.

Thank God, it's almost over.

(They all assume a pose of innocence and calm. EDNA *comes out of the bedroom.)*

EDNA. I'm sorry I was so long. I was just talking to Doctor Frankel. Mel's on his way home, he'll be here in a minute.

HARRY. How is Mel? What does the doctor say?

EDNA. Well, it's hard to tell. Mel is having a very rough time. He's in a very depressed state, he's not himself. He's completely withdrawn. He sits in that chair sometimes for hours without saying a word. You'll see when he comes in, he's a different person.

JESSIE *(wipes her eyes with a hanky, sniffs).* It hurts me every time I hear it . . .

PAULINE. So what is it, a nervous breakdown? Is it a nervous breakdown? You can tell us. We're his family. It's a nervous breakdown, isn't it?

EDNA. Yes, in a way I guess you can say it's a nervous breakdown.

PEARL. I knew it, I knew it. He had the same thing in high school.

HARRY. So what's the diagnosis? What does the doctor say?

EDNA *(shrugs).* Mel needs care and treatment. He's a very good doctor, he thinks Mel's going to be all right, but it's just going to take time.

PAULINE. How much time? A month? Two months? More than two months?

EDNA. He can't tell yet.

PAULINE. He can guess, can't he? Three months? Four months? More than four months?

EDNA. There's no way of telling yet, Pauline. It could be a month, it could be two months, it could be two *years.*

PAULINE. No, two years is out of the question. I refuse to go along with two years.

EDNA. I'm not saying it will be. I'm just saying we don't know yet.

HARRY. Can I say something? Can I get a word in?

PAULINE *(turning away from* EDNA*).* I wish you would say something, Harry. I wish you would do the talking.

HARRY. Thank you very much.

PAULINE. Because two years is ridiculous.

PEARL. Go on, Harry

HARRY. We're all very concerned, Edna. Very concerned. After all, he's our brother.

JESSIE. Since he was a baby.

HARRY. Can I please do the talking?

PEARL. Will you let him do the talking, Jessie? . . . Go on, Harry.

HARRY. We're very concerned. We appreciate that you're his wife, you're going to do all you can, but we know it's not going to be enough. We want to help. We've talked it out among ourselves and . . . we're prepared to take over the financial burden of the doctor. You take care of the apartment, the food, the miscellaneous, we'll pay the doctor bills. Whatever they come to.

EDNA. I'm . . . I'm overwhelmed . . . I'll be very truthful with you, I never expected that . . . I am deeply touched and overwhelmed. I don't know what to say . . .

HARRY. You don't have to say anything.

PAULINE. Just tell us what you think the bills will come to.

EDNA. That's very generous of you all, but I couldn't let you do that. Mel wouldn't let me do it.

HARRY. Don't be ridiculous. Where you going to get the money from, a bank? You can't put up a nervous breakdown as collateral.

EDNA. I have no idea how long Mel will be in treatment. It could run into a fortune.

HARRY. Let us worry about that. The money, we'll take care of.

EDNA. But it could run as high as twenty, twenty-five thousand dollars.

(There is a long pause. The sisters all look at HARRY.*)*

PAULINE. Harry, can I say something to you in private?

HARRY. We don't need any private discussions.

PAULINE. We just found out what X is . . . Don't you think we ought to discuss X a little further?

HARRY. It's not necessary. I don't care what it's going to cost. The three of you can contribute whatever you think you can afford, *I'll* make up the deficit . . . If it's fifteen, if it's twenty, if it's twenty-five thousand, I'll see that it's taken care of, as long as Mel has the best medical treatment. . . . That's all I have to say. *(He nods his head as though taking a little bow.)*

EDNA *(moved).* I'm—I'm speechless . . . What do I say?

HARRY. You don't say nothing.

PEARL. We just want to do the right thing.

EDNA. I know none of us have been very close the last few years.

PAULINE. Nine. Nine years was the last time we were invited.

EDNA. Has it been that long? I suppose it's been my fault. Maybe I haven't tried to understand you. Maybe you haven't tried to understand me. Anyway, I appreciate it more than you can imagine, but we really don't need it.

HARRY. What are you talking about? Certainly you need it.

EDNA. Over the years, we've managed to save something. I have some jewelry I can sell . . .

HARRY. You're not going to sell your jewelry.

PAULINE. Maybe she doesn't wear it any more. Let the woman talk.

EDNA. Mel can cash in his insurance policy and I have my job. I can manage whatever the medical expenses come to, but if you really want to help . . . What I'm worried about is Mel's future.

JESSIE. We all are, darling.

EDNA. It's not easy for a man of Mel's age to get a job today, to start all over again . . .

HARRY. If he knew lighting fixtures, I would take him in a minute.

PEARL. Certainly, my God.

EDNA. If he could just get out of New York and move to the country somewhere, he would be a hundred percent better off.

HARRY. I agree a thousand percent.

EDNA. I was thinking of a summer camp. Mel is wonderful with children and sports, I could do the cooking, the girls will help out, we can hire a small staff . . . There's a lovely place in Vermont that's for sale. We could have it for next summer. Don't you think Mel would be better off there?

HARRY. Again, a thousand percent.

EDNA. They want twenty-five thousand dollars down in cash . . . So instead of giving it to us for the doctor, would you lend it to us for the camp?

(There is a hush, a definite hush, HARRY *looks at* EDNA *in disbelief.)*

HARRY. A summer camp? . . . Twenty-five thousand dollars for a summer camp?

EDNA. The price is a hundred thousand. But they want twenty-five thousand down.

HARRY. *A hundred thousand dollars* for a *summer camp??* . . . Run by a man with a nervous breakdown?

EDNA. He'll be all right by next summer.

HARRY. Do you know what it is for a *normal* person to be responsible for that many boys and girls? The lawsuits you're open for?

EDNA. I don't understand. You were willing to give Mel the money for a doctor. Why won't you lend it to him for a camp?

HARRY. Because with a camp you can go broke. With a doctor you can go broke too, but you get better.

EDNA. All right. *You* pay for the doctor. *I'll* invest in the camp.

HARRY. You mean we should pay to get Mel healthy so you can lose your money in a camp and get him sick again? . . . Then you'll come to us for more money for another doctor?

EDNA. I thought you wanted to do something. I thought you wanted to help him.

HARRY. We *do* want to help him.

EDNA. *Then help him!*

HARRY. Not when he's sick. When he's better, we'll help him.

EDNA *(turns to the sisters).* Is that how the rest of you feel? Do you all agree with Harry? *(They all look at one another uncomfortably.)*

PAULINE *(looking into her coffee cup).* I am not familiar with Vermont.

JESSIE. I'd say yes in a minute, but Harry's the spokesman.

PEARL. I'd have to go up and see it first, but I can't travel with my leg.

EDNA. All right . . . Forget it. Forget the money, we don't need it. We'll get along without it very nicely, thank you. . . . I'm surprised you even offered it . . . It's good to know that the minute Mel is completely recovered and back on his own two strong feet again, I can count on you for help. That's just when we'll need it. *(She starts toward the bedroom.)* Will you please excuse me? I've got to make some calls before I go back to the office. . . . Just in case I don't see any of you for another nine years *(Points to the tray),* have some cookies. *(She storms into the bedroom, slamming the door behind her. They all look at one another, stunned.)*

HARRY. What did I say that was wrong? You're my witnesses, what did I say that was wrong?

PEARL. You said nothing wrong. I'm a witness.

PAULINE. The truth is, she doesn't *want* us to help him. She's jealous. And I was willing to give him *anything.*

JESSIE *(to* PEARL*).* Does that mean we're not giving for the doctor either?

PEARL *(to* JESSIE*).* Why don't you pay attention? You never pay attention.

HARRY. A man in his condition running a summer camp. I spoke to him on the phone Thursday, he could hardly say hello.

PAULINE. Why does she hate us? What did we ever do to her? It's jealousy, that's what it is.

PEARL. That's all it is.

PAULINE. Jealousy . . . I'd like to get him out of here. He could move in with me, I'd love to take care of him.

HARRY. A man in his condition running a summer camp. It would take him until August to figure out how to blow up the volleyball.

JESSIE. If nothing is settled yet, can I give my vote to Pauline? I've got shopping to do.

HARRY. *Sit down! Nothing has been settled!* . . . We'll have to settle it with Mel.

PEARL. With Mel? How can Mel make a decision in his condition?

HARRY. Him I can reason with. He's only had a nervous breakdown. *That* woman is crazy! Let me have some more coffee.

(PEARL *starts to pour* HARRY *some more coffee when suddenly we hear a key in the latch and the door opens.* MEL *enters. He looks aged. Perhaps aged isn't the right word. Distant might describe it better. His eyes are ringed and his hair is slightly unkempt; he has a glazed expression on his face. He opens the door and closes it, puts his key in his pocket, and goes across the room and into the kitchen without looking up and without noticing the others sitting there. They all look at him, puzzled and slightly horrified at his behavior. In the kitchen* MEL *pours himself a glass of water and then takes out a small vial of pills. He takes a pill, places it in his mouth and drinks the water. He comes back into the living room. He doesn't seem startled or surprised; it is as though he were sixteen again and coming into a familiar setting. When he speaks, his voice lacks emotion.)*

MEL. I just had a nice walk.

HARRY *(goes to him).* Hello, Mel.

MEL *(looks at him).* From Eighty-second and Park. *(He whispers.)* Don't tell Edna. She doesn't like me to walk too far.

HARRY. Mel? *(Points to himself)* Do you know who this is?

MEL. What do you mean, Harry?

HARRY. Nothing. Nothing. *(Points to the girls)* Look who's here to see you, Mel.

(MEL *turns and looks at the sisters.)*

MEL *(smiles).* Why shouldn't they come to see me? They're my own sisters, aren't they? Who has better sisters than I have? *(He opens up his arms to greet them and goes to PAULINE.)* Pauline! How are you? *(He kisses her. She hugs him.)*

PAULINE. Mel, darling.

MEL *(turns to* JESSIE). And Jessie. Sweet Jessica Jessie . . . *(He kisses her.)*

JESSIE. You look—wonderful, Mel. *(She sniffles and fights back the tears. His back is to* PEARL.)

MEL. Everyone's here but Pearl.

PEARL *(How could he miss her?).* Here I am, Mel.

MEL *(turns around).* There she is, hiding . . . Always hiding from your baby brother.

PEARL. I wasn't hiding, Mel. I was just sitting.

HARRY *(takes* MEL *by the arm).* Mel, sit down. We want to talk to you.

MEL *(looks at him suspiciously).* Something is wrong. Someone in the family is sick.

HARRY. No. No one is sick, Mel . . . Everybody is fine. Sit down. *(He urges* MEL *into a chair.* MEL *sits down.)*

MEL. I had such a nice walk.

JESSIE. Isn't that wonderful, Mel. You always used to like to walk.

(PEARL *gets up and goes over to the window behind* MEL. *She takes out a hanky and wipes her eyes.)*

MEL. Remember how I used to like to walk, Jessie?

JESSIE. I do, Mel, I was just saying that.

PAULINE. You're looking very well, darling.

MEL. Thank you, Pauline.

PAULINE. Are you feeling all right? *(She swallows the last word.)*

MEL. What's that, darling?

PAULINE. I said, are you feeling all right?

MEL. Am I feeling all right? . . . Yes . . . Yes, I just had a very nice walk.

PAULINE. Oh, that's nice, dear.

MEL *(looks around).* Where's Pearl? Did Pearl go home?

PEARL *(at the window, behind him).* Here I am, Mel. I didn't go home.

MEL *(turns around).* There she is. Hiding again . . . She always used to hide from me.

HARRY *(pacing).* Mel . . .

MEL. Yes, Harry?

HARRY *(stops).* Mel . . .

PEARL. Harry wants to say something to you, Mel.

MEL. What is it, Harry?

HARRY. Nothing, Mel . . . Nothing.

MEL. You don't look well to me, Harry. You're working too hard. . . . Don't work so hard, Harry.

HARRY. I won't, Mel.

MEL. You have to relax more. Three things I learned at the doctor's, Harry. You have to relax, you mustn't take the world too seriously . . . and you have to be very careful of what you say when you go out on the terrace.

(Curtain. News logo in—Six O'Clock Report*)*

VOICE OVER. This is the *Six O'Clock Report* with Stan Jennings sitting in for Roger Keating, who was beaten and mugged last night outside our studio following the *Six O'Clock Report*. . . . A Polish freighter, the six-thousand-ton *Majorska,* sailed into New York harbor in dense fog at 7:00 A.M. this morning and crashed into the Statue of Liberty. Two seamen were injured and electrical damage caused flickering in Miss Liberty's torch. It was the first recorded maritime accident involving the famed statue, although the Polish freighter had been in six previous sea collisions. . . . And today, in a midtown hotel following a convention of the National Psychiatric Society, seventeen of the leading psychiatrists in the United States were trapped between floors in an elevator for over forty-five minutes. Panic broke out and twelve of the doctors were treated for hysteria.

SCENE THREE

It is mid-December, six weeks later. It is late afternoon. As the curtain rises, EDNA *is on the phone. She is wearing a winter coat over her suit. A grocery package is in her arms. She has obviously just come in and seems rather distraught.*

———

EDNA *(into the phone).* Hello? . . . Is the superintendent there, please? . . . Mrs. Edison. 14A. I have no water. There is no water in the house . . . What do you mean he's out? Out where? I have no water. I just walked in the house . . . Well, if they're fixing the pipes, shouldn't he be in the building? He's getting paid for that, isn't he? . . . I didn't see any sign in the elevator. I have other things on my mind besides reading signs in elevators . . . I have no electricity in the kitchen . . . No, just the kitchen . . . Just—the—kitchen! I don't know why, I'm not an electrician . . . I can't wait until seven o'clock . . . My food is spoiling and you're telling me your husband is out? . . . I don't blame him. I wouldn't hang around this building either if I didn't have to. (MEL *has entered from the front door during the phone conversation. She hangs up and stands there.)* There's no water.

The water is shut off . . . They're fixing the pipes, we won't have any until five, six, seven, they're not sure when . . . And there's no electricity in the kitchen. The refrigerator's off . . . I called the super, he's out. *(She sits down. He goes to the table and puts his paints back in their box. His easel and canvas are left standing.)*

MEL. I'm not going back. I'm not going back to that doctor. He's a quack. He sits there cleaning his pipe, playing with his watch fob, and doesn't know what the hell he's talking about. The man is a quack. If I'm getting better, I'm doing it myself . . . I'm working my *own* problems out. That man sits there playing with a pipe scooper watching *me* get better for forty dollars an hour . . . I got mirrors in the house, I can watch myself get better. I could lay there for fifty minutes, if I don't say a word, he won't say a word. What would kill him *(During this, he has been going to the closet, putting his paint box, easel, and canvas away.)* to ask me a question? "What's wrong, Mr. Edison? What are you thinking about?" . . . Not him. If I don't bring it up, he don't ask. I'm curing myself, I'm telling you. I see how you look when you come home every night. Killing yourself, breaking your back and for what? To give forty dollars an hour to a pipe cleaner? I can't take it any more, Edna. I can't see you turning yourself into an old woman just for me. What's the point in it? As soon as I'm all right again, I'll be too young for you.

EDNA *(holding back tears).* Well, I don't think you have to worry about that any more, Mel. . . . We went out of business today.

MEL. Who did?

EDNA. We did. The business that I'm in is out of business. There is no business in that place any more.

MEL. They let you go?

EDNA. If *they're* not staying, what do they need me for?

MEL. You mean completely out of business?

EDNA. They went bankrupt. They overextended themselves. One of the partners may go to jail. *(She starts to cry.)*

MEL. You don't go bankrupt overnight. You must have had some inkling.

EDNA *(crying).* I had *no* inkling . . . I did, but I was afraid to think about it . . . What's happening, Mel? Is the whole world going out of business?

MEL *(goes over to her).* Okay. It's all right, Edna, it's all right.

EDNA *(sobbing).* I thought we were such a strong country, Mel. If you can't depend on America, who can you depend on?

MEL. Ourselves, Edna. We have to depend on each other.

EDNA. I don't understand how a big place like that can just go out of business. It's not a little candy store. It's a big building. It's got stone and marble with gargoyles on the roof. Beautifully hand-chiseled gargoyles, Mel. A hundred years old. They'll come tomorrow with a sledgehammer and kill the gargoyles.

MEL. It's just a job, Edna. It's not your whole life.

EDNA. You know what I thought about on the way home? One thing. I only had one thing on my mind . . . A bath. A nice, hot bath. *(Sobs again)* And now the water went out of business.

MEL. It'll come back on. Everything is going to come back on, Edna. They're not going to shut us off forever.

EDNA *(she yells).* I want my bath! I want my water! Tell them I want my bath, Mel!

MEL. It's off, Edna. What can I do? There's nothing I can do.

EDNA *(yells).* Bang on the pipes. Tell them there's a woman upstairs who needs an emergency bath. If I don't sit in some water, Mel, I'm going to go crazy. Bang on the pipes.

MEL. Edna, be reasonable . . .

EDNA *(screams). I banged for you, why won't you bang for me?*

MEL. Shh, it's all right, baby. It's all right.

EDNA *(still sobbing).* It's *not.* It's *not* all right. Why are you saying it's all right? Are you out of your mind? Oh, God, Mel, I'm sorry. I didn't mean that. Please forgive me, Mel.

MEL. It's all right, Edna . . . Please calm down.

EDNA. I don't know what I'm saying any more. It's too much for me, Mel. I have no strength left, Mel. Nothing. I couldn't open my pocketbook on the bus; a little boy had to help me.

MEL. Of course you have strength.

EDNA. I have anger, no strength. . . . If something happens to me, Mel, who's going to take care of us?

MEL. I am. I always took care of you, didn't I?

EDNA. But who's going to take care of us now, Mel?

MEL. Me, Edna. Me!

EDNA. You, Mel?

MEL. Don't you trust me, Edna? Don't you believe in me any more?

EDNA. Let's leave, Mel. Let's give up and leave . . . Let them have it. Let them have their city . . . Let them keep their garbage and their crooks and their jobs and their broken gargoyles . . . I just want to live out the rest of my life with you and see my girls grow up healthy and happy and once in a while I would like to have some water and take a bath . . . Please, Mel . . . Please.

MEL. All right, Edna . . . We'll go . . . We'll go.

(The doorbell chimes.)

EDNA *(yells).* That's the super!

MEL. I'll take care of it! Edna, you're very upset. Why don't you relax, and wait in the tub for the water to come on . . .

EDNA. All right, Mel . . . I'm sorry if I upset you. *(She turns and goes off into the bedroom. He turns, goes over to the door and opens it.* HARRY *stands there; he is carrying an attaché case.)*

HARRY. Hello, Mel . . . All right if I come in?

MEL *(surprised).* Sure, Harry, sure. I didn't know you were in New York.

HARRY *(speaks softly).* I had some business, and besides, I wanted to talk to you. How you feeling? All right?

MEL. Don't be so solemn, Harry. It's not a hospital room. I'm all right.

(HARRY enters; MEL *closes the door.)*

HARRY. I brought you some apples from the country. *(He opens his attaché case.)* Wait'll you taste these. *(He takes some apples from the case.)* You always loved apples, I remember . . . Are you allowed to eat them now?

MEL. Apples don't affect the mind, Harry. They're not going to drive me crazy. Thank you. That's very nice of you.

HARRY. Is Edna here?

MEL. Yeah, she's in the tub. She's not feeling very well.

HARRY. It's all right. She doesn't want to see me. I understand.

MEL. It's not that, Harry. She's very tired.

HARRY. The woman doesn't like me. It's all right. The whole world can't love you. . . . I feel badly that it's my brother's wife, but that's what makes horse racing. I'm only staying two minutes. I wanted to deliver this in person and then I'll go.

MEL. You came eight miles to bring me six apples? Harry, that's very sweet but it wasn't necessary.

HARRY. Not the apples, Mel. I have something a little more substantial than apples. *(Reaches in his pocket and takes out a check.)* Here. This is for you and Edna . . . The apples are separate.

(MEL *takes the check and looks at it.*)

MEL. What's this?

HARRY. It's a check. It's the money. Go buy yourself a summer camp. *(Good-naturedly)* Go. July and August, take care of six hundred running noses. Have a good time. *(He gets up to go.)*

MEL. Harry, this is twenty-five thousand dollars.

HARRY. Your sisters and I contributed equally, fifty-fifty. I'm telling them about it tomorrow.

MEL. I don't understand.

HARRY. I don't understand myself. Why would anyone want to run a summer camp? But if that gives you pleasure, then this gives me pleasure . . .

MEL. When did Edna ask you for this?

HARRY. What's the difference? It's over. Everybody got a little excited. Everyone was trying to do the right thing. Take the money, buy your crazy camp.

MEL. Harry!

HARRY. Yes?

MEL. In the first place . . . thank you. In the second place, I can't take it.

HARRY. Don't start in with me. It took me six weeks to decide to give it to you.

MEL. I can't explain it to you, Harry. But I just can't take the money.

HARRY. Why don't you let me do this for you? Why won't you let me have the satisfaction of making you happy?

MEL. You already have, by offering it. Now make me happier by tearing it up. They see this much money in this neighborhood, you'll never make it to your car.

HARRY. You let everyone else do things for you. You let everyone else take care of you. Edna, Pearl, Pauline, Jessie. Everybody but me, your brother. Why am I always excluded from the family?

MEL. They're three middle-aged widows, they're looking for someone to take care of. I made them a present, I got sick. What do you want from me, Harry?

HARRY. I had to work when I was thirteen years old. I didn't have time to be the favorite.

MEL. Harry, let's not go into that again. You want to be the favorite, I give it to you. I'll call the girls up tonight and tell them from

now on, you're the favorite.

HARRY. I'm not blaming you! I'm not blaming you. It's only natural. If there are two brothers in the family and one is out working all day, the one who stays home is the favorite.

MEL. Harry, I don't want to seem impolite. But Edna's not feeling well, we have no water, and all our food is defrosting. I'm really not in the mood to discuss why you're not the favorite.

HARRY. I lived in that house for thirty-one years, not once did anyone ever sing me "Happy Birthday."

MEL *(exasperated)*. Not true, Harry. You always had a birthday party. You always had a big cake.

HARRY. I had parties, I had cakes, no one ever sang "Happy Birthday."

MEL. All right, this year I'm going to hire a big chorus, Harry, and we're going to sing you "Happy Birthday."

HARRY. Eleven years old I was wearing long pants. Fourteen I had a little mustache. . . . At the movies I had to bring my birth certificate, they wanted to charge me adult prices.

MEL. I know, Harry. You grew up very fast.

HARRY. Did you ever see Pearl's family album? There are no pictures of me as a boy. I skipped right over it. Thousands of pictures of you on bicycles, on ponies, in barber chairs . . . one picture of me in a 1938 Buick. I looked like Herbert Hoover.

MEL. I'm sorry, Harry.

HARRY. I'm going to tell you something now, Mel. I never told this to anybody. I don't think you've got a brain for business. I don't think you know how to handle money. I don't think you can handle emotional problems. I think you're a child. A baby. A spoiled infant . . . And as God is my judge, many's the night I lay in bed envying you. . . . Isn't that something? For a man in my position to envy a man in your position? . . . Isn't that something? What I have, you'll never have . . . But what you've got, I'd like to have just once—just for an hour to see what it feels like to be the favorite.

MEL. What if I gave you a big kiss right on the mouth?

HARRY. You kiss me, I'll break every bone in your body . . . I'll call you. Listen, forget what I said. I changed my mind. I don't want to be the favorite. Not if I have to be kissed by Jessie and Pauline.

MEL. Try it, you might like it.

HARRY. I tried it, I didn't like it. . . . What if I lent you twelve thousand? You start a small camp. Five boys, two girls.

MEL. How about a little kiss on the cheek?

HARRY. You're not better yet. I don't care what your doctor says, you're not better yet. *(He leaves, closing the door behind him.)*

MEL. Edna! . . . *EDNA!*

(She comes out, wearing a bathrobe.)

EDNA. What is it, Mel? What is it?

MEL *(he paces angrily, trying to find the right words, as she stands there waiting).* You asked Harry? You asked my family for twenty-five thousand dollars for a summer camp?

EDNA. I didn't ask . . . They offered the money for a doctor . . . I told them I didn't need it for a doctor, I needed it for a camp.

MEL. Don't you see how humiliating it is for me to ask my family for money? Don't you see that?

EDNA. You didn't ask them. You weren't the one who was humiliated. *I was!* I was the one who sat here in front of the Spanish Inquisition. You were out taking a nice *tranquilized walk in the park.*

MEL. Tranquilized? Tranquilized? . . . I was sedated, Edna, not tranquilized. SEDATED!

EDNA. I don't care if you were petrified! I was the one who was humiliated . . . Next time *you* be humiliated and *I'll* be sedated!

MEL *(really loud).* You realize you're talking to a man who just had a nervous breakdown? Don't you have any regard for a man's illness?

EDNA *(yelling back).* You don't sound sick to me now. You sound like you *always* sound!

MEL. I'm not talking about *now,* I'm talking about *then!* I was sedated, Edna, not tranquilized. SEDATED!

EDNA *(yells).* Well, I wish to God you'd get sedated again so you'd stop yelling at me.

WOMAN'S VOICE *(from above).* Will you shut up down there, you hoodlums!

EDNA *(rushes out onto the terrace, yells up).* Who are you calling hoodlums?

WOMAN'S VOICE. You and your loud-mouthed husband.

EDNA *(yells up).* Don't you call us names. Your husband isn't half the man my husband is. We haven't forgotten the water. We remember the water.

(MEL goes out onto the terrace.)

WOMAN'S VOICE. My husband'll be home in an hour. If you don't shut up down there, you're gonna get more of the same.

EDNA. Ha! With what! Where are you gonna get the water? Where's your water, big mouth?

MEL *(pulling her away).* Edna, get away from there. *(He is out on the terrace now and calls up.)* I'm sorry. My wife didn't mean to yell. We were just discus—*(He gets hit with the pail of water. He reenters the room—drenched.)* They did it again . . . *(He sits down.)*

EDNA *(sitting, bewildered).* Where did they get the water? . . . Where did they get the water?

MEL. People like that always have water . . . They save it so that people like us can always get it.

(They are both seated. . . . There is silence for a few moments.)

EDNA *(looks at him).* I think you're behaving very well, Mel. I think you're taking it beautifully this time . . . That shows real progress, Mel. I think you've *grown* through this experience, Mel, I really do. *(And suddenly, behind them on the terrace, we see it begin to snow.)* Maybe you're right. Maybe you really *don't* have to go back to the doctor any more . . . I'm so proud of you, Mel, so proud . . . Because you're better than them . . . Better than all of them, Mel . . .

(Snow falls—slowly at first, but steadily increasing. MEL, *sensing something, turns and looks behind him.* EDNA *looks at* MEL, *then turns to look at the terrace to see what* MEL *is looking at. She sees the snow. They look at each other, then turn back and look at the snow again.* MEL *looks at his watch. He looks at the snow once more, then turns and slowly gets up and goes over to the closet.* EDNA *watches him. He opens the closet door and gets out his shovel. He looks at the snow once more, looks at his watch, then goes back and sits in his chair, one hand holding his shovel, the other around* EDNA's *shoulder, a contemporary* American Gothic. *Then we hear the voice of* ROGER KEATING.)

ROGER KEATING. This is Roger Keating and the *Six O'Clock Report.* . . . Heavy snow warnings have been posted along the eastern seaboard tonight, and here in New York a record forty-three inches have been forecast. . . . Snow plows were ordered out on the streets, and city residents were asked to get out their shovels in a joint effort to show how New Yorkers can live together and work together in a common cause.

CURTAIN

THE PRICE

Arthur Miller

For INGE and REBECCA

First presented by Robert Whitehead at the Morosco Theatre in New York City on February 7, 1968, with the following cast:

(In order of appearance)

VICTOR FRANZ	Pat Hingle	GREGORY SOLOMON	Harold Gary
ESTHER FRANZ	Kate Reid	WALTER FRANZ	Arthur Kennedy

Directed by Ulu Grosbard
Setting and costumes by Boris Aronson
Lighting by Paul Morrison

Arthur Miller is both a playwright and a man of conscience. He was born in Manhattan on October 17, 1915. His early background was, scholastically, not especially distinguished. However, after he had worked for a year in a warehouse and got the money to pay his tuition fees to the University of Michigan, his unusual abilities soon became apparent.

Following college he started to write radio plays, finding this discipline not only a means of making a living but also a way of honing his craftsmanship as a playwright. In 1945 he published a first novel, *Focus,* which attracted a certain amount of attention and approbation. But his heart was always set on the theatre. He had written plays all his adult life, but he did not get a professional production on Broadway until 1944 with *The Man Who Had All the Luck.* The luck, on this occasion, was not with Miller, for the play ran for only four performances. However, his next play, *All My Sons,* was destined to bring him acclamation and international fame. Opening on January 29, 1947, it ran for 328 performances on Broadway, was immensely popular in London's West End, and was produced almost everywhere else in the world.

Even more acclaim came to Miller with the production in 1949 of *Death of a Salesman.* Like *All My Sons,* this was given the award as Best Play of the Season by the Drama Critics' Circle. But it also won the 1949 Pulitzer Prize. In 1953 Miller produced what probably remains his best work to date, *The Crucible,* a historical drama about the Salem witch hunts, which also had great topical relevance, being written as it was during the McCarthy period.

The less successful *A View from the Bridge* followed in 1955. During the years that followed, Miller was beset with problems, both personal and, in a sense, political. However, when his friends Robert Whitehead and Elia Kazan started the Repertory Theatre of Lincoln Center, he was able to break his dramatic silence. The Repertory Theater was, prior to the building of the Vivian Beaumont Theater, temporarily housed in the ANTA Theatre in Washington Square. The company with all the high hopes in the world opened shop in Washington Square on January 23, 1964, and it opened with Miller's new play, *After the Fall.* This very interesting and seemingly autobiographical play was followed on December 3 of that same year by Miller's next play, *Incident at Vichy.*

Both these new plays could be seen as the exploration of guilt. In *After the Fall,* Miller was perhaps concerned with personal guilt, while in *Incident at Vichy* he returned to the theme of anti-Semitism, which had been the subject of the early novel, *Focus.* But in this play Miller was not concerned with the effects of anti-Semitism so much as its causes and responsibilities.

Miller has never been a particularly prolific playwright. In 1968 he gave us *The Price,* which was perhaps the first play that suggested that Miller really did have a sense of humor. It was very successful in New York and later repeated its success in London (where it received an even better critical response than in New York) and elsewhere in Europe. It was, however, not until the end of 1972 that he risked another play, his first comedy, *The Creation of the World and Other Business.* This somewhat pretentious comedy of creation—in this kind of play the playwright is inevitably locked into the unenviable position of playing God—flopped like a sack of Idaho potatoes. It was a nasty fall, but there was still a certain quality to it.

The Price was the important one. Indeed, in some opinions, it is Miller's best play apart from *The Crucible* and possibly *Salesman.* It opened on February 7, 1968. The play had had many difficulties on the road and in preview. Casting had to be changed, and only a few days before the premiere the man cast as Solomon (the late David Burns, who subsequently played the role on Broadway with enormous success) was taken sick and had to be instantly replaced. The replacement, Harold Gary, was very successful, but this was still one of the factors that made Miller's opening night unusually tense.

But everything worked out. The play, with its emphasis on Ibsenesque choices, went exceptionally well. Miller's theme here is that we are what we were. Our choices have been made in the past and we have to live with them.

The play is not a great one, perhaps, but it is the kind of play that makes its own contribution to the American theatre.

Arthur Miller is much more a fine man of the theatre than the consummate playwright that some of the more fervent of his admirers have taken him for. He is a good Broadway playwright rather than a figure of the stature of, say, Eugene O'Neill. Yet in terms of pure theatrical power Miller has a masterful control over his audiences. Even if his plays grip the attention at their immediate point of impact rather than providing any very solid food for thought, this is one of the theatre's most valid and exciting functions, and almost all his works have a kind of magic to them.

A fine balance of sympathy should be maintained in the playing of the roles of Victor and Walter. The actor playing Walter must not regard his attempts to win back Victor's friendship as mere manipulation. From entrance to exit, Walter is attempting to put into action what he has learned about himself, and sympathy will be evoked for him in proportion to the openness, the depth of need, the intimations of suffering with which the role is played.

This admonition goes beyond the question of theatrics to the theme of the play. As the world now operates, the qualities of both brothers are necessary to it; surely their respective psychologies and moral values conflict at the heart of the social dilemma. The production must therefore withhold judgment in favor of presenting both men in all their humanity and from their own viewpoints. Actually, each has merely proved to the other what the other has known but dared not face. At the end, demanding of one another what was forfeited to time, each is left touching the structure of his life.

The play can be performed with an intermission, as indicated at the end of Act One, if circumstances require it. But an unbroken performance is preferable.

ACT ONE

Today. New York.

Two windows are seen at the back of the stage. Daylight filters through their sooty panes, which have been X'd out with fresh whitewash to prepare for the demolition of the building.

Now daylight seeps through a skylight in the ceiling, grayed by the grimy panes. The light from above first strikes an overstuffed armchair in center stage. It has a faded rose slipcover. Beside it on its right, a small table with a filigreed radio of the twenties on it and old newspapers; behind it a bridge lamp. At its left an old wind-up Victrola and a pile of records on a low table. A white cleaning cloth and a mop and pail are nearby.

The room is progressively seen. The area around the armchair alone appears to be lived-in, with other chairs and a couch related to it. Outside this area, to the sides and back limits of the room and up the walls, is the chaos of ten rooms of furniture squeezed into this one.

There are four couches and three settees strewn at random over the floor; armchairs, wingbacks, a divan, occasional chairs. On the floor and stacked against the three walls up to the ceiling are bureaus, armoires, a tall secretary, a breakfront, a long, elaborately carved serving table, end tables, a library table, desks, glass-front bookcases, bowfront glass cabinets, and so forth. Several long rolled-up rugs and some shorter ones. A long sculling oar, bedsteads, trunks. And overhead one large and one smaller crystal chandelier hang from ropes, not connected to electric wires. Twelve dining-room chairs stand in a row along a dining-room table at left.

There is a rich heaviness, something almost Germanic, about the furniture, a weight of time upon the bulging fronts and curving chests marshalled against the walls. The room is monstrously crowded and dense, and it is difficult to decide if the stuff is impressive or merely overheavy and ugly.

An uncovered harp, its gilt chipped, stands alone downstage, right. At the back, behind a rather makeshift drape, long since faded, can be seen a small sink, a hot plate, and an old icebox. Up right, a door to the bedroom. Down left, a door to the corridor and stairway, which are unseen.

We are in the attic of a Manhattan brownstone soon to be torn down.

From the down-left door, Police Sergeant

VICTOR FRANZ *enters in uniform. He halts inside the room, glances about, walks at random a few feet, then comes to a halt. Without expression, yet somehow stilled by some emanation from the room, he lets his gaze move from point to point, piece to piece, absorbing its sphinxlike presence.*

He moves to the harp with a certain solemnity, as toward a coffin, and, halting before it, reaches out and plucks a string. He turns and crosses to the dining-room table and removes his gun belt and jacket, hanging them on a chair which he has taken off the table, where it has been set upside down along with two others.

He looks at his watch, waiting for time to pass. Then his eye falls on the pile of records in front of the phonograph. He raises the lid of the machine, sees a record already on the turntable, cranks, and sets the tone arm on the record. Gallagher and Shean sing. He smiles at the corniness.

With the record going he moves to the long sculling oar which stands propped against furniture and touches it. Now he recalls something, reaches in behind a chest, and takes out a fencing foil and mask. He snaps the foil in the air, his gaze held by memory. He puts the foil and mask on the table, goes through two or three records on the pile, and sees a title that makes him smile widely. He replaces the Gallagher and Shean record with this. It is a Laughing Record—two men trying unsuccessfully to get out a whole sentence through their wild hysteria.

He smiles. Broader. Chuckles. Then really laughs. It gets into him; he laughs more fully. Now he bends over with laughter, taking an unsteady step as helplessness rises in him.

ESTHER, *his wife, enters from the down-left door. His back is to her. A half-smile is already on her face as she looks about to see who is laughing with him. She starts toward him, and he hears her heels and turns.*

———

ESTHER. What in the world is that?

VICTOR *(surprised)*. Hi! *(He lifts the tone arm, smiling, a little embarrassed.)*

ESTHER. Sounded like a party in here! *(He gives her a peck. Of the record.)* What is that?

VICTOR *(trying not to disapprove openly)*. Where'd you get a drink?

ESTHER. I told you. I went for my checkup. *(She laughs with a knowing abandonment of good sense.)*

VICTOR. Boy, you and that doctor. I thought he told you not to drink.

ESTHER *(laughs)*. I had one! One doesn't hurt me. Everything's normal anyway. He sent you his best. *(She looks about.)*

VICTOR. Well, that's nice. The dealer's due in a few minutes, if you want to take anything.

ESTHER *(looking around with a sigh)*. Oh, dear God—here it is again.

VICTOR. The old lady did a nice job.

ESTHER. Ya—I never saw it so clean. *(Indicating the room)* Make you feel funny?

VICTOR *(shrugs)*. No, not really—she didn't recognize me, imagine?

ESTHER. Dear boy, it's a hundred and fifty years. *(Shaking her head as she stares about)* Huh.

VICTOR. What?

ESTHER. Time.

VICTOR. I know.

ESTHER. There's something different about it.

VICTOR. No, it's all the way it was. *(Indicating one side of the room)* I had my desk on that side and my cot. The rest is the same.

ESTHER. Maybe it's that it always used to seem so pretentious to me, and kind of bourgeois. But it does have a certain character. I think some of it's in style again. It's surprising.

VICTOR. Well, you want to take anything?

ESTHER *(looking about, hesitates)*. I don't know if I want it around. It's all so massive . . . where would we put any of it? That chest is lovely. *(She goes to it.)*

VICTOR. That was mine. *(Indicating one across the room)* The one over there was Walter's. They're a pair.

ESTHER *(comparing)*. Oh, ya! Did you get hold of him?

VICTOR *(rather glances away, as though this had been an issue)*. I called again this morning—he was in consultation.

ESTHER. Was he in the office?

VICTOR. Ya. The nurse went and talked to him for a minute—it doesn't matter. As long as he's notified so I can go ahead. *(She suppresses comment, picks up a lamp.)* That's probably real porcelain. Maybe it'd go in the bedroom.

ESTHER *(putting the lamp down)*. Why don't I meet you somewhere? The whole thing depresses me.

VICTOR. Why? It won't take long. Relax. Come on, sit down; the dealer'll be here any minute.

ESTHER *(sitting on a couch)*. There's just something so damned rotten about it. I can't help it; it always was. The whole thing is infuriating.

VICTOR. Well, don't get worked up. We'll sell it and that'll be the end of it. I picked up the tickets, by the way.

ESTHER. Oh, good. *(Laying her head back)*. Boy, I hope it's a good picture.

VICTOR. Better be. Great, not good. Two-fifty apiece.

ESTHER *(with sudden protest)*. I don't care! I want to go somewhere. *(She aborts further response, looking around.)* God, what's it all about? When I was coming up the stairs just now, and all the doors hanging open . . . It doesn't seem possible . . .

VICTOR. They tear down old buildings every day in the week, kid.

ESTHER. I know, but it makes you feel a hundred years old. I hate empty rooms. *(She muses.)* What was that screwball's name?—rented the front parlor, remember?—repaired saxophones?

VICTOR *(smiling)*. Oh—Saltzman. *(Extending his hand sideways.)* With the one eye went out that way.

ESTHER. Ya! Everytime I came down the stairs, there he was waiting for me with his four red hands! How'd he ever get all those beautiful girls?

VICTOR *(laughs)*. God knows. He must've smelled good. *(She laughs, and he does.)* He'd actually come running up here sometimes; middle of the afternoon—"Victor, come down quick, I got extras!"

ESTHER. And you did, too!

VICTOR. Why not? If it was free, you took it.

ESTHER *(blushing)*. You never told me that.

VICTOR. No, that was before you. Mostly.

ESTHER. You dog.

VICTOR. So what? It was the Depression. *(She laughs at the non sequitur.)* No, really—I think people were friendlier; lot more daytime screwing in those days. Like the McLoughlin sisters—remember, with the typing service in the front bedroom? *(He laughs.)* My father used to say, "In that typing service it's two dollars a copy."

(She laughs. It subsides.)

ESTHER. And they're probably all dead.

VICTOR. I guess Saltzman would be—he was well along. Although—*(He shakes his head, laughs softly in surprise.)* Jeeze, he wasn't either. I think he was about . . . my age now. Huh!

(Caught by the impact of time, they stare for a moment in silence.)

ESTHER *(gets up, goes to the harp).* Well, where's your dealer?

VICTOR *(glancing at his watch).* It's twenty to six. He should be here soon. *(She plucks the harp.) That* should be worth something.

ESTHER. I think a lot of it is. But you're going to have to bargain, you know. You can't just take what they say . . .

VICTOR *(with an edge of protest). I* can bargain; don't worry, I'm not giving it away.

ESTHER. Because they *expect* to bargain.

VICTOR. Don't get depressed already, will you? We didn't even start. *I* intend to bargain, I know the score with these guys.

ESTHER *(withholds further argument, goes to the phonograph; firing up some slight gaiety).* What's this record?

VICTOR. It's a Laughing Record. It was a big thing in the Twenties.

ESTHER *(curiously).* You remember it?

VICTOR. Very vaguely. I was only five or six. Used to play them at parties. You know —see who could keep a straight face. Or maybe they just sat around laughing; I don't know.

ESTHER. That's a wonderful idea!

(Their relation is quite balanced, so to speak; he turns to her.)

VICTOR. You look good. *(She looks at him, an embarrassed smile.)* I mean it.—I said I'm going to bargain, why do you . . . ?

ESTHER. I believe you. . . . This is the suit.

VICTOR. Oh, is that it! And how much? Turn around.

ESTHER *(turning).* Forty-five, imagine? He said nobody'd buy it, it was too simple.

VICTOR *(seizing the agreement).* Boy, women are dumb; that is really handsome. See, I don't mind if you get something for your money, but half the stuff they sell is such crap . . . *(Going to her)* By the way, look at this collar. Isn't this one of the ones you just bought?

ESTHER *(examining it).* No, that's an older one.

VICTOR. Well, even so. *(Turning up a heel)* Ought to write to Consumers Union about these heels. Three weeks—look at them!

ESTHER. Well, you don't walk straight. You're not going in uniform, I hope.

VICTOR. I could've murdered that guy! I'd just changed, and McGowan was trying to

fingerprint some bum and he didn't want to be printed; so he swings out his arm just as I'm going by, right into my container.

ESTHER *(as though this symbolized).* Oh, God . . .

VICTOR. I gave it to that quick cleaner, he'll try to have it by six.

ESTHER. Was there cream and sugar in the coffee?

VICTOR. Ya.

ESTHER. He'll never have it by six.

VICTOR *(assuagingly).* He's going to try.

ESTHER. Oh, forget it. *(Slight pause. Seriously disconsolate, she looks around at random.)*

VICTOR. Well, it's only a movie . . .

ESTHER. But we go out so rarely—why must everybody know your salary? I want an evening! I want to sit down in a restaurant without some drunken ex-cop coming over to the table to talk about old times.

VICTOR. It happened twice. After all these years, Esther, it would seem to me . . .

ESTHER. I know it's unimportant—but like that man in the museum; he really did—he thought you were the sculptor.

VICTOR. So I'm a sculptor.

ESTHER *(bridling).* Well, it was nice, that's all! You really do, Vic—you look distinguished in a suit. Why not? *(Laying her head back on the couch)* I should've taken down the name of that Scotch.

VICTOR. All Scotch is chemically the same.

ESTHER. I know; but some is better.

VICTOR *(looking at his watch).* Look at that, will you? Five-thirty sharp, he tells me. People say anything. *(He moves with a heightened restlessness, trying to down his irritation with her mood. His eye falls on a partly opened drawer of a chest, and he opens it and takes out an ice skate.)* Look at that, they're still good! *(He tests the edge with his fingernail; she merely glances at him.)* They're even sharp. We ought to skate again sometime. *(He sees her unremitting moodiness.)* Esther, I said I would bargain! . . . You see?—you don't know how to drink; it only depresses you.

ESTHER. Well, it's the kind of depression I enjoy!

VICTOR. Hot diggity dog.

ESTHER. I have an idea.

VICTOR. What?

ESTHER. Why don't you leave me? Just send me enough for coffee and cigarettes.

VICTOR. Then you'd *never* have to get out of bed.

ESTHER. I'd get out. Once in a while.

VICTOR. I got a better idea. Why don't you go off for a couple of weeks with your doctor? Seriously. It might change your viewpoint.

ESTHER. I wish I could.

VICTOR. Well, do it. He's got a suit. You could even take the dog—especially the dog. *(She laughs.)* It's not funny. Every time you go out for one of those walks in the rain I hold my breath what's going to come back with you.

ESTHER *(laughing).* Oh, go on, you love her.

VICTOR. I love her! You get plastered, you bring home strange animals, and I "love" them! I do not love that goddamned dog!

(She laughs with affection, as well as with a certain feminine defiance.)

ESTHER. Well, I want her!

VICTOR *(pause).* It won't be solved by a dog, Esther. You're an intelligent, capable woman, and you can't lay around all day. Even something part time, it would give you a place to go.

ESTHER. I don't need a place to go. *(Slight pause)* I'm not quite used to Richard not being there, that's all.

VICTOR. He's gone, kid. He's a grown man; you've got to do something with yourself.

ESTHER. I can't go to the same place day after day. I never could and I never will. Did you *ask* to speak to your brother?

VICTOR. I asked the nurse. Yes. He couldn't break away.

ESTHER. That son of a bitch. It's sickening.

VICTOR. Well, what are you going to do? He never had that kind of feeling.

ESTHER. What feeling? To come to the phone after sixteen years? It's common decency. *(With sudden intimate sympathy)* You're furious, aren't you?

VICTOR. Only at myself. Calling him again and again all week like an idiot . . . To hell with him, I'll handle it alone. It's just as well.

ESTHER. What about his share? *(He shifts; pressed and annoyed.)* I don't want to be a pest—but I think there could be some money here, Vic. *(He is silent.)* You're going to raise that with him, aren't you?

VICTOR *(with a formed decision).* I've been thinking about it. He's got a right to his half, why should he give up anything?

ESTHER. I thought you'd decided to put it to him?

VICTOR. I've changed my mind. I don't really feel he owes me anything, I can't put on an act.

ESTHER. But how many Cadillacs can he drive?

VICTOR. That's why he's got Cadillacs. People who love money don't give it away.

ESTHER. I don't know why you keep putting it like charity. There's such a thing as a moral debt. Vic, you made his whole career possible. What law said that only he could study medicine—?

VICTOR. Esther, please—let's not get back on that, will you?

ESTHER. I'm not back on anything—you were even the better student. That's a real debt, and he ought to be made to face it. He could never have finished medical school if you hadn't taken care of Pop. I mean we ought to start talking the way people talk! There could be some real money here.

VICTOR. I doubt that. There are no antiques or—

ESTHER. Just because it's ours why must it be worthless?

VICTOR. Now what's that for?

ESTHER. Because that's the way we think! We do!

VICTOR *(sharply).* The man won't even come to the phone, how am I going to—?

ESTHER. Then you write him a letter, bang on his door. This *belongs* to you!

VICTOR *(surprised, seeing how deadly earnest she is).* What are you so excited about?

ESTHER. Well, for one thing it might help you make up your mind to take your retirement.

(A slight pause.)

VICTOR *(rather secretively, unwillingly).* It's not the money been stopping me.

ESTHER. Then what is it? *(He is silent.)* I just thought that with a little cushion you could take a month or two until something occurs to you that you want to do.

VICTOR. It's all I think about right now, I don't have to quit to think.

ESTHER. But nothing seems to come of it.

VICTOR. Is it that easy? I'm going to be fifty. You don't just start a whole new career. I don't understand why it's so urgent all of a sudden.

ESTHER *(laughs).* All of a sudden! It's all I've been talking about since you became eligible—I've been saying the same thing for three years!

VICTOR. Well, it's not three years—

ESTHER. It'll be three years in March! It's *three years.* If you'd gone back to school then you'd almost have your Master's by now; you might have had a chance to get into something you'd love to do. Isn't that true? Why can't you make a move?

VICTOR *(pause. He is almost ashamed).* I'll tell you the truth. I'm not sure the whole thing wasn't a little unreal. I'd be fifty-three, fifty-four by the time I could start doing anything.

ESTHER. But you always knew that.

VICTOR. It's different when you're right on top of it. I'm not sure it makes any sense now.

ESTHER *(moving away, the despair in her voice).* Well . . . this is exactly what I tried to tell you a thousand times. It makes the same sense it ever made. But you might have twenty more years, and that's still a long time. Could do a lot of interesting things in that time. *(Slight pause)* You're so young, Vic.

VICTOR. I am?

ESTHER. Sure! I'm not, but you are. God, all the girls goggle at you, what do you want?

VICTOR *(laughs emptily).* It's hard to discuss it, Es, because I don't understand it.

ESTHER. Well, why not talk about what you don't understand? Why do you expect yourself to be an authority?

VICTOR. Well, one of us is got to stay afloat, kid.

ESTHER. You want me to pretend everything is great? I'm bewildered and I'm going to act bewildered! *(It flies out as though long suppressed.)* I've asked you fifty times to write a letter to Walter—

VICTOR *(like a repeated story).* What's this with Walter again? What's Walter going to—?

ESTHER. He is an important scientist, and that hospital's building a whole new research division. I saw it in the paper, it's his hospital.

VICTOR. Esther, the man hasn't called me in sixteen years.

ESTHER. But neither have you called him! *(He looks at her in surprise.)* Well, you haven't. That's also a fact.

VICTOR *(as though the idea were new and incredible).* What would I call him for?

ESTHER. Because, he's your brother, he's influential, and he could help—Yes, that's how people do, Vic! Those articles he wrote had a real idealism, there was a genuine human quality. I mean people do change, you know.

VICTOR *(turning away).* I'm sorry, I don't need Walter.

ESTHER. I'm not saying you have to approve of him; he's a selfish bastard, but he just might be able to put you on the track of something. I don't see the humiliation.

VICTOR *(pressed, irritated).* I don't understand why it's all such an emergency.

ESTHER. Because I don't know where in hell I am, Victor! *(To her own surprise, she has ended nearly screaming. He is silent. She retracts.)* I'll do anything if I know why, but all these years we've been saying, once we get the pension we're going to start to live. . . . It's like pushing against a door for twenty-five years and suddenly it opens . . . and we stand there. Sometimes I wonder, maybe I misunderstood you, maybe you like the department.

VICTOR. I've hated every minute of it.

ESTHER. I did everything wrong! I swear, I think if I demanded more it would have helped you more.

VICTOR. That's not true. You've been a terrific wife—

ESTHER. I don't think so. But the security meant so much to you I tried to fit into that; but I was wrong. God—just before coming here, I looked around at the apartment to see if we could use any of this—and it's all so ugly. It's worn and shabby and tasteless. And I have good taste! I know I do! It's that everything was always temporary with us. It's like we never were anything, we were always about-to-be. I think back to the war when any idiot was making so much money—that's when you should have quit, and I knew it, I knew it!

VICTOR. That's when I wanted to quit.

ESTHER. I only had one drink, Victor, so don't—

VICTOR. Don't change the whole story, kid. I wanted to quit, and you got scared.

ESTHER. Because you said there was going to be a depression after the war.

VICTOR. Well, go to the library, look up the papers around 1945, see what they were saying!

ESTHER. I don't care! *(She turns away—from her own irrationality.)*

VICTOR. I swear, Es, sometimes you make it sound like we've had no life at all.

ESTHER. God—my mother was so right! I can never believe what I see. I knew you'd never get out if you didn't during the war— I saw it happening, and I said nothing. You know what the goddamned trouble is?

VICTOR *(glancing at his watch, as he senses the end of her revolt).* What's the goddamned trouble?

ESTHER. We can never keep our minds on money! We worry about it, we talk about it, but we can't seem to *want* it. I do, but you don't. I really do, Vic. I want it. Vic? *I want money!*

VICTOR. Congratulations.

ESTHER. You go to hell!

VICTOR. I wish you'd stop comparing yourself to other people, Esther! that's all you're doing lately.

ESTHER. Well, I can't help it!

VICTOR. Then you've got to be a· failure, kid, because there's always going to be somebody up ahead of you. What happened? I have a certain nature; just as you do—I didn't change—

ESTHER. But you have changed. You've been walking around like a zombie ever since the retirement came up. You've gotten so vague—

VICTOR. Well, it's a decision. And I'd like to feel a little more certain about it. . . . Actually, I've even started to fill out the forms a couple of times.

ESTHER *(alerted).* And?

VICTOR *(with difficulty—he cannot understand it himself).* I suppose there's some kind of finality about it that . . . *(He breaks off.)*

ESTHER. But what else did you expect?

VICTOR. It's stupid; I admit it. But you look at that goddamned form and you can't help it. You sign your name to twenty-eight years and you ask yourself, Is that all? Is that it? And it is, of course. The trouble is, when I think of starting something new, that number comes up—five oh—and the steam goes out. But I'll do something. I will! *(With a greater closeness to her now)* I don't know what is is; every time I think about it all—it's almost frightening.

ESTHER. What?

VICTOR. Well, like when I walked in here before . . . *(He looks around.)* This whole thing—it hit me like some kind of craziness. Piling up all this stuff here like it was made of gold. *(He half-laughs, almost embarrassed.)* I brought up every stick; damn near saved the carpet tacks. *(He turns to the center chair.)* That whole way I was with him—it's inconceivable to me now.

ESTHER *(with regret over her sympathy).* Well . . . you loved him.

VICTOR. I know, but it's all words. What was he? A busted businessman like thousands of others, and I acted like some kind of a mountain crashed. I tell you the truth, every now and then the whole thing is like a story somebody told me. You ever feel that way?

ESTHER. All day, every day.

VICTOR. Oh, come on—

ESTHER. It's the truth. The first time I walked up those stairs I was nineteen years old. And when you opened that box with your first uniform in it—remember that? When you put it on the first time?—how we laughed? If anything happened you said you'd call a cop! *(They both laugh.)* It was like a masquerade. And we were right. That's when we were right.

VICTOR *(pained by her pain).* You know, Esther, every once in a while you try to sound childish and it—

ESTHER. I mean to be! I'm sick of the—Oh, forget it, I want a drink. *(She goes for her purse.)*

VICTOR *(surprised).* What's that, the great adventure? Where are you going all of a sudden?

ESTHER. I can't stand it in here, I'm going for a walk.

VICTOR. Now you cut out this nonsense!

ESTHER. I am not an alcoholic!

VICTOR. You've had a good life compared to an awful lot of people! You trying to turn into a goddamned teen-ager or something?

ESTHER *(indicating the furniture).* Don't talk childishness to me, Victor—not in this room! You let it lay here all these years because you can't have a simple conversation with your own brother, and I'm childish? You're still eighteen years old with that man! I mean I'm stuck, but I admit it!

VICTOR *(hurt).* Okay. Go ahead.

ESTHER *(she can't quite leave).* You got a receipt? I'll get your suit. *(He doesn't move. She makes it rational.)* I just want to get out of here.

VICTOR *(takes out a receipt and gives it to her. His voice is cold.)* It's right off Seventh. The address is on it. *(He moves from her.)*

ESTHER. I'm coming back right away.

VICTOR *(freeing her to her irresponsibility).* Do as you please, kid. I mean it.

ESTHER. You were grinding your teeth again last night. Did you know that?

VICTOR. Oh! No wonder my ear hurts.

ESTHER. I wish I had a tape recorder. I mean it, it's gruesome; sounds like a lot of rocks coming down a mountain. I wish you could hear it, you wouldn't take this self-sufficient attitude.

(He is silent, alarmed, hurt. He moves upstage as though looking at the furniture.)

VICTOR. It's okay. I think I get the message.

ESTHER (*afraid—she tries to smile and goes back toward him*). Like what?

VICTOR (*moves a chair and does a knee bend and draws out the chassis of an immense old radio*). What other message is there?

(*Slight pause.*)

ESTHER (*to retrieve the contact*). What's that?

VICTOR. Oh, one of my old radios that I made. Mama mia, look at those tubes.

ESTHER (*more wondering than she feels about radios*). Would that work?

VICTOR. No, you need a storage battery. . . . (*Recalling, he suddenly looks up at the ceiling.*)

ESTHER (*looking up*). What?

VICTOR. One of my batteries exploded, went right through there someplace. (*He points.*) There! See where the plaster is different?

ESTHER (*striving for some spark between them*). Is this the one you got Tokyo on?

VICTOR (*not relenting, his voice dead*). Ya, this is the monster.

ESTHER (*with a warmth*). Why don't you take it?

VICTOR. Ah, it's useless.

ESTHER. Didn't you once say you had a lab up here? Or did I dream that?

VICTOR. Sure, I took it apart when Pop and I moved up here. Walter had that wall, and I had this. We did some great tricks up here. (*She is fastened on him. He avoids her eyes and moves waywardly.*) I'll be frank with you, kid—I look at my life and the whole thing is incomprehensible to me. I know all the reasons and all the reasons and all the reasons, and it ends up—nothing. (*He goes to the harp, touches it.*) It's strange, you know? I forgot all about it—we'd work up here all night sometimes, and it was often full of music. My mother'd play for hours down in the library. Which is peculiar, because a harp is so soft. But it penetrates, I guess.

ESTHER. You're dear. You are, Vic. (*She starts toward him, but he thwarts her by looking at his watch.*)

VICTOR. I'll have to call another man. Come on, let's get out of here. (*With a hollow, exhausted attempt at joy*) We'll get my suit and act rich!

ESTHER. Vic, I didn't mean that I—

VICTOR. Forget it. Wait, let me put these away before somebody walks off with them. (*He takes up the foil and mask.*)

ESTHER. Can you still do it?

VICTOR (*his sadness, his distance clinging to him*). Oh, no, you gotta be in shape for this. It's all in the thighs—

ESTHER. Well, let me see, I never saw you do it!

VICTOR (*giving the inch*). All right, but I can't get down far enough any more. (*He takes position, feet at right angles, bouncing himself down to a difficult crouch.*)

ESTHER. Maybe you could take it up again.

VICTOR. Oh, no, it's a lot of work, it's the toughest sport there is. (*Resuming position*) Okay, just stand there.

ESTHER. Me?

VICTOR. Don't be afraid. (*Snapping the tip*) It's a beautiful foil, see how alive it is? I beat Princeton with this. (*He laughs tiredly and makes a tramping lunge from yards away; the button touches her stomach.*)

ESTHER (*springing back*) God! Victor!

VICTOR. What?

ESTHER. You looked beautiful.

(*He laughs, surprised and half embarrassed—when both of them are turned to the door by a loud, sustained coughing out in the corridor. The coughing increases.*

Enter GREGORY SOLOMON. *In brief, a phenomenon; a man nearly ninety but still straight-backed and the air of his massiveness still with him. He has perfected a way of leaning on his cane without appearing weak.*

He wears a worn fur-felt black fedora, its brim turned down on the right side like Jimmy Walker's—although much dustier—and a shapeless topcoat. His frayed tie has a thick knot, askew under a curled-up collar tab. His vest is wrinkled, his trousers baggy. A large diamond ring is on his left index finger. Tucked under his arm, a wrung-out leather portfolio. He hasn't shaved today.

Still coughing, catching his breath, trying to brush his cigar ashes off his lapel in a hopeless attempt at businesslike decorum, he is nodding at ESTHER *and* VICTOR *and has one hand raised in a promise to speak quite soon. Nor has he failed to glance with some suspicion at the foil in* VICTOR's *hand.*)

VICTOR. Can I get you a glass of water?

(SOLOMON *gestures an imperious negative, trying to stop coughing.*)

ESTHER. Why don't you sit down? (SOLOMON *gestures thanks, sits in the center armchair, the cough subsiding.*) You sure you don't want some water?

SOLOMON (*in a Russian-Yiddish accent*).

Water I don't need; a little blood I could use. Thank you. *(He takes deep breaths, his attention on* VICTOR, *who now puts down the foil.)* Oh, boy. That's some stairs.

ESTHER. You all right now?

SOLOMON. Another couple steps you'll be in heaven. Ah—excuse me, Officer, I am for a party. The name is . . . *(He fingers in his vest.)*

VICTOR. Franz.

SOLOMON. That's it, Franz.

VICTOR. That's me. (SOLOMON *looks incredulous.)* Victor Franz.

SOLOMON. So it's a policeman!

VICTOR *(grinning).* Uh huh.

SOLOMON. What do you know! *(Including* ESTHER) You see? There's only one beauty to this lousy business, you meet all kinda people. But I never dealt with a policeman. *(Reaching over to shake hands)* I'm very happy to meet you. My name is Solomon, Gregory Solomon.

VICTOR *(shaking hands).* This is my wife.

ESTHER. How do you do.

SOLOMON *(nodding appreciatively to* ESTHER). Very nice. *(To* VICTOR) That's a nice-looking woman. *(He extends his hands to her.)* How do you do, darling. Beautiful suit.

ESTHER *(laughs).* The fact is, I just bought it!

SOLOMON. You got good taste. Congratulations, wear it in good health. *(He lets go her hand.)*

ESTHER. I'll go to the cleaner, dear. I'll be back soon. *(With a step toward the door—to* SOLOMON) Will you be very long?

SOLOMON *(glancing around at the furniture as at an antagonist).* With furniture you never know, can be short, can be long, can be medium.

ESTHER. Well, you give him a good price now, you hear?

SOLOMON. Ah ha! *(Waving her out)* Look, you go to the cleaner, and we'll take care everything one hundred percent.

ESTHER. Because there's some very beautiful stuff here. I know it, but he doesn't.

SOLOMON. I'm not sixty-two years in the business by taking advantage. Go, enjoy the cleaner.

(She and VICTOR *laugh.)*

ESTHER *(shaking her finger at him).* I hope I'm going to like you!

SOLOMON. Sweetheart, all the girls like me, what can I do?

ESTHER *(still smiling—to* VICTOR *as she goes to the door).* You be careful.

VICTOR *(nodding).* See you later.

(She goes.)

SOLOMON. I like her, she's suspicious.

VICTOR *(laughing in surprise).* What do you mean by that?

SOLOMON. Well, a girl who believes everything, how you gonna trust her? (VICTOR *laughs appreciatively.)* I had a wife . . . *(He breaks off with a wave of the hand.)* Well, what's the difference? Tell me, if you don't mind, how did you get my name?

VICTOR. In the phone book.

SOLOMON. You don't say! The phone book.

VICTOR. Why?

SOLOMON *(cryptically).* No-no, that's fine, that's fine.

VICTOR. The ad said you're a registered appraiser.

SOLOMON. Oh, yes. I am registered, I am licensed, I am even vaccinated. (VICTOR *laughs.)* Don't laugh, the only thing you can do today without a license is you'll go up the elevator and jump out the window. But I don't have to tell you, you're a policeman, you know this world. *(Hoping for contact)* I'm right?

VICTOR *(reserved).* I suppose.

SOLOMON *(surveying the furniture, one hand on his thigh, the other on the chair arm in a naturally elegant position).* So. *(He glances about again, and with an uncertain smile.)* That's a lot of furniture. This is all for sale?

VICTOR. Well, ya.

SOLOMON. Fine, fine. I just like to be sure where we are. *(With a weak attempt at a charming laugh)* Frankly, in this neighborhood I never expected such a load. It's very surprising.

VICTOR. But I said it was a whole houseful.

SOLOMON *(with a leaven of unsureness).* Look, don't worry about it, we'll handle everything very nice. *(He gets up from the chair and goes to one of the pair of chiffoniers which he is obviously impressed with. He looks up at the chandeliers. Then straight at* VICTOR) I'm not mixing in, Officer, but if you wouldn't mind—what is your connection? How do you come to this?

VICTOR. It was my family.

SOLOMON. You don't say. Looks like it's standing here a long time, no?

VICTOR. Well, the old man moved everything up here after the '29 crash. My uncles took over the house and they let him keep this floor.

SOLOMON *(as though to emphasize that he believes it).* I see. *(He walks to the harp.)*

VICTOR. Can you give me an estimate now, or do you have to—?

SOLOMON *(running a hand over the harp frame).* No-no, I'll give you right away, I don't waste a minute, I'm very busy. *(He plucks a string, listens. Then bends down and runs a hand over the sounding board)* He passed away, your father?

VICTOR. Oh, long time ago—about sixteen years.

SOLOMON *(standing erect).* It's standing here sixteen years?

VICTOR. Well, we never got around to doing anything about it, but they're tearing the building down, so . . . It was very good stuff, you know—they had quite a little money.

SOLOMON. Very good, yes . . . I can see. *(He leaves the harp with an estimating glance.)* I was also very good; now I'm not so good. Time, you know, is a terrible thing. *(He is a distance from the harp and indicates it).* That sounding board is cracked, you know. But don't worry about it, it's still a nice object. *(He goes to an armoire and strokes the veneer.)* It's a funny thing—an armoire like this, thirty years you couldn't give it away; it was a regular measles. Today all of a sudden, they want it again. Go figure it out. *(He goes to one of the chests.)*

VICTOR *(pleased).* Well, give me a good price and we'll make a deal.

SOLOMON. Definitely. You see, I don't lie to you. *(He is pointing to the chest.)* For instance, a chiffonier like this I wouldn't have to keep it a week. *(Indicating the other chest)* That's a pair, you know.

VICTOR. I know.

SOLOMON. That's a nice chair, too. *(He sits on a dining-room chair, rocking to test its tightness.)* I like the chairs.

VICTOR. There's more stuff in the bedroom, if you want to look.

SOLOMON. Oh? *(He goes toward the bedroom.)* What've you got here? *(He looks into the bedroom, up and down.)* I like the bed. That's a very nice carved bed. That I can sell. That's your parents' bed?

VICTOR. Yes. They may have bought that in Europe, if I'm not mistaken. They used to travel a good deal.

SOLOMON. Very handsome, very nice. I like it. *(He starts to return to the center chair, eyes roving the furniture.)* Looks a very nice family.

VICTOR. By the way, that dining-room table opens up. Probably seat about twelve people.

SOLOMON *(looking at the table).* I know that. Yes. In a pinch even fourteen. *(He picks up the foil.)* What's this? I thought you were stabbing your wife when I came in.

VICTOR *(laughing).* No, I just found it. I used to fence years ago.

SOLOMON. You went to college?

VICTOR. Couple of years, ya.

SOLOMON. That's very interesting.

VICTOR. It's the old story.

SOLOMON. No, listen—What happens to people is always the main element to me. Because when do they call me? It's either a divorce or somebody died. So it's always a new story. I mean it's the same, but it's different. *(He sits in the center chair.)*

VICTOR. You pick up the pieces.

SOLOMON. That's very good, yes. I pick up the pieces. It's a little bit like you, I suppose. You must have some stories, I betcha.

VICTOR. Not very often.

SOLOMON. What are you, a traffic cop, or something . . . ?

VICTOR. I'm out in Rockaway most of the time, the airports.

SOLOMON. That's Siberia, no?

VICTOR *(laughing).* I like it better that way.

SOLOMON. You keep your nose clean.

VICTOR *(smiling).* That's it. *(Indicating the furniture)* So what do you say?

SOLOMON. What I say? *(Taking out two cigars as he glances about)* You like a cigar?

VICTOR. Thanks, I gave it up long time ago. So what's the story here?

SOLOMON. I can see you are a very factual person.

VICTOR. You hit it.

SOLOMON. Couldn't be better. So tell me, you got some kind of paper here? To show ownership?

VICTOR. Well, no, I don't. But . . . *(He half laughs.)* I'm the owner, that's all.

SOLOMON. In other words, there's no brothers, no sisters.

VICTOR. I have a brother, yes.

SOLOMON. Ah hah. You're friendly with him. Not that I'm mixing in, but I don't have to tell you the average family they love each other like crazy, but the minute the parents die is all of a sudden a question who is going to get what and you're covered with cats and dogs—

VICTOR. There's no such problem here.

SOLOMON. Unless we're gonna talk about a few pieces, then it wouldn't bother me, but to take the whole load without a paper is a—

VICTOR. All right, I'll get you some kind of statement from him; don't worry about it.

SOLOMON. That's definite; because even from high-class people you wouldn't believe the shenanigans—lawyers, college professors, television personalities—five hundred dollars they'll pay a lawyer to fight over a bookcase it's worth fifty cents—because you see, everybody wants to be number one, so . . .

VICTOR. I said I'd get you a statement. *(He indicates the room.)* Now what's the story?

SOLOMON. All right, so I'll tell you the story. *(He looks at the dining-room table and points to it.)* For instance, you mention the dining-room table. That's what they call Spanish Jacobean. Cost maybe twelve, thirteen hundred dollars. I would say—1921, '22. I'm right?

VICTOR. Probably, ya.

SOLOMON *(clears his throat)*. I see you're an intelligent man, so before I'll say another word, I ask you to remember—with used furniture you cannot be emotional.

VICTOR *(laughs)*. I haven't opened my mouth!

SOLOMON. I mean you're a policeman, I'm a furniture dealer, we both know this world. Anything Spanish Jacobean you'll sell quicker a case of tuberculosis.

VICTOR. Why? That table's in beautiful condition.

SOLOMON. Officer, you're talking reality; you cannot talk reality with used furniture. They don't like that style; not only they don't like it, they hate it. The same thing with that buffet there and that . . . *(He starts to point elsewhere.)*

VICTOR. You only want to take a few pieces, is that the ticket?

SOLOMON. Please, Officer, we're already talking too fast—

VICTOR. No-no, you're not going to walk off with the gravy and leave me with the bones. All or nothing or let's forget it. I told you on the phone it was a whole houseful.

SOLOMON. What're you in such a hurry? Talk a little bit, we'll see what happens. In a day they didn't build Rome. *(He calculates worriedly for a moment, glancing again at the pieces he wants. He gets up, goes and touches the harp.)* You see, what I had in mind—I would give you such a knockout price for these few pieces that you—

VICTOR. That's *out*.

SOLOMON *(quickly)*. Out.

VICTOR. I'm not running a department store. They're tearing the building down.

SOLOMON. Couldn't be better! We understand each other, so—*(with his charm)*—so there's no reason to be emotional. *(He goes to the records.)* These records go? *(He picks up one.)*

VICTOR. I might keep three or four.

SOLOMON *(reading a label)*. Look at that! Gallagher and Shean!

VICTOR *(with only half a laugh)*. You're not going to start playing them now!

SOLOMON. Who needs to play? I was on the same bill with Gallagher and Shean maybe fifty theatres.

VICTOR *(surprised)*. You were an actor?

SOLOMON. An actor! An acrobat; my whole family was acrobats. *(Expanding with this first opening.)* You never heard "The Five Solomons"—may they rest in peace? I was the one on the bottom.

VICTOR. Funny—I never heard of a Jewish acrobat.

SOLOMON. What's the matter with Jacob, he wasn't a wrestler?—wrestled with the Angel? (VICTOR *laughs*.) Jews been acrobats since the beginning of the world. I was a horse them days: drink, women, anything—on-the-go, on-the-go, nothing ever stopped me. Only life. Yes, my boy. *(Almost lovingly putting down the record)* What do you know, Gallagher and Shean.

VICTOR *(more intimately now, despite himself; but with no less persistence in keeping to the business)*. So where are we?

SOLOMON *(glancing off, he turns back to* VICTOR *with a deeply concerned look)*. Tell me, what's with crime now? It's up, hey?

VICTOR. Yeah, it's up, it's up. Look, Mr. Solomon, let me make one thing clear, heh? I'm not sociable.

SOLOMON. You're not.

VICTOR. No, I'm not; I'm not a businessman, I'm not good at conversations. So let's get to a price, and finish. Okay?

SOLOMON. You don't want we should be buddies.

VICTOR. That's exactly it.

SOLOMON. So we wouldn't be buddies! *(He sighs.)* But just so you'll know me a little better—I'm going to show you something. *(He takes out a leather folder which he flips open and hands to* VICTOR.) There's my discharge from the British Navy. You see? "His Majesty's Service."

VICTOR *(looking at the document).* Huh! What were you doing in the British Navy?

SOLOMON. Forget the British Navy. What does it say the date of birth?

VICTOR. "Eighteen . . . " *(Amazed, he looks up at* SOLOMON.*)* You're almost ninety?

SOLOMON. Yes, my boy. I left Russia sixty-five years ago, I was twenty-four years old. And I smoked all my life. I drinked, and I loved every woman who would let me. So what do I need to steal from you?

VICTOR. Since when do people need a reason to steal?

SOLOMON. I never saw such a man in my life!

VICTOR. Oh, yes you did. Now you going to give me a figure or—?

SOLOMON *(he is actually frightened because he can't get a hook into* VICTOR *and fears losing the good pieces).* How can I give you a figure? You don't trust one word I say!

VICTOR *(with a strained laugh).* I never saw you before, what're you asking me to trust you?!

SOLOMON *(with a gesture of disgust).* But how am I going to start to talk to you? I'm sorry; here you can't be a policeman. If you want to do business a little bit you gotta believe or you can't do it. I'm . . . I'm . . . Look, forget it. *(He gets up and goes to his portfolio.)*

VICTOR *(astonished).* What are you doing?

SOLOMON. I can't work this way. I'm too old every time I open my mouth you should practically call me a thief.

VICTOR. Who called you a thief?

SOLOMON *(moving toward the door).* No—I don't need it. I don't want it in my shop. *(Wagging a finger into* VICTOR*'s face)* And don't forget it—I never gave you a price, and look what you did to me. You see? I never gave you a price!

VICTOR *(angering).* Well, what did you come here for, to do me a favor? What are you talking about?

SOLOMON. Mister, I pity you! What is the matter with you people! You're worse than my daughter! Nothing in the world you believe, nothing you respect—how can you live? You think that's such a smart thing? That's so hard, what you're doing? Let me give you a piece advice—it's not that you can't believe nothing, that's not so hard—it's that you still got to believe it. *That's* hard. And if you can't do that, my friend—you're a dead man! *(He starts toward the door.)*

VICTOR *(chastened despite himself).* Oh, Solomon, come on, will you?

SOLOMON. No-no. You got a certain problem with this furniture but you don't want to listen so how can I talk?

VICTOR. I'm listening! For Christ's sake, what do you want me to do, get down on my knees?

SOLOMON *(putting down his portfolio and taking out a wrinkled tape measure from his jacket pocket).* Okay, come here. I realize you are a factual person, but some facts are funny. *(He stretches the tape measure across the depth of a piece.)* What does that read? *(Then turns to* VICTOR, *showing him)*

VICTOR *(comes to him, reads).* Forty inches. So?

SOLOMON. My boy, the bedroom doors in a modern apartment house are thirty, thirty-two inches maximum. So you can't get this in—

VICTOR. What about the old houses?

SOLOMON *(with a desperation growing).* All I'm trying to tell you is that my possibilities are smaller!

VICTOR. Well, can't I ask a question?

SOLOMON. I'm giving you architectural facts! Listen—*(Wiping his face, he seizes on the library table, going to it.)* You got there, for instance, a library table. That's a solid beauty. But go find me a modern apartment with a library. If they would build old hotels, I could sell this, but they only build new hotels. People don't live like this no more. This stuff is from another world. So I'm trying to give you a modern viewpoint. Because the price of used furniture is nothing but a viewpoint, and if you wouldn't understand the viewpoint is impossible to understand the price.

VICTOR. So what's the viewpoint—that it's all worth nothing?

SOLOMON. That's what you said, I didn't say that. The chairs is worth something, the chiffoniers, the bed, the harp—

VICTOR *(turns away from him).* Okay, let's forget it, I'm not giving you the cream—

SOLOMON. What're you jumping!

VICTOR *(turning to him).* Good God, are you going to make me an offer or not?

SOLOMON *(walking away with a hand at his temple).* Boy, oh boy, oh boy. You must've arrested a million people by now.

VICTOR. Nineteen in twenty-eight years.

SOLOMON. So what are you so hard on me?

VICTOR. Because you talk about everything

but money and I don't know what the hell you're up to.

SOLOMON *(raising a finger)*. We will now talk money. *(He returns to the center chair.)*

VICTOR. Great. I mean you can't blame me —every time you open your mouth the price seems to go down.

SOLOMON *(sitting)*. My boy, the price didn't change since I walked in.

VICTOR *(laughing)*. That's even better! So what's the price? (SOLOMON *glances about, his wit failed, a sunk look coming over his face.)* What's going on? What's bothering you?

SOLOMON. I'm sorry, I shouldn't have come. I thought it would be a few pieces but . . . *(Sunk, he presses his fingers into his eyes.)* It's too much for me.

VICTOR. Well, what'd you come for? I told you it was the whole house.

SOLOMON *(protesting)*. You called me so I came! What should I do, lay down and die? *(Striving again to save it)* Look, I want very much to make you an offer, the only question is . . . *(He breaks off as though fearful of saying something.)*

VICTOR. This is a hell of a note.

SOLOMON. Listen, it's a terrible temptation to me! But . . . *(As though throwing himself on* VICTOR'*s understanding)* You see, I'll tell you the truth; you must have looked in a very old phone book; a couple of years ago already I cleaned out my store. Except a few English andirons I got left, I sell when I need a few dollars. I figured I was eighty, eighty-five, it was time already. But I waited—and nothing happened—I even moved out of my apartment. I'm living in the back of the store with a hot plate. But nothing happened. I'm still practically a hundred percent—not a hundred, but I feel very well. And I figured maybe you got a couple nice pieces—not that the rest can't be sold, but it could take a year, year and half. For me that's a big bet. *(In conflict, he looks around.)* The trouble is I love to work; I love it, but—*(Giving up)* I don't know what to tell you.

VICTOR. All right, let's forget it then.

SOLOMON *(standing)*. What're you jumping?

VICTOR. Well, are you in or out!

SOLOMON. How do I know where I am! You see, it's also this particular furniture— the average person he'll take one look, it'll make him very nervous.

VICTOR. Solomon, you're starting again.

SOLOMON. I'm not bargaining with you!

VICTOR. Why'll it make him nervous?

SOLOMON. Because he knows it's never gonna break.

VICTOR *(not in bad humor, but clinging to his senses)*. Oh, come on, will you? Have a little mercy.

SOLOMON. My boy, you don't know the psychology! If it wouldn't break there is no more possibilities. For instance, you take— *(crosses to table)*—this table . . . Listen! *(He bangs the table.)* You can't move it. A man sits down to such a table he knows not only he's married, he's got to stay married—there is no more possibilities. (VICTOR *laughs.)* You're laughing, I'm telling you the factual situation. What is the key word today? Disposable. The more you can throw it away the more it's beautiful. The car, the furniture, the wife, the children—everything has to be disposable. Because you see the main thing today is—shopping. Years ago a person, he was unhappy, didn't know what to do with himself—he'd go to church, start a revolution— *something*. Today you're unhappy? Can't figure it out? What is the salvation? Go shopping.

VICTOR *(laughing)*. You're terrific, I have to give you credit.

SOLOMON. I'm telling you the truth! If they would close the stores for six months in this country there would be from coast to coast a regular massacre. With this kind of furniture the shopping is over, it's finished, there's no more possibilites, you *got* it, you see? So you got a problem here.

VICTOR *(laughing)*. Solomon, you are one of the greatest. But I'm way ahead of you, it's not going to work.

SOLOMON *(offended)*. What "work"? I don't know how much time I got. What is so terrible if I say that? The trouble is, you're such a young fella you don't understand these things—

VICTOR. I understand very well, I know what you're up against. I'm not so young.

SOLOMON *(scoffing)*. What are you, forty? Forty-five?

VICTOR. I'm going to be fifty.

SOLOMON. Fifty! You're a baby boy!

VICTOR. Some baby.

SOLOMON. My God, if I was fifty . . . ! I got married I was seventy-five.

VICTOR. Go on.

SOLOMON. What are you talking? She's still living by Eighth Avenue over there. See, that's why I like to stay liquid, because I don't want her to get her hands on this. . . . Bird she loves. She's living there with maybe a hundred birds. She gives you a plate of soup it's got feathers. I didn't work all my life for them birds.

VICTOR. I appreciate your problems, Mr. Solomon, but I don't have to pay for them. *(He stands.)* I've got no more time.

SOLOMON *(holding up a restraining hand— desperately).* I'm going to buy it! *(He has shocked himself, and glances around at the towering masses of furniture.)* I mean I'll . . . *(He moves, looking at the stuff.)* I'll have to live, that's all, I'll make up my mind! I'll buy it.

VICTOR *(he is affected as Solomon's fear comes through to him).* We're talking about everything now.

SOLOMON *(angrily).* Everything, everything! *(Going to his portfolio)* I'll figure it up, I'll give you a very nice price, and you'll be a happy man.

VICTOR *(sitting again).* That I doubt. *(Solomon takes a hard-boiled egg out of the portfolio.)* What's this now, lunch?

SOLOMON. You give me such an argument, I'm hungry! I'm not supposed to get too hungry.

VICTOR. Brother!

SOLOMON *(cracks the shell on his diamond ring).* You want me to starve to death? I'm going to be very quick here.

VICTOR. Boy—I picked a number!

SOLOMON. There wouldn't be a little salt, I suppose.

VICTOR. I'm not going running for salt now!

SOLOMON. Please, don't be blue. I'm going to knock you off your feet with the price, you'll see. *(He swallows the egg. He now faces the furniture, and, half to himself, pad and pencil poised).* I'm going to go here like an IBM. *(He starts estimating on his pad.)*

VICTOR. That's all right, take it easy. As long as you're serious.

SOLOMON. Thank you. *(He touches the hated buffet.)* Ay, yi, yi. All right, well . . . *(He jots down a figure. He goes to the next piece, jots down another figure. He goes to another piece, jots down a figure.)*

VICTOR *(after a moment).* You really got married at seventy-five?

SOLOMON. What's so terrible?

VICTOR. No. I think it's terrific. But what was the point?

SOLOMON. What's the point at twenty-five? You can't die twenty-six?

VICTOR *(laughing softly).* I guess so, ya.

SOLOMON. It's the same like secondhand furniture, you see; the whole thing is a viewpoint. It's a mental world. *(He jots down another figure for another piece.)* Seventy-five I got married, fifty-one, and twenty-two.

VICTOR. You're kidding.

SOLOMON. I wish! *(He works, jotting his estimate of each piece on the pad, opening drawers, touching everything. Peering into a dark recess, he takes out a pencil flashlight, switches it on, and begins to probe with the beam.)*

VICTOR *(he has gradually turned to watch SOLOMON, who goes on working).* Cut the kidding now—how old are you?

SOLOMON *(sliding out a drawer).* I'm eighty-nine. It's such an accomplishment?

VICTOR. You're a hell of a guy.

SOLOMON *(smiling with the encouragement and turning to Victor).* You know, it's a funny thing. It's so long since I took on such a load like this—you forget what kind of life it puts into you. To take out a pencil again . . . it's a regular injection. Frankly, my telephone you could use for a ladle, it wouldn't interfere with nothing. I want to thank you. *(He points at Victor.)* I'm going to take good care of you, I mean it. I can open that?

VICTOR. Sure, anything.

SOLOMON *(going to an armoire).* Some of them had a mirror . . . *(He opens the armoire, and a rolled-up fur rug falls out. It is about three by five.)* What's this?

VICTOR. God knows. I guess it's a rug.

SOLOMON *(holding it up).* No-no—that's a lap robe. Like for a car.

VICTOR. Say, that's right, ya. When they went driving. God, I haven't seen that in—

SOLOMON. You had a chauffeur?

VICTOR. Ya, we had a chauffeur.

(Their eyes meet. SOLOMON looks at him as though VICTOR were coming into focus. VICTOR turns away. Now SOLOMON turns back to the armoire.)

SOLOMON. Look at that! *(He takes down an opera hat from the shelf within.)* My God! *(He puts it on, looks into the interior mirror.)* What a world! *(He turns to VICTOR.)* He must've been some sporty guy!

VICTOR *(smiling).* You look pretty good!

SOLOMON. And from all this he could go so broke?

VICTOR. Why not? Sure. Took five weeks. Less.

SOLOMON. You don't say. And he couldn't make a comeback?

VICTOR. Well some men don't bounce, you know.

SOLOMON *(grunts).* Hmm! So what did he do?

VICTOR. Nothing. Just sat here. Listened to the radio.

SOLOMON. But what did he do? What—?

VICTOR. Well, now and then he was making change at the Automat. Toward the end he was delivering telegrams.

SOLOMON *(with grief and wonder).* You don't say. And how much he had?

VICTOR. Oh . . . couple of million, I guess.

SOLOMON. My God. What was the matter with him?

VICTOR. Well, my mother died around the same time. I guess that didn't help. Some men just don't bounce, that's all.

SOLOMON. Listen, I can tell you bounces. I went busted 1932; then 1923 they also knocked me out; the panic of 1904, 1898 . . . But to lay down like *that* . . .

VICTOR. Well, you're different. He believed in it.

SOLOMON. What he believed?

VICTOR. The system, the whole thing. He thought it was his fault, I guess. You—you come in with your song and dance, it's all a gag. You're a hundred and fifty years old, you tell your jokes, people fall in love with you, and you walk away with their furniture.

SOLOMON. That's not nice.

VICTOR. Don't shame me, will ya?—What do you say? You don't need to look anymore, you know what I've got here. (SOLOMON *is clearly at the end of his delaying resources. He looks about slowly; the furniture seems to loom over him like a threat or a promise. His eyes climb up to the edges of the ceiling, his hands grasping each other.)* What are you afraid of? It'll keep you busy. (SOLOMON *looks at him, wanting even more reassurance.)*

SOLOMON. You don't think it's foolish?

VICTOR. Who knows what's foolish? You enjoy it—

SOLOMON. Listen, I love it—

VICTOR. So take it. You plan too much, you end up with nothing.

SOLOMON *(intimately).* I would like to tell you something. The last few months, I don't know what it is—she comes to me. You see, I had a daughter, she should rest in peace, she took her own life, a suicide . . .

VICTOR. When was this?

SOLOMON. It was . . . 1916—the latter part. But very beautiful, a lovely face, with large eyes—she was pure like the morning. And lately, I don't know what it is—I see her clear like I see you. And every night practically, I lay down to go to sleep, so she sits there. And you can't help it, you ask yourself —what happened? What *happened?* Maybe I could have said something to her . . . maybe I *did* say something . . . it's all . . . *(He looks at the furniture.)* It's not that I'll die, you can't be afraid of that. But . . . I'll tell you the truth—a minute ago I mentioned I had three wives . . . *(Slight pause. His fear rises.)* Just this minute I realize I had four. Isn't that terrible? The first time was nineteen, in Lithuania. See, that's what I mean—it's impossible to know what is important. Here I'm sitting with you . . . and . . . and . . . *(He looks around at the furniture.)* What for? Not that I don't want it, I want it, but . . . You see, all my life I was a terrible fighter—you could never take nothing from me; I pushed, I pulled, I struggled in six different countries, I nearly got killed a couple times, and it's . . . it's like now I'm sitting here talking to you and I tell you it's a dream, it's a dream! You see, you can't imagine it because—

VICTOR. I know what you're talking about. But it's not a dream—it's that you've got to make decisions before you know what's involved, but you're stuck with the results anyway. Like I was very good in science—I loved it. But I had to drop out to feed the old man. And I figured I'd go on the Force temporarily, just to get us through the Depression, then go back to school. But the war came, we had the kid, and you turn around and you've racked up fifteen years on the pension. And what you started out to do is a million miles away. Not that I regret it all— we brought up a terrific boy, for one thing; nobody's ever going to take that guy. But it's like you were saying—it's impossible to know what's important. We always agreed, we stay out of the rat race and live our own life. That was important. But you shovel the crap out the window, it comes back in under the door —it all ends up she wants, she wants. And I can't really blame her—there's just no respect for anything but money.

SOLOMON. What're you got against money?

VICTOR. Nothing, I just didn't want to lay down my life for it. But I think I laid it down another way, and I'm not even sure anymore what I was trying to accomplish. I look back now, and all I can see is a long, brainless walk in the street. I guess it's the old story; do anything, but just be sure you win. Like my brother; years ago I was living up here with the old man, and he used to contribute five dollars a month. A *month!* And a successful surgeon. But the few times he'd come around, the expression on the old man's face—you'd think God walked in. The respect, you know what I mean? The respect! And why not? Why not?

SOLOMON. Well, sure, he had the power.

VICTOR. Now you said it—if you got that you got it all. You're even lovable! *(He laughs.)* Well, what do you say? Give me the price.

SOLOMON *(slight pause)*. I'll give you eleven hundred dollars.

VICTOR *(slight pause)*. For everything?

SOLOMON *(in a breathless way)*. Everything. *(Slight pause.* VICTOR *looks around at the furniture.)* I want it so I'm giving you a good price. Believe me, you will never do better. I want it; I made up my mind. (VICTOR *continues staring at the stuff.* SOLOMON *takes out a common envelope and removes a wad of bills.)* Here . . . I'll pay you now. *(He readies a bill to start counting it out.)*

VICTOR. It's that I have to split it, see—

SOLOMON. All right . . . so I'll make out a receipt for you and I'll put down six hundred dollars.

VICTOR. No-no . . . *(He gets up and moves at random, looking at the furniture.)*

SOLOMON. Why not? He took from you so take from him. If you want, I'll put down four hundred.

VICTOR. No, I don't want to do that. *(Slight pause)* I'll call you tomorrow.

SOLOMON *(smiling)*. All right; with God's help if I'm there tomorrow I'll answer the phone. If I wouldn't be . . . *(Slight pause)* Then I wouldn't be.

VICTOR *(annoyed, but wanting to believe)*. Don't start that again, will you?

SOLOMON. Look, you convinced me, so I want it. So what should I do?

VICTOR. *I* convinced *you?*

SOLOMON *(very distressed)*. Absolutely you convinced me. You saw it—the minute I looked at it I was going to walk out!

VICTOR *(cutting him off, angered at his own indecision)*. Ah, the hell with it. *(He holds out his hand.)* Give it to me.

SOLOMON *(wanting* VICTOR's *good will)*. Please, don't be blue.

VICTOR. Oh, it all stinks. *(Jabbing forth his hand)*. Come on.

SOLOMON *(with a bill raised over* VICTOR's *hand—protesting)*. What stinks? You should be happy. Now you can buy her a nice coat, take her to Florida, maybe—

VICTOR *(nodding ironically)*. Right, right! We'll all be happy now. Give it to me.

(SOLOMON *shakes his head and counts bills into his hand.* VICTOR *turns his head and looks at the piled walls of furniture.)*

SOLOMON. There's one hundred; two hundred; three hundred; four hundred . . . Take my advice, buy her a nice fur coat your troubles'll be over—

VICTOR. I know all about it. Come on.

SOLOMON. So you got there four, so I'm giving you . . . five, six, seven . . . I mean it's already in the Bible, the rat race. The minute she laid her hand on the apple, that's it.

VICTOR. I never read the Bible. Come on.

SOLOMON. If you'll read it you'll see—there's always a rat race, you can't stay out of it. So you got there seven, so now I'm giving you . . .

(A man appears in the doorway. In his mid-fifties, well barbered; hatless, in a camel's-hair coat, very healthy complexion. A look of sharp intelligence on his face. VICTOR, *seeing past* SOLOMON, *starts slightly with shock, withdrawing his hand from the next bill which* SOLOMON *is about to lay in it.)*

VICTOR *(suddenly flushed, his voice oddly high and boyish)*. Walter!

WALTER *(enters the room, coming to* VICTOR *with extended hand and with a reserve of warmth but a stiff smile)*. How are you, kid?

(SOLOMON *has moved out of their line of sight.)*

VICTOR *(shifts the money to his left hand as he shakes)*. God, I never expected you.

WALTER *(of the money—half-humorously)*. Sorry I'm late. What are you doing?

VICTOR *(fighting a treason to himself, thus taking on a strained humorous air)*. I . . . I just sold it.

WALTER. Good! How much?

VICTOR *(as though absolutely certain now he has been had)*. Ah . . . eleven hundred.

WALTER *(in a dead voice shorn of comment)*. Oh. Well, good. *(He turns rather deliberately—but not overly so—to* SOLOMON.) For everything?

SOLOMON *(comes to* WALTER, *his hand extended; with an energized voice that braves everything)*. I'm very happy to meet you, Doctor! My name is Gregory Solomon.

WALTER (*the look on his face is rather amused, but his reserve has possibilities of accusation.*). How do you do?

(*He shakes Solomon's hand, as Victor raises his hand to smooth down his hair, a look of near-alarm for himself on his face.*)

CURTAIN

ACT TWO

The action is continuous. As the curtain rises WALTER *is just releasing* SOLOMON's *hand and turning about to face* VICTOR. *His posture is reserved, stiffened by traditional control over a nearly fierce curiosity. His grin is disciplined and rather hard, but his eyes are warm and combative.*

WALTER. How's Esther?

VICTOR. Fine. Should be here any minute.

WALTER. Here? Good! And what's Richard doing?

VICTOR. He's at MIT.

WALTER. No kidding! MIT!

VICTOR (*nodding*). They gave him a full scholarship.

WALTER (*dispelling his surprise*). What do you know. (*With a wider smile, and embarrassed warmth*) You're proud.

VICTOR. I guess so. They put him in the Honors Program.

WALTER. Really. That's wonderful. . . . You don't mind my coming, do you?

VICTOR. No! I called you a couple of times.

WALTER. Yes, my nurse told me. What's Richard interested in?

VICTOR: Science. So far, anyway. (*With security*) How're yours?

WALTER (*moving, he breaks the confrontation*). I suppose Jean turned out best—but I don't think you ever saw her.

VICTOR. I never did, no.

WALTER. The *Times* gave her quite a spread last fall. Pretty fair designer.

VICTOR. Oh? That's great. And the boys? They in school?

WALTER. They often are. (*Abruptly laughs, refusing his own embarrassment*) I hardly see them, Vic. With all the unsolved mysteries in the world they're investigating the guitar. But what the hell . . . I've given up worrying about them. (*He walks past* SOLOMON, *glancing at the furniture.*) I'd forgotten how much he had up here. There's your radio!

VICTOR (*smiling with him*). I know, I saw it.

WALTER (*looking down at the radio, then upward to the ceiling through which the battery once exploded. Both laugh. Then he glances with open feeling at* VICTOR). Long time.

VICTOR (*fending off the common emotion*). Yes. How's Dorothy?

WALTER (*cryptically*). She's all right, I guess. (*He moves, glancing at the things, but again with suddenness turns back.*) Looking forward to seeing Esther again. She still writing poetry?

VICTOR. No, not for years now.

SOLOMON. He's got a very nice wife. We met.

WALTER (*surprised; as though at something intrusive*). Oh? (*He turns back to the furniture.*) Well. Same old junk, isn't it?

VICTOR (*downing a greater protest*). I wouldn't say that. Some of it isn't bad.

SOLOMON. One or two very nice things, Doctor. We came to a very nice agreement.

VICTOR (*with an implied rebuke*). I never thought you'd show up; I guess we'd better start all over again—

WALTER. Oh, no-no, I don't want to foul up your deal.

SOLOMON. Excuse me, Doctor—better you should take what you want now than we'll argue later. What did you want?

WALTER (*surprised, turning to* VICTOR). Oh, I didn't want anything. I came by to say hello, that's all.

VICTOR. I see. (*Fending off* WALTER's *apparent gesture with an overquick movement toward the oar*) I found your oar, if you want it.

WALTER. Oar? (*Victor draws it out from behind furniture. A curved-blade sweep*) Hah! (*He receives the oar, looks up its length, and laughs, hefting it.*) I must have been out of my mind!

SOLOMON. Excuse me, Doctor; if you want the oar—

WALTER (*standing the oar before* SOLOMON, *whom he leaves holding on to it*). Don't get excited, I don't want it.

SOLOMON. No. I was going to say—a personal thing like this I have no objection.

WALTER (*half laughing*). That's very generous of you.

VICTOR (*apologizing for* SOLOMON). I

threw in everything—I never thought you'd get here.

WALTER *(with a strained overagreeableness).* Sure, that's all right. What are you taking?

VICTOR. Nothing, really. Esther might want a lamp or something like that.

SOLOMON. He's not interested, you see; he's a modern person, what are you going to do?

WALTER. You're not taking the harp?

VICTOR *(with a certain guilt).* Well, nobody plays . . . You take it, if you like.

SOLOMON. You'll excuse me, Doctor—the harp, please, that's another story . . .

WALTER *(laughs—archly amused and put out).* You don't mind if I make a suggestion, do you?

SOLOMON. Doctor, please, don't be offended, I only—

WALTER. Well, why do you interrupt? Relax, we're only talking. We haven't seen each other for a long time.

SOLOMON. Couldn't be better; I'm very sorry. *(He sits, nervously pulling his cheek.)*

WALTER *(touching the harp).* Kind of a pity—this was Grandpa's wedding present, you know.

VICTOR *(looking with surprise at the harp).* Say—that's right!

WALTER *(to* SOLOMON). What are you giving him for this?

SOLOMON. I didn't itemize—one price for everything. Maybe three hundred dollars. That sounding board is cracked, you know.

VICTOR *(to* WALTER). You want it?

SOLOMON. Please, Victor, I hope you're not going to take that away from me. *(To* WALTER) Look, Doctor, I'm not trying to fool you. The harp is the heart and soul of the deal. I realize it was your mother's harp, but like I tried to tell—*(to* VICTOR)—you before —*(to* WALTER)—with used furniture you cannot be emotional.

WALTER. I guess it doesn't matter. *(To* VICTOR) Actually, I was wondering if he kept any of Mother's evening gowns, did he?

VICTOR. I haven't really gone through it all—

SOLOMON *(raising a finger, eagerly).* Wait, wait, I think I can help you. *(He goes to an armoire he had earlier looked into, and opens it.)*

WALTER *(moving toward the armoire).* She had some spectacular—

SOLOMON *(drawing out the bottom of a gown elaborately embroidered in gold).* Is this what you mean?

WALTER. Yes, that's the stuff! (SOLOMON *blows dust off and hands him the bottom of the gown.)* Isn't that beautiful! Say, I think she wore this at my wedding! *(He takes it out of the closet, holds it up.)* Sure! You remember this?

VICTOR: What do you want with it?

WALTER *(drawing out another gown off the rack).* Look at this one! Isn't that something? I though Jeannie might make something new out of the material. I'd like her to wear something of Mother's.

VICTOR *(a new, surprising idea).* Oh! Fine, that's a nice idea.

SOLOMON. Take, take—they're beautiful.

WALTER *(suddenly glancing about as he lays the gowns across a chair).* What happened to the piano?

VICTOR. Oh, we sold that while I was still in school. We lived on it for a long time.

WALTER *(very interestedly).* I never knew that.

VICTOR. Sure. And the silver.

WALTER. Of course! Stupid of me not to remember that. *(He half sits against the back of a couch. His interest is avid, and his energy immense.)* I suppose you know—you've gotten to look a great deal like Dad.

VICTOR. *I* do?

WALTER. It's very striking. And your voice is very much like his.

VICTOR. I know. It has that sound to me, sometimes.

SOLOMON. So, gentlemen . . . *(He moves the money in his hand.)*

VICTOR *(indicating* SOLOMON). Maybe we'd better settle this now.

WALTER. Yes, go ahead! *(He walks off, looking at the furniture.)*

SOLOMON *(indicating the money* VICTOR *holds).* You got there seven—

WALTER *(oblivious of* SOLOMON; *unable, so to speak, to settle for the status quo).* Wonderful to see you looking so well.

VICTOR *(the new interruption seems odd; observing more than speaking).* You do too, you look great.

WALTER. I ski a lot; and I ride nearly every morning. . . . You know, I started to call you a dozen times this year *(He breaks off. Indicating* SOLOMON) Finish up, I'll talk to you later.

SOLOMON. So now I'm going to give you— *(A bill is poised over* VICTOR*'s hand.)*

VICTOR *(to* WALTER*).* That price all right with you?

WALTER. Oh, I don't want to interfere. It's just that I dealt with these fellows when I split up Dorothy's and my stuff last year, and I found—

VICTOR *(from an earlier impression).* You're not divorced, are you?

WALTER *(with a nervous shot of laughter).* Yes!

(ESTHER *enters on his line; she is carrying a suit in a plastic wrapper.)*

ESTHER *(surprised).* Walter! For heaven's sake!

WALTER *(eagerly jumping up, coming to her, shaking her hand).* How are you, Esther!

ESTHER *(between her disapproval and fascinated surprise).* What are *you* doing here?

WALTER. You've hardly changed!

ESTHER *(with a charged laugh, conflicted with herself).* Oh, go on now! *(She hangs the suit on a chest handle.)*

WALTER *(to* VICTOR*).* You son of a gun, she looks twenty-five!

VICTOR *(watching for* ESTHER*'s reaction).* I know!

ESTHER *(flattered, and offended, too).* Oh, stop it, Walter! *(She sits.)*

WALTER. But you do, honestly; you look marvelous.

SOLOMON. It's that suit, you see? What did I tell you, it's a very beautiful suit.

(VICTOR *laughs a little as* ESTHER *looks conflicted by* SOLOMON*'s compliment.)*

ESTHER *(with mock affront—to* VICTOR*).* What are you laughing at? It is. *(She is about to laugh.)*

VICTOR. You looked so surprised, that's all.

ESTHER. Well, I'm not used to walking into all these compliments! *(She bursts out laughing.)*

WALTER *(suddenly recalling—eagerly).* Say! I'm sorry I didn't know I'd be seeing you when I left the house this morning—I'd have brought you some lovely Indian bracelets. I got a whole boxful from Bombay.

ESTHER *(still not focused on* WALTER*, sizing him up).* How do you come to—?

WALTER. I operated on this big textile guy and he keeps sending me things. He sent me this coat, in fact.

ESTHER. I was noticing it. That's gorgeous material.

WALTER. Isn't it? Two gallstones.

ESTHER *(her impression lingering for the instant).* How's Dorothy? Did I hear you saying you were—?

WALTER *(very seriously).* We're divorced, ya. Last winter.

ESTHER. I'm sorry to hear that.

WALTER. It was coming a long time. We're both much better off—we're almost friendly now. *(He laughs.)*

ESTHER. Oh, stop that, you dog.

WALTER *(with naïve excitement).* It's true!

ESTHER. Look, I'm for the woman, so don't hand me that. *(To Victor—seeing the money in his hand)* Have you settled everything?

VICTOR. Just about, I guess.

WALTER. I was just telling Victor *(to* VICTOR*)* when we split things up I *(to* SOLOMON*)* —you ever hear of Spitzer and Fox?

SOLOMON. Thirty years I know Spitzer and Fox. Bert Fox worked for me maybe ten, twelve years.

WALTER. They did my appraisal.

SOLOMON. They're good boys. Spitzer is not as good as Fox, but between the two you're in good hands.

WALTER. Yes. That's why I—

SOLOMON. Spitzer is vice-president of the Appraisers' Association.

WALTER. I see. The point I'm making—

SOLOMON. I used to be president.

WALTER. Really.

SOLOMON. Oh, yes. I made it all ethical.

WALTER *(trying to keep a straight face—and* VICTOR *as well).* Did you?

(VICTOR *suddenly bursts out laughing, which sets off* WALTER *and* ESTHER*, and a warmth springs up among them.)*

SOLOMON *(smiling, but insistent).* What's so funny? Listen, before me was a jungle—you wouldn't laugh so much. I put in all the rates, what we charge, you know—I made it a profession, like doctors, lawyers—used to be it was a regular snakepit. But today, you got nothing to worry—all the members are hundred percent ethical.

WALTER. Well, that was a good deed, Mr. Solomon—but I think you can do a little better on this furniture.

ESTHER *(to* VICTOR*, who has money in his hand).* How much has he offered?

VICTOR *(embarrassed, but braving it quite well).* Eleven hundred.

ESTHER *(distressed; with a transcendent protest).* Oh, I think that's . . . isn't that very low? *(She looks to* WALTER*'s confirmation.)*

WALTER *(familiarly).* Come on, Solomon.

He's been risking his life for you every day; be generous—

SOLOMON (to ESTHER). That's a real brother! Wonderful. (To WALTER). But you can call anybody you like—Spitzer and Fox, Joe Brody, Paul Cavallo, Morris White—I know them all and I know what they'll tell you.

VICTOR (striving to retain some assurance; to ESTHER). See, the point he was making about it—

SOLOMON (to ESTHER, raising his finger). Listen to him because he—

VICTOR (to SOLOMON). Hold it one second, will you? (To ESTHER and WALTER) Not that I'm saying it's true, but he claims a lot of it is too big to get into the new apartments.

ESTHER (half-laughing). You believe that?

WALTER. I don't know, Esther, Spitzer and Fox said the same thing.

ESTHER. Walter, the city is full of big, old apartments!

SOLOMON. Darling, why don't you leave it to the boys?

ESTHER (suppressing an outburst). I wish you wouldn't order me around, Mr. Solomon! (To Walter, protesting) Those two bureaus alone are worth a couple of hundred dollars!

WALTER (delicately). Maybe I oughtn't interfere—

ESTHER. Why? (Of Solomon) Don't let him bulldoze you—

SOLOMON. My dear girl, you're talking without a basis—

ESTHER (slashing). I don't like this kind of dealing, Mr. Solomon! I just don't like it! (She is near tears. A pause. She turns back to WALTER.) This money is very important to us, Walter.

WALTER (chastised). Yes. I . . . I'm sorry, Esther. (He looks about.) Well . . . if it was mine—

ESTHER. Why? It's yours as much as Victor's.

WALTER. Oh, no, dear—I wouldn't take anything from this.

(Pause)

VICTOR. No, Walter, you get half.

WALTER. I wouldn't think of it, kid. I came by to say hello, that's all.

(Pause)

ESTHER (she is very moved.) That's terrific, Walter. It's . . . really, I . . .

VICTOR. Well, we'll talk about it.

WALTER. No-no, Vic, you've earned it. It's yours.

VICTOR. (rejecting the implication). Why have I earned it? You take your share.

WALTER. Why don't we discuss it later? (To SOLOMON) In my opinion—

SOLOMON (to VICTOR). So now you don't even have to split. (To VICTOR and WALTER) You're lucky they're tearing the building down—you got together, finally.

WALTER. I would have said a minimum of three thousand dollars.

ESTHER. That's exactly what I had in mind! (To SOLOMON) I was going to say thirty-five hundred dollars.

WALTER (to VICTOR; tactfully). In that neighborhood.

(Silence. SOLOMON sits there holding back comment, not looking at VICTOR, blinking with protest. VICTOR thinks for a moment; then turns to SOLOMON, and there is a wide discouragement in his voice.)

VICTOR. Well? What do you say?

SOLOMON (spreading out his hands helplessly, outraged). What can I say? It's ridiculous. Why does he give you three thousand? What's the matter with five thousand, ten thousand?

WALTER (to VICTOR, without criticism). You should've gotten a couple of other estimates, you see, that's always the—

VICTOR. I've been calling you all week for just that reason, Walter, and you never came to the phone.

WALTER (blushing). Why would that stop you from—?

VICTOR. I didn't think I had the right to do it alone—the nurse gave you my messages, didn't she?

WALTER. I've been terribly tied up—and I had no intention of taking anything for myself, so I assumed—

VICTOR. But how was I supposed to know that?

WALTER (with open self-reproach). Yes. Well, I . . . I beg your pardon. (He decides to stop there.)

SOLOMON. Excuse me, Doctor, but I can't understand you; first it's a lot of junk—

ESTHER. Nobody called it a lot of junk!

SOLOMON. He called it a lot of junk, Esther, when he walked in here.

(ESTHER turns to WALTER, puzzled and angry.)

WALTER (reacting to her look; to SOLOMON). Now just a minute—

SOLOMON. No, please. (Indicating VICTOR) This is a factual man, so let's be factual.

ESTHER. Well, that's an awfully strange thing to say, Walter.

WALTER (intimately). I didn't mean it in that sense, Esther—

SOLOMON. Doctor, please. You said junk.

WALTER (sharply—and there is an over-meaning of much greater anger in his tone). I didn't mean it in that sense, Mr. Solomon! (He controls himself—and, half to ESTHER.) When you've been brought up with things, you tend to be sick of them . . . (To ESTHER) That's all I meant.

SOLOMON. My dear man, if it was Louis Seize, Biedermeier, something like that, you wouldn't get sick.

WALTER (pointing to a piece, and weakened by knowing he is exaggerating). Well, there happens to be a piece right over there in Biedermeier style!

SOLOMON. Biedermeier "style!" (He picks up his hat.) I got a hat it's in Borsalino style but it's not a Borsalino. (To VICTOR) I mean he don't have to charge me to make an impression.

WALTER (striving for an air of amusement). Now what's that supposed to mean?

VICTOR (with a refusal to dump SOLOMON). Well, what basis do you go on, Walter?

WALTER (reddening but smiling). I don't know . . . it's a feeling, that's all.

ESTHER (there is ridicule). Well, on what basis do you take eleven hundred, dear?

VICTOR (angered; his manly leadership is suddenly in front). I simply felt it was probably more or less right!

ESTHER (as a refrain). Oh God, here we go again. All right, throw it away—

SOLOMON (indicating VICTOR). Please, Esther, he's not throwing nothing away. This man is no fool! (To Walter as well) Excuse me, but this is not right to do to him!

WALTER (bridling, but retaining his smile). You going to teach me what's right now?

ESTHER (to VICTOR, expanding WALTER's protest). Really! I mean.

VICTOR (obeying her protest for want of a certainty of his own, he touches SOLOMON's shoulder). Mr. Solomon . . . why don't you sit down in the bedroom for a few minutes and let us talk?

SOLOMON. Certainly, whatever you say. (He gets up.) Only please, you made a very nice deal, you got no right to be ashamed . . . (To ESTHER) Excuse me, I don't want to be personal.

ESTHER (laughs angrily). He's fantastic!

VICTOR (trying to get him moving again). Whyn't you go inside?

SOLOMON. I'm going; I only want you to understand, Victor, that if it was a different kind of man (turning to ESTHER) I would say to you that he's got the money in his hand, so the deal is concluded.

WALTER. He can't conclude any deal without me, Solomon, I'm half owner here.

SOLOMON (to VICTOR). You see? What did I ask you the first thing I walked in here? "Who is the owner?"

WALTER. Why do you confuse everything? I'm not making any claim, I merely—

SOLOMON. Then how do you come to interfere? He's got the money; I know the law!

WALTER (angering). Now you stop being foolish! Just stop it! I've got the best lawyers in New York, so go inside and sit down.

VICTOR (as he turns back to escort SOLOMON). Take it easy, Walter, come on, cut it out.

ESTHER (striving to keep a light, amused tone). Why? He's perfectly right.

VICTOR (with a hard glance at her, moving upstage with SOLOMON). Here, you better hold onto this money.

SOLOMON. No, that's yours; you hold . . . (He sways. VICTOR grasps his arm. WALTER gets up.)

WALTER. You all right?

SOLOMON (dizzy, he grasps his head). Yes, yes, I'm . . .

WALTER (coming to him). Let me look at you. (He takes SOLOMON's wrists, looks into his face.)

SOLOMON. I'm only a little tired, I didn't take my nap today.

WALTER. Come in here, lie down for a moment. (He starts SOLOMON toward the bedroom.)

SOLOMON. Don't worry about me, I'm . . . (He halts and points back at his portfolio, leaning on a chest.) Please, Doctor, if you wouldn't mind—I got a Hershey's in there. (WALTER hesitates to do his errand.) Helps me. (WALTER unwillingly goes to the portfolio and reaches into it.) I'm a very healthy person, but a nap, you see, I have to have a . . . (WALTER takes out an orange.) Not the orange—on the bottom is a Hershey's. (WALTER takes out a Hershey bar.) That's a boy.

WALTER (returns to him and helps him to the bedroom). All right, come on . . . easy does it . . .

SOLOMON (as he goes into the bedroom).

I'm all right, don't worry. You're very nice people.

(SOLOMON *and* WALTER *exit into the bedroom.* VICTOR *glances at the money in his hand, then puts it on a table, setting the foil on it.)*

ESTHER. Why are you being so apologetic?

VICTOR. About what?

ESTHER. That old man. Was that his first offer?

VICTOR. Why do you believe Walter? He was obviously pulling a number out of a hat.

ESTHER. Well, I agree with him. Did you try to get him to go higher?

VICTOR. I don't know how to bargain and I'm not going to start now.

ESTHER. I wish you wouldn't be above everything, Victor, we're not twenty years old. We need this money. *(He is silent.)* You hear me?

VICTOR. I've made a deal, and that's it. You know, you take a tone sometimes—like I'm some kind of an incompetent.

ESTHER *(gets up, moves restlessly).* Well anyway, you'll get the whole amount.—God, he's certainly changed. It's amazing.

VICTOR *(without assent).* Seems so, ya.

ESTHER *(wanting him to join her).* He's so human! And he laughs!

VICTOR. I've seen him laugh.

ESTHER *(with a grin of trepidation).* Am I hearing something or is that my imagination?

VICTOR. I want to think about it.

ESTHER *(quietly).* You're not taking his share?

VICTOR. I said I would like to think . . .

(Assuming he will refuse WALTER'*s share, she really doesn't know what to do or where to move, so she goes for her purse with a quick stride.)*

VICTOR *(getting up).* Where you going?

ESTHER *(turning back on him).* I want to know. Are you or aren't you taking his share?

VICTOR. Esther, I've been calling him all week; doesn't even bother to come to the phone, walks in here and smiles and I'm supposed to fall into his arms? I can't behave as though nothing ever happened, and you're not going to either! Now just take it easy, we're not dying of hunger.

ESTHER. I don't understand what you think you're upholding!

VICTOR *(outraged).* Where have you been?!

ESTHER. But he's doing exactly what you thought he should do! What do you *want?*

VICTOR. Certain things have happened, haven't they? I can't turn around this fast, kid. He's only been here ten minutes, I've got twenty-eight years to shake off my back. . . . now sit down, I want you here. *(He sits. She remains standing, uncertain of what to do.)* Please. You can wait a few minutes for your drink.

ESTHER *(in despair).* Vic, it's all blowing away.

VICTOR *(to diminish the entire prize).* Half of eleven hundred dollars is five-fifty, dear.

ESTHER. I'm not talking about money. *(Voices are heard from the bedroom.)* He's obviously making a gesture, why can't you open yourself a little? *(She lays her head back.)* My mother was right—I can never believe anything I see. But I'm going to. That's all I'm going to do. What I see.

(A chair scrapes in the bedroom.)

VICTOR. Wipe your cheek, will you? (WALTER *enters from the bedroom.)* How is he?

WALTER. I think he'll be all right. *(Warmly)* God, what a pirate! *(He sits.)* He's eighty-nine!

ESTHER. I don't believe it!

VICTOR. He is. He showed me his—

WALTER *(laughing).* Oh, he show you that too?

VICTOR *(smiling).* Ya, the British Navy.

ESTHER. *He* was in the British Navy?

VICTOR *(building on Walter's support).* He's got a discharge. He's not altogether phony.

WALTER. I wouldn't go that far. A guy that age, though, still driving like that . . . *(As though admitting* VICTOR *was not foolish).* There *is* something wonderful about it.

VICTOR *(understating).* I think so.

ESTHER. What do you think we ought to do, Walter?

WALTER *(slight pause. He is trying to modify what he believes is his overpowering force so as not to appear to be taking over. He is faintly smiling toward* VICTOR*).* There is a way to get a good deal more out of it. I suppose you know that, though.

VICTOR. Look, I'm not married to this guy. If you want to call another dealer we can compare.

WALTER. You don't have to do that; he's a registered appraiser.—You see, instead of selling it, you could make it a charitable contribution.

VICTOR. I don't understand.

WALTER. It's perfectly simple. He puts a

value on it—let's say twenty-five thousand dollars, and—

ESTHER *(fascinated, with a laugh)*. Are you kidding?

WALTER. It's done all the time. It's a dream world but it's legal. He estimates its highest retail value, which could be put at some such figure. Then I donate it to the Salvation Army. I'd have to take ownership, you see, because my tax rate is much higher than yours so it would make more sense if I took the deduction. I pay around fifty percent tax, so if I make a twenty-five-thousand-dollar contribution I'd be saving around twelve thousand in taxes. Which we could split however you wanted. Let's say we split it in half, I'd give you six thousand dollars. *(A pause.)* It's really the only sensible way to do it, Vic.

ESTHER *(glances at VICTOR, but he remains silent)*. Would it be costing you anything?

WALTER. On the contrary—it's found money to me. *(To VICTOR)*. I mentioned it to him just now.

VICTOR *(as though this had been the question)*. What'd he say?

WALTER. It's up to you. We'd pay him an appraisal fee—fifty, sixty bucks.

VICTOR. Is he willing to do that?

WALTER. Well, of course he'd rather buy it outright, but what the hell—

ESTHER. Well, that's not his decision, is it?

VICTOR. No . . . it's just that I feel I did come to an agreement with him and I—

WALTER. Personally, I wouldn't let that bother me. He'd be making fifty bucks for filling out a piece of paper.

ESTHER. That's not bad for an afternoon. *(Pause)*

VICTOR. I'd like to think about it.

ESTHER. There's not much time, though, if you want to deal with *him*.

VICTOR *(cornered)*. I'd like a few minutes, that's all.

WALTER *(to ESTHER)*. Sure . . . let him think it over. *(To VICTOR)*. It's perfectly legal, if that's what's bothering you. I almost did it with my stuff but I finally decided to keep it. *(He laughs.)* In fact, my own apartment is so loaded up it doesn't look too different from this.

ESTHER. Well, maybe you'll get married again.

WALTER. I doubt that very much, Esther. —I often feel I never should have.

ESTHER *(scoffing)*. Why!

WALTER. Seriously. I'm in a strange business, you know. There's too much to learn and far too little time to learn it. And there's a price you have to pay for that. I tried awfully hard to kid myself but there's simply no time for people. Not the way a woman expects, if she's any kind of woman. *(He laughs.)* But I'm doing pretty well alone!

VICTOR. How would I list an amount like that on my income tax?

WALTER. Well . . . call it a gift. (VICTOR *is silent, obviously in conflict.* WALTER *sees the emotion.)* Not that it is, but you could list it as such. It's allowed.

VICTOR. I see. I was just curious how it—

WALTER. Just enter it as a gift. There's no problem. *(With the first sting of a vague resentment,* WALTER *turns his eyes away.* ESTHER *raises her eyebrows, staring at the floor.* WALTER *lifts the foil off the table—clearly changing the subject.)* You still fence?

VICTOR *(almost gratefully pursuing this diversion)*. No, you got to join a club and all that. And I work weekends often. I just found it here.

WALTER *(as though to warm the mood)*. Mother used to love to watch him do this.

ESTHER *(surprised, pleased)*. Really?

WALTER. Sure, she used to come to all his matches.

ESTHER *(to Victor, somehow charmed)*. You never told me that.

WALTER. Of course; she's the one made him take it up. *(He laughs to Victor.)* She thought it was elegant!

VICTOR. Hey, that's right!

WALTER *(laughing at the memory)*. He did look pretty good too! *(He spreads his jacket away from his chest.)* I've still got the wounds! *(To Victor, who laughs).* Especially with those French gauntlets she—

VICTOR. *(recalling)*. Say . . . ! *(Looking around with an enlivened need).* I wonder where the hell . . . *(He suddenly moves toward a bureau.)* Wait, I think they used to be in . . .

ESTHER *(to WALTER)*. *French* gauntlets?

WALTER. She brought them from Paris. Gorgeously embroidered. He looked like one of the musketeers.

(Out of the drawer where he earlier found the ice skate, Victor takes a pair of emblazoned gauntlets.)

VICTOR. Here they are! What do you know!

ESTHER *(reaching her hand out)*. Aren't they beautiful!

(He hands her one.)

VICTOR. God, I'd forgotten all about them. *(He slips one on his hand.)*

WALTER. Christmas, 1929.

VICTOR *(moving his hand in the gauntlet).* Look at that, they're still soft . . . *(To WALTER—a little shy in asking).* How do you remember all this stuff?

WALTER. Why not? Don't you?

ESTHER. He doesn't remember your mother very well.

VICTOR. I remember her. *(Looking at the gauntlet).* It's just her face; somehow I can never *see* her.

WALTER *(warmly).* That's amazing, Vic. *(To* ESTHER). She adored him.

ESTHER *(pleased).* Did she?

WALTER. Victor? If it started to rain she'd run all the way to school with his galoshes. Her Victor—my God! By the time he could light a match he was already Louis Pasteur.

VICTOR. It's odd . . . like the harp! I can almost hear the music . . . but I can never see her face. Somehow. *(For a moment, silence, as he looks across at the harp).*

WALTER. What's the problem?

(Pause. VICTOR*'s eyes are swollen with feeling. He turns and looks up at* WALTER, *who suddenly is embarrassed and oddly anxious.)*

SOLOMON *(enters from the bedroom. He looks quite distressed. He is in his vest, his tie is open. Without coming downstage).* Please, Doctor, if you wouldn't mind I would like to . . . *(He breaks off, indicating the bedroom.)*

WALTER. What is it?

SOLOMON. Just for one minute, please.

*(*WALTER *stands.* SOLOMON *glances at* VICTOR *and* ESTHER *and returns to the bedroom.)*

WALTER. I'll be right back. *(He goes rather quickly up and into the bedroom.)*

(A pause. VICTOR *is sitting in silence, unable to face her.)*

ESTHER *(with delicacy and pity, sensing his conflicting feelings).* Why can't you take him as he is? *(He glances at her.)* Well, you can't expect him to go into an apology, Vic—he probably sees it all differently, anyway. *(He is silent. She comes to him.)* I know it's difficult, but he is trying to make a gesture, I think.

VICTOR. I guess he is, yes.

ESTHER. You know what would be lovely? If we could take a few weeks and go to like . . . out-of-the-way places . . . just to really break it up and see all the things that people do. You've been around such mean, petty people for so long and little ugly tricks. I'm serious—it's not romantic. We're much too suspicious of everything.

VICTOR *(staring ahead).* Strange guy.

ESTHER. Why?

VICTOR. Well, to walk in that way—as though nothing ever happened.

ESTHER. Why not? What can be done about it?

VICTOR *(slight pause).* I feel I have to say something.

ESTHER *(with a slight trepidation, less than she feels).* What can you say?

VICTOR. You feel I ought to just take the money and shut up, heh?

ESTHER. But what's the point of going backwards?

VICTOR *(with a self-bracing tension).* I'm not going to take this money unless I talk to him.

ESTHER *(frightened).* You can't bear the thought that he's decent. *(He looks at her sharply.)* That's all it is, dear. I'm sorry, I have to say it.

VICTOR *(without raising his voice).* I can't bear that he's *decent!*

ESTHER. You throw this away, you've got to explain it to me. You can't go on blaming everything on him or the system or God knows what else! You're free and you can't make a move, Victor, and that's what's driving me crazy! *(Silence; quietly).* Now take this money. *(He is silent, staring at her.)* You take this money! Or I'm washed up. You hear me? If you're stuck it doesn't mean I have to be. Now that's it.

(Movements are heard within the bedroom. She straightens. VICTOR *smooths down his hair with a slow, preparatory motion of his hand, like one adjusting himself for combat.)*

WALTER *(enters from the bedroom, smiling, shaking his head. Indicating the bedroom).* Boy—we got a tiger here. What is this between you, did you know him before?

VICTOR. No. Why? What'd he say?

WALTER. He's still trying to buy it outright. *(He laughs.)* He talks like you added five years by calling him up.

VICTOR. Well, what's the difference, I don't mind.

WALTER *(registering the distant rebuke).* No, that's fine, that's all right. *(He sits. Slight pause).* We don't understand each other, do we?

VICTOR *(with a certain thrust, matching* WALTER*'s smile).* I am a little confused, Walter . . . yes.

WALTER. Why is that? (VICTOR *doesn't answer at once.)* Come on, we'll all be dead soon!

VICTOR. All right, I'll give you one example. When I called you Monday and Tuesday and again this morning—

WALTER. I've explained that.

VICTOR. But I don't make phone calls to pass the time. Your nurse sounded like I was a pest of some kind . . . it was humiliating.

WALTER *(oddly, he is overupset)*. I'm terribly sorry, she shouldn't have done that.

VICTOR. I know, Walter, but I can't imagine she takes that tone all by herself.

WALTER *(aware now of the depth of resentment in* VICTOR*)*. Oh, no—she's often that way. I've never referred to you like that. (VICTOR *is silent, not convinced.)* Believe me, will you? I'm terribly sorry. I'm overwhelmed with work, that's all it is.

VICTOR. Well, you asked me, so I'm telling you.

WALTER. Yes! You should! But don't misinterpret that. *(Slight pause. His tension has increased. He braves a smile.)* Now about this tax thing. He'd be willing to make the appraisal twenty-five thousand. *(With difficulty).* If you'd like, I'd be perfectly willing for you to have the whole amount I'd be saving.

(Slight pause.)

ESTHER. Twelve thousand?

WALTER. Whatever it comes to. *(Pause.* ESTHER *slowly looks to* VICTOR.*)* You must be near retirement now, aren't you?

ESTHER *(excitedly)*. He's past it. But he's trying to decide what to do.

WALTER. Oh. *(To* VICTOR—*near open embarrassment now)*. It would come in handy, then, wouldn't it? *(*VICTOR *glances at him as a substitute for a reply.)* I don't need it, that's all, Vic. Actually, I've been about to call you for quite some time now.

VICTOR. What for?

WALTER *(suddenly, with a strange quick laugh, he reaches and touches Victor's knee)*. Don't be suspicious!

VICTOR *(grinning)*. I'm just trying to figure it out, Walter.

WALTER. Yes, good. All right. *(Slight pause)*. I thought it was time we got to know each other. That's all.

(Slight pause.)

VICTOR. You know, Walter, I tried to call you a couple of times before this about the furniture—must be three years ago.

WALTER. I was sick.

VICTOR *(surprised)*. Oh . . . Because I left a lot of messages.

WALTER. I was quite sick. I was hospitalized.

ESTHER. What happened?

WALTER *(slight pause. As though he were not quite sure whether to say it)*. I broke down. *(Slight pause.)*

VICTOR. I had no idea.

WALTER. Actually, I'm only beginning to catch up with things. I was out of commisson for nearly three years. *(With a thrust of success)* But I'm almost thankful for it now— I've never been happier!

ESTHER. You seem altogether different!

WALTER. I think I am, Esther. I live differently, I think differently. All I have now is a small apartment. And I got rid of the nursing homes—

VICTOR. What nursing homes?

WALTER *(with a removed self-amusement)*. Oh, I owned three nursing homes. There's big money in the aged, you know. Helpless, desperate children trying to dump their parents —nothing like it. I even pulled out of the market. Fifty percent of my time now is in City hospitals. And I tell you, I'm alive. For the first time. I do medicine, and that's it. *(Attempting an intimate grin)* Not that I don't soak the rich occasionally, but only enough to live, really. *(It is as though this was his mission here, and he waits for Victor's comment.)*

VICTOR. Well, that must be great.

WALTER *(seizing on this minute encouragement)*. Vic, I wish we could talk for weeks, there's so much I want to tell you. . . . *(It is not rolling quite the way he would wish and he must pick examples of his new feelings out of the air.)* I never had friends—you probably know that. But I do now, I have good friends. *(He moves, sitting nearer* VICTOR, *his enthusiasm flowing.)* It all happens so gradually. You start out wanting to be the best, and there's no question that you do need a certain fanaticism; there's so much to know and so little time. Until you've eliminated everything extraneous *(he smiles)* including people. And of course the time comes when you realize that you haven't merely been specializing in something—something has been specializing in you. You become a kind of instrument, an instrument that cuts money out of people, or fame out of the world. And it finally makes you stupid. Power can do that. You get to think that because you can frighten people they love you. Even that you love them. And the whole thing comes down to fear. One night I found myself in the middle of my living room, dead drunk with a knife in my hand, getting ready to kill my wife.

ESTHER. Good Lord!

WALTER. Oh, ya—and I nearly made it, too! *(He laughs.)* But there's one virtue in going nuts—provided you survive, of course. You get to see the terror—not the screaming kind, but the slow, daily fear you call ambition, and cautiousness, and piling up the money. And really, what I wanted to tell you for some time now—is that you helped me to understand that in myself.

VICTOR. Me?

WALTER. Yes. *(He grins warmly, embarrassed.)* Because of what you did. I could never understand it, Vic—after all, you *were* the better student. And to stay with a job like that through all those years seemed . . . *(He breaks off momentarily, the uncertainty of* VICTOR's *reception widening his smile.)* You see, it never dawned on me until I got sick— that you'd made a choice.

VICTOR. A choice, how?

WALTER. You wanted a real life. And that's an expensive thing; it costs. *(He has found his theme now; sees he has at last touched something in* VICTOR. *A breath of confidence comes through now.)* I know I may sound terribly naïve, but I'm still used to talking about anything that matters. Frankly, I didn't answer your calls this week because I was afraid. I've struggled so long for a concept of myself and I'm not sure I can make it believable to you. But I'd like to. *(He sees permission to go on in* VICTOR's *perplexed eyes.)* You see, I got to a certain point where . . . I dreaded my own work; I finally couldn't cut. There are times, as you know, when if you leave someone alone he might live a year or two; while if you go in you might kill him. And the decision is often . . . not quite, but almost . . . arbitrary. But the odds are acceptable, provided you think the right thoughts. Or don't think at all, which I managed to do till then. *(Slight pause. He is no longer smiling; instead, a near-embarrassment is on him.)* I ran into a cluster of misjudgments. It can happen, but it never had to me, not one on top of the other. And they had one thing in common; they'd all been diagnosed by other men as inoperable. And quite suddenly the . . . the whole prospect of my own motives opened up. Why had I taken risks that very competent men had declined? And the quick answer, of course, is—to pull

off the impossible. Shame the competition. But suddenly I saw something else. And it was terror. In dead center, directing my brains, my hands, my ambition—for thirty years.

(Slight pause.)

VICTOR. Terror of what?

(Pause.)

WALTER *(his gaze direct on* VICTOR *now).* Of it ever happening to me *(he glances at the center chair)* as it happened to him. Overnight, for no reason, to find yourself degraded and thrown down. *(With the faintest hint of impatience and challenge)* You know what I'm talking about, don't you? (VICTOR *turns away slightly, refusing commitment.)* Isn't that why you turned your back on it all?

VICTOR *(sensing the relevancy to himself now).* Partly. Not altogether, though.

WALTER. Vic, we were both running from the same thing. I thought I wanted to be tops, but what it was was untouchable. I ended in a swamp of success and bankbooks, you on civil service. The difference is that you haven't hurt other people to defend yourself. And I've learned to respect that, Vic; you simply tried to make yourself useful.

ESTHER. That's wonderful—to come to such an understanding with yourself.

WALTER. Esther, it's a strange thing; in the hospital, for the first time since we were boys, I began to feel . . . like a brother. In the sense that we shared something. *(To* VICTOR) And I feel I would know how to be friends now.

VICTOR *(slight pause; he is unsure).* Well, fine. I'm glad of that.

WALTER *(sees the reserve but feels he has made headway and presses on a bit more urgently).* You see, that's why you're still so married. That's a very rare thing. And why your boy's in such good shape. You've lived a real life. *(To* ESTHER) But you know that better than I.

ESTHER. I don't know what I know, Walter.

WALTER. Don't doubt it, dear—believe me, you're fortunate people. *(To* VICTOR) You know that, don't you?

VICTOR *(without looking at* ESTHER). I think so.

ESTHER. It's not quite as easy as you make it, Walter.

WALTER *(hesitates, then throws himself into it).* Look, I've had a wild idea—it'll probably seem absurd to you, but I wish you'd think about it before you dismiss it. I gather you haven't decided what to do with yourself now? You're retiring . . . ?

VICTOR. I'll decide one of these days, I'm still thinking.

WALTER *(nervously)*. Could I suggest something?

VICTOR. Sure, go ahead.

WALTER. We've been interviewing people for the new wing. For the administrative side. Kind of liaison people between the scientists and the board. And it occurred to me several times that you might fit in there.

(Slight pause.)

ESTHER *(with a release of expectation)*. That would be wonderful!

VICTOR *(slight pause; he glances at her with suppression, but his voice betrays excitement)*. What could I do there, though?

WALTER *(sensing VICTOR's interest)*. It's kind of fluid at the moment, but there's a place for people with a certain amount of science who—

VICTOR. I have no degree, you know.

WALTER. But you've had analytic chemistry, and a lot of math and physics, if I recall. If you thought you needed it you could take some courses in the evenings. I think you have enough background. How would you feel about that?

VICTOR *(digging in against the temptation)*. Well . . . I'd like to know more about it, sure.

ESTHER *(as though to press him to accept)*. It'd be great if he could work in science, it's really the only thing he ever wanted.

WALTER. I know; it's a pity he never went on with it. *(Turning to VICTOR)* It'd be perfectly simple, Vic, I'm chairman of the committee. I could set it all up—

(SOLOMON *enters. They turn to him, surprised. He seems about to say something, but in fear changes his mind.)*

SOLOMON. Excuse me, go right ahead. *(He goes nervously to his portfolio, reaching into it —which was not his original intention.)* I'm sorry to disturb you. *(He takes out an orange and starts back to the bedroom, then halts, addressing Walter)* About the harp. If you'll make me a straight out-and-out sale, I would be willing to go another fifty dollars. So it's eleven fifty, and between the two of you nobody has to do any favors.

WALTER. Well, you're getting warmer.

SOLOMON. I'm a fair person! So you don't have to bother with the appraisal and deductions, all right? *(Before WALTER can answer)* But don't rush, I'll wait. I'm at your service.

(He goes quickly and worriedly into the bedroom.)

ESTHER *(starting to laugh; to VICTOR)*. Where did you *find* him?

WALTER.—that wonderful? He "made it all ethical!" (ESTHER *bursts out laughing, and* WALTER *with her, and* VICTOR *manages to join. As it begins to subside,* WALTER *turns to him.)* What do you say, Vic? Will you come by?

(The laughter is gone. The smile is just fading on VICTOR's *face. He looks at nothing, as though deciding. The pause lengthens, and lengthens still. Now it begins to seem he may not speak at all. No one knows how to break into his puzzling silence. At last he turns to* WALTER *with a rather quick movement of his head as though he had made up his mind to take the step.)*

VICTOR. I'm not sure I know what you want, Walter.

(WALTER *looks shocked, astonished, almost unbelieving. But* VICTOR's *gaze is steady on him.)*

ESTHER *(with a tone of the conciliator shrouding her shock and protest)*. I don't think that's being very fair, is it?

VICTOR. Why is it unfair? We're talking about some pretty big steps here. *(To* WALTER*)* Not that I don't appreciate it, Walter, but certain things have happened, haven't they? *(With a half laugh)* It just seems odd to suddenly be talking about—

WALTER *(downing his resentment)*. I'd hoped we could take one step at a time, that's all. It's very complicated between us, I think, and it seemed to me we might just try to—

VICTOR. I know, but you can understand it would be a little confusing.

WALTER *(unwillingly, anger peaks his voice)*. What do you find confusing?

VICTOR *(considers for a moment, but he cannot go back)*. You must have some idea, don't you?

WALTER. This is a little astonishing, Victor. After all these years you can't expect to settle everything in one conversation, can you? I simply felt that with a little goodwill we . . . we . . . *(He sees* VICTOR's *adamant poise.)* Oh, the hell with it. *(He goes abruptly and snatches up his coat and one of the evening gowns.)* Get what you can from the old man, I don't want any of it. *(He goes and extends his hand to* ESTHER, *forcing a smile.)* I'm sorry, Esther. It was nice seeing you anyway. *(Sickened, she accepts his hand.)* Maybe

I'll see you again, Vic. Good luck. *(He starts for the door. There are tears in his eyes.)*

ESTHER *(before she can think)*. Walter?

(WALTER *halts and turns to her questioningly. She looks to* VICTOR *helplessly. But he cannot think either.)*

WALTER. I don't accept this resentment, Victor. It simply baffles me. I don't understand it. I just want you to know how I feel.

ESTHER *(assuaging)*. It's not resentment, Walter.

VICTOR. The whole thing is a little fantastic to me, that's all. I haven't cracked a book in twenty-five years, how do I walk into a research laboratory?

ESTHER. But Walter feels that you have enough background—

VICTOR *(almost laughing over his quite concealed anger at her)*. I know less chemistry than most high school kids, Esther. *(To* WALTER*)*. And physics, yet! Good God, Walter. *(He laughs.)* Where you been?

WALTER. I'm sure you could make a place for yourself—

VICTOR. What place? Running papers from one office to another?

WALTER. You're not serious.

VICTOR. Why? Sooner or later my being your brother is not going to mean very much, is it? I've been walking a beat for twenty-eight years; I'm not qualified for anything technical. What's this all about?

WALTER. Why do you keep asking what it's about? I've been perfectly open with you, Victor!

VICTOR. I don't think you have.

WALTER. Why! What do you think I'm—?

VICTOR. Well, when you say what you said a few minutes ago, I—

WALTER. What did I say?!

VICTOR *(with a resolutely cool smile)*. What a pity it was that I didn't go on with science.

WALTER *(puzzled)*. What's wrong with that?

VICTOR *(laughing)*. Oh, Walter, come on, now!

WALTER. But I feel that. I've always felt that.

VICTOR *(smiling still, and pointing at the center chair; a new reverberation sounds in his voice)*. There used to be a man in that chair, staring into space. Don't you remember that?

WALTER. Very well, yes. I sent him money every month.

VICTOR. You sent him five dollars every month.

WALTER. I could afford five dollars. But what's that got to do with you?

VICTOR. What it's got to do with me!

WALTER. Yes, I don't see that.

VICTOR. Where did you imagine the rest of his living was coming from?

WALTER. Victor, that was your decision, not mine.

VICTOR. My decision!

WALTER. We had a long talk in this room once, Victor.

VICTOR *(not recalling)*. What talk?

WALTER *(astonished)*. Victor! We came to a complete understanding—just after you moved up here with Dad. I told you then that I was going to finish my schooling come hell or high water, and I advised you to do the same. In fact, I warned you not to allow him to strangle your life. *(To* ESTHER*)*. And if I'm not mistaken I told you the same at your wedding, Esther.

VICTOR *(with an incredulous laugh)*. Who the hell was supposed to keep him alive, Walter?

WALTER *(with a strange fear, more than anger)*. Why did anybody have to? He wasn't sick. He was perfectly fit to go to work.

VICTOR. Work? In 1936? With no skill, no money?

WALTER *(outburst)*. Then he could have gone on welfare! Who *was* he, some exiled royalty? What did a hundred and fifty million other people do in 1936? He'd have survived, Victor. Good God, you must know that by now, don't you?!

(Slight pause.)

VICTOR *(suddenly at the edge of fury, and caught by* WALTER*'s voicing his own opinion, he turns to* ESTHER*)*. I've had enough of this, Esther; it's the same old thing all over again, let's get out of here. *(He starts rapidly upstage toward the bedroom.)*

WALTER *(quickly)*. Vic! Please! *(He catches Victor, who frees his arm.)* I'm not running him down. I loved him in many ways—

ESTHER *(as though conceding her earlier position)*. Vic, listen—maybe you *ought* to talk about it.

VICTOR. It's all pointless! The whole thing doesn't matter to me! *(He turns to go to the bedroom.)*

WALTER. He exploited you! (VICTOR *halts, turns to him, his anger full in his face.)* Doesn't that matter to you?

VICTOR. Let's get one thing straight, Walter—I am nobody's victim.

WALTER. But that's exactly what I've tried to tell you. I'm not trying to condescend.

VICTOR. Of course you are. Would you be saying any of this if I'd made a pile of money somewhere? *(Dead stop)* I'm sorry, Walter, I can't take that. I made no choice; the icebox was empty and the man was sitting there with his mouth open. *(Slight pause)* I didn't start this, Walter, and the whole thing doesn't interest me, but when you talk about making choices, and I should have gone on with science, I have to say something. Just because you want things a certain way doesn't make them that way. *(He has ended at a point distant from* WALTER.*)*

(A slight pause.)

WALTER *(with affront mixed into his trepidation).* All right then . . . How do you see it?

VICTOR. Look, you've been sick, Walter, why upset yourself with all this?

WALTER. It's important to me!

VICTOR *(trying to smile—and in a friendly way).* But why? It's all over the dam. *(He starts toward the bedroom again.)*

ESTHER. I think he's come to you in good faith, Victor. *(He turns to her angrily, but she braves his look.)* I don't see why you can't consider his offer.

VICTOR. I said I'd consider it.

ESTHER *(restraining a cry).* You know you're turning it down! *(In a certain fear of him, but persisting)* I mean what's so dreadful about telling the truth, can it be any worse than this?

VICTOR. What "truth?" What are you—?

*(*SOLOMON *suddenly appears from the bedroom.)*

ESTHER. For God's sake, *now* what?

SOLOMON. I just didn't want you to think I wouldn't make the appraisal; I will, I'll do it—

ESTHER *(pointing to the bedroom).* Will you please leave us alone!

SOLOMON *(suddenly, his underlying emotion coming through; indicating* VICTOR*).* What do you want from him! He's a policeman! I'm a dealer, he's a doctor, and he's a policeman, so what's the good you'll tear him to pieces?!

ESTHER. Well, one of us has got to leave this room, Victor.

SOLOMON. Please, Esther, let me . . . *(Going quickly to* WALTER*)* Doctor, listen to me, take my advice—stop it. What can come of this? In the first place, if you take the deduc-tion how do you know in two, three years they wouldn't come back to you, whereby they disallow it? I don't have to tell you, the federal government is not reliable. I understand very well you want to be sweet to him *(to* ESTHER*)* but can be two, three years before you'll know how sweet they're going to allow him. *(To* VICTOR *and* WALTER*)* In other words, what I'm trying to bring out, my boys, is that—

ESTHER. —you want the furniture.

SOLOMON *(shouting at her).* Esther, if I didn't want it I wouldn't buy it! But what can they settle here? It's still up to the federal government, don't you see? If they can't settle nothing they should stop it right now! *(With a look of warning and alarm in his eyes)* Now please—do what I tell you! I'm not a fool! *(He walks out into the bedroom, shaking.)*

WALTER *(after a moment).* I guess he's got a point, Vic. Why don't you just sell it to him; maybe then we can sit down and talk sometime. *(Glancing at the furniture)* It isn't really a very conducive atmosphere. . . . Can I call you?

VICTOR. Sure.

ESTHER. You're both fantastic. *(She tries to laugh.)* We're giving this furniture away because nobody's able to say the simplest things. You're incredible, the both of you.

WALTER *(a little shamed).* It isn't that easy, Esther.

ESTHER. Oh, what the hell—I'll say it. When he went to you Walter, for the five hundred he needed to get his degree—

VICTOR. Esther! There's no—

ESTHER. It's one of the things standing between you, isn't it? Maybe Walter can clear it up. I mean . . . Good God, is there never to be an end? *(To* WALTER, *without pause)* Because it stunned him, Walter. He'll never say it, but—*(she takes the plunge)*—he hadn't the slightest doubt you'd lend it to him. So when you turned him down—

VICTOR *(as though it wearies him).* Esther, he was just starting out—

ESTHER *(in effect taking her separate road).* Not the way you told me! Please let me finish! *(To* WALTER*)* You already had the house in Rye, you were perfectly well established, weren't you?

VICTOR. So what? He didn't feel he could—

WALTER *(with a certain dread, quietly).* No, no, I . . . I could have spared the money . . . *(He sits slowly.)* Please, Vic—sit down, it'll only take a moment.

VICTOR. I just don't see any point in—

WALTER. No—no; maybe it's just as well to talk now. We've never talked about this. I think perhaps we have to. *(Slight pause. Toward* ESTHER*)* It *was* despicable; but I don't think I can leave it quite that way. *(Slight pause)* Two or three days afterward *(to* VICTOR*)* after you came to see me, I phoned to offer you the money. Did you know that?

(Slight pause)

VICTOR. Where'd you phone?

WALTER. Here. I spoke to Dad. *(Slight pause.* VICTOR *sits.)* I saw that I'd acted badly, and I—

VICTOR. You didn't act badly—

WALTER *(with a sudden flight of his voice).* It was frightful! *(He gathers himself against his past.)* We'll have another talk, won't we? I wasn't prepared to go into all this . . . (VICTOR *is expressionless).* In any case . . . when I called here he told me you'd joined the Force. And I said—he mustn't permit you to do a thing like that. I said—you had a fine mind and with a little luck you could amount to something in science. That it was a terrible waste. Etcetera. And his answer was—"Victor wants to help me. I can't stop him."

(Pause)

VICTOR. You told him you were ready to give me the money?

WALTER: Victor, you remember the . . . the helplessness in his voice. At that time? With Mother recently gone and everything shot out from under him?

VICTOR *(persisting).* Let me understand that, Walter; did you tell—?

WALTER *(in anguish, but hewing to himself).* There are conversations, aren't there, and looking back it's impossible to explain why you said or didn't say certain things? I'm not defending it, but I would like to be understood, if that's possible. You all seemed to need each other more, Vic—more than I needed them. I was never able to feel your kind of . . . faith in him; that . . . confidence. His selfishness—which was perfectly normal—was always obvious to me, but you never seemed to notice it. To the point where I used to blame myself for a lack of feeling. You understand? So when he said that you wanted to help him, I felt somehow that it'd be wrong for me to try to break it up between you. It seemed like interfering.

VICTOR. I see.—Because he never mentioned you'd offered the money.

WALTER. All I'm trying to convey is that . . . I was never indifferent; that's the whole point. I did call here to offer the loan, but he made it impossible, don't you see?

VICTOR. I understand.

WALTER *(eagerly).* Do you?

VICTOR. Yes.

WALTER *(sensing the unsaid).* Please say what you think. It's absurd to go on this way. What do you want to say?

VICTOR *(slight pause).* I think it was all . . . very convenient for you.

WALTER *(appalled).* That's all?

VICTOR. I think so. If you thought Dad meant so much to me—and I guess he did in a certain way—why would five hundred bucks break us apart? I'd have gone on supporting him; it would have let me finish school, that's all. It doesn't make any sense, Walter.

WALTER *(with a hint of hysteria in his tone.).* What makes sense?

VICTOR. You didn't give me the money because you didn't want to.

WALTER *(hurt and quietly enraged—slight pause).* It's that simple.

VICTOR. That's what it comes to, doesn't it? Not that you had any obligation, but if you want to help somebody you do it, if you don't you don't. *(He sees* WALTER*'s growing frustration and* ESTHER*'s impatience.)* Well, why is that so astonishing? We do what we want to do, don't we? (WALTER *doesn't reply.* VICTOR*'s anxiety rises.)* I don't understand what you're bringing this all up for.

WALTER. You don't feel the need to heal anything.

VICTOR. I wouldn't mind that, but how does this heal anything?

ESTHER. I think he's been perfectly clear, Victor. He's asking your friendship.

VICTOR. By offering me a job and twelve thousand dollars?

WALTER. Why not? What else can I offer you?

VICTOR. But why do you have to offer me anything? (WALTER *is silent, morally checked.)* It sounds like I have to be saved, or something.

WALTER. I simply felt that there was work you could do that you'd enjoy and I—

VICTOR. Walter, I haven't got the education, what are you talking about? You can't walk in with one splash and wash out twenty-eight years. There's a price people pay. I've paid it, it's all gone, I haven't got it anymore. Just like you paid, didn't you? You've got no wife, you've lost your family, you're rattling around all over the place? Can you go home and start all over again from scratch? This is where we are; now, right here, now. And as long as we're talking, I have to tell you that this is not what you say in front of a man's wife.

WALTER *(glancing at* ESTHER, *certainty shattered).* What have I said . . . ?

VICTOR *(trying to laugh).* We don't need to be saved, Walter! I've done a job that has to be done and I think I've done it straight. You talk about being out of the rat race, in my opinion, you're in it as deep as you ever were. Maybe more.

ESTHER *(stands).* I want to go, Victor.

VICTOR. Please, Esther, he's said certain things and I don't think I can leave it this way.

ESTHER *(angrily).* Well, what's the difference?

VICTOR *(suppressing an outburst).* Because for some reason you don't understand *anything* anymore! *(He is trembling as he turns to* WALTER.) What are you trying to tell me— that it was all unnecessary? Is that it? (WALTER *is silent.)* Well, correct me, is that the message? Because that's all I get out of this.

WALTER *(toward* ESTHER). I guess it's impossible—

VICTOR *(the more strongly because* WALTER *seems about to be allied with* ESTHER). What's impossible? . . . What do you *want,* Walter!

WALTER *(In the pause is the admission that he indeed has not leveled yet. And there is fear in his voice.)* I wanted to be of some use. I've learned some painful things, but it isn't enough to know; I wanted to act on what I know.

VICTOR. Act—in what way?

WALTER *(knowing it may be a red flag, but his honor is up).* I feel . . . I could be of help. Why live, only to repeat the same mistake again and again? I didn't want to let the chance go by, as I let it go before. (VICTOR *is unconvinced.)* And I must say, if this is as far as you can go with me, then you're only defeating yourself.

VICTOR. Like I did before. (WALTER *is silent.)* Is that what you mean?

WALTER *(hesitates, then with frightened but desperate acceptance of combat).* All right, yes; that's what I meant.

VICTOR. Well, that's what I thought. See, there's one thing about the cops—you get to learn how to listen to people, because if you don't hear right sometimes you end up with a knife in your back. In other words, I dreamed up the whole problem.

WALTER *(casting aside his caution, his character at issue).* Victor, my five hundred dollars was not what kept you from your degree! You could have left Pop and gone right on—he was perfectly fit.

VICTOR. And twelve million unemployed, What was that, my neurosis? I hypnotized myself every night to scrounge the outer leaves of lettuce from the Greek restaurant on the corner? The good parts we cut out of rotten grapefruit . . . ?

WALTER. I'm not trying to deny—

VICTOR *(leaning into* WALTER'*s face).* We were eating garbage here, buster!

ESTHER. But what is the point of—

VICTOR *(to* ESTHER). What are you trying to do, turn it all into a dream? *(To* WALTER) And perfectly fit! What about the inside of his head? The man was ashamed to go into the street!

ESTHER. But Victor, he's gone now.

VICTOR *(with a cry—he senses the weakness of his position).* Don't tell me he's gone now! *(He is wracked, terribly alone before her.)* He was here then, wasn't he? And a system broke down, did I invent that?

ESTHER. No, dear, but it's all different now.

VICTOR. What's different now? We're a goddamned army holding this city down and when it blows again you'll be thankful for a roof over your head! *(To* WALTER) How can you say that to me? I could have left him with your five dollars a month? I'm sorry, you can't brainwash me—if you got a hook in your mouth don't try to stick it into mine. You want to make up for things, you don't come around to make fools out of people. I didn't invent my life. Not altogether. You had a responsibility here and you walked out on it. . . . You can go. I'll send you your half. *(He is across the room from* WALTER, *his face turned away. A long pause)*

WALTER. If you can reach beyond anger, I'd like to tell you something. (VICTOR *does not move.)* I know I should have said this many years ago. But I did try. When you came to me I told you—remember I said, "Ask Dad for money"? I did say that.

(Pause)

VICTOR. What are you talking about?

WALTER. He had nearly four thousand dollars.

ESTHER. When?

WALTER. When they were eating garbage here.

(Pause)

VICTOR. How do you know that?

WALTER. He'd asked me to invest it for him.

VICTOR. Invest it.

WALTER. Yes. Not long before he sent you to me for the loan. (VICTOR *is silent.*) That's why I never sent him more than I did. And if I'd had the strength of my convictions I wouldn't have sent him that!

(VICTOR *sits down in silence. A shame is flooding into him which he struggles with. He looks at nobody.*)

VICTOR *(as though still absorbing the fact).* He actually had it? In the bank?

WALTER. Vic, that's what he was living on, basically, till he died. What we gave him wasn't enough; you know that.

VICTOR. But he had those jobs—

WALTER. Meant very little. He lived on his money, believe me. I told him at the time, if he would send you through I'd contribute properly. But here he's got you running from job to job to feed him—I'm damned if I'd sacrifice when he was holding out on you. You can understand that, can't you? (VICTOR *turns to the center chair and, shaking his head, exhales a blow of anger and astonishment.*) Kid, there's no point getting angry now. You know how terrified he was that he'd never earn anything anymore. And there was just no reassuring him.

VICTOR *(with protest—it is still nearly incredible).* But he saw I was supporting him, didn't he?

WALTER. For how long, though?

VICTOR *(angering).* What do you mean, how long? He could see I wasn't walking out—

WALTER. I know, but he was sure you would sooner or later.

ESTHER. He was waiting for him to walk out.

WALTER *(fearing to inflame VICTOR, he undercuts the obvious answer.)* Well . . . you could say that, yes.

ESTHER. I knew it! God, when do I believe what I see!

WALTER. He was terrified, dear, and . . . *(To VICTOR)* I don't mean that he wasn't grateful to you, but he really couldn't understand it. I may as well say it, Vic—I myself never imagined you'd go that far. (VICTOR

looks at him. WALTER *speaks with delicacy in the face of a possible explosion.*) Well, you must certainly see now how extreme a thing it was, to stick with him like that? And at such cost to you?

(VICTOR *is silent.*)

ESTHER *(with sorrow).* He sees it.

WALTER *(to erase it all, to achieve the reconciliation).* We could work together, Vic. I know we could. And I'd love to try it. What do you say?

(There is a long pause. VICTOR *now glances at* ESTHER *to see her expression. He sees she wants him to. He is on the verge of throwing it all up. Finally he turns to* WALTER, *a new note of awareness in his voice.)*

VICTOR. Why didn't you tell me he had that kind of money?

WALTER. But I did when you came to me for the loan.

VICTOR. To "ask Dad"?

WALTER. Yes!

VICTOR. But would I have come to you if I had the faintest idea he had four thousand dollars under his ass? It was meaningless to say that to me.

WALTER. Now just a second . . . *(He starts to indicate the harp.)*

VICTOR. Cut it out, Walter! I'm sorry, but it's kind of insulting. I'm not five years old! What am I supposed to make of this? You knew he had that kind of money, and came here many times, you sat here, the two of you, watching me walking around in this suit? And now you expect me to—?

WALTER *(sharply).* You certainly knew he had *something*, Victor!

VICTOR. What do you want here! What do you want here!

WALTER. Well, all I can tell you is that *I* wouldn't sit around eating garbage with *that* staring me in the face! *(He points at the harp.)* Even then it was worth a couple of hundred, maybe more! Your degree was right there. Right there, if nothing else. (VICTOR *is silent, trembling.*) But if you want to go on with this fantasy, it's all right with me. God knows, I've had a few of my own.

(He starts for his coat.)

VICTOR. Fantasy.

WALTER. It's a fantasy, Victor. Your father was penniless and your brother a son of a bitch, and you play no part at all. I said to ask him because you could see in front of your face that he had some money. You knew it then and you certainly know it now.

VICTOR. You mean if he had a few dollars left, that—?

ESTHER. What do you mean, a few dollars?

VICTOR *(trying to retract)*. I didn't know he—

ESTHER. But you knew he had something?

VICTOR *(caught; as though in a dream where nothing is explicable)*. I didn't say that.

ESTHER. Then what are you saying?

VICTOR *(pointing at WALTER)*. Don't you have anything to say to *him?*

ESTHER. I want to understand what you're saying! You knew he had money left?

VICTOR. Not four thousand dol—

ESTHER. But enough to make out?

VICTOR *(crying out in anger and for release)*. I couldn't nail him to the wall, could I? He said he had nothing!

ESTHER *(stating and asking)*. But you knew better.

VICTOR. I don't know what I knew! *(He has called this out, and his voice and words surprise him. He sits staring, cornered by what he senses in himself.)*

ESTHER. It's a farce. It's all a goddamned farce!

VICTOR. Don't. Don't say that.

ESTHER. Farce! To stick us into a furnished room so you could send him part of your pay? Even after we were married, to go on sending him money? Put off having children, live like mice—and all the time you knew he . . . ? Victor, I'm trying to understand you. Victor? —Victor!

VICTOR *(roaring out, agonized)*. Stop it! Silence. *(Then)* Jesus, you can't leave everything out like this. The man was a beaten dog, ashamed to walk in the street, how do you demand his last buck—?

ESTHER. You're still saying that? The man had *four thousand dollars! (He is silent.)* It was all an act! Beaten dog!—he was a calculating liar! And in your heart you knew it! *(He is struck silent by the fact, which is still ungraspable.)* No wonder you're paralyzed— you haven't believed a word you've said all these years. We've been lying away our existence all these years; down the sewer, day after day after day . . . to protect a miserable cheap manipulator. No wonder it all seemed like a dream to me—it *was;* a goddamned nightmare. I knew it was all unreal, I knew it and I let it go by. Well, I can't any more, kid. I can't watch it another day. *I'm* not ready to die. *(She moves toward her purse. She sits. Pause.)*

VICTOR *(not going to her; he can't. He is standing yards from her)*. This isn't true either.

ESTHER. We are dying, that's what's true!

VICTOR. I'll tell you what happened. You want to hear it? *(She catches the lack of advocacy in his tone, the simplicity. He moves from her, gathering himself, and glances at the center chair, then at WALTER.)* I did tell him what you'd said to me. I faced him with it. *(He doesn't go on; his eyes go to the chair.)* Not that I "faced" him, I just told him— "Walter said to ask you." *(He stops; his stare is on the center chair, caught by memory; in effect, the last line was addressed to the chair.)*

WALTER: And what happened?

(Pause)

VICTOR *(quietly)*. He laughed. I didn't know what to make of it. Tell you the truth *(to ESTHER)* I don't think a week has gone by that I haven't seen that laugh. Like it was some kind of a wild joke—because we *were* eating garbage here. *(He breaks off.)* I didn't know what I was supposed to do. And I went out. I went *(he sits, staring)* over to Bryant Park behind the public library. *(Slight pause)* The grass was covered with men. Like a battlefield; a big open-air flophouse. And not bums—some of them still had shined shoes and good hats, busted businessmen, lawyers, skilled mechanics. Which I'd seen a hundred times. But suddenly—you know?—I *saw* it. *(Slight pause)* There was no mercy. Anywhere. *(Glancing at the chair at the end of the table)* One day you're the head of the house, at the head of the table, and suddenly you're shit. Overnight. And I tried to figure out that laugh. How could he be holding out on me when he loved me?

ESTHER. Loved . . .

VICTOR *(his voice swelling with protest)*. He loved me, Esther! He just didn't want to end up on the grass! It's not that you don't love somebody, it's that you've got to survive. We know what that feels like, don't we! *(She can't answer, feeling the barb.)* We do what we have to do. *(With a wide gesture including her and WALTER and himself)* What else are we talking about here? If he did have something left it was—

ESTHER. "*If*" he had—

VICTOR. What does that change! I know I'm talking like a fool, but what does that change? He couldn't believe in anybody anymore, and it was unbearable to me! *(The unlooked-for return of his old feelings seems to*

anger him. Of WALTER) He'd kicked him in the face; my mother *(he glances toward* WALTER *as he speaks; there is hardly a pause)* the night he told us he was bankrupt, my mother . . . It was right on this couch. She was all dressed up—for some affair, I think. Her hair was piled up, and long earrings. And he had his tuxedo on . . . and made us all sit down; and he told us it was all gone. And she vomited. *(Slight pause; his horror and pity twist in his voice).* All over his arms. His hands. Just kept on vomiting, like thirty-five years coming up. And he sat there. Stinking like a sewer. And a look came onto his face. I'd never seen a man look like that. He was sitting there, letting it dry on his hands. *(Pause; he turns to* ESTHER.)What's the difference what you know? Do *you* do everything you know? *(She avoids his eyes, his mourning shared.)* Not that I excuse it; it was idiotic, nobody has to tell me that. But you're brought up to believe in one another, you're filled full of that crap—you can't help trying to keep it going, that's all. I thought if I stuck with him, if he could see that somebody was still . . . *(He breaks off; the reason strangely has fallen loose. He sits.)* I can't explain it; I wanted to . . . stop it from falling apart. I . . . *(He breaks off again, staring.)*
(Pause)

WALTER *(quietly).* It won't work, Vic. (VICTOR *looks at him, then Esther does.)* You see it yourself, don't you? It's not that at all. You see that, don't you?

VICTOR *(quietly, avidly).* What?

WALTER *(with his driving need).* Is it really that something fell apart? Were we really brought up to believe in one another? We were brought up to succeed, weren't we? Why else would he respect me so and not you? What fell apart? What was here to fall apart? (VICTOR *looks away at the burgeoning vision.)* Was there ever any love here? When he needed her, she vomited. And when you needed him, he laughed. What was unbearable is not that it all fell apart, it was that there was never anything here.

(VICTOR *turns back to him, fear on his face.)*

ESTHER *(as though she herself were somehow moving under the rays of judgment).* But who . . . who can ever face that, Walter?

WALTER *(to her).* You have to! *(To* VICTOR) What you saw behind the library was not that there was no mercy in the world, kid. It's that there was no love in this house.

There was no loyalty. There was nothing here but a straight financial arrangement. That's what was unbearable. And you proceeded to wipe out what you saw.

VICTOR *(with terrible anxiety).* Wipe out—

WALTER. Vic, I've been in this box. I wasted thirty years protecting myself from that catastrophe. *(He indicates the chair.)* And I only got out alive when I saw that there was no catastrophe, there had never been. They were never lovers—she said a hundred times that her marriage destroyed her musical career. I saw that nothing fell here, Vic— and he doesn't follow me any more with that vomit on his hands. I don't look high and low for some betrayal anymore; my days belong to *me* now, I'm not afraid to risk believing someone. All I ever wanted was simply to do science, but I invented an efficient, disaster-proof money-maker. You— *(To* ESTHER, *with a warm smile)* He could never stand the sight of blood. He was shy, he was sensitive . . . *(To* VICTOR) And what do you do? March straight into the most violent profession there is. We invent ourselves, Vic, to wipe out what we know. You invent a life of self-sacrifice, a life of duty; but what never existed here cannot be upheld. You were not upholding something, you were denying what you knew they were. And denying yourself. And that's all that is standing between us now—an illusion, Vic. That I kicked them in the face and you must uphold them against me. But I only saw then what you see now—there was nothing here to betray. I am not your enemy. It is all an illusion and if you could walk through it, we could meet . . . *(His reconciliation is on him.)* You see why I said before, that in the hospital—when it struck me so that we . . . we're brothers. It was only two seemingly different roads out of the same trap. It's almost as though *(he smiles warmly, uncertain still)* we're like two halves of the same guy. As though we can't quite move ahead— alone. You ever feel that? (VICTOR *is silent.)* Vic?

(Pause.)

VICTOR. Walter, I'll tell you—there are days when I can't remember what I've got against you. *(He laughs emptily, in suffering.)* It hangs in me like a rock. And I see myself in a store window, and my hair going, I'm walking the streets—and I can't remember why. And you can go crazy trying to figure it out when all the reasons disappear—when you can't even hate anymore.

WALTER. Because it's unreal, Vic, and underneath you know it is.

VICTOR. Then give me something real.

WALTER. What can I give you?

VICTOR. I'm not blaming you now, I'm asking you. I can understand you walking out. I've wished a thousand times I'd done the same thing. But, to come here through all those years knowing what you knew and saying nothing . . . ?

WALTER. And if I said—Victor, if I said that I did have some wish to hold you back? What would that give you now?

VICTOR. Is that what you wanted? Walter, tell me the truth.

WALTER. I wanted the freedom to do my work. Does that mean I stole your life? *(Crying out and standing.)* You made those choices, Victor! And that's what you have to face!

VICTOR. But what do you face? You're not turning me into a walking fifty-year-old mistake—we have to go home when you leave, we have to look at each other. What do *you* face?

WALTER. I have offered you everything I know how to!

VICTOR. I would know if you'd come to give me something! I would know that!

WALTER *(crossing for his coat)*. You don't want the truth, you want a monster!

VICTOR. You came for the old handshake, didn't you! The okay! (WALTER *halts in the doorway.*) And you end up with the respect, the career, the money, and the best of all, the thing that nobody else can tell you so you can believe it—that you're one hell of a guy and never harmed anybody in your life! Well, you won't get it, not till I get mine!

WALTER. And you? You never had any hatred for me? Never a wish to see me destroyed? To destroy me, to destroy me with this saintly self-sacrifice, this mockery of sacrifice? What will you give me, Victor?

VICTOR. I don't have it to give you. Not anymore. And you don't have it to give me. And there's nothing to give—I see that now. I just didn't want him to end up on the grass. And he didn't. That's all it was, and I don't need anything more. I couldn't work with you, Walter. I can't. I don't trust you.

WALTER. Vengeance. Down to the end. *(To* ESTHER*)* He is sacrificing his life to vengeance.

ESTHER. Nothing was sacrificed.

WALTER *(to* VICTOR*)*. To prove with your failure what a treacherous son of a bitch I am! —to hang yourself in my doorway!

ESTHER. Leave him, Walter—please, don't say any more!

WALTER *(humiliated by her. He is furious. He takes an unplanned step toward the door)*. You quit; both of you. *(To* VICTOR *as well)* You lay down and quit, and that's the long and short of all your ideology. It is all envy! (SOLOMON *enters, apprehensive, looks from one to the other.)* And to this moment you haven't the guts to face it! But your failure does not give you moral authority! Not with me! I *worked* for what I made and there are people walking around today who'd have been dead if I hadn't. Yes. *(Moving toward the door, he points at the center chair.)* He was smarter than all of us—he saw what you wanted and he gave it to you! *(He suddenly reaches out and grabs* SOLOMON*'s face and laughs.)* Go ahead, you old mutt—rob them blind, they love it! *(Letting go, he turns to* VICTOR.*)* You will never, never again make me ashamed! *(He strides toward the doorway. A gown lies on the dining table, spread out, and he is halted in surprise at the sight of it. Suddenly* WALTER *sweeps it up in his hands and rushes at* VICTOR, *flinging the gown at him with an outcry.* VICTOR *backs up at his wild approach.)*

VICTOR. Walter!

(The flicker of a humiliated smile passes across WALTER*'s face. He wants to disappear into air. He turns, hardly glancing at* VICTOR, *makes for the door, and, straightening, goes out.)*

VICTOR *(starts hesitantly to the door)*. Maybe he oughtn't go into the street like that—

SOLOMON *(stopping him with his hand)*. Let him go. (VICTOR *turns to* SOLOMON *uncertainly.)* What can you do?

ESTHER. Whatever you see, huh. (SOLOMON *turns to her, questioningly.)* You believe what you see.

SOLOMON *(thinking she was rebuking him)*. What then?

ESTHER. No—it's wonderful. Maybe that's why you're still going. (VICTOR *turns to her. She stares at the doorway.)* I was nineteen years old when I first walked up those stairs —if that's believable. And he had a brother, who was the cleverest, most wonderful young doctor . . . in the world. As he'd be soon. Somehow, some way. *(She turns to the center chair.)* And a rather sweet, inoffensive gentle-

man, always waiting for the news to come on
. . . And next week, men we never saw or
heard of will come and smash it all apart and
take it all away.—So many times I thought—
the one thing he wanted most was to talk to
his brother, and that if they could—But he's
come and he's gone. And I still feel it—isn't
that terrible? It always seems to me that one
little step more and some crazy kind of forgiveness will come and lift up everyone.
When do you stop being so . . . foolish?

SOLOMON. I had a daughter, should rest in
peace, she took her own life. That's nearly
fifty years. And every night I lay down to
sleep, she's sitting there. I see her clear like I
see you. But if it was a miracle and she came
to life, what would I say to her? *(He turns
back to* VICTOR, *paying out.)* So you got there
seven; so I'm giving you eight, nine, ten,
eleven *(he searches, finds a fifty)*—and there's
a fifty for the harp. Now you'll excuse me—
I got a lot of work here tonight. *(He gets his
pad and pencil and begins carefully listing
each piece.)*

VICTOR *(folds the money)*. We could still
make the picture, if you like.

ESTHER. Okay. *(He goes to his suit and begins to rip the plastic wrapper off.)* Don't
bother. *(He looks at her. She turns to* SOLO-
MON.*)* Good-bye, Mr. Solomon.

SOLOMON *(looks up from his pad)*. Good-
bye, dear. I like that suit, that's very nice. *(He
returns to his work.)*

ESTHER. Thank you. *(She walks out with
her life.)*

VICTOR *(buckles on his gun belt, pulls up his
tie)*. When will you be taking it away?

SOLOMON. With God's help if I'll live, first
thing in the morning.

VICTOR *(of the suit)*. I'll be back for this
later, then. And there's my foil, and the mask,
and the gauntlets. *(Puts on his uniform
jacket.)*

SOLOMON *(continuing his work)*. Don't
worry, I wouldn't touch it.

VICTOR *(extending his hand)*. I'm glad to
have met you, Solomon.

SOLOMON. Likewise. And I want to thank
you.

VICTOR. What for?

SOLOMON *(with a glance at the furniture)*.
Well . . . who would ever believe I would
start such a thing again . . . ? *(He cuts himself off.)* But go, go, I got a lot of work here.

VICTOR *(starting to the door, putting his cap
on)*. Good luck with it.

SOLOMON. Good luck you can never know
till the last minute, my boy.

VICTOR *(smiling)*. Right. Yes. *(With a last
look around at the room)*. Well . . . bye-bye.

SOLOMON *(as* VICTOR *goes out)*. Bye-bye,
bye-bye.

*(He is alone. he has the pad and pencil in
his hand, and he takes the pencil to start work
again. But he looks about, and the challenge
of it all oppresses him and he is afraid and
worried. His hand goes to his cheek, he pulls
his flesh in fear, his eyes circling the room.*

*His eye falls on the phonograph. He goes,
inspects it, winds it up, sets the tone arm on the
record, and flicks the starting lever. The
Laughing Record plays. As the two comedians
begin their routine, his depressed expression
gives way to surprise. Now he smiles. He
chuckles, and remembers. Now a laugh escapes, and he nods his head in recollection. He
is laughing now, and shakes his head back and
forth as though to say, "It still works!" And
the laughter, of the record and his own, increase and combine. He holds his head, unable
to stop laughing, and sits in the center chair.
He leans back sprawling in the chair, laughing
with tears in his eyes, howling helplessly to the
air.)*

SLOW CURTAIN

ALL OVER

Edward Albee

For BERNARD and REBECCA REIS

First presented by Richard Barr, Charles Woodward, and Edward Albee at the Martin Beck Theatre in New York City on March 27, 1971, with the following cast:

THE WIFE Jessica Tandy
THE DAUGHTER Madeleine Sherwood
THE MISTRESS Colleen Dewhurst
THE DOCTOR Neil Fitzgerald
THE SON James Ray

THE BEST FRIEND George Voskovec
THE NURSE Betty Field
TWO PHOTOGRAPHERS John Gerstad, Charles Kindl
A REPORTER Allen Williams

Directed by John Gielgud
Setting and costumes by Rouben Ter-Arutunian
Lighting by Richard Nelson

TIME: The present.

Who's Who in America suggests that Edward Albee was born on March 12, 1928. He does not say where he was born and does not give the name of his parents. His place of birth and even his ethnic background are in doubt, but at the age of two weeks he was brought from Washington, D.C., to be adopted in New York City by the wealthy Mr. and Mrs. Reed Albee, the father being the son of the celebrated Edward F. Albee, the head of the Keith-Albee theatre circuit.

Albee had a tempestuous childhood. He was brought up in the lush suburban setting of Larchmont and went to the very best schools—quite a number of them. These included Lawrenceville, Valley Forge Military Academy, and Choate. After high school graduation he went to Trinity College, Hartford, but left after a year and a half, subsequently to become that school's most famous dropout.

In his early struggles to make a living—he refused help from his adopted family—he worked as a copy boy, telegraph boy, in a lunch counter, and in the army. After his twentieth birthday times were made a little easier for him by the bequest of fifty dollars a week from a grandmother. At first he wrote in every form, including poetry and novels, but more and more his attention was taken by the theatre.

His first three professional plays were *The Zoo Story* (1958) and *The Death of Bessie Smith* and *The Sandbox* (both 1959). The very first of them was given in Berlin, in German translation, on September 28, 1958, and not given in English until its Off-Broadway production on January 14 of the following year.

By this time Albee was making a fair reputation for himself, as a kind of American absurdist, in something of the style of Eugene Ionesco or even England's N. F. Simpson. But real success did not come until October 13, 1962, with, at the Billy Rose Theatre, the world premiere of Albee's first full-evening play, *Who's Afraid of Virginia Woolf?*

Virginia Woolf led to one of those instant successes that can probably happen only on Broadway. Virtually overnight Albee was transformed from a Greenwich Village playwright of modest promise to the major American playwright of his generation. It was too much and too soon. The play's story of domestic infighting in academia, the frankness of its language, and the uninhibited savagery of its characters caused a sensation, a sensation hardly abated by secret but widespread suggestions that the two married couples in the play were in reality four men!

The play was lavishly praised by the critics, and it certainly was both well constructed and had an unerring knack at catching the sound of human speech: in this Albee was a little like his British contemporary, John Osborne. The play was the shock of the season, was produced all over the world, and was finally made into a very successful motion picture starring Elizabeth Taylor and Richard Burton.

From then on until the present, Albee was not destined to have another popular success, and this seemed to some altogether unjust. It was almost as if critics, having overpraised him once, were anxious to settle accounts by underpraising him on every subsequent outing. There was also widespread misunderstanding over what he was attempting, which was principally to bring a new sense of form and music to the play and to move away from the naturalistic forms typical of the thirties and forties but not taken over by the movies. Albee is always anxious to do in theatre precisely what cannot be done on the screen, so that, whereas all Osborne's subsequent plays seem like film scripts waiting for an offer, Albee's work is almost rigidly theatrical, loosing ideas and a verbal idiom that simply could not be accommodated by the cinema.

Apart from his three adaptations *The Ballad of the Sad Café* (1963, based on the novel by Carson McCullers), *Malcolm* (1966, based on the novel by James Purdy), and *Everything in the Garden* (1967, based on the play by Giles Cooper), Albee has written four plays since *Virginia Woolf.* These are *Tiny Alice* (1964), *A Delicate Balance* (1966), which won the Pulitzer Prize for that year, *Box-Mao-Box* (1968), and *All Over* (1971).

After the immediacy—or at least the surface immediacy—the later plays all seem a good deal more confused and have, on occasion, been called obscurantist. *Tiny Alice* deals with the soul and the spirit in very abstruse and symbolic dramatic terms, *A Delicate Balance* contains its mysteries within the pattern of a drawing room comedy, and *Box-Mao-Box* is an avantgarde attempt to use words as if they were music, and to create an abstract, virtually nonverbal, form of theatre.

Yet perhaps Albee's most important play to date is *All Over,* which had a most disappointingly brief Broadway run after having been slaughtered by most of the critics. Its subsequent successful presentation by the Royal Shakespeare Company in London a year later provided some solace for the play's admirers.

It is a moving meditation and threnody on death—and there indeed is the rub. One could hardly expect such a subject to be popular on Broadway, nor did it prove so. After its opening at the Martin Beck Theatre on March 27, 1971, the notices were almost gleefully savage, pointing out the work's melancholy mood, the special musical tonality of its texture, and its slowness, without catching its poetry and subdued passion, its operatic grace, and careful construction, its beautiful writing, and, most of all, its grave and noble sense of man's mortality. This was Albee's best play to date—but he received few thanks for it. Perhaps people do not wish to be assured that they too will one day die.

THE CHARACTERS

THE WIFE *71; small-boned, not heavy. Dresses well, if conservatively; gray-haired, probably.*
THE MISTRESS *61; auburn or dark blond hair; a great beauty fading some; more voluptuous than* THE WIFE, *maybe a bit taller; given to soft, pastel clothes.*
THE SON *52; a heavy-set man, soft features; dark hair, business clothes.*
THE DAUGHTER *45; angular; once attractive, now a little ravaged; doesn't care much about how she dresses.*
THE BEST FRIEND *73; an erect, good-looking gray-haired man, thin to middling; well dressed, well groomed.*
THE DOCTOR *86; a tiny, shrunken white-haired man; needn't be tiny, but it would be nice.*
THE NURSE *65; a large woman, gray-streaked blond hair; wears a nurse's uniform.*
TWO PHOTOGRAPHERS *and* A REPORTER; *no matter; middle-aged, or whoever understudies the male principals.*

ACT ONE

ONE IDEA OF A SET: *A paneled bed-sitting room. The bed—a huge, canopied four-poster on a raised platform to the rear. Back there, an armoire, perhaps a bureau, a hospital stand for instruments and medicines, a hospital screen hiding the occupant of the bed. In the sitting-room part, a huge fireplace in the stage-right wall, and a door leading to a bathroom upstage of it. In the stage-left wall, a door leading to the hall. The room is solid and elegant, a man's room. The furniture, all of which is good and comfortable, is most probably English. Several chairs, a sofa, side tables, lamps. A tapestry, eighteenth-century family portraits. An Oriental carpet.*
THE DOCTOR *at the bed with the patient;* THE NURSE *at the foot of the bed. The others about, the three women probably sitting,* THE SON *and* THE BEST FRIEND *maybe not.*
Unless otherwise indicated, the characters will speak in a conversational tone, without urgency, more languorously than not. But there will be no whispering; the languor is not boredom, but waiting. The fireplace has an ebbing fire in it; the room is warm.

———

THE WIFE *(gazing at the fire).* Is he dead?
THE DAUGHTER *(a gentle admonishment;*

not a rebuke). Oh, mother.
THE MISTRESS. I wish you wouldn't say that: is he dead?
THE WIFE *(too polite; small smile).* I'm *sorry.*
THE MISTRESS. It's not your curiosity I mind; it is a wifely right, and I know it's not impatience. It's the *form.* We talked about it once, I remember—he and I did—though not how it came up; I don't remember that, but let me see. He put down his fork, one lunch, at *my* house . . . what had we been talking about? Maeterlinck and that plagiarism business, I seem to recall, and we had done with that and we were examining our salads, when all at once he said to me, "I wish people wouldn't say that other people 'are dead.' " I asked him why, as much as anything to know what had turned him to it, and he pointed out that the verb to be was not, to his mind, appropriate to a state of . . . nonbeing. That one cannot . . . *be* dead. He said his objection was a quirk—that the grammarians would scoff—but that one could be dying or have died . . . but could not . . . be . . . dead.
THE WIFE *(quiet amusement).* Maeterlinck?
THE MISTRESS *(lightly).* Oh, well; that was just one day. I'm sorry for having taken issue.
THE WIFE *(gazing into the fire again).* No matter. Let me rephrase it, then. *(Raises her head, inclines it slightly toward* THE DOCTOR*)* Has he . . . *died?*
THE DOCTOR *(pause).* Not yet.
THE WIFE *(pressing a small point).* Will he die soon?
THE SON *(faint distaste). Please,* mother.
THE WIFE *(tiny laugh).* I would like to know. Merely that.
THE DOCTOR. Relatively.
THE WIFE. To?
THE DOCTOR. To the time it has taken him so far.
THE DAUGHTER. Then what was the urgency?
THE DOCTOR. Hunch.
THE BEST FRIEND *(more curiosity than reproach).* Don't you *want* to be here?
THE DAUGHTER *(considering it for the first time).* Well . . . I don't know.
(THE MISTRESS *laughs gently.*)
THE BEST FRIEND. It's not required that you *do* know. It *is* more or less required that you *be* . . . I think: here. Family. Isn't it one of our customs? That if a man has not outlived his wife and children—will not outlive them . . . they gather?

THE WIFE *(to* THE BEST FRIEND). And his closest friend, as well. (THE BEST FRIEND *bows slightly, cocks his head.* THE WIFE *indicates* THE MISTRESS.) And don't forget *her.*

THE BEST FRIEND *(matter-of-fact, but friendly).* And his . . . very special friend, too.

THE MISTRESS *(smiles).* Thank you.

THE BEST FRIEND. And we do it—custom—wanted, or not. We wait until we cannot be asked—unless there is something written, or said, refusing it—and we . . . gather, often even *if* we are refused.

THE WIFE. And is that *so?* In your lawyerish way . . .

THE BEST FRIEND. No; we have not been refused.

THE WIFE *(to* THE DOCTOR). A hunch. *Nothing* more . . . technical than that? More medical? Your hunch it will be *soon?* Your intuition if you were a woman, or are doctors graced with that? *(To her* DAUGHTER; *somewhat chiding).* We've not *come* any distance. Is it just we're in the room with him—not at the hotel, or downstairs?

THE DAUGHTER. I suppose. And that we lived here once.

THE WIFE *(to* THE DAUGHTER). That was another century. *(To* THE DOCTOR) Hunch.

THE DOCTOR *(to* THE WIFE). I can't give it to you to the minute. Did I predict when she would be born? *(Refers to* THE DAUGHTER) The hour—the day, for that matter? Or him? *(Refers to* THE SON)

THE MISTRESS *(back to the point).* Though you have *reason.*

THE DOCTOR. Yes. *(Pause)*

THE WIFE *(a little as though she were speaking to a backward child).* And what *is* it?

THE NURSE *(fact more than reproach).* You should let him die in the hospital.

THE DAUGHTER. Yes!

THE WIFE *(quietly indignant).* Hooked up?

THE NURSE *(shrugs).* Whatever.

THE MISTRESS *(soft-smiling; shaking her head; faintly ironic).* Yes, of course we should have. *(To* THE WIFE) Can you imagine it?

THE WIFE. Tubes; wires. All those machines, leading to and from? A central gadget? *(To them all, generally)* That's what he had become, with all those tubes and wires; one more machine. *(To* THE MISTRESS) Back me up.

THE MISTRESS. Oh, far more than *that.*

THE WIFE. A city seen from the air? The rail lines and the roads? Or, an octopus; the body of the beast, the tentacles electrical controls, recorders, modulators, breath and heart and brain waves, and the tubes!, in either arm and in the nostrils. Where had he gone!? In all that . . . equipment. I thought for a moment *he* was keeping *it* . . . functioning. Tubes and wires.

THE NURSE. They help to keep time, to answer your questions easier. *(Shakes her head)* That's all.

THE MISTRESS. The questions are very simple now. A stopwatch should do it, a finger on the wrist . . .

THE DAUGHTER *(fairly arch).* We are led to understand . . .

THE MISTRESS *(no nonsense).* He *said* . . . *here.*

THE DAUGHTER *(none too pleasant).* We have your word for it.

THE WIFE *(shrugs).* We have her word for *every*thing.

THE MISTRESS *(not rising to it).* He *said* . . . *here.* When it becomes hopeless . . . no, is that what he said? Pointless! When it becomes pointless, he said . . . have me brought back here. I want a wood fire, and a ceiling I have memorized, the knowledge of what I could walk about in, *were* I to. I want to leave from some place . . . I have known. *(Changed tone; to* THE DAUGHTER*)* You have my *word* for it; yes, you have only my word . . . for so very much . . . if he loved you, for example . . . any more. *(To them all; triste)* You *all* have my word, and that is all. I translate for you, as best I can; I tell you what I remember, or think I remember, and I lie sometimes, and give you what he would have said . . . *had* he: thought to . . . or bothered.

THE DAUGHTER *(dogged, but not forceful).* That will not do.

THE SON *(quiet).* Please?

THE DAUGHTER *(scoffing).* You!

THE WIFE. When I came there, to the hospital—the last time, before the . . . removal here—I said . . . *(Turns to* THE MISTRESS) you were not there, were shopping, or resting, I think . . . *(Turns back generally)* looking at him, all wired up, I stood at the foot of the bed—small talk all gone, years ago—I shook my head, and I clucked, I'm afraid—tsk-tsk-tsk-tsk—for he opened his eyes a little, baleful, as I suppose my gaze must have seemed to him, though it was merely . . . objective. This won't do at all, I said. Wouldn't you rather be somewhere else? Do you want to be here? He kept his eyes half open for a moment or so, then closed them, and nodded his head, very slowly. Well, which?, I said, for I realized I'd asked two questions, and a nod could mean either yes or no. Which is it?, I said; do you want to be here? Slow shake of the head. You *would* rather be somewhere else. Eyes opened and closed, twice, in what I know—from eons—to be impatience; then . . . nodding. Well, naturally, I said, in my bright business tone, of course you don't want to be here. Do you want to go home? No reply at all, the eyes burning at me. Your own home, I mean, not mine certainly. Or hers. Perhaps you want to go there. Shall I arrange something? Eyes still on me, no movement. Do you want *her* to arrange it? Still the eyes, still no movement. Has it been arranged? Has she arranged it already? The eyes lightened; I could swear there was a smile in them. She *has.* Well; good. If it is done, splendid. All I care is whether it is *done.* I no longer feel possessive, have not for . . . and the eyes went out—stayed open, went out, as they had . . . oh . . . so often; so far back. *(To* THE MISTRESS*)* That is one of those things . . .

THE DAUGHTER *(possessive, in a very female way).* MOTHER!

THE WIFE. Do not . . . *deflect* me.

THE DAUGHTER *(more a whine, but protective).* MOTHER.

THE WIFE *(as cool as possible).* Yes? *(Pause)* Out. Stayed open, went out.

THE MISTRESS. Ah, well; that happened often.

THE WIFE *(quiet, almost innocent interest).* Yes?

THE MISTRESS. Ah; well, yes.

THE WIFE. Odd I don't remember it. The opening and closing . . . of course, the . . . impatience, but . . . out.

THE MISTRESS *(gently).* Ah, well; perhaps you should have noticed. It must have happened.

THE WIFE *(a small smile).* Well, yes, perhaps I should have. Doubtless it did.

THE MISTRESS. It was always—for me . . .

THE DAUGHTER. Was? The past tense? Why not *is?*

THE MISTRESS *(not rising to it; calm).* He has not, for some time. You *were* a little girl. Are you still?

(THE DAUGHTER *turns away.*)

THE WIFE *(a little laugh).* Semantics from a C minus?

THE SON *(softly).* Leave her alone.

THE WIFE *(not harsh).* Was it not? At school? A C minus, if that? *You* were little

better.

THE MISTRESS. It was always—for me—an indication that . . .

THE DOCTOR *(no urgency).* Nurse. *(Some reaction from them all; not panic, but a turning of heads; a quickening)*

THE WIFE *(a little breathless).* Something?

THE DOCTOR *(looks up at them; a slight smile; some surprise).* Oh . . . oh, *no.* Just . . . business. *(Slight pause)*

THE MISTRESS *(not pressing; continuing).* . . . an indication that . . . some small fraction had gone out of him, some . . . faint shift from total engagement. Or, if not that, a warning of it: impending.

THE WIFE *(a smile).* Ah. Then I *do* know it . . . the sense of it, and probably from what you describe, without knowing I was aware of it.

THE BEST FRIEND. *I* have been aware of it.

THE WIFE *(referring to her husband).* In *him?*

THE BEST FRIEND. No. In myself.

THE WIFE *(mildly mocking).* You *have?*

THE BEST FRIEND *(smiles).* Yes; I have.

THE WIFE *(smiling, herself).* How extraordinary. *(Thinks about it)* When?

THE BEST FRIEND *(to* THE WIFE*).* In relation to my wife, when I was wavering on the divorce, during that time you and I were—how do they put it?—comforting one another; that secret time I fear that everyone knew of.

THE MISTRESS. *He* never knew of it. *I* did. I didn't tell him.

THE WIFE *(sad; smiling).* Well, there wasn't very much to tell.

THE BEST FRIEND. No; but some; briefly. It was after I decided not to get the divorce, that year . . . until I committed her. Each thing, each . . . incident—uprooting all the roses, her hands so torn, so . . . killing the doves and finches . . . setting fire to her hair . . . all . . . all those times, those things I knew were pathetic and not wanton, I watched myself withdraw, step back and close down some portion of . . .

THE MISTRESS. Ah, but that's not the same.

THE WIFE *(not unkindly; objectively).* No, not at all; she was *insane* . . . your wife.

THE MISTRESS. And that is not what we meant at all.

THE WIFE. No, not at all.

THE BEST FRIEND. It is what you were talking about.

THE MISTRESS *(laughs a little; sadly).* No.

It's when it happens calmly and in full command: the tiniest betrayal—nothing so calamitous as a lie held on to in the face of fact, or so niggling as a fantasy during the act of love, but in between—and it can be anything, or nearly nothing, except that it moves you back into yourself a little, the knowledge that all your sharing has been . . .

THE WIFE. . . . arbitrary . . .

THE MISTRESS. . . . willful, and that nothing has been inevitable . . . or even necessary. When the eyes close down; go out.

THE SON *(intense).* My father is dying!

THE WIFE *(after a tiny pause).* Yes. He is.

THE DOCTOR. If you want to go back downstairs, any of you . . .

THE DAUGHTER. . . . to the photographers? The people from the papers? I put my foot on the staircase and they're all around me: Has it happened yet? *Is* he? May we go up now? Eager. Soft voices but very eager.

THE WIFE *(soothing).* Well, they have their families . . . their wives, their mistresses.

THE DAUGHTER *(generally).* Thank you: I'll stay up here; I'll sit it out.

THE WIFE *(with a wrinkling of her nose).* Neat.

THE DAUGHTER *(slightly incredulous).* Did you say neat?

THE MISTRESS. Yes; she did.

THE DAUGHTER *(to her mother).* Because I said sit it out?

THE WIFE *(without expression; waiting).* Um-humm.

THE DAUGHTER *(startlingly shrill).* WELL, WHAT ARE YOU DOING!?

THE WIFE *(looks up at her, smiles vaguely, speaks softly).* I am waiting out a marriage of fifty years. I am waiting for my *hus*band to *die.* I am thinking of the little girl I was when he came to me. I am thinking of . . . do you want me to stop? . . . almost everything I can except the two of you—you and your . . . unprepossessing brother—*(Light, to* THE SON*) Do* forgive me. *(Back)* I am sitting it out. *I* . . . am sitting it out. *(To* THE DAUGHTER*)* And *you* are?

THE DAUGHTER. Enjoying it less than you.

THE MISTRESS *(to* THE DAUGHTER; *a quiet discovery; as if for the first time, almost).* You are not a very kind woman.

THE WIFE *(passing it off).* She has been raised at her mother's knee.

THE DAUGHTER *(to* THE MISTRESS*).* And am I suddenly *your* daughter?

THE MISTRESS. Oh; my stars! No!

THE DAUGHTER. Well, you have assumed so much . . .

THE WIFE *(announcement of a subject).* The little girl I was when he came to me.

THE MISTRESS. So much? *(To* THE WIFE*)* Interesting: it's only the mother who can ever really know whose child it is. Well, the husband knows his wife is *having* the baby . . .

THE WIFE *(laughs gaily).* He took me aside one day—before you and he had made your liaison; they were grown, though—and, rather in the guilty way of "Did I *really* back the car through the *whole* tulip bed?", asked me, his eyes self-consciously focusing just off somewhere . . . "*Did* I make these children? Was it *our* doing: the two of us alone?" I laughed, with some joy, for while we *were* winding down we were doing it with talk and presence: the silences and the goings off were later; the titans were still engaged; and I said, "Oh, yes, my darling; yes, we did; they are our very own." *(She chuckles quietly. Brief pause;* THE DAUGHTER *rises, almost languidly, walks over to where* THE WIFE *is sitting, slaps her across the face, evenly, without evident emotion, returns to where she is sitting. After a pause; to* THE MISTRESS; *small smile)* Excuse me. *(She rises, just as languidly, walks over to where* THE DAUGHTER *is sitting, slaps her across the face, evenly, without evident emotion, returns to where she is sitting. After a noncommittal sigh at* THE DAUGHTER, *who is glaring straight ahead, over her shoulder, to* THE DOCTOR*)* And what do you think now?

THE DOCTOR *(patient smile).* Are you back at my intuition again? My hunch? Your funny names for all the years I've watched you come and go? Both your parents, both of his. My sixty years of practice. *(Indicates* THE NURSE*)* The forty years she's come here with me to sit up nights with you all?

THE WIFE. Yes.

THE MISTRESS *(some wonder).* Sixty years of *some*thing.

THE WIFE *(still to* THE DOCTOR*).* Even on the chance of frightening the horses, or being taken as heartless—which I am *not*—are you holding him back, or are you seeing him through to it?

*(*THE DAUGHTER *stiffens, turns on her heel, moves to the door, opens it, exits, slams it after her.)*

THE DOCTOR *(watching this before he answers).* I've stopped the intravenous feeding. We're letting him . . . starve, if you will. He's breathing very slowly now . . . like sleep. His heart is . . . *(Shrugs)* . . . well, weak . . .

bored is close to it. He's bleeding . . . internally. Shall I go on?

THE WIFE *(no expression)*. Please do.

THE DOCTOR. If you'd like to come and look . . . he seems to have diminished every time I turn my head away and come back. There'll be precious little left for the worms.

THE MISTRESS. The flames.

THE WIFE *(having heard something on the wind)*. Oh? Yes?

THE MISTRESS. He will be burned. "And you are not to snatch my heart from the flames," he said, "for it is not a tasty organ."

THE WIFE *(schoolmarmish)*. Per*haps*. Per*haps* he will be burned.

THE BEST FRIEND *(quite serious; really!)*. Surely he didn't suggest an outdoor event . . . a funeral pyre! *(He is stopped by a concert of* THE WIFE *and* THE MISTRESS *in rather cold, knowing, helpless laughter.)*

THE SON *(finally)*. Don't you . . . *have* something? Some papers?

THE WIFE *(rather helpless in quiet, terrible laughter)*. You *must!*

THE SON *(doubtless the most intense in his life)*. You MUST!

THE MISTRESS. Yes!

THE BEST FRIEND *(after an embarrassed pause)*. There . . . are . . . papers . . . envelopes I've not opened, on instruction; there may be . . .

THE MISTRESS *(adamant; cool)*. It was a verbal . . . envelope.

THE BEST FRIEND. I will go by what is *down.*

THE WIFE *(half sardonic, half leaning)*. Of *course* he will.

THE MISTRESS *(cold; a diamond hardness, yet womanly)*. Oh, Christ; you people! You will go by what I tell you; finally; as I have told you.

THE WIFE *(almost as if improvising; bright)*. No! We will go with what *is*, with what resides. Goodness, if a man desires to go up in flames, let him put it down—on a tablet! Or shall we go over and shake him . . . wake him to the final glory before the final glory, and have two women at him, with a best friend overhead, and make him make his *mind* up! "My darling, we merely want to know! Is it flame or worm? Your mistress tells me you prefer the flame, while I, your merely wife of fifty years, the mother of your doubted children—true, oh, true, my darling—wants you to the worms. Do tell us. Yes? Open your awful lips for a moment, or do your eyes:

open and close them, put them on and out; let us . . . finally . . . misunderstand."

*(*THE MISTRESS *smiles, slowly applauds. Five sounds; seven; always an odd number. Brief pause following the applause, during which* THE WIFE *nods her head gently toward* THE MISTRESS*)*

THE DOCTOR *(to himself, but not sotto voce)*. Death is such an old disease. *(Realizes he is being listened to; speaks to* THE WIFE *and* THE MISTRESS, *laughs a little)* That being so, it must be a comfort having someone as old as I am by the bed: familiar with it, knowing it so well.

THE MISTRESS. Well, let me discomfort you. I was *not* pleased to have you. Get a younger man, I said to him . . .

THE WIFE. Be kind.

THE BEST FRIEND. There are customs . . .

THE DOCTOR *(not hurt; not angry; shrugs)*. And you had them . . . the surgeons, the consultants, younger—well, not brash, but I doubt you'd have wanted that . . .

THE WIFE. . . . some bouncy intern with a scalpel in one hand, a racquet under his arm . . .

THE MISTRESS *(mildy annoyed)*. Don't be ridiculous.

THE DOCTOR *(chuckles)*. I'm rather like a priest: you have me for the limits, for birth and dying, *and* for the minor cuts and scratches in between. If that nagging cough keeps nagging, now it's not *me* opens up the throat or the chest; not *me*. *I* send you on to *other* men . . . and very quickly. I am the most . . . general of practitioners.

THE MISTRESS. I'm sorry.

THE DOCTOR. 'Course, if you think some younger man would do better here, have him back on his feet and at the fireplace, clinking the ice in a bourbon, looking better than ever . . .

THE MISTRESS *(wants no more of it)*. No! I said I am sorry. Just . . . railing against it. *(Gently)* I *am* sorry.

THE BEST FRIEND *(to* THE MISTRESS, *really; but, to* THE DOCTOR, *and to the others)*. The custom of the house. And it *has* been, for so long. "You end up with what you start out with."

THE WIFE *(quiet, choked laughter)*. Oh; God! "The little girl I was when he came to me."

THE MISTRESS *(after a pause)*. The house? The custom of which house?

THE BEST FRIEND *(dogged, not unpleas-*

ant). Of wherever he is: the house he carries on his back, or in his head.

THE MISTRESS *(mildly assertive; slightly bewildered).* Well . . . I thought I knew it *all:* having been so . . . having participated so fully.

THE WIFE *(to* THE BEST FRIEND*)* Is it written on one of your lovely things? . . . your pieces of paper? That we end up with what we start out with? Or that *he* does?

THE BEST FRIEND *(quiet smile).* No.

THE WIFE. I thought not, for Dr. Dey, who brought him into this world . . . into all this, went down with that boat, ship, rather—the iceberg one, or was it the German sub; the iceberg, I think.

THE SON. Titanic.

THE WIFE. Thank you.

THE NURSE. Dey did not go down with a ship.

THE WIFE *and* THE BEST FRIEND *(slightly overlapping, almost simultaneously).* He did not?

THE NURSE *(to* THE DOCTOR*).* May I? . . . (THE DOCTOR *nods.)* . . . Dey went down with what we all go down with, and one *day,* you will forgive the pun, he realized the burning far too up in the chest, and the sense of the kidneys saying they can not go on, and the sudden knowledge that it has all gone on . . . from what central, possibly stoppable place—like eating that last, unwanted shard, that salad, breathing that air from the top of . . . where?—that one thing we are born to discover and never find. *(Pause)* He locused in on his killer, and he looked on it, and he said, "I will not have you." *(Pause)* And so he booked on the Titanic, of *course.*

THE SON *(abstracted).* Well . . . that is what I thought.

THE MISTRESS *(sensing something).* Of course.

THE NURSE *(lighter).* Or something like it. I mean, if the cancer's on you and you're a doctor to boot and know the chances *and* the pain, well . . . what do you do save book on a boat you think's going to run into an iceberg and sink.

THE SON *(frowning).* Oh. Then he did *not* go down on the Titanic.

THE NURSE. No; he went to Maine, to his lodge, and fished . . . for about a week. Then he killed himself.

THE WIFE. And the story of the ship . . .

THE NURSE. . . . was a fiction, invented by his wife and agreed to by his mistress, by the happy coincidence that the Titanic *did* go down when he did. Oh, nobody *believed* it, you understand; the obituaries were candid; but it became a euphemism and was eventually accepted.

THE WIFE. Poor woman.

THE MISTRESS. Poor *women.*

THE WIFE. Who was his mistress? I didn't know he had one.

THE NURSE *(casual). I* was.

THE WIFE. My gracious; you're . . . *old, aren't* you?

THE NURSE. Yes; very.

THE WIFE *(after the slightest pause).* It never occurred to me before. You've always been such a . . . presence. I don't believe a single word you've told us.

THE NURSE *(shrugs). I* don't care. *(Returns to her place by the bed. Pause)*

THE DOCTOR. You see . . .

THE MISTRESS *(quite annoyed).* You *always* say that!

THE WIFE *(not sure, but interested).* Does he?

THE DOCTOR. You see, I did my tithe all at once, in the prisons, when I was young. After my internship; I went to help.

THE WIFE. *We* never knew that.

THE MISTRESS. No.

THE DOCTOR. No? *(Shrugs, chuckles)* It was a while ago: it was before our minds had moved to the New Testament, or our reading of it. Men would die, then—for their killings —soon, if . . . well, perhaps not decently, but what passed for decently if burning a man alive survived the test . . . we were all Old Testament Jews, and we still are, two hundred million of us, save the children, for we believe what we no longer practice . . . . *if: if* the justice was merciful, for that is what sets us medicine men apart from jurors: we are not in a hurry. But, I was with them; stayed with them; helped them have what they wanted for the last time. I would be with them, and they were alone in the death cells, no access to each other, and the buggery was over, had it ever begun, the buggery and the rest; and there were some, in the final weeks, who had abandoned sex, masturbation, to God, or fear, or some enveloping withdrawal, but not all; some . . . some made love to themselves in a frenzy—indeed, I treated more than one who was bleeding from it, from so much—and several confided to me that their masturbation image was their executioner . . . some fancy of how he looked.

THE WIFE *(remembering an announce-*

ment). The little girl I was when he came to me.

THE DOCTOR. You see:

THE WIFE *(laughing a little).* You see? No one cares.

THE DOCTOR. I . . . am eighty-six . . . which, I was informed by my grandson, or perhaps my great-nephew—I confuse them, not the two, but the . . . *(Confiding)* well, they look alike, and have what I confess I think of as wigs, though I know they are not . . . *(Some, though not fruity, longing here)* . . . long, lovely . . . turning down and underneath at the shoulders . . . blond and graillike hair . . . but they said . . . or one of them did . . . *(Not loud, but emphasized)* . . . "Eighty-six! Man, that means going out!" Well, of course, I knew what they meant, but I was coy with it—and I asked them why—what does that make me? "Eighty-six and out." Does that make me . . . and suddenly I knew! I knew I wanted to lie in the long blond hair, put my lips there in the back of the neck, with the blond hair over me . . .

THE SON *(great urgency).* I don't *follow* you!

THE DOCTOR. I was completing what I had begun before: how we become enraptured by it . . . *(Small smile)* . . . by the source of our closing down. You see: I suddenly loved my executioners . . . well, figurative; and in the way of . . . nestling up against them, huddling close—for we do seek warmth, affection even, from those who tell us we are going to die, or when.

THE MISTRESS *(after a pause).* I believe in the killing; *some* of it; for *some* of them.

THE WIFE. Of *course.* Give us a theory and we'll do it in.

THE BEST FRIEND *(quiet distaste).* You *can't* believe in it.

THE WIFE. See . . . your own wife.

THE BEST FRIEND *(gut betrayal, but soft-keyed).* You *can't* do that. There was no killing there.

THE WIFE. Just . . . divorce. It wasn't *us* that did her in—our . . . late summer . . . arrangement: there had been others. *Our* . . . mercy to each other, by the lake, the city . . . *that* didn't take a wild woman who could still bake bread and give a party half the time and send her spinning back into the animal brain; no, my dear; fucking—as it is called in public by everyone these days—is not what got at her; yours and mine, I mean. Divorce: leave *alone:* So don't tell *me* you don't believe

in murder. You *do. I* do. *(Indicates* THE MISTRESS) *She* does, and admits it.

THE SON *(without moving).* I WANT TO TALK TO HIM!

THE BEST FRIEND *(to* THE WIFE, *quiet; intense).* You said she was insane. You *all* said it.

THE WIFE *(rather dreamy).* Did I? Well, perhaps I meant she was *going. (Enigmatic smile)* Perhaps we all did. *(To* THE SON) Then talk to him. You can preface every remark by saying "for the first and last time." And you'll get no argument—there's *that.* I'd not *do* it, though. *(Dry)* You'd start to cry; you've little enough emotion in you: I'd save it.

THE SON *(to his mother; frustration; controlled rage).* He's *dying!*

THE WIFE *(sad; comforting; explaining).* I *know.*

THE BEST FRIEND *(quiet; more or less to himself).* It was progressive. I *asked* them. The violence was transitional. *(To* THE WIFE) I saw her not two months ago.

THE MISTRESS *(seeing that* THE WIFE *is preoccupied).* Did you!

THE BEST FRIEND. I had been to the club, and was getting in my car; another pulled up alongside and someone said—coolly, I think —"Well; I declare." It was a voice I knew, and I turned my head and it was her sister behind the wheel, with another woman in the death seat beside her, as it is called. "I *do* declare," she said—definitely cool—and I perceived it in an instant, before I looked, that my wife was in the back, my ex-wife, and the woman in the front was from the hospital: no uniform, but an attendant of some sort. "Look who we have here!" That was the way she talked, the smile set, the eyes madder than my wife's could ever be—a sane woman, though. The attendant was smoking, I remember that. Of course I looked, and indeed she *was* there, in the back, catercorner, a fur rug half backdrop, half cocoon, and how small she was in it! "Look who's here," her sister said, this time addressing *her,* her head turned to catch both our expressions. The windows were down and I put my hands on the sill—if that *is* what car doors have—and bent down some. "Hello," I said, "how are you?" realizing as I said it that if she laughed in my face, or screamed, or went for me I would not have been surprised. She smiled, though, and stroked the fur beside her cheek with the back of her hand. Her voice was calm, and extremely . . . rested. "It's fine in here," she said, "how is it out there?" I didn't reply: I was so aware of her eyes on me, and her sister's, and the attendant not turned, but looking straight ahead, and smoking. She went on: "Oh, it would be so nice to say to you, 'Come closer, so I can whisper something to you.' That way I could put my hand to the back of your head and say very softly, 'Help me'; either that or rub my lips against your ear, the way you like, and then *grab* you with my teeth, and hold on as you pulled away, blood, and ripping." It was so . . . objective, and without rancor, I didn't move at all; the attendant did, I remember; she turned. "I can't do that, though," my wife said—sadly, I think. "Do you know why?" "No, I don't know why." "Because," she said, "when I look at your ear I see the rump and the tail of a mouse coming out from it; he must be chewing very deeply." I didn't move; my fingers stayed where they were. It could be I was trying to fashion some reply, but there *is* none to that. Her sister gunned the motor then; having seen me when she parked, she must have thought to keep it idling. "Nice to see you," she said to me, the same grim smile, mad eyes, and she backed out, curving, shifted, and moved off. And what I retain of their leaving, most of all, above the mouse, my wife, my*self*, for that matter, is the sound of her sister's bracelet clanking against the steering wheel—a massive gold chain with a disc suspended from it, a large thin disc, with her first name, in facsimile, scrawled across one face of it; that; clanking as she shifted. *(Pause)*

THE WIFE *(having listened to almost all the story)*. Then I'm sorry.

THE BEST FRIEND *(quietly; a little weary)*. It's all right. *(Pause)*

THE SON. It's not true, you know: there's more emotion in me than you think.

THE WIFE *(gentle, placating)*. Well, I hope so. *(Pause; to* THE MISTRESS*)* You're very silent.

THE MISTRESS. I was *wondering* about that; why I *was*. I'd *noticed* it and was rather puzzled. It's not my *way*.

THE WIFE *(agreeing)*. No.

THE MISTRESS. Outsider, I guess.

THE WIFE *(friendly)*. Oh, stop!

THE MISTRESS. No; really; yes. In this context. Listening to you was a capping on it, I suppose: *God;* that was effective as you did it, and I dare say you *needed* it. Maybe that's how we keep the nineteenth century going for

ourselves: pretend it exists, and . . . well . . . outsider.

THE WIFE *(objective curiosity, but friendly)*. What will you *do?*

THE MISTRESS *(thinks about that for a while)*. I don't *know*. I really don't. Give me a schedule. Who runs to the coverlet first? And who throws her arm where, and where, and where does it matter? Who grabs the shoulders, to shake the death out of them, and who collapses at the knees?

THE WIFE *(not sure, herself)*. You don't *know*.

THE MISTRESS *(laughs, so sadly)*. Oh, God, the little girl you were when he came to you.

THE WIFE *(sad truth)*. Yes!

THE MISTRESS *(sad truth)*. I don't *know*. (THE DAUGHTER *enters; her swift opening of the door jars them all to quiet attention; she chuckles a little, unpleasantly, at their reaction, and moves to the fireplace without a word; she rest her hands on the mantel, and stares into the fire.)* Ultimately, an outsider, I was *thinking* about that, and I concluded it was ritual that made it so. *(Looking about; almost amused)* This is . . . ritual, is it not? *(Normal tone)* Twenty years without it, except an awkwardness at Christmas, perhaps. *(To* THE WIFE*)* I remember one December in particular, when it was in the papers you were suing for divorce. Glad you didn't, I think; it would have forced him to marry me . . . or not. Move off. *(Generally)* He missed you all then. Oh, he always *has* . . . mildly, but *that* Christmas—we were at the lodge; it was the next year we took to the islands, to avoid the season as much as anything, though it *was* good for his back, the sun—that one in particular, we sat before the great fire, with all the snow and the pines, and I knew he missed . . . well: family. *(Small laugh)* He missed the ritual, I think. *(Not unkindly)* I doubt you were very good with Christmas, though; hardly . . . prototypical: wassail, and chestnuts.

THE SON *(slightly triste)*. Once. Chestnuts.

THE WIFE *(to* THE MISTRESS; *a smile)*. You *are* right.

THE MISTRESS. In front of the fire; Christmas Eve. We *had* been holding hands, but were *not;* not at that moment, and did he sigh? Perhaps; but there was a great . . . all of a sudden, a . . . slack, and I caught his profile as he stared into the fire, that . . . marvelous granite, and it was as if he had . . . deflated, just perceptibly. I took his hand, and he turned to me and smiled: came back. I said, "You should spend it with *them;* every *year.*" He said he thought not, and it was not for *my* sake.

THE DAUGHTER *(still staring into the fire; she intones the word, spreads it).* Drone. Drone!

THE MISTRESS *(looks up at* THE DAUGHTER*'s back, pauses a moment, looks out at nothing; continues).* It *is* the ritual, you see, that gives me the sense. The first few times I wouldn't go to his doctorates, until he *made* me do it, and the banquets when he *spoke!* Naturally, I've never thought of myself as a secret—for I am not a tart, and I would never have been good at it—but the rituals remind me of what I believe is called my . . . status. To be something so fully, and yet . . . well, no matter. *(A quick, bright laugh; the next directed to* THE WIFE*)* I wonder: if I had been *you*—the little girl you were when he came to you—would you have come along, as I did? Would *you* have come to take *my* place?

THE DAUGHTER *(as* THE WIFE *is about to speak; turns, but stays at the fireplace).* They're all down there! The cameramen, the television crews, the reporters. They gave me a container of coffee.

THE WIFE. Well, why aren't they being *looked* after? Didn't you tell them in the kitchen to see what was needed, and . . .

THE DAUGHTER. The ones out*side:* the crews with their trucks and lights. *They* gave me the coffee. *(Laughs, but it is not pleasant)* It's like a *fungus.* The TV people are on the stoop, with all their equipment on the sidewalk, and you and your tubes and wires! Like a fungus: all of those outside, and the photographers have assumed the entrance hall, like a stag line—nobody sits!—and the newspapermen have taken the library, for that is where the Scotch is.

THE WIFE *(to* THE BEST FRIEND*)*. Go down and *do* something!

THE DAUGHTER *(It is clear she's enjoying it, in a sad way).* Don't bother! It's all been set. Touch it and you'll have it on the landing. Leave it. *(Looks toward her father's bed; overplayed)* Who *is* this man?

THE WIFE *(trailing off)*. Well, I suppose . . .

THE DAUGHTER. I forgot to mention the police.

THE WIFE *(mild anxiety)*. The police!

THE DAUGHTER *(very much "on")*. For the people. Well, there aren't many there now,

people, twenty-five, maybe—the kind of crowd you'd get for a horse with sunstroke, if it were summer. The TV has brought them out, the trucks and the tubes. They're lounging, nothing better to do, and if it weren't night and a weekend, I doubt they'd linger. I mean, God, we don't have the President in here, or anything.

THE SON *(quiet, but dismayed)*. Don't talk like that.

THE WIFE *(to* THE BEST FRIEND*)*. Shouldn't you go down?

THE BEST FRIEND *(shakes his head)*. No; it's a public event; *will* be.

THE NURSE. That's the final test of fame, isn't it, the degree of it: which is newsworthy, the act of dying itself, or merely the death.

THE MISTRESS *(aghast)*. MERELY!

THE NURSE *(almost a reproach)*. I wasn't speaking for me *or* you. *Them.* The public; whether it's enough for them to read about it in the papers without a kind of anger at having missed the dying, too. They were cheated with the Kennedys, both of them, *and* with King. It happened so fast; all people could figure for themselves was they'd been clubbed in the face by history. Even poor Bobby; he took the longest, but everybody knew he was dead before he died. Christ, that loathsome doctor on the tube kept telling us. *(Imitation of a person despised)* "There's no chance at *all* as I see it; the hemorrhaging, the bullet where it is. No chance, No chance." Jesus, you couldn't even *hope.* It was a disgusting night; it made me want to be young, and a man, and violent and unreasoning—rage so that it meant something. Pope John was the last one the public could share in—two weeks of the vilest agony, and conscious to the very end, unsedated, because it was something his God wanted him to experience. I don't know, maybe a bullet *is* better. In spite of everything.

THE WIFE. Perhaps.

THE MISTRESS *(quiet sadness)*. What a sad and shabby time we live in.

THE WIFE. Yes.

THE DAUGHTER *(begins to laugh; incredulous, cruel)*. You . . . hypocrites!

THE WIFE. Oh?

THE DAUGHTER. You pious hypocrites! *(Mocking)* The sad and shabby time we live in. "Yes." You dare to sit there and shake your heads like that!? *(To* THE WIFE*)* To hell with you with your . . . affair with him, though that's not bad for sad and shabby, *is* it? *(Points to* THE MISTRESS*)* But what about *her!*

THE WIFE *(curious).* What *about* her?

THE MISTRESS *(she, too).* Yes; what *about* me?

THE DAUGHTER. Mistress is a pretty generous term for what it's all about, isn't it? So is *kept.* Isn't that *another* euphemism? And how much do you think she's gotten from him? Half a million? A million?

THE MISTRESS. There are things you do *not* know, little girl.

THE WIFE *(steel).* You live with a man who will not divorce his wife, who has become a drunkard because of him, and who is doubtless supplied with her liquor gratis from *his liquor* store—a business which is, I take it, the height of his ambition—who has taken more money from you than I like to think about, who has broken one rib that I know of, and blackened your eyes, and has *dared* . . . *dared* to come to me and suggest I intercede with your father . . .

THE DAUGHTER *(furious).* ALL RIGHT!

THE WIFE. . . . in a political matter which *stank* of the Mafia . . .

THE DAUGHTER *(a scream).* ALL RIGHT!

THE WIFE *(a change of tone to loss).* You know a lot about sad and shabby; you know far too much to turn the phrase on others, especially on those who do *not* make a point of doing what they will or must as badly as possible. That is probably what I have come to love you so little for—that *you* love yourself so little. Don't ever tell *me* how to make a life, or *anyone* who does things out of love, or even affection. *(Pause)* You were beautiful, you know. You really were. Once. (THE DAUGHTER *opens her mouth as if to respond; thinks otherwise; moves away. Silence as they think on this)*

THE MISTRESS *(some delight; really to bring them all back).* My parents are both still alive —I suddenly remember. They are neither . . . particularly *limber,* they keep to themselves more than not, and my father's eyesight is such that when he dares to drive at all it is down the center line of the road. Oh, it makes the other drivers cautious. She's learned that snapping at him does no good at all, and the one time she put her hand on the wheel, thinking—she told me later—that his drift to the left was becoming more pronounced than ever, he resisted her, and the result was weaving, and horns, and a ditch, or shoulder, whichever it is, and a good deal of heavy breathing.

THE BEST FRIEND. Why doesn't *she* drive?

THE MISTRESS *(smiles a little).* No; she could learn, but I imagine she'd rather sit there with him and see things his way.

THE DAUGHTER *(dry).* Why doesn't she walk, or take a taxi, or just not go?

THE MISTRESS *(knows she is being mocked, but prefers to teach rather than hit back).* Oh; she loves him, you see. *(Laughs again)* My *grand*father died only last *year.*

THE DAUGHTER *(spat out).* Oh, *stop* it!

THE MISTRESS *(controlled). Please* stop telling me to stop it. *(Generally)* He was a hundred and three, my mother's father, and he was not at all like those centenarians you're always reading about: full head of snow-white hair, out chopping wood all the time when they weren't burying their fourth wife or doing something worthy in the Amazon; not a bit of it. He was a wispy little man, whom none of us liked very much—not even my mother, who would be a saint one day, were it not for Luther; a tiny man, with the face of a starving child, and blond hair of the type that white does not become, and very little of that, and bones, it would appear, of the finest porcelain, for he fell, when he was seventy-two, and did to his pelvis what you would do to a teapot were you to drop it on a flagstone floor.

THE DOCTOR *(factual; nothing else).* The bones dry out.

THE MISTRESS. Indeed they must, for he took to his bed—or was taken there—and remained in it for thirty-one years. He wanted to be read to a lot.

THE WIFE. *(She tries to get the two words out sensibly, but breaks up during it into a helpless laughter; she covers her mouth, and her eyes dart from person to person; the words are:)* Poor man! *(Finally she quiets herself, but a glance at her daughter staring at her with distaste sends her into another outburst; this one she controls rather more easily.)*

THE MISTRESS *(after the second outburst has quieted; very serious).* Shh, now. As I said, he wanted to be read to a lot. (THE WIFE *smothers giggles occasionally during this.)* This was not easy for his family and fast-diminishing set of friends, for he was hard of hearing and one had to shout; *(She holds her right index finger up.)* plus; plus, everyone knew he had the eyesight of a turkey buzzard.

(THE BEST FRIEND *starts to giggle a bit, too, now.)*

THE DAUGHTER. Stop it!

THE MISTRESS. So, finally, of course, one had to start hiring people.

THE DAUGHTER *(as* THE WIFE *laughs).* Stop it!

THE WIFE. *(She can no longer control her hysteria.)* A turkey buzzard!? *(Her newest explosion of laughter is enough to set* THE SON *off as well, and, to a lesser degree,* THE DOCTOR *and* THE NURSE.)

THE DAUGHTER. Stop it!

THE WIFE. It's not *true, is* it!

THE MISTRESS *(as she breaks up, herself).* No; not a word of it!

(Note: While this laughter should have the look, to those who have watched it, and the feel, to those who have experienced it, of the self-generating laughter possible under marijuana, we should be aware that it is, in truth, produced by extreme tension, fatigue, ultimate sadness and existentialist awareness: in other words . . . the reason we always react that way. Further note: The ones who have laughed least freely should stop most precipitously, though THE SON *might keep his mirth awhile longer than most.* THE WIFE *and* THE MISTRESS *have an arm around one another.)*

THE DAUGHTER. *(She has been saying, "Stop it, stop it; stop it, you fucking bitches!" all through the ultimate laughter, mostly to* THE WIFE *and* THE MISTRESS, *but at* THE SON, THE NURSE, THE BEST FRIEND *and* THE DOCTOR *as well. Clearly, she has meant it for them all, for, as they stop, not without a whoop or two at her from time to time, her volume stays constant, so that, finally, hers is the voice we hear, and hers only.)* Stop it; stop it; stop it, you bitches, you filthy . . . you filth who allow it . . . you . . . you . . . *(Stop)*

THE WIFE. *(She is the one who stops first, becomes fixed on* THE DAUGHTER.*)* You! *You* stop it!

THE DAUGHTER. You bitches! You fucking . . . *(Stops; realizes)*

THE WIFE *(a quiet, post-hysterical smile).* Why don't you go home to your *own* filth? You . . . you . . . issue! *(Sits back, eyes her coldly)*

THE DAUGHTER *(rage only now).* Your morality is . . . it's incredible; it really is; it's a model for the world. You're smug, and excluding. You're incredible! All of you!

THE WIFE *(calm; seemingly detached).* Well, since you've nothing else to do, why don't you run downstairs and tell the waiting press about . . . *our* morality? And while you're at it . . . tell them about your own as well.

THE DAUGHTER *(so intense she can barely get it through her teeth).* This woman has come and taken . . . my . . . *father!*

THE WIFE *(after a pause; not sad; a little weary; empty, perhaps).* Yes. My *hus*band. Remember? *(Sighs)* And that makes all the difference. Perhaps your fancy man has people who care for him, who worry after him; they are not my concern. They may be *yours,* but I doubt it. *I* . . . *care;* about what happens *here.* This woman loves my husband—as *I* do—and she has made him happy; as *I* have. She is good, and decent, and she is not moved by envy and self-loathing . . .

THE DAUGHTER *(close to rage again).* . . . like some people?!! . . .

THE WIFE. . . . Indeed. Like *some* people.

THE DAUGHTER *(a stuck record).* Like *you!?* Like *you!?* Like *you!?*

THE WIFE *(shuts her eyes for a moment, as if to shut out the sound).* Somewhere, in the rubble you've made of your life so far, you must have an instinct tells you why she's part of us. No? She *loves* us. And we love *her.*

THE DAUGHTER *(a rough, deep voice).* Do *you* love *me?* (Pause; her tone becomes fiercer) Does *anyone* love *me?*

THE WIFE. *(A bright little half-caught laugh escapes her; her tone instantly becomes serious.)* Do *you* love anyone?

(A silence. THE DAUGHTER *stands for a moment, swaying, quivering just perceptibly; then she turns on her heel, opens the door and slams it behind her.)*

THE BEST FRIEND *(as* THE WIFE *sighs, reaches for* THE MISTRESS' *hand).* Will she? Will she go down and tell the waiting press?

THE WIFE *(true curiosity).* I don't *know.* I don't think she would; but I don't *know.* *(Laughs as she did before)* I laughed before, because it was so unlikely. I had an aunt, a moody lady, but with cause. She died when she was twenty-six—died in the heart, that is, or whatever portion of the brain controls the spirit; she went on, all the appearances, was snuffed out, finally, at sixty-two, in a car crash, all done up in jodhpurs and a derby, yellow scarf with the foxhead stickpin, driving in the vintage car, the old silver touring car, the convertible with the window between the front and back seats, back from the stable, from jumping, curved, bashed straight into the bread truck, Parkerhouse rolls and blood, her twenty-six-year heart emptying out of her sixty-two-year body, on the foxhead pin and the metal and the gasoline, and all the cardboard boxes sprawled on the country road. *(Slight pause)* "Does anyone love me?" she asked, once, back when I was nine, or ten. There were several of us in the room, but they were used to it. "Do *you* love anyone?" I asked her back. Slap! Then tears—hers *and* mine; mine not from the pain but the . . . effrontery; hers . . . both; effrontery *and* pain.

THE MISTRESS *(after a short silence).* Hmmmm. Yes.

(The door bursts open, and THE DAUGH-TER *catapults into the room, leaving the door wide.)*

THE DAUGHTER. *YOU* tell them!

*(*TWO PHOTOGRAPHERS *and* A REPORTER *enter tentatively; in the moment it takes for the people assembled to react, they have moved a step or two in. Then the room moves into action.* THE DOCTOR *and* THE NURSE *stay where they are, but transfixed;* THE SON *rises from his chair;* THE BEST FRIEND *takes a step or two forward;* THE WIFE *and* THE MISTRESS *rise, poised.)*

THE BEST FRIEND. Get back downstairs; you can't come . . .

(But it is THE WIFE *and* THE MISTRESS *who move.)*

THE WIFE *(a beast's voice, really).* Get . . . out . . . of . . . here! *(The two women attack, fall upon the intruders with fists and feet, and there is an animal fury within them which magnifies their strength. The struggle is brief, but intense; one of the cameramen has his camera knocked to the floor, where he leaves it as the three men retreat.* THE WIFE *forces the door shut, turns, leans against it.* THE DAUGHTER *has her back to the audience, with* THE WIFE *and* THE MISTRESS *to either side of her, facing her. No words; heavy breathing; almost a tableau. Finally; it is an animal's sound; rage, pain)* AARRRGGGHHH. *(Two seconds silence)*

CURTAIN

ACT TWO

The scene: the same as before, fifteen min-utes later. THE DOCTOR *and* THE NURSE *are at the bed, half asleep on their feet, or perhaps* THE DOCTOR *has fallen asleep on a chair near the bed.* THE BEST FRIEND *is by the fireplace, gazing into it;* THE WIFE *is dozing in a chair;* THE MISTRESS *is in a chair near the fireplace;* THE DAUGHTER *is in a chair somewhat* removed from the others, facing front; THE SON *is massaging her shoulders.*

It seems very late: the exhaustion has over-whelmed them; even awake they seem to be in a dream state. What one says is not picked up at once by another.

———

THE SON *(gently).* You shouldn't have done that. You know you shouldn't.

THE DAUGHTER *(really not anxious to talk about it).* I know I shouldn't. Gentler.

THE SON. No matter how you feel.

THE DAUGHTER. I *know.* I *said* I *know.*

THE SON. If they'd gotten in . . .

THE DAUGHTER. Not with our sentries; you'd need an army for that.

THE SON. No matter *how* you feel.

THE DAUGHTER *(languid).* I feel . . . well, how you must have felt when you were young, at school, and you'd fail, or be dis-missed, to make some point you didn't know quite what. Like that. *(Quite without emotion)* I feel like a child, rebellious, misunderstood and known oh, so very well; sated and . . . empty. I'm *on* to myself; there's no mistake there. I'm all the things you think of me, every one of you, and I'm also many more. *(An afterthought)* I wonder why they didn't kill me, the two of them.

THE SON. There's enough death going here.

THE DAUGHTER. Oh, I don't know. God knows, I can probably go my own way now, without a word or a look from any of you. Non grata *has* its compensations. Go my own way. What a relief. *(Ironic)* Back to that "degradation" of mine. Imagine her!—de-grading a family as famous as this, up by its own boot straps—well, the only one of it who mattered, anyway—all the responsibility to itself, the Puritan moral soul. How does it go? "Since we have become what we are, then the double edge is on us; we cannot back down, for we are no longer private, and the world has its eye on us." Christ, you'd think we were only nominally mortal, *he* at any rate; he's the only one who matters, and *he's* mor-tal enough, is going to prove to be. And the eye of the world! Eyes are attached to the brain, I believe, and the monster is sluggish nowadays, all confused and retreating, surly but withdrawn. *Folk* heroes, maybe, but not *his* type, too much up *here.* If you can't take it in all at once—relate to it, dear God—grant it its due, but don't dwell on it. The dust bin; anachronism. Well, I'll be glad when he's gone—no, no, not for the horrid reasons, not for all of your mistakes about me, but simply that the tintype can be thrown away, the sturdy group, and I can be what I choose to be with only half of the disapproval, no longer the public. *You* won't get in the press because you're someone's son, unless you get arrested for something serious, *or* news-worthy. Nor will I. I'll have my man—such as he is and such as I want him for—and only mother will really mind. We'll see each other less, all of us, and finally not at all, I'd imag-ine—except on . . . occasions. Whatever we disdain will be our own affair. You can, too, probably, very soon . . . when all *this* is finished.

THE SON. Do *what?*

THE DAUGHTER. Resign. . . . You'll be rich enough, or do you want to go on with it, even when he's gone? Isn't it pointless for you there? Aren't you useless?

THE SON *(wry little laugh)*. Probably. I don't like it very much; I don't feel *part* of it, though it's a way of getting through from ten to six, and avoiding all I know I'd be doing if I didn't have it . . . *(Smiles a bit)* those demons of mine.

THE DAUGHTER *(laughs a little)*. Ah, those demons. You're no different. *(Turns toward* THE BEST FRIEND) Will you keep him on— *(Mildly mocking)* at the *firm*—after . . . all this is finished, and you've no more obligation to our father, or did you make a bond to keep it up forever?

THE BEST FRIEND *(quietly)*. There's no bond; your brother isn't with me as a charity. *(To* THE SON) *You* don't think that, do you? You fill your position nicely and you're nicely paid for doing it. If you choose to leave, of course, nothing will falter, nor, for that mat-ter, will I feel any . . . particular loss, but we know that about each other, don't we. But no one's waiting to throw you down. That's your sister's manner. *(To* THE DAUGHTER) *Don't* ask me to talk about it now.

THE SON *(to* THE BEST FRIEND; *very sim-ple)*. I didn't know that you didn't care for me. I suppose I always assumed . . . well, that we were all a form of family, and . . . *(Shrugs)*

THE DAUGHTER *(sad advice)*. Don't as-sume.

THE SON. Well; no matter.

THE BEST FRIEND *(a little impatient)*. Did I say I didn't *care* for you? I thought I said I'd feel no loss if you were gone. I'm pretty much out of loss. *(He turns back to the fire.)*

THE SON. Sorry; that *is* what you said. *(To* THE DAUGHTER) Enough? More?

THE DAUGHTER. The base of the neck, and slowly, very slowly. Uh hunh. *(Sensuous, as he massages her neck)* They were animals, and I had a moment of . . . absolutely thrill-ing dread, very much as when I read of the Chinese, and how they are adept at keeping a man alive and conscious, *conscious,* for hours, while they strip the skin from his body. They tie him to a pole.

THE SON. What for?

THE DAUGHTER. So he won't wander off, I'd imagine. I'm not your usual masochist, in spite of what *she* thinks. I mean, a broken rib really *hurts,* and everybody over twelve knows what a black eye on a lady *means.* I don't fancy any of that, but I do care an awful lot about the guilt I can produce in those that do the hurting. *(Suddenly a little girl)* Mother?

THE SON. She's sleeping.

THE DAUGHTER *(turns to* THE MISTRESS). *You're* not.

THE MISTRESS *(coming back)*. Hm?

THE DAUGHTER. *You're* not, *are* you. Sleeping.

THE MISTRESS *(not hostile; still half away)*. No. I'm far too exhausted.

THE DAUGHTER *(to* THE SON; *plaintive)*. Wake mother up.

THE BEST FRIEND *(sotto voce)*. Let her sleep, for God's sake!

THE MISTRESS *(voice low; cool)*. Do you want to start in again? Do you have some new pleasure for us?

THE DAUGHTER *(heavy sigh)*. I want to tell her that I'm sorry.

THE MISTRESS. I dare say she knows that; has, for years.

THE DAUGHTER. Still . . .

THE MISTRESS. Nobody's a fool here.

THE DAUGHTER *(mildly biting)*. *You* were never a mother.

THE MISTRESS *(smiles)*. No, nor have you been, but you've been a woman.

THE DAUGHTER *(ironic)*. And the old in-stinct's always there, right?

THE MISTRESS. Right.

THE DAUGHTER. But you have been a wife, haven't you, twice as I remember, not to count your adventures in mistresshood. How many men have you gone through, hunh? No divorces, you; just bury them.

THE MISTRESS *(calm, but intent)*. Listen to me, young lady, there are things you have no idea of, matters might cross your mind were you not so . . . self-possessed. You lash out —which can be a virtue, I dare say, stridency aside, if it's used to protect and not just as a revenge . . .

THE DAUGHTER *(to cut it off).* O.K. O.K.

THE MISTRESS . . . but you're careless, not only with facts, but of your*self.* What words will you ever have left if you use them all to kill? What words will you summon up when the day *comes,* as it may, poor you, when you suddenly discover that you've been in love— oh, for a week, say, and not known it, not having been familiar with the symptoms, being such an amateur? Love with mercy, I mean, the kind you can't hold back as a reward, or use as any sort of weapon. What vocabulary will you have for that? Perhaps you'll be mute; many are—the self-conscious —in a foreign land, with only the phrases the guidebook gives them, or maybe it will be dreamlike for you—nightmarish—lock-jawed, throat constricted, knowing that whatever word you use, whatever phrase you might say will come out, not as you mean it then, but as you have meant before, that "I love you; I need you," no matter how joy-ously meant, will be the snarl of a wounded and wounding animal. You'd better go back to grade school.

THE DAUGHTER *(contempt and self-dis-gust).* Oh, I'm far too old for that, aren't I?

THE MISTRESS *(shrugs).* Perhaps you are. It would serve you right.

THE DAUGHTER. There's ignorance enough in you, too, you know. You've not been that much in touch—except with *him,* and he's hardly one to keep you up to date.

THE MISTRESS. So true. But—and I *do* hate to say it, I really do—unless you're some kind of unique, I've seen your type before.

THE DAUGHTER *(quietly).* Fuck yourself. *(To* THE SON*)* You've stopped.

THE SON *(not starting again).* Yes. My fingers ache.

THE DAUGHTER *(quietly, without emotion).* You never were much good at anything.

THE MISTRESS *(to* THE BEST FRIEND*; mock ingenuous).* How am I supposed to do that, I wonder?

THE BEST FRIEND *(dry, weary).* It's usually said to men, but even there it's a figure of speech. *(He shakes his head, turns back to the fire.) Don't* involve me; please.

(THE DOCTOR *has moved toward them; he stands for a moment.)*

THE DOCTOR *(quietly).* That's very inter-esting; it *is.*

THE SON *(soft, but frightened).* What is?

THE DOCTOR. His heart stopped beating . . . for three beats. Then it started again.

THE DAUGHTER *(to* THE SON*; anxious).* Wake mother!

THE DOCTOR *(with a gesture).* No; no; it *began* again.

THE DAUGHTER. Maybe you were asleep: you're old enough.

THE DOCTOR. Surely, but I wasn't. Fall asleep with the stethoscope to his chest, dream of stop and go? Wake immediately, jolted back by the content? No. His heart stopped beating . . . for three beats. Then it started again. Nothing less than that. I thought I'd report it. *(He starts to turn back; re-turns)* It's interesting when it happens, but it's nothing to write home about. Just thought I'd report it, that's all.

THE MISTRESS. What does it signify? It must, something.

THE DOCTOR *(thinks, shrugs).* Weakening. What did you mean, something conscious like fighting it off?

THE MISTRESS *(wistful).* Maybe.

THE DOCTOR *(gentle; a smile).* Nooooo. You're better than that. *(He moves back whence he came.)*

THE DAUGHTER. They tell you more on television. (THE MISTRESS *laughs a little.)* They do!

THE MISTRESS. In a way.

THE SON *(sober).* Just think: it could have been finished then. *(Quickly)* I don't mean anything but the wonder of it.

THE MISTRESS *(dry).* Why, don't you be-lieve in suffering?

THE DAUGHTER. Does he know he is? Suf-fering?

THE MISTRESS. I didn't mean him. *(Refers first to* THE DAUGHTER, *then* THE SON*)* I meant you . . . and you. I *do:* believe in suf-fering.

THE DAUGHTER *(quiet scorn).* What *are* you, a fundamentalist, one of those "God de-signed it so it must be right" persons, down deep beneath the silvery surface?

THE SON. She didn't mean that.

THE DAUGHTER *(Ibid.).* How would *you* know? You're not much good at anything.

THE SON *(to* THE MISTRESS*). Did* you? *Mean* that?

THE MISTRESS. I meant at least two things, as I usually do. *(To* THE DAUGHTER*)* No divorces, I just bury them? Well, what would you have me do? I know, you meant it as a way of speaking; you were trying to be unkind, but keep it in mind should your lover be rid of his wife, marry you, and die. You've been a woman, but you haven't been a wife. It isn't very nice, you know, to get it all at once—for both my deaths were sudden: heart attack, and car. *(Sighs, almost begins to laugh)* Well, maybe it's better than . . . *(Indicates the room with a general gesture)* this. It's all done at once, and you're empty; you go from that to grief without the intervening pain. You can't suffer with a man because he's dead; his dying, yes. The only horror in participating is . . . *(Thinks better of it)* . . . well, another time. *(Pause; shift of tone)* Look here! You accused me before of being—what is that old-fashioned word?—a gold digger, of having insinuated myself into . . .

THE DAUGHTER. I said you *probably!*

THE MISTRESS. Yes, of course, but you're imprecise and I know what you meant. That I am expecting something less than I have received from your father—money, in other words, a portion of what you are expecting for having permitted yourselves to be born. *(Turns to* THE BEST FRIEND, *takes his hand; he still stares into the fire)* May I engage you? *(*THE BEST FRIEND *shakes his head, leaves his hand where it is; she removes hers.)* No? All right. *(Back to* THE DAUGHTER*)* You will see, in good time. *(Laughs)* I remember a family once, two children, both well into their fifties, with a dying mother, eighty-something. These children—and there is no allegory here; read yourselves in if you want, but I hope not—these elderly children didn't like each other very much; the daughter had married perhaps not wisely for her second time— penniless, much younger than she, rather fruity to the eye and ear, but perhaps more of a man than most, you never know—but the reasons went further back, the dislike, to some genesis I came upon them too late for, and in the last months of their mother's life they did battle for a percentage of her will, for her estate. But fifty-fifty wouldn't do, and it would shift from that to sixty-forty—seventy-thirty once, I'm told! The mother, you see, had loved them both, and either one who came to her would tilt the balance. But she ended it exactly where she'd started it—half to each—and all that had happened was damage. The daughter was the one at fault, or more grievously, for she had been spoiled in

a way that sons are seldom. But all of this is to tell you that I'm not an intruder in the dollar sense. I've more than enough—I was born with it. Don't you people ever take the trouble to scout? And I told your father I wanted nothing beyond his company . . . *and* love. He agreed with me, you'll be distressed to know, said *you needed* it. So. I am not your platinum blonde with the chewing gum and the sequined dress.

THE DAUGHTER *(after a pause)*. I'm supposed to like you now, I take it, fall into your arms and cry a little and choke out words like sorry and forgive. Well, you've got the wrong lady.

THE MISTRESS *(light)*. *I* wouldn't expect it, and I really don't much care. I've more important things. *(Less light)* He taught me a sense of values, you know, beyond what I'd thought was adequate. Cold, I suppose, and right on the button. Took a little while, but I guess I knew I'd go through this someday; so I learned. And you know something else? I'll be there at the funeral, ashes if I have my way —if *he* has *his*—but either way. It's one . . . ritual I'll not defer for.

THE DAUGHTER. You wouldn't dare!

THE MISTRESS. You don't know me, child.

THE DAUGHTER. I won't *have* it.

THE SON *(gently)*. Be calm.

THE MISTRESS *(laughs a little)*. It's not a mind gone mad with power, or a dip into impropriety, or the need to reopen a wound —for the wound *is* closed, you know, your mother knows; *you* do, too; you're railing because you never saw it open; *you* can't even find a scar; you don't know where it *was;* that *must* be infuriating—none of those things, but simply that I'll not be put down by sham, and I'll *be* there, dressed in my gray and white, a friend of the family. There'll be none of your Italian melodrama, with all the buzz as to who is that stranger off to one side, that woman in black whom nobody knows, wailing louder than the widow and the family put together. None of that. I have always known my place, and I shall know it then. Don't wake her. Let her sleep.

THE DAUGHTER *(as* THE NURSE *approaches, tapping a cigarette)*. You're right: I *am* an amateur.

THE NURSE. May I join you? *(Nobody replies; she eases into a chair, clearly exhausted. She lights her cigarette, inhales, exhales with a great, slow breath.)* Sensible shoes help, but when you're well up into the 'teens, like me, there's nothing for it but this, sometimes.

THE MISTRESS *(looking away).* Any change?

THE NURSE. No; none. Well, of course, some. Procession, but nothing, really. *(Looks at* THE SON*)* You're much too fat; heavy, rather.

THE SON *(matter-of-fact).* I'm sedentary.

THE NURSE. Eat less; do isometrics. You won't last out your fifties.

THE SON *(quiet; an echo of something).* Maybe not?

THE NURSE. Well, I'm not skin and bones, myself, but it's different for a woman: our hearts are better. Eat fish and raw vegetables and fruit; avoid everything you like. *(An afterthought)* Except sex; have a lot of that: fish, raw vegetables, fruit, and sex.

THE SON *(embarrassed).* Th-thank you.

THE NURSE. Eggs, red flesh, milk-cheese-butter, nuts, most starches 'cept potatoes and rice . . . all bad for you; ignore them. Two whiskies before dinner, a glass of good burgundy *with* it, and sex before you go to sleep. That'll do the trick, keep you going.

THE SON. For?

THE NURSE *(rather surprised at his question).* Until it's proper time for you to die. No point in rushing it.

THE DAUGHTER *(eyes upward, head rolling from side to side; through her teeth).* Death; death; death; death; death . . .

THE NURSE *(taking a drag on her cigarette).* Death, yes; well, it gets us where we live, doesn't it?

(A sound startles them. It comes from THE WIFE; *it is a sharp, exhaled "Ha-ah." The first one comes while she is still asleep in her chair. She bolts upright and awake. She does it again: "Ha-ah.")*

THE WIFE *(fully awake, but still a trifle bewildered).* I was *asleep.* I *was* asleep. I was dreaming, and I dreamt I was asleep, and it wakened me. Have—have I . . . is every—every . . .

THE NURSE. It's all right; go back to sleep.

THE WIFE. No. I mustn't; I can't. *(She rises, a little unsteady, and begins to move toward* THE DOCTOR.*)* Is everything all right, is . . .

THE DOCTOR. Everything is all right. Really.

*(*THE WIFE *moves toward the grouping, sees* THE DAUGHTER, *pauses, eyes her with cold loathing, moves to* THE MISTRESS *and* THE BEST FRIEND, *puts a hand absently on* THE MISTRESS' *shoulder, looks at* THE BEST FRIEND's *back, then at* THE NURSE.*)*

THE WIFE *(to* THE NURSE; *no reproach).* Shouldn't you be back there?

THE NURSE *(smiles).* If I should be, I would be.

THE WIFE. Yes; I'm sorry. *(Generally; to no one, really)* I was dreaming of so many things, odd and . . . well, that I was shopping, for a kind of thread, a brand that isn't manufactured any more, and I knew it, but I thought that they might have some in the back, I couldn't remember the name of the maker, and of course that didn't help. They showed me several that were very much like it, one in particular that I almost settled on, but didn't. They tried to be helpful; it was what they used to call a dry goods store, and it was called that, and I remember a specific . . . not smell, but scent the place had, one that I only remember from being little, so I was clearly in the past, and when they couldn't help, I asked if I could go in the back, the stock. They smiled and said of course, and so I went through a muslin curtain, into the stock, and it was not at all what I'd expected—shelves of cardboard boxes, bales of twine, bolts of fabric, some of the boxes with labels, some with buttons pasted to the end, telling what was there—none of it; it was all canned fruit, and vegetables, peas and carrots and string beans and waxed beans, and bottles of chili sauce and catsup, and canned meats, and everything else I'd not expected and was not a help to me. So I walked back through the muslin and into the living room my family'd had when I was twelve or so, a year before we moved. It was the room my aunt had slapped me in, and I sensed that I was asleep, and it woke me.

THE SON *(moves toward a door beside the fireplace, upstage).* Excuse me.

THE MISTRESS *(wistful).* Dreams.

THE WIFE *(a little sad).* Yes. *(*THE SON *closes the door behind him.* THE WIFE *turns to* THE BEST FRIEND.*)* Are you all right?

THE BEST FRIEND *(straightens up, turns, finally, sighs).* I suppose. Trying to shut it all out helps. I felt a rush of outrage—back awhile—not over what *she* brought on, *(Indicating* THE DAUGHTER*)* or my wife's sister, or *myself,* for that matter, or *(Indicates generally)* . . . all this, but very generally, as if my brain was going to vomit, and I thought that if I was very still—as I was when I was a child, and felt I was about to be sick over something—it would go away. Well, no, not go away, but . . . recede. *(Smiles, sadly)* It has, I think; some.

THE DAUGHTER *(shy, tentative)*. Mother?

THE WIFE *(tiniest pause, to indicate she has heard; speaks to* THE BEST FRIEND*)*. I upset you, then. I'm sorry; what I said wasn't kind. You *do* understand it as well as the next.

THE DAUGHTER *(still pleading quietly, but with an edge to it)*. Mo-ther.

THE WIFE *(as before)*. And *excluding* you was never my intention, for any cruel reason, that is. Oh, I may have wanted to join the two of us together *(Indicates* THE MISTRESS*)* as close as we were but had not admitted, or discussed, certainly, for we have so much to learn from each other . . .

THE DAUGHTER *(a growl of frustration and growing anger)*. Moooootherrrr!

THE BEST FRIEND. You'd better answer her: she'll go downstairs again.

THE WIFE *(calm, smiling a little)*. No; she's done that once and won't succeed with it again, for no reason other than you wouldn't let her out the door . . . would you. *(Pause, as* THE BEST FRIEND *winces, smiles sadly)* Besides, it wouldn't be shocking any more, merely tiresome; she'd be pounding her fists on the wind.

THE DAUGHTER *(bolt upright in her chair, hands grasping the arms, neck tendons tight; a howl)*. MOOOOTHERRRRR!!

THE MISTRESS *(after a pause; gently)*. Do answer her.

THE WIFE *(pats* THE MISTRESS *gently on the shoulder; looks at* THE DAUGHTER*; speaks wistfully, eyes always on her)*. I may never speak to her again. I'm not certain now—I have other things on my mind—but there's a good chance of it: I seldom speak to strangers, and if one should try to be familiar at a time of crisis, or sorrow, I'd be enraged. *(Talks to* THE MISTRESS *now)* Well, I suppose were I to stumble on the way to the gravesite and one—she—were to take my elbow to keep me from falling, I might say thank you, looking straight ahead. Unlikely, though, isn't it . . . stumbling. *(Small smile; quietly triumphant)* No; I don't think I shall speak to her again. *(*THE DAUGHTER *rises;* THE WIFE *and* THE MISTRESS *watch.* THE DAUGHTER *seems drained and very tired; she stands for a moment, then slowly moves to the upstage chair or sofa recently abandoned by* THE WIFE*; she throws herself down on it, turns over on her back, puts one arm over her eyes, is still.)*

Softly) So much for that. *(Directly to* THE MISTRESS' *back-of-the-head)* You notice I *did* say gravesite, and I am not speaking of an urn of ashes.

THE MISTRESS *(small smile)*. I know; I heard you.

THE WIFE *(almost apologetic)*. I *will* do battle with you there, no matter what you tell me, no matter what an envelope may say, I will have my way. Not a question of faith, or a repugnance; merely an act of will.

THE MISTRESS *(gently)*. Well, I won't argue it with you now.

*(*THE SON *emerges, closes the door, leans against it, pressed flat, his head up, his eyes toward the ceiling. He is wracked by sobbing, and there is a crumpled handkerchief in his hand.)*

THE SON *(barely able to get it out, for the sobs)*. It's all . . . still there . . . all . . . just as it . . . was. *(Quite suddenly he manages to control himself. This effect is not comic. It is clear an immense effort of will has taken place. His voice is not quite steady, falters once or twice, but he is under control.)* I'm sorry; I'm being quite preposterous; I'm sorry. It's just that . . . it's all still there, just as I remember it, not from when I may have seen it last—when? twenty years?—but as it was when I was a child: the enormous sink; the strop; the paneling; the pier glass; the six showerheads and the mosaic tile; and . . . the . . . the white milkglass bottles with the silver tops, the witch hazel and cologne, the gilt lettering rubbed nearly off; and . . . *(softer; sadder)* . . . the ivory brushes, and the comb. *(Shakes his head rapidly, clearing it; full control)* Sorry; I'm sorry.

(Pause)

THE WIFE *(sighs, nods several times)*. It would take *you,* wouldn't it. Choose anything, any of the honors, the idea of a face in your mind, something from when he took you somewhere once, or came halfway round the world when you were burning up and the doctor had no way of knowing what it was, then, in those times, sat by your bed the four days till it began to slacken, *then* slept. *(Her anger, her contempt, really rising)* No! Not any of it! Give us you, and you find a BATHROOM . . . MOVING? *(Pause. Softer, a kind defeat)* Well . . . I can't expect you to be the son of your father and *be* much: it's too great a *burden;* but to be so little is . . . *(Dismisses him with a gesture, paces a little)* You've neither of you had children, thank

God, children that I've *known* of. *(Harsh)* I hope you never marry . . . *either* of you! *(Softer, if no gentler)* Let the line end where it is . . . at its zenith.

THE SON *(a rasped voice).* Mother! Be kind!

THE WIFE *(to THE MISTRESS; rather fast, almost singsong).* We made them both; remember how I told you that he asked me that? If it were true? And how I laughed, and said, oh, yes? Remember?

(THE MISTRESS nods, without looking at her.)

THE SON *(moves toward the stage-left door, stops by THE DAUGHTER; speaks to her).* I'm going across the hall, to the solarium.

(THE WIFE turns to notice this exchange.)

THE DAUGHTER *(without moving).* All right.

THE SON. So you'll know where I am.

THE DAUGHTER. All right.

THE SON. In case.

THE DAUGHTER. All right.

THE WIFE *(as THE SON reaches the door to the hallway; mocking, but without vigor).* Aren't you up to it?

THE SON *(mildly; matter-of-fact).* Not up to you, mother; never was. *(He exits.)*

THE WIFE *(at something of a loss).* Well. *(Pause)* Well. *(Pause)* Indeed.

(THE DAUGHTER speaks next; while she does, THE WIFE moves about, listening, looking at THE DAUGHTER occasionally, but generally at furniture, the floor, whatever.)

THE DAUGHTER *(never once removing her arm from across her eyes).* Dear God, why can't you leave him alone! Why couldn't you let him be, this *once*. Everyone's the target of something, something unexpected and maybe even stupid. You can shore yourself up beautifully, guns on every degree of the compass, a perfect surround, but when the sky falls in or the earth gives way beneath your feet . . . so what? It's all untended, and what's it guarding? Those movies—remember them?—way back, India, usually, or in the west, the forts against the savages: the rescue party finally got there, and there was the bastion, guns pricking out from every window and turret, the white caps of the soldiers, the flag of the regiment blowing, but something was wrong; the Max Steiner music had stopped and the only sound was the blowing of the sand; and then the head of the rescue party would shoot off his pistol as a signal to those inside, and wait; still, just the blowing of the sand, and no Max Steiner mu-

sic; they'd approach, go in, and there it all was, just as all of us except the rescue party knew it would be—every last soldier dead, propped up into position as some kind of grisly joke by the Tughees, or the Sioux, or whatever it was. Why couldn't you have just left him alone? He's spent his grown life getting set against everything, fobbing it all off, covering his shit as best he can, and so what if the sight of one unexpected, ludicrous thing collapses it all? So *what!* It's proof, isn't it? Isn't it proof he's not as . . . little as you said he was? It is, you know. *(Slight pause)* You make me as sick as I make you.

(Pause. THE WIFE looks at THE DAUGHTER for a little, opens her mouth as if to speak, doesn't, looks back at THE DOCTOR, who seems to be dozing, turns to THE NURSE.)

THE WIFE *(to THE NURSE).* You . . . *(Has to clear her throat)* . . . you'd better go back, I think; he may have fallen asleep.

THE NURSE *(swivels in her chair, looks back).* Doubt it; it's a trick he has, allows patients to think he isn't watching.

THE WIFE *(abrupt).* Don't be ridiculous!

THE NURSE *(calm).* Don't be *rude.*

THE WIFE *(sincerely).* I'm sorry.

THE DOCTOR *(from where he is, without raising his head).* If I *am* dozing—which *is* possible, though I don't think I've slept in over forty years—if I *am,* then I imagine my intuition would snap me back, if anything needed doing, wouldn't you think? My famous intuition?

THE WIFE *(sings it back to him).* Sor-ry. *(To THE MISTRESS; wryly)* That's all I seem to say. Shall I apologize to you for anything?

THE MISTRESS *(smiles; shakes her head).* No thank you.

THE WIFE. I may—just automatically—so pay no attention.

THE MISTRESS *(stretches).* You *could* answer my question, though.

THE WIFE. Have I forgotten it?

THE MISTRESS. Probably. I was wondering, musing: If I had been *you*—the little girl you were when he came to you—would you have come along as I did? Would *you* have come to take *my* place?

THE WIFE *(smiles as she thinks about it).* Hmmmmm. No; I don't think so. We function so differently. I function as a wife, and you—don't misunderstand me—you do not. Married twice, yes, you were, but I doubt your husbands took a mistress, for you were *that,* too. And no man who has a mistress for his wife will take a wife as mistress. (THE MISTRESS *laughs, softly, gaily.*) We're different kinds; whether I had children or not, I would always be a wife and mother, a symbol of stability rather than refuge. Both your husbands were married before they met you, no?

THE MISTRESS. Um; yes.

THE WIFE *(light).* Perhaps you're evil.

THE MISTRESS. No, I don't think so; I never scheme; I have never sought a man out, said, I think I will have this one. Oh, *is* he married? *I* see; well, no matter, that will fall like a discarded skin. I am not like that at all. I have cared for only three men—my own two husbands . . . and yours. My, how shocking that sounds. Well, three men and one boy. That was back, very far, fifteen and sixteen. God! We were in love: innocent, virgins, both of us, and I doubt that either of us had ever told a lie. We met by chance at a lawn party on a Sunday afternoon, and had got ourselves in bed by dusk. You may not call that love, but it was. We were not embarrassed children, awkward and puppy-rutting. No; fifteen and sixteen, and never been before, but our sex was a strong and practiced and assisting . . . "known" thing between us, from the very start. Fumbling, tears, guilt? No, not a bit of it. He was the most . . . beautiful person I have ever seen: a face I will not try to describe, a lithe, smooth swimmer's body, and a penis I could not dismiss from my mind when I was not with him—I am not one of your ladies who pretends these things are of no account. We were a man and woman . . . an uncorrupted man and woman, and we made love all the summer, every day, wherever, whenever. *(Pause)* And then it stopped. *We* stopped.

THE DAUGHTER *(after a moment; same pose).* What happened? Something tragic? Did he die, or become a priest?

THE MISTRESS *(ignoring her tone; remembering).* No, nothing like it. We had to go back to school.

THE DAUGHTER *(snorts).* Christ!

THE MISTRESS. We had to go back to *school.* Could anything be simpler?

THE DAUGHTER *(raising herself half-up on her elbows; mildly unpleasant tone).* No burning correspondence, love and fidelity sworn to eternity? Surely a weeping farewell, holding hands, staring at the ceiling, swearing your passion until Christmas holidays.

THE MISTRESS *(still calm).* No, not that at all. We made love, our last day together, kissed, rather as a brother and *sister* might,

and said: "Goodbye; I love you." "Goodbye; I love you."

THE DAUGHTER. A couple of horny kids, that's all.

THE MISTRESS *(smiles a little).* No, I think you're wrong there. Oh, we were *that,* certainly, but I also think we were very wise. "Leave it; don't touch it again." I told you; it was very simple: we had to go back to school; we were *children.*

THE DAUGHTER *(reciting the end of a fairy tale).* And you never saw him again.

THE MISTRESS. True. He was from across the country, had been visiting that summer.

THE WIFE *(very nice).* What became of him?

THE MISTRESS *(waves it away).* Oh . . . things, things I've read about from time to time; nothing.

THE DAUGHTER. Oh, come on! What became of him!?

THE MISTRESS *(irritated, but by the questioner, not the question).* Whatever you like! He died and became a priest! *What* do *you* care?

THE DAUGHTER. I don't.

THE MISTRESS. Then shut it up.

(THE DAUGHTER *sinks back to her previous position.)*

THE WIFE *(after a pause).* Four men, then.

THE MISTRESS. Hm? Oh; well, yes; yes, I suppose he *was* a man. Four men, then. Not too bad, I guess; spread out, not all bunched together.

THE WIFE. Yes. *(Slowly; something of a self-revelation)* I have loved only . . . once.

THE MISTRESS *(nods, smiles; kindly).* Yes.

THE BEST FRIEND *(swings around).* What if there *is* no paper? What if all the envelopes are business, and don't say a thing about it? What if there *are* no instructions?

THE WIFE *(dry, but sad).* Then it is in the hands of the wife . . . is it not?

THE BEST FRIEND. Yes, certainly, but . . . still.

THE WIFE *(on her guard).* Still?

THE BEST FRIEND *(pained).* After a time, it . . . after a time the prerogative becomes *only* legal.

THE WIFE. *Only,* and *legal?* Those two words *next* to each other? From you?

THE BEST FRIEND *(helpless).* *I* can't stop you.

THE WIFE. Why would you want to, and why are we playing "what if"? He's a thorough man, knows as much law as you, or certainly *some* things. I am not a speculator.

THE BEST FRIEND. Those envelopes are not from yesterday.

THE WIFE. I dare say not. How *old* were you when you became aware of death?

THE BEST FRIEND. Well . . . what it meant, you mean. *(Smiles, remembering)* The age we all became philosophers—fifteen?

THE WIFE *(mildly impatient; mildly amused)*. No, no, when you were aware of it for yourself, when you knew you were at the top of the roller-coaster ride, when you knew half of it was probably·over and you were on your *way* to it.

THE BEST FRIEND. Oh. *(Pause)* Thirty-eight?

THE WIFE. Did you make a will then?

THE BEST FRIEND *(a rueful smile)*. Yes.

THE WIFE. Instructions in it?

THE BEST FRIEND *(curiously angry)*. Yes! But not about that! Not about what was to be *done* with me. Maybe that's something women think about more.

THE WIFE *(surprised, and grudging a point)*. May-*be*.

THE BEST FRIEND *(he, too)*. And maybe it's something I never thought to *think* about.

THE WIFE. Do I sound absolutely *tribal*? Am I wearing feathers and mud, and *are* my earlobes halfway to my shoulders? I wonder! My rationale has been perfectly simple: you may lose your husband while he is alive, but when he is not, then he is yours again.

THE DAUGHTER *(same position)*. He still *is*.

(THE WIFE *opens her mouth to reply, stops herself.*)

THE BEST FRIEND. What.

THE DAUGHTER. Alive.

THE BEST FRIEND *(controlling his anger)*. We *know* that.

THE DAUGHTER. Wondered; that's all.

THE MISTRESS *(gently)*. Let's not talk about it any more. We're misunderstood.

THE BEST FRIEND. It's just that . . . well, never mind.

THE WIFE *(nicely)*. That you're his best friend in the world, and you care about what happens to him?

THE BEST FRIEND *(glum)*. Something like that.

THE WIFE. Well, there are a number of his best friends here, and we all seem quite concerned. That we differ is incidental.

THE BEST FRIEND. Hardly. I warn you: if there *is* no paper, and I doubt there is, and you persist in having your way, I'll take it to court.

THE WIFE *(steady)*. That will take a long time.

THE BEST FRIEND. No doubt.

THE WIFE. Well. *(Pause)* It was pleasant having you as my lawyer.

THE BEST FRIEND. Don't be like that.

THE WIFE *(furious)*. Don't *be* like that!? Don't *be* like that!? We are talking of *my husband*. Surely you've not forgotten. You were a guest in our house—in the days when we *had* a house together. We entertained you. Here! You and your wife spent Christmas with us; many times! Who remembered to bring you your cigars from Havana whenever we were there? Who went shopping with you to surprise your wife, to help you make sure it was right and not the folly you husbands make of so many things? Me! *Wife!* Remember!? (THE BEST FRIEND *goes to her where she sits, kneels beside her, takes her hands, puts them to his lips.*) I think I shall cry.

THE BEST FRIEND. No, now.

THE WIFE *(wrenches her hands free, looks away; weary)*. Do what you want with him; cast him in bronze if you like. I won't do battle with you: I like you both too much.

THE MISTRESS. I told you what he wants, that's all, or what he wanted when he told me. Let's not fall out over the future.

THE BEST FRIEND *(gentle)*. If I retract, will you hire me back again?

THE WIFE. You were never fired; what would I do without you? Rhetoric.

THE DAUGHTER *(same position)*. Join hands; kiss; sing.

THE WIFE *(rather light tone, to THE BEST FRIEND)*. What *is* it if you kill your daughter? It's matricide if *she* kills *you,* and infanticide if you do her in when she's a tot, but what if she's all grown up and beginning to wrinkle? Justifiable homicide, I suppose.

(THE NURSE *half emerges from behind the screen.*)

THE NURSE. *Doctor!? (He joins her, and they are only partially visible.* THE WIFE *stays where she is, grips the arms of her chair, closes her eyes.* THE MISTRESS *rises, stays put.* THE BEST FRIEND *moves toward the bed.* THE DAUGHTER *rises, stays where she is.*)

THE NURSE *(reappearing)*. Stay back; it's nothing for you. *(She goes back to the bed.* THE MISTRESS *sits again;* THE BEST FRIEND *goes into a chair.* THE DAUGHTER *returns to her sofa.*)

THE DAUGHTER. *(She pounds her hands on the sofa, more or less in time to her words; her voice is thick, and strained and angry. She must speak with her teeth clenched.)* Our Father, who art in heaven; hallowed be thy name; thy kingdom come, thy will be done on earth as it is in heaven; give us this day!

(They are all silent. THE NURSE *reappears; her uniform is spotted with blood, as if someone had thrown some at her with a paint brush. There is blood on her hands, too.)*

THE NURSE. It's all right; it's a hemorrhage, but it's all right.

THE WIFE *(eyes still closed).* Are you certain!

THE NURSE *(forceful, to quiet them).* It's all right! *(She returns to the bed.)*

THE MISTRESS *(to* THE WIFE, *after a pause).* Tell me about something; talk to me about anything—anything!

THE WIFE *(struggling for a subject).* We . . . uh . . . the . . . the garden, yes, the garden we had, when we had our house in the country, outside of Paris. We were in France for nearly three years. Did you . . . did he tell you that?

THE MISTRESS. Yes; was it lovely?

THE WIFE. He couldn't, he couldn't have taken you there. It was lovely; it burned down; they wrote us.

THE MISTRESS. What a pity.

THE WIFE. Yes; it was lovely. *(She struggles to get through it.)* It wasn't just a garden; it was a world . . . of . . . floration. Is that a word? No matter. It was a world of what it was. One didn't walk out into a garden—in the sense of when they say to you: "Come see what we've done." None of any of that. Of *course.* It had been planned, by careful minds —a woman *and* a man, I think, for it was that kind, or several; generations—and it resembled nothing so much as an environment. *(Head back, loud, to* THE DOCTOR *and* THE NURSE*)* IS ANYONE TELLING ME THE TRUTH!?

THE NURSE *(reappearing briefly).* Yes. *(Goes back)*

THE WIFE *(quietly).* Thank you.

THE MISTRESS. The garden.

THE WIFE. Yes. *(Pause, while she regathers)* The . . . the house, itself, was centuries old, rather Norman on the outside, wood laid into plaster, but not boxy in the Norman manner, small, but rambling; stone floors; huge, simple mantels, great timbers in the ceilings, a kitchen the size of a drawing room—*you* know. And all about it, clinging to it, spreading in every way, a tamed wilderness of gar-

den. No, not tamed; planned, a planned wilderness. Such profusion, and all the birds and butterflies from miles around were privy to it. *And* the bees. One could walk out and make bouquets Redon would have envied. *(Pause)* I don't think I want to talk about it any more.

*(*THE DOCTOR *appears, finishing drying his hands with a towel. He comes forward.)*

THE DOCTOR. Close, but all right; there's no predicting those. May I join you? *(He sits with* THE WIFE *and* THE MISTRESS.*)* That's better. I suddenly feel quite old . . . *(Chuckles)* . . . which could pass for a laugh, couldn't it?

THE MISTRESS. Are you going to retire, one day?

THE DOCTOR. Couldn't, now; I'm way past retirement age. I should have done it fifteen years ago. Besides, what would I do?

THE WIFE *(not looking at* THE DOCTOR*).* Did it . . . hasten it?

THE DOCTOR *(pause).* Sure. What else would you expect? Every breath diminishes; each heartbeat is taking a chance.

THE MISTRESS *(an attempt to change the subject).* I've never understood how you doctors stay so well in the midst of it all—the contagions. You must rattle from the pills and be a mass of pricks.

THE DOCTOR. Oh, it's easier now; used to be a day, though. Still, it's interesting. In Europe, in the time of the black plague—and I *read* about it, don't be thinking fresh— when eighty percent of a town would go, wiped out in a week, the doctors, such as they were, would lose only half. There wasn't much a doctor could do, in those days, against the bubonic—and especially the pneumonic—but saddling up and running wouldn't have helped, postponed, maybe, so they stayed, tried to get the buboes to break, nailed some houses shut with all the living inside if there was a case, and preceded the priests by a day or two in their rounds. The priests had the same break as the doctors, the same percentages. Might *mean* something; probably not. *(Pause)* Want some more history?

THE WIFE *(shakes her head, smiles a little).* No.

THE MISTRESS *(Ibid.).* Not really.

THE DOCTOR *(rises, with an effort).* I'll go back, then. If you do, let me know; I'm up on it. *(Starts back, passes* THE DAUGHTER, *recumbent)* Got a headache, or something? *(Moves on)*

THE DAUGHTER *(rises, swiftly; under her breath)*. Christ! *(Generally) I'll* be in the solarium, too. *(She exits, slamming the door after her. Some silence)*

THE WIFE *(to* THE MISTRESS, *gently)*. What *will* you do?

THE MISTRESS *(smiles sadly)*. I don't *know.* I've *thought* about it, of course, and nothing seems much good. I'm not a drinker, and I'm far too old for drugs. I've thought of taking a very long trip, of going places I've not been before—*we've* not been—but there's quite a lot against that, too. Do I want to forget, or do I want to remember? If the choice comes down to masochism or cowardice, then maybe best do nothing. Though, I must do *something.* The sad thing is, I've seen so many of them, the ones who are suddenly without their men, going back to places they have known together, sitting on terraces and looking about. They give the impression of wanting to be recognized, as if the crowd in Cannes that year had all the people from the time before and someone would come and say hello. They overdress, which is something they never would have done before: at three in the afternoon they're wearing frocks, and evening jewelry, and their make-up is for the dim of the cocktail lounge, and not the sun. I'm not talking of the women who fall apart. No, I mean the straight ladies who are mildly startled by everything, as if something they could not quite place were not quite right. Well, it is all the things they have come there to not admit—that the present is not the past, that they must order for themselves, and trust no one. And the groups are even worse, those three or four who make the trips together, those coveys of bewildered widows, talking about their husbands as if they'd gone to a stag, or were at the club. There's a coarsening in that, a lack of respect for oneself, ultimately. I *shall* go away; I *know* that; but it won't be to places unfamiliar, either. There are different kinds of pain, and being once more where one has been, and shared, *must* be easier than being where one *cannot* ever . . . I think what I shall do is go to where I've been, *we've* been, but I shall do it out of focus, for indeed it will be. I'll go to Deauville in October, with only the Normandie open, and take long, wrapped-up walks along the beach in the cold and gray. I'll spend a week in Copenhagen when the Tivoli's closed. And I'll have my Christmas in Venice, where I'm told it usually snows. Or maybe I'll just go to Berlin and stare at the wall. We were there when they put it up. There's so much one can do. And so little. *(Long pause; finally, with tristesse)* What will *you* do?

THE WIFE *(pause)*. It's very different. I've been practicing widowhood for so many years that I don't know what effect the fact will have on me. Maybe none. I've settled in to a life which is comfortable, interesting, and useful, and I contemplate no change. You never know, though. It may be I have told myself . . . all lies and I am no more prepared for what will happen—when? tonight? tomorrow morning?—than I would be were he to shake off the coma, rise up from his bed, put his arms about me, ask my forgiveness for all the years, and take me back. I can't predict. I know I want to feel something. I'm waiting to, and I have no idea what I'm storing up. You make a lot of adjustments over the years, if only to avoid being eaten away. Anger, resentment, loss, self-pity—*and* self-loathing—loneliness. You can't live with all that in the consciousness very long, so, you put it under, *or* it gets well, and you're never sure which. Worst might be if there's nothing there any more, if everything has been accepted. I'm not a stoic by nature, by any means—I would have killed for my children, back when I cared for them, and he could please me and hurt me in ways so subtle and complex I was always more amazed at *how* it had happened than I was by *what*. I remember once: we were in London, for a conference, and, naturally, he was very busy. *(Pause)* No; I don't want to talk about *that,* either. Something *must* be stirring: it's the second time I've balked.

THE MISTRESS *(nicely)*. *You* won't mind.

THE WIFE. Well, I won't know till it's too late, will I? *(Turns to* THE BEST FRIEND) You're going to ask me to marry you, *aren't* you.

THE BEST FRIEND *(from where he sits)*. Certainly.

THE WIFE *(smiles)*. And I shall *refuse,* shall I *not.*

THE BEST FRIEND. Certainly; I'm no bargain.

THE WIFE. Besides; fifty years married to one man, I wouldn't be settling on three or four with another—or even ten, if you outwit all the actuaries. And besides—though listen to how it sounds from someone *my* age, *my* condition—I am devoted to you, sir, but I am not in love with you. Fill my mouth with

mould for having said it, but I love my husband.

THE MISTRESS *(smiles, nicely).* Of course
you do.

THE BEST FRIEND *(as if nothing else had
entered his mind and he is not disputing it).* Of
course you do.

THE WIFE *(a bit put off by their acquies-
cence).* Yes. Well. *(Shakes her head, slowly,
sadly)* Oh, God; the little girl. *(Does she move
about? Perhaps)* Eighteen . . . *(To* THE MIS-
TRESS*)* and none of yours, no summer love-
making; no thought to it, or anything like it;
alas. *(Pause, gathers herself again)* Some
would-be beaux, but, like myself, tongue-tied
and very much their ages. They would come
to call, drink lemonade with my mother
there, an aunt or so, an uncle; they would
take me walking, play croquet, to a dance. I
didn't fancy any of them.

THE MISTRESS *(smiles).* No; you were waiting.

THE WIFE *(shakes her head, laughs).* Of
course! For Prince Charming! (THE MISTRESS
chuckles. THE WIFE *shrugs.)* And then—of
course—he came *along,* done with the university, missing the war in France, twenty-four,
already started on his fortune—just begun,
but straight ahead, and clear. We met at my
rich uncle's house, where he had come to
discuss a proposition, and he made me feel
twelve again, or younger, and . . . comfortable, as if he were an older brother, though
. . . different; very different. I had never felt
threatened, by boys, but he was a man, and
I felt secure.

THE MISTRESS. Did you fall in love at
once?

THE WIFE. Hm? *(Thinks about it)* I don't
know; I knew that I would marry him, that
he would ask me, and it seemed very . . .
right. I felt calm. Is that an emotion? I suppose it is.

THE MISTRESS. Very much.

THE WIFE *(sighs heavily).* And two years
after that we were married; and thirty years
later . . . he met *you.* Quick history. Ah,
well. *(A quickening)* Perhaps if I had been
. . . *(Realizes)* No; I don't suppose so. *(A
silence)*

THE DOCTOR *(emerging from where the bed
has hidden him; to* THE BEST FRIEND*).* Where
are the others?

THE BEST FRIEND *(rising).* In the solarium.

THE DOCTOR *(level).* You'd best have them
come in.

THE WIFE *(pathetic; lost).* No-o!

THE BEST FRIEND *(moving toward the door;
to* THE DOCTOR*).* I'll get them.

THE WIFE *(Ibid.).* Not yet!

THE BEST FRIEND *(misunderstanding).*
They should *be* here.

THE WIFE *(Ibid.).* I don't mean them!

THE BEST FRIEND *(hard to breathe).* I'll get
them. *(He exits.)*

THE WIFE *(turning back to* THE DOCTOR;
as before; pathetic, lost). Not yet!

THE MISTRESS *(takes* THE WIFE's *hand).*
Shhhhhhhhh; be a rock.

THE WIFE *(resentful).* Why!

THE MISTRESS. They need you to.

THE WIFE *(almost sneering).* Not you?

THE MISTRESS *(matter-of-fact).* I'll manage. It would help, though.

THE WIFE *(takes her hand away; hard).*
You be; *you* be the rock. I've *been* one, for all
the years; steady. It's profitless!

THE MISTRESS. Then, just a little longer.

THE WIFE *(almost snarling).* You be; *you've*
usurped! *(Pause; finally; still hard)* I'm sorry!

THE MISTRESS. That's not fair.

THE WIFE *(still hard).* Why? Because I no
longer had what you up and took?

THE MISTRESS *(her tone hard, too).* Something like that.

THE WIFE *(a sudden, hard admitting, the
tone strong, but with loss).* I don't love *you.*
(THE MISTRESS *nods, looks away.)* I don't love
anyone. (Pause) Any more. *(The door opens;*
THE DAUGHTER *enters, followed by* THE SON,
followed by THE BEST FRIEND. THE BEST
FRIEND *moves wearily, the other two shy,as if
they were afraid that by making a sound or
touching anything the world would shatter.*
THE BEST FRIEND *quietly closes the door behind him; the other two move a few paces,
stand there. On her feet, now; to* THE DAUGH-
TER, *same tone as before)* I don't love *you,* *(To*
THE SON*)* and I don't love *you.*

THE BEST FRIEND *(quietly).* Don't do that.

THE WIFE *(quieter, but merciless).* And you
know I don't love *you. (An enraged shout
which has her quivering)* I LOVE MY HUS-
BAND!! (THE NURSE *has moved forward;*
THE DAUGHTER *moves to her, buries herself in*
THE NURSE's *arms.* THE SON *falls into a chair,
covers his face with his hands, sobs. To* THE
SON*)* STOP IT!! (THE SON *abruptly ceases his
sobbing, doesn't move)*

THE MISTRESS *(steady).* You stop it.

(Silence; THE BEST FRIEND *moves to the
fireplace;* THE MISTRESS *and* THE WIFE *are
both seated;* THE SON *stays where he is;* THE
DAUGHTER *returns to the sofa;* THE DOCTOR

is by the bed; THE NURSE *stands behind the sofa and to one side, eyes steady, ready to assist or prevent. Nobody moves from these positions, save* THE DOCTOR, *from now until the end of the play.)*

THE WIFE *(calm, now, almost toneless. A slow speech, broken with long pauses).* All we've done . . . is think about ourselves. *(Pause)* There's no help for the dying. I suppose. Oh my; the burden. *(Pause)* What will become of *me* . . . and *me* . . . and *me.* *(Pause)* Well, we're the ones have got to go on. *(Pause)* Selfless love? *I* don't think so; we love to *be* loved, and when it's taken away . . . then why *not* rage . . . or pule. *(Pause)* All we've *done* is think about ourselves. Ultimately. *(A long silence. Then* THE WIFE *begins to cry. She does not move, her head high, eyes forward, hands gripping the arms of her chair. First it is only tears, but then the sounds in the throat begin. It is controlled weeping, but barely controlled.)*

THE DAUGHTER *(after a bit; not loud, but bitter and accusatory).* Why are you crying!

THE WIFE. *(It explodes from her, finally, all that has been pent up for thirty years. It is loud, broken by sobs and gulps of air; it is self-pitying and self-loathing; pain, and relief.)* Because . . . I'm . . . unhappy. *(Pause)* Because . . . I'm . . . unhappy. *(Pause)* BECAUSE . . . I'M . . . UNHAPPY! *(A silence, as she regains control. Then she says it once more, almost conversational, but empty, flat)* Because I'm unhappy.

(A long silence. No one moves, save THE DOCTOR, *who finally removes the stethoscope from* THE PATIENT*'s chest, then from his ears. He stands, pauses for a moment, then walks a few steps forward, stops.)*

THE DOCTOR *(gently).* All over.
(No one moves.)

CURTAIN

SCUBA DUBA

Bruce Jay Friedman

First presented by Ivor David Balding in association with Alvin Ferleger and Gordon Crowe for The Establishment Theatre Company at the New Theatre in New York City on October 10, 1967, with the following cast:

HAROLD WONDER	Jerry Orbach	THIEF	Judd Hirsch
CAROL JANUS	Brenda Smiley	DR. SCHOENFELD	Ken Olfson
TOURIST	Conrad Bain	CHEYENNE	Christine Norden
LANDLADY	Rita Karin	JEAN WONDER	Jennifer Warren
VOICE OF HAROLD'S MOTHER	Stella Longo	FOXTROT (FROGMAN)	Cleavon Little
GENDARME	Bernard Poulain	REDDINGTON	Rudy Challenger

Staged by Jacques Levy
Setting by Peter Larkin
Costumes by Willa Kim
Lighting by Jules Fisher
Music by Stanley Walden

TIME: The present.
PLACE: The main room of a château in southern France.

Bruce Jay Friedman, oddly enough, introduced permissiveness in language to the New York stage. He probably did not know what he was doing at the time. He was a creature of circumstance.

He was born on April 26, 1930, in the Bronx. At the University of Missouri, where he graduated in 1951, he majored in journalism. But he soon recovered from this false start. Friedman had a semi-show-business background. His father worked in women's apparel, but he apparently also moonlighted as a piano player for silent movies, while his aunt was the assistant treasurer of the Broadhurst Theatre. Perhaps, or perhaps not, this led Friedman into playwriting. At least, in his youth, he presumably got free tickets at the Broadhurst.

Friedman spent a couple of years in the Air Force, and in the mid-fifties started to make a career for himself as a free-lance writer. He started with a piece, "Wonderful Golden Rule Days," which was published by *The New Yorker* in 1953. But he was soon being published by *The New York Times Book Review, The Saturday Evening Post, Esquire, Mademoiselle, Playboy,* and *Commentary.*

He was an editor for a time, but really made his mark with two remarkable novels, *Stern* in 1962, and, more particularly, *A Mother's Kisses* in 1964. In the latter novel he was one of the many Jewish-American writers of his generation who defined and specified the role their mothers took in their lives. Unlike some of his contemporaries Mr. Friedman did it with more wit than blood, and perhaps more love than understanding.

His short story "23 Pat O'Brien Movies" was adapted by himself for a workshop production at the American Place Theatre. In 1965 he visited the French Riviera, and he started to write *Scuba Duba.*

Scuba Duba was first produced, Off Broadway, at the New Theatre, New York City, on October 10, 1967. It was an unusual production on many counts, not least because it was directed by a Broadway director, Jacques Levy, and featured a Broadway star, Jerry Orbach. Mr. Orbach was no stranger to Off-Broadway—he had started in *The Fantasticks*—but it was rare at that time for someone as well known as Mr. Orbach to go back. This was one of the first Off-Broadway shows to have a feel of Broadway to it—and that marked a difference.

Scuba Duba closed on June 8, 1969, after 692 performances. Friedman's next play, *Steambath,* was not nearly so successful. It had considerable casting difficulties and opened at the Truck and Warehouse Theatre on June 30, 1970. It was staged by Anthony Perkins, who also starred in it, and closed on October 18, 1970, after 128 performances. In between *Scuba Duba* and *Steambath,* Friedman attempted a musical version of *A Mother's Kisses,* which died on the road before reaching New York.

Scuba Duba is a very funny, very bright play. It achieves a particular place in the theatre record book because, in its particular use of language, and even its particular theme, it was the first play to take for granted expressions and attitudes that novelists had taken for granted for more than a decade. Four-letter words had been heard in the theatre before *Scuba Duba,* but *Scuba Duba* was a popular play, and this was something different.

I think I can best express the impact of *Scuba Duba* with a very simple, but true, anecdote. When I wrote my first-night notice on the play for the *New York Times,* I instantly realized that I had a certain problem. The play was using words that I could not possibly reprint in a great national newspaper. I also realized that while the words in question did not shock me, it was very possible that they could shock some of my readers.

Personally I am a believer in complete noncensorship. If people want something let them have it. But I do believe in such productions being labeled and comprehended for what they are. I think few people went to the very successful production of *Oh, Calcutta!* imagining that they were going to see a documentary play about the Bengal famines. On the other hand, people walking in from the street and hearing language that they found offensive, or being confronted with nudity they were not expecting, might well find such a performance a very special, but very special, invasion of privacy.

With this in mind I mentioned in my first-night notice of *Scuba Duba* for the *New York Times* that "the language was frequently obscene." Some months later a lady wrote to me, complaining about the play. It seems, and she made some point of this, that she had taken her maiden sister to the play, and her maiden sister had been very shocked, hurt, and offended.

I looked back triumphantly at my first-night notice, and wrote back, somewhat brusquely, to my correspondent, that I had indeed characterized some of the language as "obscene." My newfound friend instantly wrote back—on a postcard of, for some reason, Miami—that I had not pointed out *how* obscene it was. I muttered game, set, match; but on the other hand, what do you do in a family newspaper? I am the first of a new generation of drama critics, unable to report verbatim what I often hear. I would not want to say "Fuck!" in the *New York Times*. But I hear "Fuck!" all the time in the New York theatre.

ACT ONE

SCENE. *Main room of château. South of France. Early evening. Young man, thirty-five or thereabout, visibly upset, paces back and forth. He wears a bathrobe, pajamas, slippers, and holds a large gardener's scythe, but seems unaware it exists. Someone is playing a piano in a neighboring house, something loud, abrasive, in the style of Khachaturian's "Sabre Dance." He goes to the window, looks toward the source of the music.*

HAROLD WONDER. I really needed this. This is exactly what I came here for. *(He opens the window and gestures with the scythe, calling out at the same time)* Hello! Hey!

(Music stops, a young girl, quite pretty, and wearing a bikini, appears)

MISS JANUS. Hi.

HAROLD. Hey. Thanks for dropping in. I'm not allowed to leave, myself. *(Defensively)* I don't need anyone's permission. It's just better if I stay here.

MISS JANUS. I thought you might have a giant bird flying loose around here and called me over to help. Every few months someone does that to me. I seem to give the impression I'd know what to do about people's loose birds.

HAROLD *(distantly)*. I wish that's all it was. I wish I could turn the whole thing into a bird problem. *(Coming back)* I thought you'd look different. I thought you'd be a little, I don't know, a little noisier-looking. *(He has been using the scythe to accompany his speech.)* Oh this? I'm sorry. I just picked it up and started carrying it around. Well, I didn't just pick it up. Actually, we had a prowler a few nights ago. My wife opened the shutters and came face to face with him, some kind of Swede she said it was. With a frying pan on his head.

MISS JANUS *(making herself at home)*. Maybe he just wanted to go through your wife's purse. Not to steal anything, but just to see what was in it. I had a Syrian friend once who loved to do that. We had a thing where I'd fill up my purse, pretend to be asleep, and then he'd tiptoe in and go through it. I put all kinds of surprises in there for him—birth control pills, religious ornaments, surgical appliances, pictures of other Syrian guys . . .

HAROLD. I don't think he was after any of that. I think he was after much bigger stuff. Look, I'm here with my wife. Except for the slight problem that I'm suddenly not here with my wife. That she decided not to be here. *(Gesturing with scythe)* On that prowler I mentioned, it doesn't show, but I'm actually big enough under these things to take care of any trouble by myself. *(Referring to scythe)* It's just something I do. Whenever there's trouble I pick up things. A friend of mine and I once started a little fight, just for fun. Before we began, I remember unconsciously picking up a chicken. One of those ready-made roasted things. I wasn't going to use it or anything. You can imagine how much good it would do you in a fight. Fly all over the goddamned place. I just seem to need something in my hands.

MISS JANUS. You're probably a very tactile person. I am, too. *(She gets up and flicks at her bikini bottom.)* Listen, does this fit or doesn't it? I bought it today and there were some German girls who said it was too small and I was hanging out of it. They could only speak about four words of English, but they managed to get that much across. *(In imitation of German accent)* "Madame . . . from the bottom . . . you are too wide . . . " *(Resuming normal style)* They'd been trying on bikinis and *theirs* didn't fit, so it may be they were just trying to spoil mine. The proprietor said it was because they were from Düsseldorf. Düsseldorf girls try them on all day long and never buy them. That must be some city—Düsseldorf.

HAROLD. Look, I don't want to know Düsseldorf. I'm in the middle of something awful. Something that's really ripping me up. That happened tonight. But I just want you to know that your suit fits. Right out of my terribleness I know it fits. I never saw anything fit like that in my entire life.

MISS JANUS. I wish I could get to the state where I truly believed my behind was beautiful.

HAROLD. That's always a big breakthrough.

MISS JANUS. Want me to tell you something I've never told anyone in my whole life? I was working in a place in the Village when I first came to New York. They had an ad that said they only wanted girls who looked like Modigliani paintings. Well, I was *feeling* kind of Modigliani-ish, so I went over and I got the job. It was a little disappointing. I was expecting hippies, acid heads, flower-power . . . It turned out to be a hangout for electricians. Well, there were five guys with long hair who at least *looked* a little Villagey and

I'd pretend they were exotic types even though they kept talking about—what are those electric things?

HAROLD. Volts? Amperes?

MISS JANUS. That's the one, amperes. For a couple of weeks they never really said anything to me except "Another Cappuccino." And then one morning—can you imagine, it was broad daylight—they said they'd like to take some pictures of me. Even then I knew what kind of pictures they meant. When I was off at eleven, I said, very businesslike, "Okay, I'll go with you and take a few . . ." *(Trails off as though the story is over)*

HAROLD *(completely hooked).* So?

MISS JANUS. Oh! So I followed them to a brownstone and we started off with some madonnalike portraits and then, because I really knew what it was all about, I took off all my clothes without them even asking. And that was just for openers. They started moving the camera around and I started moving myself around and I was carrying on as though I were in a trance. I don't know how long it took, but then I heard a ship's horn in the harbor and I put on my clothes and went home.

HAROLD. Did you . . .

MISS JANUS. . . . Sleep with them? No. I'm not sure really whether I wanted to or whether I would have. But I didn't.

HAROLD. That's some story. I loved it and everything, but that's some story. You just walked in here and sat down and I'm your neighbor and that's the kind of story you tell? I did love it, though. I hated it and I loved it.

MISS JANUS. I know. I did, too. I hated it and I loved it and I knew you would too. I could tell.

HAROLD. Look, I'm in bad trouble. You remember that wife I mentioned earlier? She pulled something real cute on me. If I wasn't so embarrassed I'd be shaking like a leaf. I've got two kids sleeping upstairs. Until you came over I'd just been calling up people. I tried to get Dr. Schoenfeld in Monaco. Thank God, I thought of him.

MISS JANUS. Don't tell me. He's your analyst.

HAROLD. Uh-uh. I don't fool around with that stuff. He's just a guy I know who lives in my building and happens to be a psychiatrist. I talk to him a lot in elevators and I seem to just bump into him in haberdashery shops, places like that. It's the most extraordinary thing. All he has to do is say three words to

me and I feel better. *(Cutout of DR. SCHOENFELD appears.)* I was fired from a job once. It was a big argument over whether I was allowed to use the executive john. Later I started to make more money than ever—but the idea of being fired was wiping me out. So Dr. Schoenfeld says . . .

DR. SCHOENFELD'S VOICE. You're good at looking up and down, Harold, but you've never once looked at life sideways . . .

HAROLD. . . . I never once looked at life sideways. He was suggesting I start looking at my problems out of the corner of my eye. It doesn't sound like much, but I tried it . . . *(Demonstrating)* You know, there's a hell of a lot going on over there on the sides. (DR. SCHOENFELD*'s cutout disappears.)* I have to call him in a little while. Look, I feel much better now, even though that electrician story of yours got me a little nervous. I feel like a damned fool about why I called you over in the first place.

MISS JANUS. You probably wanted to borrow something.

HAROLD. Well, actually, it was the piano. It was getting me jumpy. But now that I've met you, I'm sure it wouldn't bother me. You can play all you like.

MISS JANUS. It's nice when you look at my eyes. I just realized that hardly anyone ever does that. People look at my lips, my neck, my feet . . .

HAROLD. That's what I was doing? I was looking at your eyes? The trouble was I didn't know who was playing. It might have been anyone. But now that I know you're friendly, you can bang away to your heart's content.

MISS JANUS. Say, what do you do?

HAROLD. I'm in billboards. I write the stuff on them.

MISS JANUS. I'll bet you're great at it.

HAROLD. About three years ago some Bennington girl wrote an essay for the *Partisan Review* that said the prose on my billboards was the true urban folk literature of the sixties, much more important than Faulkner . . . *(Considers this, clucks his head as though to say, "Can you imagine anything that far-fetched?")* Look, I'm expecting these phone calls. But really, you can do anything you like. You can burn incense if you like and blow it into my chimney. I mean you've gotten me through a little piece of the night and that's the whole deal. If I can just make it through to the morning I'll be able to handle things a little better.

(HAROLD WONDER's LANDLADY, *a French woman, slightly past middle age, enters with a prospective* CLIENT *for the house—presumably for the month after the* WONDERS *vacate.* CLIENT *is an American, middle-aged, robust.)*

TOURIST. Well, I like it. It's French. And you can tell it's French. It smells French. I mean the goddamned air is French. As long as you're going to be in the country I think you ought to just jump in and French it up. Like these salesgirls. Cute little biscuits, but did you ever get a whiff of them? Now ordinarily I'd haul off and tell them what I think of them, but what the hell, you're in France. I just let them go ahead and stink up the place. It's their country.

LANDLADY. Excuse me, I was just showing the château for when you leave. *(To* MISS JANUS) You are in the films, no?

MISS JANUS. No. *(Leaving)*

LANDLADY. You're not in the films?

MISS JANUS. No.

LANDLADY *(to* TOURIST). She's in the films.

MISS JANUS. 'Bye. *(She leaves.)*

LANDLADY. *Au revoir, mademoiselle.* . . . I know that face . . . *(To* TOURIST*)* Françoise Sagan has had this house. Charles Aznavour. Brigitte Bardot was down for the summer with Jacques Tati. We have had Irving de Gaulle.

TOURIST. Irving de Gaulle?

LANDLADY. He is a brother of Charles, but he stays very quiet. They say he tells Charles exactly what to do, but in a whisper so no one will know. I myself have heard him pick up the phone in this very house and tell his brother to, how you say, screw Algeria. *(Turning to* HAROLD) Excuse me, monsieur. We are through in five seconds. *(To the* TOURIST) Monsieur Wonder is here because at the last second your Steve McQueen called to say he could not make it.

HAROLD. It's a little late.

TOURIST. Now that's the kind of talk I like. It's late and you just came right out and said it was late. It's not *that* late, actually, but that's not what I'm getting at. I think you ought to call a thing what it is. I got this guy works for me and he's bald, see. Oh, he's got a little swirl of a thing sitting back there on his head and he kind of brings it forward, but for Christ's sake, the man is a skinhead, no two ways about it. Well, I could putter around and pretend I don't even notice it, you know, kind of kid him along. But I don't, see.

He comes into my office every morning with a report and I don't let two minutes go by before I say, "Hey there, Small"—that's his name—"I see you're parting your hair in the middle." Now he chokes up a little and I'm not about to say that he eats it up exactly—but for Christ's sake, I've laid the thing right out on the table instead of pretending it's not there. And, of course, to spare his feelings I've kind of blended it in with a little humor, which I believe in doing. The parting your hair in the middle part. That's humorous. It's not like I said "Get your tail in here, you bald son of a bitch," or anything. They do that in some offices. But I kind of skirt around the edges. That's how I keep my employees. You got a Chink's around here?

LANDLADY. Monsieur?

TOURIST. A Chinese restaurant.

HAROLD. There's a Vietnamese place around five miles down the road.

TOURIST. As long as they got those egg rolls I don't care what kind of Chink they are. I been all over the world, but I can't really settle into a place unless I know there's a good Chink's nearby. I understand they're opening them up all over Moscow. We got one in my town, a kind of drive-in Chink's. Night he opened up I was first in line. I said to him, "You're pretty goddamned lucky to be here, buster." He looked kind of puzzled, but he knew damned well what I was talking about. I said to him, "Let's say the dice had taken an extra roll. You could have been over there in Shanghai someplace starving to death." They got four-year-old prostitutes over there, I understand. Girl gets to be eight and she's still got her cherry, old Mao Tse-tung gives her a goddamned peace prize. You know what I'm talking about. "You'd have had beriberi by now if you'd been over there. So you just keep those egg rolls *hot,* Mr. Chinkhead, and everything'll be all right." . . . We never had any trouble with the guy. Hell, for all I know he could have been a *citizen* or something, but that gets us right to my philosophy. Lay it on the line.

HAROLD *(to* LANDLADY, *temper snapping).* Look, in case anyone forgot, this is my house until September first. I'm not interested in any Elks' Convention. Would you mind just clearing out of here? I've got some calls coming and I'd like a little privacy.

TOURIST. That's all right, son, that's frank talk. We're not really intruding, the way I see it, but you think we are and you said so. No need to apologize. I like it here. I think I'll take it. It's French. Got a little of that sales-girl smell to it. *(Leaving)* Take it easy, son, and don't take any wooden frogs' legs. (TOURIST *exists.*)

LANDLADY. Ah, wonderful. I call Charl-ton Heston immediately and tell him sorry the house is rented. *(Writing in a little book)* Alors, that takes care of September. He is charming, non? I think he is a famous actor.

HAROLD. For Christ's sake, he's *not* a fa-mous actor.

LANDLADY. No, no, I am never wrong about these things. I think he is Tony Curtis. Yes, I'm sure of it. Tony would not want to make a big fuss over it, you know how they are. I notice madame is not here. *(Primping)*

HAROLD. You notice goddamned right.

LANDLADY *(seductively, humming a little romantic refrain).* When I was a girl I was the fairest flower in all Provence. They would come from miles around to gaze at me. And when there was a man I admired, my petals would open, one by one—floop, floop, floop.

HAROLD. Look, that's the last thing I want to hear about right now.

LANDLADY. And I have a secret for you, monsieur. My petals still open, not as often perhaps, but wider than ever.

HAROLD. Look, madame, I'm sure you were a winner in the old days and that you're still standing room only. But don't you see I'm a wreck? . . . Anyway, how come you didn't do anything when I shouted last night?

LANDLADY. You mean when we had the prowler?

HAROLD. When *I* had the prowler. I had to look in the guidebook to find out how to yell for help. Didn't you hear me? *Au secours, au secours!* I felt like a goddamned jackass.

LANDLADY *(correcting pronunciation).* Se-cours. *Ours. Say! Se-Cours!*

HAROLD *(trying it). Secours.*

LANDLADY. That is much better. What about the police, monsieur?

HAROLD. Oh sure, I know about the police. I got a cop on the phone and explained what happened. He said the only way he'd come is if I drove over there and watched the station for him. They've got one cop for the whole goddamned south of France. Look, madame, I appreciate your company. I really do. But I'm in terrible trouble and I'm expecting these phone calls. I can't really talk when anyone's around. When I was a teenager I'd have to take all my calls in the closet. I'd put

all these overcoats over my head. It's the only way I feel private.

LANDLADY. All right, monsieur, I under-stand. But remember that madame has a spe-cial cure for young men. The wonders of France. Your Jimmy Cagney was in such trouble. He comes to madame and poof, he wins the Oscar.

(She leaves. He smokes, putters around nervously, looks at phone, decides against it. Goes to window with scythe. Opens shutters, hollers out au secours, au secours—*first loudly, then breaking off into a plaintive cry. Phone rings. He picks it up, still holding scythe.)*

HAROLD. New York? Yes, operator, I'll take it. *(Cutout of* MOTHER *appears.)* Hello, Mom.

MOTHER'S VOICE. Is that you, Harold?

HAROLD. Yeah, Mom, all the way from France.

MOTHER'S VOICE. What happened, sweet-heart?

HAROLD. Nothing, Mom, nothing at all. I just decided to call. But I'll have to make it fast because it's costing a goddamned fortune. I don't even know how much. Oh Christ, I can't concentrate. It's too expensive.

MOTHER'S VOICE. First tell me about the children, sweetheart.

HAROLD. They're fine.

MOTHER'S VOICE. And is it nice in France?

HAROLD. It's wonderful, Mom. A wonder-ful country.

MOTHER'S VOICE. Harold, you have some-thing heavy in your hand, don't you?

HAROLD *(looking at scythe, then dropping it).* How the hell did you know that?

MOTHER'S VOICE. I've been your mother for a long time, darling.

HAROLD. Jesus, it must have cost a grand already and I haven't even said anything. Look, Ma, I'm in lousy trouble, so I'm just calling up people. I just want it to hurry up and be tomorrow morning.

MOTHER'S VOICE. Something did happen to the children. I knew it.

HAROLD. No, Mom, I told you they're fine.

MOTHER'S VOICE. Is your wife at your side —where she belongs?

HAROLD. No, Mom, Jean is out. That's what it's all about.

MOTHER'S VOICE. I knew it. I could have predicted the whole thing. Who is she out with, darling?

HAROLD. Mom. I can hardly get it out of

my mouth. She's run off with a spade frogman.

MOTHER'S VOICE. What kind of frogman,
darling?

HAROLD. A spade. Don't you know what
that is? She's run off with a goddamned black
scuba diver!

MOTHER'S VOICE. Don't talk that way,
Harold. It's not nice.

HAROLD. All right, Mom. She's with a
dark-skinned phantom of the ocean depths. Is
that better? How do you think I feel saying
something like that on the phone and you
don't think I said it politely enough?

MOTHER'S VOICE (still calm, although news
is sinking in now). A colored frogman. That's
what she needed, a colored frogman. You
know why she's doing that, don't you, Harold? Because you didn't do enough for her.
None of us did. The whole family didn't strip
itself naked enough for her. And what did
you give her, Harold? The French Riviera?
That isn't a vacation, darling, that's a punish-
ment. Didn't you know that? That's where
you take people instead of throwing them into
dungeons. You know where I would have
taken her, Harold. I would have brought her
back to that ghetto in Baltimore where you
found her on the streets!

HAROLD (interrupting). Look, now don't
go too far. You're not exactly a bargain yourself, you know!

MOTHER'S VOICE. Harold, I think there's
something wrong with the connection. You
couldn't possibly have said what I just heard
you say.

HAROLD. How about that cello player you
took me up to see when I was seven years old?
You forgot him, eh? And that guy who made
those alligator handbags. Never heard of him,
eh? Well, I didn't forget them so easy. It
didn't exactly do me any good to be in on that
stuff, so don't go picking on Jean.

MOTHER'S VOICE. Is that why you called,
Harold? You thought your mother needed a
little filth thrown in her face. All the way
from France.

HAROLD. All right, Mom, I'm sorry. I
didn't mean to get into that.

MOTHER'S VOICE (in tears). That's all
right, Harold. I'll just consider that my pay-
ment after thirty-six years of being your
mother.

HAROLD. I think she's going to stay out the
whole night and I'm not sure I can take it.
I'm waiting for a call now. I'm all alone here.

MOTHER'S VOICE. Harold, you know what
your mother's going to do now? She's going
to quietly take a boat and she's coming right
over to France.

HAROLD. All right, all right. I'm calm now.
Look, I have to say goodbye. This call is costing around twelve grand already.

MOTHER'S VOICE. And you promise me
you'll use your head.?

HAROLD. I promise. But if you hear the
phone again from France, don't get nervous.

MOTHER'S VOICE. Believe me, sweetheart,
you forget, but I've been through much worse
than this. A mother doesn't forget. Much
worse, Harold. This is a little nothing.

HAROLD. I know, Mom. There's just something about her staying out all night in a foreign country. Listen, are you sure you're
okay?

MOTHER'S VOICE. Wonderful, Harold. I
saw this *Virginia Woolf* they're all raving
about. Frankly, I wouldn't give you two cents
for Elizabeth Taylor!

HAROLD. I got to go now, Mom.

MOTHER'S VOICE. Goodbye, darling.

(They exchange half a dozen goodbyes;
finally HAROLD hangs up, cutting her off in
the middle of one, and MOTHER cutout disappears)

HAROLD. That was a fast eighty-seven dollars for a goodbye. I don't care. I'll talk to
myself. What do I care? There's no law. As
long as it makes me feel better, that's the only
thing. (Goes to window. Shouting) Jeannie,
you bitch. France you picked to pull this on
me. Not in Queens where I have defenses.
Where I have friends. (Plaintively) Au secours,
au secours. (Hears piano playing, sweet, me-
lodic) That's okay. That's fine. It doesn't
bother me any more. Now that I know she's
friendly. . . . It's one of my favorite mazur-
kas. (Goes to the window and yells out) You
can play it all night if you like. (Music stops)

(MISS JANUS appears, still in bikini, eating
from a fruit bowl.)

MISS JANUS. Hi, could you hear me playing? I came over to find out.

HAROLD. No. I mean, I could, but it was
fine.

MISS JANUS. Want some fruit? Make you
strong.

HAROLD. I couldn't get anything down.

MISS JANUS (eating away). It's like eating
pure strength. I'm not fooling.

HAROLD. I never saw anyone eat fruit like
that. You're kind of slopping it up and eating

your fingers right along with it, and what is it? It's wonderful. *(Switching)* Look, I'm in all this trouble. You probably guessed it's about my wife. And this colored scuba diver. *(Chanting louder and louder)* Scuba duba duba. Scuba duba duba. Scuba duba duba. That's what keeps bouncing through my head.

(Cutout of giant ape-man appears for a moment. Jungle drums are heard. Cutout disappears.)

MISS JANUS. You really are upset. Would you like me to cradle your head?

HAROLD. What do you mean?

MISS JANUS *(making a cradling gesture at her bosom)*. In here. Sometimes that's all people need, people with the world's toughest exteriors.

HAROLD *(trying it but unable really to fit into a good cradle)*. I don't think I'm doing it right. Anyway, it's hard to just sail into one of those.

MISS JANUS. All right, but if at any time you feel the need . . . just signal me. *(She demonstrates with cradling pantomime.)* And we'll start right in, no formalities . . .

HAROLD. Okay, but meanwhile, if I start acting funny, just shove a little applesauce into me, It's in the kitchen. If you can just be with me awhile.

MISS JANUS. I can stay as long as you like. I was just château-sitting for my friend Abby and her new husband. Abby and I were roommates in New York while she was going with him. He's a sculptor named Nero. For three years she couldn't even get him to *talk* about marriage—until two months ago when she had her left breast removed. Suddenly Nero felt responsible as hell, wanted to marry her immediately. She hadn't come out of the ether and he had her in front of a minister. Abby wouldn't let me move out—it was almost as though she felt sorry for me for having both my breasts and having to be single. So I kind of tagged along with them to France. Something's supposed to happen between the three of us. I'm not sure what. It hasn't yet, but it's always in the air. At least once a day someone says, "What'll we do tonight?" Then the air gets very tense. I think it would have happened already, but no one knows how to start. Or who's supposed to do what to who. And then there's always Abby's breast to worry about. How are you supposed to work that in?

HAROLD *(abashed)*. You walked in here with some collection of stories . . .

MISS JANUS. Maybe some night Nero will say, "Let's go, girls," and we'll all take off our clothes. Simple as that.

HAROLD *(looking out shutters)*. You know, my wife's got the goddamned car. What am I supposed to do, take a taxi to Marseille, get out and say, "Pardon me, did you see this American woman and this black person with flippers on his feet?" He wears them out of the water, right on the goddamned sidewalk! He's graceful in them too, that's the awful part. Got one of those Jean Paul Belmondo styles, I mean, what am I supposed to do, say he looks like W. C. Fields just because he's out jazzing my wife and I'm here with two kids trying to get through the goddamned night? I'm sorry. Please go on.

MISS JANUS. I think what's supposed to happen is that Abby is going to die and then Nero and I are logically supposed to more or less blend together. Say a month or so later. None of us have ever said it, but you guess that's what it's all about. We're waiting for Abby to die. He's very attractive and everything, but I wish he'd really wait. Like yesterday, Abby was out at the beach somewhere gathering shells—she gets beautiful ones now, the most exquisite you've ever seen, almost as though they've been left for her because she's going to die. He came up behind me, put his hands very deliberately on my *two* breasts almost as though he was counting them, and asked me to inhale something he keeps in a sponge. Well, all it does is make my behind itch a little. I've taken them all—pot, mescaline, LSD—I get a little sleepy and then my behind itches.

HAROLD. Look, there's something you ought to know.

MISS JANUS. Yes?

HAROLD. I'm a married man. *(Chuckling ironically)* Some married. You know, she's had a series of these guys, not really *had* them as far as I know, but all one of them has to be is slightly worthless and she gets turned right on. *(Cutouts of three men appear in the room: one with floor-waxing equipment, a second in trunks with a swimming pool vacuum, and a third with a garbage man's trash sticker.)* The first one was a floor shellacker, then there was this guy who cleaned up swimming pools in Barbados. So help me, Christ, there was a garbage collector in Baltimore. He was a little classier than the rest of the garbage crowd. He'd only handle metal and wood. Left the mushy stuff to the other boys, but he was a garbage man all right, no matter how you slice it. It's a classical kind of deal. She can only relax with a man when she feels he isn't worth four cents. If he knows the alphabet he's finished. *(Cutouts of three men disappear, arms locked in camaraderie.)* I once tried acting a little low-down myself. I started hanging around the house in these Puerto Rican clothes. So one day Jeannie reached into my jacket and grabbed this extra inch of fat I have around my waist and wouldn't let go—she was letting me know who I was, underneath all the clothes. She wouldn't let go until I hit her. Came down hard on one of her pressure points. There's one in there, right around the shoulder blades. I used to memorize lists of pressure points and erogenous zones . . . *(Switching)* Listen, why the hell don't you just move away from your friends?

MISS JANUS. I've drifted in with them and I don't seem to be able to drift out. It's that drifting I can't get over. It was that way the first time too. Men like to hear about the first time. I was going with a boy and my father didn't really like him so one night he pointed a gun at the boy's head and went "Pow." Like a joke. Only I got very nauseous and the next thing I knew the boy and I were drifting out to the highway and we sort of drifted into this shed that was full of old magazines and newspapers from all over the world. I let him make love to me right in the middle of all those publications. I can still remember their names. *(Closing her eyes, and in a sort of religious chant, enunciating each one very deliberately)* The Philadelphia *Bulletin,* the Des Moines *Register,* the *Deutschlander Verlag, Paris-Soir,* the Sacramento *Bee,* the Newark *Star-Ledger, Variety,* the *Bulletin of Atomic Scientists* . . .

HAROLD. You know, I really love the kind of stories you tell, the kind where those things happen to you. Look, I don't know what's going to happen, you're terribly attractive, the way you eat fruit, for example, but I'm in the middle of this thing. *(Hollering out window)* Come on out and fight, you black son of a bitch. Jeannie, I dare you to produce him now that I know what his game is! *(To* MISS JANUS*)* I don't even know my own name. I've got these kids asleep upstairs. But couldn't we have this thing together in which you just tell me those stories—even if nothing else happens? They kind of sneak up on me—like a hug or something.

MISS JANUS. They never worked on Juan.

HAROLD. All right, let me sit down for this one. I'm sitting down for Juan.

MISS JANUS. He was just an eight-year-old boy in a slum school where I worked as a substitute teacher. Everyone in the whole school had tried to get through to him—but he kept on being sullen and withdrawn, wouldn't say a word, wouldn't meet your eyes. So then I took a crack at him. I told him all these stories. And at the end he was just as sullen and withdrawn as before.

HAROLD. That's the whole Juan story? That's what I sat down for? Look, I'll tell you quite frankly—I didn't like the material in that one. But I liked every one up to now. I love them even though they wreck me. I mean did you see me at the window with that black son of a bitch routine? Well, it's true. I really would like to run this thing . . . *(gesturing with scythe)* . . . right through his gizzard. But look, let's face it, you know the type of fellow I am—the straightest guy in France, right? Well, the truth is, I encouraged the whole thing. Just the way I'm getting you to tell those stories. What happened is that we met the black bastard in Cannes one afternoon, right after we got here, standing around at one of those sidewalk restaurants, with his flippers on and this black suit and that breathing equipment on his back. Wait a minute. *(Goes to slide machine)* You want to hear something? I even took pictures of the goddamn thing. *(As he is pulling a very long screen out of a very small closet)* Longest closet in France. *(Sets up slide show)* Take a seat. Any seat in the house. (MISS JANUS *complies. First slide of* FROGMAN *comes into focus.)* There he is. . . . Now, you take away the skin diving stuff and he isn't really that handsome, but he has this smile that shows up now and then. It's as though he has a zipper across his mouth. He kind of unzips that smile and when you see his teeth it kind of puts him in a different league. . . . Anyway, all summer long we'd been hearing about this wonderful loup fish, and Jeannie, who's one of the original fish-eaters, was really starved for one. Well, the restaurant was sorry but it was fresh out. So that's when this skin diver guy comes over to the table. I don't know whether he'd heard us or not, but the next thing you know, he goes flying over to the pier and heaves himself into the water, and I'll be goddamned if he doesn't come up with one of those loup fish on the end of his spear! "Voilà, babe! Compliments of Stokely Carmichael, the Honorable Martin Luther King, and Cab Calloway." Well, it really *was* a kind of charming thing to do. I mean the way he presented the damned thing. Anyway, we bought him a drink, dinner. He didn't say much except that even as a kid he'd always had these strong lungs. *(Goes up to* FROGMAN*'s image on screen, shouts)* Come on out, you son of a bitch. I'll take you on even if you have got strong lungs and I am a little afraid of that spear gun. *(Climbs down as though nothing happened)* Well, actually, he didn't seem like a bad guy, we didn't know anybody . . . so the next thing I know, Jeannie and I are in Cannes again and I find myself saying, "Let's go see old Scuba Duba." All my own idea. I have to say that for Jeannie. So far she hadn't even taken a good look at him. I was the mastermind—really brilliant the way I served him up, just like a bowl of strawberries. The way I planned it, a real Normandy Invasion. I smoked him out that second time. It wasn't easy—he was out working on shrimp boats or something—but I found him and for the next week we just went around together. I even took him along when we went to get her hair set. *(Rips out one of the slides and tears it up)* One thing I resent is paying for all those drinks, you bastard, and this has nothing to do with your being black, so don't get any ideas. *(Closes up slide equipment)* So next thing I know, she insists on being by herself one afternoon, and then a second time, a few more times, and then I get this call earlier tonight. This is it, she says. I'm with him, I'm staying with him and it isn't just for tonight, it's for always, words and music by Irving Berlin. I can go down to the Mediterranean and drain it out cup by cup as far as she's concerned and it's not going to do any good. I'm supposed to stay with the children and maybe she'll call and at a certain point she'll come and get them because she wants them. And she's not kidding either, this really *is* it. You should have heard her voice. So what am I supposed to do now, ask some spade if I can come visit my kids once in a while? Work my ass off so she can buy gold flippers for a goddamned spade frogman? What's he gonna do, send my kids to some spade school? A spade underwater school in France somewhere? *(In mock imitation)* "Now you take the flippers in one hand . . . " What am I supposed to do, start calling up girls now and ask them out on picnics?

In the condition I'm in? What do I do, go to Over Twenty-eight dances? I mean, what the hell am I supposed to do? I'm shaking like a leaf. How do you feel about men crying?

MISS JANUS. It's all right. I don't have any special theories about it. I have a feeling it would be all right if you did it.

HAROLD. I'll just turn around here for a second and try to get it over with as soon as possible. *(Turns head)* That ought to do it. It wasn't too bad, was it?

MISS JANUS. You have a beautiful neck.

HAROLD. Really? It's big, but I never thought much about it being beautiful. What a nice thing to say. I mean, if you said I was handsome that's one thing, but when you compliment a neck you've got to be serious.

MISS JANUS. What happened then?

HAROLD. Maybe I ought to show it off a little more. *(Switches)* Well, first I thought I'd get her back by insulting him. "You think you're going to be able to shop at Bendel's on what he makes with those flippers? What do you think is down at the bottom of that French ocean anyway? There's just a bunch of French shit down there. And back in the States, what'll you do, go to Freedom Marches together? Eat hominy grits? Sit around and read back issues of *Ebony?*" Well, I didn't get very far with that approach. So then I switched over to all the things we'd had together over the eight years, and you know I couldn't come up with very much. The sex you can forget about. You see, one time, when we were just married, she looked up while we were making love and saw my hand up in the air. "What's that?" she asked. "It's my hand," I said. "Well, what's it *doing* up there?" she asked. "Where's it supposed to be?" I asked. "Well, shouldn't it be *doing* something?" she said. Well, I said, the other hand was *doing* something, but she didn't see it that way and it was kind of downhill ever since then. Now the only time she gets excited is in bathrooms at other people's houses.

MISS JANUS. I never tried that. I'm not knocking it or anything. But it's funny.

HAROLD. Yeah. She goes into the toilet and she pulls me in there with her and she's as hot as a snake. All our friends know by now. We go to a party, they all stand around waiting for us to come out. Believe me, that's no sex life. So I tried to think of some other stuff and all I could come up with was a trip to Quebec we once took. "What about that trip to Quebec?" I said to her. "What about it?" she said.

"Well, wasn't it something?" "It wasn't that great," she said. I said, "Yeah, but didn't we see a ship from Israel at the waterfront that wasn't even supposed to be there?" She agreed we saw a ship from Israel, but that was no reason to keep a marriage together. I had to agree with her there. So then there wasn't much else I could do except hit her with the kids. Well, this Negro gentleman friend of hers was way ahead of me on that. He told her the kids were going to be fine, she said. Yeah. "Well, maybe that's in colored divorces," I said, "but my kids aren't going to be fine. (Hollering out window) Not with any goddamned spade frogman stepfather." I love my kids. I have this one game I play with them. I got to show you. It's called "Can't Get Out."

MISS JANUS. What do I do?

HAROLD. Oh, just pretend you're Jamie. I say to you, "Now I'm going to get you in one of the toughest grips known to the Western world. It's called the 'Double Reverse Panther Bear Pretzel Twist.' No man in history has ever been known to get out of this grip. Are you ready? Do you dare to allow me to get you into it?"

MISS JANUS. I do.

HAROLD. I do, Daddy.

MISS JANUS. I do, Daddy.

HAROLD. Well, then I spend a long time getting them into it. This kind of thing. (Twists her around, this way and that, tying up her arms, legs) "Okay," I say, "now you're in it. No man in history has ever broken out of it." Then I let them twist around for a while and gradually I let them slide out and say I "Good God, the first man in history ever to work his way out of the Double Reverse Panther Bear Pretzel Twist! Congratulations."

(She has made no effort to get out, stays twisted.)

MISS JANUS. But I can't get out.

(HAROLD kisses MISS JANUS awkwardly, then ardently, then tenderly.)

HAROLD (setting her down). Look, that isn't why I told you about the game. I wasn't working around to that, or anything.

MISS JANUS. It's a lovely game.

HAROLD. The kids love it. They can play it with me for hours. (As an afterthought) Listen, what kind of a kiss was that? I just don't know how good I'd be at kissing under the circumstances.

MISS JANUS. It was delicious. Listen, I don't want you to get the wrong idea. I've done an awful lot of drifting in and out of things, but actually I've only really had one all-out start-to-finish love thing. A writer. We were both very new with each other. What we did was wander through each other like we were the first man and woman. The sex part with him was always very quick, almost instantaneous. It was very sad. We're still friends. He married a girl who's as quick as he is—and he says they're very happy.

HAROLD. Maybe I'll get through the night. I've got this great fighting chance. . . . I once read a novel about a guy who just got divorced and what he did to get through was a lot of physical activity. Push-ups. Every morning he'd get up, light a fire, and start doing push-ups. I wonder if I ought to try a few. (Gets down on the floor and begins doing push-ups, gets up to around ten) You know, it's not bad at all. I wonder how deep knee bends would be. (Does a few) Hey, you know it's really something. I'll be goddamned if it doesn't help. (Starts to do an isometric exercise) I'll probably come up with a hernia.

MISS JANUS. Hercules had a hernia.

HAROLD. Hercules? How'd you find that out?

MISS JANUS. I saw a statue of him in the Louvre and there was a funny little hernia line nobody else noticed. I once told a boy I had a hernia. At college. He drove me out to a lake and asked me how I'd feel about some heavy petting. It sounded so heavy. So I told him I had a hernia. . . . Listen, would you like a massage?

HAROLD (with irony). Yeah, that's exactly what I'm in the mood for. I'm supposed to drift into a little massage . . .

MISS JANUS. You know, a lot of people believe it's a homosexual thing. I don't. But I don't even believe homosexual relations really exist. Certainly not between two men. Why would they bother? There are so many other things they could be out doing. I don't think it's ever really happened. Maybe in Germany once or twice, in the thirties, but that was the only time. I think it's something someone made up to play a big joke on society. A couple of fags made it up.

HAROLD. You know, for a second I thought that frogman was a fag. He's probably been keeping it up his sleeve. I just remembered something about the way he slithered into the water after that fish. (Reflecting) That's all I'd need. Losing my wife to a goddamned fag. (Quiet, desperate anger)

Boy, if I ever found that out, then I'd *really* break his head.... *(In a different mood)* I'm not sure I want to know, but where'd you learn about massages?

MISS JANUS. My father taught me how to do them. I thought it would be incestuous, but it really isn't. It just feels good.

HAROLD. How do you know it's not incestuous?

MISS JANUS. With my *father?*

HAROLD. What do I do?

MISS JANUS. Roll up your pants.

HAROLD. What do you mean?

MISS JANUS. I want to do your knees.

HAROLD. What good's that going to do?

MISS JANUS. You'll see. (HAROLD *rolls up his pants.)* They're very attractive.

HAROLD. Thank you.

(She begins to massage his knees.)

MISS JANUS *(still massaging).* I bet you were good in sports too.

HAROLD. I was about average. But I always had great form. *(Demonstrating with scythe)* I'd pick up a tennis racket or start fooling around with a basketball and I'd make these sly little moves and these great championship faces and they'd think God knows what was coming. I did a lot of losing, but it didn't seem to matter. *(Responding to massage)* Hey, you know, you're right, it *is* good. Of all things, I never even knew I *had* knees before and yet here they are, out of the clear blue skies, feeling great.

MISS JANUS. I believe some people have a special touch, don't you? That young man in the French movie who all he has to do is touch this girl on the wrist at a party and she moves right out on her millionaire husband and goes to live with him in a little cellar somewhere. And it all started with a touch.

HAROLD *(pushing her off).* I'd like to make a little announcement about my knees. My knees have just become the greatest knees in town. Everyone said they were finished, washed up, that they'd never work again. Well, you've put them back on their feet. I want to thank you for giving them another break in show business. *(They shake hands.)* But she never showed up, did she? And nothing's really changed, has it? . . . Dr. Schoenfeld. *(He picks up phone, dials.)* Dr. Schoenfeld?

(Cutout of DR. SCHOENFELD *appears.)*

DR. SCHOENFELD'S VOICE. Speaking . . .

HAROLD. Surprise. This is Harold Wonder. I'm in Cap Ferrat.

DR. SCHOENFELD'S VOICE. All right, if you want to be in France. I didn't realize you knew I was here.

HAROLD. Oh, sure. Don't you remember? In that haberdashery store? We were both trying on bathrobes. Look, I'm in terrible trouble and I'm just calling up guys. But this isn't just a call. I really have to ask you to come over here. You can make it in about twenty minutes. Look, obviously you don't *have* to come . . .

DR. SCHOENFELD'S VOICE. What's the difficulty, Harold?

HAROLD. The difficulty is that I'm climbing up the walls. It's the kind of thing you'd never get into in a million years. It's my wife. She's out with this goddamned spade frogman and I think she's going to stay the whole night. It's that whole night thing that scares me.

DR. SCHOENFELD'S VOICE. Harold, isn't the frogman just one chapter?

HAROLD. One chapter? Oh yeah, and I've been turning him into the whole Modern Library. Look, Dr. Schoenfeld, I don't want to appear ungrateful, but that capsule style just isn't enough this time. Can you come over? I've tried everything. A little while ago I started to shake. I'm afraid I'm going to blow sky high. I don't want the kids to see me that way. So could you please try to make a run over here? Please.

DR. SCHOENFELD'S VOICE. Harold, you know what your problem is—you're good at looking up and down but you've never once looked at life sideways.

HAROLD. Look, Doc, I don't want sideways now. Will you don't give me sideways.

DR. SCHOENFELD'S VOICE. No sideways, eh?

HAROLD. No. I really need you. Could you sort of come over and spend the night? I really need somebody I can depend on.

DR. SCHOENFELD'S VOICE Well, Harold, I have a friend visiting.

HAROLD. There's plenty of room. Bring your friend along. I really do need you, right this second. *(He hangs up .* DR. SCHOEN-FELD*'s cutout disappears.)* He'll be here. I know it. If it was me and I heard a guy who sounded like I did, I'd be over in a flash . . . You know, right this second, as we sit here, my wife is up on a chandelier with a spade.

MISS JANUS. You like the way that sounds, don't you?

HAROLD. What do you mean? Spade? I

guess so. Spade. It comes out so smooth. They have all the good names. *(Enunciating very deliberately)* Coon. Shine. All those n's. Wop. Kike. See? Nothing. If you ask me, I think she picked one of them just to confuse me. Or to prove something to me. She knows how mixed up I am about colored guys. There's just no right way to be about Negroes. I went down to that Freedom March a couple of years ago in Washington. All of a sudden. Actually I knew I was going, but I like to tell it as though I made up my mind on the spur of the moment. Makes me sound like more of a sympathizer. Anyway, I got down there and when the marching started it got kind of crowded and a man fainted. I stopped to see if I could help and a huge Negro in back twisted my arm up behind me and said, "Pass 'em by, pass 'em by." He kept walking me that way till we got way the hell out in a field somewhere. And he's still saying, "Pass 'em right up, pass 'em by." Finally I said, "I passed the son of a bitch by already," but he just kept marching me along saying, "You ain't really passed him all the way by yet." He finally let me go, I don't know where, someplace in Baltimore. That didn't exactly put me in the right mood for a Freedom March. I got to listen to some of the speeches anyhow—they've really got some wonderful speakers, guys you've never heard of who can knock you out of your seat.

MISS JANUS. And then something terrible happened, right?

HAROLD. You ready?

MISS JANUS. Clunk. *(She does a fastening thing at her waist, then explains.)* Safety belt.

HAROLD. Well, I'm listening to the Reverend and he's really going to town. All goose bumps, really nailing the thing down, right in front of the Lincoln Memorial, the most stirring thing you ever heard. About a third of the way through I start to look at this little colored Freedom Marcher type. She had one of those behinds you can balance things on. I couldn't take my eyes off her. I felt rotten—right in the middle of this stirring thing and I can't get my eyes off her ass. So I kind of get close to her and before long we start kidding around—in whispers—and next thing you know I've got her behind a tree. I couldn't stop myself. She was a little laundress girl from Delaware who came down by bus—her name was Eurethra—we didn't talk much. Anyway, what I'm leading up to is right through this Reverend's speech—one of the most brilliant addresses ever given—I read it next day in the *Times*—there we were, me and Eurethra behind the tree. Hell, maybe it was her fault as much as mine. I mean she was the colored one, *she* really should have been listening. I mean, what kind of guy does such a thing?

MISS JANUS. A very warm, glandular human being.

HAROLD. That'll be the day. *(Goes to shutters and cries out)* Jeannie . . . *(Then changes his mind)* I'm not going to do that any more. Listen, what do you want, anyway? You enjoy listening to a messed-up guy?

MISS JANUS. I don't know what I want. Right now I'd settle for a guarantee that I'm never going to be hairy.

HAROLD. Hairy!

MISS JANUS. Like Janine Harper, a girl in my home town. She was a beautiful redheaded girl and then one summer she got very hairy. Turned into Neanderthal man right there before everyone's eyes. She cleared up in the fall and I guess she's all right now—I hear she married an optometrist—but I never got over it. If I could just be sure that'll never happen to me. If I could have a written certificate, something I could carry around. I just don't want to have to spend a hairy summer.

HAROLD. Well *I'll* guarantee it. It'll never happen to you. Never in a million years.

MISS JANUS. And I've decided that I'd like to go to bed with you.

HAROLD. Me, you'd like to go to bed with? Oh, you crazy kid.

MISS JANUS. Listen, your wife has raced off with another man and you can't adjust to it. That's not an everyday thing, you know. It's not as though you were carrying on about urban renewal. Besides, I'd like to see what it would be like. With many men you just know, but with you . . .

HAROLD. I'll tell you what it's like. With me, it's a one-handed number. *(Changing tones)* That black bastard told us he's got beautiful paintings on the wall. I can just about imagine. I can just picture the colored shit he's got hanging up there. Haven't you heard? That's where Picasso is having all his shows these days. At that spade's apartment. The second Picasso knocks off a canvas he rushes it over there, special delivery. It's the only place he'll show his paintings. Maybe he likes the colored smell up there; it really brings out the values. *(Phone rings. He looks at her apologetically, lets it ring, goes to phone, looks back and then takes it near a clothing closet, where, standing up, he begins to pull coats over his head for privacy.)* Hello, Jeannie-and-if-it-is-don't-say-a-word-because-I'm-doing-all-the-talking. Now, Jeannie, look, I don't care what's happened. You got a little nervous, it's a foreign country, all right, I'm a little shook up, but it's over, I forgive you, and you're coming right the hell home where you belong. We'll take a few trips. Remember, we were going to use this as home base and see Barcelona? . . . It is *not* just the beginning! . . . All right then, we'll go to Liverpool. Any place you say. . . . I'm the one who *is* facing facts! . . . Jeannie, I'm all alone here. What do you think this has been like for me? . . . A strain? . . . You're holed up with a nigger frogman and you call me up and all it is is a little strain . . . Strain? *(Goes to window, yells)* I'll give you a strain, you fuckin' Mau-Mau. I'll strain your ass. *(Back to phone)* I'm not trying to put him down. . . . All right, all right. . . . Okay, he *is*. He's very nice. Nicer than I'll ever be. . . . Listen, I've been plenty nice. In my own style. . . . I use both hands too! It was just that one time. I can't explain it. *(Hardening)* Now listen, Jeannie, you get your tail the hell back here or I'm throwing you right the hell out of the house. You hear? I don't care if you're impressed or not. . . . All right, you're out. You hear that? I've thrown you out of the house. . . . I don't have to have you here to throw out of the house. You're out. *(Pacifying)* All right, Jeannie, I know. I'm sorry. Okay, if you say it's real—you say it's honest —then that's what it is. That's right, baby, with us it was filth and with your new friend it's purity all the way. . . . I know. . . . Uh-huh. That's right, baby. Will you put your clothes on now and get your white ass over here? What do you have to do, get one more of those spade screws? One more of those little screwba dewbas? Got to feel those Freedom Flippers around your toochis one more time? . . . Jeannie, I can't make it through the night . . . Jeannie, you're not home in an hour, I swear to Christ I'm walking the hell out of here. . . . I don't give a shit about the kids. . . . That's how I feel about it. I don't see you in the doorway, I'm walking right the hell out of here into the French night. . . . You just try me. . . . *(Soft)* Jeannie, do you remember Quebec? All right, forget Quebec. I'll never mention it again. I mean just come home. Will you just do that. . . . He won't

let you? *(Out the window)* You won't let her, you fag bastard. I just heard about that. It just came in over the wire. What do you mean, you won't let her? You open those goddamned doors or I'm coming over there to cut your balls off. *(To the phone)* All right, I'm calm. . . . I am . . . It's because you can't see me. I'm in complete control of myself. (THIEF *enters, pot on his head, and begins to steal things.* HAROLD *doesn't see him.* MISS JANUS *tries to warn* HAROLD, *then to reason with* THIEF. HAROLD *shouts out the window.)* You like my billboards, eh. I'll give you billboards. I'll billboard your ass when I get hold of you, you black son of a bitch. *(Into phone at same time he spots* THIEF*)* Yeah, well he can afford to be a gentleman. I'll show him dignity. I'll show him who's beneath who. Now, Jeannie, will you just come home? *(Hollering out window, ignoring* THIEF*)* You went one step too far. A lot of guys make that mistake with me. *(To* THIEF*)* Hold on a second. *(Into phone)* Hold on a second. *(Picks up scythe and as* THIEF *leaps through window hurls it after him through the shutters, then plumps down in a chair, addressing* MISS JANUS *with great casualness)* She'll be here in twenty minutes flat. Have I steered you wrong once tonight? *(Both watch curtain come down.)*

CURTAIN

ACT TWO

(The action continues directly from Act One.)

MISS JANUS. You were wonderful. I never saw anyone move that fast.

HAROLD. I love action. That's the one thing I'm crazy about. *(Door knock)* That's my wife. I know her knock.

(GENDARME *enters holding* THIEF's *arm with one hand, scythe with the other.)*

GENDARME. I'm sure you must have some explanation, monsieur.

HAROLD. Hey, you got him! That's great!

GENDARME *(taking out notebook).* Just because you Americans have everything and we nothing does not mean you can make fun of me.

HAROLD. Who's making fun? Where's the fun? *(To* MISS JANUS) Was I just making fun of him?

GENDARME. Never mind. Do not take that superior tone with me. And then as soon as I leave, the sly little jokes will begin. Just because you have your washing machines and your General Motors.

HAROLD. Look, I don't want to go into a whole thing. Will you just book this guy and get him the hell out of here.

THIEF. All men are thieves.

GENDARME. He is not entirely wrong, you know. I arrive here, you expect me to fall at your foot, to lick your boot. France is a proud nation, monsieur, something you and your General Motors will never understand. *(Pauses)* What is the salary of the American policeman?

MISS JANUS. Sixty-three hundred dollars a year. *(HAROLD is astonished.)* It was in *U.S. News and World Report,* I just happen to remember.

GENDARME *(to THIEF)*. I, Pierre Luclos, am paid forty-two francs a week and on top of that, these Americans come here and throw shit in my face!

HAROLD *(imitating Jack Benny)*. Now wait a minute!

(LANDLADY enters.)

LANDLADY *(surveying scene)*. It has not happened here. I saw nothing. It did not occur in my house. Oh, perhaps once, when the Russians were having their Yalta conference in the attic. They are terrible, the Russians. You know how long I know the Khrushchev boys? I would never have them in my house again.

HAROLD. Tonight I'm getting Yalta? I need a little Yalta?

GENDARME. Hold the horse, monsieur. I am not one of your Negroes that you can trample . . .

HAROLD. Listen, that problem is not quite as bad as it sounds. Some of them are doing pretty well. Pretty goddamned well.

THIEF. All men are thieves. The butcher is a thief. The baker. The honest man who works at the same job for forty years, from nine to six, goes home each night to his family and never steals a dime. What is he, a thief. He is cheating his loved ones. He is cheating his destiny. He is a lowly rotten scum of a thief, the worst of them all. There you have philosophy.

HAROLD. There you have garbage. *(To GENDARME)* Are you going to lock this guy up or am I supposed to wait till he kills a few of my kids?

GENDARME. When I am ready, monsieur, and only when I am ready. *(Paces the room elaborately.)* The charges, Mr. Yankee Doodle?

HAROLD. What do I know about French charges? Ask him why he wears that pot while you're at it.

THIEF. Decadence, sir. A symbol of your rotten, bourgeois Western decadence.

(GENDARME, choked with emotion, begins to sing "La Marseillaise." THIEF, LANDLADY and MISS JANUS join him while baffled HAROLD looks on.)

GENDARME. Come, my friends. We have taken enough from this man.

THIEF *(banging pot on his head)*. All men are thieves. Murderers, liars, and pederasts too. I offer you philosophy.

(THIEF, GENDARME, LANDLADY exit, all singing "La Marseillaise." DR. SCHOENFELD enters. He appears to have weekend baggage with him. He is dressed, atypically, in a very flashy manner.)

HAROLD. Dr. Schoenfeld! What a pleasure. Let me take your bags. It's amazing, I feel better already.

DR. SCHOENFELD. Good evening, Harold.

HAROLD. Didn't you bring your friend?

(Wild-looking blonde appears. This is CHEYENNE.)

CHEYENNE. Here I am, love. 'Ello there. Say, Phillsy told me about your wife. Never you mind. Soon as she runs out of money that spade'll drop her like a hot pizza.

HAROLD. Good Christ!

SCHOENFELD. Harold, I'd like you to meet Cheyenne. *(Noticing MISS JANUS)* I don't think I've had the pleasure.

MISS JANUS. Hi, Dr. Schoenfeld, I'm Carol Janus.

CHEYENNE. 'Ello lamb chop, how are you?

HAROLD *(privately to SCHOENFELD)*. This is the fancy treatment you thought up? My wife's out screwing the rules committee of SNICK and you had to come running over here with this?

SCHOENFELD. It's just one chapter.

CHEYENNE *(at bookshelves)*. Say, you got any books by Bernie Malamud? Once you get started on those urban Jews it's like eating potato chips. If you ask me, you can take C. P. Snow and shove him up your keester.

SCHOENFELD. Cheyenne, please. I have something important to say to Mr. Wonder. *(Beckoning HAROLD toward couch. MISS JANUS, CHEYENNE sit on couch, too.)* Harold, it's become obvious that we can't work with sideways any longer. Perhaps it's time we looked into our relationship. Now, I agree we've had some good times in the haberdashery store. But you know, you've never really taken our talks seriously. Do you know why, Harold? Because they've never really cost you anything.

HAROLD. Cost me anything . . .

MISS JANUS. Oh sure, it's just like figs. You know how delicious they are. But imagine, if you had all the figs in the world, they just wouldn't be delicious any more.

HAROLD. Look, hold the figs. Go ahead, Dr. Schoenfeld.

SCHOENFELD. Your friend is right. What I want you to do, before we go any further, is to give me something valuable—not money—but something you really treasure. Then I'm convinced you'll listen to me.

CHEYENNE (with pride, to MISS JANUS). He's my shrink, you know.

HAROLD (looking around). Something valuable . . . what kind of valuable?

MISS JANUS. I didn't know they dated patients.

(HAROLD exits in his search.)

CHEYENNE (to MISS JANUS). We don't start the couch bit until after the fall. This is sort of a trial period. Like exhibition baseball. Say, you've got an honest face. Shall I tell you what my problem is? Sexual climaxes.

MISS JANUS. You poor thing.

CHEYENNE. No, no, I have too many of them. He's going to try to cut me down to just five a night.

MISS JANUS. Oh, that should be plenty.

(HAROLD returns.)

HAROLD. All I could find was this muffler. My mom knitted it for me when I was around ten. There was a deaf kid who tried to take it away from me once. A strong deaf kid. A deaf bully. I had to hit him right in the mouth. It was no fun hitting a deaf guy, believe me. But it was worth it. I got it back and I've kept it ever since.

DR. SCHOENFELD. Now you're really sure you care about this muffler?

HAROLD. I really do.

DR. SCHOENFELD. All right, give me the muffler. Now, Harold, listen very carefully. When I was in the Army, I was in grain supply. As a matter of fact, I was the officer in charge of purchasing barley for the entire states of Kansas and Oklahoma. Now barley, God bless it, as we all know, gets very damp.

And damp barley means only one thing—trouble—not for the barley, but for the barley personnel. Well, sure enough, I soon came down with a respiratory ailment. Now, the Army doctors were convinced it was a rare disease common only to barley workers. Do you know what it turned out to be, Harold? It wasn't a barley disease at all. It was bronchitis. . . . Harold, do you see what I'm getting at?

HAROLD (muses awhile). Give me back the muffler.

DR. SCHOENFELD. You're not getting the muffler back.

HAROLD. Come on, hand it over.

DR. SCHOENFELD. No, Harold.

HAROLD. Give me the goddamned muffler.

(Tug of war follows, with MISS JANUS and CHEYENNE joining in. HAROLD gets muffler back.)

HAROLD (winding muffler around his neck). Y'ain't getting the muffler. Not for barley. I was better off with sideways.

DR. SCHOENFELD (collecting himself, gathering dignity). Well, Harold, it's a little late. Perhaps in the morning you'll see things differently. (Standing beside CHEYENNE) And now, if you'll show us to my room . . . (Gathers luggage)

HAROLD. Room? Yeah, that's right, I forgot. All right, go ahead. Go upstairs. Take a left at the top. Make sure it's a left. I got my kids up there.

MISS JANUS. Good night, Dr. Schoenfeld. 'Night, Cheyenne.

CHEYENNE. Nighty night, all.

DR. SCHOENFELD (at top of stairs). I don't need his muffler. It was for his own good.

CHEYENNE. C'mon love, let's have a go. (THEY enter bedroom)

HAROLD. How long have I known that guy? Now he's giving me barley.

MISS JANUS. He really let you down, didn't he?

HAROLD. No, it just seems that way, to the untutored eye.

MISS JANUS. Maybe you'd like to hear about my obscene phone call.

HAROLD. Nope. I don't know much tonight, but that's one thing I'm sure of, that I don't want to hear about your obscene phone call. Maybe when this whole thing dies down we can meet somewhere and you can tell me about it. At some little French place. I just know I'm not up to it tonight. . . . How obscene was it?

MISS JANUS. That's the whole point. It was the most timid obscene call in the world. It was from a boy at Columbia. He was studying library management and I think he'd been reading Henry Miller. He called me from the stacks. It was the shyest obscene phone call. So I asked him to meet me in the school cafeteria . . .

(CHEYENNE *appears in robe.*)

CHEYENNE. Listen, is there a crapper in this joint?

HAROLD *(gesturing).* Oh, man.

CHEYENNE *(walking toward indicated room).* I hope it has a bidet. I've been all over France and I'm the only one who hasn't seen one yet. I'm not even sure I'm looking for the right thing. *(Disappears in room.)*

HAROLD. Why'd you have to meet him? Why'd you have to meet him and then come here to France and tell me about it with what I'm going through? Why didn't you just hang up?

MISS JANUS. His face was practically all horn-rimmed glasses. I talked to him for hours. It was his first obscene phone call, just like it was mine. We went up to my room for a while . . .

HAROLD. All right, all right, hold the punchline. I knew I didn't want to hear this one. And I was right.

(CHEYENNE *appears in underwear, soaked.*)

CHEYENNE. Well, I'll be goddamned. So that's how it works. You'd think they'd at least have directions on the little stinker. *(She goes back into the bedroom.)*

HAROLD. Why didn't you call the police? That's what you're supposed to do. If everyone just invited perverts over to the house for tea like that what the hell kind of a world would it be? . . . Probably wouldn't be that bad. *(Reflecting)* Jesus, I just remembered. I made one of those calls myself.

MISS JANUS. Listen, more people than you think . . .

HAROLD. No, I was just a kid. I had a crush on a teacher named Miss Baines, so I looked up this word in the dictionary and I said it to her. "Hello, Miss Baines," I said. "Yes," she answered. "Pelvis," I said, and then I slammed down the phone. I think she knew, though. Every time I got up to recite, she put on this pelvic expression. That's something to remember, here in France, years later, and my wife's on a trapeze with the Brown Bomber . . .

(CHEYENNE *comes downstairs humming, semi-nude.*)

CHEYENNE. Hi. Phillsy likes to have a little warm milk before he gets rolling. Helps him crank up his motor. Y'know, I knew a bloke once who liked me to cover him up from head to toe with mayonnaise. Poor bastard. It was the only way he could get his rocks off. (CHEYENNE, *erupting in vulgar laughter, enters kitchen.*)

HAROLD. You want to know something *really* awful?

MISS JANUS. What's that?

HAROLD. I think I know where to find them.

MISS JANUS. Your wife?

HAROLD. Remember her? That's really something to have to come right out and admit. Eleven Rue Domergue—he said it one night and it stuck with me. So how come I'm not going anywhere? How come I'm just hollering out of windows?

MISS JANUS. You're just not ready.

HAROLD. When do I get ready? When she moves to the Congo?

(CHEYENNE *comes out of kitchen, whistling. Goes back into bedroom.*)

MISS JANUS *(stretching).* You know, it isn't that much. . . . We could just sort of drift upstairs too . . .

HAROLD *(getting up).* I don't know how it would be. . . . Maybe if you just told me a few more of those stories. Do you have any left? Just feed me a few more and we'll see what happens.

MISS JANUS. All right. *(She comes toward him, sits behind him.)* Once I was trying on dresses in a store up in Maine. I reached into the size nine rack and there was a little man all covered up inside a two-piece jersey ensemble . . . *(Light changes as though many hours have passed. Indication that it is dawn.* HAROLD *is still in his bathrobe, groggy, exhausted.* MISS JANUS *has been going on with her stories, as though she has been telling them endlessly)* . . . a Russian take-out restaurant. Anyway, I was delivering an order of borscht to a customer and I see his pockets are filled with petitions, bills, proclamations. So I put two and two together and I said, "Listen, just because you're in the House of Representatives doesn't mean I'm staying over tonight." *(Realizes how much time has gone by.)* Oh my God, I locked Nero and Abby out.

(She exits, MRS. WONDER *appears. Young, early thirties, attractive, rather forlorn at the moment, and prone to bumping into things. She is gentle in manner.)*

JEAN WONDER. Harold . . . How are you? . . .

HAROLD. What do I know? . . .

JEAN. How are the kids?

HAROLD. They're fine, under the circumstances. You all right?

JEAN. Pretty good. My arm hurts, though.

HAROLD. What happened?

JEAN. I think I got gas in it.

HAROLD. What do you mean gas? You can't have gas in your arm.

JEAN. No, that's what it is. I'm sure of it. Somehow it curled around through here and up around here and got right into my arm. It'll be all right.

HAROLD. It's not gas. Remember the party? What was it, Friends of the Middle East? You were positive you were having a heart attack. *That* was gas.

JEAN. That was a small heart attack, Harold. I just accepted it and when it was over I was grateful and that was the end of it.

HAROLD. Everything else all right?

JEAN. My neck is a little tensed up. I'm just going to have to live with that. *(She starts to dust.)* You okay?

HAROLD. Jeannie, don't dust now, will you.

JEAN. Well, what am I supposed to do, leave it there, just let it accumulate? Breathe it all in? Foreign dust. How do we know what's in it?

HAROLD. There's nothing in it. It's just a little French dust. No dusting now, okay? Will you do me that favor? I'm trying to get a little sore. There's something that happens to your shoulders—when you dust—and I don't want to get involved in that now. They get frail or something. I probably never told you, but I can't stand to see you dust. It's like I took this young, fragrant, hopeful, beautiful young girl and turned her into an old cleaning lady.

JEAN. Women like to dust, silly. It doesn't hurt them.

HAROLD. Well it hurts the hell out of me. I can't stand it.

(She stops dusting.)

JEAN. How about you? In your bathrobe. I can stand that? And making that face at me . . .

HAROLD. Which one's that?

JEAN. You know which one. There's only one. You made it at Gloria Novak's wedding reception, the first time I ever saw you. At the salad table. I looked up from my salad and I see this big guy making a face at me.

HAROLD. I don't know what you're talking about.

JEAN. Not much. That little boy face. Whenever you want something. Look at you. You can't even switch off to another one, even right now. You did it to me then and you're doing it right now.

HAROLD. What I'm doing right this second, right now?

JEAN. That's right.

HAROLD. I never made this face before in my life.

JEAN. Right. I just came in here . . . I was going to get a few things . . . *(Starts for bedroom)*

HAROLD *(intercepting her)*. No things, no things. That's one line I never want to hear. *(In British accent)* "Dudley, I've come for my things." Anybody gets their things, that's the end of their things. In this house you get your *stuff,* hear? And you don't get that either. . . . This is some mess.

JEAN. I know.

HAROLD. I think this is the worst we ever had.

JEAN. I don't know, Harold. I think when I was pregnant and we couldn't get any heat in the apartment and you had to organize a warmth committee in the building at four in the morning. I think that was worse.

HAROLD. No, I think this is worse. I had a lot of people on my side in that one. I had the whole building cheering me on. I'm all alone on this one.

JEAN. What kind of alone? You think I'm loving this? That I'm loving every second of it . . .

HAROLD. You're loving it more than I am. Anybody'd be loving it more than I am. There's not one person I can think of who wouldn't be loving this more than I am. . . . You think we'll get out of it?

JEAN. I don't know, Harold. At this point I'd settle for just getting through the morning.

HAROLD *(on his knees, cracking)*. Ah, come on, Pidge, will you just quit it right now? Will you get the hell back home? Will you just stay here? What do you want to do, ship me off to Happydale? I'm down here on the floor. I'm not a guy who does that.

JEAN *(comforting)*. I know, Harold, I know.

HAROLD *(recovering slightly)*. Look, there's just one thing I have to find out. This is important. Did you get into things like Pidge? Does he know I call you Pidge?

JEAN. That's what you consider important? That's what this is all about to you? Pidge?

HAROLD. No, seriously, I just have to know that one thing and then I'll never bother you again.

JEAN. I may have said something . . .

HAROLD (*leaping up in triumph*). You told him Pidge. That's probably the first thing you blurted out. I was just on the floor where I've never been in my life—and you had to tell him Pidge. I was hoping you'd keep one thing separate, one little private area so that maybe we could start battling our way back, inch by inch, to being a little bit together again. What you did is just fork it right over . . .

JEAN. I don't remember if I told him. . .

HAROLD (*not hearing her*). All right, number one, cancel what I just did on the floor. And number two, drag in that chocolate shithead. I've been waiting for this all night.

JEAN. Harold, could you try to be a little dignified. I can get that style from my father. I don't need it from you. I grew up with that. You know, for a second I really felt a little something—the first time in years—and then you have just heaved it right out the window.

HAROLD (*peering through window*). Is he out there?

JEAN. Yes, he's out there, Harold. But you can't see him because it's still a little dark and he has all this natural camouflage.

HAROLD (*still looking out*). Very funny. How come he's afraid to get his black ass in here?

JEAN. He couldn't possibly face you, Harold. Not after what I told him. You see, I told him about your poise. About your quiet dignity. About your finesse in handling difficult situations. He wouldn't come within ten miles of the place.

HAROLD. I'm going to be dignified. I'm going to be Dag Fucking Hammarskjold. Just get the son of a bitch in here.

JEAN. Harold, will you just listen for a second. I'm not going to ask for your full attention because I know I'm not entitled to that. Not in the short span of time that's been allotted to me on earth. But will you listen a little. I've been outside . . .

HAROLD. I don't know you've been outside? I don't have it engraved in my brain for all time—that you've been out there?

JEAN. All right, you know I've been out-side, Harold. But what you don't know is that I looked around a little. And I saw what they're doing out there. They're not hollering out of windows, Harold. They're not taking their families three thousand miles to a beautiful new country with dozens of charming little villages to roam around in—so they can stand around in bathrobes and shout things out of windows. And never see those charming villages.

HAROLD. Look, you want to know the truth? I've been trying not to say this, but you're forcing it out of me. All right, here it comes. I just don't happen to think those villages are charming. You want me to say they're charming, all right, they're charming. You got what you want. But they're not that goddamned charming. They *act* charming. No one's ever questioned it before, so they get away with it. You take Lexington Avenue and fix it up a little and you've got the same charm. And it didn't cost you thirty grand to get over here.

JEAN. Harold, let's face it. We both know there's only one charming thing in the world. You . . . in your bathrobe . . . shouting out of windows. That's the entire list. The charm lineup of our generation. . . . Let me tell you what happens to me when I'm outside, Harold. The strangest thing. You know how I trip a lot and bang my head on things and we both think it's cute, although actually it's very serious and some of the injuries will probably turn malignant at a future date— Well, I don't trip over things out there. I didn't bang myself on the head once.

HAROLD. You were supposed to get your eyes checked, Jeannie. What happened to that? Is that what you were doing out there in the bushes—with that spade—getting your eyes checked?

JEAN. There's nothing wrong with my eyes, Harold. I wish it were that. If it were an eye problem, believe me, I'd grab it. No, there's a reason that women out there don't bang into things and kill themselves. You see, they've had a breakthrough out there, Harold. They actually—and you'd better sit down for this one—they actually believe there's a difference between men and women. And here's the shocker of the year. You ready? They're doing something about it. They've come up with a separate way of treating women. They speak a little more gently to them. They actually *say* things to women. Romantic things. And it doesn't make them feel like Herbert Marshall either.

HAROLD. Look, Jeannie, we've talked about this . . . Once and for all, I can't say "Your eyes are like deep pools" unless I really believe they are a little like deep pools. Even then I can't say it.

JEAN. They don't have that trouble, Harold. They say things that are beyond your wildest imaginings. Do you know they even recite poetry to women?

HAROLD. That miserable two-bit coon recites poetry. . . . All right, get him in here.

(FROGMAN *in full undersea regalia enters casually, spear gun in hand, flippers on feet.* HAROLD *walks through door and doesn't see him.)*

HAROLD *(shouting).* I dare you to come in here and face me. *(Spots* FROGMAN.) I'm sorry, I got a little confused.

FROGMAN *(in a heightened, mocking laying-it-on-thick Negro style. This "put-on" approach continues throughout—with only one exception, indicated further on).* That's all right, sweetie-baby, it's a tough scene all around. I can tell you got a lot of heart.

HAROLD. Now look, I'm cold, I'm shaky, I've been up all night. I'm not at my best in the morning. It takes me till around noon to hit my stride. To be perfectly frank, I'm a little afraid of colored people. It's a completely irrational thing. Little girls, even old ladies. I have this feeling they were all in the Golden Gloves once. You know what I mean?

FROGMAN. Let me give you a little advice, Jim. You sass an old colored lady, she gone lean back and give you the bad eye. She gone work some roots on you, babe, then you really in a shitstorm.

HAROLD. Very cute, very cute. There's just one thing. We happen to be on *my* turf now, you son of a bitch . . . *(Using scythe,* HAROLD *begins to square off with spear-gun-carrying* FROGMAN.)

(Second Negro enters, pipe-smoking, intellectual, quite good-looking in an aesthetic way. This is REDDINGTON.)

REDDINGTON. Hi, Pidge.

HAROLD. Pidge! Everybody knows Pidge. Who the hell is this?

REDDINGTON. Is everything all right . . . *(With glance at* HAROLD) Pidge?

JEAN. I'll just be another minute.

FROGMAN. Hey baby, you made the scene just in time. We all gonna' sit down and have some chitlins.

REDDINGTON. Cool it, Foxtrot.

HAROLD. Oh, now we're getting a little "cool it." How about a little "daddy." A little "dig," a little "daddy." Who is this guy, Jeannie?

JEAN. Harold, this is Ambrose Reddington.

HAROLD. That tells me a lot.

JEAN. Harold, I'm sorry, I really wanted to avoid this. I met Ambrose a few days ago . . . A complete accident. He was very sweet to me and I take full credit for him. Foxtrot is your idea, 100 percent. A Harold Wonder special. You like him, you can't live without him. I'll tell you what—pick up the phone, make a reservation and the two of you can go flying down to Rio.

HAROLD. Hilarious.

FROGMAN. Suppose I just slip into my travelin' duds . . .

HAROLD *(threatening).* Don't push me too far, just don't push me too far. *(Recovering)* Give me a minute to adjust to this. *(Contemplates)* I can't adjust to this. *(Walks toward* REDDINGTON. *Resuming anger)* As I was just saying. *(Shouts)* We're on my turf now, you son of a bitch. We're not at any Black Muslim convention.

FROGMAN. Oh, I see where it's at.

HAROLD *(to* FROGMAN). Look. I'm sorry to have to use the racial stuff, but you'll just have to overlook it. It gives me a slight edge, but I can assure you it's got nothing to do with my true feelings. If everyone felt the way I did, you guys would have clear sailing from here on in . . . *(To* REDDINGTON, *shouting)* What's important is that I can still smell my wife on you, you bastard.

REDDINGTON. Mr. Wonder, I can see that this is a difficult situation for you, but we certainly ought to be able to deal with it as mature adults.

FROGMAN. He ain't gonna be one of them mature adults. He gonna fetch the debbil on that poor old colored man. He gonna reach around there and work some roots. Right on that poor black rascal's head. Whoooooooo-eeeee.

HAROLD. Very cute, very cute.

FROGMAN. Shame on you, babe. Just 'cause that poor old colored man went out there in the bushes and jugged your wife a few times . . .

HAROLD. Now you watch *your* ass. Just because I was wrong about you doesn't mean I was wrong about you.

FROGMAN. Shame on you, man. For shame . . .

(REDDINGTON *starts to cough.*)

JEAN. Oh my God, are you all right?

REDDINGTON. It'll pass. It's nothing.

JEAN *(to* HAROLD). Now look what you did.

HAROLD. What *I* did!

JEAN. You started his cough. Will you do something useful for a change? Where did we put the Cheracol?

HAROLD. Cheracol? You want me to nurse him back to health? It's in the medicine cabinet. Oh never mind, I'll get it. *(As he fumbles in the drawer)* I really have to congratulate you, Jeannie. I mean a little affair is one thing. But the entire Harlem Globetrotters. That's really style.

FROGMAN. Hey, Ambrose. What'd you need this shit for? You could have stayed out there in the car.

REDDINGTON. I couldn't allow Jean to face this alone.

(HAROLD *picks up medicine bottle, carries it to* REDDINGTON *and pours a spoonful.*)

HAROLD. I'm not enjoying this, you know. I'm not enjoying it one bit. I don't even know why I'm doing it. I guess that all it amounts to really *(As* REDDINGTON *swallows medicine)* is that I'm helping a guy with a bad cough.

(LANDLADY *and* TOURIST *enter,* LANDLADY *spots* FROGMAN *and runs toward him exultantly.*)

LANDLADY. Sidney . . . How marvelous. It is Sidney Poitier. *(Embracing him. Then taking in frogman get-up)* You are in a James Bond movie. I can tell . . . How come you don't write your friend, you naughty boy?

FROGMAN. I got jammed up at the Cannes Film Festival. Once you get up there on top, everybody wants a slice of the action. You got producers tryin' to get tight with you. You got them starlets . . .

LANDLADY. Ah, you rascal. *(She has unintentionally stepped on one of his flippers. He points this out and she backs away with a blush.)*

TOURIST. I got nothing against you people. What the hell, a party's a party. I'd sit around with a goddamned Yugoslav if I had to. Wouldn't blink an eyelash. I always say, if you keep alert you can even learn something from a Slav. Long as that Slav understands that when the buzzer rings I head back to my section of town and he gets up and goes back to his *Slav* side of town.

HAROLD *(to* TOURIST). I really don't need any help from you.

FROGMAN *(in mock defense of* TOURIST). Hey, don't pick on him. That's my man. Anyone mess with my man gotta hit on me first, babe. *(Confidentially, with arm around* TOURIST) You like to meet some nice colored chicks?

TOURIST. Well, actually, I'm just down here for a few weeks . . .

FROGMAN. I mean some real groovy colored chicks. I don't mean any of that street trash. Something real high class . . .

(TOURIST, *abashed, exits.* LANDLADY *follows him)*

HAROLD. Jeannie, what do you want to see, a stretcher case? A French nervous breakdown? You're going to get one, you know. I'm going to sail into one any second now.

FROGMAN. Baby, you just not getting the message. You heard about those neighborhoods that get moved in on and there's nothing you can do? You're just not facing facts. *You* the neighborhood in this case, babe.

REDDINGTON. Foxtrot, please. Mr. Wonder, I'm sorry that my friend feels it necessary to behave in this fashion, but if you'll permit me—I'm afraid he has made a valid point. Realistically speaking, your wife and I have formed a powerful attraction for one another. It has enormous meaning to both of us. It began quite innocently, I assure you.

HAROLD. I know about those innocent attractions. I could hear the bedsprings creaking all the way across the Mediterranean.

REDDINGTON. Mr. Wonder, that's not very groovy of you.

(LANDLADY *and* TOURIST *enter.)*

TOURIST *(to* LANDLADY). I sort of like the French, It's the Italians you got to watch. The important thing is to keep them away from shiny stuff. Rings, silverware, tinfoil. Drives 'em crazy. It isn't anything they can help. Something happens, inside their heads. Any time you invite an Italian person over, make sure you don't have anything around that makes a jingling sound.

(LANDLADY *and* TOURIST *go upstairs on inspection tour.)*

HAROLD. Do you actually have to handle him, Jeannie? Right in front of me. You know, if I didn't see this, maybe in thirty-three years or so I might be able to forget the thing, pretend it didn't happen. . . . Jeannie, will you do me a favor? Will you name one way in which this is helping me. One way that it's enriching my life . . .

FROGMAN. You just not taking the right

attitude, man. You could clean up. I heard about this fella, he hired another guy to jug his wife and then he sold tickets to his buddies to come down and watch. You work it that way, at least you pickin' up a little cash on the deal. Tell you what. Here's my money, I'll take five tickets down front, right now . . .

TOURIST. I've been watching you awhile, Foxtrot, and I just want to say right now that I respect you as a man. You're coming through loud and clear and nasty and I can hear you. Now I'm white and you're one of those black guys, but just one man to another—me standing here, you standing way the hell over there . . .

FROGMAN. I respect you too, man. I'm going to give you something. I'm going to give you a shine. I'm gonna shine up your ass. Hey, shine 'em up, shine 'em up.

(Chases TOURIST *out)*

LANDLADY *(wagging finger).* Sidney!

(LANDLADY *exits.)*

HAROLD *(to* REDDINGTON). If you were a Puerto Rican I'd feel the exact same way. I'm just using every weapon I can lay my hands on.

REDDINGTON. When one's masculinity is being threatened, one often resorts to . . .

HAROLD. One? What kind of one? Who talks like that? Is that the kind of poetry he recites? One. Jeannie, you know I've followed you on a lot of this, and I admit I don't walk off with the award for the Greatest Married Fellow, but I honestly don't see the big deal about this guy.

REDDINGTON *(reciting, in something of a counterattacking style).* "What matter cakes or wine or tasty bouillabaisse . . . When love lies bruised and clotted on the thin and punished lips of our American black dream . . . "

HAROLD. Big deal. LeRoi Jones, right?

REDDINGTON. No. I wrote it.

HAROLD. I'd like to see you get that junk published.

REDDINGTON. I've already heard from the *Partisan Review.*

HAROLD *(panicked).* The *Partisan?* What did they say?

REDDINGTON. They were impressed by the combination of raw power and delicacy . . .

HAROLD. Hah! You don't even know a standard *Partisan* rejection . . . "Dear Sir: Despite the raw power and delicacy of your poem, we regret . . . "

REDDINGTON. No, they bought it. It's scheduled for the fall issue.

HAROLD. Oh, well, the fall issue . . .

JEAN. Harold, you could learn a little from this. Instead of automatically hating it.

HAROLD. Learn? All right. I'm learning. Here's a little poetry. *(In a lisping, effete style)* "Intruders ye be . . . make haste, abandon this place . . . or I'll punch that spade in his colored face."

REDDINGTON *(with controlled anger).* Don't push me too far, mister.

HAROLD *(to* REDDINGTON). Push you too far . . . The main thing is I can outwrite you, I can outfight you, I can outthink you . . .

FROGMAN. Yeah, but there's one thing you can't *out* him, babe. That man there *(With a sly, sexual gesture)* is a colored man.

REDDINGTON. Foxtrot . . .

FROGMAN. Yeah, baby.

REDDINGTON. I see no point in turning this into a gutter confrontation.

FROGMAN. Shit, man, I was just holdin' up my Negritude. That man was hittin' up on you, Ambrose.

(TOURIST *and* LANDLADY *enter.)*

REDDINGTON. I can take care of myself.

HAROLD. Well, what the hell would you do? I mean, say you were in my shoes. Say I was you for a second and you were me.

FROGMAN. You askin' an awful lot, babe.

HAROLD. No, I'm serious. What the hell am I supposed to do? Let your friend just waltz off with her? Because he's colored. Throw in a few kids. Maybe some General Electric stock I've been saving up. To show I'm not prejudiced. You know this is not an easy position to be in. I'm just trying to hang in there. It's bad enough I'm not allowed to get as angry as I'd like. If I toss in a little racial slur every now and then, you'll just have to put up with it. If you don't like it, you know where the door is. *(He suddenly grabs a wine bottle and smashes it on a ledge, brandishing the jagged edge toward the group, the Negroes in particular)* All right, that's it. There's no more problem because I just solved the whole thing. Anybody comes near me they get my initials carved in their head. *(Everyone freezes in real panic and shock as* HAROLD *grabs* JEAN, *brandishing jagged bottle with great menace.)* I can't go through with the thing. *(Flings away bottle.* FROGMAN *catches it.)*

REDDINGTON *(putting out arm).* Jean . . . It's all right, Pidge, it's all right.

FROGMAN *(to* HAROLD*)*. You know, I like that—the way you whipped out that bottle and almost cut your own natural-born ass off. I liked that, man. Little more of that, you gonna be ready for One Hundred and Twenty-fifth Street.

TOURIST. Say, you fellows aren't serious about that Black Power thing, are you?

FROGMAN. You'll be the first to know, babe. We got you right at the top of the mailing list.

(Chases TOURIST *out with jungle sounds and spear gun)*

HAROLD. Look, Jeannie, I really don't want this happening right now. If you'd come in here last night when I was fresh, rested, enthusiastic, when I was at the top of my form, you'd have seen a whole different guy. I'd have settled this thing in two seconds flat and believe me everyone in this room would have walked out of here feeling like a complete winner. But, Jeannie, I can't operate in the morning, you know that. I haven't even settled into the day yet. I'm still in my bathrobe. You put me in a pair of slacks, you'll see a whole different scene. I don't even have my eyes open and you're throwing spades at me —a whole blizzard of spades. Spades—as far as the eye can see . . .

REDDINGTON. Mr. Wonder, please, a little self-control . . .

HAROLD. All right, all right. I just want you to know that I'm not entirely responsible. There's something about mornings. I assure you if it was last night you wouldn't have heard a single racial slur out of me. Maybe one or two, tops. *(To* REDDINGTON*)* Now look, you got her, all right You sneaked in there, you read poems, you're a colored guy, you did crazy things, I don't know what you did. Whatever it was, the main thing is she's yours. For the next thirty-two years she's going to be strapped to your side. At the most maybe I'll bump into her accidentally one night, have a little drink, maybe some dinner. It'll be different then. Neither of us will talk much, just as though we're total strangers. Maybe our fingers will touch accidentally, and we may even slip off to a motel together and have this exquisite evening just as though it were choreographed, everything that happens just sheer magic. And then we part at dawn, a little sadly perhaps, but without any real regret.

LANDLADY *(simultaneously with last part of* HAROLD*'s romantic fantasy timed so that last word of her speech and* HAROLD*'s come together)*. Ah, l'amour. The joy of it. The tears and the heartache. When there was only one person in the world for you. The secret meetings. The touch of a hand in the darkness. Ah, when I was a jeune fille. Floop, floop, floop.

HAROLD. Will you floop the hell out of here? Look, can I please have a couple of minutes alone with my wife? Can we empty out Grand Central for a while?

JEAN. Harold, there's nothing we can't say right out here . . .

REDDINGTON. Pidge, I think it's a reasonable request. But if you'd like me to stay here, I will.

JEAN. No. It's all right.

REDDINGTON *(reciting in a soothing manner)*. "Wait here and I'll be back, though the hours divide, and the city streets, perplexed, perverse, delay my hurrying footsteps . . ."

LANDLADY *(to* REDDINGTON. *She is still angered by* HAROLD*'s rough words)*. Take care, monsieur. Eddie Fisher has stood in this very room and played the exact same trick on Elizabeth Taylor.

*(*LANDLADY *exits.)*

REDDINGTON. Come on, Foxtrot. *(He enters kitchen,* FOXTROT *lingering slightly behind.)*

HAROLD *(to* FOXTROT*)*. Now look, can I just have a few minutes to wind up the marriage?

FROGMAN. You got any cornbread in the kitchen?

JEAN. Once and for all, will you stop putting him on, Foxtrot?

HAROLD. He can ask for cornbread. What's wrong with that? I don't happen to have any cornbread, but he can certainly ask for it.

FROGMAN *(straight, no accent, serious)*. I was born on a farm in Aiken, South Carolina, one of nine children, six boys and three girls. They called me Billy-boy in those days because no matter what happened, I'd just buck my way through. Once I was driving and I turned a car over, seven times, got out, kept walking to the post office. I stay close to one brother, George, who sees to it that I don't wise off. He says, "Maybe you're great, but let other people find it out. Don't you tell them." I lost my father on a farm accident, and didn't care much about it one way or the other. My mom's still pretty. She won a contest designing hats and my brother told the newspapermen if any of them interviewed her he'd go after them and kill them no matter where they hide. . . . I haven't got tired of the water yet. Nothing much to it. I'll just stick with it, make a few bucks, probably quit, sometime. *(He shuffles off.)*

HAROLD. What? Boy, what a pleasure to have two seconds of peace in your own home.

JEAN. All right, Harold, what's the great thing that you had to have me all alone to tell me about?

HAROLD. C'mon, Pidge. *(Spitting)* Ptuuii. I can't even call you Pidge any more. I'll have to think up a whole new name.

JEAN. Will you stop, Harold. You're hurting my hip.

HAROLD. What do you mean? I'm not touching you.

JEAN. When you act a certain way. It goes right to my hip. I've told you that a thousand times, but you never listen.

HAROLD. All right, I promise never to say anything that'll hurt your hip. *(Soft again)* Look, Jeannie, I've seen him now. I've checked out his routine. Truthfully—what has he got? What do you want, colored? All right, here's colored. *(Breaks into an elaborate shuffling dance routine in the old Bill Robinson style)* And that's without even *being* colored. It's better that way. You don't have any of the headaches. You skip the aggravation. All you have is the flashy stuff.

JEAN *(somewhat amused)*. I can't laugh, Harold. It'll start the whole sinus thing and I can't afford that now.

HAROLD. Jeannie, I know the guy now. He's not in my head, he was just *in* here. I mean, what *is* he? He's colored and he coughs. Is that what you want? That's what you're giving me up for? A colored cougher.

JEAN *(jumping up)*. All right, there's one. You wanted an example—that's one, right there. The last thing you said is the kind of remark that's complete death to my hip. You might as well take a hammer and just pound on it, right here.

HAROLD. All right, all right, you made your point. I just want to sit here one more minute, quietly, and wind up the marriage. The whole marriage that I thought was like a rock and would last a thousand years—a whole British Empire of a marriage. *(They rest a moment, silently.)* All right, what does he do?

JEAN. What do you mean?

HAROLD. You know what I mean, Jeannie.

You know. He's a colored guy, he knows stuff, he does stuff, they teach him things. Give me an idea.

JEAN. Oh, God. He doesn't do any *one* thing, Harold. People don't do *one* thing. It's a whole lot of things, if you must know. A whole collection of things.

HAROLD. Well, what are they? Can you tell me a few?

JEAN. You're really going about this the wrong way.

HAROLD. Tell me just one—one thing.

JEAN. I can't.

HAROLD. Will you come on, one lousy thing. What do you have to lose?

JEAN. I can't *do* that.

HAROLD. Jeannie, for crying out loud, the marriage is down the drain. I'm sitting here, I'm a terminal marriage fellow, will you tell me one thing . . .

JEAN. He strokes my ear . . .

HAROLD. *(leaping up)*. I can't do that? I can't outstroke that son of a bitch twenty times a day? I can't outearstroke him? Let me show you. *(He fights to stroke her ear. She struggles.)* There you are—stroke . . . stroke . . . stroke.

JEAN *(throwing him off)*. Harold!

HAROLD. There. All right, how was it?

JEAN. It was thrilling, Harold. It really turned me on. Can I go now?

HAROLD. A colored stroke is great, huh, but if I do the identical thing, the exact same stroke, it's nothing. A Caucasian nothing. In the dark you wouldn't have known one from the other.

JEAN. You almost pulled my ear off.

(HAROLD clutches her suddenly, tries to make love to her. She struggles against him.)

HAROLD. Jeannie, look, I never felt this way. I don't know what just happened to me . . . some kind of crazy new feeling . . .

JEAN. Harold, will you please . . . there are people here . . . we're not in the bathroom . . .

HAROLD *(continuing)*. I don't care where we are.

JEAN. Harold, you know I can't just do that—just leap into it . . . and you haven't said a word to me. A preliminary word . . .

HAROLD *(stops embrace)*. All right, all right . . . Jeannie . . . you've got some helluva pair of tits on you . . . *(Jumps on her again)* You want hands. A lot of hands. You couldn't live without them. Here's hands. Forty-two hands.

JEAN. Harold! *(She throws him off again after great struggle.)*

HAROLD *(with wounded dignity)*. All right, will you just go now? Will you just collect your spades and stop taking up my valuable time.

JEAN. I've been trying to, Harold, I've been trying to leave. But you've been stroking my ear.

HAROLD. Well you had your last stroke. From your old marriage. Your last broken-down, second-rate, technically lousy stroke. I just want to prepare you for something, Jeannie. So you don't hear about it second hand. So you don't read about it in the *Harlem Bugle*. When you walk out of here, I'm not folding my tent . . .

JEAN. Well I don't want you to, Harold. Is that what you think would make me happy—tent-folding?

HAROLD. What you don't see is that beneath all these layers of what you consider weakness—and maybe I'll even agree with you a little there—there's another layer that you don't know anything about. It's a little weak too, but it's toughly weak. That's the strongest kind. It's a great layer that comes from way back in my family—little villages in Budapest where these peasants would ride through the village brimming over with this tough weakness. How old am I? I've still got thirty-five good years to go. I'm a young guy. I've got great knees. I've got a terrific neck. Something you never noticed.

JEAN. I've noticed it, Harold. Many is the time I've found myself just sitting and staring out of windows, thinking about your neck. I just never could put my feelings into words. Can I go now?

HAROLD. Who's keeping you? Have I said one word? All right, a parting salute. To you I'm like an old tattered issue of *National Geographic,* right? That's how you see me. Something you find in a closet. One of those terrible issues from around 1936 with all those pictures of Borneo peasant women. With those long, endless Borneo bazooms. And I remind you of one of those issues. Are we agreed on that?

JEAN. Are we agreed on *what?*

HAROLD. But we're agreed on that, right? That I'm this old discarded guy that no woman under ninety-five would take a second look at. Oh, maybe there's a girl somewhere who's come up with a rare disease, been in a few airplane wrecks, couple of oven explo-

sions. If the thing were set up very carefully in advance, a girl like that might sit down and have a drink with me. But aside from that type, I'm dead, right? It's all over? We agreed? Okay. What if I said I could produce—voilà! right here in the middle of this French floor, before your very eyes—a young, beautiful, fascinating, non-spade-loving girl, who tells stories that if the *Partisan Review* ever knew about them they'd have a man over here with a contract by six o'clock tonight. . . . I mean *good* stories, Jeannie, I don't mean that cakes and bouillabaisse shit. All right, now you take that gorgeous girl, I don't think she's out of her teens yet—if she never saw a spade in her life she wouldn't blink an eye—you take that girl with a figure that I don't even want to get started on, a whole new kind of body for the mid-nineteen sixties, take her and imagine her in this château trying every trick in the book—and believe me, Jeannie, these new girls coming up have got plenty of new routines—this gorgeous sylphlike girl trying every trick in the book to get your husband—who supposedly doesn't know the first thing about handling ears—to get your husband into the hay with her. All right. What is that? A little fictional tidbit. A little bouillabaisse. Would you like to meet her right now?

JEAN. Did you meet her, Harold?

HAROLD. You're damned right I did.

JEAN. Well, I think one member of the family is enough. *(Starts to leave)*

HAROLD *(calls through window)*. Miss Janus . . . *(Then, for JEAN's benefit)* Carol . . . Honey.

MISS JANUS'S VOICE. Yes?

HAROLD. Can you come over for a second? I want you to settle a little argument.

MISS JANUS'S VOICE. Be right there.

HAROLD *(to JEAN)*. All right, hold still one second and you're going to see a little cornbread. You're going to see the monstrous fate that awaits your husband as soon as you take one step outside. The reason your husband has to get down on his knees and beg you not to go. (MISS JANUS *enters.)* Voilà!

MISS JANUS. Oh, hi. We had a little accident. One of Nero's sculptures fell on top of him. It's a giant carving of a dead Spanish peasant who was sitting in the stands during a bullfight and got fatally gored by accident. Nero was going to present it to the Spanish government. He was positive Franco would go wild when he heard about it.

JEAN. Is your friend all right?

MISS JANUS. Oh, yes. Luckily he's on a grease kick now. He thinks that if people keep themselves greased up as much as possible, it'll help them slide by some of their problems. Anyway, we just slid him out from under the dead peasant. You must be Mrs. Wonder.

JEAN. Yes. And Harold's been reading me your dossier. You're very pretty.

MISS JANUS. He told me all about you too, Mrs. Wonder. You're very attractive. You have this sort of mid-sixties look. No matter what I do to myself I can never look that way.

JEAN. Thank you. I've been feeling kind of mid-fifties tonight. Oh, my God!

MISS JANUS. Is anything wrong?

JEAN. Do you realize that I have walked this coastline from end to end looking for printed slacks like that? Did you buy them here?

MISS JANUS. In town. Right here in Cap Ferrat. Listen, do you think they fit? Tell me, really. Every time I try something on, I've got this pack of girls from Düsseldorf who swoop down and tell me I'm making the mistake of my life.

JEAN. They fit, they fit. Listen, with your figure . . .

MISS JANUS. *My* figure. Listen, have you looked at yourself lately? I have a marine biologist friend—if he saw you, believe me, you'd never get out of his office alive.

HAROLD. All right, time. That's it. Hold it right there. What is this, roommates at Radcliffe? It's supposed to be a tense confrontation. Where's the tense? If it can't be tense, I don't need it. I got other things to do.

(SCHOENFELD *and* CHEYENNE, *fully dressed, with luggage, come out of bedroom and make way downstairs.)*

JEAN. Oh, he's been here too. My husband's friend, the Dean of American Mental Health.

MISS JANUS. Oh, I know Dr. Schoenfeld. Hi, Dr. Schoenfeld. Hi, Cheyenne.

SCHOENFELD *(opening door).* Harold, you're on your own. I can't carry you any longer. It's time you got up on your own two feet and faked your way into the adult community. *(Exits with* CHEYENNE. FROGMAN *comes out of kitchen.)*

FROGMAN *(to* JEAN). What's shakin', baby? You 'bout ready to split? Let me call Ambrose so we can get goin'.

HAROLD *(to* MISS JANUS). My wife's interviewing gospel singers. She's got thirty more of them out in the kitchen.

MISS JANUS. He's putting me on.

FROGMAN. No, no, he ain't putting you on. *(Sings "Uncle Misery")*
I don't get no visits from my
Uncle Josh or Uncle John.
And even Uncle Andy stay away from my
   door.
The only uncle who ever come aroun' . . .
Is my Uncle Misery.
            Uncle Misery
            Uncle Misery . . .
I didn't invite you here . . .
He say "I know son,
I don't need no inivitation" . . .
(Stops singing, leaves HAROLD *trapped in song and handclapping)* Sheeeeet . . .

JEAN. Foxtrot, aren't you laying it on a little thick?

HAROLD. Don't talk to him that way, Jeannie. The man enjoys singing. Let him sing a little. What's so terrible? He's not hurting anybody. *(To* FROGMAN) C'mon, let's sing it again. I love that song.

JEAN *(to* MISS JANUS). Harold, the Great Defender of the Negro, the black man's best friend. You should see him driving. Get the picture. We're in the car on the highway and a colored person in the next lane has just gotten a little too close and forced us off the highway. Harold doesn't know it was a colored person yet and so he's gotten out on the road in his traditional style and is trying to round up ten men for a firing squad. But then Harold sees it was a colored driver. And then we have our ceremony. Harold reaches into the other car and kisses the driver on both cheeks. For being a colored driver. And for being nice enough to force us off the road.

HAROLD. Boy, you sure can lay it on thick, Jeannie. Just 'cause you've got an audience. You know damned well I've straightened out plenty of colored guys. I just don't do it in front of you. I've taken on whole moving vans full of them.

JEAN. I can just about imagine.

HAROLD. I *don't* straighten out colored guys? You're going to stick to that, right? *(Punches* FROGMAN *in the jaw, knocking him down)* All right, there! I just straightened one out.

(MISS JANUS *hides behind a couch.)*

JEAN *(running to* FROGMAN). Good Christ, Harold . . .

(HAROLD *is dancing up and down in his bathrobe, fighter style.* TOURIST *and* LANDLADY *enter.)*

TOURIST. I saw that, son. That's the only language they understand.

(HAROLD *punches* TOURIST *in jaw.* TOURIST *reels out door into* LANDLADY'*s arms.* REDDINGTON *runs in from kitchen.*)

REDDINGTON. What's going on here? *(He grabs* HAROLD, *immobilizes him.*) Mr. Wonder, control yourself.

HAROLD. Jesus, what the hell did I do? *(To* FROGMAN) Look, I'm really sorry. I just realized what happened. Will you accept my apologies? I honestly didn't mean to do that.

FROGMAN *(into fake mike, imitating Joe Louis).* I want to say hello to my folks in South Carolina, I want to say hello. He hit very hard with his left hand, he very strong with his left hand. I want to say hello. And I want to say hello . . .

HAROLD. All right, cut it out.

MISS JANUS. Maybe if I massaged his shoulders . . .

HAROLD. It won't be necessary. . . . Jesus, I really handled that beautifully.

REDDINGTON. Come on, Pidge, let's go.

JEAN. I'll be back for the children.

REDDINGTON. Mr. Wonder, I've had my fill of this vulgar exhibition. I find it truly regrettable that you couldn't have accepted this in a more gentlemanly fashion. You've blown your cool, Mr. Wonder, and you are far from a credit to your race.

HAROLD. Jeannie, please, no doors, okay? No doors. I'm not fooling around any more. You leave now, you might as well sign a death certificate for me. Just fill one and leave it over there on the couch on your way out. Jeannie, I'm about to come out with the worst thing a guy ever said in the whole history of modern recorded statements. The kind of thing that if I knew I was going to be reduced to saying it, I wouldn't have even bothered growing up. Jeannie, I have to have you in the house. And you can do whatever the hell you want. Just so long as you're here. You have to have colored guys, you got 'em. Take them upstairs with you. Close the door, I'll make the goddamned beds for you. You want a trapeze, I'll set that up too. Anything you want. I just need to have you here awhile. So I can slowly build up my strength. You want to leave then, we have a whole new situation. *(To Negroes)* Look, what do you guys have to lose? You're coughing your head off; you can hardly stand on your feet. Where you going to get a cab at this hour? You go upstairs with her, it's cool, it's comfortable, you got television, you got everything you want . . .

JEAN. Will somebody get me out of here. Right this second.

REDDINGTON. Jean. (JEAN *takes* REDDINGTON *by the arm.*)

HAROLD *(to* JEAN *on her way out).* What did I just do? I was trying to be nice to them. Well, what am I supposed to do, throw them out on their ass? Punch them in the mouth—I did that already . . . (JEAN *and two Negroes exit. Calling through door)* These people haven't had it that easy, Jeannie. They haven't had any sleigh ride. We tend to forget. They've done plenty of suffering . . . *(also through door)* Jeannie! Where you going? Hey, can't you guys get your own broads? Wait till I get my hands on you . . . You black bastards . . . What the hell did I do? Did you see me make one wrong move? Did I step out of line once? She'll be back. She just needs a few days in the sun. A different kind of sun. We get crummy sun right here around the house. You sit out there for hours, you end up white as a sheet.

MISS JANUS. You know, I think you're right. I think I'm whiter than when I started.

HAROLD. What the hell am I supposed to do now? I'm a lonely guy.

MISS JANUS. Oh, it's because she's just left. I used to feel the same way at Camp Winnetkawonta in the Berkshires when my parents just dumped me there and drove off. But then as soon as I got involved in the activities—the second I got out there on the archery court . . .

HAROLD. Look, please, don't tell me archery. It's an entirely different situation. I'm some lonely guy. I've been on my own how long . . . *(Checks watch)* Look at that, four minutes, and I'm a lonely guy. Maybe if I got out of here. Listen, do you have anything on, something where I can really celebrate being this free guy? This unattached winner . . .

MISS JANUS. I told Abby and Nero I'd help them look for shells tonight. Just before it gets dark. You could come along. If you don't mind Nero being a little greasy.

HAROLD. Who minds? I'm not going to mind. Long as I get out of here. Long as I get started in my new life.

MISS JANUS. Okay, I'll tell them. I don't like to just spring things on Nero. I like to give him plenty of lead time. . . . You be okay?

HAROLD. I'll be great. I just have to get through till around three o'clock in the afternoon. If I can just do that, I'll be in the best shape of my life.

MISS JANUS. See you later. *(She leaves.)*

HAROLD *(running to window).* Hey, you'll be there, won't you?

MISS JANUS *(returning).* Of course. *(She kisses him on cheek, exits.)*

HAROLD. Well don't worry about it. If you can't make it, put it out of your mind. Either way is okay. *(Pause. He paces back and forth, picks up scythe, looks at it, flings it aside, can't seem to get comfortable. Re-creates all activities he's tried throughout evening—calls, knee bends, etc., everything that's worked for him—but he cuts off each one in the middle. Running to door, shouting)* Jeannie, I'm going out with broads—two of them. We're going to look for shells. You met one, remember? Her friend's even better-looking—there's no comparison. You see this new girl, you forget the other one's alive. . . . I'm going out with the two of them. And this greasy guy—he's coming along too. . . . *(He turns away for an instant, then returns to window as lights dim.)* Once I go looking for shells, that's the last word you'll ever hear from me. If I find out I love it, I'll throw you right out of the house. Right out of the house. You hear me, Jeannie! *(Lights go to black.)* Right out of the God-damned house.

CURTAIN

1776

Peter Stone and Sherman Edwards

First presented by Stuart Ostrow at the Forty-Sixth Street Theatre on March 16, 1969, in New York City, with the following cast:

JOHN HANCOCK David Ford
JOSIAH BARTLETT Paul-David Richards
JOHN ADAMS William Daniels
STEPHEN HOPKINS Roy Poole
ROGER SHERMAN David Vosburgh
LEWIS MORRIS Ronald Kross
ROBERT LIVINGSTON Henry Le Clair
JOHN WITHERSPOON Edmund Lyndeck
BENJAMIN FRANKLIN Howard Da Silva
JOHN DICKINSON Paul Hecht
JAMES WILSON Emory Bass
CAESAR RODNEY Robert Gaus
THOMAS MCKEAN Bruce MacKay
GEORGE READ Duane Bodin

SAMUEL CHASE Philip Polito
RICHARD HENRY LEE Ronald Holgate
THOMAS JEFFERSON Ken Howard
JOSEPH HEWES Charles Rule
EDWARD RUTLEDGE Clifford David
LYMAN HALL Jonathan Moore
CHARLES THOMSON Ralston Hill
ANDREW MCNAIR William Duell
ABIGAIL ADAMS Virginia Vestoff
MARTHA JEFFERSON Betty Buckley
A LEATHER APRON B. J. Slater
A PAINTER William Duell
A COURIER Scott Jarvis

Music and Lyrics by Sherman Edwards
Book by Peter Stone
Based on a conception of Sherman Edwards
Scenery and lighting by Jo Mielziner
Costumes by Patricia Zipprodt
Musical direction and dance arrangements by Peter Howard
Orchestrations by Eddie Sauter
Vocal arrangements by Elise Bretton
Musical numbers staged by Onna White
Directed by Peter Hunt

THE PLACE: A single setting representing the Chamber and an Anteroom of the Continental Congress; a Mall, High Street, and Thomas Jefferson's room, in Philadelphia; and certain reaches of John Adams' mind.
THE TIME: May, June, and July, 1776.
THE SCENES: 1. The Chamber of the Continental Congress.
2. The Mall.
3. The Chamber.
4. Thomas Jefferson's room and High Street.
5. The Chamber.
6. A Congressional Anteroom.
7. The Chamber.
The action is continuous, without intermission.

In our last series of Best Plays we made a modest patch of history by including, for the first time, a musical, *Fiddler on the Roof.* This was unusual because, normally, musicals, whatever their delights, are not always remarkable for the depth of their thought or even, at times, the very literacy of their literary accomplishment. Yet there are exceptions, and the remarkable *1776,* in this series, is one of them.

The idea for *1776* came to its composer-lyricist Sherman Edwards, who worked on it for nearly a decade before bringing it to Peter Stone, who was to become the librettist.

Peter Stone was born in Los Angeles in 1930, and he was born into the Hollywood film world. His father was the late John Stone, a movie producer and screenwriter. Mr. Stone studied at Bard and Yale, where he took his MFA. Twelve years of writing in France were followed by his first Hollywood chance, *Charade,* a movie starring Audrey Hepburn and Cary Grant. Mr. Grant also starred in a later movie, *Father Goose,* which won Mr. Stone an Oscar.

Before *1776,* Mr. Stone contributed the books for two moderately unsuccessful musicals, *Kean* and *Skyscraper.* He continued to write films after the success of *1776,* including the script for the filmed version of the musical. He also wrote the book for the Broadway musical *Sugar,* which enjoyed a run of over a year, and in 1973 adapted the novelist Erich Maria Remarque's only play, *Full Circle,* for Broadway, a venture that won few critical plaudits and had a short-lived New York career.

Sherman Edwards is a New Yorker, born in 1919. He was educated at both New York University and Cornell, where he was a history major. World War II found him in the Air Force, and after the war he taught history in high school. He also pursued another career as songwriter and occasional actor. But it was history that gave him the idea for *1776.*

The research for *1776* undertaken by Mr. Edwards was formidable and unexpected. Most people regard the Founding Fathers as signatures on a piece of paper. To be sure, a few people knew about John Adams and almost everyone knew about Benjamin Franklin, but the others were all misty figures, as were their motives and intentions. Mr. Edwards worked out the faces and the hearts behind the signatures.

The best first impression of this story is perhaps given by Peter Stone himself, who has recounted that on first receiving the research: "I was enthralled. The suspense, the intrigue, the courage and compromise, the richness of the men, their vagaries, vanities and fears, the issues and convictions motivating the thirteen colonies, the factions within them, their individual pride and their collective heritage—all of it held me spellbound for over three hours."

Audiences were spellbound with it also. The musical opened on March 16, 1969, and closed on February 13, 1972, after 1,217 performances.

In many respects it was a curious musical. It was a musical where very possibly the story was more important than the music—usually a rather suspicious symptom of a musical's sickness. Furthermore, it was a story that had no suspense whatsoever. Everyone in the audience knew the outcome.

The power of the piece came partly from the simple drama of history, but, even more, from its interesting insights into events so easily taken for granted. The relationship of Adams and his young wife, Abigail, the noting of a certain frivolity in Thomas Jefferson, the intricate deals and compromises made over the issue of freedom for Americans with the continuation of slavery—all these facets helped add up to a fascinating musical. But the show also provided America with an interesting history lesson on the side. Here was how the Republic was made.

HISTORICAL NOTE
BY THE AUTHORS

The first question we are asked by those who have seen—or read—*1776* is invariably: "Is it true? Did it really happen that way?"

The answer is: Yes.

Certainly a few changes have been made in order to fulfill basic dramatic tenets. To quote a European dramatist friend of ours, "God writes lousy theater." In other words, reality is seldom artistic, orderly, or dramatically satisfying; life rarely provides a sound second act, and its climaxes usually have not been adequately prepared for. Therefore, in historical drama, a number of small licenses are almost always taken with strictest fact, and those in *1776* are enumerated in this addendum. But none of them, either separately or in accumulation, has done anything to alter the historical truth of the characters, the times, or the events of American independence.

First, however, let us list those elements of our play that have been taken, unchanged and unadorned, from documented fact.

The weather in Philadelphia that late spring and early summer of 1776 was unusually hot and humid, resulting in a bumper crop of horseflies incubated in the stable next door to the State House (now Independence Hall).

John Adams was indeed "obnoxious and disliked"—the description is his own.

Benjamin Franklin, the oldest member of the Congress, suffered from gout in his later years and often "drowsed" in public.

Thomas Jefferson, the junior member of the Virginia delegation, was entrusted with the daily weather report.

Rhode Island's Stephen Hopkins, known to his colleagues as "Old Grape and Guts" because of his fondness for distilled refreshment, always wore his round black, wide-brimmed Quaker's hat in the chamber.

Portly Samuel Chase, the gourmand from Maryland (pronounced Mary-land in those times), was referred to (behind his back, of course) as "Bacon-Face."

Connecticut's Roger Sherman always sat apart from his fellow Congressmen, sipping coffee from a saucerlike bowl.

Caesar Rodney of Delaware, suffering from skin cancer, never appeared in public without a green scarf wrapped around his face.

The dress of the Congressmen graduated from the liberal greens, golds, brocades, and laces of the conservative Southerners, to the conservative browns, blacks, mean cloth, and plain linen of the radical New Englanders.

The only two known employees of the Congress were Charles Thomson, secretary, who kept no minutes of the debates (recording only those motions which were passed), and Andrew McNair, custodian and bell-ringer.

A motion concerning Congress's liability for a certain Mr. Melchior Meng's dead mule was debated and approved prior to the motion on independence.

Ben Franklin's illegitimate son William was Royal Governor of New Jersey until he was arrested, in June 1776, and exiled to Connecticut.

The New York delegation abstained on many votes, including the final vote on independence (that tally being recorded by Mr. Thomson as twelve for, none against, and one abstaining), though later the New York Legislature (the members of which "speak very fast and very loud and nobody pays any attention to anybody else, with the result that nothing ever gets done") approved the action after the fact.

General Washington's dispatches arrived on an average of three a day, and almost all of them were "gloomy" to the point of despair.

The strength of the armed forces under Washington's command was as dismal as he reported. On May 12, 1776, for instance, the Duty Roster of the Continental Army listed:

Commissioned officers	589
Non-commissioned officers	722
Present & fit for duty	6,641
Sick but present	547
Sick but absent	352
On furlough	66
On command [A.W.O.L.]	1,122

This was the total strength of the American army.

Edward Rutledge of South Carolina, the youngest member of the Congress, was the leading proponent of individual rights for individual states.

The committee to "manage" the Declaration of Independence consisted of five Congressmen: Adams, Franklin, Roger Sherman, Robert Livingston (of New York—he wasn't available to sign the Declaration, but he obligingly sent his cousin, Philip, to affix the powerful family name), and Jefferson. The fifth member had originally been Richard Lee, the offerer of the motion of independence, but he subsequently declined in order to return to Virginia, where he had been proposed for governor of that "country" (as Virginians referred to their colony). None of the five members of this committee wanted the assignment of actually writing the Declaration, and all of them begged off for one personal reason or another. But Jefferson, whom Adams accused of being the finest writer in Congress, possessing "a happy talent for composition and a remarkable felicity of expression," was finally persuaded. Later he recalled that the purpose of the Declaration had been "to place before mankind the common sense of the subject in terms so plain and firm as to command their assent."

Jefferson was, besides being an author, lawyer, farmer, architect, and statesman, a fine violinist. His wife, Martha, a young, beautiful widow of twenty-four when they married, was often praised for her "uncommon singing voice." (She died ten years after their wedding, a full nineteen years before Jefferson inhabited the White House, and he never remarried. The Martha Jefferson who is often listed as First Lady was their daughter.)

Jefferson, during those early years in Congress, was not a loquacious man. Adams remembered him as "the most silent man in Congress. . . . I never heard him utter three sentences together."

Adams knew he would not receive his proper due from posterity. He wrote that "the whole history of this Revolution will be a lie, from beginning to end." And, equally, he knew that Franklin was the stuff of which national legends are built. They would certify that "Franklin did this, Franklin did that, Franklin did some other damned thing. . . . Franklin smote the ground and out sprang George Washington, fully-grown and on his horse. . . . Franklin then electrified him with his miraculous lightning rod and the three of them—Franklin, Washington and the horse—conducted the entire Revolution by themselves."

The seemingly endless list of Congressional committees (and their redundant titles) spoken by Secretary Thomson at the beginning of Scene 5 are all taken from his own report as it appears in the "Journal of Congress."

The Declaration of Independence was debated by the Congress for three full days. It underwent eighty-six separate changes (and withstood scores of others, including an amendment calling for clear and sovereign "fishing rights") and the deletion of over four hundred words, including a strong condemnation of that "peculiar institution" slavery (accusing King George III of waging "cruel war against human nature itself, violating its most sacred rights of life and liberty in the persons of a distant people who never offended him, carrying them into slavery in another hemisphere . . . ") which called for its abolition. This paragraph was removed to placate and appease the Southern colonies and to hold them in the Union.

Jefferson, though a slaveholder himself, declared that "nothing is more certainly written in the Book of Fate than that this people shall be free." And further: "The rights of human nature are deeply wounded by this infamous practice."

The deadlock existing within the Delaware delegation was finally and melodramatically broken by the arrival of the mortally ill Caesar Rodney, who, in great pain, had ridden all night from Dover, a distance of some eighty miles, arriving just in time to save the motion on independence from being defeated. His sacrifice was all the more remarkable in view of the fact that by voting for the motion he was abandoning forever all hope of receiving the competent medical treatment of his illness that was available in England; he had become a traitor with a price on his head.

When the motion on independence had passed, John Dickinson of Pennsylvania, the leader of the anti-independence forces (desiring reconciliation with England), refused to sign the Declaration, a document he felt he could not endorse. But, asserting a fidelity to America, he left the Congress to enlist in the Continental Army as a private—though he was entitled to a commission—and served courageously with the Delaware Militia. Some years later he was appointed to the Constitutional Convention, representing Delaware, and returned to Philadelphia to contribute greatly to the writing of that extraordinary document, the United States Constitution.

All these historical facts appear in the play. But there are, as has been stated, many other instances where changes were effected. In all cases, however, we believe they were the result of sound dramatic decisions which were aesthetically, as well as historically, justified.

These changes can be divided into five categories: things altered, things surmised, things added, things deleted, and things rearranged. Following are examples of all five categories, plus the reasons for the changes.

Things altered: Of the two main alterations that were made, one was in the interests of dramatic construction, the other for the purpose of preserving dramatic unity.

First, the Declaration, though reported back to Congress for amendments and revisions prior to the vote on independence on July 2, was not actually debated and approved until after that vote. However, had this schedule been preserved in the play, the audience's interest in the debate would already have been spent.

Second, the Declaration was not signed on July 4, 1776, the date it was proclaimed to the citizenry of the thirteen colonies. It was actually signed over a period of several months, many of the signers having not been present at the time of its ratification. The greatest number signed on August 2, but one, Matthew Thornton of New Hampshire, did not even enter Congress until November 4, and the name of Colonel Thomas McKean of Delaware, probably the last to sign, had not yet appeared on the document by the middle of January 1777. It seems fairly obvious, however, that the depiction of a July 4 signing, like the famous Pine-Savage engraving of this non-event, provides the occasion with form and allows the proper emotional punctuation to the entire spectacle.

Things surmised: Because Secretary Thomson did not keep a proper record of the debates in Congress, and because other chronicles are incomplete in certain key areas, a small number of educated suppositions had to be made in order to complete the story. These were based on consistencies of character, ends logically connected to means, and the absence of other possible explanations.

It is unknown, for instance, whether Richard Henry Lee was persuaded to go to the Virginia House of Burgesses in order to secure a motion for independence that could be introduced in Congress, or if he volunteered on his own. Certainly Adams was getting nowhere with his own efforts; he had, on twenty-three separate occasions, introduced the subject of independence to his fellows in Congress, and each time it had failed to be considered. It was also true that whenever an issue needed respectability, the influence of a Virginian was brought to bear. (Virginia was the first colony, and its citizens were regarded as a sort of American aristocracy, an honor that was not betrayed by their leaders. The Virginian Washington was given command of the army, and the Virginian Jefferson was given the assignment of writing the Declaration.) Certainly Franklin would have delighted in appealing to Lee's vanity and deflating Adams' ego at one and the same time, as Scene 2 of the play suggests. But the actual sequence of these events is unknown.

And when Lee returned from Virginia (in Scene 3) a transcript of the debate in Congress on his motion for independence was never recorded. But the positions of individual Congressmen are known, and it was possible to glean phrases, attitudes, and convictions from the many letters, memoirs, and other papers that exist in abundance, in order to reconstruct a likely facsimile of this debate. (Stick fights, such as the one occurring between Adams and Dickinson in this scene, were common during Congressional debate, and though there is no report of this particular one, the sight of the two antagonists whacking away at each other certainly would have surprised no one.)

Similarly, a record of the debate on the Declaration was never kept. But in this case there was even more to go on. Jefferson himself, in his autobiography, provided two versions of the document—as originally written and as finally approved. Who was responsible for each individual change is not known, but in most instances convincing conclusions are not too hard to draw. McKean, a proud Scot, surely would have objected to the charge of "Scotch & foreign mercenaries [sent] to invade and deluge us in blood." And John Witherspoon of New Jersey, a clergyman and the Congressional chaplain, no doubt would have supported the addition of the phrase "with a firm Reliance on the Protection of Divine Providence," which had not been present in Jefferson's original draft. Also, Edward Rutledge must be charged with leading the fight against the condemnation of slavery, being the chief proponent of that practice in Congress. And the exchange between Jefferson and Dickinson, occurring in our version of this debate, includes lines written by Jefferson on other occasions, most notably: "The right to be free comes from Nature."

The conversion of James Wilson of Pennsylvania from the "Nay" to the "Yea" column at the last minute (in Scene 7) is an event without any surviving explanation. All that is definitely known is that Wilson, a former law student of Dickinson's and certainly under his influence in Congress, as his previous voting record testifies, suddenly changed his position on independence and, as a result, is generally credited with casting the vote that decided this issue. But why? A logical solution to this mystery was found when we imagined one fear he might have possessed that would have been stronger than his fear of Dickinson's wrath—the fear of going down in history as the man who singlehandedly prevented American independence. Such a position would have been totally consistent with his well-known penchant for caution.

The final logical conjecture we made concerned the discrepancy between the appearance of the word "inalienable" in Jefferson's version of the Declaration and its reappearance as "unalienable" in the printed copy that is now in universal use. This could have been a misprint, but it might, too, have been the result of interference by Adams (he had written it as "unalienable" in a copy of the Declaration he had drafted in his own hand), who believed that this seldom-used spelling was correct. There is no doubt that the meddlesome "Massachusettensian," a Harvard graduate, was not above speaking to Mr. Dunlap, the printer.

It is also consistent with both men's behavior that Adams and Jefferson should have disagreed on this matter, as they did on most. They were to become bitter enemies for much of their lives, only to make up when they had both survived to extreme old age. Both lived long enough to be invited (by Adams' son, John Quincy, who was then occupying the White House) to the fiftieth anniversary celebration of the Declaration of Independence. But on that very date, July 4, 1826, exactly a half-century later to the day, both of these gigantic figures, Jefferson at eighty-three, Adams at ninety-one—each believing and finding solace in the thought that the other was attending the jubilee—died. Surely this was one of the greatest coincidences in all history and one which never would be believed if included in a play.

Things added: The three instances of elements that were added to the story of American independence were created in the interest of satisfying the musical-comedy form. Again, it must be stressed that none of them interferes with historic truth in any way.

The first concerns Martha Jefferson's visit to Philadelphia in Scene 4. While it is true that Jefferson missed her to distraction, more than enough to effect an unscheduled reunion, it is believed that he journeyed to Virginia to see her. The license of having her come to see him, at Adams' instigation, stemmed from our desire to show something of the young Jefferson's personal life without destroying the unity of setting.

Second, in Scene 5 of the play, Adams, Franklin, and Chase are shown leaving for New Brunswick, New Jersey, for an inspection of the military. This particular trip did not actually take place, though a similar one was made to New York after the vote on independence, during which Adams and Franklin had to share a single bed in an inn. Originally the New Jersey junket was included in the play, represented by two separate scenes (one in an inn, showing the sleeping arrangements mentioned, the other on the military training grounds, showing inspection of "a ragtag collection of provincial militiamen and irregulars" who could do nothing right until a flock of ducks flew by; the men's hunger molded them into a smoothly operating unit). These scenes were removed, however, during the out-of-town tryout, in the interests of the over-all length of the play and because they were basically cinemagraphic in concept. Needless to say, both should appear in the filmed version of *1776.*

And third, the account by General Washington's dusty young courier, at the end of Scene 5, of a battle he had witnessed, while an actual description of the village green during and after the Battle of Lexington, is a wholly constructed moment, designed to illustrate the feelings and experiences of the Americans outside the Congress, who were deeply influenced by the decisions made inside the Congress.

One further note: The tally board used throughout the play to record each vote did not exist in the actual chamber in Philadelphia. It has been included in order to clarify the positions of the thirteen colonies at any given moment, a device allowing the audience to follow the parliamentary action without confusion.

Things deleted: Certain elements that are historically true have been left out of or removed from the play for one of three separate reasons.

The first of these was the embarrassment of riches; there are just too many choice bits of information to include in one, two, or even a dozen plays. The fact that Franklin often entered the Congressional chamber in a sedan chair carried by convicts, for instance; or that, on several occasions, Indians in full regalia would appear before the Congress, petitioning for one thing or another, and accompanied by their interpreter, a full-blooded Indian who spoke with a flawless Oxford accent.

Then there was the advisability of cutting down on the number of Congressmen appearing in the play in the interests of preserving clarity and preventing overcrowding. There is, after all, a limit to an audience's ability to assimilate (and keep separate) a large number of characters, as well as the physical limits of any given stage production. For this reason several of the lesser known (and least contributory) Congressmen were eliminated altogether, and in a few cases two or more were combined into a single character. James Wilson, for example, contains a few of the qualities of his fellow Pennsylvanian, John Morton. And John Adams is, at times, a composite of himself and his cousin Sam Adams, also of Massachusetts.

But by far the most frustrating reason for deleting a historical fact was that the audiences would never have believed it. The best example of this is John Adams' reply (it was actually Cousin Sam who said it) to Franklin's willingness to drop the anti-slavery clause from the Declaration. "Mark me, Franklin," he now says in Scene 7, "if we give in on this issue, posterity will never forgive us." But the complete line, spoken in July 1776, was "If we give in on this issue, *there will be trouble a hundred years hence;* posterity will never forgive us." And audiences would never forgive *us.* For who could blame them for believing that the phrase was the author's invention, stemming from the eternal wisdom of hindsight? After all, the astonishing prediction missed by only a few years.

Things rearranged: Some historical data have been edited dramatically without altering their validity or factuality.

The first example of this would be the play's treatment of Adams' relationship with his wife, Abigail. Two separate theatrical conventions have been employed: the selection and conversion of sections of their actual letters, written to each other during this period of their separation, into dialogue; and the placing of them in close physical proximity though they remain, in reality, over three hundred miles apart. The notion for this last device sprang, oddly, from a line in one of these same letters: Adams was complaining about their continued separation and finally pleaded, "Oh, if I could only annihilate time and space!" (The description of scenes, at the beginning of the play, defines these meetings by listing the area of dramatic action as "certain reaches of John Adams' mind.")

The exchanges, spoken and sung, between John and Abigail Adams are, as has been stated, the result of distributing, as dialogue, sections and phrases from various letters. The list of their children's diseases, the constant requests for "saltpetre for gunpowder" (and the counterrequest for pins), the use of the tender salutation "Dearest friend," the catalogue of Abigail's faults, the news of the farm in Braintree failing—even certain song lyrics transferred intact

("I live like a nun in a cloister" and "Write to me with sentimental effusion")—all these were edited and rearranged in an attempt to establish a dramatically satisfying relationship.

This same process was used to construct George Washington's dispatches from the field. Literally dozens were selected, from which individual lines were borrowed and then patched together in order to form the five communiqués that now appear in the play. Therefore, though the dispatches as now constructed were not written by the Commander-in-Chief, each sentence within them is either an actual quotation ("O how I wish I had never seen the Continental Army! I would have done better to retire to the back country and live in a wigwam") or paraphrase, or comes from a first-hand report (the final line of the last dispatch, " . . . but dear God! what brave men I shall lose before this business ends!" was spoken by Washington in the presence of his adjutant, who later reported it).

And finally, John Adams' extraordinary prophecy, made on July 3, 1776, describing the way Independence Day would be celebrated by future generations of Americans and written in a letter to his wife on that date, has been paraphrased and adapted into lyric form for the song "Is Anybody There?" sung by Adams in Scene 7. The original lines are:

> I am apt to believe that it will be celebrated by succeeding generations as the great anniversary festival. It ought to be commemorated as the day of deliverance by solemn acts of devotion to God Almighty. It ought to be solemnized with pomp and parade, with shows, games, sports, guns, bells, bonfires, and illumination, from one end of this continent to the other, from this time forward for evermore.
>
> You will think me transported with enthusiasm, but I am not. I am well aware of the toil and blood and treasure that it will cost us to maintain this Declaration and support and defend these States. Yet, through all the gloom, I can see the rays of ravishing light and glory. I can see that the end is more than worth all the means. And that posterity will triumph in that day's transaction, even although we should rue it, which I trust God we shall not.

We have attempted, in the paragraphs above, to answer the question, "Is it true?" What we cannot answer, however, is how such a question could possibly be asked so often by Americans. What they want to know is whether or not the story of their political origin, the telling of their national legend, is correct as presented. Don't they know? Haven't they ever heard it before? And if not, why not? As we say, it's a question we cannot answer.

There are those who would claim that the schools just don't teach it, and we would have trouble disagreeing with them. The authors of 1776 are both products of the American public-school system—one from the West Coast, the other from the East. Both were better than average students with a deeper than average curiosity about American history. But neither of them was given any more than a perfunctory review of the major events, a roster of a few cardboard characters, and a certain number of jingoistic conclusions.

But what of the arguments, the precedents, the compromises, the personalities, the regional disputes, the perseverance, the courage, the sacrifices, the expediencies? What of the similarities between those times and these (states rights *versus* federal rights; property rights *versus* human rights; privileged rights *versus* civil rights) and the differences (if any)? What of the lessons of the past applied to the problems of the future, for what society can plan a future without an intimate knowledge of its own past?

It is presumptuous of us to assume that 1776 will be able to fill even a portion of this lamentable void (though doubtless no small portion of its success is due to the "new" information it offers); the crime is that it should even have to. The United States owes its citizens, at the very least, an educational system that describes, defines, and explains our own existence.

206

CAST OF CHARACTERS

Members of the Continental Congress

President
JOHN HANCOCK
  New Hampshire
DR. JOSIAH BARTLETT
  Massachusetts
JOHN ADAMS
  Rhode Island
STEPHEN HOPKINS
  Connecticut
ROGER SHERMAN
  New York
LEWIS MORRIS
ROBERT LIVINGSTON
  New Jersey
REVEREND JOHN WITHERSPOON
  Pennsylvania
BENJAMIN FRANKLIN
JOHN DICKINSON
JAMES WILSON
  Delaware
CAESAR RODNEY

COLONEL THOMAS MCKEAN
GEORGE READ
  Maryland
SAMUEL CHASE
  Virginia
RICHARD HENRY LEE
THOMAS JEFFERSON
  North Carolina
JOSEPH HEWES
  South Carolina
EDWARD RUTLEDGE
  Georgia
DR. LYMAN HALL
  Secretary
CHARLES THOMSON
  Custodian and bell-ringer
ANDREW MCNAIR

ABIGAIL ADAMS
MARTHA JEFFERSON
A LEATHER APRON
A PAINTER
A COURIER

SCENE ONE

In front of the curtain.

JOHN ADAMS. I have come to the conclusion that one useless man is called a disgrace, that two are called a law firm, and that three or more become a congress. And by God, I have had *this* Congress! For ten years King George and his Parliament have gulled, cullied, and diddled these Colonies with their illegal taxes—Stamp Acts, Townshend Acts, Sugar Acts, *Tea* Acts—and when we *dared* stand up like men they stopped our trade, seized our ships, blockaded our ports, burned our towns, *and* spilled our blood—and still this Congress won't grant any of my proposals on Independence even so much as the courtesy of open debate! Good God, what in hell are they waiting for?

The curtain flies up to reveal the Chamber of the Second Continental Congress in Philadelphia. At rise, Congress is in session, sweltering in the heat of a premature summer's evening. A large day-by-day wall calendar reads: "MAY 8."

CONGRESS *(singing).*
            Sit down, John!
            Sit down, John!
            For God's sake, John,
            Sit down!

            Sit down, John!
            Sit down, John!
            For God's sake, John,
            Sit down!
VOICE.
 Someone ought to open up a window!
CONGRESS.
            It's ninety degrees!
            Have mercy, John, please!
            It's hot as Hell in
            Philadel-phia!
TWO VOICES.
 Someone ought to open up a window!
JOHN.
        I say "Vote Yes!
            Vote Yes!"
        Vote for independency!
CONGRESS A.
 Someone ought to open up a window!
JOHN.
            I say "Vote Yes!"
CONGRESS.
            Sit down, John!
JOHN.
        Vote for independency!

VOICE FROM CONGRESS B.
 Someone ought to open up a window!
CONGRESS B.
            No! No! No!
            Too many flies!
            Too many flies!
CONGRESS A.
            But it's hot as Hell in
            Philadel-phia!
VOICES FROM CONGRESS A.
 Are you going to open up a window?
CONGRESS A.
            Can't we
            Compromise here?
JOHN.
            Vote Yes!
CONGRESS B.
            No, too many
            Flies here!
JOHN.
            Vote Yes!
CONGRESS, *full.*
        Oh, for God's sake, John,
        Sit down!
They freeze.
JOHN *(speaks, roaring). Good God!!* Consider yourselves fortunate that you have John Adams to abuse, for no sane man would tolerate it!
CONGRESS *(resuming action, singing).*
            John, you're a bore!
            We've heard this before!
            Now, for God's sake, John,
            Sit down!
JOHN.
            I say, "Vote Yes!"
SOME VOICES.
                No!!
JOHN.
            Vote Yes!
CONGRESS, *full.*
                No!!
JOHN.
            Vote for
            Independency!
CONGRESS A.
 Someone ought to open up a window!
JOHN.
            I say "Vote Yes!"
CONGRESS, *full.*
            Sit down, John!
JOHN.
            Vote for independency!!!
VOICE.
        Will someone shut that man up!!
JOHN *(speaking).* Never! Never! *(He storms*

from the Chamber, coming downstage, and looks to Heaven for guidance.) Dear God! For one solid year they have been sitting there—for *one year! Doing nothing! (Singing)*

I do believe you've laid a curse on
North America!
A curse that we here now rehearse in
Philadelphia!
A second Flood, a simple famine,
Plagues of locusts everywhere,
Or a cataclysmic earthquake,
I'd accept with some despair.
But, no, you've sent us Congress—
Good God, Sir, was that fair?

I say this with humility in
Philadelphia!
We're your responsibility in
Philadelphia!
If you don't want to see us hanging
On some far-off British hill,
If you don't want the voice of
  independency
Forever still,
Then, God, Sir, get Thee to it,
For Congress never will!

You see we
  Piddle, twiddle, and resolve.
  Not one damned thing do we solve.
  Piddle, twiddle, and resolve.
  Nothing's ever solved in
  Foul, fetid, fuming, foggy, filthy
Philadelphia!

(From the Chamber, rear, a Congressional voice can be heard.)

VOICE. Someone ought to open up a window!

JOHN *(speaking).* Oh, shut up!

JOHN HANCOCK. I now call the Congress' attention to the petition of Mr. Melchior Meng, who claims twenty dollars' compensation for his dead mule. It seems the animal was employed transporting luggage in the service of the Congress.

JAMES WILSON. The question, then, would appear to be one of occasion, for if the mule expired not while carrying, but after being unloaded, then surely the beast dropped dead on its own time!

JOHN. *Good God!! (Singing)*

They may sit here for years and years in
Philadelphia!
These indecisive grenadiers of
Philadelphia!
They can't agree on what is right or wrong
Or what is good or bad.
I'm convinced the only purpose

This Congress ever had
Was to gather here, specifically,
To drive John Adams mad!

You see we
  Piddle, twiddle, and resolve.
  Not one damned thing do we solve.
  Piddle, twiddle, and resolve
  Nothing's ever solved in
  Foul, fetid, fuming, foggy, filthy
Philadelphi—

ABIGAIL ADAMS, JOHN*'s wife, a handsome woman of thirty-two, now appears in* JOHN*'s imagination and interrupts.*

ABIGAIL.
  John, John!
  Is that you carrying on, John?

JOHN *(speaking).* Oh, Abigail! Abigail—I have such a desire to knock heads together!

ABIGAIL. I know, my dearest. I know. But that's because you make everything so complicated. It's all quite simple, really: *(Singing)*
  Tell the Congress to declare
  Independency!
  Then sign your name, get out of there,
  And hurry home to me!
  Our children all have dysentery,
  Little Tom keeps turning blue,
  Little Abby has the measles
  And I'm coming down with flu.
  They say we may get smallpox—

JOHN *(speaking).* Madame, what else is new? *(Music under)* Abigail, in my last letter I told you that the King has collected twelve thousand German mercenaries to send against us. I asked you to organize the ladies and make saltpetre for gunpowder. Have you done as I asked?

ABIGAIL. No, John, I have not.

JOHN. Why have you not?

ABIGAIL. Because you neglected to tell us how saltpetre is made.

JOHN *(impatient).* By treating sodium nitrate with potassium chloride, of course!

ABIGAIL *(a woman).* Oh, yes—of course.

JOHN. Will it be done, then?

ABIGAIL. I'm afraid we have a more urgent problem, John.

JOHN. *More* urgent, Madame?

ABIGAIL *(singing).*

There's one thing every woman's missed in
Massachusetts Bay—
Don't smirk at me, you egotist, pay
Heed to what I say!
We've gone from Framingham to Boston
And cannot find a pin.
"Don't you know there is a war on?"
Says each tradesman with a grin.

Well!
We will not make saltpetre
Until you send us pins!
JOHN.
    Pins, Madame? Saltpetre!
ABIGAIL.
        Pins!
JOHN AND ABIGAIL *(alternating).*
    Saltpetre!
                    Pins!
    Saltpetre!
                    Pins!
    Saltpetre!
                    Pins!
    'Petre!
                    Pins!
    'Petre!
                    Pins!
    'Petre!
                    Pins!
    'Petre!
                    Pins!

JOHN *(speaking, beaten).* Done, Madame. Done.

ABIGAIL. Done, John. *(Smiling)* Hurry home, John.

JOHN. As soon as I'm able.

ABIGAIL. Don't stop writing—it's all I have.

JOHN. Every day, my dearest friend.

ABIGAIL *(singing).*
            Till then . . .
ABIGAIL AND JOHN.
Till then,
I am, as I ever was, and ever shall be—
Yours . . .
Yours . . .
Yours . . .
Yours . . .
Yours . . .
JOHN.
    Saltpetre. *(He throws a kiss.)* John.
ABIGAIL.
    Pins. *(She throws a kiss.)* Abigail.
(She goes.)
CONGRESS *(singing).*
For God's sake, John,
Sit down!

(JOHN *turns, waves them off in disgust, then crosses.)*

JOHN *(calling).* Franklin!

SCENE TWO

The Mall. Sunlight. BENJAMIN FRANKLIN *sits on a bench, having his portrait painted.*

JOHN *discovers him.*

———

JOHN. Franklin! Where in God's name were you when I needed you?

FRANKLIN. Right here, John, being preserved for posterity. Do y'like it?

JOHN *(after examining the painting carefully).* It stinks.

(THE PAINTER *goes.)*

FRANKLIN. As ever, the soul of tact.

JOHN. The man's no Botticelli.

FRANKLIN. And the subject's no Venus.

JOHN. Franklin! You heard what I suffered in there?

FRANKLIN. Heard? Of course I heard—along with the rest of Philadelphia. Lord, your voice is piercing, John!

JOHN. I wish to heaven my arguments were. By God, Franklin, when will they make up their minds? With one hand they can raise an army, dispatch one of their own to lead it, and cheer the news from Bunker's Hill—while with the other they wave the olive branch, begging the King for a happy and permanent reconciliation. Why damn it, Fat George has declared us in rebellion—why in bloody hell can't *they?*

FRANKLIN. John, really! You talk as if independence were the rule! *It's never been done before!* No colony has ever broken from the parent stem in the history of the world!

JOHN. Dammit, Franklin, you make us sound treasonous!

FRANKLIN. Do I? *(Thinking)* Treason—"Treason is a charge invented by winners as an excuse for hanging the losers."

JOHN. I have more to do than stand here listening to you quote yourself.

FRANKLIN. No, that was a new one!

JOHN. Dammit, Franklin, we're at war!

FRANKLIN. To defend ourselves, nothing more. *We* expressed our displeasure, the English moved against us, and *we,* in turn, have resisted. Now our fellow Congressmen want to effect a reconciliation *before* it becomes a war.

JOHN. Reconciliation my ass! The *people* want independence!

FRANKLIN. The people have read Mr. Paine's *Common Sense.* I doubt the Congress has. *(He studies him.)* John, why don't you give it up? Nobody listens to you—you're obnoxious and disliked.

JOHN. I'm not promoting John Adams, I'm promoting independence.

FRANKLIN. Evidently they cannot help connecting the two.

JOHN *(suspicious)*. What are you suggesting?

FRANKLIN. Let someone else in Congress propose.

JOHN. Never! *(FRANKLIN shrugs.)* Who did you have in mind?

FRANKLIN. I don't know. I really haven't given it much thought.

(RICHARD HENRY LEE, a tall, loose-jointed Virginian aristocrat of forty-five, enters.)

LEE. You sent for me, Benjamin?

JOHN *(looking at LEE, then at FRANKLIN)*. Never!!

LEE. Halloo, Johnny.

JOHN *(nodding)*. Richard.

FRANKLIN. Richard, John and I need some advice.

LEE. If it's mine t'give, it's yours, y'know that.

FRANKLIN. Thank you, Richard. As you know, the cause that we support has come to a complete standstill. Now, why do you suppose that is?

LEE. Simple! Johnny, here, is obnoxious and disliked.

FRANKLIN. Yes, that's true. What's the solution, I wonder?

LEE *(it's obvious)*. Get someone else in Congress to propose—

FRANKLIN. Richard, that's brilliant! Wasn't that brilliant, John?

JOHN *(dully)*. Brilliant.

FRANKLIN. Yes. Now the question remains —who can it be? The man we need must belong to a delegation publicly committed to support independence, and at the present time only Massachusetts, New Hampshire, and Delaware have declared our way.

LEE. And Virginia, Benjy—don't forget Virginia.

FRANKLIN. Oh, I haven't, Richard—how could I? But strictly speaking, while Virginia's views on independence are well known, your legislature in Williamsburg has never formally authorized its delegation here in Congress to support the cause. Of course, if we could think of a Virginian with enough influence to go down there and persuade the House of Burgesses—

LEE. Damn me if *I* haven't thought of someone!

FRANKLIN AND ADAMS *(together)*. Who?

LEE. *Me!*

FRANKLIN. Why didn't I think of that!

LEE. I'll leave tonight—why, hell, right now, if y'like! I'll stop off at Stratford just long enough to refresh the missus, and then straight to the matter. Virginia, the land that gave us our glorious Commander-in-Chief— *(a short drum roll)*—George Washington, will now give the continent its proposal on independence! And when Virginia proposes, the South is bound to follow, and where the South goes the Middle Colonies go! Gentlemen, a salute! To Virginia, the Mother of American Independence!

JOHN. Incredible! We're free, and he hasn't even left yet! *(To LEE)* What makes you so sure you can do it?

(Music begins.)

LEE. *Hah!! (Singing)*
My name is Richard Henry Lee!
Virginia is my home.
My name is Richard Henry Lee!
Virginia is my home,
And may my horses turn to glue
If I can't deliver up to you
A resolution—on independency!

For I am F.F.V.
The First Family
In the Sovereign Colony of Virginia.
The F.F.V.
The Oldest Family
In the oldest colony in America!

And may the British burn my land
If I can't deliver to your hand
A resolution—on independency!

Y'see it's—
Here a Lee
There a Lee
Everywhere a Lee, a Lee!

FRANKLIN AND LEE *(alternating)*.
Social—
                                    LEE!
Political—
                                    LEE!
Financial—
                                    LEE!
Natural—
                                    LEE!
*In*ternal—
                                    LEE!
*Ex*ternal—
                                    LEE!
*Fra*ternal—
                                    LEE!
E-ternal—
                                    LEE!

(Together)
The F.F.V.,
The First Family
In the Sovereign Colony of Virginia!

LEE.
>And may my wife refuse my bed
>If I can't deliver (as I said)
>A resolution—on independency!

JOHN *(speaking)*. Spoken modest-*Lee*. God help us!

FRANKLIN. He will, John! He will!

LEE *(singing)*.
>They say that God in Heaven
>Is everybody's God.

FRANKLIN.
>Amen!

LEE.
>I'll admit that God in Heaven
>Is everybody's God.
>But I tell y', John, with pride,
>God leans a little on the side
>Of the Lees! The Lees of old Virginia!

>Y'see it's
>Here a Lee, there a Lee
>Everywhere a Lee—a Lee!

FRANKLIN AND LEE.
>Here a Lee, there a Lee
>Everywhere a Lee—

LEE.
>Look out! There's
>Arthur Lee!
>"Bobby" Lee! . . . an'
>General "Lighthorse" Harry Lee!
>Jesse Lee!
>Willie Lee!

FRANKLIN.
>And Richard H.—

LEE.
>*That's me!!*
>And may my blood stop running blue
>If I can't deliver up to you
>A resolution—on independency!
>*(He begins strutting, a military cakewalk.)*
>Yes sir, by God, it's
>Here a Lee!
>There a Lee!
>Come on, boys, join in with me!
>*(They do,* JOHN *reluctantly.)*
>Here a Lee! There a Lee!

FRANKLIN *(speaking)*. When do y'leave?

LEE *(singing)*.
>Immediate-*Lee!*
>Here a Lee! There a Lee!

FRANKLIN *(speaking)*. When will you return?

LEE *(singing)*.
>Short-*Lee!*
>Here a Lee! There a Lee!
>And I'll come back
>Triumphant-*Lee!*

FRANKLIN AND JOHN.
>Here a Lee! There a Lee!
>Ev'rywhere a Lee! A Lee!

LEE.
>Forrr-warrr . . .
>*Ho-ooo!*

*(*LEE *struts off.* FRANKLIN *and* JOHN *follow him almost as far as the wings, then drop out and return, breathless but relieved.)*

JOHN *(speaking)*. That was the most revolting display I ever witnessed.

FRANKLIN. They're a warm-blooded people, Virginians!

JOHN. Not him, Franklin—*you!* You and your infernal obsession for deviousness! If you'd come right out and asked him straight, he'd've been gone a half hour ago!

FRANKLIN. Cheer up, John. At this very moment our cause is again riding high—sitting straight in the saddle and in full gallop for Virginia!

*(*LEE *suddenly reappears.)*

LEE *(singing)*.
>—And our women are . . . serene . . .

JOHN *(speaking)*. Oh, good God!

LEE.
>Full-bosomed . . .

FRANKLIN *(perking up)*. Full-bosomed?

LEE.
>Full-bosomed, Benjy,
>Every one a queen! Why, they are . . .
>*(Music in, at tempo)*
>—Lees! Dammit!
>The Lees of old Virginia! Yes, sir! By God!
>*(Waving his riding crop, he parades around, followed by* FRANKLIN *and* JOHN.)*

ALL.
>It's here a Lee!
>There a Lee!

LEE.
>Come on, John,
>Step live-a-*Lee!*

ALL.
>Here a Lee!
>There a Lee!
>Everywhere a Lee—a Lee!

(Again LEE *starts off, strutting between, but ahead of,* JOHN *and* FRANKLIN, *who are half-heartedly marching after him. Suddenly* LEE *has still another afterthought and turns back to express it—but* JOHN *and* FRANKLIN *are ready for him this time, hooking his arms as he passes between them, and dragging the surprised and frustrated Virginian off backward.)*

SCENE THREE

The Chamber. Featured prominently, rear, is a tally board. Under three main headings (YEA, NAY, *and* ABSTAIN) *are thirteen slots, each with a shuttle containing the name of a single colony. This device, during a vote, is the province of the Secretary of the Congress. At rise, the Chamber is empty save for its aging custodian,* ANDREW MCNAIR, *who is preparing the room for the day's session with the help of a Leather Apron, a working man. The wall calendar now reads:* "JUNE 7." *Then, as* MCNAIR *sets out quill pens and fills the several inkwells from a large jar, Georgia's* DR. LYMAN HALL, *fifty-five, enters and looks around, finally clearing his throat.* MCNAIR *looks up.*

MCNAIR. Yes?

HALL. I'm Dr. Lyman Hall, new delegate from Georgia.

MCNAIR. I'm Andrew McNair, Congressional Custodian. *(He goes back to work.)* If you'll be wantin' anything at all just holler out, "McNair!" as you'll hear the others do, and there won't be too long to wait.

HALL *(looking around)*. Where does the Georgia delegation belong?

MCNAIR. Oh, they mill about over in that corner—near the two Carolinas.

HALL *(checking his watch)*. It's after ten. I was told the Congress convenes at ten.

MCNAIR. They'll be wandering' in any time now, sir—with Old Grape 'n' Guts leadin' the pack.

HALL. Old *who?*

HOPKINS' VOICE *(offstage)*. McNair!!

MCNAIR. Grape 'n' Guts.

*(*STEPHEN HOPKINS, *a thin round-shouldered man of seventy, wearing a black suit, black Quaker hat, his gray hair at shoulder length, enters.)*

HOPKINS. Fetch me a mug o' rum!

MCNAIR. Mr. Hopkins, you'll be pleased to meet Dr. Lyman Hall—

HOPKINS. I don't need a doctor, dammit—

MCNAIR. —new delegate from Georgia—

HOPKINS. Why didn't you say so? *(To* HALL) I'm Stephen Hopkins, *old* delegate from Rhode Island. McNair! *Two* mugs o' rum!

HALL. I fear it's a little early in the day—

HOPKINS. Nonsense! It's a medicinal fact that rum gets a man's heart started in the morning—I'm surprised you didn't know it. And speaking as the oldest man in the Congress—

MCNAIR. Ben Franklin's older by almost a year—

HOPKINS. *Rum!!* (MCNAIR *scurries off.)* Tell me, Dr. Hall, where does Georgia stand on the question of independence?

*(*EDWARD RUTLEDGE, *a young, handsome, dandified aristocrat of twenty-six, has entered.)*

RUTLEDGE. With South Carolina, of course.

HOPKINS *(laughing)*. Good morning, Neddy. Shake the hand of Dr. Lyman Hall from Georgia. Doctor, this here is Edward Rutledge from whichever Carolina he says he's from—God knows I can't keep 'em straight.

RUTLEDGE. A pleasure, Dr. Hall.

HALL. Your servant, Mr. Rutledge.

HOPKINS. You've met the long and short of it now, Doctor. Neddy here is only twenty-six; he's the *youngest* of us—

RUTLEDGE. Except for Ben Franklin—

HOPKINS. *McNair!!*

*(*MCNAIR *has returned and now stands at* HOPKINS' *elbow.)*

MCNAIR. Your rum.

HOPKINS. Where'd y'go for it, man—Jamaica?

*(*RUTLEDGE *and* HALL *walk away.)*

RUTLEDGE. Where *does* Georgia stand on independence at the present time, Dr. Hall?

HALL. I am here without instructions, able to vote my own personal convictions.

RUTLEDGE. And they are—?

HALL *(a pause; he examines him)*. Personal.

RUTLEDGE. Dr. Hall, the Deep South speaks with one voice. It is traditional—even more, it is historical. *(They regard one another for a moment. Then the Delaware delegation enters:* CAESAR RODNEY, *forty-eight, thin and pale, wears a green scarf tied around his face, covering some infirmity;* GEORGE READ, *forty-three, small and round, speaks with a high voice; and* COLONEL THOMAS MCKEAN, *forty-two, tall and florid, has a booming voice decorated with a Scottish brogue. As always, the three are arguing.)* Enter Delaware—*tria juncta in uno!*

MCKEAN. Speak plain, Rutledge, y'know I can't follow none o' y'r damn French!

RUTLEDGE. Latin, Colonel McKean—a tribute to the eternal peace and harmony of the Delaware delegation.

MCKEAN. What're y'sayin', man? Y'know perfectly well neither Rodney nor I can stand this little wart! *(He indicates* READ.)

RUTLEDGE. Gentlemen, gentlemen, this is

Dr. Lyman Hall of Georgia—Caesar Rodney, George Read, and Colonel Thomas McKean. *(HALL shakes hands with each in turn and they exchange greetings.)*

RODNEY. Where do you stand on independence, sir?

HALL *(a look to RUTLEDGE)*. With South Carolina, it seems.

RUTLEDGE. I leave the doctor in your excellent company, gentlemen. *(Smiling, he bows and walks away, joining another group.)*

(Slowly the Chamber has begun to fill with Congressmen: LEWIS MORRIS and ROBERT LIVINGSTON of New York; ROGER SHERMAN of Connecticut; JOSEPH HEWES of North Carolina; the portly SAMUEL CHASE of Maryland; JOSIAH BARTLETT of New Hampshire; others; and last to enter, unnoticed, THOMAS JEFFERSON of Virginia, thirty-three, six feet three, with copper-colored hair, carrying several books.)

RODNEY *(drawing HALL aside)*. Tell me, sir, would you be a doctor of medicine or theology?

HALL. Both, Mr. Rodney. Which one can be of service?

RODNEY *(good-naturedly)*. By all means the physician first! Then we shall see about the other.

HALL *(smiling)*. I'll call at your convenience, sir. *(They are joined by two members of the Pennsylvania delegation: JOHN DICKINSON, forty-four, a thin, hawkish man, not without elegance; and JAMES WILSON, thirty-three, a bespectacled, cautious little sycophant.)*

DICKINSON *(pleasantly)*. I trust, Caesar, when you're through converting the poor fellow to independency that you'll give the opposition a fair crack at him.

RODNEY. You're too late, John; once I get 'em they're got. Dr. Lyman Hall of Georgia —Mr. John Dickinson of Pennsylvania.

DICKINSON. An honor, sir.

HALL. Your servant.

WILSON *(waiting)*. Ahem.

RODNEY. Ah, Judge Wilson, forgive me— but how can anyone see you if you insist on standing in Mr. Dickinson's shadow? *(To HALL)* James Wilson, also of Pennsylvania.

WILSON. Sir.

HALL. An honor, sir.

(FRANKLIN enters, limping on a cane, one foot bandaged.)

FRANKLIN. Will you get out of my way, please? Good morning, all!

HALL *(recognizing him)*. Good Lord, do you have the honor to be Dr. Franklin?

FRANKLIN. Yes, I have that honor—unfortunately the gout accompanies the honor.

HOPKINS. Been living too high again, eh, Pappy?

FRANKLIN. Stephen, I only wish King George felt like my big toe—all over!

HOPKINS. *McNair!!* Fetch a pillow—and two more mugs o' rum!

(Now JOHN enters the Chamber and looks around, searching for someone.

It is now evident that the colors and styles of the various costumes change gradually from colony to colony—from the fancy greens and golds of the Deep South to the somber blacks of New England.)

FRANKLIN. Good morning, John!

JOHN *(joining him)*. Well, Franklin? Where's that idiot Lee? Has he returned yet? I don't see him.

FRANKLIN. Softly, John—your voice is hurting my foot.

JOHN. One more day, Franklin—that's how long I'll remain silent, and not a minute longer! That strutting popinjay was so damned sure of himself. He's had time to bring back a *dozen* proposals by now!

(DICKINSON turns to WILSON and addresses him in a loud voice, for all to hear.)

DICKINSON. Tell me, James, how do you explain the strange, monumental quietude that Congress has been treated to these past thirty days? *(Everyone, including JOHN, has turned to listen.)* Has the ill wind of independence finally blown itself out?

WILSON. If you ask me—

DICKINSON. For myself, I must confess that a month free from New England noise is more therapeutic than a month in the country! Don't you agree, James?

WILSON. Well, I—

DICKINSON *(turning)*. Mr. Adams, pray look for your voice, sir! It cannot be far, and God knows we need the entertainment in this Congress! *(Laughter from his fellow conservatives. Everyone turns to ADAMS, who is trembling with rage.)*

FRANKLIN. Congratulations, John, you've just made your greatest contribution to independence—you kept your flap shut!

JOHN. One more day . . . !

(JOHN HANCOCK, forty, takes his place at the President's desk; he is followed by CHARLES THOMSON, forty-seven, the pedantic Secretary to the Congress. HANCOCK pounds his gavel.)

HANCOCK. Gentlemen, the usual morning festivities concluded, I will now call the Congress to order. *(Gavel)* Mr. Thomson.

THOMSON *(rising and ringing a bell)*. The Second Continental Congress, meeting in the city of Philadelphia, is now in session, seventh June, seventeen seventy-six, the three hundred eightieth meeting.

MCNAIR. Sweet Jesus!

THOMSON. The Honorable John Hancock of Massachusetts Bay, President. *(He rings the bells and sits.)*

HANCOCK.Thank you, Mr. Thomson. *(He swats a fly.)* Mr. McNair, the stores of rum and other drinking spirits are hereby closed to the colony of Rhode Island for a period of three days.

MCNAIR. Yes, sir.

HOPKINS. John, y'can't do that!

HANCOCK. Sit down, Mr. Hopkins. You've abused the privilege. The Chair takes this opportunity to welcome Dr. Lyman Hall of Georgia to this Congress and hopes he will make the best of it. My God, it's hot! The Secretary will read the roll.

THOMSON. All members present with the following exceptions: Mr. Charles Carroll of Maryland; Mr. Samuel Adams of Massachusetts; Mr. Button Gwinnett of Georgia; Mr. George Wythe and Mr. Richard Henry Lee of Virginia; and the entire delegation of New Jersey.

HANCOCK. I'm concerned over the continued absence of one-thirteenth of this Congress. Where is New Jersey?

DICKINSON. Somewhere between New York and Pennsylvania.

HANCOCK. Thank you very much. Dr. Franklin, have you heard anything? Your son resides there.

FRANKLIN. Son sir? What son?

HANCOCK *(sorry he brought it up)*. The Royal Governor of New Jersey, sir.

FRANKLIN. As that title might suggest, sir, we are not in touch at the present time.

HANCOCK. Yes. Very well—uh—the weather report—Mr. Jefferson of Virginia. *(No reaction; JEFFERSON is reading a book.)* Mr. Jefferson!

JEFFERSON *(jumping to his feet)*. Present, sir!

HANCOCK. May we hear about the weather, as if it weren't speaking for itself.

JEFFERSON *(going to several gauges at the window)*. Eighty-seven degrees of temperature, thirty-point-aught-six inches of mer-cury, wind from the southwest for the rest of the day, and tonight—*(he turns)*—tonight I'm leaving for home.

HANCOCK. On business?

JEFFERSON. Family business.

HOPKINS. Give her a good one for me, young feller!

JEFFERSON *(smiling)*. Yes, sir, I will.

(A uniformed courier, dusty from his long ride, enters and approaches THOMSON, removing a communiqué from his pouch. He tosses it into the Secretary's desk and leaves wearily.)

THOMSON *(ringing his bell)*. From the Commander, Army of the United Colonies; in New York, dispatch number one thousand, one hundred and thirty-seven—

MCNAIR. Sweet Jesus!

THOMSON *(reading)*. "To the Honorable Congress, John Hancock, President. Dear Sir: It is with grave apprehension that I have learned this day of the sailing from Halifax, Nova Scotia, of a considerable force of British troops in the company of foreign mercenaries and under the command of General Sir William Howe. There can be no doubt that their destination is New York for to take and hold this city and the Hudson Valley beyond would serve to separate New England from the other colonies permitting both sections to be crushed in turn. Sadly, I see no way of stopping them at the present time as my army is absolutely falling apart, my military chest is totally exhausted, my Commissary General has strained his credit to the last, my Quartermaster has no food, no arms, no ammunition, and my troops are in a state of near mutiny! I pray God some relief arrives before the armada but fear it will not. Y'r ob'd't *(Drum roll)* G. Washington." *(During the brief silence that follows,* THOMSON *shrugs and files the dispatch.)*

MCKEAN. Mr. President!

HANCOCK *(wearily; he knows what's coming)*. Colonel McKean.

MCKEAN. Surely we've managed to promote the *gloomiest* man on this continent to the head of our troops. Those dispatches are the most depressing accumulation of disaster, doom, and despair in the entire annals of military history! And furthermore—

HANCOCK *(pounding his gavel)*. Please, Colonel McKean—it's too hot.

MCKEAN. Oh. Yes. I suppose so.

HANCOCK. General Washington will continue wording his dispatches as he sees fit, and I'm sure we all pray that he finds happier thoughts to convey in the near—*(swats a fly)* — future. Mr. Thomson, are there any resolutions?

THOMSON. Dr. Josiah Bartlett of New Hampshire.

BARTLETT *(rising and reading).* "Resolved: that for the duration of the present hostilities the Congress discourage every type of extravagance and dissipation, elaborate funerals and other expensive diversions, especially all horse-racing—" *(He is shouted down by the entire Congress. Then the door bursts open and LEE sweeps in.)*

LEE. Benjy, I'm back—I'm back Johnny! *(He lets out a Southern war whoop. In a flash, JOHN, JEFFERSON, MCKEAN, and even the hobbling FRANKLIN crowd around him.)*

MCKEAN. Richard, we're pleased t'see y'!

FRANKLIN. What news, Dickie boy, what news?

JOHN. Lee! Is it done?

LEE. First things first. *(Looking around)* Tom—where's Tom? *(Turning and seeing JEFFERSON)* Tom! Your little bride wants to know: "When's he coming home?"

JEFFERSON. I leave tonight!

JOHN *(grabbing LEE's shoulders).* Never mind that—*is it done?*

LEE. Done? *(A pause)* Why, certain—*Lee!* *(Cheers from those for independence)* Mr. President, I have returned from Virginia with the followin' resolution. *(He produces a paper and reads.)* "Resolved: that these united colonies are (and of a right ought to be) free and independent states, that they are absolved from all allegiance to the British Crown, and that all political connection between them and the state of Great Britain is (and ought to be) totally dissolved!"

JOHN. Mr. President, I second the proposal!

(A silence; HANCOCK swats a fly.)

HANCOCK. The resolution has been proposed and seconded. The Chair will now entertain debate.

DICKINSON *(rising, assuming weariness).* Mr. President, Pennsylvania moves, as always, that the question of independence be postponed—indefinitely.

WILSON. I second the motion!

HANCOCK. Judge Wilson, in your eagerness to be loved you seem to have forgotten that Pennsylvania cannot second its own motion.

READ. Delaware seconds.

MCKEAN. You would, y'little weasel!

HANCOCK. The motion to postpone has been moved and seconded. Mr. Thomson.

(THOMSON goes to the tally board. As each colony votes, he announces it and MCNAIR, in turn, mechanically records it on the board. HOPKINS, during this preparation, rises and leaves the Chamber.)

THOMSON. On the motion to postpone indefinitely the resolution of independency or proceed with the debate, all those in favor of debate say "Yea," all those for postponement say "Nay." *(Intoning)* New Hampshire—

BARTLETT. New Hampshire favors debate and says Yea.

THOMSON. New Hampshire says Yea. Massachusetts—

JOHN. Massachusetts, having borne the brunt of the King's tyranny—

THOSE AGAINST. *Shame!! Shame!!*

THOSE FOR. *Sit down, John!*

JOHN. Yes, I said *tyranny!* Massachusetts now and for all time says *Yea!*

THOMSON *(flatly).* Massachusetts says Yea. Rhode Island—Mr. Hopkins? Where's Rhode Island?

MCNAIR. Rhode Island is out visitin' the "necessary."

HANCOCK. After what Rhode Island's consumed, I can't say I'm surprised. We'll come back to him, Mr. Thomson.

THOMSON. Rhode Island passes. *(Laughter; THOMSON looks around, not understanding, then proceeds.)* Connecticut—

SHERMAN *(He holds, as he will throughout the entire play, a shallow bowl of coffee; he is never without it).* While Connecticut has, till now, been against this proposal, our legislature has instructed me that, in the event it is introduced by any colony *outside* of New England, Connecticut could not any longer withhold its support. Connecticut says Yea.

(Franklin and John exchange satisfied looks.)

THOMSON. Connecticut says Yea. New York—

MORRIS. Mr. Secretary, New York abstains—courteously.

THOMSON. New York abstains—

MORRIS. —courteously.

THOMSON. New Jersey—

HANCOCK. Absent, Mr. Secretary.

THOMSON. New Jersey is absent. Pennsylvania—

DICKINSON. Pennsylvania, for the twenty-fourth time, says Nay.

THOMSON. Pennsylvania says Nay. Delaware—

RODNEY. Delaware, as ever for independence, says Yea.

THOMSON. Delaware says Yea. Maryland—

CHASE. Mary-land would welcome independence if it were given but is highly skeptical that it can be taken. Mary-land says Nay.

THOMSON. Mary-land says Nay. Virginia—

LEE. Virginia, the First Colony, says Yea!

THOMSON. Virginia says Yea. North Carolina—

HEWES. North Carolina respectfully yields to *South* Carolina.

THOMSON. South Carolina—

RUTLEDGE. Mr. President, although we in South Carolina have never seriously considered the question of independence, when a *gentleman* proposes it, attention must be paid. However—we in the Deep South, unlike our friends in New England, have no cause for impatience at the present time. If, at some future date, it becomes the wish of *all* our sister colonies to effect a separation, we will not stand in the way. But for the time bein', South Carolina will wait—and watch. The vote is Nay.

THOMSON. South Carolina says Nay.

HEWES (*jumping up*). *North* Carolina—

THOMSON. —says Nay. Yes, Mr. Hewes, I know. Georgia—(HALL *rises, looks around, but says nothing, obviously in great uncertainty.*) Georgia—

HALL. Mr. Secretary—(*His eyes meet* RUTLEDGE*'s, then quickly look away.*) Georgia seems to be split right down the middle on this issue. The people are against it—and I'm for it. (*Understanding laughter*) But I'm afraid I'm not yet certain whether representing the people means relying on their judgment or on my own. So in all fairness, until I can figure it out, I'd better lean a little toward their side. Georgia says Nay.

THOMSON. Georgia says Nay. (*He checks the board.*) Rhode Island. (*Calling off*) Second call—Rhode Island!

HOPKINS (*offstage*). I'm comin'! I'm comin'! (*Entering*) Hold y'r damn horses!

THOMSON. We're waiting on *you* Mr. Hopkins.

HOPKINS. It won't kill you. You'd think the Congress would have its own pisser! All right, where does she stand?

THOMSON. Five for debate, five for postponement, one abstention, and one absence.

HOPKINS. So it's up to me, is it? Well, I'll tell y'—in all my years I never heard, seen, nor smelled an issue that was so dangerous it couldn't be talked about. Hell yes, I'm for debatin' anything—Rhode Island says Yea!

(*Cheers from those for, including another war whoop from* LEE *as they crowd around* HOPKINS.)

HANCOCK. McNair, get Mr. Hopkins a rum!

MCNAIR. But you said—

HANCOCK. Get him the whole damn barrel if he wants!

MCNAIR. Yes, sir!

HANCOCK. The Chair now declares this Congress a committee-of-the-whole for the purpose of debating Virginia's resolution of independence. Mr. Dickinson.

DICKINSON. Well, now. You've got your way at last, Mr. Adams—the matter may now be discussed. I confess I'm almost relieved. There's a question I've been fairly itching to ask you: why?

JOHN. Why what, Mr. Dickinson?

DICKINSON. Why independence, Mr. Adams?

JOHN. For the obvious reason that our continued association with Great Britain has grown intolerable.

DICKINSON. To whom, Mr. Adams? To you? Then I suggest you sever your ties immediately. But please be kind enough to leave the rest of us where we are. Personally, I have no objections at all to being part of the greatest empire on earth, to enjoying its protection and sharing its benefits—

JOHN. Benefits? What benefits? Crippling taxes? Cruel repressions? Abolished rights?

DICKINSON. Is that all England means to you, sir? Is that *all* the affection and pride you can muster for the nation that bore you—for the noblest, most civilized nation on the face of this planet? Would you have us forsake Hastings and Magna Carta, Strongbow and Lionhearted, Drake and Marlborough, Tudors, Stuarts, and Plantagenets? For what sir? Tell me for what? For *you? (He smiles, then turns.)* Some men are patriots, like General Washington—some are anarchists, like Mr. Paine—some even are internationalists, like Dr. Franklin. But you, sir, you are merely an *a-gi-ta-tor,* disturbing the peace, creating disorder, endangering the public welfare—and for what? Your petty little personal complaints. Your taxes are too high. Well, sir, so are mine. Come, come, Mr.

Adams, if you have grievances— and I'm sure you have—our present system must provide a gentler means of redressing them short of—*(Suddenly his manner changes as he brings his fist down on the desk with a crash.)* —*revolution!!* *(Wheeling to the Congress)* That's what *he* wants—nothing less will satisfy him! Violence! Rebellion! *Treason!* Now, Mr. Adams, are these the acts of Englishmen?

JOHN. Not Englishmen, Dickinson— Americans!

DICKINSON *(again pounding the desk).* No sir, *Englishmen!!*

FRANKLIN *(He's been asleep, his chin on his chest; now an eye opens).* Please, Mr. Dickinson—but must you start banging? How is a man to sleep?

(Laughter)

DICKINSON. Forgive me, Dr. Franklin, but must you start speaking? How is a man to stay awake? *(Laughter)* We'll promise to be quiet, sir. I'm sure everyone prefers that you remain asleep.

FRANKLIN. If I'm to hear myself called an Englishman, sir, then I assure you I'd prefer I'd remained asleep.

DICKINSON. What's so terrible about being called an Englishman? The English don't seem to mind.

FRANKLIN. Nor would I, were I given the full rights of an Englishman. But to call me one *without* those rights is like calling an ox a bull—he's thankful for the honor but he'd much rather have restored what's rightfully his.

(Laughter, FRANKLIN *laughing the longest)*

DICKINSON *(finally).* When did you first notice they were missing, sir? *(Laughter)* Fortunately, Dr. Franklin, the people of these colonies maintain a higher regard for their mother country.

FRANKLIN. Higher, certainly, than she feels for them. Never was such a valuable possession so stupidly and recklessly managed than this entire continent by the British Crown. Our industry discouraged, our resources pillaged—and, worst of all, our very character stifled. We've spawned a new race here—rougher, simpler, more violent, more enterprising, and less refined. We're a new nationality, Mr. Dickinson—we require a new nation.

DICKINSON. That may be your opinion, Dr. Franklin, but as I said, the people feel quite differently.

JOHN. What do you know about the people, Dickinson? You don't speak for the people; you represent only yourself. And that precious "status quo" you keep imploring the people to preserve for *their* own good is nothing more than the eternal preservation of *your* own property!

DICKINSON. Mr. Adams, you have an annoying talent for making such delightful words as "property" sound quite distasteful. In Heaven's name, what's wrong with property? Perhaps you've forgotten that many of us first came to these shores in order to secure rights to property—and that we hold *those* rights no less dear than the rights you speak of.

JOHN. So safe, so fat, so comfortable in Pennsylvania—

DICKINSON. And what is this independence of yours except the private grievance of Massachusetts? Why, even your own cousin, so busy now with his seditious activities in Boston that he has no time to attend this Congress, is a fugitive with a price on his head!

HANCOCK. Slowly, Mr. Dickinson, I remind you that the same price that covers Sam Adams also covers me—we are wanted together.

DICKINSON. What did you expect? You both dress up like red savages in order to commit piracy against one of His Majesty's ships—an event so embarrassing to your sister colonies that even your good friend Dr. Franklin offered to pay for all that spilt tea from his own pocket!

FRANKLIN. I'm usually able to speak for myself, Mr. Dickinson.

DICKINSON. Then tell me this: what good can come from this radicalism and civil disorder? Where can it lead except to chaos, mob rule, and anarchy? And why in God's name is it always *Boston* that breaks the King's peace? *(To the Congress)* My dear Congress, you must not adopt this evil measure. It is the work of the devil. Leave it where it belongs— in New England.

SHERMAN. Brother Dickinson, New England has been fighting the devil for more than a hundred years.

DICKINSON. And as of now, "Brother" Sherman, the devil has been winning hands down! *(Indicating* JOHN*)* Why, at this very moment he is sitting here in this Congress! Don't let him deceive you—this proposal is entirely his doing! It may bear Virginia's name, but it reeks of Adams, Adams, and more Adams! Look at him—ready to lead this continent down the fiery path of total destruction!

JOHN. Good God! Why can't you acknowledge what already exists? It has been more than a year since Concord and Lexington. Dammit, man, we're at war right now!

DICKINSON. *You* may be at war—you: Boston and John Adams—but you will never speak for Pennsylvania!

READ *(jumping up)*. Nor for Delaware!

RODNEY. Mr. Read, you represent only one-third of Delaware!

READ. The sensible third, Mr. Rodney!

MCKEAN. Sit down, y'little roach, or I'll knock y'down!

HANCOCK. Sit down, all three of you! *McNair!!* Do something about these damned flies!

HOPKINS. *McNair!!* Fetch me a rum!

HANCOCK. Get the flies first!

MCNAIR. I've only got two hands!

HANCOCK *(mopping his brow)*. Christ, it's hot! Please do go on, gentlemen; you're making the only breeze in Philadelphia.

RUTLEDGE. Mr. Adams, perhaps you could clear something up for *me:* after we have achieved independence, who do you propose would govern in South Carolina?

JOHN. The people, of course.

RUTLEDGE. Which people, sir? The people of South Carolina? Or the people of Massachusetts?

HOPKINS. Why don't you admit it, Neddy? You're against independence now, and you always will be.

MCKEAN. Aye!

RUTLEDGE. You refuse to understand us, gentlemen! We desire independence, yes—for South Carolina. That is our country. And as such we don't wish it to belong to anyone— not to England, and not to you.

JOHN. We intend to be one nation, Rutledge.

RUTLEDGE. A nation of sovereign states, Mr. Adams, united for our mutual protection, but separate for our individual pursuits. That is what we have understood it to be, and that is what we will support—as soon as *ev-ery*-one supports it.

WILSON. There you are, Mr. Adams, you must see that we need time to make certain who we are and where we stand in regard to one another—for if we do not determine the nature of the beast before we set it free, it will end by consuming us all.

JOHN. For once in your life, Wilson—take a chance. I say the time is now! It may never come again!

HEWES. Your clock is fast, Mr. Adams. I say we're not yet ripe for independence.

HOPKINS. Not ripe? Hell, we're *rotting* for want of it!

CHASE. Gentlemen, please. What in God's name is the infernal hurry? Why must this question be settled now?

RODNEY. What's wrong with now, Mr. Chase?

CHASE. General Washington is in the field. If he's defeated, as it now appears, we'll be inviting the hangman. But if, by some miracle, he should actually win, we can then declare anything we damn please!

HEWES. The sentiments of North Carolina precisely.

JOHN. Has it ever occurred to either of you that an army needs something to fight for in order *to* win—a cause, a purpose, a flag of its own?

CHASE. Mr. Adams, how can a nation of only two million souls stand up to an empire of ten million? Think of it—*ten million!* How do we *compensate* for that shortage?

FRANKLIN. It's simple, Mr. Chase—increase and multiply!

CHASE. How's that?

JOHN. We will more than compensate— with *spirit!* I tell you there's a spirit out there with the people that's sadly lacking in this Congress!

DICKINSON. Yes, of course—now it's *spirit!* Why didn't I think of that? No army, no navy, no arms, no ammunition, no treasury, no friends—but, bless our soul, *spirit! (Turning)* Mr. Lee, Mr. Hopkins, Mr. Rodney, Colonel McKean, Dr. Franklin, why have you joined this incendiary little man? This Boston radical, this *a-gi-ta-tor,* this demagogue—this *madman!*

JOHN. Are you calling me a madman, you —you—you—*fribble!!*

FRANKLIN. Easy, John!

JOHN. You and your Pennsylvania proprietors—you cool, considerate men! You keep to the rear of every issue so if we should go under you'll still remain afloat!

DICKINSON. Are you calling me a coward?

JOHN. Yes! *Coward!!*

DICKINSON. *Madman!!*

JOHN. *Landlord!!*

DICKINSON. *Lawyer!! (The battle is joined. They begin whacking away at each other with*

their walking sticks. Congress is in an uproar.)
HOPKINS. Whack him, John!
FRANKLIN. Ho, Spartacus!
CONGRESS. Stop! Go! For shame! At last!
(Et cetera.)
(RODNEY *now steps forward, between them, and pushes them apart.)*
RODNEY. Stop it! *Stop it!!* This is the Congress! Stop it, I say! The enemy is out there!
DICKINSON. No, Mr. Rodney, the enemy is here!
RODNEY. No, no, I say he's out there—England, *England,* closing in, cutting off our air—there's no time—no air—*(He is stricken.)* Thomas! *(He collapses into* MCKEAN's *arms.)*
MCKEAN. Ceasar—*Caesar!!* *(He looks around as the Congress falls silent and moves in.)* Doctor Hall?
HALL *(kneeling beside* RODNEY *and looking under the green scarf; his expression reflects what he finds).* Colonel McKean—
MCKEAN. Aye, it's the cancer.
HALL. He should go home.
RODNEY *(disgusted with himself).* Yes, a man should die in his own bed. John—John Adams—
JOHN. I'm here, Caesar.
RODNEY. I leave you a divided Delaware. Forgive me.
MCKEAN. I'll take y'home, Caesar. *(He lifts* RODNEY *and turns to* JOHN) I'll be back within the week. *(He carries* RODNEY *out.)*
(There is a moment of silence; then RUTLEDGE *steps forward.)*
RUTLEDGE. Mr. President, South Carolina calls the question.
HANCOCK *(distracted).* What's that, Mr. Rutledge?
RUTLEDGE *(walking to the tally board).* I said, Mr. President, South Carolina desires to end the debate and *(he moves the Delaware marker from the "Yea" to the "Nay" column)* call the question of independence.
READ *(glowing).* Delaware seconds!
(Again, bedlam, as everyone understands what has happened.)
CONGRESS. No! Yes! You can't do that! Call the question! *(Et cetera.)*
HANCOCK *(pounding for order).* Gentlemen, *please!* The question has been called and seconded. Mr. Secretary, you will record the vote.
JOHN *(to* FRANKLIN). Franklin, do something—*think!*
FRANKLIN. I'm thinking, I'm thinking—but nothing's coming!

THOMSON. All those in favor of the resolution on independence as proposed by the colony of Virginia signify by saying—
FRANKLIN. Mr. Secretary, would you read the resolution again? *(As everyone looks at him in surprise, he shrugs)* I've forgotten it.
(Annoyed, THOMSON *looks to* HANCOCK, *who nods; he sighs.)*
THOMSON. "Resolved: That these United Colonies are (and of a right ought to be) free and independent—"
(The REVEREND JOHN WITHERSPOON, *a lean and ascetic clergyman of fifty-four, enters.)*
WITHERSPOON. I beg your pardon, I'm the Reverend John Witherspoon, new delegate from New Jersey—? *(As everyone moves in expectantly, he draws back, then seeks out the only familiar face.)* Dr. Franklin, I regret I must be the bearer of unhappy tidings, but your son, the Royal Governor of New Jersey, is taken prisoner and has been moved under guard to the colony of Connecticut for safekeeping.
FRANKLIN. Is he unharmed, sir?
WITHERSPOON. When last I heard, he was, yes, sir.
FRANKLIN. Then why the long face? I hear Connecticut is an excellent location. Why'd they arrest the little bastard?
WITHERSPOON *(rattled).* Our—uh—New Jersey legislature has recalled the old delegation to this Congress and has sent a new one.
JOHN. Quickly, man—where do y'stand on independence?
WITHERSPOON. Oh, haven't I made that clear? No, I s'pose I haven't. But that was the reason for the change—we've been instructed to vote *for* independence.
JOHN *(quickly).* Mr. President! *(He goes to the tally board.)* Massachusetts is now ready for the vote on independence *(he records New Jersey under the "Yes" column)* and reminds the Chair of its privilege to decide all votes that are deadlocked!
HANCOCK. I won't forget, Mr. Adams. The Chair would like to welcome the Reverend Witherspoon and appoint him Congressional Chaplain if he will accept the post.
WITHERSPOON. With much pleasure, sir.
HANCOCK. Very well. Mr. Thomson, you may now *(he swats a fly)* proceed with the vote on independence.
THOMSON. All in favor of the resolution on independence as proposed by the colony of Virginia signify by saying—

DICKINSON *(jumping up)*. Mr. President, Pennsylvania moves that any vote in favor of independence must be unanimous!

JOHN. *What?*

WILSON. I second the motion!

HANCOCK *(admonishing)*. Judge Wilson—

WILSON *(chagrined)*. Oh my God.

READ. Delaware seconds, Mr. President.

JOHN. No vote's ever had to be unanimous, Dickinson, and you know it!

DICKINSON. Yes, but this one must be.

JOHN. On what grounds?

DICKINSON. That no colony be torn from its mother country without its own consent.

RUTLEDGE. Hear, hear!

JOHN. But it'll never be unanimous, dammit!

DICKINSON. If you say so, Mr. Adams.

THOMSON. It has been moved and seconded that the vote on independence must be unanimous in order to carry. All those in favor signify by saying "Yea." *(*DICKINSON, CHASE, READ, RUTLEDGE, HEWES, and HALL *say "Yea.")* Six colonies say "Yea." All those opposed signify by saying "Nay." *(*JOHN, BARTLETT, HOPKINS, SHERMAN, LEE, *and* WITHERSPOON *say "Nay.")* Six colonies say "Nay."

MORRIS. Mr. Secretary, New York abstains—courteously.

HANCOCK. Mr. Morris, why does New York constantly abstain? Why doesn't New York simply stay in New York? Very well, the vote is tied. *(He covers his eyes for a moment.)* The principles of independence have no greater advocate in Congress than its President—and that is why I must join those who vote *for* unanimity.

JOHN *(as the Congress reacts, stunned, he jumps up, horrified.)* Good God! What're y'-doing, John? You've sunk us!

HANCOCK. Hear me out. Don't you see that any colony who opposes independence will be forced to fight on the side of England—that we'll be setting brother against brother, that our new nation will carry as its emblem the mark of Cain? I can see no other way. Either we walk together or together we must stay where we are. *(A silence)* Very well. Proceed, Mr. Thomson.

THOMSON. A unanimous vote being necessary to carry, if any be opposed to the resolution on independence as proposed by the colony of Virginia, signify by saying—

JOHN. *Mr. President!!*

THOMSON. For heaven's sake, let me get through it *once!*

JOHN. Mr. President, I move for a postponement!

DICKINSON. *Ha!* I wish you the same luck *I* had with it!

FRANKLIN. Mr. Adams is right, we need a postponement!

DICKINSON. On what grounds?

FRANKLIN *(to* JOHN*)*. On what grounds?

JOHN. Mr. President, how can this Congress vote on independence without—uh—a written declaration of some sort defining it?

HANCOCK. What sort of declaration?

JOHN. Well, you know—uh—listing all the reasons for the separation and—uh—our goals and aims and so on and so forth, ditto, ditto, et cetera, et cetera.

HANCOCK *(not getting it)*. We know those, don't we?

JOHN. Well, good God, yes, we know them, but what about the rest of the world? Certainly we require the aid of a powerful nation like France or Spain, and such a declaration would be consistent with European delicacy.

CHASE. Come, now, Mr. Adams, you'll have to do better than that! Answer straight —what would be its purpose?

(A pause; for once JOHN *is at a loss for words.)*

JOHN. Yes, well—

JEFFERSON *(rising and speaking deliberately)*. To place before mankind the common sense of the subject, in terms so plain and firm as to command their assent. *(Winking at* JOHN, *he sits. A moment of surprise; then* DICKINSON *laughs.)*

DICKINSON. Mr. Jefferson, are you seriously suggesting that we publish a paper declaring to all the world that an illegal rebellion is, in reality, a legal one?

FRANKLIN. Why, Mr. Dickinson, I'm surprised at you! You should know that rebellion is *always* legal in the first person—such as "our" rebellion. It is only in the third person —"their" rebellion—that it is *ill*egal. *(Laughter)* Mr. President, I second the motion to postpone the vote on independence for a period of time sufficient for the writing of a declaration.

HANCOCK. It has been moved and seconded. Mr. Secretary—

THOMSON. All those in favor of the motion to postpone signify by saying "Yea." *(*ADAMS, BARTLETT, HOPKINS, SHERMAN, WITHERSPOON, *and* LEE *say "Yea.")* Six colonies say "Yea." Against? *(*DICKINSON, CHASE, READ, RUTLEDGE, HEWES, *and* HALL *say "Nay.")* Six colonies say "Nay."

MORRIS. Mr. Secretary, New York abstains—courteously.

HANCOCK *(threatening him with a flyswatter, then restraining himself)*. Mr. Morris! What in hell goes on in New York?

MORRIS. I'm sorry, Mr. President, but the simple fact is that our legislature has never sent us explicit instructions on anything.

HANCOCK. *Never?* That's impossible!

MORRIS. Have you ever been present at a meeting of the New York legislature? They speak very fast and very loud and nobody pays any attention to anybody else, with the result that nothing ever gets done. I beg the Congress' pardon.

HANCOCK. My sympathies, Mr. Morris. The vote again being tied, the Chair decides in favor of the postponement. *(His gavel.)* So ruled. A committee will now be formed to manage the declaration, said document to be written, debated, and approved by the beginning of July, three weeks hence, at which time Virginia's resolution on independence will finally be voted. Is that clear? *(Meeting general agreement:)* Very well. Will the following gentlemen serve on the Declaration Committee. Dr. Franklin, Mr. John Adams, Mr. Sherman, Mr. Livingston, and, of course, Mr. Lee.

LEE. Excuse me, but I must be returnin' to the sovereign country of Virginia as I have been asked to serve as governor. Therefore I must decline—respectful-*Lee!*

HANCOCK. Very well, Mr. Lee, you're excused. I suppose we could leave it a four-man committee.

JOHN. Just a moment. This business needs a Virginian. Therefore, I propose a replacement—Mr. Thomas Jefferson!

JEFFERSON. No, Mr. Adams, *no!*

HANCOCK. Very well, Mr. Adams, Mr. Jefferson will serve.

JEFFERSON. I'm going home too—to my wife!

JOHN. Move to adjourn!

JEFFERSON. No, wait—

FRANKLIN. *Second!!*

JEFFERSON. It's been six months since I've seen her!

HANCOCK. Moved and seconded—any objections?

JEFFERSON. *Yes! I* have objections!

HANCOCK *(gaveling)*. So ruled, Congress stands adjourned!

JEFFERSON *(on deaf ears)*. I need to see my wife, I tell you!

(Congress rises and goes as JOHN, FRANKLIN, SHERMAN, *and* LIVINGSTON *move downstage, with* JEFFERSON *following, still protesting. Music begins.)*

JOHN. All right, gentlemen! Let's get on with it. Which of us is going to write our declaration on independence?

FRANKLIN *(singing)*.
Mr. Adams, I say you should write it,
To your legal mind and brilliance we defer.

JOHN.
Is that so!
Well, if I'm the one to do it,
They'll run their quill pens through it.
I'm obnoxious and disliked, you know that, sir!

FRANKLIN *(speaking)*. Yes, I know.

JOHN. Then I say you should write it, Franklin, yes, you!

FRANKLIN *(singing)*.
              Hell, no!

JOHN.
        Yes, you, Dr. Franklin, you!

FRANKLIN.
                    But—

JOHN.
              You!

FRANKLIN.
                    But—

JOHN.
              You!

FRANKLIN.
But—
Mr. Adams!
But—Mr. Adams!
The things I write
Are only light extemporanea.
I won't put politics on paper.
It's a mania.
So, I refuse to use the pen—in
    Pennsylvania!

(A GLEE CLUB *is formed by* SHERMAN, LIVINGSTON, *and* FRANKLIN.*)*

GLEE CLUB.
        Pennsylvania!
        Pennsylvania!
        Refuse
        To use . . . the pen!

*(*JOHN *begins to pace, thinking.)*

JOHN.
Mr. Sherman, I say you should write it.
You are never "controversial," as it were.

SHERMAN *(speaking)*. That is true.

JOHN *(singing)*.
Whereas, if I'm the one to do it
They'll run their quill pens through it.
I'm obnoxious and disliked, you know that, sir.

SHERMAN *(speaking).* Yes, I do.

JOHN *(singing).*
Then you should write it, Roger, you.

SHERMAN *(speaking).* Good heavens, no!

JOHN *(singing).*
Yes, you, Roger Sherman, you!

SHERMAN.
                But—

JOHN.
                You!

SHERMAN.
                But—

JOHN.
                You!

SHERMAN.
But—
Mr. Adams!
But—Mr. Adams!
I cannot write with any style
Or proper etiquette.
I don't know a preposition
From a predicate.
I am just a simple cobbler
From Connecticut!

GLEE CLUB.
        Connecticut!
        Connecticut!
        A simple cobbler . . . he!

(JOHN resumes his pacing.)

JOHN.
Mr. Livingston, maybe you should write it.
You have many friends, and you're a
        diplomat.

FRANKLIN *(speaking).* Oh, that word!

JOHN *(singing).*
Whereas, if I'm the one to do it,
They'll run their quill pens through it.

GLEE CLUB.
He's obnoxious and disliked, did you know
        that?

LIVINGSTON *(speaking).* I hadn't heard—

JOHN *(singing).*
Then I say you should write it, Robert!
                Yes, you!

LIVINGSTON *(speaking).* Not me, Johnny—

JOHN *(singing).*
Yes! You, Robert Livingston—you!

LIVINGSTON.
                But—

JOHN.
                You!

LIVINGSTON.
                But—

JOHN.
                You!

LIVINGSTON.
But—
Mr. Adams!
Dear Mr. Adams!
I've been presented with a new son
By the noble stork,
So I am going home to celebrate
And pop a cork
With all the Livingstons together,
Back in old New York!

GLEE CLUB.
        New York!
        New York!
        Livingston's . . .
        Going to pop . . . a cork!

(Slowly, all eyes turn to JEFFERSON.)

JEFFERSON.
                Mr. Adams!
                Leave me Alone!!!

*(The GLEE CLUB sings a "La-la" theme,
under.)*

JOHN *(speaking firmly).* Mr. Jefferson—

JEFFERSON *(speaking).* Mr. Adams, I beg
you! I've not seen my wife these six months!

JOHN *(quoting).* " . . . and we solemnly
declare we will preserve our liberties, being
with one mind resolved to die free men—
rather than to live slaves!" *(The GLEE CLUB
stops to listen.)* Thomas Jefferson, on the
"Necessity of Taking Up Arms," seventeen
seventy-five, magnificent! You write ten times
better than any man in the Congress—including me! For a man of only thirty-three years
you possess a happy talent for composition
and a remarkable felicity of expression. Now!
Will you be a patriot? Or a lover?

JEFFERSON. A lover!

JOHN. No!

JEFFERSON *(singing).*
                But I burn, Mr. A.!

JOHN.
                So do I, Mr. J.!

(Everything stops.)

JEFFERSON *(speaking). You?*

SHERMAN. You do?

FRANKLIN. John!

LIVINGSTON. Who'd 'a' thought it?

JOHN *(singing).*
Mr. Jefferson
Dear Mr. Jefferson,
I'm only forty-one,
I still have my virility!
And I can romp through Cupid's
grove
With great agility!
But life is more than
Sexual combustibility!

GLEE CLUB.

> Bust-a-bility!
> Bust-a-bility!
> Com-bust-a-bil-i—

JOHN *(shouting).* Quiet!

(He sings.)

> Now, you'll write it, Mr. J.!

JEFFERSON *(six feet three).*

> Who will make me, Mr. A.?

JOHN *(five feet eight).*

> I!

JEFFERSON.

> You?

JOHN.

> Yes!

JEFFERSON.

> How?

JOHN *(speaking).* By—by physical force if necessary! It's your duty—*your duty, dammit!!*

JEFFERSON *(singing).*

> Mr. Adams!
> Damn you, Mr. Adams!
> You're obnoxious and disliked,
> That cannot be denied.

(This is agreed to by all.)

> Once again you stand between me
> And my lovely bride!

GLEE CLUB.

> Lovely bride!

JEFFERSON.

Oh, Mr. Adams, you are driving me . . . to Homicide!!

GLEE CLUB.

> Homicide!
> Homicide!

JOHN *(roaring).* Quiet!! *(He is furious.)* The choice is yours, Mr. Jefferson! *(He thrusts a large quill pen into* JEFFERSON*'s hand; evenly.)* Do—as—you—like—with—it.

GLEE CLUB *(gleefully).*

> We may see mur-der yet!!

*(*JOHN *goes, followed by the others.* JEFFERSON *alone, studies the pen for a moment, then turns and heads for his lodgings, still regarding the pen as he goes.)*

SCENE FOUR

JEFFERSON*'s room, above High Street. It is spare and unaffected, like the man, with a desk, a cupboard, a chair, a couch, and a music stand; a violin sits on the desk.*

JEFFERSON *mounts the steps and enters his apartment. He takes another look at the pen*

and throws it onto the desk angrily.

———

JEFFERSON. Damn the man! *(He removes his coat; then he catches sight of the pen again.)* GOD damn the man! *(Then, resigned, he sits at the desk and writes a few words. Suddenly he crumples the page and throws it on the floor. He writes some more; but again he crumples the paper and throws it on the floor. Now, merely thinking some unacceptable words, he crumples still another sheet, this one blank. Discouraged, he sits back, picks up his violin to play. Meanwhile,* JOHN *and* FRANKLIN *have appeared outside and now enter.* FRANKLIN *heads for the couch and stretches out, closing his eyes.)*

JOHN. Jefferson, are y'finished? *(There is no answer.)* You've had a whole week, man. Is it done? Can I see it? (JEFFERSON *points to all the crumpled paper on the floor.* JOHN *picks one at random and, flattening it out, reads it.)*

JOHN. "There comes a time in the lives of men when it becomes necessary to advance from that subordination in which they have hitherto remained—" this is terrible. *(Looking up.)* Where's the rest of it? *(Again* JEFFERSON *points to the floor.)* Do you mean to say it's *not* finished?

JEFFERSON. No, sir—I mean to say it's not begun.

JOHN. Good God! A whole week! The entire earth was created in a week!

JEFFERSON *(fed up, turning to* JOHN*).* Some day you must tell me how you did it.

JOHN. Disgusting! Look at him, Franklin —Virginia's most famous lover—

JEFFERSON. Virginia abstains.

JOHN. Cheer up, Jefferson, get out of the dumps. It'll come out right, I promise you. Now get back to work. Franklin, tell him to get to work.

JEFFERSON. He's asleep.

(Outside, a cloaked woman appears. She stops, looks around, then sees the door and enters. It is MARTHA, JEFFERSON*'s wife, a lovely girl of twenty-seven.)*

FRANKLIN *(sitting bolt upright on the couch).* View-hal-loo, and whose-little-girl are you? *(But* JEFFERSON *and* MARTHA *are suddenly oblivious to everything but each other as they meet and embrace. They kiss, and kiss, and will continue kissing throughout the remainder of the scene.)* John, who is she?

JOHN. His wife *(He studies them)*, I hope.

FRANKLIN *(his eyes never leaving them).* What makes y'think so?

JOHN. Because I sent for her.

FRANKLIN. Y'*what?*

JOHN. It simply occurred to me that the sooner his problem was solved, the sooner *our* problem was solved.

FRANKLIN. Good thinking, John, good thinking!

JOHN *(stepping forward).* Madame, may I present myself? John Adams. *(No reaction.)* Adams—*John Adams! (Nothing.)* And Dr. Franklin *(Nothing.)* Inventor of the stove!! *(No luck.)* Jefferson, would you kindly present me to your wife? *(No reaction.)* She *is* your wife, isn't she?

FRANKLIN. Of course she is—look how they fit! *(Starting for the door)* Come along, John, come along.

JOHN. Come along where? There's work to be done!

FRANKLIN *(with a look back over his shoulder).* Heh! Obviously!

(Outside, on the street.)

JOHN. Good God! Y'mean they—They're going to—*(He stops.)* In the middle of the afternoon?

FRANKLIN. Not everybody's from Boston, John. *(He takes* JOHN*'s arm and leads him aside.* JOHN *keeps looking back, unable to get over it.)*

JOHN. Incredible.

FRANKLIN. Well—good night, John.

JOHN. Have y'eaten, Franklin?

FRANKLIN. Not yet, but—

JOHN. I hear the turkey's fresh at the Bunch o' Grapes.

FRANKLIN. I have a rendezvous, John.

JOHN. Oh.

FRANKLIN. I'd ask you along, but talking makes her nervous.

JOHN. Yes, of course.

FRANKLIN. Good night, then.

JOHN. Good night. *(*FRANKLIN *goes. It has grown dark.* JOHN *stands for a moment, lost in thought. Then he turns and looks up at the lighted window, just as* JEFFERSON*'s violin is heard playing a lush arpeggio. An instant later the light goes out.)* Incredible. *(Music begins.)* Oh, Abigail— *(*ABIGAIL *appears, as before.)* I'm very lonely, Abigail.

ABIGAIL. Are you, John? Then as long as you were sending for wives, why didn't you send for your own?

JOHN. Don't be unreasonable, Abigail.

ABIGAIL. Now I'm unreasonable—you must add that to your list.

JOHN. List?

ABIGAIL. The catalogue of my faults you included in your last letter.

JOHN. They were fondly intended, madame!

ABIGAIL. That I play at cards badly?

JOHN. A compliment!

ABIGAIL. That my posture is crooked?

JOHN. An endearment!

ABIGAIL. That I read, write, and think too much?

JOHN. An irony!

ABIGAIL. That I am *pigeon-toed?*

JOHN. Ah, well, there you have me, Abby —I'm afraid you *are* pigeon-toed. *(Smiling)* Come to Philadelphia, Abigail—please come.

ABIGAIL. Thank you, John, I do want to. But you know it's not possible now. The children have the measles.

JOHN. Yes, so you wrote—Tom and little Abby.

ABIGAIL. Only now it's Quincy and Charles. And it appears the farm here in Braintree is failing, John—the chickens and geese have all died and the apples never survived the late frost. How do you s'pose *she* managed to get away?

JOHN *(with a glance to the shuttered window).* The winters are softer in Virginia.

ABIGAIL. And their women, John?

JOHN. Fit for Virginians, madame, but pale, puny things beside New England girls!

ABIGAIL *(pleased).* John! I thank you for that.

(A pause.)

JOHN. How goes it with you, Abigail?

ABIGAIL. Not well, John—not at all well. *(She sings).*

> I live like a nun in a cloister,
> Solitary, celibate, I hate it.
> (And you, John?)

JOHN *(singing).*

> Hm!
> I live like a monk in an abbey,
> Ditto, ditto, I hate it.

ABIGAIL.

> Write to me with sentimental effusion,
> Let me revel in romantic illusion.

JOHN.

> Do y'still smell of vanilla and spring air?
> And is my fav'rite lover's pillo' still firm
>   and fair?

ABIGAIL.

> What was there, John!
> Still is there, John!

> Come soon as you can to my cloister.
> I've forgotten the feel of your hand.

JOHN.

> Soon, Madame, we shall walk in Cupid's
>   grove together . . .

JOHN AND ABIGAIL.
And we'll fondly survey that promised
land!
Till then, till then,
I am, as I ever was, and ever shall be,
Yours . . .
Yours . . .
Yours . . .
Yours . . .
Yours . . .

ABIGAIL *(beating him to it)*. Saltpetre,
John! *(And she goes.)*

*(JOHN smiles. Now the daylight returns; it's
the next morning. FRANKLIN enters.)*

FRANKLIN. Sorry to be late, John—I was
up till all hours. Have y'been here long?

JOHN. Not long.

FRANKLIN. And what're y'doing out here?
I expected you'd be up there cracking the
whip.

JOHN. The shutters are still closed.

FRANKLIN. My word, so they are! Well, as
the French say—

JOHN. Oh, *please*, Franklin! Spare me your
bawdy mind first thing in the morning! *(They
regard the closed shutters.)* Dare we call?

FRANKLIN. A Congressman dares anything. Go ahead.

JOHN. *Me?*

FRANKLIN. Your voice is more piercing.

JOHN *(He starts, then hesitates)*. This is
positively indecent!

FRANKLIN. Oh, John, they're young and
they're in love.

JOHN. Not them, Franklin—us! Standing
out here *(He gestures vaguely at the shuttered
room)* waiting for them to—I mean, what
will people think?

FRANKLIN. Don't worry, John. The history books will clean it up.

JOHN. It doesn't matter. I won't appear in
the history books, anyway—only you. *(He
thinks about it.)* Franklin did this, Franklin
did that, Franklin did some other damned
thing. Franklin smote the ground, and out
sprang George Washington, fully grown and
on his horse. Franklin then electrified him
with his miraculous lightning rod, and the
three of them—Franklin, Washington, *and*
the horse—conducted the entire Revolution
all by themselves.

(A pause.)

FRANKLIN. I like it! *(Now the shutter opens
and MARTHA appears, dressed and radiant.
She is humming a tune.)* Look at her, John—
just look at her!

JOHN *(hypnotized)*. I am.

FRANKLIN. She's even more magnificent
than I remember! Of course, we didn't see
much of her front last night. *(Calling)* Good
morrow, madame!

(She looks down at him blankly.)

JOHN. Good morrow!

MARTHA. Is it the habit in Philadelphia for
strangers to shout at ladies from the street?

FRANKLIN. Not at all, madame, but we're
not—

MARTHA. And from men of your age it is
not only unseemly, it's unsightly.

JOHN. Excuse me, madame, but we met last
evening.

MARTHA. I spoke to no one last evening.

FRANKLIN. Indeed you did not, madame,
but nevertheless we presented ourselves. This
is Mr. John Adams and I am Dr. Franklin.
(As she stares at them, dumfounded) Inventor
of the stove?

MARTHA. Oh, please, I know your names
very well. But you say you presented yourselves?

FRANKLIN *(smiling)*. It's of no matter.
Your thoughts were well taken elsewhere.

MARTHA *(turning to the room for a moment)*. My husband is not yet up.

FRANKLIN. Shall we start over? Please join
us, madame.

MARTHA. Yes, of course. *(She disappears
from the window.)*

FRANKLIN. No wonder the man couldn't
write. Who could think of independence,
married to her?

(She appears, smiling.)

MARTHA. I beg you to forgive me. It is
indeed an honor meeting the two greatest
men in America.

FRANKLIN *(smiling back)*. Certainly the
greatest within earshot, anyway.

MARTHA. I am not an idle flatterer, Dr.
Franklin. My husband admires you both
greatly.

FRANKLIN. Then we are doubly flattered,
for we admire very much that which your
husband admires. *(A pause as they regard
each other warmly. They have hit it off.)*

JOHN *(finally; the bull in the china shop)*.
Did you sleep well, madame? *(Franklin
nudges him with his elbow.)* I mean, did you
lie comfortably? Oh, damn! Y'know what I
mean!

FRANKLIN. Yes, John, we do. Tell us about
yourself, madame; we've had precious little
information. What's your first name?

MARTHA. Martha.

FRANKLIN. Ah. Martha. He might at least have told us that. I'm afraid of your husband doesn't say very much.

JOHN. He's the most silent man in Congress. I've never heard him utter three sentences together.

FRANKLIN. Not everyone's a talker, John.

MARTHA. It's true, you know. *(She turns to look at the window.)* Tom is not—a talker. *(She sings).*

Oh, he never speaks his passions,
He never speaks his views.
Whereas other men speak volumes,
The man I love is mute.

In truth
I can't recall
Being woo'd with words
At all.

Even now . . .
(Music continues under.)

JOHN *(speaking).* Go on, madame.

FRANKLIN. How did he win you, Martha, and how does he hold onto a bounty such as you?

MARTHA. Surely you've noticed that Tom is a man of many accomplishments: author, lawyer, farmer, architect, statesman *(She hesitates)* and still one more that I hesitate to mention.

JOHN. Don't hesitate, madame—don't hesitate!

FRANKLIN. Yes, what *else* can that redheaded tombstone do?

MARTHA *(she looks at them for a moment, then leans in and sings, confidentially):*

He plays the violin
He tucks it right under his chin,
And he bows,
Oh, he bows,
For he knows,
Yes, he knows, that it's . . .

Heigh, heigh, heigh diddle-diddle,
'Twixt my heart, Tom, and his fiddle,
My strings are unstrung.
Heigh-heigh-heigh-heigh-igh-igh . . .
Heigh—I am undone!

(JOHN and FRANKLIN look at one another, not at all sure if she's putting them on or not.)

FRANKLIN *(speaking).* The *violin,* madame?

MARTHA.
I hear his violin,
And I get that feeling within,
And I sigh . . .
Oh, I sigh . . .
He draws near,

Very near, and it's . . .

Heigh, heigh, heigh diddle-diddle, and . . .
Good-by to the fiddle!
My strings are unstrung.
Heigh-heigh-heigh-heigh-igh-igh . . .
Heigh—I'm always undone!

FRANKLIN *(speaking).* That settles it, John, we're taking up the violin!

JOHN *(to MARTHA).* Very well, madame, you've got us playing the violin! What happens next?

MARTHA. Next, Mr. Adams?

JOHN. Yes! What does Tom do now?

MARTHA *(demurely).* Why, just what you'd expect. *(JOHN and FRANKLIN exchange expectant looks.)* We dance!

JOHN AND FRANKLIN *(together and to each other).* Dance?

FRANKLIN. Incredible!

MARTHA. One-two-three, one-two-three! *(And in an instant she has swept FRANKLIN off into an energetic waltz. JOHN watches them for a moment, still trying to understand.)*

JOHN. Who's playing the violin?

FRANKLIN. Oh, John—really! *(And MARTHA leaves FRANKLIN to begin waltzing with JOHN, who, to FRANKLIN's astonishment, turns out to dance expertly.)* John! You can dance!

JOHN *(executing an intricate step—he is having a grand time).* We still do a few things in Boston, Franklin! *(Finally they have twirled and spun and danced themselves out.)*

MARTHA *(singing, as she catches her breath).*

When Heaven calls to me,
Sing me no sad elegy!
Say I died
Loving bride,
Loving wife,
Loving life. Oh, it was . . .

MARTHA, JOHN, AND FRANKLIN.
Heigh, heigh, heigh diddle-diddle . . .

MARTHA.
'Twixt my heart, Tom, and his
Fiddle, and
Ever 'twill be
Heigh-heigh-heigh-heigh-igh-igh . . .
Heigh, through eternity.

FRANKLIN *(in counterpoint).*
He plays the violin . . .

JOHN *(in counterpoint).*
He plays the violin . . .

MARTHA *(in counterpoint).*
He plays the violin!

(They bow to her, and she curtsies. Now

JEFFERSON *appears, a fiddle under his arm, and stuck on the end of his bow is a paper. He collects his wife, and together they start back toward the room.)*

JOHN. Franklin, look! He's written something—he's done it! *(He dashes after them, snatches the paper off the bow, and comes back to* FRANKLIN, *delighted, and reads it.)* "Dear Mr. Adams: I am taking my wife back to bed. Kindly go away. Y'r ob'd't, T. Jefferson."

FRANKLIN. What, again?

JOHN. Incredible!

FRANKLIN. Perhaps I'm the one who should've written the declaration, after all. At my age there's little doubt that the pen is mightier than the sword. *(He sings.)*

For it's
Heigh, heigh, heigh diddle-diddle.
(Enviously).
And God bless the man who can fiddle . . .

JOHN *(ever the old warhorse).*
And independency!

JOHN AND FRANKLIN *(regaining their energy).*
Heigh-heigh-heigh-heigh-igh-igh.
Yata-ta-ta-tah!
Through eternity!
(And they exit arm in arm.)
He plays the violin! . . . Violin! . . . Violin! . . .

SCENE FIVE

The Chamber, as before.
At rise, Congress is in session, though in an exceedingly loose manner. While SECRETARY THOMSON *delivers a droning report, it is clear that no one is listening.* HANCOCK *sits at the President's table, but he is occupied reading the* Philadelphia Gazette, *his feet up on the desk; one group of Congressmen—*MORRIS, READ, WILSON, *and* DICKINSON—*sits with their heads together, talking; another group—*HOPKINS, BARTLETT, *and* SHERMAN—*stands in the rear, also conversing;* RUTLEDGE *and* HEWES *pace back and forth across the length of the Chamber as they talk;* MCKEAN *stands by the window, cleaning a long rifle;* CHASE, *a large napkin tied around his neck, sits eating a complete meal;* WITHERSPOON *is asleep at his desk, his head thrown back, his mouth open and snoring; and* MCNAIR *is kept hopping from one group to another on this errand*

and that. The wall calendar now reads: "JUNE 22."

THOMSON. . . . and what follows is a complete and up-to-date list of the committees of this Congress now sitting, about to sit, or just having sat: A committee formed to investigate a complaint made against the quality of yeast manufactured at Mr. Henry Pendleton's mill, designated as the Yeast Committee; a committee formed to consider the most effective method of dealing with spies, designated as the Spies Committee; a committee formed to think, perhaps to do, but in any case to gather, to meet, to confer, to talk, and perhaps even to resolve that each rifle regiment be allowed at least one drum and one fife attached to each company, designated as the Drum and Fife Committee; a committee formed to . . .

(FRANKLIN and DR. HALL have entered and now stand surveying the room.)

FRANKLIN. Look at it, doctor—democracy! What Plato called a "charming form of government, full of variety and disorder." I never knew Plato had been to Philadelphia.

HANCOCK *(as he reads the newspaper).* McNair! Open that damn window!

HOPKINS *(joining* FRANKLIN *and* HALL, *a mug of rum in his hand).* Ben, I want y'to see some cards I've gone 'n' had printed up that ought t'save everybody here a whole lot of time 'n' effort, considering the epidemic of bad disposition that's been going around lately. *(He reads.)* "Dear sir: You are without any doubt a rogue, a rascal, a villain, a thief, a scoundrel, and a mean, dirty, stinking, sniveling, sneaking, pimping, pocket-picking, thrice double-damned, no good son-of-a-bitch"—and y'sign y'r name. What do y'think?

FRANKLIN *(delighted).* Stephen, I'll take a dozen right now!

THOMSON. . . . a committee formed to answer all Congressional correspondence designated as the Congressional Correspondence Committee . . .

(JOHN strides in and joins FRANKLIN.)*

JOHN. All right, Franklin, enough socializing—there's work to be done!

FRANKLIN *(pointedly).* Good morning, John!

JOHN. What? Oh. *(Waving it aside)* Good morning, good morning. Now, then, let's get to it.

FRANKLIN. Let's get to what?

JOHN *(indicating the tally board).* Unanimity, of course. Look at that board—six Nays to win over in little more than a week!

THOMSON. . . . a committee formed to consider the problem of counterfeit money, designated as the Counterfeit Money Committee . . .

FRANKLIN. All right, John, where do we start?

JOHN. How about Delaware? It's a sad thing to find her on the wrong side after all this time. Is there any news of Rodney?

FRANKLIN *(pointing).* McKean's back.

JOHN. Thomas! *(They go to him.)*

THOMSON. . . . a committee formed to study the causes of our military defeat in Canada, designated as the Military Defeat Committee . . .

JOHN. How did you leave Caesar? Is he still alive?

MCKEAN. Aye, but the journey to Dover was fearful hard on him. He never complained, but I could see the poor man was sufferin'.

FRANKLIN. But you got him safely home.

MCKEAN. I did, but I doubt he'll ever set foot out of it again.

JOHN. That leaves you and Read split down the middle. Will he come over?

MCKEAN. I don't know. He's a stubborn little snot!

JOHN. Then work on him. Keep at him till you wear him down!

MCKEAN. Och, John, face facts, will y'? If it were just Read standin' in our way it wouldn't be so bad. But look for yourself, man *(Indicating the tally board)*, Mary-land, Pennsylvania, the entire South—it's impossible!

JOHN. It's impossible if we all stand around complaining about it. To work, McKean—one foot in front of the other.

FRANKLIN. I believe I put it a better way: "Never leave off till tomorrow that which you can do—"

JOHN. Shut up, Franklin!

MCKEAN. But what good will it do? Y'know Dickinson—he'll never give in! And y'haven't heard the last of Rutledge yet, either.

JOHN. Never mind about them. Your job is George Read. Talk him deaf if you have to, but bring us back Delaware!

MCKEAN. There's a simpler way. *(He holds up his rifle.)* This'll break the tie! *(He goes to talk to* READ.*)*

FRANKLIN. All right, John, who's next? *(Again they turn to study the board.)*

THOMSON. . . . a committee formed to keep secrets, designated as the Secrets Committee . . .

JOHN. Pennsylvania and Mary-land. I suggest you try to put your own house in order while I take a crack at Old Bacon Face (look at him stuff himself!), Mr. Chase! *(He goes to him.)* How about it, Chase? When are you coming to your senses?

CHASE *(sourly).* Please, Mr. Adams—not while I'm eating!

FRANKLIN *(drawing* WILSON *aside).* Mr. Wilson, it's time to assert yourself. When you were a judge, how in hell did you ever make a decision?

WILSON. The decisions I made were all based on legality and precedence. But there is no legality here—and certainly no precedent.

FRANKLIN. Because it's a new idea, you clot! We'll be setting our own precedent!

READ *(arguing with* MCKEAN*).* No, Mr. McKean—no, no, no!

MCKEAN. Damn y'r eyes, Read, y'came into this world screamin' "no," and y're determined to leave it the same way, y'little worm!

JOHN *(with* CHASE*).* The Congress is waiting on you, Chase—America's waiting—the whole *world* is waiting! What's that, kidney? *(He takes a morsel of food from* CHASE*'s plate with his fingers, but* CHASE *slaps his hand and he drops it.)*

CHASE. Leave me alone, Mr. Adams, you're wasting your time. If I thought we could win this war I'd be at the front of your ranks. But you must know it's impossible! You've heard General Washington's dispatches. His army has fallen apart.

JOHN. Washington's exaggerating the situation in order to arouse this torpid Congress into action. Why, as Chairman of the War Committee I can tell you for a fact that the army has never been in better shape! Never have troops been so cheerful! Never have soldiers been more resolute! Never have discipline and training been more spirited! *(The* COURIER *enters, dusty as ever.* JOHN *winces.)* Good God! *(The* COURIER *deposits his dispatch on* THOMSON*'s desk and goes.* HANCOCK *puts down his paper and pounds the gavel.)*

HANCOCK. May we have your ears, gentlemen? Mr. Thomson has a dispatch.

(Everyone turns to listen. WITHERSPOON *is nudged awake.)*

THOMSON (*ringing his bell*). From the Commander, Army of the United Colonies; in New York, dispatch number one thousand, one hundred and fifty-seven. "To the honorable Congress, John Hancock, President. Dear Sir: It is with the utmost despair that I must report to you the confusion and disorder that reign in every department—"

MCNAIR. Sweet Jesus!

THOMSON. "The Continental soldier is as nothing ever seen in this, or any other, century; he is a misfit, ignorant of hygiene, destructive, disorderly and totally disrespectful of rank. Only this last is understandable as there is an incredible reek of stupidity amongst the officers. The situation is most desperate at the New Jersey Training Ground in New Brunswick where every able-bodied whore—*whore*—in the Colonies has assembled. There are constant reports of drunkenness, desertion, foul language, naked bathing in the Raritan River, and an epidemic of the French disease. I have declared the town 'off-limits' to all military personnel—with the exception of officers. I beseech the Congress to dispatch the War Committee to this place in the hope of restoring some of the order and discipline we need to survive. Y'r ob'd't (*Drum roll*) G. Washington."

MCKEAN. Och! The man would depress a hyena!

HANCOCK. Well, Mr. Adams, you're Chairman of the War Committee. Do y'feel up to whoring, drinking, deserting, and New Brunswick?

WITHERSPOON. There must be some mistake. I have an aunt who lives in New Brunswick!

(*Laughter*)

DICKINSON. You must tell her to keep up the good work! (*Laughter*) Come, come, Mr. Adams, you must see that it's hopeless. Let us recall General Washington and disband the Continental Army before we are overwhelmed.

JOHN. Oh, yes, the English would like that, wouldn't they?

DICKINSON. Why not ask them yourself? They ought to be here any minute.

(*Laughter.*)

RUTLEDGE. And when they hang you, Mr. Adams, I hope you will put in a good word for the rest of us.

(*A distressed silence.*)

CHASE. Face facts, Mr. Adams—a handful of drunk and disorderly recruits against the entire British Army, the finest musketmen on earth. How can we win? How can we even hope to survive?

JOHN. Answer me straight, Chase. If you thought we *could* beat the redcoats, would Mary-land say "yea" to independence?

CHASE. Well, I suppose—

JOHN. No supposing, Chase—would you or wouldn't you?

CHASE. Very well, Mr. Adams—yes, we would.

JOHN. Then come with me to New Brunswick and see for yourself!

MCKEAN. John! Are y'mad?

BARTLETT. Y'heard what Washington said—it's a shambles!

HOPKINS. They're pushin' y'into it, Johnny!

JOHN. What do y'say, Chase?

MORRIS. Go ahead, Sam. It sounds lively as hell up there.

CHASE. All right—why not? And maybe it'll be John Adams who comes to his senses.

JOHN. Mr. President, the War Committee will heed General Washington's request! A party consisting of Mr. Chase, Dr. Franklin, and myself will leave immediately.

HANCOCK. Is that satisfactory with you, Dr. Franklin?

(*All eyes turn to* FRANKLIN, *who is asleep again.* HOPKINS *nudges him.*)

JOHN. Wake up, Franklin, you're going to New Brunswick!

FRANKLIN. Like hell I am. What for?

HOPKINS. The whoring and the drinking.

FRANKLIN (*perking up*). Why didn't you say so? *They start out.* JOHN *driving them ahead of him like a sergeant major.*

JOHN. Come on, Chase, move all that lard! We've no time to lose! Left-right, left-right, left-right—! (*And they are gone. The other liberals then go, leaving only the conservatives.* DICKINSON *looks around, then rises.*)

DICKINSON. Mr. McNair, all this talk of independence has left a certain foulness in the air. (*Laughter from the conservatives*). My friends and I would appreciate it if you could open some windows.

MCNAIR. What about the flies?

DICKINSON (*smiling*). The windows, Mr. McNair. (*As* MCNAIR *goes to the windows, the clock strikes four.* DICKINSON *takes a deep breath, surveys the Chamber, then sings.*)

Oh, say, do you see what I see?
Congress sitting here in sweet serenity.
I could cheer.
The reason's clear:

For the first time in a year
Adams isn't here!
And, look!
The sun is in the sky,
The breeze is blowing by,
And there's not a single fly!

Oh, sing Hosanna, Hosanna!
CONSERVATIVES.
    Hosanna, Hosanna!
DICKINSON.
And it's cool!

Oh, ye cool, cool conservative men,
Our like may never ever be seen again.
We have land,
Cash in hand,
Self-command,
Future planned.
Fortune thrives,
Society survives,
In neatly ordered lives
With well-endowered wives.
CONSERVATIVES.
    Come sing Hosanna, Hosanna!
DICKINSON.
    In our breeding and our manner . . .
CONSERVATIVES.
    . . . We are cool!
*(The cool, cool conservative men—*RUT-
LEDGE, WILSON, READ, MORRIS, HALL, LIV-
INGSTON, *and* HEWES *among them—ele-
gantly prepare to dance.*
DICKINSON.
Come, ye cool, cool considerate set,
We'll dance together to the same minuet,
To the right,
Ever to the right,
Never to the left,
Forever to the right,
Let our creed,
Be never to exceed,
Regulated speed,
No matter what the need!
CONSERVATIVES.
    Come sing Hosanna, Hosanna!
DICKINSON.
    Emblazoned on our banner
    Is "Keep Cool!"
(The Minuet is led by DICKINSON *and* RUT-
LEDGE, *as the conservatives dance. During this
the* COURIER *re-enters and deposits his dis-
patch, as usual, on* THOMSON's *desk.* MCNAIR
goes to him, offers him a rum, and he stays.)
CONSERVATIVES.
    To the right,
    Ever to the right,
    Never to the left,

Forever to the right.
DICKINSON.
    Hands attach,
    Tightly latch,
    Everybody match.
THOMSON *(singing).*
    I have a new dispatch . . .
*(Music stops, but the Minuet continues si-
lently.* THOMSON *speaks.)* From the Com-
mander, Army of the United Colonies; in
New York, dispatch number one thousand,
one hundred and fifty-eight. "To the honora-
ble Congress, John Hancock, President. Dear
Sir: I awoke this morning to find that Gen.
Howe has landed twenty-five thousand British regulars and Hessian mercenaries on
Staten Island and that the fleet under the
command of his brother, Admiral Lord
Howe, controls not only the Hudson and East
Rivers, but New York Harbour, which now
looks like all of London afloat. I can no
longer, in good conscience, withhold from the
Congress my certainty that the British military object at this time is Philadelphia. Happy
should I be if I could see the means of preventing them, but at present I confess I do
not. Oh, how I wish I had never seen the
Continental Army. I would have done better
to retire to the back country and live in a
wigwam. Y'r ob'd't *(Drum roll.)* G. Washington."

*(A short pause; then music begins again and
the song continues as if nothing had hap-
pened.)*
CONSERVATIVES *(singing).*
    What we do, we do rationally.
DICKINSON.
    We never ever go off half
    cocked, not we.
CONSERVATIVES.
    Why begin,
    Till we know that we can win?
    And if we cannot win,
    Why bother to begin?
RUTLEDGE.
We say this game's not of our choosing,
Why should we risk losing?
CONSERVATIVES.
    We cool, cool men.
DICKINSON *(speaking, still dancing).* Mr.
Hancock, you're a man of property—one of
us. Why don't you join us in our minuet?
Why do you persist in dancing with John
Adams? Good Lord, sir, you don't even like
him!
HANCOCK *(singing).*
    That is true,

He annoys me quite a lot,
But still I'd rather trot
To Mr. Adams' new gavotte.

DICKINSON (*speaking, continuing to dance*). But why? For personal glory? For a place in history? Be careful, sir. History will brand him and his followers as traitors!

HANCOCK. Traitors to what, Mr. Dickinson—the British Crown? Or the British *half*-crown? Fortunately, there are not enough men of property in America to dictate policy.

DICKINSON. Perhaps not, but don't forget that most men with nothing would rather protect the possibility of becoming rich than face the reality of being poor. And that is why they will follow us . . .

CONSERVATIVES.

. . . To the right,
Ever to the right,
Never to the left,
Forever to the right.
Where there's gold,
A market that will hold,
Tradition that is old,
A reluctance to be bold.

DICKINSON.

I sing Hosanna, Hosanna!
In a sane and lucid manner!

CONSERVATIVES.

We are cool!

We're the cool, cool considerate men,
Whose like may never ever be seen again!
With our land,
Cash in hand,
Self-command,
Future planned.

And we'll hold
To our gold,
Tradition that is old,
Reluctant to be bold!

We say this game's not of our choosing.
Why should we risk losing?

We Cool, Cool, Cool, Cool, Cool, Cool,
Cool, Cool, Cool, Cool, Cool, Cool,
Cool—!
Cool—!
Men!!

(*They turn and go, leaving only* MCNAIR, *the* LEATHER APRON, *and the* COURIER *in the Chamber. They are silent for a moment.*)

MCNAIR. How'd you like to try 'n' borrow a dollar from one o' them? (*To the* COURIER) Want another rum, Gen'rul?

COURIER. Gen'rul? (*He grins.*) Lord, I ain't even a *corp'l.*

MCNAIR. Yeah, well, what's the Army know? (*He pours the* COURIER *another drink, pours himself and the* LEATHER APRON *a pair, selects one of* HANCOCK *'s good clay pipes, lights it, then bangs with the gavel.*) Sit down, gentlemen. The Chair rules it's too damn hot to work! (*He occupies one chair, the* COURIER *another, and the* LEATHER APRON *still a third.*) What's it like out there, Gen'rul?

COURIER. You prob'ly know more'n me.

MCNAIR. Sittin' in here? Sweet Jesus! This is the *last* place to find out what's goin' on!

LEATHER APRON (*to the* COURIER). I'm aimin' t'join up!

MCNAIR. What're you talkin' about? You don't have to join up—you're in the Congress!

LEATHER APRON. What's that got t'do with it?

MCNAIR. Y'don't see *them* rushin' off t'get killed, do you? But they sure are great ones f'r sendin' others, I'll tell you that.

COURIER (*indicating his chair*). Who sets here?

MCNAIR. Caesar Rodney of Delaware. Where *you* from, Gen'rul?

COURIER. Watertown.

MCNAIR. Where's that?

COURIER. Massachuset.

MCNAIR. Well, then, you belong down there. (*He indicates* JOHN*'s chair.*) But be careful; there's somethin' about that chair that makes a man awful noisy.

(*The* COURIER *goes to* ADAMS' *chair and touches it reverently before he sits.*)

LEATHER APRON. You seed any fightin'?

COURIER (*proudly*). Sure did. I seed my two best friends git shot dead on the very same day! Right on the village green it was, too! (*The recollection takes hold.*) An' when they didn't come home f'r supper, their mommas went down the hill lookin' for 'em. (*Music in, softly*) Miz Lowell, she foun' Tim'thy right off, but Miz Pickett, she looked near half the night f'r Will'm cuz he'd gone 'n' crawled off the green 'fore he died. (*He is silent for a moment; then he sings.*)

Momma, hey, Momma,
Come lookin' for me.
I'm here in the meadow
By the red maple tree.
Momma, hey, Momma,
Look sharp—here I be.
Hey, Hey—
Momma, look sharp!

Them so'jurs, they fired,
Oh, Ma, did we run.

But then we turned round
An' the battle begun.
Then I went under—
Oh, Ma, am I done?
Hey, Hey—
Momma, look sharp!

My eyes are wide open,
My face to the sky.
Is that you I'm hearin'
In the tall grass nearby?
Momma, come find me
Before I do die.
Hey, Hey—
Momma, look sharp!

COURIER, MCNAIR, AND LEATHER APRON.
I'll close y'r eyes, my Billy,
Them eyes that cannot see,
An' I'll bury ya, my Billy,
Beneath the maple tree.

COURIER *(as* MCNAIR *and* LEATHER
APRON *hum quietly).*
An' never ag'in
Will y'whisper t'me,
"Hey, Hey—"
Oh, Momma, look sharp!

(The lights fade.)

SCENE SIX

*An anteroom off the main Congressional
Chamber.*

*At rise, the stage remains dark from the
previous scene as the sounds of Congress in
session are heard: first,* THOMSON's *bell, asking for attention.*

HANCOCK. The Secretary will now read the
report of the Declaration Committee. Mr.
Thomson.

THOMSON. "A Declaration by the Representatives of the United States of America in
General Congress assembled." *(Lights come
up on the anteroom. It is deserted save for*
JEFFERSON, *who stands by the door into the
Chamber, holding it ajar so he can listen to*
THOMSON *read his Declaration.)* When in the
Course of Human Events, it becomes neces-
sary for one People to dissolve the Political
Bands which have connected them with
another, and to assume among the Powers of
the Earth, the separate and equal Station to
which the Laws of Nature and of Nature's
God entitle them, a decent Respect to the
Opinion of Mankind requires that they
should declare the causes which impel them

to the Separation. We hold these Truths to be
self-evident, that all Men are created equal,
that they are endowed by their Creator with
certain inalienable Rights—"

*(JEFFERSON, having heard a sound off-
stage, closes the door, silencing* THOMSON's
voice. JOHN *and* FRANKLIN *enter from the
wings, wearing capes and hats.)*

JOHN. Jefferson! We're back and we've got
Mary-land—that is, we *will,* soon as Chase
gets through telling the Mary-land Assembly
what we saw in New Brunswick!

FRANKLIN. He's in Annapolis right now,
describing a ragtag collection of provincial
militiamen who couldn't train together, drill
together, or march together—but when a
flock of ducks flew by and they saw their first
dinner in three full days, sweet Jesus! Could
they *shoot* together! It was a slaughter!

JEFFERSON *(not listening).* They're reading
the Declaration.

JOHN. What? How far have they got?

JEFFERSON. " . . . to render the Military
independent of and superior to the Civil
Power."

(JOHN opens the door to the Chamber.)

THOMSON. " . . . independent of and superior to—"

*(JOHN closes the door. The three men pace
for a moment.)*

JOHN. Well, there's nothing to fear. It's a
masterpiece! I'm to be congratulated.

FRANKLIN. *You?*

JOHN. For making him write it.

FRANKLIN. Ah, yes—of course.

(They are silent for a moment; then . . .)

JOHN *(singing.)*
It's a masterpiece, I say.
They will cheer ev'ry word,
Ev'ry letter!

JEFFERSON.
I wish I felt that way.

FRANKLIN.
I believe I can put it better!

Now then, attend,
As friend to friend,
Our Declaration Committee—
For us I see
Immortality . . .

ALL.
In Philadelphia city.

FRANKLIN.
A farmer,
A lawyer,
And a sage!—
A bit gouty in the leg.
You know, it's quite bizarre

To think that here we are,
Playing midwives to
An egg.

JOHN *(speaking)*. Egg? What egg?

FRANKLIN. America—the birth of a new nation!

JEFFERSON. If only we could be sure of what kind of a bird it's going to be.

FRANKLIN. Tom's got a point. What sort of a bird should we choose as the symbol of our new America?

JOHN. The eagle.

JEFFERSON. The dove.

FRANKLIN. The turkey.

(JOHN and JEFFERSON look at FRANKLIN in surprise, then at each other.)

JOHN. The eagle.

JEFFERSON. The dove.

JOHN. The eagle!

JEFFERSON *(shrugging)*. The eagle.

(A pause)

FRANKLIN. The turkey.

JOHN. The eagle is a majestic bird.

FRANKLIN. The eagle is a scavenger, a thief, a coward, and the symbol of more than ten centuries of European mischief.

JOHN. And the turkey?

FRANKLIN. A truly noble bird, a native of America, a source of sustenance to our settlers, and an incredibly brave fellow *(Kettle drums)* who would not flinch from attacking an entire regiment of Englishmen singlehandedly! Therefore the national bird of America is going to be *(Drums out)*—

JOHN. The eagle.

FRANKLIN AND JEFFERSON *(shrugging)*. The eagle.

(A pause)

JOHN *(singing)*.

We're waiting for the . . .

ALL.

Chirp! chirp! chirp!
Of an eaglet being born,
Waiting for the
Chirp! chirp! chirp!
On this humid Monday morning in this
—Congressional incubator!

FRANKLIN.

God knows, the temp'rature's hot enough
To hatch a stone,
Let alone
An egg!

JOHN.

We're waiting for the . . .

ALL.

Scratch! scratch! scratch!
Of that tiny little fellow,

Waiting for the egg to hatch,
On this humid Monday morning in this
—Congressional incubator!

JOHN.

God knows the temp'rature's hot enough
To hatch a stone!

JEFFERSON.

But will it hatch
An egg?

JOHN *(speaking)*. The Declaration will be a triumph, I tell you—a triumph! If I was ever sure of anything I'm sure of that—a triumph! *(A pause)* And if it isn't, we've still got four days left to think of something else. *(He sings)*.

The eagle's going to
Crack the shell
Of the egg that England laid!

ALL.

Yessir! We can
Tell! tell! tell!
On this humid Monday morning in this
—Congressional incubator!

FRANKLIN.

And just as Tom, here, has written,
Though the shell may belong to Great Britain,
The eagle inside
Belongs to us!

ALL.

And just as Tom, here, has written
We say "To hell with Great Britain!"
The eagle inside
Belongs to us!!!

(They turn and go confidently into the Chamber.)

SCENE SEVEN

The Chamber, Congress is in session— HANCOCK, BARTLETT, HOPKINS, SHERMAN, MORRIS, LIVINGSTON, WITHERSPOON, DICKINSON, WILSON, MCKEAN, READ, HEWES, RUTLEDGE, *and* HALL *being present—and now* JOHN, FRANKLIN, *and* JEFFERSON *take their places, this action continuing from the previous scene, as* THOMSON *completes his reading of the Declaration. The calendar on the wall now reads:* "JUNE 28."

THOMSON. "—and that as Free and Independent States, they have full Power to levy War, conclude Peace, contract Alliances, establish Commerce, and to do all other Acts and Things which Independent

States may of right do. And for the support of this Declaration we mutually pledge to each other our Lives, our Fortunes, and our sacred Honor." *(Finished, he looks up. Nobody moves, nobody speaks, nobody reacts; the silence is complete and prolonged.)*

HANCOCK *(finally)*. Very well. Thank you, Mr. Thomson. The Congress has heard the report of the Declaration Committee. Are there any who wish to offer amendments, deletions, or alterations to the Declaration?

(Suddenly every hand but JOHN's, FRANKLIN's, JEFFERSON's, *and* HOPKINS's *shoots up.)*

CONGRESS. Mr. President!

Hear me, Mr. President!

I've got one!

Over here!

(Et cetera)

HANCOCK *(pounding the gavel for order)*. Gentlemen, *please!* McNair, you'd better open the window. Colonel McKean, I saw your hand first.

MCKEAN. Mr. Jefferson, it's a bonny paper y've written, but somewhere in it y've mentioned "Scottish and foreign mercenaries sent t'destroy us." *Scottish,* Tom?

JOHN. It's in reference to a Highland regiment which stood against us at Boston.

MCKEAN. Och, it was more likely Germans wearin' kilts to disguise their bein' there. I ask y'to remove the word and avoid givin' offense to a good people.

THOMSON. Mr. Jefferson?

(JEFFERSON nods and THOMSON scratches his quill pen through the word. The many hands go up again.)

HANCOCK. The Reverend Witherspoon?

WITHERSPOON. Mr. Jefferson, nowhere do you mention the Supreme Being. Certainly this was an oversight, for how could we hope to achieve a victory without His help? Therefore I must humbly suggest the following addition to your final sentence: "With a firm reliance on the protection of Divine Providence."

(Again THOMSON looks at JEFFERSON, who in turn looks at JOHN; the two patriots shrug, then JEFFERSON turns back to THOMSON and nods; the phrase is added. More hands.)

HANCOCK. Mr. Read?

READ. Among your charges against the King, Mr. Jefferson, you accuse him of depriving us of the benefits of trial by jury. This is untrue, sir. In Delaware we have always had trial by jury.

JOHN. In Massachusetts we have not.

READ. Oh. Then I suggest that the words "in many cases" be added.

THOMSON. Mr. Jefferson?

(And again JEFFERSON nods; the words are added.)

MCKEAN. "In many cases!"—och, brilliant! I s'pose every time y'see those three words y'r puny little chest'll swell up wi' pride over y'r great historical contribution!

READ. It's more memorable than your unprincipled whitewash of that race of barbarians!

HANCOCK *(pounding the gavel)*. Mr. Read, Colonel McKean—that's enough! *(The hands are raised, this time HOPKINS' among them.)* Mr. Hopkins?

HOPKINS. No objections, Johnny, I'm just trying to get a drink.

HANCOCK. I should've known. McNair, get him a rum. *(Again the hands go up.* MCNAIR *crosses to the wall calendar and removes a leaf, uncovering "JUNE 29.")* Mr. Bartlett?

BARTLETT. Mr. Jefferson. I beg you to remember that we still have friends in England. I see no purpose in antagonizing them with such phrases as "unfeeling brethren" and "enemies in war." Our quarrel is with the British King, not the British people.

JOHN. Be sensible, Bartlett. Remove those phrases, and the entire paragraph becomes meaningless. And it so happens it's among the most stirring and poetic of any passage in the entire document. *(He picks up the Declaration from THOMSON's desk, preparing to read.)*

BARTLETT. We're a Congress, Mr. Adams, not a literary society. I ask that the entire paragraph be stricken.

THOMSON. Mr. Jefferson?

(And again, after some thought this time, and with some sadness, JEFFERSON nods.)

JOHN. Good God, Jefferson! Don't you ever intend to speak up for your own work?

JEFFERSON. I had hoped that the work would speak for itself.

(THOMSON scratches out the paragraph.)

MCNAIR. Mr. Hancock.

HANCOCK. What is it, Mr. McNair?

MCNAIR. I can't say I'm very fond of the United States of America as a name for a new country.

HANCOCK. I don't care *what* you're fond of, Mr. McNair. You're not a member of this Congress! Mr. Sherman?

SHERMAN *(coffee in hand, as usual)*.

Brother Jefferson, I noted at least two distinct and direct references to the British Parliament in your Declaration. Do you think it's wise to alienate that august body in light of our contention that they have never had any direct authority over us anyway?

JOHN. This is a revolution, dammit! We're going to have to offend *some*body!

FRANKLIN. John. *(He leads* JOHN *downstage as the debate in the Chamber continues silently behind them.)* John, you'll have an attack of apoplexy if you're not careful.

JOHN. Have you heard what they're doing to it? Have *you heard?*

FRANKLIN. Yes, John, I've heard, but—

JOHN. And so far it's only been our friendsl Can you imagine what our enemies will do?

HANCOCK. The word "Parliament" will be removed wherever it occurs.

JOHN. They won't be satisfied until they remove one of the Fs from Jefferson's name.

FRANKLIN. Courage, John! It won't last much longer. *(They start back toward their seats as the hands go up again. And again* MCNAIR *goes to the calendar and removes another page; it now reads:* "JUNE 30.")

HANCOCK. Mr. Dickinson?

DICKINSON. Mr. Jefferson, I have very little interest in your paper, as there is no doubt in my mind that we have all but heard the last of it. But I am curious about one thing: why do you refer to King George as a tyrant?

JEFFERSON. Because he is a tyrant.

DICKINSON. I remind you, Mr. Jefferson, that this "tyrant" is still your King.

JEFFERSON. When a king becomes a tyrant he thereby breaks the contract binding his subjects to him.

DICKINSON. How so?

JEFFERSON. By taking away their rights.

DICKINSON. Rights that came from him in the first place.

JEFFERSON. All except one—the right to be free comes from nature.

DICKINSON. Mr. Wilson, do we in Pennsylvania consider King George a tyrant?

WILSON. Hmm? Well—I don't know. *(As he meets* DICKINSON's *stony stare.)* Oh. No—no, we don't. He's not a tyrant —in Pennsylvania.

DICKINSON. There you are, Mr. Jefferson. Your Declaration does not speak for us all. I demand the word "tyrant" be removed!

*(*THOMSON *begins scratching it out.)*

JEFFERSON. Just a moment, Mr. Thomson, I do not consent. The King is a tyrant whether we say so or not. We might as well say so.

THOMSON. But I already scratched it out.

JEFFERSON *(forcefully).* Then scratch it back in!

(A surprised silence)

HANCOCK *(finally).* Put it back, Mr. Thomsom. The King will remain a tyrant. *(Once more* MCNAIR *goes to the calendar and changes the date—to* "JULY 1." Mr. Hewes?

HEWES. Mr. Jefferson, nowhere do you mention deep-sea fishin' rights. We in North Carolina—

(Everyone throws up his hands in disgust and impatience.)

JOHN. Good God! *Fishing* rights! How long is this piddling to go on? We have been sitting here for three full days. We have endured, by my count, eighty-five separate changes and the removal of close to four hundred words. Would you whip it and beat it till you break its spirit? I tell you this document is a masterful expression of the American mind!

(There is a silence.)

HANCOCK. If there are no more changes, then, I can assume that the report of the Declaration Committee has been—

RUTLEDGE *(deliberately).* Just a moment, Mr. President.

FRANKLIN *(to* JOHN*).* Look out.

RUTLEDGE. I wonder if we could prevail upon Mr. Thomson to read again a small portion of Mr. Jefferson's Declaration—the one beginnin' "He has waged cruel war—"?

HANCOCK. Mr. Thomson?

THOMSON, *reading back rapidly to himself.* " . . . He has affected . . . He has combined . . . He has abdicated . . . He has plundered . . . He has constrained . . . He has excited . . . He has *in*cited . . . He has waged cruel war!" Ah. *(He looks up.)* Here it is. *(He clears his throat and reads.)* "He has waged cruel war against human nature itself, in the persons of a distant people who never offended him, captivating and carrying them into slavery in another hemisphere. Determined to keep open a market where men should be bought and sold, he has prostituted—"

RUTLEDGE. That will suffice, Mr. Thomson, I thank you. Mr. Jefferson, I can't quite make out what it is you're talkin' about.

JEFFERSON. Slavery, Mr. Rutledge.

RUTLEDGE. Ah, yes, You're referrin' to us as slaves of the King.

JEFFERSON. No, sir, I'm referring to *our* slaves. Black slaves.

RUTLEDGE. Ah! Black slaves. Why didn't you say so, sir? Were you tryin' to hide your meanin'?

JEFFERSON. No, sir.

RUTLEDGE. Just another literary license, then.

JEFFERSON. If you like.

RUTLEDGE. I don't like at all, Mr. Jefferson. To us in South Carolina, black slavery is our peculiar institution and a cherished way of life.

JEFFERSON. Nevertheless, we must abolish it. Nothing is more certainly written in the Book of Fate than that this people shall be free.

RUTLEDGE. I am not concerned with the Book of Fate right now, sir. I am more concerned with what's written in your little paper there.

JOHN. That "little paper there" deals with freedom for Americans!

RUTLEDGE. Oh, really! Mr. Adams is now callin' our black slaves Americans. Are-they-now?

JOHN. They are! They're people and they're here—if there is any other requirement, I've never heard of it.

RUTLEDGE. They are here, yes, but they are not people, sir, they are *property.*

JEFFERSON. No, sir! They are people who are being treated as property. I tell you the rights of human nature are deeply wounded by this infamous practice!

RUTLEDGE *(shouting).* Then see to your own wounds, Mr. Jefferson, for you are a—practitioner, are you not?

(A pause. RUTLEDGE *has found the mark.)*

JEFFERSON. I have already resolved to release my slaves.

RUTLEDGE. Then I'm sorry, for you have also resolved the ruination of your personal economy.

JOHN. Economy. Always economy. There's more to this than a filthy purse string, Rutledge. It's an offense against man and God.

HOPKINS. It's a stinking business, Mr. Rutledge—a stinking business!

RUTLEDGE. Is it really, Mr. Hopkins? Then what's that I smell floatin' down from the North—could it be the aroma of *hy*pocrisy? For who holds the other end of that filthy purse string, Mr. Adams? *(To everyone)* Our northern brethren are feelin' a bit tender toward our slaves. They don't keep slaves, no-o, but they're willin' to be considerable

carriers of slaves—to others! They are willin', for the shillin' *(rubbing his thumb and forefinger together)* or haven't y'heard, Mr. Adams? Clink! Clink! *(He sings.)*

Molasses to
Rum to
Slaves!
Oh, what a beautiful waltz!

You dance with us,
We dance with you, in
Molasses and
Rum and
Slaves!
(Afro rhythm)

Who sail the ships out of Boston,
Laden with Bibles and Rum?
Who drinks a toast
To the Ivory Coast,
"Hail, Africa! The slavers have come."
New England, with Bibles and Rum!

Then,
It's off with the Rum and the Bibles
Take on the Slaves, clink! clink!
Then,
Hail and farewell!
To the smell of the African
Coast!

Molasses to
Rum to
Slaves!
'Tisn't morals, 'tis money that saves!
Shall we dance to the sound
Of the profitable pound, in
Molasses and
Rum and
Slaves!

Who sail the ships out of Guinea,
Laden with Bibles and Slaves?
'Tis Boston can boast
To, the West Indies coast:
"Jamaica! We brung what y'craves!
Antigua! Barbados!
We brung Bibles
And Slaves!"

(He speaks, Afro rhythm continues.) Gentlemen! You mustn't think our northern friends merely see our slaves as figures on a ledger. Oh, no, sir! They see them as figures on the block! Notice the faces at the auctions, gentlemen—white faces on the African wharves—New England faces, seafaring faces: "Put them in the ships, cram them in the ships, *stuff* them in the ships!" Hurry, gentlemen, let the auction begin!

(He sings.)
 Ya-ha . . .
 Ya-ha . . . ha-ma-ha-cundahhh!
 Gentlemen, do y' hear?
 That's the cry of the auctioneer!

 Ya-ha . . .
 Ya-ha . . . ha-ma-ha-cundahhh!
Slaves, gentlemen! Black gold, livin' gold—
 gold!
 From:
 Annn-go-laah!
 Guinea-Guinea-Guinea!
 Blackbirds for sale!

 Aaa-shan-tiiii!
 Ibo! Ibo! Ibo! Ibo!

 Blackbirds for sale!
 Handle them!
 Fondle them!
 But don't finger them!
 They're prime, they're prime!

 Ya-ha . . .
 Ya-ha . . . ha-ma-ha-cundahhh!
(Music stops.)
BARTLETT *(pleading)*. For the love of God,
Mr. Rutledge, *please!*
(Music resumes.)
RUTLEDGE.
 Molasses to
 Rum to
 Slaves!

 Who sail the ships back to Boston,
 Laden with gold, see it gleam?
 Whose fortunes are made
 In the triangle trade?
 Hail, Slavery, the New England
 Dream!

 Mr. Adams, I give you a toast!
 Hail, Boston!
 Hail, Charleston!
 Who *stinketh* the most?!
*(He turns and walks straight out of the
Chamber.* HEWES *of North Carolina follows,
and* HALL *of Georgia is right behind them.)*
JOHN *(desperate)*. Mr. Rutledge! Mr.
Hewes! Dr. Hall!
*(*HALL, *the last, hesitates at the door as his
name is called. He turns, looks at* JOHN, *starts
to say something, then turns and goes after the
others.)*
WITHERSPOON. Don't worry, they'll be
back.
MCKEAN. Aye—t'vote us down.
(There is a silence. Then CHASE *bursts into
the Chamber.)*

CHASE *(elated)*. It's done! Adams, Franklin
—I have it! And the Mary-land Assembly's
approved it! I told them about one of the
greatest military engagements in history,
against a flock of—*(He runs down as the news
is greeted with less enthusiasm than expected,
and he sees the glum faces.)* What's wrong? I
thought—
DICKINSON *(cordially)*. You'll have to forgive them, Mr. Chase, they've just suffered a
slight setback. And after all, what is a man
profited, if he shall gain Mary-land, and lose
the entire South? *(Smiling as he goes)* Matthew, chapter sixteen, verse twenty-six.
*(*WILSON, READ, LIVINGSTON, *and* MOR-
RIS *follow him out.* CHASE *joins the ranks of
the depressed as* THOMSON *moves Maryland
into the "Yea" column.)*
HANCOCK *(lifelessly)*. Mr. McNair—
MCNAIR. I know, the flies.
HANCOCK. No—a rum.
JOHN *(surveying the sorry sight)*. Well?
What're you all sitting around for? We're
wasting time—precious time! *(To* MCKEAN.*)*
Thomas! I want you to ride down into Dela-
ware and fetch back Caesar Rodney!
MCKEAN. John! Are y'mad? It's eighty
miles on horseback, an' he's a dyin' man!
JOHN. No! He's a patriot!
MCKEAN. Och, John, what good'll it do?
The South's done us in.
JOHN. And suppose they change their
minds—can we get Delaware without Rod-
ney?
MCKEAN *(shaking his head)*. God! What a
bastardly bunch we are! *(He goes.)*
JOHN *(turning to* HOPKINS*)*. Stephen—
HOPKINS. I'm goin' to the tavern, Johnny.
If there's anything I can do for y'there, let me
know. *(He goes.)*
JOHN. Chase, Bartlett—
BARTLETT. What's the use, John? The
vote's tomorrow morning.
CHASE. There's less than a full day left!
(They go.)
JOHN. Roger!
SHERMAN. Face facts, John—it's finished!
WITHERSPOON. I'm sorry, John.
(And they go. JOHN *looks around, stunned
by the defection. Only* FRANKLIN, JEFFER-
SON, HANCOCK, *and* THOMSON *remain.)*
FRANKLIN. We've no other choice, John.
The slavery clause has to go.
JOHN. Franklin, what are y'saying?
FRANKLIN. It's a luxury we can't afford.
JOHN. A luxury? A half-million souls in

chains, and Dr. Franklin calls it a luxury! Maybe you should've walked out with the South!

FRANKLIN. You forget yourself, sir! I founded the first antislavery society on this continent!

JOHN. Don't wave your credentials at me! Perhaps it's time you had them renewed!

FRANKLIN *(angrily).* The issue here is independence! Maybe you've lost sight of that fact, but I have not! How dare you jeopardize our cause when we've come so far? These men, no matter how much we disagree with them, are not ribbon clerks to be ordered about; they're proud, accomplished men, the cream of their colonies—and whether you like it or not, they and the people they represent will be a part of the new country you'd hope to create! Either start learning how to live with them or pack up and go home—but in any case, stop acting like a Boston fishwife! *(And he leaves* JOHN *alone, returning upstage to join* JEFFERSON.*)*

*(*JOHN *turns and comes downstage.)*

JOHN. Good God, what's happened to me? John Adams, the great John Adams, Wise Man of the East—what have I come to? My law practice down the pipe, my farm mortgaged to the hilt—at a stage in life when other men prosper I'm reduced to living in Philadelphia. *(*ABIGAIL *appears, as before.)* Oh, Abigail, what am I going to do?

ABIGAIL. Do, John?

JOHN. I need your help.

ABIGAIL. You don't usually ask my advice.

JOHN. Yes—well, there doesn't appear to be anyone else right now.

ABIGAIL *(sighing).* Very well, John, what is it?

JOHN. The entire South has walked out of this Congress, George Washington is on the verge of total annihilation, the precious cause for which I've labored these several years has come to nothing, and it seems *(A pause),* it seems I am obnoxious and disliked.

ABIGAIL. Nonsense, John.

JOHN. That I am unwilling to face reality.

ABIGAIL. Foolishness, John.

JOHN. That I am pigheaded.

ABIGAIL *(smiling).* Ah, well, there you have me, John. I'm afraid you *are* pigheaded.

(He smiles; a pause)

JOHN. Has it been any kind of a life for you, Abby? God knows I haven't given you much.

ABIGAIL. I never asked for more. After all, I am Mrs. John Adams—that's quite a lot for one lifetime.

JOHN *(bitterly).* Is it, Abby?

ABIGAIL. Think of it, John! To be married to the man who is always first in line to be hanged!

JOHN. Yes. The ag-i-ta-tor. *(Turning to her)* Why, Abby? You must tell me what it is! I've always been dissatisfied, I know that; but lately I find that I *reek* of discontentment! It fills my throat and floods my brain, and sometimes—sometimes I fear that there is no longer a dream, but only the discontentment.

ABIGAIL. Oh, John, can you really know so little about yourself? And can you think so little of me that you'd believe I married the man you've described? Have you forgotten what you used to say to me? I haven't. "Commitment, Abby—commitment! There are only two creatures of value on the face of this earth: those with a commitment, and those who require the commitment of others." *(A pause)* Do you remember, John?

JOHN *(nodding).* I remember.

*(*MCNAIR *enters, carrying two gaily beribboned kegs, and thumps them down in front of* JOHN.*)*

MCNAIR. Mr. Adams—

JOHN. What?

MCNAIR. These're for you.

JOHN. Just a minute—what are they? What's in them? Who sent them?

(Music in, glissando.)

ABIGAIL *(singing).*

Compliments of the Concord Ladies' Coffee Club,

And the Sisterhood of the Truro Synagogue,

And the Friday Evening Baptist Sewing Circle,

And the Holy Christian Sisters of Saint Clare—

All for you John!

I am, as I ever was, and ever shall be . . .

Yours . . .

Yours . . .

Yours . . .

Yours—

JOHN *(speaking).* Just a moment, Abigail— what's in those kegs?

ABIGAIL *(singing triumphantly).*

      Saltpetre, John!

(She blows a kiss and goes.)

*(*JOHN *turns back to the Chamber.)*

JOHN. McNair! Go out and buy every damned pin in Philadelphia!

MCNAIR. Pin? What sort of pin?

JOHN. I don't know—whatever ladies use

with their sewing! And take these kegs to the armory—hurry, man! *(Turning as* MCNAIR *goes)* Franklin, Jefferson, what are you just sitting around for?

FRANKLIN. John, didn't you hear a word that I said before?

JOHN. Never mind that. Here's what you've got to do—

FRANKLIN. John! I'm not even speaking to you!

JOHN. It's too late for that, dammit! *(Music in, vigorously)* There's work to be done! *(He sings.)*

>   Time's running out!
>   Get up!
>   Get out of your chair!
>   Tomorrow is here.
>   Too late,
>   Too late to despair!
>
>   Jefferson! Talk to Rutledge, talk!
>   If it takes all night,
>   Keep talking.

JOHN AND JEFFERSON.
>   Talk and talk and talk!

JOHN *(speaking).* You're both Southern aristocrats—gentlemen. If he'll listen to anybody, he'll listen to you! *(He sings.)*
>   Franklin!
>   Time's running out!

FRANKLIN.
>   I know. Get out of my chair!
>   Do I have to talk to Wilson?

JOHN.
>   Yes, yes, you do!
>   If it takes all night,
>   Keep talking!

JOHN, FRANKLIN, AND JEFFERSON.
>   Talk and talk and talk!

JOHN *(speaking).* Get him away from Dickinson, that's the only way to do it!

(FRANKLIN and JEFFERSON go. Music under.)

HANCOCK *(coming forward).* I'm still from Massachusetts, John; you know where I stand. I'll do whatever you say.

JOHN *(considering).* No, you're the President of Congress. You're a fair man, Hancock—stay that way. *(The COURIER enters and stops short as he comes face to face with JOHN, who takes his dispatch and crosses up to THOMSON's desk, where he hands it to the SECRETARY.)* Tell me, Mr. Thomson, out of curiosity, do you stand with Mr. Dickinson, or do you stand with me?

THOMSON *(holding up the dispatch).* I stand with the General. Lately—I've had the oddest feeling that he's been—writing to *me.* *(He reads, singing.)*
>   "I have been in expectation
>   Of receiving a reply
>   On the subject of my last fifteen dispatches.
>   Is anybody there?
>   Does anybody care?
>   Does anybody care?
>   Y'r humble & ob'd't—"

(Drum roll; then it runs down as THOMSON, *unable to read the signature, rises and goes, thoroughly discouraged.*

It is growing dark outside. HANCOCK *stands by the door, watching* JOHN, *concerned.)*

HANCOCK. Are y'hungry, John?

JOHN. No, I think I'll stay.

HANCOCK. G'night, then. *(He goes.)*

(JOHN looks around the Chamber, then goes to THOMSON's desk and picks up the dispatch.)

JOHN *(singing).*
>   Is anybody there?
>   Does anybody care?

(He drops the dispatch.)
Does anybody see what I see?

>   They want me to quit,
>   They say, "John, give up the fight!"
>   Still to England I say:
>   "Good night forever, good night!"
>
>   For I have crossed the Rubicon,
>   Let the bridge be burn'd behind me!
>   Come what may, come what may . . .
>   Commitment!
>
>   The croakers all say
>   We'll rue the day,
>   There'll be hell to pay in
>   Fiery Purgatory!
>
>   Through all the gloom,
>   Through all the gloom, I can
>   See the rays of ravishing light and
>   Glory!
>
>   Is anybody there?!
>   Does anybody care?!
>   Does anybody see
>   What I see?!
>
>   I see
>   Fireworks!
>   I see the Pageant and Pomp and Parade!
>   I hear the bells ringing out!
>   I hear the cannons' roar!
>   I see Americans, *all* Americans,
>   Free! For evermore!

(He "comes to" and looks around, realizing that it's dark and that he's alone.)

How quiet . . .
How quiet the Chamber is . . .
How silent . . .
How silent the Chamber is . . .

Is anybody there—?
(He waits for an answer; there is none.)
Does anybody care—?
(Again, nothing)
Does anybody see—what I see?
(Music out)
HALL *(speaking).* Yes, Mr. Adams, I do.
(JOHN turns and discovers the Georgia delegate standing by the door, in the shadows.)
JOHN. Dr. Hall, I didn't know anyone was—
HALL. I'm sorry if I startled you. I couldn't sleep. In trying to resolve my dilemma I remembered something I'd once read—"that a representative owes the People not only his industry, but his judgment, and he betrays them if he sacrifices it to their opinion." *(He smiles.)* It was written by Edmund Burke, a member of the British Parliament. *(He walks to the tally board and moves the name of Georgia from the "Nay" to the "Yea" column. The two men regard each other for a moment.)*
It has been growing light outside and now the clock, offstage, chimes ten and the men of the Congress return silently, in single file, each with his own private thoughts, MCKEAN *supporting* RODNEY *at the end. Then* HANCOCK *pounds the gavel.)*
HANCOCK. Very well. The Congress will now vote on Virginia's resolution on independence. *(To* RODNEY*)* Thank you for coming, Caesar. And God bless you, sir. *(Foot-stamping and other signs of approval from all)* Call the roll, Mr. Thomson. And I'd remind you, gentlemen, that a single "Nay" vote will defeat the motion. Mr. Thomson?
(THOMSON goes to the tally board. During the following, FRANKLIN *is deeply engaged in silent argument with* DICKINSON *and* WILSON, *their heads remaining together.)*
THOMSON *(droning).* New Hampshire—
BARTLETT. New Hampshire says "Yea."
THOMSON. New Hampshire says "Yea." Massachusetts—
JOHN. Massachusetts says "Yea."
THOMSON. Massachusetts says "Yea." Rhode Island—
HOPKINS. Rhode Island says "Yea."
THOMSON. Rhode Island says "Yea." Connecticut—
SHERMAN. Connecticut says "Yea."

THOMSON. Connecticut says "Yea." New York—
MORRIS. New York abstains—courteously.
THOMSON. New York abstains.
MORRIS *(disgusted and ashamed).* Courteously.
THOMSON. New Jersey—
WITHERSPOON. New Jersey says "Yea."
THOMSON. New Jersey says "Yea." Pennsylvania—*(As no one responds)* Pennsylvania?
FRANKLIN. Mr. Secretary, Pennsylvania isn't ready yet. Come back to us later. *(He returns to the argument.)*
THOMSON. Pennsylvania passes. Delaware—
RODNEY *(as* MCKEAN *helps him to his feet).* Delaware, by majority vote—
MCKEAN. Aye!
RODNEY. —says "Yea."
FRANKLIN. Well done, sir.
THOMSON. Delaware says "Yea." *(And Delaware's marker on the tally board is moved into the "Yea" column.)* Mary-land—
CHASE. Mary-land says "Yea."
THOMSON. Mary-land says "Yea." Virginia—
JEFFERSON. Virginia says "Yea."
THOMSON. Virginia says "Yea." North Carolina—
HEWES. North Carolina yields to South Carolina!
THOMSON. South Carolina—
RUTLEDGE *(rising, then turning to* JOHN*).* Well, Mr. Adams?
JOHN *(returning his stare).* Well, Mr. Rutledge?
RUTLEDGE. Mr. Adams, you must believe that I will do what I have promised to do.
(A pause)
JOHN. What do y'want, Rutledge?
RUTLEDGE. Remove the offendin' passage from your Declaration.
JOHN. If we did that we'd be guilty of what we ourselves are rebelling against.
RUTLEDGE. Nevertheless, remove it or South Carolina will bury now and forever your dream of independence.
FRANKLIN *(imploring).* John, I *beg* you to consider what you're doing.
JOHN. Mark me, Franklin, if we give in on this issue, posterity will never forgive us.
FRANKLIN. That's probably true. But we won't hear a thing, John—we'll be long gone. And besides, what will posterity think we were—demigods? We're men—no more, no less—trying to get a nation started against

greater odds than a more generous God would have allowed. John, first things first! Independence! America! For if we don't secure that, what difference will the rest make?

JOHN (*looking around, uncertain*). Jefferson, say something.

JEFFERSON. What else is there to do?

JOHN. Well, man, you're the one who wrote it!

JEFFERSON. I wrote *all* of it, Mr. Adams! (*He goes to* THOMSON*'s table, takes up the quill pen, and scratches the passage from the Declaration. Then he returns to his seat.* JOHN *snatches up the Declaration, goes to* RUTLEDGE, *and waves it under his nose.*)

JOHN. There! There it is, Rutledge! You've got your slavery, and little good may it do you! Now vote, damn you!

RUTLEDGE (*unruffled*). Mr. Secretary, the fair colony of South Carolina says "Yea."

THOMSON. South Carolina says "Yea."

HEWES (*jumping up*). North Carolina says "Yea."

THOMSON. North Carolina says "Yea." (*The two markers on the tally board are moved out of the "Nay" column. Only Pennsylvania remains there.*) Georgia.

HALL. Georgia says "Yea."

THOMSON. Georgia says "Yea." Pennsylvania, second call—

DICKINSON (*rising*). Mr. President, Pennsylvania regrets all of the inconvenience that such distinguished men as Adams, Franklin, and Jefferson were put to just now. They might have kept their document intact, for all the difference it will make. Mr. President, Pennsylvania says—

FRANKLIN. Just a moment! I ask that the delegation be polled.

DICKINSON. Dr. Franklin, don't be absurd!

FRANKLIN. A poll, Mr. President. It's a proper request.

HANCOCK. Yes, it is. Poll the delegation, Mr. Thomson.

THOMSON. Dr. Benjamin Franklin—

FRANKLIN. Yea!

THOMSON. Mr. John Dickinson—

DICKINSON. Nay!

THOMSON. Mr. James Wilson— (*As there is no response*) Judge Wilson?

(*All eyes turn to* WILSON.)

FRANKLIN. There it is, Mr. Wilson, it's up to you now—the whole question of American independence rests squarely on your shoulders. An entirely new nation, Mr. Wilson, waiting to be born or to die in birth, all on your say-so. Which will it be Mr. Wilson? Every map maker in the world is waiting for your decision!

DICKINSON. Come now, James, nothing has changed. We mustn't let Dr. Franklin create one of his confusions. The question is clear.

FRANKLIN. Most questions are clear when someone else has to decide them.

JOHN (*quietly, turning the screw*). It would be a pity for a man who handed down hundreds of wise decisions from the bench to be remembered only for the one unwise decision he made in Congress.

DICKINSON. James, you're keeping everybody waiting. The Secretary has called for your vote.

WILSON (*to* DICKINSON). Please don't push me, John, I know what you want me to do. But Mr. Adams is correct about one thing. *I'm* the one who'll be remembered for it.

DICKINSON. What do you mean?

WILSON. I'm different from you, John. I'm different from most of the men here. I don't want to be remembered. I just don't want the responsibility!

DICKINSON. Yes, well, whether you want it or not, James, there's no way of avoiding it.

WILSON. Not necessarily. If I go with them, I'll only be one among dozens; no one will ever remember the name of James Wilson. But if I vote with you, I'll be the man who prevented American independence. I'm sorry, John—I just didn't bargain for that.

DICKINSON. And is that how new nations are formed—by a nonentity trying to preserve the anonymity he so richly deserves?

FRANKLIN. Revolutions come into this world like bastard children, Mr. Dickinson— half improvised and half compromised. Our side has provided the compromise; now Judge Wilson is supplying the rest.

WILSON (*to* DICKINSON). I'm sorry, John. My vote is "Yea."

FRANKLIN. Mr. Secretary, Pennsylvania says "Yea."

THOMSON. Pennsylvania says "Yea." (*There is a stunned silence as all eyes go to the tally board and Pennsylvania's marker is moved into the "Yea" column.*) The count being twelve to none with one abstention, the resolution on independence (*Surprised*) is adopted.

JOHN. It's done. It's done.

(*A pause*)

HANCOCK. Mr. Thomson, is the Declaration ready to be signed?

THOMSON. It is.

HANCOCK. Then I suggest we do so. And the Chair further proposes, for our mutual security and protection, that no man be allowed to sit in this Congress without attaching his name to it.

(All eyes now go to DICKINSON.*)*

DICKINSON. I'm sorry, Mr. President, I cannot, in good conscience, sign such a document. I will never stop hoping for our eventual reconciliation with England. But because, in my own way, I regard America no less than does Mr. Adams, I will join the Army and fight in her defense—even though I believe that fight to be hopeless. Good-by, gentlemen. *(He starts out.)*

JOHN. Gentlemen of the Congress, I say ye John Dickinson!

*(*DICKINSON *stops as the members of Congress express their admiration for him by stamping their feet and banging their walking sticks on the floor. Then he goes and* HAN-COCK *pounds the gavel.)*

HANCOCK. Gentlemen, are there any objections to the Declaration being approved as it now stands?

JOHN. I have one, Mr. Hancock.

HANCOCK. *You,* Mr. Adams?

JOHN. Yes. Mr. Jefferson, it so happens the word is *un*alienable, not *in*alienable.

JEFFERSON. I'm sorry, Mr. Adams, *in*alienable is correct.

JOHN *(his voice rising).* I happen to be a Harvard graduate—

JEFFERSON *(his voice also rising).* And *I* attended William and Mary—

HANCOCK *(pounding the gavel).* Gentlemen, please! Mr. Jefferson, will you yield to Mr. Adams's request?

(A pause)

JEFFERSON. No, sir, I will not.

JOHN. Oh, very well, I'll withdraw it.

FRANKLIN. Good for you, John!

JOHN *(privately).* I'll speak to the printer about it later.

HANCOCK. Very well, gentlemen. *(He goes to* THOMSON*'s desk and picks up the quill.)* We are about to brave the storm in a skiff made of paper, and how it will end, God only knows. *(He signs with a flourish.)*

HOPKINS. That's a pretty large signature, Johnny.

HANCOCK. So Fat George in London can read it without his glasses! *(Laughter)* All right, gentlemen, step right up, don't miss your chance to commit treason!

(Laughter)

FRANKLIN. Hancock's right. This paper is our passport to the gallows. But there's no backing out now. If we don't hang together, we shall most assuredly hang separately.

(Laughter)

MCKEAN *(patting his ample middle).* In any case hanging won't be so bad—one snap and it'll be over *(Snap!)* just like that! But look at Read, there—he'll be dancing a jig long after I'm gone!

(Laughter)

HANCOCK. Gentlemen, forgive me if I don't join in the merriment, but if we're arrested now—my name is still the only one *on* the damn thing!

(More laughter, which subsides slowly as the COURIER *enters, deposits his dispatch on* THOMSON*'s desk, and departs, turning to glance at* JOHN *as he goes.)*

THOMSON. From the Commander, Army of the United Colonies—*(He stops, looks up.)* —Army of the United States—in New York, dispatch number one thousand, two hundred and nine. "To the Hon. Congress, John Hancock, President. Dear Sir: I can now report with some certainty that the eve of battle is near at hand. Toward this end I have ordered the evacuation of Manhattan and directed our defenses to take up stronger positions on the Brooklyn Heights. At the present time my forces consist entirely of Haslet's Delaware Militia and Smallwood's Marylanders, a total of five thousand troops to stand against *(He hesitates in horrified astonishment.)* twenty-five thousand of the enemy—and I begin to notice that many of them are lads under fifteen and old men, none of whom could truly be called soldiers. One personal note to Mr. Lewis Morris of New York—I must regretfully report that his estates have been totally destroyed but that I have taken the liberty of transporting Mrs. Morris and eight of the children to Connecticut and safety. The four older boys are now enlisted in the Continental Army. As I write these words, the enemy is plainly in sight beyond the river. How it will end only Providence can direct— but dear God! what brave men—I shall lose —before this business ends. Y'r ob'd't *(Drum roll)* G. Washington."

(There is a silence, during which MCNAIR *goes to the calendar and removes the final leaf, revealing: "JULY 4."*

The light outside has dimmed; it is becoming evening.)

HANCOCK *(finally).* Very well, gentlemen. McNair, go ring the bell. *(*MCNAIR *goes.)*

MORRIS *(rising)*. Mr. President!

HANCOCK. Mr. Morris?

MORRIS. To hell with New York—I'll sign it anyway.

HANCOCK. Thank you, Mr. Morris. Stephen, sit down.

HOPKINS *(who has been standing next to the Declaration on* THOMSON's *desk)*. No—I want t'remember each man's face as he signs.

HANCOCK. Very well, Mr. Thomson—

(As each name is called, the signer rises, comes to the Secretary's desk, signs, then stands to one side. The tolling Liberty Bell begins, offstage.)

THOMSON *(in measured tones)*.

New Hampshire, Dr. Josiah Bartlett.

Massachusetts, Mr. John Adams.

Rhode Island, Mr. Stephen Hopkins.

Connecticut, Mr. Roger Sherman.

New York, Mr. Lewis Morris.

New Jersey, the Reverend John Witherspoon.

Pennsylvania, Dr. Benjamin Franklin.

Delaware, Mr. Caesar Rodney.

*(*HANCOCK *takes the Declaration to the infirm* RODNEY, *then returns it to the table.)*

Mary-land, Mr. Samuel Chase.

Virginia, Mr. Thomas Jefferson.

North Carolina, Mr. Joseph Hewes.

South Carolina, Mr. Edward Rutledge.

Georgia, Dr. Lyman Hall.

(As the last man signs, the sound of the tolling Liberty Bell in the belfry above becomes almost deafening. Then the scene freezes for a brief instant, and the pose of the familiar Pine-Savage engraving of this occasion has been captured.

A scrim curtain falls, the scene visible through it. Then as the back-light dims and the curtain is lit from the front, it becomes opaque and reveals the lower half of the Declaration, featuring the signatures.)

CURTAIN

STICKS AND BONES

David Rabe

For TÂM

First presented at Villanova University in 1969. First presented on Broadway by the New York Shakespeare Festival at the John Golden Theatre in New York City on March 1, 1972, with the following cast:

ozzie Tom Aldredge
harriet Elizabeth Wilson
david Drew Snyder

rick Cliff DeYoung
sergeant major Hector Elias
the priest Charles Siebert
the girl Asa Gim

Directed by Jeff Bleckner
Scenery by Santo Loquasto
Costumes by Theoni V. Aldredge
Lighting by Ian Calderon

time: Autumn.
place: The family home.

CAUTION: Professionals and amateurs are hereby warned that *Sticks and Bones* is subject to royalty. It is fully protected under the copyright laws of the United States of America, the British Empire, including the Dominion of Canada, and all other countries of the Copyright Union. All rights, including professional, amateur, motion picture, recitation, lecturing, public reading, radio broadcasting, television, and the rights of translation into foreign languages are strictly reserved. In its present form the play is designed for the reading public only.

Sticks and Bones is slightly restricted. For amateur and stock rights application should be made to Samuel French, Inc., at 25 West 45 St., New York, N.Y. 10036, or at 7623 Sunset Blvd., Hollywood, Calif. 90046, or to Samuel French (Canada) Ltd., 27 Grenville St., Toronto 5, Ontario, Canada. For all rights other than amateur and stock, apply to Bohan-Neuwald Agency, Inc., 905 West End Avenue, New York, N.Y. 10025.

Acknowledgment is made to Charles E. Tuttle Co., Inc., for a selection from *Vietnamese Legends* by George F. Schultz.

David Rabe was a sensation and everyone knew it. Only the wise knew that it was going to be a difficult reputation to live down. In 1971 he became the flagship of Joseph Papp's American Shakespeare Festival. The boy most likely—the savior of American drama. Mr. Papp, an impresario extraordinary, and an entrepreneur with taste, love, and, significantly, aspiration, suggested that he was the best American playwright since Eugene O'Neill.

Rabe was born in 1940 in Dubuque, Iowa. He was the son of a schoolteacher and was educated in Dubuque, at Loras Academy and at Loras College, but the more significant part of his education came with his army service. He was drafted into the army in January 1965, and he served for two years, the final year being in Vietnam. This experience had a very large influence on his life.

On his release in 1967 he studied at a writing program at Villanova, and here he produced the first drafts of his first two plays, *The Basic Training of Pavlo Hummel* and *Sticks and bones.* For a time he worked on the New Haven *Register,* before the opportunity presented itself to him to become a full-time playwright and writer.

He met Joe Papp and his entire future changed. Mr. Papp first produced *Pavlo Hummel* on May 20, 1971, at the Newman Theater of the Shakespeare Festival's Public Theater complex on Lafayette Street. It was well received and ran for a total of 363 performances, which remains a record for the Lafayette Street complex.

His second play, *Sticks and Bones,* had originally been produced in a workshop production in Villanova. In 1971, in a revised version, it was staged at the Anspacher Theater, of the Public Theater Complex, while *Pavlo Hummel* was still running. It played 121 performances downtown and then on March 1, 1972, it was moved uptown to Broadway. After 245 performances at the Golden Theatre it closed on October 1, 1972.

During this time the play was operating at a consistent loss. However, Mr. Papp and his great nonprofit-making theatre subsidized it with money coming from his Broadway musical *Two Gentlemen of Verona.* There was also a television deal for *Sticks and Bones.* It was part of the package Mr. Papp had arranged with CBS Television. The television version was made, but then CBS, fearful of public opinion and aware of governmental orthodoxy, reneged on the arrangement and canceled the showing.

More controversy was lying in wait for Mr. Rabe and, of course, Mr. Papp. His final play in his Vietnam trilogy was *The Orphan,* suggested by the Oresteia. This was very unsuccessful with the press and, it seems, the public. It opened at the Anspacher Theater on April 18, 1973, and closed on May 13.

On November 8, 1973, David Rabe's latest play, *The Boom-Boom Room,* opened Joseph Papp's first season at the Vivian Beaumont Theater at Lincoln Center—it had been chosen as the first play to demonstrate Papp's and Lincoln Center's new stand as a platform for the new, young American playwright. Its reception was exceptionally mixed. Damned in some quarters, praised in others, it became a talking point of the season. Nevertheless, this analytical story of a go-go girl in Philadelphia won a Tony nomination in 1974. And, talking of Tonys, *Sticks and Bones* actually won a Tony in 1972.

In *Sticks and Bones* Mr. Rabe takes that all-American family institution, the soap opera —even the characters are called Ozzie, Harriet, and Rick—and teases out of it a recognition of national malaise. It is a play about Vietnam, and why America had its involvement in Vietnam.

A wounded veteran returns from the war. He has been blinded, and cannot adjust to his family. But his blindness is nothing to the moral blindness of the family and, by inference, the moral blindness of America. Mr. Rabe writes on many levels. Part of his play is symbolic, with the silent, ghostlike figure of the Vietnamese girl often present but unseen by all except the returning hero.

It is a play of its time, a play that very much represented America's fears of Vietnam. It was also a pre-Watergate play—which is politically significant. I ended my first-night Broadway notice with these words: "This American nightmare deserves attention. It is no sleeping pill, but a gloriously aware play that speaks with the tongue of youth for an old America now tired of the new America." That, I think, is the way it was.

AUTHOR'S NOTE

In any society there is an image of how the perfectly happy family should appear. It is this image that the people in this play wish to preserve above all else. Mom and Dad are not concerned that terrible events have occurred in the world, but rather that David has come home to behave in a manner that makes him no longer lovable. Thus he is keeping them from being the happy family they know they must be. He attacks those aspects of their self-image in which reside all their sense of value and sanity. But, curiously, one of the requisites of their self-image is that everything is fine, and, consequently, for a long time they must not even admit that David is attacking.

Yet everything is being communicated. Often a full, long speech is used in this play where in another, more "realistic" play there would be only a silence during which something was communicated between two people. Here the communication is obvious, because it is directly spoken. Consequently the ignoring of that which is communicated must be equally obvious. David throws a yelling, screaming tantrum over his feelings of isolation and Harriet confidently, cheerfully offers Ezy Sleep sleeping pills in full faith that they will solve his problem. The actors must try to look at what they are ignoring. They must not physically ignore things —turn their backs, avert their eyes, be busy with something else. The point is not that they do not physically see or hear, but that they psychologically ignore. Though they look right at things, though they listen closely, they do not see or hear. The harder they physically focus and concentrate on an event, the clearer their psychological state and the point and nature of the play will be, when in their next moments and speeches they verbally and emotionally ignore or miss what they have clearly looked at. In addition, the actors should try not to take the play overly seriously. The characters (except for David) do not take things seriously until they are forced to, and then they do it for as short a time as they can manage. Let the audience take seriously the jolly way the people go about the curious business of their lives.

Stylization, then, is the main production problem. The forms referred to during the time of writing *Sticks and Bones* were farce, horror movie, TV situation comedy. These should have their effect, though it must be remembered that they are where form was sought, not content. What is poetic in the writing must not be reinforced by deep feeling on the part of the actors, or the writing will hollow into pretension. In a more "realistic" play, where language is thinner, subtext must be supplied or there is no weight. Such deep support of *Sticks and Bones* will make the play ponderous. As a general rule, I think it is true that when an actor's first impulse (the impulse of all his training) is to make a heavy or serious adjustment in a scene, he should reverse himself and head for a lighthearted adjustment. If his first impulse is toward lightheartedness, perhaps he should turn toward a serious tack. A major premise of the play is that stubbing your own big toe is a more disturbing event than hearing of a stranger's suicide.

At the start, the family is happy and orderly, and then David comes home and he is unhappy. As the play progresses, he becomes happier and they become unhappier. Then, at the end, they are happy.

THE SONG OF TRANG TU
Alas! This life is like a flower that forms, then fades.
My wife is dead, so I bury her; if I were dead, she would remarry.
If I had been the first to depart, what a great burst of laughter would have poured forth.
In my fields a new laborer would work; on my horse a strange rider would appear.
My wife would belong to another; my children would have to bear anger and insults.
When I think of her, my heart tightens; but I look at her without weeping.
The world accuses me of insensibility and remorselessness;
I scoff at the world for nourishing vain griefs.
If I could restore the course of things by weeping,
My tears would flow for a thousand autumns without ceasing.
—*Vietnamese legend*

Life a funny thing.
—*Sonny Liston*

ACT ONE

Place: the family home. Darkness; silence. Slides appear on both sides of the stage: the first is a black-and-white medium close-up of a young man, mood and clothing of the early 1900s; he is lean, reasonably handsome, black hair parted in the center. Voices speak. They are slow and relaxed, with an improvisational quality.

1ST CHILD'S VOICE. Who zat?

MAN'S VOICE. Grandpa Jacob's father.

(New slide: group photo, same era, eight or ten people, all ages)

2ND CHILD'S VOICE. Look at 'em all!

1ST CHILD'S VOICE. How come they're all so serious?

(New slide: small boy, black hair, black knickers)

WOMAN'S VOICE. There's Grandpa Oswald as a little boy.

1ST CHILD'S VOICE. Grandpa?

(New slide: different boy, same pose)

WOMAN'S VOICE. And that's his brother Thomas. He died real young.

MAN'S VOICE. Scarlet fever.

(New slide: young girl, seventeen or eighteen)

And that's his sister Christina.

WOMAN'S VOICE. No, that's Grandma.

MAN'S VOICE. No.

WOMAN'S VOICE. Sure.

(New slide: OZZIE and HARRIET, young, 1940s era) There's the two of them.

MAN'S VOICE. Mmmmm, you're right, because that's Grandpa.

(New slide: two boys, five and nine years old)

WOMAN'S VOICE. The taller one's David, right?

(New slide: color close-up of DAVID from the last moment of the play, a stricken look)

1ST CHILD'S VOICE. What's that one?

MAN'S VOICE. Somebody sick.

1ST CHILD'S VOICE. Boy . . . !

(New slide: color photo of OZZIE, HARRIET, and FATHER DONALD, wearing a gym suit, his back to the camera, stands holding a basketball in one hand. OZZIE and HARRIET face him, one on either side.)

2ND CHILD'S VOICE. Oh, look at that one!

MAN'S VOICE. That's a funny one, isn't it.

WOMAN'S VOICE. That's one—I bet somebody took it—they didn't know it was going to be taken.

There is a bright flash and the stage is immediately illuminated. The set is an American home, very modern, with a quality of brightness, green walls, green rug. Stairs lead up to a bedroom—not lighted now—with a hallway leading off to the rest of the upstairs beyond. There is naturalness, yet a sense of space and, oddly, a sense also that this room, these stairs, belong in the gloss of an advertisement.

Downstage, a TV on wheels faces upstage, glowing, murmuring. OZZIE, HARRIET, and FATHER DONALD—a slightly rotund, serious man—are standing as they were in the slide last seen.

FATHER DONALD. A feel for it is the big thing. A feel for the ball. You know, I mean, bouncing it, dribbling it. You don't even look at it.

(Phone rings).

OZZIE. I'll get it.

FATHER DONALD. You can do it, Harriet. Give it a try. *(He bounces the ball to HARRIET.)*

OZZIE. Hello? . . .

FATHER DONALD *(as HARRIET catches the ball).* That a girl.

HARRIET. Oh, Father . . .

OZZIE *(hanging up).* Nobody there.

FATHER DONALD. That's what I'm telling you. You gotta help kids. Keeps 'em outa trouble. We help. Organized sports activities; it does 'em a world a good. You know that. And they need you.

OZZIE. I was a track and field man. Miler. Dash man—I told you.

(Phone rings.)

FATHER DONALD. But this is basketball season. *(He moves toward HARRIET and then the door, as OZZIE goes to the phone, says "Hello," then listens intently.)* You listen to me, you get that husband of yours out there to help us. It'll do him good. Tell him he'd be a good little guard. A play maker.

HARRIET. Oh, Father Donald, bless me.

FATHER DONALD. Of course. *(He blesses her, holding the ball under his left arm.)* Bye-bye.

HARRIET *(as FATHER DONALD goes).* Good-bye, Father. *(And she turns to look for a moment at OZZIE on the phone.)* Why aren't you talking? *(Silence: she is looking at him.)* Ozzie, why aren't you talking?

OZZIE *(slowly lowering the phone).* They're gone. They hung up.

HARRIET. You didn't say a word. You said nothing.

OZZIE. I said my name.

HARRIET. What did they want?

OZZIE. I said hello.

HARRIET. Were they selling something—is that what they wanted?

OZZIE. No, no.

HARRIET. Well . . . who was it?

OZZIE. What?

HARRIET. What are we talking about?

OZZIE. The government. It was . . . you know. . . .

HARRIET. Ozzie! *(In fear)* No!

OZZIE *(some weariness in him).* No, he's all right, he's coming home!

HARRIET. Why didn't you let me speak? Who was it?

OZZIE. No, no.

HARRIET. It was David.

OZZIE. No, somebody else. Some clerk. I don't know who.

HARRIET. You're lying.

OZZIE. No. There was just all this static— it was hard to hear. But he was coming home was part of it, and they had his records and papers but I couldn't talk to him directly even though he was right there, standing right there.

HARRIET. I don't understand.

OZZIE. That's what they said. . . . And he was fine and everything. And he wanted them to say hello for him. He'd lost some weight. He would be sent by truck. I could hear truck engines in the background—revving. They wanted to know my name. I told them.

HARRIET. No more?

OZZIE. They were very professional. Very brusque . . .

HARRIET. No more . . . at all?

(The front door opens and RICK comes in. And the door slams. He is young, seventeen. His hair is long and neat, with sideburns. His clothing is elaborate—very, very up to date. He carries a guitar on his shoulder.)

RICK. Hi, Mom. Hi, Dad.

HARRIET. Hi, Rick.

OZZIE. Hi, Rick.

HARRIET. Ohhh, Ricky, Ricky, your brother's on his way home. David's coming home!

OZZIE. We just got a call.

RICK. Ohhh, boy!

HARRIET. Isn't that wonderful? Isn't it? Your father talked to him. Oh, I bet you're starving. Sit, sit.

OZZIE. I talked to *somebody,* Rick.

HARRIET. There's fudge and ice cream in the fridge; would you like that?

RICK. Oh, yeah, and could I have some soda? *(She is on her way to the kitchen, nodding.)* Wow, some news. I'm awful hungry.

OZZIE. Never had a doubt. A boy like that —if he leaves, he comes back.

RICK *(as he picks up a comic book).* How about me? What if I left?

OZZIE. Absolutely. Absolutely. *(Silence. RICK reads the comic.)* I built jeeps . . . tanks, trucks.

RICK. What?

OZZIE. In the other war, I mean. Number Two. I worked on vehicles. Vehicles were needed and I worked to build them. Sometimes I put on wheels, tightened 'em up. I never . . . served . . . is what I mean. *(Slight pause)* They got all those people—soldiers, Rick—you see what I mean? They get 'em across the ocean, they don't have any jeeps or tanks or trucks, what are they gonna do, stand around? Wait for a bus on the beachhead? Call a cab?

RICK. No public transportation in a war.

OZZIE. That's right, that's right.

(HARRIET enters, carrying fudge and ice cream.)

HARRIET. Oh, Ozzie, Ozzie, do you remember—I just remembered that time David locked himself in that old icebox. We didn't know where he was. We looked all over. We couldn't find him. And then there was this icebox in this clearing . . . out in the middle. I'll bet you don't even remember.

OZZIE. Of course I remember.

HARRIET. And he leaped to us. So frightened.

OZZIE. He couldn't even speak—he couldn't even speak—just these noises.

HARRIET. Or that time he fell from that tree.

OZZIE. My God, he was somethin'! If he wasn't fallin', he was gettin' hit.

HARRIET. And then there was that day we went out into the woods. It was just all wind and clouds. We sailed a kite!

OZZIE. I'd nearly forgotten! . . .

RICK. Where was I?

HARRIET. You were just a baby, Rick. We had a picnic.

RICK. I'm gonna get some more soda, okay?

(HARRIET touches him as he passes.)

OZZIE. What a day that was. I felt great that day.

HARRIET. And then Hank came along. Hank Grenweller. He came from out of the woods calling that—

OZZIE. That's right.

HARRIET. He was happy.

OZZIE. We were all happy. Except he'd come to tell us he was going away, leaving. And then we had that race. Wasn't that the day?

HARRIET. I don't remember.

OZZIE. Hank and me! Hank Grenweller. A foot race. And I beat him. I did it; got him.

HARRIET. Noooo.

OZZIE. It was only inches, but—

HARRIET. Ozzie, he took it easy. He wasn't trying.

OZZIE. He had to do his very best. Always. Never less. That was one thing you knew— no matter what he did or said, it was meant and true. All those long talks. Do you ever miss him?

HARRIET. He was a fine strong man.

OZZIE. I don't know why he left.

HARRIET. Do you remember when he showed us this house?

OZZIE. I remember when he showed me you.

HARRIET. You know that's not true. If it was close—and it was—that race you ran— *(This is not loud: there is intimacy; they are near one another.)* I remember now—it was because he let it be—no other reason. We were all having fun. He didn't want to make you feel badly. He didn't want to ruin all the fun. You know that. You know you do.

RICK *(calling from the kitchen)*. You people want some fudge?

HARRIET. No, Rick.

OZZIE. I don't know he didn't try. I don't know that. *(He stares at* HARRIET.*)*

HARRIET. I think I'll be going up to bed; take a little nap.

RICK. Sleepy, Mom?

HARRIET. A little. *(She is crossing toward* OZZIE.*)*

RICK. That's a good idea then.

HARRIET. Call me.

RICK. Okay.

HARRIET. Do you know, the day he left? It was a winter day. November, Ozzie. *(She moves toward the stairs.)*

OZZIE. I know.

HARRIET. I prayed; did you know that? Now he's home.

OZZIE. It was a winter day.

HARRIET *(at the top of the stairs)*. I know.

RICK *(toying with his guitar)*. Night, Mom. *(She doesn't answer but disappears down the hall. He looks up and yells after her.)* Night, Mom!

HARRIET *(from off)*. Turn off the TV, somebody.

(RICK *crosses to the TV. He turns it off and wheels it back under the stairs.* OZZIE *watches. Silence.)*

OZZIE. I knew she was praying. She moves her lips. (RICK *does not look up. He begins, softly, to strum and tune the guitar.)* And something else—yes, sir, boy, oh, boy, I tell you, huh? What a day, huh? *(Slight pause)* They got seventeen hundred million men they gotta deal with, how they gonna do that without any trucks and tanks and jeeps? But I'm some kinda jerk because I wasn't out there blastin' away, huh? I was useful. I put my time to use. I been in fights. Fat Kramer. . . . How we used to fight! (RICK *strums some notes on the guitar.* OZZIE *stares at him.)* How come I'm restless? I . . . seen him do some awful, awful things, ole Dave. He was a mean . . . foul-tempered little baby. I'm only glad I was *here* when they sent him off to do his killing. That's right. *(Silence)* I feel like I swallowed ants, that's how restless I am. Outran a bowlin' ball one time. These guys bet me I couldn't do it and I did, beat it to the pins. Got a runnin' start, then the—*(A faint, strange rapping sound has stopped him, spun him around.)* Did you do that?

RICK. Somebody knockin'.

OZZIE. Knockin'?

RICK. The door, Dad.

OZZIE. Oh.

RICK. You want me to get it?

OZZIE. No, no. It's just so late. *(He moves for the door.)*

RICK. That's all right.

OZZIE. Sure. *(He opens the door just a crack, as if to stick his head around. But the door is thrust open and a man enters abruptly. He is black or of Spanish descent, and is dressed in the uniform of a sergeant major and wearing many campaign ribbons.)*

SGT. MAJOR. Excuse me. Listen to me. I'd like to speak to the father here. I'd like to know who . . . is the father? Could . . . you tell me the address?

OZZIE. May I ask who it is who's asking?

SGT. MAJOR. I am. I'm asking. What's the address of this house?

OZZIE. But I mean, who is it that wants to know?

SGT. MAJOR. We called; we spoke. Is this seven-seventeen Dunbar?

OZZIE. Yes.

SGT. MAJOR. What's wrong with you?

OZZIE. Don't you worry about me.

SGT. MAJOR. I have your son.

OZZIE. What?

SGT. MAJOR. Your son.

OZZIE. No.

SGT. MAJOR. But he is. I have papers, pictures, prints. I know your blood and his. This is the right address. Please. Excuse me. *(He pivots, reaches out into the dark.)* I am very busy. I have your father, David. *(He draws* DAVID *in—a tall, thin boy, blond and, in the shadows, wearing sunglasses and a uniform of dress greens. In his right hand is a long, white, red-tipped cane. He moves, probing the air, as the sergeant major moves him past* OZZIE *toward the couch, where he will sit the boy down like a parcel.)*

OZZIE. Dave? . . .

SGT. MAJOR. He's blind.

OZZIE. What?

SGT. MAJOR. Blind.

OZZIE. I don't . . . understand.

SGT. MAJOR. We're very sorry.

OZZIE *(realizing)*. Ohhhhh. Yes. Ohhhh. I see . . . sure. I mean, we didn't know. Nobody said it. I mean, sure, Dave, sure; it's all right—don't you worry. Rick's here, too, Dave—Rick, your brother, tell him hello.

RICK. Hi, Dave.

DAVID *(worried)*. You said . . . "father."

OZZIE. Well . . . there's two of us, Dave; two.

DAVID. Sergeant, you said "home." I don't think so.

OZZIE. Dave, sure.

DAVID. It doesn't feel right.

OZZIE. But it is, Dave—me and Rick—Dad and Rick. Harriet! *(Calling up the stairs)* Harriet!

DAVID. Let me touch their faces. . . . I can't see. *(Rising, his fear increasing)* Let me put my fingers on their faces.

OZZIE *(hurt, startled)*. What? Do what?

SGT. MAJOR. Will that be all right if he does that?

OZZIE. Sure. . . . Sure. . . . Fine.

SGT. MAJOR *(helping* DAVID *to* OZZIE*)*. It will take him time.

OZZIE. That's normal and to be expected. I'm not surprised. Not at all. We figured on this. Sure, we did. Didn't we, Rick?

RICK *(occupied with his camera, an Instamatic)*. I wanna take some pictures, okay? How are you, Dave?

DAVID. What room is this?

OZZIE. Middle room, Dave. TV room. TV's in—

HARRIET *(on the stairs)*. David! . . . Oh, David! . . . David . . .

(And OZZIE, *leaving* DAVID, *hurries toward the stairs and looks up at her as she falters, stops, stares.* RICK, *moving near, snaps a picture of her.)*

OZZIE. Harriet . . . don't be upset. . . . They say . . . Harriet, Harriet . . . he can't see! . . . Harriet . . . they say—he—can't . . . see. That man.

HARRIET *(standing very still)*. Can't see? What do you mean?

SGT. MAJOR. He's blind.

HARRIET. No. Who says? No, no.

OZZIE. Look at him. He looks so old. But it's nothing, Harriet, I'm sure.

SGT. MAJOR. I hope you people understand.

OZZIE. It's probably just how he's tired from his long trip.

HARRIET *(moving toward him)*. Oh, you're home now, David.

SGT. MAJOR *(with a large sheet of paper waving in his hands)*. Who's gonna sign this for me, Mister? It's a shipping receipt. I got to have somebody's signature to show you got him. I got to have somebody's name on the paper.

OZZIE. Let me. All right?

SGT. MAJOR. Just here and here, you see? Your name or mark three times. *(As they move toward a table and away from* HARRIET, *who is near* DAVID*)*.

OZZIE. Fine, listen, would you like some refreshments?

SGT. MAJOR. No.

OZZIE. I mean while I do this. Cake and coffee. Of course, you do.

SGT. MAJOR. No.

OZZIE. Sure.

SGT. MAJOR. No. I haven't time. I've got to get going. I've got trucks out there backed up for blocks. Other boys. I got to get on to Chicago, and some of them to Denver and Cleveland, Reno, New Orleans, Boston, Trenton, Watts, Atlanta. And when I get back they'll be layin' all over the grass; layin' there in pieces all over the grass, their backs been broken, their brains jellied, their insides turned into garbage. One-legged boys and no-legged boys. I'm due in Harlem; I got to get to the Bronx and Queens, Cincinnati, Saint Louis, Reading. I don't have time for coffee. I got deliveries to make all across this country.

DAVID *(with* HARRIET, *his hands on her*

face, a kind of realization). Nooooooo. . . . Sergeant . . . nooo; there's something wrong; it all feels wrong. Where are you? Are you here? I don't know these people!

SGT. MAJOR. That's natural, Soldier; it's natural you feel that way.

DAVID. Nooooo.

HARRIET *(attempting to guide him back to a chair).* David, just sit, be still.

DAVID. Don't you hear me?

OZZIE. Harriet, calm him.

DAVID. The air is wrong; the smells and sounds, the wind.

HARRIET. David, please, please. What is it? Be still. Please . . .

DAVID. GODDAMN YOU, SERGEANT, I AM LONELY HERE! I AM LONELY!

SGT. MAJOR. I got to go. *(And he pivots to leave.)*

DAVID *(following the sound of the sergeant major's voice).* Sergeant!

SGT. MAJOR *(whirling, bellowing).* You shut up. You piss-ass soldier, you shut the fuck up!

OZZIE *(walking to the sergeant major, putting his hand on the man's shoulder).* Listen, let me walk you to the door. All right? I'd like to take a look at that truck of yours. All right?

SGT. MAJOR. There's more than one.

OZZIE. Fine.

SGT. MAJOR. It's a convoy.

OZZIE. Good.

(They exit, slamming the door, and RICK, *running close behind them, pops it open, leaps out. He calls from off.)*

RICK. Sure are lots a trucks, Mom!

HARRIET *(as he re-enters).* Are there?

RICK. Oh, yeah. Gonna rain some more too. *(And turning, he runs up the stairs.)* See you in the morning. Night, Dave.

HARRIET. It's so good to have you here again; so good to see you. You look . . . just . . . *(OZZIE has slipped back into the room behind her, he stands, looking.)* fine. You look —*(She senses* OZZIE's *presence, turns, immediately, speaking.)* He bewilders you, doesn't he? *(And* OZZIE, *jauntily, heads for the stairs.)* Where are you going? *(He stops; he doesn't know. And she is happily sad now as she speaks—sad for poor* OZZIE *and* DAVID, *they are so whimsical, so childlike.)* You thought you knew what was right, all those years, teaching him sports and fighting. Do you understand what I'm trying to say? A

mother knows *things* . . . a father cannot ever know them. The measles, smallpox, cuts and bruises. Never have you come upon him in the night as he lay awake and staring . . . praying.

OZZIE. I saw him put a knife through the skin of a cat. I saw him cut the belly open.

DAVID. Noooo. . . .

HARRIET *(moving toward him in response).* David, David. . . .

DAVID. Ricky! *(There is a kind of accusation in this as if he were saying* RICKY *did the killing of the cat. He says it loudly and directly into her face.)*

HARRIET. He's gone to bed.

DAVID. I want to leave. *(There is furniture around him; he is caged. He pokes with his cane.)*

HARRIET. What is it?

DAVID. Help me. *(He crashes.)*

OZZIE. Settle down! Relax.

DAVID. I want to leave! I want to leave! I want to leave. I . . . *(And he smashes into the stairs, goes down, flails, pounding his cane.)* want to leave.

OZZIE AND HARRIET. Dave! David! Davey!

DAVID. . . . to leave! Please.

(He is on the floor, breathing. Long, long silence in which they look at him sadly, until HARRIET *announces the problem's solution.)*

HARRIET. Ozzie, get him some medicine. Get him some Ezy Sleep.

OZZIE. Good idea.

HARRIET. It's in the medicine cabinet; a little blue bottle, little pink pills. *(And when* OZZIE *is gone up the stairs, there is quiet. She stands over* DAVID.*)* It'll give you the sleep you need, Dave—the sleep you remember. You're our child and you're home. Our good . . . beautiful boy.

(And front door bursts open. There is a small girl in the doorway, an Asian girl. She wears the Vietnamese ao dai, *black slacks and white tunic slit up the sides. Slowly, she enters, carrying before her a small straw hat.* HARRIET *is looking at the open door.)*

HARRIET. What an awful . . . wind. *(She shuts the door.)*

(Blackout. Guitar music.)

(A match flickers as HARRIET *lights a candle in the night. And the girl silently moves from before the door across the floor to the stairs, where she sits, as* HARRIET *moves toward the stairs and* OZZIE, *asleep sitting up in a chair, stirs.)*

HARRIET. Oh! I didn't mean to wake you.

I lit a candle so I wouldn't wake you. *(He stares at her.)* I'm sorry.

OZZIE. I wasn't sleeping.

HARRIET. I thought you were.

OZZIE. Couldn't. Tried. Couldn't. Thinking. Thoughts running very fast. Trying to remember the night David . . . was made. Do you understand me? I don't know why. But the feeling in me that I had to figure something out and if only I could remember that night . . . the mood . . . I would be able. You're . . . shaking your head.

HARRIET. I don't understand.

OZZIE. No.

HARRIET. Good night. *(She turns and leaves* OZZIE *sitting there, gazing at the dark. Arriving at* DAVID's *door, she raps softly and then opens the door.* DAVID *is lying unmoving on the bed. She speaks to him.)* I heard you call.

DAVID. What?

HARRIET. I heard you call.

DAVID. I didn't.

HARRIET. Would you like a glass of warm milk?

DAVID. I was sleeping.

HARRIET *(after a slight pause).* How about that milk? Would you like some milk?

DAVID. I didn't call. I was sleeping.

HARRIET. I'll bet you're glad you didn't bring her back. Their skins are yellow, aren't they?

DAVID. What?

HARRIET. You're troubled, warm milk would help. Do you pray at all any more? If I were to pray now, would you pray with me?

DAVID. What . . . do you want?

HARRIET. They eat the flesh of dogs.

DAVID. I know. I've seen them.

HARRIET. Pray with me; pray.

DAVID. What . . . do . . . you want?

HARRIET. Just to talk, that's all. Just to know that you're home and safe again. Nothing else; only that we're all together, a family. You must be exhausted. Don't worry; sleep. *(She is backing into the hallway. In a whisper)* Good night. *(She blows out the candle and is gone, moving down the hall. Meanwhile the girl is stirring, rising, climbing from the living room up toward* DAVID's *room, which she enters, moving through a wall, and* DAVID *sits up.)*

DAVID. Who's there? *(As she drifts by, he waves the cane at the air.)* Zung? *(He stands.)* Chào, Cô Zung. *(He moves for the door, which he opens, and steps into the hall, leaving her behind him in the room.)* Zung. Chào, Cô Zung. *(And he moves off up the hallway. She follows.)* Zung! . . .

(Blackout. Music.)

Lights up. It is a bright afternoon, and OZZIE *is under the stairs with a screwdriver in his hand, poking about at the TV set.*

OZZIE. C'mon, c'mon. Ohhhh, c'mon, this one more game and ole State's Bowl-bound. C'mon, what is it? Ohhh, hey . . . ohhhhh. . . .

HARRIET *(entering from the kitchen carrying a tray with a bowl of soup and a glass of juice).* Ozzie, take this up to David; make him eat it.

OZZIE. Harriet, the TV is broke.

HARRIET. What?

OZZIE. There's a picture but no sound. I don't—*(Grabbing her by the arm, he pulls her toward a place before the set.)*

HARRIET. Stoppit, you're spilling the soup. *(She pulls free.)*

OZZIE. It's Sunday. I want to watch it. I turned it on, picture came on just like normal. I got the volume up full blast. *(Having set the tray down,* HARRIET *now shoves the TV set deeper under the stairs, deeper into the place where it is kept when not in use.)* Hey! I want to watch it!

HARRIET. I want to talk about David.

OZZIE. David's all right. *(He turns, crosses toward the phone, picks up the phone book.)* I'm gonna call the repairman.

HARRIET *(following him).* Ozzie, he won't eat. He just lays there. I offer him food, he won't eat it. No, no. The TV repairman won't help, you silly. *(She takes the phone book from him.)* He doesn't matter. There's something wrong with David. He's been home days and days and still he speaks only when spoken to; there's no light in his eye, no smile; he's not happy to be here and not once has he touched me or held me, nor has he even shaken your hand.

*(*OZZIE *flops down in a chair.)*

OZZIE. Oh, I don't mind that. Why should I mind—

HARRIET. And now he's talking to himself! What about that? Do you mind that? He mutters in his sleep.

OZZIE *(exasperated).* Ohhhhhh.

HARRIET. Yes. And it's not a regular kind of talking at all. It's very strange—very spooky.

OZZIE. Spooky?

HARRIET. That's right.

OZZIE. I never heard him.

HARRIET. You sleep too deeply. I took a candle and followed. I was in his room. He lay there, speaking.

OZZIE. Speaking what?

HARRIET. I don't know. I couldn't understand.

OZZIE. Was it words?

HARRIET. All kind of funny and fast.

OZZIE. Maybe prayer; praying.

HARRIET. No. No, it was secret. Oh, Ozzie, I know praying when I hear it and it wasn't praying he was doing. We meant our son to be so different—I don't understand—good and strong. And yet . . . perhaps he is. But there are moments when I see him . . . hiding . . . in that bed behind those awful glasses, and I see the chalkiness that's come into—

OZZIE *(headed for the kitchen, looking for juice to drink).* Those glasses are simply to ease his discomfort.

HARRIET. I hate them.

OZZIE. They're tinted glass and plastic. Don't be so damn suspicious.

HARRIET. I'm not, I'm not. It's seeing I'm doing, not suspicion. Suspicion hasn't any reasons. It's you—now accusing me for no reason when I'm only worried.

OZZIE *(returning from the kitchen, angered).* Where's my juice?

HARRIET. I want to talk.

OZZIE. The hell with David for a minute—I want some juice.

HARRIET. Shut up. You're selfish. You're so selfish.

OZZIE *(walking to the tray and juice, attempting to threaten her.)* I'll pour it on the floor. I'll break the glass.

(She turns to move to get the juice.)

HARRIET. A few years ago you might have done that kind of thing.

OZZIE. I woke up this morning, I could see so clearly the lovely way you looked when you were young. Beside me this morning, you were having trouble breathing. You kept . . . trying . . . to breathe. *(She approaches him to hand him the juice.)* What do you give me when you give me this?

HARRIET. I always looked pretty much as I do now. I never looked so different at all.

(DAVID appears from off upstairs, dressed in a red robe, and descends toward them.)

DAVID *(sounding happy, yet moving with urgency).* Good morning.

OZZIE. Oh, David! Ohhh, good morning. Hello. How do you feel this fine bright morning; how do you feel?

DAVID. He was a big man, wasn't he?

OZZIE. What?

DAVID. Hank. You were talking about Hank Grenweller. I thought you were.

OZZIE. Oh, yes. Hank. Very big. Big. A good fine friend, ole Hank.

DAVID. You felt when he was with you he filled the room.

OZZIE. It was the way he talked that did that. He boomed. His voice just boomed.

DAVID. He was here once and you wanted me to sit on his lap, isn't that right? It was after dinner. He was in a chair in the corner.

HARRIET. That's right.

DAVID. His hand was gone—the bone showed in the skin.

OZZIE. My God, what a memory—did you hear that, Harriet? You were only four or five. He'd just had this terrible, awful auto accident. His hand was hurt, not gone.

DAVID. No. It was congenital and none of us knew.

OZZIE. What?

DAVID. That hand. The sickness in it.

OZZIE. Congenital?

DAVID. Yes.

OZZIE. What do you mean? What do you think you mean?

DAVID. I'd like some coffee. *(He is seated now, but not without tension.)*

OZZIE. Hank's parents were good fine people, David.

DAVID. I know.

OZZIE. Well, what are you saying then?

DAVID. I'd like that coffee.

HARRIET. Of course. And what else with it?

DAVID. Nothing.

HARRIET. Oh, no, no, you've got to eat. To get back your strength. You must. Pancakes? How do pancakes sound? Or wheat cakes? Or there's eggs? And juice? Orange or prune: or waffles? I bet it's eggs you want. Over, David? Over easy? Scrambled?

DAVID. I'm only thirsty.

HARRIET. Well, all right then, coffee is what you'll have and I'll just put some eggs on the side; you used to love them so; remember? *(And, picking up the tray, she is off toward the kitchen. There is a pause.)*

OZZIE. I mean, I hate to harp on a thing, but I just think you're way off base on Hank, Dave. I just think you're dead wrong.

DAVID. He told me.

OZZIE. Who?

DAVID. Hank.

OZZIE. You . . . talked to Hank?

DAVID. In California. The day before they shipped me overseas.

OZZIE. No, no. He went to Georgia when he left here. We have all his letters postmarked Georgia.

DAVID *(with great urgency)*. It was California, I'm telling you. I was in the barracks. The C.Q. came to tell me there was someone to see me. It was Hank asking did I remember him? He'd seen my name on a list and wondered if I was Ozzie's boy. He was dying, he said. The sickness was congenital. We had a long, long talk.

OZZIE. But his parents were good fine people, David.

DAVID. Don't you understand? We spoke. Why did you make me think him perfect? It was starting in his face the way it started in his hand.

OZZIE. Oh! I didn't realize—I didn't know. You weren't blind. You could see. I didn't realize, Dave.

DAVID. What?

OZZIE. Did he wanna know about me? Did he mention me?

DAVID *(after thinking a moment)*. He asked . . . how you were.

OZZIE. Well, I'm fine. Sure. You told him.

HARRIET *(entering with a cup of coffee)*. It must be so wonderful for you to be home. It must just be so wonderful. A little strange, maybe . . . just a little, but time will take care of all that. It always does. You get sick and you don't know how you're going to get better and then you do. You just do. You must have terrible, awful, ugly dreams, though.

(Slight pause.)

OZZIE. She said you probably have terrible, awful, ugly dreams . . . though.

DAVID. What?

HARRIET. Don't you remember when we spoke last night?

DAVID. Who?

HARRIET. You called to me and then you claimed you hadn't.

DAVID. I didn't.

HARRIET. Ohhh, we had a lovely conversation, David. Of course you called. You called; we talked. We talked and laughed and it was very pleasant. Could I see behind your glasses?

DAVID. What? *(Moving away, crossing in flight from them)* Do . . . what?

HARRIET. See behind your glasses; see your eyes.

OZZIE. Me too, Dave; could we?

DAVID. My eyes . . . are ugly.

OZZIE. We don't mind.

HARRIET. We're your parents, David.

DAVID. I think it better if you don't.

OZZIE. And something else I've been meaning to ask you—why did you cry out against us that first night—to that stranger, I mean, that sergeant?

HARRIET. And you do dream. You do.

OZZIE. Sure. You needn't be ashamed.

HARRIET. We all do it. All of us.

OZZIE. We have things that haunt us.

HARRIET. And it would mean nothing at all—it would be of no consequence at all—if only you didn't speak.

DAVID. I don't understand.

OZZIE. She says she heard you, Dave.

HARRIET. I stood outside your door.

DAVID. No.

OZZIE. A terrible experience for her, Dave; you can see that.

HARRIET. Whatever it is, David, tell us.

OZZIE. What's wrong?

DAVID. No.

HARRIET. We'll work it out.

OZZIE. You can't know how you hurt us.

DAVID. I wasn't asleep.

OZZIE. Not until you have children of your own.

HARRIET. What? *(Silence)* Not . . . asleep? . . .

DAVID. I was awake; lying awake and speaking.

OZZIE. Now wait a minute.

DAVID. Someone was with me—there in the dark—I don't know what's wrong with me.

HARRIET. It was me. I was with you. There's nothing wrong with you.

DAVID. No. In my room. I could feel it.

HARRIET. I was there.

(And they have him cornered in another chair.)

DAVID. No.

OZZIE. Harriet, wait!

HARRIET. What are you saying, "Wait"? I was there.

OZZIE. Oh, my God. Oh, Christ, of course. Oh, Dave, forgive us.

HARRIET. What?

OZZIE. Dave, I understand. It's buddies left behind.

DAVID. No.

OZZIE. But I do. Maybe your mother can't but I can. Men serving together in war, it's a powerful thing—and I don't mean to sound like I think I know it—all of it, I mean—I don't, I couldn't—but I respect you having had it—I almost envy you having had it, Dave. I mean . . . true comradeship.

DAVID. Dad . . .

OZZIE. I had just a taste—not that those trucks and factory were any battlefield, but there was a taste of it there—in the jokes we told and the way we saw each other first in the morning. We told dirty, filthy jokes, Dave. We shot pool, played cards, drank beer late every night, singing all these crazy songs.

DAVID. That's not right, Dad.

OZZIE. But all that's nothing, I'm sure, to what it must be in war. The things you must touch and see. Honor. You much touch honor. And then one of you is hurt, wounded . . . made blind . . .

DAVID. No. I had fear of all the kinds of dying that there are when I went from here. And then there was this girl with hands and hair like wings. *(The poetry is like a thing possessing him, a frenzy in which he does not know where he is.)* There were candles above the net of gauze under which we lay. Lizards. Cannon could be heard. A girl to weigh no more than dust.

HARRIET. A nurse, right . . . David?

OZZIE. No, no, one of them foreign correspondents—English, maybe, or French.

(Silence).

HARRIET. Oh, how lovely! A Wac or Red Cross girl? . . .

DAVID. No.

OZZIE. Redhead or blonde, Dave?

DAVID. No.

(HARRIET is shaken.)

OZZIE. I mean, what you mean is you whored around a lot. Sure. You whored around. That's what you're saying. You banged some whores . . . had some intercourse. Sure, I mean, that's my point. (DAVID, *turning away, seems about to rise).* Now Dave, take it easy. What I mean is, okay, sure, you shacked up with. I mean, hit on. Hit on, Dave. Dicked. Look at me. I mean, you pronged it, right? Right? Sure, attaboy. *(Patting* DAVID *on the shoulder)* I mean, it's like going to the bathroom. All glands and secretions. Look, Dave, what are you doing? *(A rage is building in* DAVID, *tension forcing him to stand, his cane pressing the floor.)* We can talk this over. We can talk this over. (DAVID, *heading for the stairs, crashes into* OZZIE.) Don't—goddamnit, don't walk away from me. *(He pushes* DAVID *backward.)* What the hell do you think you're doing? It's what you

did. Who the hell you think you are? You screwed it. A yellow whore. Some yellow ass. You put in your prick and humped your ass. You screwed some yellow fucking whore! *(He has chased* DAVID *backward,* HARRIET *joining in with him.)*

HARRIET. That's right, that's right. You were lonely and young and away from home for the very first time in your life, no white girls around—

DAVID. They are the color of the earth, and what is white but winter and the earth under it like a suicide? (HARRIET's *voice is a high humming in her throat.)* Why didn't you tell me what I was?

(And HARRIET *vomits, her hands at her mouth, her back turning. There is a silence. They stand.* OZZIE *starts toward her, falters, starts, reaches, stops.)*

OZZIE. Why . . . don't . . . you ask her to cook something for you, David, will you? Make her feel better . . . okay.

DAVID. I think . . . some eggs might be good, Mom.

OZZIE *(wanting to help her).* Hear that, Harriet? David wants some eggs.

HARRIET. I'm *all right.*

OZZIE. Of course you are. *(Patting her tenderly, he offers his clean white handkerchief.)* Here, here: wipe your mouth; you've got a little something—on the corner, left side. That's it. Whattayou say, David?

HARRIET. What's your pleasure, David?

DAVID. Scrambled.

OZZIE. There you go. Your specialty, his pleasure. (OZZIE, *between them, claps his hands; off she goes for the kitchen.* OZZIE, *looking about the room like a man in deep water looking for something to keep him afloat, sees a pack of cigarettes.)* How about a cigarette? *(Running to grab them, show them)* Filter, see, I switched. Just a little after you left, and I just find them a lot smoother, actually. I wondered if you'd notice. *(And speaking now, his voice and manner take on a confidence; he demonstrates; he is self-assured.)* The filter's granulated. It's an off-product of corn husks. I light up—I feel like I'm on a ship at sea. Isn't that one hell of a good tasting cigarette? Isn't that one beautiful goddamn cigarette?

(HARRIET enters with two bowls. One has a grapefruit cut in half; the second has eggs and a spoon sticking out.)

HARRIET. Here's a little grapefruit to tide you over till I get the eggs. *(And now she stirs* the eggs in preparation for scrambling them.) Won't be long, I promise—but I was just wondering, wouldn't it be nice if we could all go to church tonight? All together and we could make a little visit in thanksgiving of your coming home. (DAVID is putting his cigarette out in his grapefruit. They see.) I wouldn't ask that it be long—just— (He is rising now, dropping the grapefruit on the chair.) I mean, we could go to whatever saint you wanted, it wouldn't . . . matter . . . (He has turned his back, is walking toward the stairs.) Just in . . . just out . . . (He is climbing the stairs.) David.

OZZIE. Tired . . . Dave? (They watch him plodding unfalteringly toward his room.) Where you going . . . bathroom?

DAVID. No.

OZZIE. Oh. (DAVID disappears into his room and HARRIET whirls and heads for the telephone. OZZIE, startled, turns to look at her.) Harriet, what's up?

HARRIET. I'm calling Father Donald.

OZZIE. Father Donald?

HARRIET (dialing). We need help, I'm calling for help.

OZZIE. Now wait a minute. No; oh, no, we—

HARRIET. Do you still refuse to see it? He was involved with one of them. You know what the Bible says about those people. You heard him.

OZZIE. Just not Father Donald; please, please. That's all I ask—just— (She is obstinate, he sees. She turns her back waiting for someone to answer.) Why must everything be personal vengeance?

(The front door pops open and in comes bounding RICK, guitar upon his back.)

RICK (happy). Hi, Mom. Hi, Dad.

HARRIET (waiting, telephone in hand—overjoyed). Hi, Rick!

RICK (happy). Hi, Mom.

OZZIE (feeling fine). Hi, Rick.

RICK. Hi, Dad.

OZZIE. How you doin', Rick? (He is happy to see good ole regular RICK.)

RICK. Fine, Dad. You?

OZZIE. Fine.

RICK. Good.

HARRIET. I'll get you some fudge in just a minute, Rick!

RICK. Okay. How's Dave doin', Dad? (He is fiddling with his camera.)

OZZIE. Dave's doin' fine, Rick.

RICK. Boy, I'm glad to hear that. I'm really

glad to hear that, because, boy, I'll sure be glad when everything's back to the regular way. Dave's too serious, Dad; don't you think so? That's what I think. Whattayou think, Dad? (He snaps a picture of OZZIE, who is posing, smiling, while HARRIET waves angrily at them.)

HARRIET. SHHHHHHH! Everybody! (And then, more pleasantly she returns to the phone.) Yes, yes. Oh, Father, I didn't recognize your voice. No, I don't know who. Well, yes, it's about my son, Father, David. Yes. Well, I don't know if you know it or not, but he just got back from the war and he's troubled. Deeply. Yes. (As she listens silently for a moment, RICK, crouching, snaps a picture of her. She tries to wave him away.) Deeply. (He moves to another position, another angle, and snaps another picture.) Deeply, yes. Oh. So do you think you might be able to stop over some time soon to talk to him or not? Father, any time that would be convenient for you. Yes. Oh, that would be wonderful. Yes. Oh, thank you. And may God reward you, Father. (Hanging up the phone, she stands a moment, dreaming.)

OZZIE. I say to myself, what does it mean that he is my son? How the hell is it that . . . he . . . is my son? I mean, they say something of you joined to something of me and became . . . him . . . but what kinda goddamn thing is that? One mystery replacing another? Mystery doesn't explain mystery!

RICK (scarcely looking up from his comic). Mom, hey, c'mon, how about that fudge, will ya?

HARRIET. Ricky, oh, I'm sorry. I forgot.

OZZIE. They've got . . . diseases! . . .

HARRIET (having been stopped by his voice). What? . . .

OZZIE. Dirty, filthy diseases. They got 'em. Those girls. Infections. From the blood of their parents into the very fluids of their bodies. Malaria, TB. An actual rot alive in them . . . gonorrhea, syphilis. There are some who have the plague. He touched them. It's disgusting. It's—

RICK. Mom, I'm starving, honest to God; and I'm thirsty too.

HARRIET (as she scurries off, clapping, for the kitchen). Yes, of course. Oh, oh.

RICK. And bring a piece for Dad, too; Dad looks hungry.

OZZIE. No.

RICK. Sure, a big sweet chocolate piece of fudge.

OZZIE. No. Please. I don't feel well.

RICK. It'll do you good.

HARRIET *(entering with fudge and milk in each hand).* Ricky, here, come here.

RICK *(hurrying toward her).* What?

HARRIET *(hands him fudge and milk).* Look good? *(And she moves toward* OZZIE.)

OZZIE. And something else—maybe it could just be that he's growing away from us, like we did ourselves, only we thought it would happen in some other way, some lesser way.

HARRIET *(putting the fudge and milk into* OZZIE's *hands).* What are you talking about, "going away"? He's right upstairs.

OZZIE. I don't want that.

HARRIET. You said you did.

OZZIE. He said I did.

RICK *(having gobbled the fudge and milk).* You want me to drive you, Mom?

HARRIET. Would you, Ricky, please?

RICK *(running).* I'll go around and get the car.

HARRIET *(scolding, as* OZZIE *has put the fudge and milk down on a coffee table).* It's all cut and poured, Ozzie; it'll just be a waste.

OZZIE. I don't care.

HARRIET. You're so childish. *(She marches off toward the front door, where she takes a light jacket from a hook, starts to slip it on.)*

OZZIE. Don't you know I could throw you down onto this floor and make another child live inside you . . . now! . . .

HARRIET. I . . . doubt that . . . Ozzie.

OZZIE. You want me to do it?

HARRIET *(going out the door).* Ohhh, Ozzie, Ozzie.

OZZIE. Sure. Bye-bye. Bye-bye. *(After a pause)* They think they know me and they know nothing. They don't know how I feel. . . . How I'd like to beat Ricky with my fists till his face is ugly! How I'd like to banish David to the streets. . . . How I'd like to cut her tongue from her mouth. (DAVID *moves around upstairs.)* I was myself. *(And now he is clearly speaking to the audience, making them see his value. They are his friends and buddies, and he talks directly to them.)* I lived in a time beyond anything they can ever know —a time beyond and separate, and I was nobody's goddamn father and nobody's goddamn husband! I was myself! And I could run. I got a scrapbook of victories, a bag of medals and ribbons. In the town in which I lived my name was spoken in the factories and in the fields all around because I was the best there was. I'd beaten the finest anybody

had to offer. Summer . . . I would sit out on this old wood porch on the front of our house and my strength was in me, quiet and mine. Round the corner would come some old Model T Ford and scampering up the walk this ancient, bone-stiff, buck-toothed farmer, raw as winter and cawing at me like a crow: they had one for me. Out at the edge of town. A runner from another county. My shoes are in a brown-paper bag at my feet. I snatch 'em up. I set out into the dusk, easy as breathing. There's an old white fence and we run for the sun. . . . For a hundred yards or a thousand yards or a thousand thousand. It doesn't matter. Whatever they want. We run the race they think their specialty and I beat them. They sweat and struggle; I simply glide on, one step beyond, no matter what their effort, and the sun bleeds before me. . . . We cross rivers and deserts; we clamber over mountains. I run the races the farmers arrange and win the bets they make. And then a few days after the race, money comes to me anonymously in the mail; but it's not for the money that I run. In the fields and factories they speak my name when they sit down to their lunches. If there's a prize to be run for, it's me they send for. It's to be the-one-sent-for that I run.

(DAVID, *entering from his room, has listened to the latter part of this.)*

DAVID. And . . . then . . . you left.

OZZIE *(whirling to look at him).* What?

DAVID. I said . . . "And . . . then you left." That town.

OZZIE. Left?

DAVID. Yes. Went away; traveled.

OZZIE. No. What do you mean?

DAVID. I mean, you're no longer there; you're here . . . now.

OZZIE. But I didn't really *leave* it. I mean, not *leave.* Not really.

DAVID. Of course you did. Where are you?

OZZIE. That's not the point, Dave. Where I am isn't the point at all.

DAVID. But it is. It's everything; all that other is gone. Where are you going?

OZZIE. Groceries. Gotta go get groceries. You want anything at the grocery store? *(He looks at his watch.)* It's late. I gotta get busy.

DAVID *(as* OZZIE *exits).* That's all right, Dad. That's fine. *(Blackout.)*

The lights rise to brightness, and RICK *enters from the kitchen, carrying his guitar, plinking a note or two as* HARRIET *emerges also from the kitchen, carrying a bowl of chips and a tray of drinks, and* OZZIE *appears upstairs, coming down the hall carrying an 8-mm movie projector already loaded with film.*

HARRIET. Tune her up now, Rick.

OZZIE. What's the movie about anyway?

HARRIET. It's probably scenery, don't you think?—trees and fields and those little ponds. Everything over there's so green and lovely. Enough chips, Ricky?

(All during this, they scurry about with their many preparations.)

RICK. We gonna have pretzels too? 'Cause if there's both pretzels and chips then there's enough chips.

OZZIE *(at the projector)*. David shoot it or somebody else? . . . Anybody know? I tried to peek—put a couple feet up to the light . . .

HARRIET. What did you see?

OZZIE. Nothing. Couldn't.

HARRIET. Well, I'll just bet there's one of those lovely little ponds in it somewhere.

OZZIE. Harriet . . . you know when David was talking about that trouble in Hank's hand being congenital, what did you think? You think it's possible? I don't myself. I mean, we knew Hank well. I think it's just something David got mixed up about and nobody corrected him. What do you think? Is that what you think? Whatsamatter? Oh. *(He stops, startled, as he sees she is waving at him. Looking up the stairs, which are behind him, he sees* DAVID *is there, preparing to descend.* DAVID *wears his robe and a bright-colored tie.)*

HARRIET. Hello!

OZZIE. Oh. Hey, oh, let me give you a hand. Yes. Yes. You look good. Good to see you. *(And he is on the move to* DAVID *to help him down the stairs.)* Yes, sir. I think, all things considered, I think we can figure we're over the hump now and it's all downhill and good from here on in. I mean, we've talked things over, Dave, what do you say? The air's been cleared, that's what I mean—the wounds acknowledged, the healing begun. It's the ones that aren't acknowledged—the ones that aren't talked over—they're the ones that do the deep damage. That's always what happens.

HARRIET *(moving to* DAVID*)*. I've baked a cake, David. Happy, happy being home.

*(*DAVID*, on his own, finds his way to a chair and sits.)*

OZZIE. And we've got pop and ice and chips, and Rick is going to sing some songs.

HARRIET. Maybe we can all sing along if we want.

RICK. Anything special you'd like to hear, Dave?

OZZIE. You just sing what you know, Rick; sing what you care for and you'll do it best. *(And he and* HARRIET *settle down upon the couch to listen, all smiles.)*

RICK. How about "Baby, When I Find You"?

HARRIET. Ohhh, that's such a good one.

RICK. Dave, you just listen to me go! I'm gonna build! *(He plays an excited lead into the song.)* I'm gonna build, build, build. *(And he sings.)*

Baby, when I find you,
never gonna stand behind you,
gonna, gonna lead
softly at the start,
gently by the heart,
Sweet . . . Love! . . .

Slipping softly to the sea
you and me both mine
wondrous as a green
growing forest vine. . . .

Baby, when I find you,
never gonna stand behind you,
gonna, gonna lead you
softly at the start,
gently by the heart,
Sweet . . . Love! . . .
Baby, when I find you.

OZZIE *(as both he and* HARRIET *clap and laugh)*. Ohhh, great, Rick, great. You burn me up with envy, honest to God.

HARRIET. It was just so wonderful. Oh, thank you so much.

RICK. I just love to do it so much, you know?

OZZIE. Has he got something goin' for him, Dave? Huh? Hey! You don't even have a drink. Take this one; take mine!

(Now they hurry back and forth from DA-VID *to the table.)*

HARRIET. And here's some cake.

OZZIE. How 'bout some pretzels, Dave?

RICK. Tell me what you'd like to hear.

DAVID. I'd like to sing.

(This stops them. They stare at DAVID *for a beat of silence.)*

RICK. What?

OZZIE. What's that?

DAVID. I have something I'd like to sing.

RICK. Dave, you don't sing.

DAVID *(reaching at the air)*. I'd like to use the guitar, if I could.

HARRIET. What are you saying?

OZZIE. C'mon, you couldn't carry a tune in a bucket and you know it. Rick's the singer, Rick and your mom. *(Not really listening, thinking that his father has gotten everything back to normal,* RICK *strums and strums the guitar, drifting nearer to* DAVID.*)* C'mon, let's go, that all we're gonna hear?

DAVID. You're so selfish, Rick. Your hair is black; it glistens. You smile. You sing. People think you are the songs you sing. They never see you. Give me the guitar. *(And he clamps his hand closed on the guitar, stopping the music.)*

RICK. Mom, what's wrong with Dave?

DAVID. Give me.

RICK. Listen, you eat your cake and drink your drink, and if you still wanna, I'll let you.

*(*DAVID *stands, straining to take the guitar.)*

DAVID. Now!

HARRIET. Ozzie, make David behave.

OZZIE. Don't you play too roughly. . . .

DAVID. Ricky! . . .

RICK. I don't think he's playing, Dad.

OZZIE *(as* DAVID, *following* RICK, *bumps into a chair).* You watch out what you're doing . . .

*(*DAVID *drops his glass on the floor, grabs the guitar.)*

RICK. You got cake all over your fingers, you'll get it all sticky, the strings all sticky— *(Struggling desperately to keep his guitar)* Just tell me what you want to hear, I'll do it for you!

HARRIET. What is it? What's wrong?

DAVID. GIVE ME! *(With great anger)* GIVE ME!

OZZIE. David! . . .

(And DAVID *wrenches the guitar from* RICK*'s hands, sends* RICK *sprawling, and loops the strap of the guitar over his shoulder, smiling, smiling.)*

HARRIET. Ohhhh, no, no, you're ruining everything. What's wrong with you?

OZZIE. I thought we were gonna have a nice party—

DAVID. I'm singing! We are!

OZZIE. No, no, I mean a *nice* party—one where everybody's happy!

DAVID. I'm happy. I'm singing. Don't you see them? Don't you see them?

OZZIE. Pardon, Dave?

HARRIET. What . . . are you saying?

DAVID *(changing, turning).* I have some movies. I thought you . . . knew.

HARRIET. Well . . . we . . . do.

OZZIE. Movies?

DAVID. Yes, I took them.

RICK. I thought you wanted to sing.

OZZIE. I mean, they're what's planned, Dave. That's what's up. The projector's all wound and ready. I don't know what you had to get so angry for.

HARRIET. Let's get everything ready.

OZZIE. Sure, sure. No need for all that yelling. *(He moves to set up the projector.)*

DAVID. I'll narrate.

OZZIE. Fine, sure. What's it about anyway?

HARRIET. Are you in it?

OZZIE. Ricky, plug it in. C'mon, c'mon.

DAVID. It's a kind of story.

RICK. What about my guitar?

DAVID. No.

OZZIE. We oughta have some popcorn, though.

HARRIET. Oh, yes, what a dumb movie house, no popcorn, huh, Rick!

*(*RICK *switches off the lights.)*

OZZIE. Let her rip, Dave. *(*DAVE *turns on the projector;* OZZIE *is hurrying to a seat.)* Ready when you are, C.B.

HARRIET. Shhhhhhh!

OZZIE *(a little child playing).* Let her rip, C.B. I want a new contract, C.B.

(The projector runs for a moment. [*Note: In proscenium, a screen should be used if possible, or the film may be allowed to seem projected on the fourth wall; in three-quarter or round the screen may be necessary. If the screen is used, nothing must show upon it but a flickering of green.*]*)*

HARRIET. Ohhh, what's the matter? It didn't come out, there's nothing there.

DAVID. Of course there is.

HARRIET. Noooo. . . . It's all funny.

DAVID. Look.

OZZIE. It's underexposed, Dave.

DAVID *(moving nearer).* No. Look.

HARRIET. What?

DAVID. They hang in the trees. They hang by their wrists half-severed by the wire.

OZZIE. Pardon me, Dave?

HARRIET. I'm going to put on the lights.

DAVID. NOOOOOO! LOOK! They hang in the greenish haze afflicted by insects; a woman and a man, middle aged. They do not shout or cry. He is too small. Look—he seems all bone, shame in his eyes; his wife even here come with him, skinny also as a broom and her hair is straight and black, hanging to mask her eyes.

(The girl, ZUNG, *drifts into the room.)*

OZZIE. I don't know what you're doing, David; there's nothing there.

DAVID. LOOK! *(And he points.)* They are all bone and pain, uncontoured and ugly but for the peculiar melon-swelling in her middle which is her pregnancy, which they do not see—look! these soldiers who have found her —as they do not see that she is not dead but only dying until saliva and blood bubble at her lips. Look. . . . Yet . . . she dies. Though a doctor is called in to remove the bullet-shot baby she would have preferred . . . to keep since she was dying and it was dead. *(And* ZUNG *silently, drifting, departs.)* In fact, as it turned out they would have all been better off left to hang as they had been strung on the wire—he with the back of his head blown off and she, the rifle jammed exactly and deeply up into her, with a bullet fired directly into the child living there. For they ended each buried in a separate place; the husband by chance alone was returned to their village, while the wife was dumped into an alien nearby plot of dirt, while the child, too small a piece of meat, was burned. Put into fire, as the shattered legs and arms cut off of men are burned. There's an oven. It is no ceremony. It is the disposal of garbage! . . .

*(*HARRIET *gets to her feet, marches to the projector, pulls the plug, begins a little lecture.)*

HARRIET. It's so awful the things those yellow people do to one another. Yellow people hanging yellow people. Isn't that right? Ozzie, I told you—animals—Christ, burn them. David, don't let it hurt you. All the things you saw. People aren't themselves in war. I mean like that sticking that gun into that poor woman and then shooting that poor little baby, that's not human. That's inhuman. It's inhuman, barbaric and uncivilized and inhuman.

DAVID. I'm thirsty.

HARRIET. For what? Tell me. Water? Or would you like some milk? How about some milk?

DAVID *(shaking his head)*. No.

HARRIET. Or would you like some orange juice? All golden and little bits of ice.

OZZIE. Just all those words and that film with no picture and these poor people hanging somewhere—so you can bring them home like this house is a meat house—

HARRIET. Oh, Ozzie, no, it's not that—no —he's just young, a young boy . . . and he's been through terrible, terrible things and now he's home, with his family he loves, just trying to speak to those he loves—just—

DAVID. Yes! That's right. Yes. What I mean is, yes, of course, that's what I am—a young . . . blind man in a room . . . in a house in the dark, raising nothing in a gesture of no meaning toward two voices who are not speaking . . . of a certain . . . incredible . . . *connection!*

(All stare. RICK *leaps up, running for the stairs.)*

RICK. Listen, everybody, I hate to rush off like this, but I gotta. Night.

HARRIET. Good night, Rick.

OZZIE *(simultaneously)*. Good night.

*(*DAVID *moves toward the stairs, looking upward.)*

DAVID. Because I talk of certain things . . . don't think I did them. Murderers don't even know that murder happens.

HARRIET. What are you saying? No, no. We're a family, that's all—we've had a little trouble—David, you've got to stop—please —no more yelling. Just be happy and home like all the others—why can't you?

DAVID. You mean take some old man to a ditch of water, shove his head under, talk of cars and money till his feeble pawing stops, and then head on home to go in and out of doors and drive cars and sing sometimes. I left her like you wanted . . . where people are thin and small all their lives. *(The beginning of realization)* Or did . . . you . . . think it was a . . . place . . . like this? Sinks and kitchens all the world over? Is that what you believe? Water from faucets, light from wires? Trucks, telephones, TV. Ricky sings and sings, but if I were to cut his throat, he would no longer and you would miss him— you would miss his singing. We are hoboes! *(And it is the first time in his life he has ever thought these things.)* We make signs in the dark. You know yours. I understand my own. We share . . . coffee! *(There is nearly joy in this discovery: a hint of new freedom that might be liberation. And somewhere in the thrill of it he has whirled, his cane has come near to* OZZIE, *frightening him, though* HARRIET *does not notice. Now* DAVID *turns, moving for the stairs, thinking.)* I'm going up to bed . . . now. . . . I'm very . . . tired.

OZZIE. Well . . . you have a good sleep, Son. . . .

DAVID. Yes, I think I'll sleep in.

OZZIE. You do as you please. . . .

DAVID. Good night.

HARRIET. Good night.

OZZIE. Good night.

HARRIET. Good night. *(Slight pause)* You get a good rest. *(Silence)* Try . . . *(Silence. DAVID has gone into his room. OZZIE and HARRIET stand.)* I'm . . . hungry . . . Ozzie. . . . Are you hungry?

OZZIE. Hungry? . . .

HARRIET. Yes.

OZZIE. No. Oh, no.

HARRIET. How do you feel? You look a little peaked. Do you feel all right?

OZZIE. I'm fine; I'm fine.

HARRIET. You look funny.

OZZIE. Really. No. How about yourself?

HARRIET. I'm never sick; you know that. Just a little sleepy.

OZZIE. Well . . . that's no wonder. It's been a long day.

HARRIET. Yes, it has.

OZZIE. No wonder.

HARRIET. Good night. *(She is climbing the stairs toward bed.)*

OZZIE. Good night.

HARRIET. Don't stay up too late now.

OZZIE. Do you know when he pointed that cane at me, I couldn't breathe. I felt . . . for an instant I . . . might never breathe. . . .

HARRIET. Ohhh . . . I'm so sleepy. So . . . sooooo sleepy. Aren't you sleepy?

OZZIE *(to make her answer).* Harriet! I couldn't breathe.

HARRIET. WHAT DO YOU WANT? TEACHING HIM SPORTS AND FIGHT-ING. *(This moment—one of almost a primal rage— should be the very first shattering of her motherly self-sacrificing image.)* WHAT . . . OZZIE . . . DO YOU WANT?

OZZIE. Well . . . I was . . . wondering, do we have any aspirin down here . . . or are they all upstairs?

HARRIET. I thought you said you felt well.

OZZIE. Well, I do, I do. It's just a tiny headache. Hardly worth mentioning.

HARRIET. There's aspirin in the desk.

OZZIE *(crossing).* Fine. Big drawer?

HARRIET. Second drawer, right-hand side.

OZZIE. Get me a glass of water, would you, please?

HARRIET. Of course. *(She gets a glass from a nearby table, a drink left over from the party, and hands it to him.)*

OZZIE. Thank you. It's not much of a headache, actually. Actually it's just a tiny headache. *(He pops the tablets into his mouth and drinks to wash them down.)*

HARRIET. Aspirin makes your stomach bleed. *(He tries to keep from swallowing the aspirin, but it is too late.)* Did you know that? Nobody knows why. It's part of how it works. It just does it, makes you bleed. This extremely tiny series of hemorrhages in those delicate inner tissues. *(He is staring at her: there is vengeance in what she is doing.)* It's like those thin membranes begin, in a very minor way, to sweat blood and you bleed; inside yourself you bleed. *(She crosses away.)*

OZZIE. That's not true. None of that. You made all that up. . . . Where are you going? *(With a raincoat on, she is moving out the front door.)* I mean . . . are you going out? Where . . . are you off to? *(She is gone.)* Goddamnit, there's something going on around here, don't you want to know what it is? *(Yelling at the shut door)* I want to know what it is. *(Turning, marching to the phone, dialing)* I want to know what's going on around here. I want to; I do. Want to—got to. Police. That's right, goddamnit—I want one of you people to get on out to seven-seventeen Dunbar and do some checking, some checking at seven-seventeen—What? Ohhh—*(Hissing)* Christ! . . . *(And he is pulling a handkerchief from his pocket, and covering the mouthpiece.)* I mean, they got a kid living there who just got back from the war and something's going on and I want to know what it. . . . No, I don't wanna give my name—it's them, not me—Hey! Hey!

RICK *(popping in at the hallway at the top of the stairs).* Hey, Dad! How you doin'?

(OZZIE slams down the phone.)

OZZIE. Oh, Rick! Hi!

RICK. Hi! How you doin'? *(Guitar over his shoulder, he is heading down the stairs and toward the front door.)*

OZZIE. Fine. Just fine.

RICK. Good.

OZZIE. How you doin', Rick?

RICK. Well, I'll see you later.

OZZIE *(running).* I WANT YOU TO TEACH ME GUITAR!

RICK *(faltering).* What?

OZZIE. I want you to teach me . . . guitar! . . . To play it.

RICK *(as OZZIE pulls the guitar from his hands).* Sure. Okay.

OZZIE. I want to learn to play it. They've always been a kind of mystery to me, pianos, guitars.

RICK. Mystery?

(And OZZIE is trying, awkwardly, desperately, to play.)

OZZIE. I mean, what do you think? Do you

ever have to think what your fingers should be doing? What I mean is do you ever have to say—I don't know what—"This finger goes there and this other one does—" I mean, "It's on *this* ridge; now I chord all the strings and then switch it all." See? And do you have to tell yourself, "Now switch it all—first finger this ridge—second finger, down—third —somewhere." I mean, does that kind of thing ever happen? I mean, *How do you play it?* I keep having this notion of wanting some . . . thing . . . some material thing, and I've built it. And then there's this feeling I'm of value, that I'm on my way—I mean, moving —and I'm going to come to something eventually, some kind of achievement. All these feelings of a child . . . in me. . . . They shoot through me and then they're gone and they're not anything . . . anymore. But it's . . . a . . . wall . . . that I want . . . I think. I see myself doing it sometimes . . . all brick and stone . . . coils of steel. And then I finish . . . and the success of it is monumental and people come from far . . . to see . . . to look. They applaud. Ricky . . . teach me . . .

RICK. Ahhh . . . what, Dad?

OZZIE. Guitar, guitar.

RICK. Oh, sure. First you start with the basic C chord. You put the first finger on the second string—

OZZIE. But that's what I'm talking about. You don't do that. I know you don't.

RICK *(not understanding)*. Oh.

OZZIE. You just pick it up and play it. I don't have time for all that you're saying. That's what I've been telling you.

RICK *(on his way for the door)*. Well, maybe some other day then. Maybe Mom'll wanna learn, too.

(All this dialogue is rapid, overlapping.)

OZZIE. No, no.

RICK. Just me and you then.

OZZIE. Right. Me and you.

RICK. I'll see you later.

OZZIE. What?

RICK. Maybe tomorrow.

OZZIE. No.

RICK. Well, maybe the next day then. *(And he is gone out the door.)*

OZZIE. NOW! Now! *(And the door slams shut.)* I grew too old too quick. I had no choice. It was just a town, I thought, and no one remained to test me. I didn't even know it was leaving I was doing. I thought I'd go away and come back. Not leave. *(And he looks up at DAVID's room).* YOU SONOFA-BITCH *(running up to DAVID's room)*, NOT LEAVE! *(He bursts into the room. Silence.)* Restless, Dave; restless. Got a lot on my mind. Some of us can't just lay around, you know. You said I left that town like I was wrong, but I was right. A man proved himself out there, tested himself. So I went and then I ended up in the goddamn Depression, what about that? I stood in goddamn lines of people begging bread and soup. You're not the only one who's had trouble. All of us, by God, David; think about that a little. *(Stepping out the door, slamming it)* Just give somebody besides yourself some goddamn thought for a change. *(Pause. He talks to the audience again; they are his friends.)* Lived in goddamn dirty fields, made tents of our coats. The whole length of this country again and again, soot in our fingers, riding the rails, a bum, a hobo, but young. I remember. And then one day . . . on one of those trains, Hank was there, the first time I ever saw him. Hank, the brakeman, and he sees me hunched down in that car and he orders me off. He stands distant, ordering that I jump! . . . I don't understand and then he stops speaking . . . and . . . when he speaks again, pain is in his eyes and voice—"You're a runner," he says. "Christ, I didn't know you were a runner." And he moves to embrace me and with both hands lifts me high above his head— holds me there trembling, then flings me far out and I fall, I roll. All in the air, then slam down breathless, raw from the cinders . . . bruised and dizzy at the outskirts of this town, and I'm here, gone from that other town. I'm here. We become friends, Hank and me, have good times even though things are rough. He likes to point young girls out on the street and tell me how good it feels to touch them. I start thinking of their bodies, having dreams of horses, breasts and crotches. I remember. And then one day the feeling is in me that I must see a train go by and I'll get on it or I won't, something will happen, but halfway down to where I was thrown off, I see how the grass in among the ties is tall, the rails rusted. . . . Grass grows in abundance. No trains any longer come that way; they all go some other way . . . and far behind me Hank is calling, and I turn to see him coming, Harriet young and lovely in his hand, weaving among the weeds. I feel the wonder of her body moving toward me. She's the thing I think I'll enter to find my future. "Hank," I yell, "you sonofabitch! Bring her here. C'mon. Bring her on." *Swollen with pride, screaming and yelling, I stand there, I stand:* "I'm ready. I'm ready . . . I'm ready." *(He has come down the stairs. He stands, arms spread, yelling. Blackout. Music.)*

Lights slowly up. OZZIE *sleeps on the couch.* RICK *sits in a chair, looking at his guitar.* ZUNG *is in* DAVID's *room, sitting on the bed behind* DAVID, *who is slouched in a chair.* HARRIET, *dressed in a blue robe, enters from the upstairs hallway and comes down the stairs.*

HARRIET. Have you seen my crossword-puzzle book?

RICK. In the bathroom, Mom.

HARRIET. Bathroom? . . . Did I leave it there? *(Turning, she heads back up the stairs.)*

RICK. Guess so, Mom.

DAVID *(sitting abruptly up in his chair as if at a sudden, frightening sound).* Who's there? There's someone there? (RICK *looks up;* DAVID *is standing, poking the air with his cane.)* Who's there? *(He opens the door to his room and steps into the hallway.)*

RICK. Whatsamatter? It's just me and Dad, and Dad's sleeping.

DAVID. Sleeping? Is he?

RICK. On the davenport. . . . You want me to wake him?

DAVID. Nooo . . . nooo. *(He moves swiftly to descend to the living room.)*

RICK. Hey . . . could I get some pictures, Dave? Would you mind?

DAVID. Of course not. No.

RICK *(dashing off up the stairs, while* DAVID *gropes to find the couch).* Let me just go get some film and some flashes, okay.

DAVID *(standing behind the couch on which* OZZIE *sleeps and looking after* RICK*).* Sure . . .

OZZIE. Pardon? Par . . . don?

DAVID *(whispering into his father's ear).* I think you should know I've begun to hate you. I feel the wound of you, yet I don't think you can tell me any more, I . . . must tell you. If I had been an orphan with no one to count on me, I would have stayed there. Now . . . she is everywhere I look. I can see nothing to distract me. (OZZIE *stirs.)* You think us good, we steal all you have.

OZZIE. Good . . . ole Hank. . . .

DAVID. No, no, he has hated us always—always sick with rot.

OZZIE. Noooo . . . nooooooo. . . .

DAVID. She would tell me you would not like her. She would touch her fingers to her

eyes, and she knew how I must feel sometimes as you do.

OZZIE. Ohhh, noooo . . . sleeping. . . .

DAVID. You must hear me. It is only fraud that keeps us sane, I swear it.

OZZIE. David, sleeping! . . . Oh, oh . . .

DAVID. It is not innocence I have lost. What is it I have lost?

OZZIE. Oh . . . oh . . .

(RICK *has appeared high in the hallway and hesitates there.)*

DAVID. Don't you know? Do you see her in your sleep?

RICK *(hurrying down).* I meant to get some good shots at the party, but I never got a chance the way things turned out. You can stay right there.

DAVID *(moving toward the chair on which* RICK's *guitar rests).* I'll sit, all right?

(RICK *rushes to save the guitar.)*

RICK. Sure. How you feelin' anyway, Dave? I mean, honest ta God, I'm hopin' you get better. Everybody is. I mean . . . *(He takes a picture.)* . . . you're not gonna go talkin' anymore crazy like about that guitar and all that, are you? You know what I mean. Not to Mom and Dad anyway. It scares 'em and then I get scared and I don't like it, okay? *(He moves on, taking more pictures.)*

DAVID. Sure. That guitar business wasn't serious anyway, Rick. None of that. It was all just a little joke I felt like playing, a kind of little game. I was only trying to show you how I hate you.

RICK. Huh? *(Stunned, he stares.)*

DAVID. To see you die is why I live, Rick.

RICK. Oh.

HARRIET *(appearing from off upstairs, the crossword-puzzle book in her hands).* Goodness gracious, Ricky, it was just where you said it would be, though I'm sure I don't know how it got there because I didn't put it there. Hello, David.

DAVID. Hello.

OZZIE.   OHHHHHHHHHHHHHHH! *(Screaming, he comes awake, falling off the couch.)* Oh, boy, what a dream! Oh. . . . *(Trying to get to his feet, but collapsing)* Ohhhhhhh! God, leg's asleep. Jesus! *(And he flops about, sits there rubbing his leg).* Ohhhh, everybody. Scared hell out of me, that dream. I hollered. Did you hear me? And my leg's asleep, too. *(He hits the leg, stomps the floor.)* HARRIET *sits on the couch, working her crossword-puzzle book.* RICK, *slumped in a chair, reads a comic.* DAVID, *though, leans forward in his chair. He wants to know the effect of his whispering on his father.)* Did anybody hear me holler?

HARRIET. Not me.

RICK. What did you dream about, Dad?

OZZIE. I don't remember, but it was awful. *(Stomping the foot)* Ohhhh, wake up, wake up. Hank was in it, though. And Dave. They stood over me, whispering—I could feel how they hated me.

RICK. That really happened; he really did that, Dad.

OZZIE. Who did?

RICK. What you said.

OZZIE. No. No, I was sleeping. It scared me awful in my sleep. I'm still scared, honest ta God, it was so awful.

DAVID. It's that sleeping in funny positions, Dad. It's that sleeping in some place that's not a bed.

OZZIE. Pardon?

DAVID. Makes you dream funny. What did Hank look like?

HARRIET. Ozzie, how do you spell "Apollo"?

OZZIE. What?

RICK. Jesus, Dad, Schroeder got three home runs, you hear about that? Two in the second of the first and one in the third of the second. Goddamn, if he don't make MVP in the National, I'll eat my socks. You hear about that, Dad?

OZZIE. Yes, I did. Yes.

RICK. He's somethin'.

OZZIE. A pro.

HARRIET. Ozzie, can you think of a four letter word that starts with G and ends with B?

RICK. Glub.

HARRIET. Glub?

OZZIE *(almost simultaneously)*. Glub?

RICK. It's a cartoon word. Cartoon people say it when they're drowning. G-L-U-B.

OZZIE *(on his feet now)*. Ricky. Ricky, I was wondering . . . when I was sleeping, were my eyes open? Was I seeing?

RICK. I didn't notice, Dad.

HARRIET. *Glub* doesn't work, Rick.

RICK. Try *grub*. That's what sourdoughs call their food. It's G-R—

OZZIE. WAIT A MINUTE!

RICK. G-R—

OZZIE. ALL OF YOU WAIT A MINUTE! LISTEN! Listen. I mean, I look for explanations. I look inside myself. For an explanation. I mean, I look inside *my* self. As I

would look into water . . . or the sky . . . the ocean. They're silver. Answers . . . silver and elusive . . . like fish. But if you can catch them in the sea . . . hook them as they flash by, snatch them . . . drag them down like birds from the sky . . . against all their struggle . . . when you're adrift . . . and starving . . . they . . . can help you live. *(He falters; he stands among them, straining to go further, searching some sign of comprehension in their faces.)*

RICK. Mom . . . Dad's hungry . . . I think. He wants some fish, I—

OZZIE. SHUT UP!

RICK *(hurt deeply)*. Dad?

OZZIE. PIECE OF SHIT! SHUT UP! SHUT UP!

HARRIET. Ozzie! . . .

OZZIE *(roaring down at* DAVID*)*. I don't want to hear about her. I'm not interested in her. You did what you did and I was no part of it. You understand me? I don't want to hear any more about her! Look at him. Sitting there. Listening. I'm tired of hearing you, Dave. You understand that? I'm tired of hearing you and your crybaby voice and your crybaby stories. And your crybaby slobbering and your . . . *(And his voice is possessed with astonished loathing.)* LOOK . . . AT . . . HIM! YOU MAKE ME WANT TO VOMIT! HARRIET! YOU— *(He whirls on* HARRIET*.)* YOU! Your internal organs— your internal female organs—they've got some kind of poison in them. They're backing up some kind of rot into the world. I think you ought to have them cut out of you. I MEAN, I JUST CAN'T STOP THINKING ABOUT IT. I JUST CAN'T STOP THINKING ABOUT IT. LITTLE BITTY CHINKY KIDS HE WANTED TO HAVE! LITTLE BITTY CHINKY YELLOW KIDS! DIDN'T YOU! FOR OUR GRANDCHILDREN! *(And he slaps* DAVID *with one hand.)* LITTLE BITTY YELLOW PUFFY — *(He breaks, groping for the word.)* . . . creatures! . . . FOR OUR GRANDCHILDREN! *(He slaps* DAVID *again, again.)* THAT'S ALL YOU CARED!

*(*DAVID, *a howl in his throat, has stood up.)*

HARRIET. Ohhh, Ozzie, God forgive you the cruelty of your words. All children are God's children.

*(*DAVID *is standing rigid. The front door blows open, and in a fierce and sudden light* ZUNG *steps forward to the edge of* DAVID's *room, as he looks up at her.)*

DAVID. I didn't know you were here. I didn't know. I will buy you clothing. I have lived with them all my life. I will make them not hate you. I will buy you boots. *(And he is moving toward her, climbing the stairs.)* They will see you. The seasons will amaze you. Texas is enormous. Ohio is sometimes green. There will be time. We will learn to speak. And it will be as it was in that moment when we looked in the dark and our eyes were tongues that could speak and the hurting . . . all of it . . . stopped, and there was total understanding in you of me and in me of you . . . and . . . *(Near her now, stepping into his room through the wall, he reaches in a tentative way toward her.)* such delight in your eyes that I felt it; *(And she has begun to move away from him.)* yet . . . I *(She is moving away and down the stairs.)* discarded you. I discarded you. Forgive me. You moved to leave as if you were struggling not to move, not to leave. "She's the thing most possibly of value in my life," I said. "She is garbage and filth and I must get her back if I wish to live. Sickness. I must cherish her." Zung, there were old voices inside me I had trusted all my life as if they were my own. I didn't know I shouldn't hear them. So reasonable and calm they seemed a source of wisdom. "She's all of everything impossible made possible, cast her down," they said. "Go home." And I did as they told; and now I know that I am not awake but asleep, and in my sleep . . . there is nothing. . . . *(ZUNG is now standing before the open door, facing it, about to leave.)* Nothing! . . . What do you want from me to make you stay? I'll do it. I'll do what you want!

RICK *(in the dark before his father, camera in hand)*. Lookee here, Dad. Cheer up! Cheer up!

DAVID *(as ZUNG turns to look up at him)*. Noooooooo. . . . *(And there is a flash as RICK takes the picture.)* NOOOOOOOOOO-OOOOO! STAAAAAAAY!

And the door slams shut, leaving ZUNG still inside. A slide of OZZIE appears on the screen, a close-up of his pained and puzzled face. Music, a falling of notes. The lights are going to black. Perhaps "Intermission" is on the bottom of the slide. The slide blinks out.

ACT TWO

Blackness. Slide: color close-up of a man's ruddy, smiling, round face.

1ST CHILD'S VOICE. Who zat?

WOMAN'S VOICE. I don't know.

MAN'S VOICE. Looks like a neighbor.

WOMAN'S VOICE. How can you say it's a neighbor? You don't know.

(New slide appears: scenery, in color.)

2ND CHILD'S VOICE. Oh, that's a pretty one.

(New slide: FATHER DONALD in a boxing pose, color).

1ST CHILD'S VOICE. Oh, lookee that.

MAN'S VOICE. Father What's-his-name. You know.

(Another slide: FATHER DONALD, slightly different boxing pose).

WOMAN'S VOICE. There he is again.

2ND CHILD'S VOICE. Wow.

Lights up on the downstairs. DAVID is up in his room on his bed. Downstairs, HARRIET sits on the couch, FATHER DONALD is on a chair; OZZIE is in the chair beside him. We have the feeling they have been there a long, long time.

FATHER DONALD. I deal with people and their uneasiness on a regular basis all the time, you see. Everybody I talk to is nervous . . . one way or another . . . so . . . I anticipate no real trouble in dealing with Dave. You have no idea the things people do and then tell me once that confessional door is shut. I'm looking forward, actually, to speaking with him. Religion has been sloughed off a lot lately, but I think there's a relevancy much larger than the credit most give. We're growing—and our insights, when we have them, are twofold. I for one have come recently to understand how very often what seems a spiritual problem is in fact a problem of the mind rather than the spirit—not that the two can in fact be separated, though, in theory, they very often are. So what we must do is apply these theories to fact. At which point we would find that mind and spirit are one and I, a priest, am a psychiatrist, and psychiatrists are priests. I mean—I feel like I'm rambling. Am I rambling?

HARRIET. Oh, no, Father.

OZZIE. Nooo . . . noo.

HARRIET. Father, this is hard for me to say, but I . . . feel . . . his problem is he sinned against the sixth commandment with whores.

FATHER DONALD. That's very likely over there.

HARRIET. And then the threat of death each day made it so much worse.

FATHER DONALD. I got the impression

from our earlier talk that he'd had a relationship of some duration.

HARRIET. A day or two, wouldn't you say, Ozzie?

OZZIE, *(distracted, oddly preoccupied with his chair)*. A three-day pass I'd say . . . though I don't know, of course.

FATHER DONALD. They're doing a lot of psychiatric studies on that phenomenon right now, did you know that?

(The front door pops open, and in bounds RICK.)

HARRIET. Oh, Rick! . . .

RICK. Hi, Mom. Hi, Dad.

OZZIE. Hi, Rick.

FATHER DONALD *(rising)*. Rick, hello!

RICK. Oh, Father Donald . . . hi. *(No time for* FATHER DONALD, RICK *is speeding for the kitchen.)*

OZZIE. Look at him heading for the fudge.

FATHER DONALD. Well, he's a good big strong sturdy boy.

RICK *(as he goes out)*. Hungry and thirsty.

FATHER DONALD. And don't you ever feel bad about it, either! *(He stands for an instant, a little uncertain what to do.)* Dave's up in his room, I imagine, so maybe I'll just head on up and have my little chat. He is why I'm here, after all.

HARRIET. Fine.

OZZIE *(standing, still distracted, he stares at the chair in which* FATHER DONALD *was sitting)*. First door top of the stairs.

FATHER DONALD. And could I use the bathroom, please, before I see ole Dave? Got to see a man about a horse.

HARRIET. Oh, Father, certainly: it's just down the hall. Fifth door.

OZZIE *(stepping nearer to the chair)*. What's wrong with that chair? . . .

HARRIET. It's the blue door, Father! . . .

OZZIE. I . . . don't like that chair. I think it's stupid . . . looking. . . . *(As* RICK *enters from the kitchen, eating fudge)* Ricky, sit. Sit in that chair.

RICK. What? . . .

OZZIE. Go on, sit, sit.

*(*RICK *hurries to the chair, sits, eats.* OZZIE *is fixated on the chair.)*

HARRIET. Oh, Ricky, take your father's picture, he looks so silly.

OZZIE. I just don't think that chair is any good. I just don't think it's comfortable. Father Donald looked ill at ease all the while he was sitting there.

HARRIET. Well, he had to go to the bathroom, Ozzie, what do you expect?

OZZIE *(to* RICKY). Get up. It's just not right. (RICK *gets up and* OZZIE *flops into the chair, sits, fidgets.* RICK *goes back out to the kitchen.)* Noooooo. It's just not a comfortable chair at all, I don't know why. *(He rises and moves toward the couch.)* I don't like it. How much did we pay?

HARRIET. What do you think you're doing?

OZZIE. And this couch isn't comfortable either.

HARRIET. It's a lovely couch.

OZZIE *(tests it)*. But it isn't comfortable. Noooo. And I'm not really sure it's lovely, either. Did we pay two hundred dollars?

HARRIET. What? Oh, more.

OZZIE. How much?

HARRIET. I don't know, I told you.

OZZIE. You don't. I don't. It's gone anyway, isn't it?

HARRIET. Ozzie, what does it matter?

OZZIE *(already on the move for the stairs)*. I'm going upstairs. I'll be upstairs.

HARRIET. Wait a minute. *(As he keeps moving, up the stairs)* I want to talk to you. *I think we ought to talk! (Emotion well beneath her voice stops him, turns him.)* I mean, it's nothing to worry about or anything, but you don't know about it and it's your house, you're involved—so it's just something I mention. You're the man of the house, you ought to know. The police were here . . . earlier today.

OZZIE. What? Oh, my God.

HARRIET. The police. Two of them. Two. A big and a small . . . they— *(He is dazed; he doesn't know whether to go up or down, listen or leave. He nods.)* It was just a little bit ago; not long at all.

OZZIE. Jesus Christ. *(He descends.)*

HARRIET. Oh, I know, I know. Just out of the blue like that—it's how I felt, too. I did, I did.

OZZIE. *What—police?*

HARRIET. It was when you were gone for groceries. I mean, they thought they were supposed to be here. We wanted it, they thought.

OZZIE. No, no.

HARRIET. Somebody called them to come here. They thought it had been us. They were supposed to look through David's luggage, they thought.

OZZIE. They . . . were . . . what?

HARRIET. That's what I mean. That's exactly what I—

OZZIE. *Look through his luggage? There's nothing wrong with his luggage!*

HARRIET. Isn't it incredible? Somebody called them—they didn't know who—no name was given and it sounded muffled through a handkerchief, they said. I said, "Well, it wasn't us." Told them, "Don't you worry; we're all all right here." It must have been a little joke by somebody.

OZZIE. What about Dave?

HARRIET. No, no.

OZZIE. Or Ricky? Did you ask Ricky?

HARRIET. Ricky?

OZZIE. RICKY! RICKY!

RICK *(popping in from the kitchen, thinking he was called)*. What's up, Dad?

OZZIE. I DON'T KNOW.

RICK. I thought you called. *(He pops back out into the kitchen.)*

OZZIE *(to HARRIET)*. You ask him; you ask him. I think the whole thing's preposterous—absolutely—

HARRIET *(as RICK re-emerges to look and listen)*. Ricky, do you know anything about anybody calling the police to come here?

OZZIE *(turning and moving for the stairs)*. I'm going upstairs. I'll be upstairs.

RICK. The police? *(As HARRIET turns to look and half step after OZZIE)* Oh, no, Mom, not me. Okay if I use the car?

HARRIET. What?

FATHER DONALD *(encountering OZZIE in the upstairs hallway)*. Gonna take care of old Dave right now.

OZZIE. I'm going upstairs. I'll be upstairs. *(He exits, as HARRIET stands looking up at them.)*

RICK. Bye, Mom.

HARRIET. What? Oh. *(Looking back as RICK goes out the door)* BE CAREFUL!

FATHER DONALD *(after a slight hesitation)*. Ozzie said to tell you he was going upstairs.

HARRIET. What?

FATHER DONALD. Ozzie said to tell you he was going upstairs.

HARRIET *(stares at him a moment)*. Oh, Father, I'm so glad you're here. *(And she exits into the kitchen, leaving FATHER DONALD. He nods, knocks on DAVID's door.)*

FATHER DONALD. Dave? *(He opens the door, eases into the semidark of the room.)* Dave? It's me . . . Dave. . . . *(Finding a light, he flicks it on.)* Ohh, Dave, golly, you look just fine. Here I expected to see you all worn out and there you are looking so good. It's me, Dave, Father Donald. Let me shake

your hand. *(DAVID's rising hand comes up far off from FATHER DONALD. The priest, his own hand extended, has to move nearly around the bed before he can shake DAVID's hand.)* No, no, David. Here. Over here. Can't see me, can you? There you go. Yes, sir, let me tell you, I'm proud. A lot of people might tell you that, I know, but I mean it, and I'll stand behind it if there's anything I can do for you—anything at all.

DAVID. No. I'm all right.

FATHER DONALD. And that's the amazing part of it, Dave, you are. You truly are. It's plain as day. Golleee, I just don't know how to tell you how glad I am to see you in such high fine spirits. Would you like my blessing? *(He gets to his feet.)* Let me just give you my blessing and then we'll talk things over a little and— (DAVID *slashes with his cane and strikes the hand moving into the position to bless.)* Ohhhhhhhhhhhhhh! *(Wincing, teeth gritted)* Oh, Dave; oh, watch out what you're doing!

DAVID. I know.

FATHER DONALD. No, no, I mean, you swung it in the air, you—hit me.

DAVID. Yes.

FATHER DONALD. No, no, you don't understand, you—

DAVID. I was trying to hit you, Father.

(FATHER DONALD *stares, taking this in.)*

FATHER DONALD. What?

DAVID. I didn't send for you.

FATHER DONALD. I know, I know, your poor mother—your poor mother—

DAVID. I don't want you here, Father; get out!

FATHER DONALD. David!

DAVID. Get out, I'm sick of you. You've been in one goddamn corner or another of this room all my life making signs at me, whispering, wanting to splash me with water or mark me with oil—some goddamn hocus-pocus. I feel reverence for the air and the air is empty, Father. Now get the fuck out of here.

FATHER DONALD. No, no, no, no, David. No, no. I can't give that to you. You'll have to get that from somewhere else.

DAVID. I don't want anything from you!

FATHER DONALD. I'm supposed to react now in some foolish way—I see—some foolish, foolish way that will discredit me— isn't that right? Oh, of course it is. It's an excuse to dismiss my voice that you're seeking, an excuse for the self-destruction your anger has made you think you want, and I'm supposed to give it. I'm supposed to find all this you're doing obscene and sacrilegious instead of seeing it as the gesture of true despair that it is. You're trying to make me disappear, but it's not going to happen. No, no. No such luck, David. I understand you, you see. Everything about you.

DAVID. Do you?

FATHER DONALD. The way you're troubled.

DAVID. I didn't know that, Father.

FATHER DONALD. You say that sarcastically—"Do you? I didn't know that." As if to imply you're so complicated I couldn't ever understand you when I already have. You see, I've been looking into a few things, David, giving some things some thought. *(Producing a magazine with a colorful cover)* I have in my hand a magazine—you can't see it, I know—but it's there. A psychiatric journal in which there is an article of some interest and it deals with soldiers and some of them carried on as you did and then there's some others who didn't. It's not all just a matter of hocus-pocus any longer.

DAVID. Carried . . . on . . . Father?

FATHER DONALD. That whore. That yellow whore. You understand. You knew I was bringing the truth when I came which is why you hit me.

DAVID. I thought you didn't even know the problem. You came in here all bubbly and jolly asking how did I feel.

FATHER DONALD. That was only a little ruse, David; a little maneuver to put you off your guard. I only did that to mislead you. That's right. Your mother gave me all the basics some weeks ago and I filled in the rest from what I know. You see, if it's a fight you want, it's what you'll get. Your soul is worth some time and sweat from me. You're valued by others, David, even if you don't value yourself. *(Waving the magazine in the air)* It's all here—right here—in these pages. It was demonstrated beyond any possible doubt that people—soldiers—who are compelled for some reason not even they themselves understand to establish personal sexual relationships with whores are inferior to those who don't; they're maladjusted, embittered, non-goal-oriented misfits. The sexual acceptance of another person, David, is intimate and extreme; this kind of acceptance of an alien race is in fact the rejection of one's own race—it is in fact the rejection of one's own self—it is

sickness, David. Now I'm a religious man, a man of the spirit, but knowledge is knowledge and I must accept what is proven fact whether that fact come from science or philosophy or whatever. What kind of man are you that you think you can deny it? You're in despair, David, whether you think of it that way or not. It's only into a valley of ruin that you are trying to lock yourself. You can only die there, David. Accept me. Let God open your eyes; let Him. He will redeem you. Not I nor anyone, but only Him—yet if you reject me, you reject Him. My hand is His. His blessing. *(The hand is rising as if the very words elevate it.)* My blessing. Let me give you my blessing. *(And* DAVID's *cane hits like a snake.* FATHER DONALD *cries out in surprise and pain. He recovers and begs.)* Let me bless you. *(His hand is again rising in blessing.)* Please! (DAVID, *striking again, stands. He hits again and again.)* David! David! *(Terrified)* Stop it. Let me bless you.

(DAVID *hits* FATHER DONALD's *arm, hits his leg.)*

DAVID. I don't want you here!

FATHER DONALD. You don't know what you're saying. *(But now the blow seems about to come straight down on his head. He yells and covers his head with his arms. The blow hits. He picks up a chair, holds it up for protection.)* Stop it. Stop it. Goddamnit, stop hitting me. Stop it. You are in despair. *(He slams the chair down.)* A man who hits a priest is in despair! *(Whistling, the cane slams into his arm.)* Ohhhhh, this pain—this terrible pain in my arm—I offer it to earn you your salvation.

DAVID. Get out!

FATHER DONALD. Death! Do you understand that? Death. Death is your choice. You are in despair. *(He turns to leave.)*

DAVID. And may God reward *you,* Father.

FATHER DONALD *(turning back, as* DAVID *flops down on the bed).* Oh yes; yes of course, you're so confident now, young and strong. Look at you—full of spunk, smiling. But all that'll change. Your tune'll change in time. What about pain, Dave? Physical pain. What do you do when it comes? Now you send me away, but in a little while you'll call me back, run down by time, lying with death on your bed . . . in an empty house . . . gagging on your own spit you cannot swallow; you'll call me then, nothing left to you but fear and Christ's black judging eyes about to find and damn you; you'll call.

(Slight pause)

DAVID. That's not impossible, Father.

FATHER DONALD. I don't even like you; do you know that? I DON'T EVEN LIKE YOU!

DAVID. Tell them I hit you when you go down.

FATHER DONALD (near the door, thinking about trying to bless from there). No. No, they've pain enough already.

DAVID. Have they? You get the fuck out of here before I kill you. (As if he has read FATHER DONALD's mind and knows what the man is thinking, DAVID's cane has risen like a spear; it aims at the priest's heart.)

FATHER DONALD (moving not a muscle). THOUGH I DO NOT MOVE MY HAND, I BLESS YOU! YOU ARE BLESSED! (And he exits hurriedly; heading straight down the hall toward the bathroom. Lights up downstairs: it seems a lovely afternoon as RICK and HARRIET enter from the kitchen, chatting.)

HARRIET. So the thing I want to do—I just think it would be so nice if we could get Dave a date with some nice girl.

RICK. Oh, sure.

HARRIET. Do you think that would be a good idea?

(OZZIE, descending from the attic, pauses to peek into DAVID's room; he finds DAVID asleep, and, after a moment, continues on down.)

RICK. Sure.

HARRIET. Do you know any girls you think might get along with David?

RICK. No, but I still think it's really a good idea and I'll keep it in mind for all the girls I meet and maybe I'll meet one. Here comes Dad. Hi, Dad. Bye, Mom.

HARRIET. Oh, Ozzie, did you see what they were doing?

OZZIE. Dave's sleeping. Harriet; Father Donald's gone.

HARRIET. What? He can't be gone.

OZZIE. I thought maybe he was down here. How about the kitchen?

HARRIET. No, no, I just came out of the kitchen. Where were you upstairs? Are you sure he wasn't in David's room?

OZZIE. I was in the attic.

HARRIET. Well, maybe he saw the light and came up to join you and you missed each other on the way up and down. Why don't you go check?

OZZIE. I turned off all the lights, Harriet. The attic's dark now.

HARRIET. Well, yell up anyway—

OZZIE. But the attic's dark now, Harriet.

HARRIET. Just in case.

OZZIE. What are you trying to say? Father Donald's up in the attic in the dark? I mean, if he was up there and I turned off the lights, he'd have said something—"Hey, I'm here," or something. It's stupid to think he wouldn't. (And he sits down.)

HARRIET. No more stupid to think that than to think he'd leave without telling us what happened with David.

OZZIE. All right, all right. (Storming to the foot of the stairs) HEEEEEEYYYYYYY-YYYYYY! HEEEEYYYYYYYY! UP THEEEEERRE! ANYBODY UP THERE? (There is a brief silence. He turns toward HARRIET.)

DAVID (on his bed in his room). WHAT'S THAT, DAD?

OZZIE (falters, looks about). What?

DAVID. WHAT'S UP, DAD?

OZZIE. OH, DAVE, NO, NOT YOU.

DAVID. WHY ARE YOU YELLING?

OZZIE. NO, NO, WE JUST THOUGHT FATHER DONALD WAS UP THERE IN THE ATTIC, DAVE. DON'T YOU WORRY ABOUT IT.

DAVID. I'M THE ONLY ONE UP HERE, DAD!

OZZIE. BUT . . . YOU'RE NOT IN THE ATTIC, SEE?

DAVID. I'M IN MY ROOM.

OZZIE. I KNOW YOU'RE IN YOUR ROOM.

DAVID. YOU WANT ME TO GO UP IN THE ATTIC?

OZZIE. NO! GODDAMNIT, JUST—

DAVID. I DON'T KNOW WHAT YOU WANT.

OZZIE. I WANT YOU TO SHUT UP, DAVE, THAT'S WHAT I WANT, JUST—

FATHER DONALD (appearing from off upstairs). What's the matter? What's all the yelling?

HARRIET. Oh, Father!

OZZIE. Father, hello, hello.

HARRIET. How did it go? Did it go all right?

FATHER DONALD (coming down the steps, seeming as if nothing out of the ordinary has happened). Fine, just fine.

HARRIET. Oh, you're perspiring so, though —look at you.

FATHER DONALD (maneuvering for the door). Well, I've got a lot on my mind. It happens. Nerves. I've other appointments. Many, many.

HARRIET. You mean you're leaving? What are you saying?

FATHER DONALD. I must.

HARRIET. But we've got to talk.

FATHER DONALD. Call me.

HARRIET. Father . . . bless me! . . .

FATHER DONALD. What? . . .

HARRIET. Bless me. . . .

FATHER DONALD. Of course. *(She bows her head, and the priest blesses her, murmuring the Latin.)*

HARRIET. Ohhh, Father, thank you so much. *(Touching his hand)* Shall I walk you to your car?

FATHER DONALD *(backing for the door)*. Fine, fine. That's all right. Sure.

OZZIE *(nodding)*. DAVE, SAY GOOD-BYE TO FATHER DONALD, HE'S LEAVING NOW.

FATHER DONALD. GOOD-BYE, DAVE!

DAVID. GOOD-BYE, FATHER!

(Blackout as HARRIET and FATHER DONALD are going out the door. Music.)

OZZIE *is discovered in late night light, climbing the stairs to* DAVID'*s door, where, after hesitating an instant, he gently knocks.*

OZZIE. Dave, I'd like to come in . . . if I could. *(Easing in)* Awful dark; can I put on a light? *(Silence.)* I mean, we don't need one—not really. I just thought we might . . . I mean, first of all, I want to apologize for the way I hit you the other day. I don't know why I did it. I'm . . . gonna sit down here on the edge of the bed. Are you awake enough to understand? I am your father, you know, and I could command . . . if I wanted. I don't; but I could. I'm going to sit. *(Slight pause)* I mean, it's so sad the way you just go on and on . . . and I'd like to have time for you, but you want so much; I have important things, too. I have plans; I'm older, you know; if I fail to fulfill them, who will do it: Not you, though you could. And Rick's too busy. Do you understand? There's no evidence in the world of me, no sign or trace, as if everything I've ever done were no more than smoke. My life has closed behind me like water. But I must not care about it. I must not. Though I have inside me a kind of grandeur I can't realize, many things and memories of a darker time when we were very different—harder—nearer to the air and we thought of nothing as a gift. But I can't make you see that. There's no way. It's what I am, but it's not what you are. Even if I had the guitar, I would only stand here telling my fingers what to do, but they would do nothing. You would not see . . . I can't get beyond these hands. I jam in the fingers. I break on the bone. I am . . . lonely. I mean, oh, no, not exactly lonely, not really. That's a little strong, actually. . . . *(Silence)* I mean . . . Dave . . . *(He pulls from his back pocket* DAVID'*s overseas cap.)* What's this?

DAVID. What?

OZZIE. This cap. What is it? I cut myself on it. I was rummaging in your stuff upstairs, your bags and stuff, and I grabbed it. It cut me.

DAVID *(reaching for the cap)*. Oh . . . yes.

OZZIE. There are razors sewn into it. Why is that?

DAVID. To cut people. *(Slowly he puts the cap on his head.)*

OZZIE. Oh.

DAVID. Here . . . I'll show you. . . . *(Getting slowly to his feet)* You're on the street, see. You walk . . . and see someone who's after you. . . . You wait. . . . *(He tenses. His hand rises to the tip of the cap.)* As they get near . . . slowly you remove the hat—they think you're going to toss it aside, see? You . . . *snap it! You snap it! (Seizing the front edge of the cap between thumb and finger, he snaps it down. It whistles past* OZZIE, *who jumps.)* It cuts them. They hold their face. However you want them, they're yours. You can stomp them, kick them. This is on the street. I'd like to do that to somebody, wouldn't you?

OZZIE. Huh?

DAVID. It'd be fun.

OZZIE. Oh, sure. I . . .

DAVID. Hank told you to buy this house, didn't he?

OZZIE. What?

DAVID. "Get that house," he said. "Get it."

OZZIE. It's a good house. Solid. Not one of those prefabs, those—

DAVID. It's a coffin. You made it big so you wouldn't know, but that's what it is, and not all the curtains and pictures and lamps in the world can change it. He threw you off a fast free train, Ozzie.

OZZIE. I don't believe you saw him.

DAVID. He told you gold, he gave you shit.

OZZIE. I don't believe you saw him. You're a liar, David.

(ZUNG appears.)

DAVID. Do you know, Dad, it seemed

sometimes I would rise and slam with my fists into the walls of a city. Pointing at buildings, I turned them into fire. I took the fleeing people into my fingers and bent them to touch their heads to their heels, each screaming at the sight of their brain turning black. And now sometimes I miss them, all those screaming people. I wish they were here with us, you and Mom and Rick and Zung and me.

(Pause.)

OZZIE. Mom and Rick and who and you, Dave?

DAVID. Zung.

(ZUNG is moving nearer to them now.)

OZZIE. Zung, Dave?

DAVID. She's here. They were all just hunks of meat that had no mind to know of me until I cared for her. It was simple. We lived in a house. She didn't want to come back here, Dad; she wanted me to stay there. And in all the time I knew her, she cost me six dollars that I had to sneak into her purse. Surprised? In time I'll show you some things. You'll see them. I will be your father. *(He tosses the cap at OZZIE.)*

OZZIE *(shaken, struggling to catch the cap).* Pardon, Dave?

DAVID. What's wrong? You sound like something's terribly wrong?

OZZIE. No. No, no. I'm fine. Your poor mother—she's why I'm here. Your poor mother, sick with grief. She's mine to care for, you know. It's me you're after, yet you torment her. No more. No more. That's what I came up here to tell you.

DAVID *(getting to his feet).* Good.

OZZIE. You're phony, David—phony—trying to make up for the thousands you butchered, when if you were capable of love at all you would love us, your mother and me—not that we matter—instead of some poor little whore who isn't even here.

DAVID *(exiting the room).* I know.

OZZIE. I want her happy.

DAVID *(as OZZIE follows a little into the hall).* I know.

(And DAVID is gone. HARRIET enters slowly from the kitchen, sees OZZIE, then the room's open door.)

HARRIET. Did you have a nice talk?

OZZIE *(heading toward her).* Harriet, what would you say if I said I wanted some checking done?

HARRIET. I don't know what you mean. In what way do you mean?

OZZIE. Take a look at that. But just be careful.

HARRIET. What is it?

OZZIE. His cap. There are razor blades sewn in it; all along the edge.

HARRIET. Ozzie . . . ohhh! Goodness.

OZZIE. That's what I mean. And I was reading just yesterday—some of them bring back guns and knives. Bombs. We've got somebody living in this house who's killed people, Harriet, and that's a fact we've got to face. I mean, I think we ought to do some checking. You know that test where they check teeth against old X-rays. I think—

HARRIET. Ohhh . . . my God! . . .

OZZIE. I know, I know, it scares me, too, but what are we talking about? We're talking about bombs and guns and knives, and sometimes I don't even think it's David up there. I feel funny . . . sometimes . . . I mean, and I want his fingerprints taken. I think we should have his blood type—

HARRIET. Oh, Ozzie, Ozzie, it was you.

OZZIE. Huh?

HARRIET. You did it. You got this out of his luggage, all his baggage upstairs. You broke in and searched and called the police.

OZZIE. No. What?

HARRIET. You told them to come here, and then you lied and said you didn't.

OZZIE. What?

HARRIET. You did, and then you lied and now you're lying again.

OZZIE. Oh, no. No.

HARRIET. What's wrong with you? What's happening to you?

OZZIE. But I didn't do that. I didn't. (DAVID *appears in the upstairs hallway, moving to return to his room.*) I didn't. No, no. And even if I did, what would it mean but I changed my mind, that's all. Sure. *(Looking up at DAVID moving in the hall toward his room)* I called and then changed my mind and said I didn't when I did, and since when is there anything wrong in that? It would mean only that I have a little problem of ambivalence. I got a minor problem of ambiguity goin' for me here, is all, and you're exaggerating everything all out of proportion. You're distorting everything! All of you! *(And he whirls to leave.)* If I have to lie to live, I will! *(He runs.)*

HARRIET. Where are you going? Come back here, Ozzie. Where are you going?

OZZIE. Kitchen. Kitchen. *(He gallops away and out the front door. Blackout. Music.)*

Lights up. Bright afternoon. HARRIET *is alone, dusting.* RICK, *carrying books, enters from the kitchen and heads for the stairs to go to his room.*

HARRIET. One day, Ricky . . . there were these two kittens and a puppy all in our back yard fighting. The kittens were little fur balls, so angry, and the little puppy, yapping and yapping. I was just a girl, but I picked them up in my arms. I held them all in my arms and they got very, very quiet.

RICK. I'm going up to my bedroom and study my history and English and trigonometry, Mom.

HARRIET. Do you know, I've called Father Donald seven times now—seven times, and haven't got an answer. Isn't that funny? He's starting to act like Jesus. You never hear from him. Isn't that funny?

RICK. I'm going up to my bedroom and study my history and English and trigonometry, Mom, okay?

HARRIET. Fine, Ricky. Look in on David, would you?

RICK. Sure.

HARRIET. Good night.

RICK *(calling as he passes* DAVID's *door).* Hi, Dave.

DAVID. Hi, Rick.

RICK. DAVE'S OKAY, MOM.

(She is at the foot of the stairs. RICK *goes from view. She turns back to her work, and the front door opens and* OZZIE *enters.)*

OZZIE *(excited, upset).* Harriet! Can you guess what happened? You'll never guess what happened. *(She continues cleaning.)* Harriet, wait. Stop.

HARRIET. Ozzie, I've got work to do.

OZZIE. But I want to tell you something.

HARRIET. All right, tell me; I can clean and listen; I can do both. *(As she moves away, he rushes toward her, stretching out the lapel of his jacket to show her a large stain on it. She must see.)*

OZZIE. Lookit; look at that. What do you think that is? That spot on my coat, do you see it? That yellow?

HARRIET *(distressed, touching the spot).* Ohhhh, Ozzie! . . .

OZZIE. And the red mark on my neck.

HARRIET *(wincing).* Ohh, Ozzie, what happened? A bee sting! You got stung by a bee!

OZZIE. No, no; I was walking—thinking—trying to solve our problems. Somebody hit me with an egg. They threw it at me. I got hit with an egg. *(She stares, incredulous.)* That's right. I was just walking down the street and

—bang—I was hit. I almost blacked out; I almost fell down.

HARRIET. Ozzie, my God, who would do such a thing?

OZZIE. I don't know. That's the whole point. I've racked my brain to understand and I can't. I was just walking along. That's all I was doing.

HARRIET. You mean you didn't even see them?

OZZIE *(pacing, his excitement growing).* They were in a car. I saw the car. And I saw the hand, too. A hand. Somebody's hand. A very large hand. Incredibly large.

HARRIET. What kind of car?

OZZIE. I don't know. An old one—black— big high fenders.

HARRIET. A Buick.

OZZIE. I think so; yes. Cruising up and down, up and down.

HARRIET. Was it near here? Why don't you sit down? *(Trying to help him sit, to calm and comfort him)* Sit down. Relax.

(He obeys, hardly aware of what he is doing, sort of squatting on the couch, his body rigid with tension, as the story obsesses him.)

OZZIE. And I heard them, too. They were hollering.

HARRIET. What did they say?

OZZIE. I don't know. It was just all noise. I couldn't understand.

HARRIET *(as if the realization doubles the horror).* It was more than one? My God!

OZZIE. I don't know. Two at least, at the very least. One to drive and one to throw. Maybe even three. A lookout sort of, peering up and down, and then he sees me. "There," he says; he points me out. I'm strolling along like a stupid ass, I don't even see them. The driver picks up speed. *(And now he is rising from the couch, reliving the story, cocking his arm.)* The thrower cocks his arm . . .

HARRIET. Ozzie, please, can't you relax? You look awful.

OZZIE. Nooo, I can't relax, goddamnit! *(Off he goes, pacing again.)*

HARRIET. You look all flushed and sweating; please.

OZZIE. It just makes me so goddamn mad the more I think about it. It really does. GODDAMNIT! GODDAMNIT!

HARRIET. Oh, you poor thing.

OZZIE. Because it was calculated; it was calculated, Harriet, because that egg had been boiled to just the right point so it was hard enough to hurt but not so hard it wouldn't splatter. The filthy sonsabitches, but I'm gonna find 'em. I swear that to God, I'm gonna find 'em. I'm gonna kill 'em. I'm gonna cut out their hearts!

(RICK *appears at the top of the stairs.*)

RICK. Hey! What's all the racket? What's—

OZZIE. Ricky, come down here! . . . Goddamn 'em. . . .

HARRIET. Ricky, somebody hit your father with an egg!

RICK. Hit him? *(Descending hurriedly, worried)* Hit Dad?

OZZIE. They just threw it! Where's Dave? Dave here? *(He is suddenly looking around, moving for the stairs.)* I wanna tell Dave. DAVE!

HARRIET. Ozzie, give me your jacket! *(She follows him part way up the stairs, tugging at the jacket.)*

OZZIE. I wanna tell Dave! *(He and HARRIET struggle to get the jacket off.)*

HARRIET. I'll take the spot off.

OZZIE. I gotta tell ole Dave! *(And the jacket is in her arms. He races on up the stairs.)* DAVE? DAVE! HEY, DAVE?

(But DAVID is not in his room. While HARRIET descends and goes to a wall counter with drawers, OZZIE hurries off down the hallway. From a drawer HARRIET takes a spray container and begins to clean the jacket.)

RICK *(wandering near to her).* Boy, that's something, huh. What you got there, Mom?

HARRIET *(as RICK watches).* Meyer Spot Remover, do you know it? It gives just a sprinkling . . . like snow, which, brushed away, leaves the fabric clean and fresh like spring.

(OZZIE and DAVID rush out from the hallway and down the stairs. RICK moves toward them to take a picture.)

OZZIE. But it happened—and then there's this car tearin' off up the street. "Christ Jesus," I said, "I just been hit with an egg. Jesus Christ, that's impossible." And the way I felt—the way I feel—Harriet, let's have some beer; let's have some good beer for the boys and me. *(With a sigh, she moves to obey. As OZZIE continues, she brings beer, she brings peanuts. OZZIE now is pleased with his high energy, with his being the center of attention.)* It took me back to when I was a kid. Ole Fat Kramer. He lived on my street and we used to fight every day. For fun. Monday he'd win, and Tuesday, I'd beat him silly, my knees on his shoulders, blam, blam, blam. Later on, he grew up, became a merchant marine, sailed all over the world, and then he used to race sailboats up and down both coasts—he had one he lived on—anything that floated, he wanted to sail. And he wasn't fat either. We just called him that . . . and boy, oh boy, if he was around now—ohhhh, would we go get those punks threw that egg at me. We'd run 'em into the ground. We'd kill 'em like dogs . . . poor little stupid ugly dogs, we'd cut out their hearts.

RICK *(suddenly coughing and coughing—having gulped down beer—and getting to his feet).* Excuse me, Dad; excuse me. Listen, I've got to get going. You don't mind, do you? Got places to go; you're just talking nonsense anyway. *(He moves for the front door.)*

HARRIET. Have a good time, Rick.

RICK. I'm too pretty not to, Mom! *(And he is gone.)*

OZZIE. Where is . . . he . . . going? Where does he always go? Why does he always go and have some place to go? Always! . . .

HARRIET. Just you never mind, Ozzie. He's young and you're not. I'm going to do the dishes, but you just go right ahead with your little story and I'll listen from the kitchen. *(Gathering the beer and glasses, she goes.)*

OZZIE *(following a little after her, not knowing quite what to do).* I . . . outran a bowling ball. . . . They bet I couldn't. *(And he starts as if at a sound. He turns toward DAVID.)* What are you . . . looking . . . at? What do you think you're seeing?

DAVID. I'm not looking.

OZZIE. I feel watched; looked at.

DAVID. No.

OZZIE. Observed.

DAVID. I'm blind.

OZZIE. Did you do it? Had you anything to do with it?

DAVID. What?

OZZIE. That egg.

DAVID. I can't see.

OZZIE. I think you did. I feel like you did it.

DAVID. I don't have a car. I can't drive. How could I?

HARRIET *(hurrying in to clean up more of the party leftovers).* Ohh, it's so good to hear men's voices in the house again, my two favorite men in all the world—it's what I live for, really. Would you like some coffee? Oh, of course you would. Let me put some on. Your humble servant at your command; I do your bidding, bid me be gone. *(And she is gone without a pause, leaving OZZIE staring after her.)*

OZZIE. I could run again if I wanted. I'd . . . like . . . to want to. Christ, Fat Kramer is probably dead . . . now . . . not bouncing about in the ocean in some rattletrap, tin-can joke of a ship . . . but dust . . . locked in a box . . . held in old . . . cold hands. . . . And I just stand here, don't I? and let you talk any way you want. And Ricky gets up in the middle of some sentence I'm saying and walks right out and I let him. Because I fear him as I fear her . . . and you. Because I know the time is close when I will be of no use to any of you any longer . . . and I am so frightened that if I do not seem inoffensive . . . and pleasant . . . if I am not careful to never disturb any of your unnecessarily, you will all abandon me. I can no longer compel recognition. I can no longer impose myself, make myself seen.

HARRIET *(entering now happily with a tray of coffee).* Here you go. One for each and tea for me. Cream for David . . . *(Setting a cup for* DAVID, *moving toward* OZZIE*)* and cream and sugar for—

OZZIE. Christ how you must have beguiled me!

HARRIET. Pardon?

OZZIE. Beguiled and deceived!

HARRIET. Pardon . . . Ozzie? . . .

OZZIE. And I don't even remember. I say "must" because I don't remember, I was so innocent, so childish in my strength, never seeing that it was surrendering I was doing, innocently and easily giving to you the love that was to return in time as flesh to imprison, detain, disarm and begin . . . to kill.

HARRIET *(examining him, scolding him).* Ozzie, how many beers have you had? You've had too many beers!

OZZIE. Get away! *(He whirls to point at* DAVID *who sits on the floor facing upstage.)* Shut up! You've said enough! Detain and kill! Take and give nothing. It's what you meant, isn't it? You said it yesterday, a warning, nearly exactly this. This is your meaning!

DAVID. You're doing so well, Dad.

OZZIE *(not understanding).* What?

DAVID. You're doing so well.

OZZIE. No.

DAVID. You are.

OZZIE. Nooo, I'm doing awful. I'm doing terrible.

DAVID. This is the way you start, Dad. We'll be runners. Dad and Dave!

OZZIE. What's he saying?

HARRIET. My God, you're shaking; you're shaking.

OZZIE. I don't know what he's talking about. What's he talking about? *(To* HARRIET*)* Just let me alone. Just please let me be. I don't really mean these things I'm saying. They're not really important. They'll go away and I don't mean them; they're just coming out of me; I'm just saying them, but I don't mean them. Oh, please, please, go away.

(And DAVID, *behind them, pivots to go up the stairs. She whirls, drawn by his sudden movement.)*

HARRIET *(dismayed).* David? . . .

DAVID. I'm going upstairs.

HARRIET. Oh, yes. Of course, of course.

DAVID. Just for a while.

HARRIET. Fine. Good. Of course.

DAVID. I'll see you all later. *(And he quietly enters his room, lies down.)*

OZZIE *(coiled on the couch, constricted with pain).* I remember . . . there was a day . . . when I wanted to leave you, all of you, and I wanted desperately to leave, and Hank was there . . . with me. We'd been playing cards. "No," he told me. "No," I couldn't, he said. "Think of the children," he said. He meant something by that. He meant something and I understood it. But now . . . I don't. I no longer have it—that understanding. It's left me. What did he mean?

HARRIET *(approaching, a little fearful).* You're trembling again. Look at you.

OZZIE. For a while . . . just a while, stay away. That's all I ask.

HARRIET *(reaching to touch him).* What?

OZZIE. Stay the hell away from me!

HARRIET Stay away? How far away? Ozzie, how far away? I'll move over . . . *(And she scurries, frightened.)* Here. Is this far enough away? Ozzie . . .

OZZIE. It's my hands, my feet. There's tiredness in me. I wake up each morning, it's in my fingers . . . sleep. . . .

HARRIET. Ohhh, it's such a hateful thing in you the way you have no love for people different than yourself . . . even when your son has come home to tell you of them. You have no right to carry on this way. He didn't bring her back—didn't marry her—we have those two things to thank God for. You've got to stop thinking only of yourself. We don't matter, only the children. When are you going to straighten out your thinking? Promise. You've got to straighten out your thinking.

OZZIE. I do. I know.

HARRIET. We don't matter; we're nothing. You're nothing, Ozzie. Only the children.

OZZIE. I know. I promise.

HARRIET *(moving toward the stairs)*. All right . . . just . . . rest . . . for a little; I'll be back. . . .

OZZIE. I promise, Harriet.

HARRIET *(more to herself than to him)*. I'll go see how he is.

OZZIE *(coiled on the couch)*. It's my hands; they hurt . . . I want to wrap them; my feet . . .

HARRIET. I'll tell him for you. I'll explain —how you didn't mean those terrible things you said. I'll explain.

OZZIE. It's going to be so cold; and I hurt . . . already. . . . So cold; my ankles! . . .

HARRIET *(hesitating on the stairway)*. Oh, Ozzie, Ozzie, we're all so worried, but I just think we must hope for the fine bright day coming when we'll be a family again, as long as we try for what is good, truly for one another, please. *(And she goes upstairs. The front door pops open.)*

RICK. Hi, Mom. Hi, Dad.

OZZIE. Hi, Rick. Your mom's upstairs. You have a nice time? I bet you did.

RICK. Fine; sure. How about you?

OZZIE. Fine; sure.

RICK. Whata you doin', restin'?

OZZIE. Workin'. Measurin'. Not everybody can play the guitar, *you know*. I'm going to build a wall . . . I think—a wall. Pretty soon . . . or . . . six walls. Thinkin' through the blueprints, lookin' over the plans.

RICK *(moving for the kitchen)*. I'm gonna get some fudge, Dad; you want some?

OZZIE. No. Too busy.

RICK. I had the greatest piece a tail tonight, Dad; I really did. What a beautiful piece a ass.

OZZIE. Did you, Rick?

RICK. She was beee-uuuuu-ti-ful.

OZZIE. Who was it?

RICK. Nobody you'd know, Dad.

OZZIE. Oh. Where'd you do it—I mean, get it.

RICK. In her car.

OZZIE. You were careful, I hope.

RICK *(laughing a little)*. C'mon, Dad.

OZZIE. I mean, it wasn't any decent girl.

RICK. Hell, no. . . . *(He is still laughing, as* OZZIE *gets to his feet.)*

OZZIE *(starting for the door)*. Had a dream of the guitar last night, Rick. It was huge as a building—all flecked with ice. You swung it in the air and I exploded.

RICK. I did?

OZZIE. Yes. I was gone.

RICK. Fantastic.

OZZIE *(exaggeratedly happy, almost singing)*. Good night. *(*OZZIE *is gone out the door. Blackout. Music.)*

Late night. HARRIET *comes down the hall toward* DAVID's *room. She is wearing a bathrobe and carries a towel, soap, a basin of water. Giving just the lightest tap on the door, she enters, smiling.*

HARRIET. A little bath . . . David? A little sponge bath, all right? You must be all hot and sticky always in that bed. And we can talk. Why don't you take your shirt off? We've an awful lot to talk about. Take your shirt off, David. Your poor father . . . he has no patience, no strength. Something has to be done. . . . A little sponge bath would be so nice. Have you talked to him lately? I think he thinks you're angry, for instance, with . . . us . . . for some reason . . . I don't know. *(Tugging at his shirt a little)* Take your shirt off, David. You'll feel cool. That's all we've ever wanted, your father and me— good sweet things for you and Rick—ease and lovely children, a car, a wife, a good job. Time to relax and go to church on Sundays . . . and on holidays all the children and grandchildren come together, mingling. It would be so wonderful—everyone so happy —turkey. Twinkling lights! *(She is puzzled, a little worried.)* David, are you going to take your shirt off for me?

DAVID. They hit their children, did you know that? They hit them with sticks.

HARRIET. What?

DAVID. The yellow people. They punish the disobedience of their children with sticks. And then they sleep together, one family in a bed, limbs all entwined like puppies. They work. I've seen them . . . laugh. They go on picnics. They murder—out of petty jealousy. Young girls wet their cunts with spit when they are dry from wear and yet another GI stands in line. They spit on their hands and rub themselves, smiling, opening their arms.

HARRIET. That's not true.

DAVID. I saw—

HARRIET *(smilingly scolding him)*. None of what you say. No. No. All you did was something normal and regular, can't you see? And hundreds of boys have done it before you. Thousands and thousands. Even now. Now. Now. Why do you have to be so sick and morbid about something so ordinary?

DAVID. She wasn't always a whore. Not always. Not—

HARRIET. If she is now, she was then, only

you didn't know. You didn't know. *(She is reaching for him. He eludes her, stands above her, as she is left sitting on the bed, looking up.)* Oh, David, David, I'm sure she was a lovely little girl, but I would be insane if I didn't want you to marry someone of your own with whom you could be happy, if I didn't want grandchildren who could be free and welcome in their world. I couldn't want anything else and still think I loved you. David, think of their faces, their poor funny little faces. . . .

(And the cane is moving, slowly moving along the floor; it grazes her ankle.)

DAVID. I know . . . I know. . . .

(The cane moves now along her inner calf, rising under the hem of her robe, lifting. She tries to ignore it.)

HARRIET. The human face was not meant to be that way. A nose is a thinness—you know that. And lips that are not thin are ugly, and it is we who disappear, David. They don't change, and we are gone. It is our triumph, our whiteness. We disappear. What are you doing? *(The cane has driven her back along the bed; no longer can it be ignored. It has pressed against her.)* They take us back and down if our children are theirs—it is not a mingling of blood, it is theft. *(And she hits the cane away. In revulsion she stands, wanting only to flee.)* Oh, you don't mean these awful things you do. Your room stinks—odors come from under the door. You don't clean yourself. David, David, you've lost someone you love and it's pain for you, don't you see? I know, I know. But we will be the same, lost from you—you and us—and what will that gain for anyone? What?

Now the cane begins to scrape along the floor. It begins to lift toward her, and, shuddering, she flees down the hall. DAVID *opens the door, listens. Stepping into the hall, he carefully shuts the door before moving down the stairs. In the living room, he moves to plant himself before the front door.* HARRIET, *wearing a raincoat over her robe and a scarf on her head, comes down the stairs, when she turns toward the door and she sees* DAVID, *she stops, nods hello, and stands as he begins to advance upon her.*

DAVID. Do you remember? It was a Sunday when we had all gone to church and there was a young man there with his yellow wife and child. You spoke to us . . . Dad and Rick and me, as if we were conspirators. "I feel so sorry for that poor man—the baby looks like *her,*" you said, and your mouth twisted as if you had been forced to swallow someone else's spit.

HARRIET. No, no. You want only to hurt us, don't you? Isn't that right? That's all you want. Only to give us unhappiness. You cheat her, David. That lovely, lovely little girl you spoke of. She merits more to be done in her memory than cruelty. *(She has seated herself on the couch, clinging to some kind of normalcy, an odd and eerie calmness on both of them now.)*

DAVID. And I felt that I must go to her if I was to ever live, and I felt that to touch truly her secret stranger's tongue and mind would kill me. Now she will not forgive the way I was.

HARRIET *(standing up)*. No. No, no. No, you don't know how badly I feel. I've got a fever, the start of a cold or flu. Let me be. I can't hardly . . . *(And she is moving away from him, back toward the stairs)* move . . . or stand up. I just want to flop somewhere and not have to move. I'm so weak . . . don't hurt me anymore. Don't hurt me— no more—I've got fever; please, fever; don't hurt me. *(She is on the stairs.)*

DAVID. But I have so much to show you.

HARRIET *(stops to stare helplessly down at him)*. Who are you? I don't know who you are.

DAVID. David.

HARRIET. Noooooo.

DAVID. But I am.

HARRIET. No, no. Oh, no. *(Moving now as in a trance, she walks up the stairs and down the hallway, all slowly, while* ZUNG *comes forward in* DAVID'S *room, and* DAVID, *in the living room, calls after his mother.)*

DAVID. But it's what you want, don't you see? You can see it. Her wrists are bound in coils of flowers. Flowers are strung in her hair. She hangs from the wind and men strike and kick her. They are blind so that they may not see her, yet they howl, wanting not to hurt her but only as I do, to touch and hold her . . . and they howl. I'm home. Little David. . . . Home. *(And he is turning now to take possession of the house. As he speaks, he moves to take the space. A conquerer, he parades in the streets he has taken; among the chairs, around the lamp.)* Little Davey . . . of all the toys and tops and sailor suits, the plastic cars and Tinkertoys. Drum-player, bed-wetter, home-run-hitter, I'm home . . . now . . . and I want to drink from the toilet, wash there. *(As he climbs the stairs, he passes by* ZUNG, *who stands in his room looking out at him. He walks on down the hall in the direction* HARRIET *fled.)* And you will join me. You . . . will . . . join me!

(When he has gone, ZUNG *sits to gaze down upon the living room, as the front door opens.* OZZIE, *dressed in a suit or perhaps even a tuxedo, enters from the outside. Under his arm he carries a packet of several hundred sheets of paper. He moves now with an absolute confidence, almost smugness, as he carefully sets down the papers and proceeds to arrange three items of furniture—perhaps two chairs and a footstool—in such a way that they face him. He is cocky. Now he addresses them.)*

OZZIE *(to the large chair).* Harriet. . . . *(Nodding to the second chair)* David. . . . *(Patting the footstool)* Ricky. *(He looks them over, the three empty chairs, and then speaks in the manner of a chairman of the board addressing the members of his board, explaining his position and plan of action for total solution. This is a kind of commercial on the value of* OZZIE.*)* I'm glad we've gotten finally together here, because the thing I've decided to do—and you all, hopefully, will understand my reasoning—is to *combat* the weariness beginning in me. It's like stepping into a hole, the way I feel each morning when I awaken, I see the day and the sun and I'm looking upward into the sky with a sense of looking down. A sense of hovering over a great pit into which I am about to fall. The sky. Foolishness and deceit, you say, and I know you're right—a trick of feeling inside me being played against me, seeking to diminish me and increase itself until it is larger than me filling me and who will I be then? It. That feeling of being nothing. At first . . . at first . . . I thought the thing to do would be to learn the guitar. . . . But *that* I realized in just the nick of time was a folly that would have taken me into the very agony of frustration I was seeking to avoid. The skill to play like Ricky does is a great gift and only Ricky has it. He has no acids rotting his heart. He is all lies and music, his brain small and scaly, the brain of a snake forever innocent of the fact that it crawls. Lucky Ricky. But there are other things that people can do. And I've come at last to see the one that I must try if I am to become strong again in my opinion of myself. *(Holding up, with great confidence, one of the many packets of paper)* What I have here is an inventory of everything I own.

Everything. Every stick of furniture, pot and pan, every sock, T-shirt, pen or pencil. And opposite is its price. For instance—here—that davenport—five hundred an' twelve dollars an' ninety-eight cents. That chair—a hundred twenty ninety-nine. That table . . . *(He hurries to the table.)* . . . this table—thirty-two twenty-nine. Et cetera. Et cetera. Now the idea is that you each carry a number of these at all times. *(He is distributing more papers to the chairs, his control, however, diminishing, so that the papers are thrown about.)* Two or three copies at all times, and you are to pass them out at the slightest provocation. Let people know who I am, what I've done. Someone says to you, "Who are you?" You say, "I'm Ozzie's son." "I'm Ozzie's wife." Who?" they'll say. "Take a look at that!" you tell 'em. Spit it out, give 'em a copy, turn on your heel and walk right out. That's the way I want it; from all of you from here on out, that's the WAY I WANT IT! *(And the room goes suddenly into eerie light.* ZUNG, *high behind him in* DAVID's *room, is hit with a sudden light that makes* OZZIE *go rigid, as if some current from her has entered into him, and he turns slowly to look up at her.)* Let him alone. Let David alone.

(HARRIET is in the hallway.)

HARRIET. Is there any aspirin down there? I don't feel well . . . Ozzie, I don't feel well at all. David poked me with his cane and I don't like . . . what's . . . going on. *(OZZIE is only staring at* ZUNG.*)* I don't want what's happening to happen. *(She has halted on the stairway.)* It must be some awful flu, I'm so weak, or some awful cold. There's an odor . . .

OZZIE. I'll go to the drugstore. My eyes hurt; funny . . .

HARRIET. Oh, Ozzie . . . oh my God. It was awful. I can't help it. He's crazy—he—

OZZIE. I don't want to hear about him. I don't want to hear. Oh, no, oh, no. I can't. No more, no more. Let him do what he wants. No more of him, no more. Just you—you're all that I can see. All that I care for or want. *He has moved to her as she moved down, and they embrace.*

HARRIET. David's crazy! . . .

OZZIE. You're everything.

HARRIET. Please . . .

OZZIE. Listen; we must hide; please.

HARRIET, *(moving to kneel and he, while helping her, kneels also).* Pray with me.

OZZIE. We won't move. We'll hide by not moving.

HARRIET. We must beg God to not turn against him; convince him. Ozzie, pray. . . .

OZZIE. Yes! . . .

HARRIET. Now!. . . . *(They pray: kneeling, murmuring, and it goes on and on. The front door opens.)*

RICK. Hi, Mom. Hi, Dad. *(They continue. He stops.)* Hi . . . Mom. Hi, Dad. . . . *(Very puzzled)* Hi . . . Mom. . . . Hi . . . Dad. . . . *(He thinks and thinks.)* DAVID! *(He screams at* DAVID. *He goes running up to look in* DAVID's *room, but the room is empty.* DAVID, *in ragged combat fatigues, appears on the top of the stairs.* RICK, *frightened, backs away.)* Dave . . . what have you got to say for yourself? What can you? Honest ta God, I've had it. I really have. I can't help it, even if you are sick, and I hate to complain, but you're getting them so mixed up they're not themselves anymore. Just a minute ago—one minute—they were on their knees, do you know that? Just a minute ago—right here on the living-room floor. Now what's the point of that? They're my mom and dad, too.

DAVID. He doesn't know, does he, Dad? Did you hear him?

RICK *(as* OZZIE *and* HARRIET *are getting from their knees and struggling to sit on the couch).* Let Dad alone.

DAVID *(on the landing, looking down on them).* He doesn't know how when you finally see yourself, there's nothing really there to see . . . isn't that right? Mom?

RICK. Dave, honest to God. I'm warning you, let them alone. (DAVID *descends with* ZUNG *behind him. Calmly he speaks, growing slowly happy.)*

DAVID. Do you know how north of here, on farms, gentle loving dogs are raised, while in the forests, other dogs run wild? And upon occasion, one of those that's wild is captured and put in among the others that are tame, bringing with it the memory of when they had all been wild—the dark and terror—that had made them wolves. Don't you hear them?

(And there is a rumbling.)

RICK. What? Hear what?

(It is windlike, the rumbling of many trucks.)

DAVID. Don't you hear the trucks? They're all over town, lined up from the center of town into the country. Don't you hear? They've stopped bringing back the blind. They're bringing back the dead now. The convoy's broken up. There's no control . . .

they're walking from house to house, through the shrubbery, under the trees, carrying one of the dead in a bright blue rubber bag for which they have no papers, no name or number. No one knows whose it is. They're at the Jensens' now. Now Al Jensen's at the door, all his kids behind him trying to peek. Al looks for a long, long time into the open bag before he shakes his head. They zipper shut the bag and turn away. They've been to the Mayers', the Kellys', the Irwins' and Kresses'. They'll be here soon.

OZZIE. Nooo.

DAVID. And Dad's going to let them in. We're going to let them in.

HARRIET. What's he saying?

DAVID. He's going to knock.

OZZIE. I DON'T KNOW.

DAVID. Yes. Yes.

(A knocking sound. Is it DAVID *knocking with his fist against the door or table?)*

OZZIE. Nooooo.

RICK. Mom, he's driving Dad crazy.

(Knocking loud: it seems to be at the front door.)

OZZIE. David, will I die? *(He moves toward the door.)*

HARRIET. Who do you suppose it could be so late?

RICK *(intercepting* OZZIE, *blocking the way to the door).* I don't think you should just go opening the door to anybody this time of the night, there's no telling who it might be.

DAVID. We know who it is.

OZZIE. Oh, David, why can't you wait? Why can't you rest?

(But DAVID *is the father now, and he will explain. He loves them all.)*

DAVID. Look at her. See her, Dad. Tell her to go to the door. Tell her yes, it's your house, you want her to open the door and let them in. Tell her yes, the one with no name is ours. We'll put it in that chair. We can bring them all here. I want them all here, all the trucks and bodies. There's room. *(Handing* RICK *the guitar)* Ricky can sing. We'll stack them along the walls . . .

OZZIE. Nooo . . .

DAVID. Pile them over the floor . . .

OZZIE. No, no . . .

DAVID. They will become the floor and they will become the walls, the chairs. We'll sit in them; sleep. We will call them "home." We will give them as gifts—call them "ring" and "pot" and "cup." No, no; it's not a thing to fear. . . . We will notice them no more than all the others. *(He is gentle, happy, consoling to them.)*

OZZIE. What others? There are no others. Oh . . . please die. Oh, wait. . . . *(And he scurries to the TV where it sits beneath the stairs.)* I'll get it fixed. I'll fix it. Who needs to hear it? We'll watch it. *(Wildly turning TV channels.)* I flick my rotten life. Oh, there's a good one. Look at that one. Ohhh, isn't that a good one? That's the best one. That's the best one.

DAVID. They will call it madness. We will call it seeing. *(Calmly he lifts* OZZIE.)

OZZIE. I don't want to disappear.

DAVID. Let her take you to the door. We will be runners. You will have eyes.

OZZIE. I will be blind. I will disappear.

(Knocking is heard again. Again.)

DAVID. You stand and she stands. "Let her go," you say; "she is garbage and filth and you must get her back if you wish to live. She is sickness, I must cherish her." Old voices you have trusted all your life as if they were your own, speaking always friendly. "She's all of everything impossible made possible!"

OZZIE. Ricky . . . nooo! . . .

DAVID. Don't call to Ricky. You love her. You will embrace her, see her and—

OZZIE. He has no right to do this to me.

DAVID. Don't call to Ricky!

OZZIE *(suddenly raging, rushing at* DAVID, *pushing him).* You have no right to do this.

RICK. Noooooo! *(Savagely he smashes his guitar down upon* DAVID, *who crumples.)* Let Dad alone. Let him alone. He's sick of you. What the hell's the matter with you? He doesn't wanna talk anymore about all the stupid stuff you talk. He wants to talk about cake and cookies and cars and coffee. He's sick a you and he wants you to shut up. We hate you, goddamn you.

(Silence: DAVID *lies still.)*

ZUNG. Chào ông! (OZZIE *pivots, looks at her.)* Chào ông! Hôm nay ông manh không?

OZZIE. Oh, what is it that you want? I'm tired. I mean it. Forgive me. I'm sick of the sight of you, squatting all the time. In filth like animals, talking gibberish, your breath sick with rot. . . . And yet you look at me with those sad pleading eyes as if there is some real thing that can come between us when you're not even here. You are deceit. *(His hands, rising, have driven to her throat. The fingers close.)* I'm not David. I'm not silly and soft . . . little David. The sight of you sickens me. YOU HEAR ME, DAVID?

Believe me. I am speaking my honest true feelings. I spit on you, the both of you; I piss on you and your eyes and pain. Flesh is lies. You are garbage and filth. You are darkness. I cast you down. Deceit. Animal. Dirty animal. *(And he is over her. They are sprawled on the ground. Silence as no one moves. She lies like a rag beneath him.)*

RICK. I saw this really funny movie last night. This really . . . funny, funny movie about this young couple and they were going to get a divorce but they didn't. It was really funny.

(OZZIE *is hiding the girl. In a proscenium production, he can drag her behind the couch; in three-quarter, he covers her with a blanket brought to him by* HARRIET *which matches the rug.)*

HARRIET. What's that? What's that?

RICK. This movie I saw.

HARRIET. Anybody want to go for groceries? We need Kleenex, sugar, milk.

RICK. What a really funny movie.

OZZIE. I'll go; I'll go.

HARRIET. Good. Good.

OZZIE. I think I saw it on TV.

(They are cleaning up the house now, putting the chairs back in order, dumping all of OZZIE*'s leaflets in the waste can.)*

HARRIET. Did you enjoy it, Rick?

RICK. Oh, yeh. I loved it.

OZZIE. I laughed so much I almost got sick. It was really good. I laughed.

RICK. I bet it was; I bet you did.

OZZIE. Oh, I did.

(Even DAVID *helps with the cleaning: he gets himself off the floor and seated in a chair.)*

HARRIET. How are you feeling, Ricky?

RICK. Fine.

HARRIET. Good.

RICK. How do you feel?

HARRIET. Oh, I'm all right. I feel fine.

OZZIE. Me, too. I feel fine, too. What day is it anyway? Monday?

HARRIET. Wednesday.

RICK. Tuesday, Mom.

(Now all three are seated on the couch.)

OZZIE. I thought it was Monday.

RICK. Oh, no.

HARRIET. No, no. You're home now, David. . . .

RICK *(moving to* DAVID, *who sits alone in a chair).* Hey, Dave, listen, will you. I mean I know it's not my place to speak out and give advice and everything because I'm the youngest, but I just gotta say my honest true feelings and I'd kill myself if I were you, Dave. You're in too much misery. I'd cut my wrists. Honestly speaking, brother to brother, you should have done it long ago. (DAVID *is looking about.*) You looking for her, Dave? You looking for her? She's not here.

DAVID. What?

RICK. Nooo. She's never been here. You just thought so. You decided not to bring her, Dave, remember? You decided, all things considered that you preferred to come back without her. Too much risk and inconvenience . . . you decided. Isn't that right? Sure. You know it is. You've always known. *(Silence.* HARRIET *moves to look out the front door.)* Do you want to use my razor, Dave? *(Pulling a straight razor from his pocket)* I have one right here and you can use it if you want. (DAVID *seems to be looking at the razor.)* Just take it if you want it, Dave.

HARRIET. Go ahead, David. The front yard's empty. You don't have to be afraid. The streets, too . . . still and empty.

RICK. It doesn't hurt like you think it will. Go ahead; just take it, Dave.

OZZIE. You might as well.

RICK. That's right.

OZZIE. You'll feel better.

RICK. I'll help you now, Dave, okay?

HARRIET. I'll go get some pans and towels.

RICK *(moving about* DAVID, *patting him, buddying him).* Oh, you're so confused, you don't know what to do. It's just a good thing I got this razor, Boy, that's all I gotta say. You're so confused. You see, Dave, where you're wrong is your point of view, it's silly. It's just really comical because you think people are valuable or something and, given a chance like you were to mess with 'em, to take a young girl like that and turn her into a whore, you shouldn't, when of course you should or at least might . . . on whim . . . you see? I mean, you're all backwards, Dave —you're upside down. You don't know how to go easy and play—I bet you didn't have any fun the whole time you were over there —no fun at all—and it was there. I got this buddy Gerry, he was there, and he used to throw bags of cement at 'em from off the back a his truck. They'd go whizzin' through those villages, throwin' off these bags a cement. You could kill people, he says, you hit 'em right. Especially the kids. There was this once they knocked this ole man off his bicycle— fifty pounds a dry cement—and then the back

a the truck got his legs. It was hysterical— can't you just see that, Dave? Him layin' there howlin', all the guys in the truck bowin' and wavin' and tippin' their hats. What a goddamn funny story, huh?

(HARRIET *has brought silver pans and towels with roosters on them. The towels cover the arms of the chair and* DAVID's *lap. The pans will catch the blood. All has been neatly placed.* DAVID, *with* RICKY's *help, cuts one wrist, then the other, as they talk.)*

DAVID. I wanted . . . to kill you . . . all of you.

RICK. I know, I know; but you're hurt; too weak.

DAVID. I wanted for you to need what I had and I wouldn't give it.

HARRIET. That's not possible.

OZZIE. Nooooo.

DAVID. I wanted to get you. Like poor bug-eyed fish flung up from the brief water to the lasting dirt, I would gut you.

HARRIET. David, no, no, you didn't want that.

OZZIE. No, no.

RICK. I don't even know why you'd think you did.

OZZIE. We kill you is what happens.

RICK. That's right.

OZZIE. And then, of course, we die, too. . . . Later on, I mean. And nothing stops it. Not words . . . or walls . . . or even guitars.

RICK. Sure.

OZZIE. That's what happens.

HARRIET. It isn't too bad, is it?

RICK. How bad is it?

OZZIE. He's getting weaker.

HARRIET. And in a little, it'll all be over. You'll feel so grand. No more funny talk.

RICK. You can shower; put on clean clothes. I've got deodorant you can borrow. After Roses, Dave. The scent of a thousand roses. *(He is preparing to take a picture— crouching, aiming.)*

HARRIET. Take off your glasses, David.

OZZIE. Do as you're told.

RICK *(as* DAVID's *hands are rising toward the glasses to remove them).* I bet when you were away there was only plain water to wash in, huh? You prob'ly hadda wash in the rain. *(He takes the picture; there is a flash. A slide appears on the screen: a close-up of* DAVID, *nothing visible but his face. It is the slide that, appearing at the start of the play, was referred to as "somebody sick." Now it hovers, stricken, sightless, revealed.)* Mom, I like David like this.

HARRIET. He's happier.

OZZIE. We're all happier.

RICK. Too bad he's gonna die.

OZZIE. No, no, he's not gonna die, Rick. He's only gonna nearly die. Only nearly.

RICK. Ohhhhhhhhhh.

HARRIET. Mmmmmmmmmmmm.

(And RICK, *sitting, begins to play his guitar for* DAVID. *The music is alive and fast. It has a rhythm, a drive of happiness that is contagious. The lights slowly fade.)*

INDIANS

Arthur Kopit

For LESLIE

Indians was first performed by the Royal Shakespeare Company on July 4, 1968, at the Aldwych Theatre, London. Its American première was on May 6, 1969, at the Arena Stage, Washington, D.C. The play opened in New York at the Brooks Atkinson Theatre on October 13, 1969, with the following cast:

BUFFALO BILL Stacy Keach
SITTING BULL Manu Tupou
SENATOR LOGAN Tom Aldredge
SENATOR DAWES Richard McKenzie
SENATOR MORGAN Jon Richards
TRIAL SOLDIERS Bob Hamilton, Richard Nieves
JOHN GRASS Sam Waterston
SPOTTED TAIL James J. Sloyan
GRAND DUKE ALEXIS Raul Julia
INTERPRETER Yusef Bulos
NED BUNTLINE Charles Durning
GERONIMO Ed Rombola
WHITE HOUSE USHER Darryl Croxton
OL' TIME PRESIDENT Peter MacLean
FIRST LADY Dortha Duckworth
WILD BILL HICKOK Barton Heyman
TESKANJAVILA Dimitra Arliss
UNCAS Raul Julia

VALETS Joseph Rango, Richard Novello, Brian Donahue
ANNIE OAKLEY Pamela Grey
CHIEF JOSEPH George Mitchell
JESSE JAMES Ronny Cox
BILLY THE KID Ed Rombola
PONCHO Raul Julia
COLONEL FORSYTH Peter MacLean
LIEUTENANT Richard Novello
REPORTERS Ronny Cox, Brian Donahue, Darryl Croxton
SOLDIERS Bob Hamilton, Richard Nieves
VARIOUS INDIANS Dino Laudicina, Robert McLane, Andy Torres, Jay Fletcher, Princeton Dean, Ed Henkel, Michael Ebbin, Kevin Conway, Pascual Vaquer, Wesley Fata, Gary Weber, Peter Demaio, Ted Goodridge, Tom Fletcher, Phil Arsenault, Juan Antonio

Directed by Gene Frankel
Settings by Oliver Smith
Lighting by Thomas Skelton
Costumes by Marjorie Slaiman
Music by Richard Peaslee
Choreography by Julie Arenal

As a playwright, Arthur Kopit was practically an infant prodigy. His first play, *The Questioning of Nick*, was a one-acter written in his sophomore year at Harvard. It has subsequently been published and still stands as an unusually accomplished first effort. During his Harvard years, he wrote nine plays, five of which were produced by undergraduate groups.

Mr. Kopit was born in New York on May 10, 1937. He attended the Lawrence, Long Island, High School and graduated from Harvard in 1959. His first major play held the world's record for the longest play title, until it eventually had to relinquish this distinction to a Peter Weiss play, popularly known as *Marat/Sade*, which had twenty-four words in its full title. However, Mr. Kopit had made a brave try: his play was called *Oh Dad, Poor Dad, Mamma's Hung You in the Closet and I'm Feelin' So Sad*.

This black but very funny comedy was produced first in Cambridge, Massachusetts, had its original professional production in London in 1961—where I personally fell under its strange charms—and was, in the following year, given its famous Off-Broadway production at the Phoenix Theatre, where it was staged by Jerome Robbins. This opened on February 26 and ran for 454 performances. But an attempt to revive the play, with much the same cast and the same director, failed at the Morosco Theatre on Broadway in 1963, when it managed to rack up only forty-seven performances.

No better fortune awaited Mr. Kopit's double bill *The Day the Whores Came Out to Play Tennis* and *Sing to Me through Open Windows*, which mustered only twenty-four performances Off Broadway in March of 1965. But fortunately by this time Mr. Kopit was engaged in a major work, *Indians*, which, even more than *Poor Dad*, was to establish him as an American playwright of some individuality.

The idea for *Indians* came to Mr. Kopit in March 1966. With the assistance of a cash advance from his producer, Lyn Austin, Mr. Kopit started the considerable historical research needed for what was intended to be a picture of America's conquest of the West and its pursuit of its aims through a deliberate policy of genocide. It was Mr. Kopit's apt and pertinent point that the spirit informing the American action was much the same as that informing the Vietnam War. He was seeking to demonstrate that violence, in the words of the black militant Rap Brown, "was as American as cherry pie."

It was a remarkable concept, but for its fulfillment it needed help. Luckily some help was unexpectedly forthcoming. In the summer of 1968 the Royal Shakespeare Company in London determined upon a complete season of American plays. For the most part these were revivals, such as Paddy Chayevsky's *The Latent Heterosexual* and Edward Albee's *A Delicate Balance*, but in one instance the Royal Shakespeare Company chose a new play, Kopit's *Indians*.

It was brilliantly done, but half baked. Jack Gelber, himself a playwright and a Western buff, directed the play with a certain uncertainty. Moreover, it was beautifully acted, but with little understanding of its essential mythic values. The central character, Buffalo Bill, was entrusted to the elegant English actor, Barrie Ingham, who was almost as superb as he was wrong. But the real fault lay with Mr. Kopit himself. This story of Indian betrayal and defeat placed in the setting of Buffalo Bill's Wild West Show, had simply not been carefully enough articulated. For every moment of grandeur there was a moment of pure silliness to undercut it.

Mr. Kopit learned his lessons. When the play received its American premiere on May 6, 1969, at the Arena Stage in Washington, it had been totally refashioned and largely rewritten. In London *Indians* was exclusively focused around Buffalo Bill's Wild West Show; in Washington a counterpoised action was provided by the presidential commission sent in 1886 to investigate Indian grievances at Standing Rock Reservation.

The contrast was valuable, and in Gene Frankel's new staging the work achieved far more definition than in its London version. A further advantage was the remarkable performance given by Stacy Keach as Buffalo Bill. While Mr. Ingham in London was all immaculate technique, the rougher, tougher Mr. Keach felt the role in his saddle-sore bones. He was a mythic hero.

On October 13 of the same year, with largely the same cast and, of course, Mr. Frankel as director, *Indians* opened on Broadway. It had however, been much rewritten from its Washington production. What we are printing here is, of course, the Broadway version of the play. I only wish that it would be possible—merely as an exercise in playwriting technique —to print also the London and Washington scripts. Much could be learned from this.

(Incidentally, in 1974 yet another production of *Indians* was planned Off Broadway; it could provide yet another text.)

In commercial terms, the Broadway production was not a success—it closed on January 3, 1970, after only ninety-six performances, and it won no particular awards. The play, as you can see here, is not perfect. But it was extraordinarily original, and its comparative economic failure raised once more the question of whether Broadway is capable of handling serious theatre.

AUTHOR'S NOTE

The idea for this play occurred to me in March, 1966. Since then, there have been many persons whose help has been instrumental in the play's reaching its final form: first, my producer, Lyn Austin, to whom I described its basic concept, and who gave me an advance of money so I could afford to research the necessary historical material; then, the wonderful actors and staff of the Royal Shakespeare Company, who presented the play some two years later, and especially Jack Gelber, who directed the excellent London production, and whose firsthand knowledge of the American Indians was constantly invaluable; Zelda Fitchandler and the staff and actors of the Arena Stage, where the next and greatly rewritten version of the play was produced, which afforded me still another relatively unstressful opportunity to view what I had written; Gene Frankel, who staged the Washington and New York productions and asked a seemingly endless number of incisive, important, and fundamental questions; my agent, Audrey Wood, who—with great affection—kept urging further rewrites, and who only smiled when I said I thought this enterprise threatened to become a lifelong task. I would particularly like to thank the Rockefeller Foundation, which gave me a grant of money so my wife and I could live in Europe during the time my play was in production there, and then allowed us to go, immediately after the production, to the fantastic Villa Serbelloni, at Lake Como, where the basic rethinking and fundamental reshaping of the play was done.

CHRONOLOGY FOR A DREAMER

1846	William F. Cody born in Le Claire, Iowa, on February 26.
1866	Geronimo surrenders.
1868	William Cody accepts employment to provide food for railroad workers; kills 4,280 buffaloes. Receives nickname "Buffalo Bill."
1869	*Buffalo Bill, the King of the Border Men,* a dime novel by Ned Buntline, makes Buffalo Bill a national hero.
1872	Expedition west in honor of Grand Duke Alexis of Russia, Buffalo Bill as guide.
1876	Battle at the Little Big Horn; Custer killed.
1877	Chief Joseph surrenders.
1878	Buffalo Bill plays himself in *Scouts of the Plains,* a play by Ned Buntline.
1879	Wild Bill Hickok joins Buffalo Bill on the stage.
1883	Sitting Bull surrenders, is sent to Standing Rock Reservation.
1883	"Buffalo Bill's Wild West Show" gives first performance, is great success.
1885	Sitting Bull allowed to join Wild West Show, tours with company for a year.
1886	United States Commission visits Standing Rock Reservation to investigate Indian grievances.
1890	Sitting Bull assassinated, December 15.
1890	Wounded Knee Massacre, December 25.

The play derives, in part, from this chronology but does not strictly adhere to it.—A.K.

SCENE ONE

Audience enters to stage with no curtain. House lights dim. On stage: three large glass cases, one holding a larger-than-life-size effigy of Buffalo Bill in fancy embroidered buckskin. One, an effigy of Sitting Bull dressed in simple buckskin or cloth, no headdress, little if any ornamentation. The last case contains some artifacts: a buffalo skull, a bloodstained Indian shirt, and an old rifle. The surrounding stage is dark. The cases are lit by spotlights from above.
Strange music coming from all about. Sense of dislocation.
The house lights fade to dark.
Music up.
Lights on the cases slowly dim.
Sound of wind, soft at first.
The cases glide into the shadowy distance and disappear.
Eerie light now on stage; dim spotlights sweep the floor as if trying to locate something in space.
Brief, distorted strains of Western American music.
A VOICE *reverberates from all about the theatre.*

VOICE. Cody . . . *Cody . . . Cody! . . .*
CODY!

One of the spotlights passes something: a man on a horse. The spotlight slowly retraces itself, picks up the horse and rider. They are in a far corner of the stage; they move in slow motion.
The other spotlights now move toward them, until all converge. At first, the light is dim. As they come toward us, it gets brighter.
The man is BUFFALO BILL, *dressed as in the museum case. The horse is a glorious white artificial stallion with wild, glowing eyes.*
They approach slowly, their slow motion gradually becoming normal speed.
Vague sound of cheering heard. Music becoming rodeolike. More identifiable.
Then, slowly, from the floor, an open-framed oval fence rises and encloses them.
The horse shies.
Tiny lights, strung beneath the top bar of the fence, glitter faintly. The spotlights—multicolored—begin to crisscross about the oval.
Ghostly-pale Wild West Show banners slowly descend.
Then! It's a WILD WEST SHOW!
Loud, brassy music!
Lights blazing everywhere!
The horse rears. His rider whispers a few words, calms him.
Then, a great smile on his face, BUFFALO BILL *begins to tour the ring, one hand lightly gripping the reins, the other proudly waving his big Stetson to the unseen surrounding crowd. Surely it is a great sight; the horse prances, struts, canters, dances to the music, leaps softly through the light,* BUFFALO BILL *effortlessly in control of the whole world, the universe; eternity.*

————

BUFFALO BILL. Yessir, BACK AGAIN! That triumphant brassy music, those familiar savage drums! Should o' known I couldn't stay away! Should o' known here's where I belong! The heat o' that ol' spotlight on my face. Yessir. . . . Should o' known here's where I belong. . . . *(He takes a deep breath, closes his eyes, savors the air. A pause)* Reminded o' somethin' tol' me once by General Custer. You remember him—one o' the great dumbass men in history. Not fer nothin' that he graduated last in his class at West Point! Anyways, we was out on the plains one day, when he turned t' me, with a kind o' far-off look in his eye, an' said, "Bill! If there is one thing a man must never fear, it's makin' a personal comeback." *(He chuckles.)* Naturally, I—

VOICE *(softly).* And now, to start . . .
BUFFALO BILL *(startled).* Hm?
VOICE. *And now to start.*
BUFFALO BILL. But I . . . just . . . got up here.
VOICE. I'm sorry; it's time to start.
BUFFALO BILL. Can't you *wait a second?* WHAT'S THE RUSH? *WAIT A SECOND!* *(Silence. He takes a deep breath; quiets his horse down.)* I'm sorry. But if I seem a trifle edgy to you, it's only 'cause I've just come from a truly harrowing engagement; seems my . . . manager, a . . . rather *ancient* gentleman, made a terrible *mistake* an' booked me int' what turned out t' be a ghost town! Well! I dunno what you folks know 'bout show business, but le' me tell you, there is nothin' more depressin' than playin' two-a-day in a goddam ghost town! *(He chuckles.* INDIANS *appear around the outside of the ring. The horse senses their presence and shies;* BUFFALO BILL, *as if realizing what it means, turns in terror.)*

VOICE. Bill.
BUFFALO BILL. But—
VOICE. It's *time.*

(Pause.)

BUFFALO BILL. Be—before we start, I'd . . . just like to say—

VOICE. Bill!

(The INDIANS *slowly approach.)*

BUFFALO BILL.—*to say* that . . . I am a fine man. And anyone who says otherwise is *WRONG!*

VOICE *(softly).* Bill, *it's time.*

BUFFALO BILL. My life is an open book; I'm not *ashamed* of its bein' looked at!

VOICE *(coaxing tone).* Bill . . .

BUFFALO BILL. I'm sorry, this is very . . . hard . . . for me t' say. But I believe I . . . am a . . . hero. . . . *A GODDAM HERO!*

(Indian music. His horse rears wildly. Lights change for next scene.)

SCENE TWO

Light comes up on SITTING BULL. *He is dressed simply—no feathered headdress. It is winter.*

———

SITTING BULL. I am Sitting Bull! . . . In the moon of the first snow-falling, in the year half my people died from hunger, the Great Father sent three wise men . . . to investigate the conditions of our reservation, though we'd been promised he would come himself.

(Lights up on SENATORS LOGAN, MORGAN, *and* DAWES; *they are flanked by armed* SOLDIERS. *Opposite them, in a semicircle, are* SITTING BULL's *people, all huddling in tattered blankets from the cold.)*

SENATOR LOGAN. Indians! Please be assured that this committee has not come to punish you or take away any of your land but only to hear your grievances, determine if they are just. And if so, remedy them. For we, like the Great Father, wish only the best for our Indian children.

(The SENATORS *spread out various legal documents.)*

SITTING BULL. They were accompanied by . . . my friend, William Cody—*(Enter* BUFFALO BILL, *collar of his overcoat turned up for the wind)* in whose Wild West Show I'd once appeared . . . (BUFFALO BILL *greets a number of the* INDIANS.) in exchange for some food, a little clothing. And a beautiful horse that could do tricks.

SENATOR MORGAN. Colonel Cody has

asked if he might say a few words before testimony begins.

SENATOR LOGAN. We would be honored.

BUFFALO BILL *(to the* INDIANS). My . . . brothers. *(Pause)* I know how disappointed you all must be that the Great Father isn't here; I apologize for having said I thought I . . . could bring him. *(Pause)* However! The three men I *have* brought are by far his most trusted personal representatives. And I promise that talking to them will be the same as . . . *(Pause; softly)* . . . talking to him. *(Long pause; he rubs his eyes as if to soothe a headache.)* To . . . Sitting Bull, then . . . *(He stares at* SITTING BULL.) . . . I would like to say that I hope you can overlook your . . . disappointment. And remember what is at *stake* here. And not get angry . . . or too impatient. *(Pause)* Also, I hope you will ask your people to speak with open hearts when talking to these men. And treat them with the same great respect I have always . . . shown . . . to you, for these men have come to *help* you and your people. And I am afraid they may be the only ones left, now, who can.

SITTING BULL. And though there were many among us who wanted to speak first: men like Red Cloud! And Little Hawk! and He-Who-Hears-Thunder! And Crazy Horse! Men who were great warriors, and had counted many coups! And been with us at the Little Big Horn when we *KILLED CUSTER!* . . . *(Pause)* I would not let them speak. . . . For they were like me, and tended to get angry, easily. *(Pause)* Instead, I asked the *young* man, John Grass, who had never fought at all, but had been to the white man's school at Carlisle. And *thought* he understood . . . something . . . of their ways.

BUFFALO BILL. Sitting Bull would like John Grass to speak first.

LOGAN. Call John Grass.

BUFFALO BILL. John Grass! Come forward.

(Enter JOHN GRASS *in a black cutaway many sizes too small for him. He wears an Indian shirt. Around his neck is a medal.)*

JOHN GRASS. Brothers! I am going to talk about what the Great Father told us a long time ago. He told us to give up hunting and start farming. So we did as he said, and our people grew hungry. For the land was suited to grazing, not farming, and even if we'd been farmers, nothing could have grown. So the Great Father said he would send us food and clothing, but nothing came of it. So we asked him for the money he had promised us when we sold him the Black Hills, thinking, with this money we could *buy* food and clothing. But nothing came of it. So we grew ill and sad. . . . So to help us from this sadness, he sent Bishop Marty, to teach us to be Christians. But when we told him we did not wish to be Christians but wished to be like our fathers, and dance the sundance, and fight bravely against the Shawnee and the Crow! And pray to the Great Spirits who made the four winds, and the earth, and made man from the dust of this earth, Bishop Marty hit us! . . . So we said to the Great Father that we thought we would like to go *back* to hunting, because to live, we needed food. But we found that while we had been learning to farm, the buffalo had gone away. And the plains were filled now only with their bones. . . . Before we give you any more of our land, or move from here where the people we loved are growing white in their coffins, we want you to tell the Great Father to give us, who still live, what he promised he would! *No more than that.*

SITTING BULL. I prayed for the return of the buffalo!

(Lights fade to black on everyone but BUF-FALO BILL.

Distant gunshot heard offstage.

Pause.

Two more gunshots.

Lights to black on BUFFALO BILL.*)*

SCENE THREE

Light comes up on SPOTTED TAIL, *standing on a ledge above the plains.*

It is night, and he is lit by a pale moon.

The air is hot. No wind.

A rifle shot is heard offstage, of much greater presence than the previous shots.

SPOTTED TAIL *peers in its direction.*

Sound, offstage, of wounded bulls.

Enter an INDIAN *dressed as a buffalo, wounded in the eye and bellowing with pain. He circles the stage.*

Enter two more buffaloes, also wounded in the eyes.

The first buffalo dies.

The two other buffaloes stagger over to his side and die beside him; another buffalo (missing an eye) enters, staggers in a circle, senses the location of the dead buffaloes and heads dizzily toward them–dying en route, halfway there.

SPOTTED TAIL *crouches and gazes down at them. Then he stares up at the sky. Night creatures screech in the dark. A pause.*

———

BUFFALO BILL *(offstage but coming closer).* Ninety-three, ninety-four, ninety-five . . . ninety-six! *I DID IT! (Enter, running, a much younger* BUFFALO BILL, *rifle in hand, followed shortly by* MEMBERS OF THE U.S. CAVALRY *bearing torches, and the* GRAND DUKE's INTERPRETER.)* I did it, I did it! No one believed I could, but *I did it!* One hundred buffalo—one hundred shots! "You jus' gimme some torches," I said. "I *know* there's buffalo around us. *Here.* Put yer ear t' the ground. Feel it tremblin'? Well. You wanna see somethin' fantastic, you get me some torches. I'll shoot the reflections in their eyes. I'll shoot 'em like they was so many shiny nickels!"

INTERPRETER. I'll tell the Grand Duke you did what you said. I know he'll be pleased.

BUFFALO BILL. Well, he oughta be! I don' give exhibitions like this fer just anybody! *(Exit the* INTERPRETER*)* 'Specially as these critters're gettin' so damn hard t' find. *(To the* SOLDIERS*)* Not like the ol' days when I was huntin' 'em fer the railroads. *(He laughs, gazes down at one of the buffaloes. Pause. He looks away; squints as if in pain.)*

A SOLDIER. Are you all right, sir?

BUFFALO BILL. Uh . . . yes. Fine. *(Exit the* SOLDIERS. BUFFALO BILL *rubs his head.* SPOTTED TAIL *hops down from his perch and walks up behind* CODY *unnoticed; stares at him. Pause.* BUFFALO BILL *senses the Indian's presence and turns, cocking his rifle. The Indian makes no move.* BUFFALO BILL *stares at the Indian. Pause)*

BUFFALO BILL. *Spotted Tail!* My God. I haven't seen you in years. How . . . ya been? *(Slight laugh)*

SPOTTED TAIL. *What are you doing here? (Pause)*

BUFFALO BILL. Well, well, what . . . are *you* doing here? This isn't Sioux territory!

SPOTTED TAIL. It isn't *your* territory either.

(Pause)

BUFFALO BILL. Well I'm with . . . these *people.* I'm scoutin' for 'em.

SPOTTED TAIL. *These people* . . . must be very hungry.

INDIANS

BUFFALO BILL. Hm?

SPOTTED TAIL. To need so many buffalo.

BUFFALO BILL. Ah! Of course! You were following the buffalo *also!* . . . Well listen, I'm sure my friends won't mind you takin' some. 'Tween us, my friends don't 'specially care for the *taste* o'buffalo meat. *(He laughs.)* My God, but it's good t' see you again!

SPOTTED TAIL. *Your friends:* I have been studying them from the hills. They are very strange. They seem neither men, nor women.

BUFFALO BILL. Well! Actually, they're sort of a new *breed* o' people. Called dudes. *(He chuckles.)*

SPOTTED TAIL. You *like* them?

BUFFALO BILL. Well . . . sure. Why not? *(Pause)* I mean, obviously, they ain't the sort I've been used to. But then, things're changin' out here. An' these men are the ones who're changin' 'em. So, if you wanna be *part* o' these things, an' not left behind somewhere, you jus' plain hafta get *used* to 'em. You—uh —follow . . . what I mean? *(Silence)* I mean . . . you've got to *adjust.* To the times. Make a *plan* fer yerself. I have one. You should have one, too. Fer yer own good. Believe me. *(Long pause)*

SPOTTED TAIL. *What is your plan?*

BUFFALO BILL. Well, my plan is t' help people. Like you, ferinstance. Or these people I'm with. More . . . even . . . than that, maybe. And, and, whatever . . . it is I *do* t' help, for it, these people may someday jus' possibly name streets after me. Cities. Counties. States! I'll . . . be as famous as Dan'l Boone! . . . An' somewhere, on top of a beautiful mountain that overlooks more plains 'n rivers than any other mountain, there might even be a statue of me sittin' on a great white horse, a-wavin' my hat t' everyone down below, thankin' 'em, fer thankin' me, fer havin' done . . . whatever . . . it is I'm gonna . . . *do* fer 'em all. How . . . come you got such a weird look on yer face?

BUNTLINE *(offstage).* HEY, CODY! *STAY WHERE YA ARE!*

BUFFALO BILL. DON'T WORRY! I AIN'T BUDGIN'! *(To* SPOTTED TAIL*)* That's Mister Ned Buntline, the well-known newspaper reporter. I think he's gonna do an *article* on me! General Custer, who's in charge, an' I think is pushin' fer an article on *himself,* says this may well be the most important western expedition since Lewis 'n Clark.

BUNTLINE *(offstage).* BY THE WAY, *WHERE* ARE YA?

BUFFALO BILL. I . . . AIN'T SURE! JUST HEAD FOR THE LIGHTS! *(He laughs to himself.)*

SPOTTED TAIL. Tell me. Who is the man everyone always bows to?

BUFFALO BILL. Oh! The Gran' Duke! He's from a place called Russia. This whole shindig's in his honor. I'm sure he'd love t' meet you. He's never seen a real Indian.

SPOTTED TAIL. There are no Indians in Russia? (BUFFALO BILL *shakes his head.)* Then I will study him even more carefully than the others. Maybe if he takes me back to Russia with him, I will not end like my people will . . . end.

BUFFALO BILL *(startled).* What?

SPOTTED TAIL. I mean, like these fools here, on the ground. *(He stares at the buffalo.)*

BUFFALO BILL. *Ah* . . . Well, if ya don' mind my sayin', I think you're bein' a bit pessimistic. But you do what ya like. Jus' remember: these people you're studyin'— some folk think *they're* the fools.

SPOTTED TAIL. Oh, no! They are not fools! *No one who is a white man can be a fool. (He smiles coldly at Buffalo Bill; heraldic Russian fanfare offstage.*

Enter RUSSIAN TORCHBEARERS *and* TRUMPETERS.

BUFFALO BILL *and* SPOTTED TAIL, *in awe, back away.*

Enter with much pomp and ceremony GRAND DUKE ALEXIS *on a splendid litter carved like a horse. He is accompanied by his* INTERPRETER, *who points out the four buffaloes to the* GRAND DUKE *as he majestically circles the clearing. He is followed by* NED BUNTLINE, *who carries a camera and tripod.)*

BUFFALO BILL. My God, but that is a beautiful sight!

(The GRAND DUKE *comes to a halt. Majestic sweep of his arms to those around him)*

GRAND DUKE. *(makes a regal Russian speech)*

INTERPRETER. His Excellency the Grand Duke wishes to express his heartfelt admiration of Buffalo Bill . . . *(Music up)* . . . for having done what he has done tonight.

(The GRAND DUKE *gestures majestically. The* INTERPRETER *opens a small velvet box. Airy music. The* INTERPRETER *walks toward* BUFFALO BILL.*)*

GRAND DUKE *(gesturing for* BUFFALO BILL *to come forward).* Boofilo Beel!

*(*BUFFALO BILL *walks solemnly forward. The* INTERPRETER *takes out a medal.* BUF-

FALO BILL, *deeply moved, looks around, embarrassed.*

The INTERPRETER *smiles and holds up the medal, gestures warmly for* BUFFALO BILL *to kneel. He does so.*

The INTERPRETER *places the medal, which is on a bright ribbon, around his neck. Flashgun goes off.)*

BUNTLINE. Great picture, Cody! FRONT PAGE! My God, what a night! *What a story!* Uh . . . sorry, yer Highness. Didn't mean t' distoib ya. *(He backs meekly away. Sets up his camera for another shot. The* GRAND DUKE *regains his composure.)*

GRAND DUKE. *(Russian speech)*

INTERPRETER. His Excellency wonders how Buffalo Bill became such a deadly shot.

BUFFALO BILL. Oh, well, you know, just . . . practice. *(Embarrassed laugh)*

GRAND DUKE. *(Russian speech)*

INTERPRETER. His Excellency says he wishes that his stupid army knew how to practice.

GRAND DUKE. *(Russian speech)*

INTERPRETER. Better yet, he wishes you would come back with him to his palace and protect him yourself.

BUFFALO BILL. Oh. *(Slight laugh)* Well, I'm sure the Grand Duke's in excellent hands.

(The INTERPRETER *whispers what* BUFFALO BILL *has just said.)*

GRAND DUKE. Da! *Hands. (He holds out his hands, then turns them and puts them around his throat.)*

BUFFALO BILL. I think His Majesty's exaggeratin'. I can't believe he's not *surrounded* by friends.

GRAND DUKE. FRIENDS! *(He cackles and draws his sword, slashes the air.)* Friends! Friends! . . . *Friends! (He fights them off.)*

BUFFALO BILL *(to* BUNTLINE). I think he's worried 'bout somethin'.

BUNTLINE. Very strange behavior.

GRAND DUKE. *(nervous Russian speech)*

INTERPRETER. His Excellency wonders if Buffalo Bill has ever been afraid.

BUFFALO BILL. . . . Afraid?

GRAND DUKE. *(Russian word)*

INTERPRETER. Outnumbered.

BUFFALO BILL. Ah. *(Slight laugh)* Well, uh—

BUNTLINE. Go on, tell 'm. It'll help what I'm plannin' t' write.

BUFFALO BILL *(delighted). It will?*

BUNTLINE. Absolutely. Look: de West is

changin'—right? Well, people wanna know about it. Wanna feel . . . *part* o' things. I think *you're* what dey need. Someone t' listen to, observe, *identify* wid. No, no, really! I been studyin' you.

BUFFALO BILL. . . . You have?

BUNTLINE. I think you could be de inspiration o' dis land.

BUFFALO BILL. Now I *know* you're foolin'!

BUNTLINE. Not at all. . . . Well, go on. Tell 'm what he wants t' hear. T'rough my magic pen, others will hear also. . . . Donmentionit. De nation needs men like me, too. *(He pats* CODY *on the shoulder and shoves him off toward the* GRAND DUKE; CODY *gathers his courage.)*

BUFFALO BILL *(to the* GRAND DUKE). Well, uh . . . where can I begin? Certainly it's true that I've been outnumbered. And— uh—many times. Yes.

BUNTLINE. That's the way.

BUFFALO BILL. More times, in fact, than I can count.

BUNTLINE. Terrific.

BUFFALO BILL *(warming to the occasion).* An' believe me, I can count pretty high!

BUNTLINE. SENSATIONAL!

BUFFALO BILL. Mind you, 'gainst *me,* twelve's normally an even battle—long's I got my two six-shooters, that is.

BUNTLINE. Keep it up, keep it up!

BUFFALO BILL. THIRTEEN! If one of 'em's thin enough for a bullet t' go clean through. Fourteen if I got a huntin' knife. Fifteen if there's a hard surface off o' which I can ricochet a few shots.

BUNTLINE. *Go on!*

BUFFALO BILL. Um, twenty . . . if I got a stick o' dynamite. HUNDRED! IF THERE'S ROCKS T' START A AVALANCHE! (BUNTLINE *applauds.)* What I mean is, with *me* it's never say die! Why . . . I remember once I was ridin' for the Pony Express 'tween Laramie 'n Tombstone. Suddenly, jus' past the Pecos, fifty drunk Comanches attack. Noise like a barroom whoop-di-do, arrows fallin' like hailstones! I mean, they come on me so fast they don' have time t' see my face, notice who I am, realize I'm in fact a very good *friend* o' theirs!

GRAND DUKE. FRIEND! FRIEND!

BUNTLINE *(sotto voce).* Get off de subject!

BUFFALO BILL. Well, there was no alternative but t' fire back. Well, I'd knocked off 'bout thirty o' their number when I realized I was *out* o' bullets. Just at that moment, a arrow whizzed past my head. Thinkin' fast, I reached out an' caught it. Then, usin' it like a fly swatter, I knocked away the other nineteen arrows that were headin' fer my heart. Whereupon, I stood up in the stirrups, hurled the arrow sixty yards . . . An' killed their chief. *(Pause)* Which . . . *depressed* . . . the remainin' Indians. *(Pause)* And sent 'em scurryin' home. Well! That's sort o' what ya might call a typical day!

(Bravos from everyone except the GRAND DUKE*)*

GRAND DUKE. *(Russian speech, quite angry)*

INTERPRETER. His Excellency says he would like to kill a Comanche also.

BUFFALO BILL. Hm?

GRAND DUKE *(with obvious jealousy)*. Like Boofilo Beel!

INTERPRETER. Like Buffalo Bill!

GRAND DUKE. *(excited Russian speech)*

INTERPRETER. He will *prove* he cannot be intimidated!

GRAND DUKE. Rifle, rifle, rifle!

BUFFALO BILL *(to* BUNTLINE*)*. I think my story may've worked a bit too well.

BUNTLINE. Nonsense! This is *terrific!* *(They duck as the* GRAND DUKE*, cackling madly, scans the surrounding darkness over his rifle sight.)* Shows you've won the Grand Duke's heart.

GRAND DUKE *(pounding his chest)*. Boofilo Beel! *I* . . . am *BOOFILO BEEL! (He laughs demonically.)*

BUNTLINE. I think you'd better find 'm a Comanche.

BUFFALO BILL. Right! *Well.* Um . . . *(Slight laugh)* That *could* be a . . . problem.

GRAND DUKE. Comanche! *Comanche!*

BUFFALO BILL. Ya see, fer one thing, the Comanches live in Texas. And we're in Missouri.

GRAND DUKE. COMANCHE! *COMANCHE!*

BUFFALO BILL. Fer another, I ain't 'xactly sure what they look like.

GRAND DUKE. Ah! *(He fires into the darkness.* SPOTTED TAIL *stumbles out, collapses and dies. The* GRAND DUKE *and his* INTERPRETER *delirious with joy.* BUNTLINE *dumfounded.* BUFFALO BILL *stunned, but for vastly different reasons.)*

BUNTLINE *(approaching the body cautiously)*. My God, will you look at that? Fate must be smiling! *(He laughs weakly, stares up at the heavens in awe.* BUFFALO BILL*, almost*

in a trance, walks over to the body; stares down at it.
Weird music heard.
The lights change color, grow vague.
All movement arrested.

SPOTTED TAIL *rises slowly and moves just as slowly toward the* GRAND DUKE*; stops.)*

SPOTTED TAIL. My name is Spotted Tail. My father was a Sioux; my mother, part Cherokee, part Crow. No matter how you look at it, I'm just not a Comanche. *(He sinks back to the ground. Lights return to normal, the music ends.)*

GRAND DUKE. *(baffled Russian speech)*

INTERPRETER. His Excellency would like to know what the man he just shot has said.

(Long pause. BUFFALO BILL *looks around, as if for help; all eyes upon him.)*

BUFFALO BILL *(softly)*. He said . . . *(Pause)* "I . . . *(Pause)* should have . . . *(He looks at* BUNTLINE*, takes a deep breath.)* stayed at home in . . . Texas with the rest of my . . . Comanche tribe."

BUNTLINE. Fabulous! *(He takes* SPOTTED TAIL*'s picture; the night sky glows from the flash.)* Absolutely fabulous!

(The scene fades around BUFFALO BILL*, who stands in the center, dizzily gripping his head.)*

SCENE FOUR

Dimly we see the SENATORS *and* SITTING BULL*'s* INDIANS *glide back into view.*

———

BUFFALO BILL. If it *please* the honorable senators . . . there is something I would like to say to *them,* as well. *(Pause)* I wish to say . . . that there is far more at stake here, today, than the discovery of Indian grievances. *(Pause)* At stake are these people's lives. *(Pause)* In *some* ways, more than even that. For these are not just *any* Indians. These are *Sitting Bull's* Indians. . . . The last to surrender. *(Pause)* The last of a kind. *(Long pause)* So, in that way, you see, they are . . . perhaps more *important* for us than . . . any others. *(Pause)* For it is we, alone, who have put them on this strip of arid land. And what becomes of them is . . . our responsibility. *(*BUFFALO BILL *stares helplessly as the scene about him fades to black.)*

VOICE. And now, for your *pleasure,* BUFFALO BILL'S WILD WEST SHOW

PROUDLY PRESENTS . . . *(Lights to black; drum roll)*

SCENE FIVE

Stage dark; drum roll continues. Weirdly colored spotlights begin to crisscross on the empty stage.

VOICE. THE MOST FEROCIOUS IN-DIAN ALIVE! . . . *(The bars of a large round cage slowly emerge from the floor of the stage; then, around the bars, the Wild West Show fence seen earlier)* THE FORMER SCOURGE OF THE SOUTHWEST! . . . *(The lights on the fence begin to glow; eerie, fantastical atmosphere.*
A tunnel-cage rolls out from the wings and connects with the large central cage.
Sound of an iron grate opening offstage.
Rodeo music up.)
The one'n only . . . *GERONIMO!*
(Enter GERONIMO, *crawling through the tunnel; as soon as he is in sight, he stops, lifts his head, takes in his surroundings.*
Enter two COWBOY ROUSTABOUTS *with prods. They are enormous men—much larger than life-size. Their muscles bulge against their gaudy clothes. Their faces seem frozen in a sneer. Even their gun belts are oversized.*
They prod GERONIMO *along, raise the gate to the center cage and coax him in, closing it behind him. Then they move away.*
GERONIMO *paces about, testing the bars with his hands.)*
    GERONIMO. I AM GERONIMO! WAR CHIEF OF THE GREAT CHIRICAHUA APACHES! *(He stalks about.)* Around my neck is a string of white men's genitals! MEN I HAVE KILLED! . . . Around my waist, the scalplocks of white women's genitals! WOMEN I RAPED AND KILLED! . . . *No Indian has ever killed or raped more than I!* Even the Great Spirits cannot count the number! . . . My body is painted with blood! I am red from white men's BLOOD! . . . NO ONE LIVES WHO HAS KILLED MORE WHITE MEN THAN *I!*
*(*BUFFALO BILL, *in his fancy buckskin, enters unnoticed by* GERONIMO; *drum roll. He opens the cage door and walks inside.*
Once inside, he closes the door and stands still.
GERONIMO *senses his presence and stops moving. Lifts up his head as if to hear better. Sniffs. Turns. Stares at* BUFFALO BILL.*

Slowly, BUFFALO BILL *walks toward him. He stops just short of the Indian. Then defiantly turns his back.*
GEROMINO *practically frothing.*
Long pause. GERONIMO *does nothing.*
BUFFALO BILL *walks calmly away, opens the cage door, and exits. Disappears into the shadows.*
GERONIMO *stands trembling with frenzy.*
Lights fade to black.)

SCENE SIX

Lights come up on the Senate Committee, SITTING BULL'S INDIANS, *and* BUFFALO BILL.

SENATOR LOGAN. Mister Grass, I wonder if you could be a bit more *specific* and tell us *exactly* what you think the Great Father has promised which he has not given.
    JOHN GRASS. He promised to give us *as much as we would need, for as long as we would need it!*
    SENATOR DAWES. Where did he promise you *that?*
    JOHN GRASS. In a treaty.
    SENATOR LOGAN. *What* treaty?
    JOHN GRASS. A treaty signed some years ago, maybe five or six.
    SENATOR LOGAN. Mister Grass, many treaties were signed five or six years ago. But frankly, I've never heard of an arrangement quite like that one.
    JOHN GRASS. You took the Black Hills from us in this treaty!
    SENATOR DAWES. You mean we *bought* the Black Hills in it!
    (LOGAN *glares at* DAWES.)
    JOHN GRASS. I have nothing else to say. *(He turns and starts to walk away.)*
    SENATOR LOGAN. Mister Grass! The . . . Senator . . . *apologizes* for his . . . tone.
    (Pause; JOHN GRASS *returns.)*
    JOHN GRASS. If you *bought* the Black Hills from us, where is our money?
    SENATOR LOGAN. The money is in trust.
    JOHN GRASS. *Trust?*
    SENATOR MORGAN. He means, it's in a bank. Being *held* for you in a . . . bank. In *Washington!* Very . . . fine bank.
    JOHN GRASS. Well, we would rather hold it ourselves.
    SENATOR DAWES. The Great Father is

worried that you've not been educated enough to spend it *wisely*. When he feels you have, you will receive every last penny of it. *Plus interest.*

(JOHN GRASS *turns in fury;* LOGAN *totally exasperated with* DAWES.)

BUFFALO BILL. Mister Grass, *please!* These men have come to *help* you! But their ways are *different* from yours; you must be *patient* with them.

JOHN GRASS. You said you would bring us the Great Father.

BUFFALO BILL. I *tried!* I *told* you! But he wouldn't come; *what else could I do?*

JOHN GRASS. You told us he was your *friend.*

BUFFALO BILL. HE *IS* MY FRIEND! *Look, don't you understand?* These men are your *only hope.* If you turn away from them, it's like . . . *committing suicide.*

(Pause)

JOHN GRASS *(to the* SENATORS*).* At Fort Laramie, Fort Lyon, and Fort Rice we signed treaties, parts of which have never been fulfilled.

SENATOR DAWES. *Which* parts have never been fulfilled?

JOHN GRASS. At Fort Rice the Government advised us to be at *peace,* and said that *if we did so,* we would receive a span of horses, five bulls, ten chickens, and a wagon!

SENATOR LOGAN. You . . . really believe . . . these things were in the treaty?

JOHN GRASS. We were told they were.

SENATOR LOGAN. You . . . saw them written?

JOHN GRASS. We cannot read very well, but we were *told* they were! *(The* SENATORS *glance sadly at one another.* JOHN GRASS *grows confused. Pause)* We were also . . . promised a STEAMBOAT!

SENATOR MORGAN. A *steamboat?*

SENATOR DAWES. What in God's name were you supposed to do with a steamboat in the middle of the plains? *(He laughs.)*

JOHN GRASS. I don't know. *(He turns in confusion and stares at* BUFFALO BILL; BUFFALO BILL *turns helplessly to the* SENATORS. *As—lights begin to fade.)*

SITTING BULL. Where is the Great Father, Cody? . . . The one you said would help us. . . . The one you said you knew *so well.*

(As lights go to black, a Mozart minuet is heard.)

SCENE SEVEN

Lights come up on White House Ballroom, in the center of which is a makeshift stage. The front drop of this stage is a melodramatic western-heroic poster with "Scouts of the Plains, *by NED BUNTLINE" painted over it. The Mozart stops as a Negro* USHER *enters.*

USHER. This way, Mister President.

OL' TIME PRESIDENT *(offstage).* Thank you, George. *(Enter the* OL' TIME PRESIDENT *in white tie and tails, cigar in mouth, brandy glass in hand.)* This way, dear. They're about to start.

(Enter the FIRST LADY *in a formal gown.)*

FIRST LADY. Oh, this *is* exciting! Our *first real cowboys!*

(The USHER *leads them toward a pair of Louis XIV chairs set facing the stage. Drum roll.)*

OL' TIME PRESIDENT. Sssh. Here we go. *(They sit. Enter, from behind the canvas drop,* NED BUNTLINE. *He wears an exaggerated version of a plainsman's outfit.)*

NED BUNTLINE.
Mister President, hon'rable First Lady,
Before you stands a character most shady,
A knave whose presence darkens this bright earth,
More than does the moon's eclipsing girth.
What's that you say, I'm rude to filth espouse,
When I'm the guest of such a clean, white house?
Fear not, there's somethin' I didn't mention:
Recently, I found redemption.
Ah, forgive me, I'm sorry, Ned Buntline's the name,
It's me who's brought Bill Cody fame.
Wrote twenty-seven books with him the hero.
Made'm better known than Nero.
And though we sold'em cheap, one for a dime,
The two of us was rich in no time.
As for my soul's redemption, it came thus:
I saw the nation profit more than us.
For with each one o' my excitin' stories,
Cody grew t' represent its glories.
Also helped relieve its conscience,
By showing pessimism's nonsense.
Later, when people asked t' *see* 'm,
I wrote a play for him to be in;
A scene of which we now perform for you,
As you've so graciously implored us to.
Cody, of course, impersonates himself,
As does Yours Truly.
The Crow Maiden is Italian actress

Paula Monduli.
Our evil Pawnee Chief, the great German actor
Gunther Hookman.
Our other Indians, I'm afraid,
Come from Brooklyn.
However, as a special treat tonight,
A visitor is here,
And I've added some new dialogue,
So he might appear.
Realize though, this man's come as Cody's friend,
He's not an actor.
Though of course in *my* play, who men *are*
Is the real factor.
So get set then for anything,
May the script be damned,
An' let's give Cody an' Wild Bill Hickok
A ROUSING HAND!
(The FIRST LADY *and the* OL' TIME PRESIDENT *applaud enthusiastically.* BUNTLINE *exits.*

The canvas drop is rolled up to reveal another canvas drop—a painted forest of the worst melodramatic order.

On stage, wooden as only the worst amateur actors can be, stand CODY *and* HICKOK, *the latter with long, glorious hair, fancy buckskin leggings, two large guns and a knife in his belt.)*

BUFFALO BILL. God pray we're in time. Those Pawnee devils will do anything.
    (Silence)
BUNTLINE *(prompting from offstage). Especially* . . .
    (Silence)
BUFFALO BILL. Think that's your line, Bill.
WILD BILL HICKOK. Oh, hell's thunder.
(To BUNTLINE) Better give it-a-me agin.
BUNTLINE. Especially . . .
HICKOK. Especially.
BUNTLINE. . . . at their . . .
HICKOK. At their.
BUFFALO BILL *(sotto voce).* . . . dreadful annual . . .
HICKOK. Dreadful. Annual.
BUNTLINE. . . . Festival of the Moon.
HICKOK. Festival of the Moon. Which is . . . 'bout t' happen. As it does every . . .
    (Silence)
BUFFALO BILL. . . . year.
HICKOK. Year.
BUNTLINE. Very good.
HICKOK. Very good.
BUNTLINE. No!
HICKOK. Whose line's that?

BUFFALO BILL. No one's. He was jus' congratulatin' you.
HICKOK. Oh, Will, fer pity's sake, le' me out o' this.
BUNTLINE. *Ad-lib!*
BUFFALO BILL. Yes! Pray God we're in time to stop the Pawnee's dreadful Festival of the Moon so that I, the great Buffalo Bill, can once again—
HICKOK. Will, stop it! A man may need money, but no man needs it this bad.
(Enter BUNTLINE, *tap-dancing the sound of horse's hooves.)*
BUFFALO BILL. Hark! Ned Buntline approaches! One o' the finest sharpshooters o' the West!
HICKOK *(under his breath).* Couldn't hit a cow in the ass from two paces.
BUFFALO BILL. Who knows? Maybe *he* can help us in our dire strait.
HICKOK. Mister and Missus President, if you're still out there, believe me, I'm as plumb embarrassed by this dude-written sissyshit as you.
BUNTLINE. HAIL, BUFFALO BILL! Hail —uh—Wild Bill Hickok. What brings you to this unlikely place?
HICKOK. Good fuckin' question.
BUNTLINE. Could it be that you seek, as I do, the camp of Uncas, evil Pawnee chief?
BUFFALO BILL. Yes, verily. We seek his camp so that I, the great Buffalo Bill, can once again, save someone in distress. (HICKOK *groans.)* This time, specifically, a virgin maiden—
HICKOK. You gotta be jokin'.
BUFFALO BILL. *Will you shut up!* Named Teskanjavila! Who, 'less I save her, faces torture, sacrifice, and certain violations.
BUNTLINE. This bein' so, *let us join forces!*
HICKOK. Boy, where's your *self-respect?*
BUNTLINE *(weakly).* And save this virgin together.
BUFFALO BILL *(to* HICKOK). Will you leave me alone!
HICKOK. This ain't a *proper place* for a man t' be!
BUFFALO BILL. Well, I THINK IT *IS!* I think I'm doin' a lot o' good up here! Entertainin' people! Makin' 'em *happy!* Showin' 'em the West! Givin' 'em somethin' t' be *proud* of! *You* go spend your life in Dodge City if you want! I got *bigger* things in mind!
    (Stunned pause)
BUNTLINE *(very sheepishly).* To repeat: let us join forces and save this virgin together.

HICKOK. Buntline, if these guns were loaded, I'd—

BUNTLINE *(cueing the actors offstage).* HARK! The maiden's name is called!

NUMEROUS VOICES *(offstage).* Teskanjavila!

BUNTLINE. We must be near the camp of Uncas.

BUFFALO BILL. Evil Pawnee chief.

HICKOK. I'm gettin' sick.

BUNTLINE. Let us, therefore, approach with caution.

BUFFALO BILL. Guns ready.

BUNTLINE. Ears open.

BUFFALO BILL *(to HICKOK).* Mouths shut!

BUNTLINE. Eyes alert.

BUFFALO BILL. So that I, Buffalo Bill, may once aga—(HICKOK *has walked over and is staring into his face.)* Just *what are you doin'?*

HICKOK. What're *you* doin'?

BUFFALO BILL. I'm doin' what I'm doin', *that's* what I'm doin'!

HICKOK *(to* BUNTLINE). Always was intelligent.

BUFFALO BILL. I am doin' what my country *wants!* WHAT MY BELOVED COUNTRY *WANTS!*

HICKOK *(to the First Family).* This . . . is . . . what you want?

FIRST LADY. Absolutely!

OL' TIME PRESIDENT. Best play I've seen in years!

(HICKOK, *staggered, sits down on the stage.)*

BUFFALO BILL. When a man has a talent, a *God*-given talent, I think it's his godly duty t' make the most of it. *(Applause from the First Family.* BUFFALO BILL *nods acknowledgment. To* HICKOK) Ya see, Bill, what you fail to understand is that I'm not being false to what I *was.* I'm simply *drawin'* on what I was . . . and raisin' it to a higher level. *(He takes a conscious pause.) Now.* On with the show! *(He points to* BUNTLINE, *cueing him to give the next line.)*

BUNTLINE. AVAST, AHOY! Above yon trees see the pale moon rising! *(A cardboard moon is pulled upward.)* Feel the black night envelop us like a dark dream. (BUNTLINE *and* CODY *shiver.)* Sounds of the savage forest are heard. . . . We approach on tiptoes.

BUFFALO BILL *(to the First Family).* God pray we're in time.

(They drop to their bellies as the canvas drop is raised to reveal the camp of UNCAS. *Tied to a totem pole is* TESKANJAVILA, *writhing sensually.*

Clearly phony INDIANS *dance around her to the beat of drums.*

The heroes crawl slowly forward. HICKOK, *eyeing the girl lustfully, joins in.)*

FIRST LADY. That Hickok's rather handsome, isn't he?

OL' TIME PRESIDENT. I'm watching the girl. Note her legs. How white they are. For an Indian. One can almost see the soft inner flesh of her thighs.

FIRST LADY. *This play excites me!*

OL' TIME PRESIDENT. We really should have more things like this at the White House.

(The drums grow wilder. The INDIANS *scream;* BUNTLINE, CODY, *and* HICKOK *invade the Indian campsite. Gunshots.* INDIANS *fall dead.)*

TESKANJAVILA *(Italian accent).* Saved! A maiden's prayers are answered! And may I say, not a bit too soon! Already, my soft thighs had been pried open; my budding breasts pricked by the hot tip of an Indian spear. Yet, through it all, my maidenhead stayed secure. Here. In this pouch. Kept in this secret pocket. Where no one thought to look. Thus is innocence preserved! May Nazuma, God of Thunder, grant me happiness!

(Thunder heard.)

HICKOK. Buntline write that speech?

BUFFALO BILL. I think she changed it a little.

(UNCAS *rises from the dead.)*

UNCAS *(German accent).* I am Uncas, Chief of the Pawnee Indians, recently killed for my lustful ways. Yet, before the white men came and did me in, I had this vision: the white man is great, the red man nothing. So, if a white man kills a red man, we must forgive him, for God intended man to be as great as possible, and by eliminating the inferior, the great man carries on God's work. Thus, the Indian is in no way wronged by being murdered. Indeed, quite the opposite: being murdered is his purpose in life. This was my recent vision. Which has brought light to the darkness of my otherwise useless soul. . . . And now, I die again. *(He collapses.)*

HICKOK. Buntline write that?

BUFFALO BILL. Think Hookman changed it also. They all do it. It's our style. I dunno, people seem to like it.

HICKOK. Yeah? Well then, guess it mus' be my turn! *(He pulls out his bowie knife.)*

BUFFALO BILL. HEY!

HICKOK. Make one false move an' I'll rip you 'part, friend or no.

BUNTLINE. Bill, look—

HICKOK. As for you, Buntline, you fangless lizard, you harmless bull, you ball of—

BUNTLINE. BRING DOWN THE CURTAIN!

HICKOK. First one touches that curtain, I cuts int' mincemeat an' eats fer dinner, *raw!*

FIRST LADY. I'm trembling all over.

HICKOK. Okay, Buntline. Now we're gonna settle up the score.

BUNTLINE. Score?

HICKOK. Men jus' don' humiliate Wil' Bill Hickok.

BUNTLINE. *Hu—humiliate?*

HICKOK. Or leastways don' do it twice, bein' dead shortly after the first occasion.

BUNTLINE. Wh—what . . . 're you talkin' about?

HICKOK. 'Bout havin' to impersonate myself. 'Bout the humiliation o' havin' to impersonate my *own personal self!*

BUNTLINE. Oh.

FIRST LADY. *Fantastic!*

BUNTLINE. Well, I dunno what t' say.

HICKOK. It weren't in the deal!

BUNTLINE. Deal?

HICKOK. You said if I came here, I could play Bat Masterson!

BUNTLINE. Ah, *that!* (He chuckles.) Well, . . . if you recall, I said *maybe* you could play Bat Masterson. First, we had t' see how good you did as Hickok.

HICKOK. As *Hickok?* Chrissake, I AM Hickok!

BUNTLINE. Right.

HICKOK. Well, why in hell should I play *him* then?

BUNTLINE. Well, there's audience appeal.

FIRST LADY. There sure is!

BUNTLINE. BILL! Now—now, wait-a-second! Let's talk this over. Like gentlemen.

BUFFALO BILL. Yeah. Right. Let's . . . not get too . . . carried away. After all—

HICKOK. If you don' stay out o' this, I'm gonna slit yer stuffin' gizzard an' extract, inch by inch, what's guts in most folks, but in you is thorou' garbage.

BUFFALO BILL. Now wait-a-minute! Hold on! You—you think I'm jus' gonna stand here an'—

HICKOK. Oh, shut up! Dumb, dudelickin' FRAUD!

BUFFALO BILL. *What?*

HICKOK. If I gotta play Hickok, I'm gonna play Hickok the way Hickok should be *played!*

BUNTLINE. *Put that knife away, please!* . . . For godsakes. Cody, *HELP ME! Cody!* (BUNTLINE *falls, a knife in his back. He crawls off the front of the stage; collapses.*)

FIRST LADY. He looks kind o' dead.

(BUFFALO BILL *heads for the body, stunned.*)

HICKOK. Sorry, Will. Guess I just ain't used to show business yet. (He chuckles and turns his attention to TESKANJAVILA. BUFFALO BILL *is feeling for* BUNTLINE's *pulse.*)

TESKANJAVILA. O, *Sancta Maria,* I don' like this gleam in his eye.

HICKOK (*striking a pose*).

Hail, sweet cookie, tart of tempting flavors,
Why've I been denied your spicy favors?

TESKANJAVILA. AH! *What're you doing?* HELP!

(HICKOK *unties her from the pole, at the same time unhooking his gun belt. He works rapidly.* BUFFALO BILL *lets* BUNTLINE's *limp arm drop. He stares back at the stage, stunned.*)

FIRST LADY. Ooooh, look what he's doing now! (*The First Family climb on the stage, the Negro* USHERS *bringing their chairs for them so they can have a more comfortable view.*) Really, we must invite this theatre crowd more often.

(HICKOK *is now standing above* TESKANJAVILA, *who lies helpless at his feet.* BUFFALO BILL *watches from offstage, outside the ring. Also helpless.*)

HICKOK. Hickok, fastest shooter in the West, 'cept for Billy the Kid, who ain't as accurate; Hickok, deadliest shooter in the West, 'cept for Doc Holliday, who wields a sawed-off shotgun, which ain't fair; Hickok, shootinest shooter in the West, 'cept for Jesse James, who's absolutely indiscriminate; this Hickok, strong as an eagle, tall as a mountain, swift as the wind, fierce as a rattlesnake —a legend in his own time, or any other— this Hickok stands now above an Indian maiden—

TESKANJAVILA. I'm not an Indian and I'm not a maiden!

HICKOK. Who's not an Indian and not a maiden, but looks pretty good anyhow—an' asks those o' you watchin' t' note carefully the basic goodness of his very generous intentions, since otherwise . . . (He starts to finger her clothing.) . . . they might be mistaken for . . . (He rips open her buckskin dress.) . . . LUST!

(She is left in a frilly Merry Widow corset.)

TESKANJAVILA. Eh, bambino. If you don' mind, I'd like a little privacy. *(To the First Family)* After all, I've not rehearsed this.

(HICKOK *pulls the cord, lowering the curtain.)*

OL' TIME PRESIDENT. Good show, Cody! *Good show!*

(BUFFALO BILL, *in a daze, walks to the stage and opens the curtain.*
"Scouts of the Plains" *drop seen. He stares at it. Pulls it down.*
NO ONE THERE.
Mozart minuet heard.
He looks around in total confusion.
The stage and all the White House furniture begin to disappear.
Lights fade to black, BUFFALO BILL *spinning dizzily in the middle.*
Music fades.)

SCENE EIGHT

Lights come up again on the Senate Committee.

————

SENATOR LOGAN. Mister Grass. Let's leave aside the question of the steamboat. You mentioned the treaty at Fort Lyon and said that parts of that treaty had never been fulfilled. Well, I happen to be quite familiar with that particular treaty and happen to know that it is the Indians who did not fulfill its terms, not us.

JOHN GRASS. We did not *want* the cows you sent!

SENATOR LOGAN. You signed the treaty.

JOHN GRASS. We did not understand that we were to give up part of our reservation in exchange for these cows.

SENATOR DAWES. Why'd you think we were giving you twenty-five thousand cows?

JOHN GRASS. We were hungry. We thought it was for food.

SENATOR LOGAN. It wasn't explained that *only* if you gave us part of your reservation would you receive these cows?

JOHN GRASS. Yes. That was explained.

SENATOR MORGAN. And yet, you thought it was a gift.

JOHN GRASS. Yes.

SENATOR LOGAN. In other words, you thought you could have both the cows and the land?

JOHN GRASS. Yes.

SENATOR DAWES. Even though it was explained that you couldn't.

JOHN GRASS. Yes.

SENATOR MORGAN. This is quite hard to follow.

SENATOR LOGAN. Mister Grass, tell me, which would you prefer, cows or land?

JOHN GRASS. We prefer them both.

SENATOR LOGAN. Well, what if you can't have them both?

JOHN GRASS. We prefer the land.

SENATOR LOGAN. Well then, if you knew you had to give up some land to get these cows, why did you sign the treaty?

JOHN GRASS. The white men made our heads dizzy, and the signing was an accident.

SENATOR LOGAN. An accident?

JOHN GRASS. They talked in a threatening way, and whenever we asked questions, shouted and said we were stupid. Suddenly, the Indians around me rushed up and signed the paper. They were like men stumbling in the dark. I could not catch them.

SENATOR LOGAN. But you signed it, too.

(Long pause)

SENATOR DAWES. Mister Grass. Tell me. Do the Indians really expect to keep all this land and yet do nothing toward supporting themselves?

JOHN GRASS. We do not have to support ourselves. The Great Father promised to give us everything we ever needed; for that, we gave him the Black Hills.

SENATOR LOGAN. Mister Grass. Which do you prefer—to be self-sufficient or to be given things?

JOHN GRASS. We prefer them both.

SENATOR DAWES. Well, you can't *have* them both!

BUFFALO BILL. *Please!*

JOHN GRASS. I only know what we were promised.

SENATOR DAWES. That's *not* what you were promised!

JOHN GRASS. We believe it is.

BUFFALO BILL. *What's going on here?*

SENATOR MORGAN. Mister Grass. Wouldn't you and your people like to live like the white man?

JOHN GRASS. We are happy like the Indian!

SENATOR LOGAN. He means, you wouldn't like to see your people made *greater,* let's say?

JOHN GRASS. That is not possible! The Cheyenne and the Sioux are as great as people can be, already.

SENATOR MORGAN. Extraordinary, really.

BUFFALO BILL. Mister Grass. Surely . . . surely . . . your people would like to *improve their condition!*

JOHN GRASS. We would like what is owed us! If the white men want to give us more, that is fine also.

SENATOR LOGAN. Well, we'll see what we can do.

SENATOR MORGAN. Let's call the next. This is getting us nowhere.

JOHN GRASS. We would especially like the money the Great Father says he is holding for us!

SENATOR DAWES. I'm afraid that may be difficult, since, in the past, we've found that when an Indian's been given money, he's spent it all on liquor.

JOHN GRASS. When he's been given money, it's been so little there's been little else he could buy.

SENATOR MORGAN. Whatever, the Great Father does not like his Indian children getting drunk!

JOHN GRASS. Then tell the Great Father, who says he wishes us to live like white men, that when a n Indian gets drunk, he is merely imitating the white men he's observed!

(Laughter from the INDIANS. LOGAN *raps his gavel.)*

SENATOR DAWES. STOP IT! *(No effect.* LOGAN *raps more.)* What in God's name do they think we're doing here? STOP IT!

(Over the INDIANS' *noise, the noise of a Wild West Show is heard; lights fade to black.)*

SCENE NINE

Wild West Show music and crisscrossing multicolored spotlights. The rodeo ring rises from the stage, its lights glittering. Wild West Show banners descend above the ring.

———

VOICE. And now, ladies and gentlemen, let's hear it for Buffalo Bill's fantastic company of authentic western heroes . . . the fabulous ROUGHRIDERS OF THE WORLD! *(Enter, on heroically artificial horses, the* ROUGHRIDERS—*themselves heroically oversized. They gallop about the ring in majestic, intricate formation, whoopin' and shootin' as they do.)* With the ever-lovely . . . ANNIE OAKLEY! (ANNIE OAKLEY *performs some startling trick shots as the others ride in circles about her.)* And now, once again, here he is—the star of our show, the Ol' Scout himself; I mean the indestructible and ever-popular—*(Drum roll)*—BUFFALO BILL!

(Enter, on horseback, BUFFALO BILL. *He is in his Wild West finery. He tours the ring in triumph while his* ROUGHRIDERS *ride after him, finally exiting to leave him in the center, alone.)*

BUFFALO BILL. THANK YOU, THANK YOU! A *GREAT* show lined up tonight! With all-time favorite Johnny Baker, Texas Jack and his twelve-string guitar, the Dancin' Cavanaughs, Sheriff Brad and the Deadwood Mail Coach, Harry Philamee's Trained Prairie Dogs, the Abilene County Girls' School Trick Roping and Lasso Society, Pecos Pete and the—

VOICE. *Bill.*

BUFFALO BILL *(startled).* Hm?

VOICE. Bring on the Indians.

BUFFALO BILL. What?

VOICE. The *Indians.*

BUFFALO BILL. Ah. (BUFFALO BILL *looks uneasily toward the wings as his company of* INDIANS *enters solemnly and in ceremonial warpaint; they carry the Sun Dance pole. At its summit is a buffalo skull.)* And now, while my fabulous company of authentic . . . American Indians go through the ceremonial preparations of the Sun Dance, which they will re-create in all its death-defying goriness —let's give a warm welcome back to a courageous warrior, the magnificent Chief Joseph — *(Some* COWBOY ROUSTABOUTS *set up an inverted tub; music for* CHIEF JOSEPH's *entrance)*—who will recite his . . . celebrated speech. CHIEF JOSEPH!

(Enter CHIEF JOSEPH, *old and hardly able to walk.)*

CHIEF JOSEPH. In the moon of the cherries blossoming, in the year of our surrender, I, Chief Joseph, and what remained of my people, the Nez Percés, were sent to a prison in Oklahoma, though General Howard had promised we could return to Idaho, where we'd always lived. In the moon of the leaves falling, still in the year of our surrender, William Cody came to see me. He was a nice man. With eyes that seemed . . . frightened; I . . . don't know why. He told me I was courageous and said he admired me. Then he explained all about his Wild West Show, in which the great Sitting Bull appeared, and said if I agreed to join, he would have me released from prison, and see that my people received food. I asked what I could do, as I was not a very good rider or marksman. And he looked away and said, "Just repeat, twice a day, three times on Sundays, what you said that afternoon when our army caught you at the Canadian border, where you'd been heading, and where you and your people would have all been safe." So I agreed. For the benefit of my people. . . . And for the next year, twice a day, three times on Sundays, said this to those sitting around me in the dark, where I could not see them, a light shining so brightly in my eyes! *(Pause. He climbs up on the tub; accompanied by exaggerated and inappropriate gestures.)* "Tell General Howard I know his heart. I am tired of fighting. Our chiefs have been killed. Looking Glass is dead. The old men are all dead. It is cold and we have no blankets. The children are freezing. My people, some of them, have fled to the hills and have no food or warm clothing. No one knows where they are—perhaps frozen. I want to have time to look for my children and see how many of them I can find. Maybe I shall find them among the dead. Hear me, my chiefs. I am tired. My heart is sick and sad. From where the sun now stands, I will fight no more forever. . . ." *(He climbs down from the tub.)* After which, the audience always applauded me.

(Exit CHIEF JOSEPH; *pause)*

BUFFALO BILL. The Sun Dance . . . was the one religious ceremony common to all the tribes of the plains. The Sioux, the Crow, the Blackfeet, the Kiowa, the Blood, the Cree, the Chippewa, the Arapaho, the Pawnee, the Cheyenne. It was *their* way of proving they were . . . real Indians. *(Pause)* The bravest would take the ends of long leather thongs and hook them through their chest muscles, then, pull till they'd ripped them out. The greater the pain they could endure, the greater they felt the Spirits would favor them. Give them what they needed. . . . Grant them . . . salvation. *(Pause)* Since the Government has officially outlawed this ritual, we will merely imitate it. *(Pause)* And no one . . . will be hurt.

(He steps back. The dance begins. The IN-DIANS *take the barbed ends of long leather thongs that dangle from the top of the Sun Dance pole and hook them through plainly visible chest harnesses. Then they pull back against the center and dance about it, flailing*

their arms and moaning as if in great pain. Suddenly* JOHN GRASS *enters.* A ROUST-ABOUT *tries to stop him. The* INDIANS *are astonished to see this intruder;* BUFFALO BILL *stunned.* JOHN GRASS *pulls the* INDIANS *out of their harnesses, rips open his shirt, and sticks the barbs through his chest muscles. He chants and dances. The other* INDIANS, *realizing what he's doing, blow on reed whistles, urge him on. Finally he collapses, blood pouring from his chest. The* INDIANS *gather around him in awe.* BUFFALO BILL *walks slowly toward* JOHN GRASS; *stares down at him. The* INDIANS *remove the Sun Dance pole and trappings.* BUFFALO BILL *crouches and cradles* JOHN GRASS *in his arms. As lights fade to black.)*

SCENE TEN

Light comes up on WHITE HOUSE USHER.

————

USHER. The President is exercising in the gym, sir. This way.

(Enter BUFFALO BILL*)*

BUFFALO BILL. You're sure it's all right?

USHER. Yes, sir. He said to show you right in. Very pleased you're here. *(The* USHER *gestures for* CODY *to pass. When he does, the* USHER *bows, turns, and leaves.)*

BUFFALO BILL *stops.*

Gym noise heard.

Lights up on the OL' TIME PRESIDENT, *dressed like* HICKOK *and astride a mechanical horse pushed by another* USHER. *Near him sits an old Victrola; "On the Old Chisholm Trail" is playing.*

The OL' TIME PRESIDENT *spurs his horse onwards.*

Nearby hangs a punching bag.

BUFFALO BILL *stares at the scene, stupefied; walks cautiously forward.)*

BUFFALO BILL. Uh—

OL' TIME PRESIDENT. *Cody!* My ol' buddy! Welcome back! Long time no see!

BUFFALO BILL. Yes, sir. Long time . . . no see.

OL' TIME PRESIDENT. Wha'd'ya think o' this thing? Latest in athletic equipment. Just got it yesterday.

BUFFALO BILL. It's a . . . nice imitation.

OL' TIME PRESIDENT. More power.

USHER. Pardon?

OL' TIME PRESIDENT. *Little more power.*

(The USHER *nods; the mechanical horse bounces faster.)* Good for the figure, this bronco riding. GIDDYAP! You orn'ry sonofabitch. *(He laughs: whips his horse furiously.)*

BUFFALO BILL. Sir. What I've come t' talk t' you about is very important.

OL' TIME PRESIDENT. Can't hear ya. Speak up!

BUFFALO BILL *(pointing to the phonograph).* May I turn this down?

OL' TIME PRESIDENT. Tell me. You think I look a little bit like Hickok?

BUFFALO BILL. Mr. President, would you *please stop this?*

OL' TIME PRESIDENT. What?

BUFFALO BILL. *STOP THIS!!!*

OL' TIME PRESIDENT. Whoa, Nellie.

USHER. Pardon?

OL' TIME PRESIDENT. WHOA, NELLIE! *(The* USHER *stops the horse; shuts off the phonograph. Cold tone)* All right. What is it?

BUFFALO BILL. Well sir, I'm here t' ask if you'd come with me t' Sitting Bull's reservation.

OL' TIME PRESIDENT. *Whose* reservation?

BUFFALO BILL. Sitting Bull's. He was in my Wild West Show for a time. And naturally, I feel a sort o' . . . obligation. *(Pause)* Personal . . . obligation.

OL' TIME PRESIDENT. I see.

BUFFALO BILL. *I* figure you're just about the only one left now who can really help him. His people are in a desperate way.

OL' TIME PRESIDENT. Tell me: this—uh—Sitting Bull. Isn't he the one who wiped out Custer?

BUFFALO BILL. Uh, well, yes, he . . . is, but it was, ya know, nothin'—uh—personal. *(Weak laugh)*

OL' TIME PRESIDENT. Can't help.

BUFFALO BILL. What?

OL' TIME PRESIDENT. I'm sorry, but I can't help.

BUFFALO BILL. *You don't understand the situation!*

OL' TIME PRESIDENT. I *don't?* All right, let's say I *want* to help. *What do I do for 'em?* Do I give 'em back their land? Do I resurrect the buffalo?

BUFFALO BILL. You can do *other* things!

OL' TIME PRESIDENT. No, Cody. *Other* people can do other things. *I* . . . must do magic. Well, I can't *do* magic for *them;* it's too late.

BUFFALO BILL. I promised Sitting Bull you'd come.

OL' TIME PRESIDENT. Then you're a fool.

BUFFALO BILL. They're going to *die.*

(Long pause)

OL' TIME PRESIDENT. Tell ya what. 'Cause I'm so *grateful* to you. . . . For your Wild West Show. For what it's *done.* For this country's *pride,* its *glory. (Pause)* I'll do you a favor; I'll send a committee in my place.

BUFFALO BILL. A committee *won't be able to help!*

OL' TIME PRESIDENT. Oh, I think the gesture will mean something.

BUFFALO BILL. To *WHOM?*

(Silence)

OL' TIME PRESIDENT. Being a great President, Cody, is like being a great eagle. A great . . . *hunted* eagle. I mean, you've got to know . . . *when t' stay put. (He smiles.)* On your way out, Bill, tell the guards, no more visitors today, hm? *(He nods to the* USHER, *who starts to rock him again as* BUFFALO BILL *slowly leaves.*

Music back up.

Lights fade to black.)

SCENE ELEVEN

Lights come up on reservation, as when last seen. The INDIANS *are laughing, the* SENATORS, *rapping for silence.*

———

SENATOR DAWES. *What in God's name do they think we're doing here?*

BUFFALO BILL *(to* SITTING BULL). Please! You must tell them to stop this *noise!*

SITTING BULL. You told us you would bring the Great Father.

BUFFALO BILL. I told you! He couldn't come! It's not my fault! Besides, these men are the Great Father's representatives! Talking to them is like talking to him!

SITTING BULL. If the Great Father wants us to believe he is wise, why does he send us men who are *stupid?*

BUFFALO BILL. They're *not* stupid! They just don't see things the way *you* do!

SITTING BULL. Yes. Because they are stupid.

BUFFALO BILL. They're *not* stupid!

SITTING BULL. Then they must be blind. It is the only other explanation.

BUFFALO BILL. All right. Tell me. Do *you* understand them?

SITTING BULL. Why should I want to understand men who are stupid?

BUFFALO BILL. Because if you *don't,* your people will *starve to death. (Long pause)* All right. . . . Now. Let me try to explain some . . . *basics. (To the* SENATORS) Well, as you've just seen, the Indian can be hard t' figure. What's one thing t' us is another t' him. For example, farmin'. Now the *real* problem here is not poor soil. The real problem's plowin'. Ya see, the Indian believes the earth is sacred and sees plowin' as a sacrigious act. Well, if ya can't get 'em t' plow, how can ya teach 'em farmin'? Impossible. Fertile land's another problem. There just ain't much of it, an' what there is, the Indians prefer to use for pony racin'. Naturally, it's been explained to 'em how people can race ponies anywhere, but they *prefer* the fertile land. They say, if their ancestors raced ponies there, that's where *they* must race. . . . Another difficult problem is land itself. The majority of 'em, ya see, don't understand how land can be owned, since they believe the land was made by the Great Spirits for the benefit of everyone. So, when we do buy land from 'em, they think it's just some kind o' temporary loan, an' figure we're kind o' foolish fer payin' good money for it, much as someone 'ud seem downright foolish t' us who paid money fer the sky, say, or the ocean. Which . . . causes problems. *(Pause)* Well, what I'm gettin' at is *this:* if *their* way o' seein' is hard fer *us* t' follow, ours is just as hard fer *them.* . . . There's an old Indian legend that when the first white man arrived, he asked some Indians for enough land t' put his blanket down onto fer the night. So they said yes. An' next thing they knew, he'd unraveled this blanket till it was one long piece o' thread. Then he laid out the thread, an' when he was done, he'd roped off a couple o' square miles. Well, the Indian finds that sort o' behavior hard t' understand. That's all I have t' say. Maybe, if you think about it, some good'll finally come from all this. I dunno.

SENATOR MORGAN. Thank you. We *shall* think about it. And hope the Indians think about it, too. And cause no more disturbances like the one just now. . . . Ask Sitting Bull if he has anything to say.

BUFFALO BILL. Sitting Bull.

SITTING BULL. Of course I will speak if they desire me to. I suppose it is only such men as they desire who may say anything.

SENATOR LOGAN. Anyone here may speak.

If you have something to say, we will listen. Otherwise, sit down.

SITTING BULL. Tell me, do you know who I am, that you talk as you do?

BUFFALO BILL. SITTING BULL, PLEASE!

(Long pause)

SITTING BULL. I wish to say that I fear I spoke hastily just now. In calling you . . . stupid. For my friend William Cody tells me you are here with good intentions. So I ask forgiveness for my unthinking words, which might have caused you to wreak vengeance on my people for what was not their doing, but *mine, alone.*

SENATOR LOGAN. We are pleased you speak so . . . sensibly. You are . . . forgiven.

SITTING BULL. I shall tell you, then, what I want you to say to the Great Father for me. And I shall tell you everything that is in my heart. For I know the Great Spirits are looking down on me today and want me to tell you everything that is in my heart. For you are the only people now who can help us. *(Pause)* My children . . . are dying. They have no warm clothes, and their food is gone. The old way is gone. No longer can they follow the buffalo and live where they wish. I have prayed to the Great Spirits to send us back the buffalo, but I have not yet seen any buffalo returning. So I know the old way is gone. I think . . . my children must learn a *new* way if they are to live. Therefore, tell the Great Father that if he wishes us to live like white men, we will do so. *(Stunned reaction from his Indians; he silences them with a wave of his hand.)* For I know that if that pleases him, we will benefit. I am looking always to the benefit of my children, and so, want only to please the Great Father. . . . Therefore, tell him for me that I have never yet seen a white man starving, so he should send us food so we can live like the white man, as he wants. Tell him, also, we'd like some healthy cattle to butcher—I wish to kill three hundred head at a time. For that is the way the white man lives, and we want to please the Great Father and live the same way. Also, ask him to send us each six teams of mules, because that is the way the white men make a living, and I want my children to make as good a living. I ask for these things only because I was advised to follow your ways. I do not ask for anything that is not needed. Therefore, tell him to send to each person here a horse and buggy. And four yokes of oxen and a wagon to haul wood in, since I have never yet seen a white man dragging wood by hand. Also, hogs, male and female, and male and female sheep for my children to raise from. If I leave anything out in the way of animals that the white men have, it is a mistake, for I want every one of them! For we are great Indians, and therefore should be no less great as white men. . . . Furthermore, tell him to send us warm clothing. And glass for the windows. And toilets. And clean water. And beds, and blankets, and pillows. And fur coats, and gloves. And hats. And *pretty silk ties.* As you see, I do not ask for anything that is not needed. For the Great Father has advised us to live like white men, so clearly, this is how we should live. For it is your doing that we are here on this reservation, and it is not right for us to live in poverty. And be treated like beasts. . . . That is all I have to say.

SENATOR LOGAN. I want to say something to that man before he sits down, and I want all the Indians to listen very carefully to what I'm going to tell him. . . . Sitting Bull, this committee invited you to come here for a friendly talk. When you talked, however, you insulted them. I understand this is not the first time you have been guilty of such an offense.

SITTING BULL. Do you know who I am that you talk the way you do?

SENATOR LOGAN. I know you are Sitting Bull.

SITTING BULL. Do you really not recognize me? Do you really not know who I am?

SENATOR LOGAN. *I said, I know you are Sitting Bull!*

SITTING BULL. You know I am Sitting Bull. But do you know what *position* I hold?

SENATOR DAWES. We do not recognize any difference between you and other Indians.

SITTING BULL. Then I will tell you the difference. So you will never ever make this mistake again. I am here by the will of the Great Spirits, and by their will I am a chief. My heart is red and sweet, and I know it is sweet, for whatever I pass near tries to touch me with its tongue, as the bear tastes honey and the green leaves lick the sky. If the Great Spirits have chosen anyone to be leader of their country, know that it is not the Great Father; *it is myself.*

SENATOR DAWES. WHO IS THIS CREATURE?

SITTING BULL. I will show you. (*He raises his hand. The* INDIANS *turn and start to leave.*)

SENATOR LOGAN. Just a minute, Sitting Bull! (SITTING BULL *stops.*) Let's get something straight. You said to this committee that you were chief of all the people of this country and that you were appointed chief by the Great Spirits. Well, I want to say that you were *not* appointed by the Great Spirits. Appointments are not made that way. Furthermore, I want to say that you are arrogant and stupidly proud, for you are not a great chief of this country or any other; that you have no following, no power, no control, and no right to any control.

SITTING BULL. I wish to say a word about my not being a chief, having no authority, being proud—

SENATOR LOGAN. You are on an Indian reservation merely at the sufferance of the Government. You are fed by the Government, clothed by the Government; your children are educated by the Government, and all you have and are today is because of the Government. I merely say these things to notify you that you cannot insult the people of the United States of America or its committees. And I want to say to the rest of you that you must learn that you are the equals of other men and must not let this one man lead you astray. You must stand up to him and not permit him to insult people who have come all this way just to help you. . . . That is all I have to say.

SITTING BULL. I wish to say a word about my not being a chief, having no authority, being proud, and considering myself a great man in general.

SENATOR LOGAN. We do not care to talk with you any more today.

SENATOR DAWES. Next Indian.

SITTING BULL. I said, I wish to speak about my having no authority, being not a chief, and—

SENATOR LOGAN. I said, we've heard enough of you today!

(SITTING BULL *raises his hand; the* INDIANS *leave.* SITTING BULL *stares at* CODY.)

SITTING BULL. If a man is the chief of a great people, and has lived only for those people, and has done many great things for them, *of course he should be proud!* (*He exits. Lights fade to black.*)

SCENE TWELVE

A guitar is heard: "Chisholm Trail." *Lights up on saloon. Most of it is in shadows. Only a poker table is well lit.*
A bar is in the distance; swinging doors. Various COWBOYS *slouch about.*

JESSE JAMES *(Sings).*
Walkin' down the street in ol' Dodge City,
Wherever I look things look pretty shitty.
    Coma ti yi youpy, youpy yea, youpy yea,
    Coma ti yi youpy, youpy yea.
An' the very worst thing that I can see,
Is a dead man walkin' straight toward me.
    Coma ti yi youpy, youpy yea, youpy yea,
    Coma ti yi youpy, youpy yea.
This dead man clearly ain't feelin' well,
If you ask me I think he's just found hell.
    Coma ti yi youpy, youpy yea, youpy yea,
    Coma ti yi youpy, you

(Enter BUFFALO BILL *in an overcoat flecked with snow. Gloves. A warm scarf.)*

BUFFALO BILL. Where's Hickok? I'm told Hickok's here. . . . *Where's Hickok?*

BILLY THE KID. Hey, uh . . . stranger. *(He chuckles. Before he can draw,* BUFFALO BILL *gets the drop on him.)*

BUFFALO BILL. Who're you?

PONCHO. He . . . is the original . . . Billy the Kid. (JESSE JAMES *makes a move and* BUFFALO BILL *draws his other gun; gets the drop on him as well.)* And *he* is the original Jesse James. The original Doc Holliday is, I'm afraid, out to lunch. *(The* COWBOYS *move to encircle* BUFFALO BILL.) Who're *you?*

BUFFALO BILL. Buffalo Bill.

PONCHO. Really? (PONCHO *laughs. Enter* HICKOK)

HICKOK. Cody! My ol' buddy! *(They embrace.)* Oh, great balls o' fire! What a surprise! Why jus' this mornin' I was . . . was . . . *(Pause) picturin'* you.

BUFFALO BILL. You were?

HICKOK. So how ya been? C'mon. Tell me.

BUFFALO BILL. Oh, I been . . . fine.

HICKOK. Great!

BUFFALO BILL. An' you?

HICKOK. Never better. *Never better!*

BUFFALO BILL. Mus' say, you've sure got some . . . famous . . . people here. *(Slight laugh)*

HICKOK. Well, ya know, it's . . . that kind o' place. *(He laughs, too; slaps* CODY *on the back. He leads him to a table.)* So! . . . Whatcha doin' here? Great honor. *Great honor!*

BUFFALO BILL. I hafta . . . *talk* . . . t' you.

HICKOK. Sure thing. *(He waves the* COW-BOYS *away; they sit at the table in privacy.)*

BUFFALO BILL. I've just come from Sitting Bull's reservation.

HICKOK. Oh? *(Slight laugh)* That reservation's a far piece from here.

BUFFALO BILL. I need your help! Sitting Bull is . . . *(Pause)*

HICKOK. What?

(Long silence)

BUFFALO BILL. I'm scared. . . . I dunno what's happenin' anymore. . . . Things have gotten . . . *beyond* me. *(He takes a drink.)* I see them *everywhere. (Weak smile; almost a laugh; music;* INDIANS *appear in the shadows beyond the saloon.)* In the grass. The rocks. The branches of dead trees. *(Pause)* Took a drink from a river yesterday an' they were even there, beneath the water, their hands reachin' up, I dunno whether beggin', or t' . . . drag me under. *(Pause)* I wiped out their food, ya see. . . . Didn't *mean* to, o' course. *(He laughs to himself.)* I mean IT WASN'T MY FAULT! The railroad men needed food. They *hired* me t' *find* 'em food! Well. How was *I* t' know the goddam buffalo reproduced so slowly? *How was I to know that?* NO ONE KNEW THAT! *(Pause; the* INDIANS *slowly disappear.)* Now, Sitting Bull is . . .

(Long pause)

HICKOK. *What?*

BUFFALO BILL. The . . . hearing was a shambles. I brought these senators, you see. To Sitting Bull's reservation. It . . . was a shambles. *(Pause)* So we left. He . . . *insulted* them. *(Pause)* Then I saw the letter. *(Silence)*

HICKOK. What letter?

BUFFALO BILL. The letter to McLaughlin. The letter ordering . . . it to be . . . done. *(Pause)* So I rode back. Rode all night. Figuring, maybe . . . if I can just *warn* him. . . . But the reservation soldiers stopped me and . . . made me . . . drink with them. And by the time I got there, he . . . was dead. The greatest Indian who'd ever lived. Shot. By order of the Government. Shot with a Gatling gun. *(Pause)* While the . . . wonderful, gray horse I'd given him for . . . appearing in my show danced his repertory of tricks in the background. Since a gunshot was his cue to perform. *(He laughs. Stops. Long silence)*

HICKOK. Well now. In exactly what way did you imagine *I* could . . . *help* this . . . situation?

BUFFALO BILL. You have what I *need* . . . now.

HICKOK *(smiling slightly).* Oh?

BUFFALO BILL. I'm *scared,* you see. *(Pause)* Scared . . . not . . . so much of *dyin',* but . . . dyin' *wrong. (Slight laugh)* Dyin' . . . in the center of my arena with . . . makeup on. *(Long pause)* Then I thought of you. . . . Remembered that night in the White House. Remembered thinking, "My God! Look at Hickok. Hickok *knows just who he is!"* *(Pause) "Hickok has the answer,"* I said. . . . Hickok knows who he *is. (Pause)* I must see Hickok again.

(Long silence)

HICKOK. Well I'm glad you came. Yes. Glad . . . to be able to . . . help. *(Pause)* Funny. That night, in the White House, I remember thinking: "My God, it's *Cody* who's got the answer!"

BUFFALO BILL. . . . What?

HICKOK. Poncho!

PONCHO. *Si, señor.*

HICKOK. Bring in our . . . um . . .

PONCHO. Ah! *Si, señor! Ahorita.*

(Exit PONCHO)

HICKOK. Naturally, at first, you may be a bit startled. Put off. Not . . . exactly . . . what you *had in mind.* Yet! I'm sure that once you *think* about it, you'll agree *it's the only way.* Just like Jesse has. Billy. Doc Holliday. The boys.

BUFFALO BILL. *What are you talkin' about?*

HICKOK. Why, takin' what you were and raisin' it to a . . . higher level. *(He laughs.)* Naturally, for my services, I get a small fee. Percentage. You get 50 percent right off the top. Of course, if at any time you aren't happy, you can leave. Take your business elsewhere. That's written in. Keeps us on our toes. Mind you, this . . . *enterprise* . . . is still in its infancy. The *potential,* though . . . is unlimited. For example, think of this. The *great national good . . .* that could come from this: some of you, let's say, would concentrate strictly on theatrics. MEAN-WHILE! Others of you would concentrate on purely humanitarian affairs. Save . . . well, not Sitting Bull, but . . . some Indian down in Florida. Another up in Michigan. Perhaps expand into Canada. Mexico. Central America. SOUTH AMERICA! My God, there must be literally *millions* of people who could benefit by your presence! Your . . . *simultaneous presence!*

PONCHO. Here they are, *señor!*

(Enter a group of men dressed as BUFFALO BILL. *Their faces are covered by masks of* his face. They wear his florid buckskin clothes— if anything, even more elaborately designed.)*

HICKOK. Naturally, we've still got a few wrinkles to iron out. Color of hair. Color of eyes. That sort of thing. But with *you* here, exercising artistic control, why, we could go on like this *forever!*

(BUFFALO BILL, *stunned by the sight, fires his guns at the duplicate Codys. They fall and immediately rise again.*

They slowly surround him.

He screams as he shoots.

They disappear.

The saloon fades to black.

BUFFALO BILL *alone on stage.)*

BUFFALO BILL. AND NOW TO CLOSE! AND *NOW TO CLOSE!*

VOICE. Not *yet. (Pause)* They also killed the rest of his tribe.

(Music.

INDIANS *enter mournfully. They carry a large white sheet.*

Sound of wind.

BUFFALO BILL *watches, then moves slowly away; exits.)*

SCENE THIRTEEN

The INDIANS *cover the center area with the huge white sheet, then lie down upon it in piles.* Enter COLONEL FORSYTH, *a* LIEUTENANT, *and two* REPORTERS, *their coat collars turned up for the wind.* CODY *is with them; he carries a satchel.*

———

FIRST REPORTER. Fine time of year you men picked for this thing.

COLONEL FORSYTH. They're heathens; they don't celebrate Christmas.

FIRST REPORTER. I don't mean the date, I mean the weather.

COLONEL. Uncomfortable?

FIRST REPORTER. Aren't you?

COLONEL. One gets used to it.

SECOND REPORTER. Colonel, I gather we lost twenty-nine men, thirty-three wounded. How many Indians were killed?

COLONEL. We wiped them out.

SECOND REPORTER. Yes, I know. But how many *is* that?

COLONEL. We haven't counted.

LIEUTENANT. The snow has made it difficult. It started falling right after the battle. The bodies were covered almost at once. By night they were frozen.

COLONEL. We more than made up for Custer, though, I can tell you that.

SECOND REPORTER. But Custer was killed fifteen years ago!

COLONEL. So what?

LIEUTENANT. If there are no more questions, we'll take you to—

FIRST REPORTER. I have one! Colonel Forsyth, some people are referring to your victory yesterday as a massacre. How do you feel about that?

COLONEL. One can always find someone who'll call an overwhelming victory a massacre. I suppose they'd prefer it if we'd let more of our own boys get shot!

FIRST REPORTER. Then you don't think the step you took was harsh?

COLONEL. Of course it was harsh. And I don't like it any more than you. But had we shirked our responsibility, skirmishes would have gone on for years, costing our country millions, as well as untold lives. Of course innocent people have been killed. In war they always are. And of course our hearts go out to the innocent victims of this. But war is not a game. It's tough. And demands tough decisions. In the long run I believe what happened here at this reservation yesterday will be justified.

FIRST REPORTER. Are you implying that the Indian Wars are finally over?

COLONEL. Yes, I believe they're finally over. This ludicrous buffalo religion of Sitting Bull's people was their last straw.

SECOND REPORTER. And now?

COLONEL. The difficult job of rehabilitating begins. But that's more up General Howard's line.

LIEUTENANT. Why don't we go and talk with him? He's in the temporary barracks.

COLONEL. He can tell you about our future plans.

(They start to leave.)

BUFFALO BILL. You said you'd—

LIEUTENANT. Ah, yes, it's that one. *(He points to a body.)*

BUFFALO BILL. Thank you. *(He stays. The others leave; he stares at the grave.* SITTING BULL *has entered, unnoticed.* BUFFALO BILL *takes a sprig of pine from the satchel and is about to put it on the grave.)*

SITTING BULL. Wrong grave. I'm over here. . . . As you see, the dead can be buried, but not so easily gotten rid of.

BUFFALO BILL. Why didn't you listen to me? I *warned* you what would happen! Why didn't you *listen?*

(Long silence)

SITTING BULL. We had land. . . . You wanted it; you took it. That . . . I understand perfectly. What I cannot understand . . . is why you did all this, *and at the same time* . . . professed your love.

(Pause)

BUFFALO BILL. Well . . . well, what . . . about *your* mistakes? *Hm?* For, for example: you were very unrealistic . . . about things. For . . . example: did you *really* believe the buffalo would return? *Magically* return?

SITTING BULL. It seemed no less likely than Christ's returning, and a great deal more useful. Though when I think of their reception here, I can't see why either would really want to come back.

BUFFALO BILL. Oh, God. Imagine. For a while, I actually thought my Wild West Show would *help.* I could give you money. Food. Clothing. And also make people *understand* things . . . better. *(He laughs to himself.)* That was my reasoning. Or, anyway, *part* . . . *(Pause)* of my reasoning.

SITTING BULL *(slight smile).* Your show was very popular.

(Pause)

BUFFALO BILL. We had . . . *fun,* though, you and I. *(Pause)* Didn't we?

SITTING BULL. Oh, yes. And that's the terrible thing. We had all surrendered. We were on reservations. We could not fight, or hunt. We could do nothing. Then you came and allowed us to imitate our glory. . . . It was humiliating! For sometimes, we could almost imagine it was *real.*

BUFFALO BILL. Guess it wasn't so authentic, was it? *(He laughs slightly to himself.)*

SITTING BULL. How could it have been? You'd have killed all your performers in one afternoon.

(Pause)

BUFFALO BILL. You know what worried me most? . . . The fear that I might die, in the middle of the arena, with all my . . . makeup on. *That* . . . is what . . . worried me most.

SITTING BULL. What worried *me* most . . . was something I'd said the year before. Without thinking.

BUFFALO BILL *(softly).* What?

SITTING BULL. I'd agreed to go onto the reservation. I was standing in front of my tribe, the soldiers leading us into the fort. And as we walked, I turned to my son, who was beside me. "Now," I said, "you will never know what it is to be an Indian, for you will never again have a gun or pony. . . . " Only later did I *realize* what I'd said. These things, the gun and the pony—they came with you. And then I thought, ah, how terrible it would be if we finally owe to the white man not only our destruction, but also our glory. . . . Farewell, Cody. You were my friend. And, indeed, you still are. . . . I never killed you . . . because I *knew it would not matter. (He starts to leave.)*

BUFFALO BILL. If only I could have saved *your* life! (SITTING BULL *stops and stares at him coldly; turns and leaves. Long pause)* Well! This is it! *(He forces a weak laugh.)* Naturally, I've been thinking 'bout this moment for quite some time now. As any performer would.

VOICE. And now to close!

BUFFALO BILL. NOT YET! . . . I would . . . first . . . like to . . . say a few words in defense of my country's Indian policy, which seems, in certain circles, to be meeting with considerable disapproval. *(He smiles weakly, clears his throat, reaches into his pocket, draws out some notes, and puts on a pair of eyeglasses.)* The—uh—State of Georgia, anxious to solidify its boundaries and acquire certain valuable mineral rights, hitherto held accidentally by the Cherokee Indians, and anxious, furthermore, to end the seemingly inevitable hostilities between its residents and these Indians on the question of land ownership, initiated, last year, the forced removal of the Cherokee nation, resettling them in a lovely and relatively unsettled area west of the Mississippi, known as the Mojave Desert. Given proper irrigation, this spacious place should soon be blooming. Reports that the Cherokees were unhappy at their removal are decidedly untrue. And though many, naturally, died while marching from Georgia to the Mojave Desert, the ones who did, I'm told, were rather ill already, and nothing short of medication could have saved them.

BUFFALO BILL

The excuse that the Indian way of life is vastly different from ours, and that what seem like atrocities to us do not to them, does not hold water, I'm afraid!

Indeed, in all ways, our vast country is speedily being opened for settlement. The shipment of smallpox-infested blankets, sent by the Red Cross to the Mandan Indians, has, I'm pleased to say, worked wonders, and the Mandans are no more. Also, the Government policy of exterminating the buffalo, a policy with which I myself was intimately connected, has practically reached fruition. Almost no buffalo are now left, and soon the Indians will be hungry enough to begin farming in earnest, a step we believe necessary if they are ever to leave their barbaric ways and enter civilization. Indeed, it is for this very reason that we have begun giving rifles to the Indians as part of each treaty with them, for without armaments they could not hope to wage war with us, and the process of civilizing them would be seriously hampered in every way. Another aspect of our benevolent attitude toward these savages is shown by the Government's policy of having its official interpreters translate everything incorrectly when interpreting for the Indians, thereby angering the Indians and forcing them to learn English for themselves. Which, of course, is the first step in civilizing people. I'm reminded here of a story told me by a munitions manufacturer. It seems, by *accident,* he sent a shipment of blank bullets to the Kickapoo Indians, and . . . *(He looks around.)* Well, I won't tell it. It's too involved. I would just like to say that I am sick and tired of these sentimental humanitarians who take no account of the difficulties under which this Government has labored in its efforts to deal fairly with the Indian, nor of the countless lives we have lost and atrocities endured at their savage hands. I quote General Sheridan —*(The* INDIANS *have begun to rise from their graves; for a while they stand in silence behind* BUFFALO BILL, *where they are joined, at intervals, by the rest of the* INDIAN *company.)*—"I do not know how far these so-called humanitarians should be excused on account of their political ignorance; but surely it is the only excuse that can give a shadow of justification for their aiding and abetting such horrid crimes as the Indians have perpetrated on our people."

SITTING BULL
(very softly).
I am Sitting Bull—

(almost inaudible)—and I am— dying!

For the truth is, the Indian never had any real title to the soil of this country. We had that title. By *right of discovery!* And all the Indians were, were the *temporary occupants* of the land. They *had* to be vanquished by us! It was, in fact, our *moral obligation!*

BLACK HAWK.
Black Hawk is *dying.*

TECUMSEH.
Tecumseh is *dying.*

CRAZY HORSE.
Crazy Horse . . . is dying.

For the earth was given to mankind to support the greatest number of which it is capable; and no tribe or people have a *right* to withhold from the wants of others! For example—

RED CLOUD.
Red Cloud is *dying*

SPOTTED TAIL.
Spotted Tail . . . is dying again.

—in the case of Lone Wolf versus Hitchcock, 1902, the Supreme Court of the United States ruled that the power exists to abrogate the provisions of *any* Indian treaty if the *interests of the country demand!*

SATANTA.
Satanta is *dying.*

KIOKUK.
Kiokuk is *dying.*

Here's another one: in the case of the Seneca Indians versus the Pennsylvania Power Authority, the courts ruled that the Seneca Treaty was invalid since perpetuity was legally a vague phrase. *Vague phrase!* Yes. Ah. Here's one, even better. In the—

GERONIMO.
Geronimo . . . *is dying!*

OLD TAZA.
Old Taza *is dying!*

JOHN GRASS.
John Grass is dying.

(Long pause)

No. Wait. Got it. The one I've been looking for. In the case of Sitting Bull versus Buffalo Bill, the Supreme Court ruled that the *inadvertent* slaughter of . . . buffalo by . . . I'm sorry, I'm . . . reminded here of an amusing story told me by General Custer. You remember him— one o' the great dumbass . . .

(The INDIANS begin a soft and mournful moaning.)

(Pause)

BUFFALO BILL. Think I'd better close. I . . . just want to say that anyone who thinks we have done something wrong is *wrong!* And that I have here, in this bag, some— *(He goes and picks up his satchel; he looks up and sees the INDIANS staring at him; he turns quickly away.)* —Indian trinkets. Some . . . examples of their excellent workmanship.

Moccasins. Beads. Feathered headdresses for your children. *(He has begun to unpack these trinkets and place them, for display, on a small camp stool he has set across the front edge of the center ring.)* Pretty picture postcards. Tiny Navaho dolls. The money from the sale of these few trifling trinkets will go to help them help themselves. Encourage them a bit. You know, *raise their spirits.* . . . Ah! Wait. No, sorry, that's a—uh—buffalo skin. *(He shoves it back in the satchel.)* Yes. Here it is! Look, just look . . . at this handsome replica of an . . . Indian. Made of genuine wood. *(He puts the carved head of an Indian on the camp stool so that it overlooks all the other trinkets. The lights now slowly begin to fade on him; he sits by the trinkets, trembling.)*

CHIEF JOSEPH. Tell General Howard I know his heart. I am tired of fighting. Our chiefs have been killed. Looking Glass is dead. The old men are all dead. It is cold and we have no blankets. The children are freezing. My people, some of them, have fled to the hills and have no food or warm clothing. No one knows where they are—perhaps frozen. I want to have time to look for my children and see how many of them I can find. Maybe I shall find them among the dead. *(Almost all the lights are now gone; CHIEF JOSEPH can hardly be seen; BUFFALO BILL is but a shadow. Only the trinkets are clear in a pinspot of light, and that light, too, is fading.)* Hear me, my chiefs. I am tired. My heart is sick and sad.

From where the sun now stands, I will fight no more, forever.

(And then, very slowly, even the light on the trinkets fades.
And the stage is completely dark.
Then, suddenly, all lights blazing!
Rodeo ring up.
Rodeo music.
Enter, on horseback, the ROUGHRIDERS OF THE WORLD. *They tour the ring triumphantly, then form a line to greet* BUFFALO BILL, *who enters on his white stallion. He tours the ring, a glassy smile on his face.*
The ROUGHRIDERS *exit.*
BUFFALO BILL *alone, on his horse. He waves his big Stetson to the unseen crowd.*
Then, INDIANS *appear from the shadows outside the ring; they approach him slowly.*
Lights fade to black.
Pause.
Lights return to the way they were at the top of the show, when the audience was entering. The three glass cases are back in place.
No curtain.)

THE HOUSE OF BLUE LEAVES

John Guare

First presented by Warren Lyons and Betty Ann Besch at the Truck & Warehouse Theatre in New York City on February 10, 1971, with the following cast:

ARTIE SHAUGHNESSY Harold Gould	SECOND NUN Kay Michaels
RONNIE SHAUGHNESSY William Atherton	LITTLE NUN Alix Elias
BUNNY FLINGUS Anne Meara	M.P. Thomas F. Flynn
BANANAS SHAUGHNESSY Katherine Helmond	THE WHITE MAN Carl Hunt
CORRINNA STROLLER Margaret Linn	BILLY EINHORN Frank Converse
HEAD NUN Rita Karen	

Directed by Mel Shapiro
Setting by Karl Eigsti
Costumes by Jane Greenwood
Lighting by John Tedesco
Music and lyrics by John Guare

SCENE: A cold apartment in Sunnyside, Queens, New York City.
TIME: October 4, 1965.

It took some time for the contemporary theatre to catch up with the humor of its day—or even the seriousness of its day. Much of Broadway comedy was situation farce quite unresponsive to the potential theatre audience. For years Broadway and, for that matter, London's West End, persevered in providing poorly what television was providing well.

Many of the best comic writers deserted to television, but New York producers still gambled on television-style products that were just not good enough. So many plays were produced on this basis that the theatre was still living in the 1920s and remained a mass-entertainment medium. But slowly things changed, and a sign of the change was John Guare's anarchic tragicomedy (more comedy than tragi), *The House of Blue Leaves.*

John Guare, in common with so many American playwrights, was born in New York City on February 5, 1938. The young Guare went to Roman Catholic schools and graduated from Georgetown in 1960, before receiving his Master of Fine Arts degree from the Yale Drama School three years later. It was at Yale that he started to write plays. He also had plays produced at the Café Cino, but first drew major attention with a one-acter, *Muzeeka.* This had already been produced at the Eugene O'Neill Memorial Theater in Connecticut and the Mark Taper Forum in Los Angeles, before it turned up, in a double bill with Sam Shepard's *Red Cross,* at the Provincetown Playhouse in New York on April 28, 1968. In it, a young man was trying to do something about the spoon-fed blandness of American taped music. It ran only thirty-six performances, but it got good notices and somehow established Guare as a talent to be watched.

As with *Red Cross,* Guare's next double bill of plays, *Home Fires* and *Cop-Out,* originated at the Eugene O'Neill Memorial Theater in Waterford, Connecticut. The double bill was produced on Broadway this time, under the generic title *Cop-Out,* at the Cort Theatre on April 7, 1969. It ran for a total of eight performances, but once again it acquired a certain critical acclaim and those murmurings of intellectual approbation that can be enormously helpful to a young dramatist starting out. The first play, about a German-American family equating with the Armistice in World War I, had a certain wit but was tenuous; yet the main offering, *Cop-Out,* about cops and the women in their lives, was not only more substantial but showed a most ingenious freedom in the use of dramatic technique. It was later felt that the first-night audience, in its ritual rush up the aisle, was disconcerted by the supine body of the heroine (played by Linda Lavin) spread-eagled in their path. It was a rather amusing sight to see the cohorts of American critics delicately picking their way over Miss Lavin's supposed corpse, and pretending all the while it just was not happening. Unluckily *Cop-Out* played only eight performances, so it soon wasn't.

Guare's big success (at least so far as money was concerned) came with his adaptation with Mel Shapiro of *Two Gentleman of Verona* as a musical. Guare not only very affectionately helped to adapt the Shakespeare play, he also wrote the lyrics to Galt MacDermot's score. It was first given by the New York Shakespeare Festival in the Delacorte Theatre in Central Park on July 22, 1971. Slightly amended it opened on Broadway at the St. James Theatre on December 1 of the same year. It closed on May 20, 1973, after 613 Broadway performances. It was also produced, with moderate success, in London's West End.

However, despite all the acclaim *Two Gentleman of Verona* won for Guare, his more considerable achievement came earlier, with this present play, *The House of Blue Leaves.* It opened at the Truck and Warehouse Theatre, Off Broadway, on February 10, 1971, and it closed there, after 337 performances, on December 3 of the same year. There was a certain irony here, for the play's run was stopped by a fire. The producers tried to find another suitable theatre, to no avail. But the play's run was interrupted rather than concluded.

Blue Leaves certainly has its faults. The ending, for example, was felt by many critics, including myself, to be clumsy, and not even Guare's best friend could term the play well constructed. Yet there is a wit, a humor, here totally responsive to its times, totally honest with its material.

There is a madness here sprawling over all. The husband with the honky-tonk piano wanting to make it in show business, the wife wanting to make it like a realistically Thurber-style dog, the mistress who will give sex but not cuisine before marriage, the movie mogul eagerly watching mediocrity, the son with a bomb in his heart, and all those crazy nuns. To say nothing of the Pope—of whom Guare does, in fact, say little.

Yet behind the madness there is a society and a place. Guare knows these people, and places them with a proper, almost priestly confessional sadness, in their proper dramatic position.

It makes for a play that is both entertaining and disturbing. Whatever future generations will make of the play—and tastes do change alarmingly—I would like them to know that, whatever they may have read to the contrary, we were rather like that in February 1971. At least, we were in New York City.

AUTHOR'S FOREWORD

The House of Blue Leaves takes place in Sunnyside, Queens, one of the five boroughs of New York City. You have to understand Queens. It was never a borough with its own identity like Brooklyn that people clapped for on quiz shows if you said you came from there. Brooklyn had been a city before it became part of New York, so it always had its own identity. And the Bronx originally had been Jacob Bronck's farm, which at least gives it something personal, and Staten Island is out there on the way to the sea, and, of course, Manhattan is what people mean when they say New York.

Queens was built in the twenties in that flush of optimism as a bedroom community for people on their way up who worked in Manhattan but wanted to pretend they had the better things in life until the inevitable break came and they could make the official move to the Scarsdales and the Ryes and the Greenwiches of their dreams, the payoff that was the birthright of every American. Queens named its communities Forest Hills, Kew Gardens, Elmhurst, Woodside, Sunnyside, Jackson Heights, Corona, Astoria (after the Astors, of all people). The builders built the apartment houses in mock Tudor or Gothic or Colonial and then named them The Chateau, The El Dorado, Linsley Hall, The Alhambra. We lived first in The East Gate, then moved to The West Gate, then to Hampton Court. And the lobbies had Chippendale furniture and Aztec fireplaces, and the elevators had roman numerals on the buttons.

And in the twenties and thirties and forties you'd move there and move out as soon as you could. Your young married days were over, the promotions came. The ads in the magazines were right. Hallelujah. Queens: a comfortable rest stop, a pleasant rung on the ladder of success, a promise we were promised in some secret dream. And isn't Manhattan, each day the skyline growing denser and more crenelated, always looming up there in the distance? The elevated subway, the Flushing line, zooms to it, only fourteen minutes from Grand Central Station. Everything you could want you'd find right there in Queens. But the young marrieds become old marrieds, and the children come, but the promotions, the breaks, don't, and you're still there in your bedroom community, your life over the bridge in Manhattan, and the fourteen-minute ride becomes longer every day. Why didn't I get the breaks? I'm right here in the heart of the action, in the bedroom community of the heart of the action, and I live in the El Dorado Apartments and the main street of Jackson Heights has Tudor-topped buildings with pizza slices for sale beneath them and discount radios and discount drugs and discount records and the Chippendale-paneled elevator in my apartment is all carved up with Love To Fuck that no amount of polishing can ever erase. And why do my dreams, which should be the best part of me, why do my dreams, my wants, constantly humiliate me? Why don't I get the breaks? What happened? I'm hip. I'm hep. I'm a New Yorker. The heart of the action. Just a subway ride to the heart of the action. I want to be part of that skyline. I want to blend into those lights. Hey, dreams, I dreamed you, I'm not something you curb a dog for. New York is where it all is. So why aren't I there? When I was a kid, I wanted to come from Iowa, from New Mexico, to make the final break and leave, say, the flatness of Nebraska and get on the Greyhound and get off that Greyhound at Port Authority and you wave your cardboard suitcase at the sky: I'll Lick You Yet. How do you run away to your dreams when you're already there? I never wanted to be any place in my life but New York. How do you get there when you're there? Fourteen minutes on the Flushing line is a very long distance. And I guess that's what this play is about more than anything else: humiliation. Everyone in the play is constantly being humiliated by their dreams, their loves, their wants, their best parts. People have criticized the play for being cruel or unfeeling. I don't think any play from the Oresteia on down has ever reached the cruelty of the smallest moments in our lives, what we have done to others, what others have done to us. I'm not interested so much

311

in how people survive as in how they avoid humiliation. Chekhov says we must never humiliate one another, and I think avoiding humiliation is the core of tragedy and comedy and probably of our lives.

This is how the play got written: I went to Saint Joan of Arc Grammar School in Jackson Heights, Queens, from 1944 to 1952 (wildly pre-Berrigan years). The nuns would say, If only we could get to Rome, to have His Holiness touch us, just to see Him, capital H, the Vicar of Christ on Earth—Vicar, v.i.c.a.r., Vicar, in true spelling-bee style. Oh, dear God, help me get to Rome, the capital of Italy, and go to that special little country in the heart of the capital —v.a.t.i.c.a.n.c.i.t.y.—and touch the Pope. No sisters ever yearned for Moscow the way those sisters and their pupils yearned for Rome. And in 1965 I finally got to Rome. Sister Carmela! Do you hear me? I got here! It's a new Pope, but they're all the same. Sister Benedict! I'm here! And I looked at the Rome papers, and there on the front page was a picture of the Pope. On Queens Boulevard. I got to Rome on the day a Pope left the Vatican to come to New York for the first time to plead to the United Nations for peace in the world on October 4, 1965. He passed through Queens, because you have to on the way from Kennedy Airport to Manhattan. Like the Borough of Queens itself, that's how much effect the Pope's pleas for peace had. The Pope's no loser. Neither is Artie Shaughnessy, whom *The House of Blue Leaves* is about. They both have big dreams. Lots of possibilities. The Pope's just into more real estate.

My parents wrote me about that day that the Pope came to New York and how thrilled they were, and the letter caught up with me in Cairo because I was hitching from Paris to the Sudan. And I started thinking about my parents and me and why was I in Egypt and what was I doing with my life and what were they doing with theirs, and that's how plays get started. The play is autobiographical in the sense that everything in the play happened in one way or another over a period of years, and some of it happened in dreams and some of it could have happened and some of it, luckily, never happened. But it's autobiographical all the same. My father worked for the New York Stock Exchange but he called it a zoo and Artie in the play is a zookeeper. The Billy in the play is my mother's brother, Billy, a monstrous man who was head of casting at MGM from the thirties through the fifties. The Huckleberry Finn episode that begins Act Two is an exact word-for-word reportage of what happened between Billy and me at our first meeting. The play is a blur of many years that pulled together under the umbrella of the Pope's visit.

In 1966 I wrote the first act of the play, and, like some bizarre revenge or disapproval, on the day I finished it my father died. The first act was performed at the O'Neill Theatre Center in Waterford, Connecticut, and I played Artie. The second act came in a rush after that and all the events in that first draft are the same as you'll find in this version. But in 1966 the steam, the impetus for the play, had gone. I wrote another draft of the second act. Another. A fourth. A fifth. A sixth. A director I had been working with was leading the play into abysmal naturalistic areas with all the traps that a set with a kitchen sink in it can have. I was lost on the play until 1969 in London, when one night at the National Theatre I saw Laurence Olivier do *Dance of Death* and the next night, still reeling from it, saw him in Charon's production of *A Flea in Her Ear*. The savage intensity of the first blended into the maniacal intensity of the second, and somewhere in my head *Dance of Death* became the same play as *A Flea in Her Ear*. Why shouldn't Strindberg and Feydeau get married, at least live together, and *The House of Blue Leaves* be their child? For years my two favorite shows had been *Gypsy* and *The Homecoming*. I think the only playwrighting rule is that you have to learn your craft so that you can put on stage plays you would like to see. So I threw away all the second acts of the play, started in again, and, for the first time, understood what I wanted.

Before I was born, just before, my father wrote a song for my mother:

A stranger's coming to our house.
I hope he likes us.
I hope he stays.
I hope he doesn't go away.

I liked them, loved them, stayed too long, and didn't go away. This play is for them.

—JOHN GUARE

New York, 1971

PROLOGUE

The stage of the El Dorado Bar & Grill.
While the house lights are still on, and the
audience is still being seated, ARTIE SHAUGH-
NESSY *comes on stage through the curtains,*
bows, and sits at the upright piano in front of
the curtain. He is forty-five years old. He car-
ries sheet music and an opened bottle of beer.
He scowls into the wings and then smiles
broadly out front.

———

ARTIE *(out front; nervous).* My name is Artie Shaughnessy and I'm going to sing you
songs I wrote. I wrote all these songs. Words
and the music. Could I have some quiet,
please? *(Sings brightly)*
    Back together again,
    Back together again.
    Since we split up
    The skies we lit up
    Looked all bit up
    Like Fido chewed them,
    But they're back together again
    You can say you knew us when
    We were together;
    Now we're apart,
    Thunder and lightning's
    Back in my heart,
    And that's the weather to be
    When you're back together with me.
(Into the wings) Could you please turn the
lights down? A spotlight on me? You promised me a spotlight. *(Out front)* I got a ballad
I'm singing and you promised me a blue spotlight.
    (The house lights remain on. People are still
finding their seats.)
ARTIE *(plunges on into a ballad; sentimen-*
tally).
    I'm looking for Something,
    I've searched everywhere,
    I'm looking for something
    And just when I'm there,
    Whenever I'm near it
    I can see it and hear it,
    I'm almost upon it,
    Then it's gone.
    It seems I'm looking for Something
    But what can it be?
    I just need a Someone
    To hold close to me.
    I'll tell you a secret,
    Please keep it entre nous,

    That Someone
    I thought it was you.
(Out front) Could you please take your seats
and listen? I'm going to sing you a song I
wrote at work today and I hope you like it as
much as I do. *(Plays and sings)*
    Where is the devil in Evelyn?
    What's it doing in Angela's eyes?
    Evelyn is heavenly,
    Angela's in a devil's disguise.
    I know about the sin in Cynthia
    And the hell in Helen of Troy,
    But where is the devil in Evelyn?
    What's it doing in Angela's eyes?
    Oh, boy!
    What's it doing in Angela's eyes?
(He leaps up from the piano with his sheet
music and beer, bows to the audience. Waits
for applause. Bows. Waits. Looks. Runs off
stage.
    House lights go down).

ACT ONE

Curtain up.
    The living room of a shabby apartment in
Sunnyside, Queens. The room is filled with
many lamps and pictures of movie stars and
jungle animals.
    Upstage center is a bay window, the only
window in the room. Across the opening of the
bay is a crisscross-barred folding gate of the
kind jewelers draw across the front of their
stores at night. Outside the window is a fire
escape. A small window in the side of the bay
is close enough to the gate to be opened or
closed by reaching through the bars.
    It is late at night and a street lamp beams
some light into this dark place through the
barred window. A piano near the window is
covered with hundreds of pieces of sheet music
and manuscript paper and beer bottles. A
jacket, shirt, and pants—the green uniform of
a city employee—are draped over the end of
the piano nearest the window.
    We can see ARTIE *asleep on the couch,*
zipped tightly into a sleeping bag, snoring
fitfully and mumbling: "Pope Ronnie. Pope
Ronnie. Pope Ronald the First. Pope Ronald."
    We can see a pullman kitchen with its doors
open far stage right. Three other doors in the
room: a front door with many bolts on it, and
two doors that lead to bedrooms. Even though
Artie and his family have lived here eighteen

years now, there's still an air of transiency to the room as if they had never unpacked from the time they moved in.

Somebody is at the window, climbing down the fire escape. RONNIE, *Artie's eighteen-year-old son, climbs in the window. He gingerly pulls at the folding gate. It's locked. He stands there for a minute, out of breath. He is a young eighteen. His hair is cropped close and he wears big glasses. He wears a heavy army over-coat and under that a suit of army fatigue clothes. He reaches through the bars to his father's trousers, gets the keys out of the pocket, unlocks the lock, comes into the room and relocks the gate behind him, replaces the pants. He tiptoes past his father, who's still snoring and mumbling:* "Pope Ronnie. Pope Ronnie. Pope Ronnie."

RONNIE *opens the icebox door, careful not to let the light spill all over the floor. He takes out milk and bread.*

The doorbell buzzes. ARTIE *groans.* RONNIE *runs into his bedroom.*

Somebody is knocking on the front door and buzzing quickly, quickly, like little mosquito jabs. ARTIE *stirs. He unzips himself from his sleeping bag, runs to the door. He wears ski pajamas. A key fits into the front door. The door shakes.* ARTIE *undoes the six bolts that hold the door locked. He opens the door, dashes back to his bag, and zips himself in.*

BUNNY FLINGUS *throws open the door. The hall behind her is brilliantly lit. She is a pretty, pink, slightly plump, electric woman in her late thirties. She wears a fur-collared coat and plastic booties, and two Brownie cameras on cords clunking against a pair of binoculars. At the moment she is freezing, uncomfortable, and furious. She storms to the foot of the couch.*

———

BUNNY. You know what your trouble is? You got no sense of history. You know that? Are you aware of that? Lock yourself up against history, get drowned by the whole tide of human events. Sleep it away in your bed. Your bag. Zip yourself in, Artie. The greatest tide in the history of the world is coming in today, so don't get your feet wet.

ARTIE *(picking up his glow-in-the-dark alarm).* It's quarter-to-five in the morning, Bunny—

BUNNY. Lucky for you I got a sense of history. *(She sits on the edge of the couch; picks up the newspaper on the floor.)* You finished last night's? Oooo, it's freezing out

there. Breath's coming out of everybody's mouth like a balloon in a cartoon. *(She rips the paper into long shreds and stuffs it down into the plastic booties she wears.)*

People have been up for hours. Queens Boulevard—lined for blocks already! Cripples laid out in the streets in stretchers with earmuffs on over their bandages. Nuns—you never seen so many nuns in your life! Ordinary people like you and me in from New Jersey and Connecticut and there's a lady even drove in from Ohio—Ohio!—just for to-day! She drove four of the most crippled peo-ple in Toledo. They're stretched out in the gutter waiting for the sun to come out so they can start snapping pictures. I haven't seen so many people, Artie, so excited since the pre-miere of *Cleopatra*. It's that big. Breathe! There's miracles in the air!

ARTIE. It's soot, Bunny. Polluted air.

BUNNY. All these out-of-staters driving in with cameras and thermos bottles and you live right here and you're all zipped in like a turtle. Miss Henshaw, the old lady who's the check-out girl at A&P who gyps everybody—her nephew is a cop and she's saving us two divine places right by the curb. You're not the only one with connections. But she can't save them forever. Oh God, Artie, what a morn-ing! You should see the stars!!! I know all the stars from the time I worked for that astrono-mer and you should see Orion—O'Ryan: the Irish constellation—I haven't looked up and seen stars in years! I held my autograph book up and let Jupiter shine on it. Jupiter and Venus and Mars. They're all out! You got to come see Orion. He's the hunter and he's pulling his arrow back so tight in the sky like a Connect-the-Dots picture made up of all these burning planets. If he ever lets that ar-row go, he'll shoot all the other stars out of the sky—what a welcome for the Pope!

And right now, the Pope is flying through that star-filled sky, bumping planets out of the way, and he's asleep dreaming of the mobs waiting for him. When famous people go to sleep at night, it's us they dream of, Artie. The famous ones—they're the real peo-ple. We're the creatures of their dreams. You're the dream. I'm the dream. We have to be there for the Pope's dream. Look at the light on the Empire State Building swirling around and around like a burglar's torch looking all through the sky—Everybody's waiting, Artie—everybody!

ARTIE *(angry).* What I want to know is,

who the hell is paying for this wop's trip over here anyway—

BUNNY *(shocked)*. Artie! *(Reaches through the bars to close the window)* Ssshhh—they'll hear you—

ARTIE. I don't put my nickels and dimes in Sunday collections to pay for any dago holiday—flying over here with his robes and gee-gaws and bringing his buddies over when I can't even afford a trip to Staten Island—

BUNNY *(puzzled)*. What's in Staten Island?

ARTIE. Nothing! But I couldn't even afford a nickel ferryboat ride. I known you two months and can't even afford a present for you—a ring—

BUNNY. I don't need a ring—

ARTIE. At least a friendship ring—*(He reaches in his sleeping bag and gets out a cigarette and matches and an ashtray.)*

BUNNY *(rubbing his head)*. I'd only lose it—

ARTIE *(pulling away)*. And this guy's flying over here—not tourist—oh, no—

BUNNY *(suspicious of his bitterness)*. Where'd you go last night?

ARTIE *(back into his bag)*. You go see the Pope. Tell him hello for me.

BUNNY. You went to that amateur night, didn't you—

ARTIE *(signaling toward the other room)*. Shut up—she's inside—

BUNNY. You went to the El Dorado Bar Amateur Night, didn't you? I spent two months building you up to be something and you throw yourself away on that drivel—

ARTIE. They talked all the way through it—

BUNNY. Did you play them "Where's the Devil in Evelyn?"

ARTIE. They talked and walked around all through it—

BUNNY. I wish I'd been there with you. You know what I would've said to them? *(To us)* The first time I heard "Mairzy Doats" I realized I am listening to a classic. I picked off "Old Black Magic" and "I Could've Danced All Night" as classics the minute I heard them. *(Recites)* "Where is the devil in Evelyn? What's it doing in Angela's eyes?" I didn't work in Macy's Music Department for nix. I know what I'm talking about *(To ARTIE)* That song is a classic. You've written yourself a classic.

ARTIE. I even had to pay for my own beers.

BUNNY. Pearls before swine. Chalk it up to experience.

ARTIE. The blackboard's getting kind of filled up. I'm too old to be a young talent.

BUNNY *(opens the window through the bars)*. Smell the bread—

ARTIE. Shut the window—it's freezing and you're letting all the dirt in—

BUNNY. Miss Henshaw's saving us this divine place by the cemetery so the Pope will have to slow down—

ARTIE. Nothing worse than cold dirt—

The other bedroom door opens and BA-NANAS SHAUGHNESSY, a sick woman in a nightgown, looks at them. They don't see her.

BUNNY *(ecstatically)*. And when he passes by in his limousine, I'll call out, "Your Holiness, marry us—the hell with peace to the world—bring peace to us." And he won't hear me because bands will be playing and the whole city yelling, but he'll see me because I have been eyed by the best of them, and he'll nod and I'll grab your hand and say, "Marry us, Pope," and he'll wave his holy hand and all the emeralds and rubies on his fingers will send Yes beams. In a way, today's my wedding day. I should have something white at my throat! Our whole life is beginning—my life—our life—and we'll be married and go out to California and Billy will help you. You'll be out there with the big shots—out where you belong—not in any amateur nights in bars on Queens Boulevard. Billy will get your songs in movies. It's not too late to start. With me behind you! Oh, Artie, the El Dorado Bar will stick up a huge neon sign flashing onto Queens Boulevard in a couple of years flashing "Artie Shaughnessy Got Started Here." And nobody'll believe it. Oh, Artie, tables turn.

(BANANAS closes the door.)

(ARTIE gets out of his bag.)

ARTIE *(thoughtfully sings)*.

Bridges are for burning

Tables are for turning—

(He turns on all the lights. He pulls BUNNY by the pudgy arm over to the kitchen.)

ARTIE. I'll go see the Pope—

BUNNY *(hugging him)*. Oh, I love you!

ARTIE. I'll come if—

BUNNY. You said you'll come. That is tantamount to a promise.

ARTIE. I will if—

BUNNY. Tantamount. Tantamount. You hear that? I didn't work in a law office for nix. I could sue you for breach.

ARTIE *(seductively)*. Bunny?

BUNNY *(near tears)*. I know what you're going to say—

ARTIE (opening a ketchup bottle under her nose). Cook for me?

BUNNY (in a passionate heat). I knew it. I knew it.

ARTIE. Just breakfast.

BUNNY. You bend my arm and twist my heart but I got to be strong.

ARTIE. I'm not asking any ten-course dinner.

(BUNNY runs over to the piano where his clothes are draped to get away from his plea.)

BUNNY. Just put your clothes on over the ski p.j.'s I bought you. It's thirty-eight degrees and I don't want you getting your pneumonia back—

ARTIE (holding up two eggs). Eggs, baby. Eggs right here.

BUNNY (holding out his jingling trousers). Rinse your mouth out to freshen up and come on let's go?

ARTIE (seductively). You boil the eggs and pour lemon sauce over—

BUNNY (shaking the trousers at him). Hollandaise. I know hollandaise. (Plopping down with the weight of the temptation, glum) It's really cold out, so dress warm—Look, I stuffed the New York Post in my booties—plastic just ain't as warm as it used to be.

ARTIE. And you pour the hollandaise over the eggs on English muffins—and then you put the grilled ham on top—I'm making a scrapbook of all the foods you tell me you know how to cook and then I go through the magazines and cut out pictures of what it must look like. (He gets the scrapbook.) Look—veal parmagina—eggplant meringue.

BUNNY. I cooked that for me last night. It was so good I almost died.

ARTIE (sings, as BUNNY takes the book and looks through it with great despair).

If you cooked my words
Like they was veal
I'd say I love you
For every meal.
Take my words,
Garlic and oil them,
Butter and broil them,
Sauté and boil them—
Bunny, let me eat you!

(Speaks). Cook for me?

BUNNY. Not till after we're married.

ARTIE. You couldn't give me a little sample right now?

BUNNY. I'm not that kind of girl. I'll sleep with you anytime you want. Anywhere. In two months I've known you, did I refuse you once? Not once! You want me to climb in the bag with you now? Unzip it—go on—unzip it—Give your fingers a smack and I'm flat on my back. I'll sew those words into a sampler for you in our new home in California. We'll hang it right by the front door. Because, Artie, I'm a rotten lay and I know it and you know it and everybody knows it—

ARTIE. What do you mean? Everybody knows it—

BUNNY. I'm not good in bed. It's no insult. I took that sex test in the Reader's Digest two weeks ago and I scored twelve. Twelve, Artie! I ran out of that dentist office with tears gushing out of my face. But I face up to the truth about myself. So if I cooked for you now and said I won't sleep with you till we're married, you'd look forward to sleeping with me so much that by the time we did get to that motel near Hollywood, I'd be such a disappointment, you'd never forgive me. My cooking is the only thing I got to lure you on with and hold you with. Artie, we got to keep some magic for the honeymoon. It's my first honeymoon and I want it to be so good, I'm aiming for two million calories. I want to cook for you so bad I walk by the A&P, I get all hot jabs of chili powder inside my thighs . . . but I can't till we get those tickets to California safe in my purse, till Billy knows we're coming, till I got that ring right on my cooking finger . . . Don't tempt me . . . I love you . . .

ARTIE (beaten). Two eggs easy over?

BUNNY (shakes her head No). And I'm sorry last night went sour . . .

ARTIE (sits down, depressed). They made me buy my own beers . . .

BANANAS (calling from the bedroom). Is it light? Is it daytime already?

(ARTIE and BUNNY look at each other.)

BUNNY. I'll pour you cornflakes.

ARTIE (nervous). You better leave.

BUNNY (standing her ground). A nice bowlful?

ARTIE. I don't want her to know yet.

BUNNY. It'll be like a coming attraction.

ARTIE (pushing her into the kitchen). You're a tease, Bunny, and that's the worst thing to be. (He puts on his green shirt and pants over his pajamas.)

(BANANAS comes out of the bedroom. She's lived in her nightgown for the last six months. She's in her early forties and has been crying for as long as she's had her nightgown on. She walks uncertainly, as if hidden barriers lay scattered in her path.)

BANANAS. Is it morning?

ARTIE. *(He doesn't know how to cope with her.)* Go back to bed.

BANANAS. You're dressed and it's so dark. Did you get an emergency call? Did the lion have babies yet?

ARTIE *(checking that the gate is locked).* The lioness hasn't dropped yet. The jaguar and the cheetah both still waiting. The birds still on their eggs.

BANANAS. Are you leaving to get away from me? Tell me? The truth? You hate me. You hate my looks—my face—my clothes—you hate me. You wish I was fatter so there'd be more of me to hate. You hate me. Don't say that! You love me. I know you love me. You love me. Well, I don't love you. How does that grab you? *(She is shaking violently.)*

(ARTIE *takes pills from the piano and holds her and forces the pills in her mouth. He's accepted this as one of the natural facts of his life. There is no violence in the action. Her body shakes. The spasms stop. She's quiet for a long time. He walks over to the kitchen.* BUNNY *kisses the palm of his hand.)*

BANANAS. For once could you let my emotions come out? If I laugh, you give me a pill. If I cry, you give me a pill . . . no more pills . . . I'm quiet now . . .

(ARTIE *comes out of the kitchen and pours two pills into his hand. He doesn't like to do this.)*

BANANAS *(smiles).* No! No more—look at me—I'm a peaceful forest, but I can feel all the animals have gone back into hiding and now I'm very quiet. All the wild animals have gone back into hiding. But once—once let me have an emotion? Let the animals come out? I don't like being still, Artie. It makes me afraid . . . *(Brightly)* How are you this morning? Sleep well? You were out late last night. I heard you come in and moved over in the bed. Go back to bed and rest. It's still early . . . come back to bed . . .

ARTIE *(finishing dressing).* The Pope is coming today and I'm going to go see him.

BANANAS. The Pope is coming here?

ARTIE. Yes, he's coming here. We're going to kick off our shoes and have a few beers and kick the piano around. *(Gently, as if to a child)* The Pope is talking to the UN about Vietnam. He's coming over to stop the war so Ronnie won't have to go to Vietnam.

BANANAS. Three weeks he's been gone. How can twenty-one days be a hundred years?

ARTIE *(to the audience).* This woman doesn't understand. My kid is charmed. He gets greetings to go to basic training for Vietnam and the Pope does something never done before. He flies out of Italy for the first time *ever* to stop the war. Ronnie'll be home before you can say Jake Rabinowitz. Ronnie—what a kid—a charmed life . . .

BANANAS. I can't go out of the house . . . my fingernails are all different lengths. I couldn't leave the house. . . . Look—I cut this one just yesterday and look how long it is already . . . but this one . . . I cut it months ago right down to the quick and it hasn't moved that much. I don't understand that . . . I couldn't see the Pope. I'd embarrass him. My nails are all different. I can feel them growing . . . they're connected to my veins and heart and pulling my insides out my fingers. *(She is getting hysterical.)*

(ARTIE *forces pills down her mouth. She's quiet. She smiles at him.* ARTIE's *exhausted, upset. He paces up and down in front of her, loathing her.)*

ARTIE. The Pope takes one look at you standing on Queens Boulevard, he'll make the biggest U-turn you ever saw right back to Rome. *(Angry)* I dreamed last night Ronnie was the Pope and he came today and all the streets were lined with everybody waiting to meet him—and I felt like Joseph P. Kennedy, only bigger, because the Pope is a bigger draw than any President. And it was raining everywhere but on him and when he saw you and me on Queens Boulevard, he stopped his glass limo and I stepped into the bubble, but you didn't. He wouldn't take you.

BANANAS. He would take me!

ARTIE *(triumphant).* Your own son denied you. Slammed the door in your face and you had open-toe shoes on and the water ran in the heels and out the toes like two Rin Tin Tins taking a leak—and Ronnie and I drove off to the UN and the war in Vietnam stopped and he took me back to Rome and canonized me—made me a Saint of the Church and in charge of writing all the hymns for the Church. A hymn couldn't be played unless it was mine and the whole congregation sang "Where Is the Devil in Evelyn," but they made it sound like monks singing it. You weren't invited, Bananas. Ronnie loved only me. . . . *(He finds himself in front of the kitchen. He smiles at* BUNNY.) What a dream . . . it's awful to have to wake up. For my dreams, I need a passport and shots. I travel the whole world.

BUNNY *(whispering)*. I dreamed once I met Abraham Lincoln.

ARTIE. Did you like him?

BUNNY. He was all right. *(She opens a jar of pickles and begins eating them.)*

*(*BANANAS *sees* BUNNY'*s fur coat by* RONNIE'*s room. She opens the front door and throws the coat into the hall. She closes the door behind her.)*

BANANAS. You know what I dream? I dream I'm just waking up and I roam around the house all day crying because of the way my life turned out. And then I do wake up and what do I do? Roam around the house all day crying about the way my life turned out.

ARTIE. *(An idea comes to him; he goes to the piano; sings.)*

The day that the Pope came to New
    York
The day that the Pope came to New
    York,
It really was comical,
The Pope wore a yarmulke
The day that the Pope came to New
    York.

BANANAS. Don't be disrespectful. *(She gets up to go to the kitchen.* ARTIE *rushes in front of her and blocks her way.* BUNNY *pushes herself against the icebox trying to hide; she's eating a bowl of cornflakes.)*

ARTIE. Stay out of the kitchen. I'll get your food—

BANANAS. Chop it up in small pieces . . .

BUNNY *(in a loud, fierce whisper)*. Miss Henshaw cannot reserve our places indefinitely. Tantamount to theft is holding a place other people could use. Tantamount. Her nephew the cop could lock us right up. Make her go back to bed.

*(*ARTIE *fixes* BANANAS' *food on a plate.* BANANAS *sits up on her haunches and puts her hands, palm downwards, under her chin.)*

BANANAS. Hello, Artie!

ARTIE. You're going to eat like a human being.

BANANAS. Woof? Woof?

ARTIE. Work all day in a zoo. Come home to a zoo. *(He takes a deep breath. He throws her the food. She catches it in her mouth. She rolls on her back.)*

BANANAS. I like being animals. You know why? I never heard of a famous animal. Oh, a couple of Lassies—an occasional Trigger— but, by and large, animals weren't meant to be famous.

*(*ARTIE *storms into the kitchen.)*

BUNNY. What a work of art is a dog. How noble in its thought—how gentle in its dignity—

*(*ARTIE *buries his head against the icebox.)*

BANANAS *(smiling out front)*. Hello. I haven't had a chance to welcome you. This is my home and I'm your hostess and I should welcome you. I wanted to say Hello and I'm glad you could come. I was very sick a few months ago. I tried to slash my wrists with spoons. But I'm better now and glad to see people. In the house. I couldn't go out. Not yet. Hello. *(She walks the length of the stage, smiling at the audience, at us. She has a beautiful smile.)*

*(*BUNNY *comes out of the kitchen down to the edge of the stage.)*

BUNNY *(to us)*. You know what my wish is? The priest told us last Sunday to make a wish when the Pope rides by. When the Pope rides by, the wish in my heart is gonna knock the Pope's eye out. It is braided in tall letters, all *my* veins and arteries and aortas are braided into the wish that she dies pretty soon. *(She goes back to the kitchen.)*

BANANAS *(who has put a red mask on her head)*. I had a vision—a nightmare—I saw you talking to a terrible fat woman with newspapers for feet—and she was talking about hunters up in the sky and that she was a dream and you were a dream . . . *(She crosses to the kitchen, puts mask over her eyes and comes up behind Bunny.)* Hah!!!

*(*BUNNY *screams in terror and runs into the living room.)*

BUNNY. I am not taking insults from a sick person. A healthy person can call me anything they want. But insults from a sickie— a sicksicksickie—I don't like to be degraded. A sick person has fumes in their head—you release poison fumes and it makes me sick— dizzy—like riding the back of a bus. No wonder Negroes are fighting so hard to be freed, riding in the back of busses all those years. I'm amazed they even got enough strength to stand up straight. . . . Where's my coat? Artie, where's my coat? My binox and my camera? *(To* BANANAS*)* What did you do with my coat, Looney Tunes? *(*ARTIE *has retrieved the coat from the hallway.)* You soiled my coat! This coat is soiled! Arthur, are you dressed warm? Are you coming?

ARTIE *(embarassed)*. Bananas, I'd like to present—I'd like to meet—this is Bunny Flingus.

BUNNY. You got the ski p.j.s underneath?

You used to go around freezing till I met you. I'll teach you how to dress warm. I didn't work at ski lodges for nothing. I worked at Aspen.

BANANAS (thinks it over a moment). I'm glad you're making friends, Artie. I'm no good for you.

BUNNY (taking folders out of her purse, to BANANAS). I might as well give these to you now. Travel folders to Juarez. It's a simple procedure—you fly down to Mexico—wetback lawyer meets you—sign a paper—jet back to little old N.Y.

ARTIE. Bunny's more than a friend, Bananas.

BUNNY. Play a little music—"South of the border"—divorce Meheeco style!—

ARTIE. Would you get out of here, Bunny. I'll take care of this.

(BANANAS sings hysterically, without words, "South of the Border.")

BUNNY. I didn't work in a travel agency for nix, Arthur.

ARTIE. Bunny!

BUNNY. I know my way around.

(BANANAS stops singing.)

ARTIE (taking the folders from BUNNY). She can't even go to the incinerator alone. You're talking about Mexico—

BUNNY. I know these sick wives. I've seen a dozen like you in movies. I wasn't an usher for nothing. You live in wheelchairs just to hold your husband and the minute your husband's out of the room, you're hopped out of your wheelchair doing the Charleston and making a general spectacle of yourself. I see right through you. Tell her, Artie. Tell her what we're going to do.

ARTIE. We're going to Caliornia, Bananas.

BUNNY. Bananas! What a name!

BANANAS. A trip would be nice for you . . .

BUNNY. What a banana—

BANANAS. You could see Billy . . . I couldn't see Billy. . . . (Almost laughing) I can't see anything . . .

ARTIE. Not a trip.

BUNNY. To live. To live forever.

BANANAS. Remember the time we rode up in the elevator with Bob Hope. He's such a wonderful man.

ARTIE. I didn't tell you this, Bunny. Last week, I rode out to Long Island. (To BANANAS, taking her hand) You need help. We —I found a nice hosp . . . By the sea . . . by the beautiful sea . . . it's an old estate and

you can walk from the train station and it was raining and the roads aren't paved so it's muddy, but by the road where you turn into the estate, there was a tree with blue leaves in the rain—I walked under it to get out of the rain and also because I had never seen a tree with blue leaves and I walked under the tree and all the leaves flew away in one big round bunch—just lifted up, leaving a bare tree. Whoosh . . . It was birds. Not blue leaves but birds, waiting to go to Florida or California . . . and all the birds flew to another tree a couple of hundred feet off and that bare tree blossomed—snap! like that—with all these blue very quiet leaves. . . . You'll like the place, Bananas. I talked to the doctor. He had a moustache. You like moustaches. And the Blue Cross will handle a lot of it, so we won't have to worry about expense. . . . You'll like the place . . . a lot of famous people have had crackdowns there, so you'll be running in good company.

BANANAS. Shock treatments?

ARTIE. No. No shock treatments.

BANANAS. You swear?

BUNNY. If she needs them, she'll get them.

ARTIE. I'm handling this my way.

BUNNY. I'm sick of you kowtowing to her. Those poison fumes that come out of her head make me dizzy—suffering—look at her —what does she know about suffering . . .

BANANAS. Did you read in the paper about the bull in Madrid who fought so well they didn't let him die. They healed him, let him rest before they put him back in the ring, again and again and again. I don't like the shock treatments, Artie. At least the concentration camps—I was reading about them. Artie—they put the people in the ovens and never took them out—but the shock treatments—they put you in the oven and then they take you out and then they put you in and then they take you out . . .

BUNNY. Did you read Modern Screen two months ago? I am usually not a reader of film magazines, but the cover on it reached right up and seduced my eye in the health club. It was a picture like this (she clutches her head) and it was called "Sandra Dee's Night of Hell." Did you read that by any happenstance? Of course you wouldn't read it. You can't see anything. You're ignorant. Not you. Her. The story told of the night before Sandra Dee was to make her first movie and her mother said, "Sandra, do you have everything you need?" And she said—snapped

320   J O H N   G U A R E

back, real fresh-like—"Leave me alone, Mother. I'm a big girl now and don't need any help from you." So her mother said, "All right, Sandra, but remember I'm always here." Well, her mother closed the door and Sandra could not find her hair curlers anywhere and she was too proud to go to her mom and ask her where they were—

ARTIE: Bunny, I don't understand.

BUNNY. Shut up, I'm not finished yet—and she tore through the house having to look her best for the set tomorrow because it was her first picture and her hair curlers were nowhere! Finally at four in the A.M., her best friend, Annette Funicello, the former Mouseketeer, came over and took the hair curlers out of her very own hair and gave them to Sandra. Thus ended her night of hell, but she had learned a lesson. Suffering—you don't even know the meaning of suffering. You're a nobody and you suffer like a nobody. I'm taking Artie out of this environment and bringing him to California while Billy can still do him some good. Get Artie's songs—his music—into the movies.

ARTIE. I feel I only got about this much life left in me, Bananas. I got to use it. These are my peak years. I got to take this chance. You stay in your room. You're crying. All the time. Ronnie's gone now. This is not a creative atmosphere. . . . Bananas, I'm too old to be a young talent.

BANANAS. I never stopped you all these years . . .

BUNNY. Be proud to admit it, Artie. You were afraid till I came on the scene. Admit it with pride.

ARTIE. I was never afraid. What're you talking about?

BUNNY. No man takes a job feeding animals in the Central Park Zoo unless he's afraid to deal with humans.

ARTIE. I walk right into the cage! What do you mean?

BUNNY. Arthur, I'm trying to talk to your wife. Bananas, I want to be sincere to you and kind.

ARTIE. I'm not afraid of nothing! Put my hand right in the cage—

BUNNY (sitting down beside BANANAS, speaks to her as to a child). There's a beautiful book of poems by Robert Graves. I never read the book because the title is so beautiful there's no need to read the book: Man Does. Woman Is. Look around this apartment. Look at Artie. Look at him.

ARTIE. (muttering) I been with panthers.

BUNNY (with great kindness). I've never met your son, but—no insult to you, Artie— but I don't want to. Man does. What does Artie do? He plays the piano. He creates. What are you? What is Bananas? Like he said before when you said you've been having nightmares. Artie said, "You been looking in the mirror?" Because that's what you are, Bananas. Look in the mirror. (ARTIE is playing the piano.) Man Does. Woman Is. I didn't work in a lending library for nothing.

ARTIE. I got panthers licking out of my hands like goddam pussycats.

BUNNY. Then why don't you ever call Billy?

ARTIE. I got family obligations.

BANANAS (at the window). You could take these bars down. I'm not going to jump.

BUNNY: You're afraid to call Billy and tell him we're coming out.

BANANAS (dreamy). I'd like to jump out right in front of the Pope's car.

ARTIE. Panthers lay right on their backs and I tickle their armpits. You call me afraid? Hah!

BANANAS. He'd take me in his arms and bless me.

BUNNY. Then call Billy now.

ARTIE. It's the middle of the night!

BUNNY. It's only two in the morning out there now.

ARTIE. Two in the morning is the middle of the night!

BUNNY. In Hollywood! Come off it, he's probably not even in yet—they're out there frigging and frugging and swinging and eating and dancing. Since Georgina died, he's probably got a brace of nude starlets splashing in the pool.

ARTIE. I can't call him. He's probably not even in yet—

BUNNY. I don't even think you know him.

ARTIE. Don't know him!

BUNNY. You've been giving me a line— your best friend—big Hollywood big shot— you don't even know him—

ARTIE. Best friends stay your best friends precisely because you don't go calling them in the middle of the night.

BUNNY. You been using him—dangling him over my head—big Hollywood big-shot friend, just to take advantage of me—just to get in bed with me—casting couches! I heard about them—

ARTIE. That's not true!

BUNNY. And you want me to cook for you!

I know the score, baby. I didn't work in a theatrical furniture store for nothing! *(She tries to put her coat on to leave. He pulls it off her.)* If you can't call your best friends in the middle of the night, then who can you call—taking advantage of me in a steam bath—

BANANAS *(picking up the phone)*. You want me to get Billy on the phone?

ARTIE. You stay out of this!

BANANAS. He was always my much better friend than yours, Artie. ·

ARTIE. Your friend! Billy and I only went to kindergarten together, grammar school together, high school together till his family moved away—Fate always kept an eye out to keep us friends. *(Sings)*.

If you're ever in a jam, here I am.

BANANAS *(sings)*.

Friendship.

ARTIE *(sings)*.

If you're ever up a tree, just phone me.

(Speaks) He got stationed making training movies and off each reel there's what they call leader—undeveloped film—and he started snipping that leader off, so by the time we all got discharged, he had enough film spliced up to film Twenty Commandments. He made his movie right here on the streets of New York and Rossellini was making his movies in Italy, only Billy was making them here in America and better. He sold everything he had and he made *Conduct of Life* and it's still playing in museums. It's at the Museum of Modern Art next week—and Twentieth Century-Fox signed him and MGM signed him—they both signed him to full contracts—the first time anybody ever got signed by two studios at once. . . . You only knew him about six months' worth, Bananas, when he was making the picture. And everybody in that picture became a star and Billy is still making great pictures.

BUNNY. In his latest one, will you ever forget that moment when Doris Day comes down that flight of stairs in that bathrobe and thinks Rock Hudson is the plumber to fix her bathtub and in reality he's an atomic scientist.

BANANAS. I didn't see that . . .

ARTIE *(mocking)*. Bananas doesn't go out of the house . . .

BUNNY *(stars in her eyes)*. Call him, Artie.

ARTIE. He gets up early to be on the set. I don't want to wake him up—

BUNNY. Within the next two years, you could be out there in a black tie waiting for

the lady—Greer Garson—to open the envelope and say as the world holds its breath—"And the winner of the Oscar for this year's Best Song is—" *(She rips a travel folder very slowly.)*

ARTIE *(leaning forward)*. Who is it? Who won?

BUNNY. And now Miss Mitzi Gaynor and Mr. Franco Corelli of the Metropolitan Opera will sing the winning song for you from the picture of the same name made by his good friend and genius, Billy Einhorn. The winner is of course Mr. Arthur M. Shaughnessy. *(ARTIE goes to the telephone.)*

ARTIE *(dials once, then)*. Operator, I want to call in Bel Air, Los Angeles—

BUNNY. You got the number?

ARTIE. Tattooed, baby. Tattooed. Your heart and his telephone number right on my chest like a sailor. Not you, operator. I want and fast I want in Los Angeles in Bel Air GR2-4129 and I will not dial it because I want to speak personally to my good friend and genius, Mr. Billy Einhorn . . . E-I-N–don't you know how to spell it? The name of only Hollywood's leading director my friend and you better not give this number to any of your friends and call him up and bother him asking for screen tests.

BUNNY. When I was an operator, they made us take oaths. I had Marlon Brando's number for years and pistols couldn't've dragged it out of my head—they make you raise your right hand—

ARTIE. My number is RA 1-2276 and don't go giving that number away and I want a good connection . . . hang on, Bunny *(she takes his extended hand)* you can hear the beepbeepbeeps—we're traveling across the country—hang on! Ring. It's ringing. Ring.

BUNNY *(his palm and her palm form one praying hand)*. Oh, God, please—

ARTIE *(pulling away from her)*. Ring. It's up. Hello? Billy? Yes, operator, get off—that's Billy. Will you get off—*(to BUNNY)* I should've called station-to-station. He picked it right up and everything. Billy! This is Ramon Navarro! . . . . No, Billy, it's Artie Shaughnessy. Artie. No, New York! Did I wake you up! Can you hear me! Billy, hello! I got to tell you something—first of all, I got to tell you how bad I feel about Georgina dying—the good die young—what can I say—and second, since you, you old bum, never come back to your old stomping grounds—your happy hunting grounds, I'm thinking of coming out to see you. . . . I know you can fix up a tour of the studios and that'd be great . . . and you can get us hotel reservations— that's just fine. . . . But, Billy, I'm thinking I got to get away—not just a vacation—but make a change, get a break, if you know what I'm getting at. . . . Bananas is fine. She's right here. We were just thinking about you — NO, IT'S NOT FINE Billy, this sounds cruel to say but Bananas is as dead for me as Georgina is for you. I'm in love with a remarkable wonderful girl—yeah, she's here too—who I should've married years ago—no, we didn't know her years ago—I only met her two months ago—yeah . . . *(Secretively, pulling the phone off to the corner)* It's kind of funny, a chimpanzee knocked me in the back and kinked my back out of whack and I went to this health club to work it out and in the steam section with all the steam I got lost and I went into this steam room and there was Bunny—yeah, just towels—I mean you could make a movie out of this, it was so romantic —She couldn't see me and she started talking about the weight she had to take off and the food she had to give up and she started talking about duckling with orange sauce and oysters baked with spinach and shrimps baked in the juice of melted sturgeon eyes which caviar comes from—well, you know me and food and I got so excited and the steam's getting thicker and thicker and I ripped off my towel and kind of raped her . . . and she was quiet for a long time and then she finally said one of the geatest lines of all time. . . . She said, "There's a man in here." . . . And she was in her sheet like a toga and I was all toga'd up and I swear, Billy, we were gods and goddesses and the steam bubbled up and swirled and it was Mount Olympus. I'm a new man, Billy—a new man—and I got to make a start before it's too late and I'm calling you, crawling on my hands and knees—no, not like that, I'm standing up straight and talking to my best buddy and saying, "Can I come see you and bring Bunny and talk over old times." . . . I'll pay my own way. I'm not asking you for nothing. Just your friendship. I think about you so much and I read about you in the columns and *Conduct of Life* is playing at the Museum of Modern Art next week and I get nervous calling you and that Doris Day pic— well, Bunny and I fell out of our loge seats— no, Bananas couldn't see it—she don't go out of the house much. . . . I get nervous about calling you because, well, you know, and I'm not asking for any Auld Lang Syne treatment, but it must be kind of lonely with Georgina gone and we sent five dollars in to the Damon Runyon Cancer Fund like Walter Winchell said to do and we're gonna send more and it must be kind of lonely and the three of us—Bunny and you and me—could have some laughs. What do you say? You write me and let me know your schedule and we can come any time. But soon. Okay, buddy? Okay? No, this is my call. I'm paying for this call so you don't have to worry— talking to you I get all opened up. You still drinking rye? Jack Daniels! Set out the glasses —open the bottle—no, I'll bring the bottle— we'll see you soon. Good-night, Billy. *(The call is over.)* Soon, Billy. Soon. Soon. *(He hangs up.)*

BUNNY *(sings and dances)*.

The day that the Pope came to New York
The day that the Pope came to New York,
It really was comical,
The Pope wore a yarmulke
The day that the Pope came to New York!

ARTIE *(stunned)*. Did you hear me!

BUNNY. You made me sound like the Moon Coming Over the Mountain! So fat!

ARTIE. He said to say hello to you, Bananas.

BANANAS. Hello . . .

ARTIE *(to BUNNY)*. Get the copy of *Life* magazine with the story on his house . . . *(BUNNY gets the magazine off the top of the piano.)*

BUNNY *(thrilled)*. You made me sound so fat! So Kate Smith!

ARTIE *(taking the magazine and opening it)*. Look at his house—on the highest part of all Los Angeles—

BUNNY *(devouring the pictures)*. It's Bel Air! I know Bel Air! I mean, I don't know Bel Air, but I mean, I know Bel Air!

ARTIE and BUNNY *flop on the sofa.* BANANAS, *in the kitchen behind them, throws rice at them.*

BUNNY. Let's get out of here. She gives me the weeping willies.

BANANAS. Oh, no, I'm all right. I was just thinking how lucky we all are. You going off to California and me going off to the loony bin—

ARTIE *(correcting her)*. It's a rest place—

BANANAS. With beautiful blue trees, huh?

ARTIE. Birds—waiting to go to Florida or California—

BANANAS. Maybe it was a flock of insane bluebirds that got committed—

ARTIE *(to* BUNNY*).* I'm gonna take a shower. My shirt's all damp from the telephone call.

BUNNY *(putting her coat on).* Artie, I'll be at the corner of Forty-sixth Street near the cemetery by the TV repair store. . . . Hello, John the Baptist. That's who you are. John the Baptist. You called Billy and prepared the way—the way for yourself. Oh, Christ, the dinners I'm gonna cook for you. *(Sings).*

It really was comical,
The Pope wore a yarmulke
The day that the Pope came to New
   York.

(She blows a kiss and exits. ARTIE *yelps triumphantly. He comes downstage.)*

ARTIE. Hello, Billy. I'm here. I got all my music. *(Sings).*

I'm here with bells on,
Ringing out how I feel.
I'll ring,
I'll roar,
I'll sing
Encore!
I'm here with bells on.
Ring! Ring! Ring!

BANANAS *(very depressed).* The people downstairs . . . they'll be pumping broomsticks on the ceiling . . .

ARTIE *(jubilant).* For once the people downstairs is Bunny! *(Sings).*

For once the people downstairs is Bunny! *(He speaks now, jumping up and down on the floor.)* Whenever the conversation gets around to something you don't like, you start ringing bells of concern for the people downstairs. For once in my life, the people downstairs is Bunny and I am a free man! *(He bangs all over the keys of the piano.)* And that's a symphony for the people upstairs.

BANANAS. There's just the roof upstairs . . .

ARTIE. Yeah, and you know roofs well. I give up six months of my life taking care of you and one morning I wake up and you're gone and all you got on is a nightgown and your bare feet—the corns of your bare feet for slippers. And it's snowing out, snowing a blizzard, and you're out in it. Twenty-four hours you're gone and the police are up here and long since gone and you're being broad-

casted for in thirteen states all covered with snow—and I look out that window and I see a gray smudge in a nightgown standing on the edge of the roof over there—in a snowbank and I'm praying to God and I run out of this place, across the street. And I grab you down and you're so cold, your nightgown cuts into me like glass breaking and I carried you back here and you didn't even catch a cold—not even a sniffle. If you had just a sniffle, I could've forgiven you. . . . You just look at me with that dead look you got right now. . . . You stay out twenty-four hours in a blizzard hopping from roof to roof without even a pair of drawers on—and *I* get the pneumonia.

BANANAS. Can I have my song?

ARTIE. You're tone-deaf. *(Hits two bad notes on the piano)* Like that.

BANANAS. So I won't sing it. . . . My troubles all began a year ago—two years ago today—two days ago today? Today. (ARTIE *plays "The Anniversary Waltz.")* We used to have a beautiful old green Buick. The Green Latrine! . . . I'm not allowed to drive it anymore . . . but when I could drive it . . . the last time I drove it, I drove into Manhattan. (ARTIE *plays "In My Merry Oldsmobile.")* And I drive down Broadway—to the Crossroads of the World. (ARTIE *plays "Forty-second Street.")* I see a scene that you wouldn't see in your wildest dreams. Forty-second Street. Broadway. Four corners. Four people. One on each corner. All waving for taxis. Cardinal Spellman. Jackie Kennedy. Bob Hope. President Johnson. All carrying suitcases. Taxi! Taxi! I stop in the middle of the street—the middle of Broadway—and I get out of my Green Latrine and yell, "Get in. I'm a gypsy. A gypsy cab. Get in. I'll take you where you want to go. Don't you all know each other? Get! Get in!"

They keep waving for cabs. I run over to President Johnson and grab him by the arm. "Get in!" And pull Jackie Kennedy into my car and John-John, who I didn't see, starts crying and Jackie hits me and I hit her and I grab Bob Hope and push Cardinal Spellman into the back seat, crying and laughing, "I'll take you where you want to go. Get in! Give me your suitcases"—and the suitcases spill open and Jackie Kennedy's wigs blow down Forty-second Street and Cardinal Spellman hits me and Johnson screams and I hit him. I hit them all. And then the Green Latrine blew four flat tires and sinks and I run to protect the car and four cabs appear and all my friends run into four different cabs. And cars are honking at me to move.

I push the car over the bridge back to Queens. You're asleep. I turn on Johnny Carson to get my mind off and there's Cardinal Spellman and Bob Hope, whose nose is still bleeding, and they tell the story of what happened to them and everybody laughs. Thirty million people watch Johnny Carson and they all laugh. At me. At me. I'm nobody. I knew all those people better than me. You. Ronnie. I know everything about them. Why can't they love me? And then it began to snow and I went up on the roof . . .

ARTIE (after a long pause). Come see the Pope. Pray. Miracles happen. He'll bless you. *Reader's Digest* has an article this month on how prayer answers things. Pray? Kneel down in the street? The Pope can cure you. The *Reader's Digest* don't afford to crap around.

BANANAS. My fingernails are all different lengths. Everybody'd laugh . . .

ARTIE. We used to have fun. Sometimes I miss you so much . . .

BANANAS (smiling nervously). If I had gloves to put on my hands . . .

ARTIE. The Pope must be landing now. I'm going to turn on the television. I want you to see him. (Turns on the television) Here he is. He's getting off the plane. Bananas, look. Look at the screen. (He pulls her to the screen. He makes her kneel in front of it.) Oh, God, help Bananas. Please God? Say a prayer, Bananas. Say, "Make me better, God . . ."

BANANAS. Make me better, God . . .

ARTIE. "So Artie can go away in peace." . . . Here's the Pope. (He speaks to the screen.) Get out of the way! Let a sick woman see! There he is! Kiss him? Kiss his hem, Bananas. He'll cure you! Kiss him.

(BANANAS leans forward to kiss the screen. She looks up and laughs at her husband.)

BANANAS. The screen is so cold . . .

ARTIE (leaping). Get out of the way, you goddam newsman! (He pushes BANANAS aside and kisses the screen.) Help me—help me—Your Holiness . . .

(While he hugs the set, BANANAS leaves the room to go into her bedroom. The front door flies open. BUNNY bursts in, flushed, bubbling. She has an enormous "I Love Paul" button on her coat.)

BUNNY. He's landed! He's landed! It's on everybody's transistors and you're still here!

And the school kids!—the Pope drives by, he sees all those school kids, he's gonna come out for birth control today!! Churches will be selling Holy Diaphragms with pictures of Saint Christopher and saints on them. You mark my words. (To us, indicating her button) They ran out of "Welcome Pope" buttons so I ran downstairs and got my leftover from when the Beatles were here! I am famished! What a day! (She goes to the icebox and downs a bottle of soda.)

(BANANAS comes out of the bedroom. A coat over her nightgown. A hat cocked on her head. Two different shoes, one higher than the other. She is smiling. She is pulling on gloves. ARTIE turns off the TV. BUNNY gapes. Band music plays joyously in the distance. ARTIE goes to BANANAS and takes her arm.)

BUNNY. Now wait one minute. Miss Henshaw is going to be mighty pissed off.

ARTIE. Just for today.

BANANAS. Hold me tight . . .

ARTIE (grabbing his coat). Over the threshold . . .

(They go out.)

BUNNY. Artie, are you dressed warm? Are you dressed warm? Your music! You forgot your music! You gotta get it blessed by the Pope!!

(BANANAS appears in the doorway and grabs the music from Bunny.)

BANANAS (sings).

It really was comical,
The Pope wore a yarmulke
The day that the Pope came to New
    York.

BUNNY. You witch! You'll be in Bellevue tonight with enough shock treatments they can plug Times Square into your ear. I didn't work for Con Edison for nothing! (She storms out after them. Slams the door behind her.)

(The bedroom door RONNIE went into at the beginning of the act opens. He comes out carrying a large gift box. He comes downstage and stares at us.)

CURTAIN

ACT TWO

SCENE ONE

RONNIE is standing in the same position, staring at us. He takes two hand grenades out *of the pockets of his fatigues, wire, his father's alarm clock. He wires them together, setting the alarm on the clock at a special time. He puts the whole device into the gift box. He is very young—looks barely seventeen—his hair is cropped close all over; he is tall, skinny. He speaks with deep, suffocated, religious fervor; his eyes bulge with a strange mixture of terrifying innocence and diabolism. You can't figure out whether he'd be a gargoyle on some Gothic cathedral or a skinny cherub on some altar.)*

RONNIE. My father tell you all about me? Pope Ronnie? Charmed life? How great I am? That's how he is with you. You should hear him with me, you'd sing a different tune pretty quick, and it wouldn't be "Where Is the Devil in Evelyn?" *(He goes into his room and returns carrying a large, dusty box. He opens it and takes out an altar boy's bright red cassock and white surplice that used to fit him when he was twelve. As he puts them on, he speaks to us.)* I was twelve years old and all the newspapers had headlines on my twelfth birthday that Billy was coming to town. And *Life* was doing stories on him and *Look* and the newsreels, because Billy was searching America to find the Ideal American Boy to play Huckleberry Finn. And Billy came to New York and called my father and asked him if he could stay here—Billy needed a hideout. In Waldorf Astorias all over the country, chambermaids would wheel silver carts to change the sheets. And out of the sheets would hop little boys saying, "Hello, I'm Huckleberry Finn." All over the country, little boys dressed in blue jeans and straw hats would be sent to him in crates, be under the silver cover covering his dinner, in his medicine cabinet in all his hotel rooms, his suitcase —"Hello, Hello, I'm Huckleberry Finn." And he was coming here to hide out. Here— Billy coming here—I asked the nun in school who was Huckleberry Finn. . . . The nun in Queen of Martyrs knew. She told me. The Ideal American Boy. And coming home, all the store windows reflected me and the mirror in the tailorshop said, "Hello, Huck." The butcher shop window said, "Hello, Huck. Hello, Huckleberry Finn. All America Wants to Meet Billy and He'll Be Hiding Out in Your House." I came home—went in there —into my room and packed my bag . . . I knew Billy would see me and take me back to California with him that very day. This room smelled of ammonia and air freshener and

these slipcovers were new that day and my parents were filling up the icebox in their brand-new clothes, filling up the icebox with food and liquor as excited as if the Pope was coming—and nervous because they hadn't seen him in a long while—Billy. They told me my new clothes were on my bed. To go get dressed. I didn't want to tell them I'd be leaving shortly to start a new life. That I'd be flying out to California with Billy on the H.M.S. Huckleberry. I didn't want tears from them—only trails of envy. . . . I went to my room and packed my bag and waited. The doorbell rang. *(He starts hitting two notes on the piano.)* If you listen close, you can still hear the echoes of those wet kisses and handshakes and tears and backs getting hit and Hello, Billys, Hello. They talked for a long time about people from their past. And then my father called out, "Ronnie, guess who? Billy, we named him after your father. Ronnie, guess who?" . . . I picked up my bag and said good-bye to myself in the mirror. Came out. Billy there. Smiling . . . It suddenly dawned on me. You had to do things to get parts . . . I began dancing. And singing. Immediately. Things I have never done in my life—before or since. I stood on my head and skipped and whirled *(He cartwheels across the stage.)* spectacular leaps in the air so I could see veins in the ceiling—ran up and down the keys of the piano and sang and began laughing and crying soft and loud to show off all my emotions. And I heard music and drums that I couldn't even keep up with. And then cut off all my emotions just like that. Instantly. And took a deep bow like the Dying Swan I saw on Ed Sullivan. I picked up my suitcase and waited by the door . . . Billy turned to my parents, whose jaws were down to about there, and Billy said, "You never told me you had a mentally retarded child. You never told me I had an idiot for a godchild," and I picked up my bag and went into my room and shut the door and never came out the whole time he was here. . . . My only triumph was he could never find a Huckleberry Finn. Another company made the picture a few years later, but it flopped. . . . My father thinks I'm nothing. Billy. My sergeant. They laugh at me. You laughing at me? I'm going to fool you all. By tonight, I'll be on headlines all over the world. Cover of *Time*. *Life*. TV specials. *(He shows a picture of himself on the wall.)* I hope they use this picture of me—I look better with hair—Go ahead—

laugh. Because you know what I think of you? *(He gives us hesitant Bronx cheers.)* I'm sorry you had to hear that—pay seven or eight dollars to hear that. But I don't care. I'll show you all. I'll be too big for any of you.

(The sound of a key in the door. ARTIE *is heard singing "The Day That the Pope Came to New York."* RONNIE *exits to his room, carrying the gift box containing the bomb.)*

ARTIE. Bunny says, "Arthur, I am not talking to you but I'll say it to the breeze: Arthur, get your music. 'Bring On the Girls.' Hold up your music for when the Pope His Holiness rides by." *(To us)* You heard these songs. They don't need blessings. I hate to get all kissyass, you know? But it can't hurt. "Bring On the Girls." Where is it? Whenever Bunny cleans up in here you never can find anything. You should see the two girls holding each other up like two sisters and they're not even speaking which makes them even more like sisters. Wouldn't it be great if they fell in love and we all could stay . . .

(A beautiful girl in a fur coat stands hesitantly in the doorway. She carries flowers and liquor in her arms. She is CORRINNA STROLLER.*)*

CORRINNA. Mr. Shaughnessy?

ARTIE. Did I win something? Where'd I put those sweepstake tickets—I'll get them—

CORRINNA. Oh oh oh ohhhhh—it's just like Billy said. Oh, God, it's like walking into a photo album. Norman Rockwell. Grandma Moses. Let me look at you. Oh, I was afraid with the Pope, you'd be out, but it's just like Billy said. You're here!

ARTIE. Billy? We talked this morning . . .

CORRINNA. Billy called me just as I was checking out and told me to stop by on my way to the airport.

ARTIE. A friend of Billy's and you stay in a hotel? Don't you know any friend of Billy's has a permanent address right here. . . . Don't tell me . . .

CORRINNA. What?

ARTIE. I know your name.

CORRINNA *(very pleased)*. Oh, how could you . . .

ARTIE. You're Corrinna Stroller.

CORRINNA *(modestly)*. Oh . . .

ARTIE. I knew it. I saw that one movie you made for Billy . . .

CORRINNA. That's how we met.

ARTIE. And then you retired—

CORRINNA *(a sore point)*. Well . . .

ARTIE. You were fantastic.

CORRINNA. Well . . .

ARTIE. Why did you quit?

CORRINNA. Well . . .

ARTIE. Will you sit down for a few minutes? Just let me get my girls. If you left without seeing them . . . *(He comes down to us.)* You call Billy and he sends stars. Stars! *(To* CORRINNA*)* The icebox is yours. I'll be right back. Corrinna Stroller! *(He exits.)*

*(*CORRINNA *is alone. There is a high, loud whine. Her hands go to her ears. The whine becomes very electronic. The sound is almost painful. She pulls a hearing aid from each ear. The sound suddenly stops. She reaches into her dress and removes a receiver that the aids are wired to. She crosses to the couch and sits.)*

CORRINNA *(to us)*. Don't tell—please? I don't want them to know I'm deaf. I don't want them to think Billy's going around with some deaf girl. There was an accident on a set—a set of Billy's. . . . I can hear with my transistors. *(She shows them to us.)* I want them to know me first. So please, don't tell. Please.

*(*BUNNY *enters with* ARTIE *close behind.)*

BUNNY. Where is she? Where is she? Oh . . . Corrinna Stroller! Limos in the streets. Oh, Miss Stroller, I only saw your one movie, *Warmonger,* but it is permanently enshrined in the Loew's of my heart. *(To us)* That scene where she blows up in the landmine—so realistic. *(To* CORRINNA*)* And then you never made another picture. What happened?

CORRINA. I just dropped in to say hi—

BUNNY. Hi! Oh, Corrinna Stroller! *(to* ARTIE*)* You know that phony Mrs. Binard in 4-C who wouldn't give you the time of day—she says, "Oh, Miss Flingus, is this limo connected to you?" I'd like to put my fist through her dimple. *(She takes the newspapers out of her booties. To* CORRINNA*)* Hi, I'm Bunny, the future His. You want some snacks?

CORRINNA. I've got to catch a plane—

BUNNY. Should I send some down to the chauffeur? Oh, stay, have some snacks—

ARTIE. Are you gonna cook?

BUNNY. Just short-order snacks, while you audition . . .

ARTIE. Audition?

BUNNY. You get your ass on those tunes while the Pope's blessing is still hot on them. Artie, the Pope looked right at me! We're in solid. *(To* CORRINNA, *with a tray of celery)* Ta Ta!! That's a trumpet. Look, before we start chattering about hellos and how-are-yous and who we all are and old times and new times, bite into a celery for some quick energy and I'll get you a soda and Arthur here writes songs that could be perfect for Oscar-winning medleys and love themes of important motion-picture presentations and you should tell Billy about it. Artie being the Webster's Dictionary Definition for Mr. Shy. *Gone With the Wind. The Wizard of Oz.* That is the caliber of film that I am talking about. And His Holiness the Very Same Pope has seen these songs and given them his blessings. *(She shows the sheet music to Corrinna.)*

CORRINNA. I'd love to, but I have a very slight postnasal drip.

BUNNY. Isn't she wonderful! Go on, Artie, while Mister Magic still shimmers!

ARTIE *(at the piano, sings).*
Back together again,
Back together again, *etc.*

*(*THREE NUNS *appear at the window.* COR-RINNA *sees them and screams. Her transistors fall to the floor.)*

CORRINNA. My transistors!! *(She is down on her knees, searching for them.)*

BUNNY. Get away from here! Scat! Get away! Go! Go!

HEAD NUN. We got locked out on your roof! Please, it's fifty below and our fingers are icicles and our lips are the color of Mary—

SECOND NUN. The doorknob came right off in our hands—

ARTIE. I'm sorry, Sisters, but these are secret auditions . . .

HEAD NUN. But we missed the Pope! And we came all the way from Ridgewood! Let us see it on television!

ALL THREE NUNS. Please! Please! On television!

ARTIE *(opening the gate).* Oh, all right . . .

BUNNY. Don't do it, Arthur. *(She sees* COR-RINNA *on the floor.)* What's the matter, honey, did you drop something? It's like a regular Vatican here.

(During the scene CORRINNA *will pick up her transistors at any moment she feels she is not being observed. She keeps them in a small vial for safety.)*

SECOND NUN *(They are inside now).* We stole Monsignor Boyle's binoculars!

HEAD NUN. We couldn't see the Pope, the crowds were so thick, so we climbed up onto your roof . . .

SECOND NUN. And I put the binoculars up to my eyes and got the Pope in focus and the pressure of Him against my eyes, oh, God, the binoculars flew out of my hands like a miracle in reverse . . .

HEAD NUN. We'll be quiet.

LITTLE NUN *(in the kitchen).* Look! Peanut butter! They have peanut butter! *(To us)* We're not allowed peanut butter!

ARTIE. Put that away!

HEAD NUN *(a sergeant).* You! Get over here.

(The LITTLE NUN *obeys.* ARTIE *turns on the TV.)*

SECOND NUN. Oh, color. They don't have color!

HEAD NUN. Would you have some beers? To warm us up? We will pray for you many years for your kindness today.

BANANAS *(offstage, in the hall, terrified).* Artie? Artie, are you there? Is this my home? Artie?

ARTIE. Oh God, Bananas. Bunny, get the beers, would you?

BUNNY. What do I look like?

*(*ARTIE *runs into the hall to retrieve* BA-NANAS.*)*

BUNNY *(to* CORRINNA*).* Excuse the interruption; we're not religious as such, but his heart is the Sistine Chapel. *(She goes to the kitchen for beers.)*

BANANAS *(entering with* ARTIE*).* I didn't know where home was. Miss Henshaw showed me. And then your fat girl friend ran away. I had to ask directions how to get back.

*(*BUNNY *plunks the beers on the TV set.)*

SECOND NUN. Oh, imported! They don't have imported! We could've stayed back in Ridgewood and watched color and had imported, but no, she's got to see everything in the flesh—

HEAD NUN. You were the one who dropped the binoculars—

SECOND NUN. You were the one who stole them—

BANANAS. Artie, did you bring work home from the office?

ARTIE. They're nuns, Bananas, nuns.

HEAD NUN. We got locked out on the upstairs roof. Hi!

BANANAS. Hi!

ARTIE. This is Corrinna Stroller, Billy's girl friend. Corrinna, this is Bananas.

THE NUNS. Corinna Stroller! The movie star!

BANANAS. Hello, Billy's girl friend. God, Billy's girl friends always make me feel so shabby!

BUNNY *(to* CORRINNA*).* Arthur believes in keeping family skeletons out in the open like pets. Heel, Bananas, heel!

LITTLE NUN *(running to* CORRINNA's *side, to* CORRINNA). I saw *The Sound of Music* thirty-one times. It changed my entire life.

CORRINNA. Unitarian.

ARTIE. All right now, where were we?

BUNNY. Ta Ta! The trumpet.

ARTIE *(at the piano, sings).*
　　Back together again,
　　Back together again . . .

HEAD NUN *(screams).* There's Jackie Kennedy!!! Get me with Jackie Kennedy!!! *(She puts her arm around the TV.)*

(The LITTLE NUN *takes out her brownie with flash and takes a picture of the head nun posing with Jackie on TV.)*

SECOND NUN. There's Mayor Lindsay! Get me with him! Mayor Lindsay dreamboat! Mayor Wagner ugh!

(There is a scream from the kitchen. BANANAS *has burned herself.)*

ARTIE *(running into kitchen).* What do you think you're doing?

BANANAS. Cooking for our guests. I'm some good, Artie. I can cook.

ARTIE. What is it?

BANANAS. Hamburgers. I felt for them and I cooked them.

ARTIE. Brillo pads. You want to feed our guests Brillo pads? *(To the nuns)* Sisters, please, you're going to have to go into the other room. You're upsetting my wife. *(He unplugs the TV and hustles the nuns off into* RONNIE's *bedroom.)*

SECOND NUN. Go on with what you're doing. Don't bother about us. We're nothing. We've just given our lives up praying for you. I'm going to start picking who I pray for. *(She exits.)*

(The LITTLE NUN *crosses to the kitchen to retrieve the peanut butter.)*

BUNNY. That man is a saint. That woman is a devil.

BANANAS. I'm burned.

BUNNY. Put some vinegar on it. Some salt. Take the sting out.

HEAD NUN *(coming out of the bedroom, very pleased).* There is an altar boy in here. *(She exits.)*

BANANAS. My son was an altar boy. He kept us in good with God. But then he grew up. He isn't an altar boy anymore. *(She exits into her room.)*

BUNNY *(to* CORRINNA). Sometimes I think the whole world has gone cuckoo, don't you?

CORRINNA. For two days.

(The LITTLE NUN *goes into* RONNIE's *room as* ARTIE *comes out and downstage.)*

ARTIE *(to us).* My son Ronnie's in there! He's been picked to be the Pope's altar boy at Yankee Stadium—out of all the boys at Fort Dix! I tell you—miracles tumble down on this family. I don't want you to meet him yet. If his mother sees him, her head will go all over the wall like Spanish omelettes. *(To* CORRINNA) Are you comfortable?

BUNNY. She's adorable! And so down to earth! *(She takes* CORRINNA's *bejeweled hands.)*

CORRINNA. It's five carats. It's something, isn't it?

BUNNY *(to* CORRINNA). Sit right up here with Mister Maestro—*(She seats* CORRINNA *next to* ARTIE *at the piano.)*

ARTIE. Where was I—

BUNNY. "Like Fido chewed them." You left off there—

ARTIE *(sings as* BUNNY *dances.* BANANAS *enters and watches them.)*
　　. . . Like Fido chewed them,
　　But we're
　　Back together again.
　　you can say you knew us when
　　We were together;
　　Now we're apart,
　　Thunder and lightning's
　　Back in my heart,
　　And that's the weather to be
　　When you're back together with me.

(BUNNY *claps wildly.* CORRINNA *follows suit.* BANANAS *claps slowly.)*

BUNNY. Encore! Encore!

ARTIE *(happy now).* What should I play next?

BUNNY. Oh, God, how do you pick a branch from a whole Redwood Forest?

BANANAS *(licking her hand).* "I Love You So I Keep Dreaming."

BUNNY *(picks up the phone, but doesn't dial).* Come and get her!

BANANAS. Play "I Love You So I Keep Dreaming."

ARTIE *(pleased).* You really remember that?

BANANAS. How could I forget it . . .

BUNNY. I'm not used to being Queen of the Outsiders. What song is this?

ARTIE. I almost forgot it. It must have been like Number One that I ever wrote. The one that showed me I should go on.

BUNNY. Well, let me hear it.

ARTIE. You really surprise me, Bananas. Sometimes I miss you so much . . .

BUNNY *(a warning).* Arthur, I still haven't forgiven you for this morning.

ARTIE *(sings).*

I love you so I keep dreaming
Of all the lovely times we shared . . .

BUNNY. Heaven. That is unadulterated heaven.

BANANAS *(interrupting).* Now play "White Christmas"?

BUNNY. Shocks for sure.

BANANAS *(banging the keys of the piano).* Play "White Christmas"?

ARTIE *(to* CORRINNA*).* She's . . . not feeling too . . . hot . . .

BUNNY *(to* CORRINNA*).* In case you haven't noticed . . .

ARTIE. She keeps crawling under the weather. . . . *(He plays a run on the piano.)*

BANANAS. "White Christmas"???????

*(*ARTIE *groans; plays and sings "White Christmas.")*

BUNNY *(to* CORRINNA*).* It really burns me up all these years The Telephone Hour doing salutes to fakers like Richard Rodgers. Just listen to that. Blaaaagh.

*(*ARTIE *stops playing.)*

BANANAS. Don't you hear it?

ARTIE *(plays and sings slowly)*

I'm dreaming of a . . .
I love you so I . . .

(They are the same tune) Oh, God. Oh, God.

BANANAS *(sings desperately).*

I love you so I keep dreaming—

Are you tone deaf? Can't you hear it? *(She bangs the keys on the piano.)*

*(*ARTIE *slams the lid shut on her hand. She yells and licks her fingers to get the pain off them.)*

ARTIE: Oh, you have had it, Little Missy. All these years you knew that and made me play it. She's always trying to do that, Corrinna. Always trying to embarrass me. You have had it, Little Missy. Did Shakespeare ever write one original plot? You tell me that? *(He drags* BANANAS *down to the edge of the stage. To us)* In front of all of you, I am sorry. But you are looking at someone who has had it.

BANANAS. I am just saying your song sounds an awful lot like "White—

ARTIE. Then they can sing my song in the summertime. *(He pushes her away, and picks up the phone.)*

BANANAS. Who are you calling?

BUNNY. Do it, Arthur.

BANANAS *(terrified).* Artie, who are you calling??????

BUNNY. Do you have a little suitcase? I'll start you packing.

BANANAS *(to* CORRINNA*).* Billy's friend? Help me? Billy wouldn't want them to do this. Not to me. He'd be mad. *(Whispering desperately, grabbing* CORRINNA*'s hands)* Help me? Bluebirds. He'll tell you all about it. Me walking on the roof. Can't you say anything? You want bribes? Here—take these flowers. They're for you. Take this liquor. For you. *(She is hysterical.* BUNNY *pulls her away and slaps her.)* I'll be quiet. I'll take my pills. *(She reaches for the vial containing* CORRINNA*'s transistors and swallows them.)*

CORRINNA *(to us).* My transistors!

ARTIE *(on the telephone).* This is Mr. Shaughnessy. Arthur M. . . . I was out there last week and talked about my wife.

BANANAS. That's why my ears were burning . . .

ARTIE. I forgot which doctor I talked to.

BANANAS. He had a moustache.

ARTIE. He had a moustache. *(To his wife)* Thank you. *(Into phone)* Doctor? Hello? That's right, Doctor, could you come and . . . all that we talked about. The room over the garage is fine. Yes, Doctor. Now. Today. . . . Really? That soon? She'll be all ready. . . . *(He hangs up the phone.)*

BUNNY. Arthur, give me your hand. Like I said, today's my wedding day. I wanted something white at my throat. Look, downstairs in a pink cookie jar, I got a thousand dollars saved up and we are flying out to California with Corrinna. As soon as Bananas here is carted off, we'll step off that plane and Billy and you and I and Corrinna here will eat and dance and drink and love until the middle of the next full moon. *(To* BANANAS*)* Bananas, honey, it's not just a hospital. They got dances. *(To* CORRINNA*)* Corrinna, I'll be right back with my suitcase. *(To* ARTIE*)* Artie, start packing. All my life I been treated like an old shoe. You turned me into a glass slipper. *(Sings).*

I'm here with bells on.
Ring! Ring! Ring! Ring! Ring!

(She exits.)

ARTIE. I'm sorry. I'm sorry. *(*BANANAS *runs into her bedroom.* CORRINNA *edges toward the front door.)* Well, Corrinna, now you know everything. Dirty laundry out in the open. I'll be different out West. I'm great at a party. I never took a plane trip before. I guess that's why my stomach is all queazied up. . . . Hey, I'd better start packing. *(He exits.)*

(CORRINNA *heads for the door. The* NUNS *enter.*)

HEAD NUN. Miss Stroller! Miss Stroller! He told us all about Hollywood and Billy and Huckleberry Finn—

SECOND NUN. You tell Billy he ought to be ashamed treating a boy like that—

LITTLE NUN *(with paper and pen).* Miss Stroller, may I have your autograph?

CORRINNA. Sisters, pray for me? Pray my ears come out all right. I'm leaving for Australia—

THE NUNS. Australia?!?

CORRINNA. For a very major ear operation and I need all the prayers I can get. *(To us)* South Africa's where they do the heart work, but Australia's the place for ears. So pray for me. Pray my operation's a success.

(ARTIE *enters with his suitcase half packed.*).

ARTIE. Australia?

CORRINNA. I'm so glad I made a new friend my last day in America.

THE NUNS. She's going to Australia!

CORRINNA. Perhaps you'll bring me luck.

ARTIE. Your last day in America? Sisters, please.

CORRINNA. I'll be Mrs. Einhorn the next time you see me. . . . Billy and I are off to Australia tomorrow for two fabulous years. Billy's making a new film that is an absolute breakthrough for him—*Kangaroo—and you must—all of you—come to California.*

THE NUNS. *Kangaroo!* California!

CORRINNA. And we'll be back in two years.

ARTIE. But we're coming with you today . . .

(The NUNS *are praying for* CORRINNA.)

LITTLE NUN. Our Father, who art in heaven . . .

SECOND NUN. You shut up. I want to pray for her. Our Father—

HEAD NUN *(blows whistle).* I'll pray for her. *(Sings).*

Ave Maria—

(The THREE NUNS *sing "Ave Maria." * RONNIE *enters wearing his army overcoat over the altar boy's cassock and carrying the box with the bomb. He speaks over the singing.)*

RONNIE. Pop! Pop! I'm going!

ARTIE. Ronnie! Corrinna, this is the boy. *(To us)* He's been down at Fort Dix studying to be a general—

RONNIE. Pop, I'm going to blow up the Pope.

ARTIE. See how nice you look with your hair all cut—

(The NUNS *have finished singing "Ave Maria" and take flash pictures of themselves posing with* CORRINNA.)

RONNIE. Pop, I'm going to blow up the Pope and when *Time* interviews me tonight, I won't even mention you. I'll say I was an orphan.

ARTIE. Ronnie, why didn't you write and let me know you were coming home. I might've been in California—it's great to see you—

*(CORRINNA *runs up to the front door, then stops.)*

CORRINNA. Oh, wait a minute. The Pope's Mass at Yankee Stadium! I have two tickets for the Pope's Mass at Yankee Stadium. Would anybody like them?

(The NUNS *and* RONNIE *rush* CORRINNA *for the tickets, forcing her back against the door.* RONNIE *wins the tickets and comes downstage to retrieve his gift-wrapped bomb. When he turns around to leave, the* THREE NUNS *are advancing threateningly on him. They will not let him pass. They lunge at him. He runs into the bedroom for protection.)*

ARTIE *(at the front door).* Miss Stroller, two years? Let's get this Australia part straight. Two years? *(An* M.P. *steps between* ARTIE *and* CORRINNA *and marches into the room. The* M.P. *searches the room.)* Who are you? What are you doing here? Can I help you?

CORRINNA. Oh! This must be Ronnie! The son in the Army! I can't *wait* to hear all about you! *(She embraces the* M.P. *The* M.P. *hears the noises and fighting from* RONNIE's *room and runs in there.)*

CORRINNA *(to* ARTIE*).* He looks just like you!

ARTIE *(following the* M.P.*).* You can't barge into a house like this—where are you going?

(The LITTLE NUN *runs out of the bedroom, triumphantly waving the tickets, almost knocking* ARTIE *over.)*

LITTLE NUN. I got 'em! I got 'em!

*(RONNIE *runs out after her. The other* TWO NUNS *run after him. The* M.P. *runs after them.* RONNIE *runs into the kitchen after the* LITTLE NUN, *who leaps over the couch.* RONNIE *leaps after her. He lands on top of her. He grabs the tickets.)*

HEAD NUN *(to the* M.P.*).* Make him give us back our tickets.

M.P. *(a deep breath and then).* Ronald-V.-Shaughnessy-You-are-under-arrest-for-being-absent-without-leave.-You-have-the-right-to-remain-silent.-I-must-warn-you-that-any-thing-you-say-may-be-used-against-you-in-a-military-court-of-law.-You-have-the-right-to-counsel.-Do-you-wish-to-call-counsel?

(RONNIE *attempts escape. The* HEAD NUN *grabs him.*)

HEAD NUN. That altar boy stole our tickets!

SECOND NUN. Make him give them back to us!

(RONNIE *throws the tickets down. The* HEAD NUN *grabs them.*)

HEAD NUN (*to the* LITTLE NUN). You! Back to Ridgewood! Yahoo! (*She exits.*)

SECOND NUN (*to* CORRINNA). Good luck with your ear operation. (*She exits.*)

CORRINNA. This is an invitation—come to California.

RONNIE (*tossing the bomb to* CORRINNA). From me to Billy—

CORRINNA. Oh, how sweet. I can't wait to open it. Hold the elevator!! (*She runs out.*)

ARTIE (*to the* M.P., *who is struggling with* RONNIE). Hey, what are you doing to my boy?!?

(*A* MAN *dressed in medical whites enters.*)

WHITE MAN. I got a radio message to pick up a Mrs. Arthur M. Shaughnessy.

ARTIE. Bananas! (*He runs to her bedroom.*)

BUNNY (*dancing in through the front door, beaming and dressed like a million bucks*). Ta Ta! Announcing Mrs. Arthur M. Shaughnessy!

WHITE MAN. That's the name. Come along.

BUNNY (*to us, sings*).
I'm here with bells on,
Ringing out how I feel . . .

(*The* WHITE MAN *slips the straitjacket on* BUNNY. *She struggles. He drags her out. She's fighting wildly.*)

ARTIE. Wait. Stop.

(RONNIE *pulls him from the door as there is a terrible explosion. Pictures fly off the wall. Smoke pours in from the hall.*)

BUNNY (*entering through the smoke*). Artie? Where's Corrinna? Where's Corrinna?

ARTIE. Corrinna?

(ARTIE *runs out into the hall with* BUNNY. *The lights dim as* RONNIE *and the* M.P. *grapple in slow motion, the* LITTLE NUN *trying to pull the* M.P. *off* RONNIE. BANANAS *comes downstage into the light. An unattached vacuum hose is wrapped around her shoulders. She cleans the floor with the metallic end of the hose. She smiles at us.*)

BANANAS (*to us*). My house is a mess. . . . Let me straighten up. . . . I can do that. . . . I'm a housewife. . . . I'm good for something. . . . (*Sings as she vacuums*).
I love you so I keep dream . . .

(*Closes her eyes*) Artie, you could salvage that song. You really could.

CURTAIN

SCENE TWO

(*In the darkness after the curtain we hear the* POPE *from Yankee Stadium.*)

VOICE OF THE POPE. We feel, too, that the entire American people is here present with its noblest and most characteristic traits: a people basing its conception of life on spiritual values, on a religious sense, on freedom, on loyalty, on work, on the respect of duty, on family affection, on generosity and courage—

(*The curtain goes up. It is later that night and the only illumination in the room is the light from the television. The house is vaguely picked up but not repaired, and everything is askew; neat—things are picked up off the floor for instance—but lampshades are just tilted enough, pictures on the wall are just slanted enough, and we see that everything that had been on the floor—the clothes, the suitcases—has been jammed into corners.* ARTIE *is watching the television. Another person is sitting in the easy chair in front of the TV.*)

—safeguarding the American spirit from those dangers which prosperity itself can entail and which the materialism of our day can make even more menacing. . . . From its brief but heroic history, this young and flourishing country can derive lofty and convincing examples to encourage it all in its future progress.

(*From the easy chair, we hear sobbing. The deep sobbing of a man.* ARTIE *clicks off the television and clicks on the lights. He has put a coat and tie over his green park clothes. He's very uncomfortable and is trying to be very cheery. The* MAN *in the chair keeps sobbing.*)

———

ARTIE. I'm glad he said that. That Pope up at Yankee Stadium—some guy. Boy, isn't that Pope some guy. You ever met him in your travels? . . . You watch. That gang war in Vietnam—over tomorrow. . . . (*Brightly*) People always talking about a certain part of the anatomy of a turkey like every Thanksgiving you say give me the Pope's nose. But that Pope is a handsome guy. Not as good-looking as you and me, but clean. Business-like. *(To us)* This is the one. The only. You guessed it: this is Billy. He got here just before the eleven o'clock news. He had to identify Corrinna's body, so he's a little upset. You forgive him, okay? Billy, come on—don't take it so hard. . . . You want to take off your shoes? . . . You want to get comfortable? . . . You want a beer? . . . *(He sits at the piano; plays and sings.)*

> If there's a broken heart
> For every light on Broadway,
> Screw in another bulb . . .

You like that? . . . Look, Billy, I'm sorry as hell we had to get together this way. . . . Look at it this way. It was quick. No pain. Pain is awful but she was one of the luckies, Bill. She just went. And the apartment is all insured. They'll give us a new elevator and everything.

BILLY. The one thing she wanted was . . .

ARTIE. Come on, boy. Together. Cry, cry, get it all out.

BILLY. She wanted her footprints in Grau-man's Chinese. I'm going to have her shoes set in wet cement. A ceremony. A tribute. God knows she'd hate it.

ARTIE. Hate it?

BILLY. Ahh, ever since the ears went, she stopped having the push, like she couldn't hear her different drummer anymore, drum-ming up all that push to get her to the top. She just stopped. *(He cries. Deep sobs.)*

ARTIE *(uncomfortable)*. She could've been one of the big ones. A lady Biggie. Boy. Star-dust. Handfuls of it. All over her. Come on, boy . . . easy . . . easy . . . Bill, that's enough.

BILLY. Do you have any tea bags?

ARTIE. You want a drink? Got the bourbon here—the Jack Daniels—

BILLY. No. Tea bags. Two. One for each eye.

ARTIE. *(puzzled)*. Coming right up. . . . *(He goes into the kitchen and opens the cabi-nets.)*

BILLY. Could you wet them? My future is all ashes, Artie. In the morning, I'll fly back with Corrinna's body, fly back to L.A. and stay there. I can't work. Not for a long, long time, if ever again. I was supposed to go to Australia, but no . . . all ashes . . . *(He puts one tea bag over each eye.)* God, it's good to see you again, Artie.

ARTIE. Billy, you can't! You owe it—golly, Billy, the world—Bunny and me—we fell out of our loge seats—I'd be crazy if it wasn't for the laughs, for the romance you bring. You can't let this death stand in the way. Look what's happened to your old buddy. I've become this Dreaming Boy. I make all these Fatimas out of the future. Lourdes and Fatima. All these shrines out of the future and I keep crawling to them. Don't let that happen to you. Health. Health. You should make a musical. Listen to this. *(He goes to the piano and sings and plays.)*

> Back together again,
> Back together again . . .

(BANANAS appears in the bedroom doorway dressed in clothes that must have been very stylish and elegant ten years earlier.)

BILLY *(starts)*. Georgina!!

(ARTIE stops playing.)

BANANAS. No, Billy . . .

BILLY *(stands up)*. Oh, God—for a minute I thought it was . . .

ARTIE. Don't she look terrific . . .

BILLY. Let me look at you. Turn around. *(She does.)* Jesus, didn't Georgina have good taste.

BANANAS *(turning)*. I used to read *Vogue* on the newsstands to see what I'd be wearing in three years.

BILLY. Georgina took that dress right off her back and gave it to you. What a woman she was . . .

BANANAS. I put it on to make you happy, Billy.

(BILLY is crying again.)

ARTIE. Easy, Billy, easy . . .

BANANAS. It's a shame it's 1965. I'm like the best-dressed woman of 1954.

BILLY *(starting to laugh and cheer up)*. You got the best of them all, Artie. Hello, Ba-nanas!

BANANAS. Sometimes I curse you for giv-ing me that name, Billy.

BILLY. A little Italian girl. What else was I going to call her?

(The LITTLE NUN rushes in from the bed-room.)

LITTLE NUN. Mr. Shaughnessy! Quick—the bathtub—the shower—the hot water is steaming—running over—I can't turn it—there's nothing to turn—

(ARTIE runs into the bedroom. The LITTLE NUN looks at BILLY. BILLY smiles at her. The LITTLE NUN runs into the bedroom.)

BANANAS. I did it to burn her.

BILLY. Burn who?

BANANAS. Burn her downstairs. Have the hot water run through the ceiling and give her blisters. He won't like her so much when she's covered with blisters. Hot water can do that. It's one of the nicest properties of hot water.

BILLY. Burn who???

BANANAS. Kate Smith!!

ARTIE *(running in from the bedroom to the kitchen).* Wrench. Wrench. Screwdriver. *(He rattles through drawers. Brightly to* BILLY) God, don't seem possible. Twenty years ago. All started right on this block. Didn't we have some times? The Rainbow Room. Leon and Eddie's. I got the pictures right here.

(The pictures are framed on the wall by the front door. BILLY *comes up to them.)*

BILLY. Leon and Eddie's!

ARTIE. *(indicating another picture).* The Village Barn.

BANANAS. The Village Barn. God, I loved the Village Barn.

ARTIE. It's closed, Bananas. Finished. Like you.

LITTLE NUN. Mr Shaughnessy—please? *(*ARTIE *runs into the bedroom.)* Mr. Einhorn?

BILLY. Hello?

LITTLE NUN. I was an usher before I went in and your name always meant quality. *(She runs into the bedroom.)*

BILLY. Why—Thank you . . .

BANANAS. Help me, Billy? They're coming again to make me leave. Let me stay here? They'll listen to you. You see, they give me pills so I won't feel anything. Now I don't mind not feeling anything so long as I can remember feeling. You see? And this apartment, you see, here, right here, I stand in this corner and I remember laughing so hard. Doubled up. At something Ronnie did. Artie said. And I stand over here where I used to iron. When I could iron, I'd iron right here, and even then, the buttons, say, on button-down shirts could make me sob, cry . . . and that window, I'd stand right here and mix me a rye-and-ginger pick-me-up and watch the lights go on in the Empire State Building and feel so tender . . . unprotected. . . . I don't mind not feeling so long as I can be in a place I remember feeling. You get me? You get me? Don't look at me dead. I'm no Georgina. I'm no Corrinna. Help me? Help Ronnie?

BILLY. Ronnie's in jail.

BANANAS. I don't mind the bars, But he can't take them. He's not strong like his mom. Come closer to me? Don't let them

hear. Oh, you kept your moustache. *(She strokes his eyebrows.)* Nothing's changed. *(She sings.)*

Should auld acquaintance be forgot . . .

*(*ARTIE *comes out of the bedroom, soaking wet.)*

ARTIE. Those are eyebrows, Bananas. Eyebrows. Come on, where is it? *(He reaches behind* BANANAS' *back and pulls the silver faucet handle from her clenched fist.)* Billy, you see the wall I'm climbing. *(He goes back into the bedroom with it.)*

(The LITTLE NUN *looks out into the living room.)*

LITTLE NUN *(to Billy).* We never got introduced.

BILLY. Do I know you?

*(*BANANAS *goes into the corner by the window.)*

LITTLE NUN *(coming into the room).* No, but my two friends died with your friend today.

BILLY. I'm very sorry for you.

LITTLE NUN. No, it's all right. All they ever wanted to do was die and go to heaven and meet Jesus. The convent was very depressing. Pray a while. Scream a while. Well, they got their wish, so I'm happy.

BILLY. If your friends died with my friend, then that makes us—oh, God! Bananas! That makes us all friends! You friends and me friends and we're all friends!

BANANAS. Help Ronnie. Help him. *(She hands* BILLY *the phone.)*

BILLY *(on phone).* Operator—my friend the operator—get me person-to-person my friend General Buckley Revere in the Pentagon—202 LIncoln 5-5600.

ARTIE *(coming out of the bedroom).* No, Billy . . . no favors for Ronnie. The kid went AWOL. M.P.s dragging him out of the house. You think I like that? *(To* BANANAS) That kid's your kid, Bananas. You got the crazy monopoly on all the screwball chromosomes in that kid.

BILLY. Buck? Bill.

ARTIE *(to* BANANAS). Let him learn responsibility. Let him learn to be a man.

BILLY. Buck, just one favor: my godchild, Ron Shaughnessy. He's in the brig at Fort Dix. He wanted to see the Pope.

ARTIE *(to* BANANAS). Billy and me served our country. You think Billy could call up generals like that if he wasn't a veteran! *(To us)* I feel I got to apologize for the kid. . . . I tried to give him good strong things . . .

BILLY. Buck, has the army lost such heart that it won't let a simple soldier get a glimpse of His Holiness . . .

(The front door opens. BUNNY enters. She looks swell and great and all the Webster Dictionary synonyms for terrific. She's all exclamation points: pink and white!!! She carries an open umbrella and a steaming casserole in her pot-holder-covered hands.)

BUNNY. Arthur, are you aware the Rains of Ranchipur are currently appearing on my ceiling?

ARTIE. Ssshhhhhhh . . . *(Indicating her pot)* Is that the veal and oranges?

BUNNY. That's right, Arthur. I'm downstairs making veal and oranges and what do I get from you? Boiling drips.

ARTIE. That's Billy. . . . Billy's here. *(He takes the umbrella from her.)*

BUNNY. Billy Einhorn here? And you didn't call me? Oh, Mr. Einhorn. *(She steps into the room. She is beaming. She poses.)* And that's why the word *Voilà* was invented. Excuse my rudeness. Hi, Artie. Hi, Bananas.

BILLY *(on phone)*. Thank you, Buck, Yes, Yes, Terrific, Great. Talk to you tomorrow. Love ya. Thank you. *(He hangs up.)* Ronnie'll be all right. Buck will have him stationed in Rome with NATO. He'll do two weeks in the brig just to clear the records . . .

ARTIE. Then off to Rome? Won't that be interesting. And educational. Thank you, Billy. Thank you.

BILLY. Ronnie's lucky. Buck said everybody at Dix is skedded for Vietnam.

BUNNY. I wouldn't mind that. I love Chinese food.

ARTIE. That's the little girl from the steambath . . .

(BILLY notices BUNNY. They laugh.)

BUNNY. Hi! I'm Bunny from right down below. (BILLY *kisses her hand.*) Oohhhh . . . Artie, perhaps our grief-stricken visitor from Movieland would join us in a Snack à la Petite.

BILLY. No, no.

ARTIE. Come on, Bill.

BUNNY. Flying in on such short notice you must have all the starving people of Armenia in your tumtum, begging, "Feed me, feed me."

BILLY. Just a bite would be—

BANANAS *(comes down to us with ARTIE's scrapbook)*. What they do is they make a scrapbook of all the things she can cook, then they paste them in the book—veal par-

magina, eggplant meringue . . . (ARTIE *grabs it from her.)* Eughh . . .

ARTIE *(to BILLY)*. We make a scrapbook of all the things Bunny can cook, you see, then we paste them in the book. *(They eat. To us)* I wish I had spoons enough for all of you.

BUNNY. Mr. Einhorn, I met your friend today before Hiroshima Mon Amour happened out there and all I got to say is I hope when I go I got two Sisters of Charity with me. I don't know your persuasion God-wise, but your friend Corrinna, whether she likes it or not, is right up there in Heaven tonight.

BILLY. Artie, you were right. We are what our women make us. Corrinna: how easily deaf becomes dead. It was her sickness that held us together. Health. Health. You were always healthy. You married a wonderful little Italian girl. You have a son. Where am I?

BUNNY. Deaf starlets. That's no life.

BILLY. So how come she's dead? Who blew her up?

BANANAS. It was on the eleven o'clock news.

BUNNY. Crying and explanations won't bring her back. Mr. Einhorn, if it took all this to get you here, I kiss the calendar for today. Grief puts erasers in my ears. My world is kept a beautiful place. Artie . . . I feel a song coming on.

ARTIE. How about a lovely tune, Bill, to go with that food. *(He goes to the piano and plays.)*

BUNNY *(opens the umbrella and does a dance with it, as she sings)*.
Where is the devil in Evelyn?
What's it doing in Angela's eyes?
Evelyn is heavenly,
Angela's in a devil's disguise.
I know about the sin in Cynthia
And the hell in Helen of Troy,
But where is the devil in Evelyn?
What's it doing in Angela's eyes?
Oh, boy!
What's it doing in Angela's eyes?

BILLY. My God!

ARTIE. *Up from the piano)*. What!

BILLY. Suddenly!

BANANAS. Was it the veal?

BILLY. I see future tenses! I see I can go on! Health! I have an extra ticket. Corrinna's ticket. For Australia.

ARTIE. God, Billy, I'd love to. I have all my music . . .

BILLY *(coming to BUNNY)*. Cook for me a while? Stay with me a while? In two hours a plane leaves from Kennedy and on to a whole new world. Los Angeles. We drop off Corrinna's body. Then on to Hawaii. ᴗamoa. Nonstop to Melbourne. Someone who listens. That's what I need.

BUNNY. But my whole life is here . . .

BILLY. Chekhov was right. Work. Work. That's the only answer. All aboard??????

BUNNY. My my my my my my my . . .

ARTIE. Are you out of your head? Leaving in two hours? It takes about six months to get shots and passports—

BUNNY. Luckily two years ago I got shots and a passport in case I got luck with a raffle ticket to Paree. I'm in raffles all over the place.

ARTIE. Bunny—

BUNNY. Leave me alone, Arthur. I have to think. I don't know what to say. It's all so sudden.

(The LITTLE NUN comes out of the bedroom. She is in civvies. As a matter of fact, she has on one of GEORGINA's dresses, off the shoulder, all covered with artificial cherries. It is too big for her. She carries her wet habit.)

LITTLE NUN. I was catching a cold so I put on one of your dresses, Mrs. Shaughnessy. I have to go now. I want to thank you for the loveliest day I've ever had. You people are so lucky. You have so much. (She is near tears.) And your son is so cute. Maybe when I take my final vows I can cross my fingers and they won't count.

BILLY. How would you like to stay here?

ARTIE. Stay here?

BILLY. There'll be an empty apartment right down below and you could come up and take care of Bananas. (He takes out his wallet and gives a number of hundred-dollar bills to the LITTLE NUN.) How's this for a few months' salary?

ARTIE. What's all that money?

BILLY Artie, don't send Bananas away. Love. That's all she needs.

BANANAS. It is? (The telephone rings. She answers it.) Yes? Yes? (To ARTIE who is on his knees, trying to reason with BUNNY) It's the Zoo.

ARTIE: Tell them I'll call—what are they calling this late for?

BANANAS. The animals are all giving birth! Everything's having a baby. The leopards and the raccoons and the gorillas and the panthers and the . . .

ARTIE (taking the phone). Who is this? Al? Look, this is what you have to do. Heat the water. Lock the male elephants out. They get testy. The leopardess tends to eat her children. Watch her careful . . .

(As he talks on the phone so we can't hear him, BUNNY comes downstage and talks to us.)

BUNNY. The Pope saw my wish today. He looked me right in the eye and he winked. Hey! Smell—the bread is starting again and there's miracles in the air! The Pope is flying back through the nighttime sky and all the planets fall back into place and Orion the Hunter relaxes his bow . . . and the gang war in Vietnam will be over and all those crippled people can nowstand up and walk back to Toledo. And, Billy, in front of all these people, I vow to you I'll be the best housekeeper money can buy . . . and I'll cook for you and clean and, who knows, maybe there'll be a development. . . . And, Bananas, honey, when I get to California, I'll send you some of my clothes. I'll keep up Georgina's traditions. Sister, here are the keys to my apartment downstairs. You can write a book, I Jump Over the Wall, and, Billy, you could film it.

ARTIE (on phone). Yes! I'll be right down. I'll be right on the subway. Yes. (He hangs up.) I . . . have to go to work. . . . Billy? Bun? Would you like to come? See life starting? It's beautiful.

BUNNY (in the kitchen). Bananas, honey, could I have this copper pot? I've always had my eye on this pot.

BANANAS. Take it.

ARTIE. Listen, Bill.

BUNNY. Well, I'm packed.

ARTIE. I write songs, Bill. (He starts playing and singing "Back Together Again.")

BANANAS (to BILLY, who is on his way out). Thank you, Billy.

BILLY (coming back and sitting alongside ARTIE). Artie, can I tell you a secret? (ARTIE stops playing.) Do you know who I make my pictures for? Money? No. Prestige? No. I make them for you.

ARTIE. Me?

BILLY (coming downstage). I sit on the set and before every scene I say, "Would this make Artie laugh? Would this make Artie cry?"

ARTIE (coming to BILLY). I could come on the set and tell you personal . . .

BILLY. Oh, no, Artie. If I ever thought you and Bananas weren't here in Sunnyside, seeing my work, loving my work, I could never work again. You're my touch with reality. *(He goes to* BANANAS.) Bananas, do you know what the greatest talent in the world is? To be an audience. Anybody can create. But to be an audience . . . be an audience . . .

ARTIE *(runs back to the piano; he sings desperately).*

> I'm looking for something,
> I've searched everywhere . . .

BUNNY. Artie, I mean this in the best possible sense: You've been a wonderful neighbor.

BILLY *(to* ARTIE). I just saved your life. *(They exit.* ARTIE *plays "Where is the Devil in Evelyn" hysterically, then runs out after them.)*

ARTIE *(shouting).* Bill! Bill! I'm too old to be a young talent!!!

(The LITTLE NUN *comes downstage.)*

LITTLE NUN *(to us).* Life is this orchard and we walk beneath it and apples and grapes and cherries and mangoes all tumble down on us. Ask and you shall receive. I didn't even ask and look how much I have. Thank you. Thank you all. *(She kisses the television.)* A shrine . . . I wanted to be a Bride of Christ but I guess now I'm a young divorcee. I'll go downstairs and call up the convent. Goodbye. Thank you. *(She wrings out her wet habit, then throws it up in the air and runs out.)*

*(*ARTIE *returns. He stands in the doorway.* BANANAS *sits on the edge of the armchair. She is serene and peaceful and beautiful.* ARTIE *comes into the room slowly.)*

BANANAS. I don't blame you for that lady, Artie. I really don't. But I'm going to be good to you now. Cooking. I didn't know you liked cooking. All these years and I didn't know you liked cooking. See, you can live with a person. . . . Oh, God, Artie, it's like we're finally alone for the first time in our life. Like it's taken us eighteen years to get from the church to the hotel room and we're finally alone. I promise you I'll be different. I promise you . . . *(She sits on her haunches like a little dog smiling for food as she did in Act One.)* Hello, Artie. *(She barks. She sings.)*

> Back together again,
> Back together again.

> Since we split up
> The skies we lit up
> Looked all bit up
> Like Fido chewed them,
> But they're
> Back together again.
> You can say you knew us when . . .

(She begins barking. She crawls on all fours. She barks happily. She wags her behind. She licks ARTIE*'s hands.* ARTIE *looks at her. He touches the piano and picks up his music. She rubs her face against his pants leg, nuzzling him. She whimpers happily. She barks. She sits up, begging, her hands tucked under her chin. Her hands swing out. She knocks the music out of his hands onto the floor. She rubs her face into* ARTIE*'s legs. He pats her head. She is thrilled. He kneels down in front of her. He is crying. He touches her face. She beams. She licks his hand. He kisses her. He strokes her throat. He looks away. He holds her. He kisses her fully. She kisses him. He leans into her. As his hands go softly on her throat, she looks up at him with a beautiful smile as if she had always been waiting for this. He kisses her temples, her cheeks. His hands tighten around her throat. Their bodies blend as he moves on top of her. She smiles radiantly at him. He squeezes the breath out of her throat. She falls.*

Soft piano music plays.

The stage begins to change. Blue leaves begin to filter all over the room until it looks as though ARTIE *is standing in a forest of leaves that are blue. A blue spotlight appears downstage and he steps into it. He is very happy and smiles at us.)*

ARTIE. Hello. My name is Artie Shaughnessy and I'd like to thank you for that blue spot and to sing you some songs from the pen of. *(He sings.)*

> I'm here with bells on,
> Ringing out how I feel.
> I'll ring,
> I'll roar,
> I'll sing
> Encore!
> I'm here with bells on.
> Ring! Ring! Ring!

(The stage is filled with blue leaves.)

CURTAIN

LEMON SKY

Lanford Wilson

For JIM and JOHN

First presented on March 26, 1970, by Neal DuBrock at the Buffalo Studio Arena Theatre, Buffalo, New York with the following cast:

ALAN   Christopher Walken
DOUGLAS   Charles Durning
RONNIE   Bonnie Bartlett
PENNY   Kathryn Baumann

CAROL   Lee McCain
JERRY   Shawn McGill
JACK   Frank Martinez III

Directed by Warren Enters
Designed by Stephen Henrickson
Lighting by David Zierk
TIME: Now and the late 1950s.

Lanford Wilson was one of the first playwrights to emerge into prominence from the Off-Off-Broadway scene, and he remains one of the most interesting. People are always asking where the new young American playwrights are, and the answer is almost always the same —everywhere and anywhere but Broadway, although Wilson is one of the exceptions in once having had a play produced on Broadway.

Wilson was born in Lebanon, Missouri, and was brought up in Ozark, Missouri, and he later attended the University of Chicago. It was here that he started writing plays. He arrived in New York in 1963, where he gravitated toward the Café Cino, a pioneering, Off-Off-Broadway café theatre run by Joseph Cino.

It was at the Café Cino in 1964 that he made his professional playwrighting debut with *Home Free!,* a play that subsequently transferred to the Cherry Lane Theatre. During the following ten years, Wilson had nine plays produced in New York, and many have been given across the country and abroad. He has also written the libretto for Lee Hoiby's opera, *Summer and Smoke,* based on Tennessee Williams's play.

Before he wrote *Lemon Sky,* Wilson had a number of successes to his credit. His one-acter, *The Madness of Lady Bright,* won many plaudits both in New York and London: *The Rimers of Eldritch* had a long New York run and also won the Drama Desk Vernon Rice Award, and both *The Gingham Dog* and *Lemon Sky* were extremely well reviewed. But neither was really successful with the public.

The Gingham Dog is a particularly interesting case in point because it appeared to have everything going for it. It had a most sensitive story about a man and a woman—he is white and she is black—and the closing down of their marriage. It was most sensitively written, and rather than exploring racial issues and tensions (although these certainly symbolized and concentrated the incompatibility between the couple) Wilson wrote about two loving people for whom love is not enough. It was beautifully directed by Alan Schneider, and the acting by Diana Sands (her last Broadway appearance) and George Grizzard was impeccable. It opened on April 23, 1969, and it ran a sad total of five performances. It was one of the first indications that Broadway, except in very special circumstances, might not be hospitable to serious drama.

It must have been with this in mind that *Lemon Sky* was produced Off Broadway rather than on Broadway. *Lemon Sky* had originally been produced by the Buffalo Studio Arena Theatre, and its New York premiere, at the Playhouse Theatre on May 17, 1970, was partly produced under the Arena Theatre's auspices. Staged by Warren Enters and starring Christopher Walken as Alan, a seventeen-year-old boy trying to establish a relationship with his father, played by Charles Durning, the play ran for only seventeen performances.

Once again there was muttering and despair, for, even more than *The Gingham Dog,* this seemed to many people to be one of the best of contemporary American plays. *Lemon Sky* later moved to Chicago where it had a much longer and more successful engagement. Wilson's story does have a happy ending, however, because in 1970 he became playwright-in-residence at the Off-Off-Broadway Circle Theatre. It was there on February 4, 1973, that his *The Hot l Baltimore* was staged, and this, transferred to Off Broadway, ran for more than a year. The critics' faith in Wilson was finally justified by public response.

Wilson is a naturalistic playwright, for the most part, with an abiding interest in American themes. His concern is with contemporary American society and morals, the way we live, the way we act, the way we think. He is not experimental in his techniques but clear-sighted in his honesty and sharp in his perceptions. In a way he is an old-fashioned playwright—it is not for nothing that his *The Hot l Baltimore* has been compared with William Saroyan—but there is nothing old-fashioned about his vision of America and his remarkable skill at capturing that vision on the stage.

CHARACTERS

ALAN, *29 now, 17 when he went to California*
DOUGLAS, *his father*
RONNIE, *his father's wife*
PENNY ⎱ *both 17, wards of the state, living*
CAROL ⎰ *with Douglas's family*
JERRY ⎱ *Douglas and Ronnie's children,*
JACK ⎰ *Alan's half brothers; 12 and 8*

ACT ONE

THE SCENE: *One of the thousands of homes in the suburbs of San Diego, California. This one is in El Cajon, a city surrounded by low mountains. The home is more indicated than represented realistically. There is a back yard with redwood fences separating it from the neighbors', a low sloping roofline against a broad expanse of sky (which is never yellow); there are no walls but indicated divisions of rooms: a kitchen with a breakfast nook, refrigerator, stove, cabinets, etc.; the living room, carpeted, need only have a sofa and TV for furnishings; ALAN's bedroom, upstage; and a garage with photographic printing equipment. There is furniture in an area of the yard and a garden against the redwood fence. The kitchen and an area indicating the bathroom may have tiled floors; a patio can be surfaced in redwood or concrete or flagstone. The stage area should be open and free. Sometimes the characters move down "halls" and into "rooms" and sometimes they cut across the entire stage, paying no attention to the room divisions.*

There is no green in set or costumes; celadon, sage, anything else, but nothing green.

The lights move from area to area, defining our focus as well as the time of day and condition, and as many scenes as possible are bathed in a bright, cloudless sunlight.

(The stage is dark and undefined. All the characters are on stage, standing far upstage, just barely lighted. We should "feel" they are there without actually seeing them.)

———

ALAN. *(Comes forward from the darkness. He is twenty-nine now. Thin and light, though not blond. Enthusiastic and pensive. He speaks rapidly and at times—when talking with the other characters—with a marked midwestern accent. A little too preoccupied to begin a play, he enters a pool of light downstage and speaks to the audience.)* I've been trying to tell this story, to get it down, for a long time, for a number of years, seven years at least—closer to ten. I've had the title; I've had some of the scenes a dozen times, a dozen different ways, different starts. The times I've told it to friends as something I wanted to do, I've come home and tried to get it down—get to work on it—but the characters, the people, ignored the damn story and talked about whatever they darn well pleased and wouldn't have any part of what I wanted them to say. They sat down to coffee or some damn thing. The trouble was I wanted not to be the big deal, the hero, because I wasn't. No one was. Or how do I know who was? If it happened this way or that, who knows? But Dad—my dad— *(Quickly)* If it's all autobiographical, so, I'm sorry, there it is; what can I tell you? But how can I write about Dad? tell him? I knew him—lived with him—that I can remember, for six months. *(Quickly)* I always say I lived in California for two years, because it sounds more romantic. Bumming around the beach a couple of years, on the Coast, it sounds great. Six months is like you didn't fit in. Like why bother? Like restlessness. The title because—I don't know—it had something to do with the state. California. I mean the nut fringe; first Brown, then Reagan, and who knows what they'll come up— *(Breaking off, returning to the thought above)* But finally I said, so if you're a hero; if you can't admit that you weren't, if you've got to make a—if you can't admit that you were really as big a bastard as everybody else, if you can't admit that, for God's sake let it stay! And the fact that you can't will say more about you than if you could. Leave it be! My father, what do I know about him? If he's nothing—I mean *but nothing!*—then the fact that he comes off the short end of the stick shows something. From that you know that there's *more* there. You know? Leave it! Do it. Straight. Get it down, let it get down and let it tell itself and *mirror*—by what you couldn't say—what was really there.

DOUGLAS *(still in the shadows upstage; we cannot see him clearly. With great emotion).* Hugged me! Hugged me, by God! By God, you can't! No matter what anybody anywhere says—

ALAN *(finishing the sentence, as if recalling a quote).*—you can't separate a kid from his father.

DOUGLAS *(just a bit more visible).* Even

after—after this long a time. Even after this . . . time!

ALAN. Oh, God—

RONNIE *(faintly answering Doug; they begin to be visible).* I know, I know, Doug—

ALAN *(overlapping).*—what could I do? I got off the bus. I have a splitting headache from the altitude, from going over the Rockies and then down to sea level—like a drop of ten thousand feet. Two and a half days on a scenic-cruising Greyhound with faulty air-conditioning.

RONNIE. A migraine he said, tension—

DOUGLAS. Well, yes, tension—

ALAN *(overlapping).* Finally I had to go to a doctor; after three days I could hardly talk. He said it was tension, the change in environment, just needed acclimatization and aspirin. Maybe it was—all I know is it started while I was in the Rockies or in Arizona: I woke up and my head was splitting. Like I wanted to die there, forget it. And with this headache—the bus pulled in and I—there's only one guy standing there. A very distinguished-looking man. I think, my God, he's so handsome, he's so good-looking, so young. In this dude suit. White dinner jacket—sport jacket, but white. Wool. Sun shining. *(Sunlight beams around them)* And I said . . . Dad? *(Douglas reaches out. Alan flies into his arms, quickly, then retreats.)* I mean, what could I do? Shake his hand? But it was *right.* I felt it was right. *(Then with immediate irritation)* No, Mother hadn't said anything against him—or at least what she said I was willing to forget. All the way back in the goddamned car—

DOUGLAS. *(Douglas is a strong gray-templed man of forty-five. Oddly romantic, childish, and dogmatic, with great energy. Though considerably heavier than Alan, he is no taller, and there is a marked physical resemblance between the two. Douglas wears a white wool sport jacket and gray slacks. After he goes to work and comes back, we never see him dressed in anything but work or sport shirts again.)* Now, I know she must have told you things about me, and she's a good woman—

ALAN *(to the audience. Cutting in).* I just wanted him not to feel bad—and not to think Mother had said anything. *(To Douglas)* Really.

DOUGLAS. Hell, I wanted you out here years ago.

ALAN. Sure, you don't have to think about it, Dad. Really. I don't hold anything against

you. *(To the audience)* I almost wished I hadn't come. For a minute. It was *pain*ful! His explanations! That was over, years ago—finished.

DOUGLAS. I know, but I had to say it.

ALAN. You don't have to think about it, Dad. Really, I don't.

DOUGLAS *(loosening up).* She's a good woman. But with a man like me—Al, she was at me day and night with suspicions and limitations; I couldn't breathe. All that—she didn't let a guy breathe.

ALAN *(distantly).* I understand, really.

DOUGLAS. Ronnie is different, a different kind of woman. She *lives.* You'll love her.

ALAN. I'm anxious to meet her. *(half to the audience, half to Douglas)* And I have two brothers—half brothers—I've only seen once; I hardly know them. Not at all.

DOUGLAS. You'll see them asleep—or tomorrow. I've got to go back for the second half of the day.

ALAN *(to the audience).* He worked nights. The swing shift.

DOUGLAS. It pays better; not much, but it helps. You have the daytime to yourself; you work six hours instead of seven. I like to get out. You have some decent time to yourself. I just want you to understand.

RONNIE. *(Coming forward a step, extending her hand. She is small, attractive, blond, and perhaps thirty-eight, with a good deal of taste and poise.)* I was working in the garden—

ALAN *(to the audience, suddenly).* If it was staged . . . I mean she knew Dad was coming to get me. He called to see if the bus was on time. He said he had waited only eight minutes—

DOUGLAS. Bulova—

ALAN. —so she—

DOUGLAS. —never wrong.

ALAN.—knew I'd be in at that time. What do you do? You meet a kid. Seventeen. Just out of high school. Your stepson, you've never seen before . . . What are you going to be doing? What*ever* it is will make *some* kind of impression. You borrow a white sport coat to meet the kid, and you put on a pair of those thick, big white gloves, with dirt—from the *ground* dirt—on them, those white work gloves with blue elastic wrists, big thick things for *men,* and— *(Framing it)*—you are discovered in a garden hat so the California sun doesn't burn you and so you won't frown.

RONNIE *(coming forward a step).* I was working in the garden, pruning.

ALAN *(to the audience)*. Rose garden. The roses.

RONNIE *(showing him around the yard)*. There's the bird of paradise; it's never going to bloom. I got it because it's Jack's favorite, the only flower he likes.

ALAN *(suddenly, wanting to hug them)*. Jack! Jack! Little Jack!

RONNIE. Probably because it's very futuristic. "Spaceman" or "Jungleman."

ALAN *(back to framing the scene)*. Pruning the roses. I hear the car drive into the driveway and the gate open at the side of the house. I turn around; I come across the back yard smiling.

RONNIE *(coming to him, taking off a glove, extending her hand)*. Welcome, Alan, welcome. Hello.

ALAN. I take off a glove and extend my soft hand . . .

RONNIE. I was working in the garden, pruning.

ALAN *(to the audience)*. The roses. And a handshake; and Dad looks on beaming. *Beaming.* "You'll"—

DOUGLAS. You'll—

ALAN.—"love"—

DOUGLAS.—love—

ALAN.—"her."

DOUGLAS.—her.

ALAN. Blond hair. She looks like Blondie in the funnies; but she—you *do* love her. She's worried and planned and—

RONNIE *(cutting in)*. Do you smoke? You want a cigarette?

ALAN *(to the audience)*. And of course you smoke, but you didn't know if you should and—

DOUGLAS. A beer?

ALAN. Yes, thanks, I didn't know—

DOUGLAS. Sure, take it, drink up. Hell, Carol drinks and worse, I think. You don't have to go on binges.

ALAN. I don't, no . . .

DOUGLAS. Ronnie smokes sometimes. About one a month.

RONNIE. Not that much even.

ALAN *(to Ronnie and Douglas, with a marked midwestern accent)*. I've got this incredible headache; it's just the altitude. How high are we?

DOUGLAS. I don't know.

ALAN. Coming through the mountains . . .

RONNIE. You want some coffee?

DOUGLAS. Ronnie makes the best damn coffee in—

(They move into the breakfast area, Alan sitting, Douglas leaning against the stove.)

ALAN. Good. *(Laughs, overwhelmed, nervous)* Good, yes . . . *(to the audience, happy —without accent)* What do I say? Because I didn't *plan*. Because I didn't have a setting— it wasn't my house I was coming into. It *would be* mine, but I couldn't sit at the breakfast nook and pull up the ash tray and serve coffee out of the good cups like it was every day and lean against the stove and talk about work . . .

RONNIE. You look as I expected.

ALAN *(when speaking with them, with the accent)*. You look—do too—look like what I expected.

DOUGLAS. I've got to get along.

ALAN. How come?

RONNIE. Doug's on the night shift; so he has days off.

DOUGLAS. I still have to get in half a day.

ALAN. Good.

DOUGLAS. I told them if the bus was on time, I'd make it in; if you'd have been late, I'd have taken off.

ALAN. *(He has stood. Very joyously, throwing out his arms. Wildly)* Where are they all!? Where is it? *(looking around, as though at the surrounding landscape)* A breakfast nook and out the kitchen window all the back yards are private, with redwood fences around them. Higher than your head. And mountains all around. Out the living-room window— Mount Capitan . . .

DOUGLAS. The big one, with the bald head, that's Mount Capitan.

RONNIE *(suddenly, quietly but urgently)*. Alan, Mount McGinty is on fire, the whole sky—wake up, it's incredible—

DOUGLAS *(overlapping)*. With the brush, Mount McGinty. And the blue one in the distance—

ALAN.—Mount Otay—

DOUGLAS.—behind that, Jerry would—

ALAN *(quickly to the audience)*. My other brother.

DOUGLAS.—know that one; he knows them all. *(Turning to look out the kitchen "window")* El Cajon Mountain, Cowles Mountain, and Mount Helix.

ALAN. Out the kitchen window, with a spotlighted cross on top and expensive homes —but very expensive homes—built along the road that helixes up to the cross.

RONNIE. They turn the lights off at midnight.

ALAN. And the whole mountain disappears.

DOUGLAS. You can see it for miles.

RONNIE. We're surrounded.

DOUGLAS. Behind Mount Helix is La Mesa, the city of La Mesa, over on the other side; we can drive over there. Lemon Grove —they're all about the same. La Mesa—Grossmont may be a little more exclusive, a little more expensive.

ALAN. On the way here from downtown—

RONNIE. How do you like the traffic? Is that some drive?

ALAN. Yeah, that's something else, isn't it? I've never seen traffic like you've got here. I don't know if I'll want to drive or not.

DOUGLAS. Sure you will; you get used to it.

ALAN. But on the way out we must have passed a hundred houses that were going up. Half-constructed.

DOUGLAS. Across from the college they're building three hundred houses. Ranch types. A whole suburb. One guy. *(Almost to the audience)* A whole city: shopping centers, two theatres—one regular and a drive-in—three hundred houses. Big ranch-type houses.

RONNIE. There's supposed to be four hundred new residents in California every day.

ALAN. Every day.

DOUGLAS. It's a big state, Al; it really is. Four hundred.

RONNIE. Every day.

DOUGLAS. Don't let anybody tell you the gold rush is over out here, boy.

ALAN. I guess not.

DOUGLAS. Guys are making a killing out here.

ALAN. And the climate, I suppose—

DOUGLAS *(a brief concession)*. March is a mess. Late March into April—it rains, but that's about it for the whole year. And it's a little cooler, but outside of that—

ALAN. I don't suppose you get any—

RONNIE *(both are shaking their heads, seriously, not ironically)*. No, no snow—

DOUGLAS. Very little; up in the mountains—

RONNIE.—It seldom even freezes. Up in the mountains. The Lagunas and higher. We drive up or else the boys would never have seen snow. Of course you don't see it falling, which is half the treat. It falls during the night. It'll snow a foot and then thaw within two days.

ALAN. A foot? Overnight?

RONNIE. A lot more, sometimes.

ALAN. That's going-to-hell snowin'.

DOUGLAS. Alan, you'll love it. It's heaven. I mean it's really heaven. You'll love it here.

RONNIE. We hope you do.

DOUGLAS. You will! Hell! By God, anybody who wouldn't, sumpin's wrong with 'em er sumpin, huh?

ALAN. I think there'd have to be. I do already. We were coming through New Mexico and I didn't believe it . . . the air-conditioning wasn't working. Of course, who needs it in Nebraska? But by the time we get to El Centro, it's burning hot. Your first stop in California: El Centro. What do you do your first stop in California? You buy a glass of orange juice. Never. Whatever you do, never buy orange juice at the Greyhound bus station in El Centro, California. Yeahhh! God-awful. The worst. The worst single paper cup of orange juice I've ever had in my life. *(To the audience by now, as well as to Ronnie and Douglas)* It's not native to El Centro. Oranges can't grow there. Gila monsters you could buy. Navajo blankets, moccasins, turquoise earrings, Apache tears, you can buy. That's it. Of course, even getting to El Centro is a nightmare. You know California, you've seen the pictures: palm trees, sunsets, swimming pools, oceans, and mountain springs. The first five hours—five and a half—you are treated to the world's most barren desolation: the Mojave Desert. Telephone poles are stuck in a big hunk of asphalt to hold them upright. The asphalt is boiling. You think: this is California! Oh, wow, who does the public relations on this place! *(Back to them, exaggerating)* It's a hundred and five degrees! It's March! I want you to know. March—and it's a hundred and five. In Nebraska it's forty-seven and it's a warm day when I left.

RONNIE. I know, I remember.

DOUGLAS. She worked there.

ALAN *(to the audience, rather a different mood, straight, low; no accent)*. What I've heard about Ronnie is, Dad met her and dated her—he was still married—sometime during that time he was still married to Mother.

DOUGLAS. In Lincoln. Private secretary to the attorney of the state. State attorney, same difference, huh?

ALAN *(continuing)*. And maybe they came out here together, maybe not. He said he'd send for us—Mother and me. He ran off, out to here. O.K. She never blamed him.

RONNIE. A wonderful man, and an interesting job.

ALAN. You take shorthand and all that, then?

RONNIE. Oh, yes. I want to forget it. It's like riding a bicycle; you can't. They let the secretaries run the country, I think. From my experience.

ALAN. Probably they do.

DOUGLAS. I've got to get along.

ALAN. How come?

RONNIE. Doug's on the night shift; so he has days off.

DOUGLAS. So I can get in half a day yet.

ALAN. Good.

DOUGLAS. You darn-betcha.

ALAN. Yeah. *(Laughs)*

DOUGLAS *(embarrassingly straight and serious).* I can't tell you how much I've wanted you here.

RONNIE *(soberly).* He has, Alan.

DOUGLAS. I tried. I wrote once or twice, but your mother thought I was trying to kidnap you or some damn thing. She wouldn't let you come.

RONNIE. He cried. It's the only time I've ever seen—

ALAN *(to the audience—cutting it off).* He said he had to go, he worked on the night shift, he could get in half a day yet. That it was great having me here. Finally. He'd dreamed about it.

RONNIE *(they have moved from the kitchen; showing him around).* That's going to be your room.

ALAN. Great.

DOUGLAS *(returning to previous; soberly).* So bad. I can't tell you.

ALAN *(soberly).* I'm glad to be here. I am.

RONNIE. The patio, it will go here; you've seen the garden. The living room, the TV— it's in the cabinet; I can't stand a naked eye staring at me. We almost never watch it. Doug watches the fights and the ball games in the afternoons.

ALAN. That's right, I can watch the games.

DOUGLAS *(showing him around).* That's the darkroom.

ALAN. Wow. I didn't know that.

DOUGLAS. The mounted picture there, the second one, I won an award on last year. It's taken actually with a red filter looking straight into the sun like that—it's called sunspot—that's the sun here and the reflection here, the way the sun hits the water. It's a bitch of a shot to make because of the glare. The reflection. You have to use a filter, have to know what you're doing. *(Slapping the ta-*

ble) That's a professional enlarger; that's as good as they make them.

RONNIE. Doug went through a woodworking phase about five years ago, so we have a table saw and a lathe and all of that. He'll build the patio this summer.

DOUGLAS. Not by myself I won't. Not now that I have help.

ALAN. Right. I'd love to.

RONNIE. Dad's workroom you've seen.

ALAN. Do you develop your own film?

DOUGLAS. Develop, print, enlarge to any size, all in the same room—the whole works. It's not difficult—it's goddamned exacting; everything's timed pretty close. You have to know what the hell you're doing.

RONNIE *(pointing out).* Mount Helix with the cross, and Mount Otay; isn't that godawful? Over there—nearly in Mexico.

ALAN. All around. It's beautiful.

DOUGLAS. You'll love it.

ALAN *(enthralled).* I do. I do. I do.

DOUGLAS *(suddenly serious, man-to-man).* Carol . . . now, I want you to know, don't be embarrassed. We have these two girls living here.

(The girls can be seen dimly in the distance.)

ALAN. You wrote me; I know.

DOUGLAS. Well, Alan, they're wards of the state. They've had terrible lives; you don't know—

ALAN. Maybe I—

DOUGLAS.—Just terrible; you don't know. Penny's father left her, her mother died, she's lived in one bad foster home after another. They're happy here. The woman said we were one of the best homes in San Diego County. They live here like it's their home.

RONNIE. They really do.

DOUGLAS. They've been here—Penny a year, Carol a year now and a half. It's their home and we all get along like a family.

RONNIE. You'll have Carol's room and she can sleep with—

DOUGLAS. And Carol . . . her mother and father both died when she was too young to remember it—

RONNIE. She does, though.

DOUGLAS. She says she doesn't. Penny's good. She gets along fine. Carol. I want to talk to you man-to-man. Alan, Carol is a whore. She's promiscuous. She came here bragging she'd slept with six sailors in one night once.

RONNIE. Seven, but one more or less.

(Alan laughs.)

DOUGLAS. She has a boyfriend now; she's trying to straighten out. Hell, she was on pills, she was on God knows what. Things I hadn't even heard of.

RONNIE. But she dates this guy regularly now; he's a darn nice guy. You'll meet him.

DOUGLAS. You have to treat her like— think of her like a sister. We can't have you—

ALAN. O.K., I won't.

DOUGLAS. It's important.

ALAN. How can you keep them? They must cost . . .

DOUGLAS. Well, the state sends us sixty dollars a month toward their board—

RONNIE It's not as much as they eat, even. But we make a home for them.

ALAN *(joyous)*. Where are they? Penny! Carol! Jerry! Jack! Jerry's twelve and is a little me. A little blond me, only fatter. A little. Jack's a brush ape. A—a—renegade. Jerry and I look a little alike; Jack takes after Ronnie, except for his eyes. Penny's a dope. She's great. But she's a dope. Carol's gorgeous!

RONNIE. Not really; she's attractive. Striking. She could be a model. She has that kind of figure. Beautiful skin.

DOUGLAS. Not really, though. She knows how to fix herself up is all. She's a come-on. She's not got a personality. She's neurotic. She's had a terrible life, Alan; you don't know. *(Suddenly messing his hair)* Fella! Devil! *(To the audience, hugging Alan's head against him. Proudly)* I mean he was my kid. He looked like me. More than Jerry ever thought about. When I was his age. I was skinny like that. I had to work out. *(To Alan)* I could never gain weight. But God . . . !

RONNIE. When we were married—

DOUGLAS. I put on weight the first week. It's the air. You will, too. And Ronnie's a good cook.

ALAN. Good.

RONNIE. Which reminds me, are you hungry?

DOUGLAS *(seriously)*. They've gone out. We wanted them to, so we could meet you. Get to know each other a little first. The boys are staying with Mildred. I imagine they'll be asleep when she brings them home tonight. We told them they'd see you in the morning. One more day won't matter—you'll be here awhile. Penny'll be in. She went to a movie with Rose, I imagine.

RONNIE. Rose you've got to meet. She's unbelievable. Are you sure you can't eat?

ALAN. Really. *(To the audience)* I've got this incredible headache; a migraine, only I don't know it, and I've not had one since. Three days it lasted—all through that first day and night. It can't go on like this, of course; there'll be a scene soon. Dad had to go to work; he could get in half a day—night —yet. He always called it day . . . the working day.

DOUGLAS. I want you to go down there. You can get a job if you're going to be going to school. It costs, you know.

ALAN. I wanted to work somewhere, to pay my way—

DOUGLAS. I wish to God we could—

RONNIE.—afford to pay your way.

DOUGLAS. Alan, we can't; we just can't. I want to, but we can't that much. We'll help, sure, all we can—

ALAN. No, I want to. I said I would.

DOUGLAS. Hell, it's healthy. Everybody out at State is working part time, anyway. Earn their keep. We'll have to get you a car, won't we? You drive?

ALAN. Yeah, fairly well.

DOUGLAS. Get you a little Austin or one of those. What'd you think?

ALAN *(to the audience and them)*. What can I say? I think it's great.

DOUGLAS. We'll go over and look; you gotta have it to get you to school, doncha? I'm not going to squire you in; you don't want to have to take a bus every morning. Huh?

ALAN *(to the audience)*. There'll be a scene. Those who are confused will say, thank God, something to watch; maybe everyone will stop flying around.

(Douglas stands a moment watching, then turns with a proud smile and exits.)

RONNIE. I guess you'll want to get some sleep soon.

ALAN. Before too long. I couldn't sleep on the bus. I almost broke my neck.

RONNIE. You want to go right now?

ALAN. No, no.

RONNIE. Whenever you're ready.

ALAN. Could I have another coffee?

RONNIE *(she pours another coffee)*. He's talked about you so much. I didn't know about you at all when we were married. He told me the first night; it was quite a shock. I didn't even know he had been married. He cried. He said he wanted to bring you out here, and I wanted you too. But your mother —and she was right, don't you think?

ALAN. Yes. *(To the audience)* What could—

RONNIE. It's better this way. You're not torn apart, half in one place and half in another. He missed you so much. That's why he wanted to have another kid right away. You're not shocked or embarrassed or anything, me speaking with you frankly?

ALAN. No, God, no; it's a relief.

RONNIE. Good. I've so looked forward to knowing you. Doug's mother gives us pretty regular reports about you.

ALAN. She does?

RONNIE. Oh, sure. That's why we asked you out. She said you were out of high school; she thought it was about time you saw some of the country—and that you and Doug got reacquainted.

ALAN. She knew I wanted to go on to school.

RONNIE. What are you going to study?

ALAN. You know, I don't have any idea. Liberal arts—I don't know.

RONNIE. There's time. We'll take you up to San Diego State so you can get registered; it's a beautiful campus. Don't decide for awhile. . . . Jack has a birthday party coming up—his eighth. Two dozen local hellions. You'll want to escape from that, I imagine. Maybe you can take Jerry to a movie or something. He considers himself much too adult for that crowd.

ALAN. Of course—he's eleven.

RONNIE. No, please. Twelve. And a half: he stretches it a little; he was born Christmas Day. You knew that.

ALAN. Yes. But that's all. *(To the audience; a marked contrast as he drops the accent)* I'd seen them just once, five years ago; Jack was three, Jerry, seven. Dad and the kids came to town, and it was arranged that if a friend of Mother's went along, we'd all go to the zoo in Omaha; and we had a picnic which I remember as the most horrible experience of my younger life. Everyone worried about how I was going to react, and me not knowing what was happening. Just I didn't want any of it and I couldn't get it through my head how any of these people could be related to me. And I was freezing to death, which is all I really remember: it was November and all the animals had their winter coats and were ugly, anyway.

RONNIE *(standing, whispering—stage whisper)*. You want to see them? *(They walk to between the boys' beds.)*

ALAN *(same whisper.)* Don't wake—

RONNIE. No, you'll meet them in the morning. Jerry. He has asthma and snores like a tank. Of course, Jack could sleep through anything.

ALAN *(whisper)*. He's cute.

RONNIE *(whisper)*. Well, of course he's cute. He looks like me. He's the hairy one. He takes that from my brother; look at those arms. He has hair like that all over him.

ALAN *(whisper—to the audience)*. Blond, like a white—a little white orangutan or something.

(Penny comes in the front entrance, walks to the refrigerator door, opens it, and stands in front of it. Penny is nearly eighteen; she is slow and dull-moving and almost heartbreakingly unattractive.)

RONNIE *(hearing the noise)*. That's Penny.

ALAN *(beginning in whisper and changing into regular voice as they move out of the boys' area)*. Penny, on whom the plot will pivot, such as it is. On Penny and a photograph taken my first day in California and my first day at the ocean. First ocean, the Pacific. Real salt; I almost hadn't believed it. I had to go taste it to be sure. Jerry on one side, me in the middle, Jack on the other. A picture of the three grandchildren to send to my grandmother.

RONNIE. Doug's mother wrote back and said she couldn't believe it. That wasn't Alan between those two kids; that was Doug when he was seventeen.

ALAN. Really?

RONNIE. Oh, now he's very distinguished, very proud of the mustache and the graying temples. The whole image; the white jacket.

ALAN *(to the audience)*. He had borrowed it from a friend, but he liked it; it suited him. And it did. So he bought it from the guy.

PENNY. *(They come to her. Still with the refrigerator door open)* Pleased to meet you. I've heard a lot about you.

ALAN *(to the audience)*. And I feel like I should bow. *(To Penny)* They didn't know a thing. It was all conjecture.

RONNIE. Penny's a science major and very serious about it.

PENNY. Well, I'm not that serious about—

ALAN. What do you want to do with—

PENNY. Oh, well, I'll probably teach. *(Dead pause)* I like kids. I guess.

ALAN. I couldn't be a teacher if they paid me, and I understand they don't.

PENNY. California's not bad. They pay well here.

ALAN. I guess I've heard that.

RONNIE. Do you want something to eat?

PENNY *(closing the refrigerator door)*. No. I've got to go to bed.

RONNIE. Did you see Rose?

PENNY. Uhm. She's given up politics; she's learning to play the guitar. *(Alan laughs.)*

RONNIE. Penny dates the best-looking boy at the college.

PENNY *(pause)*. He really is. *(Shrug)*

RONNIE. He's a tennis pro.

PENNY. Not pro.

RONNIE. Well, not pro, but he will be.

PENNY. He was in the Olympics.

ALAN. They play tennis in the Olympics?

PENNY. Oh, sure. Or maybe it was skiing, because he skis. His dad's got a lodge in Colorado. Carol and I are—Carol and me—damn—Carol and I!—are both going with millionaires. Not really, but they have a lot of money. Phil drives a Pontiac convertible. It's so beautiful, I feel stupid driving around in it —especially the way he drives.

RONNIE. Why, how does he drive?

PENNY. I don't know. Conspicuously. I mean the top's never up unless it's raining. Even in the middle of winter. I've had a cold since I've known him. Do you mind if I go on to bed?

ALAN. No, if you're sleepy.

PENNY. 'Cause I am.

ALAN. I can see you tomorrow.

PENNY. Good night, Alan. Ronnie, is Carol in yet?

RONNIE. No. God knows, she's out with Sonny.

PENNY. Good night. *(Exits to bedroom)*

ALAN. And that's all of Penny that night. That first night. That was it. But more, there's more.

RONNIE. I want to tell you about Carol. It's terrible.

ALAN *(to the audience)*. Now this is funny . . . I sat there sober-faced and believed every word.

RONNIE *(to the audience)*. Well, I had to tell him something, right? I mean the girl is a whore. Let's face it: she's a nice kid but she's sick. With Sonny, Sonny is religious— that much is true.

ALAN. *(He leans against the counter and watches, smiling, listening to a favorite family joke.)* Go on, go on . . .

RONNIE *(to the audience)*. Well, I didn't know if he'd believe it or not; what do I know? He's seventeen; my boys are twelve and eight. But if I didn't say something that first night, then Carol would have him se-

duced by the next afternoon. So I told him she had this incurable "disease," that wasn't painful, but it was an impossible disgrace. I said they were trying to cure it, but it was only fifty-fifty.

ALAN. Trichinosis.

RONNIE. Well, I couldn't think of a medical-sounding name that I thought I could remember. When did you know?

ALAN. Not for years. You can lie to me; I'll believe anything.

RONNIE. Of course, I didn't know if he'd buy it or not.

ALAN. I said trichinosis was something you got from eating pork.

RONNIE *(seriously, to him)*. Well, *one* kind.

ALAN. She said this was a different kind; it was similar, but much worse.

RONNIE *(seriously, to him)*. And very rare. *(To the audience)* I thought with all those sailors he might believe she could have gotten anything. And it doesn't show up on the boy. But he passes—

ALAN *(to her)*. He's a carrier.

RONNIE. Right. And he passes it on to the next girl, who might be someone he likes very much, Alan. And respects. And—

ALAN. And I bought that.

RONNIE *(to the audience)*. And I said she wasn't sleeping with Sonny, which was true as far as any of us knew.

CAROL *(from the shadows)*. It was true.

RONNIE *(reassuringly, to her, quickly)*. No, we knew. Anyway, I described it dreadfully. All the symptoms.

ALAN *(to the audience)*. And all the time I have this pounding headache I'm practically fainting from.

RONNIE. Well, who would know? You didn't show it.

ALAN *(to the audience and her)*. I have this smile plastered on my kisser, and this look of concern. I didn't care if this girl had last-stage syphilis. I was dying there in the middle of the kitchen my first night.

RONNIE. Anyway, I made poor Carol sound like a very unattractive sleeping arrangement.

CAROL. And of course I was going balmy because I thought, why isn't anything working with this guy? Why isn't he turning on to me? How should I know he thinks I'm Typhoid Mary? I'm coming on like the Army and Navy Band with about sixty colors flying, and this cat's outrunning ostriches in the other direction. I changed toothpaste. I did, I changed my toothpaste. Twice.

RONNIE *(suddenly very sober)*. Doug used to talk about you.

ALAN. I was only five.

RONNIE. I know, but he loves children. Sometimes I think Doug should have had a girl. He'd have been a better father to her. You should see him with the neighbor girls. He really loves them. *(Long pause)*

ALAN *(to the audience)*. I didn't tell her that I had a sister. I thought about it, but I didn't say anything. That's what I was thinking about—a lot that first night.

RONNIE. No, you didn't.

ALAN *(to the audience)*. I'd had a sister who was born dead; it would have been Dad's only daughter. He was out every night until God knows what hour. He would come in with lipstick all over his shirt—and mother was pregnant—and he'd swear it was someone's sister, and mother would check his story and the guy wouldn't even have a sister—like he didn't even bother to make the story convincing, and then he'd rage at her for not believing him and spying behind his back. That's what he meant by "at him." Snooping at his heels all the time. So mother got her labor pains one night when he was out and she was walking the floor. This was eight months along only. And she called a friend of Dad's to ask if he knew where Dad was and —this guy's name was Carl. So Carl and his wife drove mother to the hospital, and the baby was born dead. Stillborn. Mom said she didn't much care at the time. It wasn't even buried—they don't—they consider it never lived. *(Pause)* I don't know. I know Carl beat the shit out of Dad, and right after that Dad left. So if Ronnie thought he was guilty about leaving *me*—or wanted another *son*—probably not.

RONNIE. He wasn't going with me.

ALAN. Even if he was, you didn't know.

RONNIE. It was a full year after that that we—

ALAN *(removed, uninterested)*. He'd been in California a year. He'd met Ronnie, but he came back afterwards and dated her; that's when they went together a year, after he'd already left. She said. I didn't ask Dad. It doesn't matter. Anyway, that's what I was thinking—or, rather, trying not to think— that night. And trying not to blame him. *(Pause)* She would have been four years younger than me.

RONNIE. Thirteen.

ALAN. Well. What time is it? It must be after midnight.

RONNIE. Are you kidding? It's one thirty or after. We talked for three hours straight.

ALAN. Briefing me on the neighborhood. Ronnie was the neighborhood confessor. Since she didn't give a wild flying damn what anyone did and didn't gossip, she got all the juiciest stories.

RONNIE. It's always been like that.

ALAN. And I liked you very much. Which is no mean trick for a stepmother.

RONNIE. And you told me about Doug being in jail.

ALAN. How did I—

RONNIE. We were just talking about anything, and you asked—

ALAN *(with an accent)*. Is Dad still interested in drawing and painting? Grandma's attic is full of stuff he did.

RONNIE. The paintings of boats and all the airplanes? I think he's always been crazy about airplanes. No, he doesn't do that any more.

ALAN. I used to go up and look at them every time I went there.

RONNIE. Well . . . he builds things . . . and you saw all the photographic equipment. I think he must have stopped painting when he was a teen-ager.

ALAN. Yes, I think Mother said he did them when he was in jail.

RONNIE *(beat)*. When he was where?

ALAN. Didn't you know that? I wouldn't want to—

RONNIE. No, it's O.K. What?

ALAN. Well, he was in on a—not a robbery but a burglary of a house with some guys when he was sixteen, and went not actually to a jail but to a reform school for a year. And that's when he did those—It was a long time ago; I guess it isn't anything necessarily that he should have told you.

RONNIE. Or that you should have been told, for that matter.

ALAN. I'm sorry; I wouldn't have—

RONNIE. No, it doesn't matter. I asked you. *(To the audience)* And he was so damned honest—I could have clubbed him.

ALAN *(to the audience)*. I was. I was.

RONNIE. You want to go to bed, don't you?

ALAN. I think so.

RONNIE. It's after two.

ALAN. I'm falling on my face.

RONNIE. Go on to bed; it's all right.

ALAN. Are you going to wait up for Dad?

RONNIE. No, no, he doesn't expect you to wait up. You won't need more covers than that.

ALAN. No, not here. *(He laughs, sits on the bed, and tucks under.)*

RONNIE. Good night, Alan.

ALAN. I'll see you tomorrow.

RONNIE. I won't wake you; Doug gets up early; he never sleeps more than four or five hours.

ALAN. Good lord.

RONNIE. I know; don't worry, we'll let you sleep. Tomorrow anyway. Everyone keeps their own hours.

(Carol approaches the front door.)

ALAN. Right.

RONNIE *(turning to the front, leaving him).* Speaking of which.

CAROL *(entering; she will soon be eighteen; tall, very thin; smashingly attractive, and quite a wreck).* I know, it's late; I wasn't watching. Where's Alan? Did he come?

RONNIE. Yes, he came.

CAROL. Doug here?

RONNIE. He went on to work.

CAROL. Went to *work?* Well, of course, he went to work, Carol. What'd you think, he stayed here with his son? How's Alan?

RONNIE. Very nice. But that isn't the subject.

CAROL. Oh, Christ, Ronnie, don't start!

RONNIE. It's two o'clock.

CAROL *(looks at her watch, puts it to her ear, shakes her arm during speech).* It isn't any—well, my watch's stopped. Damn.

RONNIE. You know I don't care, but they ask.

CAROL. We've been sitting out in front for over an hour. Didn't you hear us drive up? I thought I saw you at the window.

RONNIE. Carol, I don't care.

CAROL. Well, neither do I. He was so sweet.

RONNIE. I like Sonny.

CAROL. We talked. *(Partly to the audience)* Sonny's dad has a ranch in Texas—over twenty thousand acres, which he says is small. That's probably larger than Rhode Island. And they raise Herefords and houses and oil, and have about half the money in the country and investments everywhere. His mom and dad are paralyzed over what's going on in Cuba; apparently they own it.

RONNIE. Anyway, be that as it may, I've a vivid imagination, but it fails me when I try to conjure up what you do until—

CAROL *(cutting in violently).* Oh, Ronnie, would you stop it! Just stop it already! No, he doesn't lay me; no, never, not once. Look at my hands, for God's sake! You think I can stand it? *(Exposing her hands, which are bloody on the palms)*

RONNIE. Good God, what's wrong with—

CAROL. Well, it isn't stigmata; you can count on that! Sonny is Catholic with a vengeance, and I've never thought I could be in love with anyone. There it is! *(Rather to the audience)* Carol's problem; never thought she could cut it, and I am—very much in love with a rich Texan Catholic, and he has land, lots of land, and principles that I never even knew were principles. And I used to take "downs"; but pills are wrong, of course, so I promised him I wouldn't take them any more. No, we no longer live in a yellow submarine; we live on a red perch. And he makes out so damn beautifully, and I can't ask *him* and I can't be "bad"—his word, not mine—and I can't calm down with the pills and I claw my *hands,* the palms of my hands, apart. *(Totally breaking off—disgusted with herself)* Well, shit, Carol, there's no sense in causing a war about it. I cut them down yesterday; I'll cut them off tonight. But that won't help, because I'll bite my lip or something else if I can't get a hold of something to take to calm my damned frazzled—

RONNIE. Carol, I'm very lenient and I know you can wrap me around your little finger; I know you've had to do that in order to get anything—

CAROL. Don't make excuses for me, for God's—

RONNIE. Carol, I want to say something. I know you want to stay here for the next eight or whatever months, until you're eighteen, and I want you here; but if I see one pill, one of your tranquilizers, I'll report it. It's something I can't tolerate. I have two young sons here and I can't risk them taking something by mistake—

CAROL *(overlapping).* You don't have to tell me that. Do you think Sonny would stand for it? He's a lot better police dog than—a LOT better police dog than you, believe me—

RONNIE. There've been two different cases in the last year of kids being poisoned by taking their mother's barbiturates or someone's who had left them around the house. If I know you're taking them, I'll feel obliged to tell Sonny as well as the welfare—

CAROL *(screaming).* You don't have to tell anybody any goddamned thing! Because I PROMISED him; you know what that

MEANS? *(Regains her control; holding her hands)* That I didn't need them.

RONNIE. Do your hands hurt?

CAROL. Yes, they hurt like fire.

RONNIE. Let me put something—

CAROL. Oh, I'll do it; you're supposed to be bawling me out. You *can't*, Ronnie. I can get out of anything; I'm a master.

RONNIE. You're also a mess.

CAROL. You're telling me.

RONNIE. Let me put something on you.

CAROL *(hotly)*. No, dammit; you're not going to stain me up with iodine, thanks.

RONNIE. I'll put some salve on them, not iodine.

CAROL. They're not that bad, really. I'll do it. Are you waiting up for Doug?

RONNIE. No. He'll be in.

CAROL. Alan's in my room?

RONNIE. For tonight. We'll arrange something.

CAROL. Just let me flop somewhere.

RONNIE. Put something on your hands, that salve.

CAROL. O.K. Good night.

RONNIE. Carol. Don't. *(Pause)* Don't stay out this late. They want you in by twelve.

CAROL. I won't Ronnie. You're great. I'm sorry; I won't. *(Kisses her on the cheek)*

RONNIE *(to the audience)*. She will, and I can't blame her, of course. He's the only thing she's got—Sonny. She's on probation with the state and us and Sonny, too.

CAROL. So, I'm used to it. Don't make me out a martyr. I hate it. Besides, I can do it better. I haven't even got started on my mom and dad and poor upbringing and what a rotten life I've had. Besides, I'm a nymphomaniac—coupled with a for-all-practical-purposes eunuch in the shape of a Greek god.

RONNIE. Which isn't necessary with you, but it doesn't hurt anything.

CAROL. It hurts. It hurts. Everything. All over. Good night.

(She goes off to the girls' bedroom. Ronnie stands a moment, then goes off to her bedroom. The stage is empty for a few seconds, then Douglas enters, goes to the kitchen, takes a hunk of cheese, looks into the girls' bedroom, then Alan's, and exits into his own bedroom as the lights fade to a deep midnight blue. All is quiet for a beat, then a very slow dawn. At a nice bright sunshine the lights hold. Jerry stirs in his bed and sits up suddenly. Jumps up and sneaks down to Alan's room. Creeps in and shakes him gently.)

JERRY. Alan? *(Sits on the side of the bed, waits)* Alan? Are you awake?

ALAN *(stirring)*. Huh?

(The scene is whispered.)

JERRY. Good morning.

ALAN. Good morning. Is it morning?

JERRY. Almost.

ALAN. Do you always get up this early?

JERRY. I woke up.

ALAN. It isn't daylight yet, is it?

JERRY. Oh, yeah. *(Starts to window to pull the shades up)* It's Sunday, it's real bright out—

ALAN. NO! I believe you. That's O.K. *(Smiling, focusing on him now)* Are you Jerry or Jack?

JERRY. Don't you know?

ALAN. Yes. You're Jerry.

JERRY. Jack's asleep.

ALAN. And let's see; you would be twelve and a half, right?

JERRY. Right. I'll be thirteen—

ALAN. Christmas Day.

JERRY. Right. What's the matter with your head?

ALAN. I don't know; only it's splitting wide open. It has been all night—ever since we crossed New Mexico. I think it has something to do with the altitude. Are we at sea level?

JERRY. No, one thousand three hundred eighty feet. That's Mount Helix.

ALAN. How do you know? Are you studying geography?

JERRY. No, there's a sign on the highway. Do you want some aspirin?

ALAN. Where's the highway?

JERRY. About two blocks from here.

ALAN. Oh. Do you have any, do you think?

JERRY. What?

ALAN. Aspirin.

JERRY. Oh, I thought you meant highways, did I have any highways—

ALAN. No, aspirin—

JERRY. I'll get you one.

ALAN. Could you? Bring me three if you have plenty.

JERRY *(has run out; returns)*. You shouldn't take more than one.

ALAN. Huh? Oh, it's O.K., honey; I always take three. Two doesn't do any good and four makes me sick.

JERRY. O.K.

(As water runs)

ALAN *(calling)*. What time is it, Jerry?

JERRY. It's seven o'clock already.

ALAN *(flops down in bed).* Oh, God. Jerry, I didn't get to bed till three or something.

JERRY *(reentering).* Do adults need eight hours sleep?

ALAN *(between aspirins).* Eight or ten.

JERRY. Dad says he can't sleep but four hours. He says you shouldn't.

ALAN. Then why do I feel like this?

JERRY. Did you ride the Greyhound?

ALAN. Yeah.

JERRY. You know, I like you! *(hugs him enthusiastically)* I didn't know if I would or not, but you're nice. How come you didn't come to live with us a long time ago?

ALAN. You don't remember visiting me and the zoo? In Omaha?

JERRY. No. Mom's told me, though. It seems weird having a new brother and already he's as big as Dad. You should have been living with us when we had the farm.

ALAN. Did you have a farm?

JERRY. Your head still hurt?

ALAN. Yeah.

JERRY *(after a pause).* Jack and me called it a farm, but we just had a big open lot with a bunch of trees.

ALAN. An orchard?

JERRY. Kinda—we had some orange trees and a plum tree and a fig tree—

ALAN. You had orange trees?

JERRY. Oh, sure.

ALAN. I've never seen them growing before.

JERRY. We used to have oranges all the time. Me and Jack used to make orangeade and sell it, only nobody ever bought it, because they had more oranges than we did. Dad bought it and we drank it.

ALAN *(after a pause).* Oh, God. I like you, too. *(Squeezes him; to the audience)* So I didn't sleep, I guess. Not much, that first night. And the last thing I wanted to do, or thought of doing—

DOUGLAS *(entering).* We'll just drive in, and make your application—it'll take about ten minutes' time—and we can drive over and take a peek at the ocean you haven't seen.

ALAN *(to the audience and them, following Douglas into the kitchen for coffee).* The personnel manager at Ryan Aeronautical hated me on sight, with no love lost.

DOUGLAS. Aw, that son of a bitch, all that brass—ball-breaking office flunkies. That's all they are, Alan; ignore him, don't give him the time of day.

ALAN. Do we have to go today? I can hardly see.

DOUGLAS. He's going on a month's vacation tomorrow. They can process you while he's gone. You won't start working for a month.

CAROL. Buy now, pay later.

ALAN. Maybe I should do something else: grocery clerk or something.

DOUGLAS. Well, what do you want, boy? It's up to you. Do you want to make enough to go to school or do you want to go to the movies? We'll all go; we'll go on to the beach later.

ALAN. No, it didn't take long. He said we have two divisions of engineering personnel: temporary and full-time. I said I would much prefer the former, and he said there was a greater possibility of being hired in the *latter,* and that was that. So, providing I'm not lying about never having joined the Communist party or something, I'll be set. I'll start in a month or so.

DOUGLAS. As soon as he's back.

ALAN. At the Aeronautical Engineering Training Center riveting school.

PENNY. How can you manage full-time work and full-time school?

DOUGLAS. So he'll go part time to school until he can get on temporary at the plant.

ALAN. No, no.

DOUGLAS. Well, I say if you can cut both full time, why not? Now, if you're serious about working down there, they have a scholarship program. You can go into electrodynamics or something like that, and they'll pay the bill, all the way—

ALAN. It's my second term; I don't know what I want yet.

DOUGLAS. Well, don't be negative; give it a fair shake. Just objectively, what's happening in the world—they're putting rockets into space; they got hydrogen bombs and cobalt bombs, atomic submarines; they bounce signals off Mars and Venus and every other goddamned thing.

ALAN. I know.

DOUGLAS. Physicists are looking at the sunspots and predicting the weather. Every field. All of them, what you need—

ALAN. I don't know anything—

DOUGLAS. —is physics, by God.

CAROL. That sounds like a good book.

(Alan laughs.)

DOUGLAS. Well, you can joke around—I just want you to think about it. All I'm saying is, if I was a kid now, it wouldn't take me three minutes—three seconds—to make up my mind. Engineering, electrodynamics; you just have to open your eyes.

ALAN. And of course the head is worse— But the ocean! I've lived eight hundred miles from it all my life!

RONNIE *(coming into the kitchen with Jack)*. I wish you would, but only if you want to.

ALAN. No, I like you very— *(To the audience)* I'm embarrassed and I've no idea how to tell her. *(To Ronnie)* I'll call you Ronnie, like Dad does; I couldn't! I like you very much! You know! *(Grabbing Jack and wooling his hair)* And you! Brush ape! Nut! Huh! This is the other one. Jack. Can you see his arms? He's covered all over with white hair. He's our little white orangutan. He's had straight A's since the day he was born.

JACK. Yes.

ALAN. And he's a smart ass—I mean aleck.

JACK. Yes.

ALAN. Yes.

JACK. What's an aleck?

ALAN. I don't know, but you're one. *(To the audience)* Don't you wish you had a smart answer for all those simpleminded great questions he asks? Like, an aleck is a something or other without its watchicallit, and you're going to be one if you keep asking —Oh, Jack! Jack Jack. He's so bright the teachers think it's unhealthy. Go go go go. *(Jack and Jerry go, running off)* I won't! I promise I won't! *(To Ronnie)* And you can't either—

RONNIE. O.K., O.K., I won't—

ALAN. I won't tell you a lot of juvenile anecdotes, but I want—I want to bronze the little bastards and sit them up on the mantelpiece. One! Just one I'll tell while they're gone, one quick one. I want to get badly, badly drunk and distribute a walletful of slobbered-on and bent-up photographs all along the bar and say, notice his hair, notice that one's toes, look at those teeth. Just one little anecdote that Ronnie told me. When Jerry was five, they all went up in an airplane—big thrill for Jerry, who used to watch airplanes take off by the hour when they lived by the airport. So they're all in the plane. Jerry's on Ronnie's lap, and after they've been off the ground for a few minutes, he squirms around and whispers excitedly in Ronnie's ear: "When do we start getting small?"

DOUGLAS *(in the darkroom; red light on; projector light on)*. That's *on* now. Two three four five. *(Projector off)*

ALAN *(walking to the darkroom)*. How can you tell when to turn it off?

DOUGLAS. You have to know what you want. The less you expose it, the lighter it is; the more you expose it, the darker. You burn it in.

ALAN. When did you take this?

DOUGLAS. Couple a months ago.

ALAN. And you're just now getting around to printing them?

DOUGLAS. Aw, I got no time. Wow! Look at that! I tell you, boy, mmmm. Don't crowd, now; just don't crowd. *(Alan laughs.)* Is she a piece? Huh? Look at those boobs. Hummf. I tell you.

ALAN. She isn't the least bit overdoing it, you don't think?

DOUGLAS. What do you talk, with a butt like that?

ALAN. That's what I was looking at.

DOUGLAS. Can't miss that, huh? That's too broad for you? Hell, you got a lot to get a hold on there. Oh, yeah.

RONNIE *(to the audience as the lights brighten)*. Well, Mrs. Collins said she wouldn't let her husband out to take pictures of bare-assed girls in the woods over her dead body, and I made the mistake of saying it kept Doug off the streets.

CAROL *(to Alan)*. So she hasn't spoken to Ronnie since.

RONNIE. Really. Well, how was I to know her husband spent half his time on Delmarco Street?

ALAN. I take it that's the—

CAROL. Right.

ALAN. And now she's not speaking to you. *(Half to the audience, then fully)* San Diego is just like all other towns just under seven hundred thousand. And California. Californians. They're insane. Well, you've seen the movies they make out here; they have no idea at all what people are like. Well, it's not their fault; they've got nothing to go on—they're working in the dark. They're mad. They are. The shoes they wear, when they wear shoes; the clothes they wear, when they wear clothes. This place is impossible. Nobody walks. Nobody walks. Anywhere. Two blocks—if the old man has the car you don't go. You drive to a movie and they're all drive-ins. The food is all drive-ins—mini-hamburgers and cherry malts. The traffic is seventy miles an hour bumper-to-bumper going into town, six lanes abreast. The supermarkets. They're mad. They take up blocks. They're open twenty-four hours and they're packed jammed full with— Four in the morning, they're buying watermelon and lettuce and a ham and a gallon of Gallo port, and they've got the kids and the babies and the shopping cart and the portable radio and the whole family—the sandals flopping. They're nuts! They live on the beach. They all cook outside and eat outside and sleep outside—and of course it's a beautiful outside to do it in. Downtown San Diego is white day and night with sailors and those big fluffy moths and sea gulls and pigeons and sand, and I've finally seen the ocean. All of us, we had to beg Dad to take a picture of us. He's not taken a picture of the kids, Ronnie said, in almost two years.

RONNIE. He's got a hundred tons of cheesecake.

ALAN. All lined up, the three of us.

RONNIE. Doug's mother wrote today and said that that wasn't Alan, that was Doug when he was seventeen.

DOUGLAS. I told you! What'd I say!

RONNIE. That was Douglas when he was seventeen.

DOUGLAS. I said it was! By God! You can't —no matter what anybody anywhere says! . . . Wait till we get you flying by in a flashy MG. I tell you, sir-ee-bob!

ALAN. MG?

DOUGLAS. Or Porsche or Austin, one of those babies.

ALAN. Blue.

DOUGLAS. Red, hell, red. Man, what do you talk?

ALAN. Purple. Compromise.

DOUGLAS. Huh?

(Ronnie and Alan laugh.)

ALAN. It's beautiful. It is. I always wanted a big old family like this; it's just great. And it's not going to last. . . .

CAROL *(holding a bottle of pills, takes one with a glass of water).* Well, that ought to take the hair off!

ALAN *(to the audience).* Of course we're immediately in a conspiracy.

PENNY. What are they—dope?

CAROL. Oh, yell it out, Penny, and get us all kicked outta here—dope. Good God. You know that paint that little boys spray on little model airplanes?

PENNY. Yes. O.K., I know.

CAROL. Smells like ether; it could kill you if you breathe too deeply?

PENNY. I said Yes—

CAROL. Well, that's dope. Dope. *(Beat)* They're a very innocent sounding p-i-l-l called Mellaril. One of the seven wonder drugs, and you're going to ask what it does; well, it does wonders.

PENNY. Are they strong?

CAROL. They're stronger than I am. *(Messing with Alan's hair)* What do you think, Douglas?

PENNY. It's called a duck's tail.

DOUGLAS. What you want a duck's ass on the back of your head? *(With humor)* You want it all swirled around like that, you look like—I don't know what—like some of those high-school punks or Penny's whatsit.

CAROL. You don't like it? Doug, you're square; you can't get around it.

DOUGLAS. What the hell are you talking? He looks like a drugstore cowboy.

CAROL. Doug, you don't know your ass.

DOUGLAS *(too sharply).* Who you telling about ass?

PENNY. Phil even wears his hair like—

DOUGLAS *(enormous).* Miss Innocence, we just won't talk about the way your boyfriends . . . do anything, huh? *Huh?*

ALAN *(a long embarrassed pause; then quickly).* Dad combs his hair straight back and has since the day he was born, and that's the only way to comb your hair. It's been just twenty-four hours. And the head's still beating and it's all too fast. In six months I'll be sleeping in a park in Chicago with a letter in my pocket from Ronnie telling me that Carol is dead. But who would know that now? We're sitting down to eat. Outside. That's California. We're—

CAROL. Shhhhh! *(He stops. They listen a split second.)* No, not thunder; you feel it?

ALAN. No. Yes! I think—

CAROL. Shhhhh!

(They concentrate.)

ALAN. Yeah. Good God.

RONNIE. You get used to it. It doesn't bother the natives. If it *thunders,* they run out into the street and think the world's coming to an end.

ALAN. They don't have thunderstorms out here?

RONNIE. Almost never. I've heard it thunder maybe four times in twelve years. People nearly died of heart attack; it even scared me the last time.

ALAN. Could I have another coffee?

RONNIE. Shhhhh!

ALAN *(smiling at it, aside to the audience).*

It feels like—you've felt it in the cities—when a big loaded, lumbering diesel rolls by outside; or if you live near a subway and the whole building—all the walls, the chair you're sitting in—gives a gentle, prolonged shudder. That's it. Only there's no truck going by—it just happens of its own accord.

PENNY. Shhhhh!

RONNIE. There, feel it!

(A beat as they listen between all these lines)

ALAN *(smiling)*. Good God.

DOUGLAS. See? Isn't that sumpin?

JACK. It's silly.

PENNY. Did you hear?

CAROL. Shhhhh!

(They all concentrate, smiling, feeling the vibrations.)

RONNIE *(very gently, slowly, to them; no one changes his position)*. Feel it? *(They continue to smile, tensed, intently concentrating. Five seconds or just over)*

SLOW CURTAIN

ACT TWO

(Alan, Penny, and Carol outside. Bright sunlight. Carol is in a vivid orange robe over a bathing suit.)

ALAN *(to the audience)*. Same song, second verse, as the poet said; couldn't be better but it's gonna be worse. March. April. May. June or July or August. About. Everything goes well enough, but it's complicated. It's difficult to leave well enough alone.

CAROL. Because "well enough" is an intolerable state to be in. Take it from me.

ALAN. I'm home today for a—home. Oh, wow. And it is now. Really is. For a short time. A very short time longer. My last class is at three usually, and I go to work from school. Today is Saturday—no school, work, no school—so I can spend some time home before we leave for work at five. Penny and Carol are on vacation. . . . It's summer.

PENNY. I still don't know why you started school summer term.

ALAN. Because I was very suspicious that if I didn't, I wouldn't start at all. Two momentous events have elapsed! Dad has developed an absolute passion for milk. And he's teaching Penny photography.

PENNY. Well, not photography. There isn't anything to learn except point and snap. I'm learning developing and printing.

ALAN. You like it?

PENNY. Sure, it's fascinating. I'm a little sick of seeing that red, white, and blue bikini in every picture we print.

CAROL. Ha!

ALAN. Dad's got this bikini he takes along to his sessions with the girls—

CAROL. It's pathetic.

ALAN. —and the whole session is taken up, apparently—we only see the pictures—with first coaxing her into it and then nearly out of it. She unties it here and pushes it down there —or else she doesn't. Which is even funnier.

PENNY. It's awful. It's cotton and tacky and just ugly as it can be.

ALAN *(to Carol)*. I'm surprised he hasn't got you posing for him by now.

CAROL. Oh, honey, I'm onto that crap. He squires around those dames down to the beach with that stupid car—

ALAN. Chrysler convertible.

CAROL. Nothing but big cars in this play—

ALAN. Right, which isn't typical—some of the guys build their own, so they drive these sorta car-collages.

CAROL. But Doug squeals around in this big fat Chrysler, which is perfect, but he doesn't know it. He took a million pictures of me; I'm not photogenic—he didn't even notice it. It's all in his head—he never notices. Slobbering around: "You got nice eyes," "You got nice legs," "You got nice tits." Hell, I haven't even *got* tits, the creep.

ALAN. Probably he wanted you to—

CAROL. He wanted in my pants. It was humiliating. When a girl seventeen has to tell a man forty-five to grow up, something's wrong. I just found it repellent and I told him.

ALAN. Not in those words, I hope.

CAROL. Yes, in those words: "Doug, grow up; you're repellent." Listen, half the foster fathers I've had have tried to make me. Since I was six. It's not my scene. Men are asses. If they knew what they looked like, they'd all march into the sea in a line, like lemmicks.

PENNY. It isn't lemmicks; it's lemmings.

CAROL. You're terrific. I think you're my favorite sister. *(To Alan, who laughs)* You can go to hell, too.

ALAN. I went to one outing with Dad, and whatever you do, you have got—and have *got* —to go to an amateur photographers' meeting with cheesecake models. We went up to

Redwood—out in this cactus park with about four hundred photographers and about forty girls. Ten to one. And they're draping over every fence and adobe wall and bench in the park. I've got this thirty-five millimeter Leica that Dad's lent me, barely explaining how to work the damn thing. And all the guys are frisking around this gal—she's on a Mexican serape—and the guys are practically having heart attacks: Clickadyclickadyclickady-clickadyclickady all around like a plague of locusts, and they're all jockeying for the best angle to shoot straight down her breasts, which are pumpkins; and they're giving her: "That's it, honey. Wet your lips, baby. Wet 'em again. Give us a laugh. Now slack. Slack. Just let everything go to hell. Toss your hair. Pout. Pout. Indignant. Hate. More. Hate. Kill. Kill. . . . Thatagirl. Wet your lips, keep 'em wet—not so much. Pout. Just let it all hang—"

CAROL. That's insane.

ALAN. "Just give us a big sexy kiss!" And I'm standing there with this damn dumb Leica, saying, "Oh, I don't know, could you just sorta, maybe—smile?"

CAROL. I know that whole scene.

DOUGLAS (entering). Hey, Alan, how come you didn't show?

ALAN. Huh? Where?

DOUGLAS. This guy is impossible, isn't he? Where? I mean this wasn't important, but he'd forget it if it was. (Giving Alan's head a wrench) Is your head on tight? We wouldn't want you losing that.

ALAN. Yeah, yeah, I think. What did I forget?

DOUGLAS. Club meeting yesterday afternoon. Nothing happened. You can go to them or not; suit yourself.

ALAN (to the audience). The few times I have gone, you couldn't—

DOUGLAS (interrupting; serious afterthought). Al—hey!

ALAN. Huh?

DOUGLAS. Stanley tells me you're not coming to work. Something like three days last week you missed? Awhile back? What was that?

ALAN. Three days? No. Maybe two once, but not three.

DOUGLAS. What the hell's so important? The days I don't drive you in, you're just not showing up? I have to squire you in?

ALAN. I have been.

DOUGLAS. He says you're a good worker—

(Half to the audience) —He's a good worker; he picks things up—but you can't—

ALAN. Listen, I still do more in three days than the other guys—

DOUGLAS. They're getting their five days' pay, and you're—

ALAN. You should watch the shop steward sometime. Oh, wow. I thought your department sat around on their retired duffs. There were guys—

DOUGLAS. Retired duffs? (Mock indignation) I'll have you know—I mean a few Government Jobs that's very important stuff—

ALAN. Right, right. (To the audience) "Government Jobs" is slang for doing something of your own. (Back to Douglas) I went in the other day and two different guys were making mailboxes, and one guy was repairing his wife's Mixmaster.

DOUGLAS. Well, they're paying you to come to work five days a week, man; that's what—

ALAN. They're paying me by the hour. Maybe one week I missed two days because of tests at school I had to cram—

DOUGLAS. Well, learn to study—crap—organize yourself, man. You take a job, you go; it's a simple thing.

ALAN. Dad spoke for me down there, and he thinks I'm giving him a bad name taking off—I'm a beatnik.

DOUGLAS. They want you there five days a week. They don't give a damn if you sit on your fanny or stand on your head, man; they don't care as long as you show up.

ALAN. You know, that's true; they really don't. You should see those guys—nobody works. Nobody works. It's amazing! (Including the audience) I could tell you the name of the transportation jets we're building down there and how we're doing it—the entire aircraft industry would collapse tomorrow morning. Would you believe chewing gum? I'm not kidding. There's a little hole, no one's looking, what the hell! I don't miss that much, really.

DOUGLAS. You just see that you get whatever it is you have to do done today so we can leave on time. I'm not going to wait around for you. . . .

ALAN (to the audience). So what do you do when you hear that? You decide right there that you're not going, right?

DOUGLAS (instantly furious). You think it's funny—you want to do it now? Huh?

ALAN. Later.

DOUGLAS. You want to do it now? We'll do it now. Come on, we'll do it now.

ALAN. We'll get to it. Later.

DOUGLAS. *(looks at him a moment, then to Penny casually)*. Penny, we're gonna work right after lunch, O.K.?

PENNY. Whenever. *(Douglas exits.)* I keep asking him to print up some of his pictures of Grand Canyon or something, but it's always those darn girls—girls are so stupid to do that. Oh, I guess they think of a career, but, wow, that's so stupid. It's no worse than me, though; I'm always imagining my wedding. Do you do that?

CAROL. Do what?

PENNY. I can't pass a church some days without going through my whole wedding in it. You know, I'm running out of the door in my wedding dress with my hands over my head, keeping off the rice and trying to wave to everybody at the same time. Sometimes I'm sitting perfectly still and I catch myself tossing my bouquet at someone.

CAROL. Who are you thinking about marrying?

PENNY. Well . . . I'm not. I don't want to get married. I'd like to be a scientist just as much. I picture that too.

CAROL. Penny has a very rich fantasy life.

PENNY. Well, I do. I think it's healthy. I see myself in one of those white lab coats with a bunch of those bubbly test tubes and coils all around—analyzing blood and making notations—

CAROL. Blood? Good God, you have the most morbid goddamn sense of duty.

PENNY. Do you like being away from Sonny as much as being with him?

CAROL. What?

PENNY. Really, it's funny, but I think sometimes when I'm with Phil I'd really rather not be, so I could be away from him—*wanting* to be with him. You like Phil, don't you? He's nice, isn't he?

CAROL. Do I? I don't know him.

PENNY. You went to school with him before he graduated; I didn't. I'll bet he was popular at Grossmont, wasn't he?

CAROL *(spiritedly)*. I didn't know him. We didn't run in the same crowd. I thought he was a stuck-up jerk. He's all right. He's nice. He's beautiful. Yes, he was popular. My God, I guess he was. Aren't there any boys at your school?

PENNY. I don't go with any of them—

ALAN *(overlapping some)*. Carol goes to Grossmont; Penny goes to El Cajon.

PENNY. My gosh, why don't you like Phil? Good grief. All we can ever talk about is Sonny. . . . I don't even like Texas. I don't know what a Hereford looks like. I'll bet you don't, either. *(To Alan)* She used to talk about all of Sonny's beautiful Black Anguses. She didn't know if they were horses or automobiles. *(Beat; to Carol)* Are you going to marry Sonny?

CAROL. I hope to hell. I'm not going to come this far at such unimaginable expense and wind up—and I'm going to invite all my scores and wear white. I can't wait. *(Digging in her purse)* Goddammit! I brought a bottle of baby oil out here—I'll bet I spend a fortune just from losing— *(Penny hands her the bottle of oil from beside the chair.)* Penny, why don't you put on your swimsuit? You're going to just bake.

PENNY. No, I'm not staying.

CAROL. Well, you're driving me nuts out here dressed up like an Eskimo. *(To Alan, handing him the oil)* Get my back, will you?

ALAN. You don't need that stuff.

CAROL. I have delicate skin.

ALAN. What is that you put over your eyes? Plastic spoons? You know, I knew a girl once who went blind from sunbathing with plastic spoons over her eyes. They melted. You're going to be solid brown with white eyelids.

CAROL. Would you shut up?

ALAN *(to the audience as he rubs Carol's back)*. Ronnie, about a month ago—I came in moaning that I was failing what? Math, probably—I'm failing math every other day. And she said, "The term isn't over yet; you've got to have faith." You have to understand she was serious as hell about it. It scared us to death. I really believed it. She said, "If you have faith the size of a mustard seed, you—"

CAROL. Turn it down, why don't you?

ALAN *(stops rubbing her back)*. I'm going to stop because I think you're enjoying this in all the wrong ways. *(To the audience)* You have to understand I thought I'd probably exposed myself to trichinosis.

CAROL. You went in and washed your hands.

ALAN. I did not. How many pills today?

CAROL. Who counts any more? Three or four so far, and that's pretty far.

PENNY. You shouldn't take those and lie in the sun.

CAROL. God, the things you're opposed to. You're worse than Sonny sometimes.

PENNY. I'm not opposed to them; you just shouldn't. Maybe I should go with Sonny and you go with Phil.

CAROL *(rapidly strung together). That* does it! I'm going to take a shower. Penny, do you have any bobby pins something has to happen to—don't answer; you don't use them, right? What kind of sister are you anyway? I swear to God. You don't know *any* two-part harmony songs. You don't buy cheap perfumes I can steal, you don't use a brush, you're immoral—always suggesting we swap husbands. What the hell good are you outside of making peanut butter divinity? Jesus H. Christopher, I wish I were on the moon. I nearly am.

PENNY. Well, why do you take them? You know Ronnie will kick you out if she finds out and Sonny made it a condition.

ALAN. He didn't make it a condition; he just said he'd never speak to her again.

CAROL. It turns me off. It turns me way, way off.

ALAN. It's a kind of Norwegian Fly.

CAROL. Icelandic.

ALAN *(singing).* "Try Icelandic Fly, gets you there on time . . . "

CAROL. You couldn't possibly have said that; that song didn't come out for ages.

ALAN. That's all right; you aren't even alive. You've been dead ten years.

(They laugh.)

CAROL. I would like to thank the theatre for rescuing me from that dreary cupboard in that dreary condition.

PENNY. Dank.

ALAN. Drear.

CAROL *(overlapping them).* I want to—right—thank the drear management for the magic of the theatre, which enables me to be continually young and alive and beautiful and current—

PENNY. And here.

ALAN. Topical.

PENNY. God, yes, topical.

ALAN. We hope.

CAROL *(biting her lip, sitting down, almost in tears).* Shit.

ALAN. Hey, Carol, come on, it's all right.

CAROL. A lot you know, buddy, a lot you know.

ALAN. Really—remember those Red Skelton radio programs, and he played the mean widdle kid?

PENNY. Yeah, right—

ALAN. He used to describe something

dreadful that happened to him and start crying, "I scared me widdle self"?

CAROL. I don't remember.

ALAN. I think you scared you widdle self.

PENNY. Sure you remember. On the radio. I remember it.

ALAN. Maybe she listened to a different program: Fibber and Molly McGee. *(Beat)* Don't get maudlin, Carol.

CAROL. I'm not only locked in your god-damned sideshow, dragged out to play second fiddle in a three-ring— *(Slinging a cigarette all the way off, out the wings; walking away a few steps, furious)* Fuck!

ALAN *(calling).* Come on, come off it, munghead.

PENNY. Mung? Wow.

CAROL. I hope it burns down the theatre.

PENNY. That's the worst kind of head, munghead.

CAROL. I'm hip. *(After a deep breath she regains composure, waves it away.)* O.K., I'm back.

ALAN. She's back. *(Singing)* She's back and she's better than ever before, Campbell's Pork and Beans.

ALAN *and* PENNY *and* CAROL *(three-part harmony; quite on the patio, not for the audience).*

Back and they're better than ever before,
Back and they're better than ever before,
Back and they're better than ever before,
Campbell's Pork and Beans. Hey!

(Jerry and Jack come running in.)

ALAN *(to the audience immediately).* Most of the radio stations out here are incredible. They're three times as powerful as allowed by the FCC or whoever, but the broadcasting towers are all in Mexico, so they can get away with anything. They play rock 'n' roll all day and night, and commercials, commercials—more than you'd ever believe—and about half of them are in Spanish, so— *(To* JERRY*)* Come on. So they go like this:

JERRY. *Para refrescarse tome* Coca-Cola *frío.*

ALAN. Isn't that great? Well, what's that got to do with the story? Well . . . nothing, actually; only we feel we should throw in a little local color from time to time.

CAROL *(announcement).* Local Color!

PENNY. It takes a while for the untutored eye to recognize it, but—

CAROL. —the color green does not occur in California naturally.

ALAN *(to the audience).* Southern California is in the colors of perpetually early autumn: umber, amber, olive, sienna, ocher, orange; acres and acres of mustard and sage —the colors.

PENNY *(straight)*. The herbs, too.

ALAN. And grass dies. It has a season of winter and the weather does not. So instead of grass they plant—a lot of the lawns are planted in dichondra. A little cloverlike thing that grows about two inches high and doesn't require mowing, and it's very cute; but it isn't grass, is it? And it's green the year round.

CAROL. Only not green.

ALAN. Right. And that bright eye-breaking, bright-sun-shining-through-oak-and-maple-and-elm-onto-bright-green-ferns-and-grass green does not occur. Of course, you couldn't care less. It's something you rather gladly or at least unknowingly forfeit for nearly continual sunshine.

PENNY. Weren't we doing a play a while back?

ALAN. Right!

(Everyone listening to Ronnie, who has entered during the last sentence. Ronnie in mid-sentence. Another time, earlier)

RONNIE. . . . the size of a mustard seed, you can move mountains.

PENNY. Can you work math?

ALAN. Well, I don't seem—

RONNIE *(very seriously—mock religiously)*. No, now, I'm not kidding. The Bible says you can move mountains, and you can. And I have that faith.

PENNY. And you can move mountains?

RONNIE. It doesn't matter what you three feel, it's my faith that's important. Now, do you see Mount Helix out there?

ALAN *(as they look)*. Are you kidding?

PENNY. Come on—

RONNIE. No, now, we're all going to look away. Go on—

PENNY. That's sacri—

RONNIE. —look away now; it's a simple demonstration of my faith.

(They turn away from the mountain.)

ALAN. Right. Now what?

RONNIE. Now. When we turn around again, Mount Helix will be gone. Because I have that faith. Because I know it will be gone. In my heart. Now turn around slowly, and Mount Helix will be gone. Now.

ALAN. You.

(They don't believe, but they are a little uncertain.)

RONNIE *(turns slowly and gazes off)*. Well . . .

CAROL. What?

RONNIE. Just like I thought, there it is. Damn.

ALAN. What?

PENNY. Don't scare me.

(They laugh.)

RONNIE. I must have miscalculated. Look at it.

CAROL. Yeah, I think so.

RONNIE. I think it's even grown. My faith isn't the size of a mustard seed, it's the size of a poppy seed. And poppy seed don't move nothing.

CAROL. Poppy seed moves the world.

RONNIE. That's a different poppy seed.

CAROL *(in starting to get up, drops the bottle of pills, picks it up, nearly falls over; holding her head and trying to put the bottle into a pocket of the robe)*. Oh, wow.

RONNIE. Are you O.K.? You look like hell.

CAROL *(nearly floating away, trying to come down a little)*. Hmmm? I'm sorry, I washed my brain and I can't do a thing with it. Where are you? *(She gets the bottle into the pocket, will not look at Ronnie directly.)*

RONNIE. What's wrong? Look at me.

CAROL *(handing the robe to Penny)*. Penny, sweetheart, could you take this in?

RONNIE. What's wrong?

(Penny takes the robe in.)

CAROL. No, I'm O.K. I ate something; it didn't agree with me.

RONNIE. Look up. Is that all?

CAROL. Well, it's my *time*, as the Victorians would have it. I'm dizzy a little is all. *(She exits. Penny has taken the robe away and is back now. Ronnie looks at Alan and Penny a moment. Some tension)*

RONNIE *(rather to the audience, breaking away)*. Well, once in a while you have to admit you don't understand a thing about what kids are doing with their lives nowadays.

(All the others enter for lunch.)

PENNY. . . . because they went all the way to the top of Mount Helix and dragged down this poor palm tree.

RONNIE. I told you it wouldn't grow.

ALAN. Well, how would Jerry and I know that? This poor baby palm was thriving in the garbage heap; we transplanted it into the back yard, next to Jack's bird of paradise, and the poor little palm died before sundown. With its boots on.

CAROL. Boots off, I think.

ALAN. Well, whichever is the nobler.

RONNIE. I think it's two separate schools of thought.

JERRY. Off! "I ain't gonna die, partner, with those damn boots on!"

DOUGLAS. Jerry, don't say "damn" in front of your brother; he won't be old enough to say that for fifteen years yet.

JERRY. Why not?

RONNIE. And you've got a few years to go yourself.

JERRY. What should I say?

JACK. Say "hockey."

DOUGLAS. That's enough out of you, too—no hints from the gallery, peanut.

CAROL. He's a lady-killer.

JERRY. What can I say if I can't say that?

CAROL. How racy should it be?

JERRY Pretty racy.

CAROL. Well, you should try—

JACK. "Hanged."

JERRY. Yes! That hanged thing ain't worth the powder it'd take to blow it—

RONNIE. No, no.

JACK. Danged. Danged.

JERRY. All-fired.

RONNIE. No. Say . . . I can't think of one. Well, don't use any of them—good grief, there's at least—

JACK. Good grief!

RONNIE. No, don't say "good grief" either. There're two hundred thousand acceptable words in the language; you don't have to wallow around in the vernacular at your age.

JERRY. I don't know two hundred thousand—

DOUGLAS. Well, you better be for learning them.

JERRY. How do I know if they're acceptable?

RONNIE. O.K. You come to me and whisper them in my ear, and if they happen not to be acceptable, I'll wash your mouth out with soap.

JERRY. No.

RONNIE. See? I thought not. *(They are leaving.)* What do you say?

JACK. May we be excused?

RONNIE. Yes, you may; don't tear the house down. *(Jack and Jerry exit.)* The kids on the block have a bucket brigade of profanity. I think they have a collective mind. One of them learns a new word and everyone on the block knows it in an hour. We had an entire month of "shitfire" last year. I can't imagine where they got that one, but they loved it.

CAROL. Probably from Douglas.

RONNIE *(to Carol).* You aren't supposed to say that.

DOUGLAS. They aren't supposed to listen. Hell, I wouldn't want them to be like Alan's college buddies up at State: all potatoes and no meat. They all look like they're made out of unbaked dough. They even talk like it.

ALAN. My friends? Whatta you talk? My friends swear like sailors; it's part of the emancipated-young-adult jargon.

DOUGLAS. Well, I'd be surprised if they knew what it meant. We dropped him off the other morning—

ALAN. Yeah, yeah, last month sometime you dropped me off.

DOUGLAS. Two weeks ago Friday.

ALAN. Compromise purple. *(To the audience; aside)* Now, you see, I think that's the funniest line in the play.

DOUGLAS. And he introduced Ronnie and me to a few of them. Sasha and Joan and Owen and—don't they ever get out into the sun?

ALAN. Into the sun? Are you kidding? Oh, my God—into the sun! I've discovered there's this whole beautiful poetical intellectual coterie that wouldn't be caught dead in the sun. They're nuts, but they're great. Kinda like the Castilian Spanish: the whiter you are, the brighter you are. They're nuts, but you love them for it. A lot of the young kids out at State—

DOUGLAS. Young? Young? Young? Them? Oh, man, they're on their pensions. Who are you trying to kid? They're cadavers. Ronnie, you read—Carol, did you see that magazine thing they put out at State?

CAROL. No.

ALAN. I brought that home: I haven't even seen it yet—

DOUGLAS *(overlapping).* Well, that's what I'm talking, Ronnie. Right there. I want you to look at it some night and see if it can turn you on.

CAROL. What he's saying, Alan, is it doesn't stack up to the garage collection of the complete Erle Stanley Gardner—

DOUGLAS. Listen, twit, unless you've read those books, just don't knock them. People are a darn sight more interested in life than in those plants and those creepy ferns and creepy shadows and creepy creeps. Nobody reads that magazine except your creepy college would-be poets. Oh, man, I didn't graduate from high school, and I'll bet I can take any of them on in anything except arithmetic, huh?

ALAN. Dad and I are both rotten with figures.

DOUGLAS. Some kinds of figures.

ALAN. Probably you could.

DOUGLAS. Yeah, you damn-betcha. What do they retain? Huh? History: I'll bet you don't even know the Presidents of the country. Your own goddamned country. Do you?

ALAN. God, no. I only know the capitals of the states because I had a jigsaw puzzle.

DOUGLAS. And the vice-presidents.

ALAN. I don't know any of the vice-presidents except Truman.

DOUGLAS. Well, I don't imagine ten out of the eight thousand of them know them either. Who was Washington's vice-president?

ALAN. I don't know.

DOUGLAS. The first vice-president of the United States?

ALAN. I said no. I'm stupid.

PENNY. Adams.

DOUGLAS. Right.

PENNY. Only, that's it.

DOUGLAS (*reciting rhythmically*). Washington—Adams; Adams—Jefferson; Jefferson—Burr; Jefferson—Clinton; Madison—Clinton; Madison—Gerry; Monroe—Tompkins; Adams—Calhoun; Jackson—Calhoun; Jackson—Van Buren; Van Buren—Johnson; Harrison—*Tyler!*

ALAN. Hey, that's great. And many more, huh? Tyler of "Tippecanoe and Tyler Too" fame?

DOUGLAS. Right. . . .

ALAN. Who was Teddy Roosevelt's first vice-president?

DOUGLAS (*beat*). Cleveland—Stevenson; McKinley—Hobart; McKinley—Roosevelt; Roosevelt and nobody; Roosevelt—*Fairbanks. (Beat; then building)* Taft—Sherman; Wilson—Marshall; Harding—Coolidge; Coolidge—Dawes; Hoover—Curtis; Roosevelt—Garner; Roosevelt—Wallace; Roosevelt—*Truman!*

(*A very long pause. Silence. Everyone is still.*)

JERRY (*entering with a small postage-stamp-sized piece of photograph*). Look at me; that's terrible. Right across my ear.

RONNIE. What?

JERRY. My picture. The picture Dad took of us.

RONNIE. Doug, you didn't tear that up, did you?

DOUGLAS. What? Tear what up?

ALAN. I wanted a print of that.

DOUGLAS. What? It isn't any good.

RONNIE. Your mother loved it; I told you what she said.

DOUGLAS. Well, Mother, bless her heart, doesn't know much about photography.

ALAN. Well, I don't either, but I wanted one.

DOUGLAS. No, I tore it up; it was a bad print, anyway; it's too light. I'll print it up again.

ALAN. You never even intended to.

DOUGLAS (*quite directly*). Well, now, how do you know what I intended to do and what the hell I didn't intend to do? Huh?

RONNIE. It's the only picture we had of them; you haven't taken a picture of the boys in two years.

DOUGLAS. It was a lousy picture—I'll take another one—the light was bad. It was a snapshot, for God's sake. Penny, are you going to help me or not, huh?

PENNY. Yeah, I will.

JERRY. He tore it right across my ear.

ALAN. I really wanted it.

DOUGLAS (*much too loud for the occasion*). All right, now, will you just shut up about the goddamned *picture* now! Now I've *had it! With you! ((He exits with Penny.)*

RONNIE (*topically*). Doug and I had a terrible argument about you last night.

ALAN. What? Wait a sec—I'm not getting the drift of—

RONNIE (*going on*). Actually, he argued. He said—you should excuse the expression—you hadn't had a piece of ass since you'd been here.

ALAN. I hadn't what?

DOUGLAS (*to Ronnie as the two are suddenly isolated in the living room*). You saw that gang of dough-balls he was hanging out with at school.

RONNIE. I don't know if he's quite "hanging out" with them.

DOUGLAS. Well, I'm not saying *what* he's doing with them; I know what he's not doing. When has he been on a date? Squiring Cookie to the local movie in El Cajon and back twice, what's that supposed to mean?

RONNIE. Well, you could hardly expect him to go for Cookie; Cookie's hardly the freshest thing on the block—and it's a small block.

DOUGLAS. When's he gone out?

RONNIE. I don't know; when's he had time? Full-time work, full-time school.

DOUGLAS. Oh, time's ass. Summer term, everyone else on vacation; goddammit, he hangs around the house, he hangs around school. He hasn't had a piece of ass since he's been here.

RONNIE. Well, he's been here four or five months. I don't know.

DOUGLAS. Well nothing! He's not getting anything from that gang of dishwater dames at school, and if he is, he ought to be ashamed of himself. I can tell you that. What the hell's the matter, hasn't he got a libido?

RONNIE. I don't know if you're proud of him for—

DOUGLAS. Proud of what?

RONNIE. Well, he doesn't drink, he doesn't scoot around on a motorcycle, he's no—

DOUGLAS. Well, maybe he should! I told him he could have the car any time he wanted it. He hasn't asked for it once.

RONNIE. Well, whenever are you not using it?

DOUGLAS. Plenty is the answer to that, plenty.

RONNIE. You also told him you'd get him a new Austin. He hasn't seen that.

DOUGLAS. Not on your damn life until he shows some interest. What am I going to get a car to rust in the driveway? *(Somewhat to the audience)* Took him out to the damn lot, looked around mildly, came back saying he liked them all, and started taking a bus to school; what the hell?

RONNIE. Well, I don't want to argue.

ALAN. When would I have time?

RONNIE. That's what I said, Alan. Still.

ALAN. I can't see it's any of his business, anyway, good God.

RONNIE. I told him he didn't have a detective on your tail, how did he know?

ALLAN. Tail is funny. Oh, well.

DOUGLAS. *(continuing with* RONNIE*).* When I was his age, I knew the score all around. I'm not going to break him in like a hunting dog: stick a quail in his mouth and have him spit it out till I can teach him what it is. He isn't stupid. What kind of man doesn't know where the hunt is? Huh? I don't want to tell you! It just isn't living. Life is for living, Ronnie. The Best Is None Too Good.

ALAN *(rather rapidly).* I'll bet a hundred times Mom's told me that: "Your dad always said, 'The best is none too good, the best is none too good.'" She used to say I was like him a lot—"You're like him a lot"—and she was right, dammit, more right every day I live—

DOUGLAS. No, by God, he isn't . . . like

me! Not on your life he isn't. Maybe I got into trouble and maybe I got with some kids that were a bad influence—I don't say I was an angel—but I knew where the food was and where my hands were and my mouth and my cock and my belly; and if I knew what I had, I knew where to put it, too. And I had women. I mean real women. Hell, the first woman I had was thirty-five years old and I was a kid fifteen, and don't think she didn't teach fast. Hell, I'm younger now than he is. And I grew up in the same goddamned two-bit Nebraska town he did; so don't pull that.

RONNIE. I don't think it's at all unusual for a boy seventeen to be more—

DOUGLAS. I don't want to hear it. I'm younger now than he is now. You squeal around a corner with the girl's hair flying out, by God, and she's all over you. Wiggling her behind in your lap, by God; you pull over to the curb and let 'em have it right there. You pull into a garage. Or a lot, a parking lot. What's he going to do, take a cheap bottle of booze up to some wet hotel room? What does he know? I never went to one cheap hotel room with a bottle of cheap booze in my life. You think I'm going to sit on those sway-backed mattresses, burn-holes all over the furniture varnish? Glass circles. God knows what laid what there. Out in the damn grass alongside the road under nature's clean sky with the wind blowing and *stars!* All that smell of lipstick. Hell, the beaches at night are lined up; where's he? Huh? Goddammit, he's eighteen years old; what's he doing, jerkin' off?

RONNIE. Well, tell him, honey; don't tell me—I'm not interested in seducing young girls.

DOUGLAS. His mother stunted him. Neutered him. He's humiliating. Just looking at his damned—all right, he's a damn-all-right-looking guy, or could be. There's nothing wrong with him. He's let those two damn phony girls twist his hair up like a pretzel, all curled up like some kind of rock 'n' roll singer.

RONNIE. That's what the girls are going for nowadays, I guess.

DOUGLAS. Oh, shit, Ronnie. Nowadays. Hair that long, curled up like that, I can hardly sit at the table with him without throwing up! I'd like to snatch him bald—nowadays! Women go for men and that's all! Women go for vitality, vigor, exuberance, strength. Balls, for God's sake. What are you talking? Huh?

ALAN. You know—

DOUGLAS. Huh?

ALAN. —Dad asked me—

DOUGLAS. Aw, hell, go on! *(Exits)*

ALAN. —last night to contribute twenty-five dollars each week to the family fund. To pay my way around here . . . for room and board. For twelve years he didn't pay a red cent to my welfare, and suddenly I'm a drain on the budget. Another mouth to feed. Goddamn. I found out what the mortgage on the house is—

RONNIE. Well, I told you that. It isn't a secret, surely.

ALAN. A hundred and three dollars a month.

RONNIE. For twenty years, though.

ALAN. Unless you pay it off sooner, and you're paying a hundred twenty, which is what the two girls bring in—they just sign over the checks to the mortgage, *actually!*

RONNIE. That isn't even what they eat.

ALAN *(to the audience and* RONNIE*)*. I didn't believe it. . . . And he wants a hundred-plus a month from me as my contribution to the gas and food. I don't feel I should be working for you . . . down there for you. All I bargained for was part-time work and full-time college. I'm full-time working and I can't save the money to quit work because you people can't afford to keep me here unless I pay my own way!

RONNIE. Don't you think you should pay toward it? Because we can't. We'd like you to know that.

ALAN. I didn't think I should pay. I quite frankly didn't think I should pay. I worked down there with noise that would bring down mountains seven hours a day, when I could pull myself together after school to go, and I didn't really mind if it was doing something. All right, we're all of us selfish. If I was using it for tuition and books and school—but paying the rent on Dad's house!

RONNIE *(suddenly; quietly and seriously)*. You're an equal member of the family, Alan. The inheritance will be divided three ways equally between Doug's three kids; you'll get just as much as the kids do.

ALAN *(thrown)*. What? Well, that's a long time off—what kind of talk? Anyway—

RONNIE. I just want you to feel—I want you to know that, Alan. Truly.

DOUGLAS *(from the other side; quite heatedly and suddenly joining them. He has taken up a lunch pail and a pocket holder for pencils* with a red and green badge on it, which he carries in his shirt pocket*)*. Stay where? By God, when I say come on to work, I mean it. What the hell have—where are you sick?

ALAN. All over. I'm not sick; I don't feel like working. I don't feel well. I don't want to go. I have things to do; I don't feel good—well.

DOUGLAS. Stanley tells me you're never there five days a week. At least when you're home frisking around all day like today, by God, you can go to work. Since when didn't you feel well?

ALAN. Since now. What's wrong? What difference does it make?

DOUGLAS. Listen here, mister; if school gets in the way, then you can quit school. I don't see work getting in the way of school. Are you missing there too? Huh?

ALAN. No, not yet.

DOUGLAS. You mope around like a sick calf; now it's about time someone put a firecracker under your tail. See if there's any life in you. You and Penny—the whole lot of you. Maybe you should take liver tablets or something.

ALAN *(with some humor)*. Perhaps I should. What's wrong; can't I be sick?

DOUGLAS. If I believe it. There's no goddamned reason why you can't go in except you don't want to. . . . By God now, Alan, and I'm serious, I just want to know one thing—

ALAN. Why should I? Of what importance is the job down—

DOUGLAS. Because I told you to. I said so. . . . I told you to get ready, I wasn't having you make the whole damn carload of us late again. Now, are you coming or not?

ALAN. No, goddammit! I'm not. That's what I said. I don't feel well. I've got three chapters to read on—

DOUGLAS. *Listen here!* Now, once and for all. I'm not going to say this twice now; this has been coming. Do you want to stay here? Answer me!

ALAN *(letting down, relaxing)*. Yes, that's what I've been saying. I told you. It's as simple—

DOUGLAS. I mean, do you want to *stay* here? Live here? In this house?

ALAN *(quite thrown)*. What? I guess so. Yes—what—yes, of course I do.

DOUGLAS *(very strongly)*. Then, by God, if you do, you better know this is my home. And I say here. I call the shots here, and what

I say goes, mister. And those that don't like it can find a roof over their heads somewhere else. And you better be for learning that fast. Because I don't take any shit. None.

ALAN. I know—that—

DOUGLAS. None! Mister! Not from you or anybody else, huh? And you better be for learning that fast! *(Exits.)*

ALAN *(standing where he was; tries to speak to the audience; very upset, trying to be rational).* I—my whole body—hell, I can't do —was pounding. Well, I hadn't—he left. I— I—Ronnie went down the hall. *(She does.)* And into—I went out—blindly turned around and went out into the back yard. *(He does.)* And fell down on the ground and bawled like I never remember bawling before or since. Sobbing. I—I— *(Fighting for objectivity)* Now, what was going through my— what was I thinking? Well, of course, all the times I had wanted a father and not had one. The times I had wanted to live with Dad. The struggle Mother had had during the war, working in a garment factory. And before that, the little I could remember—of— remember of Dad, before. And what I had been told, Mom's stories. And my sister, who had been born dead while he was out with— whomever it was he was out with. That had always been my picture of him: Mom walking the floor, him coming in and her crying— Ronnie was in the house. I was very aware of that. I expected her to come out and talk to me. Something. Ronnie and I were close— friends. If I had left. Then. Where would I have gone? I couldn't consider it. This is where I had come to—right to the edge of the continent. I didn't think about going. I couldn't leave. I didn't know what we had been fighting about. I honestly didn't; not then. Well, neither here nor there. Finally I got up. Aching. And went inside.

RONNIE. I knew you went out. I knew you were crying. I didn't look out. I assumed you wanted your privacy. I wasn't going to embarrass you.

ALAN *(a kind of laugh).* Humf.

RONNIE. I just sat. Tried to sort the wash, not to listen, cleaned up the bedroom. Penny had vanished—very unlike her—nobody had seen her all afternoon. Rose finally called at eleven and said she was over there, which was all right, I suppose; at least we knew where she was.

ALAN. I went to bed about twelve. Dad came home after work. I heard him in the kitchen making scrambled eggs, I suppose, or French toast. I almost expected him to come in and apologize. All right, I did expect him to. I don't know for what. I couldn't sleep. I got up and dressed after he'd gone to bed. Actually went to a bar. Deserted bar.

RONNIE. And came home drunk as a lord.

ALAN. You shouldn't have stayed up.

RONNIE. I woke up and wondered where you'd gone.

ALAN. The next morning, bright and early, Dad's photography club went off to the mountains. And I woke up with a hangover —so we begin and end, both, with a splitting headache. And Penny came home to leave.

PENNY *(ending a very long cross to RONNIE during the above).* Ronnie? Ronnie?

RONNIE. What, Pen?

PENNY. Could I talk to you alone?

RONNIE. How come you stayed with Rose, Penny? You should call when you decide to leave like that; we were worried abo—

PENNY. I can't stay here. I love you very much, but I'll go live with Rose. I've already asked them and they said it was all right. I didn't tell them why—I wouldn't tell them that—I—

RONNIE. What's wrong, Penny? You know you can't live with Rose, Penny; that's stupid.

PENNY. With her mother, I can live with her mother. She can take me. Ronnie, yesterday afternoon—with Doug—we were in the darkroom—we were just standing there and —like always, working—and he put his arm around me, and he started talking to me about—talking to me about how I liked to help him and about how good a foster father he'd been to me and what a good relationship we had, and he kissed my cheek. I didn't know what to do. I thought of once when I was about fourteen a man tried to put his hand in my lap in a movie once. I felt the same way, and he put his hand up under my shirt, on my stomach, and tried to turn me around and kiss my mouth—with his mustache on my cheek, and I—I just pulled away and got out—went out. *(Beat; then she catches her breath.)*

RONNIE. Well, don't cry; you're O.K., aren't you?

PENNY. I want to leave here.

RONNIE. Well, I don't blame you, honey— but you don't have to do that, Penny, my God. The sky didn't fall in, Henny Penny.

PENNY. What will he do? I can't look him in the face, Ronnie. I'm going to pack now because I don't want to sleep here. You can tell the authorities that I'm still here if you want to, and they won't know the difference; they never care anyway. I don't want to tell them why.

RONNIE. Oh, Penny, stop being so much. It's all too pathetic. I mean, damn. It's just stupid. *(To the audience)* I mean, Penny, for God's sake. Look at her. She hasn't a single quality anyone would go for unless you happen to really desire pure virginity in the abstract. I mean I know her qualities, but you couldn't expect Doug to see them.

PENNY. Ronnie, I don't want to leave.

RONNIE. I said you didn't have to—

PENNY. I hate Rose! She's fat and stupid and she talks too much and I hate her boyfriends—they *all* have beards and— *(Now she does cry, and quite loudly, openly.)*

RONNIE. All right, *do* cry if you want to. Go on. It's absurd. Don't be silly.

JACK *(entering,* CAROL *just behind).* What's wrong with Penny?

CAROL *(entering).* Come on, buster.

JACK. What's wrong?

CAROL. Where do you want me to start?

RONNIE. Jack, honey, go on outside.

CAROL *(exits with* JACK*).* Come on, loverboy . . .

PENNY. Why did he do that?

RONNIE. I don't know. You're not going to leave now, Penny. You don't have to see him if you don't want to. It's only six months, Penny; don't be silly.

PENNY. Why did you tell him? You knew what he'd say. You're very bright. Why the hell did you tell him, Ronnie?

RONNIE. Penny, I'd always known pretty much what to expect from Doug. I wasn't worried about him being brought up for rape charges by those girls he ogles over; sublimation is a wonderful thing. As long as it works. *(To the audience)* But to make a creepy pass at Penny! It hadn't entered my mind. What was he trying to prove? *(Back to* PENNY*)* And you wanted to crawl away, and do you think he wouldn't know why? Doug—if the heat gets too hot—will just pick up and leave, as you, Alan, well know. And I have two kids to think about. . . . I'm sorry, Alan; are you O.K.?

ALAN. It's O.K.

RONNIE. Now, I mean, I wonder.

ALAN. It's just as well, really.

DOUGLAS *(entering).* Well, we went up into the mountains this morning—you've never seen anything like it. Some of those—

RONNIE. If you aren't the most ridiculous, childish oaf I've ever seen!

DOUGLAS. Why's that?

RONNIE. Penny's in there hysterical; she tells me you made a dumb sloppy pass at her in the garage yesterday afternoon. If you aren't an ass—to begin with for thinking she wouldn't come immediately like a shocked virgin and tell me. Confess to me. *(*DOUGLAS *stands shocked and silent.)* I can't believe you did something like that. I hope you don't delude yourself into thinking she liked it. She wants to leave is what she's thinking; she wants to go live with Rose. I told her it was stupid. If you don't know better than to upset a girl like that! I swear to God, if it's true, you ought to be ashamed of yourself. I know I am for you if you're not. Or I would be, Doug, if it weren't all so laughable.

(Beat. Beat. DOUGLAS *continues to look at her. No one moves except* CAROL *and* ALAN*.)*

CAROL. Well, that ought to be it then.

ALAN. I'd think.

CAROL. He says No, right?

ALAN. As best I recall.

CURTAIN

ACT THREE

*(*ALAN *comes forward. The stage is rather dark at the beginning, growing slowly and steadily lighter.)*

RONNIE *(from the darkness, faintly).* Alan, honey, get up, Mount McGinty is on fire, the whole sky's—

ALAN. The greatest sight while I stayed in California was something that the Californians *do* fear. Their homes, many of them—and many of the nicer ones—range up into the brush and forests in the mountains. In the fall, when it's dry—even for here—bone dry, dead, fires light the sky. Mount McGinty and Otay in the distance burned. The sky was red. The mountains were ochre with dried grass and brush one day and that night streaked with red fire and the next morning black. Houses were destroyed, timber and game and the view.

Along about this time a poet—of local fame at school—who had left State a few years earlier, came back for a day or so. I have tried to remember what he wrote, but outside of a firm conviction that he was the most brilliant person I'd ever met, and wrote more perfectly than—oh, skip it. I can't remember a word, in any case, and that's odd. It was probably more lines about creepy ferns and creepy shadows for creepy creeps. I do know we spoke, that we walked up into the mountains that had burned, around a landscape that looked like the· moon. Charred mesquite and ashes six inches deep. The brush, some of it—the fire had gone through it so quickly, some of the brush stood—like ashes on a cigarette—stood three feet high—the white negative of the brush exactly intact, and you touched it and it disintegrated. And into the woods that were saved to commune with what was left of nature. And after three afternoons of walking I skipped two days of school to stay mostly in my room, and when I went back, the poet had left—he wasn't around. It is of pertinence only as a very ironic coincidence. Ronnie said about Mount Helix: "Just like I thought, there it is." Who knows what a person is made of? I promise not to tell you if you promise not to tell me. I left Nebraska to come to the promised land because I had to. I left because I had to. This is the state I'm in. California. So much is true here, so much is open; so much is honest and so much is impossible to admit. Even of what I know is there, what I realize is there. In this state.

CAROL. It's a good enough state to be in.

ALAN. "I would like to thank the theatre"? Poor bitch.

CAROL. Right. Where else am I? Nowhere.

ALAN. You're always here, in my state. With all those possibilities, if only—

CAROL. Yes, I know. "If only" is a good state.

ALAN (ironically). California.

CAROL. Not that it matters, when you look at it from this distance, but that week—the week of the fire—I got engaged to Sonny. We will say briefly that the marriage didn't come off and the following year, quite without me giving a damn, I became a highway statistic and about as violently as one would have expected. My date for that particular night got rather too drunk, and like the idiot he was, drove us off—it's funny—it was funny then—shot like a rocket off Inspiration Point.

ALAN. And landed in the valley below.

CAROL. Hours . . . actual hours later.

ALAN. And burst into flames.

CAROL (pause). If you say so.

ALAN. Ronnie wrote me—her second and last letter—some time back.

CAROL. There should be something enormous I should say—what an opportunity. I was very good that last year. No one knows. I know it doesn't seem like it. But I was so damn good. I'm not saying I'm sorry. Goddamn, I hate people who say they're sorry.

ALAN. Right.

CAROL. Once we were engaged we didn't get along—suffice it to say without ruining the story that something came up with which Sonny violently disagreed, and we told each other to fuck off.

ALAN. And your date for that particular evening, who drove you over the cliff—

CAROL. —was a clod; forget it. I was aware that we were nowhere—I mean nowhere about to make the corner ahead. Mountain road. And I stiffened, like I was looking for the brake on my side of the car, and not a word, not a scream. Saw it all; thought: My God, some car is going to come along and see the barrier torn up on this curve and be scared to death. Saw it all. In slow motion, if you please.

ALAN. And Sonny wasn't with you?

CAROL. How do you mean wasn't with me? (Rather bitter for just a second) Well, that shows what you know, doesn't it? No, Sonny was in downtown San Diego, right?

RONNIE. Right, or so he said.

CAROL. At the time. There. Sonny was somewhere in San Diego, or so he said, getting drunk and listening to records. At the time. (Beat) Which shows that he knows, doesn't it? You didn't know right away, did you?

ALAN. No, some time. Ronnie wrote me. A reply to a request for a loan of money.

CAROL. You don't tell me your dreams, Alan, and I won't tell you mine.

ALAN. Deal.

CAROL. Deal.

RONNIE. Doug is an excellent provider, Alan; you can't see it, I know, but he is. And I'm an excellent manager, all considered. And I have Jerry and Jack, and they are more important to me than anything in the world. (Proudly) The boys are quite grown, of course, and quite normal, and I'm very proud of them. You would be, too. Jerry bowls.

ALAN. Bowls? Really? Jerry twelve. Jerry fifteen. Jerry twenty-five. Jerry thirty. Thirty-five. Forty. (Nearly crying, but recovering) Jerry, Jerry. And hairy Jack. It's like a cartoon strip, and after one artist quits, another takes over and you can hardly tell the difference—yet something—Quite normal? I had hoped—eccentric somehow.

DOUGLAS. To each his own, I guess.

ALAN. Deal.

DOUGLAS. Not at all eccentric. Not at all. Just ordinary.

RONNIE. In an extraordinary sort of way.

ALAN. Deal.

RONNIE. You were so drunk that night. I thought you'd faint right on the floor.

PENNY. I . . . *(Everyone turns to her; a pause)*

DOUGLAS. Yeah?

PENNY. I don't care, one way or the other.

RONNIE. You always wanted to be a teacher.

PENNY. No civics, I don't think. I teach civics. I'm not good with them, really; you have to be more of a disciplinarian than anything.

ALAN. Married, right?

PENNY. Oh, yeah. Kids.

CAROL. No white coat?

PENNY. No rice, really, either.

DOUGLAS. So, all those deals, some of 'em get good cards, some of 'em—

CAROL *(cutting in)*. And some of them get a lousy hand and haven't the nerve to bluff or the sense to fold. Thanks, anyway, Alan. I appreciate it. You know you hardly entered my mind. I had quite a world going for me there.

ALAN. People are always entering people's minds at inopportune times. The least I could do—

CAROL *(singing gently)*. Walk right in, sit right down; Daddy, let your hair hang down. . . .

ALAN. What are you on?

CAROL. I don't even know.

PENNY *(to* RONNIE*)*. I liked Doug, really. I'd never had a father that I remembered.

RONNIE. I know, Penny.

PENNY. I didn't want to leave.

RONNIE. You didn't have to leave, Penny, my God. The sky didn't fall in, Henny Penny.

PENNY. What will he do? I can't look him in the face, Ronnie.

CAROL. God bless us, every one.

RONNIE. Yes, indeed, Carol.

ALAN. Deal. God bless us, every one. I must have drunk about . . . *(Drunk)* . . . about . . . about . . .

RONNIE. Come on.

ALAN. About a keg of stale beer. I'll bet I really did. You know, California beer tastes like slop.

RONNIE. Right, no good at all; you shouldn't drink it.

ALAN. Now you tell me.

RONNIE. Why don't you go off to bed and get some sleep now before you wake up the whole house. Even Carol's in bed already.

ALAN. You go on to bed. The bartender kept sitting beers in front of me, and he knew I wasn't of age. I should report him for selling beer to a minor. I don't think he even charged me for the last couple, though. Just as soon as I finished, there'd be another one there, like the Sermon on the Mount. Bread and fishes. He says, "We have a couple of girls," and I said, "No, thank you, I just want to get very stoned. I haven't been stoned since I left Nebraska"—I haven't, you know.

RONNIE. I know.

ALAN. And he said, "Don't get sick, it's gonna be a scorcher tomorrow." He was from Kansas. There's no such thing as a native Californian.

RONNIE. I thought you wanted me to go on, and now you're talking.

ALAN. Did I make any sense?

RONNIE. Very little sense.

ALAN. I was so dizzy I couldn't even see the room. And . . . go on. . . .

RONNIE. O.K.: "Go on to bed; it'll be a good day tomorrow."

ALAN. And tomorrow came and the Kansan was closer.

PENNY. You can tell the authorities that I'm still here if you want to. They never care anyway.

CAROL. They never gave a wild flying damn about any of us really. Who cares about anyone?

RONNIE. It's impossible to take seriously. Penny? It's an insult to me for one thing, which of course Penny couldn't know, but I'd expect you to see that. I swear to God, you ought to be ashamed of yourself; I know I am for you if you're not; or I would be if—

DOUGLAS *(cutting in)*. It's a goddamn—

RONNIE. Oh, come on, Doug, so you tried to sneak a quick—

DOUGLAS. That lying bitch—is what I'm saying. I might want her to feel at home. Can't I put my arm around her and give her a squeeze? Goddammit, she's never had a father! Her life—the bitch. Not another night under my house, that bitch, if she thinks she can accuse me of—Alan! I want to talk with you. Now this isn't something that I want passed around, and I don't think you'll—I don't want to see her face here again. No, by God, she can go to Rose, she can go to hell for all I care. She's not spending another night under my roof.

RONNIE. Doug, it doesn't matter—of course she can—

DOUGLAS. Like hell it doesn't matter. Doesn't matter! You try to show some affection for someone—I didn't touch the tight bitch; I didn't go near her. What's she trying to pull? And by God, if you believe it, you can go to hell too. I won't have it. I won't have it, by God.

PENNY. I didn't want to cause anything—why did you tell him—I'm leaving.

DOUGLAS. The whole goddamn bunch of them can clear out for all I care. They can get out now.

ALAN. Why did you tell him?

RONNIE. I didn't say you did; I said Penny said you did. I think it's funny; there's nothing to get upset about. Good God, Doug.

ALAN. Why did you tell him?

DOUGLAS. No, by God, I never touched her.

RONNIE. She says you kissed her on the cheek. She didn't say any more than that.

DOUGLAS. Well, what the hell's wrong with that, a father kissing a daughter? *If I had!* I'm supposed to be her father—she's never had a family—what the hell would be wrong with that? If I had! Which I didn't, by God.

RONNIE. It just isn't important.

DOUGLAS. Well, something is—Alan!

ALAN. What?

DOUGLAS (*very tense—more intense than shouting*). This is important—more than that girl—as far as I'm concerned.

ALAN. What's wrong? I've not missed work any if—

DOUGLAS. Just let me talk, if you will, please now.

RONNIE. Nothing is of such importance, Doug—

DOUGLAS (*overlapping*). I said, goddammit, I'm going to talk now. Doug is gonna talk for a change now—I might know something!

ALAN (*to the audience*). He—I don't know. If I had known then what he was thinking, perhaps—

DOUGLAS (*whirling him around, cutting in; overlapping*). LOOK AT ME WHEN I'M

TRYING TO—Now you've been avoiding, conniving, and lying the whole goddamn time. Now I'm going to talk.

RONNIE. Doug, it isn't necessary to—

DOUGLAS. All right now! Penny you stay, goddammit, right there: I'll deal with your lies. (*To* ALAN) Jerry tells me that you and Phil have been sitting out at the cliffs in his sparkling Pontiac. Last night and night before that and night before that.

ALAN. With Penny and Phil, yeah. I went in to work the following day; I don't know—

DOUGLAS. That doesn't interest me! It's your job, brother; you can get fired from it if you goddamn well like—I just want to know if it's true.

ALAN. What? Is what true? I don't know what you're getting at, Dad. I haven't any idea what—

DOUGLAS. You goddamned *bast*ard, stall for time. You know, don't you?

ALAN. Well, I don't see any point in—

DOUGLAS. Yes, you are, goddammit; it all fits—everything fits; suddenly it dawns. Suddenly it dawns. Yeah, and everyone—all your friends at State know it. Well, he has to have —I'm talking about Phil; you know goddamned well what I'm saying—he has to have someone to cover for him; he can't spend *all* his time with the sailors from the queer bars downtown. Everybody else is too wise to fool. Penny wouldn't ask questions; she has to take what she can get, and she deserves just what she takes. If she's the cover-up of some rich queer, she's too stupid to ask questions . . . I feel sorry for the lying bitch if she's that stupid. But you're not dumb. I thought you had some physical problem maybe; I should have been wise, man! It's sure easy for you—going out with Penny and him. What are you—holding hands behind her back?

ALAN. Lie! That's no—

DOUGLAS. Then what are you doing?

ALAN. What are you saying?

DOUGLAS. I'm saying you're through around this house. Not with my kids—not you're not going to make sissies out of my two boys, and you're not going to breathe in my house—not my air any more!

ALAN. That's a lie! How can you say that with Penny here? She knows better—and Jerry—

DOUGLAS. Penny knows goddamn well it's true. Look at her. Ask her if he's once tried to lay her or even thought about it. Hell, ask Carol; Carol knows it and Ronnie knows it and every other goddamned person in the county knows it, and you do, too. He's famous. Everybody's so goddamned afraid to hurt, disillusion, little Penny's feelings—so they let her live in a dream world. He must be laughing himself silly. Hell, he must spit on her. He knows a good thing when he sees it.

ALAN. Ask Carol . . . *(But* CAROL *is already shaking her head, better not ask me.)* Well, if it's *true,* what do you mean saying it? What do you mean by saying that?

DOUGLAS *(this intense, not loud).* Not in my house.

ALAN. He never touched me. I don't know why you can't leave my sex interests alone or to myself.

DOUGLAS. I intend to protect my own. I'm not having it. Now, I can't take this.

ALAN. What do you mean? What are you doing?

DOUGLAS. I'm telling you to go back to where you came from—we don't need you here. It's been disturbance since you came. Now, you take your little imitation leather suitcase in there and your record player and everything you've *touched* in this goddamned house, and pack them back up into a little—

ALAN. No! By God. Damn you! I'm going to say one thing! You're lying and I don't know why! But you are and you know you are! I'm no good at this—

DOUGLAS. Well, if you think I am—

ALAN. You see! That's all I know. What you are not! You're not! You're nothing! You think the best is none too good, and you don't have any idea at all about the best! You'll never see it! And all your lies prove!

DOUGLAS. Get out. That's all I want from you, mister, that's all. That's all. That's all—just go on. Out. That's all.

ALAN. *Mur-der-er!* (Sobbing) MURDERER! I had a sister and you killed her. Killed your own daughter trying to be a man—whoring—and if that's what you want me to be like and Jerry to be like and all of us, then I may have the satisfaction.

DOUGLAS *(slaps him sharply across the face).* That's a lie! That's a lie!

ALAN. NO! You killed her! As well as if you had beat her to death. . . . Jerry's sister and Jack's sister and my sister! You drove my mother insane with your whores, and you're so proud of it! And you've come out here with her. And you're never going to forget it!

DOUGLAS. That's a goddamn lie. She never.

ALAN. She was born a bloody dead mass!

Not even human! Thrown to the trash to burn, and you did it! You know it!

DOUGLAS *(injured; quietly).* How can—you have no idea—what that did to me. No idea. You'll never know as long as you live—you couldn't—you'll never—by God—have a kid to know what it's like. Now you get your things in there, and you get out of here—in half an hour. I don't care where you go. You just get out of my sight now!

(Penny has left just before ALAN'S *line "Murderer." She goes down the hall, walks to the door of the bedroom, takes* CAROL'S *orange robe under her arm, and heads toward the bathroom. At the door of the bathroom* CAROL *reaches her.* PENNY *tries to close the door, but* CAROL *blocks it. They struggle with the bottle of pills.* CAROL'S *line comes now.)*

CAROL. No, Penny!

PENNY. No, let me—stop—stop—stop!

CAROL *(at the same time).* . . . the hell do you think you're doing, goddammit—Give THEM TO ME!

*(*PENNY *screams.* CAROL *is still struggling with her. The pills fly from the bottle across the floor, scattering all around them. Some are in* PENNY'S *hand.* PENNY *and* CAROL *both go to their knees,* CAROL *trying to hold* PENNY'S *hands away from her mouth,* PENNY *trying to stuff pills into her mouth. Struggling.)* Stop it, Penny. Stopit. . . . Stopit. . . . Give them to me. What are you trying to do?

PENNY *(at the same time).* No, don't. Get away, Carol, get away. No, let me! Carol, don't.

RONNIE *(reaches them).* Penny—stop it—did she take any?

CAROL. I don't think so.

*(*JACK *enters.)*

PENNY. Please, please, let me!

*(*RONNIE *gets a strong hold on* PENNY; JACK *picks up several of the pills.)*

CAROL. Jack, stay away, go out! Don't touch those!

RONNIE. Jack, put those back—throw them down. Every one. Now! *(He does.)* What are they?

CAROL. I don't know.

RONNIE. What are they?

CAROL. Just never mind—it isn't important—they're aspirin.

RONNIE. *What are they, Carol?*

CAROL. I said, "Never mind"; it doesn't matter. Penny, baby, come on, honey—

RONNIE. I said, goddammit, you tell me what they are!

CAROL *(screaming).* They're Mellaril, Mellaril, dope! What the goddamn hell do you

LANFORD WILSON

think they are? And I don't give a shit what—

(RONNIE *slaps her across the face.* CAROL *immediately slaps her back.* DOUGLAS *arrives, slings* CAROL *halfway across the stage.)*

DOUGLAS. Take them! Take them! All! Take them—every goddamn one!

RONNIE. It's all right. Carol, take care of her.

CAROL. I'm sorry. Let her take care of herself.

PENNY. I'm O.K. *(She turns to go.)* Leave me alone. All of you. Just don't touch me! *(*RONNIE *reaches toward her.)* Don't touch me!

*(*RONNIE *turns;* ALAN *follows her.* DOUGLAS *begins to pick up the pills.)*

ALAN. Ronnie. Ronnie—

RONNIE *(interrupting).* I didn't know you had had a sister who had been born dead, Alan. I'm very sorry. I don't know what to say.

ALAN. All—I shouldn't have said anything. I have—I don't know what to do, Ron; he's—nothing he said is true—I can't leave you and Jack and—what am I supposed to do? What am I—

RONNIE. I think you'd better go. *(She walks away, toward her room.)*

DOUGLAS *(finishing picking up the pills; going to her as she leaves* ALAN*).* Ron—Ronnie.

RONNIE. Doug, I don't want to talk to you. I want to lie down. Where's Jerry?

DOUGLAS. He's outside.

RONNIE. I just want to lie down.

DOUGLAS. Ron—Ronnie, baby—what could I do?

RONNIE. Nothing, Doug, It's all right.

DOUGLAS. Everything's going to be all right.

JACK *(going to* ALAN*).* Do you have to go?

ALAN. Yeah, I will.

DOUGLAS. Really. Forget it. It'll all be over. We're better off, Ronnie.

RONNIE. I'm sure, Doug. I don't want to think about it.

DOUGLAS *(turning, looking to him).* Alan? Alan, I want you to know—all those years . . .

ALAN. I know, Dad.

*(*DOUGLAS *and* ALAN *are very far apart;* JACK *beside* ALAN*,* Douglas *by* RONNIE*,* JERRY *alone outside;* PENNY *and* CAROL *together near their room)*

PENNY. Oh, God, Carol.

CAROL. It's all right, baby. Nothing matters.

ALAN. It's O.K., baby.

JACK. Really, don't.

(It begins to grow dark again.)

ALAN. Baby, it's good to remember that someone said that. . . .

DOUGLAS *(calling as though across time).* All those years. I wanted to help. What was I supposed to do? Alan?

(It continues to grow dark.)

JACK. Please. Take me with you, then.

ALAN. Baby, I will. Really, don't worry. You're eight years old and a little white orangutan.

JACK. Really, though, let me go with you, Alan. Can I?

ALAN. You will, Jack; I promise.

(Only the faintest light remains on ALAN *and* JACK*.* JACK *turns to go in, leaving* ALAN *alone in the spot.)*

DOUGLAS. Hugged me, by God. By God, you can't—

PENNY. Pleased to meet you; I've heard a lot about you.

DOUGLAS. —no matter what anybody anywhere says—you can't separate a kid from his father.

JERRY. Alan? Are you awake?

PENNY. Good night.

JERRY. Good morning.

(Their voices tumble over each other.)

CAROL. Thanks, anyway, Alan; I had quite a little world going for me. Walk right in, sit right down—

(Continue to end)

JERRY *(cued by* CAROL*'s "Alan").* We had orange trees and plum trees and a fig tree.

RONNIE *(cued by "orange trees").* If you have faith the size of a mustard seed, you can move mountains.

(On "faith," ALAN *laughs to himself.)*

DOUGLAS *(cued by "size").* I know she must have told you things about me.

PENNY *(cued by "told").* I'll probably teach; I like kids.

RONNIE *(cued by "teach").* Welcome, Alan, welcome. Hello.

ALAN *(crying out).* LIGHTS!

(The stage lights bounce up bright and full. Everyone is still. ALAN *turns and walks out. They follow, urgently whispering.* DOUGLAS*'s is the only voice we hear clearly.)*

DOUGLAS *(urgently).* I just want you to understand, Alan.

Alan.

Alan.

Alan.

(The stage has returned to darkness before ALAN *can escape them.)*

CURTAIN

SUBJECT TO FITS

Robert Montgomery

For DR. THOMAS HAAS and A. J. ANTOON

First presented by the New York Shakespeare Festival at the Public Theater in New York City on February 14, 1971, with the following cast:

PRINCE MYSHKIN   Andy Robinson
PARYFON ROGOZHIN   Jason Miller
LABEDEV   John Mahon
MADAME YEPANCHIN   Jean David
AGLAYA YEPANCHIN   Katherine Dunfee

GANYA IVOGLIN   James DeMarse
GENERAL IVOGLIN   Albert Quinton
IPPOLIT IVOGLIN   Jim Borrelli
NATASHA FILLIPOVNA   Sharon Laughlin

Directed by A. J. Antoon
Settings by Leo Yoshimura
Costumes by Theoni V. Aldredge
Lighting by Ian Calderon

One of the phenomena of the American theatre in the seventh decade of the twentieth century has undoubtedly been Joseph Papp—producer extraordinary, entrepreneur outrageous. Mr. Papp has established a breeding ground for young American playwrights at his Lafayette Street theatre complex where the old Astor Library used to be. There has never been anything quite like it before. Mr. Papp has a haven for playwrights, some good, some bad, but even the bad ones are interesting. His reputation is such that he gets the first offer of the best of American plays—without question.

He has encouraged some remarkable writers, including David Rabe, whose play *Sticks and Bones* is included in this anthology. Another Joe Papp protégé has been Robert Montgomery, who jumped pell-mell into public attention with his play *Subject to Fits,* which was given by Mr. Papp's New York Shakespeare Festival at the Other Stage on February 14, 1971. It was a mad, mad play that was a joy to encounter. A cerebral play of dazzling intellectuality, manic wit, and a calm literacy.

Mr. Montgomery was born in Cincinnati on December 2, 1946. He was the fifth son in a family of six boys—whatever that means psychologically. At first he was totally oriented toward sports. His father, William Montgomery, who was an engineer with Bell Telephone, encouraged all his six sons to participate in competitive sports, although he also taught them piano, guitar, and French horn. Montgomery excelled in both basketball and football, and at high school he was urged to become a professional.

Mr. Montgomery went to Dartmouth—he got his BA in 1968—and he was recruited to play football. He never did play football for Dartmouth, but he did put in a freshman year at basketball before he was diverted to the theatre. On graduation he got married and moved to Yale for a Master of Fine Arts in playwriting. It was at Yale that he began *Subject to Fits.*

The idea for *Subject to Fits* was not Montgomery's. When he was first at Yale he started writing plays—to use his own words, "seven pretty lousy plays to be exact." And then one of his instructors at Yale, Tom Haas, wanted to do some scene work based upon Dostoevski's *The Idiot.* Montgomery agreed to do the work for the project, but did not want merely to adapt the play. He read the novel some six times, and from those readings, with all the sensibilities that were suggested, emerged this play. In a note in the first-night program Mr. Montgomery explained his approach. He was not adapting the novel, he was "responding" to it. I cannot explain his approach better than he did himself, when he wrote: "It is entirely original—smacking of *The Idiot,* dreaming of *The Idiot,* but mostly taking off from where *The Idiot* drove it." The result was something absolutely thrilling—a soul trip, an adventure of the heart and mind.

These are variations on an original theme, a play that wants to play with your mind, a play that is commenting not only on life—which, of course, it is, but also most originally commenting on a literary masterpiece. For this is a view of madness, a shrewd and honest view of the outsider in society, but also, and not I think least, a view of the original artist, Dostoevski. The Dostoevski characters are here—sometimes sea-changed, sometimes not. Here is Myshkin, the perfect innocent, epileptic and pure, inheriting hero of a thousand Russian folktales placed absurdly in an urban society. A fantastic figure—a heroic misfit.

In this play Mr. Montgomery is toying with a literary masterpiece, explaining it, criticizing it, and, in a strange way, demonstrating its relevance. The director A. J. Antoon suggested it to Mr. Papp after it had been seen at a Yale Workshop. Mr. Papp jumped at it, and it was subsequently staged by the Royal Shakespeare Company in London.

Since *Subject to Fits,* Mr. Montgomery has a new musical for the New York Shakespeare Festival. Called *Lotta* it was staged on November 22, 1973, and did not enjoy much success. In May of 1974, however, Mr. Montgomery collaborated with Joseph Chaikin of the Open Theater in an investigation of *Electra,* paying attention to Sophocles, Aeschylus, and Euripides, which aroused considerable interest. But even if Mr. Montgomery were to give us nothing but *Subject to Fits,* this would remain as an absolutely fascinating exploration into a literary landscape.

AUTHOR'S NOTE

Subject to Fits is neither adaptation, dramatization, nor translation of Dostoevski's inimitable novel *The Idiot.* The greatness of Dostoevski's masterpiece is inseparable from its novelistic form, and any attempt to transpose it literally into another art form could not help but undermine its wholeness and alienate its power. *Subject to Fits* is a response to *The Idiot:* it is absolutely unfaithful to the novel; it uses the novel for its own selfish purposes; it does not hold the novel responsible. As such, it is entirely original—smacking of *The Idiot,* dreaming of *The Idiot,* but mostly, taking off from where *The Idiot* drove it.

The following should be passed out to the audience before the show, or included in the program:

Dear patient Prince,

As your analyst, I am very interested in the type of person you represent. As life uses us for its own ungodly purposes, it helps us pass the time by offering itself to our penetrating yet perfectly unthreatening analyses. How have you been? Don't you think?

My diagnosis of your present disintegration is as follows: For the past five months you haven't let go of a single thought—you've become an obsessive cranial retentive. You've hoarded every idea and experience you've chanced upon, assuming you could, in time, deal with each one exhaustively and conclusively—but time told on you, Prince. (Recent scientific experiments have found that it takes approximately 337 years to thoroughly investigate every thought that befalls the average human brain in just one hour. Five months, Prince—that would require over one million thirteen thousand years of thought! Not to mention the thoughts which would accumulate in the meantime! Makes you think, eh?)

We have this neurosis, Prince, of trying to understand everything about everybody. We come to St. Petersburg, our experiential slate clean as a baby's. In one mad day we are injected with the democratic ideas of Natasha Fillipovna; we fall in love with Aglaya; we meet a group of insane characters straight out of the contemporary Russian novel, all of whom bombard us with ideas and experiences which are in no way connected to one another; add to this epilepsy, and the large sunspots that appeared that day for the first time since the Aquarian comet—and you gather all this in, *indiscriminately,* and decide to base the rest of your life rearranging that one day into perfect harmony! You see how it fits, Prince, you see how everything fits? And now you want to dedicate yourself to Natasha because she has seen "great suffering"? What about *me*??!

Go ahead—marry her! Love her small pittance of suffering while the world is ending in agony around you! But just don't forget, I know what's wrong, I can always explain everything.

Meaningfully,

DR. RADOMSKY
Analyst

ACT ONE

Overture: Eagle's scream which turns into a fly. The music comes from an organ, a cello, and an electric bass.

Lights up on Prince Myshkin, seated cross-legged. He is simple, but worried. He spies a donkey and suddenly shows life. He imitates the donkey.

MYSHKIN. Heehaw! (*He laughs.*)

(*Blackout. Music: "Fitting," turning into a train. Myshkin is laughing, Rogozhin and Lebedev are seated next to him. Rogozhin barks at Myshkin. Myshkin stops and they look at each other; they laugh together.*)

———

ROGOZHIN. Excuse me—for some reason I've taken a strong liking to you. Forgive me —I'm somewhat delirious from a fever. I keep hearing dogs in my head.

MYSHKIN. I forgive you for liking me, and assure you, the kinship I feel with you already is deeper than the blood in your eyes, and stronger than the murder on your face. Prince Lyov Myshkin, your servant, sir.

LEBEDEV. A prince! Have you a ring to kiss, Prince?

MYSHKIN. I'm sorry, I have neither money, parents, nor baggage. I am a simple person whose only purpose is to go to St. Petersburg and get to know as many human beings as possible. I have just undergone treatment in the desert for epilepsy and—

LEBEDEV. Ohhhhhh! (*Pointing to his head*) Prince *Twitch*! Perhaps you've shaken some brains out through your ears, eh— *Prince*! Why your title alone must be worth its weight in farts! Haw-haw—

MYSHKIN (*laughing with him*). You're really remarkable—but I suppose you know far better than I how extraordinarily repulsive you are—here, there's something coming out of your nose . . .

LEDEDEV. Get away from me, you idiot!! (*Train whistle. Rogozhin shoves Lebedev.*)

ROGOZHIN. Call me Rogozhin, Prince.

LEBEDEV. *Paryfon* Rogozhin? Pray let Lebedev grovel at your wealthy feet.

ROGOZHIN (*kicking him away*). You can dance on your head in manure if you want!

LEBEDEV (*dancing*). I will! Don't give me a kopeck! I'm leaving my wife and five children just to dance on manure for you!

MYSHKIN. He's sincere!

ROGOZHIN. Hang him! When sincerity comes to that, I'll kill my best friend.

MYSHKIN. And love your enemy?

ROGOZHIN (*shivering spastically*). God-damnit, I'd better not be dying!

(*Train whistle. Blackout, sound of Aglaya giggling.*)

MME YEPANCHIN (*in darkness*). You're the one who has fits, aren't you?

(*Lights up. Myshkin visiting the Yepanchin household.*)

And you claim to be the last of the Prince Myshkins since my brother died? And you have fits.

AGLAYA. Maman, have him tell us a story!

MYSHKIN. Your face, Mme Yepanchin, tells me you are a perfect child.

MME YEPANCHIN. See how well he pronounces his words! You fascinate me, Prince —are you quiet about it or do your arms shake around?

AGLAYA. Tell us a story about the desert, Prince, or leave this house immediately.

MYSHKIN. I had just recovered from epilepsy and everthing seemed alien and hostile. I was afraid I'd be arrested if I stood on any one patch of sand too long. The fact that the sun was warm . . . worried me. And every time night came, I felt it was my fault. Then one morning I heard the braying of a donkey in a marketplace, and suddenly everything was familiar. I was sure I had seen the world before, and with a great happiness, I realized I wasn't responsible for anything.

AGLAYA (*giggling highly*). A donkey! A donkey!!

MME YEPANCHIN. Aglaya! Now what is so absurd! Many women fell in love with animals in mythology.

(*Myshkin begins laughing with Aglaya.*)

MYSHKIN. It's nice, the way I laugh sometimes, don't you think? (*To Mme Yepanchin*) And you want me to know you're very fond of Aglaya even though she's frivolous and just like you! (*Aglaya stops laughing; Myshkin and Mme Yepanchin laugh now.*) I understand you totally!

MME YEPANCHIN (*through her laughter*). I am a good person! You and I, Prince—we're the exact same child! Poor Aglaya! (*Kisses Aglaya*)

AGLAYA. Prince, teach us how to be happy.

MYSHKIN (*looking at her really for the first time, falling in love*). Pretty.

AGLAYA. Do you think you live better than anyone else?

MYSHKIN. Yes.

AGLAYA. Anyone like you should be happy forever! You'll lie in your grave thinking how lovely it is to have such nice bones for neighbors! Show you an execution or a deck of cards and you'll draw sublime conclusions from both.

MYSHKIN. I have seen an execution. The guillotine. The blade—the man heard it scraping down on his head. I saw him. As his head was falling off, it suddenly realized—it was falling off. I couldn't tell—no matter how hard I tried, I couldn't tell what that chopped head was thinking in the six seconds it remained alive, before it stopped its careful rocking and grew still.

(*Mme Yepanchin squeals; Aglaya smiles.*)

AGLAYA. You haven't told me what you think of *my* face, Prince.

(*Blackout. Knocking. Ganya enters with a lit candle.*)

MYSHKIN. Are you Ganya, Mme Yepanchin's manservant?

GANYA. Yes I am, you drooling mongoloid —what do you want?

MYSHKIN. Aglaya told me you had a room to let.

GANYA. You talked to Aglaya? She's some treasure, eh? (*Pulls out a picture of Natasha Fillipovna*) But she's worth nothing compared to this one—look at her! Her breasts alone are worth several factories!

MYSHKIN. She's seen an execution.

GANYA. A real piece of eight, if you know what I mean.

MYSHKIN. I am not a man of the world, sir.

GANYA. You're an idiot, that's what you are—gravy-brains!

MYSHKIN. Sir, you are more unlike a child than any man I have ever met. I am no more deranged than you are happy. I learn nothing new about myself from your insults. (*Turns to leave*)

GANYA. Don't go! I detest my mediocrity! Here is your room. Please, accept these kopecks as a token of my character. My drunken father will be up presently, and my disgusting little brother who is consumptive.

(*Ganya exits. Enter General Ivoglin and Ippolit.*)

GEN. IVOGLIN. What is this sight that turns these petrified eyes of mine into pudding! Could it be—yes! Yes—Prince Vitchnickskyvitchsoy MUSHKIN!! It's General Ivoglin!! (*They embrace.*) I used to hold you in my arms when you were but a wee worm of a babe! Your father and I used to save each other's lives in the wars. I would have killed him in a duel for the fair hand of your

mother, but we both missed intentionally and ended up in each other's arms, leaving your mother crying by herself in the wind as we frolicked off to the nearest vodka house!

IPPOLIT. Two months to live. Two cramped months of thin pink blood and golden fat servings of phlegm!

GEN. IVOGLIN. This is Ippolit, my son! I used to hold him in my arms when he was but a wee worm of a babe.

IPPOLIT. Should I learn a trade? Carpentry, of course! I should have time to build a toothpick. I vow, Prince, if I don't figure out, before I die, why I should be living—I shall commit suicide!

MYSHKIN. In China I was told the story of a man who contracted tuberculosis at the age of fifteen, and was told he had but eight months to live. He quit school, deserted all his friends, and began soul-searching for a reason to continue living. When the eight months were up, he was told he had but four days to live. He spent the four days contemplating suicide. On the fourth day he was told he had but eight months to live. When he was forty years old, he was told he had but four weeks to live. When he was sixty years old, he was told he had but ten years to live. Still he refused to learn or converse, so intent was he on his purpose in life. At the age of seventy, after being told he had but eight months to live, he suddenly felt as if a huge blade were hanging over his head. At seventy-two, he put a pistol to his head, held it there, thought for a while, held it there for eight hours, had a heart attack, and died. He wasn't even aware of the change.

GEN. IVOGLIN. Marvelous! Bravo! Your father and I used to tell that story to each other for hours on end! Never tire of it! Ah, Prince —Prince?! One day you shall be *King*! (*He extends his palm; Ippolit is coughing.*)

MYSHKIN. Please, General—take these kopecks and buy some white wine—for Ippolit's coughing and your own nerves.

GEN. IVOGLIN. My blessings, son—I already love you more than I loved Napoleon!

(*Ivoglin and Ippolit exit. Knocking. Music: Natasha Fillipovna theme. More insistent knocking by Natasha Fillipovna. Myshkin opens the door. He is crushed by Natasha's beauty. Natasha and Myshkin stare at each other. She flings her coat at him.*)

NATASHA. Do you realize how long I've been waiting? Some servants should be tortured! With knives! (*Myshkin drops her coat.*)

Now he's dropped my coat! Good God, you fool—if I had your hands I'd eat with my feet! Now go along and announce me. What are you carrying my coat for? (*Myshkin drags the coat back. Natasha laughs. Myshkin does too. He drops the coat.*) Ha-ha—he's dropped it again! You aren't an epileptic idiot by any chance, are you? Ha-ha-ha! (*Myshkin again laughs with her. She stamps her foot.*) What are you laughing at? Announce me! (*Myshkin goes off.*) Wait, idiot—how can you announce me if you don't know my name?

MYSHKIN. Natasha Fillipovna!

(*They stare. Natasha freezes gracefully.*)

MYSHKIN (*striding into the Ivoglins*). NATASHA FILLIPOVNA!!

(*Reenter the train scene*)

ROGOZHIN. Natasha Fillipovna is her name!

(*Reenter the Yepanchin scene*)

AGLAYA. You haven't told me what you think of my face, Prince.

ROGOZHIN. She is as beautiful as this knife —I would kill anyone who thought of her the same way I do!

(*Myshkin is bouncing and being bounced in and out of all these scenes.*)

MYSHKIN (*looking at Aglaya*). Aglaya's face is superlatively pretty—she is almost as beautiful as Natasha Fillipovna.

(*Reenter Ganya scene*)

GANYA (*showing Myshkin the portrait of Natasha Fillipovna*). This is a woman named—

MYSHKIN *and the* YEPANCHINS. NATASHA FILLIPOVNA!??

GANYA (*to Myshkin*). How did you know her name?

MYSHKIN (*to Mme Yepanchin*). Ganya showed me her portrait earlier.

AGLAYA. Our gardener's been having an affair with that woman!

LEBEDEV (*to Rogozhin and Myshkin*). In the last three months she's been seen dancing with fourteen noblemen, twelve ambassadors, six blond peasant youths, and two blacksmiths!

MYSHKIN (*to Ganya*). A man on the train called Rogozhin described her to me.

ROGOZHIN. I met her once at the opera— or was it a dance hall? No matter—my father found out and died. When she spoke to me, her breath *came* all over my face.

MYSHKIN (*to Ganya*). So I recognized her immediately.

ROGOZHIN. Since then I have not been in a room that was not filled with steam.

NATASHA. How can you announce me if you don't know my name?

(*Reenter Ivoglin scene.* [*The director should determine entrances and exits here, depending on the amount of clutter or non-clutter he wants, can afford, or can stand. The pace of the lines should be murderous, however.*])

GEN. IVOGLIN. General Mushkin—do you know anything of this Natasha Fillipopnop? Ganya has forbidden us to utter her name in this house.

MYSHKIN (*to Ganya*). I told Aglaya she was almost as beautiful as Natasha Fillipovna, so her mother wants to see that portrait.

GANYA. Did you tell them my doodle was poking about Natasha Fillipovna's soft plump purse—did you tell them that?

(*Myshkin has given the portrait to Mme Yepanchin. Aglaya looks too.*)

MME YEPANCHIN. She is somewhat fetching, Prince, but I have seen prettier things on heretical crucifixes.

GANYA (*to family and Myshkin*). She promised to declare at her birthday party tonight whether she will marry me or no. That's all—we won't speak of it any further.

NATASHA. Announce me.

AGLAYA. Almost as beautiful, indeed— China crockery.

MME YEPANCHIN. Prince, call Ganya in— either there's a bad smell of marriage in the air, or the cook burnt the cabbage again.

MYSHKIN (*to Ganya, pointing*). . . . something about Natasha Fillipovna . . .

IPPOLIT (*to Ganya*). I refuse to fritter away my dying days receiving into my family any woman with the bilious capacity to stomach such an impacted bowel as you.

MME YEPANCHIN (*to Ganya, who has been "called in"*). Whom do you plan to marry, young man? It couldn't be Aglaya— (*To Aglaya*) You couldn't possibly cram a honeymoon in this week, could you, child?

GANYA. Who? M-me? M-marry? Who? (*Mme Yepanchin shoves the picture in his face.*) Ohhh! Ha-ha! Why here's the picture I found in the gutter outside the Bolstoy House! Ha-ha! I assure you, madame, I earn a surprising salary and, er, consistently laugh at the same jokes as the highest paid officials. I must impress you, madame, that I'm too much a respectable up-and-coming young man to afford marrying a woman so bankrupt in character as this Natasha uh—Natasha . . . Fillerpurseup. (*Turning angrily to Ippo-*

lit, in another scene) Wouldn't you like a coffin when you die? Wouldn't you like a priest to sprinkle some nice pretty hardworking prayers over your sweet-smelling corpse? So how the hell do you think we're going to afford your funeral unless I marry Natasha Fillipovna and her thirty-five thousand rubles? You ought to be thankful you're still alive, yet . . . I thought I heard you die last night in the hallway. (*He imitates coughing. To Myshkin, privately*) What about this Rogozhin?

(*Rogozhin, during the above, has appeared and begun drawing his knife flirtatiously across Natasha's throat.*)

MYSHKIN. He has recently become very feverish and quite wealthy. He would marry Natasha Fillipovna tomorrow and cut her throat next week.

NATASHA (*with Rogozhin at her throat*). Announce me, idiot!

IVOGLIN (*to Ganya*). I demand you tell your father who this Fillernippup is that she considers her unrefined milk the proper food for my grandson.

LEBEDEV (*exiting*). St. Petersburg! All out for St. Petersburg and the hot breath of—

MYSHKIN (*announcing*). Natasha Fillipovna!

ROGOZHIN (*still at Natasha*). How about it, Prince—should I see if Natasha has a friend for you?

MYSHKIN. Oh no—no thank you—on account of my illness, I have never known woman.

(*Rogozhin laughs and exits.*)

MME YEPANCHIN. Goodbye, dear Prince—you and I, we're the exact same child. God sent you to St. Petersburg just for me. It was one of the nicest things he's ever done. (*She exits, with Aglaya.*)

GEN. IVOGLIN (*screaming at Ganya, who is protesting loudly, "No!" etc.*). By right of the Fourth Commandment, I hereby speak the unspeakable name: Natasha Fillerupnip!! (*Ippolit and General Ivoglin scream the name at him; Ganya is furious.*)

MYSHKIN (*entering; announcing at last for real*). NATASHA FILLIPOVNA!!

GANYA. Who?

(*Natasha enters the Ivoglin household. There is a stunned silence.*)

NATASHA. Hello, my fond little Ganya. Did you get my portrait—isn't it dreadful? I had a cold that day. (*Gives Ippolit and General Ivoglin a once-over.*) So this is the family

you'd rather not discuss. (*Gives Myshkin a tip, which he ignores.*) You may go now.

MYSHKIN (*to the stunned Ganya*). Let me get you a glass of water.

GANYA (*snapping to*). . . . What? Ha! And now, you're a doctor, eh, Prince? Why is everyone acting so confused? (*To Natasha*) This is our lodger, Prince Myshkin—he won't hurt you. Prince Myshkin, this is . . . uh—ha-ha . . . of course, it's . . . *"Jamais vu."*

MYSHKIN (*again whispering*). Natasha Fillipovna . . .

GANYA. I KNOW, YOU FOOL!! (*To Natasha*) Excuse me, he's a bit—a bit—uhhh—

NATASHA: A *prince*? (*They look at each other.*) You've seen an execution, haven't you? Do you remember why you had to keep your eyes open? Are you aware that your eyes are not shut?

MYSHKIN. I have the strange feeling I have never met you anywhere before in my entire life.

NATASHA (*after a slight pause*). My uncles never tickled me in the wrong places. My younger sisters often left long letters for me under my pillow. Sometimes my older brothers were rude to me. My father and mother told jokes to each other in the middle of their arguments. If I asked them about gladiators, they gave me picture books about Rome. When I grabbed for pineapple, they gave me lettuce. When I first menstruated, my mother and I were grinning the whole day. Whenever I laughed for no reason at all, my father would not make me explain. I have loved pineapple ever since.

MYSHKIN. You must not blame your family. They only did what they thought was best for you. Happiness bores you. (*Asking her*) Yawn. (*She does.*) Do you like me?

NATASHA (*laughing; breaking away*). And do we want to play bouncy-ball, little poo-poo face? Do you want to show me what yours looks like if I show you mine? Do we want to read each other's minds for the rest of our lives while all around us babies are being born without legs and beautiful old people are falling in love? I'm not half as interesting as everything else, Prince.

GEN. IVOGLIN. If I may say so myself, just last Sunday a vicious hyena escaped from the zoo. Rising to the occasion, I ripped the full-length dress off a nearby lady, made a sack of it, and so captured the inhuman creature!

NATASHA (*taking his arm*). That's very interesting.

GEN. IVOGLIN. Ganya, my son, gives me great pleasure; I have known him since he was a schoolboy.

NATASHA. But more interesting is the story in last Sunday's *Daily Independence* about an anonymous capture of an escaped hyena. And more interesting still is the man found recently who admits to the vulgar heroic.

GEN. IVOGLIN. Well . . . let the poor imposter have his accolades.

NATASHA. And the most interesting thing of all is his eye, which the hyena had clawed out, and his head, which is now up to its ears in pus! (*She starts laughing; General Ivoglin retreats.*)

IPPOLIT. Prince! . . . (*He sputters for words.*) . . . Hit her!

(*Ganya tries to shove Ippolit out.*)

(*Rogozhin theme. Dramatic entrance: Rogozhin.*)

ROGOZHIN You weren't expecting Paryfon Rogozhin, perhaps!

(*Dramatic entrance: Lebedev.*)

LEBEDEV. You weren't expecting Paryfon Rogozhin and Lebedev, perhaps!

(*Dramatic announcement: Natasha.*)

NATASHA. You weren't expecting Natasha Fillipovna, perhaps!

ROGOZHIN. Prince—I wasn't expecting you!

GANYA. Isn't this my house?

ROGOZHIN (*pulling a knife on Ganya, who retreats to Natasha*). Are you marrying him?

NATASHA. I shall announce everything at my birthday party tonight! Perhaps I might even marry the Prince!

GEN. IVOGLIN. Of course, Nostalgia Fillerpopnip, I believe I knew your aunt: long ago we used to picnic and watch you cavort on the grass, innocently naked . . . ahhh—how the times change . . .

GANYA (*seeing Natasha's rising irritation*). Father!! (*Pulling him away; to Natasha*) You must excuse him, he's a bit, a bit—(*Ippolit begins coughing violently.*) Good God, Ippolit! Can't you do that somewhere else—

IPPOLIT. I shall step off this floor only when she scrubs it!! (*He coughs generously in Natasha's face.*)

NATASHA (*examining what she's wiped off her face*). A fine family, Ganya—and I came here to invite them to my party.

GANYA (*to Ippolit*). You're ruining me!! (*He goes to strike Ippolit, is stopped by Myshkin.*) You again!

(*Ganya slaps Myshkin, who stares at him.*)

MYSHKIN: That's all right for me, but not Ippolit. He's thinking of writing something. (*He breaks away to a corner.*) Oh, how ashamed you'll be. (*He cries.*)

(*Natasha goes hesitatingly to him.*)

NATASHA. Prince—

MYSHKIN. And you—you know you're not really what you seem to be.

(*Rogozhin grabs Ganya.*)

ROGOZHIN. Natasha!

(*She looks.*)

ROGOZHIN (*to Ganya*). Slap me. (*Ganya does; Rogozhin turns his other cheek.*) Harder. Harder than you slapped him. (*Ganya does.*) Oh, how ashamed you'll be! (*Lebedev giggles. Ganya goes to an opposite corner, whimpering.*) (*To Natasha*) And you —you know you're not really what you seem to be!! (*He starts laughing loudly.*)

NATASHA. Very good, Rogozhin—stalemate!

ROGOZHIN (*to Myshkin*). Beware the good deed, Prince. Christianity has a way of worming into a woman's heart.

NATASHA. I'll decide whom to marry tonight! Rogozhin—perhaps a hundred thousand rubles would help me make up my mind.

LEBEDEV. A hundred thousand rubles!

ROGOZHIN (*fingering the cross around Myshkin's neck*). Perhaps we'll meet again someday, Prince. (*To Natasha*) One hundred thousand rubles? One hundred thousand rubles . . . (*Snaps fingers at Lebedev*) Come, my pet!

LEBEDEV. "Come, my pet." Stick his head in your money pocket and pet obeys! Rowf, rowf! Good God. Good dog. (*He exits with Rogozhin.*)

NATASHA. You must *all* come to my party tonight.

MYSHKIN (*alone*). When someone insults a Japanese, the Japanese goes up to him, takes out his knife—one of those curved things— and screams: "You have insulted me!"— whereupon he cuts his very own stomach out right before the insulter's eyes. I think it's Japanese—Japanese or Chinese. (*He exits.*)

(*Music: "The Russian Grub Jig." Party. All men but Rogozhin present. Natasha dancing.*)

NATASHA (*in time with the dance*). 2-4-6-8 —men-men-men-men—all touch-and-go.

(*With Ganya.*)

    Hands up my dress?
    Groping for kopecks?

(*Puts Ganya's hands up her dress.*)

    Ganya, poor Ganya, alas I confess,

there's nothing up there but my ass and some sex!

(*Slaps Ganya's hands away, laughing. Prince Myshkin enters.*) Well, well, well! Welcome, Prince! I hear you have an absolutely sensible doctor! Could you ask him for me if he reads pamphlets when he makes love, or does he make witty remarks like "Oh, my word, there go those deceptive little hormones again!"

MYSHKIN. Hello, Natasha Fillipovna.

NATASHA. Did life ever strike you as being deceptively good?

MYSHKIN. I find life perfectly normal. I've never had anything to compare it to.

NATASHA (*laughing*). Then I must convert you, Prince! Say your prayers, and I'll show you the best of evil around! Game time!! Truth game—everyone must tell the worst thing he's ever done in his life! You'll be on your honor not to lie, Lebedev! (*She determines who is to speak and for how long.*)

LEBEDEV. You're going to think I'm terrible—you'll say I'm awful—but I was young and foolish at the time and hadn't eaten in three days, so I went to the schoolyard, grabbed three small girls, took them home, raped them, slit their throats, cut them up, browned them, ate them, and threw their bones to the neighbors.

IPPOLIT. That's revolting!

GANYA. That's awful!

NATASHA. I'm sorry, Lebedev, you did nothing of the kind. I read that story in the newspaper this morning. Any more cheating, and you're out of the game. (*Points to Ganya*)

GANYA. You mean besides masturbation and things like that?

LEBEDEV. I screwed a pig once—but that doesn't count.

IPPOLIT. The worst thing I ever did happened to me when I was five years old. I was bending over to pick up this toy and I felt the first tuberculosis germ taking its first bite into a cell in my lungs.

LEBEDEV. Suckling cows, licking tongues with lambs, sucking off swans—

GANYA. I remember the day well. The sun was out and there was sunlight. I was on a park bench that was painted some color. There was a tree or two—growing, I imagine. There I was—awake. My mind was working as it does when suddenly I realized that one of the most brilliant thoughts in the history of the human head, a thought guaranteed to

yield me unimaginable riches—this thought had just run through my consciousness without me even knowing it. Something about mediocrity, I think.

LEBEDEV. Pounding nails into ears, sticking scorpions up your ass, and laughing at old ladies—

NATASHA. Those things don't shock us anymore, Lebedev.

IVOGLIN. Ganya was thirteen, Ippolit was playing under the rug like he always did. My wife had just stabbed me in the shoulder with a meat knife. I had a terrible headache. The weather outside was awful. We were having potato soup and tongue again for dinner. I was in a bad mood.

LEBEDEV. Sitting on babies' faces, sticking ear wax in your neighbor's beer, and pulling down your pants in front of grandma!

GANYA. There I was, making headway in recalling this thought, when a beggar began grabbing my attention. "Make your own living!" I yelled at him, and he . . . he . . . So I tried to get back to my thought, but all I could think of was: What if the beggar was really a rich man in disguise, waiting for someone to be kind to him, so he could repay the kindness with a big bag of money?

IVOGLIN. That was the day I did the worst thing in my life. I walked into a tavern, and decided that imagination was far far far better than reality . . . as a matter of fact—I just made up this whole story.

IPPOLIT. I felt that if I had never bent over in that one way to pick up that one toy and had never breathed the particular breath of air I breathed at that moment in the particular way I breathed it, I would never have inflicted myself with tuberculosis. But I wasn't paying attention. I was careless. Haphazard.

GANYA. For the next three weeks, the thought of the disguised philanthropist kept pushing my brilliant thought further and further out of my . . . So finally, one night I trailed the beggar to his hut just to clear my head once and for all. I saw the beggar and his old wife drink themselves out of . . . and collapse on the floor, without even vomiting. And the whole night, peeking there through the window, I was wondering: Perhaps he knew I was shadowing him, so naturally he would keep up his beggar act. I didn't know what to think. And the worst thing is, of course, the worst thing is . . . is . . .

LEBEDEV (*as Natasha chases him with the*

candle). Torturing idiots? . . . Lying about your childhood? . . . Using bad language! (*He kisses Myshkin.*) Betraying your friends. Breast spit rectum Judas Priest and Christ Almighty!

NATASHA (*laughing, stroking Lebedev*). Don't be ashamed, Lebedev—no one will remember those nasty things you've been saying when there's so much greater evil around.

IPPOLIT. I was just trying to pick up that cotton pigeon of mine that had stuffing coming out of its stomach. When I tugged at one of its eyes I could see the little red threads holding it on. The stuffing didn't have any color.

(*Pause*)

NATASHA. Prince Myshkin . . . would you care to join my religion?

MYSHKIN. Oh no, please . . . I have committed sins so evil, all of you are saints! . . . No, I cannot tell you—you couldn't forgive me.

GANYA. Trust us.

MYSHKIN (*pauses, looking at the eager faces; sighs*). Forgive me—I will. (*Dramatic pause*) I once drank an entire glass of milk. (*Puzzled reactions*) Not only that, but another time, I *ruined* an entire day sitting around waiting for my nose to clear up. Oh, I've committed sins! I've studies articles about utopia, sung love songs! I've created mucus and manufactured scabs, I've waltzed! Once I had an epileptic fit right in the middle of a dart game! (*The party is laughing now.*) (*To Lebedev*) Once I gave a lime to a child, and he started crying because it was so green. (*Laughing*) Once I called God an idiot!

LEBEDEV. I used to steal Hosts and feed them to my puppy! And guess what! I write nursery rhymes! Look! (*Pulls out a few scraps of paper and gives them to Myshkin.*)

Uggy little buggies
Get to live in ruggies;
Good goody goosie
Hangs from a noosie.
I like little duckies.

I know I'm not that good, but—

IPPOLIT. That's nothing—I left my diary in a theater once, hoping someone would find it and ask me to make a play out of it.

IVOGLIN. Sometimes I drink in front of my children.

GANYA (*to Myshkin*). You should see me cheat at solitaire. (*Laughs*)

NATASHA. Prince Myshkin . . . what is the worst thing I could do?

MYSHKIN (*reluctant*). I'm sorry.

NATASHA. Truth.

MYSHKIN. Marry Ganya.

GANYA. He wants the money for himself!

NATASHA. You'll get your money, Ganya.

GANYA. Why ask an idiot how to run your life?

(*Music: "The Grubs"*)

NATASHA (*singing*).
The grubs in the garbage are white.
The birds just flap
And drop their crap
As they twit their little ditty—
Oh shit—it's all so pretty:
The grubs in the garbage so white,
The men of our age so forthright,
So bright, so po—lite, so what!!
You're the pick of the nose of manhood!
Only one man knows it's not bad to be good,
So gentle I wince,
So ungodly human:
Prince M—

(*Rogozhin enters suddenly, dramatically, carrying a wad of money.*)

LEBEDEV (*ending song*). Rogozhin! Rogozhin!!

ROGOZHIN (*throwing the wad at Natasha's feet*). A hundred thousand birthdays, Natasha! Money!

LEBEDEV (*going for money*). One hundred thousand!

ROGOZHIN (*yanking Lebedev aside*). Back! Back! Hurry, Natasha—take it!

NATASHA. Oh, please, Rogozhin—dramatics, dramatics, dramatics! Here, Ganya—would you like a wad? A little consolation prize? Here, poochie-poochie!

ROGOZHIN. Natasha, I would kill for you. I would kiss small children, I would carry packages for lepers, I would help you commit suicide—anything!

NATASHA. Wait your turn, Rogozhin—no dramatics. Now—Ganya. I shall take these hundred thousand rubles and set fire to them. When they start burning, you may crawl to the fire. And then, using only your mouth, you may take as much money from the flames as you can stand. Ganya Ivoglin, at last face to face with pain exactly as greedy as he is!! Here we go!! (*She sets fire to the money and throws it into a glass bowl.*)

GANYA. Maybe if I proudly refused to do whatever it is she wants me to do, she'll reward me with even more money than I refuse to refuse. Maybe I'll just grow wings and flap out of here and join a circus and make millions as the only flying rich man in the world. (*He crawls to the fire.*)

LEBEDEV. Good God Holy Christ, Natasha, it burns—one hundred thousand rubles is mortal.

GANYA. If I had that money, I could turn beggars into philanthropists, stop smiling so much, buy a library of books about tuberculosis, contribute to the fire department, own a monocle, get an operation on my mouth, have money to burn.

IVOGLIN. Fillipovna—I know twenty families who live on no more than five or six grapes a day—that money—

GANYA. But I *use* my mouth! Valuable thoughts often creep into the world through my mouth. And if my head ever caught fire, how could I scream without my mouth? My mouth is almost worth a fortune to me! (*He halts.*)

IPPOLIT. That money could pay for a cure if I wanted to live.

GANYA (*motionless; to Myshkin*). You don't think I'm moving, do you? But in the head, still in the head socket, my thoughts are moving madly to maintain my immobility. I could sit here forever if you paid me enough. I could think here in my head for an eternity on whether to act or think here in my head for an eternity on whether to act or never make up my, my . . . my . . .

IPPOLIT. It could, Ganya—it could!

LEBEDEV. Ashes—a hundred thousand ashes!

(*Ganya realizes the money is gone, and slowly turns and crawls to the rocking chair, where he will barely rock, obliviously.*)

NATASHA (*to Ganya as he crawls*). Did you lose something, Ganya? Over here, Ganya— here I am. I've decided I *will* marry you after all. (*Ganya doesn't hear her; though she addresses him, she is really directing her comments to Rogozhin.*) But I must warn you— I gave away everything I own this morning. To a convent! That's right! (*She laughs at Rogozhin's reaction.*) Still no, Ganya? (*She laughs and kisses him on his blank forehead.*) Well—I think you've made the right decision. After all, I have nothing to offer. I want nothing. Who would have me now?

MYSHKIN (*singing*).
I'd have you.
You need to be taken care of.
I'd honor, respect, and wait on you.
I'd give you all my love.

If we should be poor
I'd work for you.

You'd suffer no more—
We'd eat stew.

But we won't be poor,
Our love will make us rich!
Besides I believe I'm a royal inheritor . . .
Or so says this letter from the Duke of Mackavitch . . .

IPPOLIT (*grabs letter, reads it over, ending music*). Why, it's true! He's worth millions!

NATASHA (*embracing Myshkin*). Prince! I'll be your princess. I shall impose tariffs! Prince! We shall rule the stew and read children's stories. We shall come true. . . . (*Myshkin is cold, confused, stares at Rogozhin; Natasha breaks away.*) OFF WITH HIS HEAD!!

ROGOZHIN (*to Myshkin*). Spastic virgin! Why should I kill you?

MYSHKIN. But I am giving my entire inheritance to Ippolit . . . that he may be healed . . . (*Myshkin brings letter to Ippolit; Rogozhin grabs it out of his hand.*)

ROGOZHIN. Beware the good deed, Prince. I burn your charity. (*He burns the letter. Ippolit protests, tries to save it from the fire.*) And I take these black ashes—(*from the burnt rubles*) and change them into . . . a hundred thousand rubles. (*It appears that he does.*)

MYSHKIN. How did you do that?

ROGOZHIN (*giving the creation to Ippolit*). To your health, Ippolit. . . . And now I take Natasha Fillipovna—and turn her into my wife . . .

MYSHKIN. How did you do that?

ROGOZHIN. I forgive you.

NATASHA. Goodbye, Prince—you're very silly—you're the most perfect human being I've ever met in my life. Marry the noncontroversial Aglaya Yepanchin—you're too good for me . . . too bad for you!! (*She runs off laughing with Rogozhin, followed apostolically by Lebedev.*)

IPPOLIT (*calling after them*). Thank you very much!

MYSHKIN (*examining the money*). This money's counterfeit!

(*Bass: thump, thump, thump. Ippolit begins an immense coughing fit. Ivoglin helps him and Ganya offstage.*)

MYSHKIN (*alone, lost; calling after them*). Is there anything I can say? I never say what I want to say. Like a god continually chattering about atheism! I don't understand—I am subject to epilepsy!

(*Myshkin is outside, fitful. He feels Rogozhin's eyes on him; are there crowdspeople neuterly milling about him, or are they off-stage? Natasha runs up to Myshkin frantically. Her hair is down.*)

NATASHA. I was supposed to marry Rogozhin again today. But I ditched him. He bored me. Bored me black-and-blue. Beat me stiff. To tears! Eyes! Eyes!

(*Crowdspeople Chorus, as Rogozhin shadows the haunted Myshkin, sings "Fitting."*)

CHORUS.
> Eyes
> Like handcuffs
> Shadowing you,
> Certain nerve ends splitting,
> It's all so fitting,
> Fitting!
> It's all so . . .
> So . . .
> Now where did those words go?
> Where did I put that thought?
> Simple, simple—
> I forgot . . .

(*Music and Chorus out; Myshkin at Rogozhin's door.*)

ROGOZHIN. How did you know this was my house?

MYSHKIN. The grass in front . . . the way the tree . . . (*He demonstrates how the tree looked.*) Is Natasha—

ROGOZHIN. Last night she made me chain her to the staircase. She was afraid she'd run off to you like she does on our wedding days. This morning she was gone.

MYSHKIN. Stand there. Stare at me. Use your eyes. (*He tests the stare with his back to see if it's the same stare he felt earlier: it is.*) You were following me today, I think.

ROGOZHIN. You *are* insane.

MYSHKIN. I don't think he is. Nobody is. Of course they are, but—I'm sorry—I'm . . . today I am . . . distracted . . . I feel the way I used to before my fits. (*He looks around.*) Natasha?

ROGOZHIN. But she'll come back sometime tonight, just to bitch at me about how she's loved you since that birthday party of hers. And how she'll go insane if she doesn't figure out whether to love you like her father or like you were her own child. I'll grind my teeth and think of you with dust in my mouth.

MYSHKIN. Natasha must leave St. Petersburg! Her head's a party! No music left. Too large a crowd. . . . One more puff of cigar smoke: poof. (*Rogozhin laughs loudly.*) She gags to death on fun. I'm very fond of you, Paryfon.

ROGOZHIN. What?

MYSHKIN. I'm very fond of you, Paryfon, though I'm certain you haven't laughed correctly in years. If you refuse to scream at me, I can do no good here. I'm leaving. I'll see you in heaven. . . . Goodbye. . . .

ROGOZHIN (*screaming furiously*). PLEASE STAY!! . . . When you're not right here, right before me, I hate you. I don't eat, I don't move, I don't put my clothes on, I'm so busy deciding whether I should poison you, use the knife, acid—but what kind of poison—setting fire to your bed? Naw. How about those sucking things . . . ?

MYSHKIN. Lampreys.

ROGOZHIN: No, wouldn't work. Probably poison—but what kind? (*Myshkin is playing with the knife.*) You see? When you're not here? But here you are . . .

MYSHKIN (*indicating knife*). Is this new?

ROGOZHIN (*grabbing it away*). WHY AM I SCREAMING AT YOU!! . . . Her in bed, me sleeping in the closet. I hear her fall out of bed . . . (*Natasha is present now, acting out the scene as described.*) . . . get on her knees, mumbling and moaning—

NATASHA. Oh, my Prince, forgive me, I cannot marry you, if I should die before I wake . . .

ROGOZHIN (*in the scene with Natasha now, beating her*). Prince! Prince! Prince! (*He continues to beat her as he addresses the Prince.*) And I beat her in your name. Then I'm wretched for days afterwards. She brings armies in—zookeepers, ambassadors!—then she throws me a biscuit in front of them. I sit there. I don't move until she talks to me again. Once it was a week.

NATASHA (*to Rogozhin*). What are you thinking?

ROGOZHIN. The way your legs go all the way up to the bottom of your stomach.

NATASHA. The way you beat me?

ROGOZHIN. The way your teeth show when you yawn.

NATASHA. I'll marry you, Paryfon. (*Yawning*) See my teeth?

(*As Rogozhin and Natasha start making heavy love, the Chorus, the Ivoglins, the Yepanchins, and Lebedev converge neuterly on Myshkin, singing. Myshkin dazedly toys with Rogozhin's knife.*)

CHORUS.
There's just one thing, fitting now, fitting—
> There's a dagger
> With a blade
> With a handle

With a hand—
Simple, simple,
I stagger
I bleed
I cannot stand—

(*The Chorus is off; music fades; Rogozhin grabs the knife out of Myshkin's hand; Natasha vanishes.*)

ROGOZHIN. Goddamnit, leave that alone!

MYSHKIN. It *is* new, isn't it?

ROGOZHIN. Can't I buy a letter opener if I want?

MYSHKIN. Natasha? She needs rest, peace. Oceans crushing rocks. You'll kill her. I forgive you. It is new. What is that picture? But that really *is* Christ on the cross! Is it an early photograph? (*Rogozhin laughs; Myshkin laughs and strikes a pose in imitation of the picture, playing, joking with Rogozhin. Plays with pose, to Rogozhin's laughter*) Ugly . . . He'll die in one minute. A person could lose his faith looking at that picture. In one minute.

ROGOZHIN. That's what Natasha sees in you, Prince. . . . Tell me about God.

MYSHKIN. God? I don't know. Yes I do. (*Laughs*) My God: I believe in the God of the brain cell! (*Holding his head*) Here's the infinity! There are more thoughts in the world than there are atoms in the universe! In just these last five seconds, Paryfon, you've seen this hand (*Moving his hand; footsteps are heard*) move every millionth of an inch from here . . . to here . . .

(*Crowdspeople Chorus march in a line between the staring Myshkin and Rogozhin.*)

IVOGLIN. You've known the color of my trousers—

MME YEPANCHIN. Whether you've known it or not.

IPPOLIT. You've been thinking under your breath.

NATASHA. Does Natasha think he's handsome?

GANYA. Who are we?

AGLAYA. He's a fool!

LEBEDEV. I'm getting hungry.

(*The Chorus has marched out.*)

MYSHKIN. . . . and shall you kill me. And for some ungodly reason you were thinking of —gerbils? Those little rodents?

ROGOZHIN. Right.

MYSHKIN. And over all that you were listening to me! How can all those big thoughts fit into a little head like yours? Where do they go? God takes them.

ROGOZHIN (*pointing to the cross around Myshkin's neck*). What's that cross?

MYSHKIN. Tin.

ROGOZHIN (*taking a gold cross from his own neck*). Solid gold. We'll exchange. (*Myshkin hesitates.*) It will make us brothers.

MYSHKIN. God bless you, brother Paryfon.

(*The exchange is made. Rogozhin kisses Myshkin on the mouth. Recoils; pause*)

ROGOZHIN. My mother shall bless you. Come. (*He guides Myshkin through a maze to a Headless Old Heap, who begins chanting and blessing Myshkin with its crippled hand as soon as they enter the room.*) Mother, this is Prince Myshkin. We have exchanged crosses and become brothers. Could you give him your blessing, you old hag—straight from the scales of your bony womb? You're like death stinking up my house and rotting out my floors! You'd better die soon, or I'll snap you apart and build a cabinet out of you! Ha! Ha-ha-ha! (*Myshkin is confused.*) She's blind and completely deaf. I'm always teasing her. She's not even my mother. I just found her here. But that was some thing . . . she knew you were there, and she knew I wanted you blessed! (*He yanks shawl off the Headless Old Heap, revealing the giggling Lebedev. Myshkin, stunned, begins wandering away; Lebedev sobers.*) No, no—this way, this way . . . (*Rogozhin leads the dazed Myshkin out.*)

CHORUS (*singing*).
Eagles scream and bulls give birth . . .

MYSHKIN. I've forgotten . . . haven't I forgotten something?

CHORUS.
Mars dead from the smell of earth . . .

ROGOZHIN. Go, babyface! Natasha is yours —take her then!

CHORUS.
Worms in worship of the dust,
Bloody knives turn to rust . . .

MYSHKIN. I've forgotten something!

CHORUS.
Fitting, fitting . . .

MYSHKIN. I think I've forgotten something!

CHORUS.
Fits—

ROGOZHIN. Remember Rogozhin! (*He slams the door on Myshkin, after pushing him out.*)

CHORUS WOMAN (*whispering*).
Fit!

(*Myshkin leaves the house. The Crowdspeople form a tableau about him. Rogozhin is somewhere staring at Myshkin.*)

MYSHKIN. I must forget something . . . I can't remember—what? Like a donkey. Life! Something to do with life . . . eyes!! (*He wheels around suddenly, looking for the staring eyes. He freezes in his wheelaround position. He tests the position.*) This is a nice position. Myshkin—discus thrower! Myshkin, as he was at one moment in the history of history and always will have been from here on on! Note the straining tendons in the neck, the sinewy arms uplifted, the heart like a kettledrum finishing off a symphony! Over here, fellow art lovers—we have the marvelous lifelike statue entitled: "Prekinetic Man in Crescendoing Stasis." Myshkin—gathering up all his life forces before . . . total action! Myshkin—acting like an idiot. (*He breaks the freeze.*) Playing! Idiot! Wasting God! One thought, one thought—the one thought that means—everything!

(*Music. "Fitting"*)

CROWDSPERSON 1. The aura is the pause just before the seizure, in which the epileptic experiences an extraordinary intensification of self-awareness and an extreme consciousness of existence.

MYSHKIN. The one thought—noblest feeling alive, highest extant experience—

CROWDSPERSON 2. . . . followed immediately, inseparably, by the ignobility of the ridiculous fit—

MYSHKIN. . . . trying to get rid of my body—

CROWDSPERSON 3. . . . as if being punished for overhearing God's secret formula—

(*Rogozhin still staring*)

MYSHKIN. . . . for being stared at so intensely by two cosmic eyes, suddenly seeing the eyes that have been pouring over you all your life, seeing the fire they're made of, brilliant colorless fire, constantly burning through every thought in the universe—

CROWDSPERSON 4. . . . and you have stolen one thin flame of that fire, and you must relive all of Prometheus' life in the next ten seconds—

MYSHKIN. . . . those two eyes of fire at the top of these stairs—(*I.e., Natasha's stairs—she is standing serenely at the top; Rogozhin crouches with his knife.*) I will tell Natasha the secret, the one thought over all and under all: life is everything! I am worth an infinity of thought, and there is something greater than me, two eyes that have been following me ever since I can remember. . . . Whatever happens—whatever idiocy—for this radiant moment I would give my entire life—

(*Rogozhin leaps out from the stairwell with knife raised. Natasha silent at the top of stairs. Music up; Rogozhin freezes. Myshkin sings a song.*)

I see through the eyes watching over me:
I'm alive beyond all illusion!
And each moment of life knows an
    ecstasy
Buried within our confusion.

(*Myshkin and the Chorus sing simultaneously.*)

MYSHKIN.
I see through the eyes watching over me
I'm alive beyond all illusion!
And each moment of life knows an
    ecstasy
Buried within our confusion . . .

CHORUS.
Eagles scream and bulls give birth
Mars dead from the smell of earth
Worms in worship of the dust
Bloody knives turn to rust . . .

(*On the word "confusion," Myshkin begins his epileptic scream and returns to the murder situation, Rogozhin raising his knife. The scream and the beginning of the fit frighten Rogozhin from murder. Myshkin falls down the stairs.*)

CHORUS.

Fitting!
Fitting!
Fits!
Fit!

(*Myshkin a rigid quiver. Blackout*)

ACT TWO

(*Myshkin is prostrate, as he was at end of Act One, after his fit.*)

———

MYSHKIN (*slowly raising his head*). Tomorrow is my birthday.

IPPOLIT (*crawling over to Myshkin*). I had a nightmare about you, Prince. I dreamed you had an epileptic fit and fell down a staircase. And I crawled over to you and you looked at me kindly, then more kindly, and more and more, until finally you were looking at me so kindly your forehead cracked. Then you took my hand and put it kindly through the crack and looked at me with great honesty as I lay there with my hand around your brain, and truer than tuberculosis you told me—

MYSHKIN. You're going to die, Ippolit. I understand.

IPPOLIT. And as you said that, I felt your brain cough and start twitching and I pulled it out and I was holding a piece of glass. And I looked at your brainless face and it was blank with kindness and you said—"Tomorrow is my birthday." So tell me how to die, Prince!

MYSHKIN. Leave us your life, and forgive us our happiness. (*He walks away, starts writing letters.*)

IPPOLIT. That's what you said in the dream! (*He exits.*)

ROGOZHIN (*entering with Lebedev*). Does he suspect I'm paying you to keep him at your house?

LEBEDEV. I don't know. All we talk about is my childhood.

ROGOZHIN (*paying Lebedev*). Find out who he's writing those letters to.

LEBEDEV. Yes, sir. Thank you, sir. Rogozhin—I hate talking about my childhood!

(*They exit; Mme Yepanchin enters, visits the Prince.*)

MME YEPANCHIN (*knitting*). Now, Prince —did you or did you not send Aglaya a letter this morning?

MYSHKIN. Yes. An enormous upsurge of happiness had completely dispirited me. The sun was over there. Tomorrow is my birthday. I was silent. So I wrote Aglaya, yes.

MME YEPANCHIN. This letter, did it concern you and Aglaya having a relationship?

MYSHKIN. That's all it was. Here. I'll recite it by heart. I never forget anything.

AGLAYA (*entering, with letter*). "To the living Aglaya. I am writing you this. How is it that I am? I pray, remember myself to you and together as it happens we are brought to mind. I have no particular words to write. Please be reading this now. I am—your brother, Prince Lyov Myshkin . . . " (*She looks up puzzled.*)

MME YEPANCHIN (*knitting*). Hm. Ah me —human relationships befuddle me so. Everybody has them.

MYSHKIN. Women think so highly of me.

MME YEPANCHIN. I love the Bible. I love falling asleep. I love saying things—that's how I love you. Aglaya, however, loves you precisely the same way, only in a younger manner. It's a goodly love, Prince, a very goodly love. But it's not the same love God uses to populate the earth. (*She sticks the knitting needle firmly into the ball of yarn and*

holds the sweater up against Myshkin to see how it fits.*)

AGLAYA (*to Myshkin*). I got your love letter.

MYSHKIN. Love—? Oh, no—I assure you I sent that letter only from the depths of my soul. I—

AGLAYA. You must run away from home with me. You're perfect. So am I. We're perfect for each other. You're the only reality on earth. I've never seen a single Gothic cathedral.

MYSHKIN. This is absurd, Aglaya!

AGLAYA. Do you think I'd run off with an idiot like you! (*She leaves in a huff.*)

MME YEPANCHIN (*disappointed with the fit of the sweater*). Aglaya's just like me and it worries me sick. We really don't fit our society, Prince, but for the greater honor and glory of God, we try. (*She sighs, puts the sweater and knitting equipment in her knitting bag; she prepares to leave.*) God's a bit of a misfit himself. We should all be put in a glass cage for display. Well—I'd best leave you to your thoughts. (*She busies herself off.*)

AGLAYA (*returning when Mme Yepanchin is gone*). I am being kept in a glass cage! You must run away with me! I can't even bear to look at you! Your eyes are kind. Your whole head is ugly! Natasha Fillipovna wrote me this letter.

(*Natasha appears, writing a letter. As Myshkin reads the letter silently, she reads her own letter.*)

NATASHA (*as she writes*). "Aglaya, Aglaya —I can imagine your golden body under your fine tight clothes screaming to be free. I am on fire for you. You and the Prince must marry."

(*Rogozhin enters Natasha's area and looks over her shoulder; Aglaya is looking over Myshkin's shoulder.*)

NATASHA *and* MYSHKIN (*reading the same letter in their respective areas*). "I think of you both as inseparable as two burning eyes, as silver knife and golden sheath."

ROGOZHIN (*reading over Natasha's shoulder*). "Rogozhin just laughed at what I wrote. I will marry him only when you marry the Prince. Rogozhin hides his knife among the cobwebs in his mother's bedpan."

NATASHA *and* AGLAYA. "By the end of your honeymoon, my blood will be gray. I will be dying at your defloration. Do not think of me."

AGLAYA. "Marry Myshkin! He is the resurrection! Hurry. The rats are eating something under the floor. Keep the Commandments. All my love, signed—"

MYSHKIN. "Natasha Fillipovna!"

(*Aglaya runs off. Natasha laughs fully, happily.*)

NATASHA (*to Rogozhin*). The little bitch! She has moles on her ass. Why don't you kill me before I write her another letter! (*Laughs*) Oh dear, Paryfon—you must do something for me. Ever since the Prince's fit I've been having these long periods of happiness I can't seem to snap myself out of. I've taken to sitting in trees with children and making up new words with them for whatever we can imagine. I spend an hour eating an olive. I help strangers rake their leaves, I believe in God, the Prince will marry Aglaya, I think about giraffes. (*Laughs*) I can't stand it, Paryfon. I must go pick a rose.

ROGOZHIN (*worried*). Make *me* up a word.

NATASHA (*laughing*). Counter-fit!

ROGOZHIN. How?

(*Natasha sings "Counterfitting," taking a walk with a pensive Rogozhin. Myshkin appears, shadowing them as Rogozhin shadowed him in Act One, during the singing of "Fitting."*)

NATASHA.

Stare at the sun—
Fit some warmth in your eyes.
Hear out the sound
Of a choir of flies.
Sleep deep in the earth—
Play grave in the ground,
Seize your . . .
Seize your birth . . .

(*Myshkin and Rogozhin confront each other confessionally.*)

ROGOZHIN. You know the letter you sent me—well, I burned it! Did it say you forgave me?

MYSHKIN. Remember? You tried to murder me. I had a fit. You—

ROGOZHIN. Of course, I remember! How could I forget—you scared me half to death! The letter—did it say you forgave me, that we were still brothers, and that evil was not the worst thing in the world?

MYSHKIN. No, it didn't. I was merely inquiring if I had left my hat at your house that day we exchanged crosses.

ROGOZHIN. I didn't steal your hat!

MYSHKIN. Paryfon! We're brothers. Evil is not the worst thing in the world. (*Natasha has crawled to Myshkin's feet, kisses them, humming and laughing.*) Natasha! Get up please —must I dig a hole to show you my position with respect to you?

NATASHA. Then I should dig a deeper hole.

MYSHKIN. And I a deeper.

NATASHA. I am unworthy to dig holes at your feet.

ROGOZHIN. Oh, God! (*He leads the laughing Natasha away.*)

MYSHKIN (*calling after Rogozhin*). Today is my birthday!!

LEBEDEV, GANYA, IPPOLIT, MME YEPANCHIN, *and* AGLAYA. HAPPY BIRTHDAY!!!

MME YEPANCHIN (*holding a sweater up to him*). Oh, my goodness, Prince—you *still* don't fit!

LEBEDEV. Here's a present that came for you in the mail—it's signed, "From your brother." (*He places the too-small hat on the Prince's head. Laughter.*)

MME YEPANCHIN. Oh, Prince—I swear your head must grow a pound a day!

MYSHKIN. Hello, Aglaya.

AGLAYA. Ganya—where's your father?

GANYA. He had a stroke telling lies to the Prince.

IPPOLIT (*carrying a large notebook*). Happy birthday, Prince—as you prophesied, I have written something. Please—everybody sit. It's just my life story. It'll only take about three minutes.

GANYA. Three minutes! For your life? An eternity in mine!

MME YEPANCHIN. Ganya Ivoglin!

GANYA. Well, what if it's boring? What do I do with the inside of my head in the meantime? An eternity!

MYSHKIN. Ippolit! (*He starts applauding; applause*)

IPPOLIT (*reading*). "The Summation and Conclusion of My Life, by Ippolit Ivoglin— (*Applause*)—A Consumptive in His Last Agonies."

LEBEDEV. I hope it's dirty!

IPPOLIT. "Roman numeral eye: LIFE—"

GANYA. Life??? (*He starts laughing loudly.*)

IPPOLIT. There are about four things in life not even you can laugh at, Ganya. (*Hawks and spits*) That's one of them.

(*Lebedev gets dustpan and broom.*)

GANYA: That's quite unnecessary, you know.

IPPOLIT: Unnecessary, thoughtless, and no reason for it at all—yet it's there. It's blue! (*Hawks again*) Seems to be no end to the little buggers, does there?

LEBEDEV (*sweeping up the two blobs*). Every time you come over here you have to show off your tuberculosis.

MYSHKIN. IPPOLIT! (*Begins the applause again*)

IPPOLIT. Prince Myshkin says: "It is memory that decides what we have left of our lives at death. Act memorably, and you'll die with a fuller life left you. (*Applause; the women nod appreciatively to Myshkin.*) Roman numeral eye-eye: MY LIFE, THE LIFE LEFT ME: My only two memorable memories. One—when I was first learning to read, discovering the word eye. Small ee, small why, small ee—it made a face, the look of that word. Memory two. When I was twelve when the wind blew a button off Katerina Petrovna's blouse and for two entire seconds I saw her actual breast and a real nipple issuing from the one end of it. Unwrinkled. Not a toothmark on it. And it all looked so hard and so soft and so naturally there that I coughed forty-five straight minutes without breathing once. (*Laughter*) And scattered other memories—including: Potato soup, one or two thoughts I've had in my life. Gerbil puppies. And the joke about what the ant colony said to the prostitute. That's the life left me. Everything else is covered with tuberculosis. Roman numeral eye-eye-eye: MY ULTIMATE CONCLUSION—"

GANYA. At last!

IPPOLIT. "I have a small pistol. After I am done reading this, as the sun sets, I shall shoot myself in the chest as many times as possible. Suicide is the only worthwhile project I have time to begin and conclude of my own free will. It is the only cure known for terminal tuberculosis. It is a solid kick in the crotch of God. It is my ultimate conclusion. Roman numeral eye-eye-eye-eye—"

GANYA. Oh my God, there's more!

IPPOLIT. "My last statement! No one can ever express all of what he wants to express. Everyone will die without communicating an essence to a single soul. And finally, Roman numeral eye-eye-eye-eye-eye: THE ULTIMATE QUESTION—Is it worthwhile living when you know you're definitely going to die . . . within a hundred years? THE END."

MME YEPANCHIN (*applauding, going quickly to Ippolit*). Young man, I came to this party hoping to help Prince Myshkin recover from his last fit. Obviously, I was disappointed. You would provide a more than welcome substitution. I do not find you pitiful. I enjoy helping people die with less despair. It clears my sinuses. It helps me live longer. If you would come live with us, both you and I would be eternally grateful.

MYSHKIN. Ippolit . . .

IPPOLIT. Goodbye, Prince—I only wish I had as much time for you as they do. (*He pulls his small pistol out of his pocket and runs upstairs; everyone runs after him.*)

MYSHKIN. Ippolit!!

(*Freeze—Ippolit with gun at chest. Myshkin goes to a flashback scene with General Ivoglin.*)

IVOGLIN. Come back in time with me, Prince. It's been a long life, a tall tall tale of wine, and I have some corking memories for my living—because I didn't miss a drop of it. But—I must confess everything to you, Prince—I could never have done it without Napoleon's personal help.

MYSHKIN. How did you and Napoleon meet, General?

IVOGLIN. Ahh, Prince—my greatest memory, my *raison d'être* as Napoleon's troops used to say! I shouldn't tell you, Prince—it's too exciting! (*He clutches his heart.*)

MYSHKIN. Ahhh, *mon Général—pourquoi*?

IVOGLIN (*laughing*). *Eh bien*! It's a tiny story, Prince, but so is life, *non*?

(*Party scene unfreezes. Aglaya squeals.*)

LEBEDEV. He wasn't lying!

(*Ippolit is motionless, gun at his chest.*)

GANYA. Don't move! . . . You might scare him.

LEBEDEV. I'll be goddamned if I'm sweeping up *that* mess!

(*Party scene freezes.*)

IVOGLIN. The night before I captured Napoleon, I slept in a marsh and a tiny childlike spider crawled up my nose and onto my braincase, making it impossible for me to sleep. And so, disgruntled, I rose and plodded on.

IPPOLIT (*immobile; in his head*). There should be one perfect last thought—God, don't let me waste this moment letting my mind wander. . . . Aglaya is lively. Pretty.

IVOGLIN. Right before dawn, I captured Napoleon overconfidently relieving himself into the thundering rapids outside the ken of his campsite. I had just convinced him to retreat from Moscow when seventeen guards suddenly jumped me. "*La guillotine*!" Napoleon commanded.

MYSHKIN. The guillotine! I know the guillotine!

IVOGLIN. As they prepared the blade, one thought kept running through my head—alongside my spider.

MYSHKIN. I know! I know! You were thinking: "What if I had more than one minute to live!" *Non? Non?*

IVOGLIN. *Oui! Oui!*

IPPOLIT. Thirteen seconds, the sun will set —perhaps I should do it tomorrow. One more day can't hurt! Twelve seconds.

GANYA. No one move—if we wait long enough, he'll have a coughing fit.

IVOGLIN. And—"What if I had five more minutes? Or imagine—a lifetime!" Ha-ha! Oh, Prince—this story . . . (*He is breathing hard, clutching his heart.*)

MYSHKIN. Go on, General—finish.

IPPOLIT. There very well might be an afterlife. Last thought, last thought. . . . I'm hungry.

IVOGLIN. Well . . . (*Gulping a drink, panting*) just as the executioner raised his arm, the spider fell out of my nose and Napoleon saw me smile at it! "*Cessez!*" Napoleon cried, and he ran to me, weeping: "You are free, *cher Général,* because I saw your love for life." And the sun rose!!

IPPOLIT. The sunset!! (*Pulls the trigger; no shot, a click*)

IVOGLIN. "We all know, *théoriquement,*" Napoleon went on, "that we all must die someday—but now you are one of the only living souls on earth who truly understands this beautiful inevitability."

LEBEDEV. Ohhh—He "forgot" to put the firing caps in! Ha-ha!

(*Laughter*)

IPPOLIT. Give me my gun back!!

(*The party exits. Ippolit is coughing heavily. Myshkin vacillates between Ippolit and Ivoglin.*)

IVOGLIN. "You have an eternity left to live! Go! And don't miss a moment!" And to this day I have followed his advice as loyally as his troops followed him from Moscow.

IPPOLIT. Understand, Prince! I refuse to live a life that can assume such laughable grotesque forms. (*He has a coughing fit and faints.*)

IVOGLIN. Ah, Prince, I wish you had been there. Sometimes I feel very sorry for you, Prince. I find I have nothing more to say. I've said nothing. I never met Napoleon. Oh, we exchanged a few letters . . . now and then . . . but—what else is there to talk about, then? How's life? Things? Dull factual forms.

I am not having a stroke! (*He has a stroke.*)

MYSHKIN (*between the two prostrate bodies*). I know . . . what the chopped head was thinking.

(*Lights dim*)

ROGOZHIN. Are you happy? . . . (*Natasha is heard humming "Counterfitting" in the distance.*) Natasha wants to know.

MYSHKIN. Oh no no no no no. She mustn't worry—there's no need for me to be happy.

ROGOZHIN. Lyov—I want to celebrate your birthday. We'll play death.

MYSHKIN (*laughing*). Oh yes, yes, Paryfon, I'd like that. I've been much too serious lately. How do we play? (*Laughing*) I've forgotten—it's been such a long time.

ROGOZHIN. This way, this way . . . (*He leads Myshkin to a freshly dug tomb. Natasha is heard humming in the distance.*) Happy birthday!

MYSHKIN (*delighted*). A long hole!

ROGOZHIN. Do you like it? I just dug it tonight. It's new. (*Giving Myshkin a handful of dirt*) Smell.

MYSHKIN (*smelling*). Old brain molecules . . . worms have recently held services here. (*Laughs, licks the earth*) Oh, Paryfon! I'm so glad I'm not someone else! What now?

ROGOZHIN (*pointing to the hole*). We lie. (*The two descend into the grave and lie side by side. Suppressed laughter; pause*)

ROGOZHIN. We are dead.

MYSHKIN (*bursting into laughter*). Yes, yes —I'm remembering now. Yes . . .

ROGOZHIN. Our heads begin leaking. Silkworms grub after our memory materials. Our brain cells turn to salt water and our gods trickle out into one another.

MYSHKIN. Paryfon, it's scary the way I laugh sometimes.

ROGOZHIN. Prince . . . sometimes beating Natasha and terrifying people and destroying myself—sometimes I get in moods where it all seems so empty and meaningless. I try thinking of hurricanes, measles, vivisection, talking behind people's backs—but nothing seems to inspire me until I think of your sympathy, your brainsucking. That's death, Prince, and I envy you that.

MYSHKIN. If only you could have a seizure with me . . .

ROGOZHIN (*pausing*). If we could pick each other's skulls clean as a baby's dream, and come down here every day, and not touch each other, just lie here—by God we'd figure out why there's no real reason to move . . . if it takes forever.

MYSHKIN. And Natasha?

ROGOZHIN. Are your eyes open?

MYSHKIN. I can't tell.

ROGOZHIN. Look, then. (*He reveals a dead Natasha. Myshkin starts shaking. Cello plays "Counterfitting."*)

MYSHKIN. No no no no no!

NATASHA (*resurrecting*). Marry Aglaya. (*She gives Myshkin a rose, begins humming.*)
(*Rogozhin and Natasha leave, laughing.*)

AGLAYA (*approaching the motionless Myshkin; singing*).
Behold the child!
Dying for rebirth,
Crying for delivery.
But we're out of wombs, child,
All over the earth,
We're all all out of old old wombs—
Enter a new womb with me, child!
We'll talk and we'll hide
As the world ends outside . . .
Pick me five green leaves
From the redwood tree
And I will speak the first words of my life.
Dump twelve million babies
In the deep green sea
And take me for your wife.
(*She pulls Myshkin out of his numbness, speaking to him.*) We'll play chess.

MYSHKIN (*giving her the rose*). You don't terrify me the same way Natasha does.

AGLAYA. Your move. (*Myshkin stares dumbly as Aglaya reaches over and makes a definite chess move.*) Mate!! Ha-ha-ha! You move as if you've never played before.

MYSHKIN. I haven't.

AGLAYA. Then how do you know how to move at all?

MYSHKIN. I read your mind.

AGLAYA. Ha-ha! We'll play another. My move—mate. Ha-ha-ha! I win another! You're awful! Ha-ha! Do you know how to play "Fools"?

MYSHKIN. The card game? Why, yes! In fact, I've won several medals in various "Fools" tournaments. Isn't it funny how that is so? I mean with people so dedicated to the idea that I'm a fool myself.

AGLAYA. Yes, very funny. Perhaps we should call it "Idiots" instead! Or "Ninnies"! Hee-haw—your play, donkey-ears.

MYSHKIN (*slapping down his cards triumphantly*). Fools, fools, fools, double-fools, crazy card, and fools!! . . . Frightening, isn't it? I believe I play this game flawlessly. Another?

AGLAYA (*laying down card, cheating openly*). Joker.

MYSHKIN. Trump jack, club-over, fools, nits, and underbogey! Three fools—my game! . . . You should have hidden the *other* dummy set under your foot—

AGLAYA (*getting angry*). Your deal! Three's up, double-dunce.

MYSHKIN Triple-nits!

AGLAYA. Four open, over yours.

MYSHKIN (*catching her cheating*). Under yours.

AGLAYA. Madcap.

MYSHKIN. Rummy!

AGLAYA. Joker!!

MYSHKIN. Fool!!! Ha-ha . . . I mean *fools!* You see? This game—sometimes I can hardly believe I'm so good. A virtual master.

AGLAYA. You ought to be ashamed visiting this house after running around with that Fillipovna woman. Get out!! (*Myshkin slumps off.*) Maman!

MME YEPANCHIN. Where's the Prince?

AGLAYA (*putting her games away; discovers a stuffed gerbil*). He had to go. Where's Ippolit?

MME YEPANCHIN. Over there. (*Aglaya goes to Ippolit.*) Either there's a bad smell of love in the air, or the cook put chocolate in the gravy again.

AGLAYA. Dear Ippolit—I'm so glad you forgot to put the firing caps in. Could you deliver this stuffed gerbil to the Prince, and bid him please accept it from Aglaya with her most unwavering respect. I'll pay you later.

IPPOLIT (*after a cough*). Within the month, I suppose.

AGLAYA. Go. Go!

MME YEPANCHIN (*grabbing the gerbil from Ippolit*). Aglaya! What is the meaning of this stuffed gerbil?

AGLAYA. It's a stuffed gerbil I'm sending the Prince. (*Exits*)

MME YEPANCHIN. It symbolizes something, child—you've been reading literature again! (*Music: "Stuffed Gerbil." Mme Yepanchin holds the stuffed gerbil aloft to Ippolit.*) There seems to be a motif of gerbils in the air. (*She sings.*)
What means this stuf-fed gerbil?

AGLAYA (*entering*).
Putting the paw on man's animal nature?

GANYA, IVOGLIN, LEBEDEV, *and* IPPOLIT (*as the former three enter*).
Is the soul no more than this overpuffed fur-ball?

ALL.
Is that what we're trying to say here? . . .
Gerbil.

> Gerbil, gerbil, gerbil,
> Symbol of life's gnawing mystery!
> Poor dumb thing,
> Just one squeal from you'd reveal
> All the rumbling

Message of Dostoevski!

AGLAYA.
> But no! . . . not a burble.

MME YEPANCHIN.
> Dead silent and serene.

MEN (IVOGLINS AND LEBEDEV).
> Carcass of darkness and nonsense!

WOMEN (YEPANCHINS).
> Keeper of deeper significance!

ALL.
Gerbil!
Stuf-fed gerbil . . .
What could you possibly mean??

(*Mme Yepanchin shoos everyone out save Aglaya. Myshkin enters.*)

MME YEPANCHIN. Prince Myshkin—I demand to know the meaning of this stuffed gerbil from Aglaya!

MYSHKIN. It's a stuffed gerbil Aglaya's sending me to show that she thinks enough of me to send me a stuffed gerbil.

AGLAYA. And I suppose you know what this all means, Prince—we must marry as soon as possible.

MME YEPANCHIN. Good God, the world is ending!!

MYSHKIN. Could I marry you?

MME YEPANCHIN. I refuse! I refuse!

AGLAYA (*screaming*). Maman!! Behave yourself!! (*Mme Yepanchin cowers.*) Now, Prince (*sweetly*), as the legal representative of my mother's only marriageable daughter, I must ask you some practical questions—how do you intend to support me?

MYSHKIN. I have every intention of making you happy forever. I will perhaps work as a tutor—

AGLAYA. Excellent—and during the summer you could get a part-time job as a professional athlete.

MYSHKIN. A profess—

(*Aglaya bursts out laughing, hysterically.*)

AGLAYA. Oh, God—I'm sorry—I can't help myself.

MME YEPANCHIN (*relieved*). I thought so—another joke—I knew it from the start—from the gerbil. Apologize, child.

AGLAYA. I can't—I'll die laughing . . . I'm a brat. You're lovely and I do enjoy you

so. Forgive me—I'm so young—

MME YEPANCHIN. Prince Myshkin—

AGLAYA. Don't mention that name! He smells! He drools! He looks at me!! (*She runs off.*)

MME YEPANCHIN (*sighing, looking fondly at Myshkin*). I suppose I shall have to show you her dowry now. It's obvious she thinks of you in all the various romantic ways. This is our most precious heirloom. Long ago, the head of the Myshkin line dictated in his will that the last of the Prince Myshkins have his brains placed in this vase. An old family joke. Someday, I'm sure, I *know* someday you and Aglaya will pass it on to your son and laugh about it as much as you and I have just now at this moment. (*She is unlaughing.*) Excuse me—I must tell the cook about the wedding. (*She exits.*)

(*Myshkin alone, looking at the vase; Aglaya sneaks up behind him.*)

AGLAYA. Don't break that vase!!
Myshkin starts, almost drops the vase. Aglaya laughs.)

MYSHKIN. Aglaya—everything you say is prophecy!

AGLAYA. I'll never marry you. You're as much a stranger to me as to everyone else. (*She suddenly kisses Myshkin heavily, then kisses the vase.*) I'll marry you, Prince Lyov. But not until I confront Natasha Fillipovna and get her out of your mind once and for all.

(*Music: Opera. Rogozhin escorts Natasha in and remains.*)

AGLAYA.
> Natasha Fillipovna . . .

NATASHA.
> Aglaya Yay-pumpkin . . .

NATASHA *and* AGLAYA.
> I despise you!!!!

AGLAYA.
The gnats from your womb
Gad about your perfume
And go mad and mate on the fly—
They kiss then they pop then they die—
And in their strange insectual fashion
They've covered the range of your passion!

NATASHA.
> That's a good little girl,
> Good as a well-kept abbey:
> Fecklessly neat
> While roaches eat
> Filet of baby
> In all the real places of the world.
> What do you want a man for—
> Marriage??? Hahahahahahahaha!
> All you need is a janitor

To air out your cage!
I take back everything I said in that
    letter.
MYSHKIN.
    Aglaya, please! You've upset her!
AGLAYA.
    If I had a chance I'd behead her!
(*She struggles with Natasha.*)
ROGOZHIN (*restraining Natasha*).
    Baby, I don't think you'd better!!
NATASHA.
        Ha-haha-haha-haha-haha!
        You're as weak as a titter
        Without your maid, my dear!
AGLAYA.
        Hahaha-hahaha-hahaha!
NATASHA.
        But I've only to order
        And I'm obeyed—
        Look here:
        Rogozhin!
        Go!!
(*Rogozhin starts to go.*)
AGLAYA.
        No, no! No, no!
ROGOZHIN (*facing Myshkin*).
        Myshkin . . .
(*Indicating Natasha, with resignation.*)
She enjoys playing cards in the kitchen . . .
And prefers the dog-style position.
(*He exits.*)
MYSHKIN.
        Natasha! Aglaya!
NATASHA *and* AGLAYA.
    Pick, Prince, between us!
    Quick, Prince, you promised!
    Who shall reign
    Over all your brain?
AGLAYA.
    Who will do more good for you?
NATASHA.
    Who can you do more good for?
NATASHA *and* AGLAYA.
    Tell her, Prince—
    I'm the only one in the world!
NATASHA (*to Myshkin*).
    She's weak, you must leave her.
(*Natasha faints in Myshkin's arms. Aglaya
screams.*)
AGLAYA (*overcome by this whole scene*).
    I think I'm getting . . . a fever.
(*She begins a faint exit.*)
MYSHKIN (*dazed, cradling Natasha's head
and hair, carefully*).
        One big hand
        On a thousand hairs,
        Which hair do I feel?

        There's one,
        There,
        There.
(*To the leaving Aglaya.*)
        Understand,
        There,
        There,
        There.
        I hardly feel a hair.
(*Aglaya is off. Opera ends. Natasha awakes,
shaking from a nightmare.*)
MYSHKIN. There, there. Be a child. We'll
marry tomorrow. I must see Aglaya and ex-
plain. I'll be back presently.
(*Natasha exits. Myshkin visits the Yepan-
chins.*)
MME YEPANCHIN. No! She's still delirious!
You and I, Prince, we're very different. Ex-
cuse me—the cook is burning something.
(*Exits*)
(*Music: "Counterfit Wedding March"*)
(*Myshkin, very distraught, grotesque, stag-
gers down the aisle with Natasha. The stoic
congregation contains two veiled women and
four top-hatted men. Rogozhin is the priest.
He lavabos a milky fluid into the vase, which
he will use as the consecration chalice for the
ceremony.*)
LEBEDEV (*with a noose*). Your best man,
Prince! I couldn't find a ring, but I brought
the rope. You're listening to me again,
Prince, I can tell. I'll carry it around my neck.
Here. If you want to say anything else to me,
just pull. It's good pet I am, Prince. Lead me
around on the rope, and I'm faithful forever.
No more Rogozhin!
ROGOZHIN (*intoning for the congregation*).
    Oh all-knowing God, Divine Eye of all
                ideas—
CONGREGATION.
        Have meaning on us.
ROGOZHIN (*consecrating chalice-vase*).
        For this is Thy brainmilk—
(*He gives the chalice to Natasha.*)
CONGREGATION.
        Take ye and drink.
ROGOZHIN (*as Natasha drinks*).
Pour out your Godhead unto this man—
CONGREGATION.
    That he may be known to us.
ROGOZHIN.
That we may approve his marriage—
CONGREGATION (*as Myshkin drinks*).
        And find him fit!
ROGOZHIN.
    In the name of the Logic, and of the
        Brain, and of the Holy Insight—

CONGREGATION.

Amen.

ROGOZHIN. Rise, brother, and reveal thyself, we pray thee.

(*Pause, as the Congregation sits.*)

MYSHKIN (*rising*). Many times enormous ideas possess me, wild clumps of words lying in my stomach like old dead operas. But I cannot bear to hear myself! I am only subject to fits, whereas you are subject to life! And so my message, if spoken, would be as ineffectual as the greatest art of all time. My words are only worth repeating. Love life. Watch your minds. Think of all that there is in a mere seed, and then break open your heads! (*He flings the chalice-vase against the icon, shattering it.*)

(*Sound of fly; bass: thump, thump, thump*).

AGLAYA. Who needs you? All you care about are the deepest regions of people's souls. Do you think we enjoy you rummaging around in our fondest, most unforgivable secrets? You're a cold prophet, Prince. One warm day you'll freeze to death!

MME YEPANCHIN. Nothing but a vase. Nothing but some priceless heirloom some person or another knocked over. This is only a glass joke. But people—people fall apart every day. Why, this very moment bodies are decomposing madly all over the world!

MYSHKIN. You forgive me? Not only for the vase, but for everything? I love your face —it's absurd! Ridiculousness! The root of all forgiveness, the only reason for love! The very foundation of every life in the world. Sanity itself is merely the byproduct of a ridiculously insane complex of human brain processes. Why, just think of the zillions of excited brain transactions it must take just to create catatonia!! (*Music: "Fitting" reprise*) Ridiculous! I embrace your glorious silliness! It is absurdity that makes us infinite! It is God that gives life meaninglessness!! For it is exactly what we don't know that gives us perfect reason to go on living. What a burden it would be to know everything! Our brains would have no reason to move! Time crashes, space cracks, and light turns into marble. I eat! I eat! I eat our infinite absurdities! (*Going to Natasha*) Thank brainless God we have no reason . . . (*pause, the aura*) to be . . . what we are . . . (*As he takes Natasha, he begins shaking, fitting.*)

NATASHA. Rogozhin!

Rogozhin yanks Natasha out of Myshkin's hold. Myshkin has a fit. Rogozhin jumps on

him to restrain him. Lebedev beats the rope on the floor. Myshkin almost strangles Rogozhin.

NATASHA (*screaming*). Rogozhin!!

(*Myshkin releases Rogozhin, and continues his fit. Rogozhin takes Natasha to her house and lays her out dead. All but Lebedev have exited as Myshkin finishes.*

Music climaxes, sound of a fly, the fit dies. Lebedev dangles the rope of his noose toward Myshkin.

LEBEDEV. Just pull my rope, master! I'll make you a man out of monkey sperm!

MYSHKIN (*counting clouds*). One.

LEBEDEV. I'll make a rope out of his spinal cord and give it to a child.

MYSHKIN. Two!

LEBEDEV (*offering Myshkin the rope*). Here, baby, baby! It's just a long nipple on my neck. Count to three and suck out my head.

MYSHKIN. Three! (*Lebedev barks weakly and runs off.*) I count four clouds today. Anthills! . . . Natasha? One hundred twelve ants. (*Examines brain*) Twelve, thirteen thoughts in a row . . . and there's some more! (*Looks up*) Sixteen clouds now. (*He begins counting everything at once, until Rogozhin comes up to him.*)

ROGOZHIN. Brother. Come.

MYSHKIN. Rogozhin . . . (*pointing up*) the clouds aren't making a single picture. . . . Is Natasha at your house?

ROGOZHIN (*leading Myshkin*). Yes. Here we are. Quiet as stones now.

MYSHKIN. Paryfon—

ROGOZHIN (*having a chat*). I noticed you outside—so I addressed you and brought you here, and that's all I've been doing recently up to now.

MYSHKIN. That's true . . . Natasha . . . ?

ROGOZHIN. She's in there . . . I slit her throat. On the bed. Behind the curtain.

MYSHKIN (*having gotten up to look*). I can barely see . . . oh yes . . . I found it . . .

ROGOZHIN. Prince, you'd better not have a fit. We can't afford screaming.

MYSHKIN. You've covered everything but her foot. Why her foot?

ROGOZHIN. Because if people hear you, and come in here, and see the body in that condition, I'd be arrested within a week.

MYSHKIN (*crouching*). Paryfon—I'm fairly certain I can get up . . . I have in times past gotten up, often from a similar position . . . it's the fear. We must wait. It'll go. . . . When will she start smelling?

ROGOZHIN. I thought of that! I thought of

covering her with flowers, but . . . that would be sad to see her covered with flowers . . . you know?

MYSHKIN. The knife, right? Your "letter opener"?

(*They exchange laughs.*)

ROGOZHIN. Below her breast—near the heart, you know? It went in, right? Three inches . . . maybe five inches . . . you know.

MYSHKIN (*hearing someone*). Shh! People! . . . Four people. (*Pause*) I thought you cut her throat.

ROGOZHIN. She slit her wrists.

MYSHKIN. She should start smelling any second now. It's very close in here.

ROGOZHIN (*sniffing*). Yes—there it is now. (*Gives Myshkin deck of cards*) These are the cards we always used.

MYSHKIN. I wanted to see them. (*He looks at them.*) Again and again—I'm not saying what I should be saying. I did so want to see these, but—Rogozhin? Rogozhin—look! (*He shows Rogozhin the cards.*) No use at all!! Like the one moment before the fit stretched out forever like the sun over the sky I remember my life—(*His eyes go blank.*)

A fly is heard starting and lighting fitfully. (Bass: thumping erratically)

ROGOZHIN (*cradled by Myshkin, who from time to time caresses him blankly*). Did you know she was blind in one eye?! When she was sixteen she saw two wolves eat a horse. She still has the bones! (*Laughs*) . . . Smell that? I can hear her decomposing! (*He listens closely.*) Dp! Dp! Dp! Foooom! (*Screaming*) Do you hear that, worms? (*Arming himself against the worm attack*) Try and get her, worms . . . if you dare!! I should get five years . . . mentally unfit, you know? . . . You see . . . you hear . . . you smell. . . . "Stab!" she'd say, and I'd stab. "Bark Bark!" she'd say and I'd—

Rogozhin kisses Natasha's dead mouth and howls insanely, as the rest of the characters— save Mme Yepanchin—enter, barking at Myshkin. Soon Rogozhin begins barking also.

The music grows stealthily.

Natasha is revived by Rogozhin's barking, and she begins yipping. Natasha and Rogozhin

turn their barking on Myshkin. Natasha pulls of Myshkin's left shoe and sock and begins gnawing his foot. Myshkin is blank. Rogozhin is still growling.

The other characters put a glass cube over Myshkin. His shoe and sock remain outside. Myshkin is now sitting cross-legged in the same place where he began the play.

ROGOZHIN (*his roaring turning into his final sentence*). Row, row, row—Rogozhin gets five years. (*He freezes, staring idiotically, deadly, at Myshkin.*)

Everyone, at the end of his own last line, does the same thing, ending up frozen in a stare at Myshkin.)

IPPOLIT. Ippolit dies of tuberculosissss.

IVOGLIN. General Ivoglin dies of a stroke-kk-kk!

GANYA. Ganya goes on as usual.

NATASHA. Natasha remains dead.

LEBEDEV. Lebedev hangs himself.

AGLAYA. Aglaya survives, and runs off with a lofty spasmodic homosexual of almost saintly chastity.

MME YEPANCHIN. Mme Yepanchin, the one good character in the story, sends the Prince to a Swiss mental clinic, where he never recovers, never speaks, barely moves . . . except for one day when he points to his eye and says—

MYSHKIN. Aaaaa . . .

MME YEPANCHIN. But he was probably just trying to rub it, probably saying no more than—

MYSHKIN. Aaaaa . . .

MME YEPANCHIN. And she finally breaks down, visits the Prince in Switzerland, and speaks the final lines of the show (*to the ogling statues around the glass cube*): "Well, come to your senses, you. He's not there—*we're* inside, encaged in glass around him. I'm going home—enough of these illusions!" (*She starts to exit, freezes gracefully.*)

The music increases.

Everybody catatonic, reflecting on Myshkin, who is barely wriggling, squeezed in the glass.

The music dins, then dims.

Myshkin is heard droning: "Aaaa," or is it "I"?

The music and the lights turn to nothing.

TOM PAINE

Paul Foster

Part One of this play was first performed in May, 1967, at the La Mama (E.T.C.) Experimental Theater Club, New York, by the La Mama Troupe, with sets designed by Kikuo Saito, lights designed by Laura Rambaldi, and costumes designed by Michael Warren Powell and Helen Rostagno. In addition to those listed below, the cast also included Seth Allen, Blanche Dee, and Shellie Feldman.

The entire play was first performed at the Edinburgh International Festival, September, 1967, in the Church Hill Theatre, under the auspices of the Traverse Theatre, with the following cast from the La Mama Troupe:

PART ONE

TOM PAINE'S REPUTATION John Bakos

1ST DEAF WOMAN, THE AMERICAN COMMITTEE OF SE-
CRET CORRESPONDENCE, A GREEDY, THE WOMAN
IN THE RED CLOAK Mari-Claire Charba

MAJOR DOMO, ROGER Peter Craig

SERGEANT, CAPTAIN, GENERAL, QUARTERMASTER, GOU-
VERNEUR MORRIS, KING GEORGE III OF ENGLAND
Jerry Cunliffe

GIN SELLER, 2ND DEAF WOMAN, A BRITISH SPY, A
GREEDY Claris Erickson

TOM PAINE Kevin O'Connor

PRIVATE, MATE, DRUMMER, SILAS DEANE Victor
LiPari

BEULAH, A GREEDY, COUNT DE VERGENNES Beth
Porter

BISHOP, CARON DE BEAUMARCHAIS Michael Warren
Powell

MARIE; JOHN JAY, PRESIDENT OF CONGRESS; A GREEDY
Marilyn Roberts

ALTAR BOY, QUAKER, OLD MAN, GOVERNOR, BLACK
DICK, KING LOUIS XVI OF FRANCE Rob Thirkield

PART TWO

TOM PAINE'S REPUTATION John Bakos

MARGUERITE BONVILLE Mari-Claire Charba

MAJOR DOMO Peter Craig

BURKE, SENTRY, SERGEANT, KING GEORGE III OF ENG-
LAND Jerry Cunliffe

MARY WOLLSTONECRAFT, OLD MAN, 2ND REGISTRAR
Claris Erickson

TOM PAINE Kevin O'Connor

THE SHADOW OF CROMWELL, PRIVATE, SENTRY, DRUM-
MER, THE LORD JUSTICE Victor LiPari

SIMONNE, 1ST REGISTRAR Beth Porter

BARRISTER HORSELY, CAPTAIN LAMBESC Michael
Warren Powell

QUEEN MARIE ANTOINETTE, MARIE Marilyn Roberts

BLAKE, KING LOUIS XVI OF FRANCE Rob Thirkield

A Chorus of Greedies. A Chorus of Children.
Winds and Waves.

Director and Music Composer:
Tom O'Horgan
Set designer: Hamish Henderson
Light Designer: André Tammes
Stage manager: Steve Whitson
Company manager: Bill Muir

Not so long ago the New York theatre—almost the American theatre as a whole—could be summed up as simply Broadway. No matter that few of the so-called Broadway theatres were actually on that somewhat grubby Great White Way—they were all clustered in the Broadway area around Times Square. Then came the Off-Broadway Theatre, and then the Off-Off-Broadway Theatre.

To innocents in the ways of American theatrical practice, this nomenclature can seem extremely odd. However, the distinctions it makes are not those of geography but of finance and organization. The Off-Broadway theatre buildings, always smaller and usually adapted from something else, ranging from an attic to a church, usually produced plays at a more modest level than on Broadway. Costs were deliberately kept down, experiments made, chances taken, and, generally speaking, the play rather than the profit was the thing. Actors, and everyone else connected with the theatre, were prepared to work for less, for the experience and out of a belief in what they were doing, and the unions recognized the special conditions of the Off-Broadway theatre and accordingly applied lower wage scales.

But with the rising costs of Broadway—and the rising costs of Off-Broadway—the balance shifted. Successful Off-Broadway productions, such as Mart Crowley's *The Boys in the Band,* assumed the look of Broadway productions and made about as much money. It was in these circumstances that the Off-Off-Broadway theatre developed and flourished. Here, although the actors were mostly professional, they were not paid on union scale, the idea being that these were "showcase" productions and therefore beyond the usual rules.

The Off-Off Broadway theatre was a fairly gradual development, but everyone is agreed that it began around December 1958 in the Café Cino. This was run by Joe Cino, who started a kind of theatre to supplement his coffeehouse in Greenwich Village. Another important Off-Off Broadway house was—and is—the Judson Poets' Theatre at the Judson Memorial Church in Washington Square, which opened under the direction and encouragement of Al Carmines in 1961. A year later came the most famous Off-Off Broadway theatre of them all. It has been called variously La Mama, Café La Mama, and La Mama Experimental Theatre Club, but whatever it has been called it has found its heart and soul in one woman, Ellen Stewart.

Miss Stewart founded La Mama in a basement on 321 East Ninth Street. She founded it with Paul Foster and Jim Moore. Mr. Foster wanted to write plays. The house seated twenty-five in the audience. But that was the aspiration. Mr. Foster would go out into the street to hustle up business. It has been said by Albert Poland and Bruce Mailman in their *The Off-Off Broadway Book* that, as soon as Paul found someone, he would tap the window and Ellen would start the performance—but that has to be accurately apocryphal, as it were.

Paul Foster, the son of a lawyer, was born in Pennsgrove, New Jersey, on October 15, 1931. He graduated from Rutgers with a BA in English literature, and later went on to law school at New York University. Since his first produced play, *Hurrah for the Bridge,* on September 20, 1963, Mr. Foster has kept busy in the theatre, unsuccessfully producing his play *Elizabeth I* in 1971. It is, however, his play *Tom Paine,* first directed by Tom O'Horgan, that has made the biggest impression so far. Together with a play by Rochelle Owens, *Futz,* this established the enormous European reputation of La Mama, and also helped place the American theatre in the forefront of the avant-garde in European eyes. At home we hardly knew what we had.

The first part of *Tom Paine* was originally given at La Mama on April 27, 1967, and it was an expanded version that went on the European tour. It was this expanded version that opened off Broadway on March 25, 1968. It closed on December 8, after 295 performances.

The daring and dexterity of this satiric chronicle version of Paine's life, as well as O'Horgan's imaginative staging, made this one of the landmark productions of the late sixties. It demonstrated that large audiences were ready for a style of play and a style of staging that hitherto had been thought too advanced for popular taste. In a sense *Tom Paine* help set the scene for another O'Horgan staging, the enormously popular musical, *Hair.* Incidentally, *Tom Paine* was one of the first plays to use nudity—for the most part discreetly veiled—on the legitimate Broadway stage. The play itself has enjoyed many other productions both in the United States and abroad.

DIRECTOR'S NOTE

I am trying to remember what it was first like to read the script of *Tom Paine.* Of course, my senses are not virgin to the plays of Paul Foster, having directed all but one of his plays in one medium or another, so it is impossible for me to get to where your innocence may be. But the thought of the reader having to crack the script unforewarned is somewhat disturbing.

It took us several months to understand this highly inventive play. The terrain of Foster's work is not easy to know. His theatre impulses seem to spring from earlier times and are mixed with new invention; they bear little relationship to the recent past; they never impose a secondary reality, but instead deal directly with the confrontation of the audience and the play.

Choice and chance have always played a large part in art, whether it has been in interpretations or in procedure, and in the current theatre, choice and chance have recently been reinstated in a place of dignity. In *Tom Paine,* Foster has explored more deeply into this territory than he has in his other plays, and the sense of chance operates more fully. By offering the actors improvisational "seed lines" which are to be planted in a body of improvised moments, and initiating freely improvised discussion of the play, in which, in our production, the audiences were encouraged to participate, the audience is presented with three levels of theatrical reality: the level of the text, which is tightly set down by the author to be performed exactly as written; the improvisational level, which freely uses the seed lines; and the third level of open discussion.

Another example of the audience's choice comes with Foster's view of the protagonist. In all his plays, with the exception of *The Hessian Corporal,* Foster has purposely chosen as hero a character who is beyond empathy. In *Hurrah for the Bridge,* Rover is a thoroughly destroyed man making his last journey. *The Recluse* is a fragmented old woman scrounging through the rubble of our society. In *Balls,* the two heroes are even more remote—they are abstracted as two swinging ping-pong balls. In *Tom Paine,* the audience is further distanced, not only by Foster's choosing the controversial character of Paine, who was at once one of our greatest heroes and made by some into an archvillain, but by his dividing the personality into a real self and a reputation. This inaccessibility works inversely, forcing audiences to fill the vacuum where the nature of the traditional theatrical hero usually is. The result is profoundly disturbing.

Further choice is required of the audience by the presentation of both facts and fallacies, and by the lack of time sequence. In the scenes of the Crossing to America, time and occurrences have been telescoped and invented: the thirty-seven-year-old Paine appears simultaneously as a sixteen-year-old street boy and a man in his deathbed agonies. The audience is bombarded with fragments and details of fact with subjective coloration. The viewer comes away with a subliminal residue which he has culled for himself.

For a director, the play presents the widest horizon of possibilities. More than in Foster's other plays—and most other works I have been associated with—images are allowed a kaleidoscopic freedom. Foster has come up with poetic ideas which require theatrical ingenuity on a par with *Peer Gynt* and *The Tempest.* And if some people felt our production was too richly produced, only a cursory glance at the script's requirements is necessary to realize that we even fell short of what is there.

Perhaps future productions can bring to the stage some of these images: I still do not know how to represent on stage a herd of turtles with burning candles on their backs and make them disappear as instantly as they appeared. But this is the adventure of working with a powerfully imaginative script.

The world of Paul Foster's theatre is a highly contemporary one, fragmented, burning hot and cold, offering data and facts, noncommittal, without solutions: The audience is made to feel the urgency of responsibility.

—Tom O'Horgan

TIME: 1809

PLACE: A bear pit, Lower Manhattan

CAST: An ensemble of twelve actors who play a variety of parts regardless of gender. The lines not assigned to a particular actor may be spoken by anyone, as appropriate.

BASIC COSTUME: Black—knickers, jerseys, skirts, leotards, ballet shoes.

PART ONE

Exercise your twitches, itches, limps, blinks, waddles. Specific characters begin to take shape imperceptibly and at different times.

A large barn with bales of hay, overhead hoist rope, a large rocking affair to one side that looks generic to this place.

As audience enters, actors casually bring in your own props, improvise lines about each other, your props, their locations, bus connections, etc. Seed improvisation lines with following lines on a rotational basis, a different actor each night in chance form:

————

If this is a bear pit, why all this hay?
They eat it.
EAT IT?!
They had strange diets in 1809.
The bears sleep on it.
GOGOL THE GIANT! *(Hisses)* He was the favorite.
AND KASHA! *(Cheers)* Not as big, but twice as quick.
Anybody seen the drum?
It's on my hump.
Help me with my fingernails.
(A harpsichord is placed center. The actor who plays PAINE tunes a note. Everyone tune. Sit at small stools around him. Begin to play

crumhorns, oboes, recorders, cymbals, serpent, triangle. Play GIN, GIN, GIN song, while conversation and lines continue. Make yourselves comfortable, a weird Baroque chamber concert.)
What are those birds who pick up shiny things?
Crows.
Magpies.
Oh, come on, *This* is the barn.
A bear pit.
All right, this is the bear pit. Lower Manhattan. 1809.
(Indicate beyond) There the bears. Outside, both armies slaughter each other. And in here . . . well . . .
In here another sport.
In here the fugitives.
The frayed leftovers, pick over the trappings like crows.
Like magpies.
Like *crows!*
Attracted by anything that shines.
Where's the drum?
Are they almost seated now?
I think so.
(Carry harpsichord to side. Continue to play other instruments.

Group, form crawling centipede, still singing song. Then, one by one, stand, advance and present yourself to audience. State your own name, clear, proud, stately, and bow, saying each a line.)
Tom Paine came from Thetford, England.
His father was a bastard.
His father made corsets.
He went to London. That pest hole.
He was 37 when he left.
He was exiled.
He was *not exiled!*
He went with a letter of recommendation from Benjamin Franklin.
And he bade his friends good-by.
His friends were Goldsmith and the mystic Blake.
And he made the great crossing to America.
And he lived in a bear pit in New York.
(Immediately: Two put on soldiers' hats and get rifles. PRIVATE drum a sharp roll. Silence; talk and badger these two at will.)
SERGEANT. TOM PAINE, wanted for sedition and treason, whose whereabouts are known to be in this vicinity of Five Points. All persons having information are ordered to step forth. A reward will be given. By order, General Burgoyne, Commander of this

here district. All right, Private, search this wallow! Gawd, it stinks. Never knew a place to stink up so bad.

(Group, unified animal growling)

PRIVATE. What's that?!

SERGEANT. Bears.

PRIVATE. BEARS! Gawd, I ain't enlisted to tackle no bears.

SERGEANT. They're chained, Private. They make 'em fight. And they bet on the winner. Got it? Now search.

PAINE *actor, from hay, grab his ankle.*

PRIVATE. AHH! HE'S GOT ME!

SERGEANT. All right, now what's your name, lovely?

(A wretched human, fingernails unbelievably long, hair matted to his head, dirt encrusted. Slobbering guttural animal grunts)

PRIVATE. He sounds like one of them animals.

SERGEANT. Hey, you, on your feet.

ACTOR OF PAINE. Gimme drink. *(Fall over)*

PRIVATE. I . . . I think he's dead.

SERGEANT. I think he's drunk. All right, keep it moving, Private. On your post. We'll just wait. *(Pace)* Is this some duty for a FULL sergeant? I could have been stationed at Government House tonight. No. What do I get?

PRIVATE. Five Points.

SERGEANT. The asshole of New York,

PRIVATE. Of the world. *(Pace)* Sergeant, what's he look like? I mean, how will we know we got him, if we get him?

SERGEANT. By his eyes. He's got the eyes of the Devil. He stirred up the whole mucking war. The General knows him, knows him by sight, and that's why nobody leaves till the General gets here.

PRIVATE. Gawd, it stinks.

(Improvise comments on bear pit, then on MARIE's *costume, as* MARIE, *a large woman, enters.)*

FEMALE. Marie enters and throws her weight around.

MARIE. All right. Pay up or sleep out in the snow. Nobody sleeps in my barn without cash.

(Complain)

MALE. Now the Sergeant throws his weight around. He is clearly outmatched.

SERGEANT. Hold on. Hold on! *(He cannot get attention.* PRIVATE *roll drum. Quiet for a second)* That's better. Nobody goes no place.

MARIE. You're generous with my hotel, Sergeant. Who's going to pay?

SEVERAL. The Sergeant pays.

SERGEANT. Hotel? This place ain't fittin' for animals.

ALL *(angrily).* Not fittin' for animals. You heard the Sergeant. Nobody pays.

MARIE. Then everybody sleeps out in the snow.

(Complain. Drum roll. Pick him up and carry him around.)

PRIVATE. TOM PAINE, wanted for sedition and treason, whose whereabouts are known to be in this vicinity of Five Points. All persons having information are ordered to step forth. A reward will be given. By order, General Burgoyne, Commander of this here district.

BISHOP *(addled and simple).* I know him. I KNOW HIM!

SERGEANT. Is that the truth?

MARIE. Anything's possible.

BISHOP. He used to sleep in my corner over there.

MARIE. It's an in-and-out business, Sergeant.

SERGEANT. Is he here now?

MARIE. Sergeant, we're honest people. Look at us. We'd never betray one of our own. At least not for the scrawny price you're offering.

BISHOP *(yelp up and down).* I know him!

SERGEANT. What's the matter with him?

(Gag BISHOP. *Get him into corner. Begin to dress him in ratty* BISHOP *robe.)*

MALE. He's strange.

FEMALE. Marie made him sleep out in the snow, and he got "frostbit" in the head.

(One ask if you can get frostbit in the head. The answer is either yes or no. Then at least two improvisational statements confirming, and two denying whichever answer is chosen each night. Then each a suggestion on how you would act if you did have frostbite in the head. There may be contradictions to the suggestions. From this, a composite characterization is arrived at for the role of the BISHOP.)

SERGEANT *(greatly angry).* All *RIGHT!* Then lis*TEN!* I want in-for-*MA TION!* About this trai*TOR.* This war mon*GER.*

Who dipped his pen in poison,
And writ a century off to die.

PRIVATE. WE WANT TOM PAINE!

(Repeat his name over and over. Search each other's faces for recognition. Search the theatre. It mounts to hysteria. A witch hunt emerges. The disjointed calling becomes a concerted evocation of his name. From this emerges the street jargon song.)

ALL. PAINE! PAINE!

DAMNED BE HIS NAME!
DAMNED BE HIS FAME!
AND LASTING HIS SHAME!
GOD DAMN PAINE! GOD DAMN
   PAINE!

(In mathematical rotation each night, find the "ANIMAL." Carry him onstage on a pole or rifle. Stand him on a stool. Invest him with the physical characteristics of TOM PAINE. *Each add to his character of personal filth, his matted hair, his fingernails long as a rat's, his alcoholism, his twisted nose, his stunted body. Improvise the line and select bits of costuming and paint. In a frenzy of purging anger, create a scapegoat. Seed improvisational lines with these specifics:)*

He came from Thetford.

From England.

He was Aquarius.

His father was a bastard.

His father made corsets.

He went to London. That pest hole.

He was thirty-seven when he left.

He was exiled.

He was *not exiled!*

He went with a letter of recommendation from Benjamin Franklin.

And he crossed the ocean to America.

And he bade his friends good-by.

His friends were Goldsmith and the mystic Blake.

(Lights dim. A ceremonial lifting of PAINE. *Place him center like an encircled, rutting animal.)*

And he made the great crossing.

And he lived in a bear pit in New York.

ALL. AND HE MADE THE GREAT CROSSING!

(All run off. Newly created TOM PAINE *center.* BISHOP *and* ALTAR BOY *with censer and incense, with font and evergreen branch. Chanting they go:)*

BISHOP. May this house know no evil, no demons, no spirits, no creature of darkness, no manner of black and nefarious things, no blasphemers and damned adherents of Tom Paine. His heresy, his treason, his deceits, his lies and prevarications, and his murders and rebellions, his plots, his ploys, his intrigues. Ad infinitum. *(Center,* PAINE, *pound floor or resonating box. Offstage, group take notice. Begin to pound and make catcalls, noises, and distractions.)* If Satan has cause to point him across this threshold, may flames rise up from this consecrated ground, consume him, consume his feet, hair, and bones, consume his

issue, and his issue's issue, and purify where he has trod. And may the Lord's angels who reign over these timbers and high vaults, the Lord's seraphim and cherubim who receive these prayers sent up, even as this incense is sent up to Him in the most high, may even they hear this sacred consecration and all know that herein dwells the Spirit of the most terrible and mighty Lord. *(All pound with* PAINE, *rhythmically.)*

ALTAR BOY. Hurry up your mouth.

BISHOP. I bless this house, this refuge for the homeless of the war which he has caused and brought upon us, may he burn in Hell. And I, the Lord's minion, will see that pity shall not rebuff his swinishness.

ALTAR BOY. FASTER, they're impatient!

BISHOP. I will ferret out evil even as a hog roots out truffles in this stinking barn living side by side with those miserable bears . . . Christ, I lost my place . . . His Holy war rages . . . which He in His perfectness . . . His Highness the King . . . OH, FUCK! His Holy war rages, I read that!

ALTAR BOY. MOVE YOUR JAWS! *(Throw the font at him.)*

BISHOP. In the name of the angels, the cherubim, and the seraphim, *I CONSECRATE THIS HOUSE! (Shimmy up rope to rafters. All rush in.)* SONS OF BITCHES! YOU COULDN'T WAIT TILL I WAS DONE?! COULD YOU?

(Crowd these events, rapid, overlap on each other. A simple rocking form, like a children's playground structure which volleys actors from floor to ceiling. A sign: THE LONDON PACKET. Enormous sail billows.)

(ROGER, DODGER, BEULAH *center. Sign: GIN ROW. Bilge passengers limp, run, crawl to bilge. Pack into it knife-wedge tight. Moaning, shrieking, crying, panting, gasping, pound sides for air. Arms and legs grab out like wild animals.* BISHOP *taunt them from above. All make sounds of seas, storms, groans, drumming. In this cacophony, all are sea-drunk, gin-drunk.)*

QUAKER *(in peruke).* This sea, this pit, this gutter of misery, this wallow called society . . . *(Pound gavel)*

CAPTAIN. BLOW! LOOK AT 'ER BLOW!

MARIE. The Atlantic's waves are cold and bright,
In the bilge below it's hot and tight,
From London's sewers comes a man by name,
Of fearful eye and burning roar,
He brings with him the drums of war.

QUAKER *pound gavel.* DRUMMER *louder.*
PAINE *laughs and all noises rise up. Heavy*
winds blow life into sail. The cacophony be-
gins:

CAPTAIN. Look at 'er blow! Lay out every inch of canvas you've got!

MATE. If it'll hold wind, it's stretched taut already.

CAPTAIN. Look at 'er bounce! I'll bust the record for the crossing!

MATE. I'm feared we'll bust the masts first.

CAPTAIN. Let 'em bust! She's damn near flying! It's a happy ship, ain't she mate?!

MATE. Nine weeks of bashing it out on the water. Oh, a happier ship never made the crossing, Captain.

(ROGER, *jump up and down laughing.* BEULAH *shrieking laughter;* DODGER *kneels under her skirt, bobbing voraciously. She kicks him out. All roar drunkenly.* BISHOP *above:*)

BISHOP. SHUT UP, FILTHY BLEEDERS!
(*Deluge of garbage. Roar anew.*)
ROGER. You're drunk!
DODGER. Filthy drunk!
ROGER. Cheap gin and cheap sin. I'm for Parliament and that's my platform.

DODGER. Them that ain't drunk gets hanged.
ROGER. Then drawn and quartered! Get all London screaming drunk! The whores and babies and Parliament itself. SCREAMING DRUNK!

PAINE. MARIE! MORE BRANDY FOR THE DRUMMER! THE ARMY MARCH BEHIND HIM! THEY NEED HIS BEAT! HURRY, THEIR FEET BLEED IN THE SNOW!
(*All sing. Bilge cry refrain:*)
ALL. Look around London and what do you see?
Age to the poorhouse, youth to the gallows.
Because of-ffff . . .
GIN! GIN! GIN!
Enough to float the navy in.
GIN! GIN! GIN!
It's good for everything.
GIN! GIN! GIN!
Sores and pock holes, runny wham holes.
GIN! GIN! GIN!
WASH THE BABIES IN IT!
GIN! GIN! GIN!
THE GUTTERS RUN WITH IT!
GIN! GIN! GIN!
PAINE. IF THEY STOP NOW, THEIR FEET WILL FREEZE IN THE ROAD! THE ICE TEARS THE FLESH OFF THEIR FEET! MARIE, THE ROAD IS STIFF WITH BLEEDING FLESH!
CAPTAIN. MORE SAIL! LET 'EM BUST WIDE OPEN!

(*Main area. Read gently with calm measure:*)
·(PAINE'*s body draped in Union Jack on deck. A cloth chute down side of ship.*)

OLD MAN. The bearer, Mr. Thomas Paine, is very well recommended to me as an ingenious worthy young man. He goes to Pennsylvania with a view of settling there. I request that you give him your best advice and countenance as he is quite a stranger there.

ROGER. SEND THE BASTARD DOWN HERE!

DODGER. SEND HIM DOWN!

(Measured chorus of pounding and insistence)

ALL. SEND HIM DOWN! SEND HIM DOWN!

(Intermittent cries from bilge throughout:)
Water!
Please!
God!
Gin!

BEULAH *(sings).*
If you're not blood
in England,
You are dirt,
For dirt in England,
Dirt breeds dirt.

MATE. Captain, they're rottin' in the bilge down there. This un's the fifth to go on the crossin' and the bouncin' don't help none.

CAPTAIN. Have I ever let ye down, mate, in all our crossin's?

MATE. You been good to me, Captain. I'll swear on it, but it's eatin' 'em up at a smart rate. It's the fever.

CAPTAIN. DON'T SAY THAT WORD! Now, Matey, you make out a nice new passenger list.

MATE. Showin' five less than before, Captain?

CAPTAIN. Oh, yer a bright lad!

MATE. And the finance sheet'll show a little adjustment too?

CAPTAIN. Oh, yer a bright lad.

MATE. And maybe the Captain'll see his way clear to reward the nice Matey?

CAPTAIN. Ain't you the thoughtful one. Mind, open your mouth in town and you're shark bait come the return crossin'.

(Slide PAINE's *body overboard into GIN ROW group.)*
NAKED CAME THEE OUT OF THY MOTHER'S WOMB, AND NAKED SHALL THEE RETURN THITHER! THE LORD GIVETH AND THE LORD TAKETH AWAY. BLESSED BE THE NAME OF THE LORD! WHERE'S THE GIN?!
Snatch him up, flag and all. Haul up by the feet. BISHOP *descend as counterweight.*

PAINE. BASTARDS! BASTARDS!

BEULAH. Gawd, caught him like a rat in a trap. Nabbed him proper. Lookit him. HEY! HEY!

ROGER. He's high as a kite.

BEULAH. Come on, give 'im a drink. He'll never get it up.

DODGER. Hanged man always gets it up.

ROGER. He's only sixteen.

BEULAH. I've seen it before. Come on, honey, I remember you.

(Hussahs)

ALL. HE'S GOT A HARD-ON! *(All sing.)* GIN! GIN! GIN!

Enough to float the navy in.

GIN! GIN! GIN!

It's good for everything.

PAINE. BASTARDS! BASTARDS *(Cries, moans, pleas from the bilge)* THEY'RE BURNING THE BARNS! HIDING THE CATTLE! MY ARMY WILL STARVE! MARIE, THEY'RE SCORCHING THIS FROZEN HELL! BRANDY!

(Bursts of laughter. Through the audience with electric bullhorn and lantern:)

GIN SELLER. That's for cheap gin and cheap sin. Take your choice of slow death, horrible death, or bloodsloshing screaming death. That's a messy one. Tuppence gets you roaring drunk. Mothers swear by it. Kiddies shut their foul mouths for it. Try a can for courage. Push your old pa and his matrimonial sow off the roof. The legacy'll get you a barrel of my LIGHTNING FAST GIN!

PAINE. MARIE! THE ARMY RUNS AWAY! MARIE! THEY'VE DROPPED THEIR GUNS ON THE ROAD! MARIE! BRANDY! BRANDY!

GIN SELLER. It races up your spine. Snaps your nerves and tears up your guts! OW, IT'S LOVELY STUFF! LADIES! GENTS! BABIES! Screaming fits are free. Treat yourself to a holy vision of God and all his bleedin' saints in a BLINDING, FLASHING ELECTRICAL STORM! TRY MY LIGHTNING GIN! Gawd, it's cheap enough.

(Din in every quarter)

PAINE. DAMN THEM! DAMN THEM!

QUAKER. Hush thy sinful speech. If thy right arm offend thee, cut if off. If thy tongue speak evil, cut it out. A beating will teach thee to be a better Quaker.

PAINE. If there be God, God damn them. Curse Captain. Curse King. Curse God that brought forth thy kind and his greed. We are all animals with His fever.

QUAKER. I WILL BREAK THY HEAD! If thee die on the crossing, thee'll not be laid in holy ground to infect Christians.

PAINE. CURSE THY HOLY GROUND!

QUAKER. God grant thee be taken to the Devil himself. Praise be to Him Almighty.

PAINE. BASTARDS! BASTARDS ALL!

CAPTAIN. MORE SAIL! LET 'EM BUST WIDE OPEN!

ALL. WE'RE GOING TO AMERICA. THE PROMISED LAND!

(Laughter, shrieks. Bilge floods out, moaning, crying, dazed by the light. With a long pole, pound for attention:)

MAJOR DOMO. No sooner he landed than the sulphur of discontent blew in the air, and he sniffed it. And it excited him greatly. And he saw that it was good. The city was rife with rumors of war and treason. The taverns and the coffeehouses. And yes, the slave markets; the City of Brotherly Love wasn't brotherly. God had been whipped out of him long ago, yet he prayed to God these things:

PAINE *(say very quick without a breath or pause in whole speech).* Oh, God, what I have to do, I will do. I would do these things even if I did believe in Thee. Let us keep our peace between us a little longer, between Thee and me, you ancient Faker. I will get to Thee on a latter day. For now, I will set down on my papers other hatreds, between us and that other Royal faker who sits snorting German on his English throne, and I will drag him down. His little English corporals and his hired Hessian killers. Thou will see that I do these things. *(Begin to carry him about.)* And I will shake him off that perch and I WANT MYSELF TO TAKE UP THE KNIFE IN BOTH HANDS AND RIP OPEN HIS ROYAL SEAMS FROM HEAD TO BALLS! I want my words to go out like dogs biting at his heels. I'll tree him. I'LL TREE HIM! And while horns play and dogs yelp at his heels, I will take up the knife. And I will call this little book, this keg of sulphur and powder, I will tie its title like a fuse, *Common Sense.*

MAJOR DOMO. He wrote that book and, true to his promise, the dogs were unleashed and treason ran screaming through the streets. His Reputation was born from the side of his ribs. *(Block it so that is.)* And now, it goes before him wherever he goes. (REPUTATION *in clean gray and white.)* Inside the City of Brotherly Love. Tom Paine and the Quaker.

QUAKER. This was once a good place. The City of Brotherly Love, The Peaceable Kingdom. Everyman was welcome here with open arms. Where a man could work and worship God in dignity. And the voice of the dove was heard in our land. And now . . .

PAINE. And now, Friend?

QUAKER. And now, thy black book, thine

evil thou hast spawned on us . . .

PAINE. It is only Common Sense, Friend.

QUAKER. It is Satan's sense! Three HUNDRED THOUSAND copies or more, spread into every corner and it poisons minds wherever it goes. I have come to tell ye . . .

PAINE. To tell me that you don't approve of the war. Yet you don't approve either of the dead carted into the city under your nose.

QUAKER. Ye must stop writing thy filth! Ye must end this massacre ye have begun.

PAINE. It has begun. I cannot stop it, Friend. What are we to do with the thousands of corpses fertilizing the fields around the city already? Close our eyes and bow our heads? What are we to do with the nasty details such as the 70,000 armed killers across the river, their bayonets pointed at our eyes this very minute?

QUAKER. Let the Congress settle that.

(Group run on in panicked chaos, carrying bundles, bedding, chairs. CRIERS *ring hand bells, shout through electric bullhorn:)*

CRIERS. The Congress urges everyone to stay in their homes. The roads are blocked. Stay at home! The roads are clogged. Stay at home for your own safety. CONGRESS HAS LEFT THE CITY! IT'S RUNNING FOR ITS LIFE! THE CITY IS RUNNING BEHIND IT!

PAINE. Now what is left of our army will have to slaughter itself to regain what the Congress threw away. There's the truth of it, good Friend.

QUAKER. The truth will come out by itself.

PAINE. The truth rarely comes out unless dragged by its hair. The seed crop of a whole generation dying to the last man to protect what? Those wise gentlemen who are supposed to guarantee order and happiness. They run with their tails between their legs, yelping, leaving the prize for the enemy.

(Breaking glass. Books thrown from every quarter.)

ALL. BURN THE DAMN BOOKS! BURN THEM! THROW THE TRASH IN THE STREET! THEY'RE INVADING THE CITY FROM THE NORTH! THE ROADS ARE CUT OFF! THEY'RE SHELLING THE NORTH SECTION WITH ARTILLERY! THERE HE IS! GET HIM! THROW THE BASTARD IN THE FIRE! KILL HIM! KILL PAINE! *(All attack* PAINE, MARIE *fight them off.)*

MARIE. STOP IT! STOP IT! He is laying out a blueprint for centuries to come. You want to kill him?!

PAINE. Marie, soon the angel will stalk over these hills and her cut will be clean and sure, and for so many, many, this life, this pageant, will be over.

MARIE. Go on, beat your crazy head. You're not God. You're just a man.

PAINE. That's sufficient.

REPUTATION. The war bewilders them.

PAINE. It was necessary.

(Break. Be yourself. Light a cigarette if you want to. Actors, especially REPUTATION, *ask any questions you wish of the actor playing* PAINE, *concerning his true feelings and motivations. Suggestions:*

1. *Why* PAINE *brought about the revolution?*
2. *Did he truly believe in the concept of independence enough to stir up a revolution?*
3. *Especially question why he hated the king on such an intense, personal level.*
4. PAINE *actor, answer them yourself. Conclude with:)*

ACTOR OF PAINE. He said nothing was so ridiculous as a king. He said, "Nature disapproved of kings or she wouldn't ridicule the folly so often by giving mankind an ass for a lion."

ACTOR OF REPUTATION. Do you think he would, if he could . . . like to be king himself?

ACTOR OF PAINE. That's ridiculous.

ACTOR OF MARIE. Did he hate the king . . . or did he envy him?

ACTOR OF PAINE. Neither. He believed in America. He christened the United States of America. They even picked his brains to write the Declaration of Independence!

ACTOR OF MARIE. We will see.

ACTOR OF PAINE.
Tend to your bear pit,
And leave this part to me.
I'm Tom Paine.

(Pause)

PAINE. I, Tom Paine. Land I have none. I have exiled myself from one country, without making a home of another. And sometimes, I cannot help asking myself, am I a revolutionary, or just a refugee.

*(*MAJOR DOMO *with staff of office, announce:)*

MAJOR DOMO. THE GENERAL. THE BISHOP. THE GOVERNOR. *(Bow center in elegant costumes. Chamber music group play* GIN *song sweetly on your instruments. The three minuet.)* Inside the Governor's palace.

GENERAL. Well now, just what are we to

do with this girdle maker?

GOVERNOR. We'll do nothing. The whole thing will blow over.

GENERAL. On our heads. I say arrest him.

BISHOP *(obsequiously)*. Gentlemen, the church has long experience in such matters as this. Over the centuries we have had to refine our sense of survival, and so have more experience in these matters. I say, let us wait and see.

GENERAL. Let the army arrest him and burn the damn books.

GOVERNOR. What will the people say?

GENERAL. The people! The people are like insane insects, forever rebuilding their destroyed houses. They'll survive.

BISHOP. We have to be clever. It's the book, you know. Books are dangerous. It's the book.

GOVERNOR. *Common Sense.*

GENERAL. Common Crap.

(Dance ends.)

BISHOP. Couldn't we . . . now let's see. Couldn't we somehow . . . tax the book?

BOTH. Tax?

GOVERNOR. They don't pay their other taxes. How can we collect on a book?

BISHOP. No . . . what if we tax *him*? Specifically, I mean, he sold thousands of these . . .

GENERAL. Little filth sheets.

BISHOP. We'll *invent* a tax. We'll tax his income on the book.

BOTH. What an absurd idea. A tax on income. Now this has possibilities, how did you think of that?

(Someone hold a cymbal over his head.)

BISHOP. Divine inspiration, my son.

MAJOR DOMO. Tom Paine's Reputation precedes him. (REPUTATION *kneel. They ride his back.)* The newspaper cartoons recorded the meeting. *(Two follow them with cartoon balloon. They speak as written:)*

BISHOP.

Church and Kings do bleſſ the land,
Church and ſtate go hand in hand,

"The sun never shone on a cause of greater worth. 'Tis not the affair of a city, a country, a province, or a kingdom; but of a continent—of at least one-eighth part of the habitable globe. 'Tis not the concern of a day, a year, or an age; posterity are virtually involved in the con-

GENERAL. We ſuffer their bleſſings.

GOVERNOR.

Upon our backs, the Junta rides,
So ſoft they ſit upon our hides,

GENERAL.

To feed and guide the poor and blind,
They ſuck the taxes from our labor,

ALL. God bleſſ the King!

MAJOR DOMO. Tom Paine enters in a borrowed coat.

PAINE. Gentlemen, I am Thomas Paine, my respects.

GOVERNOR. Oh, we are pleased that you consider us gentlemen.

BISHOP. Yes.

GENERAL. Yes.

PAINE. You are the church. The state. and the military. Are you not?

GOVERNOR. We are.

BISHOP. *Yes,* we are.

ALL THREE. INDEED, we are!

GOVERNOR. How kind of you to acknowledge us, you . . . *(Shrieking)* YOU REBEL!

BISHOP. FATAN! BLAFPHEMER! HEREFY!

(Grab him. Run him around.)

GOVERNOR. Your book bloſſomed treaſon!

GENERAL. You, the army will ſupreſſ and make you ſuffer!

(Throw PAINE down.)

GOVERNOR. Gentlemen! Gentlemen, we are getting over excited, and our diction gets sloppy when we get excited. NOW . . . no . . . EXCITEMENT! *(Calmly)* No ex-cite-ment. Mr. Paine, we have read your book with great interest. *(Grunts)*

PAINE. And so, my reputation speaks for me.

(Both conversations melt into each other. PAINE, drooling at the mouth as the MAJOR DOMO brings in a large brandy bottle.)

GOVERNOR. You realize the burdens of good government we have.

REPUTATION. That is precisely what I want to accomplish, good government. I have written the truth as I see it.

(PAINE's hands shake, his mouth drools. He fumbles at the bottle.)

PAINE. There they are, the fine gentlemen in their laces and lacquered pumps, their snuff-

test, and will be more or less affected even to the end of time, by the proceedings now. Now is the seed-time of continental union and faith. The least fracture now will be like a name engraved with the point of a pin on the tender rind of a young oak; the wound would enlarge with the tree, and posterity read it in full grown characters. The Cause of America is in great measure the Cause of all Mankind."

GOVERNOR. You see I have the gout, Mr. Paine. The best doctors tell me to pickle my feet. It is so good for them. *(Take off your boots as you speak.* BISHOP *pour brandy on his feet.* PAINE *drool.)*

BISHOP. A waste of good brandy.

GOVERNOR. In the interests of good government.

GENERAL. A governor in pain is apt to be a cross governor.

GOVERNOR. And it soothes the feet so. A waste of good brandy? Is that what you are thinking, Mr. Paine?

BISHOP. It shouldn't go to waste, should it, Mr. Paine?

GENERAL. Oh, don't let it go to waste.

GOVERNOR. Waste is wasteful. Go on.

GENERAL. Don't waste it. Go on, lick it up.

(PAINE *slobber over his feet.*)

BISHOP. Lick it all. Between the toes.

GENERAL. Lick it up, best brandy of Jamaica.

BISHOP. We know you appreciate good brandy.

PAINE *(to* REPUTATION*).* HYPOCRITE! Get out if you can't stand to watch!

GENERAL. We've heard you can lap up your weight in brandy.

GOVERNOR. Now dry my foot.

BISHOP. With your hair.

GOVERNOR. There sits the American Revolution.

(Change costumes laughing and grunting

ALL. *THE FIT COMES ON YOU!*

WOMAN. Fast as fire.

ALL. THE FIT COMES ON YOU!

She hovers over him.

Sucking the air from his fire.

boxes of silver and their fine court manners, and the bottle on the table between us. Warm and red. See it shine. Just a sniff. That's all. A SNIFF! Ah, I can feel its perfume oozing through the cork. Ah . . . ah. *(Fumbles a great drink)* No. No. Come away from it! Another? Just a small one. To steady my hand. I have to write all night, need a steady hand. Quick! Quick! Here they come. QUICK! ONE MORE! PLEASE!

like animals.)

MARIE. There sits Paine. A tramp. Paine a beggar. There he sits, warming his guts now for a fight. Revolution breeds like a boil in his mind to tear down whole cities, and all the continents of the fat round world will bleed from his surgery. It folds like a fist in his brain.

MALE. And sure as he promised, the armies formed sides, and death, the madwoman, ran screaming over the land.

(The RITE OF EXORCISM *begins to form. Recite lines in rotational form.)*

(PAINE, *breathlessly jerk the words out between gasps of air:)*

PAINE. The two men . . . shook hands. One had gloves. One had . . . socks over his hands. Brown wool. The two men stood. No. One was already mounted to horse. Only one man stood. The other began to curl a smile. He shook hands instead. His mouth would not smile. He was ashamed. His teeth were wood. He did not smile. OH, CHRIST, GIVE ME A DRINK!

ALL. *Go on!*

MALE. The famous woman in the red cloak enters.

WOMAN. God has sent me with a message for you.

PAINE. 'Tis a lie! He would not send his messages by such an ugly woman.

WOMAN. Recant! For your judgment is near.

PAINE. 'Tis a lie! They wished Godspeed. They departed. Slow retreat into November. The nights grow longer. THE COLD TURNED THESE

ALL. *RECANT! FOR GOD!*
They'll curse you.
They'll teach their children filth
in verse for you.
    ALL. *IN VERSE SO THEY
WON'T FORGET!*
They'll ape your face and your
long nails.
That curl around your toes.
You'll have to fight for every
inch of history you take up.
The British voyeurs watched
and giggled.
Like towel girls in a whore-
house.
    WOMAN. RECANT!
    ALL. *THE RITE OF EXOR-
CISM!*
The smell of barracks.
A woman is raped.
A boy is raped.
An army starves in the snow.
    ALL. A WHOLE ARMY!
A young boy is eaten in secret.
The cannibals weep as they eat.
    ALL. They pick his brains to
mold . . . *The United States of
America.*
They hunt him down with dogs.
    ALL. *RECANT! RECANT!*
(Surround the SERGEANT*)* The
war poor, mouths dumb with
hunger.
Too swollen to speak.
    ALL *(pointed to their mouths
like nesting birds).* Like crows.
    ALL. *Like birds!*
Stole the belts to suck the flavor.
*CANNIBAL THINGS HAP-
PENED!*
The fresh-killed soldiers . . .
*(Two soldiers carried on poles,
seminaked. Bite into them)*
. . . flung like slaughtered
sheep in the fields.
Tempting the appetite.
Tender and young.
    ALL. *TEMPTING THE
APPETITE!*
Watering juices in the mouth.

FINGERS BLUE! Retreat
drags from campfire to campfire
. . . to disintegration. Deserters
take rags from their feet. Pad
horses' hooves. Steal away on
snow. He wanted to smile, but
he was ashamed of his teeth.
They geed the horses. One went
on his journey to the South.
GODSPEED! 'TIS A LIE!
There stood the German Hes-
sians like a giant phallus, loaded
and pointed at the buttocks of
Trenton. There we, gyved up
and bound, trembling and waiting, cooking our belts for hunger's sake.
'TIS A LIE!
We, stripped naked and bare,
braced for the attack like runners in a heat, head down, hands
down, buttocks up, trembling
and waiting for the shot. The
German battering ram pounded
at us. *(Husky, very upper regis-
ters of your voice, drawing for
air, very quickly:)* I ran starving
through those icy lanes under
the arches of nut trees. Picked
clean. I saw a lone cabbage, blue
with frost. Still there. I cracked
it open like a stone and ground
it in my teeth. The whole head
of it. I crept into that house by
the nut trees. Picked clean. The
windows cataracted with frost. I
crept in past the sleepers in their
beds, and into an empty room
and gnawed the stalk of cabbage, blue with frost. And outside the bells rang, and the
bleeding feet shuffled past on the
rock hard earth. *(Say inhaling a
single breath of air. Say quickly
and staccato. Voice register
higher and higher:)* And high.
High. Hi. Hi . . . hi above.
Miles up. We below as black
ants. Creep. In the snow. De-
vour. Eat. Chew. Crack. Mar-
row. Body and blood. Of God.
Sacred. Christmas. Night. The
Star! Of. Beth. Up. Up. High.
In. Excelsis. Deo. DON'T
STAND THERE! HELP ME!

(Dialogues end together. Two women GREEDIES *wipe the feast from your mouths. Sing and dance to accompaniment. Intermittent belches of satisfied gluttony from group, as you play your instruments sweetly.)*

DUET OF THE GREEDIES.

Tom Paine came from afar,
afar,
His nose is like a blazing star.
He stirred the world around
and round.
And turned the heavens upside down.

(MAJOR DOMO *pound staff.)*

MAJOR DOMO. Filthy and drunk, he wrote the great Crisis paper.

REPUTATION. My hands sweat. How to yea-say this slaughter. All the notes. All the papers.

PAINE. Get it the way it should say.

REPUTATION. How to yea-say these things to history.

PAINE. NOT BRAY!

REPUTATION. Pray?

PAINE. CRAP THAT CRUTCH!

(REPUTATION, *speak calmly.* PAINE, *mime your mouth to the words and speak together at appropriate places.)*

REPUTATION. The treasure of the world cannot induce me to support an offensive war, for I think it murder. But if a thief breaks into my house, burns and destroys my property, and kills those that are in it, and to *"bind me in all cases whatsoever"* to his absolute kingly will, am I to suffer from it? Let them call me rebel and welcome! I feel no concern from it. But I should suffer the misery of the devil, were I to make a whore of my soul by swearing allegiance to one whose character is that of a sottish, stupid, stubborn, worthless, brutish man. I call not upon a few, but upon all; not of this state or that state, but of every state. Let it be told to the future world, that in the depth of winter when nothing but hope could survive, that the country alarmed at one common danger came forth to meet and to repulse it.

(Drum roll.)

MAJOR DOMO. And it was repeated down the line. Down the line. "Let it be told. In the depth of winter."

(Send the phrases down the line.)

MARIE. The rebels won the battle!

MAJOR DOMO. But off Sandy Hook 200 cannon had erections. And on the ships stood a thousand soldiers. And they were all erect. The Lord Admiral was in command of all these erections. And he said:

BLACK DICK *(very nasal in admiral's hat). This* is unnatural.

MAJOR DOMO. This many cannon. This many soldiers.

BLACK DICK. In *this* condition.

MAJOR DOMO. He issued a proclamation.

(Drum roll.)

DRUMMER. His Lordship, Admiral Richard Howe.

BLACK DICK. ALL RIGHT! Enough of this. Now lay down your arms. Good heavens, down. And, umm, now, you see. These soldiers and . . . ummm, SOME of these, ummmm, sailors. Mine. Umm, yes, they are mine. WE WANT TO MAKE SUE-UR-AH, THAT UMM, THIS SORT OF THING does not, umm, RE-occurah. Do you he-ah? And umm, that our-ah Lord. That is, umm George. The Thahrd I believe?

MARIE. Yes, the Thahrd.

BLACK DICK. Is paid prop-ah, an . . . ah . . . ALLEGIANCE. Yes. You see, he, umm, paid for all this. SO! That. Is, umm, my proclamation.

(Applaud him.)

MAJOR DOMO. In the streets, in Five Points, they loved it.

DRUMMER. Signed, Lord Admiral Richard Howe.

BEULAH. That's not his name.

BLACK DICK. All right, big mouth.

BEULAH. His name's Black Dick. It really was.

(Throw your hat at her. Square dance. All sing:)

ALL *(refrain).*
Who can take you serious
When your name's Black Dick.

When brains were passed around the floor,
Black Dick stood behind the door. *(Refrain)*

They put their money on his nose,
Black Dick Stood and there he froze.
(Refrain)

They bet that he would rise and shine,
Black Dick's horse was left behind. *(Refrain)*

Nobility is bound to rise,
Why should it come as a surprise.

(Crossover 1:)

QUARTERMASTER. Look, Private! You ain't gettin' no boots from my storeroom without you got the proper chit. If we had any boots. Which we ain't.

PRIVATE. I got one good one.

QUARTERMASTER. Where did you get it?

PRIVATE. From a dead Hessian. All I need is one to match it up.

QUARTERMASTER. Sorry.

PRIVATE. So I got to shoot another Hessian?

QUARTERMASTER. Yeeep.

PRIVATE. With what? I'll have to kick him to death with my one good boot.

QUARTERMASTER. Yeeep.

(Crossover 2: Two old DEAF WOMEN with ear trumpets)

1ST DEAF WOMAN. The lists show three shiploads of boots and ammunition came into port.

2ND DEAF WOMAN. What?

1ST DEAF WOMAN. It all disappeared.

2ND DEAF WOMAN. What?

1ST DEAF WOMAN. The lists are stamped Hortalez and Company.

2ND DEAF WOMAN. What?

1ST DEAF WOMAN. IT'S ALL DISAPPEARED!

2ND DEAF WOMAN. You don't have to shout.

(MAJOR DOMO. pound staff for attention.)

MAJOR DOMO. THE SILAS DEANE AFFAIR! This is the last scene in the first act. We trust it will please you. The Court of St. James and the palace of Versailles. *(Black and red patent-leather groundcloth unrolled. It is a chessboard.)* We call this chess game the Steinitz Gambit, in honor of that genius who had a fondness for the maxim, "The King is a fighting piece." You will play: *(Pound staff at presentations. Each enters in red or black velvet collars and all in large mask-peruke headpieces.)*

Monsieur Caron de Beaumarchais. (Bow.) You wrote the Marriage of Figaro but you were born to a low life and so spend the rest of your time pimping your talents at court. Red Rook. Position 1.

Mr. Silas Deane. (Bow.) A merchant to act as American agent in Paris. You are worse than a dog tick. You bloat yourself on war profits as your kind has always done. Color the blood in your veins, green for greed. *(Like a sentence of guilt:)* Black Knight. Position 2.

Mr. Arthur Lee. (Bow.) You are really a damn fool, but the author suspects you are incapable of hatching large intrigues in your small brain. Red Pawn. Position 3.

(Enter on roller skates. Face hooded. No bow for you.)

You, *A British Spy.* Oh, go on! Black Pawn. Position 4.

Ministre de France in America, Phillippe Gerard. (Bow) You are the twitching, itching, limping, blinking, skilled diplomat always in these events. Red Knight. Position 5.

Gouverneur Morris. (Bow. Red side hiss him.) You are the knife an old idea fights with but nobody sees the hand on it. It's an old trick, and you're a master of it. Black Rook. Position 6.

The Prime Minister of France, Count de Vergennes. (Bow.) Good evening, your Excellency. We are pleased you could come. Please, would you be so kind. Red Knight. Position 7.

Now let's see. *(Pause)* Oh. *The American Committee of Secret Correspondence. (Bow. Hooded.)* Black Rook. Position 8.

Mr. John Jay, President of Congress. (Bow.) You are a snob and, I suspect, a bigot. Black Pawn. Position 9.

Mister Thomas Paine. Since this scene vitally concerns you, I suggest you stand center. On the Red side. Position 10.

And now, gentlemen *(Black side to attention),* His Majesty, George III, *The King of England. (Giant wig, cloak, pumps, and crown. Black side bow low. Red side hiss and catcall.)* Gentlemen, His Majesty, Louis XVI, *The King of France. (Giant wig, cloak, pumps, and crown. Red side bow low. Black side hiss and catcall.)* As you see, there are no recognizable land masses, but on either side, ideas as firm as continents. And in between, a sea of differences. And on either shore, mankind plays at being hateful spiders. Instead of spinning silk. *(Each side hiss and insult the other side loudly.)*

LOUIS XVI. SILENCE! SILENCE!

GEORGE III. SCHWEIG! SCHWEIGEN!

(MAJOR DOMO pound your staff. Slowly, taunting.)

LOUIS XVI. 'E ees ze King of England, et 'e cannot even speek eenglish as goud as . . . me do.

GEORGE III. SCHWEINEHUND! DAS IST ZUM KNOCHEN KOTZEN!

(MAJOR DOMO do pound your staff for silence.)

LOUIS XVI *(to BEAUMARCHAIS).* What did 'e say?

BEAUMARCHAIS. Pardon, mon roi. Il a dit . . . conch.

LOUIS XVI. Conch? CONCH! CONCH LUI-MÊME!

GEORGE III. FRANZÖSISCHES SCHWEIN!

MAJOR DOMO. Count de Vergennes, advance to position, Red King 2.

(Move in the manner of the chess piece you are.)

COUNT. Sire, last night I had a dream. A divine inspiration worthy of your attention.

LOUIS XVI. Invent for me a knife big enough to cut loose that miserable little English island tied to the coast of *our France* and let it float to . . . to Terre de Fuego.

COUNT. Sire, I cannot do that. Besides, your brother-in-law owns Terre de Fuego.

LOUIS XVI. Bien, then it would be his problème.

COUNT. We can do better than that. We can keep this little war in America boiling by giving the rebels monies to purchase ammunition, gunpowder, boots, and thereby divert enough of the English armies to fight the rebels, so they will not be a threat to Your Majesty. We give this to the rebels under the fictitious name of Hortalez and Company, so the British spies will never know the money comes from us. And who knows, the rebels might even win. *And who knows,* he *(pointing to* GEORGE III) might even lose his American Colonies. What do you think that would do to his gout?

LOUIS XVI. How much will your "divine inspiration" cost us?

COUNT. About two million livres.

LOUIS XVI. DEUX MILLION! You and your divine inspiration are crazy!

COUNT. But you see, Sire, we would give the rebels all the army's outdated ammunition which we would have to melt anyway. They will do the fighting for us. And you can appreciate what the loss of America would mean to the King.

LOUIS XVI. Divine inspiration!

COUNT. I am pleased you like my plan.

LOUIS XVI. Whose plan?

COUNT. Your plan, Sire. We will use Beaumarchais.

LOUIS XVI. That clockmaker. I can't stand him.

COUNT. Exactly, Sire. If anything goes wrong, he will be the ah . . . ah . . .

BOTH. . . . . the ah . . . *(laugh)* the scapegoat.

LOUIS XVI. I love it. Call him in.

MAJOR DOMO. Beaumarchais to position Red King 2.

BEAUMARCHAIS *(stuttering)*. I-I-I will establish a fictitious company. I-I-I will call it Hortalez and Company.

MAJOR DOMO. Beaumarchais to Red Pawn 3.

BEAUMARCHAIS. Mr. Arthur Lee, American Agent in London, Hortalez and Company will give you two million livres in ammunition. Don't tell anyone it is a gift from Louis Seize, because if the English knew this, they would bomb us off the face of the earth.

MAJOR DOMO. Arthur Lee to the American Committee of Secret Correspondence. Position 2. British Spy follow him.

(Red side hiss them.)

ARTHUR LEE *(W.C. Fields delivery)*. Wonderful news. France will give us supplies free of charge.

MAJOR DOMO. Arthur Lee *check. (Off the board)* Silas Deane to Secret Committee. Position 2. Spy free to rove about.

COMMITTEE *(weasel nasal)*. Mister Deane, you will go to Paris. You will contact Hortalez and Company and get the goods.

DEANE *(drawl)*. What about mah 5 percent commission? I always get mah 5 percent commission.

COMMITTEE. Mister Deane, you are doing this for your country. You understand that, don't you Mister Deane?

DEANE. Fine. Then I get mah 5 percent commission from the country. I always get mah 5 percent commission.

COMMITTEE. Mister Deane, it is so easy to love you. Heh, heh, heh. Good-by, Mister Deane.

MAJOR DOMO. Silas Deane to Count de Vergennes. At this point the wires get crossed. Watch carefully.

COUNT. You will go to Beaumarchais and say I sent you. These vital supplies are a *gift* from France. You understand that, Mister Deane?

DEANE. I always get mah 5 percent commission.

MAJOR DOMO. Count de Vergennes *check. (Off the board)* Deane to Beaumarchais.

BEAUMARCHAIS. Ah, mais non, Monsieur! Are you crazy? A gift?

DEANE. Ah thought Mistah Lee was crazy. If this was a gift, how was ah getting mah 5 percent commission? I always get mah 5 percent commission.

BEAUMARCHAIS. Of course, if it were a gift, I would not get my 10 percent commission. Already we sent three ships of supplies. The British she confiscated two, but you can be sure I will have to charge your Congress for all three.

DEANE. Mah commission is 5 percent. I always get mah 5 percent commission, Mistah Beau-march-ais.

MAJOR DOMO. Deane to Secret Committee.

COMMITTEE. Mister Deane, you realize if this affair comes to the attention of Congress . . . well, Mister Deane, we are the SECRET Committee. We shall keep our little secret. No one must hear of this two million livres. Our little secret.

DEANE. Mistah Committee, our little two million secret is now a great big four million secret. And here's mah bill.

(SPY *to* GEORGE III)

COMMITTEE. Oh . . . no . . . Mister Deane . . .

MAJOR DOMO. Secret Committee *check.* *(Off the board)*

DEANE. And I'm going to take this heah matter to the people.

MAJOR DOMO. Silas Deane makes a public address to Congress.

DEANE. "The Address of Silas Deane to the Free and Virtuous Citizens of Amuuuurr-rrica!" *(Great noises from everyone)*

LOUIS XVI. I know nothing about this! *Beaumarchais! Idiot!*

BEAUMARCHAIS. Oui, m-m-mon roi.

(LOUIS XVI *finger across throat: "Kkkkkrrrrhhhh!")*

MAJOR DOMO. Beaumarchais, *check.* *(Off the board)* British Spy, *check.* *(Off the board)*

LOUIS XVI. SILENCE! SILENCE! And you can stop performing his plays. He does not *exist* anymore!

GEORGE III. SCHWEIG! SCHWEIGEN!

LOUIS XVI. Why don't you speek Eenglish, if you can?!

GEORGE III. FRANSÖSISCHES SCHWEIN! We will see who can spricht besser English! Your own guillotine? Kkkkkrrrrhhh! UND we will see who can spricht . . . ohne A HEAD!

LOUIS XVI. Qu-qu-qu'est-ce qu'il a dit?

GERARD. Oh, rien, mon roi.

MAJOR DOMO. Paine to John Jay, President of Congress.

J. JAY *(purse mouth at each period).* Mister Paine. I won't banter words. Everyone knows I'm no admirer of yours. But since you are Secretary of the Committee of Foreign Affairs. You should be in a position to unravel. This conundrum.

PAINE. Mr. Jay, HOW IN THE NAME OF HEAVEN . . .

J. JAY. Hear! Hear!

MORRIS. Mr. Paine, do guard your language.

PAINE. Mr. Morris, if the soldiers do not have guns, you will have to guard your private . . .

J. JAY. Mr. Paine, if you have something to say, say it with a civil tongue.

MORRIS. This Congress is composed of gentlemen.

MARIE. Tread carefully.

REPUTATION. You walk on egg shells.

PAINE. I'll walk on their heads! Mr. Jay, since I am not a gentleman . . .

MORRIS. Obviously.

PAINE. . . . you will have to guide me in those delicate matters. All that stands between this city and the 40,000 bayonets poised at our throats is a small band of freezing farmers who have to repeat out loud to themselves that they are soldiers when they know they are not. Would this august body of gentlemen tell me why the warehouses of the city are breaking with uniforms and boots and powder, guarded by private police when the soldiers are freezing to death. Daily! When those very supplies were . . .

DEANE. LIES! THE FILTHY DRUNKEN BEGGAR LIES!

PAINE. . . . were given to the army as a gift!

J. JAY. Note that down.

GERARD. The rat falls into the trap.

MORRIS. Let him hang himself.

PAINE. A GIFT! FREE AND CLEAR!

J. JAY. Remember your oath of silence.

PAINE. Silence is not in my nature. This profiteer claims he served the public. He served his pockets.

DEANE. I have been of grrrrreat service to the cause.

PAINE. God save us from what *you* have done. What any of you have done.

J. JAY. Does this accusation include the Congress, Mr. Paine?

(Pause)

MORRIS. Well, Mr. Paine? The question "tumbles" through the air.

PAINE. When the Congress should have stood their ground, did they?

J. JAY. The Congress could not be allowed to fall into enemy hands, Mister Paine.

PAINE. The Congress should have stayed in the city.

J. JAY. Note that down.

MORRIS. The trap is sprung.

DEANE. I did mah duty, and I followed orders.

PAINE. You?! You lived very well indeed

while the soldiers half-starved and half-naked waited for your supplies. And never did men grow so old in so short a time. They crowded the business of an age into a few short months while you haggled prices on those supples which were a *gift* from Louis Capet even before you arrived in France!

MAJOR DOMO. Secret revealed.

GEORGE III. SO!

LOUIS XVI. Gerard, you idiot, maneuver!

GERARD. Those supplies were no gift. They were *bought* from the King's magazines and arsenals in Paris. His Majesty did not give anything away.

LOUIS XVI. Bravo, Gerard!

GERARD. And I protest these indiscreet assertions. And I wish you to take measures suitable for divulging secrets.

REPUTATION. Now you've done it.

(Huddle and confer)

J. JAY. Mr. Paine, the Foreign Committee, I regret to say, has no further need for your services.

MORRIS. Paine. Check. And checkmate.

PAINE. I don't give a damn about the Foreign Committee. What about the supplies? The King still has his sleeve full of tricks.

J. JAY. Don't concern yourself with the King. He is our affair now.

MORRIS. Again, you go into the streets. Where you belong.

DEANE. Troublemaker.

MORRIS. You can be the king of the streets.

J. JAY. You will leave. Go away!

MORRIS. Leave!

ALL. Leave!

PAINE. Why do I do it! Jackasses dressed up in gold braid, timid mice scurrying underfoot! Eating me a piece at a time.

REPUTATION. Your work is done.

PAINE. That's what you think! I'm not done yet with the "majestic" German. Give me a drink!

(Each side menacingly to other side:)

BLACKS. No!

RED. GIVE HIM A DRINK!

MAJOR DOMO. The war in America will be over soon. He lit a fire, and now Europe is a seething caldron set to boil over and scald everything in its path. England and France are about to *crack open the face of Europe.* And nothing will ever be the same again.

(KINGS stand on shoulders and circle for battle.)

LOUIS XVI. Conch . . . conch . . . CONCH ALLEMAND!

GEORGE III. Klotz . . . klotz . . . FRANSÖSISCHER KLOTZ!

(THE BATTLE. Both sides in melée of insults, trying to drag KINGS down, defending-assaulting. KINGS fall. Each side tears crowns and regalia from other side's KING. KINGS chased off board.)

MAJOR DOMO. Exit the pomp of power!

PAINE. The revolution will be won. *Oh, it will be won!* And then . . .

REPUTATION. And then?

PAINE. Then I'll carry it to his doorstep.

ALL. To England!

REPUTATION. You're meat for his jaws.

PAINE. I'll snatch the meat from his jaws. Give me a drink!

ALL. **GIVE HIM A DRINK!**

(Revert to characters you were in the beginning of the act. Rotational lines:) You've got to be a king to fight it out with a king. *(Step center and stop action)*

SERGEANT. All right . . . ALL RIGHT! I WANT TO KNOW SOMETHING ABOUT TOM PAINE! THIS TRAITOR!

MARIE. Did this help you any, Sergeant? *(Start to dress PAINE in both kings' regalia.)*

SERGEANT. Help? I DIDN'T UNDERSTAND A DAMN WORD OF IT!

MARIE. The moment's passed, you'll understand it later. Give him this.

SERGEANT. What are you doing now?

MARIE. Give him this!

(Everyone now assist in the investiture.)

PAINE. GIVE ME A DRINK! Stop that. STOP IT!

CROWD. Get dressed. You'll love it.

It's velvet.

And ermine.

REPUTATION. What are you doing to him?! Stop this!

CROWD. He's getting good and drunk.

It's got all this gold stuff.

See it shine?

It's real . . . almost.

Just an arm.

Come on.

PAINE. GIMME 'NOTHER DRINK!

CROWD. The other arm.

BISHOP. The investiture of the King.

CROWD. The livery of royalty. *(He is drunk. Mockingly, continue to clothe him.)*

And the robes.

Red ones.

RED!

So red they're black.

PAINE. Mine must be as red as his.

They're even redder than his.

REPUTATION. STOP, YOU WITLESS FOOL! THEY'RE PUTTING WORDS IN YOUR MOUTH!

CROWD. And . . . and . . . the fingernails.

PAINE. Gilt! Gilt, please, Marie.

CROWD. They're gilded thrice over.
More gilded than even his.
And longer than even his.
And . . . and . . . the gloves of state.
That touch without being touched.
Silver gloves.
Stiff silk.
Stiffer than even his.

GIVE-ME-A-DRINK! All you ministers, get it up. ARE YOU LISTENING? Like a hanging man. I shall surely see him hang! You . . . YOU! You're not trying ! Harder! A silver bell is supposed to ring when it occurs. You're only halfway there. MINISTERS I CANNOT HEAR YOUR SILVER BELLS! *(A forceful carillon of bells. Maybe hanging pipes.)* I am ready to be horsed. *(He is lifted up.)* And the sceptre.

ALL. THE SCEPTRE!

PAINE. It must be gold.
Golder than even his.

REPUTATION. STOP THIS!

PAINE. WHERE'S MY ORB?! AND MY BRANDY?!

CROWD. Your orb.
continents than even his.

PAINE. AH! AH! AH! And . . . and . . . the dia . . . NOT DIADEM, IDIOTS! THE BASTARD NEVER WEARS A DIADEM!

REPUTATION. STOP IT, YOU FOOL! *(Try to stop them.)*

BISHOP. He wears . . . *(whisper)* the crown.

PAINE. Marie, he wears the crown. With jewels.

CRUST THEM ON ME! I am ready for . . . for . . . the . . . ah . . . ah . . . crowwwwwwnnnn.

BISHOP. The investiture is complete.

PAINE. I will go to his doorstep, and I will bring my revolution and the war and the massacre to him. Give me seven years, just seven, and I will write a Common Sense for every nation in Europe. And I will go to France, and I will decree my imprisonment in the dungeons of Luxembourg, and the fateful cross of chalk on my door, and possibly my own decapitation on the guillotine. Ohhhh, a king's a lovely thing.

SERGEANT. I DON'T UNDERSTAND A DAMN WORD OF THIS!

MARIE. Well, Sergeant, we're tired now. We'll try again later. He says he'll go to England, but before he goes, let's take a break to consider if he should.

SERGEANT. All right, but when you tell it this time, I don't want no nonsense. I want you to talk straight! Do you hear?!

ALL *(mocking).* Oh, we will, Sergeant. *(Start to straggle off singing "Tom Paine came from afar, afar." It grows and grows, louder and louder with drums, gongs, and noises.)*

SERGEANT. Allllll right. All right! ALL RIGHT! ALL RIGHT!!!

(PRIVATE try to drum them to silence. Add to the cacophony. Only PAINE and REPUTATION left on stage. He stands stunned in disarray of regalia.)

REPUTATION. "Turned the world upside down," headhunting kings. And there you are.

(REPUTATION exit, disgusted. Pause. MARIE enter. Address audience.)

MARIE. All right, you can go out for a smoke now, it's intermission.

(Leave PAINE on stage in full light throughout intermission.)

CURTAIN

SCENES IN PART TWO:

PART TWO

(Straggle on. Clear light. Rotational:)

Do you have the bag. Of turtles.
TURTLES?!
More animals in this show.
Bears. Turtles. What's next?
If there were three acts, we'd have elephants.
They didn't expect to see a bear anyway. Did you?
It's not a zoo, you know. It's just a stage.
And it's full of splinters.
And the dressing rooms are *tacky.*
Come backstage after the show, you'll see.
Oohh, Marie has had her pee.
And she's feeling ballsy.
Again.

MARIE. All right, ready for another crack at it, Sergeant?

SERGEANT. Just a minute. *Just a minute. (Get gun. Put on hat.)* Now, where were we?

MARIE. You want Tom Paine. You've come to the bear pit where he lives, in Lower Manhattan.
You've got an arrest warrant.
As long as your arm.

(Drum roll)

SERGEANT. Tom Paine wanted for sedition and treason whose whereabouts are known to be in this vicinity of Five Points. By order of General Burgoyne, Commander of this here district.

BISHOP. We went back to England.

MARIE. Wake him up.

(Wake PAINE.*)*

PAINE. Let me alone.

MARIE. Get in the boat. We're going to England.

PAINE. Oh, let me sleep.

BISHOP. It was dark when he sailed. I'm afraid of the dark.
The American Revolution is won.

MARIE. He swore he'd bring it to England.
And to France.

SERGEANT. All right, let's begin. Take out the house lights!!

BISHOP. I . . . I'm afraid in the dark.

SERGEANT. Take down the dimmers, across the light board!!

BISHOP. I . . . I'm afraid in the dark!

MARIE. Get the turtles. You'll be all right.

MAJOR DOMO. Part Two. Blake receives Paine at the coast amid the turtle stars.

(Ship rock quietly to and fro with cloaked figures. Use image of Blake's "Pity." PAINE *in black mask with burning diamond eyes and black cloak.* CHILDREN, *fore-center, take turtles from bag. Turtles have small birthday-size candles on their backs, lit. In the dark as they crawl about,* WINDS *and* WAVES *whisper-chant.* SENTRIES *stretch out arms and hold hands.)*

ALL. THE NIGHT FIXES THE EARTH BALL!

PAINE. The night fixes the earth ball, and I long to lever it round once more.

BISHOP *(sobbing). Please, it's dark, dark. Please . . . hold me.*

CHILDREN *(sing).*
Here lies the body of Jim Crow,
Who was high, but now is low.
Ye brother Crows, take warning all,
For as ye rise, so must ye fall.

WINDS AND WAVES. Oh and oh, and oh and oh, the winds sighed song for the sightless horses of the waves. The penny pot of ink sways and sways. And oh and oh, the ship a-pitch in the night, slipped in the ocean shining bright. Pad the waves, pad their hooves. His cargo is velvet black. The penny pot of ink is very black. And oh and oh, through the mists and through the waves, and on the sightless horses, two eyes burned and yearned and burned the light of madmen, to hook the coast of England in their light.

TWO SENTRIES. Two sentries on the coast of England. Our arms stretched out to tell the sea, this for you and this for us, and all of ours. Sea, this is where you leave. This patch, this rock is ours and beyond in those deeps lies yours. This coast, our arms stretched out, say to everyone, *This is England.*

WINDS AND WAVES. Wave-ferried ship in the night, outwit the stars. *To England.* And the penny pot of ink sways and sways. The bite and crack of its words still lie scrambled, jumbled-tumbled-viscous-black in the penny pot. Waiting for the dip. Of the pen. Of the man. Called Paine. *(Inhale "Ah")* Ah, but the penny pot of ink sways and sways.

TWO SENTRIES. Sea, wherever you're from, whatever you've seen, whatever you bring in your corked and salty whispers, say to brine and man alike, *This is England.*

WINDS AND WAVES. Sways and sways.

TWO SENTRIES. Ride a cocked horse to Banbury Cross to London Tower and to St. James Court. Tell the King to flail the waters, to punish the waves for their treason.

PAINE. This is an age of treason.

WINDS AND WAVES. The mystic Blake knows secret things.

(BLAKE *enter in cloak.*)

BLAKE. Solemn heave the Atlantic waves between the gloomy nations.

WINDS AND WAVES. Sways and sways.

BLAKE. A cowl of flesh grow o'er his head and scales on his back and ribs. "Things" in rustling scales rush into reptile coverts! *(Inhale "whale" and "away")*
Where wolves and tygers howl for prey,
I see a whale drinking my soul away.

(All run off except SENTRIES. KING GEORGE III *enter hurriedly and flail angrily.)*

SENTRIES. The sea trembles like a murderer and swells *to wash the shores of England clean.*

(All run before the waves. Immediately:)

MAJOR DOMO. It is now summer. The heavens continue to do their job beautifully. Rain falls, sun shines, blessings for the bounty of man continue, and nature's philanthropy is lobbied for by witch doctors and farmers around the world. Mankind accepts it all, and gripes for more. The Church in France gluts itself on over one-half of the entire land, belches its gut clear and demands in a loud voice not to be taxed.

ALL. YOU KNOW WHO PAYS THE TAXES!

MAJOR DOMO. Ancient feudal leftovers, divine rights of kings, hungry courts, a gluttonous church. France has it all. And nobody pays a sou in taxes.

ALL. YOU KNOW WHO PAYS!

MAJOR DOMO. Eat and eat and eat some more is a duty to the state.

ALL. YOU KNOW WHO EATS!

MAJOR DOMO. Louis in France. George in England. One a locksmith. One a farmer. Neither went half a mile without a swarm of toadies, overdressed and overperfumed. All eating. Every step of the way.

ALL. AND THE PEOPLE WORK OVERTIME!

MAJOR DOMO. So they could wake up and *eat* some more. Things are ripe for Paine and his fresh, hybrid, crazy way of looking at things.

ALL. BLOW SOME AIR INTO THIS LILLIPUT OF CRAP, PRETENSE, AND BULLSHIT!

MAJOR DOMO. Oh, happy is the land ruled by a king.

(Projecting frontal platforms. Union Jack over one. Fleur-de-lis over other. Two identical tables piled outrageously high with food. GEORGE III *at one.* LOUIS XVI *at other.*

Gorge yourselves, I mean shove it into your mouths and hold your hands on your mouths to hold it in. GREEDIES *sing pig song:)*

GREEDIES.
Dearly beloved brethren,
Is it not a sin,
When you peel potatoes,
To throw away the skins?
For the skins feed pigs,
And pigs feed you,
Dearly beloved brethren,
Is this not true?

(KINGS throw bones at them.)

LOUIS XVI. Why is it . . .

GEORGE III. . . . everybody who comes within speaking distance . . .

BOTH. . . . wants to wheedle us out of something? *(Eat like starved hogs. Say "und" like rooting, voracious hog.)*

GEORGE III. KARTOFFELSALAT! SCHWANZKOPF! UND, UND, *UND* FLEISCH! UND, UND, *UND* KOPF-KÄSE! UND, UND, *UND, UND* KARTOFFELN! UND, *UND, UND, UND,* BLUTWURST!

LOUIS XVI *(say "et" like panting poodle).* GRENOUILLE! CRETIN! ET, ET, *ET, ET* ESCARGOT! ET, ET, ET, *ET, ET* BOEUF! ET, *ET, ET* CÔTE DE VEAU! ET, ET, *ET, ET* CHAMPIGNONS! ET, ET, *ET, ET, ET* PÊCHES! ET, *ET, ET* POMMES! MOUTON! *(To other side)* Potatoes and pickled pike. The palette of a peasant in a palace.

(GEORGE III throw bones at him.)

GEORGE III. Slimy snails and slimy frogs and slimy eels. Your SLIMY SLOP makes you walk like a woman. You want one of my troopers to give you some good sausage?

(LOUIS XVI throw bones at him.)

LOUIS XVI. We know about your troopers. Half of them are pregnant by the other half!

GEORGE III. And your "troopers"? Women in boots and mustaches, and the men stay at home to knit!

LOUIS XVI *(suck your finger adoringly).* At least these are my people. We are French. You are not even English. My people adore me. I am their King.

(From audience, a sullen march of WOMEN*)*

GEORGE III. "My people adore me. I am their King." My English puppies hate me, but I rule them with an iron fist. *That* is how you keep order in the house, frog-eater.

(WOMEN surround LOUIS XVI angrily, sing, shout)

WOMEN. We want bread *now! (Pronounce "breahd")*

LOUIS XVI. Petit peasant, you have a visitor from over the ocean. In his lit-tle book he writes lit-tle love letters for you. And he wraps a bomb in each one! Pet your English puppies now. They'll bite your hand off!

(WOMEN lift him. Angry shouting)

WOMEN. BREAD! BREAD! BREAD!

GEORGE III. I would not touch him if he had scrofula!

LOUIS XVI *(tenderly, really not comprehending why they do not eat cake).* Mes gens, pourquoi vous ne mangez pas de gâteau?

(Bounce him on trampoline and carry him to Paris. Blackened CHIMNEY SWEEPS line up as though in street parade.)

MAJOR DOMO. Louis XVI surrounded his capital with foreign mercenaries.

ALL. Paine! Paine! Paine!

REPUTATION. Wake up!

PAINE. Oh, my head.

ALL. PAINE! PAINE! PAINE!

PAINE. Give me a drink. Just one to wake me up.

REPUTATION. Watch this! One-old-man triggers off a megaton of hate.

(CAPTAIN LAMBESC enter. Rotational with MAJOR DOMO:)

MAJOR DOMO. The German Cavalry Officer, Captain Lambesc. The Butcher of Paris. Swaggers through the poor section. The chimney sweeps crouch before him. *(OLD MAN enter.)* An old man approaches. He does not see him!

OLD MAN *(intense anger).* You learn to look quick. When they come, you learn to leave the curb and get out in the street. Or they knock you down. *Knock* you right in the mouth! Three years old or ninety. *Knock* you right down! And you *get off* the curb into the street.

MAJOR DOMO. He knocks him down with his sword! *(Pause)* Frozen hate!

REPUTATION. In the streets of Paris. WAKE UP! WATCH THIS!

OLD MAN. The world spins around. I am here in space. They won't let me land on the curb. So I got to straddle it. Legs and arms and STOP IT! Change it around so everybody walks: Out in the street. YOUNG! ONES! AND! OLD! ONES! BLACK! ONES! AND! WHITE! ONES! Out in the street and walk with me! *(Attack CAPTAIN LAMBESC and rip the clothes off his back.)* Storm the Bastille!

We SHALL overcome.

REPUTATION. The ancient, crenellated stone is attacked like a tiger ripping silk. *(Tug of war with a large rope. PAINE on one side. REPUTATION on other. Gradually, everyone take sides and tug.)* WAKE UP!

PAINE. Oh, Christ, let me be. I want to sleep.

REPUTATION. The world cracks open. Wake up. Come on. Say your line! "Wonders are many, but none is more wonderful than . . ." SAY IT!

PAINE. I want to go a-whoring like anybody else.

ALL. GET UP!

PAINE. I'll be so old I can't get it up. Who would want you? You'd be surprised.

ALL. WAKE UP!

REPUTATION. Have you forgotten somewhere in London, in Paris, all those wretches starved by the thousands, cauterizing their guts with hot gin, sleeping twelve in a room, working for sixpence a day. He wants a mistress. The revolution is your mistress.

PAINE. Let me alone. Say the lines the writer wrote for you.

REPUTATION *(very quickly).* "Here sits the typewriter with its keys staring at me, ready to sprinkle millions of letters over an acre of paper. My head breaking with Tom Paine's war." He wants to go a-whoring too, but he sips coffee. Drags a cigarette. NOW HE HAS the line for you. The telephone rings. Let it! He has the line for you, Paine.

ALL. SAY IT! WONDERS ARE MANY, BUT NONE IS MORE WONDERFUL THAN . . .

PAINE. Man. And yet . . . *(All giggle.)* And yet . . . *(All giggle.)* And yet . . .

REPUTATION. That's it! Come on! More lines! Many more! Say them!

PAINE *(blurt out in one breath).* And yet animals and insect things laugh at such two-legged pomposity.

(Cheers)

REPUTATION. Go on! Move it!

PAINE. Now see what miracles insects perform with their royalty. The king becomes the . . . becomes the . . . becomes the . . .

ALL. BREAD AND CAKE QUEEN!

(Tug of war ends.)

MAJOR DOMO. The termites of Paris march to the bread and cake queen.

REPUTATION. Now write your second book.

ALL. THE RIGHTS OF MAN!

(PAINE and REPUTATION *write this with large paint brushes on the wall. Lift* BREAD AND CAKE QUEEN *on one's shoulders. She wears enormous cloth. Group under cloth, clawing outward.)*

PAINE *and* REPUTATION *rotational:*

Why is it that such vast classes of mankind are called the ignorant mob? They arise as the unavoidable consequences of old governments! By distortedly exalting some men, others are distortedly debased, till the whole is out of nature. A vast mass of mankind is degraded in the human picture to bring forth with greater glare, the puppet show of state and aristocracy. The mob learns to punish from the governments they live under, and retaliate the punishments they have been accustomed to behold. It signifies nothing to a man what is done to him after he is dead, but it signifies much to the living. It hardens their hearts and instructs them how to punish when power falls into their hands. LAY THE AXE TO THE ROOT, AND TEACH GOVERNMENTS HUMANITY! It is their sanguinary punishments which corrupt mankind. Their hanging, their drawing and quartering, tearing to pieces by horses! Who does not remember them? This is an age of revolutions in which everything may be looked for. All false governments are military. War is their trade, plunder and revenue their objects. The history of these governments is a disgustful picture of human wretchedness. Wearied with war, and tired with human butchery . . .

Rotational:
The strangest sight in history.
There is vice in the weather today.
RAIN!!
A droning deluge of rain across the hot July fields.
Nine miles to Versailles.
RAIN!!
The termite queen bloats on eggs. She's the size of a skyscraper.
Stuffed with eggs.
Rain! March in the rain!
The stuff of love bloats her gut.
Lick her sides. Salivate to lubricate,
One hundred billion eggs of state.
The will of the termites!
ILS VEULENT!
Feed her tiny orifice of taste,
And lick away the eggs of state.
The land is barren of bread and cake,
To feed the termite queen of state.
The termite women march!
In the *driving rain!*
Hungry. Angry.
Eight thousand midwives march the steamy July fields.
To Versailles!
To lick the enormous queen,
To lick the mother-bearer clean.
Of eggs!
Their staff of life!
THEIR BREAD!
BREAD!!
(Childbearing shriek)
EAT! CAKE!
The eggs are finished. She has no more to give. And yet . . .
(All giggle.)
and yet . . .
(All giggle.)
And yet . . .
(All giggle.)
They continue to lick her . . . to death.

(Dialogues end together. Pause)

ALL. . . . they sit down to rest. And call it peace. *(Sing)*

Tom Paine talked of here and now,
Why should one man's stomach growl,
(Talk)
And another man say, "You work and slave, and I'll eat the bread!"
(Sing)
Why should one man in a palace reside,
(Talk)
And another man live in a wallow!
(Sing)
Sometimes living side by side.
Sometimes living side by side.

Mary talks of other things,
The genocide of despotic kings,
(Talk)
An old man's calumny,
And Frankenstein's monstery.
(Sing)
Tom Paine talked of here and now,
Why should one man's stomach growl?

MARY W. His brain aches. He goes to soak it. In warm gin. Said Mary Wollstonecraft.

REPUTATION. Put down your bottle. Your brain's pickled.

BLAKE. A suckled red cherry. Said the mystic Blake.

REPUTATION. You hallucinate on genocide . . .

BLAKE & MARY W. . . . of a gaggle of kings.

PAINE. The book planted in London, in Bristol, In Edinburgh, in Dublin, even in London Tower his soldiers read it. This is here and now. Hallucinations don't carry pistols. His island is honeycombed. Wherever he walks, the ground gives way under him from Hebrides to Land's End. He shakes like a toy rattle. (PAINE *drink and fondle the orb.* REPUTATION *throw it away.)*

REPUTATION. Let loose the King from your head. He is a madman with a crown.

PAINE. I don't want *HIM!*

BLAKE & MARY W. What do you want? *(Litany:)*

BLAKE. What do you want? From Hebrides to Land's End?

PAINE. I don't know.

BLAKE & MARY W. We suspicion.

BLAKE. I see a whale drinking your soul away.

ALL. We suspicion.

MARY W. My daughter, unborn and gestating, will dwell on Frankenstein's monster, running in the forests silent and gigantic with cataracts FOR EYES!

REPUTATION. What are you conjuring?!

BLAKE & MARY W. The shadow of Cromwell.

SHADOW. I want . . .

PAINE. I want . . .

BLAKE & MARY W. We suspicion.

SHADOW. The Hebrides to Land's End.

PAINE. 'TIS A LIE!

SHADOW. Ye brother crows,
          Take warning all,
          As ye rise,
          So must ye fall.

PAINE. My brain aches.

BLAKE. A suckled red cherry.

REPUTATION. OH, GOD 'TIS A LIE!

BLAKE. Soldiers of the king!

MARY W. The channel boat. Dover to Calais.

BLAKE. Things in rustling scales rush into reptile coverts.

PAINE. The Rights of Man go with us! *(Exit to cheering group in France. Put tricolor cockade in his hat. Two, hold flags either side of stage, French and English. Immediately lights)*

MAJOR DOMO. Do let us pause and cool the stage for the trial in absentia. The puppet show of state and aristocracy. *Bow, present yourselves:* Barrister Horsely.

ALL. HEAR! HEAR!

MAJOR DOMO. Barrister Edmund Burke.

ALL. HEAR! HEAR!

MAJOR DOMO. The Lord Justice!

ALL. HEAR! HEAR!

LORD JUSTICE. Damn noisy in here.

MAJOR DOMO *(with fervor).* OYEZ! OYEZ! Lord Justice of the Court of the King's Bench. Guildhall, London. December 18, 1792. God bless the King! Shatter his enemies and make them fall! Confound their politics! *Frustrate their knavish tricks.* . . .

LORD JUSTICE. Aren't you getting carried away?

HORSELY. American accents rattle on the eardrum so.

MAJOR DOMO. The Lord Justice opens the trial for libelous passages in the book called *The Rights of Man.*

LORD JUSTICE. Now, gentlemen, his latest book is a unique case. This time he is messing about with our laws.

HORSELY. The laws are already confused enough without him mucking about.

BURKE. Of course. They were written that way for a purpose. For the people's sake.

LORD JUSTICE. Precisely. If you can't convince them, what do you do?

BURKE. Confuse them.

(Stamp BURKE's *forehead with big, black rubber stamp)*

JUSTICE & HORSELY. Right.

LORD JUSTICE. A basic principle of law and order.

HORSELY. I don't know what the mass of people in any country have to do with the laws. Except to obey them.

MAJOR DOMO. The Lords temporal said:

(Stamp HORSELY*)*

JUSTICE & BURKE. RIGHT.

HORSELY. *They* are noted for their mono-syllables.

BURKE. Paine is a robustious anarchist who is for tearing everything up by the roots, for prostrating government by violence and inflicting upon a nation the heaviest calamities.

HORSELY. *He* is noted for his polysyllables.

LORD JUSTICE. Well now, it is a clear-cut case. It's either yes or no. No or yes. And when you line up the Yesses and the Noseses in some kind of order, except when it's sometimes, of course, *littered* with Maybes and Perhapseses, then you line *all those up* and you take your choice of the various Yesseses and Noseses, the Maybes and the Perhapseses and ah . . . OH! You leave it at that!

ALL THREE. Ahhh, the divine mysteries of the law.

HORSELY. That settles that.

BURKE. However. . . .

HORSELY. Now you're going to confuse it, I know.

BURKE. It's not *really* a Perhapseses, as we understand it, by established precedent.

HORSELY. Didn't I tell you?

BURKE. As in the case of the Crown versus . . .

(Stamp BURKE*)*

JUSTICE & HORSELY. WRONG.

HORSELY. That case was clear-cut. Clear as crystal. A *straightforward* case: of Maybe.

BURKE. Ahhhhh, yes, yes.

LORD JUSTICE. No, no, not Yesseses!

BURKE *(obsequiously)*: Oh, Noseses, my Lord.

HORSELY. No, no! It wasn't Noseses! It was MAYBESES! *(Softly)* Am I right?

(Stamp HORSELY*)*

JUSTICE & BURKE. WRONG.

LORD JUSTICE. Or was it Now that I think about it, maybe it was a case of Noseses. Yesseses! It was Noseses. *(Stamp* LORD JUSTICE*)*

BURKE & HORSELY. RIGHT.

LORD JUSTICE *(acidly)*. Thank you.

BURKE. It is a difficult decision.

ALL. IT IS a difficult decision.

HORSELY. They're always difficult. Decisions!

LORD JUSTICE. Decisionseses!

BURKE. My lords, it's the only way. Let's flip for it.

LORD JUSTICE. Brilliant man!

HORSELY. A pillar of the Empire!

LORD JUSTICE. An ornament! *(Try to one-up each other. End hitting each other)*

HORSELY. A sparkling jewel!

LORD JUSTICE. A BREATH OF AIR!

HORSELY. A SILVER TONGUE!

LORD JUSTICE. TWO TURTLE DOVES!

HORSELY. THREE FRENCH HENS!

ALL THREE *(sing)*.

FIVE GOLDEN RINGS!
Three French hens,
Two turtle doves,
And a partridge in a pear tree. *(Pause)*
Ahhhhh, lovely the mysteries of the law.

BURKE. Shall we? Ready then.

LORD JUSTICE. What we won't do for justice.

HORSELY. Do the people really appreciate it?

LORD JUSTICE. My lords, FLIP!

(On your heads)

BURKE. Now it's clear as day.

HORSELY. It's so obvious.

LORD JUSTICE. Why didn't we think of it before?

PAINE. My lords.

ALL THREE. Sssssh! We are probing the mysteries of the law.

LORD JUSTICE. My lords, have you touched the mysteries?

BURKE & HORSELY. We have. GUILTY!

LORD JUSTICE. Gentlemen, UNflip. *(You do.)* Call in the prisoner.

(REPUTATION *forward. Indicating* PAINE *on French side)*

BURKE. He's drunk.

PAINE. I'm drunk and you're crazy. Tomorrow I'll be sober, but you'll be crazy the rest of your life.

HORSELY. Sharp-tongues beast, isn't he?

LORD JUSTICE. Well now, Mr. Paine, you have been a busy lit-tle man since you arrived, haven't you?

BURKE. You, at your lit-tle table, with your lit-tle penny pot of ink, hmmmmm?

HORSELY. How did you do it, Mr Paine?

Saaaaavvve it up? Hmmmm? A ha'penny at
a time, and put the two together, and trot to
the stationers, giggling to yourself.

BURKE. Put down your penny on the counter and say:

LORD JUSTICE. A penny pot of ink, please.
I'm going to topple an empire.

BURKE. Is that how it's done?

HORSELY. Make the Lords temporal and
the Lords spiritual quake before your lit-tle
penny pot of ink?

BURKE. This prodigy of human intellect,
this product of ever-renewed intoxication,
this leader of the sanguinary rabble of France
whose hands are clotted with blood. He staggers under a LOAD OF RUM! Sneaking off
to France.

LORD JUSTICE. Since Paine has fled from
England . . .

BURKE. The coward.

HORSELY. The spoilsport.

(REPUTATION *forward)*

LORD JUSTICE. We will condemn this
shadow of him.

ALL. In high absentia.

BURKE. It's a clear-cut case of Yesseses.

LORD JUSTICE. Let's not get started on that
again, or we'll be flipping all day. *(Pause)* Mr.
Paine, impartial justice has weighed you in its
blindfolded scales and found you wanting.

REPUTATION. I have written the truth. *The
Rights of Man* will do for Europe what *Common Sense* has done for America.

LORD JUSTICE. And what, pray tell us, is
that besides blood and war?

PAINE. To defend the right of all men to
choose their own rulers, to make their own
governments, and to get rid of those rulers if
they choose.

BURKE. The English people utterly dis-
claim such a right, and they will resist the
assertion with their lives.

REPUTATION. That men should take up
arms and spend their lives to maintain they
have no rights is a new species of discovery
suited to the paradoxical genius of Mr.
Burke.

(Quacking, honking, gaggle)

ALL THREE. GUILTY! GUILTY!
GUILTY!

LORD JUSTICE. You never imagined we'd
countenance a revolution. Really, Mr. Paine,
we are British, you know.

BURKE. He will cover England with human gore!

BURKE. Look at France!

HORSELY. Sure, look at her.

LORD JUSTICE. Yes, yes, they're worse
than we are.

BURKE. Now, what shall we do with him?

HORSELY. Burn him at the stake!

LORD JUSTICE. We can't start a fire on
stage.

HORSELY. We will put him down! *(Do so)*

BURKE. And we will blacken his reputation.

LORD JUSTICE. He has fled to France!
(Stamp REPUTATION)

ALL. RIGHT!

HORSELY. He stirs up trouble there!

ALL. RIGHT!

BURKE. He plots with Condorcet and the
Rabble!

ALL. RIGHT!

LORD JUSTICE. King Louis' sacred person
is holed up!

BURKE & HORSELY. WRONG!

HORSELY. He's not holed up. He's still in
a palace of 2,000 rooms.

LORD JUSTICE. And not one toilet!

BURKE. The French don't need such
things. They use perfume.

JUSTICE & HORSELY. Oh.

BURKE. He called us frauds.

HORSELY. He called us corrupt.

(Quickly stamp REPUTATION *all over angrily)*

LORD JUSTICE. Well, there he sits, a mass
of contradictions.

ALL. Ahhh, the divine mysteries of the law.

*(Pause a beat. Now, an unnerving, grinding
sound of butcher knife honing. Quick, nervous
scurrying, whispers, tocks of wood on wood.*
ALL *whisper, "Quick.")*

REPUTATION. Events rush. Quick! Paris.
Quick! Quick! Explosive. Words of petrol.
Nod of the head. Death! QUICK! The guillo-
tine. Flash. Explosive. Quick! QUICK! Ex-
plosive. Finger itches. QUICK! To strike the
match. The King sweats his life. QUICK!
QUICK! He cries. QUICK! Pisses himself.
Fear. QUICK! Fear. Explosive. QUICK!
PARIS. 1793. THE CONVENTION DE-
CIDES IF LOUIS WILL LIVE OR IF HE
WILL DIE. THE COMMITTEE OF THE
CONVENTION:

(Grinding louder. Roll call rotational)

BRISSOT!
VERGNIAUD!
GENSONNÉ!
BARÈRE!
VILLENEUVE!
CONDORCET!

DANTON!
SIEYÈS!
PAINE!
    (Pound, roar:)
KILL THE KING!
    (Dead quiet. LOUIS *weep in center. Begin as* PAINE *begins: grinding, catcalls, yells)*
    PAINE *(breathless rapidity).* Kings have trained the human race to blood. The people must not follow the example by vengeance. Save his life. *(Dead quiet.* LOUIS *weeps.* ALL *begin again.)* France is the first to abolish kings. Let her be the first to abolish the death vengeance. Save his life. *(Dead quiet.* LOUIS *weeps.* ALL *begin again.)* Could I speak the French language I would descend to your bar. In your language, beg you not to sever his head. *(Dead quiet.* LOUIS *weeps.* ALL *begin again.)* Guard him. Detain him until the war ends. Send him in perpetual banishment to America. Save him! *(Dead quiet.* LOUIS *weeps.)* Save the king!
    ALL. KILL THE KING!
    (A great noise. Light man, do brilliant things. LOUIS *carried off. Now, a single light on* PAINE *only)*
    PAINE. The Committee of the Convention? Marie? Marie, where are they now? Brissot.
    ALL. Guillotined.
    PAINE. Vergniaud.
    ALL. Guillotined.
    PAINE. Gensonné?
    ALL. Guillotined.
    PAINE. Barère?
    ALL. Guillotined.
    PAINE. *Villeneuve?!*
    ALL. Eaten by wolves.
    PAINE. CONDORCET?
    ALL. Suicide.
    PAINE *(softly).* Danton.
    ALL. Guillotined.
    PAINE *(very softly).* Sieyès?
    MARIE. Everyone died, except Sieyès, and he changed sides.
    REPUTATION. And except Paine, who was lucky. If you can call it that. He rots in Luxembourg's dungeons and waits for the glittering knife to lift above his neck. The cross is the signal!
    (Large iron grill center stage slams down. PAINE *circles like a rat in a maze. Hysterical lifting and slamming down a stool with hypnotic compulsion.* PAINE, *say roller-coaster fast:)*
    PAINE. The iron cage shut. It swings in and out. Up and down. Locked. SLAM! LOCK! CROSS OF CHALK! STOP!! STOP!!! Iron cage. Swings in. OUT!! Sometimes swings out. OUT!!! Cross of chalk on the door. MARK! BASTARD!! BASTARD, SWING OUT!! Oh, please, BASTARD! IN! OUT!! Oh, Christ, it's shut. IRON SHUT!!! Oh, fuck. Oh, Christ! A jail. CAGE!! THE KNIFE!! I know why I'm here. I KNOW!! Cross of chalk. Oh, iron. IRON!! Oh, Christ, the knife. IT'S SHARP! The bastard. The FUCKING BASTARD! SHARP!! BANG! On my neck. Chink it up. CHINK!! Chink. Chink. Chink a chain up. SLAM!! BANG! DOWN! BANG! On my neck, oh, Christ, dirty bastard. IRON!! SHARP!!! Chink it up again. Chink, chink, chink, chink a chain up. OH, CHRIST! HELP! HOLD IT!!!! Neck down. A block. BASTARD, LAUGH!! Wait. WAIT!!! HOLD IT! STOP!!! Oh, God, here it comes. CLOSE YOUR EYES!!! BITE YOUR TEETH!!! Up and down. Iron. SHARP! Oh, my, wait, wait, wait, wait. HERE IT COMES!!!! It's heavy. Oh, Christ it's heavy. Scaffold trembles. BANG!! SHARP!!! Oh, my, neck, it hurts. Wait. CHRIST, HOLD IT!!! Iron. SHARP!! Here it comes. HERE IT COMES!!!! Iron cage. OPEN! Swing out. Goes in. Must go out. OUT!!! OUT!!! BASTARD!!! Oh, God, it's clean. THEY CLEANED IT!!! Help. CHUNK! HERE IT COMES!!! Don't look up. Down. Down. DOWN!! CLOSE YOUR EYES!! Oh, Christ, help. MOVE! CAN'T MOVE! Ears. Please. Please. Please. NOT MY EARS!!! Make a fist. Shut your eyes. Hold your breath. BITE YOUR TEETH!! HERE IT COMES!! WHOOSEH! HERE IT COMES!!! WHOOSEH!! HERE IT COMES!!! HELP! OH GOD! JESUS CHRIST! DON'T LOOK UP!! DOWN! DOWN!! DOWN!!! DOWN!!!! WHOOSEH HERE IT COMES!!!!
    ALL. CHUNK!
    REPUTATION *(flatly).* One hundred and sixty-eight people are taken out of the Luxembourg each night. One hundred and sixty of them are guillotined the next day. The signal is a cross of chalk on the door of those chosen. For the next day. The guards wait until night. When the prisoners sleep. To mark the signal. So there will be: no panic. In their department. Everyone waits. *(One, mark a large cross of chalk. Hang it on the grate.)* The prisoners learn self-control. It has been known, in a room full of people, one will start to cry. Then a second. Then a third. Another. And soon, the whole room will cry, silently.

(Rotational:)
How do you bury a severed body?
Do they bury the head with it?
Do they place the head on the chest? In the hands?
On the neck? Between the legs?
Do they put the right head with the right body?
Does it matter?
Do they dig separate graves?
Do they make a trench?
Does it matter?
Where are they all buried?
Does *anyone* know?
Does it make a *difference* to know?

SIMONNE. My name is Simonne. My hair is brown. My eyes are blue. My skin is soft, and in summer it turns brown when it's hot. And in summer, in Lyons, where I live, I walk in the fields. The fields near Lyons have yellow flowers. I walk there in summer, when it's hot, with Jean-Jacques. And our skin turns brown. Together. I want to know. *I* hope it is a field of yellow flowers. I hope . . . please, Bon Dieu . . . let it be. (SIMONNE *weeps. Then* ALL.)

REPUTATION. Then a second. Then a third. Another. And soon. All.

(Guitar music start.)

MAJOR DOMO. A curious twist of fate, the cross of chalk on the iron plate was turned around and the avenging angel passed him by. The world flies through space attracting meteors. Notre Dame, the great cathedral, is now a dance hall. A clean sweep has made even the calendar obey. And the revolution supplants Jesus as the reckoning day. So it is the Year One. The earth is as pure again as when Adam said "Begin." Madame Bonville teaches Monsieur Paine the new calendar at Number 4, rue du Théâtre Français.

ALL. And it's September in a kissproof world.

MARGUERITE. The days of the month are thirty. The months of the year are twelve. What passes in between can be whatever you want it to be. It's simple.

PAINE *(speak English)*. MARGUERITE *(sing French)*.

September.
Vendémiaire.
The month of grapes.
Le mois vendange.

October.
Brumaire.
The month of mists.
Le mois brumeux.

November.
Frimaire.
The freezing month.
Lemois des vents froids.

December.
Nivose.
The month of snow.
Le mois neigeux.

January.
Pluviose.
The month of rains.
Le mois pluvieux.

February.
Ventose.
The month of winds.
Le mois éventé.

March.
Germinal.
The month of seeds.
Le mois des semences.

April.
Floreal.
The month of flowers.
Le mois fleuri.

May.
Prairial.
The pastoral month.
Le mois champêtre.

June.
Messidor.
The good month.
Le mois du bien-être.

July.
Thermidor.
The hot month.
Le mois des grandes chaleurs.

August.
Fructidor.
The month of fruitful things.
Le mois des fruits.

MAJOR DOMO. That year, Thomas Paine Bonville was born. Some say the child was his. Some say not. Marguerite only smiled. It's a thing called style.

MARGUERITE. And then what did you do?

PAINE. Then? Old and sick from the prison. I try to remember. I lay in bed. I try to remember, but the more I try . . .

MARIE. Then you went back to New York.

PAINE. To the bear pit.

MARGUERITE. No, not yet. You went back to New York. I went with you.

PAINE. Can't remember. Give me a drink, please. Please . . . Marie.

REPUTATION. You went back to your farmhouse alone. And the mob taunted you. And they threw rocks at your windows. And the toughs baited you. And they pushed you in the mud.

(Rotational:)

Damned if he'll sleep in the same barn with us.

Filthy creep.

He denied God in his black book.

PAINE. *The Age of Reason* does not deny God.

(Rotational:)

It says religion is set up for plunder and profit. If that don't deny God, what does? And it gets worse page by page.

And the country you named, ganged up.

(Push, shove, taunt him. ALL *chant street jargon)*

Make a revolution, blood and flame, I'm the one who does it. My name is Paine. I should have gone to the guillotine, AND LET THE KNIFE CHOP OFF YOUR LYING HEAD TO LEARN VARIOUS AND ASSORTED OTHER PERSONAGES WHO MURDER AND ARE INCENDIARIES AND REVOLUTIONISTS AND WHO OUR GREAT SOCIETY DISLIKES TO PUT UP WITH!

PAINE. MARIE! MARIE, then I went to the bear pit to be left in peace?!

MARIE. You went to your farmhouse. Alone. You lit the fire at night, and the drums and the fifes crackled and licked at your memory, marching feet of comrades all gone.

(Rotational:)

Paine we need guns.

Paine we need powder.

Cannon, shot and more than balls.

We need meat.

We'll settle for hardtack.

We need boots.

We can't fight the damned war on good intentions.

ONE. Paine the quartermaster blames the paymaster.

ONE & TWO. The paymaster blames the generals.

ONE, TWO & THREE. The generals blame the congress.

ONE, TWO, THREE & FOUR. The congress blames the traitors.

ALL. AND THE TRAITORS SAY, GET STUFFED!

PAINE. Leave me alone! Marie, let me go to the bear pit. NOW?!

MARIE. You went to vote.

PAINE. Oh, Christ, give me a drink!

MARGUERITE. Then what happened?

REPUTATION. You went to vote. You left the farmhouse. You walked to town. In the nation you named. In the nation you made. Four million people are your credentials. You stand in line. There is a table. The registrars sit before it. They smile. They stroke their noses. They narrow their eyes. They smile. They look at each other. They smile. They look at you.

(Each REGISTRAR *on someone's shoulders. Large black robes to floor cover them. Each wears a peruke.)*

REGISTRAR 1. Your name?

REPUTATION. They look at your fierce hooked nose. Your twisted eyes. Your filth. Your rumpled clothes.

PAINE. My name?! My name is Thomas Paine.

REGISTRAR 1. Do be serious. Voting is serious business.

REGISTRAR 2. This trembling old man is the thundering revolutionist?

REGISTRAR 1. Absurd.

PAINE. I want to register.

REGISTRAR 1. Indeed.

REGISTRAR 2. I'm afraid you cannot vote.

REGISTRAR 1. You are not a citizen.

REGISTRAR 2. You are a foreigner.

REGISTRAR 1. You are not a citizen of the United States.

PAINE. I am Thomas Paine. I have given the name to this country which I have come to love above all else. I have spent my life forging its principles and spreading those principles to the world.

REGISTRAR 2. Yes, yes, that's splendid, but can you prove you are a citizen?

REGISTRAR 1. Were you ever formally made a citizen?

PAINE. Formalities? No, no, my life has been spent breaking down formalities.

REGISTRAR 2. Ah, then you are still English.

MARIE. He can't return to England. They'll hang him on sight.

REGISTRAR 1. So we understand.

REGISTRAR 2. Then you cannot vote anywhere.

REGISTRAR 1. You are an alien.

REGISTRAR 2. A refugee.

REGISTRAR 1. You really have no country, Mr. Paine.

PAINE. BUT I HAVE THE RIGHT TO VOTE!!

REGISTRAR 2. YOU HAVE NO RIGHTS AT ALL, DRUNKEN FOOL! DO YOU WANT TO GO TO PRISON?!

PAINE. No . . . not prison again. But I am Thomas Paine, returned home to the country I love and fought for.

(Laughter)

REGISTRAR 1. We do not register foreigners.

REGISTRAR 2. You are not a citizen.

REGISTRAR 1. You cannot vote.

REGISTRAR 2. You are holding up the line.

REGISTRAR 1. Move on, old man.

(Laughter)

PAINE. What am I to do now? Marie, MA-RIE, THE BEAR PIT, NOW?!

MARIE. Now it is the time for that.

PAINE. Give me a drink.

REPUTATION. First the bear pit. Then the sickness. And then you lay a-dying and the swarms of do-good-greedies flocked about to catch the plum of converting the great Paine back to the fold.

(A heartbeat, steady and rhythmic, louder and louder and quicker and quicker)

(DO-GOOD-GREEDIES' rotational:)

Mr. Paine, do you wish to ask God's forgiveness?

Mr. Paine, do you want to recant?

Mr. Paine, do you hear me?

Mr. Paine, do you still persist in heresy?

(From here, start to emerge from characters back to yourselves as indicated; and at varying times)

ACTOR OF REPUTATION. Oh, they put a bad mouth on him and hacked him up and they did him most bad. And there wasn't a mother who would waste spit on him. *(To SERGEANT)* And what can he do now? Well, his heart will break open. And it will float away.

SERGEANT. Whaaaaat? Oh, come on, cut the theatrical nonsense.

PRIVATE. Tell the story straight.

ACTOR OF REPUTATION. And his heart broke open. And it floated away in the air.

SERGEANT. Hey. HEY! Come on, wake up! I got my orders to bring him in. HEY, YOU! HEY, CUT THAT OUT!

(Heartbeat reaches a peak and stops. Red balloons fly out from him and float over the entire audience to the ceiling.)

ACTOR OF REPUTATION. Now you did it.

ACTOR OF MAJOR DOMO. Poor old drunk.

ACTRESS OF MARIE. Well, Sergeant, did the second act help you?

SERGEANT. What's the matter with you people? Can't anybody tell a straight story any more? I asked for Tom Paine, not this beggar you created.

ACTRESS OF MARIE. We tried, [*use name of actor*].

ACTOR OF MAJOR DOMO. Let's say he was ahead of his time for his country. And the way things look, he's getting farther and farther ahead.

ACTOR OF SERGEANT. Well, did he want to be a king, or didn't he?!

ACTOR OF GEORGE III. That's an easy way to explain him away.

ACTOR OF REPUTATION. IT'S A COP-OUT!

ACTOR OF LOUIS XVI. Well, that's the end. There's no more script left.

(Rotational:)

Anybody seen the drum?

It's on my hump, over by [*use name of actress*].

Come on, let's get these props offstage.

Who's going for coffee?!

Oh, give us some music to end this or we'll all leave sad.

(Start to straggle off singing "Tom Paine came from afar, afar." It grows and grows, louder and louder with drums, gongs, and noises.)

What about him?

He'll sober up.

One of the turtles escaped.

Switch off the light board.

Put the turtles in the water tank.

One of them escaped!

More animals in this show.

(Nasally, mocking a bad line:)

If there were three acts . . . . . . we'd have elephants.

(Light fading, and music growing louder and louder.)

ACTOR OF PAINE. And the raw stuff, the raw stuff that moved the pen was dumped into a hole in an empty field. Then, Marie, one last act of revenge. In the night, they invaded the farm and they hacked the trees and ripped up the few flowers and with iron hammers they broke the stone above his head, and dug up his very bones and they shoveled them into a sack and they threw them aboard a ship bound for London to hang upside down before the jeering mobs. And when they were done, the bones, the raw stuff that moved the pen, were thrown into the street. And nobody knows where they are today. So went Tom Paine who shook continents awake. And today, right now, his small statue is splashed in red paint in a small farm in a small town in a nation growing smaller and smaller *(light fading)* and smaller and smaller and smaller. *(And the music growing louder and louder and louder and louder)*

CURTAIN

MORNING

Israel Horovitz

NOON

Terrence McNally

NIGHT

Leonard Melfi

(three one-act plays)

First presented by Circle in the Square on Broadway on November 28, 1968, at the Henry Miller's Theatre in New York City with the following cast:

(In order of appearance)

MORNING by Israel Horovitz

GERTRUDE Charlotte Rae
UPDIKE Sorrell Booke
SISSY Jane Marla Robbins

JUNIOR Robert Klein
TILLICH John Heffernan

NOON by Terrence McNally

KERRY John Heffernan
ASHER Robert Klein
ALLEGRA Jane Marla Robbins

BERYL Charlotte Rae
CECIL Sorrell Booke

NIGHT by Leonard Melfi

MISS INDIGO BLUE Jane Marla Robbins
ROBIN BREAST WESTERN John Heffernan
FILIGREE BONES Charlotte Rae

FIBBER KIDDING Sorrell Booke
MAN Robert Klein

Directed by Theodore Mann
Music by John Hall
Lyrics by Israel Horovitz
Scenery and Costumes by Michael Annals
Lighting by Martin Aronstein

SYNOPSIS OF SCENES

MORNING by Israel Horovitz
THE PLACE: Harlem.
THE TIME: Now.

NOON by Terrence McNally
THE PLACE: A large loft.
THE TIME: Now.

NIGHT by Leonard Melfi
THE PLACE: Somewhere outdoors in any American cemetery,
and perhaps other places, too.
THE TIME: Now.

Normally this series celebrates success. Most of the plays collected in these volumes have enjoyed a decent Broadway or, nowadays just as likely, an Off-Broadway run, probably been revived, been produced all over the world, anthologized, and acclaimed. This is not true of *Morning, Noon and Night.* This was not even a play—it was a series of three playlets by three different authors; it opened on November 28, 1968, and closed on January 11, 1969, after only fifty-two performances. At the time it was regarded as rather daring—which is all the more ironic because it was one of the very last legitimate offerings at the charming Miller Theatre. This has now become a prominent New York home for homosexual skin-flicks, so daring was as daring did.

The reason I have chosen *Morning, Noon and Night* is partly personal, partly sociological, and partly artistic. I myself really enjoyed the evening—so much for the personal touch. I realize that in the cold light of print the brilliance of these playlets is somewhat dimmed, but see them in the theatre with a gallimaufry of accomplished clowns and I think they will once more come to life.

Now for the sociological reasons. Ever since the beginning of the Off-Broadway theatre it had been set apart from Broadway—not merely by union contracts (which do indeed differ) but by standards of quality, of taste, of aspiration and, even, of seriousness. By the end of the sixties this artificial boundary was already breaking down. Major playwrights, producers, and actors were willing to brave Off-Broadway, and critics started to pay Off-Broadway much the same attention as they gave Broadway itself.

What gave a special interest to *Morning, Noon and Night* was that it represented a direct Broadway invasion by Off-Broadway, or, to be more realistic, an invasion by Off-Off-Broadway, for all three of the young playwrights were graduates of the Café La Mama, Café Cino, and so forth, circuit that was gathering in strength and interest during the sixties in New York. In addition, the director of the program and the producing organization were Theodore Mann and the Circle in the Square, one of the most reverential haunts of the Off-Broadway theatre. Mr. Mann wanted to establish an uptown branch and, with his organization, leased the Henry Miller Theatre. (It all had a happy ending. Although the Circle in the Square lost their shirt and blue jeans on this venture, in 1973 a good fairy called Joseph E. Levine gave it an entirely new and beautiful uptown home in the same building as the new Uris Theatre and called, appropriately enough, the Circle in the Square–Joseph E. Levine Theatre.)

These three playlets—all variations on a theme of outrage—were not only good work in themselves, but brought to Broadway (two of them for the first time) three interesting American playwrights, Israel Horovitz, Terrence McNally, and Leonard Melfi. These were three of the young, irreverent talents who gave real flavor to the American theatre at the end of the sixties.

Mr. Horovitz had almost literally burst onto the New York theatre scene the year before. During the 1967/68 season he had four plays produced—three of them one-acters: *Line,* the one full-evening play, *Its's Called the Sugar Plum, The Indian Wants the Bronx,* and *Rats.* It was *The Indian Wants the Bronx* that really drew attention to Horovitz, and to its young, then unknown star, Al Pacino.

Horovitz was born in Wakefield, Massachusetts, in 1939 and he was educated in Boston. Quite early on he spent some time in London, studying at the Royal Academy of Dramatic Art, and serving as one of the resident playwrights to the Royal Shakespeare Company.

After his Broadway debut he produced a number of New York plays, including *The Honest-to-God Schnozzola;* a new one-acter, *Acrobats;* and a new version of *Line.* He also worked on film scripts, notably *The Strawberry Statement,* a film about student unrest that was to the rear of its time. In 1973 he had a marked success with his first novel, *Cappella.*

Terrence McNally is a Texan, but disguises the fact quite successfully. He was reared in Corpus Christi and first came to New York to study at Columbia. In 1960 he graduated with a BA in English. In 1965 he made a premature but promising Broadway debut with *And Things That Go Bump in the Night.* The things bumped for few nights, but Mr. McNally was noticed.

Since then he has had a number of successes and a few failures. His one-act play *Next* was a big Off-Broadway hit, *Sweet Eros* was rather less successful, but *Where Has Tommy Flowers Gone* attracted attention both at the Yale Repertory Theatre and later Off Broadway. Early in 1974 Mr. McNally had a major success with *Bad Habits,* a couple of one-acters, each more funny than cynical, but both are very funny, and both pretty cynical.

427

Horovitz is a Jew, McNally is an Irishman; it needed something else ethnic to round out this New York trio. Leonard Melfi is Italian, of course. He was born and educated in Binghamton, New York, and later attended St. Bonaventure University, the American Academy of Dramatic Arts, and the Herbert Berghof–Uta Hagen School. Originally he wanted to be an actor. He spent two years in Europe with the United States Army, came back, and, abandoning acting, decided to be a poet. Then he decided to become a playwright, and supported himself with odd jobs. Through a chance meeting with Paul Foster at La Mama Experimental Theatre Club, Mr. Melfi got to know Ellen Stewart, the club's founder. He has worked on films, but his career is still dedicated to the theatre, and his plays have been produced all over the world.

For me *Morning, Noon and Night* was a symbol of a new kind of theatre making it to Broadway. And its comparative failure was both an indication that Broadway was not yet ready for it, and also a warning that Broadway itself might be obsolescent.

These three plays are cheeky and cheerful. I commend the clever originality of Horovitz, the Jesuitical sense of unredeemable pleasure that McNally proffers, and, finally, the poetic night music of Melfi, a soft speculation about Christ and relationships. Here are three very different views of an even then changing world. Use them as time-markers to history.

MORNING

Israel Horovitz

With love, to DORIS

SCENE ONE: MORNING BEGINS

The lights fade up, revealing a large raked platform on which a smaller, identically shaped platform is set, center, dressed as an enormous bed, with black sheets and blankets.
UPDIKE *is in bed dressed in black pajamas. He is barely awake. He is white.*
There is a door unit downstage right, at the foot of the platform, a window unit downstage left. All the scenery is black. A four-man rock band is assembled on the stage, center left of the platform. They watch the action of the play.
GERTRUDE *stands just stage left of the bed. She calls to* UPDIKE. *She is white.*

———

GERTRUDE *(fiercely)*. Come on, Updike. You worthless white nigger! Get your black ass out of that fucking black bed!

BLACKOUT

SCENE TWO: THE CREATION OF MAN

In the blackout, GERTRUDE, SISSY, JUNIOR *and* UPDIKE *stand across the apron of the stage. The lights fade up. They deliver their lines as television-commercial announcers, smiling empty smiles directly at the audience. The rock group plays soupy-church-rock music softly. The entire family wears black clothing.*

———

GERTRUDE. In the beginning, there was only God on Earth. And the sunshine.
SISSY. Now God walked in the sunshine daily. He walked in the sunshine and sometimes would lie in the sunshine for hours. Dreaming of ways to create man. Dreaming of ways to create trees. Dreaming of ways to kill time. So God wouldn't get bored just hanging around by himself in the sunshine.
JUNIOR. God, being a wise and educated man, realized all that sunshine was causing his skin to burst forth with itchy sun blisters and a scratchy rash, so first God created Coppertone, and then Bain de Soleil.

GERTRUDE. And then God would lie in the sunshine in great comfort.
UPDIKE. When God turned a bronze and beautiful brown, He created man in the image of Himself.
JUNIOR. At first, man was ravaged by itchy skin blisters and scratchy rash, so God gave unto man His Coppertone and Bain de Soleil.
UPDIKE. And when man had turned a bronze and beautiful brown, he prayed to God to create woman. Man was ready.
GERTRUDE. And God created woman.
SISSY. The women of the Earth lay in the sun until their skin burst forth with itchy skin blisters and scratchy rash.
GERTRUDE. So God gave unto woman His Coppertone and Bain de Soleil as well.
SISSY. And once the women of the Earth turned a bronze and beautiful brown, they lay in the sun in great comfort.
UPDIKE. And the men of the Earth then lay in the women of the Earth in great comfort as well.
JUNIOR *(stepping forward as a preacher)*. So tired did God grow from watching the men of the Earth lay the women of the Earth, He fell asleep.
GERTRUDE. While God was asleep, the women of the Earth gave birth to new men and new women, who lay in the sun until their skin burst forth with itchy skin blisters and scratchy rash. But because God was resting, there was not Coppertone nor Bain de Soleil. So the new men and women of the Earth had to choose between hiding beneath and behind God's new shade trees, or face a life of prickly heat.
UPDIKE. They, being wise and educated men, hid beneath and behind the shade trees until their itchy sun blisters and scratchy rash disappeared, leaving only the first men and women of the Earth to be a bronze and beautiful brown.
GERTRUDE. As time passed, those in the dark did grow lighter.
UPDIKE. And so, beneath and behind the shade trees, the light men lay the light women, and new light men and new light women were born to Earth.
SISSY. As the years passed, the men and women of the shade and the men and women of the sun sought new lands.
JUNIOR. The black men sought lands of clear sun for laying, while the light men sought lands of shady trees and rocks for laying, without threat of prickly heat.

UPDIKE. So happy was the black man laying under God's own sun, he learned to make music and dance.

JUNIOR. So unhappy was the light man in the dark of God's own shade trees, he stopped laying, now and then, and invented the wheel, the automobile, the jet plane, Coppertone and Bain de Soleil. But while the wheel and the automobile and the jet plane served him well, the Coppertone and the Bain de Soleil came too late to ever catch the bronze and beautiful brown, gone to black, of the black man.

SISSY. And the light man grew discontent with his machinery and his light white women, and began to lay the bronze and brown-to-black women, who could then only sing and dance and lay. And so discontent did grow the light man when he discovered that the black man sang and danced and lay better than he, with all his intricate machinery, and he hated the black man and put him into captivity.

ALL. But God did not sleep forever!

GERTRUDE. He awoke one morning, but grew so tired of watching the white men lay the black women and the black men lay the white women, not to mention the black men laying the black women and the white men laying the white women, and all those in between . . . he fell back into his deep and holy rest at once.

UPDIKE. And then he awoke again to create Moses and Christ and the Caesars and the Kings and the Kennedys, but the white man had created weapons modeled after the black man's spears, so Moses and Christ and the Caesars and the Kings and the Kennedys were betrayed and dead so quickly, that God could only sleep again.

GERTRUDE. In his sleep, God was reached by a small fat Jewish man who runs a pawnshop on East 126th Street, and has a certain secret interest in a store called Bloomingdale's. In God's half-sleep—for although black, God is a light sleeper—this man took His six pills that are antidotes to the original sin of Coppertone and Bain de Soleil. He took these six pills from God and returned to Earth to distribute the pills, at great profit, among the bronze and beautiful brown-turned-to-black, who wished to liken themselves to those who have lingered so long in the dark, beneath and behind the shade trees.

SISSY. In his journey from Heaven to 126th Street, two of the pills spilled from his pocket and were lost forever.

GERTRUDE. He told me so.

ALL. Indeed, sir!

GERTRUDE. And so, with just four pills, he returned to 126th Street, where he sold them to me. One for me and one for my master. *(Pointing to* UPDIKE*)* Him. And one for each of my two children. *(Pointing to* SISSY *and* JUNIOR*)* Them. Last night, before we went to rest to lay, my man and I and each of our two children swallowed a pill with a bit of wine, and the wafer-thin curtains of our poor flat, flat held the heat in and the cool breezes out, while we lay in rest and waited to wake. And wake we did as you can see. No longer bronze and brown, but free and ready to face the world this day as those who have lived forever in the shade.

ALL *(but* GERTRUDE*)*. Not a trace of bronze or brown on my skin. Not a trace of bronze or brown in my mind.

GERTRUDE. I can take my place this morning at the complaint window of E. J. Korvette's, and Lord! The man will listen! I can discuss the size of a bedroom in a low-income controlled city flat on 98th and Riverside, and Lord! the man won't stare down my dress and try to lay me on the bedroom floor, on the bedroom floor plans. I can do any*thing* and any*one* my lily-white heart pleases, because I am free of the bronze and the brown. Not a trace of bronze or brown on my skin! Not a trace of bronze or brown in my mind! God can go straight on sleeping forever, because I'm free of the bronze and the brown.

ALL. Free! Free, forever, Lord! I'm free.

GERTRUDE. Free! Free, forever, Lord! I'm free.

BLACKOUT

SCENE THREE: WAKING UP WHITE

GERTRUDE *stands beside the bed.* UPDIKE *pretends to be sleeping. They are alone.*

———

GERTRUDE *(disgusted)*. Kiss me. C'mon. Kiss me?

UPDIKE *(gruff)*. I ain't even brushed my teeth yet.

GERTRUDE *(strong)*. Kiss me.

UPDIKE *(surprised, still gruff)*. You ain't asked me to kiss you for twenty years.

GERTRUDE. I know.

UPDIKE *(sitting up)*. After twenty years,

don't you think I ought to brush my teeth first?

GERTRUDE *(angry).* This is such a special morning and that's all you can think about? "Don't you think I ought to brush my teeth first?" I'll bet I can find plenty of men this morning that'll kiss me without brushing their teeth. Plenty of men that'll kiss me so terrific, they won't even have any teeth left after they get done kissing me, 'cause they'll lose all their teeth in their passion.

UPDIKE *(annoyed).* Gimme the blankets back, huh? I got a couple of minutes left. I could get some more rest for a couple of minutes.

GERTRUDE. Kiss me, or so help me God, I'll beat you black and blue.

UPDIKE *(turns away).* That's a joke, huh? Black and blue, huh?

GERTRUDE *(hurt).* I didn't mean it to be funny.

UPDIKE *(wounded).* Well, it ain't funny.

GERTRUDE *(furious).* Damn you! You haven't kissed me! You haven't said one special word about how special I look! You haven't made one mention of nothing, damn you. Nothing!

UPDIKE *(martyred).* And what's so special about what you've been saying to me? What's so motherfucking special about what you've been sayin' to me? "Get up, Updike! Kiss me, Updike!" Have you said one word about how terrifically terrific I look this morning, huh? One little word?

GERTRUDE *(quizzically).* How the hell would you know what you look like? You been asleep ever since you took the pill. You haven't even seen yourself, let alone taken one little peek at me!

UPDIKE *(awake now).* Buullshit, woman. That's what I got to say to you. Buuuuuuullllllshiiiiiitttt. You just go rappin' on and on about how fantastically terrifically beautifully magnificently wonderfully wonderful you look, right? And you haven't said fuck-all about Updike, have you? Anything about Updike?

GERTRUDE *(amazed).* But you been asleep since you took the pill?

UPDIKE *(proud).* While you was sleeping in bed, woman. This black bed right here? I was up and around and staring at things. Staring out the window at the stars. Staring at the walls. Staring at the blankets and the bed. I even lifted off the blankets.

GERTRUDE *(surprised, almost stunned).* While I was sleeping?

UPDIKE *(enormous pride, success).* I even lifted off the blankets and I sat staring at you. Right there. Right over there I sat. Right there in that chair just staring at you and digging the hell out of you. I didn't stop there either. You got a lipstick kiss on your stomach. That's how close you looked at yourself. That's how close you were payin' attention to yourself . . . let nothin' to me! You got a lipstick kiss on your stomach.

GERTRUDE *(laughing, a defense).* You're crazy.

UPDIKE *(strong).* I'll bet you all my week's gin money against two extra minutes of sleep you got a lipstick kiss on your belly, 'cause I put it there when I got up.

GERTRUDE *(honestly curious).* I'm a light sleeper. I would have heard you, let alone feel you. What do you mean a "lipstick kiss"?

UPDIKE *(delighted).* You think I didn't know how you'd behave this morning, huh? I figured it out! I know my little Gertrude-honey. Twenty-two years don't pass with me learning nothing, Gertrude. I put your lipstick on and I kissed your belly sure as there was a moon last night and sure as the sun beat the hell out of it at dawn.

GERTRUDE *(delighted, as well).* That's crazy talk.

UPDIKE *(laughing).* Look at your belly!

GERTRUDE *(opens her robe and screams).* Lipstick!

(A "lipstick kiss," cut from bright red plastic tape, is seen.)

UPDIKE *(laughing and prancing like a prize pony in the winner's circle).* Hot shit, Trudy, huh? That's what I told you, didn't I? Huh? Ain't that lipstick, huh? Ain't that the prettiest lipstick kiss you ever seen?

GERTRUDE *(pleased).* Why'd you do a crazy thing like that? Why'd you do a crazy thing like that?

UPDIKE *(sexy).* Yesterday morning would that lipstick'd shined like that, huh? Would that lipstick kiss shined out glowin' like that, huh? That's a coming-out present from Updike, Trudy. That's the present I promised you. Beats the hell out of that process job you wanted, right?

GERTRUDE *(absolutely thrilled).* I'm gonna' give you a lipstick kiss like that straight back, too.

(They roll about kissing and hugging, about to make love, when their son, JUNIOR, bursts into the room. They jump up sharply.)

UPDIKE *(caught).* Why the hell ain't you out on the street, Junior?

GERTRUDE *(concerned).* What happened to you?

UPDIKE *(angry).* Answer your mother, Junior. Why ain't you outside?

JUNIOR. *(He's been beaten up.)* I got mugged!

UPDIKE. By who?

JUNIOR *(furious).* I can't count that high. *(Pauses)* Everybody.

UPDIKE *(amazed).* That's crazy.

JUNIOR *(looking out the window to see if he's safe).* They wouldn't believe me.

GERTRUDE *(stunned).* You told them?

JUNIOR *(angry).* 'Course I told them. They're my brothers.

UPDIKE *(furious).* You're crazy. *(To* GERTRUDE) He's crazy.

GERTRUDE *(pulls* JUNIOR *so he faces her).* Why'd you tell them?

JUNIOR. They're my brothers!

GERTRUDE *(horror-struck).* What did you tell them? The pill? Did you tell them about the pill?

JUNIOR. Yep.

UPDIKE *(exasperated).* Oh, my God. He's crazy. Gertrude. Your son's crazy.

GERTRUDE *(tough, strong, angry).* Say that again, boy. You told them about the pill?

JUNIOR *(smart-assed).* They didn't believe me. It's okay.

UPDIKE *(can't believe it).* What do you mean?

JUNIOR *(smart-assed, bitchy).* What do you mean, "What do you mean?"

UPDIKE *(furious).* Don't get smart with me, Junior. Give me a straight answer.

JUNIOR *(as angry, hostile).* I gave you a straight answer, but you didn't listen. I told them about the pill and they didn't believe me.

UPDIKE *(amazed).* How'd they think you got white???

JUNIOR *(simply).* Paint.

GERTRUDE *(quickly, a sound).* Paint?

UPDIKE *(the same).* Paint?

JUNIOR *(the same).* Paint.

GERTRUDE *(shocked).* They figured you *painted* yourself? *(Pauses)* That's terrific.

JUNIOR *(very hostile).* One morning white Uptown, and your Super-Tom skin pills got me mugged. And *washed* more times in one morning than I would have washed all next year. They stole my wallet, then they washed up one side of my head and right down the other. *(Pauses, humiliated and furious)* They checked me all over, man. *All* over.

UPDIKE *(curious).* What did they find?

JUNIOR *(disgusted).* What did they find?

UPDIKE *(quickly).* You heard me!

GERTRUDE *(quickly, tough).* Answer your father.

JUNIOR *(whining).* They pulled off my underpants. What do you think they found?

GERTRUDE *(thrilled).* We're home free, Updike! Home free!

JUNIOR *(pulls away).* You're all crazy, you know that? You're all fuckin' crazy!

UPDIKE *(scolding).* Mind your fuckin' filthy tongue 'round your mother, boy.

GERTRUDE *(double-checks).* They didn't believe you, huh?

JUNIOR *(annoyed).* I said that clear enough.

GERTRUDE *(joyously).* We're home free, Updike. Home free. Ain't nobody gonna' believe we was anything 'cept what we look. What you depressed about?

JUNIOR *(wants attention).* I take one fuckin' walk with my sister, man, and I get my ass whupped and my head whupped and my legs and everything scrubbed so clean I'm about to break open . . . and I'm supposed to be overjoyed, right? Well, hot shit. Nobody whupped me yesterday. Nobody whupped Sissy, neither.

UPDIKE *(upset).* Sissy. Where is she?

GERTRUDE *(upset).* Where's Sissy?

JUNIOR *(pleased).* They were whuppin' hell out of her. That's how I got into the middle of it. They knocked her down and stole her pocketbook.

GERTRUDE *(frightened).* Where is she?

JUNIOR *(calming).* She's okay. She ran off like I told her to. She's probably visiting. She's okay.

UPDIKE *(disgusted).* He's nuts. He's plain nuts.

JUNIOR *(wants love).* I need a Band-Aid for my finger.

UPDIKE *(curious).* Let's have a look at it. *(*JUNIOR *extends his hurt finger, bloody, for his father's careful scrutiny.* UPDIKE *is delighted.)*

JUNIOR *(rather proud, as a soldier).* There.

UPDIKE *(delighted, almost thrilled).* Ain't that something?

GERTRUDE *(amazed).* It's pretty.

JUNIOR *(disgusted, hostile, tense).* Have you gone looney? That's my blood you're lovin'!

(Suddenly TILLICH *screams from behind the audience.)*

TILLICH. Niggers! (TILLICH *rushes down*

*the aisle from the back of the theatre scream-
ing.)* Niggers! Black bastards! *(He rushes up
on to the stage, sees them and stops, stunned.
They all run to hiding positions and freeze for
a moment before peeking their heads out at
him.)* Hey. What the hell's goin' on here?
Where are the niggers?

UPDIKE. *(His accent goes from "black" to
"white": almost clipped.)* The what?

TILLICH *(regains his fury)*. The niggers.
There were four niggers living here yesterday.
A man, a woman and two black kids. A boy
and a girl. Where'd they go off to?

UPDIKE *(very British now)*. What'd you
want them for?

TILLICH *(too quickly)*. My daughter's pregnant. The nigger-boy that lives here knocked
her up. *(Realizes)* Oh, Jesus. Now I went and
said it out loud. You got me so rattled, seeing
you here instead of niggers. I never would
have said it out loud.

*(The family freezes. The lights fade out on
the set and crossfade up on the apron.* TILLICH
takes a hand microphone.)

SCENE FOUR: TILLICH'S NIGHTMARE

The lights close in to a pinspot on TILLICH.
*He speaks first, then breaks into a talk-sing-
song: a straightforward satire of Bob Dylan.
The song should build slowly, until the final
"angel-chorus," with the family and the rock
group joining in sweetly.*

TILLICH *walks to the audience and tells his
story.*

————

TILLICH. I never would have said it out
loud. Never. My name is Tillich. We live
Midtown. Near the river. I'm in communica-
tions. My daughter, Alice, is pregnant. She's
going to have a baby. *(Sucks in his breath and
tells the truth)* A black baby. She goes to
school with a black kid. I mean, she used to
go to school with him. He hasn't been around
the school at all. Not since she told us. I
would have gotten him there. But he stopped
going to school. That's where they met. At
the school. They bussed the little black bastard right into her. *(Very emotional now)*
Look, I know how I stand. I've seen *Guess
Who's Coming to Dinner? Twice!* But she's
pregnant. Pregnant. I've seen the kid. Seen
him maybe twenty or thirty times. I didn't

know what to do. I've been coming up here
daily. Just staring at this place. Just staring
from outside and trying like the dickens to
figure something out. But last night she told
me. She told me what she felt. What she
wanted. She didn't leave me any choice. *(He
takes a pistol from his pocket and shows it to
the audience.)* I had to buy this. Twenty-nine
ninety-five for this. *(Music vamps in slowly.*
TILLICH *begins his song, "Tillich's Nightmare.")*

I am average weight and height.
I have average kids and sight.
I have average means and way.
On the average, I'm okay. Hooray.
My average daughter Alice
Fucks on the average twice a day,
With an average spade named Junior;
Now she's in the family way.
Oh, my God.
In your average shotgun marriage,
You know exactly what to do.
You make an average family wedding.
Then you wipe your hands, you're through.
But when your average dummy daughter
Expects and wants a mocha child,
Forget your average rules, sir.
You're super-average wild
To kill that little black spade rapist
In an awful average way.
You buy a gun to blow his brains out
Then you kill the goddamn day.
Wondering why the hell she did it:
Why she screwed and screwed you up.
Why she layed and then betrayed you.
Why she . . . Why you? Why you? . . .
    (The family steps in as an "angel chorus."
TILLICH *now has a gun in one hand and a wad
of dollars in the other. He sees the money and
sings, ever so sweetly.)*
Polytechnics. Basic dynamics.
Positive forward thrust.
I love America.
America.
Oh God, I love America.
    (Really big climax here)
ALL. Oh, God, I trust!

BLACKOUT

SCENE FIVE: IN BIG TROUBLE

Lights up on the set. TILLICH *walks on, gun
and money in hand.*

UPDIKE *(very British again; pulls* TILLICH

back into the scene). Is that loaded? That sidearm. Is that a loaded thing?

TILLICH *(furious).* You bet your ass it is!

JUNIOR *(not so "white"; concerned).* Is she all right? Your daughter? Is she okay?

UPDIKE *(pushing JUNIOR fiercely).* You get the fuck out of here, you goddamned fool. *(To* TILLICH) The boy's too young for this grown-up talk.

GERTRUDE *(grand).* Ain't it time for you to take a walk, Junior? *(She bends JUNIOR's arm.* TILLICH *sees it.* GERTRUDE *explains.)* The boy's got a terrible nervous condition. The doctor says he's supposed to take a long walk every morning. So he doesn't get too nervous. What time is it?

TILLICH *(quickly).* Nine thirty.

GERTRUDE *(a shove).* It's time, Junior.

TILLICH *(the name's familiar; too familiar).* Junior?

JUNIOR *(thinks he's being asked a question).* What?

TILLICH *(furious).* Is that your name? Junior?

JUNIOR *(tense; a lie).* No. That's my nickname.

TILLICH *(introspective).* That's a hell of a coincidence.

UPDIKE *(interrupting, frightened).* How so?

TILLICH *(to all).* A hell of a coincidence. Strange. Junior.

UPDIKE *(reasonably).* Ain't nothin' strange about a white boy bein' called Junior. John Kennedy's little one's called Junior. Abe Lincoln's boy was called Junior.

TILLICH *(turns on UPDIKE).* Abe Lincoln? He had a son named Junior?

UPDIKE *(caught).* Junior Lincoln. Terrific kid.

TILLICH. *(After a pause, he sits.)* I don't understand this. Excuse me, But I think I'm losing my mind.

JUNIOR. *(Right at TILLICH, laughing; JUNIOR's seen enough.)* Hot shit! Terrific!

GERTRUDE *(fist in JUNIOR's mouth).* Don't pay any attention to him. He's strange.

JUNIOR *(pulling free).* Hot shit! Hot shit! Hee-hee.

(JUNIOR dances around the bed, laughing. UPDIKE *hits him on the back of his head fiercely, with a slap.* JUNIOR *stops.)*

UPDIKE. You'll be dead, you jerk. Now shut up! *(To* TILLICH) We told you this boy was strange. We got problems in our house too, mister. This boy's one of them. Doesn't know anything. Stupid. *(Hits JUNIOR)* You're

stupid, right? Tell the man how stupid you are!

TILLICH. Don't make the same mistake I did. I didn't think my middle one knew anything. I didn't think she knew anything at all. The boy probably knows more than any of us, don't you, boy?

JUNIOR *(leaps at him).* What did you call me?

TILLICH *(doesn't see or hear).* It's all very "in" now, you know. The way they mix it up. I wouldn't give a damn if they played cards or something like that. But she's knocked up.

GERTRUDE *(a real mum).* How old is she?

TILLICH *(crybaby, whines).* Alice? She's fourteen. That's all she is. Just a baby. A baby? Hell, that's what she's having!

GERTRUDE *(has an idea).* How do you know the boy did it?

JUNIOR *(can't believe it; to GERTRUDE).* You too? Damn it. We got him three to one.

UPDIKE *(aside).* He's got a gun.

TILLICH *(hears a sound).* Huh?

UPDIKE *(smiling; sick with anxiety).* I was just explaining to the boy that you're upset enough to kill someone, that's all.

TILLICH *(angry).* Goddamned right I am! How'd you feel if your daughter got knocked up by some nigger?

UPDIKE *(a long, slow, silent stare into space).* Well . . .

TILLICH. God forgive me for having to say it out loud.

JUNIOR *(tough).* Yeah?

UPDIKE *(angry, terrified, trapped).* That's enough. That's enough.

(SISSY walks slowly down the aisle and into the room, crying.)

SISSY. Them dirty motherfucking mothers whupped my head. Them dirty motherfucking motherfuckers. *(She sees TILLICH.)* Is that an ofay, or you been passing out our pills, boy?

TILLICH *(amazed, stands, stares).* Who's that?

UPDIKE *(in a sealed box, buying time).* I'll be damned if I know. Who are you, girl? This is Mr. WHITE. Was that your name?

TILLICH *(confused).* Mr. *Who?* Tillich. Till —icchh. Tillich.

UPDIKE *(anxious beyond description).* This man I just called Mr. WHITE by accident, has a gun, and he's come up here to shoot and kill some dumb-assed little nigger, what's knocked up his little girl, girl. *(Pauses)* Who are you?

SISSY *(rudely).* What do you mean, "Who are you?"

UPDIKE *(out of control, then in).* What do you mean, "What do you mean?" This here Mr. WHITE . . .

TILLICH *(corrects him).* Tillich.

UPDIKE *(lays it out carefully).* Mr. Tillich . . . here. This Mr. Tillich's little girl, who happens to be about your age, has just been made with child in her stomach by some little black nigger boy, who happens to be about your brother's age. And this here Mr. WHITE, er . . .

TILLICH. Tillich.

UPDIKE *(a false laugh, then screams).* . . . Mr. Tillich's got a loaded gun that kills people deader than a couple of whups on the head, you stupid little shit. *(Quickly to TILLICH)* She's our adopted daughter, and she has a terrible filthy mouth. She's crazy, too. We adopted her from a crazy house. Her mother and father were crazies. *(To GERTRUDE)* Get her out of here.

TILLICH *(thinks he knows).* Wait a minute! Hey. Wait a goddamn minute. The girl and the boy. The ages. And you two. The same size. The apartment. Wait a minute.

GERTRUDE *(a try).* What's going through your head?

TILLICH *(sure he knows).* This apartment. The boy. The girl.

GERTRUDE *(a grand white lady).* Mr. Tillich! I've been standing over there just being very quiet and ladylike, and I've been listening to you use some terrible, terrible language on my youngest and my oldest. And worst of all, on ME, Mr. Tillich. Now, I wouldn't want to think of coming around up your place and talking that way on *your* innocent little children . . . especially the one that got RAPED by some black boy . . . and corrupt their innocent little bellies. Especially the swollen belly. I wouldn't go pointing guns and using filthy language or any of that shit!

TILLICH *(can't believe it).* Something's crazy here.

GERTRUDE *(thinks she's got it made, slapping TILLICH's face).* Manners, Mr. Tillich. Mind your manners.

SISSY *(overlapping, a sound).* Manners.

JUNIOR *(overlapping, a sound).* Manners.

TILLICH *(overlapping, a sound).* I heard her.

GERTRUDE *(overlapping, a sound).* Manners.

TILLICH *(overlapping, a sound).* I heard you.

JUNIOR *(overlapping, a sound).* He heard you.

UPDIKE *(from nowhere, an answer).* Well, there, Mr. Tillich. I know what's going on here. You gotta be looking for the niggers in Four-B. Four-B*eeee*, Tillich.

TILLICH *(his brain is boggled).* Huh?

UPDIKE *(thrilled, grand, understated).* You got the wrong apartment. There are niggers in Four-B. A little black boy.

JUNIOR *(amazed).* Jesus? He's a Cuban.

UPDIKE *(annoyed at the distraction).* Cuban, Puerto Rican, Nigger. It's all the same, ain't it, Tillich?

JUNIOR *(continues his amazement).* But Jesus ain't home! He's back in Havana.

UPDIKE *(angry).* He was home when she got pregnant, though, wasn't he, Tillich? When did she get pregnant, Tillich?

TILLICH *(a limp reply).* Three months ago.

UPDIKE *(furiously, to JUNIOR).* Three months ago, you jerk. *(Back to TILLICH, he mimes his answer softly.)* I think I hear him rattling around in there now, Tillich. Yes, I do. Sounds like they're eating grits in there. Eating *soul* food! You suppose that's the boy you want to talk to, huh?

TILLICH *(stunned).* Jesus? His name is Jesus?

UPDIKE *(pours it on).* That's his nickname. That's what the neighborhood kids call him. Just for the hell of it. What is the kid's name? The kid you're looking for?

TILLICH *(simply an explanation).* Updike. *(They freeze.)*

UPDIKE *(terrified).* That sounds like Jesus.

TILLICH *(can't believe what he's heard).* What are you talking about?

UPDIKE *(as a machine—rapid fire).* You take the *J* in Jesus. The next letter is *K*. There's a *K* in Updike. You take the *S* in Jesus. Two letters over, there's a *U*. Like in Updike. *E* in Jesus comes after the *D* in Updike. *J* in Jesus after the *I* in Updike. What's left?

SISSY *(from nowhere).* Pee.

UPDIKE *(quickly).* One Letter? Kill me for one lousy letter?

TILLICH *(overlapping).* I smell a rat.

UPDIKE *(overlapping).* I know. It's a problem up here.

(They unfreeze.)

TILLICH *(taunting).* "Jesus"? My little Alice is knocked up by a black boy named "Jesus"? If I had a sense of humor, I'd think that was pretty funny. Goddamned funny!

UPDIKE (helpless, confused). What's so funny?

TILLICH (quiet rage). "Jesus." The whole idea of a black boy being called "Jesus" strikes me as being a funny thing. Doesn't it strike you as being a funny thing?

UPDIKE (trapped, a false laugh). Oh, yeah. Sure. Strikes me, all right.

TILLICH (to JUNIOR). How's that strike you?

JUNIOR (spits). Dirty motherfucker!

UPDIKE. (He slaps JUNIOR sharply on the back of his head.) How does that strike you, the man wants to know?

JUNIOR (vomits). Motherfucking bastard!

UPDIKE (hits him again). Every time I ask you how that strikes you, I'm gonna strike you again.

TILLICH (boggled again). What's going on here?

UPDIKE (threatens). Now you answer the man, Junior, or I'll whup your head black and blue, boy. Black and blue.

JUNIOR (straight at UPDIKE). Black is beautiful, man. Beautiful. (UPDIKE and GERTRUDE smile at TILLICH as though JUNIOR is insane. SISSY giggles. JUNIOR continues to scream. The tension is incredible.) Black is beautiful. Black is love. Black is God. Jesus is black. Jesus is black. Jesus is black. Jesus is black. Jesus is black. Jesus is blaaaaaaaaaaccccccccccckkkk!!

(UPDIKE takes a pillow from the bed and slams JUNIOR to the bed. He covers JUNIOR's face with the pillow until JUNIOR's words are muffled. He continues chanting softly under the pillow.)

UPDIKE (simply). The boy is trying to tell you that Jesus is black.

TILLICH. What the hell's going on?

UPDIKE (quickly, smiling helplessly). Jesus is black. Jesus. The black boy from Four-B, what's knocked up your little girl, mister.

TILLICH (ferociously). I've been watching this apartment, not Four-Bee! This is the apartment where the niggers live, not Four-Bee! Now somebody tell me what got into that boy and what the hell's got into this apartment.

GERTRUDE (simply). Ain't no niggers got into this apartment.

UPDIKE (as simply). Ain't none here. Can you see any here?

JUNIOR (unmuffled for a moment). Jesus is black!

UPDIKE (muffling him again). Now if you'll listen to my boy carefully, he's been tellin' you that there's a black boy next door named Jesus. Time and time again this boy of mine's been tellin' you just that. Now you go straight around to Four-B and you knock up that door.

TILLICH (shows the gun; a cowboy). Take the pillow off of his face, mister.

GERTRUDE (ferociously). Now you listen here, mister. I told you that you can't come running up here into the home of us white people just like you and come busting things up and screaming and pointing guns. (Pauses) You got a permit for that gun? Huh?

TILLICH (strangely concerned). Huh?

GERTRUDE (angrily). That's a plain enough question. You got a permit for that gun? Or maybe I got to call the fuzz to find out the answer to my question?

TILLICH (strangely frightened). What are you driving at?

GERTRUDE (goes with it). Sissy. Call the fuzz.

SISSY (amazed). You gone crazy, woman?

GERTRUDE (strongly). Do as your mother tells you, Sissy. This here what's-his-name thinks he can come busting up our place, maybe he can tell the fuzz exactly why. Why he thinks he can do these kind of things.

TILLICH (terrified). Wait a minute.

GERTRUDE (goes on with it). No "wait a minutes." Call them, Sissy.

SISSY (begins, but really whispers). Fuzz! Help! Fuzz!

UPDIKE (ashen). Not so loud, you goddamned fool.

GERTRUDE (confidently). Go on, Sissy. Go on.

SISSY. (Now she screams.) FUZZZ! FUZZZ! FUUUUZZZZZ!

TILLICH (a command more than a plea). Hold it!

SISSY. FUZZZ!

GERTRUDE. (Races over and jams her hand over SISSY's mouth. UPDIKE still has JUNIOR pinned under the pillow. They all freeze waiting for TILLICH's reply.) Yes?

TILLICH (quietly). Four-B?

UPDIKE (a sound). Yeah.

TILLICH (simply). Next door?

UPDIKE (a simple reply, quickly). Right next door.

TILLICH (softly). You sure?

GERTRUDE (softly). Positive.

TILLICH (backing up). Jesus?

UPDIKE (quickly). That's right.

TILLICH (quickly). Jesus?

GERTRUDE *(quickly).* Uh-huh.

TILLICH *(softly).* OK. *(Starts out, down the aisle, turns back to them)* "Jesus," then. Next door. *(Runs off, screaming)* Jesus! You dirty black bastard. I'm coming after you, Jesus, you oversexed buck son-of-a-bitch!

(They slowly come back to life after TILLICH*'s exit. First* SISSY *screams, then* JUNIOR.*)*

SISSY. You chicken-shit . . . (GERTRUDE *smacks her viciously.)*

JUNIOR. *Motherfucker!* I'll be a dirty son-of-a-bitch! (UPDIKE *smacks him viciously.)*

GERTRUDE *(undone).* Knock it off. What are we gonna do?

(The lights fade out on the set. Lights cross-fade up on the apron of the stage.)

SCENE SIX: IN MY SOUL

JUNIOR *and* SISSY *take hand microphones and face the audience. The rock group stands at the microphone behind them.*

———

JUNIOR *and* SISSY.
Mum and daddy's in the back room
Stoned out on gin.
Us up front stretched out on grass.
Set our asses at the table and we rap about the gap.
Between us and around us. Between us and around.
All between and all around.
CHORUS (JUNIOR *and* SISSY *are "answered" by the rock group.)*
Uncle Martin. Uncle Martin. Uncle Martin's in my soul.
Uncle Martin. Uncle Martin. Uncle Martin's in my soul.
JUNIOR.
 I don't want to be a white man,
 But, man, I don't want the black.
 All I want is for the war to end,
 I just want my babies black.
 I don't want to be a white man.
 But, man, I don't want the black.
 All I want is for the war to end.
 That's the war that's got to end.
 Man, I want my babies black.
CHORUS.
Uncle Martin. Uncle Martin. Uncle Martin's in my soul.
Uncle Martin. Uncle Martin. Uncle Martin's in my soul.
JUNIOR *and* SISSY *(talk-sing).*
How do you freak out?
How do you drop out?

How do you work out how you love?
Can't you see it? Can't you see it?
 (Sung)
Can't you see it, man, it's real?
 CHORUS.
 Uncle Martin. Uncle Martin. Uncle Martin's in my soul.
 Uncle Martin. Uncle Martin. Uncle Martin's in my soul. My soul.

(The lights switch off with JUNIOR *and* SISSY *standing on the apron of the stage, staring into the audience hatefully. They have each chosen separate people in the audience to "fix" on during the song. The song ends abruptly.)*

BLACKOUT

SCENE SEVEN: THE MORNING CONTINUES

The lights fade up again in the room. JUNIOR *and* SISSY *re-enter through the front of the set. The play is again "naturalistic." They stare at each other for a brief moment, then speak.*

———

SISSY *(furiously).* I'm going to kill that white cracker bastard.

UPDIKE. *(He's had it.)* You ain't killing nobody, girl. You're as white as that cracker bastard and you ain't got a gun like he's got. That's *power,* girl. Gun power.

JUNIOR *(a spade cat).* I'll buy a piece on the street, man, and I'll go up the side of his head and I'll blow his cracker brains out.

UPDIKE *(a king).* Fuck, you will, boy! You done knocked up his little girl surer than shit. Piece on the street. You had your piece.

GERTRUDE *(after a huge pause, furiously).* You been fucking white girls, huh?

JUNIOR *(the son again; embarrassed).* Alice? She fucks for everybody, Mama.

GERTRUDE *(outraged).* Goddamn this! Goddamn everybody. Goddamn you, especially. *(To* JUNIOR) You and your white girls? White girls!

SISSY *(checks herself).* What do I look like? A tub of shit?

UPDIKE. Mind your mouth, girl.

JUNIOR *(explaining).* Alice's been on her back more times this year than somebody dead in a coffin. And she's just about that good, too.

UPDIKE *(an idea).* Hey! Wait a minute. Wait a goddamned minute.

GERTRUDE *(gigantically disgusted)*. Yeah? What you got to say, you fast-talkin' worthless white nigger?

UPDIKE *(disgusted)*. Shut up, woman. If that there Alice girl—Tillich's little honey—if that there Alice been packin' 'em all in like you say, how come Tillich figures you for the one what made her swell up?

JUNIOR *(sweet, soft)*. Alice likes me.

GERTRUDE *(amazed)*. What?

JUNIOR *(softly)*. Alice likes me.

GERTRUDE *(wants to be sure)*. Speak up, boy. Speak up loud and clear so you Mama can hear you!

JUNIOR *(loud and clear; proud)*. Alice is in love with me!

UPDIKE *(delighted)*. Well, hot shit! At your age. With a cracker girl, too. At your age. *(Pauses)* How old are you, boy?

JUNIOR. Sixteen.

UPDIKE *(hugs JUNIOR, confidentially)*. Shee-ittt. When I was ten, I had me my first cracker. And she was like dead fish too. Just laying there, waiting for me to set her afire with my rhythm, man.

JUNIOR *(softly, giggling)*. I love Alice.

UPDIKE *(shocked)*. Say that again, boy. I think you just said a crazy thing.

JUNIOR *(louder)*. I love Alice.

UPDIKE *(almost faints)*. Gertrude, your boy's gone crazy.

GERTRUDE *(strong)*. What did you say, boy?

JUNIOR *(angry now)*. Damn it! You all heard me. I love Alice. I don't care what you say. She's got creamy white skin, man, and beautiful boobies. And she talks real pretty. All the time. She's beautiful, man. *(To SISSY)* And you are a tub of shit, man. That's just what you are.

SISSY *(clobbering him)*. You motherfucking son-of-a-bitch!

UPDIKE *(breaking up the fight)*. No fighting here and none of your fucking filthy language in this here house. Huh? You get me? Just knock off the shit!

SISSY *(quickly)*. You hear what that motherfucker called me?

UPDIKE. I heard him. *(To JUNIOR)* Say you're sorry, boy.

JUNIOR *(confused)*. For what?

UPDIKE *(quickly)*. For calling your only sister a tub of shit, that's what. Everybody knows she looks just like her mother. That's a bad thing, Junior.

GERTRUDE. *(Leaning at the window, she stands up sharply.)* Apologize, Junior.

SISSY *(mocking)*. Yeah, Junior. Let's kiss and make up. I ain't never kissed a cracker before.

UPDIKE *(angry)*. Lay off that shit. As if we ain't got enough trouble here already without you actin' like a racist!

SISSY *(a "take")*. Huh?

UPDIKE *(very "black")*. Look, I hate to be the one to say it, but pill or no pill, "ya-all" is acting like a pack of niggers. And that's all there is to that.

GERTRUDE *(taunts)*. "Ya-all"?

UPDIKE *(caught)*. In varying degrees. Granted, you ain't actin' quite so Nee-grow as your babies. What with Sissy's "them motherfuckin' motherfuckers" every other word out of her mouth. And Junior here acting like the word "boy" wasn't in Webster's Dictionary. And, shee-it, woman. You is actin' a mite tougher than your average white-assed cracker.

GERTRUDE *(sits on the bed, disgusted)*. Don't "shee-it, woman" me, you Swaheelee bum.

UPDIKE *(insulted)*. Who you callin' "bum"?

SISSY *(Uncle Tom, mocking)*. It ain't me, Babe!

UPDIKE *(furiously, to SISSY)*. Come off the shit, girl, 'fore I whup you like you never been whupped before.

JUNIOR *(dancing)*. Whup. Whup. Whup. That's the way them white folks talk all the time. Whup, whup, whup. I'll whup ya' like ya' never done been whupped before, mother. Yes, zer!

UPDIKE *(distressed)*. Well . . . shee-it. That's the appreciation I get for bringing the pill into this house. Well, shee-it.

GERTRUDE *(Uncle-Toms it like mad)*. You didn't bring no pill into this house, Updike. I washed and scrubbed them floors every Wednesday through Wednesday—yez, ma'am. Sure thing, ma'am. Bet your sweet ass, I scrubbed them floors, baby, not you. I brought them green bucks right into this house surer than shit so's we could buy them wonderful pills. Now didn't I, children?

SISSY *(revivalist)*. Oh, yes. Oh, yes!

GERTRUDE *(proud, grand, "black")*. Don't sass me, Sissy.

JUNIOR *(false "white")*. I hear this 'xact conversation taking place in twenty million white homes just like ours all 'cross the country right now.

GERTRUDE *(angry)*. Don't sass me with

your wise-ass school talk neither, boy, 'cause I didn't get the benefits what your father and your mother slaved away to get you . . . that don't give you no sassin' rights.

JUNIOR *(as angry; plays rhythm—"Hot shit, Ben-a-fit")*. Well, hot shit, benefit! What'd you do for all I got? You didn't even vote for the mayor what passed the bussin' law so I get bussed.

UPDIKE *(almost weeping)*. And a good fuckin' thing too. That cracker bussed you Downtown, man, and look at the mess you made. One day, that's all it took. One day Downtown and look at the mess you done made. *Oooooo. Ooooooo.*

JUNIOR *(imitating him)*. *Ooooo. Ooooo.* *(Pauses)* Shee-it. *(Walks directly to audience. A public speaker. He smiles quietly.)* I'm sick all this infightin' and outfightin'. *(Very middle-class "white" speech imitation)* I'm going to grow up to be just like you, Dad. I'm leaving this impoverished neighborhood so's I can grow up to go to college—maybe Harvard—then become a surgeon. My lifelong desire. Then I'll have a nice apartment on the Lower West Side. *(Very Southern Negro)* Wid a motherfuckin' view of da ribba', baby! Shee-it! *(Runs back into set)*

UPDIKE *(very "black")*. Hee. Hee. Hee. Hee. The boy's got a good black brain inside that white head of his. And black is beautiful.

JUNIOR *(as "black")*. Yez, sah!

SISSY *(the same)*. Indeed, sah!

GERTRUDE *(the same)*. Shee-it. You all jist puttin' me on, ain't ya?

UPDIKE *(laughing)*. Shee-it. We can't 'ford no infightin' or outfightin' like the young man sez. 'Cause we's crackers now!

(They all laugh and slap each other's hands. JUNIOR runs "through" the set and grabs a hand microphone for GERTRUDE. The lights fade down to a spot on the front apron.)

SCENE EIGHT: GERTRUDE'S DREAM

GERTRUDE *takes the microphone and begins to sing "White Like Me." The family stands behind her, as a chorus. The rock group walks into the play. All dance and sing. GERTRUDE begins the song very "white." Slowly, during the song, she goes through the gradations of gray, from white to black, and completes the song as a soul singer.*

GERTRUDE *(singing sweet and cool)*.

I'll sashaye into Saks
And the man will say "GOOD
    MORNIN'."
Slither into Schrafft's
And have a frappe.
I'll mince my way through Macy's
And get thirty-day credit.
No—*oooooo* one will give me crap.
(She struts.)
Move over, Mrs. Robinson.
You ain't nothin' any more.
Startin' this mornin', chippie-child,
I don't wash another floor!
Fuck off, Selma Robinson.
Honey-chile', can't you see?
You ain't a rat's-ass better.
You're just white like me!

(The family steps in with the rock group. THEY sing the chorus, while GERTRUDE ad libs.)

FAMILY.

White like me. White like me. White like me.

(Repeated while GERTRUDE sings)

GERTRUDE.

White like me.
It ain't like yesterday.
Uh-uh, honey. Nooo.
The world is *mine* today.
Uh-huh.

(The chorus ends. GERTRUDE continues.)

GERTRUDE.

I'll send my boy to Harvard and
My Sissy to the 'Cliffe.
Take Spanish at the New School.
Won't I speak terrific
Phrases in six languages.
Sometimes they rhymes.
I . . . I . . . I'll read *The New York
    Times!*
(Strutting)
Move over, Mrs. Robinson.
You ain't nothin' any more.
Starting this mornin' chippie-child.
I don't wash another floor.
(On her knees, swinging)
Fuck off! Selma Robinson.
Honey-chile! Can't you see?
You ain't a rat's-ass better,
You're just white like me.

FAMILY *(as a chorus)*.

White like me. White like me. White like me.

(Repeated while GERTRUDE sings)

GERTRUDE *(ad-libbing on top)*.

It ain't like yesterday.
The world is mine today.

The world is mine.
I'll tell ya' why.
I'll tell ya' why.
I'll tell ya' why. Why. Why.
Because I'm White! White! White!
(Screams a soul scream)
           W - H - I - T - E!
(Just a shriek)
           AHHHHHHHHHH!
ALL *(soul-brother climax)*.
           Oh-oh-oh, Yeah-yeah-yeah.
(If a reprise is called for, the final chorus, starting with "Move over, Mrs. Robinson . . ." should be used, through the finish of the song. Then blackout and hold until applause ends.)

BLACKOUT

SCENE NINE: NEARING NOW

After the audience applause stops, the lights fade up. The family is dancing. The rock group plays quietly, faintly. The dialogue and accent are very "Amos and Andy"—until TILLICH's entrance.

———

UPDIKE *(laughing)*. Dance, woman. You got rhythm.
SISSY *(very "black" and happy)*. Somebody gotta tell this mother he's black inside. He's steppin' all over my toes.
UPDIKE. Hee-hee. Hee-hee. This is terrific.
GERTRUDE *(screaming her delight)*. You all want to see my lipstick kiss?
UPDIKE *(proudly)*. Yeah. Show 'em, Trudy.
(They continue the dance throughout this scene. The music fades under slightly.)
SISSY. What you rappin' 'bout?
GERTRUDE. Your pa done give me a lipstick kiss, that's what. Right down here. *(She opens her robe so SISSY and JUNIOR can see the lipstick mark)* Ain't that the prettiest damn thing he's ever done?
JUNIOR *(enchanted)*. Hee-hee. You did that, Pa?
UPDIKE *(a bad joke)*. You don't think your mama's got a girl friend, do ya?
JUNIOR *(thrilled)*. Hee-hee. That's a pretty thing, Mama.
SISSY *(jealous)*. I want one. Huh? I want one too.
GERTRUDE. Go on, Junior. Give your sister Sissy what your pa gived me. Where's my lipstick, Updike?
UPDIKE. *(Pulls out a tube of lipstick. He throws it to JUNIOR. They all continue to laugh and dance.)* Here ya are, boy!
(JUNIOR puts on the lipstick and dances to SISSY. He dances down her body.)
JUNIOR *(giggling)*. Hold still, lovely.
SISSY *(out of control, overlapping)*. Shee-it! Shee-it!
JUNIOR *(surfacing)*. Hee-hee.
SISSY *(laughing, thrilled, embarrassed)*. Shee-it! I never been kissed low down or even up by no cracker before. Shee-it. You don't look like my brother.
JUNIOR *(delighted)*. Sissy's gettin' hot, Updike.
UPDIKE *(a sound)*. Hee-hee. Hee-hee.
SISSY *(arguing)*. I am not, ya son-of-a-bitch.
JUNIOR *(giggling)*. Yes, ya are. Ya are. Admit it.
SISSY *(quickly)*. Well, you don't look like the brother I knew yesterday, you white-assed bastard. And you know it.
JUNIOR *(loudly)*. Hee-hee. Sissy's hotter 'n' hell. Just like Alice.
UPDIKE *(runs to the rock group)*. Alice! Holy shit! Alice! Stop the music!
(The music stops)
GERTRUDE *(continues to dance)*. What are you doin', Updike? I'm dancing happy.
UPDIKE *(tense)*. You're crazy, woman. That cracker's been over with Jesus for a couple of hours now.
JUNIOR *(cool)*. Jesus ain't home, man.
UPDIKE *(anxious)*. Jesus is too home, ya jerk. He come home wid his folks this mornin'. They all made up and they're back livin' together. Just this mornin'. I seen 'em in the hallway, man. Before you all woke up.
GERTRUDE *(still dancing)*. I was dancin' happy.
UPDIKE *(disgusted, frightened)*. Kee-riiist! The woman's high on hope! *(He slaps GERTRUDE lightly.)* Don't hit me, Trudy. You was just high and I had to bring you down.
GERTRUDE *(angry, stops dancing)*. What'd you do that for, Updike? Huh? What'd you hit me for?
UPDIKE *(helpless)*. 'Splain it to her.
SISSY *(not really concerned)*. Pa think the cracker's comin' back to shoot us.
JUNIOR *(explaining)*. Jesus come home this mornin'. The cracker's over with him now.
GERTRUDE. The cracker'll shoot Jesus 'stead of you.
JUNIOR *(satirically)*. Well, hell. We gotta stop that injustice right now, ain't we? He's

killin' the wrong man. Go get the cracker, Sissy, so's he can shoot me, 'stead of Jesus. Fair's fair, huh?

UPDIKE *(really frightened)*. Don't talk crazy. This here's a serious situation.

(TILLICH *reappears down the aisle. Quietly, he answers* UPDIKE.)

TILLICH *(tough)*. Very serious, mister.

UPDIKE *(ashen)*. Shee-it.

(They all freeze as TILLICH *walks into the room.)*

TILLICH *(takes a long, angry walk across, staring at each of them—*JUNIOR *last)*. Why's the boy wearing lipstick?

UPDIKE *(after they turn to* JUNIOR*)*. The boy's a bit peculiar.

TILLICH *(straight mockery)*. I just had a long long talk with Jesus.

SISSY *(revivalist, to* TILLICH*)*. Glory be.

UPDIKE *(to* SISSY*)*. Shut your fuckin' mouth.

TILLICH *(pours it out)*. Jesus is Cuban.

JUNIOR *(hostile)*. Communist, too, probably.

UPDIKE *(to* JUNIOR*)*. You shut your fuckin' mouth, too.

TILLICH *(he's rolling)*. Jesus is a black Cuban.

GERTRUDE *(a gasping try)*. That sounds like the Jesus we know.

TILLICH *(keeps rolling)*. Jesus is a black Cuban and his father's blacker still.

UPDIKE *(futile)*. Just what I was sayin' to my family. Ain't that the truth?

SISSY *(revivalist)*. It's the truth. It's the truth.

TILLICH *(he knows)*. Jesus is a black Cuban and his father's even blacker. I'd say his father is just about the blackest bastard I've ever seen.

JUNIOR. *(He knows he knows.)* Oh, wow!

TILLICH *(stopped)*. Huh?

JUNIOR *(a rapid explanation; a put-down)*. I just said "Oh, wow." I say that a lot. I put on lipstick, see. Once I get the lipstick on, I can't seem to stop myself from sayin' things like "Oh, wow." That's all.

UPDIKE *(flatly)*. Well, then. You met Jesus.

TILLICH *(as flatly)*. That's right.

UPDIKE *(a sound)*. Yep.

TILLICH *(a sound)*. Yep.

GERTRUDE *(politely, simply)*. Nice of you to drop back and tell us.

TILLICH *(won't stop now)*. What would you say if I told you that Jesus never laid his eyes on Alice? Jesus never laid his hands on Alice?

UPDIKE *(helpless, scared)*. Jesus never laid Alice?

TILLICH *(a wicked smile)*. That's right.

UPDIKE *(the last try)*. That rules Jesus out, don't it? What other sex-crazed friends you got, Junior?

TILLICH. *(Taking out the pistol, he steps back and aims it at* UPDIKE*'s head.)* Come here.

GERTRUDE *(her last try)*. You can't come bustin' in here and . . .

TILLICH *(fiercely)*. SHUT UP! I'm gonna blow his brains out if I don't get a straight answer. *(He walks to* UPDIKE *and puts the end of the pistol in* UPDIKE*'s left ear.* UPDIKE *is not happy.)* Now what is going on here?

UPDIKE *(an aphorism)*. You've got that gun in my ear.

TILLICH *(a greater truth)*. Yes, I do.

UPDIKE *(a plea)*. Gertrude?

GERTRUDE *(feebly)*. You just can't come bustin' in like this. Sissy, call the fuzz.

TILLICH. *(He isn't kidding.)* If you do, I'll blow his head off.

UPDIKE. (UPDIKE *knows.)* Don't call them, Sissy. Let it go. *(Tries to cool it)* Now, Tillich. Tillich. Let's be reasonable.

TILLICH. (TILLICH *knows he knows.)* I'm a reasonable man, Updike. Reasonable enough to listen to my little Alice. I listened to my little Alice tell me about Junior and Sissy and Updike and Junior's mother, Gertrude. Alice says that Junior likes you a lot, Gertrude.

GERTRUDE *(an attempt)*. We like Alice a lot, too.

UPDIKE *(terrified)*. Are you crazy, woman? Shee—it.

TILLICH *(archly)*. How do you say that? "Shee-it"? Is that right?

UPDIKE *(a simple reply)*. That's about it. Yeah.

TILLICH *(the nitty-gritty)*. How'd you get white?

JUNIOR *(getting furious)*. Fuck. Let me throw this son-of-a-bitch right out . . .

TILLICH *(fiercely)*. I'll blow your Pa's head off if you as much as open your mouth, boy.

UPDIKE *(simply, terrified)*. Please don't open your mouth, Junior. Please.

TILLICH *(again)*. Now let's answer some questions. How'd you get white?

SISSY *(furious, ashamed)*. We was born white. Same as you. You're makin' one hell of a mistake. *(To* JUNIOR*)* Motherfucker.

TILLICH *(taunting)*. Jesus says different. Jesus says you was born black as coal. Jesus says you was all born black. And you turned white. Now I believe him. He's a good boy, Jesus. He's been away.

JUNIOR *(a quick reply)*. I'll get that bastard.

TILLICH *(enjoying his power)*. Shut your mouth, boy, or I'll blow your old man's head right off. Then I'll blow your head off. Then I'll think about the ladies. The way you thought about my Alice.

JUNIOR *(an angry reaction)*. I love Alice.

UPDIKE *(undone)*. Shut your mouth.

TILLICH *(pleased)*. Now we're gettin' somewhere. Go on, boy.

JUNIOR *(can't get the words back)*. I didn't say nothin'.

TILLICH *(won't let up)*. I said, go on, boy!

JUNIOR *(introverted)*. There's nothin' to go on with.

UPDIKE *(flatly, ashen)*. The boy tells the truth.

TILLICH *(presses)*. Why are you wearing lipstick?

SISSY *(pauses, gets an idea; pulling up her skirt)*. 'Cause he gave me a lipstick kiss right here.

(TILLICH *stares, stunned.*)

GERTRUDE *(sees what's happening)*. I got a lipstick kiss right here.

(She pulls up her skirt as well. TILLICH *drops his guard.* UPDIKE *simply takes the gun out of his hand.)*

UPDIKE *(amazed)*. I got the fuckin' gun!

TILLICH *(panic; he screams)*. Help! Police! The nigger's got a gun! (JUNIOR *runs and takes the gun from* UPDIKE *and shoves it into* TILLICH*'s ear.* TILLICH *continues to scream for help until he slowly realizes there's a gun in his ear.)* Help! Help! Help! Police! Help! *(Pauses)* You've put the gun in my ear.

JUNIOR *(a cat)*. No shit. You're a whiz.

TILLICH *(terrified)*. What are you going to do?

GERTRUDE *(tension is relieved)*. Shee-it. Hee-hee. Shee-it! That school's done that child a world of good.

UPDIKE *(faints)*. Oooooowwwwww.

GERTRUDE *(strongly, quickly)*. Push the piece further in his ear, and you, Tillich, you shut your mouth. Sissy, get your Pa some water. He fainted.

SISSY *(walks over to* UPDIKE *and slaps his face gently)*. Pa? Pa? You okay?

UPDIKE. Am I dead? *(Stares at his hands)* Holy Christ, I've turned fucking white. I'm dead. Sissy! You're all white too.

SISSY *(slaps him fiercely)*. Hey!

UPDIKE. What you hit me like that for, girl? You just like your Ma. *(Sees what's happening)* Well, hot shee-it. We done got ourselves a captive. *(Pauses)* What we gonna do wid him?

JUNIOR *(taunting)*. Maybe we'll blow his brains out, huh?

SISSY *(joining quickly)*. He ain't got no brains.

TILLICH *(pleads)*. Please. I didn't mean to . . .

JUNIOR *(softly, viciously)*. Shut the fuck up, cracker.

TILLICH *(flatly)*. Yes. Of course.

UPDIKE *(pressing)*. The worm's turned, ain't it, cracker?

TILLICH *(a sound)*. Yes.

JUNIOR *(quickly)* I told you to shut your mouth, man.

TILLICH *(a plea)*. That gun is loaded, you know. You could kill somebody.

JUNIOR *(a sound, a laugh)*. Who?

TILLICH *(falls to his knees)*. Please.

SISSY *(tough)*. Push the piece in a little harder, Junior. Cracker needs to get his ear bent the way he's been bending ours.

UPDIKE *(laughing)*. Hee-hee. We done got ourselves one hell of a prisoner.

GERTRUDE *(from nowhere, fiercely)*. SHUT UP! *(Takes a long pause. Everybody freezes. Silence. She speaks.)* What were you gonna do, cracker? Huh? Were you gonna blow our brains out? Were you gonna shoot Pa's head off? Then Junior? Maybe grab a little ass from me and the little girl before you went home? Huh, cracker?

TILLICH *(almost sobbing)*. No. Of course not.

JUNIOR *(quickly)*. Was you planning to integrate our neighborhood, man? Is that what you came up for?

SISSY *(overlapping)*. He was gonna fuck up the neighborhood.

JUNIOR *(overlapping)*. Real estate prices would skyrocket!

GERTRUDE *(overlapping)*. Hee-hee. That school's done the boy a world of good, Updike. I told you I was right!

UPDIKE *(overlapping)*. Shee-it. Hee-hee. Shee-it!

TILLICH *(clearly)*. I'm sorry. Please. I'm really sorry.

JUNIOR *(a cat)*. Man, I got a piece of real power in my hands, ain't I? If I pull this thing . . . what do you call it? A trigger *(rhymes with "nigger")*, mister? If I pull the *trigger* on this piece of power, will you believe me like you believe Alice, mister?

TILLICH *(great sincerity)*. I believe you. I believe you.

JUNIOR *(savors his position)*. But I ain't told you nothin' yet! What's to believe?

SISSY *(a sound)*. Power, baby.

UPDIKE *(overlapping; a sound)*. Hee-hee. Power.

TILLICH *(babbling, sobbing)*. Look. I'm a very liberal guy. I mean I *believe* in integration. I want to help you people. It's just that my Alice got pregnant that way. I've been donating money and working on fair-housing committees . . . Hell, I never would act like this.

GERTRUDE *(with tremendous authority)*. Stand over there, cracker. Over there. There. Stop. Right there. That's just where I want you. *(Walking over to* TILLICH *and inspecting him)* Let's see your white skin, mister. (*To* JUNIOR) I want to see a little skin.

(JUNIOR *stares at his mother blankly.)*

JUNIOR *(wise-ass)*. Roll over nice for my Mama, cracker.

(TILLICH *rolls)*

GERTRUDE *(fiercely, pauses)*. Looks pretty stupid, don't it? Looks pretty stupid when all that white skin's down on its knees just beggin' for mercy.

JUNIOR *(taunting)*. Right, Mama. It looks pretty dumb to me.

TILLICH *(terrified)*. Please. What are you going to do to me?

GERTRUDE *(stronger still)*. I think you better keep your mouth tight-up closed.

TILLICH *(flatly, softly)*. Sure. Yes. Sure.

GERTRUDE *(laughing)*. That's the stuff.

SISSY *(overlapping)*. *Cracker's scared shit, ain't he?*

UPDIKE *(proudly)*. Well, hot shit. You figure it out, Trudy. *(To* TILLICH) She's tough, Cracker. You're in a rotten situation, I know.

GERTRUDE *(disgusted)*. Jesus. There ain't nothin' slower than a worthless white nigger. Shut up, Updike.

JUNIOR *(a cat)*. Hey, man. I'm carrying a piece of States' Rights. Right here in my hand. I didn't even know it either. Want me to kill him, Mama?

GERTRUDE *(surprised)*. Huh?

JUNIOR *(a killer)*. You heard me. Want me to blow Cracker's brains out?

SISSY *(an accomplice)*. I told you he ain't got no brains.

TILLICH *(feels the threat completely)*. Please don't. I got kids. I got a family. Please. I'll do anything for you. Honest to God. Don't shoot me.

GERTRUDE *(taunting, to* TILLICH). You're very scared now, ain't you, boy?

TILLICH *(a plea)*. Yes. Wouldn't you be?

GERTRUDE *(flip)*. Yep. I'd be scared all right.

JUNIOR *(presses for permission)*. Shit. Mama. We got one. We'll pretend he's all of them. *(Pauses, then he pleads viciously)* Let me kill him, Mama?

GERTRUDE *(stunned)*. I don't know. I don't know.

SISSY *(slowly, clearly)*. Mama. I'm sick to my stomach, Mama. I feel like I'm gonna throw it all up.

GERTRUDE *(watches)*. Wait a minute, honey. I'll think of somethin'.

JUNIOR *(means it)*. I feel sick to my stomach, Mama.

GERTRUDE *(confused)*. I'll think of something, honey. I'll think of something.

UPDIKE *(retching)*. I'm sick too. Christ! It's comin' up on me. I'm sick too!

GERTRUDE *(reeling, pained)*. Christ! I'm sick to my stomach now too. It's comin' up! *(As she walks to the window)* Updike. Damn it. Updike.

(GERTRUDE *walks to the window and stares outside)*

UPDIKE *(ill)*. What you up to, woman?

GERTRUDE *(a matriarch)*. The sun's almost straight above us, Updike. The morning's almost gone. We been white one morning, darling. *(Pauses, then softly)* Remember what you did this morning?

UPDIKE *(slowly)*. The lipstick-kiss?

GERTRUDE *(with enormous pride)*. Uh-huh. I don't want it, darlin'. Not that I don't love you. I love you more now than when I met you. More this morning than ever before. Even though you're a stupid shit, darlin'. You are, *too*. But I'm stupid, too, huh? *(She rubs her dress against her belly)* Do as I'm doing, Sissy. Rub your lipstick-kiss off. Off! Off! Off! (SISSY *does)* That's my little girl.

(GERTRUDE *begins to weep. Then she cries. Sobbing.* TILLICH *stares.* SISSY *begins to weep. Then* JUNIOR *too. Finally* UPDIKE)

UPDIKE. *(Weeping openly, he hugs her.)* Darlin'. My black beautiful darlin'. Oh shit, honey. Honey, I love you.

(They kiss a long, loving kiss. A tape recording of the Creation of Man begins to play and they all pause, listening to their own voices.)

GERTRUDE *(on tape).* In the beginning, there was only God on Earth. And the sunshine.

JUNIOR *(on tape).* At first, man was ravaged by scratchy rash and itchy skin blisters.

UPDIKE *(on tape).* When God turned a bronze and beautiful brown, He created man in the image of Himself.

SISSY *(on tape).* In his journey from Heaven to 126th Street, two of the pills spilled from his pocket and were lost forever.

GERTRUDE *(screams to the tape-recorded voice).* Say that again!

SISSY *(on tape).* In his journey from Heaven to 126th Street, two of the pills spilled from his pocket and were lost forever.

GERTRUDE *(screams violently to* SISSY*).* Say that again.

SISSY *(simply, explaining).* Two of the pills spilled from his pocket and were lost forever.

(She begins to realize. She stares at TILLICH*.)*

TILLICH *(explaining, desperately).* Please, brothers. Let me explain. Please. I'm black too. Brothers. Please. Let me explain. I'm black too, I'm black too.

SISSY *(reeling backwards).* A pill.

JUNIOR *(the same).* One of the missing pills!

TILLICH *(weeping).* After all this time. My Alice. A black baby. Please. Don't you understand? Please, brothers. Please . . . My wife. My kids. They don't know. They don't know. They never knew. They never knew.

GERTRUDE *(after a huge ugly silence in which they all freeze and stare at* TILLICH *begging; violently).* MAKE HIM BLACK! MAKE HIM BLACK! PAINT THE BASTARD AND MAKE HIM BLACK! *(Music, very loud, is heard. There are buckets of black paint and brushes under the bed.* GERTRUDE *dives after them and passes out brushes to all.* UPDIKE *brings out three buckets also. They grab* TILLICH, *throw him down and dance around him, chanting and painting him with the black paint.* TILLICH *tries to flick the paint from his body as though he were being covered with stinging insects. Spoken mechanically)* Black is beautiful.

SISSY *(a sound).* Black is beautiful.

JUNIOR *(a sound).* Black is beautiful.

UPDIKE *(a sound).* Black is beautiful.

GERTRUDE *(a sound).* Black is Jesus.

SISSY *(a sound).* Black is Jesus.

JUNIOR *(a sound).* Black is Jesus.

UPDIKE *(a sound).* Black is Jesus.

GERTRUDE *(a sound).* Black is love!

SISSY *(a sound).* Black is love.

JUNIOR *(a sound).* Black is love.

UPDIKE *(a sound).* Black is love.

(They continue blackening TILLICH. *They blacken themselves as well. They dance as they scream, laugh, and cry—all at the same time.* TILLICH *is frozen with horror. He tries to escape the paint. He can't)*

GERTRUDE *(spitting fire).* Black is black is black is black.

ALL. *(Chanting and crying, they repeat the phrase in turn, not in unison.)* BLACK IS BLACK IS BLACK. BLACK IS BLACK IS BLACK. BLACK IS BLACK IS BLACK.

(The chanting becomes a frenzied fugue.)

GERTRUDE. Kill the white man!

ALL. KILL THE WHITE MAN. KILL THE WHITE MAN. KILL THE WHITE MAN.

GERTRUDE. BLACK IS BEAUTIFUL.

ALL *(overlapping).* BLACK IS BEAUTIFUL.

GERTRUDE. Kill the white man.

ALL *(overlapping).* Kill the white man.

GERTRUDE. Black is love.

ALL *(overlapping).* Black is love.

GERTRUDE. BLACK IS BLACK IS BLACK. BLACK IS BLACK IS BLACK. BLACK IS BLACK IS BLACK.

ALL. BLACK IS BLACK IS BLACK. BLACK IS BLACK IS BLACK. BLACK IS BLACK IS BLACK.

GERTRUDE. KILL THE WHITE MAN. KILL THE BLACK MAN.

ALL. KILL THE WHITE MAN. KILL THE BLACK MAN.

GERTRUDE. KILL. KILL. KILL. KILL. KILL. KILL.

ALL. KILL. KILL. KILL. KILL. KILL. KILL.

TILLICH *(screams in frantic horror).* NO! *(The chanting and music stop.)*

GERTRUDE *(simply).* Yes.

(In the three buckets previously brought out from under the bed by UPDIKE *are catsup, and bits of black fabric cut into squares. All the buckets look exactly the same. Music comes on in the beginning of the chant. The stage manager cues as follows: On* TILLICH*'s scream "No!", the music bumps out. On* GERTRUDE*'s "Yes," all flip brushes at* TILLICH, *giving him final black streaks on his clothing. At the flip of the brushes, the lights switch from the stage to special lights focused on the audience. The stage is in blackness now, as the pistol is fired. Blam! Blam! A second shot.*

Blam! The final shot. During the shots SISSY *sets the catsup bucket near* TILLICH, *who, during the BLACKOUT on stage, scoops catsup into his mouth. LIGHTS switch from the audience to the stage.* GERTRUDE *and* UP- DIKE *throw buckets of black fabric at the audience. Precisely when the fabric leaves the buckets, the lights switch from the stage into the audience's eyes again. During this blackout on the stage,* TILLICH *turns on his back, dead, with his head over the lip of the stage, his face, upsidedown, facing the audience with a hideous stare. The lights quickly switch from the audience to a special on* TILLICH's *face. Blood slowly trickles from his mouth.* JUNIOR *walks calmly to* TILLICH *and photographs him with a flash camera. Then the family poses over* TILLICH's *body as hunters with a slain lion. They are photographed. Then they all photograph the audience. There is a pinspot on* TILLICH. *The lights fade.)*

CURTAIN

NOON

Terrence McNally

For ANTHONY DeSANTIS

While the house lights are still up, we hear a phone ringing—ringing and ringing and ringing. Endlessly. Just when the play is about to begin, the person on the other end gives up and the ringing stops.

We are in a large room, maybe a loft, no furniture, perhaps a few crates to sit on if necessary.

KERRY, *in his early thirties, medium build, pleasantly outgoing, enters. He carries a flight bag. He's out of breath from climbing stairs.*

KERRY. Christ! oi vey! and mamma mia! *(Catches his breath)* Somebody ought to report this place to the Red Cross. *Whoof!* I thought there were laws about this sort of thing. I mean this beats Mexico City. Dear God! My heart! *(Calls)* Hello! I'm here. You said after twelve and . . . *(Looks at his watch)* well, you know what the early bird catches! *(Pause)* Hey? Anybody home? Dale? *(BONG. BONG. Enormously loud tolling sounds as a*

clock somewhere nearby begins to tell the hour. BONG. BONG. BONG.) Ow! *(Covers his ears. The clock continues to toll.* ASHER, *in his early twenties, tall, thin and nervous, will come up the stairs and into the room during the following. He is carrying several books. It is impossible to talk over the tolling, but* KERRY *tries to get a word in whenever he can.)* I thought Big Ben was in London! *(BONG. BONG)* I'll be with you in a minute! *(BONG. BONG)* The door was open! *(BONG)* I took the liberty! *(BONG)* I hope you don't mind! *(BONG)* I SAID THE DOOR WAS OPEN, AND I TOOK THE LIBERTY OF JUST WALKING IN! *(The clock has stopped tolling.)* Hey, friend, you got the time? *(He laughs.)*

ASHER *(he looks at his wrist watch).* It's just noon.

KERRY. No kidding! *(Shaking hands)* Hi. I'm Kerry.

ASHER. Hello.

KERRY. Nice place you got. All you need is a ski lift and earplugs. Did you check for nosebleed?

ASHER. This isn't my place.

KERRY. You don't live here?

ASHER. No.

KERRY. Good! I can stop feeling sorry for you. And if I didn't have to worry about getting my tail back down, I could even stop feeling sorry for me.

ASHER. Oh. The stairs. Yes. They're really something.

KERRY. I don't have to ask if you do this often. You'd be up on manslaughter charges. *(Reading from an imaginary headline)* "Large numbers have heart attacks climbing stairs. Dale is charged." *(He laughs.)*

ASHER. It's quite a climb, all right.

KERRY. Just out of curiosity, what was wrong with your place?

ASHER. Hunh?

KERRY. Your place. What's wrong with there?

ASHER. Nothing.

KERRY. Got a roommate, hunh? Me too. She's a bitch about things like this. Come to think of it, she's a bitch, period.

ASHER. I don't have a roommate.

KERRY. No?

ASHER. I mean a lover.

KERRY. Oh.

ASHER. Mistress is what I'm trying to say!

KERRY. Then you're married?

ASHER. Me?

KERRY. You keep a very large dog then?

ASHER. What dog?

KERRY. You can't be *that* ashamed of your place . . .

ASHER. I'm not.

KERRY. You *do* have a place, don't you?

ASHER. Well, sure.

KERRY. 'Cause I'd sure as hell love to know what was wrong with it. If it's any worse than this, you ought to write your congressman. How are you fixed for time?

ASHER. Fine.

KERRY. I'm supposed to be on a business lunch. *(Sits on a crate)* Dale what?

ASHER. Hunh?

KERRY. Not that it really matters, but anyway, Dale what?

ASHER. Dale what?

KERRY. You. Your last name.

ASHER. I'm not Dale.

KERRY. I thought you said Dale.

ASHER. No, it's Asher.

KERRY. On the phone it sounded like Dale.

ASHER. What phone?

KERRY. My phone. Your phone. Last night.

ASHER. I think you're confusing me with someone else. My name's Asher.

KERRY *(shaking hands).* Hi, Asher. I'm still Kerry.

ASHER. Hello.

KERRY. Do we start all over again?

ASHER. This isn't my place.

KERRY. I think we've pretty well established that.

ASHER. I'm supposed to be meeting someone here.

KERRY. No kidding?

ASHER. Hunh?

KERRY. After all those stairs, it figures you're meeting *someone* up here. Unless you're some kind of calf-nut.

ASHER. What?

KERRY *(slapping at his leg).* Calf-nut. Here! Leg muscles.

ASHER. No. Not especially.

KERRY. Me either. I'm a chest-and-biceps man. You work out?

ASHER. In a gym? No.

KERRY. At home? You know, those Royal Canadian Air Force exercises really work. I took an inch off here with isometrics.

ASHER. I don't work out anywhere.

KERRY. How come?

ASHER. I . . . just . . . don't.

KERRY. You should.

ASHER. I know.

KERRY. You look like you work out.

ASHER. Thank you.

KERRY. You look like you work out a lot.

ASHER *(beet red by now).* They said right after twelve.

KERRY. You're right on time. *(Loosening a few buttons)* It's hot up here.

ASHER. I know.

KERRY. Take your jacket off.

ASHER. I know I'm right on time!

KERRY. We both are.

ASHER. It's my problem. I'm never late for anything. Everybody else always is and I'm always waiting. Sometimes I think I'm the only person in the world who thinks right after twelve means right after twelve. God knows, girls never do. They're always late. I have a theory why.

KERRY. I like your trousers.

ASHER. Hunh?

KERRY. Your pants. They're nice.

ASHER. Oh.

KERRY. They're a good fit. Nice and snug on you.

ASHER. They're just off the rack.

KERRY. It's a nice fabric, too.

ASHER. I guess.

KERRY. Lightweight.

ASHER. They're just summer pants.

KERRY. Clinging, though.

ASHER. What?

KERRY. Clinging. It's a good clinging fabric.

ASHER. They shrunk a little.

KERRY *(shaking his head).* Then they'd just be tight. No, yours cling.

ASHER. They're just pants.

KERRY. Well, I'd sure as hell love to get my hands on a pair like yours.

ASHER. Ordinary summer pants. They sell them anywhere.

KERRY. Not with that clinging quality.

ASHER. Sears and Roebuck.

KERRY *(still shaking his head).* Your usual lightweight summer trousers don't give you support like that. Not anymore.

ASHER. What?

KERRY. Support. Here. Keep the whang from waggling. It's a problem.

ASHER *(taking off the jacket).* You're right.

KERRY. You hang out all over the place, too?

ASHER. It's hot up here! *(Suddenly)* Can I ask you something?

KERRY. Sure.

ASHER. Are you—

KERRY *(at once).* Unh-hunh!

ASHER. . . . Are you meeting someone named Dale too?

KERRY *(momentarily deflated)*. Oh. I *thought* I was meeting someone named Dale. Why?

ASHER. I think we both are.

KERRY. Dale gets around.

ASHER. Do you know Dale?

KERRY. No. Do you?

ASHER. No.

KERRY. Does it matter?

ASHER. I guess not.

KERRY. 'Cause any friend of Dale's is a friend of mine.

ASHER. You just said you didn't know Dale.

KERRY. All right, screw Dale!

ASHER. That's what I had in mind.

KERRY. Ditto! *(Pause.* ASHER *paces.)* I guess you don't even need shorts with trousers like that.

ASHER. Shorts?

KERRY. Underwear. B.V.D.s. Skivvies.

ASHER. Sure you do.

KERRY. Well, whatever you've got on under there, they're doing a fantastic job.

ASHER. What?

KERRY. Of keeping you in place.

ASHER. Oh.

KERRY. Are they boxers?

ASHER. What?

KERRY. Are you wearing boxer-type shorts or jockeys?

ASHER. Jockey. Boxer. The baggy-type ones!

KERRY *(solemn agreement)*. Yeah, they give you more mobility. Now your jockeys are more for support. It's a real choice. I switch back and forth myself.

ASHER *(trying to change the subject)*. Do you know Dale the way I know Dale?

KERRY *(not really letting him)*. I thought we'd just agreed that neither of us had had the pleasure. Yours, of course, are as fantastic as your trousers.

ASHER. My what are fantastic!

KERRY. Your shorts. It doesn't look like you're wearing any and that's the whole secret, of course.

ASHER. I mean, did you put one of those ads in one of those papers and someone named Dale answered?

KERRY. What do you think?

ASHER. Maybe one of us ought to leave.

KERRY. I don't follow.

ASHER. Well, you were here first. I mean, it might be awkward, three of us.

KERRY. That depends on Dale, wouldn't you think?

ASHER. You see, I hadn't planned on an . . . *(Almost swallowing the word)* an orgy.

KERRY. Do you mind if I ask what make they are?

ASHER. Make?

KERRY. Your fabulous undershorts. What brand are they?

ASHER. I couldn't tell you, I'm sure.

KERRY. Where'd you pick them up, then?

ASHER. I don't remember.

KERRY. A men's specialty store?

ASHER. I wouldn't think so.

KERRY. Because if they're from a men's specialty store, they're probably a French or German import. The French are fantastic with men's underwear. The work with nylon has been extraordinary.

ASHER. I'm sure these are just Fruit of the Loom.

KERRY. Oh.

ASHER. Or something like that!

KERRY. I bet not, though.

ASHER. I don't think I've ever been in a men's specialty store.

KERRY. You probably have and didn't know it. They're popping up all over the place lately.

ASHER. I don't even know what a men's specialty store is!

KERRY. Do you always pace in little circles?

ASHER. Only when I'm nervous.

KERRY. I'm not making you nervous, am I?

ASHER. No, this does! Even my palms are sweating.

KERRY. What?

ASHER. This. Up here. I've never done it before.

KERRY. Now you're really putting me on.

ASHER. Why? Have you?

KERRY. You couldn't tell?

ASHER. I don't mean sex. Sex doesn't make me nervous. I love sex.

KERRY. Only your palms sweat.

ASHER. Taking an ad to have sex and then some girl answering it makes my palms sweat! I may never do this again. I'm a wreck already!

KERRY. Oh! I thought you were trying to tell me you were a virgin.

ASHER. A virgin! Hah! That's a good one. A virgin! Hah!

KERRY. I wouldn't have minded.

ASHER. Well I would! A virgin! Jeez! I can't

think of anything I'm more definitely not. A virgin. Ha!

KERRY. Some people have all the luck.

ASHER. Luck?

KERRY. Fruit of the Loom and a fit like that!

ASHER. I wasn't thinking about that!

KERRY. Of course you weren't. Why should you? If I could find summer pants and shorts like that, I wouldn't think about it either. I guess I'll just have to stick with these until something better comes along. Talk about hot! I don't think it's possible to have hotter pants than I do. They've actually steamed up on me! My knees are roasting. And they're tight, too! I mean, here's your real difference between lightweight summer-clinging and plain goddam tight. I feel like I'm going to burst out of these half the time. Look at the thighs alone. Tight as two sausages in these. And support! I don't even want to go into that. Hell, it's like flying buttresses in here. I'm so supported I could split. *(He's standing right in front of* ASHER.)

ASHER. Why don't you buy bigger pants?

KERRY. They're no answer. It's all in the fabric and the kind of shorts.

ASHER. Oh.

KERRY. No, I'll just bide my time with these until the right fabric and pair of shorts come winging my way.

(During the following he will take an air mattress out of his flight bag and begin to inflate it with a pump. ASHER *will try not to notice.)*

ASHER. What made you think I was a virgin, anyway? Jeez! I kissed my cherry goodbye way back in the eighth grade. Whatever men call it, I lost it. After a hayride around White Rock Lake. It's in Dallas. That's where I grew up. Her name was Mary Beth Page. She was a little tubby, but still she was pretty. And she wasn't any town pump, either. It was her first time, too.

KERRY *(still pumping).* Are you sure those are Fruit of the Looms?

ASHER. I told you I thought so.

KERRY. But you're not sure? The only reason I ask is I'd hate to go out and invest in a pair and then get home and find out I wasn't getting the same kind of support.

ASHER. I'm pretty sure that's what they are.

KERRY. I wish you could be more definite.

ASHER. Well, when I get home I suppose I could look and call you, if you want.

KERRY. I won't be in.

ASHER. Tomorrow then.

KERRY. I'm leaving town. I don't know how long I'll be away.

ASHER. I'm sorry.

*(*KERRY *has finished pumping. The mattress is just lying there now.)*

KERRY. I don't suppose you'd? . . . I know it's an imposition, but I'd really appreciate getting this thing settled for once and for all.

ASHER. There's no place to . . . !

KERRY. We're just two men.

ASHER. What if Dale walked in? I'd look ridiculous.

KERRY *(explosive).* Got it! *(He leaps toward* ASHER.)

ASHER. Hunh?

KERRY. Turn around.

ASHER. Turn? . . .

KERRY. I can just pull the waistband up and read the label right off.

ASHER *(pulling his shirt out of his pants).* Well, if it's really that important to you! . . .

KERRY. Hey, your shirt's nice, too! What is that? Cotton percale?

ASHER. Really, I don't know! Please, hurry up.

KERRY. You try reading upside down.

ASHER. Fruit of the Loom uses an insignia. A cornucopia, I think.

KERRY. A.R.S.? Arse?

ASHER. That's my laundry mark!

KERRY. You know something? You've got your shorts on backwards. Either that or the brand name's up front.

ASHER. Backwards?

KERRY. Backwards! I can feel the fly crotch opening.

ASHER. My underwear's on backwards?

KERRY *(laughing).* All these years of looking for the one underwear with the perfect support, and his trick is to wear them backwards! It's incredible!

ASHER. I've never put my underwear on backwards in my life!

KERRY. You did this morning, God bless you! And I think we've found something. This is it, baby, this is it! *(He's turning* ASHER *around.)*

ASHER. What are you doing?

KERRY. Front or backwards, I still want to know what make they are.

ASHER. I can do it!

KERRY. Stand still.

ASHER. Really I can!

KERRY. J. C. Penney!

ASHER. That's *like* Fruit of the Loom.

KERRY. J. C. Penney cotton boxers worn backwards! A rank amateur gets his drawers on cockeyed and successfully and single-handedly dynamites every theory of male genital support going. Like I said, it's incredible! *(He's undone* ASHER'*s belt, unzipped his fly.* ASHER'*s pants drop to his knees.)* Shoes.

ASHER. Hey!

KERRY. You can't get your pants off with your shoes on. Dummy!

ASHER. I don't want my pants off!

KERRY. What are you? Some kind of faggot?

ASHER. Faggot?

KERRY. Or are you trying to call me one? For Christ's sake, I just want to see you in your shorts.

ASHER. I know, but . . .

KERRY. Guys are guys.

ASHER. Hunh?

KERRY. You're a guy, aren't you?

ASHER. Well of course I am.

KERRY. Be proud of it!

ASHER. I am!

KERRY. You'd never know it.

ASHER *(half trips, half stumbles out of his pants).* All right?

KERRY. How can I tell?

ASHER. Hunh?

KERRY. Your shirt.

ASHER. My shirt?

KERRY. It's in the way. I can't see you or your shorts.

ASHER *(pulls his shirt up).* Okay?

KERRY. Just take it all the way off, hunh?

ASHER. I . . .

KERRY. You're sure acting like a faggot. And a faggot virgin at that.

ASHER. Well, I'm not. Either one!

KERRY. I said you were *acting* like . . .

ASHER. All right! *(Takes off his shirt)* There. Okay?

KERRY. Turn around. Slowly! *(While* ASHER'*s back is turned,* KERRY *gathers his clothes and hides them.)* Again.

ASHER. I feel like a . . . a . . .

KERRY. What do you do?

ASHER. A model!

KERRY. You're a model?

ASHER. I feel like a model. I'm a writer.

KERRY. Figures.

ASHER. Hunh?

KERRY. What else do you do?

ASHER. What else? . . .

KERRY. God, you're exasperating. In bed. What do you do in bed?

ASHER. Everything.

(He's scratching his head, puzzled, looking around for his clothes. KERRY *is putting a 45 rpm record on his portable phonograph. The music is a Jackie Gleason "Music for Lovers Only"-type selection.)*

KERRY. Everything?

ASHER. You know . . . everything. I'm not inhibited, if that's what you're asking. My ad said it. "Culmination of your most sensuous desires."

KERRY *(sniffing an amyl nitrate capsule).* Keep talking!

ASHER. Say, have you seen my? . . . *(Sees* KERRY *sniffing)* What's that?

KERRY. "Have poppers." That's what my ad said. *(Long ecstatic moan)* Oooooooooooh! *(He offers a sniff to* ASHER.)

ASHER. No, thank you.

KERRY. I thought you did everything.

ASHER. In bed.

KERRY. That's what this is for.

ASHER. You mean? . . .

KERRY. Gets those colored lights going.

ASHER. *Streetcar.*

KERRY. Hunh? Now you've got me doing it.

ASHER. *A Streetcar Named Desire.* Colored lights going. Tennessee Williams.

KERRY. Tennessee Williams uses poppers?

ASHER. I wouldn't be surprised at anything Tennessee Williams uses. Did you ever read his plays?

KERRY *(offering a "popper" again).* Here. Relax. Fly with me.

ASHER. I guess they're a lot like marijuana and opium and stuff like that?

KERRY. You'll see! You'll see!

ASHER. I don't really approve of drugs . . . *any* artificial stimulus, for that matter . . . but I think a writer has to leave himself open to any new experience. Don't you?

KERRY *(putting the "popper" in* ASHER'*s hand).* Wide open.

ASHER. Look at George Plimpton! *(Sniffs)* Wow! *(Sniffs again, laughs)* You know something? I don't see my pants. *(Sniffs again)* You know something else? I don't care. *(Sniffs again)* I'm getting a headache. *(Sniffs again)* Hey, it's gone already! *(Reeling happily)* Hoo! Do I feel wild and randy! Randy and wild!

KERRY *(getting* ASHER *onto the air mattress. It's a job).* Just lie back. It's going to be beautiful.

ASHER *(lying down now, eyes closed).* Where's Dale?

KERRY *(quickly stripping to flowered bikini shorts).* "Young gay man, mid-twenties"— that's me, baby—"digs groovy sex with hung horny bisexual guys over eighteen." *(A snore from* ASHER; KERRY *bends over him.)* Asher? (ALLEGRA*'s voice offstage is heard calling brightly:* "Bonjour!") Shit!

(He hides quickly as ALLEGRA, *early twenties, with a nice face and body, taut-nerved, bounds into the room. She seems unaffected by the stairs.)*

ALLEGRA. Bonjour! Bonjour! *(Her accent is execrable.) Je regrette d'être en retard. . . .* (sorry to be late!) . . . *Le trafic, ça c'est formidable . . .* (The traffic was terrible.) . . . *but me voici tout de même. . . .* (I'm here all the same!) *Bonjour! Bonjour!* (ASHER *mumbles something in his daze.) Ne parle pas anglais, mauvais garçon. . . .* (bad boy) *Il faut parler français tous les temps . . .* (all the time) . . . *si vous vraiment voulez parler comme un native. . . .* (really want to speak like a native) (ASHER *mumbles again.) Non, non, non et non!* (ASHER *regards her with a glassy stare.) Je m'appelle Allegra. Allegra. . . .* (That's Italian for full of pep!) *J'ai lu votre avertissement . . .* (read your ad) *. . . et je suis allée dehors de ma tête . . .* (went out of my head!) You want French lessons? You're going to get French lessons! *Fou du sexe! . . .* (sex maniac!) *(Moves away from him. His dazed eyes are never off her.) Premiere leçon français. Les articles des habits! . . .* (articles of clothing!) I'm double-parked, so we'd better get right to it, *mon élève. . . .* (you student, you!) *(Pointing out each article of clothing) Voici la blouse. Voici les boutons de la blouse. J'ai un . . .* (Unbuttoning as she counts them) *. . . deux . . . trois . . . quatre boutons. (Her blouse is open.) J'enleve ma blouse. (Takes off her blouse) Voici la lupe. Voici le zipper de la lupe. (Unzips her skirt) Adieu à la lupe. (Steps out of her skirt) Voici les nylons. (Takes off her stockings, sings the* "Marseillaise" *while she does so) Patriotique chanson français! (Stands in front of* ASHER) *Maintenant je suis presque nu . . .* (nearly naked) *. . . mais pas encore. . . .* (not yet, brown-eyes) *Je reste dans brassiere et panties pour le temps. . . .* (I'm keeping these on for a while.) *Il faut savoir d'abord . . .* (first) *. . . les parts du corps . . .* (parts of the body . . . yours and mine, long lashes!) *(Comes right next to him) La bouche. (She kisses him.) Les cuisses. (Hand on his thighs) La poitrine. (Other hand on his chest) Le coq. (Points this time) Le chat. (Points at herself,* then laughs wildly) *Je ne suis pas vraiment nymphomanique . . .* (I'm not really a nympho) *. . . mais . . .* can we drop the French lesson a minute? There's something I really want to tell you. I've never done anything like this in my life. Honest. I've wanted to, but I come from a pretty conservative background. Dull, you'd call it. *Seducteur! (Gives him a playful nudge)* But when I read your ad in that paper, it like turned me on. Turned me on? I'm a girl on fire! *(Moving around the room now)* You see, I'm stuck out in Flushing with this creep-liberal-intellectual-lawyer husband, who likes to talk about it all the time, and I'm going out of my mind out there with him and all his damn books. It's his fault I'm here. His and Grove Press. He's a big liberal about all sorts of things, but especially Grove Press. Those books can warp a girl. But try telling him that. "The only obscene word in the English language is the word obscene." Him, Carlton Schapiro, and he's the Oscar Wilde of Greater Flushing! I didn't even want to read them at first. But he was always nagging at me. "They're not dirty," he'd say, "they're not dirty." Fuck him, they're not dirty! I practically had a nervous breakdown over the last one he gave me. *Moist,* it's called. Just *Moist.* It's about an American girl tourist in Spain who ends up on a breeding ranch . . . out there on the pampas, with the bulls she's doing it! . . . But Carlton says it's an allegory. I could just kill him. I mean, he's down at the Civil Liberties Union or the NAACP half the time, and I'm stuck in Flushing reading Grove Press stuff and climbing the walls. I've tried branching out with him. You know, wilder stuff, like I've been reading about. And he says, "What's the matter with you, Allegra? My mother said you dancers were all sick in the head and sex maniacs." (I'm a dancer, I guess you noticed.) I said, "Dancing has nothing to do with it, Carlton. It's what I'm reading in those books." I wish you could have heard him. "That's only in books. Real people don't do things like that. You're a sensitive, intelligent girl." I could have slugged him for that crack. I'm so sick of being a sensitive, intelligent girl after reading Grove Press, I could spit. I mean, I'm still a nice girl deep down inside, but I can't be a nice girl twenty-four hours a day. Not after what I went through last weekend with *Moist.* Your ad saved my life. You see, Carlton got me started reading those kinds of newspapers, too. I think he subscribes to every one of them. It took a lot of nerve to call you—thank God, you're a stranger, that makes it okay at least—but when I finally got my nerve up and dialed and then you sounded so . . . well, sexy, just like your ad . . . I mean like I flipped. *(Pause)* You don't waste much time chatting a girl up, do you, Dale? It's better you don't talk. I came here to degrade myself. Treat me bad, Dale, treat me really bad. (ASHER *is starting to come out of it.)* I know. Keep it in French. "Beginner in French needs female with firm, clean, shapely body to practice on. No charge for this service. Special attention given to handicapped girls." That last part is so Grove Press! I hope these'll do for handicaps. *She starts to remove her bra)*

ASHER *(fully awake, in horror at what he sees approaching him).* Aaaaaaaaaaaaaaaaa! *(He runs screaming from the room.)*

ALLEGRA. Dale? *Merde!*

(BERYL, *fortyish, handsome, large-boned, has come into the room.)*

BERYL. Thanks for telling us about the stairs!

ALLEGRA. The . . . ?

BERYL. My husband's having a stroke on one of the goddamn landings!

ALLEGRA. Your . . . ?

BERYL. I told you we'd be bringing equipment!

ALLEGRA. Equip—?

BERYL. Now get your pink little tuch down there and help him!

ALLEGRA. I . . .

BERYL. Look, you little chippy, no lip!

ALLEGRA *(beside herself).* Yes! *(She runs out of the room.)*

BERYL *(scowling at the room).* A two-hundred-thousand-dollar home in Westchester County with special rooms for this sort of thing and we have to come here! I swear I'm going to divorce that man one day . . . divorce him so fast he won't know what hit him! *(She's seen the phone, dials a number.)* Hello, Mrs. Firth? It's me again. I forgot to tell you. Caroline has a dance class at one thirty. Someone will be by for her, but see that she's got her leotard on this time. (ASHER *has edged back into the room. She sees him.)* What are you doing, you little nit? They're on the stairs. Give them a hand!

ASHER. Who? . . .

BERYL. You heard me! (ASHER *hurries off.)* And Mrs. Firth, if the man calls about the pony for Johnny's birthday tomorrow, tell

him to have the little beast there at two . . .

(KERRY *has come back into the room. She sees him.)*

KERRY. Hello.

BERYL. Well don't just stand there, newt! They need you.

KERRY. Who?

BERYL. Them. On the stairs. Now go to it!

KERRY. Yes, ma'am. *(He hurries out.)*

BERYL. Is the baby sleeping? . . . Well, tell the nanny she *can't* go on strike! I swear, Mrs. Firth, I swear, being a suburban mother is even harder than being a city one. . . . I appreciate your solicitude. It's what we're paying you for! *(Hangs up)* God, God, God. What's to become of us all? (ALLEGRA *has returned. She is struggling with a large trunk.)* How is he?

ALLEGRA. Fine, I guess.

BERYL. You guess, you little tramp?

ALLEGRA. I offered to help him and he beat me off with his cane.

BERYL. And you loved it! He's a forceful man, my husband. Over there! (ALLEGRA *drops the trunk; crashing metallic sounds.)* You'll pay for that, my pet.

ALLEGRA. I'll? . . .

BERYL. Not so fast! You'll have to wait for it. Beg.

ALLEGRA. Hunh?

BERYL. I'll have my martini. Eight-to-one. With a twist.

ALLEGRA. Your martini?

BERYL. You thought that was a purse, didn't you, you silly bitch?

ALLEGRA. It looks like a purse.

BERYL. Of course it looks like a purse! It's a portable bar. They're the rage in Westchester. Now hop to it. *(While* ALLEGRA *mixes)* Pretty deplorable diggings, if you ask me.

ALLEGRA. You know something?

BERYL. I don't remember addressing you, whore.

ALLEGRA. You're pretty forceful yourself.

BERYL. Thank you.

ALLEGRA. I mean, I don't even know you and you've got me waiting on you hand and foot. That plus the insults.

BERYL. The fault, my dear Dale, is in your nature. Yours is a submissive one.

ALLEGRA. I'm not Dale. My name is Allegra.

BERYL. But you're willing to serve. Submission and discipline, that's the ticket! *(Toasting with her martini)* Discipline° and submission! *(Spits it out)* I said eight-to-one, you jelly-slimed harlot! You left baggage, you painted tart! You bloated lymph node, you raven-trussed hussy!

ALLEGRA. Tressed. You mean raven-tressed.

BERYL. Silence, bitch, when I'm reviling you!

ALLEGRA. Oh, now really, Beryl!

BERYL. Beryl?

ALLEGRA. It's what they call you, isn't it?

BERYL. You dare use my name?

ALLEGRA. It's stenciled right on the bag. Beryl and Cecil.

BERYL. I'll blind you first! With white-hot tongs. Pluck those eyes from your head with pincers.

ALLEGRA. If you're not careful, you're going to hit someone with that riding crop.

BERYL. You! You!

ALLEGRA. I wouldn't recommend that. I know karate.

BERYL. Bravo! I love a slave with spunk.

ALLEGRA. I'm very good at it, in fact.

BERYL. Cecil should be here for this.

ALLEGRA. I'm a black belt!

BERYL. He adores black belts!

ALLEGRA. I'm warning you!

(*They struggle, but it's more like shadow-boxing. No real contact is made.* BERYL *flailing at the air with her riding crop;* ALLEGRA *warding her off with a few karate chops*)

BERYL (*huffing*). Don't try so hard! I'm not a teenybopper!

ALLEGRA. You started it!

BERYL. I'm just trying to turn you on.

ALLEGRA. With a riding crop?

BERYL. Our ad *specified.*

ALLEGRA. What ad?

BERYL. The one you answered!

ALLEGRA. I'm here for French lessons!

(CECIL *has entered the room in a sedan chair borne by* KERRY *and* ASHER. *He's just in time to see* BERYL *lunge at* ALLEGRA, *only to trip and fall instead.*)

CECIL. Seize that woman! (ASHER *lets his end of the chair drop, spilling* CECIL *onto the floor.*) Unh!

(ASHER *has taken* BERYL*'s arm and is helping her up.*)

BERYL. Not me, you idiot! Not the queen. Her!

ALLEGRA (*to* ASHER). Where have you been? I told you I was double-parked!

ASHER. Hunh?

BERYL (*deflated, to* ALLEGRA). You didn't have to take *all* the fun out of it!

KERRY (*attending to* CECIL). Mister! Hey, mister! (*To* BERYL) Hey, lady, is this your husband?

BERYL. Well, he's not my *lover!*

KERRY. He's blacked out.

BERYL. Of course he has! He does this to me all the time. Can't wait till he gets there, and then I'm the one with egg on her face. (*She joins* KERRY *and* CECIL.)

ALLEGRA (*to* ASHER). I wish you'd told me how many people would be here.

ASHER. I wish you had.

ALLEGRA. Hunh?

ASHER. Is your name Dale?

ALLEGRA. Isn't yours?

ASHER. I'm Asher.

ALLEGRA. I'm Allegra.

ASHER. Who's Dale?

ALLEGRA. That's Beryl and he's Cecil.

ASHER. And he's Kerry.

ALLEGRA. Oh, dear.

(*They are both suddenly aware of their lack of clothes, but there's not much they can do about it gracefully.*)

BERYL. Cecil, wake up, Cecil! You're causing a scene.

KERRY. He's out like a light.

BERYL. You're making a fool of yourself, Cecil, in front of *them!*

KERRY. Wait! I think he's . . .

BERYL. Nobody obeys *fainting nellies,* Cecil!

KERRY. Yes! He's coming around!

CECIL (*opens eyes, looks around, gets to his feet, everyone in the room is watching him. He speaks with a German accent*). All stripped down, are we?

BERYL. That's my Cecil!

ASHER. Well, you see, I—

CECIL. All stripped down and ready to have a go at it, were we? (*He's methodically tearing his clothes off. Underneath he's wearing black leather underwear and high leather boots.*)

BERYL. They were, Cecil, they were! I caught them at it!

ALLEGRA. I only—

CECIL. All stripped down and ready to have a go at it without waiting for Cecil and Beryl, were we? Were we?

BERYL. Punish them, Cecil, punish them!

CECIL. Swine! Pigs! Dogs! (*He blacks out again.*)

ALLEGRA. What was that all about?

ASHER. Is he mad at someone?

BERYL. I'm terribly sorry. What can I say?

You said right after twelve . . . we show up half an hour late . . . the traffic was unbelievable, it gets worse all the time . . . and now this. I'm sorry and that's the long and the short of it. Shall we get started? He'll wake up. *(She has started to undress.)* I'm delighted there's more than one of you. Of course it was naughty of you not to mention it. One of you will pay for that. By the way, I'm Beryl. Which one of you is Dale?

ALLEGRA. What unusual lingerie!

BERYL. It's lizard, you tacky trollop!

ASHER. Hey, now just a minute!

BERYL. Shut up, slime!

KERRY. Who the hell do you think you are?

BERYL. You, too, you little blob! Now which one of you is Dale?

ALLEGRA. None of us is.

BERYL *(thrown).* You're joking. You must be joking.

ALLEGRA. I'm Allegra.

ASHER. I'm Asher.

KERRY. I'm Kerry.

BERYL. Oh, God.

ALLEGRA. I think you owe us all an apology.

BERYL *(in great and sudden panic).* Cecil! Wake up, Cecil! We're in the wrong place!

CECIL *(responding).* Our subject for today is leather.

BERYL *(mortified).* Cecil, please, they can hear you!

CECIL *(starting to rave).* What is leather? What are its origins? Its uses?

ASHER. I know!

BERYL. Must you humor him? Can't you see he's a sick man? *(Urgent, to* CECIL*)* It's the wrong place, Cecil!

CECIL *(shaking her off, moving about the room).* Why is leather the symbol of intellectual genius?

ASHER. I never heard that before.

BERYL. I could just die, I'm so embarrassed. Cecil, sshh!

ASHER *(to* ALLEGRA *and* KERRY*).* I'm a writer. It seems to me I would have heard about leather being a symbol of genius.

CECIL *(railing at them).* All the great geniuses have belonged to the leather cult!

ASHER. I can't think of one.

CECIL. Goethe, Schiller, Beethoven, Thomas Mann!

ASHER. All Germans.

CECIL. And all leatherists! What do you think Goethe was wearing when he wrote his *Faust?* Cotton? Was Schiller in silk when he created his masterpieces? Would the world have Beethoven's nine symphonies had he been wearing satin? Can you mention Thomas Mann and wool in the same breath? You cannot!

ASHER. What about Mozart?

CECIL *(apoplectic).* Mozart! Mozart was Austrian, you *dummkopf!* All great art is German, and German art is leather!

KERRY. Leather?

CECIL. Leather! Leather, I tell you!

ALLEGRA *(to* ASHER*).* I like Mozart, too.

CECIL. Beryl, Beryl, who are these people? Must they be disciplined like all the others? *Ach! Mein Herz* is heavy! *(He's getting a whip out of the trunk.)*

BERYL. If you'd just listen to me!

CECIL. Speak, *Liebchen,* speak.

BERYL. I've been trying to! We're in the wrong place.

CECIL *(stunned).* What do you mean? . . . the wrong place? . . .

BERYL. They're not our kind of people.

CECIL. Not our kind? . . .

BERYL. Just look at them.

CECIL *(as if transformed; all trace of German accent vanishing).* Well . . . hello there . . . I guess I got a little carried away just then . . . hah, hah, hah! . . . Cecil's the name . . . you're right, it's warm up here. Kind of makes you delirious . . . well, I guess the missus and I better shove off now . . . the kids'll be wanting their supper . . . hah, hah, hah! . . . Whew! Sure is warm! . . . Hell of a day for a ballgame!

BERYL. Cecil has these little attacks, you see.

CECIL. Never know when they're gonna hit me.

BERYL. It could be anywhere.

CECIL. Let's face it, I'm a dying man.

BERYL. We certainly hope we haven't inconvenienced you . . . interrupted anything . . . barging in like this.

CECIL. I told Beryl it didn't look like the place. Hah, hah, hah!

(Awkward silence)

KERRY. May I say something?

BERYL. I wish somebody would.

KERRY. I think we should all put our cards on the table.

BERYL. Stop pussyfooting?

KERRY. Exactly. Now we all came here expecting to meet someone named Dale. Right? *(Embarrassed assents, much head-hanging)* Right after twelve, he said.

ASHER. She. It was a she.

KERRY. I don't think that matters much at this point.

ASHER. To me it does.

KERRY. The fact is, this Dale person called all of us, conveniently forgetting to mention he-or-she had spoken to the others.

CECIL. When we saw the three of you, naturally we thought . . . hah, hah, hah!

BERYL. Cecil, please!

KERRY. And now Dale doesn't show.

ASHER (looking at his watch). It's still only . . . I mean, maybe he . . . she's still on he way.

KERRY. Not very likely.

CECIL. Do you suppose? . . . No, it couldn't possibly.

BERYL. What?

CECIL. Right after twelve meant right after midnight?

BERYL. Don't be ridiculous.

ASHER. It is the more usual time for it.

ALLEGRA. It?

ASHER (gulping). You know!

KERRY. I think it's a pretty safe assumption someone's played a trick on us.

BERYL. No!

KERRY. I'm afraid so.

BERYL. What kind of sick mind would do a thing like that?

ASHER. It takes all kinds of people to make up a world!

BERYL. But what kind of perverted, twisted, warped, maimed, mutilated mind would play a joke like that?

CECIL (shaking his head). I don't know, I don't know what people are coming to anymore.

ALLEGRA. What a spooky weirdo this Dale must be!

ASHER. And noon's such an inconvenient time for . . . I mean, people are busy at noon! I had a deadline with my publisher. I write textbooks.

ALLEGRA. What about me, all the way in from Flushing?

BERYL. We drove in from Westchester in this heat and traffic!

KERRY. Listen, I don't know if I still have a job when I get back.

CECIL. Morning, noon, or night, wild horses couldn't drag me up here again.

KERRY. All right then let's put the *rest* of our cards on the table. Since we're all here . . . and at no little inconvenience . . . I suggest we try working something out.

CECIL (brightening at the prospect). You mean? . . .

KERRY. I mean!

CECIL. What do you think, honey?

BERYL (weighing it). Well . . .

KERRY (persuasive). After all, we did all come here for the same thing. Hell, we even advertised, we wanted it so bad.

ALLEGRA. I beg your pardon! I answered an ad. I never took one. There's a big difference!

KERRY. Really? What?

ASHER. Are you people talking about an . . . (Gulping on the word again) orgy?

BERYL (becoming convinced). I hate to see an afternoon wasted.

CECIL (agreeing). I had work, too. I mean I'm not exactly unemployed, you know.

KERRY. Asher?

ASHER. (bluff bravado). Sure, sure! Why the hell not?

KERRY. You, Allegra?

ALLEGRA. It's certainly worth a try. Even if you're not Dale, you're both kind of sexy. I mean we could . . . wow!

ASHER. Don't talk like that.

ALLEGRA. What's wrong with you?

ASHER. Nice girls don't say things like that.

ALLEGRA. Wait a minute! Are you that "sensitive writer, Harvard Ph.D., who's seeking a grownup girl to share wonderful conversation and Bach," who's been advertising like mad lately?

ASHER. It's a Columbia Ph.D., actually.

ALLEGRA. That's the creep!

ASHER. What's wrong with that?

ALLEGRA. Give Carlton a toot on the phone next time. You two were made for each other. (To KERRY) I guess that makes it us. What do you say? *Qu'est-ce que vous dites?*

KERRY (nodding toward ASHER). I want him actually.

ALLEGRA. Him?

KERRY. He turns me on, what can I tell you?

ALLEGRA. *Ecch!*

BERYL. Tolerance, dear, a little tolerance for God's creatures.

ASHER. *You* were the queer!

KERRY. Elementary, my dear Watson.

ASHER. You could have fooled me!

KERRY. Well? What do you say?

ASHER. You mean? . . . Of course not!

KERRY. It doesn't exactly hurt, you know.

ASHER. I said no!

KERRY. Come to think of it, you're not masculine enough.

ASHER *(aghast).* Not . . . masculine enough!?

KERRY *(appraising* CECIL *now).* I like a man with balls in his voice, hair on his chest . . .

ASHER *(to* ALLEGRA). I've got hair on my chest.

ALLEGRA. Drop dead!

KERRY. A guy with nice musky male smells.

CECIL *(so affably).* You see this fist, fruit?

KERRY *(smiling at him).* It was worth a try, wasn't it?

(They laugh and shake hands.)

BERYL. Cecil?

CECIL *(for both of them).* "Extremely attractive Westchester couple—"

BERYL *(he's left a word out).* White!

CECIL. " . . . both of dominant nature, seek couples and singles who would enjoy serving as our slave—"

BERYL. Any combination of you would do.

CECIL. "Must be of submissive nature and be willing to serve."

(A pause)

BERYL *(still hopeful).* Discretion assured!

ALLEGRA. I've read *The Story of O,* thank you.

BERYL. And didn't you like it?

ALLEGRA. I thought it was funny.

BERYL. Funny? Funny!

KERRY. You don't go my route, I don't go yours.

CECIL. I think we've . . . as the saying has it . . . bombed out, Beryl.

KERRY *(his turn to be affable).* I'm sorry, but I specifically stated no disciplinarians.

ASHER *(dawning on him).* I know what that means. Oh, gosh. Oh, gosh!

BERYL *(trying to figure something out).* Maybe if we . . . you and she could . . . no! Cecil and him . . . and then . . . *no.*

CECIL *(eagerly).* What, Beryl?

BERYL. Nothing, Just a wild thought.

ASHER *(to no one in particular).* All I want is a sensitive girl I can relate to. What's so unusual about that?

ALLEGRA *(a voice in the wilderness).* Fucking, anyone?

KERRY *(after a beat).* Well, *that* . . . as the other saying has it . . . would seem to be *that.*

BERYL. And I'm getting dressed.

ALLEGRA. I think we'd all better.

ASHER. I've had it with advertising. I'm going back to hanging around the Village. NYU's down there.

KERRY. The next time I meet anyone, it's going to be at my place.

ALLEGRA. I'm so mad I could spit.

CECIL. Can we give anyone a lift?

ASHER. Do you go up the West Side?

BERYL. My dear, we stay as far away from the West Side as we possibly can.

(Ring. The telephone. Everybody freezes.)

ASHER. Hey, the phone's ringing.

(Ring)

CECIL. Did you tell Mrs. Firth where we'd be?

(Ring)

KERRY. It's not for me.

(Ring)

BERYL. Don't move, anybody. Just stay put.

(Ring. Ring. Ring)

ALLEGRA. Maybe it's Dale.

BERYL. Oh, my God! Quick! *(They race for the phone.* BERYL *gets it.)* Hello . . . who is this? *(To the others)* It's Dale! It's Dale! *(They gather around her.)* Yes, this is Beryl . . . my husband? He's right beside me . . . *(To* CECIL) he said hello, Cecil.

CECIL. Well, you tell that practical joker he can just—

BERYL. Yes, Allegra's here, too . . . *(To* ALLEGRA) He said *"bonjour."*

ALLEGRA. Tell him *va aux enfers!* Go to hell!

BERYL. Yes, they're both here, too. . . . Of course they didn't hit it off!

ASHER *(recoiling at the thought).* You can say that again!

KERRY *(trying to get the phone).* I'll tell that bitch a thing or two!

BERYL. Let me handle it.

CECIL. She's terrific at this.

BERYL *(into the phone).* Listen, you, wherever you are . . . Paramus! . . . I *know* where Paramus is; now you just listen to me. You have some nerve, getting us all here and then not showing up. I suppose you think that's pretty funny. Well, let me tell you something—

CECIL *(so proudly to the others).* What'd I tell you?

BERYL *(sudden delight).* You couldn't make it because you're all tied up? *(Sotto voce)* Cecil! *(Back into the phone cooing)* What do you mean, you're all tied up? *(Angry again)* Oh, you're just busy, you mean! *(Resuming her tirade)* Well, let me tell you—*(She listens, then to the others)* Do we want to go to Paramus?

CECIL. Out of the question.

ASHER. Paramus, that's in New Jersey.

KERRY. I'd rather cruise Hackensack.

BERYL *(back into the phone, with great dignity)*. We're afraid not. Nothing could get us out there. Not after this. *(She listens.)*

CECIL. I guess that's telling him.

BERYL *(hushing CECIL, then into the phone)*. What? You're disciplining someone? . . . Where? . . . A bowling alley? At this time of day? What. kind of bowling alley is that? . . . *OH!*

CECIL *(on the alert)*. What? What?

BERYL. Sshh! *(Back into the phone)* Who? . . . a young man . . . yes . . .

KERRY *(eagerly)*. Keep talking!

BERYL. And he wants a young girl to practice German lessons with? *(Looking at ALLEGRA)* Will French do?

ALLEGRA. Don't split hairs! I'm very lingual.

BERYL. And he's got his sensitive sister with him? *(She's looking at ASHER.)* A poetess?

ASHER. A poetess? Oh, wow!

BERYL *(businesslike now, getting the facts)*. Now let me get this straight. You're in Paramus, at a bowling alley, disciplining a young man who wants a young girl to practice German lessons with, and he's got his sensitive poetess sister with him? *(To CECIL)* How soon can we get there?

CECIL. Fifteen minutes.

BERYL. We can make it in ten! *(Into the phone)* What's the address?

ALLEGRA. Ten minutes? In this traffic?

CECIL. Just watch us.

BERYL *(writing it down)*. 143. Got it. Now hold everything and just sit tight. . . . *(Harsh)* Ten minutes, half an hour, just wait for us! *(Listens)* You'll answer for that, pig. *(Sweetly)* Yes, of course we'll hurry. *(Listens, looks at KERRY)* What? . . . Don't bring the fag. You hate fags. He wouldn't fit in. Of course I understand. *(Looks away, rambling on)* Tell me something, are they being very naughty? *(She relishes the answer.)* We're on our way! *(She hangs up.)* Don't just stand there, Cecil. Pack.

(There is a great flurry of activity now as they make ready to leave.)

ASHER. Are you people talking about another orgy?

BERYL *(making haste)*. The branding irons, Cecil. Don't mix them with the tongs!

ALLEGRA. I'll be right behind you. It's a blue Plymouth.

BERYL. Cecil drives like a bat out of hell.

ALLEGRA. I'll keep up.

ASHER *(watching them get ready)*. Hey! Hey! Everybody! What about me? I'm willing to try it, at least. I've never been to an orgy, orgy! ORGY! before. See? I'm losing my inhibitions. To be frank, I could use the experience!

BERYL. Take the trunk.

ASHER. Wow! Thanks a lot! A poetess. Oh, wow! *(He goes down the stairs.)*

ALLEGRA *(following)*. Paramus, *ici je viens!* Paramus, here I come!

(They are both gone.)

BERYL. Paramus! Whoever dreamed I'd end up in Paramus!

CECIL *(on the stairs)*. Say, isn't that where Dot and Hugh live?

BERYL. I wouldn't put it past them. (CECIL *is gone. She sees KERRY.)* Come on, anyway.

KERRY *(mustering up all the dignity he can)*. I've been on my goose chase for the day, thank you.

BERYL. But a bowling alley! I'm sure we can whip something up for you.

KERRY. No, thank you.

BERYL. Well, just don't get too depressed. Promise? Something will turn up. It always does. Hope! We can't live with it and we can't live without it! *(She runs down the stairs. We hear them all laughing as their voices die away.)*

KERRY *(shouting down the stairs)*. Sure, go ahead, laugh! You'll get *there* and nothing'll happen either! I bet there's no such thing as Dale! *(Paces, yells down again)* And thanks a lot. I was here first, just remember. Hell, I wasn't going to hurt anybody. *(Pauses, paces, yells again. He's been hurt, you see.)* I hope you get stuck in the tunnel. *(Realizes they're gone)* I hope it caves in on you!

(He is alone in the room. Slowly, sadly, he begins to gather his things and make ready to leave. And then—at a great distance—we hear a VOICE *on the stairs.)*

VOICE *(from afar)*. Dale? (KERRY *freezes.)* Dale? . . . (KERRY *goes to the stairwell, looks down.)* Dale? (KERRY *runs his fingers through his hair, generally spruces himself up. The* VOICE *is getting closer.)* Dale? (KERRY *has started to smile. The future is his.)* Dale?

(Slow fade)

CURTAIN

NIGHT

Leonard Melfi

To GAY *and* NAN

The stage is almost in complete darkness. Eventually, the jet black sky begins to fill with a quiet splattering of bright twinkling scattered stars. Now we hear familiar organ music for a funeral, coming from somewhere onstage. The organ music should be real and alive; for that matter, all the music that is called for in the play should be real and alive. As the music plays, the lights begin to come up somewhat slowly onstage.

We are in a rather vast part of a rather vast cemetery. At first the lights reveal a simple wooden black coffin, closed, somewhere in the precise far background center of the stage, possibly between two soft columns. The simple black coffin is resting on a skeleton-type brass support that has four legs and is waist-high. It is situated so that the foot of it faces the audience. To the immediate right and to the immediate left of the coffin there is an array of sprays of various colorful flowers and small radiant floral wreaths. It would be good if the sprays and the wreaths consisted of real leaves and ferns and authentic flowers. To our right, about stage center, we notice an old worn wheelbarrow, all by itself, half filled with a tiny pile of real fresh dirt, with a large beat-up-looking shovel extending from it. The rest of the stage is bare.

Presently, MISS INDIGO BLUE, *who is about nineteen or twenty, all dressed up in flashy and very sexy miniskirted red, from long flowing hair to thin young feet: all the very same shade of bright blazing red, appears from our left. She is carrying a little cluster of fresh flowers. She goes to the foot of the coffin and places the flowers down before it. She then disappears into the blackness of the black apron of the stage and remains there. She is instantly followed by* ROBIN BREAST WESTERN, *about twenty-one or twenty-two, and who is all dressed up in complete glaring grazing forest green clothes, who performs the exact same ritual. He is instantly followed by* FILIGREE BONES, *about forty-nine or fifty, who is all dressed up in the fanciest and most confusing mess of matching and nonmatching colors you ever saw in your whole life: a gaudy-walking, somewhat joyous-suggesting, rainbow from all over America. She does the precise same thing*

that they both have done. Finally, it is FIBBER KIDDING, *fifty-one or fifty-two, and who is also dressed up in the same puzzle of colors as* FILIGREE BONES: *another gaudy-walking, somewhat joyous-suggesting, rainbow from all over America too, whom we see; he goes through the identical ritual. The music begins to die away, and as it does, the lights—soft delicate blue lights—come up on the four of them, bathing everything, and the star-jammed sky becomes a beautiful midnight blue.*

MISS INDIGO BLUE. I've never been to a funeral at nighttime.

ROBIN BREAST WESTERN. That's the way he wanted it.

MISS INDIGO BLUE. The cocky little bastard!

FILIGREE BONES. But, honey . . . ?

MISS INDIGO BLUE. What?

FILIGREE BONES. He wasn't so little! His name wasn't *Cock Certain* for nothing! It's true: he was a cocky bastard, but he wasn't a *little* bastard! He just simply was not a *little* one!

MISS INDIGO BLUE. You're not telling me anything I didn't already know, Filigree Bones!

FILIGREE BONES. Cock Certain was a very certain cocky little bastard who was very *very big* . . . indeed!

MISS INDIGO BLUE. I know all about it.

(FIBBER KIDDING *is becoming restless.*)

ROBIN BREAST WESTERN. I've never been to a funeral at nighttime.

MISS INDIGO BLUE. That's the way he wanted it.

FILIGREE BONES. The cocky little bastard!

MISS INDIGO BLUE. But honey . . . ?

FILIGREE BONES. What?

MISS INDIGO BLUE. He wasn't so *little*! His name wasn't *Cock Certain* for nothing! It's true: he was a cocky bastard, but he wasn't a *little* bastard! He just simply was not a *little* one!

FILIGREE BONES. You're not telling me anything I didn't already know, Miss Indigo Blue!

MISS INDIGO BLUE. Cock Certain was a very certain cocky little bastard who was very *very big* . . . indeed!

FILIGREE BONES. I know all about it.

(FIBBER KIDDING *is very restless now.* ROBIN BREAST WESTERN *leaves his rather stiff position. He moves far away from the three of them.*)

ROBIN BREAST WESTERN. The one thing about everything is that you should always enjoy yourself whenever you're doing anything that has to do with everything. *(Runs to* MISS INDIGO BLUE *and stands behind her)* I love to sleep a lot. There's absolutely nothing like good sound sleep. *(He pinches* MISS INDIGO BLUE *on the ass.)*

MISS INDIGO BLUE *(enjoying it).* You pinched me . . . there!

ROBIN BREAST WESTERN. I told you I love to sleep a lot. There's absolutely nothing like good sound sleep. *(Pinches her on the other side of her ass.)*

MISS INDIGO BLUE *(enjoying it even more).* Now you pinched me . . . *there!*

ROBIN BREAST WESTERN. I told you I love to sleep a lot. There's abolutely nothing like good sound sleep.

*(*ROBIN BREAST WESTERN *goes and sits on an imagined large gray rock-boulder.)*

MISS INDIGO BLUE. Filigree Bones doesn't like what you're doing to me. I can tell that she'd much rather have you do it to her. *(*MISS INDIGO BLUE *takes out her imagined makeup kit and then begins to make up.)*

FILIGREE BONES. I've never been to a funeral at nighttime. *(*ROBIN BREAST WESTERN *takes an imagined bright red transistor radio out of his breast pocket.)* But honey . . . ? What! He wasn't so *little!* His name wasn't *Cock Certain* for nothing! It's true: he was a cocky bastard, but he wasn't a *little* bastard! He just simply was not a *little* one! *(*ROBIN BREAST WESTERN *turns the radio on. A raunchy rock melody is playing. Over the music)* You're not telling me anything I didn't already know, Miss Indigo Blue! *(*FILIGREE BONES *begins to dance with the music. She is slow and careful and not too certain, because of her age, perhaps. Dancing)* Cock Certain was a very certain cocky little bastard who was very *big* . . . indeed! I know all about it.

*(*FIBBER KIDDING *looks as though he is going to blow up any second now.)*

ROBIN BREAST WESTERN. He was such a good little guy. I mean, I'm sorry: but he was such a good little BIG GUY! I was really jealous of the cocky cunning cute little bastard. I mean, the cocky cunning cute little BIG BASTARD! He could eat for days and nights without ever stopping, and yet he would still never gain an extra pound. He was such a thin and very agile beautiful son-of-a-bitch. And he loved me . . .

*(*MISS INDIGO BLUE *begins to dance while she applies her makeup. She is very free and full of fast sensual movements.)*

MISS INDIGO BLUE. He liked you a lot, that's all, Robin Breast Western. He liked you a lot and I think you should say that: I think you should say that he liked you a lot . . . I certainly do not think that you should say that he loved you. He didn't love you, Robin Breast Western. *He loved me!* He . . . liked . . . you.

ROBIN BREAST WESTERN. That's *your* fantasy.

MISS INDIGO BLUE. It's *your* fantasy! *(*MISS INDIGO BLUE *dances more intensely.)*

FILIGREE BONES *(dancing).* You're both full of it completely right up to your purple pairs of dirty deaf ears! He was fond of the two of you. Fond! It's a good word. Fond! Did you both hear me? Fond! It's nothing to be ashamed of. Fond! He was fond of the two of you. *He loved me!* Did you hear what I just said! HE LOVED ME! *(A pause)* He was such a bright bastard, wasn't he?

ROBIN BREAST WESTERN. Yeah?

FILIGREE BONES. Yeah!

MISS INDIGO BLUE. Yeah?

FILIGREE BONES. Yeah!

*(*MISS INDIGO BLUE *is trying to outdo and outdance* FILIGREE BONES. *She is younger, and so it is easier for her to suceed at this.)*

ROBIN BREAST WESTERN. Yeah, yeah, yeah! *(He goes around almost like a half-mad person; he motions fast masturbation.)* YEAH! YEAH! YEAH!

*(*FIBBER KIDDING *is standing away from them now; he is over near the coffin; he begins to tremble violently.)*

FILIGREE BONES. Cock Certain loved me!

MISS INDIGO BLUE. It was me!

ROBIN BREAST WESTERN. You're both so wrong. You're both so full of modern shit. Really and truly full of pure modern shit! *(He stamps his feet like a child throwing a temper tantrum.)* IT WAS ME!

FILIGREE BONES. ME!

MISS INDIGO BLUE. ME!

*(*FIBBER KIDDING *begins to run around the whole stage area now in great incredible steps. He is almost completely wild. None of them pay attention to him.)*

ROBIN BREAST WESTERN. ME!

*(*FIBBER KIDDING *is beside himself. He runs over to* ROBIN BREAST WESTERN *and turns off the transistor radio. He flings it to the ground.* MISS INDIGO BLUE *and* FILIGREE BONES *stop their individual dancing. They are like statues now.)*

FIBBER KIDDING. All I need is a gun! A good gun! All I need is a rifle! A right rifle! All I need is a bomb! A big bomb! All I need really is just one simple little weapon that will do its duty, that will perform the duty I want it to perform, that duty being the very simple and very noncomplex duty of killing! Murdering! Murdering the three of you right here on the spot in the middle of this cemetery during the middle of this night.

ROBIN BREAST WESTERN. You've gone out of your mind, Fibber Kidding.

FIBBER KIDDING. I'll kill all of you! Here in this cemetery! It will all be so easy, quick! Slaughtered in a graveyard! Perfect! Sudden death for the three of you, and then, very logically, of course: an instant funeral . . . because of the circumstances, because of where we're all at!

ROBIN BREAST WESTERN. You've gone out of your mind, Fibber Kidding.

FIBBER KIDDING. Kill the lousy three of you!

ROBIN BREAST WESTERN. This is a sacred place, you old bastard.

FIBBER KIDDING. I'm not so old! Do you understand? I'm not so old! He made me feel young. He made me look young. He made me young, period. I went out and bought a sports car because of him. I slept with a fifteen-year-old teen-aged girl because of him. After that she won a beauty contest in her high school in Seattle. She was a full flower after she knew me. And he was responsible. *He was so young!* AND HE LOVED ME! COCK CERTAIN LOVED ME! (FIBBER KIDDING *runs to the coffin and throws himself up against it; and then he slowly slides down to the ground.*)

ROBIN BREAST WESTERN. Now take it easy, Fibber Kidding, take it easy . . .

MISS INDIGO BLUE. Please take it easy, Fibber Kidding . . .

FILIGREE BONES. They're both so right: for your own safety and health and protection, and everything else that goes with it, take it easy, Fibber Kidding . . . please?

(They all go to him the way a mother and her two children would go to the man of the house.)

ROBIN BREAST WESTERN. Everything's going to be okay, Fibber . . .

MISS INDIGO BLUE. Honest-to-God it is, honey . . .

FILIGREE BONES. Oh, darling little baby Fibber of mine . . . (FILIGREE BONES *hugs and kisses* FIBBER KIDDING.)

ROBIN BREAST WESTERN. I've never been to a funeral at nighttime.

MISS INDIGO BLUE. That's the way he wanted it.

FILIGREE BONES. The cocky little bastard!

FIBBER KIDDING. I've never been to a funeral at nighttime! That's the way he wanted it! The cocky little bastard! The three of you are trying to drive me out of my mind! I want peace of mind, peace of soul, and the three of you are giving me just the opposite of what I want! All I want is peace of mind and peace of soul! Peace! THAT BIG LITTLE, LITTLE BIG, COCKY CUNNING CUTE LITTLE BIG BASTARD LOVED ME MOST OF ALL! I WAS LIKE A FATHER TO HIM!

ROBIN BREAST WESTERN. I WAS LIKE A BROTHER! From Kansas, maybe.

MISS INDIGO BLUE. I WAS LIKE A SISTER! From . . . well, from Niagara Falls, perhaps.

FILIGREE BONES. I WAS LIKE A MOTHER! From . . . well, I suppose, well, I guess from . . . Miami Beach, Florida, maybe.

FIBBER KIDDING. Do you know what I was really like to him? I was really like a lover to him! That's right: A LOVER! And I'm not ashamed of it, either!

ROBIN BREAST WESTERN. I was his lover . . . in a strange invisible masculine way.

FIBBER KIDDING. Bullshit!

MISS INDIGO BLUE. Did you ever meet his wife, Filigree Bones?

FILIGREE BONES. I loved his wife.

MISS INDIGO BLUE. I did too. She was so young. I loved her because she was so young.

FILIGREE BONES. She loved me, his young wife. She loved me the way a woman can love another woman. It's so special: that sort of love.

MISS INDIGO BLUE. It was her mind that was so young. If I were a man I would have loved to have been her lover.

FILIGREE BONES. She was like a cellophane lover to me.

FIBBER KIDDING. You two women are sick.

FILIGREE BONES. You two men are sick.

ROBIN BREAST WESTERN. I'm going to miss Cock Certain so much.

MISS INDIGO BLUE. Well, how do you think I feel?

FIBBER KIDDING. The poor little bastard!

FILIGREE BONES. I want to die.

ROBIN BREAST WESTERN. He really was such a great big beautiful person to know!

MISS INDIGO BLUE. We know, we know!

FIBBER KIDDING. It's a funny world full of funny freaks. You can't plan on anything. It's all so stupid in the end. I can't do anything any more. All I want to do is sleep now; and eat now; and drink now; and smoke now; and bet now; and bowl now; and fuck now. I don't want to do anything else any more. Just those things.

FILIGREE BONES. We really shouldn't bury him. Let's take him back home with us. Let's not bury him.

MISS INDIGO BLUE. I like that idea.

ROBIN BREAST WESTERN. It's not a bad idea.

FIBBER KIDDING. We'll take him back to the house, okay?

FILIGREE BONES. But it just won't be the same. It will always be awful now. It will never be nice any more. It will always be insane now. I just don't know what I'm going to do. I just don't know what any of us are going to do.

FIBBER KIDDING. We won't bury him, that's all. It's very simple.

ROBIN BREAST WESTERN. It's against the law.

FIBBER KIDDING. We'll change the law. Christ, they're even changing the law in Rhode Island now.

ROBIN BREAST WESTERN. Okay.

MISS INDIGO BLUE. Oh, I think that's wonderful!

FILIGREE BONES. What is?

MISS INDIGO BLUE. The idea of changing the law!

FILIGREE BONES. But can we do it?

ROBIN BREAST WESTERN. Why not? They're doing it in North Dakota, aren't they?

MISS INDIGO BLUE. Yes, why not? I heard in New Hampshire, too.

FIBBER KIDDING. Aw, but we're talking crazy. We can't do that.

ROBIN BREAST WESTERN. Why not?

FIBBER KIDDING. Because the cocky cunning cute perfect little big bastard is dead. He's cold stone dead here in the cold stone-dead cemetery, the hard-rock hard-tree hard-dirt hard-heaven graveyard! IT'S NO USE!

FILIGREE BONES. Now you stop that sort of talk, do you hear me? And you calm down, and you relax, and just take it easy, and you just take care of yourself.

FIBBER KIDDING. IT'S NO USE!

FILIGREE BONES. I told you to stop that sort of talk.

FIBBER KIDDING. IT'S NO GODDAMN USE!

MISS INDIGO BLUE. Oh, that's terrible!

FIBBER KIDDING. IT'S NO GODDAMN USE, USE, USE!

MISS INDIGO BLUE. Oh, that's terrible!

ROBIN BREAST WESTERN. C'mon, Fibber Kidding: stop that sort of talk, will you?

FIBBER KIDDING. Stop it, huh! NO!

FILIGREE BONES. I've never been to a funeral at nighttime.

FIBBER KIDDING. It's no use . . .

ROBIN BREAST WESTERN. You're not making things easy for any of us, Fibber Kidding.

FIBBER KIDDING. So what!

MISS INDIGO BLUE. I'm going back to Chicago.

FIBBER KIDDING. Go!

ROBIN BREAST WESTERN. You stay right here, Miss Indigo Blue.

FIBBER KIDDING. No. Let her go back to Denver. She might be better off in the end. I'm staying here because I was born here.

FILIGREE BONES. You're terrible, Fibber Kidding.

FIBBER KIDDING. Why am I terrible?

FILIGREE BONES. You're absolutely terrible!

FIBBER KIDDING. Why don't you go back to where you came from then, huh? Why don't you go back, Filigree Bones? Where you from, anyway, Filigree Bones?

FILIGREE BONES. I'm from Saint Louis.

FIBBER KIDDING. Then go back there. Go back to Boston.

FILIGREE BONES. But I want to stay here with you.

FIBBER KIDDING. Go back to Vermont!

ROBIN BREAST WESTERN. This is the first time I've ever been to a funeral at nighttime.

MISS INDIGO BLUE. That's the way he wanted it.

FILIGREE BONES. The cocky little bastard!

FIBBER KIDDING. I was like a father to him, see? The cocky little BIG BEAUTIFUL BASTARD! Just the way I'm like a father to you, Miss Indigo Blue. Just the way I'm like a father to you, Robin Breast Western. Just the way I'm like a father and a lover and a brother and a husband to you, Filigree Bones.

(ROBIN BREAST WESTERN *and* MISS INDIGO BLUE *go to* FIBBER KIDDING, *who is now hugging* FILIGREE BONES.)

FILIGREE BONES. We all know, Fibber Kidding. We all know.

(They all begin to surround FIBBER KIDDING *now: a protective little mountain of three people.)*

ROBIN BREAST WESTERN. We love you, man.

MISS INDIGO BLUE. We love you so much, darling.

FILIGREE BONES. We love you, we love you so much, because we just do, that's all . . .

*(*ROBIN BREAST WESTERN *stands behind* FIBBER *and places his hands on his shoulders.)*

ROBIN BREAST WESTERN. We just love you . . .

*(*MISS INDIGO BLUE *grabs* FIBBER*'s right hand.)*

MISS INDIGO BLUE. We just simply do . . .

*(*FILIGREE BONES *grabs* FIBBER*'s left hand.)*

FILIGREE BONES. Love you . . . !

(There is a short pause.)

FIBBER KIDDING. I believe you. I believe the three of you.

ROBIN BREAST WESTERN *(desperately).* We love you, man, we love you!

FIBBER KIDDING *(becoming desperate now too: but a rather contented sort of desperation).* I believe you!

MISS INDIGO BLUE *(desperately).* We really love you, darling!

FIBBER KIDDING *(the same as before).* I really believe you!

FILIGREE BONES *(desperately).* You have no idea how much we all love you!

*(*FIBBER KIDDING *tries in vain to break away from their overly loving hold.)*

FIBBER KIDDING *(almost impatiently now).* But I do! I do have an idea. I really do!

(For a brief moment there is a brief dead silence wherein FIBBER *seems to be totally engulfed by the three of them. He is both annoyed and joyful at the very same time. Finally,* ROBIN BREAST WESTERN *is the first to break away.* MISS INDIGO BLUE*'s eyes follow* ROBIN BREAST WESTERN.)*

MISS INDIGO BLUE. What time is it?

ROBIN BREAST WESTERN. I don't know exactly. But I do know that it's late.

MISS INDIGO BLUE *(breaking away).* Does anyone have the exact time?

ROBIN BREAST WESTERN. No.

*(*FILIGREE BONES *comes out of her kiss with* FIBBER KIDDING.)*

FILIGREE BONES. No.

FIBBER KIDDING *(coming out of the kiss too).* No.

(Another short pause)

ROBIN BREAST WESTERN. What does it matter, anyway? . . .

FIBBER KIDDING. What's the use!

ROBIN BREAST WESTERN. Aw, please don't start up with that again, please, Fibber Kidding?

FIBBER KIDDING. What's the use!

MISS INDIGO BLUE. Please, Fibber Kidding?

FIBBER KIDDING. What's the use!

FILIGREE BONES. Please, Fibber Kidding?

(The three of them stand there with their hands sort of up in the air in dismay at FIBBER KIDDING.)*

FIBBER KIDDING. All right, all right, all right . . . what's the use! . . . I mean I'm a bit sorry. . . . I'm meaning really to say to all of you here that I am a bit sorry and I would like to apologize and everything else.

ROBIN BREAST WESTERN. Well, now, that's a whole lot better.

MISS INDIGO BLUE. Yes, it certainly is.

FILIGREE BONES. Thank you, Fibber Kidding. When I meet you in Atlantic City the next time you're there and I'm there, I'll buy you a nice cool refreshing alcoholic drink.

MISS INDIGO BLUE. Isn't that funny? I mean it's such a small world. I used to live in Virginia Beach.

FILIGREE BONES. You don't say? Yes, it is a small world then, isn't it? I've spent many of my summers in Far Rockaway too.

(They slowly begin to spread far apart from each other.)

FIBBER KIDDING *(finally).* I've never been to a funeral at nighttime. . . . *(*FIBBER *immediately covers his mouth with his hands. The three of them glare at him, but then the glare suddenly turns into a rapid gaze of terrible sadness.)*

MISS INDIGO BLUE *(finally).* This is certainly a long funeral.

ROBIN BREAST WESTERN. This is certainly a long funeral.

MISS INDIGO BLUE. I just said that.

ROBIN BREAST WESTERN. But it'll be over soon.

FILIGREE BONES. How long do you think?

ROBIN BREAST WESTERN. Soon. And when it's over I'm going back to Atlanta.

FILIGREE BONES. Only soon? Can't you be more exact?

MISS INDIGO BLUE. He said soon. Isn't that enough?

FILIGREE BONES. Well, I'm tired of funerals!

ROBIN BREAST WESTERN. We all are.

MISS INDIGO BLUE. You're not the only one, Filigree Bones.

FILIGREE BONES. And this is such a *sad* funeral.

MISS INDIGO BLUE. It's much *too* sad.

FIBBER KIDDING. All of the funerals have been sad recently.

(*There is a slight pause. The four of them by now have found their own private little areas of the cemetery in which to be all by themselves. The lights begin to grow darker all around: everywhere, even on the jet black wooden coffin, which is a sort of strange bright green now.*)

ROBIN BREAST WESTERN (*sitting remotely by himself*). Poor Cock Certain. Poor beautiful fucking guy: rich and beautiful loving lion, rich and beautiful loving bull. Son-of-a-bitch . . . I'm so down, man! Oh, man, oh, man, I am so far down, so far deep down. So far down, down, down, in this deep far down stone-cold-dead graveyard!

MISS INDIGO BLUE (*overlapping*). I just want to go home and go to sleep after all of this. I mean I very sincerely want to sleep for at least a week after this, or a whole month perhaps, or even an entire year after all of this. Now a year surely isn't that long. I'll wake up a year from now, a whole year later from now, I'll wake up again and then maybe everything will be nice again.

FILIGREE BONES (*overlapping*). It's enough to drive a sane person insane. It's enough to think that you're not able to think any more. It's enough to think that you believe that you might just be going stark raving mad. It's enough to make you think that you shouldn't be around any more either. (*Begins to sob*) It's enough . . . it's enough, enough, enough . . . *BASTA!* (*She falls down on her knees. Now* MISS INDIGO BLUE *begins to sob too.* ROBIN BREAST WESTERN *goes to* FILIGREE BONES *and comforts her; he is trying to hold back his desperate tears. There is a quick horrible pause.*)

FIBBER KIDDING. I've never been to a funeral at nighttime. (FIBBER KIDDING *drops to his knees near where* MISS INDIGO BLUE *is sitting. He tries to comfort her as he also tries to hold back his tears, but he is not as good at it as* ROBIN BREAST WESTERN *is. The lights begin to come up again, just a tiny bit brighter, but enough to be noticed and enough to be comforting. And now* MAN *appears, stage right. He is just about thirty, and all dressed up in dazzling white, with a little bit of amazing gold and silver specks also: a very modern, star-looking guy.*)

MAN. This looks like a very good place, a very good place. Actually, it looks like a very perfect sort of place: a very good and very perfect place. (MAN *is carrying an old woman's shawl of silk and fringe that is worn and faded in color. The shawl contains something. He is also carrying two long-stemmed single flowers, freshly cut and brightly colored. He walks about the area of the coffin; then he looks all about the vast section of the cemetery; finally, he stops and looks at the four of them. He places the bulging silk shawl gently down on the ground near the coffin. He keeps the two flowers in his hands.*) I like the way the four of you people look. You look very good to me. Actually, you look very good and very perfect to me. Maybe that's why this place looks like the right place: because of the four of you, sitting here like this underneath the twinkling stars. I like the fact that you people are here.

ROBIN BREAST WESTERN. Are you having a funeral too?

MAN. Yes, I am.

MISS INDIGO BLUE. Who are you burying?

FILIGREE BONES. Do we know him?

MISS INDIGO BLUE. Yes, do we?

ROBIN BREAST WESTERN. Maybe it's not a him. Maybe it's a her. Is it a her?

FIBBER KIDDING. It's probably a him.

MAN. It's a him.

ROBIN BREAST WESTERN. Some guy killed in the war?

FIBBER KIDDING. Some guy shot at a birthday party?

MISS INDIGO BLUE. Some guy shot at his wedding?

FILIGREE BONES. Some guy shot at his graduation from high school? Or college, maybe?

(MAN *simply smiles at them all.*)

MAN. Would you like to hold this flower for me until I'm ready, please? (MAN *hands a flower to* MISS INDIGO BLUE.)

MISS INDIGO BLUE. Oh, yes, of course, (*She takes the flower.* MAN *goes toward the wheelbarrow.*) It's a very pretty-looking flower. Terribly tiny, but very pretty-looking. Where did you pick it?

MAN (*returning*). Salt Lake City.

MISS INDIGO BLUE. I've never been there.

MAN. Would you like to hold this other flower for me until I'm ready, please? (MAN *hands the other flower to* FILIGREE BONES.)

FILIGREE BONES. Oh, yes, of course. *(Takes the flower.* MAN *goes back to the wheelbarrow. He begins to wheel it out toward all of them.)* It's a very lovely-looking flower. Awfully small, but very lovely-looking. Where did you pick it?

MAN. Annapolis.

FILIGREE BONES. I've never been there.

ROBIN BREAST WESTERN. I've never been to a funeral at nighttime.

MISS INDIGO BLUE. Me either.

FILIGREE BONES. Me too.

FIBBER KIDDING. It's rather nice because it's so peaceful at night, here in the graveyard. It's a nice experience. I like the experience of it a whole lot.

(MAN goes to where the coffin is. He takes the bulging shawl up in his arms. He comes down to where the four of them are sitting.)

ROBIN BREAST WESTERN. What's your late friend's name?

MAN. Dog.

MISS INDIGO BLUE. Dog?

MAN. Dog.

FILIGREE BONES. It's such a simple name.

MISS INDIGO BLUE. And so obvious.

FIBBER KIDDING. I like it.

MAN. He's a tiny little fellow.

MISS INDIGO BLUE. Is that him in there? *(She points to the bulging shawl.)*

MAN. That's him.

FILIGREE BONES. He really is a tiny little fellow.

MAN. But he had a big heart.

FIBBER KIDDING. That's true lots of times.

MAN. I don't know: I think it's true most of the time.

ROBIN BREAST WESTERN. How did the little fellow die?

MAN. Natural causes.

MISS INDIGO BLUE. You mean he was shot?

MAN. No.

ROBIN BREAST WESTERN. Killed in the war then?

MAN. No.

FILIGREE BONES. Automobile collision?

MAN. No.

FIBBER KIDDING. Gas chamber? Electric chair?

MISS INDIGO BLUE. Airplane crash? Drugs? What?

MAN. None of those things. I told you: natural causes. He died of old age. He was eighteen years old. He dropped dead all of a sudden early this afternoon in front of a fruit-and-vegetable market outdoors in the heart of the East Village of Manhattan City. Dog's old sad master cried like a wild little baby. His sad old master had to be taken home by two sad old ladies who didn't speak American and who had big solid hearts and who were carrying fat shopping bags full of potatoes and cabbage and carrots and onions and fresh sprigs of bright green parsley and more potatoes. One of them kissed me on the forehead and the other one gave me this shawl here. And so I took it from her and then I bent over and picked Dog up in my arms from out of the dirty windy gutter. I wrapped Dog up in the sad old lady's cozy-looking shawl here. I almost threw up, but I didn't. I got nervous too. It all made me very nervous: the whole situation. But I'm always nervous anyway. Who isn't always nervous anyway? And so then I took Dog up the avenue all wrapped up in the sad old lady's cozy-looking shawl here, and I walked until I could finally hail a taxicab down. I solidly had promised the sobbing old man that Dog would have the proper funeral, the proper burial, and everything else that was proper in the bloodshot eyes of the sad old master. *(*MAN *then takes the bulging shawl and unties it at the top where the knot is. He opens it out and reveals the small still body of the gray, little old dead hound dog. The four of them move in a bit closer in order to get a better look at the body of Dog.)*

ROBIN BREAST WESTERN. He was a good-looking dog, wasn't he?

MAN. Yes, he was, come to think of it.

MISS INDIGO BLUE. He's cute, too. *(She cries a little.)*

MAN. Don't feel too bad.

MISS INDIGO BLUE. I can't help it. *(She wipes her tears.)*

FILIGREE BONES. I love dogs. I love all kinds of pets. I feel terrible. *(She cries too.)*

MAN. Well, I guess I'd better do my job now. (MAN *goes to the wheelbarrow and takes hold of the shovel.)*

FIBBER KIDDING. Do you need any help, sir?

MAN. No, but thanks very much anyway.

FIBBER KIDDING. You're welcome, sir.

*(*MAN *takes a heaping shovelful of the real dirt and drops it over the body of Dog.)*

MISS INDIGO BLUE. But shouldn't he be in a box?

FILIGREE BONES. Or a blanket?

ROBIN BREAST WESTERN. Or something?

FIBBER KIDDING. Anything!

MAN. I really don't think so. I think it's all right this way. I'm certain that Dog would have liked it this way. In fact, I'm very certain that he *does* like it this way. The dirt is so fresh and cool! (MAN *has just about covered the body of Dog completely now. He drops the shovel in the wheelbarrow. Then he goes and takes up two full handfuls of the fresh dirt from the wheelbarrow.*) And so warm and cool. (MAN *goes and hands each one of the four of them a nice portion of the dirt. They all accept it happily and without any questions.*) It's soft and it tickles so nicely. And it has such a deep and impressively fantastic smell. Can't you all just smell every juicy second of it? It's such a gradual-beginning sort of smell. It makes you want to live and sleep and think and breathe and dream all at the same time: if, of course, that's at all possible. (MAN *sniffs at the remaining dirt in his hands with great relish. The four of them all go to Dog's grave and stand over it, along with* MAN.)

ROBIN BREAST WESTERN. I guess you're right, sir.

FIBBER KIDDING. I'm willing to buy it.

(MAN *drops his handful of dirt onto Dog's grave. Then the four of them do the same thing with their handfuls of dirt.*)

MAN. I think it's all right this way. I think Dog likes it this way. (MAN *finishes covering up Dog with the shovel.*)

MISS INDIGO BLUE. Let me know when you want the flower.

FILIGREE BONES. Let me know when you want my flower too.

(MAN *tosses the last shovelful of dirt onto Dog's tiny grave.*)

MAN. What are you people doing afterwards?

ROBIN BREAST WESTERN (*walking away from them all*). That's always a problem.

MISS INDIGO BLUE (*leaving them*). It's always the hardest part of all.

FILIGREE BONES (*moving into the foreground*). It's the most horrible part of it all.

FIBBER KIDDING (*moving about nervously*). I don't know what we'll be doing afterwards.

(MAN *bends over and begins to make the small pile of dirt which is Dog's grave into a very neat-looking vision by packing and smoothing the dirt with his hands.*)

MISS INDIGO BLUE (*coming back to them immediately*). Do you want my flower now?

MAN. Yes.

(MISS INDIGO BLUE *goes to* MAN *and hands him the flower. He plants it lightly but confidently on top of the pile of dirt.*)

ROBIN BREAST WESTERN. It looks like a pretty picture.

MAN. Yeah, it's okay.

FILIGREE BONES (*moving back to them*). Here's my flower. (FILIGREE BONES *gives her flower to* MAN.)

MAN. Thank you. (MAN *plants it on top of the pile of dirt. There is a pause. They all stare at the grave of Dog.*)

ROBIN BREAST WESTERN (*finally*). It's a very good idea to have a funeral at nighttime.

MISS INDIGO BLUE. It's very special.

FILIGREE BONES. I'm glad I came.

FIBBER KIDDING. It's a very good idea, and it is very special, and I'm also glad that I came.

(MAN *brushes off the dirt from his hands. He stands very bright and tall.*)

MAN (*very fast*). It's a very good idea to have a funeral at nighttime. It is very special. I'm glad I came too. (*He looks at all of them with a vast beaming smile.*) Would any of you like to join me?

ROBIN BREAST WESTERN. Doing what?

MAN. Looking for a new dog for the old man who lives in my neighborhood.

(*The four of them all turn half away from him; the idea is somewhat depressing for them.*)

MISS INDIGO BLUE (*quietly*). No. . . .

FILIGREE BONES (*softly*). I don't think so. . . .

(ROBIN BREAST WESTERN *moves far to our right;* FIBBER KIDDING *moves far to our left;* MISS INDIGO BLUE *shakes her head in slight confusion;* FILIGREE BONES *wipes some more of her new tears.* MAN *stops to look at them all. He picks up his vast beaming smile again. He moves so that he can be seen by them all, despite where they are standing. He snaps his fingers: then he spreads his arms like a marvelous and very friendly human bird.*)

MAN. Hey, let's have a little private champagne party, okay? White champagne and pink champagne and midnight blue champagne. And all sorts of fresh delectable fruit to go with it: sweet-tasting and ripe-looking fruit. The grapes will be the kind of grapes that will knock you out and then bring you way up to where you're at.

(*He mimes eating the grapes. No one moves.*) Listen . . . I've got this, this *camel*, waiting all by himself outside the front gates of this graveyard.

FILIGREE BONES. A camel . . . ?

MISS INDIGO BLUE. A camel?!

MAN. We'll sip and gulp the champagne and munch and suck on the fruit, and we'll ride everywhere we can, until it gets light again, on the back of my great camel. Okay? *(No one moves, but they all look at* MAN, *not knowing what to really think. Instantly,* MAN *moves about them, and as he does so, he counts off real fast, pointing to each one of them and then ending up with himself.)* One, two, three, four, five! Why, it's really perfect, it's really fine. You see, my great camel is also a very special camel. Most camels have one hump on their backs; some have two; but mine has five. We can all go out to the iron gates of this graveyard where we can all ascend the five phoenix humps on the back of my great waiting camel. (MAN *begins to walk slowly about the graveyard as though he were riding the camel. He goes up and down in gentle slow motion. Now we begin to hear light and very fantastically beautiful music somewhere in the background. The lights begin to change: a radiant yellow is coming into the deep midnight blue, very slowly and very definitely.* MAN *pushes the wheelbarrow very far out of the way. The four of them continue to stand and watch and listen to* MAN.*)* We'll ride up to Niagara Falls and then we'll cross the Rainbow Bridge. The honeymooners will laugh and smile. We'll trot down to Atlantic City and move the sunny way of the beach and boardwalk. The bathers will giggle and talk and walk alongside the five of us and our great camel. We'll cross the great Mississippi on a floating barge, and we'll climb the orange rocks of the orange-bird Rockies. (MAN *begins to really ride the five-humped camel now. And he has now seduced the four of them into riding the camel too: up and down they all go in easy slow motion.)* We'll burn up the roads in Nevada until we come to Las Vegas! The people of Las Vegas will be real people again! We'll drink in Los Angeles and dine in Detroit and we'll camp overnight in the quiet stockyards of old Chicago! *(The five of them are going a bit faster now; they are all having a very good time.)* We'll dance in New York City and we'll breathe in the New England country! (MAN *slows the great five-humped camel down to a long and soft halt. They all remain, one by one, behind* MAN, *still on the back of the camel. Then* MAN *takes them all in his arms.)* Our great five-humped camel is the oldest camel of the entire world. And so we'd better hurry now, we'd better move now, because—it's the right time, the exact time, the precise time, the correct time, the absolutely accurate and *perfect time . . . to go now!*

(The lights become brighter. The music becomes louder. They all cheer.)

MISS INDIGO BLUE *(running about).* I've never been to a funeral at nighttime . . .

ROBIN BREAST WESTERN *(running after* MISS INDIGO BLUE*).* That's the way he wanted it . . .

FILIGREE BONES *(chasing* FIBBER KIDDING*).* The cocky little bastard . . .

FIBBER KIDDING *(now chasing* FILIGREE BONES*).* It's a nice experience. I like the experience of it a whole lot . . . !

(The four of them all make a joyous and celebrating exit to our left. MAN *goes and picks a great bright yellow flower from one of the floral sprays. Then he goes down to the center of the stage.)*

MAN *(to the audience).* I've never been to a funeral at nighttime. I like the fact that you people are here. (MAN *holds the long-stemmed flower over his shoulder. And then he exits, following after* ROBIN BREAST WESTERN, MISS INDIGO BLUE, FILIGREE BONES, *and* FIBBER KIDDING. *The lights swell into brilliant sunshine; and the music swells into brilliant party time.)*

CURTAIN

LITTLE MURDERS

Jules Feiffer

First presented by Alexander H. Cohen at the Broadhurst Theatre in New York City on April 25, 1967. A second production opened at the Circle In The Square on January 5, 1969, with the following cast:

KENNY NEWQUIST Jon Korkes	ALFRED CHAMBERLAIN Fred Willard
MARJORIE NEWQUIST Elizabeth Wilson	JUDGE STERN Shimen Ruskin
CAROL NEWQUIST Vincent Gardenia	REVEREND DUPAS Paul Benedict
PATSY NEWQUIST Linda Lavin	LT. PRACTICE Andrew Duncan

Directed by Alan Arkin
Settings by Ed Wittstein
Costumes by Albert Wolsky
Lighting by Neil Peter Jampolis

SYNOPSIS OF SCENES

ACT ONE. SCENE ONE: The Newquist apartment. SCENE TWO: The Newquist apartment, one month later. SCENE THREE: The Newquist apartment, two months later.
ACT TWO. SCENE ONE: The Newquist apartment, four hours later. SCENE TWO: The Newquist apartment, six months later.

How many cartoonists have ever become dramatists? That is what is known as a rhetorical question. (If I had been asked the same question about critics I could have replied, Max Beerbohm, but that doesn't count.) Yet the difference is not so great. As a cartoonist Mr. Feiffer was always a dramatist. His cartoons are either dialogues or monologues. His characters are always saddened refugees from either urban culture or urbane living. And they spell out their problems as if they were on a couch. Mr. Feiffer looks at modern living the way a microbiologist looks at life.

He was born in New York City on January 26, 1929. After studying at the Art Students League and Pratt Institute, both in New York City, he served in the Army from 1951 to 1953. It was in 1956 that the turning point came in his career. It was then he became a contributing cartoonist to a new paper, *The Village Voice*. He helped make *The Village Voice* and *The Village Voice* helped make him. After all these years the two of them are still morosely together.

Feiffer's cartoons took the pulse of a new and strange city creature. Oversensitive, overexposed, and probably overeducated, Feiffer's new hero suffered all the slings and arrows of outrageous neurosis. His people were recognizable creatures of our time—and they proved as recognizable in London as they were in New York. There is nothing quite like Feiffer as a cartoonist unless, in an odd way, it be Charles Schulz and Peanuts. The comparison is not precise. Feiffer, properly salted, is more of a cashew than a peanut. He is nothing if not sophisticated. But equally he is nothing if not honest. His strip cartoons provided a peep-show history of our times.

He was for many years a writer. He published a great many short stories, and one novel, *Harry the Rat with Women*. His first play, a one-acter called *Creeping Arnold,* was produced in 1961, but it was not until April 1967 that he staged his first full-length play on Broadway. This was *Little Murders,* and it ran four or five days after chilling reviews. A few weeks later it was staged in London by the Royal Shakespeare Company, and there it was far better received.

In 1969 his play *God Bless* was also produced in London, but, although it was subsequently seen in a production by the Yale Repertory Company, it still awaits its New York premiere. However, in 1970 his latest play, *The White House Murder Case,* was given off Broadway at the Circle in the Square, where it ran for 119 performances. In 1972 Mr. Feiffer turned his attention to screen-writing and wrote the script for Mike Nichols's film, *Carnal Knowledge.*

So far Mr. Feiffer's reputation as a dramatist rests solidly on *Little Murders.* Interestingly, the production details of *Little Murders* lend credence to the contention that critics can never kill a good play—they merely bruise it a little. The play was originally produced at the Broadhurst Theatre, Broadway, on April 25, 1967, and it ran for seven performances. I did not see this production, but it seems to have been a misconception of the play. Also, this rigorously anti-Establishment work could hardly be expected to feel at home in a Broadway theatre. However, the story had a happy ending.

Theodore Mann, artistic director of the Circle in the Square, had faith in the play, and he persuaded Alan Arkin to stage a new Off-Broadway production of *Little Murders*. It was triumphant—the notices this time round were good and the play, which opened on January 5, 1969, closed on November 30 of the same year after four hundred performances. The time, the place, and the cast were all right.

The play itself is a particularly savage satire on that violence which we have been told is as American as apple pie. It is a striking play that is both funny and bitter. Its corrosive portraits of American archetypes and its casual killings are horrifying and yet maintain the good-natured tone of a TV soap opera. It is perhaps this tone, even, level, and convincing, that is the play's final horror and achievement.

"Two, four, six, eight—
who do we assassinate?"

—New York children's
street chant, circa 1964

ACT ONE

Scene One

A view of the Newquist apartment. The living room, dining area, foyer, and front door slowly fade into view (by means of a scrim or any other workable method), in sync with the rising sound of city street noises. The apartment is typically Upper West Side, dominated by overstuffed furniture, enormous multipaned windows and walls with too much molding. At the moment, mid-morning, it is empty. As the apartment fades into view the level of noise rises—morning noise: construction, traffic, and helicopters. In the next few minutes both light and noise change: shadows shift, lengthen, and darken in sync with the fading of construction sounds, replaced by the late afternoon cries of children at play. This too fades into the quieter monotone of early evening traffic.

The apartment darkens accordingly and we may even see the setting sun as reflected in the apartment windows across the street. (The only view of the world outside is of other buildings, other windows.) What we see is comparable to a stop-motion camera's view of the apartment, from mid-morning to dusk. Throughout, a steady patina of soot has drifted in through one of the half-open windows, and specks of plaster may now and then drop from the ceiling. The telephone rings. Other sounds: police sirens, fire engines, etc. The front door unlocks; this takes time, since there are two double locks on the door. The door slowly pushes open, revealing two enormous shopping bags. Almost completely hidden behind them is MARJORIE, small, energetic, in her fifties. She switches on the foyer light with an elbow and bustles across to the kitchen.

———

MARJORIE. Don't let a draft in! *(As she disappears through the swinging door that leads to the kitchen,* KENNY *enters reading a*

paperback. *He is listless, in his early twenties. Leaving the door open he starts slowly across the room, engrossed in his reading. On the return swing of the kitchen door,* MARJORIE *reappears sans coat and shopping bags, this time carrying a folded tablecloth and a large sponge.)* I'm going to need your help, young man. *(*KENNY *enters bathroom, closes door loudly.)* Don't dawdle! *(*MARJORIE *runs sponge across dining-room table. It comes up pitch black.)* Filth! *(She unfolds tablecloth in one motion. It falls perfectly into place.)* They'll be here any minute, Kenny! *(She disappears into kitchen with sponge, reappears on return swing of door with serving cart piled high with dishes and silver. She is about to set table when an explosion of automobile horns drives her to window, which she slams shut with great effort. She hastens to other window and switches on air conditioner—a loud hum.* CAROL *enters, carrying brief case. He is a short, thickset, energetic man in his fifties, about* MARJORIE's *size.)*

CAROL. What the hell is that for? This is February! *(Switches off air conditioner)*

MARJORIE *(a cheerful but uninterested hug).* It drowns out the traffic.

CAROL *(slips out of embrace).* All right, when we don't have guests. We don't want people to think we're crazy. Did the liquor come?

MARJORIE. It came. *(Suspicious)* Why are you so interested in liquor?

CAROL. Don't worry. You've got nothing to worry about.

MARJORIE. You called up twice from the office to ask about the liquor.

CAROL. That's all right. That's perfectly all right. *(Evades her stare)* You can find out a lot more about somebody, you know, when he's a little—*(He flutters his hand to indicate tipsiness.)*

MARJORIE *(shocked).* Carol, you're not going to get that poor boy *drunk!*

CAROL. That poor boy wants to marry my Patsy! And don't call me *Carol!*

(Sounds of toilet flush and door slam. KENNY *enters from bathroom, reading.)*

MARJORIE. But—dear—you haven't even met him!

KENNY *(matter-of-fact).* He's an artsy-fartsy photographer. Patsy says he's thirty-six, but I know he's forty.

CAROL *(to* KENNY). Are you *reading* again? *(He grabs paperback.)* Harlots of Venus! Is that what I spend seven thousand a year on graduate school for? Get dressed!

KENNY. You lost my place! (KENNY *exits.*)

CAROL. Why is she doing this to me?

MARJORIE. He'll be a fine boy. I know it in my bones.

CAROL. What are you talking about? Do you have the slightest idea what you're talking about? She's only known him three weeks! I bet he's a fag!

MARJORIE. Carol!

CAROL (*vicious*). I *hate* that name! I told you never to call me that name. You deliberately do that to annoy me! (*Shouts*) Call me *dear!* (*Subsides*) You refuse to look at the facts. This whole family. That's the trouble with it. I'm the only one who looks at the facts. What was the name of that interior decorator she went to Europe with?

MARJORIE. Howard. He was—delicate.

CAROL. Swish! And that *actor,* the one who she went camping up in Maine with?

MARJORIE. Roger. He was very muscular.

CAROL. Swish! And the musician. And the stockbroker. And the Jewish novelist!

MARJORIE. Oh, *they're* not like that—

CAROL. Swish! Swish! Swish! I can spot 'em a mile away. She draws 'em like flies. Too strong for real men. Too much stuff! (*Proudly*) She's got *too much stuff!* Wait, you'll see. This new one—what's his name?

MARJORIE. Alfred.

CAROL A swish name if I ever heard one. You'll see. He'll come in. Be very polite. Very charming. Look handsome. Well-dressed. Have a strong handshake. Look me right in the eye. Smile a lot. Have white teeth. Shiny hair. Look very regular. But after two or three drinks—look at his wrists—he'll have trouble keeping 'em straight. Watch his lips. He'll start smacking his lips with his tongue. Watch his eyes. He'll start rolling his eyes. And his legs will go from being crossed like this—(*Wide-legged*) to this (*Close-legged*). And when he gets up to start walking—(*He is about to mimic walk. Offstage sound of shots.* CAROL *and* MARJORIE *rush to window. He struggles, but can't get it open.*) Damn! Goddamn!

MARJORIE. Hurry! (*Shots fade. Offstage siren, loud, then fading*) They're miles away by now. You take forever.

(*Doorbell*)

PATSY'S VOICE. Hey, everybody!

(CAROL *outpaces* MARJORIE *to door.* PATSY *and* ALFRED *enter. Much excitement, laughter.* CAROL *is more involved with his daughter than* MARJORIE, *who is just a touch restrained.*

PATSY *is all-consuming. Tall, blond, vibrant, the All-American Girl.* ALFRED *is big, heavy-set, and quite dour. He is in his middle thirties. Two cameras hang from straps around his neck.* PATSY, MARJORIE, *and* CAROL *speak in unison. None of the following is intelligible.*)

PATSY. Daddy, Mother, I love your hair! Daddy, you're putting on weight, Mother, Daddy.

MARJORIE. Hello, dear, how are you, what's wrong with my hair, you're putting on weight.

CAROL. Patsy, Patsy, my little girl! My baby girl, you look like a million dollars! I'll tell the world.

PATSY. This is Alfred!

CAROL (*ignoring* ALFRED, *to* PATSY). Hey, you weren't in that business down there?

PATSY. What business?

CAROL. Well, from now on just be more careful.

MARJORIE (*her eyes on* ALFRED). I don't think we need worry any longer, dear. Patsy's finally got herself a *man!*

(CAROL *scowls.*)

PATSY. Where's my Kenny? (*Offstage sound of toilet flush and door slam.* KENNY *enters, adjusting trousers.* PATSY *swoops down on him.* PATSY *and* KENNY *speak in unison. None of the following is intelligible.*)

PATSY. Kenny! My baby brother! Isn't he the absolute cutest? I could eat him alive! Kenny!

KENNY. Ah, come on, cut it out! Quit all the hugging! Quit it! Boy, oboy, oboy.

MARJORIE (*somewhat catty*). Alfred, have you ever seen such a madhouse?

(ALFRED *smiles diffidently.*)

CAROL. He's in the house for three minutes and she's already putting him on the spot. Have you ever seen anything like it, Alfred?

(ALFRED *smiles diffidently.*)

PATSY Kenny! You're so handsome! I can't get over it! (*To* ALFRED) I've always had a mad thing on my kid brother! (KENNY *clowns embarrassment,* PATSY *and* MARJORIE *laugh,* ALFRED *smiles diffidently,* CAROL *looks annoyed. To* ALFRED) He breaks me up!

CAROL (*nastily*). Kenny's the *comedian* around here. (KENNY *sobers immediately. To* ALFRED) What's your pleasure, young fellow?

PATSY. Mother, what have you done to this room?

(*Lights flicker and black out in apartment, and in windows across the street.*)

MARJORIE (lighting candles). Nothing special. A little bit of this. A little bit of that. (Offstage sirens begin.)

CAROL (self-pityingly). If you bothered to come here more often—

MARJORIE (studying PATSY's face by candlelight). I don't like your looks.

CAROL (studying PATSY). What's the matter? The day that girl doesn't look like a million dollars—

MARJORIE. You've got black rings under your eyes.

PATSY. Mother, that's eyeliner.

MARJORIE. Makes you look exhausted.

KENNY (studying PATSY). I like it.

MARJORIE. Always together!

CAROL. Do you have the slightest idea what you're talking about? She looks like a million dollars!

MARJORIE. I know. It's what they're wearing today. I'm out of step. As usual.

(Lights come back on. MARJORIE blows out candle.)

CAROL (a little nervous; to ALFRED). What's your pleasure, young fellow?

MARJORIE (critical). Why don't you wear your other outfit?

PATSY. What other outfit?

CAROL. Will you stop criticizing?

PATSY. What other outfit, Mother?

MARJORIE. I can't be expected to remember everything. It's not as if you still lived here.

KENNY. Hey, Al, want to see Patsy's old room?

PATSY. Alfred, Kenny. And he's not interested in that!

KENNY. I bet he is! Want to?

ALFRED. Maybe later.

KENNY (rejected). Why should I care?

CAROL (to KENNY). He doesn't want to! Stop acting silly! (To ALFRED) What's your pleasure, young fellow?

MARJORIE. Alfred, may I shake your hand? My mother taught us that you could tell a lot about a person by the way he shakes hands. (Shakes his hand) You have a good hand. (Flirtatious) Better look out, Patsy! I'll steal your boy friend! (Releases ALFRED's hand. Short laugh. To ALFRED) I'm only joking.

KENNY. Let me try. (Shakes ALFRED's hand) You don't squeeze so hard. (Disengages) Dad?

CAROL This is the silliest business I've ever heard of! I think we all need drinks. What's your pleasure, young fellow?

MARJORIE. Alfred, is something the matter with your face?

ALFRED (to PATSY). Is there?

PATSY (subdued annoyance). Just the usual assortment of bruises, Mother.

MARJORIE. What kind of talk is that? Modern talk?

PATSY (not overjoyed to be on the subject). Alfred is always getting beat up, Mother. At least once a week. (To ALFRED) Or is it more?

ALFRED (shakes his head to indicate it is not more). I don't get hurt.

MARJORIE. You don't get hurt? Carol, look at that boy! His face is a mass of bruises!

CAROL. I have asked you repeatedly never to call me Carol. (To PATSY) I hate that name Carol!

MARJORIE. I have to call you something, dear.

CAROL. I don't care what you call me. Just don't call me Carol!

KENNY. Call him Harriet! (Laughs) Harriet! Harriet! Yoohoo! Harriet! (Convulses himself)

PATSY. You're not being funny, Kenny. (He sobers immediately.) I love your name. I know lots of men named Carol.

KENNY. Sure. Sure. Name one.

(CAROL glares at him.)

PATSY (thinking). Carol—

KENNY. Chessman! (Screams with laughter)

PATSY. King Carol of Rumania!

CAROL. That's right! King Carol! Damn it, that's right! Say, I feel like a drink. Anyone join me?

MARJORIE. I want to know why Alfred gets into these fights. I don't think that's the least bit funny.

PATSY (resigned). Ask him!

ALFRED (not interested but making an effort, mindful that this is his first attempt at conversation). Look. (Long pause. Others stir uncomfortably.) There are lots of little people who like to start fights with big people. They hit me for a couple of minutes, they see I'm not going to fall down, they get tired and they go away.

MARJORIE (after an embarrassed pause). So much tension. Rush. Rush. Rush. My mother taught me to take dainty, little steps. She'd kill me if she saw the stride on Patsy.

CAROL (puzzled; the beginnings of contempt). Don't you defend yourself?

ALFRED. I ask them not to hit my cameras. They're quite good about that. (Cheerful) Surprising!

CAROL. Let me get this straight. You just stand there and let these hooligans do whatever they want to you?

ALFRED. I'm quite strong, so you needn't worry about it. At the risk of sounding arrogant, this has been going on for ten years and I've yet to be knocked unconscious.

CAROL. But why don't you fight back?

ALFRED. I don't want to.

CAROL. Christ Jesus, you're not a pacifist?

PATSY *(warning)*. Daddy—

ALFRED *(slowly shakes his head)*. An apathist. *(Blank stares from* CAROL *and* MARJORIE*)* I want to do what I want to do, not what *they* want me to do.

CAROL. So you just stand there.

ALFRED. It doesn't hurt.

CAROL. Getting your face beat in doesn't hurt?

ALFRED. Not if you daydream. I daydream all through it. About my work. I imagine myself standing there, in the same spot, clicking off roll after roll of film, humming to myself with pleasure. I hum to myself when I work. There are times when I get so carried away that I think I'm actually doing what I'm only dreaming I'm doing. Muggers tend to get very depressed when you hum all the while they're hitting you. It's not something I choose to happen. It's just one of those things you learn to live with.

PATSY *(to family)*. Look, this is an old argument and it doesn't really concern you. Why don't we get on something else?

CAROL *(indignant)*. It certainly does concern me, young lady!

PATSY *(placating)*. Oh, Daddy—

CAROL. I want you to know it concerns me very much. *(To* ALFRED*)* How do you get into these things? You must do something to get them mad—

ALFRED. No—

CAROL. Well, goddamnit, you're getting *me* mad!

MARJORIE *(taking the heat off)*. Alfred, do you try *talking* to them?

ALFRED *(the patient old pro)*. There's no way of talking someone out of beating you up if that's what he wants to do.

KENNY *(to* PATSY*)*. This guy's a riot!

(She slaps at him. He playfully eludes her.)

PATSY. Haven't we had enough of this? I'm going to make some drinks.

KENNY. Vodka and tonic.

MARJORIE. Just *one,* young man.

CAROL. I'll make them!

PATSY. No, Daddy. I want to get my hands busy. Alfred?

ALFRED. Nothing right now.

CAROL. You don't drink either. Is that right?

ALFRED. I drink beer.

CAROL. Get him a beer, Kenny.

KENNY. Why is it always my turn?

ALFRED. Not now, thanks.

CAROL. He doesn't drink.

ALFRED. I'll drink later.

CAROL. You don't drink. You don't fight.

PATSY. I fight, Daddy!

MARJORIE. Carol, leave the poor boy alone.

CAROL *(shouts)*. *How many times do I have to tell you—*

MARJORIE *(hurt)*. I'm sorry. Whatever I do is wrong.

KENNY *(doing Bogart)*. Hey. What's dat? Dat my best goil talking? Hey. *(He hugs her from behind.)*

MARJORIE *(kittenish)*. Kenny! What will Alfred think? He'll think you're always making love to your mother!

CAROL *(sourly)*. He *is* always making love to his mother.

MARJORIE. Well, someone has to—*(She smiles into* CAROL*'s glare.)* dear.

PATSY *(serving drinks)*. What's this? What's this? I thought I was your best girl, Kenny?

*(*KENNY *tries to release* MARJORIE *and go to* PATSY. *She grabs his arms and holds on.)*

MARJORIE *(to* ALFRED*)*. When Patsy lived at home we used to go on like this all the time.

KENNY *(whining)*. Let go, Mom!

CAROL. Stop all this silliness and drink your liquor!

*(*MARJORIE *releases* KENNY, *who goes over to* PATSY.*)*

MARJORIE *(flirtatious)*. You're an intelligent-sounding man, Alfred. I would think if you spoke to these people quietly and sensibly they'd realize the sort of person you were and go away.

ALFRED. What can you say that's sensible to a drunk who you haven't been staring at, when he shoves you in the chest and says, "Who do you think you're staring at, fatface?" If you deny you've been staring at him, you've as much as called him a liar. For that you get hit. If you stutter in confusion, you've as much as admitted your guilt. For that you get hit. If you tell him you were staring at him because he reminds you of a kid you went to school with in Chicago, he turns out to *hate* Chicago. And for that you get hit.

MARJORIE *(to* PATSY). I didn't know he went to school in Chicago. Nobody tells me anything. *(To* ALFRED) We went to Chicago in 1946. Whereabout did you live in Chicago, Alfred?

ALFRED. The South Side.

MARJORIE. I'm not comfortable eating away from home. Well, that's another story. Does your family still live there?

ALFRED. I don't know.

CAROL. You don't know! What kind of answer is that? You don't know! That's the silliest answer I've ever heard!

ALFRED. I haven't kept up contact.

(CAROL *frowns, disapproving.*)

MARJORIE. There seems to be so little cohesiveness in families today. *We* never went anywhere. We were too unsophisticated to know that home wouldn't serve. *(At* PATSY) Today they run off here, they run off there—

KENNY *(hugs her).* I'll never leave you, Mom.

CAROL. Will you two break it up? How about another round? Name your poison, Alfred.

MARJORIE *(sadly).* We've had our share of tragedy—

PATSY *(warning).* Mother—

(Phone rings. CAROL *starts for it.* MARJORIE *beats him to it.)*

MARJORIE. Let me, dear. It's never for you. Hello. *(Amplified sound of heavy breathing)* Hello. Hello. Who is this? Hello. (PATSY *starts toward her.)* The most curious business. Hello.

(PATSY *takes phone, listens and hangs up.)*

PATSY *(to* MARJORIE). You get it too.

CAROL. What? (PATSY *looks toward* MARJORIE, *who smiles but does not answer.)* What?

MARJORIE. Never mind, dear. It's not important.

(CAROL *frustrated.* PATSY *goes to him.)*

PATSY. The Breather, Daddy. Do you get many of these, Mother?

MARJORIE. He's the pleasantest of the lot. You should hear the ones who *talk!* I grit my teeth, turn my ears *right* off, and wait politely for them till they've finished their business.

CAROL *(exasperated).* Will somebody please explain to me—

PATSY. I get them every night. You know, Daddy—these oddballs who call you up at all hours and just *breathe* at you.

CAROL *(appalled).* Late at night? They breathe at you? *(To* ALFRED) And you don't fight back?!

(Doorbell)

MARJORIE. I'll get it! *(She crosses to door and opens peephole.)* Who is it? I'm sorry, I can't understand you! Will you please stand closer to the peephole? I can't see you—take your hand off the peephole. I warn you, I'm calling the doorman! (PATSY *starts for door.* MARJORIE *shuts peephole and intercepts her. She returns, musing.)* If it happens once, it happens a dozen times a day. And we gave that doorman fifteen dollars for Christmas.

(PATSY *protectively puts her arms around her.* MARJORIE *lightly shrugs it off.)*

CAROL *(to* ALFRED). *What are you going to do if you're on the street with my daughter?*

PATSY. Don't be silly, Daddy. I'm quite capable of taking care of myself.

KENNY *(proudly).* She's as strong as an OX. When we were kids we used to wrestle all the time. I always lost.

PATSY *(enjoying herself).* Daddy, I assure you, no one's going to pick on me. I'm a big, strapping girl! I don't daydream, and I *do* hit back. When I take Alfred home every night, I guarantee you there's no trouble.

CAROL. You let *her* take you home?

PATSY. He doesn't *let* me. He doesn't have anything to say about it. Every time I leave him alone somebody in this crazy city mugs him. Once I have him safely married (CAROL *and* KENNY *wince.),* I won't let him out of my sight for five minutes. *(Pinches* ALFRED) He's too cute to get beat up—by anyone but me. *(She throws a playful but entirely masculine punch at* ALFRED. *He smiles happily as it connects.* KENNY *exits. Offstage door slam)*

MARJORIE. Aren't they adorable?

CAROL *(quietly to* MARJORIE). What did I tell you about him, huh? Didn't I predict?

MARJORIE. I think he's very sweet.

CAROL. That's a sure sign. You think they're *all* sweet. I'll be damned *(Louder)* if I'd let myself stand by and let a woman fight my battles for me.

PATSY *(hugging* CAROL *from behind).* They don't make frontier fighters like my father any more.

MARJORIE *(looks about).* Kenny! *(Shakes her head in exasperation and smiles seductively at* ALFRED) Alfred, would you mind giving me a hand? *(They exit.)*

CAROL *(delighted).* Come on. Stop being silly. Cut it out.

PATSY *(playful, squeezing tighter).* Let's see how good you are, tiger. Break my grip! Come on!

(Momentary look of panic in CAROL*'s eyes.* PATSY *releases him. They laugh.)*

CAROL *(slaps her cheek playfully).* Who's my baby girl, eh? *(Suddenly serious)* I wish you had as much brains as you have brawn.

PATSY. You don't like him, do you, Daddy?

CAROL. Don't put words in my mouth.

PATSY. Then you *do* like him?

CAROL I want to know more about him before I make up my mind—

PATSY. Not to like him.

CAROL. Don't bully me, young lady. You know I don't like it when you bully me.

PATSY. You *love* it when I bully you.

CAROL *(chuckles).* You're too damned fast for the old man. *(Slaps her cheek playfully)* But I know a thing or two. *(Deadly serious)* Never settle for less.

PATSY. Daddy, I'm *not!*

CAROL. Never sell yourself short.

PATSY. Oh, Daddy, when have I *ever*—

CAROL. The right man will come along.

PATSY. Daddy, I'm twenty-seven. The right men all got married two years ago. They won't get their first divorce for another five years, and I just don't have the time, the inclination, or the kind of looks that can afford to wait.

CAROL. I don't want to hear you knocking yourself. You've got ten people working under you! *(Proudly)* You're five foot eight!

PATSY. After a while it doesn't *matter* that you can do everything better than everyone else. I've been the best for years now, and all it comes down to is that I'm efficient.

CAROL. You don't know what you're talking about. You're very popular.

PATSY. When they want a woman they can collapse without shame in front of—they come to me.

CAROL. Why not? You're trusted!

PATSY. Oh, to meet a man who *is* ashamed to collapse in front of me! Daddy, I get dizzy spells from being so strong; I get migraine from being so damnably dependable. I'm tired of being Mother Earth! Daddy, Alfred's the *only* man I know who isn't waiting for me to save him. Don't you know how that makes me feel? God help me, I've got to save him! *(She embraces* CAROL, *who blissfully returns embrace.* ALFRED *enters uncorking the wine and surveys scene.* CAROL *quickly disengages.)*

MARJORIE *(enters wheeling serving cart).* Come an' git it! *(To* ALFRED *as she starts serving)* My mother always used to say that to us children at mealtimes. I've always found it a charming family tradition. So I say, "Come an' git it!" to our children. I dream of the day when I can hear Patsy say, "Come an' git it!" to her children. *(To* KENNY, *who is offstage)* Kenny! Didn't you hear me say come an' git it, or do you need a special invitation?

KENNY *(still offstage).* In a minute!

MARJORIE. Not a minute, young man! Right now! *(To* ALFRED) It's so stuffy in here. Alfred, would you open a window like a good fellow? *(Sounds of toilet flush, offstage door slam.* CAROL *rises.)* No, I asked Alfred, dear.

*(*KENNY *enters with paperback, passes* CAROL, *who outpaces* ALFRED *to window.)*

CAROL *(struggling with window).* It's all right. It's perfectly all right. *(Gives up) Son of a bitch! (To* ALFRED) The son of a bitch refuses to open!

*(*ALFRED *gives strong jerk. Window opens. Traffic, construction, and airplane noise)*

MARJORIE. Thank you, Alfred. *(To* CAROL) You see, I had my reasons.

(Light film of soot wafts through window.)

CAROL. I loosened it!

KENNY. He loosened it! That's a riot! *(Convulses himself.)*

CAROL *(slams window shut; to* KENNY). Now *you* open it! *(*KENNY *airily dismisses him.)* No, you're the smart one around here! Let's see you open it!

MARJORIE. I spent the whole day cooking. Can't we eat now and open and close windows later?

CAROL. It won't take a second. Well, young man, are you going to try or are you just going to sit back and laugh at the earnest efforts of your betters? *(*KENNY, *with arrogant mockery, rises, tries, and fails to open window. He shrugs, smiles, and ambles back to table.* ALFRED *and* CAROL *follow. All sit.)* You're not so smart now, are you?

MARJORIE. Will someone please open the window? *(*PATSY *leaps up before* ALFRED *can rise, strides to window, kicks off heels, jerks window open. Noise and dust.* KENNY *and* CAROL *bend over their plates, embarrassed.* PATSY *returns to table.)* When Patsy lived at home I always knew I had someone to do my heavy lifting for me. I was always too petite. *(*PATSY *shrinks over her plate. All quietly eat.)* You don't know what a pleasure it is to have my family all together this way. *(Lights flicker and black out, as before. Sounds of eating)* Do you know that in the *big* power failure some people stood in the subways, in total darkness, for as long as four hours without bringing their newspapers down from in front of their faces? *(Long silence. Eating sounds.* MARJORIE *lights candles.)* It would be nice if someone else, on occasion, would think of lighting the candles. Kenny, come back here! *(Offstage door slam.* KENNY *returns carrying paperback.)* I'm the watchdog around here, Alfred. I can imagine what Patsy must have told you about me.

PATSY *(bored).* Must you, Mother?

(They exchange long stares. MARJORIE *rises and exits. Door slam. Lights go on.)*

CAROL *(up quickly).* I'm going to make myself another drink.

KENNY. Make me one.

PATSY. Me too.

ALFRED. Scotch neat.

*(*CAROL *stops, stares at him, goes over to bar, grinning. Offstage sounds of toilet flush, door slam)*

MARJORIE *(enters carrying photographs).* It's gotten a little chilly in here. . . . *(*KENNY *up before anyone can move. He slams down window.* CAROL *serves drinks.* MARJORIE *frowns as* PATSY *accepts drink.)* That's your second tonight, isn't it? And I suppose you're still smoking as much? *(*PATSY *salutes with glass. Drains it)* Drinks like a fish. Smokes like a chimney. *(*PATSY *has mock cough spasm.)* It's the ones who think they're indestructible who do the most damage to themselves. Kenny, is that a new drink? *(*KENNY *bolts drink.* MARJORIE *shakes head, looks warily at* CAROL. *He bolts drink, scratches his hand nervously. To* ALFRED, *with photographs)* You're a photographer, Alfred, so I thought you'd be interested in seeing these pictures of Patsy's dead brother, Steve.

*(*PATSY *covers her face with her hands.)*

ALFRED. He looks very handsome in his swimsuit.

MARJORIE. He won five gold cups. He was ten years older than Patsy.

KENNY. Fifteen years older than me.

ALFRED. He looks very handsome in his baseball uniform.

MARJORIE. He only pitched no-hitters.

ALFRED *(handing back pictures).* Thank you for letting me see them.

MARJORIE. This one was taken after he came home from the war, a hero.

ALFRED. He looks very handsome in his uniform. What do these double bars signify?

MARJORIE. He was a captain. A hero. He bombed Tokyo. When his country called on him to serve again he bombed Korea. A brilliant future in electronics, not an enemy in the world, whoever dreamed he'd be shot down in his tracks on the corner of Ninety-seventh Street and Amsterdam Avenue. *(Gathers up pictures)* But I won't bore you with our tragedy.

PATSY *(explodes).* Damn it, Mother! Must I go through this every time I bring a man home to dinner? *(*MARJORIE *sobs, rushes off. Door slam)* Patsy's done it again!

KENNY *(admiring).* Boy, I'd be killed if I ever talked like that.

CAROL. I don't approve of your behavior, young lady. Your mother worked long and hard and imaginatively over this dinner. *(*PATSY *puts a cigarette in her mouth.)* And she's right about your smoking too much, goddamnit!

*(*PATSY *turns to* CAROL, *cigarette in mouth, waiting for a light. He resists for a moment, then lights it.)*

PATSY *(in command).* Thank you. *(*CAROL *scratches his hand. Softly to* ALFRED*)* I'm sorry you had to be subjected to this, honey. *(To* CAROL, *taking his hand, placating)* Alfred knows all about Steve, Daddy.

*(*CAROL *revives.)*

ALFRED. They still don't have any idea who did it?

CAROL. That's all right. The boys down at Homicide have worked long and hard and imaginatively on this case. *(With pride)* Many have become close personal friends.

(Toilet flush, door slam. MARJORIE *enters, eyes red but smiling. She is clutching a handkerchief.* KENNY *rises and exits in her direction. Door slam)*

MARJORIE *(at serving cart).* We can't disappoint our guest with only one helping.

ALFRED. No, thank you, Mrs. Newquist. I've had plenty.

PATSY *(ingratiating).* It was delicious, Mother!

CAROL. It was delicious!

MARJORIE. Kenny! Where are you?

KENNY *(offstage, muffled).* It was delicious!

MARJORIE *(to* ALFRED*).* A big man like you. Now, don't just stand on politeness—

ALFRED. No. I'm really quite stuffed, thank you.

MARJORIE *(to* PATSY*).* Well, then I'll have to turn to my best customer.

PATSY. I couldn't eat another bite, Mother. It was delicious.

CAROL. I couldn't eat another bite. It was delicious.

KENNY (offstage, muffled). I couldn't eat another bite. It was delicious! (Toilet flush. Door slam. He enters carrying paperback.) I could use another drink, though. (He detours on his way back from bar to surreptitiously pick up PATSY's heels in front of window. Takes them to his seat.)

CAROL (rises). I think I'll have another. (At the bar) Patsy?

PATSY (rises). Leave out the water this time. (She goes to bar.)

ALFRED. Scotch neat.

MARJORIE (not really approving). Well, it's a special occasion.

PATSY (looks around). Where the devil did I leave my shoes?

(KENNY looks away.)

MARJORIE (gathering photographs from table). I'd better put these in a safe place before someone spills liquor on them. I'm sorry to have taken your time, Alfred. Knowing you were a photographer I thought you'd be interested. (Waits for response; there is none) Exactly what sort of work do you do? Portraits?

ALFRED. No.

PATSY (returns protectively; hands ALFRED drink). Stop cross-examining him, Mother.

MARJORIE. I don't know why everything I do is wrong. Alfred, do you object to my asking you about your work?

ALFRED. It's not all that interesting, actually.

MARJORIE. You don't do portraits?

ALFRED. No.

MARJORIE. Do you do magazine photography?

ALFRED. No.

PATSY. Has somebody got a cigarette?

MARJORIE (to PATSY). Must you? Can't you give in to me just this once? (CAROL sits, hands PATSY cigarette. KENNY lights it. Barely in control, to ALFRED) Advertising photography?

ALFRED. Well, I used to. I don't any more.

CAROL. Fashion photography? (He nudges KENNY.)

KENNY (rolls his eyes). Woo! Woo!

(CAROL and KENNY exchange joyful glances. Stifle laughs)

ALFRED. It's sort of complicated. Are you sure you want to hear?

PATSY (resigned). You may as well—

ALFRED. Well, I began as a commercial photographer—

PATSY. He began as a painter.

ALFRED. A very bad painter.

PATSY. Says you!

CAROL. For Christ sakes, will you let the boy finish!

(All, including CAROL, are surprised by outburst.)

ALFRED. I began as a commercial photographer, and was doing sort of well at it.

PATSY. Sort of well! You should see his portfolio. He's had work in Holiday, Esquire, The New Yorker, Vogue—

CAROL. Vogue!

KENNY (rolls his eyes). Woo! Woo! (He and CAROL, exchange nudges, joyful glances. PATSY glares. They subside.)

ALFRED. It's an overrated business. But after a couple of years of doing sort of well (PATSY slaps his hand lightly) at it, things began to go wrong. I began losing my people. Somehow I got my heads chopped off. Or out of focus. Or terrible expressions on my models. I'd have them examining a client's product like this (Expression of distaste)—the agencies began to wonder if I didn't have some editorial motive in mind. Well, it wasn't true. But once they'd planted the idea—I couldn't help thinking of plane crashes every time I shot an airline ad, or deaths on the highway every time I shot an automobile ad, or price-rigging every time I shot a pharmaceutical ad—and power failures when I shot Con Edison ads.

(Lights go out.)

MARJORIE. I don't mean to interrupt, dear. (Lights match and candles) "How far better it is to light a match than curse the darkness." My mother told us that. Go on.

ALFRED. Well, my career suffered. But there was nothing I could do about it. The harder I tried to straighten out, the fuzzier my people got and the clearer my objects. Soon my people disappeared entirely, they just somehow never came out. But the objects I was shooting—brilliantly clear. (Snaps fingers. Lights come back on.) So I began to do a lot of catalogue work. (MARJORIE blows out candles.) Pictures of medical instruments, things like that. There was—well, the best way to describe it is—a seductiveness I was able to draw out of inanimate things that other photographers didn't seem to be able to get. I suppose the real break came with the I.B.M. show. They had me shoot thirty of their new models. They hired a gallery and had a computer show. One hundred and twenty color pictures of computers. It got some very strange *(Whimsical smile)* notices, the upshot of which was that the advertising business went "thing" crazy, and I became commercial again.

MARJORIE. You must be extremely talented.

ALFRED *(more to himself than to family)*. I got *sick* of it! Where the hell are standards? That's what I kept asking myself. Those people will take anything! Hell, if I gave them a picture of *shit* they'd give me an award for it!

(All stiffen. PATSY *looks wary.)*

MARJORIE. Language! young man!

ALFRED. Mm? So that's what I do now.

CAROL *(hesitantly)*. What?

ALFRED. Take pictures of shit.

MARJORIE. Language! Language! This is *my* table!

ALFRED. I don't mean to offend you, Mrs. Newquist. I've been shooting shit for a year now, and I've already won a half-dozen awards.

MARJORIE *(slowly thaws)*. Awards?

ALFRED. And *Harper's Bazaar* wants me to do its spring issue.

KENNY *(rolling his eyes)*. Woo! Woo!

CAROL *(angry, to* KENNY*)*. *Don't kid!*

MARJORIE. That's a very respectable publication. *(Rises shakily, gathers up dishes)* It all sounds very impressive. *(She exits with serving cart.)*

CAROL *(up quickly, about to speak, when phone rings. He goes for it, all the while glaring at* ALFRED*)*. Hello. *(Amplified breathing)* Look, I don't know who you are, but you're not dealing with helpless women now! *You people!* You young people today! Destroy! Destroy! When are you going to find time to build? In my day we couldn't afford telephones to breathe in! You ought to get down on your hands and knees and be grateful! Why isn't anybody GRATEFUL—(PATSY *takes receiver away, hangs up.)* Excuse me. *(He exits.)*

PATSY. Kenny, would you mind—

KENNY *(grins)*. It's my house.

PATSY *(threatening)*. Kenny! (PATSY *starts for him. He jumps up from table, grabbing his drink, and runs out. He has on* PATSY*'s heels. Door slams. Offstage sound of distant sirens)* Well, my friend—

ALFRED. They asked me what I did for a living. *(Shrugs)*

PATSY *(gives him a long stare)*. I don't know what to do with you. You're the toughest reclamation job *I've* ever had.

ALFRED. You might try retiring on your laurels. You've reformed five fags in a row, why press your luck with a nihilist?

PATSY. *Because you're wrong! (Calms herself)* Alfred, *every* age has problems. And people somehow manage . . . *to be happy!* I'm sorry, I don't mean to bully you. . . . Yes, I do mean to bully you. Alfred, do you know how I wake up every morning of my life? With a smile on my face! And for the rest of the day I come up against an unending series of challenges to wipe that smile off my face. The Breather calls . . . ex-boy friends call to tell me they're getting married . . . someone tries to break into the apartment while I'm dressing . . . there's a drunk asleep in the elevator . . . three minutes after I'm out on the street my camel coat turns brown . . . the subway stalls . . . the man standing next to me presses his body against mine . . . the up elevator jams . . . rumors start buzzing around the office that we're about to be automated . . . the down elevator jams . . . all the taxis are off duty . . . the air on Lexington Avenue is purple . . . a man tries to pick me up on the bus . . . another man follows me home . . . I step in the door and the Breather's on the phone . . . isn't that enough to wipe the smile off anybody's face? Well, it doesn't wipe it off *mine!* Because for every bad thing there are two good things— no—*four* good things! There are friends . . . and a wonderful job . . . and tennis . . . and skiing . . . and traveling . . . and musicals . . . and driving in the country . . . and flying your own airplane . . . and staying up all night to see the sun rise. (ALFRED *goes into his daydream.)* Alfred, come back here! *(Long pause)* Alfred, if everything is so hopeless—why do anything?

ALFRED. Okay.

PATSY. That's why you don't hit back.

ALFRED. There isn't much point, is there?

PATSY *(explodes)*. Do you know what you're talking about? Do you have the slightest idea *(Catches herself, shakes her head)*—I always talk like my father when I'm in this house. Alfred . . . if you feel that way about things . . . why get *married?*

ALFRED. You said you wanted to.

PATSY *(turns away)*. I find this a very unpleasant conversation.

ALFRED *(dryly)*. Patsy, let's not turn this

into a "critical conversation," just because you're not getting your way. *I'm* for getting married.

PATSY *(dryly)*. Thanks.

ALFRED *(after a long, tense pause)*. So it is a "critical conversation." *(He starts off.)*

PATSY. Where do you think you're going? *(He exits.)* Alfred! *(Starts after him, muttering to herself)* He doesn't know how to fight; *that's* why I'm not winning. *(Exits and brings him back)* Damn it! Aren't you willing to battle over *anything*? Even *me*? *(She anticipates what he is about to say.)*

ALFRED *and* PATSY. There isn't much point, is there? *(She bear-hugs him.)*

PATSY. At least say you love me.

ALFRED *and* PATSY. I'm not sure I know what love is.

PATSY *(slaps him in the stomach)*. Okay. The gauntlet's flung! You've had it, buster! I'm going to marry you, make you give me a house, entrap you into a half-dozen children, and seduce you into a life so remorselessly satisfying that within two years under my management you'll come to me with a camera full of baby pictures and say: "Life can be beautiful!"

ALFRED. And ugly. More often ugly.

PATSY. You'll give me a piano to sing around. And a fireplace to lie in front of. And each and every Christmas we will send out *personalized* Christmas cards—with a group family portrait on the front—taken by *Alfred Chamberlain*. Daddy! Mother! I have an announcement! (CAROL *and* MARJORIE *rush in. Sounds of toilet flush, door slam.* KENNY *rushes in, adjusting his trousers.)* Alfred and I are getting married! (CAROL *and* KENNY *freeze.)* Next week!

(CAROL *sits down heavily.)*

MARJORIE *(beaming)*. I've always dreamed of a wedding in my living room! Oh, there's so much to do. *(Kisses them)* You've got yourself a fine young man. And so accomplished! We'll have to let Dr. Paterson know right away—

ALFRED *(to PATSY)*. Who?

PATSY. The minister, dopey.

ALFRED *(to MARJORIE, picking up phone)*. Mrs. Newquist—*(Sound of amplified breathing.* MARJORIE *quickly hangs up. Picks up again and begins to dial)* Mrs. Newquist, when you speak to the minister, you'd better tell him—we don't want any mention of God in the ceremony.

CAROL. I'm going to have him arrested.

(All freeze, stare at ALFRED. *Blackout. Street noises, sirens, etc.)*

SCENE TWO

The Newquist apartment, one month later. ALFRED, PATSY, CAROL, *and* MARJORIE *sit quietly.* CAROL *looks at his watch, rises, begins to pace.* PATSY *places a calming hand on* ALFRED's *arm.* MARJORIE, *the only one unperturbed, smiles gamely. Doorbell.* CAROL *crosses to door.*

———

MARJORIE. Ask who it is first!

(CAROL *opens door. The* JUDGE *enters, a portly, well-dressed man of about* CAROL's *age.)*

CAROL *(softly, as if at a wake)*. Jerry. You don't know how I appreciate this.

(The JUDGE *nods, accepts* CAROL's *handshake, looks at his watch.)*

JUDGE *(softly)*. Nice to see you again, Mrs. Newquist. Are these the youngsters? (CAROL *nods.)* No God in the ceremony. Does she live away from home? (CAROL *nods.)* It begins there.

MARJORIE *(softly)*. You'll have to pardon the mess, Judge Stern.

JUDGE. You have a second girl, don't you, Carol?

CAROL. A boy.

JUDGE. A son!

CAROL. A boy.

MARJORIE *(to PATSY and ALFRED)*. Children, this is—

CAROL. I'll do it! Judge Jerome M. Stern, one of my oldest and dearest—

JUDGE. I don't have much time. If the grownups will please excuse us— *(Looks to* CAROL *and* MARJORIE, *who reluctantly start to exit as* KENNY *enters)*

MARJORIE. Out, young man!

KENNY. Why can't I ever—

(MARJORIE *shoves him. They exit together.)*

JUDGE *(stares at* ALFRED *and* PATSY *for a long moment)*. Sit down, please. *(They remain standing.)* I can't talk unless I'm the tallest. (PATSY *sits, and eases* ALFRED *down beside her.)* No God in the ceremony, mm? Getting a lot of turn-downs, aren't you? Surprising, isn't it, how the name of God is still respected in this town. *(Studies* PATSY) Carol Newquist's daughter. *(Sighs)* Your father and me go back a long ways, young lady. He's done me a lot of favors. Got me tickets to shows—*(Sighs. Shakes his head)* I'd *like* to help him out *(Shakes his head)*—My mother, thank God she's not alive today, landed in this country sixty-five years ago. Four infants in her arms. Kissed the sidewalk the minute she got off the boat, she was so happy to be out of Russia alive. Across the ocean alive. More dead than alive, if you want to know the truth. Sixteen days in the steerage. Fifteen people got consumption. Five died. My father, thank God he's not alive today, came over two years earlier, sixty-seven years ago. Worked like a son of a bitch to earn our passage *(To* PATSY)—pardon my French. You don't want God in the ceremony, so you're probably familiar with it. My father worked fourteen hours a day in a sweatshop on lower Broadway. Number three-fifteen. Our first apartment was a five-flight walk-up, four-and-a-half-room cold-water flat. With the bathtub in the kitchen and the toilet down the hall. One-forty-two Hester Street. Three families used the toilet. An Italian family. A colored family. A Jewish family. Three families with different faiths, but one thing each of those families had in common. They had in common the sacrifices each of them had to make to get where they were. What they had in common was *persecution.* So they weren't so *glib* about God. God was in my mother's every conversation about how she got her family out of Russia, thank God, in one piece. About the pogroms. The steerage. About those who *didn't* make it. Got sick and died. Who could they ask for help? If not God, then *who? The Great Society? The Department of Welfare? Travelers Aid?* Mind you, I'm a good Democrat, I'm not knocking these things. Although sometimes—there weren't any handouts in those days. This city was a —a—*concrete jungle* to the families that came here. They had to carve homes and lives out of *concrete*—cold *concrete!* You think they didn't call on God, these poor suffering greenhorns? You see the suit I'm wearing? Expensive? Custom-made? My father, thank God he's not alive today, worked sixteen hours a day in a shop on Broome Street, and his artistry for a tenth of what you pay today makes meat loaf out of this suit. One-forty-five dash one-forty-seven Broome Street. So tired, so broken in spirit, when he climbed the six flights of stairs each night to the three-room unheated cold-water flat the five of us were crowded in—one-seventy-one Attorney Street—that he did not have the strength to

eat. *The man did not have the strength to eat.* Turning thinner and yellower by the day for lack of *what?* A well-balanced diet? Too much cholesterol? Too many carbohydrates and starchy substances in his blood? Not on your sweet life! For lack of *everything!* What was God to my father? I'll tell you—sit down, I'm not finished!—I'll tell you what God was to my father! God got my father up those six and a half flights of stairs, not counting the stoop, every night. God got my mother, worn gray from lying to her children about a better tomorrow she didn't believe in, up each morning with enough of the failing strength that finally deserted her last year in Miami Beach at the age of ninety-one, to face another day of hopelessness and despair. Thirty-one-thirty-five Biscayne Boulevard. God. Do you know how old I was when I first had to go out and work? Look at these hands? The hands of a professional man? Not on your sweet life! The hands of a *worker!* I *worked!* These hands toiled from the time I was nine—strike that, *seven.* Every morning up at five, dressing in the pitch black to run down seven flights of stairs, thirteen steps to a flight—I'll never forget them—to run five blocks to the Washington market, unpacking crates for seventy-five cents a week. A dollar if I worked Sundays. Maybe! Based on the goodness of the bosses' hearts. Where was my God then? Where, on those bitter cold mornings, with my hands so blue with frostbite they looked like ladies' gloves, was God? Here! In my heart! Where He was, has been, will always be! Till the day they carry me feet first out of these chambers—knock wood, God grant it's soon. My first murder trial— where are you going? I'm not finished!

ALFRED *(at the door).* You're not going to marry us.

JUDGE. I'm not finished! Don't be a smart punk! (ALFRED *exits.)* You're a know-it-all wise guy smart punk, aren't you? I've seen your kind! *You'll come up before me again!* (PATSY *exits.* CAROL *and* MARJORIE *enter. The* JUDGE *looks at his watch. Very coldly, after a long pause)* He made me very late.

BLACKOUT

SCENE THREE

The lights come up. The Newquist apartment is decorated for a wedding. The guests are gathered around the wedding cake, having their picture taken. Ad-lib laughter on the camera flash. Two gunshots are heard coming from the window. The guests rush to the window.

———

FIRST GUEST. Where is it—

SECOND GUEST. Up there!

THIRD GUEST. Where?

FOURTH GUEST. There!

SECOND GUEST. He's got a rifle!

FIFTH GUEST. Somebody call the police!

SECOND GUEST. He's only a kid!

THIRD GUEST. Kids can kill.

FOURTH GUEST. I think somebody should call the police!

FIFTH GUEST. I think Carol should call the police.

SIXTH GUEST. An old lady got murdered in my building in front of thirty witnesses.

THIRD GUEST. And everybody just stood there, right?

FIRST GUEST. Call the police.

(Guests have begun to drift away from the window. Two more gunshots, which they ignore)

THIRD GUEST. I learned to kill with the edge of a rolled-up newspaper.

FIRST GUEST. I carry a hunting knife.

(The family enters and the guests applaud.)

CAROL *(to FIRST GUEST).* Nothing like a little excitement— *(Loses smile as he watches* PATSY *cross to* ALFRED *and hug him. Scattered cheers, drinks raised in toast)*

MARJORIE *(to SECOND GUEST).* Aren't they an attractive couple? He's so big. It's wonderful to marry a big man. There are so many complications when you marry a man shorter than yourself.

CAROL *(to THIRD GUEST).* I gave them twenty-five hundred. It's just a token.

MARJORIE *(to SECOND GUEST).* And she's so big herself. Many's the time I gave up hope she'd find a man bigger than she is.

CAROL *(to FOURTH GUEST).* Twenty-five hundred—

MARJORIE *(to SECOND GUEST).* Or heavier. It's always amazed me the size of her. I've always been such a little peanut.

ALFRED *(to FIFTH GUEST).* No. My family's not here.

MARJORIE *(to SECOND GUEST).* You'd think almost anybody I'd married would have to be bigger than me; well, that's the way life works out.

KENNY *(to SIXTH GUEST).* I haven't made up my mind. I may go into teaching.

MARJORIE *(to THIRD GUEST).* He's a world-famous photographer, you know. He does collages for *Harper's Bazaar.* *(General laughter.* MARJORIE *looks around to see what she's missing.)* And he's terribly independent. I always thought Patsy was independent, but this time I think she's met her match.

PATSY *(to SECOND GUEST).* Well, the first year at least we'll live at my place.

MARJORIE *(to THIRD GUEST).* No God in the ceremony, he says. Yes, God in the ceremony, she says. Well, you see who won that one.

CAROL. Twenty-five hundred—

ALFRED *(to FIRST GUEST).* No. My family isn't here.

MARJORIE *(to THIRD GUEST).* I would never have the nerve to stand up to her. Her father has never stood up to her. Her brother has never stood up to her. But this time she didn't get her way. *(Gaily)* There's not going to be any God in the ceremony.

KENNY *(to SECOND GUEST).* What I really want to do is direct films.

MARJORIE *(to FOURTH GUEST).* Poor children, these past few weeks they've really had a rough time of it. Nobody wanted to marry them. Even the state of New York has God in the ceremony. They looked everywhere.

ALFRED *(to SECOND GUEST).* No. My family's not here.

MARJORIE *(to FOURTH GUEST).* Ethical Culture told them they didn't have to have God in the ceremony, but they had to have ethical culture in the ceremony.

PATSY *(to FIRST GUEST).* I plan to go on working into my eighth month.

MARJORIE *(to FOURTH GUEST).* Finally, they found this man *(Doorbell. All pause tensely.* CAROL *checks peephole, unlocks door.* DUPAS *enters.)*—there he is now—Alfred found him, really—Reverend Dupas. *(Pronounced Doo-pah)*

ALFRED *(escorting PATSY over to DUPAS).* Henry.

(Mimed greetings and handshakes)

MARJORIE *(to FOURTH GUEST).* He doesn't have much of a handshake, but Alfred says he's very well established in Greenwich Village. He's pastor of the First Existential Church—the one that has that sign in front that says—

DUPAS *(to ALFRED).* My bike wouldn't start up.

MARJORIE *(to* FOURTH GUEST, *quoting).* "Christ died for our sins. Dare we make his martyrdom meaningless by not committing them?"

CAROL *(to* DUPAS, *with feigned good cheer).* No atheists in foxholes these days, eh, Reverend? They've all gone into the ministry.

MARJORIE *(to* FOURTH GUEST). Two Sundays ago he gave a sermon on the moral affirmation in Alfred's photographs.

CAROL. Can I see you for a minute in private, Reverend? *(He leads him off.)*

KENNY *(starts off).* Hey, that's *my* room!

PATSY *(looking after them, puzzled).* They'll be right out.

MARJORIE. They'll be right out, dear.

KENNY. How do they know I don't have to go in there? *(Starts off.* MARJORIE *blocks his way.)* I need a *handkerchief!* *(Tries to get around her but is blocked)* I've got a right to go into my own room!

MARJORIE *(conciliatory).* Why don't you go into the bathroom, dear?

KENNY *(to* PATSY). Why can't you do your things in your own room?

PATSY. Kenny—*(Reaches for him. He turns away.)* Why are you mad at me?

(KENNY *storms away. The phone rings.* KENNY *gets it. Amplified breathing)*

KENNY *(into phone).* Faggot! *(Hangs up. Sound of gunshots. All ignore them.* CAROL *enters with his arm around* DUPAS, *who disengages and crosses to* ALFRED.)

DUPAS *(to* ALFRED). Your father-in-law wants me to sneak the deity into the ceremony.

ALFRED. What did you tell him?

DUPAS. He offered me a lot of money. I told him I'd make my decision in a few minutes. (DUPAS *checks* CAROL's *whereabouts. He is across room being congratulated, scratching his hand and staring intently at* DUPAS.) If it's all right with you I'd like to take the money, and then *not* mention the deity. First Existential can use the money.

ALFRED. He'll stop the check.

DUPAS. I thought he might. Still, it would serve as a lesson . . .

ALFRED. I don't know what to tell you, Henry.

DUPAS. Well, we'll see. *(He crosses over to* CAROL. *They exit.)*

KENNY *(starts off).* I need something out of my bedroom.

MARJORIE. Kenny! *(Blocks his way.* KENNY *tries to charge past her. She intercepts*

and they begin to struggle. *With forced gaiety)* Ha! Ha! Look, everybody! We're dancing!

(CAROL *and* DUPAS *enter—wrestling match breaks up.* CAROL, *hiding triumph, crosses over to* ALFRED.)

CAROL *(slaps him on back).* Nervous, young fellow?

(ALFRED *turns to look for* PATSY. CAROL *takes him by the arm.)* I've been looking forward to this day for a long, long time. It would only take one thing more to make it perfect. (ALFRED *smiles politely, looks for* PATSY. CAROL *squeezes his arm.)* To hear you call me Dad.

ALFRED. I didn't call my own father Dad.

CAROL. What did you call him?

ALFRED. I didn't call him anything. The occasion never came up. *(Amiably)* I could call you Carol.

CAROL *(winces).* Look, if it's this God business that's bothering you, I'm willing to be open-minded. I wouldn't let this on to Marjorie or the kids—*(Winks)* I don't believe in God. But to me it's not a matter of belief in God. It's a matter of belief in institutions. I have great belief in institutions. You couldn't concede me *one* Dad? *(No response)* Not all the time—but every once in a while, "Hello, Dad," "How are you, Dad?"

DUPAS. May we proceed?

CAROL. "You like some of my tobacco, Dad?" (ALFRED *tries to free his arm.* CAROL *hangs on, hisses.)* I want an *answer!* (PATSY *crosses, kisses* CAROL, *takes* ALFRED *away. All take their positions for the ceremony.)*

DUPAS *(in a gentle, folksy manner).* You all know why we're here. There is often so much sham about this business of marriage. Everyone accepts it. Ritual. That's why I was so heartened when Alfred asked me to perform this ceremony. He has certain beliefs that I assume you all know. He is an atheist, which is perfectly all right. Really it is. I happen not to be, but inasmuch as this ceremony connotates an abandonment of ritual in the search for truth, I agreed to perform it. First, let me state frankly to you, Alfred, and to you, Patricia, that of the two hundred marriages I have performed, all but seven have failed. So the odds are not good. We don't like to admit it, especially at the wedding ceremony, but it's in the back of all our minds, isn't it? How long will it last? We all think that, don't we? We don't like to bring it out in the open, but we all think that. Well, I say why *not* bring it out in the open? *Why* does one decide to marry? Social pressure? Boredom? Loneliness? Sexual appeasement? Um, Love? I do not put any of these reasons down. Each, in its own way, is adequate. Each is all right. I married a musician last year who wanted to get married in order to stop masturbating. *(Guests stir)* Please don't be startled. I am not putting it down. That marriage did not work. But the man tried. Now the man is separated, and still masturbating—but he is at peace with himself. He tried society's way. So you see, it was not a mistake, it turned out all right. Last month I married a novelist to a painter, with everyone at the wedding under the influence of hallucinogenic drugs. The drug quickened our mental responses but slowed our physical responses. It took two days to perform the ceremony. But never had the words so much meaning. *That* marriage should last. Still, if it does not—well, that will be all right. For, don't you see, *any* step that one takes is useful, is positive, *has*to be positive, because it is part of life. And negation of the previously taken step is positive. It too is part of life. And in this light, and *only* in this light, should marriage be regarded. As a small, single step. If it works—fine! If it fails —fine! Look elsewhere for satisfaction. Perhaps to more marriages—fine! As many as one likes—fine! To homosexuality—fine! To drug addiction—I won't put it down. Each of these is an *answer*—for *somebody*. For Alfred, today's answer is Patsy. For Patsy, today's answer is Alfred. I won't put them down for that. So what I implore you both, Alfred and Patricia, to dwell on as I ask the questions required by the State of New York in order to legally bind you—sinister phrase, that—is that not only are the *legal* questions I ask you meaningless but so, too, are those *inner* questions you ask of yourselves meaningless. Failing one's partner does *not* matter. Sexual disappointment does *not* matter. Nothing can hurt if we do not see it as hurtful. Nothing can destroy if we will not see it as destructive. It is all part of life. Part of what we are. So now, Alfred. Do you take Patricia as your lawfully wedded wife, to love —whatever *that* means—to honor—but is not dishonor, in a sense, a *form* of honor?— to keep her in sickness, in health, in prosperity and adversity—what nonsense!— Forsaking all others—what a shocking invasion of privacy! Rephrase that to more sensibly say: if you *choose* to have affairs you won't feel guilty about them—as long as you both shall live—or as long as you're not bored with each other?

ALFRED *(numb).* I do.

DUPAS. So. Patricia. Do you take Alfred here as your lawfully wedded husband, to love—that harmful word—can't we more wisely say: communicate?—to honor—meaning, I suppose, you won't cut his balls off. Yet some men like that. And to obey—well, my very first look at you told me you were not the type to obey, so I went through the thesaurus and came up with these alternatives: to be loyal, to show fealty, to show devotion, to answer the helm—general enough, I would think, and still leave plenty of room to dominate, in sickness, in health, and all the rest of that gobbledegook, as long as you both shall live?

PATSY *(struggling to suppress her fury).* I do.

DUPAS. Alfred and Patsy. I know now that whatever you do will be all right. And Patsy's father, Carol Newquist—I've never heard that name on a man before, but I'm sure it's all right—I ask you, sir, not to feel guilt over the $250 check you gave me to mention the deity in this ceremony. What you have done is all right. It is part of what you are, what we all are. And I beg you not to be overly perturbed when I do not mention the deity in this ceremony. Betrayal, too, is all right. It is part of what we all are. And Patsy's brother, Kenneth Newquist, in whose bedroom I spent a few moments earlier this afternoon and whose mother proudly told me the decoration was by your hand *entirely:* I beg of you to feel no shame; homosexuality is all right—

(KENNY *and* CAROL, *followed by* MARJORIE *and* GUESTS, *charge* DUPAS. *Outraged screams and cries as they mob and beat him.* PATSY *staggers off as* DUPAS, *crying, "It's all right, it's all right," is driven out the door.* CAROL *turns on* ALFRED *and begins to slug away at his body.* ALFRED, *unflinching, begins to hum.)*

CURTAIN

ACT TWO

SCENE ONE

Four hours later. The Newquist apartment is strewn with wedding litter. ALFRED *and* CAROL *have not moved since last scene. They stand in half dark,* CAROL *sluggishly pounding away at* ALFRED, *who is humming obviously in a dream world. The phone rings several times.* PATSY *enters, answers phone—amplified breathing.*

———

PATSY *(into phone).* You're all we need today. *(Hangs up. To* CAROL*)* Daddy, you've been at it for hours. Will you please come away from there? *(She helps* CAROL *off.* ALFRED *doesn't move. She reenters, stares a long while at him.)* Mother's hysterical, Daddy's collapsed, and Kenny's disappeared with my wardrobe. I hope you're pleased with your day's work. *(She goes to him.)* You can stop daydreaming, Alfred. Nobody's hitting— *(Stops. Takes off wedding glove. Cocks back fist. Holds, undecided. Distant gunshot)*

ALFRED *(coming out of trance).* I thought it was a very nice ceremony. *(She drops fist.)* A little hokey—

PATSY *(controlling herself).* Alfred? *(Waves hand in front of his face)* What's going to become of us if you go on this way? Weren't you *there?* Weren't you *listening?* I wanted a *wedding!* What in God's name do you use for feelings?

ALFRED. I feel.

PATSY. You don't feel.

ALFRED. Have it your way.

PATSY. There you go again! You won't fight!

ALFRED. You knew I wouldn't fight before you married me. I didn't realize it was a prerequisite.

PATSY. Well, maybe it is. More and more I think it is. If you don't fight you don't feel. If you don't feel you don't love.

ALFRED. I don't know—

PATSY *(finishing his sentence).* What love is. Of course you don't know! Because you don't feel.

ALFRED. I feel what I want to feel.

PATSY *(an impulsive kiss).* It's like kissing white bread. You *don't* feel. Alfred, what is it with you? It gets worse instead of better! I've never had a man do this to me before. It's not just pain you don't feel, you don't feel *pleasure!*

ALFRED. I do feel pleasure.

PATSY. About what?

ALFRED. A lot of things.

PATSY. Name one.

ALFRED *(pause).* My work.

PATSY. Name another.

ALFRED *(pause).* Sleeping.

PATSY. Work and sleeping! That's just great! What about sex?

ALFRED *(pause).* It helps you sleep better.

PATSY. Alfred, do you mean half the things you say? You *must* feel something! *(No response. Snaps her fingers in his face. No response. Holds her head)* Jesus Christ! *(Very tired)* Alfred, why did you marry me?

ALFRED *(pause).* You're comfortable.

PATSY. *I've never made men comfortable!* I'm popular because I make them *uncertain. You don't understand the first thing about me!*

ALFRED. Patsy, you're screaming.

PATSY. *Screaming! You son of a bitch, I'll tear you limb from limb! I married you because I wanted to mold you. I loved the man I wanted to mold you into! But you're not even there! How can I mold you if you're not there?*

ALFRED. Everything I say makes you unhappy. We used to get along so well—

PATSY. Because *I* did all the talking! My God! That's why you were always so quiet! You weren't listening—

ALFRED. Sure I was.

PATSY. Don't lie, Alfred. I used to stare into those eyes of yours, so warm, so complete with understanding—and now I remember where I've seen those eyes since—when my father was hitting you! *That's* the way you look when you're daydreaming!

ALFRED. You don't get hurt that way.

PATSY. Honey, I don't want to hurt you. I want to change you. I want to make you see that there is some value in life, that there is some beauty, some tenderness, some things *worth* reacting to. Some things *worth* feeling *(Snaps fingers in front of his eyes)*—Come back here! I swear, Alfred, *nobody* is going to kill you. *(Distant gunshots)* But you've got to take some *chances* some time! What do you want out of life? Just *survival?*

ALFRED *(nods).* And to take pictures.

PATSY. Of shit? It's not enough! It's not, not, not enough! I'm not going to have a surviving marriage, I'm going to have a flourishing marriage! I'm a *woman!* Or, by Jesus, it's about time I became one. I want a *family!* Oh, Christ, Alfred, this is my wedding day. *(Pause. Regains composure)* I want—I want to be married to a big, strong, protective, vital, virile, self-assured man. Who I can protect and take care of. Alfred, honey, you're the first man I've ever gone to bed with where I didn't feel *he* was a lot more likely to get pregnant than I was. *(Desperate)* You owe me something! I've invested everything I believe in you. You've *got* to let me mold you. *Please let me mold you. (Regains control)* You've got me begging. You've got me whining, begging and crying. I've never behaved like this in my life. Will you look at this? *(Holds out finger)* That's a tear. I never cried in my life.

ALFRED. Me neither.

PATSY. You never cried because you were too terrified of everything to let yourself *feel!* You'd have to learn crying from a manual! Chop onions! I never cried because I was too tough—but I felt *everything.* Every slight, every pressure, every vague competition—but I *fought.* And I *won!* There hasn't been a battle since I was five that I haven't won! And the people I fought were happy that I won! Happy! After a while. Alfred, do you have any idea how many people in this town *worship* me? *(To herself, quickly)* Maybe that's the attraction—you don't worship me. Maybe I'd quit loving you if you *did* worship me. Maybe I'd lose all respect for you if you did all the things I want you to do. *(Thinks about it)* Alfred, you've got to change! *(Regains calm)* Listen . . . I'm not saying I'm better or stronger than you are. It's just that we—you and I—have different temperaments. *(Explodes) And my temperament is better and stronger than yours! (No reaction)* You're a wall! *(Circles around him)* You don't fight! You hardly even listen! Dear God, will somebody please explain to me why I think you're so beautiful? *(Phone rings. She picks it up. Amplified breathing)* Leave me alone! What do you want out of me? Will you please leave me alone?

(ALFRED, *startled by outbursts, takes phone away.* PATSY *buries her head in her hands.)*

ALFRED *(into phone).* She can't talk now.

(Hangs up. Distant siren. PATSY *brings hands down from her face: all life has been drained out of it)*

PATSY *(empty).* Alfred, it's all shit. How come I never noticed before?

ALFRED. Patsy—

PATSY *(empty).* You were right. I'm just dense. *I'm* the one who doesn't feel. It's all terrible. Terrible. Terrible

ALFRED. Come on, Patsy.

PATSY *(empty).* No more reason for *anything.*

ALFRED *(uncomfortably, weakly).* Mrs. Newquist!

PATSY *(flat).* The only true feeling is no feeling. The only way to survive. You're one hundred percent right. Hold my hand. (AL-

FRED *backs away.* PATSY *drops hand.)* I'm sorry. I'm not this weak, really. You know how tough I am. I'll be just as tough again, I promise. I just have to learn to be tough about shit. And I will.

(ALFRED *backs off to a chair.)*

ALFRED. I feel weak.

PATSY *(flat).* Alfred, we can't both feel weak at the same time.

ALFRED. Patsy, you're beginning to get me nervous. You have to listen to me for a minute—

PATSY *(flat).* You're right. I'm wrong. Everything is the way you say. *(Begins to withdraw)* You sit. *(Sits)* You get old. *(Freezes)* You die. *(Stares as if in one of* ALFRED's *daydreams.* ALFRED *goes to her. Touches her head. No reaction. Lifts her arm. It drops limply to her side. He stares at her horrified, then goes into his daydream stare. He slides into the chair opposite hers. Both stare blankly into space. Phone rings. Many rings.* ALFRED *finally rises, crosses to phone, numbly lifts it. Amplified breathing)*

ALFRED *(dazed, into phone).* Thanks. I'm up. *(Hangs up. Stares thoughtfully at* PATSY. *Then, slowly, deliberately)* During Korea—I was in school then—the government couldn't decide whether I was a security risk or not—I wore a beard—so they put a mail check on me. *(Passes a hand in front of her eyes. No reaction)* Every day the mail would come later and later. And it would be bent. Corners torn. Never sealed correctly. Like they didn't give a damn whether I knew they were reading my mail or not. I was more of a militant in those days, so I decided to fight fire with fire. I began writing letters to the guy who was reading my mail. I addressed them to myself, of course, but inside they went something like: "Dear Sir: I am not that different from you. All men are brothers. Tomorrow, instead of reading my mail in that dark, dusty hall, why not bring it upstairs where we can check it out together." I never got an answer. So I wrote a second letter. "Dear Sir: There are no heroes, no villains, no good guys, no bad guys. The world is more complicated than that. Come on up where we can open a couple of beers and talk it all out." *(Checks* PATSY. *No reaction)* Again no answer. So then I wrote: "Dear Sir: I've been thinking too much of my own problems, too little of yours. Yours cannot be a happy task—reading another man's mail. It's dull, unimaginative. A job—and let's not mince words—for a hack. Yet, I wonder—can this be the way you see yourself? Do you see yourself as a hack? Do you see yourself as the office slob? Have you ever *wondered* why they stuck *you* with *this* particular job, instead of others who have *less* seniority? Or was it, do you think, that your supervisor looked around the office to see who he'd stick for the job, saw *you* and said, 'No one will miss *him* for a month!'" *(Checks* PATSY*) That* letter never got delivered to me. So *then* I wrote: "Dear Friend: Just a note to advise you—you may retain my letters as long as you deem fit. Reread them. Study them. Think them out. Who back at the home office is *out to get you?* Who, at this *very* moment, is sitting at *your* desk, reading *your* mail? I do not say this to be cruel, but because I am the only one left you can *trust* —" No answer. *But,* the next day a man, saying he was from the telephone company, showed up—no complaint had been made— to check the phone. Shaky hands. Bloodshot eyes. A small quaver in the voice. And as he dismembered my phone he said, "Look. What nobody understands is that everybody has his job to do. I got my job. In this case it's repairing telephones. I like it or I don't like it, but it's my job. If I had another job— say, for example, with the F.B.I. or someplace, putting in a wiretap, for example, or reading a guy's mail—*like it or don't like it, it would be my job!* Has anyone got the right to *destroy* a man for doing his job?" I wrote one more letter—expressing my deep satisfaction that he and I had at last made contact, and informing him that the next time he came, say, to read the meter, I had valuable information, photostats, recordings, names, and dates, about the conspiracy against him. This letter showed up a week after I mailed it, in a crumpled, grease-stained, and Scotch-taped envelope. The letter itself was torn in half and then clumsily glued together again. In the margin, on the bottom, in large, shaky letters was written the word: "Please!" I wasn't bothered again. It was after this that I began to wonder: If they're *that* unformidable, why bother to fight back? (PATSY *stirs.*) It's very dangerous to challenge a system unless you're completely at peace with the thought that you're not going to miss it when it collapses. Patsy—you can't be the one to change. (PATSY *stares, uncomprehending.*) I'm the one who has to change.

PATSY *(tired).* Alfred, what are you talking about?

ALFRED. When I first met you I remember thinking, this is the most formidable person I have ever known. I don't stand a chance! I'll try to stay the way I am. I'll try desperately! *(Happily)* But I *don't stand a chance!* It's only a matter of time. Very soon now I'll be *(Smiles)—different.* I'll be able to look at half-empty glasses of water and say, This glass isn't half empty. This glass is half *full! You* can't be the one to sell out. *I* was supposed to sell out. *(Stares miserably at the disheveled, slumped-over* PATSY *he's created)* Why doesn't somebody beat me up now? *(Starts off)* I'm going out to Central Park! *(He exits.)*

PATSY *(watches him go; slowly straightens).* Alfred—*come back here!* (A long pause, then ALFRED *enters, uncertain.)* You see what happens when you start fooling around with the rules? *(Recovering, holds out her arms)* It begins with weddings and it ends with—well, there's no telling where it ends. *(More affirmative)* There are reasons for doing things the old way. *(With growing assurance she takes his hands.)* Don't look for trouble and trouble won't look for you. *(Very strong)* I don't say there aren't problems but you have to fight. You are going to fight. *(Squeezes her arms around him)* Starting now. Is that right? *(Pause. Finally he nods.)* And you are going to feel. Starting right now. Is that right? *(Pause. He finally nods.)* I don't want a nod. I want an answer. Say, "Yes, Patsy."

ALFRED. Yes, Patsy.

PATSY. Yes, Patsy, what?

ALFRED. Yes, Patsy—I'm going to feel.

PATSY. Starting when?

ALFRED. Starting as soon as I can manage it.

PATSY. Starting *when?*

ALFRED. Starting now.

PATSY. And what's your first feeling?

ALFRED. It's sort of distant.

PATSY. Don't be ashamed ot it.

ALFRED. It's worship.

PATSY. Of God?

ALFRED. Of you.

PATSY. You're doing fine. *(Kisses him. Puts her arms around him)* My lover. *(Kisses him)* My hero! *(Kisses him.* ALFRED *tentatively responds. Embrace builds.* CAROL *and* MARJORIE *enter. React with warm surprise. They put their arms around each other.)*

MARJORIE. Aren't they an attractive couple?

(Sound of gunshot. Window shatters. Ex-

plosion of blood as PATSY's *hand flies up to her head. She drops.* CAROL *and* MARJORIE *freeze.* ALFRED *stares down at* PATSY, *then melting into his daydream pose, slowly turns away. The street noise is loud through the shattered window.)*

BLACKOUT

SCENE TWO

The Newquist apartment, six months later. There have been changes. Heavy blackout drapes cover the windows. Large photographic blowups of PATSY's *eyes, nose, hair, smiling lips and teeth are hung unframed on the walls, and are in evidence in several two- and three-foot-high stacks on the floor. (These pictures can be premounted on the reverse sides of the molded sections of the walls and pivoted about during the scene change.)*

ALFRED *is bent over a small photo stand, shooting away with a camera, humming to himself. He looks happy. Sporadic gunfire is heard in the background. He pays no attention. Doorbell.* ALFRED *takes a quick last look at the work on the stand, goes to the door, detouring past the couch to pick up a long cardboard carton and shove it out of sight under the couch. He has the beginnings of a black eye.*

——

ALFRED. One minute. *(He checks through keyhole and unlocks door. There are now four different kinds of locks and bolts on door, including a police bar.)* One more minute. *(Opens door)* Hi, Dad!

CAROL *(enters carrying bulging brief case).* It's murder out there.

*(*ALFRED *tries to relieve him of brief case.* CAROL *brusquely pushes him aside.)*

ALFRED Hey, Dad, you're limping!

CAROL *(shouts). How many times have I told you not to call me Dad!*

ALFRED. I can't call you "Dad." I can't call you "Carol." What can I call you? "Dear"?

(Long exchange of stares, ALFRED's *good-humored,* CAROL's *sullen)*

CAROL. Call me "Mr. Newquist."

ALFRED. You're just in a bad mood, Dad. Let me fix you a drink. *(Crosses to bar)*

CAROL *(sits).* I don't want you to fix me—Bourbon.

ALFRED *(serving drink).* The family that drinks together sinks together.

CAROL *(drinks).* Maybe I'd feel better if you turned on the air conditioner. It blots out the sound of the shooting. Agh, the hell with it. It's here to stay. I might as well get used to it. *(Conspiratorial)* I dropped by police headquarters this afternoon. That's why I'm late.

ALFRED. Are you late?

CAROL *(annoyed). Yes, I'm late!* I'm four hours late. I told you I'd be finished with my deliveries at one. Any calls?

ALFRED. The Breather, once or twice. He's picking up the pace again.

CAROL *(mutters).* Asthmatic bastard!

ALFRED. I never told you, but the day after Patsy died he rang up. I went a little crazy—I started screaming, "Didn't you hear the news? No need to call any more! Patsy's dead!" In no more than ten seconds, he called back. And he *spoke!* He said, "I don't know what to say. I'm terribly sorry." And then before hanging up he said, "What can we do? The world's gone crazy!" Not another breath out of him until this week. In mourning, I suppose.

CAROL. You sure it's the same one?

ALFRED. You think we're on a mailing list? God, I *hope* it's the same one.

CAROL. This damned business! *(Conspiratorial)* Keep this under your hat, but I paid an unexpected call on police headquarters this afternoon.

ALFRED. I'm surprised they didn't shoot you.

CAROL. They did shoot me. *(Rubs his leg)* It was my own damned fault. I didn't give the password. *(Hands empty glass to* ALFRED, *who pours drink)* I feel sorry for those poor bastards. I know a lot of them by their first names. I call them Jimmy, and Mac and Phil. They call me Carol. *(Quickly)* It sounds different when *they* say it. I had a fifteen-minute talk with Lieutenant Practice. Busy as hell but he found fifteen minutes to talk to me. He's convinced they're closing in on the conspiracy.

ALFRED. What conspiracy?

CAROL. Three hundred and forty-five unsolved murders in six months. There's got to be a conspiracy! *(*ALFRED *shrugs.)* There's *got* to be some logic behind all this. Any other calls?

ALFRED. You mean orders? No.

CAROL. I have to admit to you these new

pictures are really catching on! Fifty orders of Patsy Number Seven last week, ten orders so far this week of Patsy Number Eight and Fifteen, and five orders from an uptown gallery for the entire Patsy series. *(Thickly)* We wouldn't have come through this without you, Alfred.

ALFRED *(shrugs)*. I had to do *something* after I abandoned my shit series.

CAROL *(emotional)*. But you didn't have to put *me* to work. Nobody asked. *(Suddenly defensive) I* didn't ask—

ALFRED. You're a top-notch salesman, Dad.

CAROL. I'm an order taker and a messenger boy. But when I get back on my feet—

ALFRED. It'll be no time.

CAROL. Who knows if they'll even want me back at the office. Six months— *(Shakes his head)* You've been very good—to us.

ALFRED. Forget it.

CAROL *(nods)*. I'll do that. *(A pained sigh)* I wish I resented you less.

ALFRED. Keep up the fight, tiger.

CAROL *(sadly)*. Patsy used to call me tiger. Everything you say these days reminds me of Patsy.

ALFRED *(thoughtful, a little sad)*. I owe Patsy a lot. *(Cheerful again)* Why shouldn't I talk like her?

CAROL. Just as long as you don't dress like her. Where's Kenny?

ALFRED. In her closet.

CAROL. Little son of a bitch! Christ, I hope it's only a phase. I don't see where that Doctor Harm is helping any—

ALFRED. Doctor Good.

CAROL. Yeah? Well, I suppose he must be good. Otherwise he'd take a hell of a kidding. *(Depressed)* Agh—I don't understand anything any more. You know how I get through the day?—don't say a word of this to Marjorie—in planned segments. I get up in the morning and I think, Okay, a sniper didn't get me for breakfast, let's see if I can go for my morning walk without being mugged. Okay, I finished my walk, let's see if I can make it back home without having a brick dropped on my head from the top of a building. Okay, I'm safe in the lobby, let's see if I can go up in the elevator without getting a knife in my ribs. Okay, I made it to the front door, let's see if I can open it without finding burglars in the hall. Okay, I made it to the hall, let's see if I can walk into the living room and not find the rest of my family dead. *This goddamned city!*

ALFRED *(with sympathy)*. Got to fight, tiger.

CAROL. You do enough fighting for one family. Where'd you get that eye? *(He indicates* ALFRED*'s mouse.)*

ALFRED. Some kid was staring at me in the park. I hit him.

CAROL *(tired)*. Another fight?

ALFRED. What could I do? The little bastard was *staring* at me! (CAROL *turns away in disgust. Placating)* I beat the crap out of him —(CAROL *reluctantly smiles.* ALFRED *starts to spar with him.)* Let's go a couple of quick ones, tiger.

CAROL *(retreating)*. Come now. Cut it out. Cut it out.

ALFRED *(sparring)*. Pow! Pow! Pow! Boy if Patsy could have only been there! *(Mimes a wicked kick)* And she said I didn't feel. Every time I get into one of these things, I think of her—I think of her alive and me coming home weary, every night—you know, after I beat somebody up, and she meets me at the door, looking up at me with eyes full of pride, and she takes my swollen fists in her hands, and she kisses my knuckles—what a dream. Why is it we only learn when it's too late? *(Spars)* Pow! Pow! It was my fourth fight this week. I suppose all that euphoria takes something out of you. Anyhow, I got very faint, so I sat down on a park bench to rest—and I found *this* lying there. *(He holds up the* Daily News.)*

CAROL *(reading.)* "Hippie Minister Slain at Church Happening." They're sure giving the son of a bitch a hell of a lot of free publicity!

ALFRED. It wasn't so much the story that interested me. I don't have the patience for facts, or any of that nonsense any more. What interested me was *(Shows* CAROL *newspaper)* this photograph of the body—what does it look like?

CAROL. That son of a bitch. With his eyes closed.

ALFRED *(excited)*. No! Look closer! *(He raises newspaper to* CAROL*'s face.)*

CAROL. What do I want to look for? This is the silliest—

ALFRED. Don't you see the dots?

CAROL. What dots?

ALFRED. Here! The little black dots that make up the photograph. Use your eyes, Dad!

CAROL *(pushes paper away)*. Okay. I see them! So what!

ALFRED. Keep staring at them. *(Raises paper closer to* CAROL*'s face)* You see how they slowly begin to move? *(Takes paper away from* CAROL*)* I was sitting on the park bench looking at this photograph of the body and the little black dots began to break apart—they began detaching themselves from the body—the dots that make up his eyes—the little black dots that make up his mouth—and the top of his head—they just lifted off his body—and broke apart. Until it wasn't the body of Henry Dupas I was staring at, but millions of little black dots coming at me until I thought I was going to be sucked in alive. I panicked! I wanted to close off! But then I thought, Wait a minute, that's the *old* you, the *pre-Patsy* you. So I let go and I was swallowed. Into a free-floating constellation of dots. Fantastic! I swung my eyes away from the photograph—I looked up at a tree. Do you know how many trillions of dots there are in one Central Park tree? And then the dots that made up the tree merged with the dots that made up the sky merged with the dots that made up the park bench and the grass and the dirt path and the three colored kids walking toward me carrying bicycle chains. Do you know the wild arrangement of dots that's made every time you punch somebody out? Those poor kids must've thought I was crazy—humming as I beat their heads against the sidewalk. *(Offstage muffled shot)* I've been studying this newspaper for hours now trying to figure out a way of decomposing everything into dots.

CAROL. I don't know why you want to fool around. We're doing *extremely* well with our current line.

ALFRED. There gets to be something ultimately stifling about taking photographs of old photographs.

CAROL *(reasonably).* You enlarge them.

ALFRED. It's limited! I want to do *life!* If I could somehow make people see themselves as trillions upon trillions of free-wheeling, interchanging dots—*(Loses himself in thought.* CAROL *shakes his head, says nothing. Doorbell.* ALFRED *puts an arm on* CAROL's *shoulder and goes to door.)* One minute. *(Looks through peephole. Begins the process of unlocking the door)* One more minute.

MARJORIE *(enters, flushed, carrying leaking shopping bag).* Will you look at this mess? They shot a hole in my shopping bag.

CAROL *(stricken).* You could have been killed!

MARJORIE *(annoyed).* I get shot at every day. We all do, Carol. Don't make more of it

than it is. *(To* ALFRED*)* I saw that nice Lieutenant Practice in the lobby. He looks simply awful. I invited him up for coffee just as soon as he gets finished investigating the new murder.

CAROL. What new murder?

MARJORIE *(bored).* I don't know. It's in the other wing.

*(*ALFRED *reaches under couch and slides out long carton he concealed at start of scene. It is not the box he intended to pull out. He slides it back and reaches for a smaller box, which he hands to* MARJORIE*.)*

ALFRED. Mom.

MARJORIE *(opens box).* Alfred. Oh, Alfred! *(Removes flowers)* Aren't they beautiful! Look, Carol, they're flowers! *(Clutches them to her. Cries)* I'm sorry—there is so little thought left of giving today that I've forgotten how to receive. *(Drops flowers. Rushes offstage, holding her hands to her face. Offstage)* Kenny! Let me in there!

(Offstage toilet flush, door slams. KENNY *camps in, wearing dark glasses, carrying* Vogue. CAROL, *who cannot look at him, exits.* KENNY *sees flowers on floor. He picks them up.)*

ALFRED. You want 'em?

KENNY *(drops flowers).* What do I want with your fruity flowers?

*(*ALFRED *returns to camera stand.* MARJORIE *enters.)*

MARJORIE *(staring down at flowers).* Alfred, you are a love. *(*ALFRED, *distracted, waves from camera stand.)* When I was twelve-and-a-half my mother and father would cart the whole pack of us out to the country and we would always picnic near the flowers. There were so many more flowers in those days. We'd pick every last one and bring it back to the city. *(To* KENNY *as she stoops for flowers)* No one does the cleaning up around here except me. *(Doorbell.* KENNY *starts for door.)* I'll get it. *(*KENNY *spots protruding edge of the carton under the couch.)* Who is it? Will you step a little closer and turn your face into the light, please? *(She checks peephole, starts to unlock door.* KENNY *slides out carton, is about to lift lid.)*

ALFRED *(still peering into the camera on stand).* That's—not—a—good—idea—

KENNY *(whirls).* Who died and made you boss? *(Shot splinters window near* KENNY's *head just as* LIEUTENANT PRACTICE *enters.* KENNY *shakes fist at window, screams.)* Fags!

MARJORIE *(to* PRACTICE*).* You'll have to pardon the mess.

CAROL *(enters, glances over to* KENNY *at window, hurries over to* PRACTICE, *shakes his hand).* Well, well, well. This is an unexpected pleasure. Alfred, look who's decided to pay us a visit. Lieutenant Practice! (ALFRED, *at work, gives a perfunctory wave of hand.* CAROL *whispers.)* He's working. Goes on day and night. It's no accident he's successful.

PRACTICE. And I'm not. Is that it?

CAROL *(takes his arm).* I didn't mean that. You're making great strides. Nobody expects very much anyway. (PRACTICE *draws arm away.)* Nobody's complaining.

MARJORIE *(cheerful).* We certainly haven't complained. And if anyone has a right to—

PRACTICE *(sad).* Can I please have a glass of milk, Mrs. Newquist? *(He sits down.)*

MARJORIE. Of course, dear.

PRACTICE. And a cookie. Jeez, I'm depressed. There's got to be some logical explanation to all of this.

(MARJORIE *exits.)*

CAROL. You've got nothing to be ashamed of. You'll figure it out.

PRACTICE *(hands* CAROL *envelope).* I really stopped by to return this. I don't know what got into me this afternoon.

CAROL *(looks nervously around).* It's all right. It's yours! Forget it!

PRACTICE. I *can't* accept a $250 check. I know your heart was in the right place, Mr. Newquist, but believe me, it's not gonna make us find your daughter's murderer any quicker.

CAROL. Keep it! Keep it! You never can tell—

MARJORIE *(enters with glass of milk).* Drink this. You'll feel better. Carol, are you giving money away again? You know, Lieutenant, every time we pass a policeman he hands him five dollars.

CAROL. I just want the boys on the beat to know somebody still has faith in them.

PRACTICE *(drinks).* I needed this. (ALFRED *slides carton back under couch;* KENNY *watches with interest.* PRACTICE *examines hand holding glass. It has a tremor.)* I wasn't like this when I met you six months ago, was I? Wasn't I a lot more self-confident? Jeez, the way I used to enter the scene of a crime! Like I owned the goddamned world! Can you put a little Scotch in this milk, please? And a piece of cheese on this cookie? There's going to be a shake-up, you know. When there are three hundred and forty-five murders and none of them get solved. *(Angry)* Somebody

has to be elected fall guy! *(Accepts drink)* Thank you. Maybe a piece of ice like a good fellow. *(Hands drink back)* Somewhere there's a logical pattern to this whole business. There *has* to be. *(Accepts cookie)* I didn't ask for butter on the cookie, just cheese. *(Hands cookie back)* Thank you. And these damned vigilante groups—they're not helping matters. Black against white. White against black. What ever became of human dignity? *(Accepts drink)* Oh, for Christ sakes, only *one* piece of ice? Let's get it right, huh? Say, what kind of cheese is this? Sharp cheddar? You ought to know by now with my stomach I can't take sharp cheddar! Come on! *Will you shape up? (Reflective)* Sooner or later there's a pattern. Sooner or later everything falls into place. I believe that. If I didn't believe that I wouldn't want to wake up to see the sun tomorrow morning. (CAROL *and* MARJORIE *scrambling from different directions with drink and cheese)* Is *this* what I asked for? Goddamnit, *I want some cooperation! (A shot—milk glass explodes in his hand. All except* PRACTICE *stare toward window. He stares at remnant of glass in his hand)* Every crime has its own pattern of logic. Everything has an order. If we can't find that order it's not because it doesn't exist, but only because we've incorrectly observed some vital piece of evidence. Let us examine the evidence. *(Places glass in handkerchief, handkerchief in pocket)* Number one. In the last six months three hundred and forty-five homicides have been committed in this city. The victims have ranged variously in sex, age, social status, and color. Number two. In none of the three hundred and forty-five homicides have we been able to establish motive. Number three. All three hundred and forty-five homicides remain listed on our books as unsolved. So much for the evidence. A subtle pattern begins to emerge. What is this pattern? What is it that each of these three hundred and forty-five homicides have in common? They have in common three things: a) that they have nothing in common; b) that they have no motive; c) that, consequently, they remain unsolved. The pattern becomes clearer. Orthodox police procedure dictates that the basic question you ask in all such investigations is: 1) who has the most to gain? What could possibly be the single unifying motive behind three hundred and forty-five unconnected homicides? When a case does not gel it is often not because we lack the necessary facts, but because we have observed our facts incorrectly. In each of these three hundred and forty-five homicides we observed our facts incorrectly. Following normal routine we looked for a cause. And we could find no cause. Had we looked for effect we would have had our answer that much sooner. What is the effect of three hundred and forty-five unsolved homicide cases? The effect is loss of faith in law-enforcement personnel. That is our motive. The pattern is complete. We are involved here in a far-reaching conspiracy to undermine respect for our basic beliefs and most sacred institutions. Who is behind this conspiracy? Once again ask the question: Who has the most to gain? People in high places. Their names would astound you. People in low places. Concealing their activities beneath a cloak of poverty. People in all walks of life. Left wing and right wing. Black and white. Students and scholars. A conspiracy of such ominous proportions that we may not know the whole truth in our lifetime, and we will never be able to reveal all the facts. We are readying mass arrests. *(Rises to leave)* I'm going to try my best to see that you people get every possible break. If there is any information you wish to volunteer at this time it will be held in the strictest confidence. *(Waits for response. There is none. Crosses to door and opens it)* I strongly advise against any of you trying to leave town. *(Quickly exits)*

CAROL *(gradually exploding)*. What's left? What's there left? I'm a reasonable man. Just explain to me what I have left to believe in. I swear to God the tide's rising! Two hundred and fifty dollars. Gimme, gimme. We need honest cops! People just aren't being protected any more! We need a revival of honor. And trust! We need the Army! We need a giant fence around every block in the city. An electrically charged fence. And everyone who wants to leave the block has to have a pass. And a haircut. And can't talk with a filthy mouth! We need respect for a man's reputation. TV cameras! That's what we need! In every building lobby, in every elevator, in every apartment, in every room. Public servants who *are* public servants! And if they catch you doing anything funny—to yourself, or anybody—they break down the door and beat the living— A return to common sense! We have to have lobotomies for anyone who earns less than ten thousand a year. I don't like it but it's an emergency. Our side needs

weapons too. Is it fair that they should have all the weapons? We've got to train ourselves! And steel ourselves! It's freedom I'm talking about! There's a fox loose in the chicken coop! *Kill him!* I want my *freedom! (He collapses.)*

ALFRED. Let's get him inside.

(ALFRED *and* MARJORIE *carry* CAROL *off.* KENNY *watches after them, quickly crosses to box, slides it out and lifts lid as* MARJORIE *enters.* KENNY *slams down lid.* MARJORIE *grabs bottle from bar and exits.* KENNY *lifts rifle out of box, goes to window, parts curtain slightly, aims—*ALFRED *enters.* KENNY, *startled, holds rifle out to him.)*

KENNY. I thought it was more flowers.

ALFRED. Use it.

KENNY. What do I want to use it for? I've only been in analysis four months. I've never fired one of these in my life.

ALFRED. Me too.

KENNY *(suspicious)*. Why'd you get it?

ALFRED *(shrugs)*. It was on sale. *(Stares at rifle in* KENNY's *hands. Goes to door, relocks it. To* KENNY) Put it away—(KENNY *begins to)* No. (ALFRED *crosses to* KENNY, *takes rifle, studies it.)* You notice, if you stare at it long enough it breaks into dots?

KENNY *(studies rifle)*. No—

ALFRED *(turns rifle in his hand)*. Trillions of dots—*(Pulls trigger. A loud click)* It's not loaded. *(Puts it down)*

KENNY. Why don't you load it?

ALFRED. I don't know how. *(Hands rifle to* KENNY, *who backs away from it)*

KENNY *(shakes his head)*. The Army rejected me four times. The fifth time they said if I ever came around again they'd have me arrested. *(Reaches into box. Takes out instruction booklet, turns page, reads)* "Nomenclature." *(Turns page)* "Trigger housing group." *(Turns page)* "To load: hold the weapon by the forearm of the stock with left hand. Rotate the safety to its 'on' position. Lock the bolt open. With right hand insert the magazine into the magazine opening and push up."

MARJORIE *(enters; looks over* ALFRED's *shoulder as he struggles to insert magazine clip)*. I don't know about these things, dear, but I found the best way to deal with the unfamiliar is to think things back to their source. *(She takes rifle out of his hands.)* Now, it would seem to me that *this* goes in— *(Struggles.* CAROL *enters. Observes)* Damn it! They must have given you the wrong— *(CAROL *takes rifle out of her hands, expertly loads it, tosses it to* ALFRED. MARJORIE *is very impressed.) Dear!*

ALFRED *(hands rifle back to* CAROL*)*. Go on, Dad. You loaded it. You go first.

CAROL *(solemnly hands rifle back)*. It's yours.

KENNY. Where'd you learn that, Dad? It's a trick, right?

(CAROL stares scornfully at KENNY, *takes rifle.* ALFRED *parts curtains.)*

ALFRED. Can you see well enough?

(CAROL aims, fires.)

KENNY. I think you got somebody.

MARJORIE. Let me see! I never can see! *(ALFRED boosts her)* Yes! Yes! Somebody's lying there!

CAROL *(to* ALFRED*)*. Why don't you try *your* luck? *(Hands over rifle)*

ALFRED *(hands rifle to* KENNY*)*. You first, Kenny.

KENNY. Gee.

ALFRED *(reassuring)*. I'll go right after you.

(KENNY quickly gets up with rifle. Fires out window)

CAROL. Miss!

KENNY. You made me nervous! You were *looking!*

CAROL *(takes rifle)*. It's Alfred's turn.

KENNY. No fair! You shook my arm.

ALFRED. Let him have another shot.

(KENNY aims carefully, fires.)

CAROL *(looking into street; very proud)*. Son of a bitch!

MARJORIE *(hugs him)*. You did it! You did it!

(CAROL reloads, hands rifle to ALFRED.*)*

KENNY *(cool, manly)*. Dad and I got *our* two.

(CAROL puts his arm around KENNY's *shoulder.* ALFRED *aims out window, fires.)*

CAROL. You know who I think he got?

MARJORIE. Lieutenant Practice!

(All jump up and down in self-congratulations—ad-lib shouts, Texas yells. ALFRED, CAROL, *and* KENNY *in unison; none of the following is intelligible.)*

ALFRED. Fantastic! What a picture! Unbelievable! Fantastic! What a picture!

CAROL. Some hell of a team, eh, boys! Now we're moving! Now we'll show 'em! Show the whole Goddamn world!

KENNY. Son of a bitch! Bastard! See me, Dad? Goddamn! Son of a bitch! Goddamn! See me, Alfred?

(During all this MARJORIE *has made a sprightly exit, instantly reentering, wheeling serving cart. She lights candles on dining-room table.)*

MARJORIE. Come an' get it!

(The others, wrestling, horsing around, move slowly toward table.)

MARJORIE. Boys!

(Amidst great noise, bustle, serving of drinks, they finally sit. More ad-lib cries, friendly shoving)

ALFRED *(over the others)*. Hey, how about Mom trying her luck after dinner?

(Cheers, ad-lib agreement)

MARJORIE *(serving)*. It's so nice to have my family laughing again. You know, for a while I was really worried.

(General merriment)

CURTAIN

THE BOYS IN THE BAND

Mart Crowley

For
HOWARD JEFFREY
and
DOUGLAS MURRAY

First presented on the New York stage by Richard Barr and Charles Woodward, Jr., at Theatre Four on April 14, 1968, with the following cast:

MICHAEL	Kenneth Nelson	BERNARD	Reuben Greene
DONALD	Frederick Combs	COWBOY	Robert La Tourneaux
EMORY	Cliff Gorman	HAROLD	Leonard Frey
LARRY	Keith Prentice	ALAN	Peter White
HANK	Laurence Luckinbill		

Directed by Robert Moore
Designed by Peter Harvey

The play is divided into two acts. The action is continuous and occurs one evening within the time necessary to perform the script.

Quite a number of the plays in this volume represent breakthroughs in the American theatre, but perhaps few so marked as Mart Crowley's *The Boys in the Band*. For years homosexuality had been delicately skirted in the theatre, in plays such as *The Green Bay Tree* or Robert Anderson's considerable Broadway hit, *Tea and Sympathy*. Some critics—Stanley Kauffmann for example, who expressed his view in a vigorous Sunday article in the *New York Times*—also felt that certain homosexual playwrights were in their plays translating their own sexual connotations and experiences into heterosexual terms, often with unsatisfactory results. Then, on April 14, 1968, came *The Boys in the Band*.

A few years later Gay Liberationists (as militant workers for homosexual rights were called) were to develop a phrase "coming out of the closet," indicating the process by which the secret homosexual (the so-called "closet queen") would openly acknowledge his or her sexual inclinations. With *The Boys in the Band* homosexual New York theatre came out of the closet—and sensationally.

The author Mart Crowley was born on August 21, 1935, in Vicksburg, Mississippi. His father owned a pool hall, and the young Crowley was brought up as a Catholic. After high school in Vicksburg he went to Washington, D.C., where he attended Catholic University. Having scripted a few TV shows, he became a member of Theatre 1968's Playwrights Unit. It was for this showcase organization that a first version of *The Boys in the Band* was produced.

The Boys in the Band was one of Off-Broadway's biggest ever hits. It closed on September 6, 1970, after precisely one thousand performances. But this was, in a sense, only a beginning to the story. Road companies took it across the country, and it appeared, with the original New York cast, in London's West End, and the same cast went on to make the successful, and almost equally controversial, movie. *The Boys in the Band* must have been a difficult act to follow. Certainly Mr. Crowley found it so.

In 1970 his second play, *Remote Asylum,* was given by the Center Theater Group of Los Angeles but did not find much favor with the local critics and did not proceed farther. On October 16, 1973, Mr. Crowley's latest play, *A Breeze from the Gulf,* was staged Off Broadway. Seemingly partly autobiographical in content, the play described an adolescent growing up into manhood faced with two difficult and warring parents. Much of the writing proved exceptionally sharp, and Mr. Crowley's enormous ability to make his stage alive with people was as evident here as it was in *The Boys in the Band*. But weak construction and a certain monotony of tone resulted in very mixed reviews from the New York critics.

Nevertheless, Mr. Crowley seems to be a natural playwright. The dialogue in *The Boys in the Band* snaps, crackles, and pops, like a new and yeasty brand of breakfast cereal. And the characters are completely real and seemingly embedded in their bitchy kind of humanity. For the first time the critics were faced with witty dialogue they could not possibly repeat in a family newspaper. The critics of both *Time* and *Newsweek* vied with one another to get into print the line "Well, one thing you can say for masturbation—you certainly don't have to look your best," but both, understandably, lost.

The play was an enormous success in many respects, but it did offend some members of the homosexual community. In a sense the play does offer a heterosexually reassuring view of homosexuality—every homosexual is depicted as morally lame, unhappy, and, fundamentally, sick. But one cannot deny the cute and camp remarks that spin across the stage iridescent and deadly, or the considerable dramatic power of the piece. *The Boys in the Band* is admittedly a very funny play, but it is also among the most powerful Broadway melodramas of recent times.

CHARACTERS

MICHAEL	Thirty, average face, smartly groomed
DONALD	Twenty-eight, medium blond, wholesome American good looks
EMORY	Thirty-three, small, frail, very plain
LARRY	Twenty-nine, extremely handsome
HANK	Thirty-two, tall, solid, athletic, attractive
BERNARD	Twenty-eight, Negro, nice-looking
COWBOY	Twenty-two, light blond, muscle-bound, too pretty
HAROLD	Thirty-two, dark, lean, strong limbs, unusual Semitic face
ALAN	Thirty, aristocratic Anglo-Saxon features

ACT ONE

A smartly appointed duplex apartment in the East Fifties, New York, consisting of a living room and, on a higher level, a bedroom. Bossa nova music blasts from a phonograph.

MICHAEL, *wearing a robe, enters from the kitchen, carrying some liquor bottles. He crosses to set them on a bar, looks to see if the room is in order, moves toward the stairs to the bedroom level, doing a few improvised dance steps en route. In the bedroom, he crosses before a mirror, studies his hair—sighs. He picks up comb and a hair drier, goes to work.*

The downstairs front-door buzzer sounds. A beat. MICHAEL *stops, listens, turns off the drier. More buzzing.* MICHAEL *quickly goes to the living room, turns off the music, opens the door to reveal* DONALD, *dressed in khakis and a Lacoste shirt, carrying an airline zipper bag.*

————

MICHAEL. Donald! You're about a day and a half early!

DONALD *(enters)*. The doctor canceled!

MICHAEL. Canceled! How'd you get inside?

DONALD. The street door was open.

MICHAEL. You wanna drink?

DONALD *(going to bedroom to deposit his bag)*. Not until I've had my shower. I want something to work out today—I want to try to relax and enjoy *something*.

MICHAEL. You in a blue funk because of the doctor?

DONALD *(returning)*. Christ, no. I was depressed long before I got *there*.

MICHAEL. Why'd the prick cancel?

DONALD. A virus or something. He looked awful.

MICHAEL *(holding up a shopping bag)*. Well, this'll pick you up. I went shopping today and bought all kind of goodies. Sandalwood soap . . .

DONALD *(removing his socks and shoes)*. I feel better already.

MICHAEL *(producing articles)*. . . . Your very own toothbrush because I'm sick to death of your using mine.

DONALD. How do you think *I* feel.

MICHAEL. You've had worse things in your mouth. *(Holds up a cylindrical can)* And, also for you . . . something called "Control." Notice nowhere is it called hair spray—just simply "Control." And the words "For Men" are written about thirty-seven times all over the goddamn can!

DONALD. It's called Butch Assurance.

MICHAEL. Well, it's *still* hair spray—no matter if they call it *"Balls"!* *(DONALD laughs.)* It's all going on your very own shelf, which is to be labeled: Donald's Saturday Night Douche Kit. By the way, are you spending the night?

DONALD. Nope. I'm driving back. I still get very itchy when I'm in this town too long. I'm not that well yet.

MICHAEL. That's what you say every weekend.

DONALD. Maybe after about ten more years of analysis I'll be able to stay one night.

MICHAEL. Maybe after about ten more years of analysis you'll be able to move back to town permanently.

DONALD. If I live that long.

MICHAEL. You will. If you don't kill yourself on the Long Island Expressway some early Sunday morning. I'll never know how you can tank up on martinis and make it back to the Hamptons in one piece.

DONALD. Believe me, it's easier than getting here. Ever had an anxiety attack at sixty miles an hour? Well, tonight I was beside myself to get to the doctor—and just as I finally make it, rush in, throw myself on the couch, and vomit out how depressed I am, he says, "Donald, I have to cancel tonight—I'm just too sick."

MICHAEL. Why didn't you tell him you're sicker than he is.

DONALD. He already knows *that.* (DON-

ALD *goes to the bedroom, drops his shoes and socks.* MICHAEL *follows.)*

MICHAEL. Why didn't the prick call you and cancel. Suppose you'd driven all this way for nothing.

DONALD *(removing his shirt).* Why do you keep calling him a prick?

MICHAEL. Whoever heard of an analyst having a session with a patient for two hours on Saturday evening?

DONALD. He simply prefers to take Mondays off.

MICHAEL. Works late on Saturday and takes Monday off—what is he, a psychiatrist or a hairdresser?

DONALD. Actually, he's both. He shrinks my head and combs me out. *(Lies on the bed)* Besides, I had to come in town to a birthday party anyway. Right?

MICHAEL. You had to remind me. If there's one thing I'm not ready for, it's five screaming queens singing Happy Birthday.

DONALD. Who's coming?

MICHAEL. They're really all Harold's friends. It's *his* birthday and I want everything to be just the way he'd want it. I don't want to have to listen to him kvetch about how nobody ever does anything for anybody but themselves.

DONALD. Himself.

MICHAEL. Himself. I think you know everybody anyway—they're the same old tired fairies you've seen around since the day one. Actually, there'll be seven, counting Harold and you and me.

DONALD. Are you calling me a screaming queen or a tired fairy?

MICHAEL. Oh, I beg your pardon—six tired screaming fairy queens and one anxious queer.

DONALD. You don't think Harold'll mind my being here, do you? Technically, I'm *your* friend, not his.

MICHAEL. If she doesn't like it, she can twirl on it. Listen, I'll be out of your way in just a second. I've only got one more thing to do.

DONALD. Surgery, so early in the evening?

MICHAEL. Sunt! That's French, with a cedilla. *(Gives him a crooked third finger, goes to mirror)* I've just got to comb my hair for the thirty-seventh time. Hair—that's singular. My hair, without exaggeration, is clearly falling on the floor. And *fast,* baby!

DONALD. You're totally paranoid. You've got plenty of hair.

MICHAEL. What you see before you is a masterpiece of deception. My hairline starts about here. *(Indicates his crown)* All this is just tortured forward.

DONALD. Well, I hope, for your sake, no strong wind comes up.

MICHAEL. If one does, I'll be in terrible trouble. I will then have a bald head and shoulder-length fringe. *(Runs his fingers through his hair, holds it away from his scalp, dips the top of his head so that* DONALD *can see.* DONALD *is silent.)* Not good, huh?

DONALD. Not the best.

MICHAEL. It's called, "getting old." Ah, life is such a grand design—spring, summer, fall, winter, death. Who*ever* could have thought it up?

DONALD. No one *we* know, that's for sure.

MICHAEL *(turns to study himself in the mirror, sighs).* Well, one thing you can say for masturbation . . . you certainly don't have to look your best. *(Slips out of the robe, flings it at* DONALD; DONALD *laughs, takes the robe, exits to the bath.* MICHAEL *takes a sweater out of a chest, pulls it on.)*

MICHAEL. What are you so depressed about? I mean, other than the usual *everything. (A beat)*

DONALD *(reluctantly).* I really don't want to get into it.

MICHAEL. Well, if you're not going to tell me, how can we have a conversation *in depth* —a warm, rewarding, meaningful friendship?

DONALD. Up yours!

MICHAEL *(Southern accent).* Why, Cap'n Butler, how you talk!

(Pause. DONALD *appears in the doorway holding a glass of water and a small bottle of pills.* MICHAEL *looks up.)*

DONALD. It's just that today I finally realized that I was *raised* to be a failure. I was *groomed* for it. *(A beat)*

MICHAEL. You know, there was a time when you could have said that to me and I wouldn't have known what the hell you were talking about.

DONALD *(takes some pills).* Naturally, it all goes back to Evelyn and Walt.

MICHAEL. Naturally. When doesn't it go back to Mom and Pop. Unfortunately, we all had an Evelyn and a Walt. The crumbs! Don't you love that word—crumb? Oh, I love it! It's a real Barbara Stanwyck word. *(A la Stanwyck's frozen-lipped Brooklyn accent)* "Cau'll me a keab, you kr-rumm."

DONALD. Well, I see all vestiges of sanity

for this evening are now officially shot to hell.

MICHAEL. Oh, Donald, you're so serious tonight! You're fun-starved, baby, and I'm eating for two!

(Sings)

"Forget your troubles, c'mon get happy!
You better chase all your blues away.
Shout, 'Hallelujah!' c'mon get happy . . . "

(Sees DONALD *isn't buying it)*—what's more boring than a queen doing a Judy Garland imitation?

DONALD. A queen doing a Bette Davis imitation.

MICHAEL. Meanwhile—back at the Evelyn and Walt Syndrome.

DONALD. America's Square Peg and America's Round Hole.

MICHAEL. Christ, how sick analysts must get of hearing how mommy and daddy made their darlin' into a fairy.

DONALD. It's beyond just that now. Today I finally began to see how some of the other pieces of the puzzle relate to them—like why I never finished anything I started in my life . . . my neurotic compulsion to not succeed. I've realized it was always when I failed that Evelyn loved me the most—because it displeased Walt, who wanted perfection. And when I fell short of the mark she was only too happy to make up for it with her love. So I began to identify failing with winning my mother's love. And I began to fail on purpose to get it. I didn't finish Cornell—I couldn't keep a job in this town. I simply retreated to a room over a garage and scrubbing floors in order to keep alive. Failure is the only thing with which I feel at home. Because it is what I was taught at home.

MICHAEL. Killer whales is what they are. Killer whales. How many whales could a killer whale kill . . .

DONALD. A lot, especially if they get them when they were babies. *(Pause.* MICHAEL *suddenly tears off his sweater, throws it in the air, letting it land where it may, whips out another, pulls it on as he starts down the stairs for the living room.* DONALD *follows.)* Hey! Where're you going?

MICHAEL. To make drinks! I think we need about thirty-seven!

DONALD. Where'd you get *that* sweater?

MICHAEL. This clever little shop on the right bank called Hermes.

DONALD. I work my ass off for forty-five lousy dollars a week *scrubbing* floors and you waltz around throwing cashmere sweaters on them.

MICHAEL. The one on the floor in the bedroom is vicuña.

DONALD. I *beg* your pardon.

MICHAEL. You could get a job doing something else. Nobody holds a gun to your head to be a charwoman. That is, how you say, your neurosis.

DONALD. Gee, and I thought it's why I was born.

MICHAEL. Besides, just because I *wear* expensive clothes doesn't necessarily mean they're paid for.

DONALD. That is, how you say, *your* neurosis.

MICHAEL. I'm a spoiled brat, so what do I know about being mature? The only thing mature means to me is *Victor* Mature, who was in all those pictures with Betty Grable.

(Sings à la Grable)

"I can't begin to tell you, how much you mean to me . . . "

Betty sang that in 1945. '45?—'43. No, '43 was "Coney Island," which was remade in '50 as "Wabash Avenue." Yes, "Dolly Sisters" was in '45.

DONALD. How did I manage to miss these momentous events in the American cinema? I can understand people having an affinity for the stage—but movies are such garbage, who can take them seriously?

MICHAEL. Well, I'm sorry if your sense of art is offended. Odd as it may seem, there wasn't any Shubert Theatre in Hot Coffee, Mississippi!

DONALD. However—thanks to the silver screen, your neurosis has got style. It takes a certain flair to squander one's unemployment check at Pavillon.

MICHAEL. What's so snappy about being head over heels in debt? The only thing smart about it is the ingenious ways I dodge the bill collectors.

DONALD. Yeah. Come to think of it, you're the type that gives faggots a bad name.

MICHAEL. And you, Donald, *you* are a credit to the homosexual. A reliable, hard-working, floor-scrubbing, bill-paying fag who don't owe nothin' to nobody.

DONALD. I am a model fairy.

*(*MICHAEL *has taken some ribbon and paper and begun to wrap* HAROLD's *birthday gift.)*

MICHAEL. You think it's just nifty how I've always flitted from Beverly Hills to Rome to Acapulco to Amsterdam, picking up a lot of one-night stands and a lot of custom-made duds along the trail, but I'm here to tell you that the only place in all those miles—the only place I've ever been *happy*—was on the goddamn plane. *(Puffs up the bow on the package, continues)* Bored with Scandinavia, try Greece. Fed up with dark meat, try light. Hate tequila, what about slivovitz. Tired of boys, what about girls—or how about boys and girls mixed and in what combination? And if you're sick of people, what about poppers? Or pot or pills or the hard stuff. And can you think of anything else the bad baby would like to indulge his spoiled-rotten, stupid, empty, boring, selfish, self-centered self in? Is that what you think has style, Donald? Huh? Is that what you think you've missed out on—my hysterical escapes from country to country, party to party, bar to bar, bed to bed, hangover to hangover, and all of it, hand to mouth! *(A beat)* Run, charge, run, buy, borrow, make, spend, run, squander, beg, run, run, run, waste, waste, *waste!* *(A beat)* And why? And why?

DONALD. Why, Michael? Why?

MICHAEL. I really don't want to get into it.

DONALD. Then how can we have a conversation in depth?

MICHAEL. Oh, you know it all by heart anyway. Same song, second verse. Because my Evelyn refused to let me grow up. She was determined to keep me a child forever and she did one helluva job of it. And my Walt stood by and let her do it. *(A beat)* What you see before you is a thirty-year-old infant. And it was all done in the name of love—what *she* labeled love and probably sincerely believed to be love, when what she was really doing was feeding her own need—satisfying her own loneliness. *(A beat)* She made me into a girl-friend dash lover. *(A beat)* We went to all those goddamn cornball movies together. I picked out her clothes for her and told her what to wear and she'd take me to the beauty parlor with her and we'd both get our hair bleached and a permanent and a manicure. *(A beat)* And Walt let this happen. *(A beat)* And she convinced me that I was a sickly child who couldn't run and play and sweat and get knocked around—oh, no! I was frail and pale and, to hear her tell it, practically female. I can't tell you the thousands of times she said to me, "I declare, Michael, you should have been a girl." And I guess I should have—I was frail and pale and bleached and curled and bedded down with hot-water bottles and my dolls and my paper

dolls, and my doll clothes and my doll houses! *(Quick beat) And Walt bought them for me!* *(Beat. With increasing speed)* And she nursed me and put Vicks salve on my chest and cold cream on my face and told me what beautiful eyes I had and what pretty lips I had. She bathed me in the same tub with her until I grew too big for the two of us to fit. She made me sleep in the same bed with her until I was fourteen years old—until I finally flatly refused to spend one more night there. She didn't want to prepare me for life or how to be out in the world on my own or I might have left her. But I left anyway. This goddamn cripple finally wrenched free and limped away. And here I am—unequipped, undisciplined, untrained, unprepared and unable to live! *(A beat)* And do you know until this day she still says, "I don't care if you're seventy years old, you'll always be my baby." And can I tell you how that drives me mad! Will that bitch never understand that what I'll always *be* is her son—but that I haven't been her baby for twenty-five years! *(A beat)* And don't get me wrong. I know it's easy to cop out and blame Evelyn and Walt and say it was *their* fault. That we were simply the helpless put-upon victims. But in the end, we are responsible for ourselves. And I guess—I'm not sure—but I want to believe it—that in their own pathetic, *dangerous* way, they just loved us too much. *(A beat)* Finis. Applause. (DONALD *hesitates, walks over to* MICHAEL, *puts his arms around him and holds him. It is a totally warm and caring gesture.)* There's nothing quite as good as feeling sorry for yourself, is there?

DONALD. Nothing.

MICHAEL *(à la Bette Davis).* I adore cheap sentiment. *(Breaks away)* Okay, I'm taking orders for drinks. What'll it be?

DONALD. An extra-dry-Beefeater-martini-on-the-rocks-with-a-twist.

MICHAEL. Coming up.

(DONALD *exits up the stairs into the bath;* MICHAEL *into the kitchen. Momentarily,* MICHAEL *returns, carrying an ice bucket in one hand and a silver tray of cracked crab in the other, singing "Acapulco" or "Down Argentine Way" or some other forgotten Grable tune. The telephone rings.)*

MICHAEL *(answering it).* Backstage, "New Moon." *(A beat)* Alan? My God, I don't believe it. How *are* you? *Where* are you? In town! Great! When'd you get in? Is Fran with you? Oh. What? No. No, I'm tied up tonight.

No, tonight's no good for me.—You mean, *now?* Well, Alan, ole boy, it's a friend's birthday and I'm having a few people.—No, you wouldn't exactly call it a birthday party— well, yes, actually I guess you would. I mean, what else would you call it. A *wake,* maybe. I'm sorry I can't ask you to join us—but— well, kiddo, it just wouldn't work out. —No, it's not place cards or anything. It's just that —well, I'd hate to just see you for ten minutes and . . . Alan? Alan? What's the matter? — Are you—are you crying?—Oh, Alan, what's wrong?—Alan, listen, come on over. No, no, it's perfectly all right. Well, just hurry up. I mean, come on by and have a drink, okay? Alan . . . are you all right? Okay. Yeah. Same old address. Yeah. Bye. *(Slowly hangs up, stares blankly into space;* DONALD *appears, bathed and changed. He strikes a pose.)*

DONALD. Well. Am I stunning?

(MICHAEL *looks up.*)

MICHAEL *(tonelessly).* You're absolutely stunning. You *look* like shit, but I'm absolutely stunned.

DONALD *(crestfallen).* Your grapes are, how you say, sour.

MICHAEL. Listen, you won't believe what just happened.

DONALD. Where's my drink?

MICHAEL. I didn't make it—I've been on the phone.

(DONALD goes to the bar, makes himself a martini.)

MICHAEL. My old roommate from Georgetown just called.

DONALD. Alan what's-his-name?

MICHAEL. McCarthy. He's up here from Washington on business or something and he's on his way over here.

DONALD. Well, I hope he knows the lyrics to Happy Birthday.

MICHAEL. Listen, asshole, what am I going to do? He's *straight.* And *Square City! ("Top Drawer" accent through clenched teeth)* I mean, he's rally vury proper. Auffully good family.

DONALD *(same accent).* That's *so* important.

MICHAEL *(regular speech).* I mean, they look down on people in the *theatre*—so whatta you think he'll feel about this *freak show* I've got booked for dinner?

DONALD *(sipping his drink).* Christ, is that good.

MICHAEL. Want some cracked crab?

DONALD. Not just yet. Why'd you invite him over?

MICHAEL. He invited himself. He said he had to see me tonight. *Immediately.* He absolutely lost his spring on the phone—started crying.

DONALD. Maybe he's feeling sorry for himself too.

MICHAEL. Great heaves and sobs. Really boo-hoo-hoo-time—and that's not his style at all. I mean, he's so pulled-together he wouldn't show any emotion if he were in a plane crash. What am I going to do?

DONALD. What the hell do you care what he thinks?

MICHAEL. Well, I don't really but . . .

DONALD. Or are you suddenly ashamed of your friends?

MICHAEL. Donald, *you* are the only person I know of whom I am truly ashamed. Some people *do* have different standards from yours and mine, you know. And if we don't acknowledge them, we're just as narrow-minded and backward as we think they are.

DONALD. You know what you are, Michael? You're a *real* person.

MICHAEL. Thank you and fuck you. *(* MICHAEL *crosses to take a piece of crab and nibble on it.)* Want some?

DONALD. No, thanks. How could you ever have been friends with a bore like that?

MICHAEL. Believe it or not, there was a time in my life when I didn't go around *announcing* that I was a faggot.

DONALD. That must have been before speech replaced sign language.

MICHAEL. Don't give me any static on that score. I didn't come out until I left college.

DONALD. It seems to me that the first time we tricked we met in a gay bar on Third Avenue during your *junior* year.

MICHAEL. Cunt.

DONALD. I thought you'd never say it.

MICHAEL. Sure you don't want any cracked crab?

DONALD. *Not yet! If you don't mind!*

MICHAEL. Well, it can only be getting colder. What time is it?

DONALD. I don't know. Early.

MICHAEL. Where the hell is Alan?

DONALD. Do you want some more club soda?

MICHAEL. What?

DONALD. There's nothing but club soda in the glass. It's not gin—like mine. You want some more?

MICHAEL. No.

DONALD. I've been watching you for several Saturdays now. You've actually stopped drinking, haven't you?

MICHAEL. And smoking too.

DONALD. And smoking too. How long's it been?

MICHAEL. Five weeks.

DONALD. That's amazing.

MICHAEL. I've found God.

DONALD. It *is* amazing—for you.

MICHAEL. Or is God dead?

DONALD. Yes, thank God. And don't get panicky just because I'm paying you a compliment. I can tell the difference.

MICHAEL. You always said that I held my liquor better than anybody you ever saw.

DONALD. I could always tell when you were getting high—one way.

MICHAEL. I'd get hostile.

DONALD. You seem happier or something now—and that shows.

MICHAEL *(quietly)*. Thanks.

DONALD. What made you stop—the analyst?

MICHAEL. He certainly had a lot to do with it. Mainly, I just didn't think I could survive another hangover, that's all. I don't think I could get through that morning-after ick attack.

DONALD. Morning-after what?

MICHAEL. Icks! Anxiety! Guilt! Unfathomable guilt—either real or imagined—from that split second your eyes pop open and you say, "Oh, my God, what did I do last night!" and ZAP, Total recall!

DONALD. *Tell* me about it!

MICHAEL. Then, the coffee, aspirin, Alka-Seltzer, Darvon, Daprisal, and a quick call to I.A.—Icks Anonymous.

DONALD. "Good morning, I.A."

MICHAEL. "Hi! Was I too bad last night? Did I do anything wrong? I didn't do anything terrible, did I?"

DONALD *(laughing)*. How many times! How many times!

MICHAEL. And from then on, that struggle to live till lunch, when you have a double Bloody Mary—that is, if you've *waited* until lunch—and then you're half pissed again and useless for the rest of the afternoon. And the only sure cure is to go to bed for about thirty-seven hours, but who ever does that? Instead, you hang on till cocktail time, and by then you're ready for what the night holds—which hopefully is another party, where the whole goddamn cycle starts over! *(A beat)* Well, I've been on that merry-go-round long enough

and I either had to get off or die of centrifugal force.

DONALD. And just how does a clear head stack up with the dull fog of alcohol?

MICHAEL. Well, all those things you've always heard are true. Nothing can compare with the experience of one's faculties functioning at their maximum natural capacity. The only thing is . . . I'd *kill* for a drink.

(The wall-panel buzzer sounds.)

DONALD. Joe College has finally arrived.

MICHAEL. Suddenly, I have such an ick! *(Presses the wall-panel button)* Now listen, Donald . . .

DONALD *(quick)*. Michael, don't insult me by giving me any lecture on acceptable social behavior. I promise to sit with my legs spread apart and keep my voice in a deep register.

MICHAEL. Donald, you are a real *card-carrying cunt*.

(The apartment door buzzes several times. MICHAEL goes to it, pauses briefly before it, tears it open to reveal EMORY, LARRY, and HANK. EMORY is in Bermuda shorts and a sweater. LARRY has on a turtleneck and sandals. HANK is in a dark Ivy League suit with a vest and has on cordovan shoes. LARRY and HANK carry birthday gifts. EMORY carries a large covered dish.)

EMORY *(bursting in)*. ALL RIGHT THIS IS A RAID! EVERYBODY'S UNDER ARREST! *(This entrance is followed by a loud raucous laugh as EMORY throws his arms around MICHAEL and gives him a big kiss on the cheek. Referring to dish)* Hello, darlin'! Connie Casserole. Oh, Mary, don't ask.

MICHAEL *(weary already)*. Hello, Emory. Put it in the kitchen.

(EMORY spots DONALD.)

EMORY. Who is the exotic woman over here?

MICHAEL. Hi, Hank. Larry.

(They say, "Hi," shake hands, enter. MICHAEL looks out in the hall, comes back into the room, closes the door.)

DONALD. Hi, Emory.

EMORY. My dear, I thought you had perished! Where have you been hiding your classically chiseled features?

DONALD *(to EMORY)*. I don't live in the city any more.

MICHAEL *(to LARRY and HANK, referring to the gifts)*. Here, I'll take those. Where's yours, Emory?

EMORY. It's arriving later. *(EMORY exits to the kitchen. LARRY and DONALD's eyes have met.* HANK *has handed* MICHAEL *his gift—* LARRY *is too preoccupied.)*

HANK. Larry!—Larry!

LARRY. What!

HANK. Give Michael the gift!

LARRY. Oh. Here. *(To* HANK*)* Louder. So my mother in Philadelphia can hear you.

HANK. Well, you were just standing there in a trance.

MICHAEL *(to* LARRY *and* HANK *as* EMORY *reenters).* You both know Donald, don't you?

DONALD. Sure. Nice to see you. *(To* HANK*)* Hi.

HANK *(shaking hands).* Nice to meet you.

MICHAEL. Oh, I thought you'd met.

DONALD. Well . . .

LARRY. We haven't exactly met but we've. . . . Hi.

DONALD. Hi.

HANK. But you've what?

LARRY. . . . *Seen* . . . each other before.

MICHAEL. Well, *that* sounds murky.

HANK. You've never met but you've seen each other.

LARRY. What was wrong with the way *I* said it.

HANK. Where?

EMORY *(loud aside to* MICHAEL*).* I think they're going to have their first fight.

LARRY. The first one since we got out of the taxi.

MICHAEL *(referring to* EMORY*).* Where'd you find this trash.

LARRY. Downstairs leaning against a lamppost.

EMORY. With an orchid behind my ear and big wet lips painted over the lipline.

MICHAEL. Just like Maria Montez.

DONALD. Oh, *please!*

EMORY *(to* DONALD*).* What have you got against Maria—she was a good woman.

MICHAEL. Listen, everybody, this old college friend of mine is in town and he's stopping by for a fast drink on his way to dinner somewhere. But, listen, he's *straight,* so . . .

LARRY. *Straight!* If it's the one I met, he's about as straight as the Yellow Brick Road.

MICHAEL. No, you met Justin Stuart.

HANK. I don't remember anybody named Justin Stuart.

LARRY. Of course you don't, dope. *I* met him.

MICHAEL. Well, this is someone else.

DONALD. Alan McCarthy. A very close to-tal stranger.

MICHAEL. It's not that I care what he would think of me, really—it's just that *he's* not ready for it. And he never will be. You understand that, don't you, Hank?

HANK. Oh, sure.

LARRY. You honestly think he doesn't know about you?

MICHAEL. If there's the slightest suspicion, he's never let on one bit.

EMORY. What's he had, a lobotomy? *(He exits up the stairs into the bath.)*

MICHAEL. I was super-careful when I was in college and I still am whenever I see him. I don't know why, but I am.

DONALD. Tilt.

MICHAEL. You may think it was a crock of shit, Donald, but to him I'm sure we were close friends. The closest. To pop that balloon now just wouldn't be fair to him. Isn't that right?

LARRY. Whatever's fair.

MICHAEL. Well, of course. And if that's phony of me, Donald, then that's phony of me and make something of it.

DONALD. I pass.

MICHAEL. Well, even you have to admit it's much simpler to deal with the world according to its rules and then go right ahead and do what you damn well please. You do understand *that,* don't you?

DONALD. Now that you've put it in lay-man's terms.

MICHAEL. I was just like Alan when I was in college. Very large in the dating department. Wore nothing but those constipated Ivy League clothes and those ten-pound cordovan shoes. *(To* HANK*)* No offense.

HANK. Quite all right.

MICHAEL. I butched it up quite a bit. And I didn't think I was lying to myself. I really thought I was straight.

EMORY *(coming downstairs tucking a Klee-nex into his sleeve.)* Who do you have to fuck to get a drink around here?

MICHAEL. Will you *light* somewhere? *(*EM-ORY *sits on steps.)* Or I thought I thought I was straight. I know I didn't come out till after I'd graduated.

DONALD. What about all those weekends up from school?

MICHAEL. I still wasn't out. I was still in the "Christ-was-I-drunk-last-night syn-drome."

LARRY. The *what?*

MICHAEL. The Christ-was-I-drunk-last-night syndrome. You know, when you made it with some guy in school and the next day when you had to face each other there was always a lot of shit-kicking crap about, "Man, was I drunk last night! Christ, I don't remember a thing!"

(Everyone laughs.)

DONALD. You were just guilty because you were Catholic, that's all.

MICHAEL. That's not true. The Christ-was-I-drunk-last-night syndrome knows no religion. It has to do with immaturity. Although I will admit there's a high percentage of it among Mormons.

EMORY. Trollop.

MICHAEL. We all somehow managed to justify our actions in those days. I later found out that even Justin Stuart, my closest friend . . .

DONALD. Other than Alan McCarthy.

MICHAEL *(a look to* DONALD*).* . . . was doing the same thing. Only Justin was going to Boston on weekends.

*(*EMORY *and* LARRY *laugh.)*

LARRY *(to* HANK*).* Sound familiar?

MICHAEL. Yes, long before Justin or I or God only knows how many others *came out,* we used to get drunk and "horse around" a bit. You see, in the Christ-was-I-drunk-last-night syndrome, you really *are* drunk. That part of it is true. It's just that you also *do remember everything. (General laughter)* Oh God, I used to have to get loaded to go in a gay bar!

DONALD. Well, times certainly have changed.

MICHAEL. They *have.* Lately I've gotten to despise the bars. Everybody just standing around and standing around—it's like one eternal intermission.

HANK *(to* LARRY*).* Sound familiar?

EMORY. I can't stand the bars either. All that cat-and-mouse business—you hang around *staring* at each other all night and wind up going home alone.

MICHAEL. And pissed.

LARRY. A lot of guys have to get loaded to have sex. *(Quick look to* HANK*, who is unamused)* So I've been told.

MICHAEL. If you remember, Donald, the first time we made it I was so drunk I could hardly stand up.

DONALD. You were so drunk you could hardly *get* it up.

MICHAEL *(mock innocence).* Christ, I was so drunk I don't remember.

DONALD. Bullshit, you remember.

MICHAEL *(sings to* DONALD*).* "Just friends, lovers no more . . . "

EMORY. You may as well be. Everybody thinks you are anyway.

DONALD. We never *were—really.*

MICHAEL. We didn't have time to be—we got to know each other too fast. *(Door buzzer sounds.)* Oh, Jesus, it's Alan! Now, please everybody, do me a favor and cool it for the few minutes he's here.

EMORY. Anything for a sis, Mary.

MICHAEL. That's *exactly* what I'm talking about, Emory. *No camping!*

EMORY. Sorry. *(Deep, deep voice to* DONALD*)* Think the Giants are gonna win the pennant this year?

DONALD *(deep, deep voice).* Fuckin' A, Mac.

*(*MICHAEL *goes to the door, opens it to reveal* BERNARD, *dressed in a shirt and tie and sport jacket. He carries a birthday gift and two bottles of red wine.)*

EMORY *(big scream).* Oh, it's only another queen!

BERNARD. And it ain't the Red one, either.

EMORY. It's the queen of spades! *(*BERNARD *enters.* MICHAEL *looks out in the hall.)*

MICHAEL. Bernard, is the downstairs door open?

BERNARD. It was, but I closed it.

MICHAEL. Good.

*(*BERNARD *starts to put wine on bar.)*

MICHAEL *(referring to the two bottles of red wine).* I'll take those. You can put your present with the others. *(*MICHAEL *closes the door.* BERNARD *hands him the gift. The phone rings.)*

BERNARD. Hi, Larry. Hi, Hank.

MICHAEL. *Christ of the Andes!* Donald, will you bartend, please. *(*MICHAEL *gives* DONALD *the wine bottles, goes to the phone.)*

BERNARD *(extending his hand to* DONALD*).* Hello, Donald. Good to see you.

DONALD. Bernard.

MICHAEL *(answers phone).* Hello? Alan?

EMORY. Hi, Bernardette. Anybody ever tell you you'd look divine in a hammock, surrounded by louvres and ceiling fans and lots and lots of lush tropical ferns?

BERNARD *(to* EMORY*).* You're *such* a fag. You take the cake.

EMORY. Oh, what *about* the cake—whose job was that?

LARRY. Mine. I ordered one to be delivered.

EMORY. How many candles did you say put on it—eighty?

MICHAEL. . . . What? Wait a minute.

There's too much noise. Let me go to another phone. *(Presses the hold button, hands up, dashes toward stairs)*

LARRY. Michael, did the cake come?

MICHAEL. No.

DONALD *(to* MICHAEL *as he passes).* What's up?

MICHAEL. Do *I* know?

LARRY. Jesus, I'd better call. Okay if I use the private line?

MICHAEL *(going upstairs).* Sure. *(Stops dead on stairs, turns)* Listen, everybody, there's some cracked crab there. Help yourselves.

*(*DONALD *shakes his head.* MICHAEL *continues up the stairs to the bedroom.* LARRY *crosses to the phone, presses the free-line button, picks up receiver, dials Information.)*

DONALD. Is everybody ready for a drink?

*(*HANK *and* BERNARD *say, "Yeah.")*

EMORY *(flipping up his sweater).* Ready! I'll be your topless cocktail waitress.

BERNARD. Please spare us the sight of your sagging tits.

EMORY *(to* HANK, LARRY*).* What're you having, kids?

MICHAEL *(having picked up the bedside phone).* . . . Yes, Alan . . .

LARRY. Vodka and tonic. *(Into phone)* Could I have the number for the Marseilles Bakery in Manhattan.

EMORY. A vod and ton and a . . .

HANK. Is there any beer?

EMORY. Beer! Who drinks beer before dinner?

BERNARD. Beer drinkers.

DONALD. That's telling him.

MICHAEL. . . . No, Alan, don't be silly. What's there to apologize for?

EMORY. Truck drivers do. Or . . . or wallpaperers. Not school teachers. They have sherry.

HANK. This one has beer.

EMORY. Well, maybe school teachers in *public* schools. *(To* LARRY*)* How can a sensitive artist like you live with an insensitive bull like that?

LARRY *(hanging up the phone and redialing).* I can't.

BERNARD. Emory, you'd live with Hank in a minute, if he'd ask you. In fifty-eight seconds. Lord knows, you're *sss*ensitive.

EMORY. Why don't you have a piece of watermelon and hush up!

MICHAEL. . . . Alan, don't be ridiculous.

DONALD. Here you go, Hank.

HANK. Thanks.

LARRY. Shit. They don't answer.

DONALD. What're you having, Emory?

BERNARD. A Pink Lady.

EMORY. A vodka martini on the rocks, please.

LARRY *(hangs up).* Well, let's just hope.

*(*DONALD *hands* LARRY *his drink—their eyes meet again. A faint smile crosses* LARRY*'s lips.* DONALD *returns to the bar to make* EMORY*'s drink.)*

MICHAEL. Lunch tomorrow will be great. One o'clock—the Oak Room at the Plaza okay? Fine.

BERNARD *(to* DONALD*).* Donald, read any new libraries lately?

DONALD. One or three. I did the complete works of Doris Lessing this week. I've been depressed.

MICHAEL. Alan, forget it, will you? Right. Bye. *(Hangs up, starts to leave the room—stops. Quickly pulls off the sweater he is wearing, takes out another, crosses to the stairs)*

DONALD. You must not work in Circulation any more.

BERNARD. Oh, I'm still there—every day.

DONALD. Well, since I moved, I only come in on Saturday evenings. *(Moves his stack of books off the bar)*

HANK. Looks like you stock up for the week.

*(*MICHAEL *rises and crosses to steps landing.)*

BERNARD. Are you kidding—that'll last him two days.

EMORY. It would last *me* two years. I still haven't finished *Atlas Shrugged,* which I started in 1912.

MICHAEL *(to* DONALD*).* Well, he's not coming.

DONALD. It's just as well now.

BERNARD. Some people eat, some people drink, some take dope . . .

DONALD. I read.

MICHAEL. And read and read and read. It's a wonder your eyes don't turn back in your head at the sight of a dust jacket.

HANK. Well, at least he's a constructive escapist.

MICHAEL. Yeah, what do I do—take planes. No, I don't do that any more. Because I don't have the *money* to do that any more. I go to the baths. That's about it.

EMORY. I'm about to do both. I'm flying to the West Coast—

BERNARD. You still have that act with a donkey in Tijuana?

EMORY. I'm going to *San Francisco* on a well-earned vacation.

LARRY. No shopping?

EMORY. Oh, I'll look for a few things for a couple of clients, but I've been so busy lately I really couldn't care less if I never saw another piece of fabric or another stick of furniture as long as I live. I'm going to the Club Baths and I'm not out till they announce the departure of TWA one week later.

BERNARD *(to EMORY)*. You'll never learn to stay out of the baths, will you. The last time Emily was taking the vapors, this big hairy number strolled in. Emory said, "I'm just resting," and the big hairy number said, "I'm just *arr*esting!" It was the vice! *(Everybody laughs.)*

EMORY. You have to tell everything, don't you? *(DONALD crosses to give EMORY his drink.)* Thanks, sonny. You live with your parents?

DONALD. Yeah. But it's all right—they're gay. *(EMORY roars, slaps HANK on the knee, HANK gets up, moves away. DONALD turns to MICHAEL.)* What happened to Alan?

MICHAEL. He suddenly got terrible icks about having broken down on the phone. Kept apologizing over and over. Did a big about-face and reverted to the old Alan right before my very eyes.

DONALD. Ears.

MICHAEL. Ears. Well, the cracked crab obviously did not work out. *(Starts to take away the tray)*

EMORY. Just put that down if you don't want your hand slapped. I'm about to have some.

MICHAEL. It's really very good. *(Gives DONALD a look)* I don't know why everyone has such an aversion to it.

DONALD. Sometimes you remind me of the Chinese water torture. I take that back. Sometimes you remind me of the *relentless* Chinese water torture.

MICHAEL. Bitch. *(HANK has put on some music.)*

BERNARD. Yeah, baby, let's hear that sound.

EMORY. A drumbeat and their eyes sparkle like Cartier's. *(BERNARD starts to snap his fingers and move in time with the music. MICHAEL joins in.)*

MICHAEL. I wonder where Harold is.

EMORY. Yeah, where *is* the frozen fruit?

MICHAEL *(to DONALD)*. Emory refers to Harold as the frozen fruit because of his former profession as an ice skater.

EMORY. She used to be the Vera Hruba Ralston of the Borscht Circuit.

(MICHAEL and BERNARD are now dancing freely.)

BERNARD *(to MICHAEL)*. If your mother could see you now, she'd have a stroke.

MICHAEL. Got a camera on you?

(The door panel buzzes. EMORY lets out a yelp.)

EMORY. Oh my God, it's Lily Law! Everybody three feet apart!

(MICHAEL goes to the panel, presses the button. HANK turns down the music. MICHAEL opens the door a short way, pokes his head out.)

BERNARD. It's probably Harold now.

(MICHAEL leans back in the room.)

MICHAEL. No, it's the delivery boy from the bakery.

LARRY. Thank God.

(MICHAEL goes out into the hall, pulling the door almost closed behind him.)

EMORY *(loudly)*. Ask him if he's got any hot-cross buns!

HANK. Come on, Emory, knock it off.

BERNARD. You can take her anywhere but out.

EMORY *(to HANK)*. You remind me of an old-maid school teacher.

HANK. You remind me of a chicken wing.

EMORY. I'm sure you meant that as a compliment.

(HANK turns the music back up.)

MICHAEL *(in hall)*. Thank you. Good night. *(MICHAEL returns with a cake box, closes the door, and takes it into the kitchen.)*

LARRY. Hey, Bernard, you remember that thing we used to do on Fire Island? *(LARRY starts to do a kind of Madison.)*

BERNARD. That was "in" so far back I think I've forgotten.

EMORY. *I* remember. *(Pops up—starts doing the steps. LARRY and BERNARD start to follow.)*

LARRY. Yeah. That's it.

(MICHAEL enters from the kitchen, falls in line with them.)

MICHAEL. Well, if it isn't the Geriatrics Rockettes.

(Now they all are doing practically a precision routine. DONALD comes to sit on the arm of a chair, sip his drink, and watch in fascination. HANK goes to the bar to get another beer.

The door buzzer sounds. No one seems to hear it. It buzzes again. HANK turns toward the door, hesitates. Looks toward MICHAEL, who is now deeply involved in the intricacies of the dance. No one, it seems, has heard the buzzer but HANK, *who goes to the door, opens it wide to reveal* ALAN. *He is dressed in black tie.*

The dancers continue, turning and slapping their knees and heels and laughing with abandon. Suddenly MICHAEL *looks up, stops dead.* DONALD *sees this and turns to see what* MICHAEL *has seen. Slowly he stands up.* MICHAEL *goes to the record player, turns it off abruptly.* EMORY, LARRY, *and* BERNARD *come to out-of-step halts, look to see what's happened.)*

MICHAEL. I thought you said you weren't coming.

ALAN. I . . . well, I'm sorry . . .

MICHAEL *(forced lightly).* We were just—acting silly . . .

ALAN. Actually, when I called I was in a phone booth around the corner. My dinner party is not far from here. And . . .

MICHAEL. Emory was just showing us this . . . silly dance.

ALAN. Well, then I walked past and your downstairs door was open and . . .

MICHAEL. This is Emory. (EMORY *curtsies.* MICHAEL *glares at him.)* Everybody, this is Alan McCarthy. Counterclockwise, Alan: Larry, Emory, Bernard, Donald, and Hank. *(They all mumble "Hello," "Hi.")* Would you like a drink?

ALAN. Thanks, no. I . . . I can't stay . . . long . . . really.

MICHAEL. Well, you're here now, so stay. What would you like?

ALAN. Do you have any rye?

MICHAEL. I'm afraid I don't drink it any more. You'll have to settle for gin or Scotch or vodka.

DONALD. Or beer.

ALAN. Scotch, please

(MICHAEL *starts for bar.)*

DONALD. I'll get it. *(Goes to bar)*

HANK *(forced laugh).* Guess I'm the only beer drinker.

ALAN *(looking around group).* Whose . . . birthday . . . is it?

LARRY. Harold's.

ALAN *(looking from face to face).* Harold?

BERNARD. He's not here yet.

EMORY. She's never been on time . . .

(MICHAEL *shoots* EMORY *a withering glance.)* He's never been on time in his . . .

MICHAEL. Alan's from Washington. We went to college together. Georgetown.

(A beat. Silence)

EMORY. Well, isn't that fascinating.

(DONALD *hands* ALAN *his drink.)*

DONALD. If that's too strong, I'll put some water in it.

ALAN *(takes a quick gulp).* It's fine. Thanks. Fine.

HANK. Are you in the government?

ALAN. No. I'm a lawyer. What . . . what do you do?

HANK. I teach school.

ALAN. Oh. I would have taken you for an athlete of some sort. You look like you might play sports . . . of some sort.

HANK. Well, I'm no professional, but I was on the basketball team in college and I play quite a bit of tennis.

ALAN. I play tennis too.

HANK. Great game.

ALAN. Yes. Great. *(A beat. Silence)* What . . . do you teach?

HANK. Math.

ALAN. Math?

HANK. Yes.

ALAN. Math. Well.

EMORY. Kinda makes you want to rush out and buy a slide rule, doesn't it.

MICHAEL. Emory. I'm going to need some help with dinner and you're elected. Come on!

EMORY. I'm *always* elected.

BERNARD. You're a natural-born domestic.

EMORY. Said the African queen! You come on, too—you can fan me while I make the salad dressing.

MICHAEL *(glaring; phony smile).* RIGHT THIS WAY, EMORY! (MICHAEL *pushes the swinging door aside for* EMORY *and* BERNARD *to enter. They do and he follows. The door swings closed, and the muffled sound of* MICHAEL's *voice can be heard.) (Offstage)* You son of a bitch!

EMORY *(offstage).* What the hell do you want from me?

HANK. Why don't we all sit down.

ALAN. . . . Sure.

(HANK *and* ALAN *sit on the couch.* LARRY *crosses to the bar, refills his drink.* DONALD *comes over to refill his.)*

LARRY. Hi.

DONALD. . . . Hi.

ALAN. I really feel terrible—barging in on you fellows this way.

LARRY *(to* DONALD). How've you been?

DONALD. Fine, thanks.

HANK *(to* ALAN). . . . Oh, that's okay.

DONALD *(to* LARRY). . . . And you?

LARRY. Oh . . . just fine.

ALAN *(to* HANK*).* You're married?

(LARRY *hears this, turns to look in the direction of the couch.* MICHAEL *enters from the kitchen.)*

HANK *(watching* LARRY *and* DONALD*).* What?

ALAN. I see you're married. *(Points to* HANK*'s wedding band)*

HANK. Oh.

MICHAEL *(glaring at* DONALD*).* Yes. Hank's married.

ALAN. You have any kids?

HANK. Yes. Two. A boy nine, and a girl seven. You should see my boy play tennis— really puts his dad to shame.

DONALD *(avoiding* MICHAEL*'s eyes).* I better get some ice. *(Exits to the kitchen)*

ALAN *(to* HANK*).* I have two kids too. Both girls.

HANK. Great.

MICHAEL. How *are* the girls, Alan?

ALAN. Oh, just sensational. *(Shakes his head)* They're something, those kids. God, I'm nuts about them.

HANK. How long have you been married?

ALAN. Nine years. Can you believe it, Mickey?

MICHAEL. No.

ALAN. Mickey used to go with my wife when we were all in school.

MICHAEL. Can you believe that?

ALAN *(to* HANK*).* You live in the city?

LARRY. Yes, we do. (LARRY *comes over to the couch next to* HANK*.)*

ALAN. Oh.

HANK. I'm in the process of getting a divorce. Larry and I are—roommates.

MICHAEL. Yes.

ALAN. Oh. I'm sorry. Oh, I mean . . .

HANK. I understand.

ALAN *(gets up).* I . . . I . . . I think I'd like another drink . . . if I may.

MICHAEL. Of course. What was it?

ALAN. I'll do it . . . if I may. *(Gets up, starts for the bar. Suddenly there is a loud crash offstage.* ALAN *jumps, looks toward swinging door.)* What was that?

(DONALD *enters with the ice bucket.)*

MICHAEL. Excuse me. Testy temperament out in the kitch! (MICHAEL *exits through the swinging door.* ALAN *continues to the bar— starts nervously picking up and putting down bottles, searching for the Scotch.)*

HANK *(to* LARRY*).* Larry, where do you know that guy from?

LARRY. What guy?

HANK. *That* guy.

LARRY. I don't know. Around. The bars.

DONALD. Can I help you, Alan?

ALAN. I . . . I can't seem to find the Scotch.

DONALD. You've got it in your hand.

ALAN. Oh. Of course. How . . . stupid of me.

(DONALD *watches* ALAN *fumble with the Scotch bottle and glass.)*

DONALD. Why don't you let me do that?

ALAN *(gratefully hands him both).* Thanks.

DONALD. Was it water or soda?

ALAN. Just make it straight—over ice.

(MICHAEL *enters.)*

MICHAEL. You see, Alan, I told you it wasn't a good time to talk. But we . . .

ALAN. It doesn't matter. I'll just finish this and go . . . *(Takes a long swallow)*

LARRY. Where can Harold be?

MICHAEL. Oh, he's always late. You know how neurotic he is about going out in public. It takes him hours to get ready.

LARRY. Why *is* that?

(EMORY *breezes in with an apron tied around his waist, carrying a stack of plates which he places on a drop-leaf table.* MICHAEL *does an eye roll.)*

EMORY. Why is what?

LARRY. Why does Harold spend hours getting ready before he can go out?

EMORY. Because she's a sick lady, that's why. *(Exits to the kitchen.* ALAN *finishes his drink.)*

MICHAEL. Alan, as I was about to say, we can go in the bedroom and talk.

ALAN. It really doesn't matter.

MICHAEL. Come on. Bring your drink.

ALAN. I . . . I've finished it.

MICHAEL. Well, make another and bring it upstairs.

(DONALD *picks up the Scotch bottle and pours into the glass* ALAN *has in his hand.* MICHAEL *has started for the stairs.)*

ALAN *(to* DONALD*).* Thanks.

DONALD. Don't mention it.

ALAN *(to* HANK*).* Excuse us. We'll be down in a minute.

LARRY. He'll still be here. *(A beat)*

MICHAEL *(on the stairs).* Go ahead, Alan. I'll be right there.

(ALAN *turns awkwardly, exits to the bedroom.* MICHAEL *goes into the kitchen. A beat)*

HANK *(to* LARRY*).* What was *that* supposed to mean?

LARRY. What was what supposed to mean?

HANK. You know.

LARRY. You want another beer?

HANK. No. You're jealous, aren't you? (HANK *starts to laugh.* LARRY *doesn't like it.*)

LARRY. I'm Larry. *You're* jealous. (*Crosses to* DONALD) Hey, Donald, where've you been hanging out these days? I haven't seen you in a long time . . .

(MICHAEL *enters to witness this disapprovingly. He turns, goes up the stairs. In the bedroom* ALAN *is sitting on the edge of the bed.* MICHAEL *enters, pauses at the mirror to adjust his hair. Downstairs,* HANK *gets up, exits into the kitchen.* DONALD *and* LARRY *move to a corner of the room, sit facing upstage and talk quietly.*)

ALAN (*to* MICHAEL). This is a marvelous apartment.

MICHAEL. It's too expensive. I work to pay rent.

ALAN. What are you doing these days?

MICHAEL. Nothing.

ALAN. Aren't you writing any more?

MICHAEL. I haven't looked at a typewriter since I sold the very very wonderful, very very marvelous *screenplay* which never got produced.

ALAN. That's right. The last time I saw you, you were on your way to California. Or was it Europe?

MICHAEL. Hollywood. Which is not in Europe, nor does it have anything whatsoever to do with California.

ALAN. I've never been there but I would imagine it's awful. Everyone must be terribly cheap.

MICHAEL. No, not everyone. (ALAN *laughs. A beat.* MICHAEL *sits on the bed.*) Alan, I want to try to explain this evening . . .

ALAN. What's there to explain? Sometimes you just can't invite everybody to every party and some people take it personally. But I'm not one of them. I should apologize for inviting myself.

MICHAEL. That's not exactly what I meant.

ALAN. Your friends all seem like very nice guys. That Hank is really a very attractive fellow.

MICHAEL. . . . Yes. He is.

ALAN. We have a lot in common. What's his roommate's name?

MICHAEL. Larry.

ALAN. What does *he* do?

MICHAEL. He's a commercial artist.

ALAN. I liked Donald too. The only one I didn't care too much for was—what's his name—Emory?

MICHAEL. Yes. Emory.

ALAN. I just can't stand that kind of talk. It just grates on me.

MICHAEL. What kind of talk, Alan?

ALAN. Oh, you know. His brand of humor, I guess.

MICHAEL. He can be really quite funny sometimes.

ALAN. I suppose so. If you find that sort of thing amusing. He just seems like such a goddamn little pansy. (*Silence. A pause*) I'm sorry I said that. I didn't mean to say that. That's such an awful thing to say about *any-one*. But you know what I mean, Michael—you have to admit he *is* effeminate.

MICHAEL. He is a bit.

ALAN. A bit! He's like a . . . a butterfly in heat! I mean, there's no wonder he was trying to teach you all a dance. He *probably* wanted to dance *with* you! (*Pause*) Oh, come on, man, you know me—you know how I feel—your private life is your own affair.

MICHAEL (*icy*). No. I *don't* know that about you.

ALAN. I couldn't care less what people do —as long as they don't do it in public—or— or try to force their ways on the whole damned world.

MICHAEL. Alan, what was it you were crying about on the telephone?

ALAN. Oh, I feel like such a fool about that. I could shoot myself for letting myself act that way. I'm so embarrassed I could die.

MICHAEL. But, Alan, if you were genuinely upset—that's nothing to be embarrassed about.

ALAN. All I can say is—please accept my apology for making such an ass of myself.

MICHAEL. You must have been upset or you wouldn't have said you were and that you wanted to see me—*had* to see me and had to talk to me.

ALAN. Can you forget it? Just pretend it never happened. I know *I* have. Okay?

MICHAEL. Is something wrong between you and Fran?

ALAN. Listen, I've really got to go.

MICHAEL. Why are you in New York?

ALAN. I'm dreadfully late for dinner.

MICHAEL. *Whose* dinner? Where are you going?

ALAN. Is this the loo?

MICHAEL. Yes.

ALAN. Excuse me. (*Quickly goes into the bathroom, closes the door.* MICHAEL *remains silent—sits on the bed, stares into space. Downstairs,* EMORY *pops in from the kitchen to discover* DONALD *and* LARRY *in quiet, intimate conversation.)*

EMORY.   What's-going-on-in-here-oh-Mary-don't-ask! *(Puts a salt cellar and pepper mill on the table.* HANK *enters, carrying a bottle of red wine and a corkscrew. Looks toward* LARRY *and* DONALD. DONALD *sees him, stands up.)*

DONALD. Hank, why don't you come and join us?

HANK. That's an interesting suggestion. Whose idea is that?

DONALD. Mine.

LARRY *(to* HANK*).* He means in a conversation.

*(*BERNARD *enters from the kitchen, carrying four wine glasses.)*

EMORY *(to* BERNARD*).* Where're the rest of the wine glasses?

BERNARD. Ahz workin' as fas' as ah can!

EMORY. They have to be told everything. Can't let 'em out of your sight. *(Breezes out to the kitchen.* DONALD *leaves* LARRY*'s side and goes to the coffee table, helps himself to the cracked crab.* HANK *opens the wine, puts it on the table.* MICHAEL *gets up from the bed and goes down the stairs. Downstairs,* HANK *crosses to* LARRY.*)*

HANK. I thought maybe you were abiding by the agreement.

LARRY. We have no agreement.

HANK. We *did.*

LARRY. *You* did. I never agreed to anything!

*(*DONALD *looks up to see* MICHAEL, *raises a crab claw toward him.)*

DONALD. To your health.

MICHAEL. Up yours.

DONALD. Up my health?

BERNARD. Where's the gent?

MICHAEL. In the gent's room. If you can all hang on for five more minutes, he's about to leave. *(The door buzzes.* MICHAEL *crosses to it.)*

LARRY. Well, at last!

*(*MICHAEL *opens the door to reveal a muscle-bound young* MAN *wearing boots, tight Levi's, a calico neckerchief, and a cowboy hat. Around his wrist there is a large card tied with a ribbon.)*

COWBOY *(singing fast).*
"Happy birthday to you,
Happy birthday to you,
Happy birthday, dear Harold.
Happy birthday to you."
(And with that, he throws his arms around

MICHAEL *and gives him a big kiss on the lips. Everyone stands in stunned silence.)*

MICHAEL. Who the hell are you?

*(*EMORY *swings in from the kitchen.)*

EMORY. She's Harold's present from me and she's *early!* *(Quick, to* COWBOY*)* And that's not even Harold, you *idiot!*

COWBOY. You said whoever answered the door.

EMORY. But *not until midnight!* *(Quickly, to group)* He's supposed to be a *midnight cowboy!*

DONALD. He *is* a midnight cowboy.

MICHAEL. He looks right out of a William Inge play to me.

EMORY *(to* COWBOY*).* . . . Not until midnight and you're supposed to sing to the right person, for Chrissake! I *told* you Harold has very, very tight, tight, black curly hair. *(Referring to* MICHAEL*)* This number's practically bald!

MICHAEL.Thank you and fuck you.

BERNARD.It's a good thing *I* didn't open the door.

EMORY. Not that tight and not that black.

COWBOY. I forgot. Besides, I wanted to get to the bars by midnight.

MICHAEL. He's a class act all the way around.

EMORY. What do you mean—get to the bars! Sweetie, I paid you for the whole night, remember?

COWBOY. I hurt my back doing my exercises and I wanted to get to bed early tonight.

BERNARD. Are you ready for this one?

LARRY *(to* COWBOY*).* That's too bad, what happened?

COWBOY. I lost my grip doing my chin-ups and I fell on my heels and twisted my back.

EMORY. You shouldn't *wear* heels when you do chin-ups.

COWBOY *(oblivious).* I shouldn't do chin-ups—I got a weak grip to begin with.

EMORY. A weak grip. In my day it used to be called a limp wrist.

BERNARD. Who can remember that far back?

MICHAEL. Who was it that always used to say, "You show me Oscar Wilde in a cowboy suit, and I'll show you a gay caballero."

DONALD. I don't know. Who *was* it who always used to say that?

MICHAEL *(Katharine Hepburn voice).* I don't know. Somebody.

LARRY *(to* COWBOY*).* What does your card say?

COWBOY *(holds up his wrist).* Here. Read it.

LARRY *(reading card).* "Dear Harold, bang, bang, you're alive. But roll over and play dead. Happy birthday, Emory."

BERNARD. Ah, sheer poetry, Emmy.

LARRY. And in your usual good taste.

MICHAEL. Yes, so conservative of you to resist a sign in Times Square.

EMORY *(glancing toward stairs).* Cheese it! Here comes the socialite nun.

MICHAEL. Goddamnit, Emory!

(ALAN comes down the stairs into the room. Everybody quiets.)

ALAN. Well, I'm off. . . . Thanks, Michael, for the drink.

MICHAEL. You're entirely welcome, Alan. See you tomorrow?

ALAN. . . . No. No, I think I'm going to be awfully busy. I may even go back to Washington.

EMORY. Got a heavy date in Lafayette Square?

ALAN. What?

HANK. Emory.

EMORY. Forget it.

ALAN *(sees* COWBOY*).* Are you . . . Harold?

EMORY. No, he's not Harold. He's *for* Harold.

(Silence. ALAN *lets it pass. Turns to* HANK*)*

ALAN. Goodbye, Hank. It was nice to meet you.

HANK. Same here. *(They shake hands.)*

ALAN. If . . . if you're ever in Washington —I'd like for you to meet my wife.

LARRY. That'd be fun, wouldn't it, Hank.

EMORY. Yeah, they'd love to meet him—her. I have such a problem with pronouns.

ALAN *(quick, to* EMORY*).* How many esses are there in the word pronoun?

EMORY. How'd you like to kiss my ass—that's got two or more *essessss* in it!

ALAN. How'd you like to blow me!

EMORY. What's the matter with your *wife,* she got lockjaw?

ALAN *(lashes out).* Faggot, fairy, pansy . . . *(Lunges at* EMORY*)* . . . queer, cocksucker! *I'll kill you, you goddamn little mincing swish! You goddamn freak!* FREAK! FREAK!

(Pandemonium. ALAN *beats* EMORY *to the floor before anyone recovers from surprise and reacts.)*

EMORY. Oh, my God, somebody help me! Bernard! He's killing me!

*(*BERNARD *and* HANK *rush forward.* EMORY *is screaming. Blood gushes from his nose.)*

HANK. Alan! ALAN! ALAN!

EMORY. Get him off me! Get him off me! Oh, my God, he's broken my nose! I'M BLEEDING TO DEATH!

*(*LARRY *has gone to shut the door. With one great, athletic move,* HANK *forcefully tears* ALAN *off* EMORY *and drags him backward across the room.* BERNARD *bends over* EMORY*, puts his arm around him and lifts him.)*

BERNARD. Somebody get some ice! And a cloth!

*(*LARRY *runs to the bar, grabs the bar towel and the ice bucket, rushes to put it on the floor beside* BERNARD *and* EMORY*.* BERNARD *quickly wraps some ice in the towel, holds it to* EMORY*'s mouth.)*

EMORY. Oh, my face!

BERNARD. He busted your lip, that's all. It'll be all right.

*(*HANK *has gotten* ALAN *down on the floor on the opposite side of the room.* ALAN *relinquishes the struggle, collapses against* HANK*, moaning and beating his fists rhythmically against* HANK*'s chest.* MICHAEL *is still standing in the same spot in the center of the room, immobile.* DONALD *crosses past the* COWBOY*.)*

DONALD *(to* COWBOY*).* Would you mind waiting over there with the gifts. *(*COWBOY *moves over to where the gift-wrapped packages have been put.* DONALD *continues past to observe the mayhem, turns up his glass, takes a long swallow. The door buzzes.* DONALD *turns toward* MICHAEL*, waits.* MICHAEL *doesn't move.* DONALD *goes to the door, opens it to reveal* HAROLD*.)* Well, Harold! Happy birthday. You're just in time for the floor show, which, as you see, is on the floor. *(To* COWBOY*)* Hey, you, *this* is Harold!

*(*HAROLD *looks blankly toward* MICHAEL*.* MICHAEL *looks back blankly.)*

COWBOY *(crossing to* HAROLD*).*

"Happy birthday to you,
Happy birthday to you,
Happy birthday, dear Harold.
Happy birthday to you."

(Throws his arms around HAROLD *and gives him a big kiss.* DONALD *looks toward* MICHAEL*, who observes this stoically.* HAROLD *breaks away from* COWBOY*, reads the card, begins to laugh.*

MICHAEL *turns to survey the room.* DONALD *watches him. Slowly* MICHAEL *begins to move. Walks over to the bar, pours a glass of gin, raises it to his lips, downs it all.* DONALD *watches silently as* HAROLD *laughs and laughs and laughs.)*

CURTAIN

ACT TWO

A moment later. HAROLD *is still laughing.* MICHAEL, *still at the bar, lowers his glass, turns to* HAROLD.

———

MICHAEL. What's so fucking funny?

HAROLD *(unintimidated; quick hand to hip)*. Life. Life is a goddamn laff-riot. You remember life.

MICHAEL. *You're stoned.* It shows in your arm.

LARRY. Happy birthday, Harold.

MICHAEL *(to* HAROLD*)*. Your're stoned and you're late! You were supposed to arrive at this location at approximately eight-thirty dash nine o'clock!

HAROLD. What I *am,* Michael, is a thirty-two-year-old, ugly, pockmarked Jew fairy— and if it takes me a while to pull myself together and if I smoke a little grass before I can get up the nerve to show this face to the world, it's nobody's goddamn business but my own. *(Instant switch to chatty tone)* And how are *you* this evening?

(HANK *lifts* ALAN *to the couch.* MICHAEL *turns away from* HAROLD, *pours himself another drink.* DONALD *watches.* HAROLD *sweeps past* MICHAEL *over to where* BERNARD *is helping* EMORY *up off the floor.* LARRY *returns the bucket to the bar.* MICHAEL *puts some ice in his drink.)*

EMORY. Happy birthday, Hallie.

HAROLD. What happened to *you?*

EMORY *(groans)*. Don't ask!

HAROLD. Your lips are turning blue; you look like you been rimming a snowman.

EMORY. That piss-elegant kooze hit me! *(Indicates* ALAN. HAROLD *looks toward the couch.* ALAN *has slumped his head forward into his own lap.)*

MICHAEL. Careful, Emory, that kind of talk just makes him s'nervous.

(ALAN *covers his ears with his hands.)*

HAROLD. Who is she? Who was she? Who does she hope to be?

EMORY. Who knows, who cares!

HANK. His name is Alan McCarthy.

MICHAEL. Do forgive me for not formally introducing you.

HAROLD *(sarcastically, to* MICHAEL*)*. Not the famous college *chum.*

MICHAEL *(takes an ice cube out of his glass, throws it at* HAROLD*)*. Do a figure eight on that.

HAROLD. Well, well, well. I finally get to meet dear ole Alan after all these years. And in black tie too. Is this my surprise from you, Michael?

LARRY. I think Alan is the one who got the surprise.

DONALD. And, if you'll notice, he's absolutely speechless.

EMORY. I *hope* she's in *shock!* She's a beast!

COWBOY *(indicating* ALAN*)*. Is it his birthday too?

EMORY *(indicates* COWBOY *to* HAROLD*)*. *That's* your surprise.

LARRY. Speaking of beasts.

EMORY. From me to you, darlin'. How do you like it?

HAROLD. Oh, I suppose he has an interesting face and body—but it turns me right off because he can't talk intelligently about art.

EMORY. Yeah, ain't it a shame.

HAROLD. I could never *love* anyone like that.

EMORY. Never. *Who could?*

HAROLD. I could and *you* could, that's who could! Oh, Mary, she's *gorgeous!*

EMORY. She may be dumb, but she's all yours!

HAROLD. In affairs of the heart, there are no rules! Where'd you ever find him?

EMORY. Rae knew where.

MICHAEL *(to* DONALD*)*. Rae is Rae Clark. That's R-A-E. She's Emory's dike friend who sings at a place in the Village. She wears pinstriped suits and bills herself "Miss Rae Clark —Songs Tailored To Your Taste."

EMORY. Miss Rae Clark. Songs tailored to your taste!

MICHAEL. Have you ever heard of anything so crummy in your life?

EMORY. Rae's a fabulous chanteuse. I adore the way she does: "Down in the Depths on the Ninetieth Floor."

MICHAEL. The faggot national anthem. *(Exits to the kitchen singing "Down in the Depths" in a butch baritone)*

HAROLD *(to* EMORY*)*. All I can say is thank God for Miss Rae Clark. I think my present is a super-surprise. I'm so thrilled to get it I'd kiss you but I don't want to get blood all over me.

EMORY. Ohhh, look at my sweater!

HAROLD. Wait'll you see your face.

BERNARD. Come on, Emory, let's clean you up. Happy birthday, Harold.

HAROLD *(smiles).* Thanks, love.

EMORY. My sweater is ruined!

MICHAEL *(from the kitchen).* Take one of mine in the bedroom.

DONALD. The one on the floor is vicuña.

BERNARD *(to* EMORY). You'll feel better after I bathe your face.

EMORY. Cheer-up-things-could-get-worse-I-did-and-they-did. (BERNARD *leads* EMORY *up the stairs.)*

HAROLD. Just another birthday party with the folks.

(MICHAEL *returns with a wine bottle and a green crystal white-wine glass, pouring en route.)*

MICHAEL. Here's a cold bottle of Pouilly-Fuissé I bought especially for you, kiddo.

HAROLD. Pussycat, all is forgiven. You can stay. No. You can stay, but not all is forgiven. Cheers.

MICHAEL. I didn't want it this way, Hallie.

HAROLD *(indicating* ALAN). Who asked Mr. Right to celebrate my birthday?

DONALD. There are no accidents.

HAROLD *(referring to* DONALD). And who asked *him?*

MICHAEL. *Guilty again.* When I make problems for myself, I go the whole route.

HAROLD. Always got to have your crutch, haven't you.

DONALD. I'm *not* leaving. *(Goes to the bar, makes himself another martini)*

HAROLD. Nobody ever thinks completely of somebody else. They always please themselves; they always cheat, if only a little bit.

LARRY *(referring to* ALAN). Why is he sitting there with his hands over his ears?

DONALD. I think he has an ick. (DONALD *looks at* MICHAEL. MICHAEL *returns the look, steely.)*

HANK *(to* ALAN). Can I get you a drink?

LARRY. How can he hear you, dummy, with his hands over his ears?

HAROLD. He can hear every word. In fact, he wouldn't miss a word if it killed him. (ALAN *removes his hands from his ears.)* What'd I tell you?

ALAN. I . . . I . . . feel sick. I think . . . I'm going to . . . throw up.

HAROLD. Say that again and I won't have to take my appetite depressant.

(ALAN *looks desperately toward* HANK.)

HANK. Hang on. (HANK *pulls* ALAN's *arm around his neck, lifts him up, takes him up the stairs.)*

HAROLD. Easy does it. One step at a time.

(BERNARD *and* EMORY *come out of the bath.)*

BERNARD. There. Feel better?

EMORY. Oh, Mary, what would I do without you? (EMORY *looks at himself in the mirror.)* I am not ready for my close-up, Mr. De Mille. Nor will I be for the next two weeks.

(BERNARD *picks up* MICHAEL's *sweater off the floor.* HANK *and* ALAN *are midway up the stairs.)*

ALAN. I'm going to throw up! Let me go! Let me go! *(Tears loose of* HANK, *bolts up the remainder of the stairs. He and* EMORY *meet head-on.* EMORY *screams.)*

EMORY. Oh, my God, he's after me again! (EMORY *recoils as* ALAN *whizzes past into the bathroom, slamming the door behind him.* HANK *has reached the bedroom.)*

HANK. He's sick.

BERNARD. Yeah, sick in the head. Here, Emory, put this on.

EMORY. Oh, Mary, take me home. My nerves can't stand any more of this tonight. (EMORY *takes the vicuña sweater from* BERNARD, *starts to put it on. Downstairs,* HAROLD *flamboyantly takes out a cigarette, takes a kitchen match from a striker, steps up on the seat of the couch and sits on the back of it.)*

HAROLD. TURNING ON! *(With that, he strikes the match on the sole of his shoe and lights up. Through a strained throat)* Anybody care to join me? *(Waves the cigarette in a slow pass)*

MICHAEL. Many thanks, no.

(HAROLD *passes it to* LARRY, *who nods negatively.)*

DONALD. No, thank you.

HAROLD *(to* COWBOY). How about you, Tex?

COWBOY. Yeah. (COWBOY *takes the cigarette, makes some audible inhalations through his teeth.)*

MICHAEL. I find the sound of the ritual alone utterly humiliating. *(Turns away, goes to the bar, makes another drink)*

LARRY. I hate the smell poppers leave on your fingers.

HAROLD. Why don't you get up and wash your hands?

(EMORY *and* BERNARD *come down the stairs.)*

EMORY. Michael, I left the casserole in the oven. You can take it out any time.

MICHAEL. You're not going.

EMORY. I couldn't eat now anyway.

HAROLD. Well, *I'm* absolutely ravenous. I'm going to eat until I have a fat attack.

MICHAEL *(to* EMORY*)*. I said, you're *not going.*

HAROLD *(to* MICHAEL*)*. Having a cocktail this evening, are we? In my honor?

EMORY. It's your favorite dinner, Hallie. I made it myself.

BERNARD. *Who* fixed the casserole?

EMORY. Well, *I* made the sauce!

BERNARD. Well, *I* made the salad!

LARRY. Girls, please.

MICHAEL. Please *what!*

HAROLD. Beware the hostile fag. When he's sober, he's dangerous. When he drinks, he's lethal.

MICHAEL *(referring to* HAROLD*)*. Attention must *not* be paid.

HAROLD. I'm starved, Em, I'm ready for some of your Alice B. Toklas' opium-baked lasagna.

EMORY. Are you really? Oh, that makes me so pleased maybe I'll just serve it before I leave.

MICHAEL. *You're not leaving.*

BERNARD. I'll help.

LARRY. I better help too. We don't need a nosebleed in the lasagna.

BERNARD. When the sauce is on it, you wouldn't be able to tell the difference anyway. (EMORY, BERNARD, *and* LARRY *exit to the kitchen.)*

MICHAEL *(proclamation)*. Nobody's going anywhere!

HAROLD. You are going to have schmertz tomorrow you wouldn't believe.

MICHAEL. May I kiss the hem of your schmata, Doctor Freud?

COWBOY. What are you two talking about? I don't understand.

DONALD. He's working through his Oedipus complex, sugar. With a machete.

COWBOY. Huh?

(HANK *comes down the stairs.)*

HANK. Michael, is there any air spray?

HAROLD. Hair spray! You're supposed to be holding his head, not doing his hair.

HANK. *Air* spray, not *hair* spray.

MICHAEL. There's a can of floral spray right on top of the john.

HANK. Thanks. (HANK *goes back upstairs.)*

HAROLD *(to* MICHAEL*)*. Aren't you going to say, "If it was a snake, it would have bitten you."?

MICHAEL *(indicating* COWBOY*)*. That is something only your friend would say.

HAROLD *(to* MICHAEL*)*. I am turning on and you are just turning. *(To* DONALD*)* I keep my grass in the medicine cabinet. In a Band-Aid box. Somebody told me it's the safest place. If the cops arrive, you can always lock yourself in the bathroom and flush it down the john.

DONALD. *Very cagey.*

HAROLD. It makes more sense than where I *was* keeping it—in an oregano jar in the spice rack. I kept forgetting and accidentally turning my hateful mother on with the salad. *(A beat)* But I think she liked it. No matter what meal she comes over for—even if it's breakfast—she says, "Let's have a salad!"

COWBOY *(to* MICHAEL*)*. Why do you say I would say, "If it was a snake, it would have bitten you."? I think that's what I *would* have said.

MICHAEL. Of course you would have, baby. That's the kind of remark your pint-size brain thinks of. You are definitely the type who still moves his lips when he reads and who sits in a steam room and says things like "Hot enough for you?"

COWBOY. I never use the steam room when I go to the gym. It's bad after a workout. It flattens you down.

MICHAEL. Just after you've broken your back to blow yourself up like a poisoned dog.

COWBOY. Yeah.

MICHAEL. You're right, Harold. Not only can he not talk intelligently about art, he can't even follow from one sentence to the next.

HAROLD. *But he's beautiful.* He has *un-natural* natural beauty. *(Quick palm upheld)* Not that that means anything.

MICHAEL. It doesn't mean *everything.*

HAROLD. Keep telling yourself that as your hair drops out in handfuls. *(Quick palm upheld)* Not that it's not *natural* for one's hair to recede as one reaches seniority. Not that those wonderful lines that have begun creasing our countenances don't make all the difference in the world because they add so much *character.*

MICHAEL. Faggots are worse than women about their age. They think their lives are over at thirty. Physical beauty is not that goddamned important!

HAROLD. Of course not. How could it be—it's only in the eye of the beholder.

MICHAEL. And it's only skin deep—don't forget that one.

HAROLD. Oh, no, I haven't forgotten that one at all. It's only skin deep and it's *transitory* too. It's *terribly* transitory. I mean, how long does it last—thirty or forty or fifty years at the most—depending on how well you take care of yourself. And not counting, of course, that you might die before it runs out anyway. Yes, it's too bad about this poor boy's face. It's tragic. He's absolutely cursed! *(Takes* COWBOY's *face in his hands)* How can *his* beauty ever compare with *my* soul? And although I have never seen my soul, I understand from my mother's rabbi that it's a knockout. I, however, cannot seem to locate it for a gander. And if I could, I'd sell it in a flash for some skin-deep, transitory, meaningless beauty!

*(*ALAN *walks weakly into the bedroom and sits on the bed. Downstairs,* LARRY *enters from the kitchen with salad plates.* HANK *comes into the bedroom and turns out the lamps.* ALAN *lies down. Now only the light from the bathroom and the stairwell illuminates the room)*

MICHAEL *(makes sign of the cross with his drink in hand)*. Forgive him, Father, for he know not what he do.

*(*HANK *stands still in the half darkness.)*

HAROLD. Michael, you kill me. You don't know what side of the fence you're on. If somebody says something pro-religion, you're against them. If somebody denies God, you're against *them.* One might say that you have some problem in that area. You can't live with it and you can't live without it.

*(*EMORY *barges through the swinging door, carrying the casserole.)*

EMORY. Hot stuff! Comin' through!

MICHAEL *(to* EMORY). One could murder you with very little effort.

HAROLD *(to* MICHAEL). You hang on to that great insurance policy called The Church.

MICHAEL. That's right. I believe in God, and if it turns out that there really isn't one, okay. Nothing lost. But if it turns out that there *is*—I'm covered.

*(*BERNARD *enters, carrying a huge salad bowl. He puts it down, lights table candles.)*

EMORY *(to* MICHAEL). Harriet Hypocrite, that's who you are.

MICHAEL. Right. I'm one of those truly rotten Catholics who gets drunk, sins all night, and goes to Mass the next morning.

EMORY. Gilda Guilt. It depends on what you think sin is.

MICHAEL. Would you just shut up your goddamn minty mouth and get back to the goddamn kitchen!

EMORY. Say anything you want—*just don't hit me! (Exits. A beat)*

MICHAEL. Actually, I suppose Emory has a point—I only go to confession before I get on a plane.

BERNARD. Do you think God's power only exists at thirty thousand feet?

MICHAEL. It must. On the ground, I *am* God. In the air, I'm just one more scared son of a bitch. *(A beat)*

BERNARD. I'm scared on the ground.

COWBOY. Me, too. *(A beat)* That is, when I'm not high on pot or up on acid.

*(*HANK *comes down the stairs.)*

LARRY *(to* HANK). Well, is it bigger than a breadstick?

HANK *(ignores last remark; to* MICHAEL). He's lying down for a minute.

HAROLD. How does the bathroom smell?

HANK. Better.

MICHAEL. Before it smelled like somebody puked. Now it smells like somebody puked in a gardenia patch.

LARRY. And how does the big hero feel?

HANK. Lay off, will you. *(*EMORY *enters with a basket of napkin-covered rolls, deposits them on the table.)*

EMORY. *Dinner is served!*

*(*HAROLD *comes to the buffet table.)*

HAROLD. Emory, it looks absolutely fabulous.

EMORY. I'd make somebody a good wife. *(*EMORY *serves pasta.* BERNARD *serves the salad, pours wine.* MICHAEL *goes to the bar, makes another drink.)* I could cook and do an apartment and entertain . . . *(Grabs a long-stem rose from an arrangement on the table, clenches it between his teeth, snaps his fingers and strikes a pose)* Kiss me quick, I'm Carmen! *(*HAROLD *just looks at him blankly, passes on.* EMORY *takes the flower out of his mouth.)* One really needs castanets for that sort of thing.

MICHAEL. And a getaway car.

*(*HANK *comes up to the table.)*

EMORY. What would you like, big boy?

LARRY. Alan McCarthy, and don't hold the mayo.

EMORY. I can't keep up with you two *(indicating* HANK, *then* LARRY)—I thought you were mad at him—now he's bitchin' you. What gives?

LARRY. Never mind.

*(*COWBOY *comes over to the table.* EMORY *gives him a plate of food.* BERNARD *gives him salad and a glass of wine.* HANK *moves to the*

couch, sits and puts his plate and glass on the coffee table. HAROLD *moves to sit on the stairs and eat.)*

COWBOY. What is it?

LARRY. Lasagna.

COWBOY. It looks like spaghetti and meatballs sorta flattened out.

DONALD. It's been in the steam room.

COWBOY. It has?

MICHAEL *(contemptuously).* It looks like spaghetti and meatballs sorta flattened out. Ah, yes, Harold—truly enviable.

HAROLD. As opposed to you who knows so much about *haute cuisine. (A beat)* Raconteur, gourmet, troll. (LARRY *takes a plate of food, goes to sit on the back of the couch from behind it.)*

COWBOY. It's good.

HAROLD *(quick).* You like it, eat it.

MICHAEL. Stuff your mouth so that you can't say anything.

(DONALD *takes a plate.)*

HAROLD. Turning.

BERNARD *(to* DONALD). Wine?

DONALD. No, thanks.

MICHAEL. Aw, go on, kiddo, force yourself. Have a little *vin ordinaire* to wash down all that depressed pasta.

HAROLD. Sommelier, connoisseur, pig.

(DONALD *takes the glass of wine, moves up by the bar, puts the glass of wine on it, leans against the wall, eats his food.* EMORY *hands* BERNARD *a plate.)*

BERNARD *(to* EMORY). Aren't you going to have any?

EMORY. No. My lip hurts to much to eat.

MICHAEL *(crosses to table, picks up knife).* I hear if you puts a knife under de bed it cuts de pain.

HAROLD *(to* MICHAEL). I hear if you put a knife under your chin it cuts your throat.

EMORY. Anybody going to take a plate up to Alan?

MICHAEL. The punching bag has now dissolved into Flo Nightingale.

LARRY. Hank?

HANK. I don't think he'd have any appetite.

(ALAN, *as if he's heard his name, gets up from the bed, moves slowly to the top of the stairwell.* BERNARD *takes his plate, moves near the stairs, sits on the floor.* MICHAEL *raps the knife on an empty wine glass.)*

MICHAEL. Ladies and gentlemen. Correction: Ladies and ladies, I would like to announce that you have just eaten Sebastian Venable.

COWBOY. Just eaten *what?*

MICHAEL. Not *what,* stupid. *Who.* A character in a play. A fairy who was eaten alive. I mean the chop-chop variety.

COWBOY. Jesus.

HANK. Did Edward Albee write that play?

MICHAEL. No. Tennessee Williams.

HANK. Oh, yeah.

MICHAEL. Albee wrote *Who's Afraid of Virginia Woolf?*

LARRY. Dummy.

HANK. I know that. I just thought maybe he wrote that other one too.

LARRY. Well, you made a mistake.

HANK. So I made a mistake.

LARRY. That's right, you made a mistake.

HANK. What's the difference? You can't add.

COWBOY. Edward who.

MICHAEL *(to* EMORY). How much did you pay for him?

EMORY. He was a steal.

MICHAEL. He's a ham sandwich—fifty cents any time of the day or night.

HAROLD. King of the Pig People. (MICHAEL *gives him a look.* DONALD *returns his plate to the table.)*

EMORY *(to* DONALD). Would you like some more?

DONALD. No, thank you, Emory. It was very good.

EMORY. Did you like it?

COWBOY. I'm not a steal. I cost twenty dollars.

(BERNARD *returns his plate.)*

EMORY. More?

BERNARD *(nods negatively).* It was delicious—even if I did make it myself.

EMORY. Isn't anybody having seconds?

HAROLD. I'm having seconds and thirds and maybe even fifths. *(Gets up off the stairs, comes toward the table)* I'm absolutely desperate to keep the weight up.

(BERNARD *bends to whisper something in* EMORY*'s ear.* EMORY *nods affirmatively and* BERNARD *crosses to* COWBOY *and whispers in his ear. A beat.* COWBOY *returns his plate to the buffet and follows* EMORY *and* BERNARD *into the kitchen.)*

MICHAEL *(parodying* HAROLD). You're *absolutely* paranoid about *absolutely* everything.

HAROLD. Oh, yeah, well, why don't you *not* tell me about it.

MICHAEL. You starve yourself all day, living on coffee and cottage cheese so that you can gorge yourself at one meal. Then you feel guilty and moan and groan about how fat you are and how ugly you are when the truth is you're no fatter or thinner than you ever are.

EMORY. Polly Paranoia. (EMORY *moves to the coffee table to take* HANK's *empty plate.)*

HANK. Just great, Emory.

EMORY. Connie Casserole, no-trouble-at-all-oh-Mary, D.A.

MICHAEL (to HAROLD). . . . And this pathological lateness. It's downright *crazy.*

HAROLD. Turning.

MICHAEL. Standing before a bathroom mirror for hours and hours before you can walk out on the street. And looking no different after Christ knows how many applications of Christ knows how many ointments and salves and creams and masks.

HAROLD. I've got bad skin, what can I tell you.

MICHAEL. Who wouldn't after they deliberately take a pair of tweezers and *deliberately* mutilate their pores—no wonder you've got holes in your face after the hack job you've done on yourself year in and year out!

HAROLD (coolly but definitely). You hateful sow.

MICHAEL. Yes, you've got scars on your face—but they're not that bad and if you'd leave yourself alone you wouldn't have any more than you've already awarded yourself.

HAROLD. You'd really like me to compliment you now for being so honest, wouldn't you. For being my best friend who will tell me what even my best friends won't tell me. Swine.

MICHAEL. And the pills! (Announcement to group) Harold has been gathering, saving, and storing up barbiturates for the last year like a goddamn squirrel. Hundreds of Nembutals, hundreds of Seconals. All in preparation for and anticipation of the long winter of his death. (Silence) But I tell you right now, Hallie. When the time comes, you'll never have the guts. It's not always like it happens in plays, not all faggots bump themselves off at the end of the story.

HAROLD. What you say may be true. Time will undoubtedly tell. But, in the meantime, you've left out one detail—the cosmetics and astringents are *paid* for, the bathroom is *paid* for, the tweezers are *paid* for, and the pills *are paid for!*

(EMORY *darts in and over to the light switch, plunges the room into darkness except for the light from the tapers on the buffet table, and*

begins to sing "Happy Birthday." Immediately BERNARD *pushes the swinging door open and* COWBOY *enters carrying a cake ablaze with candles. Everyone has now joined in with "Happy birthday, dear Harold, happy birthday to you." This is followed by a round of applause.* MICHAEL *turns, goes to the bar, makes another drink.)*

EMORY. Blow out your candles, Mary, and make a wish!

MICHAEL (to himself). Blow out your candles, *Laura.*

(COWBOY *has brought cake over in front of* HAROLD. *He thinks a minute, blows out the candles. More applause)*

EMORY. Awwww, she's thirty-two years young!

HAROLD (groans, holds his head). Ohh, my God!

(BERNARD *has brought in cake plates and forks. The room remains lit only by candlelight from the buffet table.* COWBOY *returns the cake to the table and* BERNARD *begins to cut it and put the pieces on the plates.)*

HANK. Now you have to open your gifts.

HAROLD. Do I have to open them here?

EMORY. Of course you've got to open them here. (Hands HAROLD *a gift.* HAROLD *begins to rip the paper off.)*

HAROLD. Where's the card?

EMORY. Here.

HAROLD. Oh. From Larry. (Finishes tearing off the paper) It's heaven! Oh, I just love it, Larry. (HAROLD *holds up a graphic design —a large-scale deed to Boardwalk, like those used in a Monopoly game.)*

COWBOY. What is it?

HAROLD. It's the deed to Boardwalk.

EMORY. Oh, gay pop art!

DONALD (to LARRY). It's sensational. Did you do it?

LARRY. Yes.

HAROLD. Oh, it's super, Larry. It goes up the minute I get home. (HAROLD *gives* LARRY *a peck on the cheek.)*

COWBOY (to HAROLD). I don't get it—you cruise Atlantic City or something?

MICHAEL. Will somebody get him out of here!

(HAROLD *has torn open another gift, takes the card from inside.)*

HAROLD. Oh, what a nifty sweater! Thank you, Hank.

HANK. You can take it back and pick out another one if you want to.

HAROLD. I think this one is just nifty.

(DONALD *goes to the bar, makes himself a brandy and soda.*)

BERNARD. Who wants cake?

EMORY. Everybody?

DONALD. None for me.

MICHAEL. I'd just like to sleep on mine, thank you.

(HANK *comes over to the table.* BERNARD *gives him a plate of cake, passes another one to* COWBOY *and a third to* LARRY. HAROLD *has torn the paper off another gift. Suddenly laughs aloud*)

HAROLD. Oh, Bernard! How divine! Look, everybody! Bejeweled knee pads! (*Holds up a pair of basketball knee pads with sequin initials*)

BERNARD. Monogrammed!

EMORY. Bernard, you're a camp!

MICHAEL. Y'all heard of Gloria DeHaven and Billy de Wolfe, well, dis here is Rosemary De Camp!

BERNARD. Who?

EMORY. I never miss a Rosemary De Camp picture.

HANK. I've never heard of her.

COWBOY. Me neither.

HANK. Not all of us spent their childhood in a movie house, Michael. Some of us played baseball.

DONALD. And mowed the lawn.

EMORY. Well, *I* know who Rosemary De Camp is.

MICHAEL. You would. It's a cinch you wouldn't recognize a baseball or a lawnmower.

(HAROLD *has unwrapped his last gift. He is silent. Pause*)

HAROLD. Thank you, Michael.

MICHAEL. What? (*Turns to see the gift*) Oh. (*A beat*) You're welcome. (MICHAEL *finishes off his drink, returns to the bar.*)

LARRY. What is it, Harold? (*A beat*)

HAROLD. It's a photograph of him in a silver frame. And there's an inscription engraved and the date.

BERNARD. What's it say?

HAROLD. Just . . . something personal.

(MICHAEL *spins round from the bar.*)

MICHAEL. Hey, Bernard, what do you say we have a little music to liven things up!

BERNARD. Okay.

EMORY. Yeah, I feel like dancing.

MICHAEL. How about something good and ethnic, Emory—one of your specialties, like a military toe tap with sparklers.

EMORY. I don't do that at birthdays—only

on the Fourth of July. (BERNARD *puts on a romantic record.* EMORY *goes to* BERNARD. *They start to dance slowly.*)

LARRY. Come on, Michael.

MICHAEL. I only lead.

LARRY. I can follow. (*They start to dance.*)

HAROLD. Come on, Tex, you're on. (COWBOY *gets to his feet, but is a washout as a dancing partner.* HAROLD *gives up, takes out another cigarette, strikes a match. As he does, he catches sight of someone over by the stairs, walks over to* ALAN. *Blows out match*) Wanna dance?

EMORY (*sees* ALAN). Uh-oh. Yvonne the Terrible is back.

MICHAEL. Oh, hello, Alan. Feel better? This is where you came in, isn't it? (ALAN *starts to cross directly to the door.* MICHAEL *breaks away.*) Excuse me, Larry . . . (ALAN *has reached the door and has started to open it as* MICHAEL *intercepts, slams the door with one hand, and leans against it, crossing his legs.*) As they say in the Deep South, don't rush off in the heat of the day.

HAROLD. Revolution complete.

(MICHAEL *slowly takes* ALAN *by the arm, walks him slowly back into the room.*)

MICHAEL. You missed the cake—and you missed the opening of the gifts—but you're still in luck. You're just in time for a party game. (*They have reached the phonograph.* MICHAEL *rejects the record. The music stops, the dancing stops.* MICHAEL *releases* ALAN, *claps his hands.*)Hey, everybody! Game time! (ALAN *starts to move.* MICHAEL *catches him gently by the sleeve.*)

HAROLD. Why don't you just let him go, Michael?

MICHAEL. He can go if he wants to—but not before we play a little game.

EMORY. What's it going to be—movie-star gin?

MICHAEL. That's too faggy for Alan to play—he wouldn't be any good at it.

BERNARD. What about Likes and Dislikes?

(MICHAEL *lets go of* ALAN, *takes a pencil and pad from the desk.*)

MICHAEL. It's too much trouble to find enough pencils, and besides, Emory always puts down the same thing. He dislikes artificial fruit and flowers and coffee grinders made into lamps—and he likes Mabel Mercer, poodles, and *All About Eve*—the screenplay of which he will then recite *verbatim*.

EMORY. I put down other things sometimes.

MICHAEL. Like a tan out of season?

EMORY. I just always put down little "Chi-Chi" because I adore her so much.

MICHAEL. If one is of the masculine gender, a poodle is the *insignia* of one's deviation.

BERNARD. You know why old ladies like poodles—because they go down on them.

EMORY. *They do not!*

LARRY. We could play B for Botticelli.

MICHAEL. We *could* play *Spin* the Botticelli, but we're not going to. *(A beat)*

HAROLD. What would you like to play, Michael—the Truth Game? (MICHAEL *chuckles to himself.)*

MICHAEL. Cute, Hallie.

HAROLD. Or do you want to play Murder? You all remember that one, don't you?

MICHAEL *(to* HAROLD). Very, very cute.

DONALD. As I recall, they're quite similar. The rules are the same in both—you kill somebody.

MICHAEL. In affairs of the heart, there are no rules. Isn't that right, Harold?

HAROLD. That's what I always say.

MICHAEL. Well, that's the name of the game. The Affairs of the Heart.

COWBOY. I've never heard of that one.

MICHAEL. Of course you've never heard of it—I just made it up, baby doll. Affairs of the Heart is a combination of both the Truth Game and Murder—with a new twist.

HAROLD. I can hardly wait to find out what that is.

ALAN. Mickey, I'm leaving. *(Starts to move)*

MICHAEL *(firmly, flatly).* Stay where you are.

HAROLD. Michael, let him go.

MICHAEL. He really doesn't *want* to. If he did, he'd have left a long time ago—or he wouldn't have come here in the first place.

ALAN *(holding his forehead).* Mickey, I don't *feel* well!

MICHAEL *(low tone, but distinctly articulate).* My name is Michael. I am called Michael. You must never call anyone called Michael Mickey. Those of us who are named Michael are very nervous about it. If you don't believe it—try it.

ALAN. I'm sorry. I can't think.

MICHAEL. You can think. What you can't do—is leave. It's like watching an accident on the highway—you can't look at it and you can't look away.

ALAN. I . . . feel . . . weak . . .

MICHAEL. You are weak. Much weaker than I think you realize. *(Takes* ALAN *by the* arm, leads him to a chair. Slowly, deliberately, pushes him down into it)* Now! Who's going to play with Alan and me? Everyone?

HAROLD. I have no intention of playing.

DONALD. Nor do I.

MICHAEL. Well, not everyone is a participant in *life.* There are always those who stand on the sidelines and watch.

LARRY. What's the game?

MICHAEL. Simply this: we all have to call on the telephone the *one person* we truly believe we have loved.

HANK. I'm not playing.

LARRY. Oh, yes, you are.

HANK. You'd like for me to play, wouldn't you?

LARRY. You bet I would. I like to know who you'd call after all the fancy speeches I've heard lately. Who would you call? Would you call me?

MICHAEL *(to* BERNARD). Sounds like there's, how you say, trouble in paradise.

HAROLD. If there isn't, I think you'll be able to stir up some.

HANK. And who would *you* call? Don't think for one minute it would be me. Or that one call would do it. You'd have to make several, wouldn't you? About three long-distance and God only knows how many locals.

COWBOY. I'm glad I don't have to pay the bill.

MICHAEL. Quiet!

HAROLD *(loud whisper to* COWBOY). Oh, don't worry, Michael won't pay it either.

MICHAEL. Now, here's how it works.

LARRY. I thought you said there were no rules.

MICHAEL. That's right. In Affairs of the Heart, there are no rules. This is the goddamn point system! *(No response from anyone. A beat)* If you make the call, you get one point. If the person you are calling answers, you get two more points. If somebody else answers, you get only one. If there's no answer at all, you're screwed.

DONALD. You're screwed if you make the call.

HAROLD. You're a *fool*—if you screw yourself.

MICHAEL. When you get the person whom you are calling on the line—if you tell them who you are, you get two points. And then— if you tell them that you *love* them—you get a bonus of five more points!

HAROLD. Hateful.

MICHAEL. Therefore you can get as many as ten points and as few as one.

HAROLD. You can get as few as none—if you know how to work it.

MICHAEL. The one with the highest score wins.

ALAN. Hank. Let's get out of here.

EMORY. Well, now. Did you hear that!

MICHAEL. Just the two of you together. The pals . . . the guys . . . the buddy-buddies . . . the he-men.

EMORY. I think Larry might have something to say about that.

BERNARD. Emory.

MICHAEL. The duenna speaks. *(Crosses to take the telephone from the desk, brings it to the group)* So who's playing? Not including Cowboy, who, as a gift, is neuter. And, of course, le voyeur. *(A beat)* Emory? Bernard?

BERNARD. I don't think I want to play.

MICHAEL. Why, Bernard! Where's your fun-loving spirit?

BERNARD. I don't think this game is fun.

HAROLD. It's absolutely hateful.

ALAN. Hank, leave with me.

HANK. You don't understand, Alan. I can't. You can . . . but I can't.

ALAN. Why, Hank? Why can't you?

LARRY *(to HANK)*. If he doesn't understand, why don't you explain it to him?

MICHAEL. *I'll* explain it.

HAROLD. I had a feeling you might.

MICHAEL. Although I doubt that it'll make any difference. That type refuses to understand that which they do not wish to accept. They reject certain facts. And Alan is decidedly from The Ostrich School of Reality. *(A beat)* Alan . . . Larry and Hank are lovers. Not just roommates, *bed*mates. *Lovers.*

ALAN. Michael!

MICHAEL. No man's still got a *roommate* when he's over thirty years old. If they're not lovers, they're sisters.

LARRY. Hank is the one who's over thirty.

MICHAEL. Well, you're pushing it!

ALAN. . . . Hank? *(A beat)*

HANK. Yes, Alan. Larry is my lover.

ALAN. But . . . but . . . you're married.

(MICHAEL, LARRY, EMORY, and COWBOY are sent into instant gales of laughter.)

HAROLD. I think you said the wrong thing.

MICHAEL. Don't you love that quaint little idea—if a man is married, then he is automatically heterosexual. *(A beat)* Alan—Hank swings both ways—with a definite preference. *(A beat)* Now. Who makes the first call? Emory?

EMORY. You go, Bernard.

BERNARD. I don't want to.

EMORY. I don't want to either. I don't want to at all.

DONALD *(to himself)*. There are no accidents.

MICHAEL. Then, may I say, on your way home I hope you *will* yourself over an embankment.

EMORY *(to BERNARD)*. Go on. Call up Peter Dahlbeck. That's who you'd like to call, isn't it?

MICHAEL. Who is Peter Dahlbeck?

EMORY. The boy in Detroit whose family Bernard's mother has been a laundress for since he was a pickaninny.

BERNARD. I worked for them too—after school and every summer.

EMORY. It's always been a large order of Hero Worship.

BERNARD. I think I've loved him all my life. But he never knew I was alive. Besides, he's straight.

COWBOY. So nothing ever happened between you?

EMORY. Oh, they finally made it—in the pool house one night after a drunken swimming party.

LARRY. With the right wine and the right music there're damn few that aren't curious.

MICHAEL. Sounds like there's a lot of Lady Chatterley in Mr. Dahlbeck, wouldn't you say, Donald?

DONALD. I've never been an O'Hara fan myself.

BERNARD. . . . And afterwards we went swimming in the nude in the dark with only the moon reflecting on the water.

DONALD. Nor Thomas Merton.

BERNARD. It was beautiful.

MICHAEL. How romantic. And then the next morning you took him his coffee and Alka-Seltzer on a tray.

BERNARD. It was in the afternoon. I remember I was worried sick all morning about having to face him. But he pretended like nothing at all had happened.

MICHAEL. Christ, he must have been so drunk he didn't remember a thing.

BERNARD. Yeah. I was sure relieved.

MICHAEL. Odd how that works. And now, for ten points, get that liar on the phone.

(A beat. BERNARD picks up the phone, dials.)

LARRY. You *know* the number?

BERNARD. Sure. He's back in Grosse Pointe, living at home. He just got separated from his third wife.

(All watch BERNARD *as he puts the receiver to his ear, waits. A beat. He hangs up quickly.)*

EMORY. D.A. or B.Y.?

MICHAEL. He didn't even give it time to find out. *(Coaxing)* Go ahead, Bernard. Pick up the phone and dial. You'll think of something. You know you want to call him. You know that, don't you? Well, go ahead. Your curiosity has got the best of you now. So . . . go on, call him.

(A beat. BERNARD *picks up the receiver, dials again. Lets it ring this time)*

HAROLD. Hateful.

COWBOY. What's D.A. or B.Y.?

EMORY. That's operator lingo. It means "Doesn't Answer" or "Busy."

BERNARD. Hello?

MICHAEL. One point. *(Efficiently takes note on the pad)*

BERNARD. Who's speaking? Oh . . . Mrs. Dahlbeck.

MICHAEL *(taking note)*. One point.

BERNARD. . . . It's Bernard—Francine's boy.

EMORY. *Son,* not *boy.*

BERNARD. . . . How are you? Good. Good. Oh, just fine, thank you. Mrs. Dahlbeck . . . is . . . Peter . . . at home? Oh. Oh, I see.

MICHAEL *(shakes his head)*. Shhhhiiii . . .

BERNARD. . . . Oh, no. No, it's nothing important. I just wanted to . . . to tell him . . . that . . . to tell him I . . . I . . .

MICHAEL *(prompting flatly)*. I love him. That I've always loved him.

BERNARD. . . . that I was sorry to hear about him and his wife.

MICHAEL. No points!

BERNARD. My mother wrote me. Yes. It is. It really is. Well. Would you just tell him I called and said . . . that I was . . . just . . . very, very sorry to hear and I . . . hope . . . they can get everything straightened out. Yes. Yes. Well, good night. Goodbye. *(Hangs up slowly.* MICHAEL *draws a definite line across his pad, makes a definite period.)*

MICHAEL. Two points total. Terrible. Next! *(*MICHAEL *whisks the phone out of* BERNARD*'s hands, gives it to* EMORY*.)*

EMORY. Are you all right, Bernard?

BERNARD *(almost to himself)*. Why did I call? Why did I do that?

LARRY *(to* BERNARD*)*. Where was he?

BERNARD. Out on a date.

MICHAEL. Come on, Emory. Punch in.

*(*EMORY *picks up the phone, dials information. A beat)*

EMORY. Could I have the number, please —in the Bronx—for a Delbert Botts.

LARRY. A Delbert Botts! How many can there be!

BERNARD. Oh, I wish I hadn't called now.

EMORY. No, the residence number, please. *(Waves his hand at* MICHAEL, *signaling for the pencil.* MICHAEL *hands it to him. He writes on the white plastic phone case.)* . . . Thank you. *(A beat. And he indignantly slams down the receiver.)* I do wish information would stop calling me "Ma'am"!

MICHAEL. By all means, scribble all over the telephone. *(Snatches the pencil from* EM-ORY*'s hands)*

EMORY. It comes off with a little spit.

MICHAEL. Like a lot of things.

LARRY. Who the hell is Delbert Botts?

EMORY. The one person I have always loved. *(To* MICHAEL*)* That's who you said call, isn't it?

MICHAEL. That's right, Emory board.

LARRY. How could you love anybody with a name like that?

MICHAEL. Yes, Emory, you couldn't love anybody with a name like that. It wouldn't look good on a place card. Isn't that right, Alan? *(*MICHAEL *slaps* ALAN *on the shoulder.* ALAN *is silent.* MICHAEL *snickers.)*

EMORY. I admit his name is not so good— but he is absolutely beautiful. At least, he was when I was in high school. Of course, I haven't seen him since and he was about seven years older than I even then.

MICHAEL. Christ, you better call him quick before he dies.

EMORY. I've loved him ever since the first day I laid eyes on him, which was when I was in the fifth grade and he was a senior. Then, he went away to college and by the time he got out I was in high school, and he had become a dentist.

MICHAEL *(with incredulous disgust)*. A dentist!

EMORY. Yes. Delbert Botts, D.D.S. And he opened his office in a bank building.

HAROLD. And you went and had every tooth in your head pulled out, right?

EMORY. No. I just had my teeth cleaned, that's all.

*(*DONALD *turns from the bar with two drinks in his hands.)*

BERNARD *(to himself)*. Oh, I shouldn't have called.

MICHAEL. Will you shut up, Bernard! And take your boring, sleep-making icks somewhere else. *Go!* (MICHAEL *extends a pointed finger toward the steps.* BERNARD *takes the wine bottle and his glass and moves toward the stairs, pouring himself another drink on the way.*)

EMORY. I remember I looked right into his eyes the whole time and I kept wanting to bite his fingers.

HAROLD. Well, it's absolutely mind boggling.

MICHAEL. Phyllis Phallic.

HAROLD. It absolutely boggles the mind.

(DONALD *brings one of the drinks to* ALAN. ALAN *takes it, drinks it down.*)

MICHAEL (*referring to* DONALD). Sara Samaritan.

EMORY. . . . I told him I was having my teeth cleaned for the Junior-Senior Prom, for which I was in charge of decorations. I told him it was a celestial theme and I was cutting stars out of tin foil and making clouds out of chicken wire and angel's hair. (*A beat*) He couldn't have been less impressed.

COWBOY. I got angel's hair down my shirt once at Christmas time. Gosh, did it itch!

EMORY. I told him I was going to burn incense in pots so that white fog would hover over the dance floor and it would look like heaven—just like I'd seen it in a Rita Hayworth movie. I can't remember the title.

MICHAEL. The picture was called *Down to Earth.* Any *kid* knows that.

COWBOY. . . . And it made little tiny cuts in the creases of my fingers. Man, did they sting! It would be terrible if you got that stuff in you . . . (MICHAEL *circles slowly toward him.*) I'll be quiet.

EMORY. He was engaged to this stupid-ass girl named Loraine whose mother was truly Supercunt.

MICHAEL. Don't digress.

EMORY. Well, anyway, I was a wreck. I mean a total mess. I couldn't eat, sleep, stand up, sit down, *nothing.* I could hardly cut out silver stars or finish the clouds for the prom. So I called him on the telephone and asked if I could see him alone.

HAROLD. Clearly not the coolest of moves.

(DONALD *looks at* ALAN. ALAN *looks away.*)

EMORY. He said okay and told me to come by his house. I was so nervous my hands were shaking and my voice was unsteady. I couldn't look at him this time—I just stared straight in space and blurted out why I'd come. I told him . . . I wanted him to be my friend. I said that I had never had a friend who I could talk to and tell everything and trust. I asked him if he would be my friend.

COWBOY. You poor bastard.

MICHAEL. Shhhhhh!

BERNARD. What'd he say?

EMORY. He said he would be glad to be my friend. And any time I ever wanted to see him or call him—to just call him and he'd see me. And he shook my trembling wet hand and I left on a cloud.

MICHAEL. One of the ones you made yourself.

EMORY. And the next day I went and bought him a gold-plated cigarette lighter and had his initials monogrammed on it and wrote a card that said "From your friend, Emory."

HAROLD. Seventeen years old and already big with the gifts.

COWBOY. Yeah. And cards too.

EMORY. . . . And then the night of the prom I found out.

BERNARD. Found out what?

EMORY. I heard two girls I knew giggling together. They were standing behind some goddamn corrugated cardboard Greek columns I had borrowed from a department store and had draped with yards and yards of goddamn cheesecloth. Oh, Mary, it takes a fairy to make something pretty.

MICHAEL. *Don't digress.*

EMORY. This girl who was telling the story said she had heard it from her mother—and her mother had heard it from Loraine's mother. (*To* MICHAEL) You see, Loraine and her mother were not beside the point. (*Back to the group*) Obviously, Del had told Loraine about my calling and about the gift. (*A beat*) Pretty soon everybody at the dance had heard about it and they were laughing and making jokes. Everybody knew I had a crush on Doctor Delbert Botts and that I had asked him to be my friend. (*A beat*) What they didn't know was that I *loved* him. And that I would go on loving him years after they had all forgotten my funny secret. (*Pause*)

HAROLD. Well, I for one need an insulin injection.

MICHAEL. *Call him.*

BERNARD. Don't, Emory.

MICHAEL. Since when are you telling him what to do!

EMORY (*to* BERNARD) What do I care— I'm pissed! I'll do anything. Three times.

BERNARD. Don't. *Please!*

MICHAEL. I said call him.

BERNARD. Don't! You'll be sorry. Take my word for it.

EMORY. What have I got to lose?

BERNARD. Your dignity. That's what you've got to lose.

MICHAEL. Well, *that's* a knee-slapper! I love *your* telling *him* about dignity when you allow him to degrade you constantly by Uncle Tom-ing you to death.

BERNARD. *He* can do it, Michael. *I* can do it. But *you can't* do it.

MICHAEL. Isn't that discrimination?

BERNARD. I don't like it from him and I don't like it from me—but I do it to myself and I let him do it. I let him do it because it's the only thing that, to him, makes him my equal. We both got the short end of the stick —but I got a hell of a lot more than he did and he knows it. I let him Uncle Tom me just so he can tell himself he's not a complete loser.

MICHAEL. How very considerate.

BERNARD. It's his defense. You have your defense, Michael. But it's indescribable. (EMORY *quietly licks his finger and begins to rub the number off the telephone case*)

MICHAEL (*to* BERNARD). Y'all want to hear a little polite parlor jest from the liberal Deep South? Do you know why *Nigras* have such big lips? Because they're always going "P-p-p-a-a-a-h!" (*The labial noise is exasperating with lazy disgust as he shuffles about the room.*)

DONALD. Christ, Michael!

MICHAEL (*unsuccessfully tries to tear the phone away from* EMORY). I can do without your goddamn spit all over my telephone, you nellie coward.

EMORY. I may be nellie, but I'm no coward. (*Starts to dial*) Bernard, forgive me. I'm sorry. I won't ever say those things to you again. (MICHAEL *watches triumphant.* BERNARD *pours another glass of wine. A beat*) B.Y.

MICHAEL. It's busy?

EMORY (*nods*). Loraine is probably talking to her mother. Oh, yes, Delbert married Loraine.

MICHAEL. I'm sorry, you'll have to forfeit your turn. We can't wait. (*Takes the phone, hands it to* LARRY, *who starts to dial*)

HAROLD (*to* LARRY). Well, you're not wasting any time.

HANK. Who are you calling?

LARRY. Charlie. (EMORY *gets up, jerks the phone out of* LARRY'S *hands.*)

EMORY. I refuse to forfeit my turn! It's *my* turn and I'm taking it!

MICHAEL. That's the spirit, Emory! *Hit that iceberg—don't miss it! Hit it! Goddamnit!* I want a smash of a finale!

EMORY. Oh, God, I'm drunk.

MICHAEL. A falling-down-drunk-nellie-queen.

HAROLD. Well, that's the pot calling the kettle beige!

MICHAEL (*snapping; to* HAROLD). *I am not drunk!* You cannot tell that I am drunk! Donald! I'm not drunk! Am I!

DONALD. *I'm* drunk.

EMORY. So am I. I am a *major drunk.*

MICHAEL (*to* EMORY). Shut up and dial!

EMORY (*dialing*). I am a major drunk of this or any other season.

DONALD (*to* MICHAEL). Don't you mean shut up and *deal.*

EMORY. . . . It's ringing. It is no longer B.Y. Hello?

MICHAEL (*taking note*). One point.

EMORY. . . . Who's speaking? Who? . . . Doctor Delbert Botts?

MICHAEL. Two points.

EMORY. Oh, Del, is this really you? Oh, nobody. You don't know me. You wouldn't remember me. I'm . . . just a friend. A falling-down drunken friend. Hello? Hello? Hello? (*Lowers the receiver*) He hung up. (EMORY *hangs up the telephone.*)

MICHAEL. Three points total. You're winning.

EMORY. He said I must have the wrong party.

(BERNARD *gets up, goes into the kitchen.*)

HAROLD. He's right. We have the wrong party. We should be somewhere else.

EMORY. It's your party, Hallie. Aren't you having a good time?

HAROLD. Simply fabulous. And what about you? Are you having a good time, Emory? Are you having as good a time as you thought you would?

(LARRY *takes the phone.*)

MICHAEL. If you're bored, Harold, we could sing Happy Birthday again—to the tune of Havah Nageelah.

(HAROLD *takes out another cigarette.*)

HAROLD. Not for all the tea in Mexico. (*Lights up*)

HANK. My turn now.

LARRY. It's my turn to call Charlie.

HANK. No. Let me.

LARRY. Are *you* going to call Charlie?

MICHAEL. The score is three to two. Emory's favor.

ALAN. Don't, Hank. Don't you see—Bernard was right.

HANK (*firmly, to* ALAN). I want to. (*A beat. Holds out his hand for the phone*) Larry? (*A beat*)

LARRY (*gives him the phone*). Be my eager guest.

COWBOY (*to* LARRY). Is he going to call Charlie for you? (LARRY *breaks into laughter.* HANK *starts to dial.*)

LARRY. Charlie is all the people I cheat on Hank with.

DONALD. With whom I cheat on Hank.

MICHAEL. The butcher, the baker, the candlestick maker.

LARRY. Right! I love 'em all. And what he refuses to understand—is that I've got to *have* 'em all. I am *not* the marrying kind, and I never will be.

HAROLD. Gypsy feet.

LARRY. Who are you calling?

MICHAEL. Jealous?

LARRY. Curious as hell!

MICHAEL. And a little jealous too.

LARRY. Who are you calling?

MICHAEL. Did it ever occur to you that Hank might be doing the same thing behind your back that you do behind his?

LARRY. I wish to Christ he would. It'd make life a hell of a lot easier. Who are you calling?

HAROLD. Whoever it is, they're not sitting on top of the telephone.

HANK. Hello?

COWBOY. They must have been in the tub.

MICHAEL (*snaps at* COWBOY). Eighty-six! (COWBOY *goes over to a far corner, sits down.* BERNARD *enters, uncorking another bottle of wine. Taking note*) One point.

HANK. . . . I'd like to leave a message.

MICHAEL. Not in. One point.

HANK. Would you say that Hank called. Yes, it is. Oh, good evening, how are you?

LARRY. Who the hell *is* that?

HANK. . . . Yes, that's right—the message is for my roommate, Larry. Just say that I called and . . .

LARRY. It's our answering service!

HANK. . . . and said . . . I love you.

MICHAEL. *Five points!* You said it! You get five goddamn points for saying it!

ALAN. Hank! Hank! . . . Are you crazy?

HANK. . . . No. You didn't hear me incorrectly. That's what I said. The message is for Larry and it's from me, Hank, and it is just as I said: *I . . . love . . . you.* Thanks. (*Hangs up*)

MICHAEL. Seven points total! Hank, you're ahead, baby. You're way, way ahead of everybody!

ALAN. Why? . . . Oh, Hank, why? Why did you do that?

HANK. Because I do love him. And I don't care who knows it.

ALAN. Don't say that.

HANK. Why not? It's the truth.

ALAN. I can't believe you.

HANK (*directly to* ALAN). I left my wife and family for Larry.

ALAN. I'm really not interested in hearing about it.

MICHAEL. Sure you are. Go ahead, Hankola, tell him all about it.

ALAN. No! I don't want to hear it. It's disgusting! (*A beat*)

HANK. Some men do it for another woman.

ALAN. Well, I could understand *that*. That's *normal*.

HANK. It just doesn't always work out that way, Alan. No matter how you might want it to. And God knows, nobody ever wanted it more than I did. I really and truly felt that I was in love with my wife when I married her. It wasn't altogether my trying to prove something to myself. I did love her and she loved me. But . . . there was always that something there . . .

DONALD. You mean your attraction to your own sex.

HANK. Yes.

ALAN. Always?

HANK. I don't know. I suppose so.

EMORY. I've known what I was since I was four years old.

MICHAEL. Everybody's always known it about *you*, Emory.

DONALD. I've always known it about myself too.

HANK. I don't know when it was that I started admitting it to myself. For so long I either labeled it something else or denied it completely.

MICHAEL. Christ-was-I-drunk-last-night.

HANK. And then there came a time when I just couldn't lie to myself any more . . . I thought about it but I never did anything about it. I think the first time was during my wife's last pregnancy. We lived near New Haven—in the country. She and the kids still live there. Well, anyway, there was a teachers' meeting here in New York. She didn't feel up to the trip and I came alone. And that day on the train I began to think about it and think about it and think about it. I thought of nothing else the whole trip. And within fifteen minutes after I had arrived I had picked up a guy in the men's room of Grand Central Station.

ALAN *(quietly)*. Jesus.

HANK. I'd never done anything like that in my life before and I was scared to death. But he turned out to be a nice fellow. I've never seen him again and it's funny I can't even remember his name any more. *(A beat)* Anyway. After that, it got easier.

HAROLD. Practice makes perfect.

HANK. And then . . . sometime later . . . not very long after, Larry was in New Haven and we met at a party my wife and I had gone in town for.

EMORY. And your real troubles began.

HANK. That was two years ago.

LARRY. Why am I always the goddamn villain in the piece! If I'm not thought of as a happy-home wrecker, I'm an impossible son of a bitch to live with!

HAROLD. Guilt turns to hostility. Isn't that right, Michael?

MICHAEL. Go stick your tweezers in your cheek.

LARRY. I'm fed up to the teeth with everybody feeling so goddamn sorry for poor shat-upon Hank.

EMORY. Aw, Larry, everybody knows you're Frieda Fickle.

LARRY. I've never made any promises and I never intend to. It's my right to lead my sex life without answering to *anybody*—Hank included! And if those terms are not acceptable, then we must not live together. Numerous relations is a part of the way I am!

EMORY. You don't have to be gay to be a wanton.

LARRY. By the way I am, I don't mean being gay—I mean my sexual appetite. And I don't think of myself as a wanton. Emory, you are the most promiscuous person I know.

EMORY. I am not promiscuous at all!

MICHAEL. Not by choice. By design. Why would anybody want to go to bed with a flaming little sissy like you?

BERNARD. Michael!

MICHAEL *(to EMORY)*. Who'd make a pass at you—I'll tell you who—nobody. Except maybe some fugitive from the Braille Institute.

BERNARD *(to EMORY)*. Why do you let him talk to you that way?

HAROLD. Physical beauty is not everything.

MICHAEL. Thank you, Quasimodo.

LARRY. What do you think it's like living with the goddamn gestapo! I can't breathe without getting the third degree!

MICHAEL. Larry, it's your turn to call.

LARRY. I can't take all that let's-be-faithful-and-never-look-at-another-person routine. It just doesn't work. If you want to promise that, fine. Then do it and stick to it. But if you *have* to promise it—as far as I'm concerned—nothing finishes a relationship faster.

HAROLD. Give me Librium or give me Meth.

BERNARD *(intoxicated now)*. Yeah, freedom, baby! Freedom!

LARRY. You gotta have it! It can't work any other way. And the ones who swear their undying fidelity are lying. Most of them, anyway—ninety percent of them. They cheat on each other constantly and lie through their teeth. I'm sorry, I can't be like that and it drives Hank up the wall.

HANK. There is that ten percent.

LARRY. The only way it stands a chance is with some sort of an understanding.

HANK. I've tried to go along with that.

LARRY. Aw, *come on!*

HANK. I agreed to an agreement.

LARRY. Your agreement.

MICHAEL. What agreement?

LARRY. A ménage.

HAROLD. The lover's agreement.

LARRY. Look, I know a lot of people think it's the answer. They don't consider it cheating. But it's not my style.

HANK. Well *I* certainly didn't want it.

LARRY. Then who suggested it?

HANK. It was a compromise.

LARRY. Exactly.

HANK. And you agreed.

LARRY. I didn't agree to anything. You agreed to your own proposal and *informed me* that I agreed.

COWBOY. I don't understand. What's a me . . . menaa . . .

MICHAEL. A ménage à trois, baby. Two's company—three's a ménage.

COWBOY. Oh.

HANK. It works for some.

LARRY. Well, I'm not one for group therapy. I'm sorry, I can't relate to anyone or anything that way. I'm old-fashioned—I like 'em all, but I like 'em one at a time!

MICHAEL (to LARRY). Did you like Donald as a single side attraction? (Pause)

LARRY. Yes. I did.

DONALD. So did I, Larry.

LARRY (to DONALD, referring to MICHAEL). Did you tell him?

DONALD. No.

MICHAEL. It was perfectly obvious from the moment you walked in. What was that song and dance about having seen each other but never having met?

DONALD. It was true. We saw each other in the baths and went to bed together but we never spoke a word and never knew each other's name.

EMORY. You had better luck than I do. If I don't get arrested, my trick announces upon departure that he's been exposed to hepatitis!

MICHAEL. In spring a young man's fancy turns to a fancy young man.

LARRY (to HANK). Don't look at me like that. You've been playing footsie with the Blue Book all night.

DONALD. I think he only wanted to show you what's good for the gander is good for the gander.

HANK. That's right.

LARRY (to HANK). I suppose you'd like the three of us to have a go at it.

HANK. At least it'd be together.

LARRY. That point eludes me.

HANK. What kind of an understanding do you want!

LARRY. Respect—for each other's freedom. With no need to lie or pretend. In my own way, Hank, I love you, but you have to understand that even though I do want to go on living with you, sometimes there may be others. I don't want to flaunt it in your face. If it happens, I know I'll never mention it. But if you ask me, I'll tell you. I don't want to hurt you but I won't lie to you if you want to know anything about me.

BERNARD. He gets points.

MICHAEL. What?

BERNARD. He said it. He said "I love you" to Hank. He gets the bonus.

MICHAEL. He didn't call him.

DONALD. He called him. He just didn't use the telephone.

MICHAEL. Then he doesn't get any points.

BERNARD. He gets five points!

MICHAEL. He didn't use the telephone. He doesn't get a goddamn thing!

(LARRY goes to the phone, picks up the receiver, looks at the number of the second line, dials. A beat. The phone rings.)

LARRY. It's for you, Hank. Why don't you take it upstairs? (The phone continues to ring. HANK gets up, goes up the stairs to the bedroom. Pause. He presses the second-line button, picks up the receiver. Everyone downstairs is silent.)

HANK. Hello?

BERNARD. One point.

LARRY. Hello, Hank.

BERNARD. Two points.

LARRY. . . . This is Larry.

BERNARD. Two more points!

LARRY. . . . For what it's worth, I love you.

BERNARD. Five points bonus!

HANK. I'll . . . I'll try.

LARRY. I will too. (Hangs up. HANK hangs up.)

BERNARD. That's ten points total!

EMORY. Larry's the winner!

HAROLD. Well, that wasn't as much fun as I thought it would be.

MICHAEL. THE GAME ISN'T OVER YET! (HANK moves toward the bed into darkness.) Your turn, Alan. (MICHAEL gets the phone, slams it down in front of ALAN.) PICK UP THE PHONE, BUSTER!

EMORY. Michael, don't!

MICHAEL. STAY OUT OF THIS!

EMORY. You don't have to, Alan. You don't have to.

ALAN. Emory . . . I'm sorry for what I did before. (A beat)

EMORY. . . . Oh, forget it.

MICHAEL. Forgive us our trespasses. Christ, now you're both joined at the goddamn hip! You can decorate his home, Emory—and he can get you out of jail the next time you're arrested on a morals charge. (A beat) Who are you going to call, Alan? (No response) Can't remember anyone? Well, maybe you need a minute to think. Is that it? (No response)

HAROLD. I believe this will be the final round.

COWBOY. Michael, aren't you going to call anyone?

HAROLD. How could he? He's never loved anyone.

MICHAEL (sings the classic vaudeville walk-off to HAROLD).
"No matter how you figger,
It's tough to be a nigger,
(Indicates BERNARD)

But it's tougher
To be a Jeeeew-ooouu-oo!"

DONALD. My God, Michael, you're a charming host.

HAROLD. Michael doesn't have charm, Donald. Michael has countercharm.

(LARRY *crosses to the stairs.*)

MICHAEL. Going somewhere?

(LARRY *stops, turns to* MICHAEL.)

LARRY. Yes. Excuse me. *(Turns, goes up the stairs)*

MICHAEL. You're going to miss the end of the game.

LARRY *(pauses on stairs)*. You can tell me how it comes out.

MICHAEL. I never reveal an ending. And no one will be reseated during the climactic revelation.

LARRY. With any luck, I won't be back until it's all over. *(Turns, continues up the stairs into the dark)*

MICHAEL *(into* ALAN's *ear)*. What do you suppose is going on up there? Hmmm, Alan? What do you imagine Larry and Hank are doing? Hmmmmm? Shooting marbles?

EMORY. Whatever they're doing, they're not hurting anyone.

HAROLD. And they're minding their own business.

MICHAEL. And you mind yours, Harold. I'm warning you! *(A beat)*

HAROLD *(coolly)*. Are you now? Are you warning *me? Me?* I'm Harold. I'm the one person you don't warn, Michael. Because you and I are a match. And we tread very softly with each other because we both play each other's game too well. Oh, I know this game you're playing. I know it very well. And I *play* it very well. You play it very well too. But you know what, I'm the only one that's better at it than you are. I can beat you at it. So don't push me. I'm warning *you. (A beat.* MICHAEL *starts to laugh.)*

MICHAEL. You're funny, Hallie. A laff riot. Isn't he funny, Alan? Or, as you might say, isn't he amusing. He's an amusing faggot, isn't he? Or, as you might say, freak. That's what you called Emory, wasn't it? A freak? A pansy? My, what an antiquated vocabulary you have. I'm surprised you didn't say sodomite or pederast. *(A beat)* You'd better let me bring you up to date. Now it's not so new, but it might be new to you—*(A beat)* Have you heard the term "closet queen"? Do you know what that means? Do you know what it means to be "in the closet"?

EMORY. Don't, Michael. It won't help anything to explain what it means.

MICHAEL. He already knows. He knows very, very well what a closet queen is. Don't you, Alan? *(Pause)*

ALAN. Michael, if you are insinuating that I am homosexual, I can only say that you are mistaken.

MICHAEL. Am I? *(A beat)* What about Justin Stuart?

ALAN. . . . What about . . . Justin Stuart?

MICHAEL. You were in love with him, that's what about him. *(A beat)* And *that* is who you are going to call.

ALAN. Justin and I were very good friends. That is all. Unfortunately, we had a parting of the ways and that was the end of the friendship. We have not spoken for years. I most certainly will not call him now.

MICHAEL. According to Justin, the friendship was quite passionate.

ALAN. What do you mean?

MICHAEL. I mean that you slept with him in college. Several times.

ALAN. That is not true!

MICHAEL. Several times. One time, it's youth. Twice, a phase maybe. Several times, *you like it!*

ALAN. IT'S NOT TRUE!

MICHAEL. Yes, it is. Because Justin Stuart *is* homosexual. He comes to New York on occasion. He calls me. I've taken him to parties. Larry "had" him once. *I* have slept with Justin Stuart. And he has told me all about *you.*

ALAN. Then he told you a lie. *(A beat)*

MICHAEL. You were obsessed with Justin. That's all you talked about, morning, noon, and night. You started doing it about Hank upstairs tonight. What an attractive fellow he is and all that transparent crap.

ALAN. He *is* an attractive fellow. What's wrong with saying so?

MICHAEL. Would you like to join him and Larry right now?

ALAN. I said he was attractive. That's all.

MICHAEL. How many times do you have to say it? How many times did you have to say it about Justin: what a good tennis player he was; what a good dancer he was; what a good body he had; what good taste he had; how bright he was—how *amusing* he was—how the girls were all mad for him—what close friends you were.

ALAN. We . . . we . . . were . . . very close . . . very good . . . friends. *That's all!*

MICHAEL. It was *obvious*—and when you did it around Fran it was downright embarrassing. Even she must have had her doubts about you.

ALAN. *Justin . . . lied.* If he told you that, he lied. It is a lie. A vicious lie. He'd say anything about me now to get even. He could never get over the fact that *I* dropped *him*. But I had to. I had to because . . . he told me . . . he told me about himself . . . he told me that he wanted to be my lover. And I . . . I . . . told him . . . he made me sick . . . I told him I pitied him. *(A beat)*

MICHAEL. You ended the friendship, Alan, because you couldn't face the truth about yourself. You could go along, sleeping with Justin, as long as he lied to himself and you lied to yourself and you both dated girls and labeled yourselves men and called yourselves just fond friends. But Justin finally had to be honest about the truth, and you couldn't take it. You couldn't take it and so you destroyed the friendship and your friend along with it. (MICHAEL *goes to the desk and gets address book.)*

ALAN. No!

MICHAEL. Justin could never understand what he'd done wrong to make you cut him off. He blamed himself.

ALAN. No!

MICHAEL. He did until he eventually found out who he was and what he was.

ALAN. No!

MICHAEL. But to this day he still remembers the treatment—the scars he got from you. *(Puts address book in front of* ALAN *on coffee table.)*

ALAN. NO!

MICHAEL. Pick up this phone and call Justin. Call him and apologize and tell him what you should have told him twelve years ago. *(Picks up the phone, shoves it at* ALAN)

ALAN. NO! HE LIED! NOT A WORD IS TRUE!

MICHAEL. CALL HIM! (ALAN *won't take the phone.)* All right then, *I'll dial!*

HAROLD. You're so helpful.

(MICHAEL *starts to dial.)*

ALAN. Give it to me. (MICHAEL *hands* ALAN *the receiver.* ALAN *takes it, hangs up for a moment, lifts it again, starts to dial. Everyone watches silently.* ALAN *finishes dialing, lifts the receiver to his ear.)* . . . Hello?

MICHAEL. One point.

ALAN. . . . It's . . . it's Alan.

MICHAEL. Two points.

ALAN. . . . Yes, yes, it's *me.*

MICHAEL. Is it Justin?

ALAN. . . . You sound surprised.

MICHAEL. I should hope to think so—after twelve years! Two more points.

ALAN. I . . . I'm in New York. Yes. I . . . I won't explain now . . . I . . . I just called to tell you . . .

MICHAEL. THAT I LOVE YOU, GOD-DAMNIT! I LOVE YOU!

ALAN. I love you.

MICHAEL. You get the goddamn bonus. TEN POINTS TOTAL! JACKPOT!

ALAN. I love you and I beg you to forgive me.

MICHAEL. Give me that! *(Snatches the phone from* ALAN) Justin! Did you hear what that son of a bitch said! *(A beat.* MICHAEL *is speechless for a moment.)* . . . Fran? *(A beat)* Well, of course I expected it to be you! . . . *(A beat)* How are you? Me, too. Yes, yes . . . he told me everything. Oh, don't thank *me.* Please . . . Please . . . *(A beat)* I'll . . . I'll put him back on. *(A beat)* My love to the kids . . .

ALAN. . . . Darling? I'll take the first plane I can get. Yes. I'm sorry too. I love you very much. *(Hangs up, stands, crosses to the door, stops. Turns around, surveys the group)* Thank you, Michael. *(Opens the door and exits. Silence.* MICHAEL *slowly sinks down on the couch, covering his face. Pause)*

COWBOY. Who won?

DONALD. It was a tie. (HAROLD *crosses to* MICHAEL.)

HAROLD *(calmly, coldly, clinically).* Now it is my turn. And ready or not, Michael, here goes. *(A beat)* You are a sad and pathetic man. You're a homosexual and you don't want to be. But there is nothing you can do to change it. Not all your prayers to your God, not all the analysis you can buy in all the years you've got left to live. You may very well one day be able to know a heterosexual life if you want it desperately enough—if you pursue it with the fervor with which you annihilate—but you will always be homosexual as well. Always, Michael. Always. Until the day you die. *(Turns, gathers his gifts, goes to* EMORY. EMORY *stands up unsteadily.)* Oh, friends, thanks for the nifty party and the super gift. *(Looks toward* COWBOY) It's just what I needed. (EMORY *smiles.* HAROLD *gives him a hug, spots* BERNARD *sitting on the floor, head bowed)* . . . Bernard, thank you. *(No response. To* EMORY) Will you get him home?

EMORY. Don't worry about her. I'll take care of everything.

(HAROLD *turns to* DONALD, *who is at the bar making himself another drink.*)

HAROLD. Donald, good to see you.

DONALD. Good night, Harold. See you again sometime.

HAROLD. Yeah. How about a year from Shavuoth? (HAROLD *goes to* COWBOY.) Come on, Tex. Let's go to my place. (COWBOY *gets up, comes to him.*) Are you good in bed?

COWBOY. Well . . . I'm not like the average hustler you'd meet. I try to show a little affection—it keeps me from feeling like such a whore. *(A beat.* HAROLD *turns.* COWBOY *opens the door for them. They start out.* HAROLD *pauses.)*

HAROLD. Oh, Michael . . . thanks for the laughs. Call you tomorrow. *(No response. A beat.* HAROLD *and* COWBOY *exit.)*

EMORY. Come on, Bernard. Time to go home. (EMORY, *frail as he is, manages to pull* BERNARD*'s arm around his neck, gets him on his feet.*) Oh, Mary, you're a heavy mother.

BERNARD *(practically inaudible mumble).* Why did I call? Why?

EMORY. Thank you, Michael. Good night, Donald.

DONALD. Goodbye, Emory.

BERNARD. Why . . .

EMORY. It's all right, Bernard. Everything's all right. I'm going to make you some coffee and everything's going to be all right.

(EMORY *virtually carries* BERNARD *out.* DONALD *closes the door. Silence.* MICHAEL *slowly slips from the couch onto the floor. A beat. Then slowly he begins a low moan that increases in volume—almost like a siren. Suddenly he slams his open hands to his ears.)*

MICHAEL *(in desperate panic).* Donald! Donald! DONALD! DONALD! (DONALD *puts down his drink, rushes to* MICHAEL. MICHAEL *is now white with fear and tears are bursting from his eyes. He begins to gasp his words.)* Oh, no! No! What have I done! Oh, my God, what have I done! (MICHAEL *writhing.* DONALD *holds him, cradles him in his arms.)*

DONALD. Michael! Michael!

MICHAEL *(weeping).* Oh, no! NO! It's beginning! The liquor is starting to wear off and the anxiety is beginning! Oh, NO! No! I feel it! I know it's going to happen. Donald!! Donald! Don't leave me! Please! Please! Oh, my God, what have I done! Oh Jesus, the guilt! I can't handle it any more. I won't make it!

DONALD *(physically subduing him).* Michael! Michael! Stop it! Stop it! I'll give you a Valium—I've got some in my pocket!

MICHAEL *(hysterical).* No! No! Pills and alcohol—I'll die!

DONALD. I'm not going to give you the whole bottle! Come on, let go of me!

MICHAEL *(clutching him).* NO!

DONALD. Let go of me long enough for me to get my hand in my pocket!

MICHAEL. Don't leave! (MICHAEL *quiets down a bit, lets go of* DONALD *enough for him to take a small plastic bottle from his pocket and open it to give* MICHAEL *a tranquilizer.)*

DONALD. Here.

MICHAEL *(sobbing).* I don't have any water to swallow it with!

DONALD. Well, if you'll wait one goddamn minute, I'll get you some! (MICHAEL *lets go of him. He goes to the bar, gets a glass of water and returns.)* Your water, Your Majesty. *(A beat)* Michael, stop that goddamn crying and take this pill! (MICHAEL *straightens up, puts the pill into his mouth amid choking sobs, takes the water, drinks, returns the glass to* DONALD.)

MICHAEL. I'm like Ole Man River—tired of livin' and scared o' dyin'. (DONALD *puts the glass on the bar, comes back to the couch, sits down.* MICHAEL *collapses into his arms, sobbing. Pause)*

DONALD. Shhhhh. Shhhhhh. Michael. Shhhhhh. Michael. Michael. (DONALD *rocks him back and forth. He quiets. Pause)*

MICHAEL. . . . If we . . . if we could just . . . not hate ourselves so much. That's it, you know. If we could just *learn* not to hate ourselves quite so very much.

DONALD. Yes, I know. I know. *(A beat)* Inconceivable as it may be, you used to be worse than you are now. *(A beat)* Maybe with a lot more work you can help yourself some more—if you try.

(MICHAEL *straightens up, dries his eyes on his sleeve.)*

MICHAEL. Who was it that used to always say, "You show me a happy homosexual, and I'll show you a gay corpse."

DONALD. I don't know. Who was it who always used to say that?

MICHAEL. And how dare you come on with that holier-than-thou attitude with me! "A lot more work," "if I try," indeed! You've got a long row to hoe before you're perfect, you know.

DONALD. I never said I didn't.

MICHAEL. And while we're on the subject —I think your analyst is a quack. (MICHAEL *is sniffling.* DONALD *hands him a handkerchief. He takes it and blows his nose.)*

DONALD. Earlier you said he was a prick.

MICHAEL. That's right. He's a prick quack. Or a quack prick, whichever you prefer.

(DONALD *gets up from the couch, goes for his drink.*)

DONALD *(heaving a sigh).* Harold was right. You'll never change.

MICHAEL. Come back, Donald. Come back, Shane.

DONALD. I'll come back when you have another anxiety attack.

MICHAEL. I need you. Just like Mickey Mouse needs Minnie Mouse—just like Donald Duck needs Minnie Duck. Mickey needs Donnie.

DONALD. My name is Donald. I am called Donald. You must never call anyone named Donald Donnie . . .

MICHAEL *(grabs his head, moans).* Ohhhhh . . . icks! Icks! Terrible icks! Tomorrow is going to be an ick-packed day. It's going to be a Bad Day at Black Rock. A day of nerves, nerves, and more nerves! (MICHAEL *gets up from the couch, surveys the wreckage of the dishes and gift wrappings.)* Do you suppose there's any possibility of just burning this room? *(A beat)*

DONALD. Why do you think he stayed, Michael? Why do you think he took all of that from you?

MICHAEL. There are no accidents. He was begging to get killed. He was dying for somebody to let him have it and he got what he wanted.

DONALD. He could have been telling the truth—Justin could have lied.

MICHAEL. Who knows? What time is it?

DONALD. It seems like it's day after tomorrow.

(MICHAEL *goes to the kitchen door, pokes his head in. Comes back into the room carrying a raincoat)*

MICHAEL. It's early. *(Goes to a closet door, takes out a blazer, puts it on)*

DONALD. What does life *hold?* Where're you doing?

MICHAEL. The bedroom is ocupado and I don't want to go to sleep anyway until I try to walk off the booze. If I went to sleep like this, when I wake up they'd have to put me in a padded cell—not that that's where I don't belong. *(A beat)* And . . . and . . . there's a midnight mass at St. Malachy's that all the show people go to. I think I'll walk over there and catch it.

DONALD *(raises his glass).* Well, pray for me.

MICHAEL *(indicates bedroom).* Maybe they'll be gone by the time I get back.

DONALD. Well, *I* will be—just as soon as I knock off that bottle of brandy.

MICHAEL. Will I see you next Saturday?

DONALD. Unless you have other plans.

MICHAEL. No. *(Turns to go)*

DONALD. Michael?

MICHAEL *(stops, turns back).* What?

DONALD. Did he ever tell you why he was crying on the phone—what it was he *had* to tell you?

MICHAEL. No. It must have been that he'd left Fran. Or maybe it was something else and he changed his mind.

DONALD. Maybe so. *(A beat)* I wonder why he left her. *(A pause)*

MICHAEL. . . . As my father said to me when he died in my arms, "I don't understand any of it. I never did." *(A beat.* DONALD *goes to his stack of books, selects one, and sits in a chair.)* Turn out the lights when you leave, will you? (DONALD *nods.* MICHAEL *looks at him for a long silent moment.* DONALD *turns his attention to his book, starts to read.* MICHAEL *opens the door and exits.)*

CURTAIN

CEREMONIES IN DARK OLD MEN

Lonne Elder III

To
My son, David Dubois Elder
My wife, Judith Ann
To the memory of my life's teacher,
    Dr. William E. B. Dubois
To the memory of Dr. Martin Luther King
To the Negro Ensemble Company

First presented by the Negro Ensemble Company at the St. Marks Playhouse in New York City on February 4, 1969, with the following cast:

MR. RUSSELL B. PARKER Douglas Turner
MR. WILLIAM JENKINS Arthur French
THEOPOLIS PARKER William Jay
BOBBY PARKER David Downing

ADELE ELOISE PARKER Rosalind Cash
BLUE HAVEN Samuel Blue, Jr.
YOUNG GIRL Judyann Elder

Directed by Edmund Cambridge
Setting by Whitney LeBlanc
Costumes by Gertha Brock
Lighting by Shirley Prendergast

Lonne Elder III was not the first black playwright to win distinction—anything but. Lorraine Hansberry, with her *Raisin in the Sun,* was one of the pioneers, as was Charles Gordone with his Pulitzer Prize-winning *No Place to Be Someone,* which was produced originally by Joseph Papp's New York Shakespeare Festival. But Mr. Elder's *Ceremonies in Dark Old Men* seemed to explore a new vein in blackness. Originally produced by the Negro Ensemble Company, it seemed to be essentially a black play for black audiences rather than a black propaganda play for white audiences.

In his play Mr. Elder is not really trying to prove anything. He is showing a realistic situation, and very much attempting to show black life as it is. It is a play that black audiences can readily identify with, and white audiences observe with a brotherly interest. The black experience has always been apart from the white experience, but on certain common grounds —such as poverty and aspiration—black and white can see to some degree alike.

Mr. Elder was born in Americus, Georgia, but received his education at the New Jersey State University. He once said that he was introduced to the theatre by the work of Douglas Turner Ward, one of the founders and directors of the Negro Ensemble Company. Mr. Elder has said: "I met Douglas Turner Ward in Harlem—and upon reading a play of Mr. Ward's I made my decision to write exclusively for the theatre."

After he came North, Mr. Elder supported himself in a diversity of ways, including that of actor. But he was also a dockworker, a time and motion study man, a professional political activist, a professional gambler, a waiter, and a numbers runner. He wrote many plays, including *Ceremonies in Dark Old Men.* It is ironic that this play won the Stanley Drama Award in 1965 and was instrumental in obtaining its playwright a John Hay Whitney Fellowship in playwriting. But the play itself was not produced until February 4, 1969, when it was one of the first big hits of the Negro Ensemble Company.

The Negro Ensemble Company was founded by Douglas Turner Ward and Robert Hooks in 1967. It found a theatre on St. Marks Place, and with Ford Foundation funding and much private help, it began to develop seriously the young black actor and the young black playwright. That the American black theater is in such a healthy state today is largely due to the efforts of the N.E.C. There were other black theatres that played an important role— notably the New Lafayette Theatre in Harlem run by the black playwright Ed Bullins—but the N.E.C. has kept hammering away at the world in a true, cohesive effort to create a true black theatre, in which every black artist would have the opportunity to have his voice heard.

One of the interesting aspects of the first generation of black playwrights—such as Mr. Elder or Mr. Gordone—was the way in which they espoused the naturalistic play. It was almost like the Group Theater again, and black writers espoused a realism that their white colleagues were nervous of. The reason for this is, I think, far simpler than usually imagined. Some years ago there was a public interest advertisement emblazoned across New York buses. It said, with some grave simplicity: "In the Ghetto it is still the 1930s." This happened to be one of the profounder comments of drama criticism during the period. It caught at once the black need for dramatic reality, the simple necessity to tell it as it is, to put in on the line for all to see.

Mr. Elder has written many other plays but none it seems with quite the effect of *Ceremonies.* Indeed nowadays Mr. Elder works more in movies and television, and he was responsible for the film script of the award-winning *Sounder,* a film by Martin Ritt, based on the novel by William Armstrong.

Yet Mr. Elder's reputation is still largely based on *Ceremonies.* The strength of Mr. Elder's play is partly as a cry of pain in a dark night, partly as an American document, a very sad American document. It is a play about the rituals, or the ceremonies, of survival. The fabric of the play is wonderfully diversified as Mr. Elder piles on tragedy, melodrama, and even slapstick comedy into a dramatic mixture as inconsistent as life itself. On its first night with the N.E.C. it reminded me irresistibly of Sean O'Casey's *Juno and the Paycock.* Its mood, poised between comedy and tragedy, is identical, its intensity of feeling and love of language are similar, and there is finally common cause in its undercurrents of rebellion.

ACT ONE

SCENE ONE

Early spring, about 4:30 in the afternoon, now.

A small, poverty-stricken barbershop on 126th Street between Seventh and Lenox avenues, Harlem, U.S.A.

There is only one barber's throne in this barbershop. There is a not too lengthy mirror along the wall, and a high, broad shelf in the immediate area of the throne. There are two decks of shelves of equal width projecting just below the main shelf. These shelves are covered by small, sliding panels. On the far left corner of the shop is the street door, and on the far right corner is a door leading to a back room. Just to the right of the door, flush against the wall, is a card table and two chairs. Farther right is a clothes rack. Against the wall to the far left of the shop, near the door, are four chairs lined up uniformly.

The back room is like any back room in a poverty-stricken barbershop. It has an old refrigerator, an even older antique-type desk, and a medium-size bed. On the far right is a short flight of stairs leading up. A unique thing about this room: a door to stairs coming up from a small basement.

The action of the play takes place in the barbershop and the back room.

As the curtain rises, MR. RUSSELL B. PARKER *is seated in the single barber's throne, reading the* Daily News. *He is in his early or middle fifties. He rises nervously, moves to the window, and peers out, his right hand over his eyebrows. He returns to the chair and continues to read. After checking his watch, he rises again and moves to the window for another look. Finally he sees the right person coming and moves to the door to open it.* MR. WILLIAM JENKINS *enters: early fifties, well dressed in a complete suit of clothes, and carrying a newspaper under his arm.*

———

MR. PARKER. Where have you been?

MR. JENKINS. Whatcha mean? You know where I was.

MR. PARKER. You want to play the game or not?

MR. JENKINS. That's what I came here for.

MR. PARKER (*slides open a panel in the counter*). I wanted to get in at least three games before Adele got home, but this way we'll be lucky if we get in one.

MR. JENKINS. Stop complaining and get the board out—I'll beat you, and that will be that.

MR. PARKER. I can do without your bragging. (*Pulls out a checkerboard and a small can, quickly places them on the table, then shakes up the can.*) Close your eyes and take a man.

MR. JENKINS (*closing his eyes*). You never learn. (*Reaches into the can and pulls out a checker.*) It's red.

MR. PARKER. All right, I get the black. (*Sits at the table and rushes to set up his men*) Get your men down, Jenkins!

MR. JENKINS (*sits*). Aw, man, take it easy, the checkers ain't gon' run away! (*Setting his men up*) If you could play the game I wouldn't mind it—but you can't play! — Your move.

MR. PARKER. I'll start here—I just don't want Adele to catch us here playing checkers. She gave me and the boys a notice last week that we had to get jobs or get out of the house.

MR. JENKINS. Don't you think it's about time you got a job? In the five years I've been knowing you, I can count the heads of hair you done cut in this shop on one hand.

MR. PARKER. This shop is gon' work yet; I know it can. Just give me one more year and you'll see. . . . Going out to get a job ain't gon' solve nothing—all it's gon' do is create a lot of bad feelings with everybody. I can't work! I don't know how to! (*Moves checker*)

MR. JENKINS. I bet if all your children were living far from you like mine, you'd know how to. That's one thing I don't understand about you, Parker. How long do you expect your daughter to go on supporting you and those two boys?

MR. PARKER. I don't expect that! I just want some time until I can straighten things out. My dear Doris understood that. She understood me like a book. (*Makes another move*)

MR. JENKINS. You mean to tell me your wife enjoyed working for you?

MR. PARKER. Of course she didn't, but she never worried me. You been married, Jenkins: you know what happens to a man when a woman worries him all the time, and that's what Adele been doing, worrying my head off! (*Makes another move*)

MR. JENKINS. Whatcha gon' do about it?

MR. PARKER. I'm gon' get tough, evil, and bad. That's the only sign a woman gets from a man. *(Makes move)*

(THEOPOLIS PARKER *enters briskly from street. He is in his twenties, of medium height, and has a lean, solid physique. His younger brother* BOBBY *follows, carrying a huge paper bag whose contents are heavy and fragile.)*

THEO. That's the way I like to hear you talk, Pop, but she's gon' be walking through that door soon, and I wants to see how tough you gon' be.

MR. PARKER. Leave me alone, boy.

THEO. Pop, we got six more days. You got to do something!

MR. PARKER. I'll do it when the time comes.

THEO. Pop, the time is *now.*

MR. PARKER. And right now I am playing a game of checkers with Mr. Jenkins, so leave me alone!

THEO. All right—don't say I didn't warn you when she locks us out of the house! *(*THEO *and* BOBBY *rush through the back room.* BOBBY *places the brown bag in the old refrigerator as they dart up the stairs leading to the apartment.* PARKER *makes another move.)*

MR. PARKER. *You're trapped, Jenkins!* *(Pause)*

MR. JENKINS *(pondering).* Hmmmmmm . . . It looks that way, don't it?

MR. PARKER *(moves to the door).* While you're moaning over the board, I'll just make a little check to see if Adele is coming . . . Don't cheat now! *(He backs toward the window, watching that his adversary does not cheat. He quickly looks out the window.)* Uh-uh! It's Adele! She's in the middle of the block, talking to Miss Thomas! *(Rushes to take out a towel and spreads it over the checkerboard)* Come on, man! *(Drags* MR. JENKINS *by the arm toward the back room.)*

MR. JENKINS. *What are you doing, Parker!*

MR. PARKER. You gon' have to hide out in the back room, 'cause if Adele comes in here and sees you, she'll think that we been playing ckeckers all day!

MR. JENKINS. I don't care about that!

MR. PARKER. You want to finish the game, don't you?

MR. JENKINS. Yeah, but—

MR. PARKER. All you have to do, Jenks, is lay low for a minute, that's all. She'll stop in and ask me something about getting a job, I'll tell her I got a good line on one, and then

she'll go on upstairs. There won't be nobody left here but you and me. Whatcha say, Jenks?

MR. JENKINS *(pause).* All right, I'll do it. I don't like it, but I'll do it, and you better not mention this to nobody, you hear!

MR. PARKER. Not a single soul in this world will know but you and me.

MR. JENKINS *(moves just inside the room and stands).* This is the most ridiculous thing I ever heard of, hiding in somebody's back room just to finish up a checker game.

MR. PARKER. Stop fighting it, man!

MR. JENKINS. All right!

MR. PARKER. Not there!

MR. JENKINS. What in the hell is it now!

MR. PARKER. *You've got to get under the bed!*

MR. JENKINS. No, I'm not gettin' under nobody's bed!

MR. PARKER. Now look . . . Adele never goes through the front way. She comes through the shop and the back room, up the basement stairs to the apartment. Now you want her to catch you hiding in there, looking like a fool?

MR. JENKINS. No, I can take myself out of here and go home!

MR. PARKER *(pushes* JENKINS *over to the table and uncovers the checkerboard).* Look at this! Now you just take a good look at this board! *(Releases him)*

MR. JENKINS. I'm looking, so what?

MR. PARKER. *So what?* I got you and you know it! There ain't no way in the world you'll ever get out of that little trap I got you in. *And it's your move.* How many years we been playing against each other?

MR. JENKINS. Three.

MR. PARKER. Never won a game from you in all that time, have I?

MR. JENKINS. That ain't the half of it. You ain't gon' win one either.

MR. PARKER. Now that I finally got you, that's easy talk, comin' from a running man. All right, go on. Run. *(Moves away)*

MR. JENKINS. Go on, hell! All I gotta do is put my king here, give you this jump here, move this man over there, and you're dead!

MR. PARKER. *(Turns to him)* Try me then. Try me, or are you scared at last I'm gon' beat you?

MR. JENKINS. I can't do it now, there ain't enough time!

MR. PARKER *(strutting like a sport).* Run, rabbit, run . . .

MR. JENKINS. All right! I'll get under the bed. But I swear, Parker, I'm gon' beat you silly! *(They move into the back room.)*

MR. PARKER. Hurry it up then. We ain't got much time.

(As MR. PARKER *struggles to help* MR. JENKINS *get under the bed in the back room,* ADELE *comes in from the street. She is in her late twenties, well dressed in conventional New York office attire. She is carrying a smart-looking handbag and a manila envelope. She stops near the table on which checkerboard is hidden under towel.* MR. PARKER *enters from the back room.)*

MR. PARKER. Hi, honey.

(She doesn't answer, instead busies herself putting minor things in order.)

ADELE. You looked for work today?

MR. PARKER. All morning . . .

(Pause)

ADELE. No luck in the morning, and so you played checkers all afternoon.

MR. PARKER. No, I've been working on a few ideas of mine. My birthday comes up the tenth of the month, and I plan to celebrate it with an idea to shake up this whole neighborhood, and then I'm gon' really go to the country!

ADELE. Don't go to the country—go to work, huh? *(Moves toward back room)* Oh, God, I'm tired!

MR. PARKER *(rushing to get her away from bed).* Come on and let me take you upstairs. I know you must've had yourself a real tough day at the office . . . and you can forget about cooking supper and all of that stuff.

ADELE *(breaks away, moves back into shop toward counter).* Thank you, but I've already given myself the privilege of not cooking your supper tonight.

MR. PARKER. You did?

ADELE. The way I figure it, you should have my dinner waiting for me.

MR. PARKER. But I don't know how to cook.

ADELE *(turns sharply).* You can learn.

MR. PARKER. Now look, Adele, if you got something on your mind, say it, 'cause you know damn well I ain't doin' no cooking.

ADELE *(pause).* All right, I will. A thought came to me today as it does every day, and I'm damn tired of thinking about it—

MR. PARKER. What?

ADELE. —and that is, I've been down at that motor-license bureau so long, sometimes I forget the reasons I ever took the job in the first place.

MR. PARKER. Now look, everybody knows you quit college and came home to help your mama out. Everybody knows it! What you want me to do? Write some prayers to you?

(The two boys enter the back room from upstairs.)

ADELE. I just want you to get a job!

(The boys step into shop and stand apart from each other.)

BOBBY. Hey, Adele.

ADELE. Well! From what cave did you fellows crawl out of? I didn't know you hung around barbershops. . . . Want a haircut, boys?

THEO. For your information, this is the first time we been in this barbershop today. We been upstairs thinking.

ADELE. With what?

THEO. With our *minds,* baby!

ADELE. If the two of you found that house upstairs so attractive to keep you in it all day, then I can think of only three things: the telephone, the bed, and the kitchen.

BOBBY. The kitchen, that's it: we been washing dishes all day!

ADELE. I don't like that, Bobby!

THEO. And I don't like your attitude!

ADELE. Do you like it when I go out of here every morning to work?

THEO. There you go again with that same old tired talk: work! Mama understood about us, I don't know why you gotta give everybody a hard time . . .

ADELE. That was one of Mama's troubles: understanding everybody.

THEO. Now don't start that junk with me!

ADELE. I have got to start that, *Mr. Theopolis Parker!*

MR. PARKER. Hold on now, there's no need for all this . . . Can't we settle this later on, Adele? . . .

ADELE. We settle it now. You got six days left, so you gotta do something, and quick. I got a man coming here tomorrow to change the locks on the door. So for the little time you have left, you'll have to come by me to enter this house.

THEO. Who gives you the right to do that?

ADELE. Me, Adele Eloise Parker, black, over twenty-one, and the only working person in this house! *(Pause)* I am not going to let the three of you drive me into the grave the way you did Mama. And if you really want to know how I feel about that, I'll tell you: Mama killed herself because there was no kind of order in this house. There was nothing but her old-fashion love for a bum like you, Theo—and this one *(points to* BOBBY*)* who's got nothing better to do with his time but to shoplift every time he walks into a department store. And you, Daddy, you and those fanciful stories you're always ready to tell, and all the talk of the good old days when you were the big vaudeville star, of hitting the numbers big. How? How, Daddy? The money you spent on the numbers you got from Mama. . . . In a way, you let Mama make a bum out of you—you let her kill herself!

MR. PARKER. That's a terrible thing to say, Adele, and I'm not going to let you put that off on me!

ADELE. But the fact remains that in the seven years you've been in this barbershop you haven't earned enough money to buy two hot dogs! Most of your time is spent playing checkers with that damn Mr. Jenkins.

THEO *(breaks in)*. Why don't you get married or something! We don't need you—Pop is here, it's HIS HOUSE!

ADELE. You're lucky I don't get married and—

THEO. Nobody wants you, baby!

ADELE. (THEO'*s remark stops her for a moment. She resettles herself.)* All right, you just let someone ask me, and I'll leave you with *Pop,* to starve with Pop. Or, there's another way: why don't the three of you just leave right now and try making it on your own? Why don't we try that!

MR. PARKER. What about my shop?

ADELE. Since I'm the one that has to pay the extra forty dollars a month for you to keep this place, there's going to be no more shop. It was a bad investment and the whole of Harlem knows it!

MR. PARKER *(grabbing her by the arm, in desperation)*. I'm fifty-four years old!

ADELE *(pulling away)*. Don't touch me!

MR. PARKER. You go ahead and do what you want, but I'm not leaving this shop! *(Crosses away from her)*

ADELE. Can't you understand, Father? I can't go on forever supporting three grown men! *That ain't right!*

(Long pause)

MR. PARKER *(shaken by her remarks)*. No, it's not right—it's not right at all.

ADELE. —It's going to be *you* or me.

BOBBY *(after a pause)*. I'll do what I can, Adele.

ADELE. You'll do *more* than you can.

BOBBY. I'll do more than I can.

ADELE. Is that all right by you, Mr. Theopolis?

THEO. Yes.

(Pause)

ADELE. That's fine. Out of this house tomorrow morning—before I leave here, or with me—suit your choice. And don't look so mournful *(gathers up her belongings at the shelf)*, smile. You're going to be happier than you think, earning a living for a change. *(Moves briskly through the back room and up the stairs)*

BOBBY. You do look pretty bad, Theo. A job might be just the thing for you.

(MR. JENKINS *comes rushing from the bed into the shop.)*

MR. PARKER. Jenkins! I plumb forgot—

MR. JENKINS. I let you make a fool out of me, Parker!

MR. PARKER. We can still play!

MR. JENKINS *(gathering his jacket and coat)*. We can't play nothing, I'm going home where I belong!

MR. PARKER. Okay, okay, I'll come over to your place tonight.

MR. JENKINS. That's the only way. I ain't gon' have my feelings hurt by that daughter of yours.

MR. PARKER. I'll see you tonight—about eight.

MR. JENKINS *(at the door)*. And, Parker, tell me something?

MR. PARKER. Yeah, what, Jenks?

MR. JENKINS. Are you positively sure Adele is your daughter?

MR. PARKER. Get out of here! (MR. JENKINS *rushes out.)* Now what made him ask a silly question like that?

THEO. I think he was trying to tell you that you ain't supposed to be taking all that stuff from Adele.

BOBBY. Yeah, Pop, he's right.

(MR. PARKER *starts putting his checker set together.)*

THEO *(to* BOBBY*)*. I don't know what you talking about—you had your chance a few minutes ago, but all you did was poke your eyes at me and nod your head like a fool.

BOBBY. I don't see why you gotta make such a big thing out of her taking charge. Somebody's gotta do it. I think she's right!

THEO. I know what she's up to. She wants us to get jobs so she can fix up the house like she always wanted it, and then it's gon' happen.

BOBBY. What's that?

THEO. She gon' get married to some konk-head out on the Avenue, and then she gon' throw us out the door.

BOBBY. She wouldn't do that.

THEO. She wouldn't, huh? Put yourself in her place. She's busting thirty wide open. *Thirty years old*—that's a lot of years for a broad that's not married.

BOBBY. I never thought of it that way . . .

THEO (in half confidence). And you know something else, Pop? I sneaked and peeped at her bank book, and you know what she got saved?

MR. PARKER and BOBBY (simultaneously, turning their heads). How much!?

THEO. Two thousand two hundred and six-ty-five dollars!

BOBBY. WHAT!!!

MR. PARKER. I don't believe it!

THEO. You better—and don't let her hand you that stuff about how she been sacrificing all these years for the house. The only way she could've saved up that kind of money was by staying right here!

MR. PARKER. Well, I'll be damned—two thousand dollars!

THEO. She better watch out is all I gotta say, 'cause I know some guys out there on that Avenue who don't do nothing but sit around all day figuring out ways to beat working girls out of their savings.

MR. PARKER. You oughta know, 'cause you're one of them yourself. The way I figure it, Theo, anybody that can handle you the way she did a few minutes ago can very well take care of themselves. (He occupies himself putting checkers and board away and cleaning up.)

THEO. That's mighty big talk coming from you, after the way she treated you.

MR. PARKER. Lay off me, boy.

THEO. You going out to look for a job?

MR. PARKER. I'm giving it some serious thought.

THEO. Well, I'm not. I ain't wasting myself on no low, dirty, dead-end job. I got my paintings to think about.

BOBBY. Do you really think you're some kind of painter or something?

THEO. You've seen them.

BOBBY. Yeah, but how would I know?

THEO (rushes into the back room, takes paintings from behind the refrigerator). All right, look at 'em.

BOBBY. Don't bring that stuff in here to me —show it to Pop!

(THEO holds up two ghastly, inept paintings to his brother. MR. PARKER, sweeping the floor, pays no attention.)

THEO. Look at it! Now tell me what you see.

BOBBY. Nothing.

THEO. You've got to see something—even an idiot has impressions.

BOBBY. I ain't no idiot.

THEO. All right, fool then.

BOBBY. Now look, you better stop throwing them words "fool" and "idiot" at me any time you feel like it. I'm gon' be one more fool, and then my fist is gonna land right upside your head!

THEO. Take it easy now—I tell you what: try to see something.

BOBBY. Try?

THEO. Yeah, close your eyes and really try.

BOBBY (closes his eyes). Okay, I'm trying, but I don't know how I'm gon' see anything with my eyes closed!

THEO. Well, open them!

BOBBY. They open.

THEO. Now tell me what you see.

BOBBY. I see paint.

THEO. I know you see paint, stupid.

BOBBY (slaps him ferociously across the face). Now I told you about that! Every time you call me out of my name, you get hit!

THEO. You'll never understand!

BOBBY. All I know is that a picture is sup-posed to be pretty, but I'm sorry, that mess you got there is downright ugly!

THEO. You're hopeless.—You understand this, don't you, Pop? (Holding the painting for him to see)

MR. PARKER (not looking at the painting). Don't ask me—I don't know nothing about no painting.

THEO. You were an artist once.

MR. PARKER. That was a different kind.

THEO. Didn't you ever go out on the stage with a new thing inside of you? One of them nights when you just didn't want to do that ol' soft-shoe routine? You knew you had to do it—after all, it was your job—but when you did it, you gave it a little bite here, a little acid there, and still, with all that, they laughed at you anyway. Didn't that ever hap-pen to you?

MR. PARKER. More than once. . . . But you're BSn', boy, and you know it. You been something new every year since you quit school. First you was going to be a racing-car driver, then a airplane pilot, then a office big shot, and now it's a painter. As smart a boy as you is, you should've stayed in school, but who do you think you're fooling with them pictures?—It all boils down to one thing: you don't want to work. But I'll tell you something, Theo: time done run out on you. Adele's not playing, so you might as well put all that junk and paint away.

THEO. Who the hell is Adele? You're my father, you're the man of the house.

MR. PARKER. True, and that's what I intend to be, but until I get a job, I'm gon' play it cool.

THEO. You're going to let her push you out into the streets to hustle up a job. You're an old man. You ain't used to working, it might kill you.

MR. PARKER. Yeah, but what kind of leg do I have to stand on if she puts me out in the street?

THEO. She's bluffing!

MR. PARKER. A buddy of mine who was in this same kind of fix told me exactly what you just said. Well, the last time I saw him, he was standing on the corner of Eighth Avenue and 125th Street at four o'clock in the morning, twenty-degree weather, in nothing but his drawers, mumbling to himself, "I could've sworn she was bluffing!"

THEO. Hey, Pop! Let me put it to you this way: if none of us come up with anything in that two-week deadline she gave us—none of us, you hear me?

MR. PARKER. I hear you and that's just about all.

THEO. Don't you get the point? That's three of us—you, me, and Bobby. What she gon' do? Throw the three of us out in the street? I tell you, she ain't gon' do that!

MR. PARKER. If you want to take that chance, that's your business, but don't try to make me take it with you. Anyway, it ain't right that she has to work for three grown men. It just ain't right.

THEO. Mama did it for you.

MR. PARKER (sharply). That was different. She was my wife. She knew things about me you will never know. We oughtn' talk about her at all.

THEO. I'm sorry, Pop, but ever since Mama's funeral I've been thinking. Mama was the hardest-working person I ever knew, and it killed her! Is that what I'm supposed to do? No, that's not it, I know it's not. You know what I've been doing? I've been talking to some people, to a very important person

right here in Harlem, and I told him about this big idea of mine—

MR. PARKER. You're loaded with ideas, boy—bad ideas! (Puts broom away)

THEO. WHY DON'T YOU LISTEN TO WHAT I HAVE TO SAY!

MR. PARKER. Listen to you for what? Another con game you got up your sleeve because your sister's got fed up with you lying around this house all day while she's knocking herself out. You're pulling the same damn thing on me you did with those ugly paintings of yours a few minutes ago.

THEO. Okay, I can't paint. So I was jiving, but now I got something I really want to do —something I got to do!

MR. PARKER. If you're making a point, Theo, you've gotta be smarter than you're doing to get it through to me.

THEO (goes to back room, opens refrigerator, and takes out brown-paper bag, then comes back into the shop). Pop, I got something here to show how smart I really am. (Lifts an old jug out of the bag) Check this out, Pop! Check it out!

MR. PARKER. What is it?

THEO. Whiskey—corn whiskey—you want some?

MR. PARKER (hovers). Well, I'll try a little bit of it out, but we better not let Adele see us.

THEO (starts unscrewing cork from jug). That girl sure puts a scare in you, Pop, and I remember when you wouldn't take no stuff off Mama, Adele, or nobody.

MR. PARKER. God is the only person I fear.

THEO (stops unscrewing the jug). God! Damn, you're all alike!

MR. PARKER. What are you talking about, boy?

THEO. You, the way Mama was—ask you any question you can't answer, and you throw that Bible stuff at us.

MR. PARKER. I don't get you.

THEO. For instance, let me ask you about the black man's oppressions, and you'll tell me about some small nation in the East rising one day to rule the world. Ask you about pain and dying, and you say, "God wills it." . . . Fear?—and you'll tell me about Daniel, and how Daniel wasn't scared of them lions. Am I right or wrong?

MR. PARKER. It's all in the book and you can't dispute it.

THEO. You wanta bet? If that nation in the East ever do rise, how can I be sure they won't be worse than the jokers we got running things now?—Nobody, but nobody, wills me to pain and dying, not if I can do something about it. That goes for John, Peter, Mary, J.C., the whole bunch of 'em! And as for ol' Daniel: sure, Daniel didn't care nothing about them lions—*but them lions didn't give a damn about him either! They tore him into a million pieces!*

MR. PARKER. That's a lie! That's an ungodly, unholy lie! *(Takes his Bible from the shelf)* And I'll prove it!

THEO. What lie?

MR. PARKER. *(moving from the counter, thumbing through Bible)*. You and those bastard ideas of yours. Here, here it is! *(Reading from Bible)* "And when he came near unto the den to Daniel, he cried with a pained voice; The King spoke and said to Daniel: 'O Daniel, servant of the living God, is thy God, whom thou servest continually, able to deliver thee from the lions?' Then said Daniel unto the King: 'O King, live forever! My God hath sent his angel, and hath shut the lions' mouths, and they have not hurt me; for as much as before him innocence was found in me, and also before thee, O King, have I done no hurt.' Then was the King exceeding glad, and commanded that they should take Daniel up out of the den. So Daniel was taken up out of the den, and no manner of hurt was found upon him, because he trusted his God!!!" *(Slams the book closed, triumphant)*

THEO. Hollywood, Pop, Hollywood!

MR. PARKER. Damn you! How I ever brought something like you into this world, I'll never know! You're no damn good! Sin! That's who your belief is! Sin and corruption! With you, it's nothing but women! Whiskey! Women! Whiskey! *(While he is carrying on,* THEO *pours out a glass of corn and puts it in* MR. PARKER's *hand.)* Women! Whiskey! *(Takes a taste)* Whisk—Where did you get this from? *(Sits on barber's throne)*

THEO *(slapping* BOBBY's *hand)*. I knew you'd get the message, Pop—I just knew it!

MR. PARKER. Why, boy, this is the greatest corn I ever tasted!

BOBBY. And Theo puts that stuff together like he was born to be a whiskey maker!

MR. PARKER. Where did you learn to make corn like this?

THEO. Don't you remember? You taught me.

MR. PARKER. By George, I did! Why, you weren't no more'n nine years old—

THEO. Eight. Let's have another one. *(Pours another for* PARKER) Drink up. Here's to ol' Daniel. You got to admit one thing—he had a whole lot of heart!

MR. PARKER *(drinks up and puts his hand out again)*. Another one, please . . .

THEO *(pouring)*. Anything you say, Pop! You're the boss of this house!

MR. PARKER. Now that's the truth if you ever spoke it. *(Drinks up)* Whew! This is good! *(Putting his glass out again, slightly tipsy)*

THEO. About this idea of mine, Pop: well, it's got something to do with this corn.

MR. PARKER *(drinks up)*. Wow! Boy, people oughta pay you to make this stuff.

THEO. Well, that's what I kinda had in mind. I tested some of it out the other day, and I was told this corn liquor could start a revolution—that is, if I wanted to start one. I let a preacher taste some, and he asked me to make him a whole keg for him.

MR. PARKER *(pauses; then, in a sudden change of mood)*. God! Damnit!

BOBBY. What's wrong, Pop?

MR. PARKER. I miss her, boy, I tell you, I miss her! Was it really God's will?

THEO. Don't you believe that—*don't you ever believe that!*

MR. PARKER. But I think, boy—I think hard!

THEO. That's all right. We think hard too. We got it from you. Ain't that right, Bobby?

BOBBY. Yeah.

MR. PARKER *(pause)*. You know something? That woman was the first woman I ever got close to—your mama . . .

BOBBY. *How old were you?*

MR. PARKER. Twenty.

BOBBY. Aw, come on, Pop!

MR. PARKER. May God wipe me away from this earth . . .

THEO. Twenty years old and you had never touched a woman? You must've been in bad shape.

MR. PARKER. I'll tell you about it.

THEO. Here he goes with another one of his famous stories!

MR. PARKER. I can always go on upstairs, you know.

THEO. No, Pop, we want to hear it.

MR. PARKER. Well, I was working in this circus in Tampa, Florida—your mother's hometown. You remember Bob Shepard—well, we had this little dance routine of ours we used to do a sample of outside the tent.

One day we was out there doing one of our numbers, when right in the middle of the number I spied this fine, foxy-looking thing, blinking her eyes at me. 'Course ol' Bob kept saying it was him she was looking at, but I knew it was *me*—'cause if there was one thing that was my specialty, it was a fine-looking woman.

THEO. You live twenty years of your life not getting anywhere near a woman, and all of a sudden they become *your specialty?*

MR. PARKER. Yeah, being that—

THEO. Being that you had never had a woman for all them terrible years, naturally it was on your mind all the time.

MR. PARKER. That's right.

THEO. And it being on your mind so much, you sorta became a specialist on women?

MR. PARKER. Right again.

THEO *(laughs)*. I don't know. But I guess you got a point there!

MR. PARKER. You want to hear this or not!?

BOBBY. Yeah, go on, Pop. *I'm* listening.

MR. PARKER. Well, while I was standing on the back of the platform, I motions to her with my hand to kinda move around to the side of the stand, so I could talk to 'er. She strolled 'round to the side, stood there for a while, and you know what? Ol' Bob wouldn't let me get a word in edgewise. But you know what she told him; she said Mister, you talk like a fool! *(All laugh.)*

BOBBY. That was Mama, all right.

MR. PARKER. So I asked her if she would like to meet me after the circus closed down. When I got off that night, sure enough, she was waiting for me. We walked out to the main section of town, off to the side of the road, 'cause we had a hard rain that day and the road was full of muddy little ponds. I got to talking to her and telling her funny stories and she would laugh—boy, I'm telling you that woman could laugh!

THEO. That was your technique, huh? Keep 'em laughing!

MR. PARKER. Believe it or not, it worked—'cause she let me kiss her. I kissed her under this big ol' pecan tree. She could kiss too. When that woman kissed me, somethin' grabbed me so hard and shook me so, I fell flat on my back into a big puddle of water! *And that woman killed herself laughing! (Pause)* I married her two weeks later.

THEO. And then you started making up for lost time. I'm glad you did, Pop—'cause if you hadn't, I wouldn't be here today.

MR. PARKER. If I know you, you'd have made some kind of arrangement.

BOBBY. What happened after that?

MR. PARKER. We just lived and had fun—and children too, that part you know about. We lived bad and we lived good—and then my legs got wobbly, and my feet got heavy, I lost my feeling, and everything just stayed as it was. *(Pause)* I only wish I had been as good a haircutter as I was a dancer. Maybe she wouldn't have had to work so hard. She might be living today.

THEO. Forget it, Pop—it's all in the gone by. Come on, you need another drink. *(Pouring)*

MR. PARKER. Get me to talking about them old days. It hurts, I tell you, it—

THEO. Pop, you have got to stop thinking about those things. We've got work to do!

MR. PARKER. You said you had an idea . . .

THEO. Yes—you see, Pop, this idea has to do with Harlem. It has to do with the preservation of Harlem. That's what it's all about. So I went to see this leader, and I spoke to him about it. He thought it was great and said he would pay me to use it!

MR. PARKER. Who wants to preserve this dump! Tear it down, is what I say!

THEO. But this is a different kind of preserving. Preserve it for black men—preserve it for men like you, me, and Bobby. That's what it's all about.

MR. PARKER. That sounds good.

THEO. Of course I told this leader, I couldn't promise to do anything until I had spoken to my father. I said, after straightening everything out with you I would make arrangements for the two of you to meet.

MR. PARKER. Meet him for what?

THEO. For making money! For business! *This man knows how to put people in business!*

MR. PARKER. All right, I'll meet him. What's his name?

THEO.—But first you gotta have a showdown with Adele and put her in her place once and for all.

MR. PARKER. Now wait just a minute. You didn't say Adele would have anything to do with this.

THEO. Pop, this man can't be dealing with men who let women rule them. Pop, you've got to tell that girl off or we can't call ourselves men!

MR. PARKER *(pause)*. All right. If she don't like it, that's too bad. Whatever you have in mind for us to do with this leader of yours, we'll do it.

THEO. Now that's the way I like to hear my old man talk! Take a drink, Pop! *(Starts popping his fingers and moves dancing about the room)*

> We're gonna show 'em now
> We're gonna show 'em how
> All over
> This ol' Harlem Town!

(THEO *and* BOBBY *start making rhythmic scat sounds with their lips as they dance around the floor.)*—Come on, Pop, show us how you used to cut one of them things!

BOBBY *(dancing).* This is how he did it!

THEO. Nawwww, that's not it. He did it like this!

MR. PARKER *(rising).* No, no! Neither one of you got it! Speed up that riff a little bit . . . *(The two boys speed up the riff, singing, stomping their feet, clapping their hands. Humped over,* MR. PARKER *looks down on the floor concentrating.)* Faster! *(They speed it up more.)*

THEO. Come on now, Pop—let 'er loose!

MR. PARKER. Give me time . . .

BOBBY. *Let that man have some time!*

(MR. PARKER *breaks into his dance.)*

THEO. Come on, Pop, take it with you!

BOBBY. Work, Pop!

THEO. DOWNTOWN!

(MR. PARKER *does a coasting "camel walk.")*

BOBBY. NOW BRING IT ON BACK UP-TOWN!

(MR. PARKER *really breaks loose: a rapid series of complicated dance steps.)*

THEO. YEAHHHHHHH!

BOBBY. That's what I'm talkin' about!

(ADELE *enters, stops at the entrance to the shop, observes the scene, bemused.* PARKER, *glimpsing her first, in one motion abruptly stops dancing and reaches for the broom.* BOBBY *looks for something to busy himself with.* THEO *just stares.)*

ADELE. Supper's ready, fellows!

CURTAIN

SCENE TWO

Six days later. Late afternoon. BOBBY *is seated in the barber's throne, munching on a sandwich.* THEO *enters from the front of the shop.*

——

THEO. Did Pop get back yet?

(BOBBY *shrugs shoulders.)*

THEO. You eating again? Damn. *(Calling upstairs)* Pop! *(No answer;* THEO *checks his watch, steps back into shop, looks through window, then crosses to* BOBBY *and snatches the sandwich from his mouth.)* You eat too damn much!

BOBBY. What the fuck you do that for?

THEO *(handing the sandwich back).* 'Cause you always got a mouth full of peanut butter and jelly!

BOBBY. I'm hungry! And let me tell you something: don't you *ever* snatch any food from my mouth again.

THEO. You'll hit me—you don't care nothing about your brother. One of these days, I'm gon' hit back.

BOBBY. *Nigger!* The day you swing your hand at me, you'll draw back a nub.

THEO. You see! That's exactly what I mean. Now when Blue gets here tonight, I don't want you talking like that, or else you gon' blow the whole deal.

BOBBY. I know how to act. I don't need no lessons from you.

THEO. Good. I got a job for you.

BOBBY. A job? Shit!

THEO. Don't get knocked out now—it ain't no real job. I just want you to jump over to Smith's on 125th Street and pick me up a portable typewriter.

BOBBY. Typewriter—for what?

THEO. Don't ask questions, just go and get it.

BOBBY. Them typewriters cost a lotta money.

THEO. You ain't gon' use money.

BOBBY. You mean—

THEO.—I mean you walk in there and take one.

BOBBY. Naw, you don't mean I walk into nowhere and take nothing!

THEO. Now, Bobby.

BOBBY. No!

THEO. Aw, come on, Bobby. You the one been bragging about how good you are, how you can walk into any store and get anything you wanted, provided it was not too heavy to carry out.

BOBBY. I ain't gon' do it!

THEO. You know what day it is?

BOBBY. Thursday.

THEO. That's right. Thursday, May 10th.

BOBBY. What's that suppose to mean, Thieves' Convention on 125th Street?

THEO. It's Pop's birthday!

BOBBY. I didn't know he was still having them.

THEO. Well, let me tell you something: Adele remembered it and she's planning on busting into this shop tonight with a birthday cake to surprise him.

BOBBY. She suppose to be throwing us out today. That don't make no sense with her buying him a birthday cake.

THEO. He's been looking for work, I guess she changed her mind about him. Maybe it's gon' be just me and you that goes.

BOBBY (pause). What's he gon' type?

THEO. Them lies he's always telling—like the one about how he met Mama. Pop can tell some of the greatest lies you ever heard of and you know how he's always talking about writing them down.

BOBBY. Pop don't know nothing 'bout writing—specially no typewriting!

THEO (takes out his father's notebook). Oh no? take a look at this. (Hands book to BOBBY) All he has to do is put it down on paper the way he tells it. Who knows, somebody might get interested in it for television or movies, and we can make ourselves some money, and besides, I kinda think he would get a real charge out of you thinking about him that way—don't you?

BOBBY (pause). Well, ain't no use in lettin' you go over there, gettin' yourself in jail with them old clumsy fingers of yours.

THEO. Good boy, Bobby! (MR. PARKER enters the shop.) Hey, Pop! Did you get that thing straightened out with Adele yet?

MR. PARKER. What?

THEO. Adele?

MR. PARKER. Oh, yeah, I'm gon' take care of that right away. (Shoves BOBBY out of throne and sits)

THEO. Where you been all day?

(BOBBY moves into back room.)

MR. PARKER. Downtown, seeing about some jobs.

THEO. You sure don't care much about yourself.

MR. PARKER. I can agree with you on that, because lookin' for a job can really hurt a man. I was interviewed five times today, and I could've shot every last one of them interviewers—the white ones and the colored ones too. I don't know if I can take any more of this.

THEO. Yeah, looking for a job can be very low-grading to a man, and it gets worse after you get the job. Anyway, I'm glad you got

back here on time, or you would've missed your appointment. (No response from PARKER) Now don't tell me you don't remember! The man, the man that's suppose to come here and tell you how life in Harlem can be profitable.

MR. PARKER (steps out of throne, edging toward back room). Oh, that.

THEO (following him). Oh, that—my foot! Today is the day we're suppose to come up with those jobs, and you ain't said one word to Adele about it—not one single word! All you do is waste your time looking for work! Now that don't make no sense at all, Pop, and you know it.

MR. PARKER Look, son. Let me go upstairs now and tell her about all the disappointments I suffered today, soften her up a bit, and then I'll come on back down here to meet your man. I promise, you won't have to worry about me going downtown any more—not after what I went through today. And I certainly ain't giving up my shop for nobody! (Exits upstairs)

THEO (turns to BOBBY, who's at the mirror). Now that's the way I like to hear my old man talk! Hey, baby, don't forget that thing. It's late, we ain't got much time.

BOBBY. All right!

(A jet-black-complexioned young man comes in. He is dressed all in blue and wears sunglasses. He carries a gold-top cane and a large salesman's valise. He stops just inside the door.)

THEO. Blue, baby!

BLUE. Am I late?

THEO. No, my father just walked in the door. He's upstairs now, but he'll be right back down in a few minutes. Let me take your things. (Takes BLUE's cane and valise) Sit down, man, while I fix you a drink. (Places BLUE's things on the table and moves into back room; BOBBY enters shop.)

BLUE. Hey, Bobby. How's the stores been treating you?

BOBBY. I'm planning on retiring next year. (Laughs)

THEO (returning with jug and two glasses; moves to the table and pours). I was thinking, Blue—we can't let my old man know about our "piano brigade." I know he ain't going for that, but we can fix it where he will never know a thing.

BLUE. You know your father better than I do. (Takes a drink)

BOBBY. What's the "piano brigade"?

THEO. Blue here has the best thieves and store burglars in this part of town, and we plan to work on those businesses over on 125th Street until they run the insurance companies out of business.

BOBBY. You mean breaking into people's stores at night and taking their stuff?

THEO. That's right, but not the way you do it. We'll be organized, we'll be revolutionary.

BOBBY. If the police catch you, they ain't gon' care what you is, and if Pop ever finds out, the police gon' seem like church girls! *(Slips out the front door)*

THEO *(after him)*. You just remember that the only crime you'll ever commit is the one you get caught at! *(Pause)* Which reminds me, Blue—I don't want Bobby to be a part of that "piano brigade."

BLUE. If that's the way you want it, that's the way it shall be, Theo. How's your sister?

THEO. You mean Adele?

BLUE. You got a sister named Mary or something?

THEO. What's this with Adele?

BLUE. I want to know, how are you going to get along with her, selling bootleg whiskey in this place?

THEO. This is not her place, it's my father's. And once he puts his okay on the deal, that's it. What kind of house do you think we're living in, where we gon' let some woman tell us what to do? Come here, let me show you something. *(Moves into back room.* BLUE *follows.)* How you like it—ain't it something?

BLUE *(standing in doorway)*. It's a back room.

THEO. Yeah, I know. But I have some great plans for reshaping it by knocking down this wall, and putting—

BLUE. Like I said, it's a back room. All I wanta know is, will it do the job? It's a good room. You'll do great with that good-tasting corn of yours. You're going to be so busy here, you're going to grow to hate this place —you might not have any time for your love life, Theopolis!

THEO *(laughing)*. Don't you worry about that—I can manage my sex life!

BLUE. Sex! Who's talking about sex? You surprise me, Theo. Everyone's been telling me about how you got so much heart, how you so deep. I sit and talk to you about life, and you don't know the difference between sex and love.

THEO. Is it that important?

BLUE. Yes, it is, ol' buddy, if you want to hang out with me, and you do want to hang out with me, don't you?

THEO. That depends—

BLUE. It depends upon you knowing that sex's got nothing to do with anything but you and some woman laying up in some funky bed, pumping and sweating your life away all for one glad moment—you hear that, *one moment!*

THEO. I'll take that moment!

BLUE. With every woman you've had?

THEO. One out of a hundred!

BLUE *(laughing, and moving back into shop)*. One out of a hundred! All that sweat! All that pumping and grinding for the sake of one little dead minute out of a hundred hours!

(MR. PARKER *comes in from upstairs.)*

THEO *(pause; stopping* PARKER*)*. Pop, you know who this is?

MR. PARKER. I can't see him.

THEO. This is Blue!

MR. PARKER. Blue who?

THEO. The man I was telling you about . . . *Mr. Blue Haven.*

MR. PARKER *(extends his hand to shake* BLUE*'s)*. Please to make your acquaintance, Mr. Haven.

BLUE *(shaking* MR. PARKER*'s hand)*. Same to you, Mr. Parker.

THEO. You sure you don't know who Blue Haven is, Pop?

MR. PARKER. I'm sorry, but I truly don't know you, Mr. Haven. If you're a celebrity, you must accept my apology. You see, since I got out of the business, I don't read the *Variety* any more.

THEO. I'm not talking about a celebrity.

MR. PARKER. Oh, no?

THEO. He's the leader!

MR. PARKER. Ohhhhh!

THEO. Right here in Harlem.

MR. PARKER. Where else he gon' be but in Harlem? We got more leaders within ten square blocks of this barbershop than they got liars down in City Hall. That's why you dressed up that way, huh, boy? So people can pick you out of a crowded room?

THEO. Pop, this is serious!

MR. PARKER. All right, go on, don't get carried away—there are some things I don't catch on to right away, Mr. Blue.

THEO. Well, get to this: I got to thinking the other day when Adele busted in here showing everybody around—I was thinking about this barbershop, and I said to myself:

Pop's gon' lose this shop if he don't start making himself some money.

MR. PARKER. Now tell me something I don't know. *(Sits on throne)*

THEO. Here I go. What would you say if I were to tell you that Blue here can make it possible for you to have a thriving business going on, right here in this shop, for twenty-four hours a day?

MR. PARKER. What is he—some kind of hair grower!

THEO. Even if you don't cut but one head of hair a week!

MR. PARKER. Do I look like a fool to you?

THEO *(holds up his jug). Selling this!*

MR. PARKER *(pause)*. Well, well, well. I knew it was something like that. I didn't exactly know what it was, but I knew it was something. And I don't want to hear it!

THEO. Pop, you've always been a man to listen—even when you didn't agree, even when I was wrong, you listened! That's the kind of man you are! You—

MR. PARKER. Okay, okay, I'm listening!

THEO *(pause)*. Tell him who you are, Blue.

BLUE. I am the Prime Minister of the Harlem De-Colonization Association.

MR. PARKER *(pause)*. Some kind of organization?

BLUE. Yes.

MR. PARKER *(as an aside, almost under his breath)*. They got all kinds of committees in Harlem. What was that name again, "De"?

THEO. De-Colo-ni-zation! Which means that Harlem is owned and operated by Mr. You-Know-Who. Let me get this stuff—we gon' show you something . . . *(Moves to the table and opens BLUE's valise)*

BLUE. We're dead serious about this project, Mr. Parker. I'd like you to look at this chart.

THEO. And you'll see, we're not fooling. *(Hurriedly pins charts taken from BLUE's valise on wall out in the shop)*

MR. PARKER *(reading from center chart)*. The Harlem De-Colonization Association, with Future Perspective for Bedford Stuyvesant. *(Turns to BLUE)* All right, so you got an organization. What do you do? I've never heard of you.

BLUE. The only reason you've never heard of us is because we don't believe in picketing, demonstrating, rioting, and all that stuff. We always look like we're doing something that we ain't doing, but we are doing something— and in that way nobody gets hurt. Now you

may think we're passive. To the contrary, we believe in direct action. We are doers, enterprisers, thinkers—and most of all, we're businessmen! Our aim is to drive Mr. You-Know-Who out of Harlem.

MR. PARKER. Who's this Mr. You-Know-Who?

THEO. Damn, Pop! The white man!

MR. PARKER. Oh, himmm!

BLUE. We like to use that name for our members in order to get away from the bad feelings we have whenever we use the word "white." We want our members to always be objective and in this way we shall move forward. Before we get through, there won't be a single Mr. You-Know-Who left in this part of town. We're going to capture the imagination of the people of Harlem. And that's never been done before, you know.

MR. PARKER. Now, tell me how?

BLUE *(standing before the charts, pointing with his cane)*. You see this here. This is what we call a "brigade." And you see this yellow circle?

MR. PARKER. What's that for?

BLUE. My new and entertaining system for playing the numbers. You do play the numbers, Mr. Parker?

MR. PARKER. I do.

BLUE. You see, I have a lot of colors in this system and these colors are mixed up with a whole lot of numbers, and the idea is to catch the right number with the right color. The right number can be anything from one to a hundred, but in order to win, the color must always be black. The name of this game is called "Black Heaven." It's the color part that gives everybody all the fun in playing this game of mine.

MR. PARKER. Anybody ever catch it?

BLUE. Sure, but not until every number and every color has paid itself off. The one thing you'll find out about my whole operation: you can't lose. *(Pause for effect)*

MR. PARKER. Keep talking.

BLUE. Now over here is the Red Square Circle Brigade, and this thing here is at the heart of my dream to create here in Harlem a symbolic life-force in the heart of the people.

MR. PARKER. You don't say . . .

BLUE. Put up that target, Theo. (THEO *hurriedly pins on wall a dart target with the face of a beefy, Southern-looking white man as bull's-eye.)*

MR. PARKER. Why, that's that ol' dirty sheriff from that little town in Mississippi!

BLUE *(taking a dart from* THEO*).* That's right—we got a face on a target for every need. We got governors, mayors, backwood crackers, city crackers, Southern crackers, and Northern crackers. We got all kinds of faces on these targets that any good Harlemite would be willing to buy for the sake of slinging one of these darts in that bastard's throat! *(Throws dart, puncturing face on board)*

MR. PARKER. Let me try it one time. *(Rising, takes dart from* BLUE *and slings it into the face on the target)* Got him! *(A big laugh)*

BLUE. It's like I said, Mr. Parker: the idea is to capture the imagination of the people!

MR. PARKER. You got more? Let me see more!

BLUE. Now this is our green circle—that's Theo and his corn liquor—for retail purposes will be called "Black Lightning." This whiskey of Theo's can make an everlasting contribution to this life-force I've been telling you about. I've tested this whiskey out in every neighborhood in Harlem, and everybody claimed it was the best they ever tasted this side of Washington, D.C. You see, we plan to supply every after-hours joint in this area, and this will run Mr. You-Know-Who and his bonded product out of Harlem.

THEO. You see, Pop, this all depends on the barbershop being open night and day so the people can come and go as they please, to pick up their play for the day, to get a bottle of corn, and to take one of them targets home to the kiddies. They can walk in just as if they were getting a haircut. In fact, I told Blue that we can give a haircut as a bonus for anyone who buys two quarts.

MR. PARKER. What am I suppose to say now?

THEO. You're suppose to be daring. You're suppose to wake up to the times, Pop! These are urgent days—a man has to stand up and be counted!

MR. PARKER. The police might have some counting of their own to do.

THEO. Do you think I would bring you into something that was going to get us in trouble? Blue has an organization! Just like Mr. You-Know-Who. He's got members on the police force! In the city government, the state government.

BLUE. Mr. Parker, if you have any reservations concerning the operation of my association, I'd be only too happy to have you come to my summer home, and I'll let you in on everything—especially our protective system against being caught doing this thing.

THEO. Did you hear him, Pop, *he's got a summer home!*

MR. PARKER. Aw, shut up, boy! Let me think! *(Turns to* BLUE.*)* So you want to use my place as a headquarters for Theo's corn, the colored numbers, and them targets?

BLUE. Servicing the area of 125th to 145th, between the east and west rivers.

MR. PARKER *(pause).* I'm sorry, fellows, but I can't do it. *(Moves into back room)*

THEO *(following* MR. PARKER*).* Why?

MR. PARKER. It's not right.

THEO. Not right! What are you talking about? Is it right that all that's out there for us is to go downtown and push one of them carts? I have done that, and I ain't gon' do it no more!

MR. PARKER. That still don't make it right.

THEO. I don't buy it! I'm going into this thing with Blue, with or without you!

MR. PARKER. Go on, I don't care! You quit school, I couldn't stop you! I asked you to get a job, you wouldn't work! You have never paid any attention to any of my advice, and I don't expect you to start heeding me now!

THEO. Remember what you said to me about them paintings, and being what I am—well, this is me! At last I've found what I can do, and it'll work—I know it will. Please, Pop, just—

MR. PARKER. Stop begging, Theo. *(Crosses back into shop, looks at* BLUE*)* Why?

BLUE. I don't get you.

MR. PARKER. What kind of boy are you that you went through so much pain to dream up this cockeyed, ridiculous plan of yours?

BLUE. Mr. Parker, I was born about six blocks from here, and before I was ten I had the feeling I had been living for a hundred years. I got so old and tired I didn't know how to cry. Now you just think about that. But now I own a piece of this neighborhood. I don't have to worry about some bastard landlord or those credit crooks on 125th Street. Beautiful, black Blue—they have to worry about me! *(Reaches into his pocket and pulls out a stack of bills; places them in* PARKER*'s hands)* Can't you see, man—I'm here to put you in business! (MR. PARKER *runs his fingers through the money.)* Money, Mr. Parker—brand-new money . . .

(After concentrated attention, MR. PARKER *drops money on table and moves into back room.* THEO *hurriedly follows.* MR. PARKER *sits on bed, in deep thought.)*

THEO. That's just to get us started. And if we can make a dent into Mr. You-Know-Who's going-ons in Harlem, nobody's going to think of us as crooks. We'll be heroes from 110th Street to Sugar Hill. And just think, Pop, you won't have to worry about jobs and all that. You'll have so much time for you and Mr. Jenkins to play checkers, your arms will drop off. You'll be able to sit as long as you want, and tell enough stories and lies to fit between the covers of a 500-page book. That's right! Remember you said you wanted to write all them stories down! Now you'll have time for it! You can dress up the way you used to. And the girls—remember how you used to be so tough with the girls before you got married? All that can come back to you, and some of that you never had. It's so easy! All you have to do is call Adele down those stairs and let her know that you're going into business and if she don't like it she can pack up and move out, because you're not going to let her drive you down because you're a man, and—

MR. PARKER. All right! (Moves back into shop, where BLUE is putting away his paraphernalia) I'll do it! (Pause) I'll do it under one condition—

BLUE. And that is?

MR. PARKER. If my buddy Jenkins wants to buy into this deal, you'll let him.

BLUE. Theo?

THEO. It's all right.

MR. PARKER (extending his hand to BLUE). Then you got yourself some partners, Mr. Haven!

BLUE. Welcome into the association, Mr. Parker.

MR. PARKER. Welcome into my barbershop!

THEO (jubilantly). Yehhhhhhhhhh!

(BLUE checks his watch. ADELE comes into the back room.)

BLUE. Well, I have to check out now, but I'll stop over tomorrow and we will set the whole thing up just as you want it, Mr. Parker. See you later, Theo.

MR. PARKER (to BLUE as he is walking out the front door). You should stick around awhile and watch my polish!

THEO. Pop, don't you think it would be better if you would let me give the word to Adele?

MR. PARKER. No. If I'm going to run a crooked house, I'm going to run it, and that goes for you as well as her.

THEO. But, Pop, sometimes she kinda gets by you.

MR. PARKER. Boy, I have never done anything like this in my life, but since I've made up my mind to it, you have nothing to say—not a word. You have been moaning about me never making it so you can have a chance. Well, this time you can say I'm with you. But let me tell you something: I don't want no more lies from you, and no more conning me about painting, airplane piloting, or nothing. If being a crook is what you want to be, you're going to be the best crook in the world—even if you have to drink mud to prove it.

THEO (pause). Okay, Pop.

MR. PARKER (moves toward back room). Well, here goes nothing. Adele! (Just as he calls, ADELE steps out of the back room, stopping him in his tracks.)

ADELE. Yes, Father.

MR. PARKER. Oh, you're here already. Well, I want to talk to—well, I, er—

ADELE. What is it?

MR. PARKER (pause). Nothing. I'll talk to you later. (He spots BOBBY entering from the outside with a package wrapped in newspaper.) What you got there?

BOBBY. Uh . . . uh . . . —fish!

MR. PARKER. Well, you better get them in the refrigerator before they stink on you.

THEO (going over to BOBBY and taking package from him). No, no. Now, Bobby, I promised Pop we would never lie to him again. It ain't fish, Pop. We've got something for you. (Puts the package on the table and starts unwrapping it. The two boys stand over the table, and as the typewriter is revealed, both turn to him.)

THEO and BOBBY. Happy Birthday!

MR. PARKER. Birthday? Birthday?

THEO and BOBBY. Yes, Happy Birthday!

MR. PARKER. Now hold on just a minute!

BOBBY. What are we holding on for, Pop?

MR. PARKER (pause). That's a good question, son. We're—we're holding on for a celebration! (Laughs loudly) Thanks, fellows! But what am I going to do with a typewriter! I don't know nothing about no typing!

ADELE. I would like to know where they got the money to buy one!

THEO (ignoring her). You know what you told me about writing down your stories—now you can write them down three times as fast!

MR. PARKER. But I don't know how to type!

THEO. With the money we're gonna be having, I can hire somebody to teach you!

ADELE. What money you going to have?

THEO. We're going into business, baby—right here in this barbershop!

MR. PARKER. Theo—

THEO *(paying no attention)*. We're going to sell bootleg whiskey, numbers, and—

ADELE. You're what!?

MR. PARKER. Theo—

THEO. You heard me, and if you don't like it you can pack your bags and leave!

ADELE. Leave? I pay the rent here!

THEO. No more! I pay it now!

MR. PARKER. Shut up, Theo!

THEO. We're going to show you something, girl. You think—

MR. PARKER. *I said shut up!*

ADELE. Is he telling the truth?

MR. PARKER. Yes, he is telling the truth.

ADELE. You mean to tell me you're going to turn this shop into a bootleg joint?

MR. PARKER. I'll turn it into anything I want to!

ADELE. Not while I'm still here!

MR. PARKER. The lease on this house has my signature, not yours!

ADELE. I'm not going to let you do this!

MR. PARKER. You got no choice, Adele. *You don't have a damn thing to say!*

ADELE *(turns sharply to* THEO*)*. You put him up to this!

MR. PARKER. Nobody puts me up to anything I don't want to do! These two boys have made it up in their minds they're not going to work for nobody but themselves, and the thought in my mind is *why should they!* I did like you said, I went downtown, and it's been a long time since I did that, but *you're* down there every day, and you oughta know by now that I am too old a man to ever dream I . . . could overcome the dirt and filth they got waiting for me down there. I'm surprised at you, that you would have so little care in you to shove me into the middle of that mob.

ADELE. You can talk about caring? What about Mama? She *died* working for you! Did you ever stop to think about that! In fact, *did you ever love her?* No!!!

MR. PARKER. That's a lie!

ADELE. I hope that one day you'll be able to do one good thing to drive that doubt out of my mind. *But this is not it!* You've let this hoodlum sell you his twisted ideas of making a short cut through life. But let me tell you something—this bastard is going to ruin you!

THEO *(into her face)*. Start packing, baby!

ADELE *(strikes him across the face)*. Don't you talk to me like that!

(He raises his hand to strike her back.)

MR. PARKER. Drop your hand, boy! (THEO *does not respond.*) I said, drop your goddamn hand!

THEO. She hit me!

MR. PARKER. I don't care if she had broken your jaw. If you ever draw your hand back to hit this girl again—*as long as you* live! You better not be in my hand reach when you do, 'cause *I'll split your back in two!* (To ADELE) We're going into business, Adele. I have come to that and I have come to it on my own. I am going to stop worrying once and for all whether I live naked in the cold or whether I die like an animal, unless I can live the best way I know how to. I am getting old and I oughta have some fun. I'm going to get me some money, and I'm going to spend it! I'm going to get drunk! I'm going to dance some more! *I'm getting old! I'm going to fall in love one more time before I die!* So get to that, girl, and if it's too much for you to bear, I wouldn't hold it against you if you walked away from here this very minute—

ADELE *(opens the door to the back room to show him the birthday surprise she has for him)*. Happy birthday!

MR. PARKER *(goes into the room and stands over table where birthday cake is)*. I guess I fooled all of you. Today is not my birthday. It never was. *(Moves up the stairs)*

ADELE. It's not going to work! You're going to cut your throat—you hear me! You're going to rip yourself into little pieces! *(Turns to* THEO*)* It's not going to be the way you want it—because I know Mr. Blue Haven, and he is not a person to put your trust in. (THEO *turns his back on her, heads for the shop door.*) . . . I am talking to you!

THEO *(stops and turns)*. Why don't you leave us alone. You're the one who said we had to go out and do something. Well, we did, but we're doing it our way. Me and Bobby, we're men—if we lived the way you wanted us to, we wouldn't have nothing but big fat veins popping out of our heads.

ADELE. I'll see what kind of men you are every time a cop walks through that door, every time a stranger steps into this back room and you can't be too sure about him, and the day they drag your own father off and throw him into a jail cell.

THEO. But, tell me, what else is there left

for us to do. You tell me and I'll do it. You show me where I can go to spin the world around before it gets too late for somebody like Mama living fifty years just to die on 126th Street! *You tell me of a place where there are no old crippled vaudeville men!*

ADELE. There is no such place. *(Pause)* But you don't get so hung up about it you have to plunge a knife into your own body. You don't bury yourself here in this place; you climb up out of it! Now that's something for you to wonder about, boy.

THEO. I wonder all the time—how you have lived here all your whole life on this street, and you haven't seen, heard, learned, or felt a thing in all those years. I wonder how you ever got to be such a damn fool!

CURTAIN

ACT TWO

Scene One

Two months later. It is about 9 P.M.

As the curtain rises, the lights come up in the back room. BOBBY *is there, listening to a record of James Brown's "Money Won't Change You, But Time Will Take You On." As he is dancing out to the shop,* THEO *appears from the cellar, which has been enlarged by taking out a panel in the lower section of the wall and houses the whiskey-making operation.* THEO *brings in two boxes filled with bottles of corn whiskey and shoves them under the bed.*

BOBBY *moves past* THEO *into the shop, carrying a target rolled up in his hand, and two darts. He is wearing a fancy sports shirt, new trousers, new keen-toed shoes, and a stingy, diddy-bop hat. He pins the target up on the wall of the shop. In the center of the target is the face of a well-known American racist.*

———

BOBBY *(moves away from the target, aims and hurls the dart).* That's for Pop! Huh! *(Throws another)* And this is for me! Huh! *(Moves to the target to pull darts out.* THEO *cuts record off abruptly. A knock at the door)*

THEO *(calling out to* BOBBY *from the back room).* Lock that door!

BOBBY. Lock it yourself!

THEO *(with quick but measured steps moves toward front door).* I'm not selling another bottle, target, or anything, till I get some help! *(Locks door in spite of persistent knocking)* We're closed!

BOBBY. I don't think Blue is gon' like you turning customers away. *(Sits in barber chair, lighting up cigar)*

THEO. You can tell Blue I don't like standing over that stove all day, that I don't like him promising me helpers that don't show up. There are a lot of things I don't go for, like Pop taking off and not showing up for two days. I make this whiskey, I sell it, I keep books, I peddle numbers and those damn targets. *And I don't like you standing around here all day not lifting a finger to help me!*

BOBBY *(taking a big puff on his cigar).* I don't hear you.

THEO. Look at you—all decked out in your new togs. Look at me: I haven't been out of these dungarees since we opened this place up.

BOBBY *(jumps out of chair).* I don't wanta hear nothing! You do what you wanta do, and leave me alone!

THEO. What am I supposed to be, a work mule or something?

BOBBY. You're the one that's so smart—you can't answer your own stupid questions?

THEO. You done let Blue turn you against me, huh?

BOBBY. You ask the questions, and you gon' answer them—but for now, stop blowing your breath in my face!

THEO. You make me sick. *(Moves into back room; sits on bed)*

ADELE *(enters from upstairs, dressed in a smart Saks Fifth Avenue outfit).* Getting tired already, Theo?

THEO. No, just once in a while I'd like to have some time to see one of my women!

ADELE. You being the big industrialist and all that, I thought you had put girls off for a year or two!

THEO. Get away from me. *(Crosses to desk and sits)*

ADELE. I must say, however—it is sure a good sight to see you so wrapped up in work. I never thought I'd live to see the day, but—

THEO. Don't you ever have anything good to say?

ADELE. I say what I think and feel. I'm honest.

THEO. Honest? You're just hot because Pop decided to do something my way for a change.

ADELE. That's a joke, when you haven't seen him for two whole days. Or, *do* you know where he has gone to practically every night since you opened up this little store.

THEO. He's out having a little sport for himself. What's wrong with that? He hasn't had any fun in a long time.

ADELE. Is fun all you can think of? When *my* father doesn't show up for two days, I worry.

THEO. You're not worried about nobody but yourself—I'm on to your game. You'd give anything in the world to go back just the way we were, because you liked the idea of us being dependent on you. Well, that's all done with, baby. We're on our own. So don't worry yourself about Pop. When Blue gets here tonight with our money, he'll be here!

ADELE. If my eyes and ears are clear, then I would say that Father isn't having the kind of money troubles these days that he must rush home for your pay day.

THEO. What do you mean by that?

ADELE. I mean that he has been dipping his hands into that little drawer of yours at least two or three times a week.

THEO. You ain't telling nothing I don't know.

ADELE. What about your friend Blue?

THEO. I can handle him.

ADELE. I hope so, since it is a known fact that he can be pretty evil when he thinks someone has done him wrong—and it happened once, in a bar uptown, he actually killed a man.

THEO. You're lying. *(He moves quickly to shop entrance.)* Bobby, have you heard anything about Blue killing a man? (BOBBY, *seated in the barber's chair, looks at him, then turns away, not answering.* THEO *returns to the back room.)*

ADELE. Asking him about it is not going to help you. Ask yourself a few questions and you will know that you are no better than Blue—because it is you two who are the leaders of those mysterious store raids on 125th Street, and your ace boy on those robberies is no one other than your brother, Bobby Parker!

THEO. Bobby!

ADELE. I don't know why that should surprise you, since he is known as the swiftest and coolest young thief in Harlem.

THEO. I didn't know about Bobby—*who told you!*

ADELE. As you well know by now, I've been getting around lately, and I meet people, and people like to have something to talk about, and you know something: this place is becoming the talk along every corner and bar on the Avenue!

THEO. You're just trying to scare me.

ADELE. I wish to God I was. *(Starts out)*

THEO. Where are you going?

ADELE *(stops, turns abruptly)*. Out. Do you mind?

THEO. *That's all you ever do!*

ADELE. Yes, you're right.

THEO. They tell me you're going with Wilmer Robinson?

ADELE. Yes, that's true. *(Moving through shop toward door;* BOBBY *doesn't move from the barber's throne and buries his nose in a comic book.)*

THEO *(following behind her)*. He's a snake.

ADELE. No better or worse than someone like you or Blue.

THEO. He'll bleed you for every dime you've got!

ADELE. So what. He treats me like a woman, and that's more than I can say for any man in this house!

THEO. He'll treat you like a woman until he's gotten everything he wants, and then he's gon' split your ass wide open!

ADELE *(turns sharply at door)*. Theooooooooooo! *(Pause)* You talk like that to me because you don't know how to care for the fact that I am your sister.

THEO. But why are you trying to break us up? Why?

ADELE. I don't have to waste that kind of good time. I can wait for you to bust it up yourself. Good night! *(Slams the door behind herself)*

(THEO *stands with a long, deep look in his eye, then goes down cellar.* MR. PARKER *steps into the shop, all dapper, dressed up to a fare-thee-well, holding a gold-top cane in one hand and a book in the other.* BOBBY *stares at him, bewildered.)*

BOBBY. What's that you got on?

MR. PARKER. What does it look like?

BOBBY. Nothing.

MR. PARKER. You call this nothing!

BOBBY. Nothin—I mean, I didn't mean nothing when I asked you that question.

MR. PARKER. Where's Theo?

BOBBY. In the back, working.

MR. PARKER. Good! Shows he's got his mind stretched out for good and great things. *(Hangs up hat and puts away cane)*

BOBBY. He's been stretching his mind out to find out where you been.

MR. PARKER. Where I been is none of his business, Blue is the man to think about. It's pay day, and I wanta know, where the hell is he! *(Checks his watch, taps* BOBBY, *indicating he should step down from chair)*

BOBBY *(hops down from chair;* PARKER *sits).* Whatcha reading?

MR. PARKER. A book I picked up yesterday. I figured since I'm in business I might as well read a businessman's book.

BOBBY. Let me see it. *(Takes the book in his hand) The Thief's Journal,* by Jean Gin-nett. *(Fingering through pages)* Is it a good story?

MR. PARKER. So far—

BOBBY *(hands it back).* What's it all about?

MR. PARKER. A Frenchman who was a thief.

BOBBY. Steal things?

MR. PARKER. Uh-huh.

BOBBY. Where did he get all that time to write a book?

MR. PARKER. Oh, he had the time all right, 'cause he spent most of it in jail.

BOBBY. Some thief!

MR. PARKER. The trouble with this bird is that he became a thief and then he became a thinker.

BOBBY. No shucking!

MR. PARKER. No shucking. But it is my logicalism that you've got to become a thinker and then you become a crook! Or else, why is it when you read up on some of these politicians' backgrounds you find they all went to one of them big law colleges? That's where you get your start!

BOBBY. Well, I be damned!

MR. PARKER *(jumps down out of the chair, moves briskly toward door).* Now where is Blue! He said he would be here nine thirty on the nose! *(Opens the door and* JENKINS *comes in.)* Hey, Jenkins! What's up!

MR. JENKINS. That Blue fellow show up yet?

MR. PARKER. No, he didn't, and I'm gon' call him down about that too.

MR. JENKINS. It don't matter. I just want whatever money I got coming, and then I'm getting out of this racket.

MR. PARKER. Don't call it that, it's a committee!

MR. JENKINS. This committee ain't no committee. It ain't nothing but a racket, and I'm getting out of it!

MR. PARKER. You put your money into this thing, man. It ain't good business to walk out on an investment like that.

MR. JENKINS. I can, and that's what I'm doing before I find myself in jail! Man, this thing you got going here is the talk in every bar in this neighborhood.

MR. PARKER. There ain't nothing for you to be scared of, Jenkins. Blue guaranteed me against ever being caught by the police. Now that's all right by me, but I've got some plans of my own. When he gets here tonight, I'm gon' force him to make me one of the leaders in this group, and if he don't watch out, I just might take the whole operation over from him. I'll make you my right-hand man, and not only will you be getting more money, and I won't just guarantee you against getting caught, but I'll guarantee you against being scared!

MR. JENKINS. There's nothing you can say to make me change my mind. I shouldn't've let you talk me into this mess in the first place. I'm getting out, and that's it! *(Starts for the door)* And if he gets back before I do, you hold my money for me! *(Exiting)*

MR. PARKER *(pursuing him to door).* Suit yourself, but you're cutting your own throat. This little setup is the biggest thing to hit this neighborhood since the day I started dancing! *(Slams door)* Fool! *(Takes off coat, hangs it up; goes to mirror to primp)*

BOBBY. Going somewhere again?

MR. PARKER. Got myself a little date to get to if Blue ever gets here with our money—*and he better get here with our money!*

BOBBY. You been dating a lot lately—nighttime dates, and day ones too—and Theo's not happy about it. He says you don't stay here long enough to cut Yul Brynner's hair.

MR. PARKER. He can complain all he wants to. I'm the boss here, and he better not forget it. He's the one that's got some explaining to do: don't talk to nobody no more, don't go nowhere, looking like he's mad all the time. . . . I've also noticed that he don't get along with you any more.

BOBBY. Well, Pop, that's another story.

MR. PARKER. Come on, boy, there's something on his mind, and you know what it is.

BOBBY *(moving away).* Nothing, except he wants to tell me what to do all the time. But I've got some ideas of my own. I ain't no dumbbell; I just don't talk as much as he do. If I did, the people I talk to would know just as much as I do. I just want him to go his way, and I'll go mine.

MR. PARKER. There's more to it than that, and I wanta know what it is.

BOBBY. There's nothing.

MR. PARKER. Come on now, boy.

BOBBY. That's all, Pop!

MR. PARKER *(grabs him)*. It's not, and you better say something!

BOBBY. He—I don't know what to tell you, Pop. He just don't like the way things are going—with you, me—Adele. He got in a fight with her today and she told him about Blue killing a man.

MR. PARKER. Is it true?

BOBBY. Yeah. Blue killed this man one time for saying something about his woman, and this woman got a child by Blue but Blue never married her and so this man started signifying about it. Blue hit him, the man reached for a gun in his pocket, Blue took the gun from him, and the—man started running, but by that time Blue had fire in his eyes, and he shot the man three times.

MR. PARKER. Well . . .

BOBBY. Blue got only two years for it!

MR. PARKER. Two years, hunh? That's another thing I'm gon' throw in his face tonight if he tries to get smart with me. Ain't that something. Going around bumping people off, and getting away with it too! What do he think he is, white or something! (THEO *comes in and sits at desk.* MR. PARKER *checks his watch.)* I'm getting tired of this! *(Moves into back room)* Where's that friend of yours!? I don't have to wait around this barbershop all night for him. It's been two months now, and I want my money! When I say be here at nine thirty, I mean be here!

THEO *(rising from desk)*. Where have you been, Pop?

MR. PARKER. That's none of your business! Now where is that man with my money!

THEO. Money is not your problem—you've been spending it all over town! And you've been taking it out of this desk!

MR. PARKER. So? I borrowed a little.

THEO. You call four hundred dollars a little! Now I've tried to fix these books so it don't show too big, and you better hope Blue don't notice it when he starts fingering through these pages tonight.

MR. PARKER. To hell with Blue! It's been two months now, and he ain't shown us a dime!

THEO. What are you doing with all that money, Pop?

MR. PARKER. I don't have to answer to you! I'm the boss here. And another thing, there's a lot about Blue and this association I want to know about. I want a position! I don't have to sit around here every month or so, waiting for somebody to bring me *my* money.

THEO. Money! Money! That's all you can think about!

MR. PARKER. Well, look who's talking. You forget this was all your idea. Remember what I told you about starting something and sticking with it. What is it now, boy? The next thing you'll tell me is that you've decided to become a priest or something. What's the new plan, Theo?

THEO. No new plans, Pop. I just don't want us to mess up. Don't you understand—things must be done right, or else we're going to get ourselves in jail. We have to be careful, we have to think about each other all the time. I didn't go into this business just for myself, I wasn't out to prove how wrong Adele was. I just thought the time had come for us to do something about all them years we laid around here letting Mama kill herself!

MR. PARKER. I have told you a thousand times I don't wanta hear any talk about your mama. She's dead, damnit! So let it stay that way! *(Moves toward shop)*

THEO. All right, let's talk about Adele then.

MR. PARKER *(stopping at steps)*. What about her?

THEO. She's out of this house every night.

MR. PARKER. Boy, you surprise me. What do you think she should do, work like a dog all day and then come to this house and bite her fingernails all night?

THEO. She's got herself a boy friend too, and—

MR. PARKER *(crossing to counter)*. Good! I got myself a girl friend, now that makes two of us!

THEO *(following him)*. But he's—aw, what's the use. But I wish you'd stay in the shop more!

MR. PARKER. That's too bad. I have things to do. I don't worry about where you're going when you leave here.

THEO. I don't go anywhere and you know it. If I did, we wouldn't do an hour's business. *But we have been doing great business!* And you wanta know why? They love it! *Everybody* loves the way ol' Theo brews corn! Every after-hours joint is burning with it! And for us to do that kind of business, I've had to sweat myself down in this hole for something like sixteen hours a day for two whole months!

MR. PARKER. What do you want from me?

THEO. I just want you here in the shop with me, so at least we can pretend that this is a barbershop. A cop walked through that door today while I had three customers in here, and I had to put one of them in that chair and cut his hair!

MR. PARKER. How did you make out?

THEO. Pop, I don't need your jokes!

MR. PARKER. All right, don't get carried away. *(Goes to* THEO *and puts his arm around the boy's shoulders)* I'll make it my business to stay here in the shop with you more.

THEO. And make Blue guarantee me some help.

MR. PARKER. You'll get that too. But you've got to admit one thing, though—you've always been a lazy boy. I didn't expect you to jump and all of a sudden act like John Henry!

THEO. I have never been lazy. I just didn't wanta break my back for the man!

MR. PARKER. Well, I can't blame you for that. I know, because I did it. I did it when they didn't pay me a single dime!

BOBBY. When was that?

MR. PARKER. When I was on the chain gang!

BOBBY. Now you know you ain't never been on no chain gang!

MR. PARKER *(holds up two fingers)*. Two months, that's all it was. Just two months.

BOBBY. Two months, my foot!

MR. PARKER. I swear to heaven I was. It was in 19-something, I was living in Jersey City, New Jersey . . . *(Crosses to throne and sits)*

BOBBY. Here we go with another story!

MR. PARKER. That was just before I started working as a vaudeville man, and there was this ol' cousin of mine we used to call "Dub," and he had this job driving a trailer truck from Jersey City to Jacksonville, Florida. One day he asked me to come along with him for company. I weren't doing nothing at the time, and—

BOBBY. As usual.

MR. PARKER. I didn't say that! Anyway, we drove along. Everything was fine till we hit Macon, Georgia. We weren't doing a thing, but before we knew it this cracker police stopped us, claiming we'd ran through a red light. He was yelling and hollering and,

boyyy, did I get mad—I was ready to get a hold of that cracker and work on his head until . . .

BOBBY. Until what?

MR. PARKER. Until they put us on the chain gang, and the chain gang they put us on was a chain gang and a half! I busted some rocks John Wayne couldn't've busted! I was a rock-busting fool! *(Rises and demonstrates how he swung the hammer)* I would do it like this! I would hit the rock, and the hammer would bounce—bounce so hard it would take my hand up in the air with it—but I'd grab it with my left hand and bring it down like this: Hunh! *(Carried away by the rhythm of his story, he starts twisting his body to the swing of it.)* It would get so good to me, I'd say: Hunh! Yeah! Hunh! I'd say, Ooooooooooooo-weeeee! I'm wide open now! *(Swinging and twisting)* Yeah, baby, I say, Hunh! Sooner or later that rock would crack! Old Dub ran into a rock one day that was hard as Theo's head. He couldn't bust that rock for nothing. He pumped and swung, but that rock would not move. So finally he said to the captain: "I'm sorry, Cap, but a elephant couldn't break this rock." Cap didn't wanna hear nothing. He said, "Well, Dub, I wanna tell you something —your lunch and your supper is in the middle of that rock." On the next swing of the hammer, Dub busted that rock into a thousand pieces! *(Laughs)* I'm telling you, them crackers is mean. Don't let nobody tell you about no Communists, Chinese, or anything: there ain't nothing on this earth meaner and dirtier than an American-born cracker! We used to sleep in them long squad tents on the ground, and we was all hooked up to this one big long chain: the guards had orders to shoot at random in the dark if ever one of them chains would rattle. You couldn't even turn over in your sleep! *(Sits on throne)*

BOBBY. A man can't help but turn over in his sleep!

MR. PARKER. Not on this chain gang you didn't. You turn over on this chain gang in your sleep and your behind was shot! But if you had to, you would have to wake up, announce that you was turning over, and then you go back to sleep!

BOBBY. What!

MR. PARKER. Just like this. *(Illustrating physically)* "Number 4 turning over!" But that made all the chains on the other convicts rattle, so they had to turn over too and shout: "Number 5 turning over! Number 6 turning over! Number 7!"

THEO. Why don't you stop it!

MR. PARKER. I ain't lying!

BOBBY. Is that all?

MR. PARKER. Yeah, and I'm gon' get Adele to type that up on my typewriter! *(Goes to the window.)* Now where the hell is that Blue Haven!

MR. JENKINS *(rushing in).* Did he show up yet?

MR. PARKER. Naw, and when he does, I'm—

MR. JENKINS. I told you I didn't trust that boy—who knows where he is! Well, I'm going out there and get him! *(Starts back out)*

MR. PARKER *(grabs him by the arm).* Now don't go out there messing with Blue, Jenkins! If there's anybody got a reason for being mad with him, it's me. Now take it easy. When he gets here, we'll all straighten him out. Come on, sit down and let me beat you a game one time. *(Takes board out quickly)*

BOBBY. Tear him up, Pop!

MR. JENKINS *(pause).* Okay, you're on. *(Moves toward* MR. PARKER *and the table)* It's hopeless. I been playing your father for three solid years, and he has yet to beat me one game!

MR. PARKER. Yeah! But his luck done come to past!

MR. JENKINS. My luck ain't come to past, 'cause my luck is skill. *(Spelling the word out)* S-K-I-L-L.

MR. PARKER *(shakes up the can).* Come on now, Jenkins, let's play the game. Take one. (MR. JENKINS *pulls out a checker.)* You see there, you get the first move.

MR. JENKINS. You take me for a fool, Parker, and just for that I ain't gon' let you get a king.

MR. PARKER. Put your money where your lips is. I say I'm gon' with this game!

MR. JENKINS. I don't want your money, I'm just gon' beat you!

MR. PARKER. I got twenty dollars here to make a liar out of you! *(Slams down a twenty-dollar bill on the table)* Now you doing all the bragging about how I never beat you, but I'm valiant enough to say that, from here on in, you can't win air, and I got twenty dollars up on the table to back it up.

MR. JENKINS. Oh, well, he ain't satisfied with me beating him all the time for sport. He wants me to take his money too.

MR. PARKER. But that's the difference.

MR. JENKINS. What kind of difference?

MR. PARKER. We're playing for money, and I don't think you can play under that kind of pressure. You do have twenty dollars, don't you?

MR. JENKINS. I don't know what you're laughing about, I always keep some money on me. *(Pulls out change purse and puts twenty dollars on the table)* You get a little money in your pocket and you get carried away.

MR. PARKER. It's your move.

MR. JENKINS. Start you off over here in this corner.

MR. PARKER. Give you that little ol' fellow there.

MR. JENKINS. I'll take him.

MR. PARKER. I'll take this one.

MR. JENKINS. I'll give you this man here.

MR. PARKER. I'll jump him—so that you can have this one.

MR. JENKINS. I'll take him.

MR. PARKER. Give you this man here.

MR. JENKINS. All right. *(He moves.)*

MR. PARKER. I'll take this one. *(Series of grunts and groans as they exchange men)* And I'll take these three. *(Jumping* MR. JENKINS*'s men and laughing loud)* Boom! Boom! Boom! *(The game is now definitely in favor of* MR. PARKER. MR. JENKINS *is pondering over his situation. Relishing* MR. JENKINS*'s predicament)* Study long, you study wrong. I'm afraid that's you, ol' buddy . . . I knew it, I knew it all the time—I used to ask myself: I wonder how ol' Jenks would play if he really had some pressure on him? You remember how the Dodgers used to raise hell every year until they met the Yankees in the World Series, and how under all that pressure they would crack up? *(Laughs)* That pressure got him!

MR. JENKINS. Hush up, man. I'm trying to think!

MR. PARKER. I don't know what you could be thinking about, 'cause the rooster done came and wrote, skiddy biddy!

MR. JENKINS *(finally makes a move).* There!

MR. PARKER *(in sing-song).* That's all— that's all . . . *(Makes another jump)* Boom! Just like you say, Bobby—"tear him up!" *(Rears his head back in ecstatic laughter)*

MR. JENKINS *(makes a move).* It's your move.

MR. PARKER. *(His laughter trails off sickly as he realizes that the game is now going his opponent's way.)* Well, I see. I guess that kinda changes the color of the game. . . . Let me see now . . .

MR. JENKINS *(getting his revenge).* Why don't you laugh some more? I like the way you laugh, Parker.

MR. PARKER. Shut up, Jenkins. I'm thinking!

MR. JENKINS. Thinking? Thinking for what? The game is over! *(Now he is laughing hard.* MR. PARKER *ruefully makes his move.)* Uh-uh! Lights out! *(Still laughing, answers* PARKER*'s move).* Game time, and you know it! Take your jump! (MR. PARKER *is forced to take his jump.* JENKINS *takes his opponent's last three men.)* I told you about laughing and bragging in my game! Boom! Boom! Boom!

MR. PARKER *(rises abruptly from the table and dashes to coat rack).* DAMNIT!!!

MR. JENKINS. Where you going—ain't we gon' play some more?

MR. PARKER *(putting on coat).* I don't wanta play you no more. You too damn lucky!

MR. JENKINS. Aw, come on, Parker. I don't want your money, I just want to play!

MR. PARKER. You won it, you keep it—I can *afford* it! But one of these days you're going to leave that voodoo root of yours home, and that's gonna be the day—you hear me, you sonofabitch!

BOBBY. Pop!

MR. PARKER. I don't want to hear nothing from you!

MR. JENKINS *(realizing that* PARKER *is really upset).* It's only a game—and it don't have nothing to do with luck. . . . But you keep trying, Parker, and one of these days you're going to beat me. And when you do, it won't have nothing to do with luck—it just might be the unluckiest and worst day of your life. You'll be champion checker player of the world. Meanwhile, I'm the champ, *and you're gonna have to' live with it.*

MR. PARKER *(smiling, grudgingly moves toward him with his hand extended).* All right, Jenkins! You win this time, but I'm gon' beat you yet. I'm gon' whip your behind until it turns white!

BOBBY. That's gon' be some strong whipping! *(There's a tap at the door.)* That must be Blue. *(Rushes to the door and opens it)*

MR PARKER. About time. (BLUE *enters.)* Hey, boy, where have you been?

BLUE *(moves in, carrying an attaché case).* I got stuck with an emergency council meeting.

MR. PARKER. What kind of council?

BLUE. The council of the Association. I see you're sporting some new clothes there, Mr. P. You must be rolling in extra dough these days.

MR. PARKER. Just a little something I picked up the other day. All right, where is the money, Blue?

BLUE. You'll get your money, but first I want to see those books. *(Moves to the desk in the back room and starts going over the books; in the shop an uneasy silence prevails.* JENKINS, *out of nervousness, sets up the checkers for another game.)*

BLUE. I see. *(Takes out pencil and pad and starts scribbling on a sheet of paper)* Uh-huh. Uh-huh . . . *(Re-enters shop)*

MR. PARKER. Well?

BLUE. Everything seems to be okay.

MR. PARKER. Of course everything is all right. What did you expect? *(Angry, impatient)* Now come on and give me my money.

BLUE. Take it easy, Mr. Parker! *(Takes a white envelope from his case and passes it on to* PARKER*)* Here's your money.

MR. PARKER. Now this is what I like to see!

BLUE *(passes some bills to* MR. JENKINS*).* And you, Mr. Jenkins.

MR. JENKINS. Thank you, young man. But from here on in, you can count me out of your operation.

BLUE. What's the trouble?

MR. JENKINS. No trouble at all. I just want to be out of it.

BLUE. People and headaches—that's all I ever get from all the Mr. Jenkinses in this world!

MR. JENKINS. Why don't you be quiet sometime, boy?

MR. PARKER. I'm afraid he's telling you right, Blue.

BLUE. *He's telling me that he is a damn idiot, who can get himself hurt!*

THEO. Who's going to hurt him?

(They all stare at BLUE.*)*

BLUE *(calming down).* I'm sorry. I guess I'm working too hard these days. I got a call today from one of them "black committees" here in Harlem . . .

THEO. What did they want?

BLUE. They wanted to know what we did. They said they had heard of us, but they never see us—meaning they never see us picketing, demonstrating, and demanding something all the time.

MR. PARKER. So?

BLUE. They want us to demonstrate with them next Saturday, and I have decided to set up a demonstrating committee, with you in charge, Mr. Parker.

MR. PARKER. You what!

BLUE. You'd be looking good!

MR. PARKER. You hear that! *(Cynical laughter)* I'd be looking good! Count me out! When I demonstrate, it's for real!

BLUE. You demonstrate in front of any store out there on that street, and you'll have a good sound reason for being there!

MR. PARKER. I thought you said we was suppose to be different, and we was to drive out that Mr. You-Know-Somebody—well, ain't that what we doing? Two stores already done put up "going out of business" signs.

BLUE. That's what we started this whole thing for, and that's what we're doing.

MR. PARKER. I got some questions about that, too. I don't see nothing that we're doing that would cause a liquor store, a clothing store, and a radio store to just all of a sudden close down like that, unless we've been raiding and looting them at night or something like that.

(BOBBY *quickly moves out of the shop into the back room and exits upstairs.*)

BLUE. It's the psychological thing that's doing it, man!

MR. PARKER. Psychological? Boy, you ain't telling me everything, and anyway I wanta know who made this decision about picketing.

BLUE. The council!

MR. PARKER. Who is on this council?

BLUE. You know we don't throw names around like that!

MR. PARKER. I don't get all the mystery, Blue. This is my house, and you know everything about it from top to bottom. I got my whole family in this racket!

BLUE. You're getting a good share of the money—ain't that enough?

MR. PARKER. Not when I'm dealing with you in the dark.

BLUE. You're asking for something, so stop beating around corners and tell me what it is you want!

MR. PARKER. All right! You been promising my boy some help for two months now, and he's still waiting. Now I want you to give him that help starting tomorrow, and I want you to put somebody in this shop who can cut hair to relieve me when I'm not here. And from here on in, I want to know everything that's to be known about this "de-colonization committee"—how it works, who's in it,

who's running it—*and I want to be on that council you was talking about!*

BLUE. NO!

MR. PARKER. Then I can't cooperate with you any more!

BLUE. What does that mean?

MR. PARKER. It means we can call our little deal off, and you can take your junk out of here!

BLUE. Just like that?

MR. PARKER. Just any ol' way you want it. I take too many risks in this place, not to know where I stand.

BLUE. Mr. Parker—

MR. PARKER. All right, let me hear it and let me hear it quick!

BLUE. There is an opening on our council. It's a—

MR. PARKER. Just tell me what position is it!

BLUE. President.

MR. PARKER. President?

BLUE. The highest office on our council.

MR. PARKER Boy, you're gonna have to get up real early to get by an old fox like me. A few minutes ago you offered me nothing, and now you say I can be president—that should even sound strange to *you!*

BLUE. There's nothing strange. A few minutes ago you weren't ready to throw me out of your place, but now *I've got no other choice!*

MR. PARKER *(pointing his finger at him and laughing).* That's true! You don't! All right, I'll give you a break—I accept! Just let me know when the next meeting is. *(Checks watch and grabs his hat).* Come on, Jenkins, let's get out of here! *(Starts out with* MR. JENKINS*).*

THEO. Hey, Pop—you're going out there with all that money in your pocket.

MR. PARKER. Don't worry about it. I'm a grown man, I can take care of myself.

THEO. But what about our part of it?

MR. PARKER. Look, son, he held me up—I'm late already. You'll get yours when I get back.

THEO. But, Pop—

MR. PARKER. Good night, Theo! *(Bolts out the door, with* MR. JENKINS *following)*

THEO *(rushes to the door).* Pop, you better be careful! I'll be waiting for you! I don't care if it's till dawn!

BLUE. You're becoming a worrier, Theo! *(Pause)* But that's the nature of all things. . . . I'm forever soothing and pacifying someone. Sometimes I have to pacify myself.

You don't think that president stuff is going to mean anything, do you? He had me uptight, so what I did was to bring him closer to me so I would be definitely sure of letting him know less and having more control over him—and over you, too.

THEO. What do you mean by that?

BLUE. It didn't take me more than one glance into those books to know that he's been spending money out of the box. And to think—you didn't bother to tell me about it.

THEO. Why should I? I trust your intelligence.

BLUE. Please don't let him do it any more.

THEO. Why don't you hire your own cashier and bookkeeper? *(He goes into back room.)*

BLUE *(following him).* That's an idea! What about Adele! Now that was a thought in the back of my mind,, but I'm putting that away real quick. Seems this sweet, nice-girl sister of yours has took to partying with the good-time set and keeping company with a simple ass clown like Wilmer Robinson. No, that wouldn't work, would it? I'd have more trouble with her than I'm having with you. When a girl as intelligent as your sister, who all of a sudden gets into things, and hooked up to people who just don't go with her personality, that could mean trouble. To be honest with you, I didn't think this thing was going to work, but *it is working,* Theo! I've got three places just like this one, and another on the way. A man has to care about what he does. Don't you want to get out of this place?

THEO. Yes, but lately I've been getting the feeling that I'm gonna have to hurt someone.

BLUE. I see.

THEO. You think the old man was asking you those questions about stores closing down as a joke or something?

BLUE. He asks because he thinks, but he is still in the dark!

THEO. He was playing with you! And when my father holds something inside of him and plays with a man, he's getting meaner and more dangerous by the minute.

BLUE. I don't care what he was doing—he is messing with my work! He has gotten himself into a "thing" with one of the rottenest bitches on the Avenue, who happens to be tight with a nigger who is trying to fuck up my business. Now that's something you had better get straight: it's your turn to soothe and pacify!

THEO. Why should I do anything for you when you lied to me and sent my brother out with that band of thieves of yours?

BLUE. He said he needed the money, and I couldn't stop him.

THEO. But I told you I didn't want that!

BLUE. Let's face it, baby! Bobby's the greatest thief in the world! He's been prancing around stores and stealing all of his life! And I think that's something to bow down to —because he's black and in trouble, just like you and me. So don't ride me so hard, Theo! *(They cross back into shop. He picks up attaché case, preparing to leave.)*

THEO. Blue! Now I don't care what kind of protection you got, but I say those store raids are dangerous and I don't want my brother on them, and I mean it!

BLUE. When we first made our plans, you went along with it—you knew somebody had to do it. What makes you and your brother so special?

THEO. Well, you better—

BLUE. *To hell with you, Theo!* I could take this hand and make you dead! You are nothing but what I make you be!

THEO *(pause).* That just might be. But what if tomorrow this whole operation were to bust wide open in your face because of some goof-up by my father or sister—something that would be just too much for you to clean up. What would you do? Kill them?

BLUE *(pause; then calmly and deliberately).* The other day I went up on the hill to see my little boy. I took him out for a ride and as we were moving along the streets he asked me where all the people were coming from. I said from work, going home, going to the store, and coming back from the store. Then we went out to watch the river and then he asked me about the water, the ships, the weeds— everything. That kid threw so many questions at me, I got dizzy—I wanted to hit him once to shut him up. He was just a little dark boy discovering for the first time that there are things in the world like stones and trees. . . . It got late and dark, so I took him home and watched him fall asleep. Then I took his mother into my arms and put her into bed. I just laid there for a while, listening to her call me all kinds of dirty mother-fuckers. After she got that out of her system, I put my hands on her and before long our arms were locked at each other's shoulders and then my thighs moved slowly down between her thighs and then we started that sweet rolling until the both of us were screaming as if the last piece of love was dying forever. After that, we just laid there, talking soft up into the air. I would tell her she was the loveliest bitch that ever lived, and all of a sudden she was no longer calling me a dirty mother-fucker, she was calling me a sweet mother-fucker. It got quiet. I sat up on the edge of the bed with my head hanging long and deep, trying to push myself out of the room and back into it at one and the same time. She looked up at me and I got that same question all over again. Will you marry me and be the father of your son! I tried to move away from her, but she dug her fingernails into my shoulders. I struck her once, twice, and again and again—with this hand! And her face was a bloody mess! And I felt real bad about that. I said, I'll marry you, *Yes! Yes! Yes! (Pause)* I put my clothes on and I walked out into the streets, trembling with the knowledge that now I have a little boy who I must walk through the park with every Sunday, who one day just may blow my head off—and an abiding wife who on a given evening may get herself caught in the bed of some other man, and I could be sealed in a dungeon until dead! I was found lying in a well of blood on the day I was born! But I have been kind! I have kissed babies for the simple reason they were babies! I'm going to get married to some bitch and that gets me to shaking all over! *(He moves close to* THEO.) The last time I trembled this way *I killed a man! (Quickly and rhythmically takes out a long, shiny switchblade knife. It pops open just at* THEO's *neck.* BLUE *holds it there for a moment, then withdraws and closes it. Puts it away. Then he collects his belongings, then calmly addresses* THEO.) Things are tight and cool on my end, Theo, and that's how you should keep it here. If not, everything gets messy and I find myself acting like a policeman, keeping order. I don't have the time for that kind of trick. (BLUE *exits.*)

THEO *(after a moment of silent thought, moves decisively to the back-room stairs and calls).* Bobby! (BOBBY *comes downstairs.*)

THEO. I want you to stay away from those store raids, Bobby.

BOBBY. Not as long as I can get myself some extra money. *(Moving close to him)* You didn't say nothing to me before, when I was stealing every other day and giving you half of everything I stole. You didn't think nothing that day you sent me for that typewriter!

THEO. I don't know what you're going to do from here on in, because I'm calling the whole affair off with Blue.

BOBBY. That won't stop me, and you know it!

THEO. What is it, Bobby—we used to be so close! Bobby, don't get too far away from me!

BOBBY *(heatedly).* What do you want me to do? Stick around you all the time? Hell, I'm tired of you! I stick by you and I don't know what to do! I steal and that puts clothes on my back and money in my pockets! *That's* something to do! But I sit here with you all day just thinking about the next word I'm going to say—I'm not stupid! I sit here all day thinking about what I'm going to say to you. I stuck by you and I hoped for you because whatever you became, I was gonna become. I thought about that, and that ain't shit! *(He leaves the shop.* THEO *is alone with his troubled thoughts. Suddenly he rushes into back room, gets hat and shirt, puts them on, and goes out into the street.)*

MR. PARKER *(stepping down into the back room from the apartment upstairs).* Come on, girl! *(A very attractive, well-dressed* YOUNG GIRL *in her early twenties follows him into the shop.)*

MR. PARKER. You wanted to see it. Well, here it is.

GIRL *(looking about the place).* So this is where you do your business. Like I keep asking you, Russell, what kind of business is it for you to make all that money you got?

MR. PARKER *(heading toward the refrigerator in the back room).* Come on in here, sweetheart. I'll fix us a drink!

GIRL *(moves briskly after him).* I asked you a question, Russell.

MR. PARKER. *(still ignoring her question, he takes a jug out of refrigerator and grabs two glasses.)* I'm going to make you a special drink, made from my own hands. It's called "Black Lightning."

GIRL *(surveys the room as* PARKER *pours drink).* That should be exciting.

MR. PARKER. Here you go. *(Hands her the drink) Toujours l'amour!*

GIRL *(gasping from the drink).* What the fuck is this! What *is* this, Russell?

MR. PARKER *(patting her on the back).* Knocks the tail off of you, don't it! But it gets smoother after the second swallow. . . . Go on, drink up!

GIRL. Okay. *(Tries it again and scowls; moves away as he sits on bed)*

MR. PARKER. Now, did you think about what I asked you last night?

GIRL. About getting married?

MR. PARKER. Yes.

GIRL. Why do you want to marry me, Russell?

MR. PARKER. Because I love you, and I think you could make me happy.

GIRL. Well, I don't believe you. When I asked you a question about your business, you deliberately ignored me. It was like you didn't trust me, and I thought that love and trust went together.

MR. PARKER. I'm not so sure about that. My son Theo, I'm wild about him, but I wouldn't trust him no farther 'n I could throw a building.

GIRL. I'm not your son!

MR. PARKER. What is it you wanta know?

GIRL. Where you gettin' all that money from?

MR. PARKER. Oh, that. That's not for a girl to know, baby doll.

GIRL. Then it's time for me to go. I'm not gettin' myself hooked up with no mystery man! *(Moves as if to leave; PARKER stops her, then pauses for a moment.)*

MR. PARKER. All right, I'll tell you. I'm partners in a big business, which I'm the president of.

GIRL. Partners with who, Russell?

MR. PARKER. That's not important, baby.

GIRL. Partners with who, Russell?

MR. PARKER. Mr. Blue Haven.

GIRL. *Blue Haven!* Then it's crooked business.

MR. PARKER. Oh no, baby, it's nothing like that. It's real straight.

GIRL. What does that mean?

MR. PARKER. That what we're doing is right!

GIRL. Tell me about it, then.

MR. PARKER. I've said enough. Now let's leave it at that! *(Tries to embrace her)*

GIRL *(wards him off, sits on bed)*. All you take me for is something to play with.

MR. PARKER. That's not true, I wanna marry you. *(Sits beside her)*

GIRL. You say you want to marry me, but how do you expect me to think about marrying somebody who won't confide in me about what they're doing? How do I know I'm not letting myself in for trouble?

MR. PARKER *(ponders for a moment, then rises)*. All right, I'll tell you! We peddle a variety of products to the community and we sell things to people at a price they can't get nowhere else in this city. Yes, according to the law it's illegal, but we help our people, our own people. We take care of business and at the same time we make everybody happy. We take care of our people. Just like I been taking care of you.

GIRL. You take care of me? How? You've never given me more than ten dollars in cash since I've known you.

MR. PARKER. Well, I've got a big present for you coming right out of this pocket and I'm gon' take you downtown tomorrow and let you spend till the store runs out.

GIRL. Taking me to a store and giving me spending change makes me feel like a child and I don't like it and I'm not gonna stand for it any more.

MR. PARKER. Then take this and you do whatever you want with it.

GIRL *(taking the money and putting it away)*. Now don't get the idea I'm just in love with your money.

MR. PARKER. Now I want you to stop talking to me about money. I've got *plenty* of it! You've got to understand—I'm the most different man you ever met. I've been around this world, I danced before the King and Queen of England. I've seen and heard many a thing in my lifetime—and you know what: I'm putting it all down on paper—my story!

GIRL. Your story!

(MR. PARKER moves into shop, gets notebook from behind one of the sliding panels. During his absence GIRL checks under the bed)

MR. PARKER *(re-enters)*. Here it is, right here. *(Sits next to her on the bed, giving her the notebook)*

GIRL *(thumbing through the pages)*. You write things too?

MR. PARKER. I certainly do—and I've been thinking about writing a poem about you.

GIRL. A poem about me!

MR. PARKER *(taking book from her and dropping it on floor)*. I'm gon' do it tonight before I go to sleep. *(He kisses her neck and reaches for the hem of her dress.)*

GIRL *(breaking out of his embrace)*. No, Russell, not here!

MR. PARKER. Why not?

GIRL. Just because there's a bed wherever we go don't mean that we have to jump into it. You don't understand, Russell! You've got to start treating me the same as if I was your wife.

MR. PARKER. *That's exactly what I'm trying to do!*

GIRL *(rising)*. Don't yell at me!

MR. PARKER. All right. I tell you what: I'm

kinda tired, let's just lie down for a while and talk. I ain't gon' try nothing.

GIRL. Russell—

MR. PARKER. May the Lord smack me down this minute into hell—I swear I won't do nothing.

GIRL. What are the three biggest lies men tell to women, Russell?

MR. PARKER. I ain't just any man—I'm the man you gon' spend your life with.

GIRL. Okay, Russell, we'll lie down, but you've got to keep your word. If I'm the girl you want to marry, you've got to learn to keep your word. *(They lie on bed. To her surprise,* PARKER *is motionless, seemingly drifting off to sleep. After a moment she takes the initiative and begins love-making. He responds, and once his passion has reached an aggressive peak she breaks off abruptly.)* Where do you get these things you sell to people?

MR. PARKER. What are you talking about?

GIRL. You know what I'm saying. I overheard you tell Mr. Jenkins you suspected your son was robbing stores.

MR. PARKER. You heard no such thing!

GIRL *(desperately).* Where do they keep the stuff?

MR. PARKER. Now, baby, you've got to relax and stop worrying about things like that! *(Pulls her by the shoulders; she does not resist.)* Come here. *(He pulls her down to the bed, takes her into his arms and kisses her, reaching again for the hem of her dress.)*

GIRL *(struggling, but weakening to his ardor).* Russell, you said you wouldn't do nothing!

MR. PARKER. I ain't! I just want to get a little closer to you!

GIRL. Russell, not here!

MR. PARKER. Just let me feel it a little bit!

GIRL. You swore to God, Russell! (THEO *comes in the front door and heads toward back room.)*

MR. PARKER. I ain't gon' do nothing!

GIRL *(hears* THEO). Russell! Russell! Somebody is out there!

MR. PARKER. *(Jumps up quickly.* THEO *stands before him.)* What are you doing here?

THEO. The question is, *what are you doing!*

MR. PARKER. I have been having a private talk with a good friend of mine. Now get out of here!

(GIRL *jumps up, moving past* MR. PARKER)

MR. PARKER *(stopping her).* Where are you going?

GIRL. Home!

MR. PARKER. Hold it now, honey!

GIRL. I never should have come here in the first place!

MR. PARKER. No, you're not going anywhere. This is my place and you don't have to run off because of this Peeping Tom!

THEO. Pop, it's time to give us our money.

MR. PARKER. You'll get your share tomorrow and not before!

THEO. I want it now before you give it all to that girl. Pop, cut that broad loose!

MR. PARKER. What was that?

THEO. I said, cut her loose! She don't need an old man like you, she's just pumping you for information. That bitch is a hustler!

MR. PARKER *(slaps* THEO *with the back of his hand).* Bite your tongue!

GIRL. I think I better go, Russell. *(Heads for the front door)*

MR. PARKER *(following her).* Okay, but I'll be right with you as soon as I get things straight here. You will be waiting for me, won't you?

GIRL. Sure!

MR. PARKER. You run along now and I'll be right over there. (GIRL *exits.* PARKER *whirls back into shop.)* What do you think you're doing, boy?

THEO. Just be careful, Pop. Please be careful.

MR. PARKER. If there's anybody I got to be careful of, it's you! You lying selfish sonofabitch! You think I don't know about you and Blue running that gang of thieves—about you sending your own brother out there with them?

THEO. I didn't do that!

MR. PARKER. If Bobby gets hurt out on them streets, I'm gonna kill you, boy! I'm gonna kill you. *(Hurriedly collects hat and coat)*

THEO. You're not worried about Bobby! All you can think of is the money you're rolling in. The clothes. And that stupid outfit you've got on.

(ADELE *comes in from the street, obviously distraught.)*

MR. PARKER. What's wrong with you? Are you drunk? *(Moves in.* ADELE *doesn't answer, so he moves off.)*

THEO. Of course she's drunk. What did you expect—did you think everything would stop and stand still while you were being reborn again!

MR. PARKER. What do you want from me? Call this whole thing off? It was your idea, not mine! But now that I've got myself something—I'm not going to throw it away for nobody!

THEO. But can't you see what's happening here?

MR. PARKER. If she wants to be a drunken wench, let her! I'm not going to take the blame. And as for you—*(Fumbles in his coat pocket)* If you want this money, you can take it from me—I can throw every dollar of it into the ocean if I want to! You can call me a fool too, but I'm a *burning fool!* I'm going to marry that little girl. She is not a whore! She is a woman! And I'm going to marry her! And if the two of you don't like it, you can kiss my ass! *(Bolts out into the street)*

THEO. You're not drunk. What happened?

ADELE *(heading for the back room).* What does it look like? Wilmer hit me.

THEO *(following).* Why?

ADELE *(sits on bed).* He caught me in Morgan's with a friend of his after I had lied about going bowling with the girls. He just walked in and started hitting me, over and over again. His friend just stood there pleading with him not to hit me, but he never did anything to stop him. I guess he figured, "Why should I risk getting myself killed over just another piece of ass?" I thought he was going to kill me but then Blue came in with some of his friends and they just grabbed him by the arms and took him away.

THEO. Was Bobby with them?

ADELE. I couldn't tell.

THEO. Damnit! Everything gets fucked up!

ADELE. It had to, because you don't think. If you're going to be a crook, you don't read a comic book for research, you don't recruit an old black man that's about to die!

THEO. No matter what you do, he's gon' die anyway. This whole place was built for him to die in—so you bite, you scratch, you kick: you do anything to stay alive!

ADELE. Yes, you bite! You scratch, you steal, you kick, and you get killed anyway! Just as I was doing, coming back here to help Mama.

THEO. Adele, I'm sick and tired of your talk about sacrifices. You were here because you had no other place to go. You just got scared too young and too soon.

ADELE. You're right. All I was doing was waiting for her to die so I could get on with what I thought I wanted to do with myself. But, God, *she took so long to die!* But then I found myself doing the same things she had done, taking care of three men, trying to shield them from the danger beyond that door, *but who the hell ever told every black woman she was some kind of goddamn savior!* Sure, this place was built for us to die in, but if we aren't very careful, Theo—that can actually happen. Good night. *(Heads for the stairs)*

THEO. Adele—*(She stops in her tracks and turns.)* I've decided that there's going to be no more of Blue's business here. It's over. We're getting out.

ADELE *(after a long pause).* Theo, do you really mean it? (THEO *nods yes.)* What about Daddy?

THEO. He will have to live with it. This setup can't move without me.

ADELE. And Bobby?

THEO. I'll take care of him.

ADELE. That's fine, Theo. We'll throw the old things into the river—and we'll try something new: I won't push and you won't call me a bitch! *(Goes upstairs.* THEO *picks up his father's notebook from the floor beside the bed. A knock at the door)*

THEO. We're closed!

(The knocking continues.)

THEO. WE'RE CLOSED!

(The knocking turns to banging and a voice calls out to THEO. *He rushes to the door and opens.)*

THEO. I SAID WE'RE CLOSED! Oh, I'm sorry, Mr. Jenkins, I didn't know that was you. . . . What are you doing here this time of night?

MR. JENKINS. I want to speak to Parker.

THEO. You know him—he's been keeping late hours lately . . .

MR. JENKINS. I'll wait for him.

THEO. Suit yourself, but don't you have to work tomorrow?

MR. JENKINS. I have something to tell him, and I'll wait if it takes all night.

THEO. In that case, you can tell me about it.

(ADELE *comes downstairs and stops on steps leading to shop, looking about confusedly. She has a deadly, almost blank look on her face.)*

THEO. What's wrong with you?

ADELE *(pause).* Some—somebody just called me.

THEO. What did they call you about? *(She does not answer.* JENKINS *rises and seats her gently on bed.)* Didn't you hear me—what about? *(She still does not respond.)* WHAT IS IT, ADELE!!!

MR. JENKINS. THEO!!! (THEO *turns to* MR. JENKINS.) I think she probably just heard that your brother Bobby has been killed in a robbery by a night watchman.

THEO. Uh-uh, nawww, nawww, that's not true.

MR. JENKINS. Yes, it is, son.

ADELE. Yes.

THEO. No.

MR. JENKINS. Yes! (*Moves toward the shop door*)

THEO. *I don't believe you!*

MR. JENKINS. I saw him, boy, I saw him. (*Dead silence as* MR. JENKINS *slowly moves toward the street exit*)

THEO. You should've seen this dude I caught the other day on Thirty-second Street. He had on a bright purple suit, gray shirt, yellow tie, and his hair was processed with bright purple color. What a sight he was! But I have to say one thing for him—he was clean. (*The lights are slowly dimming.*) Used to be a time when a dude like that came in numbers, but you don't see too many of them nowadays. I have to say one thing for him—he was clean. You don't see too many like—he was clean. He was—he was clean—

BLACKOUT

SCENE TWO

About two hours later, in the shop.
MR. PARKER *and* MR. JENKINS *enter the shop.* MR. PARKER *is drunk, and* MR. JENKINS *helps him walk and finally seats him on the barber's throne.*

———

MR. PARKER. Thank you, Jenkins. You are the greatest friend a man can have. They don't make 'em like you any more. You are one of the last of the great friends, Jenkins. Pardon me, Mister Jenkins. No more will I ever call you Jenks or Jenkins. From now on, it's Mister Jenkins!

MR. JENKINS. Thank you, but when I ran into Theo and Adele tonight, they said they had something important to say to you, and I think you oughta see them.

MR. PARKER. I know what they want. They want to tell me what an old fool I am.

MR. JENKINS. I don't think that's it, and you should go on upstairs and—

MR. PARKER. Never! Upstairs is for the people upstairs!

MR. JENKINS. Russell, I—

MR. PARKER. I am downstairs people! You ever hear of downstairs people?

MR. JENKINS (*pause*). No.

MR. PARKER. Well, they're the people to watch in this world.

MR. JENKINS. If you say so.

MR. PARKER. *Put your money on 'em!*

MR. JENKINS. Come on, Mister Parker: why don't you lie down in the back room and—

MR. PARKER Oh!—No you don't think I'd have you come all the way over here just for me to go to bed, do you? I wouldn't do a thing like that to you, Jenkins. I'm busy—Mister Jenkins. Just stay with me for a little while. . . . (*His tone changes.*) Why did that girl lock me out? She said she would be waiting for me, but she locked me out. Why did she do a thing like that? I give her everything—money, clothes, pay her rent. I even love her!

MR. JENKINS. Russell—

MR. PARKER (*rising precariously*). Tell me something, Mister Jenkins—since you are my friend—why do you think she locked me out?

MR. JENKINS (*steadying him*). I don't know.

MR. PARKER. I'll tell you why. I'm an old man, and all I've got is a few dollars in my pocket. Ain't that it?

MR. JENKINS. I don't know. . . . Good night, Parker. (*Starts out*)

MR. PARKER (*grabs his arm*). You think a man was in that room with my girl?

MR. JENKINS. *Yes!*

MR. PARKER. *Goddamnit! Goddamnit!*

MR. JENKINS. Russell—

MR. PARKER. I don't believe it! When I love 'em, they stay loved!

MR. JENKINS. Nobody's got that much love, man!

MR. PARKER (*pause*). No, no—you're wrong. My wife—my dear Doris had more love in her than life should've allowed. A hundred men couldn't have taken all that love.

MR. JENKINS. We ain't talking about Doris, Russell.

MR. PARKER. Aw, forget it! (*Crossing toward table*) Goddamnit! You stumble around like an old black cow and you never get up again . . .

I have had my fun!
If I don't get well no more!
I have had my fun!
If I—

(PARKER *falls down.*) Get up, old bastard! Get up! (*Rises to his feet, aided by* JENKINS) Get up and fall back down again. Come on,

Mister Jenkins, let's play ourselves a game of checkers.

MR. JENKINS. I don't want to play no damn checkers.

MR. PARKER. Why do you curse my home, Mister Jenkins?

MR. JENKINS (pause). I apologize for that.

MR. PARKER. Come on, have a game of checkers with your good friend. (Sits at table)

MR. JENKINS (moves to the table). All right, one game and then I'm going home.

MR. PARKER. One game. (Pausing while JENKINS sits down.) I said a lot of dirty things to my children tonight—the kind of things you have to live a long time to overcome.

MR. JENKINS. I know exactly what you mean. (JENKINS sets up jumps for PARKER. PARKER seems unaware of it. They play briefly. PARKER stops.)

MR. PARKER. Theo is a good boy, and a smart one too, but he lets people push him around. That's because he's always trying to con somebody out of something—you know the kind: can't see for looking. And Bobby? He wouldn't hurt a flea. A lot of people think that boy is dumb, but just let somebody try to trick or fool him if they dare! (Begins a series of checker jumps. Pause) Got a story for you.

MR. JENKINS. No stories tonight, Parker . . .

MR. PARKER. Mister Parker. (The last move is made, the game is over. His conquest slowly sinks in. And MR. PARKER is at long last the victor. Rising from the table.) Call me champ! (THEO and ADELE enter shop from outside, and stand just inside the door. PARKER is laughing.) You're beat! I beat you! I beat you! (MR. PARKER throws his arm around MR. JENKINS's waist and holds him from behind.) . . . You fall down and you never get up! (Still laughing) Fall down, old man! Fall down! (Releases JENKINS upon seeing ADELE and THEO) You hear that, children, I beat him! I beat him! (His laughter subsides as he realizes they are not responding to him. Guilt-ridden, he approaches THEO, looks at him intently, then reaches into his inside coat pocket and pulls out the money.) Here, Theo, here's the money, here's all of it. Take it, it's yours. Go out and try to get happy, boy. (THEO does not move or take the money from his father's outstretched hand. He turns to ADELE. Her face is almost a blank.) WHY DON'T SOMEBODY SAY SOMETHING! (ADELE attempts to speak but PARKER cuts her off.) I know you have some trouble with me . . . (PARKER spies the notebook in the throne, takes it in his hand, and approaches ADELE.) You have a woman, you love her, you stop loving her, and sooner or later she ups and dies and you sit around behaving like you was a killer. I didn't have no more in me. I just didn't have no more in me! (Pause) I know you don't believe I ever loved your mother, but it's here in this book —read it . . . (She does not respond.) You wanta read something, boy! (THEO turns away. PARKER slowly crosses, hands the book to MR. JENKINS, and addresses his remarks to him.) I got sour the day my legs got so trembly and sore on the stage of the Strand Theatre—I couldn't even walk out to take a proper bow. It was then I knew nobody would ever hire me to dance again. I just couldn't run downtown to meet the man the way she did—not after all those years of shuffling around like I was a dumb clown, with my feet hurting and aching the way they did, having my head patted as if I was some little pet animal: back of the bus, front of the train, grinning when I was bleeding to death! . . . After all of that I was going to ask for more by throwing myself into the low drag of some dusty old factory in Brooklyn. All I could do was to stay here in this shop with you, my good friend. And we acted out the ceremony of a game. And you, boy (Turns to THEO) . . . You and Blue with your ideas of overcoming the evil of white men. To an old man like me, it was nothing more than an ounce of time to end my dragging about this shop. All it did was to send me out into those streets to live a time—and I did live myself a time for a while. I did it amongst a bunch of murderers—all kinds of 'em—where at times it gets so bad till it seems that the only thing that's left is for you to go out there and kill somebody before they kill you. That's all— that's out there! (Goes to ADELE) Adele, as for that girl that was here tonight, she's probably no good, but if at my age I was stupid enough to think that I could have stepped out of here and won that little girl, loved her, and moved through the rest of my days without killing anybody, that was a victory! (Moves to center stage, stands silently, then does a little dance) Be a dancer—any kind of dancer you wanta be—but dance it! (Tries out a difficult step, but can't quite make it) Uh-uhhh! Can't make that one no more. (Continues to dance) Be a singer—sing any song you wanta sing, but sing! *(Stops in his tracks) And you've got enough trouble to take you to the graveyard!* *(Pause)* But think of all that life you had before they buried you. *(Breaks into a frantic dance, attempting steps that just cross him up; he stumbles about until he falls. Everyone in the room rushes to help him up.)* . . . I'm okay, I'm okay. . . . *(He rises from the floor, slowly.)* I'm tired, I'm going to bed and by the time tomorrow comes around, let's see if we can't all throw it into the river. *(Moves into the back room, singing)*

I have had my fun!
If I don't get well no more

I have had my fun
If I don't get well no more—
(A thought strikes him. He turns and moves back to where JENKINS *is standing at the entrance to the back room.)* Jenkins, you said that the day I beat you playing checkers, you said it could be the unluckiest day of my life. But after all that's happened today—I'm straight—I feel just great! *(Moves to the stairs leading up, suddenly stops, turns and briskly moves back to the doorway leading to the shop)* Say, where's Bobby?

CURTAIN

PLAY IT AGAIN, SAM

Woody Allen

First presented on February 12, 1969, by David Merrick in association with Jack Rollins and Charles Joffe at the Broadhurst Theatre in New York City, with the following cast:

(In order of appearance)

ALLAN FELIX Woody Allen
NANCY Sheila Sullivan
BOGART Jerry Lacy
DICK CHRISTIE Anthony Roberts
LINDA CHRISTIE Diane Keaton
DREAM SHARON Barbara Brownell

SHARON LAKE Diana Walker
GINA Jean Fowler
VANESSA Cynthia Dalbey
GO-GO GIRL Lee Anne Fahey
INTELLECTUAL GIRL Barbara Press
BARBARA Barbara Brownell

Directed by Joseph Hardy
Setting by William Ritman
Lighting by Martin Aronstein
Costumes by Ann Roth
Associate Producer Samuel Liff

SYNOPSIS OF SCENES

The entire action of the play takes place in the apartment of Allan Felix on West 10th Street in New York.
ACT ONE. SCENE ONE: A late summer afternoon. SCENE TWO: Later that night.
ACT TWO. Two weeks later.
ACT THREE. The following morning.

Woody Allen is possibly the most unlikely playwright in this series. Unlikely not through any lack of talent, for the protean Mr. Allen has achieved success in many fields, but simply because for most people "playwright" is probably not the first word to pop into the head on mention of his name. Mr. Allen has done so much, and done it extremely.

He is a New Yorker by birth and almost by profession. He was born December 1, 1935, and attended New York University and City College. While at school he started sending jokes to columnists and very soon moved on to providing material for radio and television comedians.

He wrote material for many shows and comedians, including Peter Lind Hayes and Carol Channing, but his association with Sid Caesar, where he joined such writers as Neil Simon and Mel Brooks, in producing gags and situations for one of the most inventive and gifted of contemporary comedians, was a turning point in his career.

Mr. Allen soon began writing for himself. He got a very successful night-club act going, where his morose literacy was both charming and compelling. He soon established himself as a most winning loser, with the most ghastly sexual aspirations and the most horrendous sexual hang-ups. Most writers present a special dimension of themselves, but Mr. Allen has always had a natural comedian's gift for presenting all his writing as a specific aspect of his own public personality.

His first movie appeared in 1965. It was *What's New, Pussycat?* and though it was not a tremendous success the baroque impossibilities of his script were at the very least endearing. A year later, in 1966, Mr Allen was ready for Broadway, and oddly enough it seems that Broadway was ready for him. His play was called *Don't Drink the Water,* and it could hardly have been worse received by the New York critics had it been a commercial for typhoid fever. Yet—largely on the playwright's own reputation—it managed to run for nearly a year. On February 12, 1969, he produced his second play called *Play It Again, Sam.* This marked Mr. Allen's own Broadway debut—in fact, I think, his stage debut, and it became a very considerable hit. After a year, however, Mr. Allen left the cast, his place being taken by a very amusing TV comedian, Bob Denver. This proved two things. First it demonstrated that the play was not, as had been suggested, merely a vehicle for the very special comedy talents of Mr. Allen himself. Second, and rather sadly, it also demonstrated that it was those special talents—rather than the play—that the public was paying to see, for, although Mr. Denver succeeded, the play itself failed and closed soon after Mr. Allen's departure.

Since *Play It Again, Sam,* Mr. Allen has been chiefly concerned with movies, writing them, directing them, and playing in them. *Play It Again, Sam* itself became a successful movie (this one was directed by Herbert Ross), and other Allen movies have included *Bananas,* and *Everything You Wanted to Know About Sex But Were Afraid to Ask.*

Versatility is one of the keynotes of Mr. Allen's career. He still has his stand-up comedy act, he records, he occasionally plays his clarinet in a New York jazz club, and he is an accomplished and witty essayist. His brilliance is almost unnerving. For example, he once wrote an essay for *The New Yorker* consisting of nothing but spoofed-up ballet scenarios. Now, anyone could have done this, and it might have amused anyone who knew nothing about ballet. Mr. Allen did it with such deadly accuracy and apparently inside knowledge that it became the talk of the dance world in both New York and London.

Play It Again, Sam is an enormously accomplished comedy that probably plays better than it reads. The title is that mythical phrase (for no one actually says the words in the movie) that legend has it Humphrey Bogart said in the movie *Casablanca.* This is fair enough because Bogart himself is one of the mythical characters in the play.

The hero is Allan Felix, a movie critic and even more movie buff, who has lost his wife and mislaid such sexual confidence as he ever had. His problems are eventually resolved by the spectral Bogart who advises on how to woo and, at least temporarily, lay the wife of his overpreoccupied best friend. The play is entertaining rather than moral—as so many things are.

At the end of 1972 Mr. Allen was reportedly engaged for a couple of one-act plays for production Off Broadway, but at the time of this writing, more than six months later, nothing has yet materialized. Personally I hope it will. Mr. Allen is a one-man Renaissance and an amiable zany whom the theatre can well use. Play it again, Woody!

ACT ONE

SCENE ONE

The house lights dim and we hear the voices of Humphrey Bogart and Mary Astor in a scene from The Maltese Falcon. *Presently the curtain rises on* ALLAN FELIX *watching the movie on his TV set in the living room of his apartment on 10th Street, between Fifth and Sixth avenues, in New York City.*

The living room is one of three rooms, the other two being a small but adequate bedroom and small but adequate kitchen, both of which are offstage in opposite directions. Up left there is a door which is the entrance to the apartment and which opens right in on a railed platform which serves as an office area; there are two sets of steps leading down to the living room, and between them, under the railing, a padded bench.

The living room itself is a reasonably spacious room, typical of the type found in old Village brownstones: cheery, with good-sized windows that overlook a tree-lined block from the second floor. It has a wood-burning fireplace and is furnished with a youthful warmth that includes books and records, a large photo of Bogart, comfortable chairs and an inviting sofa. It is an apartment that rents for about a hundred and sixty-five dollars a month and has been furnished and lived in for the past two years by the Felixes, a young married couple.

ALLAN FELIX *is a slight, bespectacled young man of about twenty-eight or twenty-nine who looks as if he just stepped out of a Jules Feiffer cartoon. He earns a decent living as a writer of articles and reviews, some literary but mostly cinematic, as he is a film buff, for a little intellectual film magazine. He daydreams of someday doing something important in either literature or film.*

ALLAN *daydreams a lot, in fact, his mind is a hyperactive mass of preposterously neurotic contradictions that make the world a little too much for him. He is nervous, shy, insecure, and has been in and out of psychotherapy for years.*

At the rise of the curtain ALLAN *is alone in a swivel chair watching* The Maltese Falcon. *The film is in the final sequence wherein Bogey tells a surprised Mary Astor that he is going to turn her in despite the fact that he loves her. The soundtrack precedes the curtain for a line or two. . . . He watches a bit after the curtain is up, sighs, crosses to the set and turns it off.*

——

ALLAN. How does he do it? What's the secret? It's the movies that's the secret. Maybe if I took two more aspirin I'd feel better. That's two—four—six aspirin. *(He picks up an empty aspirin bottle on the coffee table.)* I'm turning into an aspirin junkie. Next thing you know I'll be boiling the cotton at the top of the bottle to get the extra. What's the matter with me—why can't I relax? I never should have signed those papers. *(He sits on the swivel-chair hassock.)* Let her take me to court. Two years of marriage down the drain . . . like that . . . I couldn't believe it when she told me two weeks ago. She was like a stranger, not like my wife, like a total stranger.

(Dream light rises in the office area. NANCY *appears in a wrapper, drying her hair with a towel, and crosses to the end of the railing on the platform.)*

NANCY. I don't want any alimony. You can have everything. I just want out.

ALLAN. Can't we discuss it?

NANCY. We've discussed it fifty times. It's no use.

ALLAN. Why?

NANCY. I don't know. I can't stand the marriage. I don't find you fun. I feel you suffocate me. I don't feel any rapport with you, and I don't dig you physically. For God's sake, don't take it personal! *(She exits; the light fades.)*

ALLAN*(rises and paces left and right).* Oh, I won't take it personal. I'll just kill myself, that's all. If only I knew where my damn analyst was vacationing. Where do they go every August? They leave the city. Every summer New York is full of people who are crazy till Labor Day. And so what? What if I reach him? No matter what I say, he tells me it's a sexual problem. Isn't that silly? How can there be a sexual problem? We weren't even having relations. Well, once in a while. But she used to watch television during it . . . and change channels with the remote-control switch. *(He sits in the swivel hassock.)* What's the matter with me? Why can't I be cool? What's the secret?

(Dream light rises. BOGART *appears in a trench coat.)*

BOGART. There's no secret, kid. Dames are simple. I never met one who didn't understand a slap in the mouth or a slug from a forty-five.

ALLAN. I could never hit Nancy. It's not that type of relationship.

BOGART. Relationship? Where'd you learn that word? From one of those Park Avenue headshrinkers?

ALLAN. I'm not like you. At the end of *Casablanca,* when you lost Ingrid Bergman, weren't you crushed?

BOGART *(crosses up the left steps).* Nothing that a little bourbon and soda wouldn't fix.

ALLAN. See, I don't drink. My body will not tolerate alcohol.

BOGART. Take my advice and forget this fancy relationship stuff. The world is full of dames. All you got to do is whistle. (BOGART *exits and the dream light fades.)*

ALLAN *(pacing).* He's right. You give 'em an inch and they step all over you. Why can't I develop that attitude? Nothing a little bourbon and soda couldn't heal. I have one thimble full of bourbon, I run out and get tattooed. On the other hand, why should a divorce bother me so? What the hell—maybe I'm better off without her. Why not? I'm young . . . I'm healthy . . . I got a good job . . . this could be an opportunity to step out a little . . . if she can swing, so can I. I'll get broads up here like you wouldn't believe. I'll turn this place into a night club. Swingers, freaks, nymphomaniacs . . . salesgirls from Paraphernalia . . . She didn't want me—I'm not going to push myself on her. *(He sits in the swivel chair.)* I couldn't believe the things she said to me the day she left.

(Dream light rises in the office area. NANCY *enters with bag, gloves, and scarf.)*

NANCY. I want a new life. I want to go discothequing and skiing and to the beach. I want to drive through Europe on a motorcycle. All we ever do is see movies.

ALLAN. I write for a film magazine, they send me. Besides, I happen to like movies.

NANCY. You like movies because you're one of life's great watchers. I'm not like that. I'm a doer. I want to participate. I want to laugh. We never laugh together.

ALLAN. How can you say that? I don't know about you, but I'm constantly laughing —I chuckle, I giggle, I guffaw occasionally. Besides, why didn't any of this come up while we were dating?

NANCY. Things were different—you were more aggressive.

ALLAN. Everybody is during courtship. It's only natural. You try and impress the other person. You can't expect me to keep up that level of charm. I'd have a heart attack.

NANCY. Good-by, Allan. My lawyer will call your lawyer.

ALLAN. I don't have a lawyer . . . have him call my doctor. (NANCY *exits and the dream light fades.* ALLAN *paces.)* She thinks she's some hot stuff. She's no swinger. She's a product of the City College cafeteria. Next thing you know she'll be smoking pot—she'll think it's hip. I smoked pot once. Had a bad reaction . . . tried to take my pants off over my head. It's 'cause I'm guilty. I'm always so guilty over everything. She leaves me and I'm worried how she'll make out. *(The door buzzer sounds.)* There's Dick and Linda. Thank God for Dick. He's my best friend, but I must not use him as a crutch. *(There is another buzz.)* I'll use him as a crutch. *(He opens the door.* DICK, *a nice-looking young executive type, and his lovely wife* LINDA *enter.)*

DICK *(moving along the railing).* Allan, are you all right?

LINDA *(closes the door and crosses to the end of the railing).* Oh, you poor thing.

DICK. Why didn't you call us as soon as she left?

ALLAN. I didn't want to bother you.

DICK. Not bother us! For God's sake, what are friends for?

LINDA. What reason did she give for wanting a divorce?

ALLAN *(he moves to the swivel chair, then sits on the corner bench).* She wants to laugh. She doesn't laugh enough. Insufficient laughter, that's grounds for divorce. And skiing— she wants to go skiing. She wants to ski down a mountain laughing like an idiot.

DICK. Just let me call my office and let them know where I am. I rushed right out of a business meeting the minute you called. They must've thought I was crazy.

LINDA *(she places her purse on the bench).* Have you heard from her?

ALLAN. I heard from the firm of Schulman and Weiss; they had me sign some papers, and Nancy went to Mexico. It's funny. We went to Mexico on our honeymoon. Spent the entire two weeks in bed. I had dysentery.

(During the above and the following speeches, LINDA *puts books from the floor by the coffee table on a shelf above the bar; she puts magazines from the sofa corner on a table behind the sofa; she gets a mug from the bar, a sweater from the end of the sofa, TV trays and the aspirin bottle from the coffee table, and in general cleans up the place.)*

DICK *(into the phone)*. Hello, George? Did they agree to the terms? Oh hell. Well, if we blow it, we blow it.

LINDA. Don't you cook anything but TV dinners?

ALLAN. Who cooks 'em? I suck 'em frozen.

DICK. Let me tell you where you can reach me. I'll be at Gramercy 7-9205 for a while, then I'll be at Murray Hill 5-4774 for fifteen minutes, then I'll be at Templeton 8-5548, then I'll be home, that's LE 5-8343. Right, George.

LINDA. There's a phone booth on the corner—you want me to run down and get the number—you'll be passing it. *(She exits into the kitchen.)*

DICK. I'm sorry, Allan.

ALLAN. She wants to be a swinger. All of a sudden married life is no good.

DICK. Don't get all worked up.

(LINDA enters from the kitchen with paper toweling, which she puts on the desk, and continues to tidy up the apartment as the two men talk. She dusts around the office area, then puts the papers from the floor around the wastebasket into the wastebasket, and the wastebasket under the desk.)

ALLAN. I gave her a home with affection and security. This was a little girl I found waiting on tables at the Hip Bagel. I used to come in every night and overtip her. A dollar fifty on a thirty-five-cent check!

(LINDA takes the robe off the railing, and the towel and T-shirt off the desk chair.)

DICK. Nancy was impulsive. We all knew that about her.

ALLAN. She didn't leave impulsively. She talked about it for months. I just couldn't believe she'd go through with it. I'm such a naïve jerk. I'm lying in bed with her and she's looking up lawyers in the yellow pages.

DICK. It's good you found out now. You're young. You can make new lives.

(LINDA takes the things into the bedroom.)

ALLAN. Young? I'm twenty-nine. The height of my sexual potency was ten years ago.

DICK. Look at the bright side. You're free. You'll go out. You'll meet exciting new girls, you'll flirt, there'll be parties, you'll have affairs with married women, sexual relations with girls of every race, creed, and color.

(LINDA comes out of the bedroom, moves down toward the steps, picks up a plastic pillow and puts it on the bench.)

ALLAN. Ah, you get tired of that. Besides, those things never happen to me. I managed to fool one girl into loving me and now she's gone.

DICK. See how he downgrades himself? Don't you think there are plenty of women in the world who would find him attractive?

LINDA. Huh? . . . Oh, er . . . of course.

DICK *(sits on the sofa)*. The world is full of eligible women.

ALLAN. Not like Nancy. She was a lovely thing. I used to lie in bed at night and watch her sleep. Once in a while she'd wake up and see me. She'd let out a scream.

LINDA. He really loved her. I feel like crying.

DICK. Why do you feel like crying? A man makes an investment—it doesn't pay off.

LINDA. Could I get an aspirin? I'm getting a little headache.

DICK. He's having a breakdown and you're getting sick.

LINDA. Don't get upset.

DICK. I'm not getting upset. I had a very rough day today.

ALLAN. *You* want an aspirin?

DICK. No.

ALLAN. I ate all the aspirins. What about Darvon?

LINDA. That's okay. My analyst once suggested Darvon when I had migraines.

ALLAN. I used to get migraines, but my analyst cured me. Now I get tremendous cold sores.

LINDA. I still do. Big ugly ones—from tension.

ALLAN. I don't think analysis can help me. I may need a lobotomy.

LINDA. With mine on vacation, I feel paralyzed.

DICK. The two of you should get married and move into a hospital.

ALLAN. You want a Fresca with your Darvon?

LINDA. Unless you have apple juice.

ALLAN. Oh, apple juice and Darvon are fantastic together.

LINDA. Have you ever had Librium and tomato juice?

ALLAN. I haven't personally, but another neurotic tells me they're unbelievable.

DICK. Could I get a Coke with nothing in it?

(ALLAN exits to the bedroom; LINDA puts the papers in the hall.)

LINDA. He's suffering for her so. It's kind of sweet in a way. Would you suffer for me like that?

DICK. Sure I'd suffer, but I wouldn't go crazy. You're like him. The two of you can get emotionally wrapped up in a weather report.

LINDA. He never should have married Nancy.

DICK. He never mentioned anything. I thought they were getting along.

LINDA. That's because you're so busy all the time. You never see what's going on around you. Didn't you think it was strange he was married and yet he still couldn't get a date for New Year's Eve?

DICK. Why are you getting so overwrought?

LINDA. These things upset me. I'm experiencing a wave of insecurity.

DICK. You're experiencing a wave of insecurity? May I tell you what happened to me today? I bought one hundred acres of land in Florida this morning. It turns out ninety-eight of them have quicksand. My syndicate wanted to build a golf course. Now what? The only thing we can do is build a three-hole golf course with the biggest sand trap in the world. Why did this have to come up when I'm on the verge of a million things?

LINDA. You're always on the verge of a million things.

DICK. I can't help it. That's what I do, Linda. I look for openings, I keep on my toes, I play to market, I make brilliant deals like this quicksand thing.

LINDA. Dick, you're doing brilliantly. You're only twenty-nine years old and you've already filed for bankruptcy twice.

DICK. Oh, come on, darling, don't get upset. Could I be any more crazy about you? Jesus, I tell him to take it easy . . . If I was in his shoes I'd go nuts. Now come on, we've got to get him over this.

LINDA. If I knew a nice girl for him.

DICK. You know models. There must be somebody in your agency.

LINDA. Not that many single ones.

DICK. What about Carol?

LINDA. Engaged.

DICK. And Doreen?

LINDA. She's living with a priest.

DICK (he has a brainstorm). What about Zorita? That model at Don's party?

LINDA. For Allan? My God, she'd eat him alive. There'd be nothing left but his glasses. No, this is going to be a little problem.

(ALLAN enters with the pills and drinks.)

ALLAN. Y'know, I'm glad you two came over. I'm feeling a little better.

DICK. Listen, Allan, Linda and I are going out for dinner tonight. We'll invite some nice girl, and the four of us will go together.

ALLAN. Oh no, I don't think so.

DICK. Come on, you've got to get out of the house.

ALLAN. I haven't looked at another woman in two years. I'm out of practice. When I was in practice I was out of practice.

DICK. Come on, Allan. You've invested your emotions in a losing stock, it was wiped out, dropped off the board. What do you do? You reinvest . . . maybe in a more stable stock . . . something with long-term growth possibilities.

ALLAN. Who are you going to fix me up with—Merrill, Lynch, Pierce, Fenner, and Smith?

DICK. Come on, Allan, shape up.

ALLAN. A pretty girl? Because she'd have to be damn good to do anything for my morale at all.

DICK. Who can we get for him?

ALLAN. You mean you don't even have anybody in mind?

DICK. We've got several people in mind.

LINDA. What kind do you like?

DICK. He likes neurotics.

ALLAN. I like blondes. Little blondes with long hair and short skirts and big chests and boots and bright and witty, and perceptive.

DICK. Don't set yourself ridiculous standards.

LINDA. She must be beautiful? With long hair and a big bust?

ALLAN. Oh—and a good behind. Something I can sink my teeth into.

DICK. He was always very fussy.

ALLAN. That's right, but look at the result.

DICK. That's right, you never went out.

LINDA. Sally Keller is blonde and has a good-sized chest.

ALLAN. What's good-sized?

LINDA (makes a gesture with her hands). I don't know—like this.

DICK. She's not the brightest girl in the world.

ALLAN. What does she do?

LINDA. She dances in a cage at a discotheque.

ALLAN. Forget it.

DICK. Come on, you might even be able to get her into bed.

ALLAN. Into bed! With my luck, I wouldn't be able to get her into a chair.

LINDA. Well, the girls that look the way

you want them to don't usually have great minds.

DICK. I don't know why we're making such a fuss over a little pleasant dinner companionship.

ALLAN. I don't even want that. I'm still too attached to Nancy.

DICK. Allan, forget Nancy. She's gone.

ALLAN. That's true. She wanted to be free to swing.

DICK. Come on, honey, think of someone.

ALLAN. I can just picture what she's been up to.

NANCY *(enters)*. Oh, Jeffrey, take me in your arms, hold me. To think that we two could meet here in a little town like Juarez, you divorcing Celia, me getting rid of what's-his-name. It's such a pleasure to be made love to by a tall, strong, handsome, blond, blue-eyed man. *(She exits.)*

ALLAN. We're divorced two weeks, she's dating a Nazi.

LINDA. Hey, what about Sharon?

DICK *(it strikes him)*. What about Sharon?

ALLAN. I like the name.

LINDA. Sharon Lake. She works for Jack Edelman, the photographer. She's his assistant.

DICK. She's a bright girl and very cute.

ALLAN. Okay. Let's go.

DICK *(to* LINDA*)*. Call her.

LINDA *(goes to the phone)*. Perfect.

ALLAN *(beginning to falter)*. What are you going to tell her?

LINDA *(dials)*. I'm going to see if she's free for dinner.

ALLAN *(getting panicky)*. Don't tell her anything about the divorce. Maybe you better tell her my wife's dead.

DICK. Leave it to us.

ALLAN. I don't know if we should go through with this. *(Begins pacing)* The old tension is setting in. My stomach is jumping.

LINDA *(into the phone)*. Sharon Lake please. Linda Christie.

ALLAN *(puts his hands up to his ears, blocking out the sound, and prowls nervously)*. I don't want to hear this. *La-ummmmmmm-de-ummmmmmmmmmm* . . .

LINDA. Sharon? Hi. Linda. How are you? Good. Listen—

ALLAN. *Ummmm-ummmmmmm* . . .

LINDA. Dick and I are having dinner with a friend tonight and we thought you might want to join us.

ALLAN. *Ummmm-ummmmmmm* . . .

LINDA. No, that's nothing. We have the radio on. *(She beckons to* DICK *to help. He silences* ALLAN.*)* Allan Felix. You don't know him. He's a friend of Dick's.

ALLAN *(prompting)*. Attractive. A writer. A widow—widower—my wife died in a mine-shaft explosion . . .

LINDA. He's a lot of fun. I think you'll like him.

ALLAN. Listen, if she doesn't want to— forget it. I don't need this aggravation.

LINDA. Okay. We'll pick you up with the car. Eight o'clock. A simple dress, oh, sure . . . flats are okay.

ALLAN. Let her wear heels, what am I— Toulouse-Lautrec?

LINDA. Okay. . . . We'll pick you up. Okay. Bye. *(She hangs up.)* You're set.

ALLAN *(he can hardly suppress his excitement)*. I have very mixed feelings. What if I have this chick in bed and Nancy comes in? Hoo-hoo.

DICK. Let's not hope for too much this first night, Allan.

ALLAN *(to* LINDA*)*. Did she say anything about me?

LINDA. She doesn't know you. How could she say anything?

ALLAN. You know, you never said I was a widower.

LINDA *(as she takes the Coke and Fresca into the kitchen)*. I got you the date. You tell her the part about your wife's death.

ALLAN. Ooh, I'm excited.

DICK *(dials the phone)*. We'll pick Sharon up because she lives two blocks from us and then the three of us will pick you up. See you about ten after eight. I can't stay out late though, I have a business meeting tomorrow morning.

*(*LINDA *comes out of the kitchen with the four clean glasses and takes them to the bar.)*

LINDA. Listen, if there's anything at all you want—if the dishes pile up or if you need a bed made . . .

DICK *(into the phone)*. Hello, this is Mr. Christie. I'm leaving the Gramercy number now and proceeding due north to the Murray Hill number.

ALLAN. Let's eat at Tavern on the Green. It's a perfect night to dine out in Central Park.

LINDA. Wonderful, it's so romantic there.

DICK. I hate the food there. Besides I think it's going to rain. *(To* ALLAN*)* You be all right? *(*DICK *and* LINDA *stop at the door.)*

ALLAN. Sure—I'll be fine—I'll shower and douse my body with Canoe. . . . Now I'm kind of looking forward to it. I'm excited.

DICK. Good-by.

ALLAN. I'm better . . . (Closes the door; the expression on his face becomes serious) I'm scared.

BLACKOUT

SCENE TWO

It is nearly eight that night. ALLAN *emerges from the bedroom, tie around his neck, and goes to the mirror over the bar. He is a mixture of anticipatory excitement, guilt, and nerves as he tries to get his hair to fall satisfactorily.*

ALLAN. I cannot get my damn hair to stay down . . . this hot weather is murder on it. I'm not a bad-looking guy . . . chin's a little weak . . . what the hell . . . she shouldn't be disappointed. What does she expect? Rock Hudson? I'm a normal decent-looking guy . . . maybe slightly below normal. I wish she'd seen me before . . . I hate to be there on a blind date when the girl sets eyes on me. What if she looks at me and laughs or screams? Will you relax! Has a girl ever once reacted by laughing or screaming? Once. That little coed from Brooklyn College came to the door, saw me, and passed out . . . but she was weak from dieting. What the hell . . . Bogart was short . . . didn't bother anybody.

BOGART (appearing at the archway). You're starting off on the wrong foot, kid.

ALLAN. Negative, you mean?

BOGART. Sure. You're letting her get the best of you before the game starts. What's that stuff you were putting on your face?

ALLAN. Canoe. It's an aftershave lotion.

BOGART. And the other stuff?

ALLAN. That was Mennen spray deodorant, Lavoris, and Johnson and Johnson baby powder.

BOGART. For Christ's sake, you're going to smell like a French cathouse.

ALLAN. I need them.

BOGART. Why? You ashamed to sweat?

ALLAN. I want to make an impression.

BOGART. Y'know, kid, somewhere in life you got turned around. It's her job to smell nice for you. And whatever you do, don't tell her you don't drink. She'll think you're a Boy Scout. And don't get nervous—the only bad break you could get is if she turns out to be a virgin or a cop. (He exits.)

ALLAN. With my luck she'll turn out to be both. He's right. A lot of girls get turned on by a masculine, earthy quality. I shouldn't have put so much Binaca under my arms. I want to create a good subliminal impression without being too pushy. Hey, I better memorize some photography terms, if she's a photographer's assistant. (He crosses to the magazine rack and pulls out a magazine, crossing back to the coffee table as he reads) " 'Not only is there a great qualitative difference between my Nikon and my other cameras,' says ace photographer Greg Barnett, 'but my Nikon is built sturdy enough to withstand the throwing around I give it when the outdoor shooting gets rough.' " (Drops the magazine on the coffee table) I'm going to charm this girl. Wouldn't it be great if Sharon and I hit it off at first sight? Sure, why not? They say dames are simple. I never met one who didn't respond to a slap in the mouth or a slug from a forty-five. C'mere, Sharon.

(DREAM SHARON appears from the slot, slightly disheveled; she is wearing no shoes or stockings. "As Time Goes By" plays softly on the piano.)

DREAM SHARON. Oh, Allan, you are fantastic . . . up until tonight, the doctors had said that I was frigid. I want to thank you for proving them wrong.

ALLAN. If you've got any friends with the same problem, bring them around.

DREAM SHARON. When Dick and Linda spoke of you, they used terms like genius and brilliant. They never said you were also an animal.

ALLAN. I'm sorry I had to slap you around, sweetheart, but you got hysterical when I said, "No more."

DREAM SHARON. Oh, Allan . . . Allan.

(The lights change, the music fades and the buzzer sounds simultaneously. DREAM SHARON disappears.)

ALLAN. Yes?

LINDA (offstage). It's Linda.

ALLAN. Linda?

LINDA. I'm alone. (ALLAN opens the door. LINDA enters with a jar of cocktail nuts in a bag.) Sharon's with Dick. They're parking. He sent me ahead just to make sure everything's okay.

ALLAN. Everything's fine . . . I didn't realize it was so late.

LINDA *(takes two bowls out of the cabinet and puts nuts into each).* Hey! What did you do? Break a bottle of shaving lotion?

ALLAN. You're kidding! I'm wearing too much?

LINDA. It's a touch strong . . . not terrible. Once we get into the air, you won't even notice it.

ALLAN *(closes the bedroom door).* I just want to set up the place quickly.

LINDA *(places a nut bowl on the coffee table).* The place is fine. We're only going to have a quick drink and go.

ALLAN *(taking a book from the desk shelf and moving it to the downstage bench).* A few carefully placed objects will create the proper impression.

LINDA *(she puts the second bowl of nuts on the hassock).* You're not going to leave half-open books around like you're reading them?

ALLAN. Why not? It creates a certain image.

LINDA. You don't need an image . . .

ALLAN *(takes a medal from the bar drawer).* I've got just the thing . . . my hundred-yard-dash medal.

LINDA. You're joking! You're not going to leave out a track medal?

ALLAN *(puts the medal on the swivel hassock).* Why not? I paid twenty dollars for it!

LINDA. Just be yourself. She'll like you.

ALLAN *(takes a Bartok record from the shelf above the desk).* I've got a big decision to make. Do I go with Thelonius Monk or Bartok's String Quartet Number Five?

LINDA. Why don't you put on Thelonius Monk and leave Bartok carelessly strewn about?

ALLAN *(puts the Bartok record against the rail on the bench).* Brilliant! That's exactly what I'll do.

LINDA *(gets bottles out of the bar and puts them on top).* I've never seen anyone go through so much trouble to impress a date. Particularly such a casual date. If you devoted this much interest and care with Nancy, I don't see why she left you.

ALLAN *(finding a Monk record on the shelf).* Oh, I did. I used to write her poems. And take her to little candlelight restaurants and order in French and then the waiter would bring all the wrong things.

LINDA *(at the corner of the bench).* Maybe if you had leaned across the candlelight and kissed her . . .

ALLAN. I tried, and she'd say, "Christ, not here, people are staring." Then once at a great little bistro on Second Avenue, my sleeve caught fire. *(Puts the Monk record on the phonograph and plays it.* LINDA *laughs.)* So you laugh at it, it's funny, right? She took it as a symbol of my clumsiness, which I guess it was. *(The door buzzer sounds.* ALLAN *snaps to attention.)* Finesse . . . tremendous poise . . . I'm an absolute master.

LINDA. Right. I'll get the ice. *(She exits to the kitchen as* ALLAN *answers the door.* DICK *enters with* SHARON LAKE, *a very nice girl, attractive, but not the sex machine of* ALLAN*'s vision. However,* ALLAN *is sufficiently impressed to be rendered speechless.)*

DICK. Allan, this is Sharon.

SHARON. Hello.

ALLAN. Ah . . . er . . . *(He stands dumbfounded, his hand on the door.* DICK *directs* SHARON *to the living room, thumps on the door to release* ALLAN*'s hold and closes the door.)*

SHARON *(sitting on the left end of the sofa).* I was just telling Dick, I have some friends on this block. In the house across the street. Do you know the Gibsons?

ALLAN . . . the Gibsons? . . . No . . . *(*DICK *gives* ALLAN *a push into the room.)*

SHARON. Hal and Eleanor Gibson. They're a great couple. He's an interior decorator.

ALLAN *(at the sofa).* Oh really? That's sort of a hobby of mine.

SHARON *(looking around, not overly impressed).* Oh . . . uh-huh . . .

ALLAN. The key to decorating is to avoid looking like you used a decorator.

DICK *(at the railing).* I've got to make one fast call.

LINDA *(entering from the kitchen with a water pitcher and ice bucket; she goes to the bar).* Hi!

SHARON. Hi! . . . Linda?

LINDA. Yes?

SHARON. Are you wearing Jasmine?

LINDA. Me? No . . . *(*LINDA *and* ALLAN *realize simultaneously that the pervading scent is from* ALLAN.*)* What are we drinking?

DICK. J and B on the rocks.

SHARON. I'll just have a little Harvey's Bristol Cream, please.

ALLAN. The usual. *(*LINDA *looks at him quizzically.)* Bourbon and water.

*(*LINDA *goes to the bar and pours the drinks.)*

SHARON. Oh . . . a bourbon man.

ALLAN. Yeah, I gotta cut down on it. I'm putting away a quart a day. *(He sits on the sofa.)*

DICK *(into the phone).* Hello, this is Mr. Christie. I'm no longer at Lehigh 5-8343. I'll be at . . . What? Did he leave a message? *(DICK sits at the desk to take a few notes.)*

LINDA *(delivering a glass of sherry to* SHARON *and moving back to the bar).* Sharon did a movie.

ALLAN. Oh?

SHARON. Underground.

ALLAN. A stag film?

SHARON. Underground. You know—very arty sixteen-millimeter.

LINDA *(taking a drink to* DICK *at the desk and going back to the bar).* Allan's interested in cinema.

SHARON. What do you do?

ALLAN. I'm a writer. Nothing major. For *Film Quarterly.* You know—essays, criticism . . . reviews . . .

SHARON. This film I made got very good reviews. And I got singled out. Of course, I was the only girl in it with nine men.

ALLAN. Oh, really? What was the film called, maybe I saw it?

SHARON. "Gang Bang." They have the raunchiest titles, but it wasn't a bit sexy . . .

DICK *(finished at the desk, he crosses to join* SHARON *and* ALLAN*).* This is ridiculous. I have to get a phone for my car, Volkswagen or not.

ALLAN. Volkswagen!

(The music starts to build.)

LINDA *(delivering a glass to* ALLAN*).* You were all out of bourbon, so I made it straight water. *(She joins the group, sitting on the hassock with her own drink.)* It's so humid. I think it's going to rain.

SHARON. Maybe that's why I have this headache; I get sinus attacks.

ALLAN. Really? You should have them drained.

(The music builds.)

DICK *(sits in the swivel chair).* That's why it's silly to go to Tavern on the Green.

SHARON. Do you think you could turn the music down a bit?

(ALLAN crosses to the office area.)

DICK. What's the point of going to an outdoor restaurant if it's going to rain?

LINDA. You used to like to take me walking in the rain.

ALLAN. I love the rain . . . it washes memories off the sidewalk of life . . .

(As this purple prose hangs in the air, AL-LAN *turns to the phonograph, where he accidentally knocks the tone arm, causing an ear-splitting scratch. All cringe.* DICK *spins around in the swivel chair.)*

LINDA. Gee . . . you really have a delicate touch.

DICK *(rising and crossing to the hassock; he takes a nut).* Allan's a little tense. He's had a little misfortune with his wife . . .

SHARON. His WIFE?

*(ALLAN *takes the Monk jacket and replaces the record, keeping the record jacket in his hands.)*

LINDA. Dick . . .

DICK. Ex-wife . . . she's gone . . .

ALLAN. She's dead.

SHARON. How awful!

LINDA. Well, no, she's not dead.

ALLAN. Technically not dead . . . but we're not dating.

DICK. She left him.

SHARON. I'm sorry.

DICK *(crossing to the phone).* Why don't I call and make a reservation at the Hong Fat Noodle Company in Chinatown.

LINDA *(joining* DICK*).* Here, I have the phone number in my purse.

ALLAN *(joining* SHARON *on the sofa, the record jacket still in his hand).* I don't know if you like Thelonius Monk or not, but to me he has a wry, mirthful quality that's not at all accommodating to the casual listener, although his harmonic conceptions are often haunting.

SHARON. You sound like the back of a record jacket. (ALLAN *tosses the album in back of the sofa.)* Er . . . have you known Dick and Linda long?

ALLAN. I've known Dick for years. I don't know Linda nearly as well. Dick's a great guy. A little overambitious, maybe, but he's always been that way. He's like a kid brother to me. I'm always helping him out of one jam or another. He kind of looks up to me. (AL-LAN *crosses his legs, hooking his toe under the coffee table and tipping it, scattering nuts and debris.* DICK *and* LINDA *rush to set things right.* ALLAN *backs off in dismay.)*

DICK *(turning to* ALLAN*).* We're all set at the Hong Fat Noodle Company.

ALLAN. Just let me get my sport jacket. *(He limps off to the bedroom.)*

SHARON . . . . Is he on anything?

LINDA. Um . . . oh . . . no.

DICK. I'm just going to call my service and tell them where I'll be.

LINDA *(clearing up the mess).* I hope you like Chinese food.

SHARON. Oh, sure . . . Linda, I've just got to make it an early evening . . . I've got a terrible day tomorrow.

LINDA. Oh, I'm sorry.

DICK *(into the phone).* Hello. This is Mr. Christie. If Mr. Milton from the Chase Manhattan Bank calls, I'll be at the Hong Fat Noodle Company in Chinatown. That's Canal 8-6321.

(LINDA *hands* SHARON *the photography magazine from the floor.* LINDA *puts her and* SHARON'S *glasses on the bar.* DICK *crosses to* LINDA *and gives her his glass.)*

SHARON. Hey! Look at this! Greg Barnett. You remember Greg? . . . Jack's old partner . . . *(She reads.)* " 'There is a great qualitative difference between my Nikon and my other cameras,' says ace photographer Greg Barnett, 'but my Nikon is built sturdy enough to withstand the throwing around I give it when the outdoor shooting gets rough.' " I wonder how much they paid him to say that?

ALLAN *(enters from the bedroom and crosses to* SHARON). I'm ready! And you've gotta let me order because I'm an expert on Chinese food.

SHARON. Good! I'm starved . . . we had such a rough day today trying to photograph little children.

ALLAN *(giving his arm as they start out).* Oh really? Photography is a hobby of mine. In fact, I've been having a little trouble with my cameras lately. See, I feel there is a great qualitative difference between my Nikon and my other cameras, but my Nikon is built sturdy enough to withstand the throwing around I give it when . . .

CURTAIN

ACT TWO

The curtain rises on ALLAN. *It is two weeks later, and he has had a pretty discouraging time of it. He is at the sofa, with the phone on the coffee table, as he thumbs through an old address book.*

———

ALLAN. Mildred Denberg . . . can't even remember her. Marion Drayson . . . she sat behind me in Civics. Toby Kovack . . . yeah . . . I remember her! She was a pushover, with those great legs and those freaky parties. *(He dials.)* Hello? Is this the Kovack residence? Ah . . . how can I get in touch with Toby? Oh, she is? I see. No. thanks, let it go, forget it. *(Hangs up)* The wife of Rabbi Kaplan! I'm cursed. I cannot get a break. *(Thumbs through the book)* Marilyn Perry. The queen of Dubrow's. *(Dials)* Hello, is this the Perry residence? Ah, is Marilyn there? *(Rises and crosses)* You know where I can reach her? An old friend from Midwood High School—Allan Felix. I dated her once. Do you remember? I'm stunned! It was eleven years ago . . . that's right . . . short, with red hair, and glasses—no, that's cleared up. How can I get in touch with her? Oh really? She still feels that way? You know, it's been eleven years now. When did you speak to her? Last week . . . and she specified she didn't want you to give me the number? Well, goodby, Mrs. Perry. No, that's all right. *(Hangs up and puts the phone on the bench)* I don't know how much longer I can take this. I miss being married. These past two weeks have been terrible. At least Linda's been fixing me up with some of her friends. But with every girl something goes wrong. First there was that photographer's assistant, Sharon. I made a mess of that. Then the next night there was Gina.

(GINA *enters as the lights change and* ALLAN *falls into step with her as they cross to the downstage railing.)*

GINA. Good night, Allan. *(He moves to embrace her.)* Don't !

ALLAN. Why not?

GINA. I'm Catholic.

ALLAN. I'll convert.

GINA. Besides, I didn't take my pill today. *(She exits through the bedroom door, slamming it behind her.)*

ALLAN. That's all right . . . I took an extra one! *(The lights are restored.)* What'd I do wrong? She treated me cold from the second I showed up at her door with a Whitman Sampler. And what about Vanessa? That was only a week ago . . . you'd think by then my luck would have begun to change.

(The lights dim to a late-night romantic mood. VANESSA, *exotically dressed, appears and glides to the sofa, where she reclines. Soft music plays in the background.* ALLAN *joins her.)*

VANESSA. I've had many men . . . my first at twelve. After that it was an endless stream. Poets, writers. I lived in a house with five actors. Some were gay, but what does it matter? I straightened them out. It was a challenge. My life was a continual round of orgies. I took on the entire Tau Epsilon Phi Fraternity at Yale in three hours. It's still a record in New Haven. I've always thought of sex as something wonderful and open . . . to be enjoyed as fully and frequently as possible. (ALLAN, *increasingly aroused, finally can restrain himself no longer and lunges for her. She screams and jumps up.*) Aaaaagh! What do I take me for? (*She exits as the lights are restored.*)

ALLAN. How did I misread those signs? . . . What am I going to do? I've practically used up every friend Linda has. I may have to resort to desperate measures to meet women . . . like going up to East Hampton or hanging around Bloomingdale's stocking counter. Ah . . . I'm too shy to do those things alone. Linda would come with me even if Dick's busy. Dick and Linda sure have been great. I've dragged them everywhere to help me find girls. Linda seems to like it. I know she enjoyed that evening at the discotheque.

(*He sits on a corner of the bench. The lights dim.* DICK *and* LINDA *join* ALLAN *and sit at the corner of the bench. On the platform behind them a fantastic little blonde in a glittering dress is bumping and jerking to drive you crazy. The music blares.*)

LINDA. Gee, this is fun. We haven't been to a discotheque in such a long time.

ALLAN. I'm getting a heart attack. I can't believe that girl.

DICK (*into the phone*). I'm at Lehigh 4-3605.

ALLAN. She's a doll! I would sell my mother to the Arabs for that girl!

LINDA. Well, ask her to dance. You've been staring at her for an hour.

ALLAN. I can't . . . I don't know her.

DICK (*puts the phone down, and turns to them*). Come on. I can't stay any longer. I have to get up early tomorrow and sue some friends.

LINDA. You want to dance one dance, honey?

DICK. We can't do those dances. They're undignified. You've got to be under sixteen to look good. But you two can stay, just don't get home too late. Good luck. (DICK *exits through the kitchen.*)

ALLAN. I love you, Miss—whoever you are —I want to have your child.

(*The music segues to a relatively slow number.*)

LINDA. Get up and do it.

ALLAN. I can't dance—have you ever seen my body move? It's like a printing press.

LINDA (*dragging him to the platform*). Come on . . .

ALLAN. I'm scared—please—no—no . . .

LINDA. Start dancing . . . that's it . . . keep count . . . one . . . two . . . one . . . two. Now talk to her. Go ahead.

ALLAN. One . . . two . . . one . . . two . . .

LINDA. Try something more meaningful.

ALLAN. Three . . . four . . . three . . . four . . .

LINDA. No! . . . Go on . . .

ALLAN. Er . . . good evening, Miss. Would you be interested in dancing?

GO-GO GIRL. Sure!

(*The music switches abruptly to a wild rock rhythm as the* GO-GO GIRL *thrashes appropriately. In a desperate effort to look good* AL-LAN *attempts a few vaguely Spanish fandangos.* LINDA *has slipped offstage at the start of this. The* GO-GO GIRL *dances her way toward the center of the stage, sees* ALLAN *and erupts into derisive laughter, backing off. The lights restore and the music fades.*)

ALLAN. What I need is a more intellectual girl . . . that's where my appeal is . . . that's why last Monday afternoon the Museum of Modern Art seemed such a good idea . . .

(*The lights fade, leaving an aisle of light across the forestage.* LINDA *enters wearing a raincoat.* ALLAN *joins her.*)

LINDA. Um . . . look at that Salvador Dali . . . if you could have any painting in the world, what would you pick? (*Through these speeches they drift toward the left of the stage.*)

ALLAN. A Van Gogh. Any Van Gogh.

LINDA. Me too. I feel some kind of mystical attraction for Van Gogh. Why is that?

ALLAN. All I know is that he's a great, great painter and he cut his ear off for a girl he loved.

LINDA. That's the kind of thing you'd do for a girl.

ALLAN. Yeah . . . (*Embarrassed*) I'd really have to like her a lot.

LINDA. I wonder if Dick would cut his ear off for me.

ALLAN. I don't think you better ask him. He's been very busy lately.

LINDA. It must be fantastic to be loved so intensely.

ALLAN. I guess we may as well split and see if there's any action at the Guggenheim.

(*A pretty blonde, the* INTELLECTUAL GIRL,

wearing low-cut jeans and a shirt tied high, exposing a lovely midriff, wearing moccasins and a shoulder bag, enters.)

LINDA. Here comes one.

ALLAN. Ah . . . she is one.

LINDA. Go ahead . . . speak to her.

ALLAN. I'll get arrested.

LINDA. Go ahead before the room gets crowded and you feel ashamed.

ALLAN *(to the* INTELLECTUAL GIRL). Uh . . . that's quite a lovely Franz Kline, isn't it?

GIRL. Yes, it is.

ALLAN. What does it say to you? (LINDA *sits in the swivel chair and turns upstage.)*

GIRL. It restates the negativeness of the universe. The hideous, lonely emptiness of existence—nothingness—the predicament of man, forced to live in a barren, Godless eternity, like a tiny flame flickering in an immense void—with nothing but waste, horror, and degradation—forming a useless, bleak straitjacket in a black, absurd cosmos.

ALLAN. What are you doing Saturday night?

GIRL *(exiting)*. Committing suicide.

ALLAN. What about Friday night? Intellectual women are a pain in the neck—got to be the right mixture of brains and passion. Now Linda's got it all. She's so easy to be with . . . like that day last week in Central Park . . . she was sweet, and friendly, and tried her best to be helpful. (ALLAN *moves to the hassock, sits and starts to mime rowing a boat. Appropriate sounds are heard.* LINDA *has been sitting in the swivel chair and spins around to face front.)*

LINDA. Don't you understand, Allan? You have a lot going for you. You're bright and funny and even romantic, if you could only believe it. You put on a false mask as soon as you meet a girl.

ALLAN. It's different around you. You're my friend's wife. I'm not trying to impress you.

LINDA. I keep telling you . . . be yourself. The girl will fall in love with you.

ALLAN. Listen, you've been so nice this past week, spending your time with me. (AL-LAN *stops rowing and pulls a small tissue-wrapped object from his pocket.)*

LINDA. I'll tell you the truth, I'm having a ball.

ALLAN *(takes the present from his pocket)*. I wanted to get you this because it's your birthday.

LINDA. How did you know it was my birthday?

ALLAN. You mentioned it one day and I remembered it because it's the same date my mother had her hysterectomy.

LINDA *(moving to kneel on the hassock just behind him)*. It's lovely—it's beautiful—a tiny plastic skunk.

ALLAN. It looked so cute in F. A. O. Schwarz and I heard you say skunks are your favorite animals . . . it doesn't function . . . it just exists . . .

LINDA. I'm so touched. I don't know what to say. (LINDA *sits back in the swivel chair, swings around to face upstage, and exits.* AL-LAN *goes back to rowing; then, as the lights change, he finds himself back in his living room.)*

ALLAN. Linda's a great girl. I think Dick kind of neglects her. Hell, I told him so the other night. If I'm his friend, I've got to speak candidly to him. He's gotta learn to take it easy and treat her a little better.

(The lights change and DICK *enters.)*

DICK *(crosses to the sofa, puts his briefcase on the coffee table)*. How could you get her a birthday present and I forget? Why didn't you warn me?

ALLAN. She's your wife. I assumed you knew.

DICK *(crosses to the phone on the bench)*. I'm up to my ears in work. I purchased fifty lots for building in Tennessee, it turns out they're radioactive. I'm taking a beating. *(He dials.)*

ALLAN. Maybe if you just took Linda out once in a while.

DICK. That's the farthest thing from my mind. Besides, I went to a discotheque with both of you last week.

ALLAN. That was one night, two weeks ago, and you left early, and you wouldn't dance with her, and you forgot her birthday.

DICK. I didn't forget completely. I was late. My secretary picked her up some jewelry.

ALLAN. Your secretary? That's not very personal. Women like personal junk . . .

DICK. You know what it is to be stuck with fifty lots that are radioactive? What am I going to build, an X-ray center? *(Into the phone)* Hello, Miss Carson? What are the figures on the new contract, fifteen hundred or eighteen hundred? . . . Thank you. *(He hangs up and crosses back to the sofa.)*

ALLAN. So once in a while you take her dancing or on a picnic.

DICK. Maybe, who knows . . . maybe I got married too young. She was so beautiful . . .

first in her class at Bard College. I'll never forget that prom weekend, there was moonlight, and soft music, I looked at her with her hair spilling down her shoulders and thought —she's the perfect corporate image for a young executive.

ALLAN. I hate to tell you, pal, but that sounds a little callous.

DICK. Oh, come on, Allan, she knows I love her. Christ, I'm crazy about her, and have been since the second I met her. Meanwhile, between my quicksand and my radioactivity, I'll be driving a cab soon.

(The lights change and DICK *vanishes.)*

ALLAN. Some guys don't know a good thing when they have one. *(He rises from the hassock and crosses to the desk.)* Well, I gotta stop daydreaming . . . I'm going to lose my job if I don't finish my essay on Anna May Wong. *(The doorbell buzzes. He answers it and it is* LINDA.*)* Hi.

LINDA. Hi.

ALLAN. What's the matter?

LINDA. I hope I'm not bothering you . . . what do you have for an anxiety attack? I need a tranquilizer.

ALLAN. I got everything. I'm a drugstore.

LINDA. I have a throbbing in the pit of my stomach.

ALLAN. How do you know it's anxiety? How do you know it's not fear?

LINDA. My stomach feels jumpy.

ALLAN. You find it hard to breathe?

LINDA. A little—I feel frightened, and I don't know over what.

ALLAN. I get that.

LINDA. Is it fear or anxiety?

ALLAN. Homosexual panic. *(He exits to the bedroom.)*

LINDA. Oh . . . I always get this way when Dick goes on a business trip.

ALLAN *(offstage)*. Oh?

LINDA. He had to fly to Cleveland for the day. I got up, helped him pack, drove him to the airport, and threw up in the United Airlines terminal.

ALLAN *(returning with a pill and a glass of water)*. That's a good terminal. I've thrown up there.

LINDA. I don't know what it is that upsets me so.

ALLAN. Fear of separation. It's an interesting psychological phenomenon. I had to go to Washington once when I was married, and even though I was the one leaving, I got sick. Yet when I returned, my wife threw up. *(He returns the glass to the bedroom.)*

LINDA. My analyst would say I'm feeling guilty because I really want him to go.

ALLAN *(reenters from the bedroom)*. Come on . . . I don't understand you . . . you got everything going for you. You're bright . . . people photograph you for magazines, so you know you're beautiful. You read, you play Bach on the recorder, you're happily married. I mean, why should you be a mass of symptoms?

LINDA. Well, you've got a lot going for you, and you're a mass of symptoms. I guess it happens to us when we're children . . . you know, you think you're ugly and your parents get divorced . . . you feel abandoned . . . you must have had the same thing.

ALLAN. My parents didn't get divorced . . . although I begged them to.

LINDA *(sits on the sofa)*. Do you really think I've got a lot going for me?

ALLAN. I do. And I'm fussy. I don't know how I can afford to be, but I am.

LINDA. It's funny. I never thought you liked me very much. You know, when I married Dick.

ALLAN. I thought you didn't like me so much. I thought maybe you thought I was an oddball.

LINDA. I never really knew you. I mean, we never spent any time together. Dick described you as the first guy who sat through *The Maltese Falcon* twelve times in two weeks. Then when the four of us went out together we acted differently than now. I feel I've really gotten to know you in the past few weeks and I've come to a very interesting conclusion. You definitely are an oddball . . . but you're one of the best people I've ever known.

ALLAN. That's nice. Because you're the only really platonic friend I've ever had.

LINDA. I like a platonic relationship. They're so much less complicated. Not that I'm down on male-female relationships—although marriage is a tough proposition at best.

ALLAN. It's disastrous.

LINDA. I know. Dick and I are constantly, quote, reappraising our marriage.

ALLAN. Are you?

LINDA. Sure. Especially in the last year. You know, he's gotten deeper and deeper into his work and my interests have gone in another area. That is, they always were. There are certain things we both need that we don't give each other.

ALLAN. Marriage can be a very lonely

thing. But not so lonely as I've been since I've been single.

LINDA. Hey, no date tonight?

ALLAN. Ah . . . I had a date but she called it off . . . some kind of Polish holiday.

LINDA. Well, why don't we go out to dinner and maybe a movie?

ALLAN. I got a better idea. Why don't we have dinner here and see what's on the "Late Show"?

LINDA. You have anything here for me to cook?

ALLAN. I have some frozen steaks and a bottle of champagne.

LINDA. What are you doing with champagne? You going to launch a ship?

ALLAN. I tried cooking here last week—to impress a date. I tried to make beef stroganoff in the pressure cooker.

LINDA. How'd it taste?

ALLAN. I don't know. It's still on the wall.

LINDA. Is the grocery on the corner still open?

ALLAN. Yes.

LINDA *(rises and takes her purse from the coffee table)*. I'll be right back. I'll get us some asparagus and salad and dessert. I love to cook and I never get the chance—Dick's so busy all the time.

ALLAN. And get some candles. I love to eat by candlelight.

LINDA. I'll cook and you open the champagne. But not if I'm going to be the only one who drinks it.

ALLAN. I'll drink one or two with you, but you've got to promise to put me to bed if I try and dance naked. (LINDA *exits.)* Hey, this'll be fun! I have a terrific rapport with Linda. I hate to see her depressed. It'll be cozy. *(Puts pillows from the couch by the fireplace)* Spending an evening in . . . nice summer rain outside . . . *(Closes the shutters)* It's just damp enough to have a small fire. Adjust the lighting in here. *(Turns on a light on the bar)* Create a little atmosphere. *(Picks up the address book from the coffee table, puts it on the desk shelf, starts for the kitchen)* Get out the champagne . . . Women are suckers for champagne . . . it makes them crazy. *(Out from the kitchen)* Wait a minute . . . what the hell am I doing! Women are suckers for champagne. This is Linda. Dick's wife. Linda. Remember? Gee, I got carried away for a minute. What the hell was I thinking?

(LINDA *enters. Soft music plays in the background. They meet on the sofa.)*

LINDA. Dinner was wonderful, Allan. The steaks were superb, the champagne perfect. I'm so glad we decided to stay home and spend a quiet evening together. You're the only man I've ever met who really holds my interest.

ALLAN. You should feel flattered. Not many women are deep enough to know what it is I'm all about.

LINDA *(kissing him)*. I'm sorry for acting like a schoolgirl—I couldn't help myself. I've wanted to do that for so long now.

ALLAN. We mustn't. It's forbidden.

LINDA. But these things happen. Nobody plans them.

ALLAN. Yes, but you're not free.

LINDA. In my heart I'm free. I can't repress it any longer. At first I thought you were just a helpless, mixed-up child, but I didn't really know you then. Now I believe you're everything I ever dreamed of loving.

ALLAN. You poor thing. How you must've suffered—wanting me so.

LINDA. My darling, I need you. I need to possess you body and soul.

ALLAN. Which would you like to begin with?

LINDA *(rises and crosses to the mantel)*. We were meant for each other. If we miss this opportunity we'll regret it as long as we live.

ALLAN. My head says it's insane, but my heart says, don't believe your head, it's a lying head. (LINDA *vanishes.)* This is terrible. I'm sitting here making love to my best friend's pillow.

BOGART *(enters)*. So, you finally fell in love with her.

ALLAN. I just got carried away for a minute.

BOGART. Come on, kid, you don't have to feel guilty.

ALLAN. Guilty over what? Two lonely people with a tremendous amount in common have dinner together. We're platonic friends.

BOGART. There's nothing platonic about the way she feels about you.

ALLAN. How can you tell?

BOGART. What do you want her to do—attack you?

ALLAN. She's my friend's wife.

NANCY *(enters)*. Of course she is. She'll tell Dick and he'll beat you to a pulp.

BOGART. Look, she loves you, not him.

NANCY. He's not the romantic type.

BOGART. He could be if he tried.

NANCY. Don't listen to him.

BOGART. Don't listen to her.

ALLAN. I'm getting a headache.

(NANCY *and* BOGART *exit.*)

DICK *(enters).* Allan, I want you to do me a favor.

ALLAN. Yes?

DICK. I've fallen in love with another woman. Don't ask me how—it just happened. We're going off together to live in Alaska. Oh, she's an Eskimo. I know that you and Linda have always been fond of one another and I thought perhaps after I'm gone you might look after her. It would mean a lot to me.

ALLAN. Of course.

DICK. Well, I'm off to Alaska. If you need me I'll be at Frozen Tundra 7-0659. *(He vanishes.)*

ALLAN. She is always complimenting me. I know she likes me. But does she like me that way? What the hell? I could test her. I could maybe make an advance . . . what could possibly go wrong?

(The dream lights go on. LINDA *appears and crosses to the sofa. Music plays in the background.)*

LINDA. Dinner was wonderful, Allan. The steaks were superb, the champagne perfect. *(She sits on the sofa.)*

ALLAN *(crosses to sit on the sofa).* Linda, tonight the earth shook.

LINDA. What?

ALLAN. Linda darling . . .

LINDA. Don't . . .

ALLAN. It was meant to be . . .

LINDA. Allan, take your hands off me, you must be crazy.

ALLAN. Linda, my love . . .

LINDA. Allan, I'm a married woman. Rape!

ALLAN. Shhhh . . . you'll wake up the whole house!

LINDA. Think of Dick—he's your best friend. *(They rise.)*

ALLAN. My sleeve is caught on your zipper!

LINDA. Thank God, Dick gave me this tear-gas pen! *(She mimes the pen business as a loud jet spray sound is heard;* LINDA *exits.* ALLAN *covers his face, coughing as the lights are restored.)*

ALLAN *(pacing).* Look, let's not get carried away. I'm not an appealing guy. The thought that a girl like Linda could go for me . . . I'm kidding myself. Where the hell is she? By now she could have had her steak and been home!

(The doorbell buzzes. ALLAN *opens the door.* LINDA *enters for real with a bag of groceries.)*

LINDA. I feel so light. That Librium is beginning to work.

ALLAN *(takes the bag).* Maybe you better not have any champagne.

LINDA *(takes the candles from the bag).* Oh no, what the hell—if I get too out of hand you can always call the police.

ALLAN *(goes into the kitchen with the bag).* How long did you say Dick was out of town for?

LINDA. He'll be back tomorrow.

ALLAN *(enters from the kitchen).* There's a new Godard film at the Sutton . . . I thought maybe we could go—

LINDA *(gets the candlesticks from a shelf above the bar).* Come on—you're kidding . . . we're all set for here. . . . Besides, it's starting to rain. Besides, I remembered that great Ida Lupino movie is on Channel Four . . . you know, where she's married and she suddenly becomes involved with her husband's best friend.

ALLAN. How does it end?

LINDA *(sits on the sofa and puts the candles in the holders).* She kills them and herself.

ALLAN *(crosses to the sofa).* Let's go out.

LINDA *(puts the candles on the mantel, turns on the sconce switch, them picks up some pillows near the fireplace).* I want to see that Ida Lupino movie. It's a fascinating theme. You think it's possible to love two people at once?

ALLAN *(moves to the center of the sofa).* What do you mean?

LINDA *(crosses to* ALLAN *at the sofa and puts one pillow on the sofa).* A wife, happily married, suddenly finds she loves another man . . . not that she doesn't love her husband . . . just that . . . she loves someone else . . . you think it's very possible?

ALLAN. Do you?

LINDA. Very. Very possible and probably very common. Love is such a strange phenomenon . . . strange and exquisite . . .

BOGART *(appears).* Go ahead. Make your move.

ALLAN. Uh—

BOGART *(crosses to* ALLAN *on the sofa).* Go ahead. Take her and kiss her.

ALLAN. Uh—*(Paralyzed to act on this advice)* Uh—

LINDA. Is something wrong?

BOGART. Go ahead. She wants it.

ALLAN. Wrong? No—I—

LINDA. I better begin our food.

BOGART. Go ahead. Kiss her.

LINDA. Yes?

BOGART. Hurry! Before she moves out of position.

ALLAN. I—can't do it.

BOGART. Kiss her, kid!

ALLAN. I—I—can't!

LINDA. I'll be right back. *(She turns and goes off to the kitchen, putting another pillow on the sofa.)*

BOGART *(sits in the swivel chair)*. Well, kid! You blew it.

ALLAN. I can't do it. She'll misunderstand it. I invite her over and I come on like a sex degenerate! How does it look? What am I, a rapist?

BOGART. You're getting carried away. You think too much. Just do it.

ALLAN. We're platonic friends. I can't spoil that by suddenly coming on. She'll slap my face.

BOGART. I've had my face slapped plenty of times.

ALLAN. Yeah, but your glasses don't go flying across the room.

BOGART *(rises and crosses to the corner of the sofa)*. You're going to disappoint her.

(LINDA *enters with two glasses of champagne.)*

LINDA. Here we are. Start on this. *(Hands him a glass and crosses below the coffee table to the other corner of the sofa)* Hey, did you read in the papers, another Queens woman was raped?

(ALLAN *practically spits up his first swallow.)*

ALLAN. Oh really? I was nowhere near Queens. Do they know who did it?

LINDA *(sits on the sofa)*. No. They haven't a clue. He must be very clever.

ALLAN *(sits on the opposite end of the sofa)*. You've got to have something on the ball to rape so many women and get away with it. Ah-ha . . . *(He's trying to be light. He looks at BOGART, who doesn't smile.)*

LINDA. I think if anyone ever tried to rape me I'd pretend to go along with it and them right in the middle pick up the nearest heavy object and let him have it. (BOGART *and* ALLAN *look troubled.)* Unless, of course, I was enjoying it.

(Both men brighten.)

ALLAN. They say it's the secret desire of every woman.

LINDA. Well, I guess it depends on who does the raping.

ALLAN. Well look, why dwell on morbid things? Odds are you'll never get raped.

LINDA. Not with my luck. *(Closes her eyes happily)* Um—I feel so light. The drink went right to my head. I'm floating.

ALLAN *(agreeing)*. Um.

BOGART. Go ahead, kiss her.

ALLAN. I can't.

BOGART. She's ready.

ALLAN. How do you know?

BOGART. Believe me. I know.

ALLAN. She'll pull back. I feel it.

BOGART. She's sitting and waiting. Don't screw up.

ALLAN. Okay—I'm going to try. . . . But I'm gonna go slow . . . *(He begins inching into position. Very scared)* If she jumps I'll pretend it was a joke.

BOGART. Hurry.

ALLAN. She better laugh. *(Just as he's about to strike, the phone rings with shattering clarity and he jumps with a near heart attack.)* Ohmigod! Didn't expect that! *(He goes to pick up the phone.)* What a start . . . *(Into the phone)* Hello? Dick? Hi . . . What? Yes . . . she is. She dropped over—very unexpectedly. I had a Polish date. Two good friends—we're going to have one fast dinner, then right out . . . Huh? Yes, I'm all right. I'm fine. Say, aren't you in Cleveland? Oh, then this call is costing you money . . . I'll put her on . . . *(Offers her the phone)* He wants to speak to you. From Cleveland.

(BOGART *crosses above the sofa.)*

LINDA *(to ALLAN, en route to the phone)*. Are you upset over anything?

ALLAN. Oh no . . . I was just startled . . . (LINDA *sits on the bench and speaks into the phone.* ALLAN *crosses to one end of the sofa.)* This is ridiculous. I'm going to cause an international incident. I want her out. I can't handle this.

LINDA. Hello, darling.

ALLAN. Hello, darling. She loves him. What am I kidding myself?

BOGART *(crosses to the sofa)*. Will you relax? You're as nervous as Lizabeth Scott was before I blew her brains out. All you gotta do is make your move and you're home free.

ALLAN. This is crazy. We'll all wind up on the front page of the *National Enquirer.*

LINDA. Okay. Good-by. I will. *(She hangs up.)* Dick sounded a little down. I think he's having some trouble in Cleveland.

ALLAN. How come he never takes you with him when he goes on those out-of-town trips?

LINDA *(crosses to the sofa)*. I'm afraid to

fly. My analyst thinks that's an excuse. He never asks me along, though. Who knows? Maybe he's got something going on the side. *(This last said jokingly)*

ALLAN *(sits on the sofa, left of LINDA).* Would that bother you?

LINDA. Sure. I mean, not if I didn't know.

ALLAN. I know he'd be very hurt if you ever had a casual affair with somebody else.

LINDA. I don't think I could have a casual affair.

ALLAN. No?

LINDA. I don't take those things lightly. If I fell for another man there'd have to be something more there than a little fling. I'd have to feel something more serious, in which case my marriage would be in question. Are you shaking?

ALLAN. I'm chilly.

LINDA. It's not very cold. I'm not the type, though. I don't think I could take the excitement involved. Anyway, I'm not glamorous enough.

ALLAN. Oh, you are. You're uncommonly beautiful.

LINDA. When I go to a discotheque and see all those beautiful young girls I feel like life has passed me by. I should be selling chocolates at Fanny Farmer.

ALLAN. You're crazy! Those girls are not in your league.

LINDA. Keep talking. You're saving my life. I have such an inferiority complex.

BOGART. Say, you're handling yourself very well. Now kiss her.

ALLAN. Please—

BOGART. You built up to it beautifully.

ALLAN. I just don't have the nerve.

BOGART. Tell her how beautiful she is again.

ALLAN. I just told her!

BOGART. Again.

ALLAN. Y'know, you are really one of the most beautiful girls I've ever known.

LINDA. I don't know what to say to that.

ALLAN. I mean really beautiful—unbelievably beautiful—fantastically beautiful—

BOGART. All right already.

LINDA. It's been so long since anybody said that to me.

BOGART. Now move closer to her.

ALLAN. How close?

BOGART. The length of your lips.

ALLAN. That's very close.

BOGART. Come on. Move. (ALLAN *does.*)

ALLAN. Now what?

BOGART. Tell her that she moves something in you that you can't control.

ALLAN. Your're kidding.

BOGART. Go ahead.

ALLAN. From me it's corny.

BOGART. She'll love it.

ALLAN. It's like Fred Astaire looks great in tails, I look silly.

BOGART. Leave Fred Astaire out of this. Say something.

ALLAN. I love the time we've spent together.

LINDA. So have I.

ALLAN. Was that all right? I don't want to use your other line about moving something in me.

BOGART. You're doing fine, kid. Tell her she has the most irresistible eyes you've ever seen.

ALLAN. Eyes you—you eyes—you—you have the *most* eyes of anybody . . .

LINDA. Your hand is trembling.

ALLAN. It is?

BOGART. That's because you're near.

ALLAN. Pardon me?

BOGART. Tell her that!

ALLAN. That's because you're near.

LINDA. You always know what to say, don't you?

BOGART. Tell her you've met a lot of dames but she's really something special.

ALLAN. That she won't believe.

BOGART. No?

ALLAN. I've met a lot of dames but you are really something special.

LINDA. Really?

ALLAN. She bought it.

BOGART. Now put your right hand around her shoulder and draw her near.

ALLAN. I don't want to—I'm afraid.

BOGART. Go ahead. (ALLAN *does it.*) Now get ready for the big move and do exactly as I tell you.(NANCY *enters with a gun.)*

NANCY. I warned you to leave my ex-husband alone. *(She shoots BOGART. NANCY and BOGART exit.)*

LINDA. Well, I guess I'll start the steaks.

ALLAN. Linda, your eyes are like two thick steaks. *(He has summoned his courage and tries to kiss her. She bangs backwards, knocking over the standing lamp on the sofa table.)*

LINDA. Allan, don't! I'll pay for the lamp.

ALLAN. It's all right! I think I love you!

LINDA. I insist on paying for the lamp!

ALLAN *(still in a wrestle).* Forget the lamp!

LINDA. I'm so clumsy—will you take ten dollars!

ALLAN *(still going for her bobbing head).* Forget the damn lamp! Give me five bucks, we'll call it square!

LINDA *(disengaged, she rises and gets her purse from the bench).* Allan—don't—

ALLAN. Don't get the wrong idea—it was a joke—I was testing you—you don't think—I meant a platonic kiss—not a whole kiss—here—

LINDA. I better go.

ALLAN *(following).* Linda . . .

LINDA. I really better go.

ALLAN. Linda.

LINDA. Please. I'll be fine. *(Awkwardly, she goes.)*

ALLAN *(alone, frantic).* I attacked her! What did I do? I'm a vicious jungle beast! She's going to tell Dick! She's panicky now! By the time she gets home she'll be hysterical! She'll probably go right to police headquarters! What kind of idiot am I to try a fool thing like that! I'm not Bogart. I never will be Bogart. What'll I tell Dick? I'm a disgrace to my sex. I should work in an Arabian palace as a eunuch. *(The doorbell buzzes.)* There's the Vice Squad. *(He turns and opens the door. LINDA enters.)*

LINDA. Did you say you love me? *(They kiss.)*

ALLAN. Play it again, Sam! *(The music becomes louder.)*

CURTAIN

ACT THREE

The curtain rises on ALLAN *and* LINDA, *the following morning, after they have "done it." It has been a mixed thing for them—beautiful and traumatic. They are on the sofa with coffee mugs.*

———

ALLAN. Two lonely people with a tremendous amount in common thrown together continually—before we know what's happening, we're in love . . . we fight it as long as possible, we're alone on a rainy summer evening, Dick's a thousand miles away, we couldn't fight it any longer, I took you in my arms, and we made love. Then we each got upset stomachs. The main thing is that we're honest.

LINDA. I still can't believe it.

ALLAN. I haven't slept that well in years. Is it noon yet?

LINDA. It's seven.

ALLAN. Seven? I didn't realize it was so early. You were fantastic last night.

LINDA. Thanks.

ALLAN. How do you feel now?

LINDA. I think the Pepto-Bismol helped. What were you thinking of while we were doing it?

ALLAN. Willie Mays.

LINDA. You always think of baseball players when you're making love?

ALLAN. It keeps me going.

LINDA. I couldn't figure out why you kept yelling, "Slide!"

ALLAN. I think it'd probably be best if you told Dick.

LINDA. Dick?

ALLAN. I guess it'll come as a surprise, but . . .

LINDA. Oh . . . it'll be a surprise all right . . .

ALLAN. Make sure you tell him on a day that Wall Street closes high.

LINDA. Gee . . . the whole thing is complicated.

ALLAN. Listen, it happened, it happened—can't help that. It happened. It's not my fault. It's not your fault. The point is—you felt like a woman, and I felt like a man, and that's what those kind of people do.

LINDA. I did feel like a woman. You were wonderful.

ALLAN. I have a fantastic craving for breakfast.

LINDA. I'll make some. What are you in the mood for?

ALLAN. Steak and eggs, pancakes, butter and syrup, biscuits, and a big pot of coffee.

LINDA *(rising).* Well! In that case, I'd better go downstairs and pick up a few things.

ALLAN. Don't bother . . . we'll go out.

LINDA *(gets her purse from the bench).* No . . . no . . . I'll go. I need a little fresh air.

ALLAN. Take my raincoat, there's money in the pocket.

LINDA. Wait'll my analyst comes back from his vacation and finds out about this. He'll become a chiropodist. *(She exits.)*

ALLAN. You killer! You were incredible in bed last night . . . like Toscanini. Nancy should have been there—she'd have seen a master in action . . .

NANCY *(appears in dream light).* Oh Allan, word's out all over Europe that you're the best thing in bed the United States has to offer.

ALLAN. You could have had some of this and you threw it away.

NANCY. I made a mistake. I know that now. Can't we start over?

ALLAN. It's too late. Linda and I are in love. We're going away.

NANCY. I've been a fool. *(Organ music plays.)* Good-by, Allan, I'm going to become a nun. If I can't have you, the next best thing is God. *(She vanishes.)*

ALLAN. She's got a point there. Gee, I can't believe it. This bright, beautiful woman is in love with me. Of course she's in love with me Why shouldn't she be? I'm bright, amusing . . . sensitive face . . . fantastic body. Dick'll understand. Hell, we're two civilized guys. In the course of our social encounters a little romance has developed. It's a very natural thing to happen amongst sophisticated people.

DICK *(appearing in dream light)*. You sent for me?

ALLAN. Yes.

DICK. Good.

ALLAN. Drink?

DICK. Quite.

ALLAN. Scotch?

DICK. Fine.

ALLAN. Neat?

DICK. Please.

ALLAN. Soda?

DICK. A dash.

ALLAN. Linda and I are in love.

DICK. It's just as well. I've come from my doctor. He gives me two months to live.

ALLAN. Good, then you don't mind?

DICK. Not a bit.

ALLAN. Cheers.

DICK. Cheers. *(He vanishes.)*

ALLAN *(rises)*. Sure . . . things are going to be okay. Hell, Dick and I have been through tougher situations than this. Dick and I have been through a lot together. He's my best friend. This is terrible. This is going to hurt him . . . I know it.

DICK *(enters in dream light)*. Thanks a lot.

ALLAN. Dick . . .

DICK *(crosses left of the sofa)*. How could you? My wife and my best friend. I trusted you both. I feel I've been made such a fool of. I love you. I love you. Why didn't I see it coming? Me—who had the foresight to buy Polaroid at eight and a half! *(He disappears.)*

ALLAN. This is awful . . . he'll do something rash. Dick's an emotional guy. He'll kill himself. Kill himself? Did you ever think

what he might do to you? Didn't you ever hear of the unwritten law? You take a guy's wife . . . you humiliate him. You've seen enough Italian movies. Dick's got a temper!

DICK *(enters in undershirt and scarf)*. Bastado! Pezzo di curnutu. Tu mai tradutto me!

ALLAN *(backing up the steps onto the platform)*. Ma non e vero.

DICK. Tu mi pigli per stupido!

ALLAN. Non e curpa mia.

DICK *(leaps over the railing)*. Bugiardo! Proco! Carogna! Imbesile! *(He draws a dagger.)*

ALLAN. No . . . no . . .

DICK. Solo chisto me tuo sadisfari mio onore. *(He stabs ALLAN.)*

ALLAN. Oh boy, that hurt! (DICK *exits.* ALLAN *stands at the railing.)* This is ridiculous! What am I going to do? I love her. She loves me. We could have a wonderful life together. Why does Dick have to be in the picture? Hell, take it easy. Why do you have to make everything into a Warner Brothers production? She'll come back, we'll have breakfast together. Shape up. She'll be back in a minute. You'll spend the day together . . .

(The doorbell rings. ALLAN *opens the door to find* DICK *with his suitcase and coat.)*

DICK *(leaves his coat and case at the railing)*. I had to come home, Allan. I have to speak to you. Allan, I think Linda's having an affair. I just called home. She's not there. These past few weeks she's seemed distracted, distant, little things only a husband would notice. You've seen her a lot these past couple of weeks . . . she's changed. The other night she talked about an affair in her sleep.

ALLAN. Did she mention any names?

DICK. Only yours. When I woke her and questioned her she said it was just a nightmare. *(He crosses up the steps and onto the platform.)* I try to think of who it might be. It has to be someone I don't know . . . some guy she met through work . . . an agent, a photographer, some ad executive, or actor.

ALLAN. Why are you so upset . . . I thought she was just your corporate image?

DICK. I love her. If she leaves me I'll kill myself.

ALLAN. Since when are you so emotional?

DICK. I've never been in love with anyone before. If I find out who the guy is I'll kill him, I swear. I've neglected her and now she's involved with some stud! (ALLAN *sits in the swivel hassock;* DICK *sits on the edge of the coffee table.)* If I haven't already lost her to someone, I'm going to make up for everything to her. I'm going to change. I'm going to do everything I can to make her life with me exciting and fun because without her it wouldn't be worth living. I was up all last night in a Cleveland hotel room. I figured, all right, I'm losing her . . . too bad . . . I'll survive. Then I panicked and phoned her. She was out. When I called her here last night she said she was going home. Where'd she stay?

ALLAN *(rising)*. Calm yourself.

DICK *(rises, crosses, then moves back to AL-LAN)*. I've got to find her. I've got to stop her and beg her forgiveness before it's too late. I want her to get on that plane with me and fly back to Cleveland. I want her with me all the time. I want to pamper her. I want to hear her laugh and speak . . . I'm sorry for carrying on like this, Allan, but you're the only friend in the world who would understand.

ALLAN. I . . . I understand.

DICK. Look, if she calls, tell her I'll see her home. Tell her I've got to speak to her, will you?

ALLAN. Sure . . . sure.

DICK. Thanks . . . thanks a lot. *(He gets his coat and suitcase and exits.)*

ALLAN *(sits on the coffee table)*. I'm going to faint. How could I tell him? The guy's desperately in love with her. I never realized how much. He never realized how much. I couldn't do that to a stranger, much less a friend. But what if it's too late? What if Linda's really hooked on me now? You know, once a woman's been made love to by somebody who can really do it great! I was fantastic last night! I never once had to sit up and consult the manual. Love is very different for a woman. It's a complicated phenomenon. I don't know what to expect. I've never broken off with a woman before.

(The dream lights go on. LINDA enters in a trench coat and goes up the steps to the railing end.)

LINDA. So you think it's as simple as that?

ALLAN *(goes up the platform to LINDA)*. We have no choice.

LINDA. You told me you loved me.

ALLAN. Try to take it gracefully.

LINDA. But the time we spent together, the closeness, the promises.

ALLAN. Please, Linda . . .

LINDA. You mean too much to me. I can't let you go.

ALLAN. Linda, don't be difficult . . . I'm sorry.

LINDA. Sorry's not enough . . . you think I'm a play toy.

ALLAN. What can I say?

LINDA *(Bette Davis with a gun)*. Give me the letter.

ALLAN. What letter?

LINDA. Philip, give me the letter. (LINDA *backs* ALLAN *up through all this.)*

ALLAN. There is no letter.

LINDA. I want the letter. Philip, give me the letter.

ALLAN. Linda, you're going crazy.

LINDA. You can't treat me that way.

ALLAN. Don't pull the trigger—I'm a bleeder. *(The light fades and she vanishes. AL-LAN crosses.)* She'll kill me. Women are violence-prone. Bette Davis, Barbara Stanwyck . . . they're killers . . . I'll go away—I'll join the circus. I'll be a clown . . . I'll never take off my makeup . . . Like Jimmy Stewart.

(The dream lights go on. BOGART appears.)

BOGART *(at the end of the railing)*. Pull yourself together, kid, you're hysterical.

ALLAN. I'm going to join the circus.

BOGART. You should feel encouraged. When you weren't coming on phony, you got a pretty good dame to fall for you. You never thought you could make it with dames. Well, you can.

ALLAN. But now it's got to end and I can't do it.

BOGART. It's not that hard, kid. Watch. (LINDA *enters. Music plays in the background.)* C'mere, sweetheart.

LINDA *(goes up the steps onto the platform with BOGART)*. Yes, darling?

BOGART. It's over.

LINDA. What is?

BOGART. Us.

LINDA. Over?

BOGART. That's right, toots. Over. *Kaput.*

LINDA. That simple, eh?

BOGART. That's right.

LINDA. Supposing I say no?

BOGART. Won't do you any good.

LINDA *(pulls out a pistol and sticks it in his face)*. And will this?

BOGART *(takes the gun and slaps her in one cool move)*. Come off it, Sugar. You never could use a rod.

LINDA *(sobbing)*. But why does it have to end before it can begin? Tell me why?

BOGART. You play too rough for me, Sugar. It was you that killed Johnson. Parker found out about it so you killed him too. But that wasn't good enough for you. You wanted to finish me off. You knew you couldn't do it while I was facing you, so you figured you'd get me to turn my back. But not me, Sugar. Now come on. You're taking the fall. (LINDA *exits, sobbing.*) That's all there is to it.

ALLAN. For you, because you're Bogart.

BOGART. Everybody is, kid. At certain times. You're doing something now I didn't think you had in you. You're passing up a real tomato because you don't want to hurt a guy. If I did that there wouldn't be a dry eye in the house.

ALLAN. Yeah, but I'm brokenhearted over it.

BOGART. That's all the more reason you can be proud of it.

ALLAN. You think so?

BOGART. Sure. Listen, kid, There's other things in life besides dames and one of 'em is to know you did a right thing for a pal. Think it over.

(*The doorbell buzzes.* ALLAN *goes to the door. It is* LINDA. BOGART *moves down the steps.*)

ALLAN. Er—grocery store not open yet?

LINDA. No.

BOGART. Tell her.

ALLAN. What?

BOGART. Tell her. Now. (*He exits.*)

ALLAN. Linda . . .

LINDA. Allan, do you realize what a wonderful thing has happened?

ALLAN. Linda . . .

LINDA. Allan, the most beautiful thing in the world has occurred right under our noses. We've had a wonderful experience. Doesn't that surprise you? You didn't have to do anything. Didn't have to leave any half-open books lying around . . . you didn't have to put on the proper mood music. I even saw you in your underwear with the days of the week written on them.

ALLAN. Look, Linda, we've . . . got to call it quits.

LINDA. Yes, I know. While I was out, suddenly everything became very clear, and when I asked myself do I really want to break up my marriage . . . the answer was no. I love Dick, and while someone as wonderful as you is very tempting . . . I can't think of my life without him.

ALLAN. You can't?

LINDA. He needs me. Allan . . . and in some unexplainable way . . . I need him.

ALLAN. I know he needs you.

LINDA. This is the first time I've ever been affected by anyone besides Dick—I'm already a little in love with you—and unless I stop it now I'll find myself too deeply involved to go back to him. I don't regret one second of what's happened because what it's done for me is to reaffirm my feelings for Dick.

ALLAN. Go home, Linda. . . . He's home waiting for you.

LINDA. He is?

ALLAN. He came by while you were out. He wants you to go back to Cleveland with him. He'll explain it. Meanwhile, we'll just be good friends . . . I think I'd like that.

LINDA. You're sure? You're not saying that to make things easy?

ALLAN (*piano music starts in the background*). I'm saying it because it's true. Inside of us we both know you belong with Dick. (*Music*) You're part of his work, the thing that keeps him going. If that plane leaves the ground and you're not with him, you'll regret it. Maybe not today, maybe not tomorrow, but soon and for the rest of your life.

LINDA. That's beautiful.

ALLAN. It's from *Casablanca.* I waited my whole life just to say it.

LINDA (*goes up the steps and kisses* ALLAN). Good-bye. (*She exits.*)

NANCY (*enters*). Poor Allan—I told you this would happen.

ALLAN (*crosses to the sofa*). Are you kidding? She was in love with me—you heard her.

NANCY. Meanwhile she's back with Dick.

ALLAN. I gave him a pretty good run for his money . . . without even trying—that's the key.

BOGART (*enters*). You tell her, kid—it's all yours now.

ALLAN. I'm going to do something I should have done a long time ago. I'm going to forget you.

NANCY. What! Allan don't—no—don't—don't, nooo . . . (*She gives a long wail as she backs out.*)

BOGART. Gee, kid, that was great. I'd have slapped her around a little myself, but you've got your own style.

ALLAN. I do have a little style.

BOGART. Well, kid, so long.

ALLAN. You're leaving?

BOGART. You don't need me any more. There's nothing I could show you, you don't already know.

ALLAN. I guess that's right. The secret's not being you, it's being me. True, you're not too tall and kinda ugly. But I'm short enough and ugly enough to succeed by myself.

BOGART. Here's looking at you, kid. *(He exits. The doorbell buzzes. The piano music fades.* ALLAN *opens the door.)*

BARBARA. I'm sorry for bothering you. My name is Barbara Tyler. I just moved in upstairs and I'm all alone and I locked myself out. Could I use your phone?

ALLAN. Sure, it's right over there.

BARBARA. Thank you. *(Noticing* Film Quarterly *on the desk)* Film Quarterly! You're not *the* Allan Felix who writes for *Film Quarterly,* are you?

ALLAN. Yes, I am.

BARBARA. I just did my Ph.D. on cinema for the New School, and I used some of your articles for reference. They're very clever.

ALLAN *(piano music starts).* Thank you.

BARBARA. I particularly liked the article you wrote on *The African Queen.*

ALLAN. That was one of my favorite movies.

BARBARA. It was quite a departure for Bogart.

ALLAN. Well, you see, the thing about Bogart that most people don't know is that . . .

CURTAIN